NEW WORLDS
OF
LITERATURE

Writings from
America's Many Cultures

Second Edition

NEW WORLDS
OF
LITERATURE

Writings from
America's Many Cultures

Second Edition

JEROME BEATY
Emory University

J. PAUL HUNTER
The University of Chicago

W · W · NORTON & COMPANY

New York • London

PHOTO CREDITS

Opposite page 1: © Bern Keating. Used courtesy of Black Star.
Page 114: © Puerto Rican family from Buffalo's Lower West Side.
Photograph by Milton Rogovin.
Page 182: © Peter Byron. Used courtesy of Black Star.
Page 256: © Paul Chesley / Photographers Aspen.
Page 360: © Arthur Tress / Magnum Photos.
Page 464: © J. Bruce Baumann. Used courtesy of Black Star.
Page 604: © Michael Carpenter.
Page 718: © Tony Savino / The Image Works.
Page 804: © Dixie D. Vereen: "This Far by Faith."
Cover illustration: Ralph Fasanella (born 1914), *Sunday Afternoon*, 1953.
Private collection. Reproduced by permission of the artist.

Since this page cannot legibly accommodate all the copyright notices,
pages 961–67 constitute an extension of the copyright page.

The text of this book is composed in Janson,
with display type set in Centaur.
Composition by Vail-Ballou. Manufacturing by R. R. Donnelley.
Book design by Suzanne Bennett.

Library of Congress Cataloging-in-Publication Data
New worlds of literature : writings from America's many cultures /
[edited by] Jerome Beaty, J. Paul Hunter. — 2nd ed.
p.   cm.
Includes bibliographical references and index.
1. American literature—Minority authors.   2. Ethnic groups—
United States—Literary collections.   3. Ethnic groups—Canada—
Literary collections.   4. Canadian literature—Minority authors.
5. Caribbean literature (English)   I. Beaty, Jerome, 1924–   .
II. Hunter, J. Paul, 1934–   .
PS153.M56N48   1994
810.8'0920693—dc20   93-9921
ISBN 0-393-96354-3

W. W. Norton & Company, Inc., 500 Fifth Avenue, New York, N. Y. 10110
W. W. Norton & Company Ltd., 10 Coptic Street, London WC1A 1PU
4 5 6 7 8 9 0

CONTENTS

5   ALIENS   361

9

INTRODUCTION

This book is intended as an introduction to literature and also as a text
for courses in composition, multicultural literature, multiculturalism, or contemporary American literature. It is, too, a collection of enjoyable, informative, and stimulating readings.

When the first edition of *New Worlds of Literature* was created, there
was no major collection of modern American multicultural literature; so
much of the introduction to the first edition argued for the legitimacy of
such an anthology. In many quarters that argument has been won, but
there are still those who fear that a collection like this is meant to replace
the canonical Great Books and Authors. For them, and for those more
familiar with traditional authors and works than with those here included,
let us briefly rehearse our position.

Great Works, we believe, are too often approached archaeologically, as
museum pieces, monolithic Cultural Monuments. In order to be able to
read the great works of the past in anything other than an antiquarian way
and to make them a meaningful part of our own lives and experiences, most
of us first need to be enthralled and informed by the works of the here and
now. The *here* is America, the New World: all the pieces in this book are by
writers of the United States, Canada, and the Caribbean, and all are written in English. The *now* is the last quarter of the twentieth century; only a
very few works in this anthology were published more than twenty-five
years ago.

Each new generation looks at its past from a different perspective. New works change the tradition, give a new perspective on and vitality to the works of the past. To hear the sound of African or Asian rhythms come through traditional Anglo-American forms, as in a poem by Audre Lorde or Cathy Song, is to hear the new, to hear the future. It will also change the past. We will read the poetry and prose and drama of the past with new eyes and ears—*our* eyes and ears. Thus in each chapter there is a piece of student writing on one of the works or topics in that chapter to illustrate how these contemporary works speak to present-day students.

The selections in this anthology are not meant to *replace* but to invigorate your reading of the masterpieces of Western culture. An hour spent reading Maya Angelou does not mean you have no time for Aristophanes. And when you come to him or Melville or Montaigne, you will be better prepared to understand and enjoy. The editors' intention is both to open you up to a whole new world of literature, one that you may not have been introduced to in high school or other college courses, and by the excitement of these texts to make you enthusiastic about reading literature.

This book presents recent, stimulating, American writing while representing more fully than has been done previously the works of new and otherwise marginalized Americans—those who keep the New World new and who illustrate the ethnic diversity of America toward the end of the twentieth century as the cross-cultural experience becomes more and more central to our lives. Indeed, Mitsuye Yamada insists that there is a new look to Americans (and America) nowadays:

MIRROR MIRROR

People keep asking where I come from
says my son
Trouble is   I'm american on the inside
             and oriental on the outside
   No Doug
Turn that outside in
THIS is what American looks like.

The cultural diversity of the selections is a rich *literary* experience, but it is also an enriching experience that will prepare you for the many cross-cultural experiences that are inevitable in modern American life. For the stereotypes exist and persist in life as well as in literature, and they influence us even when we know better, even it seems when we are the people being stereotyped. Barbara Cameron, in an essay entitled "Gee, You Don't Seem Like an Indian from the Reservation," tells of her feelings when she was three years old: "My family took me to my first pow-wow. I kept asking my grandmother, 'Where are the Indians? Where are the Indians? Are they going to have bows and arrows?' I was very curious and strangely excited about the prospect of seeing real live Indians even though I myself was one."

If there is a political slant to this book it is the emphasis on the "cross-" in cross-cultural. As you will have noticed, the chapters are not arranged by ethnic or gender ghettos but by topics that suggest aspects or elements of life common to all—home, family, heritage, and so on. Rather than deny the distinctiveness of cultures, their experiences, and responses, this arrangement, we feel, suggests that the elements, problems, and joys are parallel or analogous if not identical. It can be both thrilling and at times comforting to recognize the common humanity and common experiences across what seem to be unbridgeable cultural divides. There are a number of pieces that center upon cross-cultural experiences, especially in the second half of the volume (from "Aliens" on). Some of these acknowledge, lament, or protest the height and thickness of the walls between cultures; the power, pain, and cruelty of prejudice and repression, which are all too familiar a part of our modern American experience. Others celebrate, sometimes with surprise and usually with joy and a sense of expanding horizons, the possibility of crossing such boundaries. A touching and amusing example is Gary Soto's autobiographical "Like Mexicans." The Chicano author has, quite surprisingly to himself, fallen in love with a Japanese woman. He is afraid to visit her family, but does so, and is relieved to find "newspapers piled in corners, dusty cereal boxes and vinegar bottles in corners. The wallpaper was bubbled from rain that had come in from a bad roof. Dust. Dust lay on lamp shades and window sills. These people were just like Mexicans, I thought. Poor people." Successful encounters may not mean the necessary loss of heritage or melting. As the first-person narrator of Bharati Mukherjee's short story "Hindus" says, she sees America as "a vast sea in which new Americans [read "any American"] like myself could disappear and resurface at will." Without shying away from the difficulties of a multicultural society, of entrenched interests and power, resistance to change, prejudice, and even hatred, this anthology's "political" slant is that though nobody says it will be easy, yes, we can all get along. And there is or may be someday an America without hyphens.

New Worlds of Literature generally moves outward in space, time, and community. The first two chapters include works that chiefly deal with home and family, the next with the cultural community and its forebears and traditions. The fourth chapter focuses on language as an aspect of the individual's sense of identity, as a bond for the ethnic culture, and as a barrier in the larger society. Chapter 5 centers on aliens, strangers, or our own experience of being the stranger. The next chapter deals with encounters across ethnic, racial, or sexual conflicts or barriers, and chapter 7 with the crossing of those barriers, for better or worse. In chapter 8, "new" or minority Americans seek to understand or search for a role in the larger society. The works in the final chapter suggest varieties of ways in which Americans relate to whatever is beyond self and society.

The selections within each chapter are arranged by literary genre: three or four short stories, eight to twelve poems, a play (in six of the nine chapters), and three or four essays and autobiographical narratives. One can choose to read (or teach) first (or only) fiction or poetry, drama, or nonfiction prose. There are 28 stories, which, supplemented with a few novels, could make up a course in cross-cultural fiction, or, supplemented with so-called "mainstream" stories, could constitute a course of contemporary short fiction; the 90 poems go a long way toward setting up a course in cross-cultural poetry; etc.

The headnotes to each chapter seek to lead you into experiencing the works that follow and at the same time relating the experiences in the works to those in your own life. Brief biographies of the author come before each piece, occasionally with a statement of the author's about his or her own work.

Each piece is followed by one or more study questions. We have tried to avoid asking "What am I holding in my hand?" questions as well as "Don't you think so, too?" ones. The aim is to stimulate your perceptions and thought as well as, in some instances, to urge you to relate the experiences within the work to your own experiences. As is the practice in Norton anthologies, there are informational—not interpretive—footnotes; we have not footnoted words that can be quickly found in a college dictionary, and we have chosen not to footnote certain words where context and careful reading make the sense clear.

Following the selections in each chapter is an "Afterword" that deals with an aspect or element of literature—"Setting," "Characterization," etc. These are intended particularly for those using the text as an introduction to literature, though they should prove generally useful for thinking, talking, or writing about literature.

The thematic and experiential organization of the text seems particularly appropriate to a course in which frequent student writing is a central element. The poems, stories, plays, and nonfiction prose pieces, given their subject matter and their relevance to contemporary American experience, should inevitably stimulate student themes: personal essays related to the experiences of the literary works, comparisons and contrasts of pieces with similar content, argument, research papers (particularly, but not only, on the cross-cultural conditions and issues in our society), imitations or parodies, as well as literary analysis. Each chapter includes suggestions for paper topics and writing projects.

The nine pieces of student writing offer a wide range of models. There is at least one student paper in the text that treats in essay form a short story, a poem, a play, or an essay in the relevant chapter, as well as two original poems in imitation of selections or on the subject of the chapter, and a parody of a story. A new section on writing about literature is included at the end of the book.

You may be using this book as a reader for writing, as an anthology inviting you into the serious and enjoyable study of literature, or even as a rich but unsystematic exploration of contemporary American society through literature. Whatever your aim, may the journey be intellectually, psychologically, sociologically, and emotionally stimulating and profitable. And fun.

Jerome Beaty

J. Paul Hunter

ACKNOWLEDGMENTS

The editors wish to thank Agha Shahid Ali, Paula Gunn Allen, Andrew Beaty, Shawn Beaty, the late John Benedict, Suzanne Bennett, Clark Blaise, Susan Brekka, J. Douglas Canfield, Judith Ortiz Cofer, Martha Cook, Peter Dowell, Pam Durban, Larry Eby, Marianne Eismann, Elizabeth Freebairn, Carol Hollar-Zwick, Ellen Harris, Debra Hunter, Kathryn Hunter, Irwin Hyatt, Roger Kaplan, Anna Karvellas, Juliet Kono, Tato Laviera, Ruth Looper, Michael Lund, John Mardirosian, Ricardo Gutierrez Mouat, Bharati Mukherjee, Diane O'Connor, Nancy Palmquist, Walter Reed, Carter Revard, Laura Reyes, Alberto Ríos, Lawrence Rothfield, Harry Rusche, Ronald Schuchard, Barbara Thompson, Lib Triplett, Helena Maria Viramontes, and Melissa Walker. We would like to thank our reviewers: William T. Cotton (Loyola University), Joseph Leopold (St. Petersburg Junior College), Thomas Miller (University of Arizona), Quandra Prettyman (Barnard College), Swarup Raman (Delaware County Community College), Daniel Reardon (University of Missouri), Nancy Tynan (University of Houston), and George Wolf (University of Nebraska). Finally, we wish to thank Carolina Hospital and Carlos Medina of Miami Dade Community College for their work on the Instructor's Guide.

Special thanks to the late Barry Wade, without whose guidance and support this work would not have begun, much less been completed.

In Memorium
Barry K. Wade, 1951–1993
Our all-too silent partner

NEW WORLDS
OF
LITERATURE

Writings from
America's Many Cultures

Second Edition

I

HOME

"Home" is many things to many people. Quite beyond a particular place with specific memories and associations, home is a feeling, a state of mind. To be "at home" means to feel comfortable, at ease, secure in familiar surroundings. "At home" usually suggests satisfaction more than it indicates an address. Home can, of course, mean lots of unpleasant things as well, especially for those who had difficult childhoods or who felt hurt by their families, playmates, or communities. Even when home is not unpleasant it can feel restrictive, and many of us could not wait to get out of there as part of growing up. Though home does not always feel good, it always feels familiar.

Home, however, is more than a feeling; it is also a specific place (or sometimes more than one place) for every one of us: it may be the place we live now, or the place where we were born, or the place our parents or ancestors came from, or the place where, for better or worse, the presence of relatives and friends makes us feel most as if we belong.

Thinking of home is often accompanied by nostalgia—the absence or loss of loved ones, the remoteness of the homeplace or its physical demolition. Some of us are, for political or economic reasons, cut off from our childhood home—are exiles. And the rest of us can perhaps understand, since we are all "exiles" from our past, our childhood, that universal "home."

Home is usually a certain house, apartment, or room, but it also often means a block or neighborhood, town or city, region, country, or culture.

We are from Elm Street, East Harlem, the North End, or Los Angeles; we identify ourselves as Chicagoans, Floridians, Chicanas, Barbadians; or we may say we are Mexican, Greek, Welsh, or Korean—not necessarily meaning that we ourselves ever lived in another country but that "our people" came from there at some time in the past. When we say we feel at home in Maine, or San Antonio, or Jamaica, or Japan, we mean that something about it feels "right" to us, that the people and their ways seem familiar, or that the landscape, vegetation, or buildings prompt our memories.

Every experience of home—whether positive and based on feelings of pleasure and belonging, or negative and based on feelings of pressure and disappointment—is highly personal and based on specific places and details and very particular, often very private, feelings. Sometimes it is difficult to communicate just what our home was like and how we feel about it to someone who has never been there, especially if that person is from a different family background and grew up with different habits and experiences, or if that person is from another region or another country with different customs. Still, certain kinds of feelings about home—both good and bad—are widely shared across places and cultures, and the particular details of growing up in one place often generate the same feelings as similar experiences in a home halfway across the world or in a different kind of family or culture.

Trying to understand what home is like for someone else can be difficult, but it may give us, for a moment, a sense of what it might be like to be someone different with different expectations from life. Someone else's experience about home can also make us more aware of our own home, and what it means to us, giving us a richer and more exact sense of ourselves, how we live, and what we value. What place we call home—where it is, what it looks like, who is there, and how it makes us feel—tells us a lot about us as people. In literature, as in life, home often becomes a fabric of emotions and an index of values as well as a specific place.

Michael Anthony

O ne of the best-known Caribbean writers, Michael Anthony was born in Trinidad in 1932, and, except for four years in England and two years in Brazil, he has continued to live there. He is the author of many stories about growing up in Trinidad, but considers himself "essentially a novelist"; his most familiar books include *The Games Were Coming* (1963), *Green Days by the River* (1967), *Streets of Conflict* (1976), and *All That Glitters* (1981). Anthony has also written several history books, the most recent of which is *The Golden Quest: The Four Voyages of Christopher Columbus* (1992), the first study of Columbus from a Carribean perspective.

SANDRA STREET

Mr Blades, the new teacher, was delighted with the compositions we wrote about Sandra Street. He read some aloud to the class. He seemed particularly pleased when he read what was written by one of the boys from the other side of the town.

"Sandra Street is dull and uninteresting," the boy wrote. "For one half of its length there are a few houses and a private school (which we go to) but the other half is nothing but a wilderness of big trees." Mr Blades smiled from the corners of his mouth and looked at those of us who belonged to Sandra Street. "In fact," the boy wrote, "*it* is the only street in our town that has big trees, and I do not think it is a part of our town at all because it is so far and so different from our other streets."

The boy went on to speak of the gay attractions on the other side of the town, some of which, he said, Sandra Street could never dream to have. In his street, for instance, there was the savannah where they played football and cricket, but the boys of Sandra Street had to play their cricket in the road. And to the amusement of Mr Blades, who also came from the other side of the town, he described Sandra Street as a silly little girl who ran away to the bushes to hide herself.

Everyone laughed except the few of us from Sandra Street, and I knew what was going to happen when school was dismissed, although Mr Blades said it was all a joke and in fact Sandra Street was very fine. I did not know whether he meant this or not, for he seemed very much amused and I felt this was because he came from the other side of the town.

He read out a few more of the compositions. Some of them said very $_5$ nice things about Sandra Street, but those were the ones written by ourselves. Mr Blades seemed delighted about these, too, and I felt he was trying to appease us when he said that they showed up new aspects of the beauty of Sandra Street. There were only a few of us who were appeased, though, and he noticed this and said all right, next Tuesday we'll write about the other side of the town. This brought fiendish laughter from some of us from Sandra Street, and judging from the looks on the faces of those from the other side of the town, I knew what would happen next Tuesday, too, when school was dismissed. And I felt that whatever happened it wasn't going to make any difference to our side or to the other side of the town.

Yet the boy's composition was very truthful. Sandra Street was so dif- $_6$ ferent from the other streets beyond. Indeed, it came from the very quiet fringes and ran straight up to the forests. As it left the town there were a few houses and shops along it, and then the school, and after that there were not many more houses, and the big trees started from there until the road trailed off to the river that bordered the forests. During the day all would be very quiet except perhaps for the voice of one neighbour calling to another, and if some evenings brought excitement to the schoolyard, these did very little to disturb the calmness of Sandra Street.

Nor did the steel band gently humming from the other side of the town. $_7$ I had to remember the steel band because although I liked to hear it I had to put into my composition that it was very bad. We had no steel bands in Sandra Street, and I thought I could say that this was because we were decent, cultured folk, and did not like the horrible noises of steel bands.

I sat in class recalling the boy's composition again. Outside the window $_8$ I could see the women coming out of the shops. They hardly passed each other without stopping to talk, and this made me laugh. For that was exactly what the boy had written—that they could not pass without stopping to talk, as if they had something to talk about.

I wondered what they talked about. I did not know. What I did know $_9$ was that they never seemed to leave Sandra Street to go into the town. Maybe they were independent of the town! I chuckled a triumphant little chuckle because this, too, would be good to put into my composition next Tuesday.

Dreamingly I gazed out of the window. I noticed how Sandra Street $_{10}$ stood away from the profusion of houses. Indeed, it did not seem to belong to the town at all. It stood off, not proudly, but sadly, as if it wanted peace and rest. I felt all filled up inside. Not because of the town in the distance but because of this strange little road. It was funny, the things the boy had written; he had written in anger what I thought of now in joy. He had spoken of the pleasures and palaces on the other side of the town. He had said why they were his home sweet home. As I looked at Sandra Street, I, too, knew why it was my home sweet home. It was dull and uninteresting to him but it meant so much to me. It was . . .

"Oh!" I started, as the hand rested on my shoulder. $_{11}$

"It's recess," said Mr Blades.

"Oh! . . . yes, sir." The class was surging out to the playground. I didn't seem to have heard a sound before.

Mr Blades looked at me and smiled. "What are you thinking of?" he said.

He seemed to be looking inside me. Inside my very mind. I stammered out a few words which, even if they were clear, would not have meant anything. I stopped. He was still smiling quietly at me. "You are the boy from Sandra Street?" he said.

"Yes, sir."

"I thought so," he said.

What happened on the following Tuesday after school was a lot worse than what had ever happened before, and it was a mystery how the neighbours did not complain or Mr Blades did not get to hear of it. We turned out to school the next morning as if all had been peaceful, and truly, there was no sign of the battle, save the little bruises which were easy to explain away.

We kept getting compositions to write. Mr Blades was always anxious to judge what we wrote but none gave him as much delight as those we had written about Sandra Street. He had said that he knew the other side of the town very well and no one could fool him about that, but if any boy wrote anything about Sandra Street he would have to prove it. And when he had said that, he had looked at me and I was very embarrassed. I had turned my eyes away, and he had said that when the mango season came he would see the boy who didn't speak the truth about Sandra Street.

Since that day I was very shy of Mr Blades, and whenever I saw him walking towards me I turned in another direction. At such times there would always be a faint smile at the corners of his mouth.

I stood looking out of the school window one day thinking about this and about the compositions when again I felt a light touch and jumped.

"Looking out?" Mr Blades said.

"Yes, sir."

He stood there over me and I did not know if he was looking down at me or looking outside, and presently he spoke; "Hot, eh?"

"Yes," I said.

He moved in beside me and we both stood there looking out of the window. It was just about noon and the sun was blazing down on Sandra Street. The houses stood there tall and rather sombre-looking, and there seemed to be no movement about save for the fowls lying in the shadows of the houses. As I watched this a certain sadness came over me and I looked over the houses across to the hills. Suddenly my heart leapt and I turned to Mr Blades, but I changed my mind and did not speak. He had hardly noticed that I looked up at him. I saw his face looking sad as his eyes wandered about the houses. I felt self-conscious as he looked at the houses for they no longer were new and the paint had been washed off them by the rains and they had not been repainted. Then, too, there were no gates and no fences around them as there were in the towns, and sometimes, with a great flurry, a hen would scamper from under one house to another leaving dust behind in the hot sun.

I looked at Mr Blades. He was smiling faintly. He saw me looking at him. "Fowls," he said. 27

"There are no gates," I apologized. 28

"No, there are no gates." And he laughed softly to himself. 29

"Because . . ." I had to stop. I did not know why there were no gates. 30

"Because you did not notice that before." 31

"I noticed that before," I said. 32

Looking sharply at me he raised his brows and said slowly: "You noticed that before. Did you put that in your composition? You are the boy from Sandra Street, are you not?" 33

"There are more from Sandra Street." 34

"Did you notice the cedar grove at the top?" he went on. "You spoke of the steel band at the other side of the town. Did you speak of the river? Did you notice the hills?" 35

"Yes." 36

"Yes?" His voice was now stern and acid. His eyes seemed to be burning up from within. 37

"You noticed all this and you wrote about Sandra Street without mentioning it, eh? How many marks did I give you?" 38

"Forty-five." 39

He looked surprised. "I gave you forty-five for writing about the noises and about the dirty trams of the town? Look!" he pointed, "do you see?" 40

"Mango blossoms," I said, and I felt like crying out: "*I wanted to show it to you!*" 41

"Did you write about it?" 42

"No." I just wanted to break out and run away from him. He bent down to me. His face looked harder now, though kind, but I could see there was fury inside him. 43

"There is something like observation, Steve," he said. "*Observation*. You live in Sandra Street, yet Kenneth writes a composition on your own place better than you." 44

"He said Sandra Street was soppy," I cried. 45

"Of course he said it was soppy. It was to his purpose. He comes from the other side of the town. What's he got to write on—gaudy houses with gates like prisons around them? High walls cramping the imagination? The milling crowd with faces impersonal as stone, hurrying on buses, hurrying off trams? Could he write about that? He said Sandra Street was soppy. Okay, did you prove it wasn't so? Where is your school and his, for instance?" 46

I was a little alarmed. Funny how I did not think of that point before. "Here," I said. "In Sandra Street." 47

"Did you mention that?" 48

Mercifully, as he was talking, the school bell sounded. The fowls, star- 49
tled, ran out into the hot sun across the road. The dust rose, and above the
dust, above the houses, the yellow of mango blossom caught my eye.

"The bell, sir." 50

"Yes, the bell's gone. What's it now—Geography?" 51

"Yes, sir," I said. And as I turned away he was still standing there, 52
looking out into the road.

It was long before any such thing happened again. Though often when 53
it was dry and hot I stood at the window looking out. I watched the freedom
of the fowls among the tall houses, and sometimes the women talked to each
other through the windows and smiled. I noticed, too, the hills, which were
now streaked with the blossoms of the poui, and exultantly I wondered how
many people observed this and knew it was a sign of the rains. None of the
mango blossoms could be seen now, for they had already turned into fruit,
and I knew how profuse they were because I had been to the hills.

I chuckled to myself. *There is something like observation, Steve.* And how I 54
wished Mr Blades would come to the window again so I could tell him what
lay among the mango trees in the hills.

I knew that he was not angry with me. I realized that he was never angry 55
with any boy because of the parts the boy came from. We grew to like him,
for he was very cheerful, though mostly he seemed dreamy and thoughtful.
That is, except at composition time.

He really came to life then. His eyes would gleam as he read our com- 56
positions and whenever he came to a word he did not like he would frown
and say any boy was a sissy to use such a word. And if a composition pleased
him he would praise the boy and be especially cheerful with him and the boy
would be proud and the rest of us would be jealous and hate him.

I was often jealous. Mr Blades had a passion for compositions, and I was 57
anxious to please him to make up for that day at the window. I was anxious
to show him how much I observed and often I noted new things and put
them into my compositions. And whenever I said something wonderful I
knew it because of the way Mr Blades would look at me, and sometimes he
would take me aside and talk to me. But many weeks ran out before we spoke
at the window again.

I did not start this time because I had been expecting him. I had been 58
watching him from the corners of my eyes.

"The sun's coming out again," he said. 59

"It's cloudy," I said. 60

The rains had ceased but there were still great patches of dark cloud in 61
the sky. When the wind blew they moved slowly and cumbersomely, but if
the sun was free of one cloud there would soon be another. The sun was
shining brightly now, although there was still a slight drizzle of rain, and I
could smell the steam rising from the hot pitch and from the galvanized roofs.

"Rain falling sun shining," Mr Blades said. And I remembered that they 62 said at such times the Devil fought his wife, but when Mr Blades pressed me to tell what I was laughing at I laughed still more and would not say. Then thoughtfully he said, "You think they're all right?"

"What, sir?" 63

"In the 'mortelle root." 64

I was astonished. I put my hands to my mouth. How did he know? 65

He smiled down at me: "You won't be able to jump over now." And the 66 whole thing came back. I could not help laughing. I had put into my composition how I had gone into the hills on a Sunday evening, and how the mango trees were laden with small mangoes, some full, and how there were banana trees among the immortelle and poui. I had written, too, about the bunch of green bananas I had placed to ripen in the immortelle roots and how afterwards I had jumped across the river to the other bank.

"They're all right," I said, and I pretended to be watching the steam 67 rising from the hot pitch.

"I like bananas," said Mr Blades. I was sure that he licked his lips as he 68 looked towards the hills.

I was touched. I felt as one with him. I liked bananas, too, and they 69 always made me lick my lips. I thought now of the whole bunch which must be yellow by now inside the immortelle roots.

"Sir . . ." I said to him, hesitating. Then I took the wild chance. And 70 when he answered, a feeling of extreme happiness swept over me.

I remember that evening as turning out bright, almost blinding. The 71 winds had pushed away the heavy clouds, and the only evidence of the rains was the little puddles along Sandra Street. I remember the hills as being strange in an enchanted sort of way, and I felt that part of the enchantment came from Mr Blades being with me. We watched the leaves of the cocoa gleaming with the moisture of the rains, and Mr Blades confessed he never thought there was so much cocoa in the hills. We watched the cyp, too, profuse among the laden mango trees, and the redness of their rain-picked flowers was the redness of blood.

We came to the immortelle tree where I had hidden the bananas. I watched 72 to see if Mr Blades licked his lips but he did not. He wasn't even watching.

"Sir," I said in happy surprise, after removing the covering of trash from 73 the bunch. Mr Blades was gazing across the trees. I raised my eyes. Not far below, Sandra Street swept by, bathed in light.

"The bananas, sir," I said. 74

"*Bananas!*" he cried, despairingly. "Bananas are all you see around you, 75 Steve?"

I was puzzled. I thought it was for bananas that we had come to the 76 hills.

"Good heavens!" he said with bitterness. "To think that you instead of 77 Kenneth should belong to Sandra Street."

STUDY QUESTIONS

1. List all the things we learn about Steve. In what ways does he change as the story develops? How old is he at the time of the episode? Is he the same age when he tells the story? What indications are there in the story for your answer?

2. What functions does Mr. Blades perform for Steve? for the story? In what ways do his attitudes affect your evaluation of what is attractive about Sandra Street? Why is it significant that he lives on the other side of town? How do Steve's perceptions of his teacher change? What does Mr. Blades's memory for the details in Steve's composition suggest about him?

3. According to Kenneth, what are the virtues of his own "home sweet home"? What features of Steve's home, in Sandra Street, are implied in the opening three paragraphs of the story? What do we later learn about the neighborhood that extends our sense of what life is like in Sandra Street?

4. How does the fight after school relate to Steve's feelings about Sandra Street? to the main THEMES* of the story?

5. What details make it clear that the story takes place on a Caribbean island? Besides the fruit and vegetation, what features of the place are important to the story? What customs of the people seem distinctive to the culture on the island? Which customs are crucial to the effects of the story?

6. How do the differences in people's habits—conversations, street customs, the ways their houses are built and their lawns are kept—express the values of the two different cultures in the town? Which side of town do you like better? Which details in the story are most important to making you feel that way?

7. What skills of observation does Steve learn by writing about his street? What does he fail to notice until the end? What does his preoccupation with bananas in the final scene reveal about his limits as an observer?

8. The changing relationship between Steve and Mr. Blades is important to our understanding of Steve, and much of the action involves conversation and interaction between the two. Does the story keep our central attention on Steve and his perceptions of himself or on the teacher? on the relationship between the two or on the boy's understanding of where he came from? What values implicit in Sandra Street are still mysteries to the boy at the end of the story? Do you think the NARRATOR of the story would be as kind to Mr. Blades if the episode described in the story had not happened long ago?

9. What kind of person does the story suggest that Steve turned out to be? What evidence is there in the story itself?

*Words in small capitals are defined in the Glossary.

Amy Tan

Amy Tan was born in Oakland, California, in 1952, just two and a half years after her parents immigrated there from China. She has worked as a consultant to programs for disabled children and as a freelance writer. In 1987 she visited China for the first time—"As soon as my feet touched China, I became Chinese"—and returned to write her first book, *The Joy Luck Club* (1989). Her second novel, *The Kitchen God's Wife*, was published in 1991.

A PAIR OF TICKETS

The minute our train leaves the Hong Kong border and enters Shenzhen, China, I feel different. I can feel the skin on my forehead tingling, my blood rushing through a new course, my bones aching with a familiar old pain. And I think, My mother was right. I am becoming Chinese.   1

"Cannot be helped," my mother said when I was fifteen and had vigorously denied that I had any Chinese whatsoever below my skin. I was a sophomore at Galileo High in San Francisco, and all my Caucasian friends agreed: I was about as Chinese as they were. But my mother had studied at a famous nursing school in Shanghai, and she said she knew all about genetics. So there was no doubt in her mind, whether I agreed or not: Once you are born Chinese, you cannot help but feel and think Chinese.   2

"Someday you will see," said my mother. "It's in your blood, waiting to be let go."   3

And when she said this, I saw myself transforming like a werewolf, a mutant tag of DNA suddenly triggered, replicating itself insidiously into a *syndrome*, a cluster of telltale Chinese behaviors, all those things my mother did to embarrass me—haggling with store owners, picking her mouth with a toothpick in public, being color-blind to the fact that lemon yellow and pale pink are not good combinations for winter clothes.   4

But today I realize I've never really known what it means to be Chinese. I am thirty-six years old. My mother is dead and I am on a train, carrying with me her dreams of coming home. I am going to China.   5

We are going to Guangzhou, my seventy-two-year-old father, Canning Woo, and I, where we will visit his aunt, whom he has not seen since he was   6 ten years old. And I don't know whether it's the prospect of seeing his aunt or if it's because he's back in China, but now he looks like he's a young boy, so innocent and happy I want to button his sweater and pat his head. We are sitting across from each other, separated by a little table with two cold cups of tea. For the first time I can ever remember, my father has tears in his eyes, and all he is seeing out the train window is a sectioned field of yellow, green, and brown, a narrow canal flanking the tracks, low rising hills, and three people in blue jackets riding an ox-driven cart on this early October morning. And I can't help myself. I also have misty eyes, as if I had seen this a long, long time ago, and had almost forgotten.

In less than three hours, we will be in Guangzhou, which my guidebook tells me is how one properly refers to Canton these days. It seems all the cities I have heard of, except Shanghai, have changed their spellings. I think they are saying China has changed in other ways as well. Chungking is Chongqing. And Kweilin is Guilin. I have looked these names up, because after we see my father's aunt in Guangzhou, we will catch a plane to Shanghai, where I will meet my two half-sisters for the first time.

They are my mother's twin daughters from her first marriage, little babies she was forced to abandon on a road as she was fleeing Kweilin for Chungking in 1944. That was all my mother had told me about these daughters, so they had remained babies in my mind, all these years, sitting on the side of a road, listening to bombs whistling in the distance while sucking their patient red thumbs.

And it was only this year that someone found them and wrote with this joyful news. A letter came from Shanghai, addressed to my mother. When I first heard about this, that they were alive, I imagined my identical sisters transforming from little babies into six-year-old girls. In my mind, they were seated next to each other at a table, taking turns with the fountain pen. One would write a neat row of characters: *Dearest Mama. We are alive.* She would brush back her wispy bangs and hand the other sister the pen, and she would write: *Come get us. Please hurry.*

Of course they could not know that my mother had died three months before, suddenly, when a blood vessel in her brain burst. One minute she was talking to my father, complaining about the tenants upstairs, scheming how to evict them under the pretense that relatives from China were moving in. The next minute she was holding her head, her eyes squeezed shut, groping for the sofa, and then crumpling softly to the floor with fluttering hands.

So my father had been the first one to open the letter, a long letter it turned out. And they did call her Mama. They said they always revered her as their true mother. They kept a framed picture of her. They told her about their life, from the time my mother last saw them on the road leaving Kweilin to when they were finally found.

And the letter had broken my father's heart so much—these daughters calling my mother from another life he never knew—that he gave the letter to my mother's old friend Auntie Lindo and asked her to write back and tell my sisters, in the gentlest way possible, that my mother was dead.

But instead Auntie Lindo took the letter to the Joy Luck Club and discussed with Auntie Ying and Auntie An-mei what should be done, because they had known for many years about my mother's search for her twin daughters, her endless hope. Auntie Lindo and the others cried over this double tragedy, of losing my mother three months before, and now again. And so they couldn't help but think of some miracle, some possible way of reviving her from the dead, so my mother could fulfill her dream.

So this is what they wrote to my sisters in Shanghai: "Dearest Daughters, I too have never forgotten you in my memory or in my heart. I never gave up hope that we would see each other again in a joyous reunion. I am only sorry it has been too long. I want to tell you everything about my life since I last saw you. I want to tell you this when our family comes to see you in China. . . ." They signed it with my mother's name.

It wasn't until all this had been done that they first told me about my sisters, the letter they received, the one they wrote back.

"They'll think she's coming, then," I murmured. And I had imagined my sisters now being ten or eleven, jumping up and down, holding hands, their pigtails bouncing, excited that their mother—*their* mother—was coming, whereas my mother was dead.

"How can you say she is not coming in a letter?" said Auntie Lindo. "She is their mother. She is your mother. You must be the one to tell them. All these years, they have been dreaming of her." And I thought she was right.

But then I started dreaming, too, of my mother and my sisters and how it would be if I arrived in Shanghai. All these years, while they waited to be found, I had lived with my mother and then had lost her. I imagined seeing my sisters at the airport. They would be standing on their tiptoes, looking anxiously, scanning from one dark head to another as we got off the plane. And I would recognize them instantly, their faces with the identical worried look.

"*Jyejye, Jyejye*. Sister, Sister. We are here," I saw myself saying in my poor version of Chinese.

"Where is Mama?" they would say, and look around, still smiling, two flushed and eager faces. "Is she hiding?" And this would have been like my mother, to stand behind just a bit, to tease a little and make people's patience pull a little on their hearts. I would shake my head and tell my sisters she was not hiding.

"Oh, that must be Mama, no?" one of my sisters would whisper excitedly, pointing to another small woman completely engulfed in a tower of presents. And that, too, would have been like my mother, to bring mountains of gifts, food, and toys for children—all bought on sale—shunning thanks, saying the gifts were nothing, and later turning the labels over to show my sisters, "Calvin Klein, 100% wool."

I imagined myself starting to say, "Sisters, I am sorry, I have come alone 22
. . ." and before I could tell them—they could see it in my face—they were
wailing, pulling their hair, their lips twisted in pain, as they ran away
from me. And then I saw myself getting back on the plane and coming
home.

After I had dreamed this scene many times—watching their despair turn 23
from horror into anger—I begged Auntie Lindo to write another letter. And
at first she refused.

"How can I say she is dead? I cannot write this," said Auntie Lindo 24
with a stubborn look.

"But it's cruel to have them believe she's coming on the plane," I said. 25
"When they see it's just me, they'll hate me."

"Hate you? Cannot be." She was scowling. "You are their own sister, 26
their only family."

"You don't understand," I protested. 27

"What I don't understand?" she said. 28

And I whispered. "They'll think I'm responsible, that she died because 29
I didn't appreciate her."

And Auntie Lindo looked satisfied and sad at the same time, as if this 30
were true and I had finally realized it. She sat down for an hour, and when
she stood up she handed me a two-page letter. She had tears in her eyes. I
realized that the very thing I had feared, she had done. So even if she had
written the news of my mother's death in English, I wouldn't have had the
heart to read it.

"Thank you," I whispered. 31

The landscape has become gray, filled with low flat cement buildings, 32
old factories, and then tracks and more tracks filled with trains like ours
passing by in the opposite direction. I see platforms crowded with people
wearing drab Western clothes, with spots of bright colors: little children
wearing pink and yellow, red and peach. And there are soldiers in olive green
and red, and old ladies in gray tops and pants that stop mid-calf. We are in
Guangzhou.

Before the train even comes to a stop, people are bringing down their 33
belongings from above their seats. For a moment there is a dangerous shower
of heavy suitcases laden with gifts to relatives, half-broken boxes wrapped in
miles of string to keep the contents from spilling out, plastic bags filled with
yarn and vegetables and packages of dried mushrooms, and camera cases.
And then we are caught in a stream of people rushing, shoving, pushing us
along, until we find ourselves in one of a dozen lines waiting to go through
customs. I feel as if I were getting on a number 30 Stockton bus in San
Francisco. I am in China, I remind myself. And somehow the crowds don't
bother me. It feels right. I start pushing too.

I take out the declaration forms and my passport. "Woo," it says at the 34
top, and below that, "June May," who was born in "California, U.S.A.," in

1951. I wonder if the customs people will question whether I'm the same person as in the passport photo. In this picture, my chin-length hair is swept back and artfully styled. I am wearing false eyelashes, eye shadow, and lip liner. My cheeks are hollowed out by bronze blusher. But I had not expected the heat in October. And now my hair hangs limp with the humidity. I wear no makeup; in Hong Kong my mascara had melted into dark circles and everything else had felt like layers of grease. So today my face is plain, unadorned except for a thin mist of shiny sweat on my forehead and nose.

Even without makeup, I could never pass for true Chinese. I stand five-foot-six, and my head pokes above the crowd so that I am eye level only with other tourists. My mother once told me my height came from my grandfather, who was a northerner, and may have even had some Mongol blood. "This is what your grandmother once told me," explained my mother. "But now it is too late to ask her. They are all dead, your grandparents, your uncles, and their wives and children, all killed in the war, when a bomb fell on our house. So many generations in one instant."

She had said this so matter-of-factly that I thought she had long since gotten over any grief she had. And then I wondered how she knew they were all dead.

"Maybe they left the house before the bomb fell," I suggested.

"No," said my mother. "Our whole family is gone. It is just you and I."

"But how do you know? Some of them could have escaped."

"Cannot be," said my mother, this time almost angrily. And then her frown was washed over by a puzzled blank look, and she began to talk as if she were trying to remember where she had misplaced something. "I went back to that house. I kept looking up to where the house used to be. And it wasn't a house, just the sky. And below, underneath my feet, were four stories of burnt bricks and wood, all the life of our house. Then off to the side I saw things blown into the yard, nothing valuable. There was a bed someone used to sleep in, really just a metal frame twisted up at one corner. And a book, I don't know what kind, because every page had turned black. And I saw a teacup which was unbroken but filled with ashes. And then I found my doll, with her hands and legs broken, her hair burned off. . . . When I was a little girl, I had cried for that doll, seeing it all alone in the store window, and my mother had bought it for me. It was an American doll with yellow hair. It could turn its legs and arms. The eyes moved up and down. And when I married and left my family home, I gave the doll to my youngest niece, because she was like me. She cried if that doll was not with her always. Do you see? If she was in the house with that doll, her parents were there, and so everybody was there, waiting together, because that's how our family was."

The woman in the customs booth stares at my documents, then glances at me briefly, and with two quick movements stamps everything and sternly nods me along. And soon my father and I find ourselves in a large area filled with thousands of people and suitcases. I feel lost and my father looks help-less.

"Excuse me," I say to a man who looks like an American. "Can you tell me where I can get a taxi?" He mumbles something that sounds Swedish or Dutch.

"Syau Yen! Syau Yen!" I hear a piercing voice shout from behind me. An old woman in a yellow knit beret is holding up a pink plastic bag filled with wrapped trinkets. I guess she is trying to sell us something. But my father is staring down at this tiny sparrow of a woman, squinting into her eyes. And then his eyes widen, his face opens up and he smiles like a pleased little boy.

"*Aiyi! Aiyi!*"—Auntie Auntie!—he says softly.

"Syau Yen!" coos my great-aunt. I think it's funny she has just called my father "Little Wild Goose." It must be his baby milk name, the name used to discourage ghosts from stealing children.

They clasp each other's hands—they do not hug—and hold on like this, taking turns saying, "Look at you! You are so old. Look how old you've become!" They are both crying openly, laughing at the same time, and I bite my lip, trying not to cry. I'm afraid to feel their joy. Because I am thinking how different our arrival in Shanghai will be tomorrow, how awkward it will feel.

Now Aiyi beams and points to a Polaroid picture of my father. My father had wisely sent pictures when he wrote and said we were coming. See how smart she was, she seems to intone as she compares the picture to my father. In the letter, my father had said we would call her from the hotel once we arrived, so this is a surprise, that they've come to meet us. I wonder if my sisters will be at the airport.

It is only then that I remember the camera. I had meant to take a picture of my father and his aunt the moment they met. It's not too late.

"Here, stand together over here," I say, holding up the Polaroid. The camera flashes and I hand them the snapshot. Aiyi and my father still stand close together, each of them holding a corner of the picture, watching as their images begin to form. They are almost reverentially quiet. Aiyi is only five years older than my father, which makes her around seventy-seven. But she looks ancient, shrunken, a mummified relic. Her thin hair is pure white, her teeth are brown with decay. So much for stories of Chinese women looking young forever, I think to myself.

Now Aiyi is crooning to me: "*Jandale.*" So big already. She looks up at me, at my full height, and then peers into her pink plastic bag—her gifts to us, I have figured out—as if she is wondering what she will give to me, now that I am so old and big. And then she grabs my elbow with her sharp pincerlike grasp and turns me around. A man and a woman in their fifties are shaking hands with my father, everybody smiling and saying, "Ah! Ah!" They are Aiyi's oldest son and his wife, and standing next to them are four other people, around my age, and a little girl who's around ten. The introductions go by so fast, all I know is that one of them is Aiyi's grandson, with his wife, and the other is her granddaughter, with her husband. And the little girl is Lili, Aiyi's great-granddaughter.

Aiyi and my father speak the Mandarin dialect from their childhood, but the rest of the family speaks only the Cantonese of their village. I understand only Mandarin but can't speak it that well. So Aiyi and my father gossip unrestrained in Mandarin, exchanging news about people from their old village. And they stop only occasionally to talk to the rest of us, sometimes in Cantonese, sometimes in English. 51

"Oh, it is as I suspected," says my father, turning to me. "He died last summer." And I already understood this. I just don't know who this person, Li Gong, is. I feel as if I were in the United Nations and the translators had run amok. 52

"Hello," I say to the little girl. "My name is Jing-mei." But the little girl squirms to look away, causing her parents to laugh with embarrassment. I try to think of Cantonese words I can say to her, stuff I learned from friends in Chinatown, but all I can think of are swear words, terms for bodily functions, and short phrases like "tastes good," "tastes like garbage," and "she's really ugly." And then I have another plan: I hold up the Polaroid camera, beckoning Lili with my finger. She immediately jumps forward, places one hand on her hip in the manner of a fashion model, juts out her chest, and flashes me a toothy smile. As soon as I take the picture she is standing next to me, jumping and giggling every few seconds as she watches herself appear on the greenish film. 53

By the time we hail taxis for the ride to the hotel, Lili is holding tight onto my hand, pulling me along. 54

In the taxi, Aiyi talks nonstop, so I have no chance to ask her about the different sights we are passing by. 55

"You wrote and said you would come only for one day," says Aiyi to my father in an agitated tone. "One day! How can you see your family in one day! Toishan is many hours' drive from Guangzhou. And this idea to call us when you arrive. This is nonsense. We have no telephone." 56

My heart races a little. I wonder if Auntie Lindo told my sisters we would call from the hotel in Shanghai? 57

Aiyi continues to scold my father. "I was so beside myself, ask my son, almost turned heaven and earth upside down trying to think of a way! So we decided the best was for us to take the bus from Toishan and come into Guangzhou—meet you right from the start." 58

And now I am holding my breath as the taxi driver dodges between trucks and buses, honking his horn constantly. We seem to be on some sort of long freeway overpass, like a bridge above the city. I can see row after row of apartments, each floor cluttered with laundry hanging out to dry on the balcony. We pass a public bus, with people jammed in so tight their faces are nearly wedged against the window. Then I see the skyline of what must be downtown Guangzhou. From a distance, it looks like a major American 59 city, with highrises and construction going on everywhere. As we slow down in the more congested part of the city, I see scores of little shops, dark inside, lined with counters and shelves. And then there is a building, its front laced with scaffolding made of bamboo poles held together with plastic strips. Men and women are standing on narrow platforms, scraping the sides, working without safety straps or helmets. Oh, would OSHA[1] have a field day here, I think.

Aiyi's shrill voice rises up again: "So it is a shame you can't see our village, our house. My sons have been quite successful, selling our vegetables in the free market. We had enough these last few years to build a big house, three stories, all of new brick, big enough for our whole family and then some. And every year, the money is even better. You Americans aren't the only ones who know how to get rich!"

The taxi stops and I assume we've arrived, but then I peer out at what looks like a grander version of the Hyatt Regency. "This is communist China?" I wonder out loud. And then I shake my head toward my father. "This must be the wrong hotel." I quickly pull out our itinerary, travel tickets, and reservations. I had explicitly instructed my travel agent to choose something inexpensive, in the thirty-to-forty-dollar range. I'm sure of this. And there it says on our itinerary: Garden Hotel, Huanshi Dong Lu. Well, our travel agent had better be prepared to eat the extra, that's all I have to say.

The hotel is magnificent. A bellboy complete with uniform and sharp-creased cap jumps forward and begins to carry our bags into the lobby. Inside, the hotel looks like an orgy of shopping arcades and restaurants all encased in granite and glass. And rather than be impressed, I am worried about the expense, as well as the appearance it must give Aiyi, that we rich Americans cannot be without our luxuries even for one night.

But when I step up to the reservation desk, ready to haggle over this booking mistake, it is confirmed. Our rooms are prepaid, thirty-four dollars each. I feel sheepish, and Aiyi and the others seem delighted by our temporary surroundings. Lili is looking wide-eyed at an arcade filled with video games.

Our whole family crowds into one elevator, and the bellboy waves, saying he will meet us on the eighteenth floor. As soon as the elevator door shuts, everybody becomes very quiet, and when the door finally opens again, everybody talks at once in what sounds like relieved voices. I have the feeling Aiyi and the others have never been on such a long elevator ride.

Our rooms are next to each other and are identical. The rugs, drapes, bedspreads are all in shades of taupe. There's a color television with remote-control panels built into the lamp table between the two twin beds. The bathroom has marble walls and floors. I find a built-in wet bar with a small refrigerator stocked with Heineken beer, Coke Classic, and Seven-Up, mini-bottles of Johnnie Walker Red, Bacardi rum, and Smirnoff vodka, and pack-

---

1. Occupational Safety and Health Administration.

ets of M & M's, honey-roasted cashews, and Cadbury chocolate bars. And again I say out loud, "This is communist China?"

My father comes into my room. "They decided we should just stay here and visit," he says, shrugging his shoulders. "They say, Less trouble that way. More time to talk." 66

"What about dinner?" I ask. I have been envisioning my first real Chinese feast for many days already, a big banquet with one of those soups steaming out carved winter melon, chicken wrapped in clay, Peking duck, the works. 67

My father walks over and picks up a room service book next to a *Travel & Leisure* magazine. He flips through the pages quickly and then points to the menu. "This is what they want," says my father. 68

So it's decided. We are going to dine tonight in our rooms, with our family, sharing hamburgers, french fries, and apple pie à la mode. 69

Aiyi and her family are browsing the shops while we clean up. After a hot ride on the train, I'm eager for a shower and cooler clothes. 70

The hotel has provided little packets of shampoo which, upon opening, I discover is the consistency and color of hoisin sauce.[2] This is more like it, I think. This is China. And I rub some in my damp hair. 71

Standing in the shower, I realize this is the first time I've been by myself in what seems like days. But instead of feeling relieved, I feel forlorn. I think about what my mother said, about activating my genes and becoming Chinese. And I wonder what she meant. 72

Right after my mother died, I asked myself a lot of things, things that couldn't be answered, to force myself to grieve more. It seemed as if I wanted to sustain my grief, to assure myself that I had cared deeply enough. 73

But now I ask the questions mostly because I want to know the answers. What was that pork stuff she used to make that had the texture of sawdust? What were the names of the uncles who died in Shanghai? What had she dreamt all these years about her other daughters? All the times when she got mad at me, was she really thinking about them? Did she wish I were they? Did she regret that I wasn't? 74

At one o'clock in the morning, I awake to tapping sounds on the window. I must have dozed off and now I feel my body uncramping itself. I'm sitting on the floor, leaning against one of the twin beds. Lili is lying next to me. The others are asleep, too, sprawled out on the beds and floor. Aiyi is seated at a little table, looking very sleepy. And my father is staring out the window, tapping his fingers on the glass. The last time I listened my father was telling Aiyi about his life since he last saw her. How he had gone to Yenching University, later got a post with a newspaper in Chungking, met my mother there, a young widow. How they later fled together to Shanghai to try to find my mother's family house, but there was nothing there. And then they 75

---

2. Sweet brownish-red sauce made from soybeans, flour, sugar, water, spices, garlic, and chili.

traveled eventually to Canton and then to Hong Kong, then Haiphong and finally to San Francisco. . . .

"Suyuan didn't tell me she was trying all these years to find her daughters," he is now saying in a quiet voice. "Naturally, I did not discuss her daughters with her. I thought she was ashamed she had left them behind." 76

"Where did she leave them?" asks Aiyi. "How were they found?" 77

I am wide awake now. Although I have heard parts of this story from my mother's friends. 78

"It happened when the Japanese took over Kweilin," says my father. 79

"Japanese in Kweilin?" says Aiyi. "That was never the case. Couldn't be. The Japanese never came to Kweilin." 80

"Yes, that is what the newspapers reported. I know this because I was working for the news bureau at the time. The Kuomintang[3] often told us what we could say and could not say. But we knew the Japanese had come into Kwangsi Province. We had sources who told us how they had captured the Wuchang-Canton railway. How they were coming overland, making very fast progress, marching toward the provincial capital." 81

Aiyi looks astonished. "If people did not know this, how could Suyuan know the Japanese were coming?" 82

"An officer of the Kuomintang secretly warned her," explains my father. "Suyuan's husband also was an officer and everybody knew that officers and their families would be the first to be killed. So she gathered a few possessions and, in the middle of the night, she picked up her daughters and fled on foot. The babies were not even one year old." 83

"How could she give up those babies!" sighs Aiyi. "Twin girls. We have never had such luck in our family." And then she yawns again. 84

"What were they named?" she asks. I listen carefully. I had been planning on using just the familiar "Sister" to address them both. But now I want to know how to pronounce their names. 85

"They have their father's surname, Wang," says my father. "And their given names are Chwun Yu and Chwun Hwa." 86

"What do the names mean?" I ask. 87

"Ah." My father draws imaginary characters on the window. "One means 'Spring Rain,' the other 'Spring Flower,' " he explains in English, "because they born in the spring, and of course rain come before flower, same order these girls are born. Your mother like a poet, don't you think?" 88

I nod my head. I see Aiyi nod her head forward, too. But it falls forward and stays there. She is breathing deeply, noisily. She is asleep. 89

"And what does Ma's name mean?" I whisper. 90

" 'Suyuan,' " he says, writing more invisible characters on the glass. "The way she write it in Chinese, it mean 'Long-Cherished Wish.' Quite a fancy name, not so ordinary like flower name. See this first character, it means something like 'Forever Never Forgotten.' But there is another way 91

---

3. "National People's Party" led by General Chiang Kai-shek (1887–1975).

to write 'Suyuan.' Sound exactly the same, but the meaning is opposite." His finger creates the brushstrokes of another character. "The first part look the same: 'Never Forgotten.' But the last part add to first part make the whole word mean 'Long-Held Grudge.' Your mother get angry with me, I tell her her name should be Grudge."

My father is looking at me, moist-eyed. "See, I pretty clever, too, hah?"   92

I nod, wishing I could find some way to comfort him. "And what about   93 my name," I ask, "what does 'Jing-mei' mean?"

"Your name also special," he says. I wonder if any name in Chinese is   94 not something special. " 'Jing' like excellent *jing*. Not just good, it's something pure, essential, the best quality. *Jing* is good leftover stuff when you take impurities out of something like gold, or rice, or salt. So what is left— just pure essence. And 'Mei,' this is common *mei*, as in *meimei*, 'younger sister.' "

I think about this. My mother's long-cherished wish. Me, the younger   95 sister who was supposed to be the essence of the others. I feed myself with the old grief, wondering how disappointed my mother must have been. Tiny Aiyi stirs suddenly, her head rolls and then falls back, her mouth opens as if to answer my question. She grunts in her sleep, tucking her body more closely into the chair.

"So why did she abandon those babies on the road?" I need to know,   96 because now I feel abandoned too.

"Long time I wondered this myself," says my father. "But then I read   97 that letter from her daughters in Shanghai now, and I talk to Auntie Lindo, all the others. And then I knew. No shame in what she done. None."

"What happened?"   98

"Your mother running away—" begins my father.   99

"No, tell me in Chinese," I interrupt. "Really, I can understand."   100

He begins to talk, still standing at the window, looking into the night.   101

After fleeing Kweilin, your mother walked for several days trying to find a   102 main road. Her thought was to catch a ride on a truck or wagon, to catch enough rides until she reached Chungking, where her husband was stationed.

She had sewn money and jewelry into the lining of her dress, enough,   103 she thought, to barter rides all the way. If I am lucky, she thought, I will not have to trade the heavy gold bracelet and jade ring. These were things from her mother, your grandmother.

By the third day, she had traded nothing. The roads were filled with   104 people, everybody running and begging for rides from passing trucks. The trucks rushed by, afraid to stop. So your mother found no rides, only the start of dysentery pains in her stomach.

Her shoulders ached from the two babies swinging from scarf slings.   105 Blisters grew on the palms from holding two leather suitcases. And then the blisters burst and began to bleed. After a while, she left the suitcases behind, keeping only the food and a few clothes. And later she also dropped the bags of wheat flour and rice and kept walking like this for many miles, singing songs to her little girls, until she was delirious with pain and fever.

Finally, there was not one more step left in her body. She didn't have the strength to carry those babies any further. She slumped to the ground. She knew she would die of her sickness, or perhaps from thirst, from starvation, or from the Japanese, who she was sure were marching right behind her. [106]

She took the babies out of the slings and sat them on the side of the road, then lay down next to them. You babies are so good, she said, so quiet. They smiled back, reaching their chubby hands for her, wanting to be picked up again. And then she knew she could not bear to watch her babies die with her. [107]

She saw a family with three young children in a cart going by. "Take my babies, I beg you," she cried to them. But they stared back with empty eyes and never stopped. [108]

She saw another person pass and called out again. This time a man turned around, and he had such a terrible expression—your mother said it looked like death itself—she shivered and looked away. [109]

When the road grew quiet, she tore open the lining of her dress, and stuffed jewelry under the shirt of one baby and money under the other. She reached into her pocket and drew out the photos of her family, the picture of her father and mother, the picture of herself and her husband on their wedding day. And she wrote on the back of each the names of the babies and this same message: "Please care for these babies with the money and valuables provided. When it is safe to come, if you bring them to Shanghai, 9 Weichang Lu, the Li family will be glad to give you a generous reward. Li Suyuan and Wang Fuchi." [110]

And then she touched each baby's cheek and told her not to cry. She would go down the road to find them some food and would be back. And without looking back, she walked down the road, stumbling and crying, thinking only of this last hope, that her daughters would be found by a kind-hearted person who would care for them. She would not allow herself to imagine anything else. [111]

She did not remember how far she walked, which direction she went, when she fainted, or how she was found. When she awoke, she was in the back of a bouncing truck with several other sick people, all moaning. And she began to scream, thinking she was now on a journey to Buddhist hell. But the face of an American missionary lady bent over her and smiled, talking to her in a soothing language she did not understand. And yet she could somehow understand. She had been saved for no good reason, and it was now too late to go back and save her babies. [112]

When she arrived in Chungking, she learned her husband had died two weeks before. She told me later she laughed when the officers told her this [113] news, she was so delirious with madness and disease. To come so far, to lose so much and to find nothing.

I met her in a hospital. She was lying on a cot, hardly able to move, her dysentery had drained her so thin. I had come in for my foot, my missing toe, which was cut off by a piece of falling rubble. She was talking to herself, mumbling. 114

"Look at these clothes," she said, and I saw she had on a rather unusual dress for wartime. It was silk satin, quite dirty, but there was no doubt it was a beautiful dress. 115

"Look at this face," she said, and I saw her dusty face and hollow cheeks, her eyes shining black. "Do you see my foolish hope?" 116

"I thought I had lost everything, except these two things," she murmured. "And I wondered which I would lose next. Clothes or hope? Hope or clothes?" 117

"But now, see here, look what is happening," she said, laughing, as if all her prayers had been answered. And she was pulling hair out of her head as easily as one lifts new wheat from wet soil. 118

It was an old peasant woman who found them. "How could I resist?" the peasant woman later told your sisters when they were older. They were still sitting obediently near where your mother had left them, looking like little fairy queens waiting for their sedan to arrive. 119

The woman, Mei Ching, and her husband, Mei Han, lived in a stone cave. There were thousands of hidden caves like that in and around Kweilin so secret that the people remained hidden even after the war ended. The Meis would come out of their cave every few days and forage for food supplies left on the road, and sometimes they would see something that they both agreed was a tragedy to leave behind. So one day they took back to their cave a delicately painted set of rice bowls, another day a little footstool with a velvet cushion and two new wedding blankets. And once, it was your sisters. 120

They were pious people, Muslims, who believed the twin babies were a sign of double luck, and they were sure of this when, later in the evening, they discovered how valuable the babies were. She and her husband had never seen rings and bracelets like those. And while they admired the pictures, knowing the babies came from a good family, neither of them could read or write. It was not until many months later that Mei Ching found someone who could read the writing on the back. By then, she loved these baby girls like her own. 121

In 1952 Mei Han, the husband, died. The twins were already eight years old, and Mei Ching now decided it was time to find your sisters' true family. 122

She showed the girls the picture of their mother and told them they had been born into a great family and she would take them back to see their true mother and grandparents. Mei Ching told them about the reward, but she swore she would refuse it. She loved these girls so much, she only wanted 123 them to have what they were entitled to—a better life, a fine house, educated ways. Maybe the family would let her stay on as the girls' amah. Yes, she was certain they would insist.

Of course, when she found the place at 9 Weichang Lu, in the old French 124 Concession, it was something completely different. It was the site of a factory building, recently constructed, and none of the workers knew what had become of the family whose house had burned down on that spot.

Mei Ching could not have known, of course, that your mother and I, 125 her new husband, had already returned to that same place in 1945 in hopes of finding both her family and her daughters.

Your mother and I stayed in China until 1947. We went to many differ- 126 ent cities—back to Kweilin, to Changsha, as far south as Kunming. She was always looking out of one corner of her eye for twin babies, then little girls. Later we went to Hong Kong, and when we finally left in 1949 for the United States, I think she was even looking for them on the boat. But when we arrived, she no longer talked about them. I thought, At last, they have died in her heart.

When letters could be openly exchanged between China and the United 127 States, she wrote immediately to old friends in Shanghai and Kweilin. I did not know she did this. Auntie Lindo told me. But of course, by then, all the street names had changed. Some people had died, others had moved away. So it took many years to find a contact. And when she did find an old schoolmate's address and wrote asking her to look for her daughters, her friend wrote back and said this was impossible, like looking for a needle on the bottom of the ocean. How did she know her daughters were in Shanghai and not somewhere else in China? The friend, of course, did not ask, How do you know your daughters are still alive?

So her schoolmate did not look. Finding babies lost during the war was 128 a matter of foolish imagination, and she had no time for that.

But every year, your mother wrote to different people. And this last 129 year, I think she got a big idea in her head, to go to China and find them herself. I remember she told me, "Canning, we should go, before it is too late, before we are too old." And I told her we were already too old, it was already too late.

I just thought she wanted to be a tourist! I didn't know she wanted to 130 go and look for her daughters. So when I said it was too late, that must have put a terrible thought in her head that her daughters might be dead. And I think this possibility grew bigger and bigger in her head, until it killed her.

Maybe it was your mother's dead spirit who guided her Shanghai 131 schoolmate to find her daughters. Because after your mother died, the schoolmate saw your sisters, by chance, while shopping for shoes at the Number One Department Store on Nanjing Dong Road. She said it was like a dream, seeing these two women who looked so much alike, moving down the stairs together. There was something about their facial expressions that reminded the schoolmate of your mother.

She quickly walked over to them and called their names, which of course, they did not recognize at first, because Mei Ching had changed their names. But your mother's friend was so sure, she persisted. "Are you not Wang Chwun Yu and Wang Chwun Hwa?" she asked them. And then these double-image women became very excited, because they remembered the names written on the back of an old photo, a photo of a young man and woman they still honored, as their much-loved first parents, who had died and become spirit ghosts still roaming the earth looking for them.

At the airport, I am exhausted. I could not sleep last night. Aiyi had followed me into my room at three in the morning, and she instantly fell asleep on one of the twin beds, snoring with the might of a lumberjack. I lay awake thinking about my mother's story, realizing how much I have never known about her, grieving that my sisters and I had both lost her.

And now at the airport, after shaking hands with everybody, waving good-bye, I think about all the different ways we leave people in this world. Cheerily waving good-bye to some at airports, knowing we'll never see each other again. Leaving others on the side of the road, hoping that we will. Finding my mother in my father's story and saying good-bye before I have a chance to know her better.

Aiyi smiles at me as we wait for our gate to be called. She is so old. I put one arm around her and one arm around Lili. They are the same size, it seems. And then it's time. As we wave good-bye one more time and enter the waiting area, I get the sense I am going from one funeral to another. In my hand I'm clutching a pair of tickets to Shanghai. In two hours we'll be there.

The plane takes off. I close my eyes. How can I describe to them in my broken Chinese about our mother's life? Where should I begin?

"Wake up, we're here," says my father. And I awake with my heart pounding in my throat. I look out the window and we're already on the runway. It's gray outside.

And now I'm walking down the steps of the plane, onto the tarmac and toward the building. If only, I think, if only my mother had lived long enough to be the one walking toward them. I am so nervous I cannot feel my feet. I am just moving somehow.

Somebody shouts, "She's arrived!" And then I see her. Her short hair. Her small body. And that same look on her face. She has the back of her hand pressed hard against her mouth. She is crying as though she had gone through a terrible ordeal and were happy it is over.

And I know it's not my mother, yet it is the same look she had when I was five and had disappeared all afternoon, for such a long time, that she was convinced I was dead. And when I miraculously appeared, sleepy-eyed, crawling from underneath my bed, she wept and laughed, biting the back of her hand to make sure it was true.

And now I see her again, two of her, waving, and in one hand there is   141
a photo, the Polaroid I sent them. As soon as I get beyond the gate, we run toward each other, all three of us embracing, all hesitations and expectations forgotten.

"Mama, Mama," we all murmur, as if she is among us.   142

My sisters look at me, proudly. "*Meimei jandale*," says one sister proudly   143
to the other. "Little Sister has grown up." I look at their faces again and I see no trace of my mother in them. Yet they still look familiar. And now I also see what part of me is Chinese. It is so obvious. It is my family. It is in our blood. After all these years, it can finally be let go.

My sisters and I stand, arms around each other, laughing and wiping   144
the tears from each other's eyes. The flash of the Polaroid goes off and my father hands me the snapshot. My sisters and I watch quietly together, eager to see what develops.

The gray-green surface changes to the bright colors of our three images,   145
sharpening and deepening all at once. And although we don't speak, I know we all see it: Together we look like our mother. Her same eyes, her same mouth, open in surprise to see, at last, her long-cherished wish.

STUDY QUESTIONS

1. How do the NARRATOR's names—Jing-mei and June May—relate to the SETTING? to the THEME? Why does the story begin not in the United States or China but in Hong Kong? June May literally returns to her "mother land"; how is this element of the story modified by the fact that all the Chinese place-names have been changed since her mother left China? How does the setting of Mr. Woo's story of her mother's escape from Kweilin relate to the various uses of settings in the story?

2. What is the relationship of the time of action in paragraphs 1 and 2? What other time shifts are there in the story? Can you explain why time is handled as it is in the story? What relationship does it have to the theme? to the raising and modifying of our EXPECTATIONS? What is the time setting in Mr. Woo's story of how June May's sisters were abandoned? What is the historical background of that incident? How much of it did you know before you read the story? How much have you learned since? What misconceptions did you have of that historical setting? How is history related to June May's failure to understand her mother? How does learning her mother's story change her understanding of her relationship to her mother?

3. How are the relationships between "blood," place, family, and identity defined in the story? Explain the final sentence of paragraph 143: "After all these years, it can finally be let go."

Richard Dokey

A native of Stockton, California, and a graduate of the University of California, Berkeley, Richard Dokey has worked as a laborer on a railroad, in a shipyard, for a soft drink bottling company, and for an ink factory, but he now teaches philosophy at San Joachin Delta Community College in Stockton, California. His works include *August Heat* (1982), *Funeral: A Play* (1982), and *Sánchez and Other Stories* (1981). His novel, *The Adidas Kid*, was published in 1993.

SÁNCHEZ

That summer the son of Juan Sánchez went to work for the Flotill Cannery in Stockton. Juan drove with him to the valley in the old Ford. 1

While they drove, the boy, whose name was Jesús, told him of the greatness of the cannery, of the great aluminum buildings, the marvelous machines, and the belts of cans that never stopped running. He told him of the building on one side of the road where the cans were made and how the cans ran in a metal tube across the road to the cannery. He described the food machines, the sanitary precautions. He laughed when he spoke of the labeling. His voice was serious about the money. 2

When they got to Stockton, Jesús directed him to the central district of town, the skid row where the boy was to live while he worked for the Flotill. It was a cheap hotel on Center Street. The room smelled. There was a table with one chair. The floor was stained like the floor of a public urinal and the bed was soiled, as were the walls. There were no drapes on the windows. A pall spread out from the single light bulb overhead that was worked with a length of grimy string. 3

"I will not stay much in the room," Jesús said, seeing his father's face. "It is only for sleep. I will be working overtime, too. There is also the entertainment." 4

Jesús led him from the room and they went out into the street. Next to the hotel there was a vacant lot where a building had stood. The hole which was left had that recent, peculiar look of uprootedness. There were the remains of the foundation, the broken flooring, and the cracked bricks of tired red to which the gray blotches of mortar clung like dried phlegm. But the ground 5 had not yet taken on the opaqueness of wear that the air and sun give it. It gleamed dully in the light and held to itself where it had been torn, as earth does behind a plow. Juan studied the hole for a time; then they walked up Center Street to Main, passing other empty lots, and then moved east toward Hunter Street. At the corner of Hunter and Main a wrecking crew was at work. An iron ball was suspended from the end of a cable and a tall machine swung the ball up and back and then whipped it forward against the building. The ball was very thick-looking, and when it struck the wall the building trembled, spurted dust, and seemed to cringe inward. The vertical lines of the building had gone awry. Juan shook each time the iron struck the wall.

"They are tearing down the old buildings," Jesús explained. "Redevelopment," he pronounced. "Even my building is to go someday." 6

Juan looked at his son. "And what of the men?" he asked. "Where do the men go when there are no buildings?" 7

Jesús, who was a head taller than his father, looked down at him and then shrugged in that Mexican way, the head descending and cocking while the shoulders rise as though on puppet strings. "¿*Quien sabe?*"[1] 8

"And the large building there?" Juan said, looking across the rows of parked cars in Hunter Square. "The one whose roof rubs the sky. Of what significance?" 9

"That is the new courthouse," Jesús said. 10

"There are no curtains on the windows." 11

"They do not put curtains on such windows," Jesús explained. 12

"No," sighed Juan, "that is true." 13

They walked north on Hunter past the new Bank of America and entered an old building. They stood to one side of the entrance. Jesús smiled proudly and inhaled the stale air. 14

"This is the entertainment," he said. 15

Juan looked about. A bar was at his immediate left, and a bald man in a soiled apron stood behind it. Beyond the bar there were many thick-wooded tables covered with green material. Men crouched over them and cone-shaped lights hung low from the ceiling casting broad cones of light downward upon the men and tables. Smoke drifted and rolled in the light and pursued the men when they moved quickly. There was the breaking noise of balls striking together, the hard wooden rattle of the cues in the racks upon the wall, the humming slither of the scoring disks along the loose wires overhead, the explosive cursing of the men. The room was warm and dirty. Juan shook his head. 16

"I have become proficient at the game," Jesús said. 17

"This is the entertainment," Juan said, still moving his head. 18

Jesús turned and walked outside. Juan followed. The boy pointed across the parked cars past the courthouse to a marquee on Main Street. "There are also motion pictures," Jesús said. 19

1. Who knows?

Juan had seen a movie as a young man working in the fields near Fresno. He had understood no English then. He sat with his friends in the leather seats that had gum under the arms and watched the images move upon the white canvas. The images were dressed in expensive clothes. There was laughing and dancing. One of the men did kissing with two very beautiful women, taking turns with each when the other was absent. This had embarrassed Juan, the embracing and unhesitating submission of the women with so many unfamiliar people to watch. Juan loved his wife, was very tender and gentle with her before she died. He never went to another motion picture, even after he had learned English, and this kept him from the Spanish films as well. 20

"We will go to the cannery now," Jesús said, taking his father's arm. "I will show you the machines." 21

Juan permitted himself to be led away, and they moved back past the bank to where the men were destroying the building. A ragged hole, like a wound, had been opened in the wall. Juan stopped and watched. The iron ball came forward tearing at the hole, enlarging it, exposing the empty interior space that had once been a room. The floor of the room teetered at a precarious angle. The wood was splintered and very dry in the noon light. 22

"I do not think I will go to the cannery," Juan said. 23

The boy looked at his father like a child who has made a toy out of string and bottle caps only to have it ignored. 24

"But it is honorable work," Jesús said, suspecting his father. "And it pays well." 25

"Honor," Juan said. "Honor is a serious matter. It is not a question of honor. You are a man now. All that is needed is a room and a job at the Flotill. Your father is tired, that is all." 26

"You are disappointed," Jesús said, hanging his head. 27

"No," Juan said. "I am beyond disappointment. You are my son. Now you have a place in the world. You have the Flotill." 28

Nothing more was said, and they walked to the car. Juan got in behind the wheel. Jesús stood beside the door, his arms at his sides, the fingers spread. Juan looked up at him. The boy's eyes were big. 29

"You are my son," Juan said, "and I love you. Do not have disappointment. I am not of the Flotill. Seeing the machines would make it worse. You understand, niño?"[2] 30

"Sí, Papa," Jesús said. He put a hand on his father's shoulder. 31

"It is a strange world, niñito," Juan said. 32

"I will earn money. I will buy a red car and visit you. All in Twin Pines will be envious of the son of Sánchez, and they will say that Juan Sánchez has a son of purpose." 33

"Of course, Jesús mío," Juan said. He bent and placed his lips against the boy's hand. "I will look for the bright car. I will write regardless." He 34

2. Son. *Niñito:* dear son. *Querido:* dear one.

smiled, showing yellowed teeth. "Goodbye, *querido*," he said. He started the car, raced the engine once too high, and drove off up the street.

When Juan Sánchez returned to Twin Pines, he drove the old Ford to the top of Bear Mountain and pushed it over. He then proceeded systematically to burn all that was of importance to him, all that was of nostalgic value, and all else that meant nothing in itself, like the extra chest of drawers he had kept after his wife's death, the small table in the bedroom, and the faded mahogany stand in which he kept his pipe and tobacco and which sat next to the stuffed chair in the front room. He broke all the dishes, cups, plates, discarded all the cooking and eating utensils in the same way. The fire rose in the blue wind carrying dust wafers of ash in quick, breathless spirals and then released them in a panoply of diluted smoke, from which they drifted and spun and fell like burnt snow. The forks, knives, and spoons became very black with a flaky crust of oxidized metal. Then Juan burned his clothing, all that was unnecessary, and the smoke dampened and took on a thick smell. Finally he threw his wife's rosary into the flames. It was a cheap one, made of wood, and disappeared immediately. He went into his room then and lay down on the bed. He went to sleep.

When he woke, it was dark and cool. He stepped outside, urinated, and then returned, shutting the door. The darkness was like a mammoth held breath, and he felt very awake listening to the beating of his heart. He would not be able to sleep now, and so he lay awake thinking.

He thought of his village in Mexico, the baked white clay of the small houses spread like little forts against the stillness of the bare mountains, the men with their great wide hats, their wide, white pants, and their naked, brown-skinned feet, splayed against the fine dust of the road. He saw the village cistern and the women all so big and slow, always with child, enervated by the earth and the unbearable sun, the enervation passing into their very wombs like the acceptance, slow, silent blood. The men walked bent as though carrying the air or sky, slept against the buildings in the shade like old dogs, ate dry, hot food that dried them inside and seemed to bake the moisture from the flesh, so that the men and women while still young had faces like eroded fields and fingers like stringy, empty stream beds. It was a hard land. It took the life of his father and mother before he was twelve and the life of his aunt, with whom he then lived, before he was sixteen.

When he was seventeen he went to Mexicali because he had heard much of America and the money to be obtained there. They took him in a truck with other men to work in the fields around Bakersfield, then in the fields near Fresno. On his return to Mexicali he met La Belleza, as he came to call her: loveliness. He married her when he was nineteen and she only fifteen. The following year she had a baby girl. It was stillborn and the birth almost killed her, for the doctor said the passage was oversmall. The doctor cautioned him (warned him, really) La Belleza could not have children and live, and he went outside into the moonlight and wept.

He had heard much of the liveliness of the Sierra Nevada above what was called the Mother Lode, and because he feared the land, believed almost that it possessed the power to kill him—as it had killed his mother and father, his aunt, was, in fact, slow killing so many of his people—he wanted to run away from it to the high white cold of the California mountains, where he believed his heart would grow, his blood run and, perhaps, the passage of La Belleza might open. Two years later he was taken in the trucks to Stockton in the San Joaquin Valley to pick tomatoes, and he saw the Sierra Nevada above the Mother Lode.

It was from a distance, of course, and in the summer, so that there was no snow. But when he returned he told La Belleza about the blueness of the mountains in the warm, still dawn, the extension of them, the aristocracy of their unmoving height, and that they were only fifty miles away from where he had stood.

He worked very hard now and saved his money. He took La Belleza back to his village, where he owned the white clay house of his father. It was cheaper to live there while he waited, fearing the sun, the dust, and the dry, airless silence, for the money to accumulate. That fall La Belleza became pregnant again by an accident of passion and the pregnancy was very difficult. In the fifth month the doctor—who was an atheist—said that the baby would have to be taken or else the mother would die. The village priest, a very loud, dramatic man—an educated man who took pleasure in striking a pose—proclaimed the wrath of God in the face of such sacrilege. It was the child who must live, the priest cried. The pregnancy must go on. There was the immortal soul of the child to consider. But Juan decided for the atheist doctor, who did take the child. La Belleza lost much blood. At one point her heart had stopped beating. When the child was torn from its mother and Juan saw that it was a boy, he ran out of the clay house of his father and up the dusty road straight into a hideous red moon. He cursed the earth, the sky. He cursed his village, himself, the soulless indifference of the burnt mountains. He cursed God.

Juan was very afraid now, and though it cost more money, he had himself tied by the atheist doctor so that he could never again put the life of La Belleza in danger, for the next time, he knew with certainty, would kill her.

The following summer he went again on the trucks to the San Joaquin Valley. The mountains were still there, high and blue in the quiet dawn, turned to a milky pastel by the heat swirls and haze of midday. Sometimes at night he stepped outside the shacks in which the men were housed and faced the darkness. It was tragic to be so close to what you wanted, he would think, and be unable to possess it. So strong was the feeling in him, particularly during the hot, windless evenings, that he sometimes went with the other men into Stockton, where he stood on the street corners of skid row and talked, though he did not get drunk on cheap wine or go to the whores, as did the other men. Nor did he fight.

They rode in old tilted trucks covered with canvas and sat on rude benches staring out over the slats of the tail gate. The white glare of headlights crawled up and lay upon them, waiting to pass. They stared over the whiteness. When the lights swept out and by, the glass of the side windows shone. Behind the windows sometimes there would be the ghost flash of an upturned face, before the darkness clamped shut. Also, if one of the men had a relative who lived in the area, there was the opportunity to ride in a car.

He had done so once. He had watched the headlights of the car pale, 45 then whiten the back of one of the trucks. He saw the faces of the men turned outward and the looks on the faces that seemed to float upon the whiteness of the light. The men sat forward, arms on knees, and looked over the glare into the darkness. After that he always rode in the trucks.

When he returned to his village after that season's harvest, he knew they 46 could wait no longer. He purchased a dress of silk for La Belleza and in a secondhand store bought an American suit for himself. He had worked hard, sold his father's house, saved all his money, and on a bright day in early September they crossed the border at Mexicali and caught the Greyhound for Fresno.

Juan got up from his bed to go outside. He stood looking up at the stars. 47 The stars were pinned to the darkness, uttering little flickering cries of light, and as always he was moved by the nearness and profusion of their agony. His mother had told him the stars were a kind of purgatory in which souls burned in cold, silent repentance. He had wondered after her death if the earth too were not a star burning in loneliness, and he could never look at them later without thinking this and believing that the earth must be the brightest of all stars. He walked over to the remains of the fire. A dull heat came from the ashes and a column of limp smoke rose and then bent against the night wind. He studied the ashes for a time and then looked over the tall pine shapes to the southern sky. It was there all right. He could feel the dry char of its heat, that deeper, dryer burning. He imagined it, of course. But it was there nevertheless. He went back into the cabin and lay down, but now his thoughts were only of La Belleza and the beautiful Sierra Nevada.

From Fresno all the way up the long valley to Stockton they had been 48 full with pride and expectation. They had purchased oranges and chocolate bars and they ate them laughing. The other people on the bus looked at them, shook their heads, and slept or read magazines. He and La Belleza gazed out the window at the land.

In Stockton they were helped by a man named Eugenio Mendez. Juan 49 had met him while picking tomatoes in the delta. Eugenio had eight children and a very fat but very kind and tolerant wife named Anilla. He had helped them find a cheap room off Center Street, where they stayed while determining their next course of action. Eugenio had access to a car, and it was he who drove them finally to the mountains.

It was a day like no other day in his life: to be sitting in the car with La 50 Belleza, to be in this moving car with his Belleza heading straight toward the high, lovely mountains. The car traveled from the flatness of the valley into the rolling brown swells of the foothills, where hundreds of deciduous and evergreen oaks grew, their puffball shapes like still pictures of exploding holiday rockets, only green, but spreading up and out and then around and down in nearly perfect canopies. At Jackson the road turned and began an immediate, constant climb upward.

It was as though his dream about it had materialized. He had never seen so many trees, great with dignity: pines that had gray bark twisted and stringy like hemp; others whose bark resembled dry, flat ginger cookies fastened with black glue about a drum, and others whose bark pulled easily away; and those called redwoods, standing stiff and tall, amber-hued with straight rolls of bark as thick as his fist, flinging out high above great arms of green. And the earth, rich red, as though the blood of scores of Indians had just flowed there and dried. Dark patches of shadow stunned with light, blue flowers, orange flowers, birds, even deer. They saw them all on that first day.

"¿*A dónde vamos?*" Eugenio had asked. "Where are we going?"

"*Bellísima,*" Juan replied. "Into much loveliness."

They did not reach Twin Pines that day. But on their return a week later they inquired in Jackson about the opportunity of buying land or a house in the mountains. The man, though surprised, told them of the sawmill town of Twin Pines, where there were houses for sale.

Their continued luck on that day precipitated the feeling in Juan that it was indeed the materialization of a dream. He had been able in all those years to save two thousand dollars, and a man had a small shack for sale at the far edge of town. He looked carefully at Juan, at La Belleza and Eugenio and said "One thousand dollars," believing they could never begin to possess such a sum. When Juan handed him the money, the man was so struck that he made out a bill of sale. Juan Sanchez and his wife had their home in the Sierra.

When Juan saw the cabin close up, he knew the man had stolen their money. It was small, the roof slanted to one side, the door would not close evenly. The cabin was gradually falling downhill. But it was theirs and he could, with work, repair it. Hurriedly they drove back to Jackson, rented a truck, bought some cheap furniture and hauled it back to the cabin. When they had moved in, Juan brought forth a bottle of whiskey and for the first time in his life proceeded to get truly drunk.

Juan was very happy with La Belleza. She accepted his philosophy completely, understood his need, made it her own. In spite of the people of the town, they created a peculiar kind of joy. And anyway Juan had knowledge about the people.

Twin Pines had been founded, he learned, by one Benjamin Carter, who lived with his daughter in a magnificent house on the hill overlooking town. This Benjamin Carter was a very wealthy man. He had come to the mountains thirty years before to save his marriage, for he had been poor once and loved when he was poor, but then he grew very rich because of oil discovered on his father's Ohio farm and he went away to the city and became incapable of love in the pursuit of money and power. When he at last married the woman whom he had loved, a barrier had grown between them, for Ben Carter had changed but the woman had not. Then the woman became ill and Ben Carter promised her he would take her West, all the way West away from the city so that it could be as it had been in the beginning of their love. But the woman was with child. And so Ben Carter rushed to the California mountains, bought a thousand acres of land, and hurried to build his house before the rain and snows came. He hired many men and the house was completed, except for the interior work and the furnishings. All that winter men he had hired worked in the snow to finish the house while Ben Carter waited with his wife in the city. When it was early spring they set out for California, Ben Carter, his wife, and the doctor, who strongly advised against the rough train trip and the still rougher climb by horse and wagon from Jackson to the house. But the woman wanted the child born properly, so they went. The baby came the evening of their arrival at the house, and the woman died all night having it. It was this Ben Carter who lived with that daughter now in the great house on the hill, possessing her to the point, it was said about his madness, that he had murdered a young man who had shown interest in her.

Juan learned all this from a Mexican servant who had worked at the great house from the beginning, and when he told the story to La Belleza she wept because of its sadness. It was a tragedy of love, she explained, and Juan—soaring to the heights of his imagination—believed that the town, all one hundred souls, had somehow been infected with the tragedy, as they were touched by the shadow of the house itself, which crept directly up the highway each night when the sun set. This was why they left dead chickens and fish on the porch of the cabin or dumped garbage into the yard. He believed he understood something profound and so did nothing about these incidents, which, after all, might have been the pranks of boys. He did not want the infection to touch him, nor the deeper infection of their prejudice because he was Mexican. He was not indifferent. He was simply too much in love with La Belleza and the Sierra Nevada. Finally the incidents stopped.

Now the life of Juan Sánchez entered its most beautiful time. When the first snows fell he became delirious, running through the pines, shouting, rolling on the ground, catching the flakes in his open mouth, bringing them in his cupped hands to rub in the hair of La Belleza, who stood in the doorway of their cabin laughing at him. He danced, made up a song about snowflakes falling on a desert and then a prayer which he addressed to the Virgin of Snowflakes. That night while the snow fluttered like wings against the bedroom window, he celebrated the coming of the whiteness with La Belleza.

He understood that first year in the mountains that love was an enlargement of himself, that it enabled him to be somehow more than he had ever been before, as though certain pores of his senses had only just been opened. Whereas before he had desired the Sierra Nevada for its beauty and contrast to his harsh fatherland, now he came to acquire a love for it, and he loved it as he loved La Belleza; he loved it as a woman. Also in that year he came to realize that there was a fear or dread about such love. It was more a feeling than anything else, something which reached thought now and then, particularly in those last moments before sleep. It was an absolutely minor thing. The primary knowledge was of the manner in which this love seemed to assimilate everything, rejecting all that would not yield. This love was a kind of blindness.

That summer Juan left La Belleza at times to pick the crops of the San Joaquin Valley. He had become good friends with the servant of the big house and this man had access to the owner's car, which he always drove down the mountain in a reckless but confident manner. After that summer Juan planned also to buy a car, not out of material desire, but simply because he believed this man would one day kill himself, and also because he did not wish to be dependent.

He worked in the walnuts near the town of Linden and again in the tomatoes of the rich delta. He wanted very much to have La Belleza with him, but that would have meant more money and a hotel room in the skid row, and that was impossible because of the pimps and whores, the drunks and criminals and the general despair, which the police always tapped at periodic intervals, as one does a vat of fermenting wine. The skid row was a place his love could not assimilate, but he could not ignore it because so many of his people were lost there. He stayed in the labor camps, which were also bad because of what the men did with themselves, but they were tolerable. He worked hard and as often as he could and gazed at the mountains, which he could always see clearly in the morning light. When tomato season was over he returned to La Belleza.

Though the town would never accept them as equals, it came that summer to tolerate their presence. La Belleza made straw baskets which she sold to the townspeople and which were desired for their beauty and intricacy of design. Juan carved animals, a skill he had acquired from his father, and these were also sold. The activity succeeded so well that Juan took a box of these things to Jackson, where they were readily purchased. The following spring he was able to buy the Ford.

Juan acquired another understanding that second year in the mountains. It was, he believed, that love, his love, was the single greatness of which he was capable, the thing which ennobled him and gave him honor. Love, he became convinced, was his only ability, the one success he had accomplished in a world of insignificance. It was a simple thing, after all, made so painfully simple each time he went to the valley to work with his face toward the ground, every time he saw the men in the fields and listened to their talk and watched them drive off to the skid row at night. After he had acquired this knowledge, the nights he had to spend away from La Belleza were occupied by a new kind of loneliness, as though a part of his body had been separated from the whole. He began also to understand something more of the fear or dread that seemed to trail behind love.

It happened late in the sixth year of their marriage. It was impossible, 66
of course, and he spent many hours at the fire in their cabin telling La Belleza
of the impossibility, for the doctor had assured him that all had been well
tied. He had conducted himself on the basis of that assumption. But doctors
can be wrong. Doctors can make mistakes. La Belleza was with child.

For the first five months the pregnancy was not difficult, and he came 67
almost to believe that indeed the passage of La Belleza would open. He prayed
to God. He prayed to the earth and sky. He prayed to the soul of his mother.
But after the fifth month the true sickness began and he discarded prayer
completely in favor of blasphemy. There was no God and never could be
God in the face of such sickness, such unbelievable human sickness. Even
when he had her removed to the hospital in Stockton, the doctors could not
stop it, but it continued so terribly that he believed that La Belleza carried
sickness itself in her womb.

After seven months the doctors decided to take the child. They brought 68
La Belleza into a room with lights and instruments. They worked on her for
a long time and she died there under the lights with the doctors cursing and
perspiring above the large wound of her pain. They did not tell him of the
child, which they had cleaned and placed in an incubator, until the next day.
That night he sat in the Ford and tried to see it all, but he could only remember the eyes of La Belleza in the vortex of pain. They were of an almost eerie
calmness. They had possessed calmness, as one possesses the truth. Toward
morning he slumped sideways on the seat and went to sleep.

So he put her body away in the red earth of the town cemetery beyond 69
the cabin. The pines came together overhead and in the heat of midday a
shadow sprinkled with spires of light lay upon the ground so that the earth
was cool and clean to smell. He did not even think of taking her back to
Mexico, since, from the very beginning she had always been part of that
dream he had dreamed. Now she would be always in the Sierra Nevada,
with the orange and blue flowers, the quiet, deep whiteness of winter, and
all that he ever was or could be was with her.

But he did not think these last thoughts then, as he did now. He had 70
simply performed them out of instinct for their necessity, as he had performed the years of labor while waiting for the infant Jesús to grow to manhood. Jesús. Why had he named the boy Jesús? That, perhaps, had been
instinct too. He had stayed after La Belleza's death for the boy, to be with
him until manhood, to show him the loveliness of the Sierra Nevada, to
instruct him toward true manhood. But Jesús. Ah, Jesús. Jesús the American. Jesús of the Flotill. Jesús understood nothing. Jesús, he believed, was
forever lost to knowledge. That day with Jesús had been his own liberation.

For a truth had come upon him after the years of waiting, the ultimate 71
truth that he understood only because La Belleza had passed through his life.
Love was beauty, La Belleza and the Sierra Nevada, a kind of created or
made thing. But there was another kind of love, a very profound, embracing
love that he had felt of late blowing across the mountains from the south and

that, he knew now, had always been there from the beginning of his life, disguised in the sun and wind. In this love there was blood and earth and, yes, even God, some kind of god, at least the power of a god. This love wanted him for its own. He understood it, that it had permitted him to have La Belleza and that without it there could have been no Belleza.

Juan placed an arm over his eyes and turned to face the wall. The old 72 bed sighed. An image went off in his head and he remembered vividly the lovely body of La Belleza. In that instant the sound that loving had produced with the bed was alive in him like a forgotten melody, and his body seemed to swell and press against the ceiling. It was particularly cruel because it was so sudden, so intense, and came from so deep within him that he knew it must all still be alive somewhere, and that was the cruelest part of all. He wept softly and held the arm across his eyes.

In the dark morning the people of the town were awakened by the blaze 73 of fire that was the house of Juan Sánchez. Believing that he had perished in the flames, several of the townspeople placed a marker next to the grave of his wife with his name on it. But, of course, on that score they were mistaken. Juan Sánchez had simply gone home.

STUDY QUESTIONS

1. In two or three words each, describe the central district of Stockton and the "entertainment." How does it appear to Juan? to Jesús? to you?

2. Why does Juan refuse to visit the cannery? What does he mean by his being "beyond disappointment"?

3. Why did Juan, years earlier, want to leave his native village in Mexico? Why did he choose the Sierra Nevada above Stockton as his new home?

4. Why does the man offer to sell Juan a cabin for a thousand dollars? What does the clause "the man was so struck that he made out a bill of sale" (paragraph 55) imply about the man's ATTITUDE toward Juan?

5. What might be the reason—if there is one—for the brief history of Ben Carter in the middle of this story?

6. "Jesús. Why had he named the boy Jesús? That, perhaps, had been instinct too" (paragraph 70). Why *had* he named the boy Jesús? Is this blasphemy? What is meant here by his "instinct"?

7. Sánchez has been unable to instruct Jesús in "true manhood. . . . Jesús, he believed, was forever lost to knowledge. That day with Jesús had been his own liberation" (paragraph 70). Explain.

8. What is the "other kind of love" that Juan discovers?

9. "Believing that he had perished in the flames, several of the townspeople placed a

marker next to the grave of his wife with his name on it. But, of course, on that score they were mistaken. Juan Sánchez had simply gone home" (paragraph 73). Explain.

Vanessa Howard

Vanessa Howard wrote this poem in the sixties, when she was a teenager growing up in New York.

ESCAPE THE GHETTOS OF NEW YORK

escaping the ghettos of New York
they trip
off they go into a paradise of
LSD, heroin, pot and speed
fantasy   5
the ecstasy of drugs

escaping the ghettos of New York
they drink
off they go into a paradise of
wine, beer, scotch, and gin   10
fantasy
the ecstasy of alcohol

to break through
only to return
yes, only to return to the   15
hell of an empty wine bottle
crushed beside the wall
in anger
no little drop left
to free a straining soul   20
to the hell of

an empty needle or a smoked down
red all dreams gone up
in smoke

escaping the ghettos of New York   25
they leave for a while
but they always always
return

STUDY QUESTIONS

1. Is the poem's title advice, command, or simply statement? How can you tell?

2. The poem pictures life in "the ghettos of New York" as alternating between "paradise" (lines 3, 9) and "hell" (lines 16, 21). Explain how the IMAGERY of the poem connects the two in order to suggest that they involve the same things. Explain fully the implications of "fantasy" (lines 5, 11), "ecstasy" (lines 6, 12), and "dreams" (line 23).

3. What do the last two lines of the poem mean?

Luis Cabalquinto

B orn in the Philippines, Luis Cabalquinto was educated at the University of the Philippines and at Cornell University and now divides his writing time between his hometown, Magarao, in the Philippines, and New York City. He is the author of three collections of poetry: *The Dog-eater and Other Poems* (1989), *The Ibalon Collection* (1991), and *Dreamwanderer* (1992), all published by Kalikasan Press, Manila. Cabalquinto's poetry and fiction have appeared in many anthologies published in the United States, the Philippines, Hong Kong, France, and Australia, and he is the recipient of several writing awards and fellowships.

HOMETOWN

After a supper of mountain rice
And wood-roasted river crab

I sit on a long bench outside
The old house, looking at a river

Alone, myself, again away   5
From that other self in the city
On this piece of ancestor land
My pulses slowed, I am at peace

I have no wish but this place
To remain here in a stopped time   10
With stars moving on that water
And in the sky a brightness

Answering: I want nothing else
But this stillness filling me
From a pure darkness over the land   15
That smells ever freshly of trees

The night and I are quiet now
But for small laughter from a neighbor
The quick sweep of a winged creature
And a warm dog, snuggled by my feet   20

STUDY QUESTIONS

1. The poem is full of details and images of things in motion, and yet it emphasizes a stillness in which nothing, including time, moves at all. How do you explain the contradiction? How do the several sights, smells, and sounds contribute to the poem's quiescence? to its tranquillity? How does the punctuation—or lack of it—contribute?

2. Why are the specific details of supper presented? Why the detail about how the crab is roasted? What does the supper imply about the person who speaks the poem? What other details help to characterize the SPEAKER?

3. Why is an "other self" (line 6) mentioned? What kind of contrast does the mention of the city imply? What other absences help to set the mood of the poem?

4. How long has the speaker been attached to this place? In the absence of specific facts about years, how is the impression of permanence created? What different IMAGES of satisfaction does the poem present?

5. Are you surprised that the poet now lives in the United States rather than the Philippines? Does the fact affect your reading of the poem in any way? your appreciation of it? What does the fact of his exile or immigration suggest about his sense of roots? Do you think that a person's sense of "home" is likely to be weakened or strengthened by living in a "foreign" place?

Maurice Kenny

Maurice Kenny, of Mohawk ancestry, was born in 1929 and reared in northern New York State near the St. Lawrence River. He is currently poet in residence at North Country Community College in Saranac, New York, and visiting professor at Oklahoma State University. His first book of poetry, *Dead Letters Sent*, was published in 1959, and he has published ten volumes, including *The Mama Poems*, which won the 1985 American Book Award, *Between Two Rivers* (1987), and *Rain and Other Fictions* (1990). His most recent work, *Tekonwatouti: Molly Brant*, was published in 1992.

GOING HOME

The book lay unread in my lap
snow gathered at the window
from Brooklyn it was a long ride
the Greyhound followed the plow
from Syracuse to Watertown   5
to country cheese and maples
tired rivers and closed paper mills
home to gossipy aunts . . .
their dandelions and pregnant cats . . .
home to cedars and fields of boulders   10
cold graves under willow and pine
home from Brooklyn to the reservation
that was not home
to songs I could not sing
to dances I could not dance   15
from Brooklyn bars and ghetto rats
to steaming horses stomping frozen earth
barns and privies lost in blizzards
home to a Nation, Mohawk
to faces, I did not know   20
and hands which did not recognize me
to names and doors
my father shut

STUDY QUESTIONS

1. Why does the description of the journey "home" mix sights along the road with personal memories? Which lines describe which?

2. Why does "the book [lie] unread in my lap" (line 1)? With what aspects of the SPEAKER's life is the book connected? What substitutes for the book on the trip?

3. Why is the reservation said to be "not home" (line 13)? List all of the things mentioned in the poem that cut the speaker off from the reservation. What things tie him to it? How is Brooklyn characterized? Explain the emotional effects of the contrast between rats and horses (lines 16, 17); between bars and "barns and privies lost in blizzards" (lines 16, 18).

4. How much do we know about the father? What seems to have been involved in his shutting of doors?

5. Describe the attitudes of the speaker toward his upstate "home." What contradictions do you find in his attitude? Do the contradictions mean that he is insincere? confused? that his feelings are complicated? that he is torn between deep loyalties from the past and feelings from his own limited personal experience?

6. Do you think the speaker is likely to leave Brooklyn and move to upstate New York? What evidence does the poem provide?

7. In speaking of this poem, Kenny has written:

> So I travel home/north to the re-birth of chicory, burdock, tadpoles, otters and the strawberry. I fly with geese who, like myself, have wintered in a more southern clime, or salmon who have matured in the ocean. I travel home to those natal waters. "Home" is with your people who stand on that earth and partake of its nourishment, spiritual and corporeal. And though some, like yourself, have wandered they too cannot refrain from returning at picking time. Once fingers have been lowered to the earth they cannot be retracted.

How do you explain the strong attraction to land and the earth in someone who has spent most of his life in a city of concrete and busy populous streets?

Lorna Dee Cervantes

Born in San Francisco in 1954, Lorna Dee Cervantes is of Mexican descent. She has published two books of poems, *Emplumada* (1981) and *From the Cables of Genocide: Poems of Love and Hunger* (1991). She was educated at San Jose City College and San Jose State University and is the founder of Mango Publications, a small press that publishes books and a literary magazine. She currently teaches creative writing at the University of Colorado at Boulder.

FREEWAY 280

Las casitas[1] near the gray cannery,
nestled amid wild abrazos[2] of climbing roses
and man-high red geraniums
are gone now. The freeway conceals it
all beneath a raised scar.   5

But under the fake windsounds of the open lanes,
in the abandoned lots below, new grasses sprout,
wild mustard remembers, old gardens
come back stronger than they were,
trees have been left standing in their yards.   10
Albaricoqueros, cerezos, nogales . . .[3]
Viejitas[4] come here with paper bags to gather greens.
Espinaca, verdolagas, yerbabuena . . .[5]

I scramble over the wire fence
that would have kept me out.   15
Once, I wanted out, wanted the rigid lanes
to take me to a place without sun,
without the smell of tomatoes burning
on swing shift in the greasy summer air.

Maybe it's here   20
en los campos extraños de esta ciudad[6]
where I'll find it, that part of me
mown under
like a corpse
or a loose seed.   25

1. Little houses. [Author's note]
2. Bear hugs.
3. Apricot trees, cherry trees, walnut trees. [Author's note]
4. *Viejitas:* old women.
5. Spinach, purslane, mint. [Author's note]
6. In the strange fields of this city. [Author's note]

STUDY QUESTIONS

1. How much do we know about the places the poem describes? How much do we know about the SPEAKER? Make a list of all the facts we are given about people and places. What relationships between people and land are implied?

2. Find all the places in the poem where nature is contrasted with artificial or man-made things; where wildness is contrasted with restraint; where growth is contrasted with death.

3. What "facts" are we given about the freeway? What words used to describe the freeway tend to color our emotional responses to it? What effect does it seem to have on the landscape? on people? How are these effects dramatized? How did the speaker formerly feel about the freeway (lines 16–19)? What seems to have changed her mind? How is her attitude toward "home" different now from what it was when she "wanted out" (line 16)?

4. How do the human characteristics described in the last half of the poem relate to the characteristics of nature in the first part? What is the common enemy?

5. What does each of the four STANZAS accomplish? Although there are four stanzas, the poem breaks into two main parts. Where, exactly, does the break occur? How is the break indicated? Describe the relationship between the two parts.

6. What terms and IMAGES earlier in the poem are summarized in the contrast between "corpse" and "loose seed" (lines 24–25)?

Carter Revard

Carter Revard, part Osage on his father's side, grew up on the Osage Reservation in Oklahoma and attended Buck Creek rural school (one room, eight grades), working as a farm laborer and a greyhound trainer before earning a B.A. in English at the University of Tulsa. In 1952 he was given his Osage name, Nompewathe, which means "fear-inspiring," and went to Oxford University (as a Rhodes Scholar), later earning a Ph.D. from Yale in Middle English literature. He is professor of English at Washington University, St. Louis, and a board member of the American Indian Center of Mid-America in St. Louis. He has published three collections of poems: *Ponca War Dancers* (1980), from which "Driving in Oklahoma" is taken, *Cowboys and Indians, Christmas Shopping* (1992), and *An Eagle Nation* (1993).

DRIVING IN OKLAHOMA

On humming rubber along this white concrete
    lighthearted between the gravities
of source and destination like a man
      halfway to the moon
    in this bubble of tuneless whistling   5
at seventy miles an hour from the windvents,
      over prairie swells rising
    and falling, over the quick offramp
that drops to its underpass and the truck
      thundering beneath as I cross   10
with the country music twanging out my windows,
    I'm grooving down this highway feeling
technology is freedom's other name when
              —a meadowlark
    comes sailing across my windshield   15
      with breast shining yellow
and five notes pierce
      the windroar like a flash
      of nectar on mind
gone as the country music swells up and   20
    drops me wheeling down
my notch of cement-bottomed sky
    between home and away
          and wanting
to move again through country that a bird   25
    has defined wholly with song
      and maybe next time see how
he flies so easy, when he sings.

STUDY QUESTIONS

1. What does it mean to be "between the gravities / of source and destination" (lines 2–3)? How does this expression relate to line 23?

2. How, exactly, does the second half of the poem contradict the conclusion that "technology is freedom's other name" (line 13)?

3. What formal features in the poem contribute to the sense of speed: line divisions? lack of punctuation? word choices? Which word choices seem to you particularly important to the rapid pace of the first part of the poem? Explain how the pacing of the poem is controlled.

4. How many different sounds does the poem describe? Which visual IMAGES are most important to the effects of the poem?

5. Which sounds in the poem are the sounds of "home"? Which are the sounds of "away"?
6. Explain how the last two lines sum up the poem's ACTION and connect its THEMES.

Edward Hirsch

Edward Hirsch teaches at the University of Houston. His poems have appeared in many journals and magazines and have been collected in *For the Sleepwalkers* (1981), *Wild Gratitude* (1986), and *The Night Parade* (1989). He has held fellowships from the John Simon Guggenheim Foundation, the American Council of Learned Societies, and the National Endowment for the Arts, and he has won a number of prestigious awards for his poetry, including several from the American Academy of Poets. Born in Chicago in 1950, he comes from a family with roots in Eastern Europe.

IN A POLISH HOME FOR THE AGED (CHICAGO, 1983)

It's sweet to lie awake in the early morning
Remembering the sound of five huge bells
Ringing in the village at dawn, the iron
Notes turning to music in the pink clouds.

It's nice to remember the flavor of groats   5
Mixed with horse's blood, the sour tang
Of unripe peppers, the smell of garlic
Growing wildly in Aunt Stefania's garden.

I can remember my grandmother's odd claim
That her younger brother was a mule   10
Pulling an ox-cart across a lapsed meadow
In the first thin light of a summer morning;

Her cousin, Irka, was a poorly-planted tree
Wrapping itself in a dress of white blossoms.

I could imagine an ox-cart covered with flowers,   15
The sound of laughter rising from damp branches.

Some nights I dream that I'm a child again
Flying through the barnyard at six a.m.:
My mother milks the cows in the warm barn
And thinks about her father, who died long ago,   20

And daydreams about my future in a large city.
I want to throw my arms around her neck
And touch the sweating blue pails of milk
And talk about my strange, childish nightmares.

God, you've got to see us to know how happy   25
We were then, two dark caresses of sunlight.
Now I wake up to the same four walls staring
At me blankly, and the same bare ceiling.

Somehow the morning starts over in the home:
Someone coughs in the hall; someone calls out   30
An unfamiliar name, a name I don't remember;
Someone slams a car door in the distance.

I touch my feet to the cold tile floor
And listen to my neighbor stirring in his room
And think about my mother's peculiar words   35
After my grandmother died during the war:

"One day the light will be as thick as a pail
Of fresh milk, but the pail will seem heavy.
You won't know if you can lift it anymore,
But lift it anyway. Drink the day slowly."   40

STUDY QUESTIONS

1. What does "home" mean in the title? What does "Polish home" come to mean in the course of the poem? How do the two meanings of "home" help define the THEME and TONE of the poem?

2. What "facts" are we given about the SPEAKER? What memories of childhood are presented? How much do we know about family? about places of origin?

3. How much are we told about the "village" (line 3) of long ago? What clues are there about where the village was? What customs help define the village and the family? How far away does the village seem to be in time? in place?

4. How much do we know about the speaker's present life? What seem to be the speaker's primary emotions now? How much do we know about the place where the speaker lies awake?

5. What is accomplished by having the poem set in the speaker's waking moment?

6. What does the advice in the final STANZA of the poem mean? How does it relate to the speaker's present state of mind and situation? to the opening lines of the poem?

Agha Shahid Ali

Originally from Kashmir (and a graduate of the University of Kashmir), Agha Shahid Ali moved to New Delhi and then to the United States to receive his advanced degrees (M.A., University of Delhi, 1970; M.F.A., University of Arizona, 1985; Ph.D., Penn State, 1984). He has written poetry exclusively in English since the age of ten. A scholar as well as a poet, Ali is the author of *T. S. Eliot as Editor* (1986); his three volumes of poetry are *A Walk Through the Yellow Pages* (1986), *The Half-Inch Himalayas* (1987), from which "Postcard from Kashmir" is taken, and *A Nostalgist's Map of America* (1991). He has taught at Hamilton College and now teaches at the University of Massachusetts, Amherst.

POSTCARD FROM KASHMIR

(for Pavan Sahgal)

Kashmir shrinks into my mailbox,
my home a neat four by six inches.

I always loved neatness. Now I hold
the half-inch Himalayas in my hand.

This is home. And this the closest   5
I'll ever be to home. When I return,
the colors won't be so brilliant,

the Jhelum's waters[1] so clean,
so ultramarine. My love
so overexposed.   10

And my memory will be a little
out of focus, in it
a giant negative, black
and white, still undeveloped.

STUDY QUESTIONS

1. The present in the poem quickly fades into the past and then leaps into the future. What aspects of the past seem now to be lost forever? Why, if there is to be a "return" to Kashmir later (line 6), is the postcard "the closest I'll ever be to home" (lines 5–6)? Why is it important to the poem that the Himalayan scene is miniaturized? that it is idealized?

2. How much do we know about the SPEAKER? How does the miniaturization of his homeland lead him to think about old feelings? Why will the colors be lessened and the water not be so clean when the speaker actually does return?

3. Explain how the language of photography works in the poem. What does it mean that love, in future times, will not be "so overexposed" (line 10)? that memory will be "out of focus" (line 12)? "undeveloped" (line 14)? that in it will be "a giant negative" (line 13)?

4. What, besides a particular place, does home mean to the speaker?

Audre Lorde

Audre Lorde authored nine books (mostly collections of poetry, such as *Coal* [1976], *The Black Unicorn* [1978], and *Undersong* [1992], and a fictionalized memoir she called a "biomythography," *Zami: A New Spelling of My Name* [1982]). Born in New York in 1934 to West Indian parents, she taught at the John Jay College of Criminal Justice and at Hunter College. She died in November 1992.

1. The river Jhelum runs through Kashmir and Pakistan.

HOME

We arrived at my mother's island
to find your mother's name in the stone
we did not need   to go to the graveyard
for affirmation
our own genealogies   5
the language of childhood wars.

Two old dark women
in the back of the Belmont lorry
bound for L'Esterre
blessed us   greeting   10
Eh Dou-Dou you look *too* familiar
to you   to me
it no longer mattered.

STUDY QUESTIONS

1. How much do we know about the "we" in the poem? about the SPEAKER herself?
   about her companion? What clues does the poem give about the occasion for the
   visit to the island?

2. What details in the poem make it possible to determine which island is involved in
   the episode? What does the poem imply about the distinctiveness of language on
   the island? How does the recording of dialogue in the second STANZA relate to
   THEMES introduced in the first stanza?

3. What does the fact that the strangers look familiar to the two old women have to
   do with facts introduced in the poem's opening lines?

4. Is it significant that the poem is cast in the past tense? Why does the visual recognition of the two old women "no longer" matter? What does the title of the poem
   mean?

Elías Miguel Muñoz

Elías Miguel Muñoz was born in Cuba in 1954. After immigrating to the United
States, he attended the University of California at Irvine, where he received

his Ph.D. in 1984. Muñoz has published scholarship on the work of Manuel Puig; a study of Cuban poets in exile; two novels in English, *Crazy Love* (1988) and *The Greatest Performance* (1991); and two collections of poems, *En estas tierras / In This Land* (1989) and *No fue posible el sol* (1989).

RETURNING

While in the barrio no one spoke
of leaving or of telegrams
And we all dreamed about apples
and mint-flavored chewing gum.
Remember?   5

The rice and black beans
no longer satisfied us.
Without the eternal summer,
without dirt streets and sugar cane
we would no longer have dark skin.   10
The lines would end,
and so would the *quimbumbia*,
the *yuca*.
and the mud puddles.

So we could sing, later,   15
to a different beat.
So we could forget your
conga player's outfit.
So we could chew away
until we had no teeth.   20
So we could speak of the things
we lost,
things we never had.
So that later,
under the Northern skies,   25
we could begin to dream
about returning.

STUDY QUESTIONS

1. What is the time SETTING of the first two STANZAS of the poem? At that time, what time is thought about, dreamed about, or talked about? How is that "dreamed

about" time related to the present time of the poem? How does the time element or setting change in the final stanza? What is the time dreamed about in the final line of the poem? How does the time STRUCTURE relate to the stanzaic structure of the poem? the title? to the THEME?

2. What indications are there of place in the first two stanzas? in the final stanza? How do the details evaluate the two places? The word "home" is never mentioned, but how would you infer it is defined by the poem? by the last word and title?

Lucille Clifton

Born in Depew, New York, in 1936, Lucille Clifton attended Howard University and Fredonia State Teacher's College. The author of numerous books for children and a memoir, *Generations* (1976), in which she recounts the genealogical stories that animate so much of her writing, Clifton is also the author of the *Good News About the Earth* (1972), *Two-Headed Woman* (1980), and *Quilting* (1991).

IN THE INNER CITY

in the inner city
or
like we call it
home
we think a lot about uptown
and the silent nights
and the houses straight as
dead men
and the pastel lights
and we hang on to our no place
happy to be alive
and in the inner city
or
like we call it
home

STUDY QUESTION

The first four lines are repeated at the end of this short poem. To what extent does calling the inner city "home" seem IRONIC or sad early in the poem? how does our understanding of the lines change between their first and last appearance? Why does the SPEAKER prefer the inner city to "uptown"?

Wakako Yamauchi

Born in 1924 in California (where she still lives), Wakako Yamauchi is best known as a writer of short stories, which have been widely anthologized.

AND THE SOUL SHALL DANCE

CHARACTERS

MURATA, 40, Issei[1] farmer.
HANA, Issei wife of Murata.
MASAKO, 11, Nisei daughter of the Muratas.
OKA, 45, Issei farmer.
EMIKO, 30, wife of Oka.
KIYOKO, 14, Oka's daughter.

PLACE AND TIME

The action of the play takes place on and between two small farms in Southern California's Imperial Valley in the early 1930s.

ACT I

Scene 1

Summer 1935, afternoon. Interior of the Murata house. The set is spare. There is a kitchen table, four chairs, a bed, and on the wall, a calendar indicating the year and

1. First-generation Japanese-American. *Nisei:* second-generation.

month: June, 1935. There is a doorway leading to the other room. Props are: a bottle of sake, two cups, a dish of chiles, a phonograph, and two towels hanging on pegs on the wall. A wide wooden bench sits outside.

The bathhouse has just burned to the ground due to the carelessness of MASAKO, *Nisei daughter,* 11. *Off stage there are sounds of* MURATA, 40, *Issei farmer, putting out the fire.*

Inside the house HANA MURATA, *Issei wife, in a drab house dress, confronts* MASAKO *(wearing summer dress of the era).* MASAKO *is sullen and somewhat defiant.* HANA *breaks the silence.*

HANA: How could you be so careless, Masako? You know you should be extra careful with fire. How often have I told you? Now the whole bathhouse is gone. I told you time and again, when you stoke a fire, you should see that everything is swept into the fireplace.

    [MURATA *enters. He's dressed in old work clothes. He suffers from heat and exhaustion.*]

MURATA: [*Coughing.*] Shack went up like a match box . . . This kind of weather dries everything . . . just takes a spark to make a bonfire out of dry timber.

HANA: Did you save any of it?

MURATA: No. Couldn't . . .

HANA: [*To* MASAKO.] How many times have I told you . . .

    [MASAKO *moves nervously.*]

MURATA: No use crying about it now. *Shikata ga nai.* It's gone now. No more bathhouse. That's all there is to it.

HANA: But you've got to tell her. Otherwise she'll make the same mistake. You'll be building a bathhouse every year.

    [MURATA *removes his shirt and wipes off his face. He throws his shirt on a chair and sits at the table.*]

MURATA: *Baka!* Ridiculous!

MASAKO: I didn't do it on purpose.

    [*She goes to the bed, opens a book.* HANA *follows her.*]

HANA: I know that but you know what this means? It means we bathe in a bucket . . . inside the house. Carry water in from the pond, heat it on the stove . . . We'll use more kerosene.

MURATA: Tub's still there. And the fireplace. We can still build a fire under the tub.

HANA: [*Shocked.*] But no walls! Everyone in the country can see us!

MURATA: Wait 'til dark then. Wait 'til dark.

HANA: We'll be using a lantern. They'll still see us.

MURATA: Angh! Who? Who'll see us? You think everyone in the country waits to watch us take a bath? Hunh? You know how stupid you sound? Ridiculous!

HANA: [*Defensively.*] It'll be inconvenient.

    [HANA *is saved by a rap on the door.* OKA, *Issei neighbor,* 45, *enters. He is short and stout, dressed in faded work clothes.*]

OKA: Hello! Hello! Oi! What's going on here? Hey! Was there some kind of fire?

[HANA *rushes to the door to let* OKA *in. He stamps the dust from his shoes and enters.*]

HANA: Oka-san![2] You just wouldn't believe . . . We had a terrible thing happen.

OKA: Yeah. Saw the smoke from down the road. Thought it was your house. Came rushing over. Is the fire out?

[MURATA *half rises and sits back again. He's exhausted.*]

MURATA: [*Gesturing.*] Oi, oi. Come in . . . sit down. No big problem. It was just our bathhouse.

OKA: Just the *furoba*, eh?

MURATA: Just the bath.

HANA: Our Masako was careless and the *furoba* caught fire. There's nothing left of it but the tub.

[MASAKO *looks up from her book, pained. She makes a very small sound.*]

OKA: Long as the tub's there, no problem. I'll help you with it. [*He starts to roll up his sleeves.* MURATA *looks at him.*]

MURATA: What . . . now? Now?

OKA: Long as I'm here.

HANA: Oh, Papa. Aren't we lucky to have such friends?

MURATA: [*To* HANA.] Hell, we can't work on it now. The ashes are still hot. I just now put the damned fire out. Let me rest a while. [*To* OKA.] Oi, how about a little *sake*? [*Gesturing to* HANA.] Make *sake* for Oka-san. [OKA *sits at the table.* HANA *goes to prepare the* sake. *She heats it, gets out the cups and pours it for the men.*] I'm tired . . . I am *tired.*

HANA: Oka-san has so generously offered his help . . .

[OKA *is uncomfortable. He looks around and sees* MASAKO *sitting on the bed.*]

OKA: Hello, there, Masako-chan. You studying?

MASAKO: No, it's summer vacation.

MURATA: [*Sucking in his breath.*] Kids nowadays . . . no manners . . .

HANA: She's sulking because I had to scold her.

[MASAKO *makes a small moan.*]

MURATA: Drink, Oka-san.

OKA: [*Swallowing.*] Ahhh, that's good.

MURATA: Eh, you not working today?

OKA: No . . . no . . . I took the afternoon off today. I was driving over to Nagatas' when I saw this big black cloud of smoke coming from your yard.

HANA: It went up so fast . . .

MURATA: What's up at Nagatas'? [*To* HANA]. Get the chiles out. Oka-san loves chiles.

[HANA *opens a jar of chiles and puts them on a plate. She serves the men and gets*

2. A suffix indicating polite address, roughly equivalent to Mr., Mrs., Ms. The suffixes *-chan* and *-kun* (below) are affectionate or diminutive.

her mending basket and walks to MASAKO. MASAKO *makes room for her on the bed.*]

OKA: [*Helping himself.*] Ah, chiles. [MURATA *looks at* OKA, *the question unanswered.*] Well, I want to see him about my horse. I'm thinking of selling my horse.

MURATA: Sell your horse!

OKA: [*He scratches his head.*] The fact is, I need some money. Nagata-san's the only one around made money this year, and I'm thinking he might want another horse.

MURATA: Yeah, he made a little this year. And he's talking big . . . big! Says he's leasing twenty more acres this fall.

OKA: Twenty acres?

MURATA: Yeah. He might want another horse.

OKA: Twenty acres, eh?

MURATA: That's what he says. But you know his old woman makes all the decisions. [OKA *scratches his head.*]

HANA: They're doing all right.

MURATA: Henh. Nagata-kun's so hen-pecked, it's pathetic. Peko-peko. [*He makes motions of a hen pecking.*]

OKA: [*Feeling the strain.*] I better get over there.

MURATA: Why the hell you selling your horse?

OKA: I need cash.

MURATA: Oh, yeah. I could use some too. Seems like everyone's getting out of the depression but the poor farmers. Nothing changes for us. We go on and on planting our tomatoes and summer squash and eating them . . . Well, at least it's healthy.

HANA: Papa, do you have lumber?

MURATA: Lumber? For what?

HANA: The bath.

MURATA: [*Impatiently.*] Don't worry about that. We need more *sake* now. [HANA *rises to serve him.*]

OKA: You sure Nagata-kun's working twenty more acres?

MURATA: Last I heard. What the hell; if you need a few bucks, I can loan you . . .

OKA: A few hundred. I need a few hundred dollars.

MURATA: Oh, a few hundred. But what the hell you going to do without a horse? Out here a man's horse is as important as his wife.

OKA: [*Seriously.*] I don't think Nagata will buy my wife. [*The men laugh, but* HANA *doesn't find it so funny.* MURATA *glances at her. She fills the cups again.* OKA *makes a half-hearted gesture to stop her.* MASAKO *watches the pantomine carefully.* OKA *swallows his drink in one gulp.*] I better get moving.

MURATA: What's the big hurry?

OKA: Like to get the horse business done.

MURATA: Ehhhh . . . relax. Do it tomorrow. He's not going to die, is he?

OKA: [*Laughing.*] Hey he's a good horse. I want to get it settled today. If Nagata-kun won't buy, I got to find someone else. You think maybe Kawaguchi . . . ?

MURATA: Not Kawaguchi . . . Maybe Yamamoto.

HANA: What is all the money for, Oka-san? Does Emiko-san need an operation?

OKA: Nothing like that . . .

HANA: Sounds very mysterious.

OKA: No mystery, Mrs. No mystery. No sale, no money, no story.

MURATA: [*Laughing.*] That's a good one. "No sale, no money, no . . ." Eh, Mama. [*He points to the empty cups.* HANA *fills the cups and goes back to* MASAKO.]

HANA: [*Muttering.*] I see we won't be getting any work done today. [*To* MASAKO.] Are you reading again? Maybe we'd still have a bath if you . . .

MASAKO: I didn't do it on purpose.

MURATA: [*Loudly.*] I sure hope you know what you're doing. Oka-kun. What'd you do without a horse?

OKA: I was hoping you'd lend me yours now and then . . . [*He looks at* HANA.] I'll pay for some of the feed.

MURATA: [*Emphatically waving his hand.*] Sure! Sure!

OKA: The fact is, I need that money. I got a daughter in Japan and I just got to send for her this year.

[HANA *comes to life. She puts down her mending and sits at the table.*]

HANA: A daughter? You have a daughter in Japan? Why, I didn't know you had children. Emiko-san and you . . . I thought you were childless.

OKA: [*Scratching his head.*] We are. I was married before.

MURATA: You son-of-a-gun!

HANA: Is that so? How old is your daughter?

OKA: Kiyoko must be . . . fifteen now. Yeah, fifteen.

HANA: Fifteen! Oh, that *would* be too old for Emiko-san's child. Is Kiyoko-san living with relatives in Japan?

OKA: [*Reluctantly.*] Yeah, with grandparents. With Shizue's parents. Well, the fact is, Shizue, that's my first wife, and Emiko were sisters. They come from a family with no sons. I was a boy when I went to work for the family . . . as an apprentice . . . they're blacksmiths. Later I married Shizue and took on the family name—you know, *yoshi*—because they had no sons.[3] My real name is Sakakihara.

MURATA: Sakakihara! That's a great name!

HANA: A magnificent name!

OKA: No one knows me by that here.

MURATA: Should have kept that . . . Sakakihara.

OKA: [*Muttering.*] I don't even know myself by that name.

HANA: And Shizue-san passed away and you married Emiko-san?

OKA: Oh, yeah. Shizue and I lived with the family for a while and we had

---

3. Yoshi is a procedure wherein a man is married into a family that has no sons and is obliged to carry the wife's family name and continue the lineage. [Author's note]

the baby . . . that's, you know, Kiyoko . . . [*The liquor has affected him and he's become less inhibited.*] Well, while I was serving apprentice with the family, they always looked down their noses at me. After I married, it got worse . . . That old man . . . Angh! He was terrible! Always pushing me around, making me look bad in front of my wife and kid. That old man was mean . . . ugly!

MURATA: Yeah, I heard about that apprentice work—*detchi-boko* . . . Heard it was damned humiliating.

OKA: That's the God's truth!

MURATA: Never had to do it myself. I came to America instead. They say *detchi-boko* is bloody hard work.

OKA: The work's all right. I'm not afraid of work. It's the humiliation! I hated them! Pushing me around like I was still a boy . . . Me, a grown man! And married to their daughter! [MURATA *groans in sympathy.*] Well, Shizue and I talked it over and we decided the best thing was to get away. We thought if I came to America and made some money . . . you know, send her money until we had enough, I'd go back and we'd leave the family . . . you know, move to another province . . . start a small business, maybe in the city, a noodle shop or something.

MURATA: That's everyone's dream. Make money, go home and live like a king.

OKA: I worked like a dog. Sent every penny to Shizue. And then she died. She died on me!

[HANA *and* MURATA *observe a moment of silence in respect for* OKA's *anguish.*]

HANA: And you married Emiko-san.

OKA: I didn't marry her. They married her to me! Right after Shizue died.

HANA: But Oka-san, you were lucky . . .

OKA: Before the body was cold! No respect! By proxy. The old man wrote me they were arranging a marriage by proxy for me and Emiko. They said she'd grown to be a beautiful woman and would serve me well.

HANA: Emiko-san *is* a beautiful woman.

OKA: And they sent her to me. Took care of everything! Immigration, fare, everything.

HANA: But she's your sister-in-law—Kiyoko's aunt. It's good to keep the family together.

OKA: That's what I thought. But hear this: Emiko was the favored one. Shizue was not so pretty, not so smart. They were grooming Emiko for a rich man—his name was Yamoto—lived in a grand house in the village. They sent her to schools; you know, the culture thing: tea ceremony, you know, all that. They didn't even like me, and suddenly they married her to me.

MURATA: Yeah. You don't need all that formal training to make it over here. Just a strong back.

HANA: And a strong will.

OKA: It was all arranged. I couldn't do anything about it.

HANA: It'll be all right. With Kiyoko coming . . .

OKA: [*Dubiously.*] I hope so . . . I never knew human beings could be so cruel. You know how they mistreated my daughter? You know after Emiko came over, things got from bad to worse and I *never* had enough money to send to Kiyoko.

MURATA: They don't know what it's like here. They think money's picked off the ground here.

OKA: And they treated Kiyoko so bad. They told her I forgot about her. They told her I didn't care—they said I abandoned her. Well, she knew better. She wrote to me all the time and I always told her I'd send for her . . . soon as I got the money. [*He shakes his head.*] I just got to do something this year.

HANA: She'll be happier here. She'll know her father cares.

OKA: Kids tormented her for not having parents.

MURATA: Kids are cruel.

HANA: Masako will help her. She'll help her get started at school. She'll make friends . . . she'll be all right.

OKA: I hope so. She'll need friends. [*He considers he might be making a mistake after all.*] What could I say to her? Stay there? It's not what you think over here? I can't help her? I just have to do this thing. I just have to do this one thing for her.

MURATA: Sure . . .

HANA: Don't worry. It'll work out fine.

   [MURATA *gestures to* HANA. *She fills the cup.*]

MURATA: You talk about selling your horse, I thought you were pulling out.

OKA: I wish I could. But there's nothing else I can do.

MURATA: Without money, yeah . . .

OKA: You can go into some kind of business with money, but a man like me . . . no education . . . there's no kind of job I can do. I'd starve in the city.

MURATA: Dishwashing, maybe. Janitor . . .

OKA: At least here we can eat. Carrots, maybe, but we can eat.

MURATA: All the carrots we been eating 'bout to turn me into a rabbit.

   [*They laugh.* HANA *starts to pour more wine for* OKA *but he stops her.*]

OKA: I better not drink any more. Got to drive to Nagata-san's yet. [*He rises and walks over to* MASAKO.] You study hard, don't you? You'll teach Kiyoko English, eh? When she gets here . . .

HANA: Oh, yes. She will.

MURATA: Kiyoko-san could probably teach her a thing or two.

OKA: She won't know about American ways . . .

MASAKO: I'll help her.

HANA: Don't worry, Oka-san. She'll have a good friend in our Masako. [*They move toward the door.*]

OKA: Well, thanks for the *sake*. I guess I talk too much when I drink. [*He scratches his head and laughs.*] Oh. I'm sorry about the fire. By the way, come to my house for your bath . . . until you build yours again.

HANA: [*Hesitantly.*] Oh, uh . . . thank you. I don't know if . . .

MURATA: Good! Good! Thanks a lot. I need a good hot bath tonight.

OKA: Tonight, then.

MURATA: We'll be there.

HANA: [*Bowing.*] Thank you very much. *Sayonara.*

OKA: [*Nodding.*] See you tonight.

[OKA *leaves.* HANA *faces her husband as soon as the door closes.*]

HANA: Papa, I don't know about going over there.

MURATA: [*Surprised.*] Why?

HANA: Well, Emiko-san . . .

MURATA: [*Irritated.*] What's the matter with you? We need a bath and Oka's invited us over.

HANA: [*To* MASAKO.] Help me clear the table. [MASAKO *reluctantly leaves her book and begins to clear the table.*] Papa, you know we've been neighbors already three, four years and Emiko-san's never been very hospitable.

MURATA: She's shy, that's all.

HANA: Not just shy . . . she's strange. I feel like she's pushing me off . . . she makes me feel like—I don't know—like I'm prying or something.

MURATA: Maybe you are.

HANA: And never put out a cup of tea . . . If she had all that training in the graces . . . why, a cup of tea . . .

MURATA: So if you want tea, ask for it.

HANA: I can't do that, Papa. She's strange . . . I don't know . . . [*To* MASAKO.] When we go there, be very careful not to say anything wrong.

MASAKO: I never say anything anyway.

HANA: [*Thoughtfully.*] Would you believe the story Oka-san just told? Why, I never knew . . .

MURATA: There're lot of things you don't know. Just because a man don't . . . talk about them, don't mean he don't feel . . . don't think about . . .

HANA: [*Looking around.*] We'll have to take something . . . There's nothing to take . . . Papa, maybe you can dig up some carrots.

MURATA: God, Mama, be sensible. They got carrots. Everybody's got carrots.

HANA: Something . . . maybe I should make something.

MURATA: Hell, they're not expecting anything.

HANA: It's not good manners to go empty-handed.

MURATA: We'll take the *sake.*

[HANA *grimaces.* MASAKO *sees the record player.*]

MASAKO: I know, Mama. We can take the Victrola! We can play records for Mrs. Oka. Then nobody has to talk.

[MURATA *laughs.*]

Fade out.

Scene 2

That evening. We see the exterior wall of the Okas' weathered house. There is a work-able screen door and a large screened window. Outside there is a wide wooden bench that can accommodate three or four people. There is one separate chair and a lantern stands against the house.

The last rays of the sun light the area in a soft golden glow. This light grows gray as the scene progresses and it is quite dark at the end of the scene.

Through the screened window, EMIKO OKA, *Issei woman, 30, can be seen walk-ing erratically back and forth. She wears a drab cotton dress but her grace and femi-ninity come through. Her hair is bunned back in the style of Issei women of the era.*

OKA *sits cross-legged on the bench. He wears a Japanese summer robe (yukata) and fans himself with a round Japanese fan.*

The Muratas enter. MURATA *carries towels and a bottle of sake.* HANA *carries the Victrola, and* MASAKO *a package containing their* yukatas.

OKA: [*Standing to receive the Muratas.*] Oh, you've come. Welcome!

MURATA: Yah . . . Good of you to ask us.

HANA: [*Bowing.*] Yes, thank you very much. [*To* MASAKO.] Say "hello," Masako.

MASAKO: Hello.

HANA: And "thank you."

MASAKO: Thank you.

> [OKA *makes motion of protest.* EMIKO *stops her pacing and watches from the window.*]

HANA: [*Glancing briefly at the window.*] And how is Emiko-san this evening?

OKA: [*Turning toward the house.*] Emi! Emiko!

HANA: That's all right. Don't call her out. She must be busy.

OKA: [*Half rising.*] Emiko!

> [EMIKO *comes to the door.* HANA *starts a deep bow toward the door.*]

MURATA: *Konbanwa!* (*"Good evening!"*)

HANA: *Konbanwa,* Emiko-san. I feel so bad about this intrusion. Your hus-band has told you, our bathhouse was destroyed by fire and he graciously invited us to come use yours.

> [EMIKO *shakes her head.*]

OKA: I didn't have a chance to . . .

> [HANA *recovers and nudges* MASAKO.]

HANA: Say hello to Mrs. Oka.

MASAKO: Hello, Mrs. Oka.

> [HANA *lowers the Victrola on the bench.*]

OKA: What's this? You brought a phonograph?

MASAKO: It's a Victrola.

HANA: [*Laughing indulgently.*] Yes. Masako wanted to bring this over and play some records.

MURATA: [*Extending the wine.*] Brought a little *sake* too.

OKA: [*Taking the bottle*] Ah, now that I like. Emiko, bring out the cups.

[*He waves at his wife, but she doesn't move. He starts to ask again, but decides to get them himself. He enters the house and returns with two cups.* EMIKO *seats herself on the single chair. The Muratas unload their paraphernalia;* OKA *pours the wine, the men drink,* HANA *chatters and sorts the records.* MASAKO *stands by, helping her.*]

HANA: Yes, our Masako loves to play records. I like records too . . . and Papa, he . . .

MURATA: [*Watching* EMIKO.] They take me back home. The only way I can get there . . . in my mind.

HANA: Do you like music, Emiko-san? [EMIKO *looks vague but smiles faintly.*] Oka-san, you like them, don't you?

OKA: Yeah. But I don't have a player. No chance to hear them.

MURATA: I had to get this for them. They wouldn't leave me alone until I got it. Well . . . a phonograph . . . what the hell, they got to have *some* fun.

HANA: We don't have to play them, if you'd rather not . . .

OKA: Play. Play them.

HANA: I thought we could listen to them and relax. [*She extends some records to* EMIKO.] Would you like to look through these, Emiko-san? [EMIKO *doesn't respond. She pulls out a sack of Bull Durham and starts to roll a cigarette.* HANA *pushes* MASAKO *to her.*] Take these to her. [MASAKO *moves toward* EMIKO *with the records.* MASAKO *stands watching her as she lights her cigarette.*] Some of these are very old. You might know them, Emiko-san. [*She sees* MASAKO *watching* EMIKO.] Masako, bring those over here. [*She laughs uncomfortably.*] You might like this one, Emiko-san . . . [*She starts the player.*] Do you know it?

[*The record whines out "Kago No Tori."*[4] EMIKO *listens with her head cocked. She smokes her cigarette. She becomes wrapped in nostalgia and memories of the past.* MASAKO *watches her carefully.*]

MASAKO: [*Whispering.*] Mama, she's crying.

[*Startled,* HANA *and* MURATA *look toward* EMIKO.]

HANA: [*Pinching* MASAKO.] Shhh. The smoke is in her eyes.

MURATA: Did you bring the record I like, Mama?

[EMIKO *rises abruptly and enters the house.*]

MASAKO: There were tears, Mama.

HANA: From yawning, Masako. [*Regretfully, to* OKA.] I'm afraid we've offended her.

OKA: [*Unaware.*] Hunh? Aw . . . no . . . pay no attention . . . no offense . . .

[MASAKO *looks toward the window.* EMIKO *stands forlornly and slowly drifts into a dance.*]

HANA: I'm very sorry. Children, you know . . . they'll say anything, anything that's on their minds.

[MURATA *notices* MASAKO *watching* EMIKO *through the window and tries to divert her attention.*]

MURATA: The needles. Masako, where're the needles?

4. See lyrics, p. 91.

MASAKO: [*Still watching.*] I forgot them.

[HANA *sees what's going on.* OKA *is unaware.*]

HANA: Masako, go take your bath now. Masako . . .

[MASAKO *reluctantly picks up her towel and leaves.*]

OKA: Yeah, yeah . . . take your bath.

MURATA: [*Sees* EMIKO *still dancing.*] Change the record, Mama.

OKA: [*Still unaware.*] That's kind of sad.

MURATA: No use to get sick over a record. We're supposed to enjoy.

[HANA *stops the record.* EMIKO *disappears from the window.* HANA *selects a lively* ondo—"*Tokyo Ondo.*"]

HANA: We'll find something more fun. [*The three begin to tap to the music.*] Can't you just see the festival? The dancers, the bright kimonos, the paper lanterns bobbing in the wind, the fireflies . . . How nostalgic . . . Oh, how nostalgic . . .

[*From the side of the house* EMIKO *appears. Her hair is down, she wears an old straw hat. She dances in front of the Muratas. They're startled. After the first shock, they watch with frozen smiles. They try to join* EMIKO's *mood but something is missing.* OKA *is grieved. He finally stands as though he's had enough.* EMIKO, *now close to the door, ducks into the house.*]

HANA: That was pretty . . . very nice . . .

[OKA *settles down and grunts.* MURATA *clears his throat and* MASAKO *returns from her bath.*]

MURATA: You're done already? [*He's glad to see her.*]

MASAKO: I wasn't very dirty. The water was too hot.

MURATA: Good! Just the way I like it.

HANA: Not dirty?

MURATA: [*Picking up his towel.*] Come on, Mama . . . scrub my back.

HANA: [*Laughing embarrassedly.*] Oh, oh . . . well . . . [*She stops the player.*] Masako, now don't forget . . . crank the machine and change the needle now and then.

MASAKO: I didn't bring them.

HANA: Oh. Oh . . . all right. I'll be back soon . . . don't forget . . . crank.

[*She leaves with her husband.* OKA *and* MASAKO *are alone.* OKA *is awkward and falsely hearty.*]

OKA: So! So you don't like hot baths, eh?

MASAKO: Not too hot.

OKA: [*Laughing.*] I thought you like it real hot. Hot enough to burn the house down. That's a little joke. [MASAKO *busies herself with the records to conceal her annoyance.*] I hear you're real good in school. Always top of the class.

MASAKO: It's a small class. Only two of us.

OKA: When Kiyoko comes, you'll help her in school, yeah? You'll take care of her . . . a favor for me, eh?

MASAKO: Okay.

OKA: You'll be her friend, eh?

MASAKO: Okay.

OKA: That's good. That's good. You'll like her. She's a nice girl too. [OKA *stands, yawns, and stretches.*] I'll go for a little walk now.

[*He touches his crotch to indicate his purpose.* MASAKO *turns her attention to the records and selects one, "The Soul Shall Dance,"*[5] *and begins to sway to the music. The song draws* EMIKO *from the house. She looks out the window, sees* MASAKO *is alone and begins to slip into a dance.*]

EMIKO: Do you like that song, Masa-chan? [MASAKO *is startled and draws back. She remembers her mother's warning. She doesn't know what to do. She nods.*] That's one of my favorite songs. I remember in Japan I used to sing it so often . . . my favorite song . . . [*She sings along with the record.*]

> Akai kuchibiru
> Kappu ni yosete
> Aoi sake nomya
> Kokoro ga odoru . . .

Do you know what that means, Masa-chan?

MASAKO: I think so . . . The soul will dance?

EMIKO: Yes, yes, that's right.

> The soul shall dance. Red lips against a glass
> Drink the green . . .

MASAKO: Wine?

EMIKO: [*Nodding.*] Drink the green wine.

MASAKO: Green? I thought wine is purple.

EMIKO: [*Nodding.*] Wine is purple . . . but this is a green liqueur. [EMIKO *holds up one of the china cups as though it were crystal, and looks at it as though the light were shining through it and she sees the green liquid.*] It's good . . . it warms your heart.

MASAKO: And the soul dances.

EMIKO: Yes.

MASAKO: What does it taste like? The green wine . . .

EMIKO: Oh, it's like . . . it's like . . .

[*The second verse starts. "Kurai yoru yume, Setsunasa yo, Aoi sake nomya, Yume mo odoru . . ."*]

MASAKO: In the dark night . . .

EMIKO: Dreams are unbearable . . . insufferable . . . [*She turns sad.*]

MASAKO: Drink the . . .

EMIKO: [*Nodding.*] Drink the green wine . . .

MASAKO: And the dreams will dance.

EMIKO: [*Softly.*] I'll be going back one day . . .

MASAKO: To where?

5. Full lyrics are given on p. 91.

EMIKO: My home . . . Japan . . . my real home. I'm planning to go back.

MASAKO: By yourself?

EMIKO: [*Nodding.*] Oh, yes. It's a secret. You can keep a secret?

MASAKO: Unhn. I have lots of secrets . . . all my own . . . [*The music stops.* EMIKO *sees* OKA *approaching and disappears into the house.* MASAKO *attends to the record and does not know* EMIKO *is gone.*] Secrets I never tell anyone.

OKA: Secrets? What kind of secrets? What did she say?

MASAKO: Oh. Nothing.

OKA: What did you talk about?

MASAKO: Nothing . . . Mrs. Oka was talking about the song. She was telling me what it meant . . . about the soul.

OKA: [*Scoffing.*] Heh! What does she know about soul? [*Calming down.*] Ehhh . . . some people don't have them . . . souls.

MASAKO: [*Timidly.*] I thought . . . I think everyone has a soul. I read in a book . . .

OKA: [*Laughing.*] Maybe . . . maybe you're right. I'm not an educated man, you know . . . I don't know too much about books. When Kiyoko comes you can talk to her about it. Kiyoko is very . . . [*From inside the house, we hear* EMIKO *begin to sing loudly at the name* KIYOKO *as though trying to drown it out.* OKA *stops talking. Then resumes.*] Kiyoko is very smart. You'll have a good time with her. She'll learn your language fast. How old did you say you are?

MASAKO: Almost twelve.

> [*By this time* OKA *and* MASAKO *are shouting, trying to be heard above* EMIKO's *singing.*]

OKA: Kiyoko is fifteen . . . Kiyoko . . . [OKA *is exasperated. He rushes into the house seething.* MASAKO *hears* OKA's *muffled rage. "Behave yourself" and "kitchigai" come through.* MASAKO *slinks to the window and looks in.* OKA *slaps* EMIKO *around.* MASAKO *reacts to the violence.* OKA *comes out.* MASAKO *returns to the bench in time. He pulls his fingers through his hair and sits next to* MASAKO. *She very slightly draws away.*] Want me to light a lantern?

MASAKO: [*Shaken.*] No . . . ye- . . . okay . . .

OKA: We'll get a little light here . . .

> [*He lights the lantern as the Muratas return from their bath. They are in good spirits.*]

MURATA: Ahhhh . . . Nothing like a good hot bath.

HANA: So refreshing . . .

MURATA: A bath should be taken hot and slow. Don't know how Masako gets through so fast.

HANA: She probably doesn't get in the tub.

MASAKO: I do. [*Everyone laughs.*] Well I do.

> [EMIKO *comes out. She has a large purple welt on her face. She sits on the separate chair, hands folded, quietly watching the Muratas. They look at her with alarm.* OKA *engages himself with his fan.*]

HANA: Oh! Emiko-san . . . what . . . ah-ah . . . whaa . . . [*She draws a deep breath.*] What a nice bath we had . . . such a lovely bath. We do appreciate your hos . . . pitality. Thank you so much.

EMIKO: Lovely evening, isn't it?

HANA: Very lovely. Very. Ah, a little warm, but nice . . . Did you get a chance to hear the records? [*Turning to* MASAKO.] Did you play the records for Mrs. Oka?

MASAKO: Ye- . . . no . . . The needle was . . .

EMIKO: Yes, she did. We played the records together.

MURATA: Oh, you played the songs together?

EMIKO: Yes . . . yes . . .

MURATA: That's nice . . . Masako can understand pretty good, eh?

EMIKO: She understand everything . . . everything I say.

MURATA: [*Withdrawing.*] Oh, yeah? Eh, Mama, we ought to be going . . . [*He closes the player.*] Hate to bathe and run but . . .

HANA: Yes, yes. Tomorrow is a busy day. Come, Masako.

EMIKO: Please . . . stay a little longer.

MURATA: Eh, well, we got to be going.

HANA: Why, thank you, but . . .

EMIKO: It's still quite early.

OKA: [*Indicating he's ready to say goodbye.*] Enjoyed the music. And the *sake.*

EMIKO: The records are very nice. Makes me remember Japan. I sang those songs . . . those very songs . . . Did you know I used to sing?

HANA: [*Politely.*] Why, no . . . no. I didn't know that. You must have a very lovely voice.

EMIKO: Yes.

HANA: No, I didn't know that. That's very nice.

EMIKO: Yes, I sang. My parents were very strict . . . they didn't like it. They said it was frivolous. Imagine?

HANA: Yes, I can imagine. Things were like that . . . in those days singing was not considered proper for nice . . . I mean, only for women in the profess- . . .

MURATA: We better get home, Mama.

HANA: Yes, yes. What a shame you couldn't continue with it.

EMIKO: In the city I did do some classics: the dance, and the *koto,* and the flower, and, of course, the tea . . . [*She makes the proper gesture for the different disciplines.*] All those. Even some singing . . . classics, of course.

HANA: [*Politely.*] Of course.

EMIKO: All of it is so disciplined . . . so disciplined. I was almost a *natori.*[6]

HANA: Oh! How nice.

EMIKO: But everything changed.

HANA: Oh!

EMIKO: I was sent here to America. [*She glares at* OKA.]

HANA: Oh, too bad . . . I mean, too bad about your *natori.*

6. Certified artiste.

MURATA: [*Loudly to* OKA.] So did you see Nagata today?

OKA: Oh, yeah. Yeah.

MURATA: What did he say? Is he interested?

OKA: Yeah. Yeah. He's interested.

MURATA: He likes the horse, eh?

OKA: Ah . . . yeah.

MURATA: I knew he'd like him. I'd buy him myself if I had the money.

OKA: Well, I have to take him over tomorrow. He'll decide then.

MURATA: He'll buy . . . he'll buy. You'd better go straight over to the ticket office and get that ticket. Before you—ha-ha—spend the money.

OKA: Ha-ha. Yeah.

HANA: It'll be so nice when Kiyoko-san comes to join you. I know you're looking forward to it.

EMIKO: [*Confused.*] Oh . . . oh . . .

HANA: Masako is so happy. It'll be good for her too.

EMIKO: I had more freedom in the city . . . I lived with an aunt and she let me . . . She wasn't so strict.

[MURATA *and* MASAKO *have their gear together and stand ready to leave.*]

MURATA: Good luck on the horse tomorrow.

OKA: Yeah, thanks.

HANA: [*Bowing.*] Many, many thanks.

OKA: [*Nodding toward the* sake.] Thanks for the *sake*.

HANA: [*Bowing again.*] Goodnight, Emiko-san. We'll see you again soon. We'll bring the records too.

EMIKO: [*Softly.*] Those songs . . . those very songs . . .

MURATA: Let's go, Mama.

[*The Muratas pull away. Light follows them and grows dark on the Okas. The Muratas begin walking home.*]

HANA: That was uncomfortable.

MASAKO: What's the matter with . . .

HANA: Shhhh!

MURATA: I guess Oka has his problems.

MASAKO: Is she really *kitchigai*?

HANA: Of course not. She's not crazy. Don't say that word, Masako.

MASAKO: I heard Mr. Oka call her that.

HANA: He called her that?

MASAKO: I . . . I think so.

HANA: You heard wrong, Masako. Emiko-san isn't crazy. She just likes her drinks. She had too much to drink tonight.

MASAKO: Oh.

HANA: She can't adjust to this life. She can't get over the good times she had in Japan. Well, it's not easy . . . but one has to know when to bend . . . like the bamboo. When the winds blow, bamboo bends. You bend or crack. Remember that, Masako.

MURATA: [*Laughing wryly.*] Bend, eh? Remember that, Mama.

HANA: [*Softly.*] You don't know . . . it isn't ever easy.

MASAKO: Do you want to go back to Japan, Mama?

HANA: Everyone does.

MASAKO: Do you, Papa?

MURATA: I'll have to make some money first.

MASAKO: I don't. Not me. Not Kiyoko . . .

HANA: After Kiyoko-san comes, Emiko will have company and things will straighten out. She has nothing to live on but her memories. She doesn't have any friends. At least I have my friends at church . . . at least I have that. She must get awful lonely.

MASAKO: I know that. She tried to make friends with me.

HANA: She did? What did she say?

MASAKO: Well, sort of . . .

HANA: What did she say?

MASAKO: She didn't say anything. I just felt it. Maybe you should be her friend, Mama.

MURATA: Poor woman. We could have stayed longer.

HANA: But you wanted to leave. I tried to be friendly. You saw that. It's not easy to talk to Emiko. She either closes up, you can't pry a word from her, or else she goes on and on . . . all that . . . that . . . about the *koto* and tea and the flower . . . I mean, what am I supposed to say? She's so unpredictable. And the drinking . . .

MURATA: All right, all right, Mama.

MASAKO: Did you see her black eye?

HANA: [*Calming down.*] She probably hurt herself. She wasn't very steady.

MASAKO: Oh, no. Mr. Oka hit her.

HANA: I don't think so.

MASAKO: He hit her. I saw him.

HANA: You saw that? Papa, do you hear that? She saw them. That does it. We're not going there again.

MURATA: Aww . . . Oka wouldn't do that. Not in front of a kid.

MASAKO: Well, they didn't do it in front of me. They were in the house.

MURATA: You see . . .

HANA: That's all right. You just have to fix the bathhouse. Either that or we're going to bathe at home . . . in a bucket. We're not going . . . we'll bathe at home. [MURATA *mutters to himself.*] What?

MURATA: I said all right, it's the bucket then. I'll get to it when I can.

[HANA *passes* MURATA *and walks ahead.*]

Fade out.

Scene 3

Same evening. Lights crossfade to the exterior of the Oka house. The Muratas have just left. EMIKO *sits on the bench. Her back is to* OKA. OKA, *still standing, looks at her contemptuously as she takes the bottle and one of the cups to pour herself a drink.*

OKA: Nothing more disgusting than a drunk woman. [EMIKO *ignores him.*] You
    made a fool of yourself. *Washi baka ni shite!* You made a fool of me! [EMIKO
    doesn't move.]

EMIKO: One can only make a fool of one's self.

OKA: You learn that in the fancy schools, eh? [EMIKO *examines the pattern on her
    cup.*] Eh? Eh? Answer me! [EMIKO *ignores.*] I'm talking to you. Answer me!
    [*Menacing.*] You don't get away with that. You think you're so fine . . .
    [EMIKO *looks off into the horizon.* OKA *turns her roughly around.*] When I talk,
    you listen! [EMIKO *turns away again.* OKA *pulls the cup from her hand.*] God-
    damnit! What'd you think my friends think of you? What kind of ass they
    think I am? [*He grabs her shoulders.*]

EMIKO: Don't touch me . . . don't touch me.

OKA: Who the hell you think you are? "Don't touch me, don't touch me."
    Who the hell! High and mighty, eh? Too good for me, eh? Don't put on
    the act for me . . . I know who you are.

EMIKO: Tell me who I am, Mister Smart Peasant.

OKA: Shut your fool mouth, goddamnit! Sure! I'll tell you. I know all about
    you . . . Shizue told me. The whole village knows.

EMIKO: Shizue!

OKA: Yeah! Shizue. Embarrassed the hell out of her, your own sister.

EMIKO: Embarrassed? I have nothing to be ashamed of. I don't know what
    you're talking about.

OKA: [*Derisively.*] You don't know what I'm talking about. I know. The whole
    village knows. They're all laughing at you. At me! Stupid Oka got stuck
    with a second-hand woman. I didn't say anything because . . .

EMIKO: I'm not second-hand!

OKA: Who you trying to fool? I know. Knew long time ago . . . Shizue wrote
    me all about your affairs in Tokyo. The men you were mess- . . .

EMIKO: Affairs? Men?

OKA: That man you were messing with . . . I knew all along. I didn't say
    anything because you . . . I . . .

EMIKO: I'm not ashamed of it.

OKA: You're not ashamed! What the hell! Your father thought he was pulling
    a fast one on me . . . thought I didn't know nothing . . . thought I was
    some kind of dumb ass . . . I didn't say nothing because Shizue's dead . . .
    Shizue's dead. I was willing to give you a chance.

EMIKO: [*Laughing.*] A chance?

OKA: Yeah! A chance! Laugh! Give a *joro* another chance. Sure, I'm stupid
    . . . dumb.

EMIKO: I'm not a whore. I'm true . . . he knows I'm true.

OKA: True! Ha!

EMIKO: You think I'm untrue just because I let . . . let you . . . There's only
    one man for me.

OKA: Let me [*Obscene gesture.*] you? I can do what I want with you. Your
    father palmed you off on me—like a dog or cat—an animal . . . couldn't

do nothing with you. Even that rich dumb Yamoto wouldn't have you. Your father—greedy father—so proud . . . making big plans for you . . . for himself. Ha! The whole village laughing at him . . . [EMIKO *hangs her head.*] Shizue told me. And she was working like a dog . . . trying to keep your goddamn father happy . . . doing my work and yours.

EMIKO: My work?

OKA: Yeah, your work too! She killed herself working! She killed herself . . . [*He has tender memories of his dull, uncomplaining wife.*] Up in the morning getting the fires started, working the bellows, cleaning the furnace, cooking, and late at night working with the sewing . . . tending the baby . . . [*He mutters.*] The goddamn family killed her. And you . . . you out there in Tokyo with the fancy clothes, doing the [*He sneers.*] dance, the tea, the flower, the *koto*, and the . . . [*Obscene gesture.*]

EMIKO: [*Hurting.*] Achhhh . . .

OKA: Did you have fun? Did you have fun on your sister's blood? [EMIKO *doesn't answer.*] Did you? He must have been a son-of-a-bitch . . . What would make that goddamn greedy old man send his prize mare to a plow horse like me? What kind of bum was he that your father . . .

EMIKO: He's not a bum . . . he's not a bum.

OKA: Was he Korean? Was he *Etta*? That's the only thing I could figure.

EMIKO: I'm true to him. Only him.

OKA: True? You think he's true to you? You think he waits for you? Remembers you? *Aho!* Think he cares?

EMIKO: [*Nodding quietly.*] He does.

OKA: And waits ten years? *Baka!* Go back to Japan and see. You'll find out. Go back to Japan. *Kaire!*

EMIKO: In time.

OKA: In time? How about now?

EMIKO: I can't now.

OKA: Ha! Now! Go now! Who needs you? Who needs you? You think a man waits ten years for a woman? You think you're some kind of . . . of . . . diamond . . . treasure . . . he's going to wait his life for you? Go to him. He's probably married with ten kids. Go to him. Get out! Goddamn *joro* . . . Go! Go!

[OKA *sweeps* EMIKO *off the bench.*]

EMIKO: [*Hurting.*] Ahhhh! I . . . I don't have the money. Give me money to . . .

OKA: If I had money I would give it to you ten years ago. You think I been eating this *kuso* for ten years because I like it?

EMIKO: You're selling the horse . . . Give me the . . .

OKA: [*Scoffing.*] That's for Kiyoko. I owe you nothing.

EMIKO: Ten years, you owe me.

OKA: Ten years of what? Misery? You gave me nothing. I give you nothing. You want to go, pack your bag and start walking. Try cross the desert. When you get dry and hungry, think about me.

EMIKO: I'd die out there.

OKA: Die? You think I didn't die here?

EMIKO: I didn't do anything to you.

OKA: No, no you didn't. All I wanted was a little comfort and . . . you . . . no, you didn't. No. So you die. We all die. Shizue died. If she was here, she wouldn't treat me like this . . . [*He thinks of his poor dead wife.*] Ah, I should have brought her with me. She'd be alive now. We'd be poor but happy . . . like . . . like Murata and his wife . . . and the kid . . .

EMIKO: I wish she were alive too. I'm not to blame for her dying. I didn't know . . . I was away. I loved her. I didn't want her to die . . . I . . .

OKA: [*Softening.*] I know that. I'm not blaming you for that . . . And it's not my fault what happened to you either . . . [EMIKO *is silent and* OKA *mistakes that for a change in attitude. He is encouraged.*] You understand that, eh? I didn't ask for you. It's not my fault you're here in this desert . . . with . . . with me . . . [EMIKO *weeps.* OKA *reaches out.*] I know I'm too old for you. It's hard for me too . . . but this is the way it is. I just ask you be kinder . . . understand it wasn't my fault. Try make it easier for me . . . for yourself too.

[OKA *touches her and she shrinks from his touch.*]

EMIKO: Ach!

OKA: [*Humiliated again.*] Goddamn it! I didn't ask for you! *Aho!* If you was smart you'd done as your father said . . . cut out that *saru shibai* with the *Etta* . . . married the rich Yamoto. Then you'd still be in Japan. Not here to make my life so miserable. [EMIKO *is silent.*] And you can have your *Etta* . . . and anyone else you want. Take them all on . . . [OKA *is worn out. It's hopeless.*] God, why do we do this all the time? Fighting, fighting all the time. There must be a better way to live . . . there must be another way.

[OKA *waits for a response, gives up, and enters the house.* EMIKO *watches him leave and pours herself another drink. The storm has passed, the alcohol takes over. She turns to the door* OKA *disappeared into.*]

EMIKO: Because I must keep the dream alive . . . the dream is all I live for. I am only in exile now. Because if I give in, all I've lived before . . . will mean nothing . . . will be for nothing . . . Because if I let you make me believe this is all there is to my life, the dream would die . . . I would die . . . [*She pours another drink and feels warm and good.*]

Fade out.

ACT II

Scene 1

Mid-September, afternoon. Muratas' kitchen. The calendar reads September. MASAKO *is at the kitchen table with several books. She thumbs through a Japanese magazine.* HANA *is with her sewing.*

MASAKO: Do they always wear kimonos in Japan, Mama?

HANA: Most of the time.

MASAKO: I wonder if Kiyoko will be wearing a kimono like this?

HANA: [*Peering into* MASAKO's *magazine.*] They don't dress like that . . . not for every day.

MASAKO: I wonder what she's like.

HANA: Probably a lot like you. What do you think she's like?

MASAKO: She's probably taller.

HANA: Mr. Oka isn't tall.

MASAKO: And pretty . . .

HANA: [*Laughing.*] Mr. Oka . . . Well, I don't suppose she'll look like her father.

MASAKO: Mrs. Oka is pretty.

HANA: She isn't Kiyoko-san's real mother, remember.

MASAKO: Oh. That's right.

HANA: But they are related. Well, we'll soon see.

MASAKO: I thought she was coming in September. It's already September.

HANA: Papa said Oka-san went to San Pedro a few days ago. He should be back soon with Kiyoko-san.

MASAKO: Didn't Mrs. Oka go too?

HANA: [*Glancing toward the Oka house.*] I don't think so. I see lights in their house at night.

MASAKO: Will they bring Kiyoko over to see us?

HANA: Of course. First thing, probably. You'll be very nice to her, won't you?

[MASAKO *leaves the table and finds another book.*]

MASAKO: Sure. I'm glad I'm going to have a friend. I hope she likes me.

HANA: She'll like you. Japanese girls are very polite, you know.

MASAKO: We have to be or our Mamas get mad at us.

HANA: Then I should be getting mad at you more often.

MASAKO: It's often enough already, Mama. [*She opens a hardback book.*] Look at this, Mama . . . I'm going to show her this book.

HANA: She won't be able to read at first.

MASAKO: I love this story. Mama, this is about people like us—settlers—it's about the prairie. We live in a prairie, don't we?

HANA: Prairie? Does that mean desert?

MASAKO: I think so.

HANA: [*Nodding and looking bleak.*] We live in a prairie.

MASAKO: It's about the hardships and the floods and droughts and how they have nothing but each other.

HANA: [*Nodding.*] We have nothing but each other. But these people—they're white people.

MASAKO: [*Nodding.*] Sure, Mama. They come from the east. Just like you and Papa came from Japan.

HANA: We come from the far far east. That's different. White people are different from us.

MASAKO: I know that.

HANA: White people among white people . . . that's different from Japanese among white people. You know what I'm saying?

MASAKO: I know that. How come they don't write books about us . . . about Japanese people?

HANA: Because we're nobodies here.

MASAKO: If I didn't read these, there'd be nothing for me . . .

HANA: Some of the things you read, you're never going to know.

MASAKO: I can dream, though.

HANA: [*Sighing.*] Sometimes the dreaming makes the living harder. Better to keep your head out of the clouds.

MASAKO: That's not much fun.

HANA: You'll have fun when Kiyoko-san comes. You can study together, you can sew, and sometime you can try some of those fancy American recipes.

MASAKO: Mama, you have to have chocolate and cream and things like that.

HANA: We'll get them.

[*We hear the putt-putt of* OKA's *old car.* MASAKO *and* HANA *pause and listen.* MASAKO *runs to the window.*]

MASAKO: I think it's them!

HANA: The Okas?

MASAKO: It's them! It's them!

[HANA *stands and looks out. She removes her apron and puts away her sewing.*]

HANA: Two of them. Emiko-san isn't with them. Let's go outside.

[OKA *and* KIYOKO, *14, enter.* OKA *is wearing his going-out clothes: a sweater, white shirt, dark pants, but no tie.* KIYOKO *walks behind him. She is short, chunky, broadchested and very self-conscious. Her hair is straight and banded into two shucks. She wears a conservative cotton dress, white socks and two-inch heels.* OKA *is proud. He struts in, his chest puffed out.*]

OKA: Hello, hello . . . We're here. We made it! [*He pushes* KIYOKO *forward.*] This is my daughter, Kiyoko. [*To* KIYOKO.] Murata-san . . . remember I was talking about? My friends . . .

KIYOKO: [*Barely audible, bowing deeply.*] Hajime mashite yoroshiku onegai shimasu . . .

HANA: [*Also bowing formally.*] I hope your journey was pleasant.

OKA: [*While the women are still bowing, he pushes* KIYOKO *toward* MASAKO.] This is Masako-chan; I told you about her . . .

[MASAKO *is shocked at* KIYOKO's *appearance. The girl she expected is already a woman. She stands with her mouth agape and withdraws noticeably.* HANA *rushes in to fill the awkwardness.*]

HANA: Say hello, Masako. My goodness, where are your manners? [*She laughs apologetically.*] In this country they don't make much to-do about manners. [*She stands back to examine* KIYOKO.] My, my, I didn't picture you so grown up. My, my . . . Tell me, how was your trip?

OKA: [*Proudly.*] We just drove in from Los Angeles just this morning. We spent the night in San Pedro and the next two days we spent in Los Angeles . . . you know, Japanese town.

HANA: How nice!

OKA: Kiyoko was so excited. Twisting her head this way and that—couldn't see enough with her big eyes. [*He imitates her fondly.*] She's from the country, you know . . . just a big country girl. Got all excited about the Chinese dinner—we had a Chinese dinner. She never ate it before.

[KIYOKO *covers her mouth and giggles.*]

HANA: Chinese dinner!

OKA: Oh, yeah. Duck, pakkai, chow mein, seaweed soup . . . the works!

HANA: A feast!

OKA: Oh, yeah. Like a holiday. Two holidays. Two holidays in one.

HANA: [*Pushes* MASAKO *forward.*] Two holidays in one! Kiyoko-san, our Masako has been looking forward to meeting you.

KIYOKO: [*Bowing again.*] *Hajime mashite* . . .

HANA: She's been thinking of all sorts of things she can do with you: sewing, cooking . . .

MASAKO: Oh, Mama.

[KIYOKO *covers her mouth and giggles.*]

HANA: It's true, Kiyoko-san. She's been looking forward to having a best friend.

[KIYOKO *giggles again and* MASAKO *pulls away.*]

OKA: Kiyoko, you shouldn't be so shy. The Muratas are my good friends and you should feel free with them. Ask anything, say anything . . . right?

HANA: Of course, of course. [*She is slightly annoyed with* MASAKO.] Masako, go in and start the tea. [MASAKO *enters the house.*] I'll call Papa. He's in the yard. Papa! Oka-san is here! [*To* KIYOKO.] Now tell me, how was your trip? Did you get seasick?

KIYOKO: [*Bowing and nodding.*] *Eh* ("yes"). A little . . .

OKA: Tell her. Tell her how sick you got.

[KIYOKO *covers her mouth and giggles.*]

HANA: Oh, I know, I know. I was too. That was a long time ago. I'm sure things are improved now. Tell me about Japan . . . what is it like now? They say it's so changed . . . modern . . .

OKA: Kiyoko comes from the country . . . backwoods. Nothing changes much there from century to century.

HANA: Ah! That's true. That's why I love Japan. And you wanted to leave. It's unbelievable. To come here!

OKA: She always dreamed about it.

HANA: Well, it's not really that bad.

OKA: No, it's not that bad. Depends on what you make of it.

HANA: That's right. What you make of it. I was just telling Masako today . . .

[MURATA *enters. He rubs his hands to take off the soil and comes in grinning. He shakes* OKA's *hand.*]

MURATA: Oi, oi . . .

OKA: Yah . . . I'm back. This is my daughter.

MURATA: No! She's beautiful!

OKA: Finally made it. Finally got her here.

MURATA: [*To* KIYOKO.] Your father hasn't stopped talking about you all summer.

HANA: And Masako too.

KIYOKO: [*Bowing.*] *Hajime mashite* . . .

MURATA: [*Acknowledging with a short bow.*] Yah. How'd you like the trip?

OKA: I was just telling your wife—had a good time in Los Angeles. Had a couple of great dinners, took in the cinema—Japanese pictures, bought her some American clothes.

HANA: Oh, you bought that in Los Angeles.

MURATA: Got a good price for your horse, eh? Lots of money, eh?

OKA: Nagata's a shrewd bargainer. Heh. It don't take much money to make her happy. She's a country girl.

MURATA: That's all right. Country's all right. Country girl's the best.

OKA: Had trouble on the way back.

MURATA: Yeah?

OKA: Fan belt broke.

MURATA: That'll happen.

OKA: Lucky I was near a gasoline station. We were in the mountains. Waited in a restaurant while it was getting fixed.

HANA: Oh, that was good.

OKA: Guess they don't see Japanese much. Stare? Terrible! Took them a long time to wait on us. Dumb waitress practically threw the food at us. Kiyoko felt bad.

HANA: Ah! That's too bad . . . too bad. That's why I always pack a lunch when we take trips.

MURATA: They'll spoil the day for you . . . those barbarians!

OKA: Terrible food too. Kiyoko couldn't swallow the dry bread and bologna.

HANA: That's the food they eat!

MURATA: Let's go in . . . have a little wine. Mama, we got wine? This is a celebration.

HANA: I think so . . . a little . . . [*They enter the house talking.* MASAKO *has made the tea, and* HANA *begins to serve the wine.*] How is your mother? Was she happy to see you?

KIYOKO: Oh, she . . . yes . . .

HANA: I just know she was surprised to see you so grown up. Of course, you remember her from Japan, don't you?

KIYOKO: [*Nodding.*] *Eh* ("yes"). I can barely remember. I was very young . . .

HANA: Of course. But you do, don't you?

KIYOKO: She was gone most of the time . . . at school in Tokyo. She was very pretty, I remember that.

HANA: She's still very pretty.

KIYOKO: *Eh.* She was always laughing. She was much younger then.

HANA: Oh now, it hasn't been that long ago.

[MASAKO *leaves the room to go outside. The following dialogue continues muted as light goes dim in the house and focuses on* MASAKO. EMIKO *enters, is drawn to the* MURATA *window and listens.*]

OKA: We stayed at an inn on East First Street. *Shizuokaya.* Whole inn filled with Shizuoka people . . . talking the old dialect. Thought I was in Japan again.

MURATA: That right?

OKA: Felt good. Like I was in Japan again.

HANA: [*To* KIYOKO.] Did you enjoy Los Angeles?

KIYOKO: [*Nodding.*] Eh.

OKA: That's as close as I'll get to Japan.

MURATA: *Mattakuna!* That's for sure.

[*Outside* MASAKO *becomes aware of* EMIKO.]

MASAKO: Why don't you go in?

EMIKO: Oh. Oh. Why don't you?

MASAKO: They're all grown-ups in there. I'm not grown up.

EMIKO: [*Softly.*] All grown-ups . . . Maybe I'm not either. [*Her mood changes.*] Masa-chan, do you have a boy friend?

MASAKO: I don't like boys. They don't like me.

EMIKO: Oh, that will change. You will change. I was like that too.

MASAKO: Besides, there're none around here . . . Japanese boys . . . There are some at school, but they don't like girls.

HANA: [*Calling from the kitchen.*] Masako . . .

[MASAKO *doesn't answer.*]

EMIKO: Your mother is calling you.

MASAKO: [*Answering her mother.*] *Nani?* ("What?")

HANA: [*From the kitchen.*] Come inside now.

EMIKO: You'll have a boy friend one day.

MASAKO: Not me.

EMIKO: You'll fall in love one day. Someone will make the inside of you light up, and you'll know you're in love. [*She relives her own experience.*] Your life will change . . . grow beautiful. It's good, Masa-chan. And this feeling you'll remember the rest of your life . . . will come back to you . . . haunt you . . . keep you alive . . . five, ten years . . . no matter what happens . . . keep you alive.

HANA: [*From the kitchen.*] Masako . . . come inside now.

[MASAKO *turns aside to answer and* EMIKO *slips away.*]

MASAKO: What, Mama?

[HANA *comes out.*]

HANA: Come inside. Don't be so unsociable. Kiyoko wants to talk to you.

MASAKO: [*Watching* EMIKO *leave.*] She doesn't want to talk to me. You're only saying that.

HANA: What's the matter with you? Don't you want to make friends with her?

MASAKO: She's not my friend. She's your friend.

HANA: Don't be so silly. She's only fourteen.

MASAKO: Fifteen. They said fifteen. She's your friend. She's an old lady.

HANA: Don't say that.

MASAKO: I don't like her.

HANA: Shhh! Don't say that.

MASAKO: She doesn't like me either.

HANA: Ma-chan. Remember your promise to Mr. Oka? You're going to take her to school, teach her the language, teach her the ways of Americans.

MASAKO: She can do it herself. You did.

HANA: That's not nice, Ma-chan.

MASAKO: I don't like the way she laughs.

[*She imitates* KIYOKO *holding her hand to her mouth and giggling and bowing.*]

HANA: Oh, how awful! Stop that. That's the way the girls do in Japan. Maybe she doesn't like your ways either. That's only a difference in manners. What you're doing now is considered very bad manners. [*She changes tone.*] Ma-chan . . . just wait—when she learns to read and speak, you'll have so much to say to each other. Come on, be a good girl and come inside.

MASAKO: It's just old people in there, Mama. I don't want to go in.

[HANA *calls* KIYOKO *away from the table and speaks confidentially to her.*]

HANA: Kiyoko-san, please come here a minute. Maybe it's better for you to talk to Masako alone. [KIYOKO *leaves the table and walks to* HANA *outside.*] Masako has a lot of things to tell you about . . . what to expect in school and things . . .

MURATA: [*Calling from the table.*] Mama, put out something . . . chiles . . . for Oka-san.

[HANA *leaves the two girls and enters the house.* KIYOKO *and* MASAKO *stand awkwardly,* KIYOKO *glancing shyly at* MASAKO.]

MASAKO: Do you like it here?

KIYOKO: [*Nodding.*] Eh.

[*There's an uncomfortable pause.*]

MASAKO: School will be starting next week . . .

KIYOKO: [*Nodding.*] Eh.

MASAKO: Do you want to walk to school with me?

KIYOKO: [*Nodding.*] Ah.

[MASAKO *rolls her eyes and tries again.*]

MASAKO: I leave at 7:30.

KIYOKO: Ah.

[*There's a long pause.* MASAKO *finally gives up and moves off stage.*]

MASAKO: I have to do something.

[KIYOKO *watches her leave and uncertainly moves back to the house.* HANA *looks up at* KIYOKO *coming in alone, sighs, and quietly pulls out a chair for her.*]

Fade out.

Scene 2

November night. Interior of the Murata house. Lamps are lit. The family is at the kitchen table. HANA *sews,* MASAKO *does her homework,* MURATA *reads the paper. They're dressed in warm robes and having tea. Outside thunder rolls in the distance and lightning flashes.*

HANA: It'll be *ohigan* ("an autumn festival") soon.

MURATA: Something to look forward to.

HANA: We will need sweet rice for *omochi* ("rice cakes").

MURATA: I'll order it next time I go to town.

HANA: [*To* MASAKO.] How is school? Getting a little harder?

MASAKO: Not that much. Sometimes the arithmetic is hard.

HANA: How is Kiyoko-san doing? Is she getting along all right?

MASAKO: She's good in arithmetic. She skipped a grade already.

HANA: Already? That's good news. Only November and she skipped a grade! At this rate she'll be through before you.

MASAKO: Well, she's older.

MURATA: Sure, she's older, Mama.

HANA: Has she made any friends?

MASAKO: No. She follows me around all day. She understands okay, but she doesn't talk. She talks like, you know . . . she says "ranchi" for lunch and "ranchi" for ranch too, and like that. Kids laugh and copy behind her back. It's hard to understand her.

HANA: You understand her, don't you?

MASAKO: I'm used to it. [MURATA *smiles secretly.*]

HANA: You should tell the kids not to laugh; after all, she's trying. Maybe you should help her practice those words . . . show her what she's doing wrong.

MASAKO: I already do. Our teacher told me to do that.

MURATA: [*Looking up from his paper.*] You ought to help her all you can.

HANA: And remember when you started school you couldn't speak English either.

MASAKO: I help her.

[MURATA *rises and goes to the window. The night is cold. Lightning flashes and the wind whistles.*]

MURATA: Looks like a storm coming up. Hope we don't have a freeze.

HANA: If it freezes, we'll have another bad year. Maybe we ought to start the smudge pots.

MURATA: [*Listening.*] It's starting to rain. Nothing to do now but pray.

HANA: If praying is the answer, we'd be in Japan now . . . rich.

MURATA: [*Wryly.*] We're not dead yet. We still have a chance. [HANA *glares at this small joke.*] Guess I'll turn in.

HANA: Go to bed . . . go to bed. I'll sit up and worry.

MURATA: If worrying was the answer, we'd be around the world twice and in Japan. Come on, Mama. Let's go to bed. It's too cold tonight to be mad. [*There's an urgent knock on the door. The family react to it.*] Dareh da! ("Who is it!") [MURATA *goes to the door and pauses.*] Who is it!

KIYOKO: [*Weakly.*] It's me . . . help me . . .

   [MURATA *opens the door and* KIYOKO *enters. She's dressed in a kimono with a shawl thrown over. Her legs are bare except for a pair of straw* zori. *Her hair is stringy from the rain and she trembles from the cold.*]

MURATA: My God! Kiyoko-san! What's the matter?

HANA: Kiyoko-san! What is it?

MURATA: What happened?

KIYOKO: [*Gasping.*] They're fighting . . . they're fighting.

MURATA: Ah . . . don't worry . . . those things happen. No cause to worry. Mama, make tea for her. Sit down and catch your breath. I'll take you home when you're ready.

HANA: Papa, I'll take care of it.

MURATA: Let me know when you're ready to go home.

HANA: It must be freezing out there. Try to get warm. Try to calm yourself.

MURATA: Kiyoko-san . . . don't worry.

   [HANA *waves* MASAKO *and* MURATA *off.* MURATA *leaves.* MASAKO *goes to her bed in the kitchen.*]

HANA: Papa, I'll take care of it.

KIYOKO: [*Looking at* MURATA's *retreating form.*] I came to ask your help.

HANA: You ran down here without a lantern? You could have fallen and hurt yourself.

KIYOKO: I don't care . . . I don't care.

HANA: You don't know, Kiyoko-san. It's treacherous out there . . . snakes, spiders . . .

KIYOKO: I must go back . . . I . . . I . . . you . . . please come with me.

HANA: First, first, we must get you warm . . . Drink your tea.

KIYOKO: But they might kill each other. They're fighting like animals. Help me stop them!

   [HANA *goes to the stove to warm a pot of soup.*]

HANA: I cannot interfere in a family quarrel.

KIYOKO: It's not a quarrel . . . it's a . . .

HANA: That's all it is. A family squabble. You'll see. Tomorrow . . .

   [KIYOKO *rises and puts her hand on* HANA's *arm.*]

KIYOKO: Not just a squabble . . . please! [*She starts toward the door but* HANA *restrains her.*]

HANA: Now listen. Listen to me, Kiyoko-san. I've known your father and mother a little while now. I suspect it's been like this for years. Every family has some kind of trouble.

KIYOKO: Not like this . . . not like this.

HANA: Some have it better—some worse. When you get married, you'll understand. Don't worry. Nothing will happen. [*She takes a towel from the*

wall and dries KIYOKO's *hair.*] You're chilled to the bone. You'll catch your
death . . .

KIYOKO: I don't care . . . I want to die.

HANA: Don't be silly. It's not that bad.

KIYOKO: They started drinking early in the afternoon. They make some kind
of brew and hide it somewhere in the desert.

HANA: It's illegal to make it. That's why they hide it. That home brew is
poison to the body . . . and the mind too.

KIYOKO: It makes them crazy. They drink it all the time and quarrel constantly. I was in the other room studying. I try so hard to keep up with
school.

HANA: We were talking about you just this evening. Masako says you're doing
so well . . . you skipped a grade?

KIYOKO: It's hard . . . hard . . . I'm too old for the class and the children . . .
[*She remembers all her problems and starts to cry again.*]

HANA: It's always hard in a new country.

KIYOKO: They were bickering and quarreling all afternoon. Then something
happened. All of a sudden I saw them on the floor . . . hitting and . . .
and . . . He was hitting her in the stomach, the face . . . I tried to stop
them, but they were so . . . drunk.

HANA: There, there . . . It's probably all over now.

KIYOKO: Why does it happen like this? Nothing is right. Everywhere I go . . .
Masa-chan is so lucky. I wish my life was like hers. I can hardly remember
my real mother.

HANA: Emiko-san is almost a real mother to you. She's blood kin.

KIYOKO: She hates me. She never speaks to me. She's so cold. I want to love
her but she won't let me. She hates me.

HANA: I don't think that's true, Kiyoko-san.

KIYOKO: I know it's true.

HANA: No. I don't think you have anything to do with it. It's this place. She
hates it. This place is so lonely and alien.

KIYOKO: Then why didn't she go back? Why did they stay here?

HANA: You don't know. It's not so simple. Sometimes I think . . .

KIYOKO: Then why don't they make the best of it here? Like you?

HANA: That isn't easy either. Believe me. [*She goes to the stove to stir the soup.*]
Sometimes . . . sometimes the longing for homeland fills me with despair.
Will I never return again? Will I never see my mother, my father, my
sisters again? But what can one do? There are responsibilities here . . .
children . . . [*She draws a sharp breath.*] And another day passes . . . another
month . . . another year. Eventually everything passes. [*She takes the soup
to* KIYOKO.] Did you have supper tonight?

KIYOKO: [*Bowing gratefully.*] Ah. When my . . . my aunt gets like this, she
doesn't cook. No one eats. I don't get hungry anymore.

HANA: Cook for yourself. It's important to keep your health.

KIYOKO: I left Japan for a better life here . . .

HANA: It isn't easy for you, is it? But you must remember your filial duty.

KIYOKO: It's so hard.

HANA: But you can make the best of it here, Kiyoko-san. And take care of yourself. You owe that to yourself. Eat. Keep well. It'll be better, you'll see. And sometimes it'll seem worse. But you'll survive. We do, you know . . . we do . . . [*She looks around.*] It's getting late.

KIYOKO: [*Apprehensively.*] I don't want to go back.

HANA: You can sleep with Masako tonight. Tomorrow you'll go back. And you'll remember what I told you. [*She puts her arms around* KIYOKO, *who is overcome with self-pity and begins to weep quietly.*] Life is never easy, Kiyoko-san. Endure. Endure. Soon you'll be marrying and going away. Things will not always be this way. And you'll look back on this . . . this night and you'll . . .

> [*There is a rap on the door.* HANA *exchanges glances with* KIYOKO *and goes to answer it. She opens it a crack.* OKA *has come looking for* KIYOKO. *He's dressed in an overcoat and holds a wet newspaper over his head.*]

OKA: Ah! I'm sorry to bother you so late at night . . . the fact is . . .

HANA: Oka-san . . .

OKA: [*Jovially.*] Good evening, good evening . . . [*He sees* KIYOKO.] Ah . . . there you are . . . Did you have a nice visit?

HANA: [*Irritated.*] Yes, she's here.

OKA: [*Still cheerful.*] Thought she might be. Ready to come home now?

HANA: She came in the rain.

OKA: [*Ignoring* HANA'*s tone.*] That's foolish of you, Kiyoko. You might catch cold.

HANA: She was frightened by your quarreling. She came for help.

OKA: [*Laughing with embarrassment.*] Oh! Kiyoko, that's nothing to worry about. It's just we had some disagreement . . .

HANA: That's what I told her, but she was frightened all the same.

OKA: Children are . . .

HANA: Not children, Oka-san. Kiyoko. Kiyoko was terrified. I think that was a terrible thing to do to her.

OKA: [*Rubbing his head.*] Oh, I . . . I . . .

HANA: If you had seen her a few minutes ago . . . hysterical . . . shaking . . . crying . . . wet and cold to the bone . . . out of her mind with worry.

OKA: [*Rubbing his head.*] Oh . . . I . . . don't know what she was so worried about.

HANA: You. You and Emiko fighting like you were going to kill each other.

OKA: [*There's nothing more to hide. He lowers his head in penitence.*] Aaaaaachhhhhhh . . .

HANA: I know I shouldn't tell you this, but there're one or two things I have to say: You sent for Kiyoko-san and now she's here. You said yourself she had a bad time in Japan, and now she's having a worse time. It isn't easy for her in a strange new country; the least you can do is try to keep her from worrying . . . especially about yourselves. I think it's terrible what you're doing to her . . . terrible!

OKA: [*Bowing in deep humility.*] I am ashamed . . .

HANA: I think she deserves better. I think you should think about that.

OKA: [*Still in his bow.*] I thank you for this reminder. It will never happen again. I promise.

HANA: I don't need that promise. Make it to Kiyoko-san.

OKA: [*To* KIYOKO.] Come with Papa now. He did a bad thing. He'll be a good Papa from now. He won't worry his little girl again. All right? All right? [*They move to the door.*]

KIYOKO: Thank you so much. [*She takes* MURATA's *robe and tries to return it.*]

OKA: Madam. I thank you again.

HANA: [*To* KIYOKO.] That's all right. You can bring it back tomorrow. [*Aside to* KIYOKO.] Remember . . . remember what we talked about. [*Loudly.*] Goodnight, Oka-san.

> [*They leave.* HANA *goes to* MASAKO, *who lies on the bed. She covers her.* MURATA *appears from the bedroom. He's heard it all. He and* HANA *exchange a glance and together they retire to their room.*]

Fade out.

Scene 3

The next morning. The Murata house and yard. HANA *and* MURATA *have already left the house to examine the rain damage in the fields.* MASAKO *prepares to go to school. She puts on a coat and picks up her books and lunch bag. Meanwhile,* KIYOKO *slips quietly into the yard. She wears a coat and carries* MURATA's *robe and sets it on the outside bench.* MASAKO *walks out and is surprised to see* KIYOKO.

MASAKO: Hi. I thought you'd be . . . sick today.

KIYOKO: Oh. I woke up late.

MASAKO: [*Scrutinizing* KIYOKO's *face.*] Your eyes are red.

KIYOKO: [*Averting her eyes.*] Oh. I . . . got . . . sand in it. Yes.

MASAKO: Do you want to use eye drops? We have eye drops in the house.

KIYOKO: Oh . . . no. That's all right.

MASAKO: That's what you call bloodshot.

KIYOKO: Oh.

MASAKO: My father gets it a lot. When he drinks too much.

KIYOKO: Oh . . .

> [MASAKO *notices* KIYOKO *doesn't have her lunch.*]

MASAKO: Where's your lunch bag?

KIYOKO: I . . . forgot it.

MASAKO: Did you make your lunch today?

KIYOKO: Yes. Yes, I did. But I forgot it.

MASAKO: Do you want to go back and get it?

KIYOKO: No, that's all right. [*They are silent for a while.*] We'll be late.

MASAKO: Do you want to practice your words?

KIYOKO: [*Thoughtfully.*] Oh . . .

MASAKO: Say, "My."

KIYOKO: My?

MASAKO: Eyes . . .

KIYOKO: Eyes.

MASAKO: Are . . .

KIYOKO: Are.

MASAKO: Red.

KIYOKO: Red.

MASAKO: Your eyes are red. [KIYOKO *doesn't repeat it.*] I . . . [KIYOKO *doesn't cooperate.*] Say, "I."

KIYOKO: I.

MASAKO: Got . . .

KIYOKO: Got.

MASAKO: Sand . . . [KIYOKO *balks.*] Say, "I."

KIYOKO: [*Sighing.*] I.

MASAKO: Reft . . .

KIYOKO: Reft.

MASAKO: My . . .

KIYOKO: My.

MASAKO: Runch . . .

KIYOKO: Run . . . Lunch. [*She stops.*] Masako-san, you are mean. You are hurting me.

MASAKO: It's a joke! I was just trying to make you laugh!

KIYOKO: I cannot laugh today.

MASAKO: Sure you can. You can laugh. Laugh! Like this! [*She makes a hearty laugh.*]

KIYOKO: I cannot laugh when you make fun of me.

MASAKO: Okay, I'm sorry. We'll practice some other words then, okay? [KIYOKO *doesn't answer.*] Say, "Okay."

KIYOKO: [*Reluctantly.*] Okay . . .

MASAKO: Okay, then . . . um . . . um . . . [*She still teases and talks rapidly.*] Say . . . um . . . "She sells sea shells on the sea shore." [KIYOKO *turns away indignantly.*] Aw, come on, Kiyoko! It's just a joke. Laugh!

KIYOKO: [*Imitating sarcastically.*] Ha-ha-ha! Now you say, "*Kono kyaku wa yoku kaki ku kyaku da!*"

MASAKO: Sure! I can say it! Kono kyaku waki ku kyoku kaku . . .

KIYOKO: That's not right.

MASAKO: Koki kuki kya . . .

KIYOKO: No.

MASAKO: Okay, then. You say, "Sea sells she shells . . . shu . . . sss . . ."

[*They both laugh,* KIYOKO *with her hands over her mouth.*]

MASAKO: [*Taking* KIYOKO's *hands from her mouth.*] Not like that! Like this! [*She gives a big belly laugh.*]

KIYOKO: Like this? [*She imitates* MASAKO.]

MASAKO: Yeah, that's right! You're not mad anymore?

KIYOKO: I'm not mad anymore.

MASAKO: Okay. You can share my lunch today because we're . . .

KIYOKO: "Flends?"

[MASAKO *looks at* KIYOKO, *they giggle and move on.* HANA AND MURATA *come in from assessing the storm's damage. They are dressed warmly.* HANA *is depressed.* MURATA *tries hard to be cheerful.*]

MURATA: It's not so bad, Mama.

HANA: Half the ranch is flooded . . . at least half.

MURATA: No-no. A quarter, maybe. It's sunny today . . . it'll dry.

HANA: The seedlings will rot.

MURATA: No, no. It'll dry. It's all right—better than I expected.

HANA: If we have another bad year, no one will lend us money for the next crop.

MURATA: Don't worry. If it doesn't drain by tomorrow, I'll replant the worst places. We still have some seed left. Yeah, I'll replant . . .

HANA: More work.

MURATA: Don't worry, Mama. It'll be all right.

HANA: [*Quietly.*] Papa, where will it end? Will we always be like this—always at the mercy of the weather—prices—always at the mercy of the Gods?

MURATA: [*Patting* HANA's *back.*] Things will change. Wait and see. We'll be back in Japan by . . . in two years . . . guarantee . . . Maybe sooner.

HANA: [*Dubiously.*] Two years . . .

MURATA: [*Finds the robe on the bench.*] Ah, look, Mama. Kiyoko-san brought back my robe.

HANA: [*Sighing.*] Kiyoko-san . . . poor Kiyoko-san . . . and Emiko-san.

MURATA: Ah, Mama. We're lucky. We're lucky, Mama.

[HANA *smiles sadly at* MURATA.]

Fade out.

Scene 4

The following spring, afternoon. Exterior of the Oka house. Oka is dressed to go out. He wears a sweater, long-sleeved white shirt, dark pants, no tie. He puts his foot on the bench to wipe off his shoe with the palm of his hand. He straightens his sleeve, removes a bit of lint and runs his fingers through his hair. He hums under his breath. KIYOKO *comes from the house. Her hair is frizzled with a permanent wave, she wears a gaudy new dress and a pair of new shoes. She carries a movie magazine—*Photoplay *or* Modern Screen.

OKA: [*Appreciatively.*] Pretty. Pretty.

KIYOKO: [*Turning for him.*] It's not too *badeh?*[7] I feel strange in colors.

OKA: Oh no. Young girls should wear bright colors. There's time enough to wear gray when you get old. Old lady colors. [KIYOKO *giggles.*] Sure you want to go to the picture show? It's such a nice day . . . shame to waste in a dark hall.

KIYOKO: Where else can we go?

OKA: We can go to the Muratas.

KIYOKO: All dressed up?

OKA: Or Nagatas. I'll show him what I got for my horse.

KIYOKO: [*Laughing.*] Oh, I love the pictures.

OKA: We don't have many nice spring days like this. Here the season is short. Summer comes in like a dragon . . . right behind . . . breathing fire . . . like a dragon. You don't know the summers here. They'll scare you. [*He tousles* KIYOKO's *hair and pulls a lock of it. It springs back. He shakes his head in wonder.*] Goddamn. Curly hair. Never thought curly hair could make you so happy.

KIYOKO: [*Giggling.*] All the American girls have curly hair.

OKA: Your friend Masako like it?

KIYOKO: [*Nodding.*] She says her mother will never let her get a permanent wave.

OKA: She said that, eh? Bet she's wanting one.

KIYOKO: I don't know about that.

OKA: Bet she's wanting some of your pretty dresses too.

KIYOKO: Her mother makes all her clothes.

OKA: Buying is just as good. Buying is better. No trouble that way.

KIYOKO: Masako's not so interested in clothes. She loves the pictures, but her mother won't let her go. Some day, can we take Masako with us?

OKA: If her mother lets her come. Her mother's got a mind of her own . . . a stiff back.

KIYOKO: But she's nice.

OKA: [*Dubiously.*] Oh, yeah. Can't be perfect, I guess. Kiyoko, after the harvest I'll have money and I'll buy you the prettiest dress in town. I'm going to be lucky this year. I feel it.

KIYOKO: You're already too good to me . . . dresses, shoes, permanent wave . . . movies . . .

OKA: That's nothing. After the harvest, just wait . . .

KIYOKO: Magazines . . . You do enough. I'm happy already.

OKA: You make me happy too, Kiyoko. You make me feel good . . . like a man again . . . [*That statement bothers him.*] One day you're going to make a young man happy. [KIYOKO *giggles.*] Someday we going to move from here.

KIYOKO: But we have good friends here, Papa.

7. Gaudy.

OKA: Next year our lease will be up and we got to move.

KIYOKO: The ranch is not ours?

OKA: No. In America, Japanese cannot own land. We lease and move every two, three years. Next year we going to go someplace where there's young fellows. There's none good enough for you here. [*He watches* KIYOKO *giggle.*] Yeah. You going to make a good wife. Already a good cook. I like your cooking.

KIYOKO: [*A little embarrassed.*] Shall we go now?

OKA: Yeah. Put the magazine away.

KIYOKO: I want to take it with me.

OKA: Take it with you?

KIYOKO: Last time, after we came back, I found all my magazines torn in half.

OKA: [*Looking toward the house.*] Torn?

KIYOKO: This is the only one I have left.

OKA: [*Not wanting to deal with it.*] All right. All right.

[*The two prepare to leave when the door opens.* EMIKO *stands there, her hair is unkempt and she looks wild. She holds an empty can in one hand, the lid in the other.*]

EMIKO: Where is it?

[OKA *tries to make a hasty departure.*]

KIYOKO: Where is what?

[OKA *pushes* KIYOKO *ahead of him, still trying to make a getaway.*]

EMIKO: Where is it? Where is it? What did you do with it? [EMIKO *moves toward* OKA. *He can't ignore her and he stops.*]

OKA: [*With false unconcern to* KIYOKO.] Why don't you walk on ahead to the Muratas?

KIYOKO: We're not going to the pictures?

OKA: We'll go. First you walk to the Muratas. Show them your new dress. I'll meet you there.

[KIYOKO *picks up a small package and exits.* OKA *sighs and shakes his head.*]

EMIKO: [*Shaking the can.*] Where is it? What did you do with it?

OKA: [*Feigning surprise.*] With what?

EMIKO: You know what. You stole it. You stole my money.

OKA: *Your* money?

EMIKO: I've been saving that money.

OKA: Yeah? Well, where'd you get it? Where'd you get it, eh? You stole it from me! Dollar by dollar . . . You stole it from me! Out of my pocket!

EMIKO: I saved it!

OKA: From my pocket!

EMIKO: It's mine! I saved for a long time . . . Some of it I brought from Japan.

OKA: *Bakayuna!* [8] What'd you bring from Japan? Nothing but some useless kimonos. [OKA *starts to leave but* EMIKO *hangs on to him.*]

EMIKO: Give back my money! Thief!

8. Stupid woman.

OKA: [*Swings around and balls his fists but doesn't strike.*] Goddamn! Get off me!

EMIKO: [*Now pleading.*] Please give it back . . . please . . . please . . . [*She starts to stroke him.* OKA *pulls her hands away and pushes her from him.*] Oni!

OKA: [*Seething.*] *Oni?* What does that make you? *Oni baba?* Yeah, that's what you are . . . a devil!

EMIKO: It's mine! Give it back . . .

OKA: The hell! You think you can live off me and steal my money too? How stupid you think I am?

EMIKO: [*Tearfully.*] But I've paid . . . I've paid . . .

OKA: With what?

EMIKO: You know I've paid.

OKA: [*Scoffing.*] You call that paying?

EMIKO: What did you do with it?

OKA: I don't have it.

EMIKO: It's gone? It's gone?

OKA: Yeah! It's gone. I spent it. The hell! Every last cent.

EMIKO: The new clothes . . . the curls . . . restaurants . . . pictures . . . shoes . . . My money . . . my going-home money . . .

OKA: You through?

EMIKO: What will I do? What will . . .

OKA: I don't care what you do. Walk. Use your feet. Swim to Japan. I don't care. I give you no more than you gave me. Now I don't want anything. I don't care what you do. [*He walks away.*]

> [EMIKO *still holds the empty can. Off stage we hear* OKA's *car door slam and the sound of his old car starting off. Accustomed to crying alone, she doesn't utter a sound. Her shoulders begin to shake, her dry soundless sobs turn to a silent laugh. She wipes the dust gently from the can as though comforting a friend. Her movements become sensuous, her hands move on to her own body, around her throat, over her breasts, to her hips, caressing, soothing, reminding her of her lover's hands.*]

Fade out.

Scene 5

Same day, late afternoon. Exterior of the Murata house. The light is soft. HANA *is sweeping the yard;* MASAKO *hangs a glass wind chime on the exposed wall.*

HANA: [*Directing* MASAKO.] There . . . there. That's a good place.

MASAKO: Here?

HANA: [*Nodding.*] It must catch the slightest breeze. [*Sighing and listening.*] It brings back so much . . . That's the reason I never hung one before. I guess it doesn't matter much any more . . .

MASAKO: I thought you liked to think about Japan.

HANA: [*Laughing sadly.*] I didn't want to hear that sound so often . . . get too used to it. Sometimes you hear something too often, after a while you don't hear it anymore . . . I didn't want that to happen. The same thing happens to feelings too, I guess. After a while you don't feel any more. You're too young to understand that yet.

MASAKO: I understand, Mama.

HANA: Wasn't it nice of Kiyoko-san to give us the *furin?*

MASAKO: I love it. I don't know anything about Japan, but it makes me feel something too.

HANA: Maybe someday when you're grown up, gone away, you'll hear it and remember yourself as this little girl . . . remember this old house, the ranch, and . . . your old mama . . .

MASAKO: That's kind of scary.

[EMIKO *enters unsteadily. She carries a bundle wrapped in a colorful scarf "furoshiki." In the packages are two beautiful kimonos.*]

HANA: Emiko-san! What a pleasant surprise! Please sit down. We were just hanging the *furin.* It was so sweet of Kiyoko-san to give it to Masako. She loves it.

[EMIKO *looks mildly interested. She acts as normal as she can throughout the scene, but at times drops her facade, revealing her desperation.*]

EMIKO: Thank you. [*She sets her bundle on the bench but keeps her hand on it.*]

HANA: Your family was here earlier. [EMIKO *smiles vaguely.*] On their way to the pictures, I think. [*To* MASAKO.] Make tea for us, Ma-chan.

EMIKO: Please don't . . .

HANA: Kiyoko-san was looking so nice—her hair all curly . . . Of course, in our day, straight black hair was desirable. Of course, times change.

EMIKO: Yes.

HANA: But she did look fine. My, my, a colorful new dress, new shoes, a permanent wave—looked like a regular American girl. Did you choose her dress?

EMIKO: No . . . I didn't go.

HANA: You know, I didn't think so. Very pretty, though. I liked it very much. Of course, I sew all Masako's clothes. It saves money. It'll be nice for you to make things for Kiyoko-san too. She'd be so pleased. I know she'd be pleased . . . [*While* HANA *talks,* EMIKO *plucks nervously at her package. She waits for* HANA *to stop talking.*] Emiko-san, is everything all right?

EMIKO: [*Smiling nervously.*] Yes.

HANA: Masako, please go make tea for us. See if there aren't any more of those crackers left. Or did you finish them? [*To* EMIKO.] We can't keep anything in this house. She eats everything as soon as Papa brings it home. You'd never know it, she's so skinny. We never have anything left for company.

MASAKO: We hardly ever have company anyway.

[HANA *gives her daughter a strong look, and* MASAKO *goes into the house.* EMIKO *is lost in her own thoughts. She strokes her package.*]

HANA: Is there something you . . . I can help you with? [*Very gently.*] Emiko-san?

EMIKO: [*Suddenly frightened.*] Oh no. I was thinking . . . Now that . . . now that . . . Masa-chan is growing up . . . older . . .

HANA: [*Relieved.*] Oh, yes. She's growing fast.

EMIKO: I was thinking . . . [*She stops, puts the package on her lap and is lost again.*]

HANA: Yes, she *is* growing. Time goes so fast. I think she'll be taller than me soon. [*She laughs weakly, stops and looks puzzled.*]

EMIKO: Yes.

[EMIKO'*s depression pervades the atmosphere.* HANA *is affected by it. The two women sit in silence. A small breeze moves the wind chimes. At the moment light grows dim on the two lonely figures.* MASAKO *comes from the house with a tray of tea. The light returns to normal again.*]

HANA: [*Gently.*] You're a good girl.

[MASAKO *looks first to* EMIKO *then to her mother. She sets the tray on the bench and stands near* EMIKO, *who seems to notice her for the first time.*]

EMIKO: How are you?

[HANA *pours the tea and serves her.*]

HANA: Emiko-san, is there something I can do for you?

EMIKO: There's . . . I was . . . I . . . Masa-chan will be a young lady soon . . .

HANA: Oh, well, now I don't know about "lady."

EMIKO: Maybe she would like a nice . . . nice . . . [*She unwraps her package.*] I have kimonos . . . I wore in Japan for dancing . . . maybe she can . . . if you like, I mean. They'll be nice on her . . . she's so slim . . .

[EMIKO *shakes out a robe.* HANA *and* MASAKO *are impressed.*]

HANA: Ohhhh! Beautiful!

MASAKO: Oh, Mama! Pretty! [HANA *and* MASAKO *finger the material.*] Gold threads, Mama.

HANA: Brocade!

EMIKO: Maybe Masa-chan would like them. I mean for her school programs . . . Japanese school . . .

HANA: Oh, no! Too good for country. People will be envious of us . . . wonder where we got them.

EMIKO: I mean for festivals . . . *Obon, Hana Matsuri* . . .

HANA: Oh, but you have Kiyoko-san now. You should give them to her. Has she seen them?

EMIKO: Oh . . . no . . .

HANA: She'll love them. You should give them to her . . . not our Masako.

EMIKO: I thought . . . I mean I was thinking of . . . if you could give me a little . . . if you could pay . . . manage to give me something for . . .

HANA: But these gowns, Emiko-san—they're worth hundreds.

EMIKO: I know, but I'm not asking for that. Whatever you can give . . . only as much as you can give.

MASAKO: Mama?

HANA: Masako, Papa doesn't have that kind of money.

EMIKO: Anything you can give . . . anything . . .

MASAKO: Ask Papa.

HANA: There's no use asking. I know he can't afford it.

EMIKO: [*Looking at* MASAKO.] A little at a time.

MASAKO: Mama?

HANA: [*Firmly.*] No, Masako. This is a luxury. [HANA *folds the gowns and puts them away.* MASAKO *is disappointed.* EMIKO *is devastated.* HANA *sees this and tries to find some way to help.*] Emiko-san, I hope you understand . . . [EMIKO *is silent trying to gather her resources.*] I know you can sell them and get the full price somewhere. Let's see . . . a family with a lot of growing daughters . . . someone who did well last year . . . Nagatas have no girls . . . Umedas have girls but no money . . . Well, let's see . . . Maybe not here in this country town. Ah . . . You can take them to the city, Los Angeles, and sell them to a store . . . or Terminal Island . . . lots of wealthy fishermen there. Yes, that would be the place. Why, it's no problem, Emiko-san. Have your husband take them there. I know you'll get your money. He'll find a buyer. I know he will.

EMIKO: Yes.

[EMIKO *finishes folding and ties the scarf. She sits quietly.*]

HANA: Please have your tea. I'm sorry . . . I really would like to take them for Masako but it just isn't possible. You understand, don't you? [EMIKO *nods.*] Please don't feel so . . . so bad. It's not really a matter of life or death, is it? Emiko-san?

[EMIKO *nods again.* HANA *sips her tea.*]

MASAKO: Mama? If you could ask Papa . . .

HANA: Oh, the tea is cold. Masako could you heat the kettle?

EMIKO: No more. I must be going. [*She picks up her package and rises slowly.*]

HANA: [*Looking helpless.*] So soon? Emiko-san, please stay. [EMIKO *starts to go.*] Masako will walk with you. [*She pushes* MASAKO *forward.*]

EMIKO: It's not far.

HANA: Emiko-san? You'll be all right?

EMIKO: Yes . . . yes . . . yes . . .

HANA: [*Calling as* EMIKO *exits.*] I'm sorry, Emiko-san.

EMIKO: Yes . . .

[MASAKO *and* HANA *watch as* EMIKO *leaves. The light grows dim as though a cloud passed over.* EMIKO *exits.* HANA *strokes* MASAKO's *hair.*]

HANA: Your hair is so black and straight . . . nice . . .

[*They stand close. The wind chimes tinkle; light grows dim. Light returns to normal.* MURATA *enters. He sees this tableau of mother and child and is puzzled.*]

MURATA: What's going on here?

[*The two women part.*]

HANA: Oh . . . nothing . . . nothing . . .

MASAKO: Mrs. Oka was here. She had two kimo- . . .

HANA: [*Putting her hand on* MASAKO's *shoulder.*] It was nothing . . .

MURATA: Eh? What'd she want?

HANA: Later, Papa. Right now, I'd better fix supper.

MURATA: [*Looking at the sky.*] Strange how that sun comes and goes. Maybe I didn't need to irrigate—looks like rain. [*He remembers and is exasperated.*] Ach! I forgot to shut the water.

MASAKO: I'll do it, Papa.

HANA: Masako, that gate's too heavy for you.

MURATA: She can handle it. Take out the pin and let the gate fall all the way down. All the way. And put the pin back. Don't forget to put the pin back.

HANA: And be careful. Don't fall in the canal.

    [MASAKO *leaves.*]

MURATA: What's the matter with that girl?

HANA: Nothing. Why?

MURATA: Usually have to beg her to do . . .

HANA: She's growing up.

MURATA: Must be that time of the month.

HANA: Oh, Papa, she's too young for that yet.

MURATA: [*Genially as they enter the house.*] Got to start some time. Looks like I'll be out-numbered soon. I'm out-numbered already.

    [HANA *glances at him and quietly sets about preparations for supper.* MURATA *removes his shirt and sits at the table with a paper. Light fades slowly.*]

Fade out.

Scene 6

Same evening. Exterior, desert. There is at least one shrub. MASAKO *appears, walking slowly. From a distance we hear* EMIKO *singing the song "And the Soul Shall Dance."* MASAKO *looks around, sees the shrub and crouches under it.* EMIKO *appears. She's dressed in her beautiful kimono tied loosely at her waist. She carries a branch of sage. Her hair is loose.*

EMIKO: *Akai kuchibiru / Kappu ni yosete / Aoi sake nomya / Kokoro ga odoru . . .*
  Kurai yoru no yume / Setsu nasa yo . . .

    [*She breaks into a dance, laughs mysteriously, turns round and round, acting out a fantasy.* MASAKO *stirs uncomfortably.* EMIKO *senses a presence. She stops, drops her branch and walks off stage singing as she goes.*]

EMIKO: *Aoi sake nomya / Yume mo odoru . . .*

    [MASAKO *watches as* EMIKO *leaves. She rises slowly and picks up the branch* EMIKO *has left. She looks at the branch, moves forward a step and looks off to the point where* EMIKO *disappeared. Light slowly fades until only the image of* MASAKO's *face remains etched in the mind.*]

Fade out.

KOKORO GA ODORU

AND THE SOUL SHALL DANCE

Akai kuchibiru
Kappu ni yosete
Aoi sake nomya
Kokoro ga odoru

Red lips
Press against a glass
Drink the green wine
And the soul shall dance

Kurai yoru no yume
Setsu nasa yo
Aoi sake nomya
Yume mo odoru

Dark night dreams
Are unbearable
Drink the green wine
And the dreams will dance

Asa no munashisa
Yume wo chirasu
Sora to kokoro wa
Sake shidai

Morning's reality
Scatter the dreams
Sky and soul
Depend on the wine

Futari wakare no
Samishisa yo
Hitori sake nomya
Kokoro ga odoru

The loneliness of
The two apart
Drink the wine alone
And the soul shall dance

LYRICS BY WAKAKO YAMAUCHI

KAGO NO TORI

THE CAGED BIRD
(She)

Aitasa, mita sa ni
Kowa sa wo wasure
Kurai yomichi wo
Tada hitori

   In the desire to meet her
   And the wish to see her
   He forgets his fear and
   Walks the dark streets alone.

(He)

Aini kita no ni
Naze dete awanu?
Boku no yobu koye
Wasure taka?

   Though I've come to tryst
   Why do you not come out?
   My voice calling you—
   Have you forgotten it?

(She)

Anata no yobu koye
Wasure ma senu ga
Deru ni derareru
Kago no tori

   Your voice calling me
   I have not forgotten, but
   To leave, to be able to leave—
   No choice for the caged bird.

POPULAR SONG

STUDY QUESTIONS

1. How does the play establish on the stage the sense of importance that the home has to each family? How personal to each family is the sense of place in the family

house? What indications are there that the invitation to share the bathhouse is a very personal, almost intimate act?

2. How does each of the CHARACTERS feel about Japan? In each case, how are his or her feelings revealed? Which characters show the most interest in American ways and in adapting to life in America? Who resists most?

3. What did you learn about Japanese farmers in California in the 1930s by reading the play? What happened to Japanese Americans a few years after the time in which the play is set? For those who are not Japanese Americans, imagine reading the play in the late thirties, the early forties, the late forties, and compare all the likely attitudes you would have toward Japan and Japanese Americans at the time of these readings to your attitude now. For those who are Japanese Americans, trace how your attitudes would have shifted toward life and your place in America in these past fifty-five or sixty years. Talk to the various generations in your family, and ask how it was "in their time." What emotions are aroused by this exercise of historical imagination?

4. What facts about the life of Japanese farmers in America in the 1930s emphasize the rootlessness felt by the two families? In what ways does the action of the play emphasize the lack of a sense of permanence? In what ways does the SETTING emphasize the transience of things? of a sense of place? of loyalties?

5. What do the two families have in common? How are they different? How are the differences dramatized?

6. In what specific ways are the two young girls alike? How does the scene in which Masako makes fun of Kiyoko's language and giggling emphasize their similarity? What TONAL function does the scene perform?

7. How important to the mood of the play is the kind of set provided for the performance? What specific directions in the text seem crucial to creating the possibilities of mood? If you were staging the play, how would you light the stage for the final scene? What other scenes would pose the biggest staging challenges? How would you stage the scene differently if you were adapting the play for television? for a film?

8. What props, beyond those absolutely necessary to the PLOT and ACTION, would you use onstage to remind the audience that the main characters are constantly thinking of life in Japan?

9. How does the setting concretely indicate the passage of time? If you were turning the play into a film, what alternatives might you use to indicate changing seasons and passing time? How important to the THEME of the play is the audience's sense that time has passed and seasons have changed?

10. The accidental burning of the bathhouse serves, early in the play, as a reason for the two families to interact and for scenes to take place in the Okas' house. Does the destruction of the bathhouse perform other dramatic functions as well?

Elise Sprunt Sheffield

B orn and raised in rural Virginia, Elise Sprunt Sheffield received her undergrad-
uate education at Mt. Holyoke College and Brown University. After serving
two years in the Peace Corps in Africa, she took a master's degree from Harvard
Divinity School, and she currently lives in Virginia. The following essay was her
first published piece.

THE "GENTLE WHOLENESS" OF HOME

A year ago with stamp-choked passport and two Ivy diplomas, I came home   1
to rural Virginia—not to visit, but to stay. The cows kept on grazing, the
dogs continued to loll about the porch, and local folks greeted my return as
if it were a natural thing.

But coming home wasn't part of my original plan. The Blue Ridge   2
Mountains may be beautiful, but years in their shadows had left me aching
for wider horizons. Hence Brown, and all that followed: short-term service
projects across the nation, and work abroad. By the time I joined the Peace
Corps in 1985, Africa was but the latest port-of-call in my life of moving on.

Sent to the tiny mountain kingdom of Lesotho in southern Africa to   3
teach high school, I began a two-year residence in the traditional village of
Ha Poli (meaning "Home of the Goats"), a hilltop cluster of sixty com-
pounds, innumerable animals, and one Catholic mission. Bounded by 10,000-
foot ridges, Ha Poli is cut off from much of Western development. Vehicles
are rare; electricity and telephone non-existent. Mail takes weeks.

As the only white person in the village, I settled into my hut with great   4
anticipation. Giddy with culture, only slowly did I come to recognize the
great irony at the heart of my foreign assignment. I began to see that all my
expansive notions of the exotic were to be lived, actually, in the tight confines
of a single goat village. So I committed myself to the ordinary. Like my
Basotho neighbors, I hauled water, hung laundry, gossiped. I celebrated birth,
marked death, humored drunks, deflected proposals, tangled with kids. I
borrowed eggs, loaned flour, dug a garden, prayed for rain. I waited.

And then it happened. The very qualities I had rejected in rural life 5
returned to me with an intensity that was no longer suffocating, but rather
deeply sustaining. In the parameter of Ha Poli's particularity, I discovered
community; in neighborly commitments, great freedom; in the humdrum of
our days together, gentle wholeness. The paradox stunned me: how could
such abundant living spring from so limited a life?

Many of my Brown-inspired assumptions about my life fell away. The 6
aspiration to stand out gave way to a groping desire to join in—to find community, get stuck, stay. By freeing us from past reference points and claims,
by setting us on individual paths of knowledge and responsibility, the university, I think, calls us to be a people on the move, in life and work. But
deep in Africa, I heard a different call.

Which is why, seven years after graduating from Brown, and one year 7
after a master's degree from Harvard, the only "track" I find myself on is the
dirt road winding past my home in western Virginia.

In search of community, my husband, Eric, and I have returned not 8
only to these familiar hills and hollows, but to the very house in which I was
raised. By choice, we live with my parents. While sanity requires that the
Sprunts and the Sheffields run separate households, we know ourselves at
the same time to be caught up in a single dance, needing each other in com-
plementary, mutually necessary ways. So far, it works.

I am amazed, and greatly relieved. As one who takes pride in her self- 9
sufficiency, I regarded coming home to be as perilous as going to Africa. But
a year after our leap, it feels good to be home. It feels very good, also, to
have had a choice. Africa's lessons were taught to me by people who, for the
most part, can't choose. Poverty keeps the rural Basotho close to the land
and to each other, and poverty is far different from the path of simplicity I
have chosen.

As woodworker and teacher, respectively, Eric and I believe we can find 10
a niche here on RFD[1] One. But it has been a humbling year. I've discovered
that getting a job in the public schools is harder than getting into Brown. So
I make do: some part-time teaching, a little substituting, even waitressing at
the local burger place. Commitment to place first, and job second, has given
me the patience to wait and the freedom to try new things.

The job market may be frustrating, but joining the community in other 11
ways has been a revelation. Suddenly I find myself speaking up at public
hearings, writing letters to the editor, ranting about unregulated growth,
coal-fired plants, school conditions . . . small things, mostly, but important
to the present and future life of this place and its people. Never an activist at
Brown, I am surprised by these initiatives, grateful for the clarity of vision
and strength of purpose this new rootedness seems to bring.

Sometimes when I think of my past wanderings, all this born-again 12
parochialism makes me laugh. When, at eighteen, I tossed myself into the

---

1. Rural Free Delivery, indicating postal address for unnumbered houses on unnamed streets.

sea of adventure, little did I intend, at thirty, to return with the tide. And yet, washed up, I know this is the place I both need and want to be.

"*Motho ke motho ka batho ba ba bang*," say the Basotho; "one is human only by, with, and through others." I hold these words before me like a lantern. I doubt I'll ever recreate the feeling of wholeness I found in Ha Poli; our cultures are just too different. Nevertheless, as an American with a taste of Africa as rich and full as honey on my tongue, I try.

STUDY QUESTIONS

1. How did the SPEAKER's experience in the African village of Ha Poli change the attitudes about life and place that she had had at Brown University? What is IRONIC about the meaning of the name Ha Poli ("Home of the Goats")? Compare her commitment "to the ordinary" (paragraph 4) in Ha Poli and her parental home in the Virginia Blue Ridge Mountains.

2. What are the values of "home" that Sheffield implies? What is the irony in the final sentence?

Elena Padilla

E ducated at the Universities of Puerto Rico and Chicago and at Columbia University, Elena Padilla is professor of public administration at New York University. The following selection is taken from the final chapter from Padilla's 1958 study *Up from Puerto Rico.*

MIGRANTS: TRANSIENTS OR SETTLERS?

Many Hispanos see their lives and those of their children as unfolding in this country. To them, Puerto Rico is something of the past, and for many of the children who are growing up or have grown up in the United States, Puerto Rico is less than an echo; it is a land they have never visited, a "foreign country." Some migrants consciously decide at some point or other to make their homes here, to stay in this country permanently, never again turning back to look at Puerto Rico. These are to be found even among recent migrants.

They are the people who view their future as being tied up with whatever life in New York may offer. We can call these Hispanos settlers, and can distinguish them from transients or those who regard their future life as gravitating toward Puerto Rico and who hope to return to live there later on, after their children have grown up or when they have enough savings to buy a house or start a business.

Settlers who have migrated to New York as adults are those who have lost or who give little importance to their relationships with their home towns, their friends and relatives who are still in Puerto Rico or are recent migrants to New York. They have cut off their emotional ties with the homeland, but they may still have significant interpersonal relationships with their kin and within cliques that may consist largely of persons from their own home town who are residents of New York. The settler fulfills or expects to fulfill his social needs in relation to living in New York.

One sort of settler has in his formative years moved away from his home town, rural or urban, in Puerto Rico to another town or city in the island itself. He started to break away from the primary relations and bonds of his home town then. By the time he comes to New York, he has already experienced life situations in which primary groups derived from his home town contexts have no longer operated for him, in which he has developed new social bonds, wherever he may have been. The primary group relationships of this kind of settler lack the continuity and history of those of the settler who, throughout his life, whether in Puerto Rico or New York, has been able to continue depending and relying on persons known to him for many years.

The consequent social adjustments that the settlers here have made are the outcome of a gradual process of adaptation to living in New York, and of recognizing that home, friends, and other interests are here and not in Puerto Rico. The settler may be oriented within the ethnic group of Puerto Ricans in New York, partially by his participation in the cliques and other small groups of people from his home town and in those of his New York neighbors. But the one who has lost his primary ties with a home town and has been exposed to a greater variety of group experiences in Puerto Rico through moving about there is likely to become involved in New York in groups and cliques that are not derived from any particular home town context. The kinds of adjustments he can make to these changing group situations is related to his own background experiences as a migrant in Puerto Rico itself. There he may have reacted to and resolved the social stresses of the uprooting he underwent as a migrant, acquiring as a result the social techniques for making it easier to establish satisfactory social relationships outside of home town and family settings.

The migrant who is essentially a transient, on the other hand, still maintains ties with the homeland: he has a strong feeling of having a country in Puerto Rico, a national identity there, and there he has friends and relatives whom he writes, visits, and can rely upon. "If things get bad" (*si las cosas se ponen malas)*, he can go back to Puerto Rico and get sympathy and help from those he grew up with. The transient migrants can be expected to feel obligated to their Puerto Rican friends and relatives, should these come to New York. The settler, on the other hand, is likely to say that he will "not return to Puerto Rico even if I have to eat stones in New York," and he will feel less bound to friends and relatives left in the island.

But becoming a settler does not necessarily involve a conscious decision. Transients may change into settlers as life orientations and social relations that are satisfactory and meaningful to them become part of their life in New York. The fundamental difference between settlers and transients is that the settler's life is organized in New York, while that of the transient is both in New York and in Puerto Rico. 6

In New York the lives of Puerto Ricans must, obviously, undergo profound changes. For those who learn American life in a slum like Eastville, the experience is one thing. For Puerto Ricans who were in better circumstances and had better life-chances in the island, it is another: they can begin life in New York as members of the middle class and avoid the particular cultural and social difficulties that beset the residents of Eastville. Yet all have their difficulties. Many overcome them. Many Eastvillers have made their way out of the slum into satisfactory fulfillment of their aspirations for themselves and their children. Others have returned to Puerto Rico. 7

One of the matters that concern Eastville Puerto Ricans is what has happened and is happening to Puerto Ricans in New York. Among migrants, social and cultural changes among Hispanos are a conscious preoccupation. They see the results of change in their own lives and in those of their friends. It is on this basis that they evaluate social behavior. Their awareness also reflects the conflicting values, orientations, and ambivalence of New York Hispanos. 8

True, old migrants and Hispanos who have grown up in New York regard recent migrants as representing a departure from their culture and as being socially inferior; on the other hand, recent migrants, in turn, express discontent with the ways Hispanos "are"—behave—in this country. George Espino, a New York–born man of Puerto Rican parents, voiced a sentiment frequently heard from others who like himself have grown up in New York: "The Puerto Ricans that are coming over today, well, they're the most hated people . . . the most hated people." Migrants, particularly those who have come as adults, contrast and evaluate the changes they experienced in their lives in Puerto Rico with those they are experiencing in New York. To them, changes here in family life, in the expectancies of what family members can demand of each other, in the ways children are brought up, in marital behavior, and in the behavior of men, women, and children—all these factors that govern daily life—are of concern. Migrants are conscious of these changes and speak of how they have something to do both with modern life and with living in New York. Some of these changes are acceptable and "good," while others are disapproved of and considered "bad." 9

Migrants write of their experiences in New York, tell of them on visits   10
to Puerto Rico, or show in their behavior the new ways they have adopted.
In Puerto Rico some of these types of behavior are considered to be for the
best, others for the worst. Potential migrants in the island know their future
life in New York is going to be different from their life in Puerto Rico. How,
and to what extent, however, is part of the adventure and "changing environment" they will find in New York.

The impact of New York life on Puerto Rican migrants is described in   11
fact and popular fancy, but whether it is described glowingly, soberly, or
depressingly depends on the aspirations, frustrations, hopes, and anxieties of
the one who is speaking. Men, women, and children change in New York,
it is said. How?

Clara Fredes, now a mother of three, who migrated after the Second   12
World War when she was a teen-ager, replied to a member of the field team
when asked if there were any differences between "the way people act here
and in Puerto Rico," that "when women get here they act too free. They go
out and stand in the street and don't cook dinner or anything. Puerto Rican
women in New York City are bad. They talk to other men beside their
husband, and just aren't nice. They boss the men. In Puerto Rico a wife
obeys her husband, and keeps house, and takes care of her children. But here
they run wild. [They are] all day long in the candy store talking and forgetting about their houses. Men here don't always support their wives and children. They are too free to. They think they can get away with everything,
but I think it's the women's fault. They are so bad. They don't take care of
the children right. The children [are] out on the streets at all hours of the
night."

Another informant, Gina Ortiz, said that Puerto Rican women in New   13
York like to go dancing the mambo and drinking and that "they don't do it
in Puerto Rico. In Puerto Rico the woman who smokes and drinks is a bad
woman."

Rose Burgos also explained changes in the behavior of women migrants.   14
"[It is] because they work and they have too much freedom. In Puerto Rico
the wife is always in the house. Here they go out, they go to work, get
together with another girl, drink beer, and so on. In Puerto Rico they don't
do that."

Women who want to be rated as "good" do not admit to having changed   15
in these directions. They would claim that they do not drink, smoke, or work
outside the home, though they may acknowledge having changed in such
areas as child-rearing, including giving greater freedom to their children.

Among changes that men undergo in New York, Dolores Miro men-   16
tioned that "some of them take friends. The friends like to drink and have
women in the street. They change. They like to do same thing the friends
do. . . . In Puerto Rico they have the same friends always, but here they
have friends from other places, other towns. Some of them are good friends,
some bad."

Good men are expected not to change in New York, but to continue   17 recognizing their obligations to their wives and children. They may say they do not have friends in New York because friends get a man in trouble.

A couple that consider themselves good and as having a satisfactory rela- [18] tionship with each other and their children may deny changes in their lives in New York. Manuel and Sophia Tres, in telling a fieldworker about themselves, said, "We don't have any change. We still the same." Manuel continued, "Some of them [Hispanos] when they come here they want to go to the bar and drink, are drunk people and have plenty girl friends," to which Sophia added, "because they make more money to spend. We are not changed, we have the same customs."

In New York children also change, in a variety of ways. It is more [19] difficult to make them respect their parents and elders, and one must keep them upstairs in order to prevent their becoming too uncontrollable and bad. For Juana Roman: "In Puerto Rico the fathers don't want the children to do what they want. They are strict; is better there. In Puerto Rico if your kids do anything wrong, the father punishes. Here you can't punish a big boy. . . . One day my boy went with another boy and they took a train and got lost, and when I got to the Children's Shelter, the lady said, 'Don't punish the boy,' and I said, 'Oh yes [I will punish him], I don't want him to do it again.' I see many kids that they do what they want."

Antonia Velez, now in her mid-thirties, finds that in this country people [20] are nice to old people, but says that in Puerto Rico old people are more respected. Her children do not respect in the same way she respected her father and mother in Puerto Rico when she was a child. Yet she is acceptant to some of the changes in patterns of respect she finds among her children. Says she, "Everybody is nice with the old people here in this country. They take care better of the old people and the children. I didn't pay too much attention to it in Puerto Rico. They are nice too. Everybody respects old people. The children are more respectful to old people in Puerto Rico than here . . . I know. I never used to argue with my mother in Puerto Rico. If she had a reason or no, I keep quiet. And with my father too. The word that he said was the only word to me. If he said not to go to a movie, I didn't discute [argue] that with him. I didn't go. No here. The children are more free here. Tommy, when I say, do that, and he don't want to and he explains me why, I don't mind that. I think it is better for him. You know, we didn't do that but it was not good inside. I think so, because they are human beings too. I love my father and mother because they are so good to me. If I didn't go to movies they may have the reason to say no, but I don't know it. Maybe that way, if I know it, I would have been better."

Children who have migrated recently at ages when they had friends and [21] were allowed to play in the yards and streets in their home towns and now are being reared "upstairs in the home" speak of their past life in Puerto Rico with nostalgia. Lydia Rios, age twelve, says that "here one cannot do anything," referring to having to remain at home, sitting and watching from a window the play of other children, except when she goes to church or school.

Advantages listed of living in New York are the higher wages and income, [22] better opportunities to educate the children, better medical care, more and better food, more and better clothes, furniture, and material things here than in Puerto Rico. In New York one can even save money to go back to Puerto Rico and purchase a house. Which place is better to live in is contingent on whether the migrant has realized or is on his way to realizing the aspirations and hopes connected with his coming to New York.

For Emilio Cruz it is better to live in New York than in Puerto Rico. "I think life in New York is better. We have better living in New York and can give the children the food they want and need. When we work we have more money. We spend more here but we earn more so we can live better. In Puerto Rico we rent a house [for] $10.00 or $12.00 a month, and here we [pay] so much [more] money and [must have] a lease too, [of] two or three years in New York." 23

Migrants speak of the future with reference to a good life, and a good life can be realized either in New York or in Puerto Rico, though one must search for it. As Rafael Dorcas put it, "A good life is when we work and we has the things we need for all the family. I think that's a good life." 24

STUDY QUESTIONS

1. What kinds of evidence does Padilla use to demonstrate the various points she makes? What kind of research has apparently gone into the study?

2. What kind of person, according to Padilla, is most likely to return to Puerto Rico? to look back upon earlier years in Puerto Rico with nostalgia or regret? What kind of person adapts most readily to mainland ways?

3. What are the characteristic ways in which Puerto Ricans find life different, according to Padilla, in New York? In what ways are those who move to New York most likely to change?

4. Choose one of the people quoted by Padilla, and analyze the words that person uses to express the fears and hopes of the migration experience. In what ways are that person's values expressed? How can you tell, from the words the person uses, what he or she cares most about?

5. How can you tell, for the people quoted in this essay, where "home" really is?

Edward Said

Born in Jerusalem, Palestine, in 1935, Edward Said attended Princeton and Harvard Universities and now teaches at Columbia University, where he was awarded the Lionel Trilling Award in 1976 for academic excellence. Said is the author of several books of literary criticism and theory, including *Orientalism* (1978), *The World, the Text, and the Critic* (1983), and *Culture and Imperialism* (1993), as well as books and essays on foreign relations.

REFLECTIONS ON EXILE

Exile is strangely compelling to think about but terrible to experience. It is the unhealable rift forced between a human being and a native place, between the self and its true home: its essential sadness can never be surmounted. And while it is true that literature and history contain heroic, romantic, glorious, even triumphant episodes in an exile's life, these are no more than efforts meant to overcome the crippling sorrow of estrangement. The achievements of exile are permanently undermined by the loss of something left behind for ever.

1

Exiles look at non-exiles with resentment. *They* belong in their surroundings, you feel, whereas an exile is always out of place. What is it like to be born in a place, to stay and live there, to know that you are of it, more or less for ever?

2

Although it is true that anyone prevented from returning home is an exile, some distinctions can be made between exiles, refugees, expatriates and émigrés. Exile originated in the age-old practice of banishment. Once banished, the exile lives an anomalous and miserable life, with the stigma of being an outsider. Refugees, on the other hand, are a creation of the twentieth-century state. The word 'refugee' has become a political one, suggesting large herds of innocent and bewildered people requiring urgent international assistance, whereas 'exile' carries with it, I think, a touch of solitude and spirituality.

3

Expatriates voluntarily live in an alien country, usually for personal or social reasons. Hemingway and Fitzgerald were not forced to live in France. Expatriates may share in the solitude and estrangement of exile, but they do not suffer under its rigid proscriptions. Émigrés enjoy an ambiguous status. Technically, an émigré is anyone who emigrates to a new country. Choice in the matter is certainly a possibility. Colonial officials, missionaries, technical experts, mercenaries and military advisers on loan may in a sense live in exile, but they have not been banished. White settlers in Africa, parts of Asia and Australia may once have been exiles, but as pioneers and nation-builders the label 'exile' dropped away from them.

4

Much of the exile's life is taken up with compensating for disorienting loss by creating a new world to rule. It is not surprising that so many exiles seem to be novelists, chess players, political activists, and intellectuals. Each

5

of these occupations requires a minimal investment in objects and places a great premium on mobility and skill. The exile's new world, logically enough, is unnatural and its unreality resembles fiction. Georg Lukács, in *Theory of the Novel*, argued with compelling force that the novel, a literary form created out of the unreality of ambition and fantasy, is *the* form of 'transcendental homelessness'. Classical epics, Lukács wrote, emanate from settled cultures in which values are clear, identities stable, life unchanging. The European novel is grounded in precisely the opposite experience, that of a changing society in which an itinerant and disinherited middle-class hero or heroine seeks to construct a new world that somewhat resembles an old one left behind for ever. In the epic there is no *other* world, only the finality of *this* one. Odysseus returns to Ithaca after years of wandering; Achilles will die because he cannot escape his fate. The novel, however, exists because other worlds *may* exist, alternatives for bourgeois speculators, wanderers, exiles.

No matter how well they may do, exiles are always eccentrics who *feel* 6
their difference (even as they frequently exploit it) as a kind of orphanhood. Anyone who is really homeless regards the habit of seeing estrangement in everything modern as an affectation, a display of modish attitudes. Clutching difference like a weapon to be used with stiffened will, the exile jealously insists on his or her right to refuse to belong.

This usually translates into an intransigence that is not easily ignored. 7
Wilfulness, exaggeration, overstatement: these are characteristic styles of being an exile, methods for compelling the world to accept your vision—which you make more unacceptable because you are in fact unwilling to have it accepted. It is yours, after all. Composure and serenity are the last things associated with the work of exiles. Artists in exile are decidedly unpleasant, and their stubbornness insinuates itself into even their exalted works. Dante's vision in *The Divine Comedy* is tremendously powerful in its universality and detail, but even the beatific peace achieved in the *Paradiso* bears traces of the vindictiveness and severity of judgement embodied in the *Inferno*. Who but an exile like Dante, banished from Florence, would use eternity as a place for settling old scores?

James Joyce *chose* to be in exile: to give force to his artistic vocation. In 8
an uncannily effective way—as Richard Ellmann has shown in his biography—Joyce picked a quarrel with Ireland and kept it alive so as to sustain the strictest opposition to what was familiar. Ellmann says that 'whenever his relations with his native land were in danger of improving, [Joyce] was to find a new incident to solidify his intransigence and to reaffirm the rightness of his voluntary absence.' Joyce's fiction concerns what in a letter he once described as the state of being 'alone and friendless'. And although it is rare to pick banishment as a way of life, Joyce perfectly understood its trials.

But Joyce's success as an exile stresses the question lodged at its very 9
heart: is exile so extreme and private that any instrumental use of it is ultimately a trivialization? How is it that the literature of exile has taken its place

as a *topos*[1] of human experience alongside the literature of adventure, education or discovery? Is this the *same* exile that quite literally kills Yanko Goorall[2] and has bred the expensive, often dehumanizing relationship between twentieth-century exile and nationalism? Or is it some more benign variety?

Much of the contemporary interest in exile can be traced to the somewhat pallid notion that non-exiles can share in the benefits of exile as a redemptive motif. There is, admittedly, a certain plausibility and truth to this idea. Like medieval itinerant scholars or learned Greek slaves in the Roman Empire, exiles—the exceptional ones among them—do leaven their environments. And naturally 'we' concentrate on that enlightening aspect of 'their' presence among us, not on their misery or their demands. But looked at from the bleak political perspective of modern mass dislocations, individual exiles force us to recognize the tragic fate of homelessness in a necessarily heartless world.

A generation age, Simone Weil[3] posed the dilemma of exile as concisely as it has ever been expressed. 'To be rooted,' she said, 'is perhaps the most important and least recognized need of the human soul.' Yet Weil also saw that most remedies for uprootedness in this era of world wars, deportations and mass exterminations are almost as dangerous as what they purportedly remedy. Of these, the state—or, more accurately, statism—is one of the most insidious, since worship of the state tends to supplant all other human bonds.

Weil exposes us anew to that whole complex of pressures and constraints that lie at the centre of the exile's predicament, which, as I have suggested, is as close as we come in the modern era to tragedy. There is the sheer fact of isolation and displacement, which produces the kind of narcissistic masochism that resists all efforts at amelioration, acculturation and community. At this extreme the exile can make a fetish of exile, a practice that distances him or her from all connections and commitments. To live as if everything around you were temporary and perhaps trivial is to fall prey to petulant cynicism as well as to querulous lovelessness. More common is the pressure on the exile to join—parties, national movements, the state. The exile is offered a new set of affiliations and develops new loyalties. But there is also a loss—of critical perspective, of intellectual reserve, of moral courage.

It must also be recognized that the defensive nationalism of exiles often fosters self-awareness as much as it does the less attractive forms of self-assertion. Such reconstitutive projects as assembling a nation out of exile (and this is true in this century for Jews and Palestinians) involve constructing a national history, reviving an ancient language, founding national institutions like libraries and universities. And these, while they sometimes promote strident ethnocentrism, also give rise to investigations of self that inevitably go far beyond such simple and positive facts as 'ethnicity'. For example, there

---

1. An oft-repeated scene or situation; type.

2. Castaway in Joseph Conrad's *Typhoon* (1903).

3. French philosopher (1909–1943). Author of *Enracinement (The Need for Roots)*.

is the self-consciousness of an individual trying to understand why the histories of the Palestinians and the Jews have certain patterns to them, why in spite of oppression and the threat of extinction a particular ethos remains alive in exile.

Necessarily, then, I speak of exile not as a privilege, but as an *alternative* to the mass institutions that dominate modern life. Exile is not, after all, a matter of choice: you are born into it, or it happens to you. But, provided that the exile refuses to sit on the sidelines nursing a wound, there are things to be learned: he or she must cultivate a scrupulous (not indulgent or sulky) subjectivity.

Perhaps the most rigorous example of such subjectivity is to be found in the writing of Theodor Adorno, the German-Jewish philosopher and critic. Adorno's masterwork, *Minima Moralia,* is an autobiography written while in exile; it is subtitled *Reflexionen aus dem beschädigten Leben (Reflections from a Mutilated Life).* Ruthlessly opposed to what he called the 'administered' world, Adorno saw all life as pressed into ready-made forms, prefabricated 'homes'. He argued that everything that one says or thinks, as well as every object one possesses, is ultimately a mere commodity. Language is jargon, objects are for sale. To refuse this state of affairs is the exile's intellectual mission.

Adorno's reflections are informed by the belief that the only home truly available now, though fragile and vulnerable, is in writing. Elsewhere, 'the house is past. The bombings of European cities, as well as the labour and concentration camps, merely precede as executors, with what the immanent development of technology had long decided was to be the fate of houses. These are now good only to be thrown away like old food cans.' In short, Adorno says with a grave irony, 'it is part of morality not to be at home in one's home.'

To follow Adorno is to stand away from 'home' in order to look at it with the exile's detachment. For there is considerable merit in the practice of noting the discrepancies between various concepts and ideas and what they actually produce. We take home and language for granted; they become nature, and their underlying assumptions recede into dogma and orthodoxy.

The exile knows that in a secular and contingent world, homes are always provisional. Borders and barriers, which enclose us within the safety of familiar territory, can also become prisons, and are often defended beyond reason or necessity. Exiles cross borders, break barriers of thought and experience.

Hugo of St Victor, a twelfth-century monk from Saxony, wrote these hauntingly beautiful lines:

> It is, therefore, a source of great virtue for the practised mind to learn, bit by bit, first to change about invisible and transitory things, so that afterwards it may be able to leave them behind altogether. The man who finds his homeland sweet is still a tender beginner; he to whom every soil is as his native one is already strong; but he is perfect to whom the entire world is as a foreign land. The tender soul has fixed his love on one spot in the world;

the strong man has extended his love to all places; the perfect man has extinguished his.

Erich Auerbach, the great twentieth-century literary scholar who spent the war years as an exile in Turkey, has cited this passage as a model for anyone wishing to transcend national or provincial limits. Only by embracing this attitude can a historian begin to grasp human experience and its written records in their diversity and particularity; otherwise he or she will remain committed more to the exclusions and reactions of prejudice than to the freedom that accompanies knowledge. But note that Hugo twice makes it clear that the 'strong' or 'perfect' man achieves independence and detachment by *working through* attachments, not by rejecting them. Exile is predicated on the existence of, love for, and bond with, one's native place; what is true of all exile is not that home and love of home are lost, but that loss is inherent in the very existence of both.

Regard experiences as if they were about to disappear. What is it that anchors them in reality? What would you save of them? What would you give up? Only someone who has achieved independence and detachment, someone whose homeland is 'sweet' but whose circumstances make it impossible to recapture that sweetness, can answer those questions. (Such a person would also find it impossible to derive satisfaction from substitutes furnished by illusion or dogma.)

This may seem like a prescription for an unrelieved grimness of outlook and, with it, a permanently sullen disapproval of all enthusiasm or buoyancy of spirit. Not necessarily. While it perhaps seems peculiar to speak of the pleasures of exile, there are some positive things to be said for a few of its conditions. Seeing 'the entire world as a foreign land' makes possible originality of vision. Most people are principally aware of one culture, one setting, one home; exiles are aware of at least two, and this plurality of vision gives rise to an awareness of simultaneous dimensions, an awareness that— to borrow a phrase from music—is *contrapuntal*.

For an exile, habits of life, expression or activity in the new environment inevitably occur against the memory of these things in another environment. Thus both the new and the old environments are vivid, actual, occurring together contrapuntally. There is a unique pleasure in this sort of apprehension, especially if the exile is conscious of other contrapuntal juxtapositions that diminish orthodox judgement and elevate appreciative sympathy. There is also a particular sense of achievement in acting as if one were at home wherever one happens to be.

This remains risky, however: the habit of dissimulation is both wearying and nerve-racking. Exile is never the state of being satisfied, placid, or secure. Exile, in the words of Wallace Stevens, is 'a mind of winter'[4] in which the pathos of summer and autumn as much as the potential of spring

4. From "The Snow Man" by Wallace Stevens (1879–1955).

are nearby but unobtainable. Perhaps this is another way of saying that a life of exile moves according to a different calendar, and is less seasonal and settled than life at home. Exile is life led outside habitual order. It is nomadic, decentred, contrapuntal; but no sooner does one get accustomed to it than its unsettling force erupts anew.

STUDY QUESTIONS

1. What are the differences between an exile, a refugee, an expatriate, and an émigré?

2. Why do exiles become intellectuals, novelists, political activists, and chess players, according to Said? Why do artists in exile tend to be unpleasant?

3. Explain why Said believes that though the lack of roots is a curse, the "cure," especially loyalty to a state, is almost as bad (paragraph 11). What are some of the other "remedies" (paragraph 12)?

4. What possible benefit or positive alternative to modern life can come from being an exile? Explain the clause Said quotes from Theodor Adorno: "it is part of morality not to be at home in one's home" (paragraph 16). Explain Hugo St. Victor's assertion that that person is "perfect to whom the entire world is as a foreign land" (paragraph 19); be sure to incorporate Said's explanation in that paragraph and the two that follow, and, especially, to define what he means by "contrapuntal." Apply what Said says concerning the positive things about the life of an exile to the study of other cultures.

5. After you finish the essay return to the opening paragraphs: to what extent has the "terrible experience" of exile been modified? reinforced? defined?

6. Said says the exile asks "What is it like to be born in a place, to stay and live there, to know that you are of it, more or less for ever?" (paragraph 2). Do you live where you were born—in the same country? city? neighborhood? house? Can you answer that question? Or have you returned to your home after living elsewhere? What works in this chapter celebrate (enjoy) the homeplace, which look back on it nostalgically or longingly? Do any celebrate instead what Sheffield suggests are the values she learned at Brown—"the aspiration to stand out," the freedom from the past and the gaining of new knowledge and responsibility, the call to be different and on the move?

AFTERWORD

SETTING

Both time and place are crucially important in literature, especially—but not only—in narratives. In most of the selections in this chapter, some particular place that is, was, or is discovered to be home was, is, or becomes central to a person's identity, his or her sense of self. Though she has never been to China and considers herself very American, the central CHARACTER in "A Pair of Tickets" finds when she visits China that she *is* indeed Chinese, more than she realized, and in a special sense, China is her "home." The boy who tells the story of "Sandra Street" learns about his street and about how to look around and locate himself and appreciate what he sees. He comes to understand what his street and his neighborhood mean to him, and its features which had before seemed ordinary take on significance and personal value. In Audre Lorde's "Home" the power of place helps to define the SPEAKER even though she seems never to have been to that place before and is at least a generation removed from it. She is returning to her roots, to a place that has influenced her because her mother was born there, not because she herself remembers personal experiences there. But the details of that place are important to her and important to the effects the poem has on us as readers.

Sometimes more than one place is "home," each home having a differ-ent, and sometimes changing, value or set of values. In "Sánchez," for example, his village in Mexico is his first home, Twin Pines in the Sierra Nevada another home, and their values change during the story. The speaker in Cabalquinto's "Hometown" seems two different people when he is in the two places he calls home—his childhood home and his home where he lives as a working adult. Often we leave our childhood home and sometimes even our homeland, and what we feel about that place is altered or intensified by time. We see such feelings in some of the poems in this chapter—for example, "In a Polish Home for the Aged" and "Postcard from Kashmir." There is a special feeling, too, in returning home, as we see in "Returning." That feeling is not always pleasant—the speaker in "Going Home" has some bitter memories—just as home itself is not always pleasant, as in "Escape the Ghettos of New York."

Time is equally important in most of the selections here, especially in the narratives. Poems, because they are short and may not tell a story, are often more concerned just to establish a mood or set of attitudes, and time may sometimes be less important to them; but they still need to be "placed" both temporally and spatially. In the accounts of "home" here, two different—and contrasting—versions of time are often important. One time frame involves the period remembered—usually a period in childhood or youth in which sense impressions were powerful and some sort of personal expectations were set. The other time frame is that of the present—that is, the time from which the person looks back, as in "Postcard from Kashmir." Sometimes, as in "Freeway 280" or "In a Polish Home for the Aged," the selection is clear about the double time setting—present adulthood and remembered past, separated by at least several decades—and at other times the contrast is implicit.

Both time and place are matters of SETTING—that is, the context where the ACTION takes place. Setting locates the action in a particular room or in a certain city and gives us a certain year or season or time of day. Setting is almost always important to the way a piece of literature affects us and thus is an important element to consider in reading—and in your own writing. At the least, setting establishes MOOD or gives particularity to the action, but often setting makes the action possible, believable, or meaningful. In plays, the setting is usually described explicitly in the beginning; we are told what the stage looks like and what the audience is to imagine as the time and place of action. In narratives, the setting may be less obvious but often is just as important. In "Sandra Street," for example, place becomes very much the subject of the narrative itself, and in "Sanchez" particular features of the location of the opening of the story (a section of

Stockton, California) are crucial to an understanding of the characters and their values.

And so is time. For "Sandra Street" the impressionable age of the person having the experience is crucial to the discovery—he must be young and unsure of his values for the story to work. In *And the Soul Shall Dance* the setting in the 1930s—before World War II—is essential to our understanding of the situation.

Even in poems, where action is often less explicit and where location sometimes may seem arbitrary, it is a good idea to try to be clear about setting. It is, in fact, a good rule of thumb, when beginning to read any piece of literature, to ask basic questions about where and when, as well as who and why. The particular location of the speaker who is reading the postcard is not specified in "Postcard from Kashmir," but Kashmir, the place from which the card comes, is all important. In "Hometown" the nighttime is essential to the mood and even the subject.

Setting is, however, not necessarily simple. In "In a Polish Home for the Aged" the events in the poem are remembered from a much later perspective, and the temporal setting is really a double one—that of events experienced as a young boy and remembered as an old man. To fully appreciate the poem, you must not only imagine the speaker's feelings but also recognize that memory, in literature as in life, is not always accurate, nor perspective reliable. Sometimes there is a tension between events and events remembered. Sometimes there is a tension between recollection and reality.

Setting is a part of the complex perspective on people and action that is offered to a reader; it helps set TONE and mood and it helps to realize both character and PLOT. It is one of the basic *elements* of literature (some of which are discussed briefly at the end of individual chapters in this book and defined in the Glossary at the end of the book). Interacting with one another, elements often bring about a complexity that goes beyond the identifiable effect of any single element alone.

WRITING
ABOUT THE READING

PERSONAL ESSAYS AND NARRATIVES

1. Think about the place you consider home: the room, the house or apartment build-ing, the street, the neighborhood, the city or town. Write an essay in which you describe, for someone of your own age and background, your home and what it means to you. Be sure to include physical details that help to demonstrate the things you value most. Be sure, too, to provide a sense of yourself in the way you describe your surroundings. Before beginning to write, consider carefully what aspects of your home are most important to you, what means the most to you emotionally; think carefully about how you are going to convey a sense of your feelings about home. Try to provide this sense without commenting directly on how much you like or dislike particular things.

2. Write a letter to a friend describing the place you live while you are at college. Choose one object in your room to concentrate on as an example of what is impor-tant to you in your present life. Provide enough detail about how you use that object to suggest some revealing things about yourself as a person. Be sure to fit the description to your assumed "audience"—that is, describe your room and the details of your life in ways that would be interesting to the particular person you have chosen as the receiver of your letter.

3. Write a letter (as in #2 above) to an uncle or grandmother (or some other relative you don't live with) or to some adult friend of your family's. Pretend that you have received a present, something that will be useful to you in school, and that you are writing to say thank you and at the same time to provide a picture of what your daily life is like at your college. Give a detailed picture of some SETTING that is important to you nearly every day at college—a place where you study, or go to class, or talk with friends, or take time to play and relax.

4. Think of some important event in your childhood that took place in the house you were then living in. Write a story about that event, paying particular attention to show the role that your home had in the story. Try to capture a sense of what you felt like at the time, how you saw things (did objects, for example, seem to you much larger then than they do now?), and how much you then understood of the "meaning" of the event. Try to figure out a way to convey a contrast between your present evaluation of the event and the value you put upon it at the time.

IMITATIONS AND PARODIES

1. Write an imitation of "Sandra Street." You will want to see your neighborhood (or a neighborhood you invent) with the eyes of an outsider, but tell the story in your own voice.

2. Write a poem on the subject of home as does Bao Gia Tran, an imitation of Kenny's "Going Home" or Cabalquinto's "Hometown," or a parody of "Postcard from Kashmir" ("Postcard from Detroit," ". . . Hope, Arkansas," ". . . Washington, D.C.," etc.).

3. Write a parodic scenario of Muñoz's return to the barrio.

ARGUMENTATIVE PAPERS

1. Write a brief speech of the kind you would like to deliver at the school assembly of a town near yours, proving that your hometown is superior to the one in which you are delivering the speech.

2. Write a reply to a friend who has written to ask you what kind of neighborhood you like best. In no more than 200 or 300 words, describe the kind of ideal community you would like to live in, suggesting both what kind of mix of people you would want to have living there and what kinds of buildings, open spaces, and businesses you would want there.

3. Imagine a debate (straight or parodic) between Vanessa Howard and Lucille Clifton.

RESEARCH PAPERS

1. In the library, look up at least three books or other sources of information on a place where you used to live. (If you have always lived in the same place, choose a city or country that you have always wanted to live in.) Find out the population, details of climate, ethnic and racial mix, basis of its economy, employment statistics, tax rates, transportation systems. Then look up the same information for the place you live in. Write a paragraph of no more than 100 words comparing the features of the two places in *one* category.

2. On the basis of the information you have discovered, write a brief historical account of your hometown from its founding to the present time. Limit yourself to 500 words, and choose the details carefully to try to suggest the "character" of the town as you know it.

3. Write a biographical paper on one of the writers featured in this chapter, going into more depth and detail than do the headnotes.

Student Writing

MY HOME

Bao Gia Tran

My home is not as vast as
a cowboy's "home on the range . . ."
Nor is my home as immense as John Lennon's "imagine."
It's not the Wailing Wall,
Nor is it Mecca.   5
It's not the YMCA,
Nor is it the nursing home of the forgotten elders.

*   *   *

My home is unique.
It is days in the first grade,
When I awkwardly copied those first letters in my life,   10
Shouldering my parents' wish,
To see me become a dignified man.
It is my mother whipping me,
The day I cut class to run after dragonflies.
My home   15
Is evenings and mornings spent on the river bank,
Watching the tide ebb and flow.
It is lullabies vaguely heard,
Those hot and humid afternoons.
It is also a rainy night,   20
A homeless boy holding his baby brother,
sitting under the shade of a house.
So cold, so wet, so tender.
They taught me love.
My home   25
is the war we were exposed to,
which we could never understand.
Friends came and went abruptly
We were braided together, like a rope, stretched;
Even the slightest touch would vibrate us all,   30
Warriors with tears.
My home
is the month of May,
as I strolled amid the ancient capital,
I inhaled, deeply inhaled the scent of leaves.   35
The night was clear, violet, and tranquil,

And I knew I was going to escape.

* * *

My home is in me, simple and complete.
Although it's been so far away,
Whenever I feel like a bird with sore wings,   40
I wish I could fly back to my nest.
Whenever chilly smiles in this land of vanity hit me,
I return home.

2

FAMILY

Everyone is part of a family of one kind or another. Even the most solitary person in the world is apt to be defined—in literature or in life—in relation to a family. That family may be absent or unknown; it may not fit the old stereotype of television families—a bread-winning father, 2.8 children, a dog named Spot, and a house in the suburbs. Still, we have all had to deal with emotions involving mother and father—whether biological or adoptive, absent or present—sisters and brothers, daughters and sons. We often resemble our relatives physically and mentally, for better or worse. We look like Dad. We have Mother's sense of humor. We have a way of turning our head that is just like Aunt Maria.

Sometimes our physical, social, and emotional bonds to our family cause embarrassment, resentment, and anger, but almost always a very special love as well. We are tied to family, yet we are different: we are ourselves. Belonging to another generation from that of our parents, we have different tastes in music; different preferences in clothes and forms of entertainment; different experiences, ideas, and beliefs. There often develops a division, sometimes a failure of understanding, a generation gap, even in the most close-knit of families. And between even the closest of siblings there usually arises some sort of rivalry or competition for attention, affirmation, and love. Emotions in a family setting tend to be intense. Perhaps that is why so many writers, trying to portray feelings and make them come to life, situate the people they describe within a family.

These family emotions are especially strong when we live in times of great social change. In twentieth-century North America, where change has been rapid and great and the population mobile, the generation gap sometimes seems very wide indeed. Few of us live in the same town from birth to marriage(s), even fewer in the house or town or on the farm that has been in the family for generations. Our parents may have been part of a totally different culture—rural, perhaps, while we are urban; inhabiting a racially segregated society while we are in transition toward some form of integration. The gap is even more dramatic when we are the children of migrants or immigrants, citizens of a different national or ethnic culture, perhaps with different beliefs and values as well as different food, clothing, language. Even sisters and brothers may differ as to whether they should retain some of the old language and customs of their parents or become wholly "American," as defined by their friends at school and other people their own age or those they see in films or on television.

The selections in this chapter deal with mothers and fathers and children; they are expressions of love and pride, of debt and regret. They explore the search to accommodate the self, the family, and the larger society. Like those in the first chapter, they are concerned with "home," but here the focus is not on a place but on the people who make that place home.

Tony Ardizzone

C hicagoan Tony Ardizzone has published two novels, *In the Name of the Father* and *Heart of the Order* (winner of the Virginia Prize for fiction), and two volumes of short stories, *The Evening News*, which won the Flannery O'Connor Award and from which "My Mother's Stories" is taken, and *Larabi's Ox: Stories of Morocco* (1992).

MY MOTHER'S STORIES

They were going to throw her away when she was a baby. The doctors said she was too tiny, too frail, that she wouldn't live. They performed the baptism right there in the sink between their pots of boiling water and their rows of shining instruments, chose who would be her godparents, used water straight from the tap. Her father, however, wouldn't hear one word of it. He didn't listen to their *she'll only die anyway* and *please give her to us* and *maybe we can experiment.* No, the child's father stood silently in the corner of the room, the back of one hand wiping his mouth and thick mustache, his blue eyes fixed on the black mud which caked his pants and boots.

Nein,[1] he said, finally. *Nein,* die anyvay.

With this, my mother smiles. She enjoys imitating the man's thick accent. She enjoys the sounds, the images, the memory. Her brown eyes look past me into the past. She draws a quick breath, then continues.

You can well imagine the rest. How the farmer took his wife and poor sickly child back to his farm. How the child was nursed, coddled, fed cow's milk, straight from the tops of the buckets—the rich, frothy cream. How the child lived. If she hadn't, I wouldn't be here now in the corner of this room, my eyes fixed on her, my mother and her stories. For now the sounds and pictures are *my* sounds and pictures. Her memory, my memory.

I stand here, remembering. The family moved. To Chicago, the city by the Great Lake, the city of jobs, money, opportunity. Away from northwestern Ohio's flat fields. The child grew. She is a young girl now, enrolled in school, Saint Teresa's, virgin. Chicago's Near North Side. The 1930s.

1. No (German).

And she is out walking with her girlfriend, a dark Sicilian. Spring, late afternoon. My mother wears a small pink bow in her brown hair.

Then from across the black pavement of the school playground comes a   6
lilting stream of foreign sound, language melodic, of the kind sung solemnly at High Mass. The Sicilian girl turns quickly, smiling. The voice is her older brother's, and he too is smiling as he stands inside the playground fence. My mother turns but does not smile. She is modest. Has been properly, strictly raised. Is the last of seven children and, therefore, the object of many scolding eyes and tongues. Her name is Mary.

Perhaps our Mary, being young, is somewhat frightened. The boy behind   7
the high fence is older than she, is in high school, is finely muscled, dark, deeply tanned. Around his neck hang golden things glistening on a thin chain. He wears a sleeveless shirt—his undershirt. Mary doesn't know whether to stay with her young friend or to continue walking. She stays, but she looks away from the boy's dark eyes and gazes instead at the worn belt around his thin waist.

That was my parents' first meeting. His name is Tony, as is mine. This   8
is not a story she tells willingly, for she sees nothing special in it. All of the embellishments are mine. I've had to drag the story out of her, nag her from room to room. Ma? Ask your father, she tells me. I ask my father. He looks up from his newspaper, then starts to smile. He's in a playful mood. He laughs, then says: I met your mother in Heaven.

She, in the hallway, overhears. Bull, she says, looking again past me.   9
He didn't even know I was alive. My father laughs behind his newspaper. I was Eva's friend, she says, and we were walking home from school— I watch him, listening as he lowers the paper to look at her. She tells the story.

She knows how to tell a pretty good story, I think. She's a natural. She   10
knows how to use her voice, when to pause, how to pace, what expressions to mask her face with. Her hand slices out the high fence. She's not in the same room with you when she really gets at it; her stories take her elsewhere, somewhere back. She's there again, back on a 1937 North Side sidestreet. My father and I are only witnesses.

Picture her, then. A young girl, frightened, though of course for no   11
good reason—my father wouldn't have harmed her. I'll vouch for him. I'm his first son. But she didn't know that as the afternoon light turned low and golden from between distant buildings. Later she'd think him strange and rather arrogant, flexing his tanned muscles before her inside the fence, like a bull before a heifer. And for years (wasted ones, I think) she didn't give him a second thought, or so she claims—the years that she dated boys who were closer to her kind. These are her words.

Imagine those years, years of *ja Fräulein, ja, bitte, entschuldigen Sie,*[2] years   12
of pale Johnnys and freckled Fritzes and hairy Hermans, towheads all, who take pretty Mary dancing and roller-skating and sometimes downtown on

---

2. Yes miss, yes, please, excuse me.

the El to the movie theaters on State Street to see Clark Gable, and who buy popcorn and ice cream for her and, later, cups of coffee which she then drank with cream, and who hold her small hand and look up at the Chicago sky as they walk with her along the dark city streets to her father's flat on Fremont. Not *one* second thought? I cannot believe it. And whenever I interrupt to ask, she waves me away like I'm an insect flying between her eyes and what she really sees. I fold my arms, but I listen.

She was sweeping. This story always begins with that detail. With broom 13 in hand. Nineteen years old and employed as a milliner and home one Saturday and she was sweeping. By now both her parents were old. Her mother had grown round, ripe like a fruit, like she would. Her father now fashioned wood. A mound of fluff and sawdust grows in the center of the room and she is humming, perhaps something from Glenn Miller, or she might have sung, as I've heard her do while ironing on the back porch, when from behind the locked back screen door there was suddenly a knock and it was my father, smiling.

She never tells the rest of the details. But this was the afternoon he 14 proposed. Why he chose that afternoon, or even afternoon at all, are secrets not known to me. I ask her and she evades me. *Ask your father.* I ask him and he says he doesn't know. Then he looks at her and laughs, his eyes smiling, and I can see that he is making up some lie to tell me. I watch her. Because I loved her so much I couldn't wait until that night, he says. My mother laughs and shakes her head. No, he says, I'll tell you the truth this time. Now you really know he's lying. I was just walking down the street and the idea came to me. See, it was awful hot. His hand on his forehead, he pretends he had sunstroke. My mother laughs less.

There were problems. Another of her stories. They follow one after the 15 next like cars out on the street—memories, there is just no stopping them. Their marriage would be mixed. Not in the religious sense—that would have been unthinkable—but in terms of language, origin, tradition. Like mixing your clubs with your hearts, mixing this girl from Liechtenstein with this boy from Sicily. Her family thought she was, perhaps, lowering herself. An Italian? Why not your kind? And his family, likewise, felt that he would be less than happy with a non-Sicilian girl. She's so skinny, they told him. *Misca!* [3] Mary's skin and bones. When she has the first baby she'll bleed to death. And what will she feed you? Cabbages? *Marry your own kind.*

At their Mass someone failed to play "Ave Maria." Since that was the 16 cue for my mother to stand and then to place a bouquet of flowers on Mary's side altar, she remained at the center altar, still kneeling, waiting patiently for the organist to begin. He was playing some other song, not "Ave Maria." The priest gestured to her. My mother shook her head.

She was a beautiful bride, and she wore a velvet dress. You should see 17 the wedding photograph that hangs in the hallway of their house in Chicago.

3. Gracious!

Imagine a slender brown-haired bride in white velvet shaking her head at the priest who's just married her. No, the time is not yet for the young woman to stand, for her to kneel in prayer before the altar of the Virgin. This is her wedding day, remember. She is waiting for "Ave Maria."

She is waiting to this day, for the organist never did play the song, and the priest again motioned to her, then bent and whispered in her ear, and then, indignant, crushed, the young bride finally stood and angrily, solemnly, sadly waited for her maid of honor to gather the long train of her flowing velvet dress, and together the two marched to the Virgin's side altar. 18

She tells this story frequently, whenever there is a wedding. I think that each time she begins the story she is tempted to change the outcome, to make the stupid organist suddenly stop and slap his head. To make the organist begin the chords of "Ave Maria." That kind of power isn't possible in life. The organist didn't stop or slap his head. 19

I wonder if the best man tipped him. If my father was angry enough to complain. If the muscles in his jaws tightened, if his hands turned to fists, if anyone waited for the organist out in the parking lot. I am carried away. 20

Details *are* significant. Literally they can be matters of life and death. An organist makes an innocent mistake in 1946 and for the rest of her life a woman is compelled to repeat a story, as if for her the moment has not yet been fixed, as if by remembering and then speaking she could still influence the pattern of events since passed. 21

Life and death— 22

I was hoping the counterpart wouldn't be able to work its way into this story. But it's difficult to keep death out. The final detail. Always coming along unexpectedly, the uninvited guest at the banquet, acting like you were supposed to have known all along that he'd get there, expecting to be seated and for you to offer him a drink. 23

My father called yesterday. He said he was just leaving work to take my mother again to the hospital. Tests. I shouldn't call her yet. No need to alarm her, my father said. Just tests. We'll keep you posted. My mother is in the hospital. I am not Meursault.[4] 24

I must describe the counterpart, return, begin again. With 1947, with my mother, delirious, in labor. Brought to the hospital by my father early on a Saturday, and on Monday laboring still. The doctors didn't believe in using drugs. She lay three days, terrified, sweating. On Monday morning they brought my father into the room, clad in an antiseptic gown, his face covered by a mask. She mistook him for one of the doctors. When he bent to kiss her cheek she grabbed his arm and begged him. Doctor, doctor, can you give me something for the pain? 25

That Monday was Labor Day. Ironies exist. Each September now, on my older sister Diana's birthday, my mother smiles and tells that story. 26

---

4. Narrator of Albert Camus's *The Stranger* (1942).

Each of us was a difficult birth. Did my father's family know something   27
after all? The fourth, my brother Bob, nearly killed her. He was big, over
ten pounds. The doctors boasted, proudly, that Bob set their personal record.
The fifth child, Jim, weighed almost ten-and-a-half pounds, and after Jim
the doctors fixed my mother so that there wouldn't be a sixth child. I dislike
the word *fixed*, but it's an appropriate word, I think.

When I was a child my mother once took Diana and me shopping, to   28
one of those mom-and-pop stores in the middle of the block. I remember a
blind man who always sat on a wooden milk crate outside the store with his
large dog. I was afraid of the dog. Inside the store we shopped, and my
mother told us stories, and the three of us were laughing. She lifted a carton
of soda as she spoke. Then the rotted cardboard bottom of the carton gave
way and the soda bottles fell. The bottles burst. The sharp glass bounced.
She shouted and we screamed, and as she tells this story she makes a point
of remembering how worried she was that the glass had reached our eyes.
But then some woman in the store told her she was bleeding. My mother
looked down. Her foot was cut so badly that blood gushed from her shoe. I
remember the picture, but then the face of the blind man's dog covers up the
image and I see the wooden milk crate, the scratched white cane.

The middle child, Linda, is the special one. It was on a Christmas morn-   29
ing when they first feared she was deaf. Either Diana or I knocked over a
pile of toy pans and dishes—a pretend kitchen—directly behind the one-
year-old child playing on the floor, and Linda, bright and beautiful, did not
move. She played innocently, unaffected, removed from the sound that had
come to life behind her. Frantic, my mother then banged two of the metal
dinner plates behind Linda's head. Linda continued playing, in a world by
herself, softly cooing.

What I can imagine now from my mother's stories is a long procession   30
of doctors, specialists, long trips on the bus. Snow-covered streets. Waiting
in sterile waiting rooms. Questions. Answers. More questions. Tests. Hope.
Then, no hope. Then guilt came. Tony and Mary blamed themselves.

Forgive the generalities. She is a friendly woman; she likes to make oth-   31
ers laugh. Big-hearted, perhaps to a fault, my mother has a compulsion to
please. I suspect she learned that trait as a child, being the youngest of so
many children. Her parents were quite old, and as I piece her life together I
imagine them strict, resolute, humorless. My mother would disagree were
she to hear me. But I suspect that she's been bullied and made to feel inferior,
by whom or what I don't exactly know, and, to compensate, she works very
hard at pleasing.

She tells a story about how she would wash and wax her oldest brother's   32
car and how he'd pay her one penny. How each day, regardless of the weather,
she'd walk to a distant newsstand and buy for her father the *Abendpost*.[5] How
she'd be sent on especially scorching summer days by another of her brothers

5. Evening Post, a German-language newspaper.

for an ice cream cone, and how as she would gingerly carry it home she'd take not one lick. How could she resist? In my mother's stories she's always the one who's pleasing.

Her brown eyes light up, and like a young girl she laughs. She says she used to cheat sometimes and take a lick. Then, if her brother complained, she'd claim the ice cream had been melted by the sun. Delighted with herself, she smiles. Her eyes again twinkle with light. 33

I am carried away again. If it were me in that story I'd throw the cone to the ground and tell my brother to get his own damn ice cream. 34

You've seen her. You're familiar with the kind of house she lives in, the red brick two-flat. You've walked the tree-lined city street. She hangs the family's wash up in the small backyard, the next clothespin in her mouth. She picks up the squashed paper cups and the mustard-stained foot-long hot dog wrappers out in the front that the kids from the public school leave behind as they walk back from the Tastee-Freeze on the corner. During the winter she sweeps the snow. Wearing a discarded pair of my father's earmuffs. During the fall she sweeps leaves. She gets angry when the kids cut through the backyard, leaving the chain-link gates open, for the dog barks then and the barking bothers her. The dog, a female schnauzer mutt, is called Alfie. No ferocious beast—the plastic BEWARE OF DOG signs on the gates have the harsher bite. My mother doesn't like it when the kids leave the alley gate open. She talks to both her neighbors across both her fences. Wearing one of Bob's old sweaters, green and torn at one elbow, she bends to pick up a fallen autumn twig. She stretches to hang the wash up—the rows of whites, then the coloreds. She lets Alfie out and checks the alley gate. 35

Summer visit. Over a mug of morning coffee I sit in the kitchen reading the *Sun-Times*. Alfie in the backyard barks and barks. My mother goes outside to quiet her. I turn the page, reading of rape or robbery, something distant. Then I hear the dog growl, then again bark. I go outside. 36

My mother is returning to the house, her face red, angry. Son of a B, she says. I just caught some punk standing outside the alley gate teasing Alfie. She points. He was daring her to jump at him, and the damn kid was holding one of the garbage can lids over his head, just waiting to hit her. My mother demonstrates with her hands. 37

I run to the alley, ready to fight, to defend. But there is no one in the alley. 38

My mother stands there on the narrow strip of sidewalk, her hands now at her sides. She looks tired. Behind her in the yard is an old table covered with potted plants. Coleus, philodendron, wandering Jew. One of the planters, a statue of the Sacred Heart of Jesus. Another, Mary with her white ceramic hands folded in prayer. Mother's Day presents of years ago. Standing in the bright morning sun. 39

And when I came out, my mother continues, the punk just looked at me, real snotty-like, like he was *daring* me, and then he said come on and hit 40 me, lady, you just come right on and hit me. I'll show you, lady, come on. And then he used the *F* word. She shakes her head and looks at me.

Later, inside, as she irons one of my father's shirts, she tells me another ₄₁ story. It happened last week, at night. The ten o'clock news was on. Time to walk Alfie. She'd been feeling lousy all day so Jim took the dog out front instead.

So he was standing out there waiting for Alfie to finish up her business ₄₂ when all of a sudden he hears this engine and he looks up, and you know what it was, Tony? Can you guess, of all things? It was this car, this *car*, driving right down along the sidewalk with its lights out. Jim said he dove straight for the curb, pulling poor Alfie in the middle of number two right with him. And when they went past him they swore at him and threw an empty beer can at him. She laughs and looks at me, then stops ironing and sips her coffee. Her laughter is from fear. Well, you should have heard your little brother when he came back in. Boy was he steaming! They could have killed him they were driving so fast. The cops caught the kids up at Tastee-Freeze corner. We saw the squad car lights from the front windows. It was a good thing Jim took the dog out that night instead of me. She sprinkles the shirt with water from a Pepsi bottle. Can you picture your old mother diving then for the curb?

She makes a tugging gesture with her hands. Pulling the leash. Saving ₄₃ herself and Alfie. Again she laughs. She tells the story again when Jim comes home.

At first the doctors thought she had disseminated lupus erythematosus. ₄₄ Lupus means wolf. It is primarily a disease of the skin. As lupus advances, the victim's face becomes ulcerated by what are called butterfly eruptions. The face comes to resemble a wolf's. Disseminated lupus attacks the joints as well as the internal organs. There isn't a known cure.

And at first they made her hang. My mother. They made her buy a ₄₅ sling into which she placed her head, five times each day. Pulling her head from the other side was a heavy water bag. My father put the equipment up on the door of my bedroom. For years when I went to sleep I stared at that water bag. She had to hang for two-and-a-half hours each day. Those were the years that she read every book she could get her hands on.

And those were the years that she received the weekly shots, the corti- ₄₆ sone, the steroids, that made her puff up, made her put on the weight the doctors are now telling her to get rid of.

Then one of the doctors died, and then she had to find new doctors, and ₄₇ then again she had to undergo their battery of tests. These new doctors told her that she probably didn't have lupus, that instead they thought she had severe rheumatoid arthritis, that the ten years of traction and corticosteroids had been a mistake. They gave her a drugstore full of pills then. They told her to lose weight, to exercise each night.

A small blackboard hangs over the kitchen sink. The markings put there ₄₈ each day appear to be Chinese. Long lines for these pills, dots for those, the letter *A* for yet another. A squiggly line for something else.

The new doctors taught her the system. When you take over thirty pills a day you can't rely on memory.   49

My father called again. He said there was nothing new. Mary is in the hospital again, and she'd been joking that she's somewhat of a celebrity. So many doctors come in each day to see her. Interns. Residents. They hold conferences around her bed. They smile and read her chart. They question her. They thump her abdomen. They move her joints. They point. One intern asked her when she had her last menstrual cycle. My mother looked at the young man, then at the other doctors around her bed, then smiled and said twenty-some years ago but I couldn't for the life of me tell you which month. The intern's face quickly reddened. My mother's hysterectomy is written there in plain view on her chart.   50

They ask her questions and she recites her history like a litany.   51

Were the Ohio doctors right? Were they prophets? *Please give her to us. Maybe we can experiment.*   52

My father and I walk along the street. We've just eaten, then gone to Osco for the evening paper—an excuse, really, just to take a walk. And he is next to me suddenly bringing up the subject of my mother's health, just as suddenly as the wind from the lake shakes the thin branches of the trees. The moment is serious, I realize. My father is not a man given to unnecessary talk.   53

I don't know what I'd do without her, he says. I say nothing, for I can think of nothing to say. We've been together for over thirty years, he says. He pauses. For nearly thirty-four years. Thirty-four years this October. And, you know, you wouldn't think it, but I love her so much more now. He hesitates, and I look at him. He shakes his head and smiles. You know what I mean? he says. I say yes and we walk for a while in silence, and I think of what it must be like to live with someone for thirty-four years, but I cannot imagine it, and then I hear my father begin to talk about that afternoon's ball game—he describes at length and in comic detail a misjudged fly ball lost in apathy or ineptitude or simply in the sun—and for the rest of our walk home we discuss what's right and wrong with our favorite baseball team, our thorn-in-the-side Chicago Cubs.   54

I stand here, not used to speaking about things that are so close to me. I am used to veiling things in my stories, to making things wear masks, to telling my stories through masks. But my mother tells her stories openly, as she has done so all of her life—since she lived on her father's farm in Ohio, as she walked along the crowded 1930 Chicago streets, to my father overseas in her letters, to the five of us children, as we sat on her lap, as we played in   55 the next room while she tended to our supper in the kitchen. She tells them to everyone, to anyone who will listen. She taught Linda to read her lips.

I learn now to read her lips.   56

And I imagine one last story.   57

Diana and I are children. Our mother is still young. Diana and I are   58
outside on the sidewalk playing and it's summer. And we are young and full of play and happy, and we see a dog, and it comes toward us on the street. My sister takes my hand. She senses something, I think. The dog weaves from side to side. It's sick, I think. Some kind of lather is on its mouth. The dog growls. I feel Diana's hand shake.

Now we are inside the house, safe, telling our mother. Linda, Bob, and   59
Jim are there. We are all the same age, all children. Our mother looks outside, then walks to the telephone. She returns to the front windows. We try to look out the windows too, but she pushes the five of us away.

No, she says. I don't want any of you to see this.   60

We watch her watching. Then we hear the siren of a police car. We   61
watch our mother make the sign of the Cross. Then we hear a shot. Another. I look at my sisters and brothers. They are crying. Worried, frightened, I begin to cry too.

Did it come near you? our mother asks us. Did it touch you? Any of   62
you? Linda reads her lips. She means the funny dog. Or does she mean the speeding automobile with its lights off? The Ohio doctors? The boy behind the alley gate? The shards of broken glass? The wolf surrounded by butterflies? The ten-and-a-half-pound baby?

Diana, the oldest, speaks for us. She says that it did not.   63

Our mother smiles. She sits with us. Then our father is with us. Bob   64
cracks a smile, and everybody laughs. Alfie gives a bark. The seven of us sit closely on the sofa. Safe.

That actually happened, but not exactly in the way that I described it.   65
I've heard my mother tell that story from time to time, at times when she's most uneasy, but she has never said what it was that she saw from the front windows. A good storyteller, she leaves what she has all too clearly seen to our imaginations.

I stand in the corner of this room, thinking of her lying now in the   66
hospital.

I pray none of us looks at that animal's face.   67

STUDY QUESTIONS

1. What is the occasion of the NARRATOR* retelling his mother's stories? The mother's stories are presented more or less chronologically according to when in her

*Words in small capitals are defined in the Glossary.

life they occurred. What other reason is there for beginning, as the narrator does, with "They were going to throw her away when she was a baby" (paragraph 1)? Why does the mother enjoy this story?

2. The narrator says his mother is good at telling stories, and that he and his father "are only witnesses" (paragraph 10) to her stories. Why are they only witnesses? Why does that make her a good storyteller?

3. In what sense is the marriage of the mother and father "mixed" (paragraph 15)?

4. Why does the narrator wonder if the best man at his mother and father's wedding tipped the organist who forgot to play "Ave Maria," and describe how his father reacted (paragraph 20)? Why does he think his mother is compelled to repeat that story so often?

5. What phrase in paragraph 21 makes the narrator shift from speaking of the wedding that took place thirty-four years earlier to the present?

6. Why is the story of the narrator's birth the "counterpart" (paragraph 25) to his mother's situation at present?

7. What does the narrator mean when he says, in paragraph 35, "You've seen her [my mother]"?

8. How does the narrator describe the difference between his stories and his mother's stories (paragraph 55)? Why is this story, "My Mother's Stories," more like his mother's stories than his own?

9. In the story of the mad dog that the narrator tells—not exactly as it happened— his mother asks, "Did it touch you? Any of you?" Linda—or the narrator—says, "She means the funny dog," but he then goes on to ask if she meant a number of other things (paragraph 62). What do these things have in common? What, then, does the question "Did it touch . . . [a]ny of you?" mean?

10. The narrator says his mother is a good storyteller, and a good storyteller leaves some things she knows and has seen to the imagination. Is the narrator a good storyteller? If so, what does he seem to know but not tell, to leave to your imagination?

11. What do you understand the last sentence of the story to mean?

Cynthia Kadohata

Cynthia Kadohata was hailed as an important young writer when her first novel, *The Floating World*, was published in 1989. Apparently autobiographical, it is the story of a Japanese-American family traversing the country and experiencing an ordinary yet magical world of backwater towns, gas stations, and truck stops. In 1991 she received a Whiting Writers' Award. Her second novel, *In the Heart of the Valley of Love* (1992), paints a dark picture of Los Angeles, where she now lives, in the year 2052.

CHARLIE-O

When I was fifteen, I was almost as tall as the man I have always thought of as my father. He was five feet three, and his name was Charles Osaka—Charlie-O to everyone except my mother, who called him Charles when she didn't like him and Chuck when she did, just as she called me Olivia or Livvie, depending on my behavior. Charlie-O was almost always cheerful, and he had a childlike joie de vivre that would not quite have fit a larger man. My mother's mother forced my mother to marry him, though I didn't know that until I'd grown up. I don't know how exactly my grandmother found him, but I later heard she'd first brought him to Fresno to meet my mother when my mother was seven months pregnant with me. Charlie-O came from a small town in Oregon called Florence. When I was older, he used to keep a picture on his bureau of my mother on prom night, when she was seventeen, and sometimes I wonder whether that was the picture my grandmother first sent him to get him to Fresno. He married my mother when she was eight months pregnant, and in time they had three sons, making me the only girl. But I think that I was always Charlie-O's favorite, and that if he'd loved me less he would have spoiled me the way I sometimes felt he wanted to. My real father had visited me several times, but he was married and had other children, and we never became close. So I was devoted to Charlie-O and followed him everywhere when I was quite young—he even took me to his poker games—and sometimes I brought him to Parents' Day at my school, where, starting in the fifth grade, he was shorter than some of my classmates. As I grew older, though, I no longer cared about poker games or Parents' Days, and Charlie-O and I began to grow apart. That hurt him. By the time I was fifteen, my allegiances had shifted to my mother. At thirty-three, she was graceful and pensive and sincere—things I wanted to be when I grew up. Charlie-O was loud, undignified.

I was born in Fresno, but shortly after my birth Charlie-O took my mother and me to his home in Florence. I loved it there, but when I was fifteen we moved, suddenly and very much against my will. I was furious with Charlie-O for taking us from Oregon. I had friends, babysitting jobs, and my first boyfriend, and during the summer, when the windows were always open, the ocean air would drift through our house, so that I could feel its touch when I woke in the mornings. I would go for walks not long after first light, but sometimes Charlie-O, an amateur painter, would already be outside painting on the beach. I would look back at our house and see tendrils of fog moving into the windows, and it seemed as if we lived in a house in the clouds. I knew that after I left Florence my friends would still build fires on the beaches at night, my boyfriend would soon find a new girlfriend, and by the following week my employers would have found new babysitters—maybe better ones than I. I resented not just that I would lose my old life in Oregon but that I was replaceable. I wanted to grow up to be like my mother, who struck me as a woman who couldn't be replaced.

We were moving to, of all places, the Ozarks. Charlie-O said he wanted   3
to move to Arkansas because he had a chance to buy into a garage a friend of his owned. In Oregon he worked in a garage for somebody else.

We put our furniture in a trailer and drove to Arkansas. Our arrival was   4
inauspicious. It was almost midnight when Charlie-O announced that, first, he believed we were in Arkansas; second, he believed we were lost; and, third, we had run out of gas. I was the only one awake.

"How do you know we're in Arkansas if we're lost?" I said. I put on my   5
longest face.

"Don't worry, honey-dog," he said. He smiled, but his eyes didn't look   6
happy. His eyes looked uncertain, and they seemed to be asking me something—nothing specific, just asking.

I got out a map. "Where's the highway?" I said.   7

He didn't know. It was raining hard, and the rain formed rivers down   8
the windshield. The raindrops made the windows look like textured glass. Charlie-O got out, and I pressed my nose against the back-seat window and watched him squint into the darkness as the rain splashed on his face. He was looking down the road, but I didn't see why he couldn't look from inside the dry car. It was as if he were under a spell. I lowered the window. The air was warmer than I'd expected.

"What are you doing?"   9

"Just seeing what's what," he said. "I'm gonna walk down a ways and   10
try to get us some gas." As he set off, he appeared as sturdy as always but even smaller than usual. In the car my three brothers and my mother slept on. I rolled up the window and ran after Charlie-O, almost slipping in the mud as I hurried. He walked on surefootedly.

"If I were me, I wouldn't be doing this," I said. "I would just wait in   11
the car."

We went a long way, but we never thought of turning back. We were   12
both very stubborn. We'd always been alike that way. There was nothing but bush around us, and sometimes—maybe it was the play of sky light off the rain—I would think I saw lights in the leaves. Charlie-O didn't look either right or left as he walked, and I thought how much more scared I would be without him.

We got gas at a gas station and returned to the car. My youngest brother   13 had awoken. He cringed from me. "You're all wet," he said, as if my wetness were a contagious disease.

"Just a little water," boomed Charlie-O. "Ain't nothing to have a cow about."

In front of my friends, his way of talking had lately embarrassed me, but it didn't now. He was wet and tired, and though it had been he who'd decided we would leave Oregon, he'd lived there a long time and I suddenly realized that he was losing a lot, too.

We found a highway after a while, and then a motel. I'd heard my parents say the day before that they would take two rooms tonight—one for me and my brothers, Ben, Walker, and Peter, and one for themselves. I knew it was so that they could make love. Only a couple of years earlier, I wouldn't have understood completely why it was so important for them to get their own room, as they sometimes did on vacations.

A tired-looking man with rollers in his hair registered us at the motel. Lightning lit the sky like a flash of sunlight. When I watched my parents at the counter, they seemed to be the same person. Maybe it was just that they lived in the same world, bought their clothes at the same stores, ate the same foods. In any case, they matched. Yet I knew that sometimes my mother felt lonely and my father felt alone. And though my mother was barely taller than Charlie-O, she always struck me as womanly, whereas my father was boyish.

"One room?" said the man.

"Yes, plus cots, if you have any," said my mother.

The man got a cot. "Only have one. I won't charge you. We usually charge a dollar, but I understand. I've got seven of my own." A cry came from a back room. "There's one now," the man said with a sigh. He yawned and shook his head, and a loose roller jiggled.

Charlie-O turned and winked at me, and when we got outside he said, "Remember—you can always trust a man with seven children and the nerve to wear rollers in his hair." Charlie-O carried the cot to the room. Then he and I went to a coffee shop, where he got coffee and stole packets of sugar and containers of ersatz cream to give to my brothers, because they couldn't come. They were too young to be out so late. Ben was ten, Walker nine, and Peter four.

Back in the room, the lights were off, and everyone was already asleep— my mother in the bed and the boys on the floor. I wondered why my mother had decided to take just one room. Did it mean that my parents weren't getting along in ways I couldn't see? Everything changed so quickly, and without my noticing.

I thought I remembered a time when my parents had been unable to keep their hands off one another, always walking arm in arm, or stopping to kiss lightly. But the memory was there and then not there. On the way down from Oregon, we'd taken only one motel room whenever we stopped, but somewhere in Utah my parents had made love anyway—quietly—probably after they thought that we were all asleep. I thought they'd *had* to make love or they wouldn't have—not with me and my brothers in the room. They'd never made love on vacations when we'd taken only one room. Something about their lovemaking that night, about the sound of it, seemed to me somehow hopeless. I had to go to the bathroom badly, and by the time they finally fell asleep and I could get up, I had decided that if it came to that I would wet my bed before I would let them know I was awake. It was not the sex that I thought I ought not to have heard but the hopelessness.

I was on the cot, and my eyes were closed. I heard my mother and Charlie-O begin speaking, though I couldn't hear what they were saying. Finally she said something, and my father didn't answer. I heard the sheets rustle. I thought they were going to make love, but they didn't. Then they did. I opened my eyes and saw their bodies moving beneath the sheets. I felt guilty for watching, so I closed my eyes again and averted my face. But I couldn't help listening closely; they were almost as silent as if they were asleep. 24

Afterward, my mother said, "It doesn't make any sense." I had no idea what she was talking about, but she sounded fearful, disappointed—a way she rarely sounded, or allowed herself to sound. Yet sometimes I thought she was disappointed with her life, and I wondered how much of that might be due to me and my brothers—maybe we weren't the kind of children she would have hoped for. For a moment I began to drift off, and as I drifted I thought that I would rather have her be unhappy with me than with Charlie-O. Then I woke up again, and wondered why I had thought that. 25

My parents fell asleep. The cot squeaked softly as I shook my feet up and down, back and forth. I lay still then and realized that Walker, on the floor in the corner near the cot, wasn't breathing evenly—he was awake. The others were asleep. Walker had probably heard our parents making love. I wished he hadn't. It seemed to me a burden to have heard, and I didn't want him to have that burden. 26

"Walk?" I said. 27

"Huh." 28

"Good night." 29

He didn't answer, but I knew that he felt comforted not to be alone, and soon he fell asleep. So did I. Maybe I felt comforted, too. 30

Arkansas was humid, and the clouds at night were unnaturally white, as if someone had spilled bleach on the black sky. I liked to sit late in the back yard, and in bed each night my arms and legs would be covered with mosquito bites, some of them as big and round as quarters, others longer, thinner, like welts. We lived near the outside of our town in one of a cluster of old houses close to some apple orchards. My father was a big believer in organizations, and he joined a bowling team, a golf club, and a group of small-business owners, which was really sort of a poker club. After he'd bought a half interest in his garage, he subscribed to a business newsletter, 31 and whenever he was reading it we would all have to be very quiet around the house. I tried to make friends with some of the children of my parents' new friends, but it was hard, and whenever I didn't fit in I would hate Charlie-O, because I thought it meant that I was more like him than like my mother. There was a boy I liked in our town. I didn't think he liked me, but just his being there made me hopeful for a future that was as lush as I lately imagined my mother's past—I knew she'd loved my real father a great deal, and I thought she loved Charlie-O. My mother was amused by my crush. "You forget everything so easily when you're fifteen," she said, referring to my forgotten Oregon boyfriend. She was right about him but wrong about my memory. There were many things that I remembered. For instance, I remembered that my grandmother, before she died, had frequently told me that if I hoped to get what I wanted in the future I would always have to take great care with what meagre looks I had. At night I would take off my clothes and stand on the rim of the bathtub so that I could see my body in the medicine-cabinet mirror. But I knew that if I didn't get what I wanted in life it wouldn't be because my skin was not the smoothest, or my hair not the blackest and straightest—not because I didn't look the best. I knew that much about my future.

The first time I spent more than a few minutes with a boy I liked was about half a year after we'd arrived, when Charlie-O and my mother were driving him, his parents, and me to a party—children were always invited to the parties of my parents' new friends. I sat next to the boy in the car, and I was nervous and chewing my fingernails. Charlie-O laughed and said. "I remember when you were little you used to chew your toenails."

I felt mortified, but the boy didn't seem to have heard. I slunk down in my seat.

Charlie-O continued, "And then after you'd bit them off you used to swallow them."

I considered flinging myself out of the car to my death, but we were going only thirty miles an hour, and I probably would have just got a concussion. I looked at the boy and he smiled, and for the first time I thought he might like me.

Charlie-O had just resumed his art interest, and on Saturdays he would take me when he went painting landscapes. In Oregon I would never go painting with him, though he asked all of us to. Since I didn't really feel close to him any longer, perhaps it was two-faced of me to make such a turn-around, here where I had no friends and needed company—any company.

He was not a good painter. He painted pictures of forests, with solid yellow sunbeams plunging through the trees like missiles from heaven, and his clouds were applied in thick globs, "for texture." But it was fun to go painting with him. At the time, I wanted to be a biologist, and I would take along my microscope and examine insects, blades of grass, whatever I came upon. Other times, I would paint. Charlie-O showed me how to hold a brush—

not like a pencil but the way you would hold a brush to paint a house. That, he said, is how the Impressionists held brushes.

Though his paintings were dreadful, he hung them up in the garage and offered them for sale. Sometimes he painted me and my brothers, and hung up those pictures as well. Once, when I stopped by the garage, he told a customer that he'd painted pictures of all his children. 38

The customer pointed to a picture of four-year-old Peter. "Is that you?" she said to me. 39

"That's my brother," I said. "But my brother and I look a *lot* alike. People *always* get us mixed up." 40

The woman said. "How nice." 41

"Have you ever sold a painting?" I asked Charlie-O after she'd left. 42

"Oh, sure," he said. He winked and pointed to his head with his forefinger. "I've sold lots of paintings." In his imagination, he meant. 43

My mother had had an affair in Oregon, but I didn't find that out until almost a year after we'd come to Arkansas. I walked into the living room one day and came upon Charlie-O and my mother standing in the center of the room, doing nothing, saying nothing. I hadn't heard any shouting, but something in the room felt the way it did when there'd just been a big fight in the house. Peter had been peeking out the window, but he turned when he heard me walk in. He appeared pleased to see me. 44

"What's going on?" I said. 45

"There's a man out there waiting for Mom." 46

My parents still didn't move, and I went to the window. On the walkway stood a man I'd seen around in Florence—a friend of my mother's. At first I didn't know why he was out there—why he didn't come in. Understanding came to me physically before it came mentally; my whole body flushed and grew tense, and then I understood who the man was: my mother's lover. 47

"Who is it?" whispered Peter. Though young, he had an instinctive ability to detect when something had gone wrong. 48

"The enemy," I whispered back. I suddenly hated that man. "Remember, Peter," I whispered fiercely, "if you ever see that man, he's the *enemy*." Peter looked scared, and I wished I hadn't spoken. 49

First Charlie-O went outside to talk to the man, then my mother went, and then the man left. The house was extra quiet. My parents went into the bedroom to talk. We were supposed to go to a party later—it was a local novelist's birthday—but I figured now we wouldn't go. But after a while my mother went into the bathroom to get ready. I worked with my microscope. I studied dust, hair, tap water, spit. I studied dirt, fly wings, a seashell from Oregon. As I worked I kept thinking of a fight I'd overheard a few weeks before we left Oregon. My mother had been crying, and she said, "I tell you I *am* grateful. But now—Do you still want me?" Charlie-O said he didn't 50 know. "I don't know if you *should* still want me," she said. "And I don't know if I want you to."

Charlie-O had a few beers, and when we got in the car he took a wrong 51 turn almost immediately. It was easy to do. The town we lived in was green. There was the wild green of sprawling oaks and maples, the honeysuckle vines in untended fields. Each street looked like the one before: green everywhere.

At one corner Charlie-O said, "Should I make a right here?" 52

"No," I said. 53

He turned anyway, too sharply, and we ended up in a ditch. 54

"Whoops, sweetie-dog," he said, "I thought you said yes. I thought she 55 said yes."

We sat there for several minutes, as if we'd simply come to a very long 56 traffic light. Eventually, Charlie-O said, "All right," and got out of the car, slipping almost immediately and falling to the ground. My mother and I got out to help him. He lay on the ground with his eyes open, blinking. We lifted him into the car, then patted down the dirt around the wheels. We weren't sure whether that was what we were supposed to do, but it made us feel better. I pushed in back with my brothers while our mother accelerated, the wheels whipping dirt into the air. The car didn't budge. Despite protests from my mother, my father got out of the car. "Aw, I can help," he said. He pushed with my brothers and me. I found myself pushing harder than before. My legs stretched out as I tried to get into a good position, and my cheek rested against the cool metal of the trunk. The effort took me over, and I realized how badly I wanted my father to be able to say later that he had helped to get us out of the ditch. I thought that that would help the marriage somehow. But it was no good. The car remained stuck. Finally, my mother and I found a house and a man came to help us, and my mother took over the driving.

The novelist, whom Charlie-O played golf with sometimes, owned a 57 small farm. The boy I liked was at the party, and he stood out back and talked with me while the grown-ups, mostly the fathers, got drunk. Some of the drunk men took off their blazers and dress shirts and got into a field and started chasing some animals—a few sheep and pigs and a goat. There was a dog, too. After a while a couple of the women and some of the kids joined in. In fact, the man who owned the farm was running around with his wife and two kids. Everybody was chasing without actually trying to catch anything—they just felt like whooping and having fun. Some of the drunker men actually seemed to have taken on the running style of the animals; for instance, one man began taking little steps, like the short-legged sheep.

A couple of women were talking next to where the boy and I stood. 58 They watched serenely, as if their husbands and friends were playing croquet or badminton.

"I adore that dress Marie is wearing," said one of them. Marie was the daughter of the novelist. She was having a great time running around. 59

"Isn't she getting married soon?" said the other woman. 60

"Yes." 61

"When is she getting married?" 62

"Oh," said the first woman, watching Marie fall on her face. "Some Saturday, I guess." 63

The boy frowned and bit his lip, as if he didn't understand something, and then his face lit up with discovery. "Life is funny," he said. 64

I really liked that boy. 65

Charlie-O tackled the dog. "Got me a pig!" He looked at the animal in his arms. "Got me a dog," he said. 66

There was a tussle with the dog, and then everyone was up and chasing the animals again. Over the field, fleets of bleached clouds raced through the sky, and above the sounds of shouting rose the ubiquitous chirp of crickets. 67

Charlie-O, tired, walked over to me. His mouth was bleeding a bit—I guess from the struggle with the dog—but he was sweaty and happy, not happy with his life or with himself but happy with his exertion. He wiped his mouth. "Did you see that?" he said. "Thought I had me a pig." 68

The animals suddenly all spread out, running every which way, and there was general confusion in the field. 69

My father wasn't watching anymore. He had turned the other way, and was gazing past me. I turned, too, and saw my mother coming forward. Charlie-O didn't move, but she walked over. They stood for an instant facing each other, and he gave her that look—the one with the question in it. He seemed confused, and then he said, "Thought I had me a pig." 70

My mother was lovely and radiant, and suddenly she reached out to touch his face. The touch was sad, and also loving—sad because loving but not in love. "The boys are asleep," she said gently. "I think we'd better get going." She tugged at my hair affectionately and walked inside. 71

Charlie-O wiped his mouth again and turned to the field. 72

"Aren't we leaving?" I said. 73

He put his arm around the boy's shoulders. "So you like my daughter?" he said. 74

The boy's jaw dropped, almost imperceptibly, and then he sort of hunched up one shoulder and averted his eyes. 75

"She's a honey-dog, ain't she?" said Charlie-O. 76

"She is," the boy mumbled. He smiled with embarrassment, and he looked cute and silly. 77

Then Charlie-O put his arm around me, too, and we stood and watched the end of the chase. A couple of people hoisted a pig into the air. 78

"Poor thing," said the boy. "I'm glad I ain't a pig." 79

Someone fell down, and the boy looked at me. "My dad," he said. He went off to help. 80

"Are you O.K., Dad?" I heard him say. 81

"Never felt better," said his father as he got up. 82

Charlie-O watched, not seeing. I looked down and saw a cricket hop 83
onto his foot. "I never saw a cricket do that before," I said.

Charlie-O nodded abstractedly, and his face looked old in the same light 84
that had made my mother so radiant. He still had his arm around me. "Promise me something," he said.

"O.K." 85

"Promise me you'll never break anyone's heart." 86

STUDY QUESTIONS

1. What do you think Charlie-O's motivation was in marrying the NARRATOR's mother
when she was already eight months pregnant with someone else's baby? Why do
you think he favors the narrator over his own three sons? How do you feel about
his favoring her?

2. What is it that makes the narrator and Charlie-O grow apart?

3. Why do they suddenly move away from Florence, Oregon?

4. What does the episode with the car in the ditch contribute to your understanding
of the story? of Charlie-O?

5. What does the last sentence of the story imply? How do you feel about the narrator's mother?

John Edgar Wideman

John Edgar Wideman—Rhodes scholar, basketball star at the University of Pennsylvania, and author of almost a dozen highly regarded books—was born in 1941
in Washington, D.C. He grew up in a black neighborhood (Homewood) in Pittsburgh, and much of his fiction (like the short story here) is set there and involves
family histories of individuals who, despite powerful rivalries and reverses, care deeply
for each other. One of his most powerful books, *Brothers and Keepers* (1984), recounts
Wideman's relationship with his brother, Robby, who was sentenced to life in prison
for armed robbery. The short story that follows—entirely in dialogue, with no external narrative point of view—is from *Fever*, a collection published in 1989.

LITTLE BROTHER

For Judy

Penny, don't laugh. Come on now, you know I love that little critter. ₁
And anyway, how you so sure it didn't work?

Tylenol? ₂

Yep. Children's liquid Tylenol. The children's formula's not as strong ₃
and he was only a pup. Poured two teaspoons in his water dish. I swear it
seemed to help.

Children's Tylenol. ₄

With the baby face on it. You know. Lapped it up like he understood it ₅
was good for him. He's alive today, ain't he? His eye cleared up, too.

You never told me this story before. ₆

Figured you'd think I was crazy. ₇

His eye's torn up again. ₈

You know Little Brother got to have his love life. Out tomcatting around ₉
again. Sticking his nose in where it don't belong. Bout once a month he
disappears from here. Used to worry. Now I know he'll be slinking back in
three or four days with his tail dragging. Limping around spraddle-legged.
Sleeping all day cause his poor dickie's plumb wore out.

Geral. ₁₀

It's true. Little Brother got it figured better than most people. Do it till ₁₁
you can't do it no more. Come home half dead and then you can mind your
own business for a while.

Who you voting for? ₁₂

None of them fools. Stopped paying them any mind long time ago. ₁₃

I hear what you're saying, but this is special. It's for president. ₁₄

One I would have voted for. One I would have danced for buck naked ₁₅
up on Homewood Avenue, is gone. My pretty preacher man's gone. Shame
the way they pushed him right off the stage. The rest them all the same.
Once they in they all dirty dogs. President's the one cut the program before
I could get my weather stripping. Every time the kitchen window rattles and
I see my heat money seeping out the cracks, I curse that mean old Howdy
Doody turkey-neck clown.

How's Ernie? ₁₆

Mr. White's fine. ₁₇

Mama always called him Mr. White. And Ote said *Mr. White* till we ₁₈
shamed him out of it.

I called Ernie that too before we were married. When he needed teasing. ₁₉
Formal like Mama did. *Mr. White.* He was *Mr. White* to her till the day she
died.

But Mama loved him. ₂₀

Of course she did. Once she realized he wasn't trying to steal me away. ₂₁

Thing is she never had that to worry about. Not in a million years. I'd have never left Mama. Even when Ote was alive and staying here. She's been gone all these years but first thing I think every morning when I open my eyes is, You OK, Mama? I'm right here, Mama. Be there in a minute, to get you up. I still wake up hoping she's all right. That she didn't need me during the night. That I'll be able to help her through the day.

Sometimes I don't know how you did it. 22

Gwan, girl. If things had been different, if you didn't have a family of your own, if I'd had the children, you would have been the one to stay here and take care of Mama. 23

I guess you're right. Yes. I would. 24

No way one of us wouldn't have taken care of her. You. Ote. Sis or me. Made sense for me and Ote to do it. We stayed home. If you hadn't married, you'd have done it. And not begrudged her one moment of your time. 25

Ote would have been sixty in October. 26

I miss him. It's just Ernie and me and the dogs rattling around in this big house now. Some things I have on my mind I never get to say to anybody because I'm waiting to tell them to Ote. 27

He was a good man. I can still see Daddy pulling him around in that little wagon. The summer Ote had rheumatic fever and the doctor said he had to stay in bed and Daddy made him that wagon and propped him up with pillows and pulled him all over the neighborhood. Ote bumping along up and down Cassina Way with his thumb in his mouth half sleep and Daddy just as proud as a peacock. After three girls, finally had him a son to show off. 28

Ote just about ran me away from here when I said I was keeping Little Brother. Two dogs are enough, Geraldine. Why would you bring something looking like that in the house? Let that miserable creature go on off and find a decent place to die. You know how Ote could draw hisself up like John French. Let you know he was half a foot taller than you and carrying all that John French weight. Talked like him, too. *Geraldine*, looking down on me saying all the syllables of my name like Daddy used to when he was mad at me. *Geraldine*. Run that miserable thing away from here. When it sneaks up under the porch and dies, you won't be the one who has to get down on your hands and knees and crawl under there to drag it out. 29

But he was the one wallpapered Little Brother's box with insulation, wasn't he? The one who hung a flap of rug over the door to keep out the wind. 30

The one who cried like a baby when Pup-pup was hit. 31

Didn't he see it happen? 32

Almost. He was turning the corner of Finance. Heard the brakes screech. The bump. He was so mad. Carried Pup-pup and laid him on the porch. Fussing the whole time at Pup-pup. You stupid dog. You stupid dog. How many times have I told you not to run in the street. Like Pup-pup could hear him. Like Pup-pup could understand him if he'd been alive. Ote stomped in 33 the house and up the stairs. Must have washed his hands fifteen minutes. Running water like we used to do when Mama said we better not get out of bed once we were in the bed so running and running that water till it made us pee one long last time before we went to sleep.

What are you girls doing up there wasting all that water? I'ma be up   34 there in ten minutes and you best be under the covers.

Don't be the last one. Don't be on the toilet and just starting to pee good   35 and bumpty-bump here she comes up the steps and means what she says. Uh ohh. It's Niagara Falls and you halfway over and ain't no stopping now. So you just sit there squeezing your knees together and work on that smile you don't hardly believe and she ain't buying one bit when she brams open the door and Why you sitting there grinning like a Chessy cat, girl. I thought I told youall ten minutes ago to get in bed.

Ote washed and washed and washed. I didn't see much blood. Pup-pup   36 looked like Pup-pup laid out there on the porch. Skinny as he was you could always see his ribs moving when he slept. So it wasn't exactly Pup-pup because it was too still. But it wasn't torn up bloody or runned-over looking either.

Whatever Ote needed to wash off, he took his time. He was in the bath-   37 room fifteen minutes, then he turned off the faucets and stepped over into his room and shut the door but you know how the walls and doors in this house don't stop nothing so I could hear him crying when I went out in the hall to call up and ask him if he was all right, ask him what he wanted to do with Pup-pup. I didn't say a word. Just stood there thinking about lots of things. The man crying on his bed was my baby brother. And I'd lived with him all my life in the same house. Now it was just the two of us. Me in the hall listening. Him on his bed, a grown man sobbing cause he's too mad to do anything else. You and Sis moved out first. Then Daddy gone. Then Mama. Just two of us left and two mutts in the house I've lived in all my life. Then it would be one of us left. Then the house empty. I thought some such sorrowful thoughts. And thought of poor Pup-pup. And that's when I decided to say yes to Ernie White after all those years of no.

Dan. If you want a slice of this sweet potato pie you better come in here   38 now and get it. It's leaving here fast. They're carting it away like sweet potato pie's going out of style.

It's his favorite.   39

That's why I bake one every time old Danny boy's home from school.   40

Did he tell you he saw Marky at Mellon Park?   41

No.   42

Dan was playing ball and Marky was in a bunch that hangs around on   43 the sidelines. He said Marky recognized him. Mumbled hi. Not much more than that. He said Marky didn't look good. Not really with the others but sitting off to the side, on the ground, leaning back against the fence. Dan went over to him and Marky nodded or said hi, enough to let Danny know it really was Marky and not just somebody who looked like Marky, or Marky's ghost because Dan said it wasn't the Marky he remembered. It's the Marky who's been driving us all crazy.

At least he's off Homewood Avenue. 44

That's good I suppose. 45

Good and bad. Like everything else. He can move hisself off the Avenue 46 and I'm grateful for that but it also means he can go and get hisself in worse trouble. A healthy young man with a good head on his shoulders and look at him. It's pitiful. Him and lots the other young men like zombies nodding on Homewood Avenue. Pitiful. But as long as he stays on Homewood the cops won't hassle him. What if he goes off and tries to rob somebody or break in somebody's house? Marky has no idea half the time who he is or what he's doing. He's like a baby. He couldn't get away with anything. Just hurt hisself or hurt somebody trying.

What can we do? 47

We kept him here as long as we could. Ernie talked and talked to him. 48 Got him a job when he dropped out of school. Talked and talked and did everything he could. Marky just let hisself go. He stopped washing. Wore the same clothes night and day. And he was always such a neat kid. A dresser. Stood in front of the mirror for days arranging himself just so for the ladies. I don't understand it. He just fell apart, Penny. You've seen him. You remember how he once was. How many times have I called you and cried over the phone about Marky? Only so much any of us could do, then Ernie said it was too dangerous to have him in the house. Wouldn't leave me here alone with Marky. I about went out my mind then. Not safe in my own house with this child I'd taken in and raised. My husband's nephew who'd been like my own child, who I'd watched grow into a man. Not safe. Nothing to do but let him roam the streets.

None of the agencies or programs would help. What else could you do, 49 Geral?

They said they couldn't take him till he did something wrong. What 50 kind of sense does that make? They'll take him after the damage is done. After he freezes to death sleeping on a bench up in Homewood Park. Or's killed by the cops. Or stark raving foaming at the mouth. They'll take him then. Sorry, Mrs. White, our hands are tied.

Sorry, Mrs. White. Just like the receptionist at Dr. Franklin's. That skinny, 51 pinched-nosed *sorry, Mrs. Whatever-your-name-is* cause they don't give a good goddamn they just doing their job and don't hardly want to be bothered, especially if it's you, and you're black and poor and can't do nothing for them but stand in line and wait your turn and as far as they're concerned you can wait forever.

Did I tell you what happened to me in Dr. Franklin's office, Penny? 52 Five or six people in the waiting room. All of them white. Chattering about this and that. They don't know me and I sure don't know none of them but cause they see my hair ain't kinky and my skin's white as theirs they get on colored people and then it's niggers after they warm up awhile. Ain't niggers enough to make you throw up? Want everything and not willing to work a lick. Up in your face now like they think they own the world. Pushing past you in line at the A&P. Got so now you can't ride a bus without taking your life in your hands. This city's not what it used to be. Used to be a decent place to live till they started having all those nigger babies and now a white person's supposed to grin and bear it. It's three women talking mostly and the chief witch's fat and old as I am. And listen to this. She's afraid of being raped. She hears about white women attacked every day and she's fed up. Then she says, It's time somebody did something, don't you think? Killing's too good for those animals. Looking over at me with her head cocked and her little bit of nappy orange hair got the nerve to google at me like she's waiting for me to wag my head and cluck like the rest of those hens. Well I didn't say a word but the look I gave that heifer froze her mouth shut and kept it shut. Nobody uttered a word for the half hour till it was my turn to see Dr. Franklin. Like when we were bad and Mama'd sit us down and dare us to breathe till she said we could. They're lucky that's all I did. Who she think want to rape her? What self-respecting man, black, white, green or polka dot gon take his life in his hands scuffling with that mountain of blubber?

Geral.   53

Don't laugh. It wasn't funny. Rolling her Kewpie-doll eyes at me. Ain't   54
niggers terrible? I was about to terrible her ass if I heard *nigger* one more time in her mouth.

Listen at you. Leave that poor woman alone. How old's Little Brother   55
now?

We've had him nine years. A little older than that. Just a wee thing   56
when he arrived on the porch. *Geraldine*. You don't intend bringing that scrawny rat into the house, do you?

And the funny thing is Little Brother must have heard Ote and been   57
insulted. Cause Little Brother never set foot inside the front door. Not in the whole time he's lived here. Not a paw. First he just made a bed in the rags I set out by the front door. Then the cardboard box on the front porch. Then when he grew too big for that Ote built his apartment under the porch. I just sat and rocked the whole time Ote hammering and sawing and cussing when the boards wouldn't stay straight or wouldn't fit the way he wanted them too. Using Daddy's old rusty tools. Busy as a beaver all day long and I'm smiling to myself but I didn't say a mumbling word, girl. If I had let out so much as one signifying I-told-you-so peep, Ote woulda built another box and nailed me up inside. Little Brother went from rags to his own private apartment and in that entire time he's never been inside the house once. I coaxed him, Here, puppy, here, puppy, puppy, and put his food inside the hallway but that's one stubborn creature. Little Brother'd starve to death before he'd walk through the front door.

He about drove Pup-pup crazy. Pup-pup would sneak out and eat Little   58
Brother's food. Drag his rags away and hide them. Snap and growl but Little

Brother paid him no mind. Pup-pup thought Little Brother was nuts. Living outdoors in the cold. Not fighting back. Carrying a teddy bear around in his mouth. Peeing in his own food so Pup-pup wouldn't bother it. Pup-pup was so jealous Went to his grave still believing he had to protect his territory. Pup-pup loved to roam the streets, but bless his heart, he became a regular stay-at-home. Figured he better hang around and wait for Little Brother to make his move. Sometimes I think that's why Pup forgot how to act in the street. In such a hurry to get out and get back, he got himself runned over.

That reminds me of Maria Indovina. Danny wanted me to walk around 59 the neighborhood with him. He wanted to see the places we're always talking about. Mr. Conley's lot. Klein's store. Aunt Aida's. Hazel and Nettie's. Showed him the steps up to Nettie's and told him she never came down them for thirty years. He said, In youall's tales these sounded like the highest, steepest steps in creation. I said they were. Told him I'd follow you and Sis cause I was scared to go first. And no way in the world I'd be first coming back down. They didn't seem like much to him even when I reminded him we were just little girls and Aunt Hazel and Cousin Nettie like queens who lived in another world. Anyway, we were back behind Susquehanna where we used to play and there's a high fence back there on top of the stone wall. It's either a new fence or newly painted but the wall's the same old wall where the bread truck crushed poor Maria Indovina. I told him we played together in those days. Black kids and white kids. Mostly Italian then. Us and the Italians living on the same streets and families knowing each other by name. I told him and he said that's better than it is today. Tried to explain to him we lived on the same streets but didn't really mix. Kids playing together and Hello, how are you, Mr. So-and-so, Mrs. So-and-so, that and a little after-hours undercover mixing. Only time I ever heard Mama curse was when she called Tina Sabettelli a whorish bitch.

John French wasn't nobody's angel. 60

Well, I wasn't discussing none of that with Dan. I did tell him about the 61 stain on the wall and how we were afraid to pass by it alone.

Speaking of white people how's your friend from up the street? 62

Oh, Vicki's fine. Her dresses are still too mini for my old fuddy-duddy 63 taste. But no worse than what the other girls wearing. Her little girl Carolyn still comes by every afternoon for her piece of candy. She's a lovely child. My blue-eyed sweetheart. I worry about her. Auntie Gerry, I been a good girl today. You got me a sweet, Auntie Gerry? Yes, darling, I do. And I bring her whatever we have around the house. She'll stand in line with the twins from next door, and Becky and Rashad. They're my regulars but some the others liable to drop by, too. Hi, Aunt Gerry. Can I have a piece of candy, please? When they want something they're so nice and polite, best behaved lil devils in Homewood.

Yes, my friend Vicki's fine. Not easy being the only white person in the 64 neighborhood. I told Fletcher and them to leave her alone. And told her she better respect herself a little more cause they sure won't if she don't. Those jitterbugs don't mean any harm, but boys will be boys. And she's not the smartest young lady in the world. These slicksters around here, you know how they are, hmmph. She better be careful is what I told her. She didn't like hearing what I said but I've noticed her carrying herself a little different when she walks by. Saw her dressed up real nice in Sears in East Liberty last week and she ducked me. I know why, but it still hurt me. Like it hurts me to think my little sugar Carolyn will be calling people niggers someday. If she don't already.

Did you love Ernie all those years you kept him waiting? 65

Love? 66

You know what I mean. Love. 67

Love love? 68

Love love love. You know what I'm asking you. 69

Penny. Did you love Billy? 70

Five children. Twenty-seven years off and on before he jumped up and left for good. I must have. Some of the time. 71

Real love? Hootchy-gootchy cooing and carrying on? 72

What did you say? Hootchy-koo? Is that what you said? To tell the truth I can't hardly remember. I must of had an operation when I was about eleven or twelve. Cut all that romance mess out. What's love got to do with anything, anyway. 73

You asked me first. 74

Wish I'd had the time. Can you picture Billy and Ernie dancing the huckle-buck, doing the hootchy-koo? 75

Whoa, girl. You gonna start me laughing. 76

Hootchy-gootchy-koo. Wish I'd had the time. Maybe it ain't too late. Here's a little hootchy-gootchy-koo for you. 77

Watch out. You're shaking the table. Whoa. Look at my drink. 78

Can't help it. I got the hootchy-goos. I'm in love. 79

Hand me one of those napkins. 80

Gootchy-gootchy-goo. 81

Behave now. The kids staring at us. Sitting here acting like two old fools. 82

So you think I ought to try Tylenol? 83

Two things for sure. Didn't kill Little Brother. And Princess is sick. Now the other sure thing is it might help Princess and it might not. Make sure it's the baby face. Kids' strength. Try that first. 84

I just might. 85

No you won't. You're still laughing at me. 86

No I'm not. I'm smiling thinking about Ote hammering and sawing an apartment for Little Brother and you rocking on the porch trying to keep your mouth shut. 87

Like to bust, girl. 88

But you didn't. 89

Held it in to this very day. Till I told you. 90

Hey, youall. Leave a piece of sweet potato pie for your cousin, Dan. It's 91 his favorite.

STUDY QUESTIONS

1. Who is Little Brother? Why is he called that? Who else in the story is a "little brother"? When does the dialogue in the story take place? How old are the two main participants in the dialogue? How can you tell?

2. Who is Mr. White? Why is he called by that name? How important to the story are the men with whom the SPEAKERS are involved? Where are these men now?

3. What are the most important relationships in the lives of the two speakers? What evidence does the dialogue present that the two care deeply for each other? What other kinds of "love" are presented in the story?

4. How long does it take you to sort out who the speakers are and exactly what the situation is? When do you become aware of when the action is set? How much do we know about other characters in the story? How important are the two dogs?

5. Why are the ailments of the dogs compared to the plight of humans in the story?

Simon J. Ortiz

Simon J. Ortiz, of the Acoma Pueblo in New Mexico, earned his master's degree at the University of Iowa, has taught at several universities, and edits the Navajo publication *Rough Rock News*. Among his published books are *A Good Journey; Going for the Rain; Fight Back: For the Sake of the People, for the Sake of the Land; Howbah Indians;* and *From Sand Creek* (which won the Pushcart Prize in 1982). In 1989 he was awarded a humanitarian award for literary achievement by the New Mexico Humanities Council. In 1991 he published *Woven Stone*, a volume of poetry and prose.

MY FATHER'S SONG

Wanting to say things,
I miss my father tonight.
His voice, the slight catch,
the depth from his thin chest,

the tremble of emotion   5
in something he has just said
to his son, his song:

    We planted corn one Spring at Acu—
    we planted several times
    but this one particular time   10
    I remember the soft damp sand
    in my hand.

    My father had stopped at one point
    to show me an overturned furrow;
    the plowshare had unearthed   15
    the burrow nest of a mouse
    in the soft moist sand.

    Very gently, he scooped tiny pink animals
    into the palm of his hand
    and told me to touch them.   20
    We took them to the edge
    of the field and put them in the shade
    of a sand moist clod.

    I remember the very softness
    of cool and warm sand and tiny alive mice   25
    and my father saying things.

STUDY QUESTIONS

1. Who is the SPEAKER of the final four verse paragraphs? Who is the father in those paragraphs?

2. What are the significance and effect of the repetition of the word "sand"?

Rhoda Schwartz

Rhoda Schwartz, daughter of a Russian-Jewish father and Midwestern mother, was born in Atlantic City and grew up in Elmira, New York. She has been co-editor of *The American Poetry Review*.

OLD PHOTOGRAPHS

1.

We are returning together. The train is late at every
stop on the way, detained by the banging of switchmen and
flares. It's the dead of winter. Snow has made bones
out of the trees. The huts are covered by drifts so
white our eyes hurt in the morning. Our conversation is   5
disjointed. We won't be able to stand it when the
train gets in. Candles burn in the aisles. We are
lurching towards the next day and the next. You keep
telling me I should go back to Russia. The train is
a black holocaust going through the mountains. Tomorrow,   10
we will be there. It is never the same. Someday, tell
me how beautiful it was when we went back together.
Say my name.

2.

My Russian great-grandmother: I would not be surprised to see
a crow sitting on her shoulder. Black silk dress—pleats heavy   15
and twisted like the rills of the Caucasus, she stands erect in
her garden—the long, slender hands touching the knob of the
summer chair. Is she brown with age or is it the old sepia
photograph? She is frowning. She says, to no one in particular,
what can I do with the 15-year-old upstart, my grandson,   20
in Bialystok prison for six months because he hates the Tsar, loves
Chekhov and marched in a parade before the revolution?

My father's friends are throwing rolls to him over the prison
walls with messages. He laughs. I love him.

He told me his grandmother hit him with Russian birch twigs to   25
subdue him. When he tried to row across the Dnieper
in a boat smaller than a toy, they laughed.
Father, when you hid your books in the hayloft, and argued with
Gogol late at night, I was there in your sperm waiting to hear your story.

The ship that brought you to America had no library. You cursed its   30
keel—the hunger—the gold slipped through your fingers when you
disembarked. The shore was lonely. I want you to know I would have
loved you if I could have loved you, still hidden in your sperm
with Gogol and Pushkin. What a foursome. I would have
lost to you on purpose. I wish I could tear   35
down every Russian birch tree that hurt you before I could say I was sorry.

3.

The walls were taller than the prison
at Bialystok. You were shorter than the guards. Did you ever spit
at them—kick the dirt and yell down with the Tsar, or did you eat
your black bread quietly, pee in a trench, dig holes   40
for posts and think about the time you would leave for America?

4.

I am dreaming of you sitting in a buggy with your uncle,
holding the reins of an old horse. The reins look like
dried tobacco leaves. I think of your wallet, the same
color and texture, whenever I reach into a drawer of silk   45
scarves and suddenly touch it. I am old
and wrinkled as the tobacco leaf. I swim into daydreams about you.
You are smiling because you are young and your hair is black
and curly and Pushkin is waiting for you back in the hayloft.
You were a romantic; a sensualist even then. Sometimes,   50
I wake up crying because I've seen you in a pine box, eyes
closed against living. You told me to always
be full of love and gentle with men. I try to remember.

5.

When you came to America, why did you think
the St. Lawrence river was like the Dnieper and try to row   55
across it in a rowboat? You were too slight
to do it, but you did it
while the steamships blew their horns in anger.
You told me the fog was rolling in like puffs of black cotton
and you were scared.   60
They let you off with a warning—
You sold expensive things to millionaires
and became a capitalist.
I used to pretend your name was Marco Polo
when you opened the packing crates   65
and showed me Italian linens, Spanish shawls and Chinese
vases. We put them all in a row and talked about them.
I was your best audience. It was hard for either
one of us to spell Czechoslovakia.

STUDY QUESTIONS

1. How many photographs are there? Describe them.

2. How much of the SPEAKER's father's life story can you reconstruct from the poem?

3. What seem to be the qualities in her father that the speaker loves?

Eric Chock

E ric Chock, who works in the Poets-in-the-Schools program in Hawaii, has published poems in many magazines. His work was included in the Pushcart Prize volume in 1991–92. His latest book, *Last Days Here*, was published by Bamba Ridge Press in 1989.

CHINESE FIREWORKS BANNED IN HAWAII

for Uncle Wongie, 1987

Almost midnight, and the aunties
are wiping the dinner dishes
back to their shelves,
cousins eat jook[1] from the huge vat
in the kitchen, and small fingers   5
help to mix the clicking ocean
of mah jong[2] tiles, so the uncles can play
through another round of seasons.
And you put down your whiskey
and go outside to find your long bamboo pole   10
so Uncle Al can help you tie on
a ten foot string of good luck,
red as the raw fish we want
on our plates every New Year's.
As you hang this fish over the railing   15
Uncle Al walks down the steps
and with his cigarette lighter
ignites it and jumps out of the way.
You lean back and jam the pole
into the bottom of your guts,   20

1. Rice porridge.
2. A Chinese game played with tiles, similar to dominoes.

waving it across the sky,
whipping sparks of light from its tail,
your face in a laughing Buddha smile
as you trace your name in the stars
the way we teach our kids to do   25
with their sparklers.
This is the family picture
that never gets taken, everyone
drawn from dishes and food and games
and frozen at the sound   30
of 10,000 wishes filling our bodies
and sparkling our eyes.
You play the fish till its head explodes
into a silence that echoes,
scattering red scales to remind us of spirits   35
that live with us in Hawaii.
Then, as we clap and cheer,
the collected smoke of our consciousness
floats over Honolulu, as it has
each year for the last century.   40
But tonight, as we leave,
Ghislaine stuffs her styrofoam tea cup
full of red paper from the ground.
This is going to be history, she says.
Let's take some home.   45

STUDY QUESTIONS

1. Explain the poem's title.

2. In what ways would the "photograph" here, if it were to be taken, differ from the photographs in the Schwartz poem, "Old Photographs"?

3. Describe the TONE of the family gathering here. What kind of family role does Uncle Al play? What other family members here have specific, expected roles to play?

4. How important is the sense of ritual in this poem? to this family gathering? What does ritual have to do with the title of the poem?

Li-Young Lee

Li-Young Lee was born in 1957 in Jakarta, Indonesia, to Chinese parents "who were classically educated and in the habit of reciting literally hundreds of ancient Chinese poems." His father was jailed by then-dictator Sukarno for nineteen months, seventeen of them in a leper colony. After his escape, the family fled from country to country, and then settled in western Pennsylvania, where his father became a Presbyterian minister. Lee has published two volumes of poems, *Rose* (1986) and *The City in Which I Love You* (1990). "I . . . believe the King James Bible to contain some of the greatest poetry in the world," he says, "and I hope to own some of its simplicity, glory, and mystery in my own writing one day."

THE GIFT

To pull the metal splinter from my palm
my father recited a story in a low voice.
I watched his lovely face and not the blade.
Before the story ended he'd removed
the iron sliver I thought I'd die from.   5

I can't remember the tale
but hear his voice still, a well
of dark water, a prayer.
And I recall his hands,
two measures of tenderness   10
he laid against my face,
the flames of discipline
he raised above my head.

Had you entered that afternoon
you would have thought you saw a man   15
planting something in a boy's palm,
a silver tear, a tiny flame.
Had you followed that boy
you would have arrived here,
where I bend over my wife's right hand.   20

Look how I shave her thumbnail down
so carefully she feels no pain.
Watch as I lift the splinter out.
I was seven when my father
took my hand like this,   25
and I did not hold that shard
between my fingers and think,
Metal that will bury me,
christen it Little Assassin,
Ore Going Deep for My Heart.   30
And I did not lift up my wound and cry,
Death visited here!
I did what a child does
when he's given something to keep.
I kissed my father.   35

STUDY QUESTIONS

1. What is the SPEAKER doing in the present tense of the poem?

2. Of what from the past does his action remind him?

3. What is "the gift"?

Jimmy Santiago Baca

Born in New Mexico in 1952, Jimmy Santiago Baca wrote the poems in his collection *Immigrants in Our Own Land* (1979), from which "Ancestor" is taken, while he was in prison. His second collection, *Martin & Meditations on the South Valley* (1987), won the 1987 Before Columbus Foundation American Book Award. His most recent book, *Black Mesa Poems*, was published in 1989. He now lives on a small farm outside Albuquerque.

ANCESTOR

It was a time when they were afraid of him.
My father, a bare man, a gypsy, a horse

with broken knees no one would shoot.
Then again, he was like the orange tree,
and young women plucked from him sweet fruit.   5
To meet him, you must be in the right place,
even his sons and daughter, we wondered
where was papa now and what was he doing.
He held the mystique of travelers
that pass your backyard and disappear into the trees.   10
Then, when you follow, you find nothing,
not a stir, not a twig displaced from its bough.
And then he would appear one night.
Half covered in shadows and half in light,
his voice quiet, absorbing our unspoken thoughts.   15
When his hands lay on the table at breakfast,
they were hands that had not fixed our crumbling home,
hands that had not taken us into them
and the fingers did not gently rub along our lips.
They were hands of a gypsy that filled our home   20
with love and safety, for a moment;
with all the shambles of boards and empty stomachs,
they filled us because of the love in them.
Beyond the ordinary love, beyond the coordinated life,
beyond the sponging of broken hearts,   25
came the untimely word, the fallen smile, the quiet tear,
that made us grow up quick and romantic.
Papa gave us something: when we paused from work,
my sister fourteen years old working the cotton fields,
my brother and I running like deer,   30
we would pause, because we had a papa no one could catch,
who spoke when he spoke and bragged and drank,
he bragged about us: he did not say we were smart,
nor did he say we were strong and were going to be rich someday.
He said we were good. He held us up to the world for it to see, 35
three children that were good, who understood love in a quiet way,
who owned nothing but calloused hands and true freedom,
and that is how he made us: he offered us to the wind,
to the mountains, to the skies of autumn and spring.
He said, "Here are my children! Care for them!"   40
And he left again, going somewhere like a child
with a warrior's heart, nothing could stop him.
My grandmother would look at him for a long time,
and then she would say nothing.
She chose to remain silent, praying each night,   45
guiding down like a root in the heart of earth,
clutching sunlight and rains to her ancient breast.

And I am the blossom of many nights.
A threefold blossom: my sister is as she is,
my brother is as he is, and I am as I am.   50
Through sacred ceremony of living, daily living,
arose three distinct hopes, three loves,
out of the long felt nights and days of yesterday.

STUDY QUESTIONS

1. The first five lines offer a series of contradictions: the SPEAKER's father is a mere ("bare") man, and rather worthless ("a horse / with broken knees"), but he is loved by young women, and feared by "them." Can you reconcile these contradictions? put them together to make a composite picture? What is the portrait that emerges? the effect?

2. In lines 6–19, it is chiefly the father's long absences that are described, and what he did not give or do for his family. How do you feel about him at this point in the poem? If your response is not entirely negative, even here, try to explain in terms of the words of the text just how the speaker manages to make you accept this "unfatherly" behavior.

3. To what does the speaker attribute the fact that he and his brother and sister grew up "quick and romantic" (line 27)?

4. Why does the father think his children, whom he sees rather rarely, are "good" (line 35)?

5. Are you convinced by this poem that the father was a good and loving father and that his "child rearing" was successful?

Elías Miguel Muñoz

Elías Miguel Muñoz was born in Cuba in 1954. After immigrating to the United States, he attended the University of California at Irvine, where he received his Ph.D. in 1984. Muñoz has published scholarship on the work of Manuel Puig; a study of Cuban poets in exile; two novels in English, *Crazy Love* (1988) and *The Greatest Performance* (1991); and two collections of poems, *En estas tierras / In This Land* (1989) and *No fue posible el sol* (1989).

LITTLE SISTER BORN IN THIS LAND

When you slip
slowly and lovingly

through my fingers
I cannot hold you
and explain a thousand things   5
Each time you smile
and show me your shoes with buckles
or tell me a story
of space flights
(How you would love to be a princess   10
in those absurd and bloody wars)
Each time you intrigue me
with your riddles
with your words
that will always be foreign   15
to our experience

It isn't a reproach
sister
Little sister born in this land
It's just that you will never know   20
of hens nesting
(Is there anywhere in your childhood
a similar feeling?)
Once upon a time
there was a boy   25
on paving stones so white
and excursions on foot
toys made of tin
There was also mystery
in the ravines   30
There were evil pirates
and brave corsairs
There were lessons
for carving men
out of stone   35
There was caramel candy
and sweet potato pudding

It isn't a reproach
sister
Little sister born in this land   40
It's just that you have only
the joy of Disney heroes
Because you will smile
when the ingenious man
behind the cartoons   45

makes of you
of every child
a little clown
plastic and ridiculous

When you slip away   50
slowly and lovingly
I cannot invent
another childhood for you
cannot offer you mine
also nourished by heroes   55
but tasting of palm leaf
and *mamoncillo*
It did not suffer the mockery
of expensive toys
that the deceptive   60
ghost of December
brings to you

When you slip away
slowly and lovingly
we cannot bury together   65
in the backyard
(That warm and always
open earth)
the models
that will take hold of you   70
that already stalk you
from their cardboard boxes
and their printed letters
on a glass of milk
or Coca Cola   75

It isn't a reproach
Sister
Little Sister born in this land

STUDY QUESTIONS

1. How does the SPEAKER feel about his/her childhood compared to that of the little sister?

2. What experiences and images characterize the speaker's childhood? What experiences and images characterize that of the little sister?

3. How and why is "little sister" slipping away?

4. What is the TONE of the poem?

5. Which childhood experience here is closest to your own?

Sherley Williams

Born in Bakersfield, California, in 1944, Sherley Williams was educated at California State University at Fresno, Howard University, and Brown University. She has taught at Federal City College, California State University at Fresno, and the University of California, San Diego, where she is now professor of literature. A highly regarded poet, she is the author of *Give Birth to Brightness* (1972), *The Peacock Poems* (1975), the novel *Dessa Rose* (1986), and *Working Cotton* (1992), a fictional work on African-American migrant labor and family life.

SAY HELLO TO JOHN

I swear I ain't done what Richard
told me bout jumpin round and stuff.
And he knew I wouldn't do nothin to make the baby
come, just joke, say I'mo cough

this child up one day.   5
So in the night when I felt the water tween
my legs, I thought it was pee and I laid
there wonderin if maybe I was in a dream.

Then it come to me that my water broke and I went
in to tell Ru-ise. *You been havin pains?*   10
she ask. I hear her fumblin for the light.
Naw, I say. Don't think so. The veins

stand out along her temples. *What time
is it?* Goin on toward four o'clock.
Nigga, I told you: 15
You ain't havin no babies, not

in the middle of the night.
Get yo ass back to bed.
That ain't nothin but pee. And what
I know bout havin kids cept what she said?　　　　　　20

Second time it happen, even she
got to admit this mo'n pee.
And the pain when it come, wa'n't bad
least no mo'n I eva expect to see

again. I remember the doctor smilin,　　　　　　　　25
sayin, Shel, you got a son.
His bright black face above me
sayin, Say hello to John.

STUDY QUESTIONS

1. Who is Richard? Why does he recommend that the SPEAKER "[jump] round" (line 2)?

2. What can you infer about Ru-ise and her relationship to the speaker? From that conversation, what do you learn about the speaker?

3. What are all the implications and emotions that surround "hello" in the final line?

Naomi Long Madgett

Author of more than a half-dozen volumes of poetry, including *Songs to a Phantom Nightingale* (1941), *One and the Many* (1956), *Star by Star* (1965), *Pink Ladies in the Afternoon* (1972), and *Exits and Entrances* (1978), Naomi Long Madgett is professor emeritus of English at Eastern Michigan University. She won a Creative Achievement Award in 1988 from the College Language Association for her collection of poems, *Octavia and Other Poems*. She cooperated in the publication of a compilation of poems entitled *Adam of Ife: Black Women in Praise of Black Men* (1992).

OFFSPRING

I tried to tell her:
　　This way the twig is bent.

Born of my trunk and strengthened by my roots,
You must stretch newgrown branches
    Closer to the sun   5
    Than I can reach.
I wanted to say:
    Extend my self to that for atmosphere
    Only my dreams allow.

But the twig broke,   10
And yesterday I saw her
Walking down an unfamiliar street,
    Feet confident,
    Face slanted upward toward a threatening sky,
And   15
    She was smiling
    And she was
    Her very free,
    Her very individual,
    Unpliable   20
    Own.

STUDY QUESTIONS

1. What is it that the SPEAKER tried to tell her daughter? Does the speaker now think that she was right or wrong?

2. What does it mean that the twig "broke" (line 10)? What is implied by "threatening sky" (line 14)? What earlier words in the poem refer to the sky or something in or like the sky?

3. What is the TONE of the poem? How does the speaker seem to feel about her daughter's present, grown-up self? What is the force or significance of the last word in the poem?

Simon J. Ortiz

Simon J. Ortiz, of the Acoma Pueblo in New Mexico, earned his master's degree at the University of Iowa, has taught at several universities, and edits the Navajo publication *Rough Rock News*. Among his published books are *A Good Journey; Going for the Rain; Fight Back: For the Sake of the People, for the Sake of the Land; Howbah Indians;* and *From Sand Creek* (which won the Pushcart Prize in 1982). In 1989 he was awarded a humanitarian award for literary achievement by the New Mexico Humanities Council. In 1991 he published *Woven Stone*, a volume of poetry and prose.

SPEAKING

I take him outside
under the trees,
have him stand on the ground.
We listen to the crickets,
cicadas, million years old sound.   5
Ants come by us.
I tell them,
"This is he, my son.
This boy is looking at you.
I am speaking for him."   10

The crickets, cicadas,
the ants, the millions of years
are watching us,
hearing us.
My son murmurs infant words,   15
speaking, small laughter
bubbles from him.
Tree leaves tremble.
They listen to this boy
speaking for me.   20

STUDY QUESTIONS

1. Each STANZA of this brief poem contains ten lines. The first three lines of the first stanza and the final three lines of the second make up a "frame." Inside that frame are two seven-line sections, each made up of two or three sentences. Compare the first sentences of each (lines 4–7 and 11–14). What is the function of the opening frame (lines 1–3)? What is the function of the closing frame (lines 18–20)?

2. The insects and the years listen and respond to the boy's babble but not to the father's language. What does this suggest about the relationship of humankind to nature?

Merle Woo

A writer of both fiction and drama, Merle Woo has lectured in Asian-American studies at the University of California, Berkeley. Her work has been published in *Bridge*, *Hanai*, and *This Bridge Called My Back*.

LETTER TO MA

January, 1980

Dear Ma,

I was depressed over Christmas, and when New Year's rolled around, do you know what one of my resolves was? Not to come by and see you as much anymore. I had to ask myself why I get so down when I'm with you, my mother, who has focused so much of her life on me, who has endured so much; one who I am proud of and respect so deeply for simply surviving.

I suppose that one of the main reasons is that when I leave your house, your pretty little round white table in the dinette where we sit while you drink tea (with only three specks of Jasmine) and I smoke and drink coffee, I am down because I believe there are chasms between us. When you say, "I support you, honey, in everything you do except . . . except . . ." I know you mean except my speaking out and writing of my anger at all those things that have caused those chasms. When you say I shouldn't be so ashamed of Daddy, former gambler, retired clerk of a "gook suey" store, because of the time when I was six and saw him humiliated on Grant Avenue by two white cops, I know you haven't even been listening to me when I have repeatedly said that I am not ashamed of him, not you, not who we are. When you ask, "Are you so angry because you are unhappy?" I know that we are not talking to each other. Not with understanding, although many words have passed between us, many hours, many afternoons at that round table with Daddy out in the front room watching television, and drifting out every once in a while to say "Still talking?" and getting more peanuts that are so bad for his health.

We talk and talk and I feel frustrated by your censorship. I know it is unintentional and unconscious. But whatever I have told you about the classes I was teaching, or the stories I was working on, you've always forgotten within a month. Maybe you can't listen—because maybe when you look in my eyes, you will, as you've always done, sense more than what we're actually saying, and that makes you fearful. Do you see your repressed anger manifested in me? What doors would groan wide open if you heard my words with complete understanding? Are you afraid that your daughter is breaking out of our shackles, and into total anarchy? That your daughter has turned into a crazy woman who advocates not only equality for Third World people, for women, but for gays as well? Please don't shudder, Ma, when I speak of homosexuality. Until we can all present ourselves to the world in our completeness, as fully and beautifully as we see ourselves naked in our bedrooms, we are not free.

After what seems like hours of talking, I realize it is not talking at all, but the filling up of time with sounds that say, "I am your daughter, you are my mother, and we are keeping each other company, and that is enough." But it is not enough because my life has been formed by your life. Together we have lived one hundred and eleven years in this country as yellow women, and it is not enough to enunciate words and words and words and then to have them only mean that we have been keeping each other company. I desperately want you to understand me and my work, Ma, to know what I am doing! When you distort what I say, like thinking I am against all "caucasians" or that I am ashamed of Dad, then I feel anger and more frustration and want to slash out, not at you, but at those external forces which keep us apart. What deepens the chasms between us are our different reactions to those forces. Yours has been one of silence, self-denial, self-effacement; you believing it is your fault that you never fully experienced self-pride and freedom of choice. But listen, Ma, only with a deliberate consciousness is my reaction different from yours.

When I look at you, there are images: images of you as a little ten-year-old Korean girl, being sent alone from Shanghai to the United States, in steerage with only one skimpy little dress, being sick and lonely on Angel Island[1] for three months; then growing up in a "Home" run by white missionary women. Scrubbing floors on your hands and knees, hauling coal in heavy metal buckets up three flights of stairs, tending to the younger children, putting hot bricks on your cheeks to deaden the pain from the terrible toothaches you always had. Working all your life as maid, waitress, salesclerk, office worker, mother. But throughout there is an image of you as strong and courageous, and persevering: climbing out of windows to escape from the Home, then later, from an abusive first husband. There is so much more to these images than I can say, but I think you know what I mean. Escaping out of windows offered only temporary respites; surviving is an everyday chore. You gave me, physically, what you never had, but there was a spiritual, emotional legacy you passed down which was reinforced by society: self-contempt because of our race, our sex, our sexuality. For deeply

1. The largest island in San Francisco Bay, formerly used, like Ellis Island in New York, as an entry point for immigrants.

ingrained in me, Ma, there has been that strong, compulsive force to sink into self-contempt, passivity, and despair. I am sure that my fifteen years of alcohol abuse have not been forgotten by either of us, nor my suicidal depressions.

Now, I know you are going to think that I hate and despise you for your self-hatred, for your isolation. But I don't. Because in spite of your withdrawal, in spite of your loneliness, you have not only survived, but been beside me in the worst of times when your company meant everything in the world to me. I just need more than that now, Ma. I have taken and taken from you in terms of needing you to mother me, to be by my side, and I need, now, to take from you two more things: understanding and support for who I am now and my work. 6

We are Asian American women and the reaction to our identity is what causes the chasms instead of connections. But do you realize, Ma, that I could never have reacted the way I have if you had not provided for me the opportunity to be free of the binds that have held you down, and to be in the process of self-affirmation? Because of your life, because of the physical security you have given me: my education, my full stomach, my clothed and starched back, my piano and dancing lessons—all those gifts you never received—I saw myself as having worth; now I begin to love myself more, see our potential, and fight for just that kind of social change that will affirm me, my race, my sex, my heritage. And while I affirm myself, Ma, I affirm you. 7

Today, I am satisfied to call myself either an Asian American Feminist or Yellow Feminist. The two terms are inseparable because race and sex are an integral part of me. This means that I am working with others to realize pride in culture and women and heritage (the heritage that is the exploited yellow immigrant: Daddy and you). Being a Yellow Feminist means being a community activist and a humanist. It does not mean "separatism," either by cutting myself off from non-Asians or men. It does not mean retaining the same power structure and substituting women in positions of control held by men. It does mean fighting the whites and the men who abuse us, straightjacket us and tape our mouths; it means changing the economic class system and psychological forces (sexism, racism, and homophobia) that really hurt all of us. And I do this, not in isolation, but in the community. 8

We no longer can afford to stand back and watch while an insatiable elite ravages and devours resources which are enough for all of us. The obstacles are so huge and overwhelming that often I do become cynical and want to give up. And if I were struggling alone, I know I would never even attempt to put into action what I believe in my heart, that (and this is primarily because of you, Ma) Yellow Women are strong and have the potential to be powerful and effective leaders. 9

I can hear you asking now, "Well, what do you mean by 'social change and leadership'? And how are you going to go about it?" To begin with we must wipe out the circumstances that keep us down in silence and self-efface- 10 ment. Right now, my techniques are education and writing. Yellow Feminist means being a core for change, and that core means having the belief in our potential as human beings. I will work with anyone, support anyone, who shares my sensibility, my objectives. But there are barriers to unity: white women who are racist, and Asian American men who are sexist. My very being declares that those two groups do not share my complete sensibility. I would be fragmented, mutilated, if I did not fight against racism and sexism together.

And this is when the pain of the struggle hits home. How many white women have taken on the responsibility to educate themselves about Third World people, their history, their culture? How many white women really think about the stereotypes they retain as truth about women of color? But the perpetuation of dehumanizing stereotypes is really very helpful for whites; they use them to justify their giving us the lowest wages and all the work they don't want to perform. Ma, how can we believe things are changing when as a nurse's aide during World War II, you were given only the tasks of changing the bed linen, removing bed pans, taking urine samples, and then only three years ago as a retired volunteer worker in a local hospital, white women gave themselves desk jobs and gave you, at sixty-nine, the same work you did in 1943? Today you speak more fondly of being a nurse's aide during World War II and how proud you are of the fact that the Red Cross showed its appreciation for your service by giving you a diploma. Still in 1980, the injustices continue. I can give you so many examples of groups which are "feminist" in which women of color were given the usual least important tasks, the shitwork, and given no say in how that group is to be run. Needless to say, those Third World women, like you, dropped out, quit.

Working in writing and teaching, I have seen how white women condescend to Third World women because they reason that because of our oppression, which they know nothing about, we are behind them and their "progressive ideas" in the struggle for freedom. They don't even look at history! At the facts! How we as Asian American women have always been fighting for more than mere survival, but were never acknowledged because we were in our communities, invisible, but not inaccessible.

And I get so tired of being the instant resource for information on Asian American women. Being the token representative, going from class to class, group to group, bleeding for white women so they can have an easy answer—and then, and this is what really gets to me—they usually leave to never continue their education about us on their own.

To the racist white female professor who says, "If I have to watch everything I say I wouldn't say anything," I want to say, "Then get out of teaching."

To the white female poet who says, "Well, frankly, I believe that politics and poetry don't necessarily have to go together," I say, "Your little taste of white privilege has deluded you into thinking that you don't have to fight against sexism in this society. You are talking to me from your own isolation and your own racism. If you feel that you don't have to fight for me, that you don't have to speak out against capitalism, the exploitation of human and natural resources, then you in your silence, your inability to make connections, are siding with a system that will eventually get you, after it has gotten me. And if you think that's not a political stance, you're more than simply deluded, you're crazy!"

This is the same white voice that says, "I am writing about and looking for themes that are 'universal.' " Well, most of the time when "universal" is used, it is just a euphemism for "white": white themes, white significance, white culture. And denying minority groups their rightful place and time in U.S. history is simply racist. [16]

Yes, Ma, I am mad. I carry the anger from my own experience and the anger you couldn't afford to express, and even that is often misinterpreted no matter how hard I try to be clear about my position. A white woman in my class said to me a couple of months ago, "I feel that Third World women hate me and that *they* are being racist; I'm being stereotyped, and I've never been part of the ruling class." I replied, "Please try to understand. Know our history. Know the racism of whites, how deep it goes. Know that we are becoming ever more intolerant of those people who let their ignorance be their excuse for their complacency, their liberalism, when this country (this world!) is going to hell in a handbasket. Try to understand that our distrust is from experience, and that our distrust is power*less*. Racism is an essential part of the status quo, power*ful*, and continues to keep us down. It is a rule taught to all of us from birth. Is it no wonder that we fear there are no exceptions?" [17]

And as if the grief we go through working with white women weren't enough; so close to home, in our community, and so very painful, is the lack of support we get from some of our Asian American brothers. Here is a quote from a rather prominent male writer ranting on about a Yellow "sister": [18]

> . . . I can only believe that such blatant sucking off of the identity is the work of a Chinese American woman, another Jade Snow Wong Pochahontas yellow. Pussywhipped again. Oh, damn, pussywhipped again.

Chinese American woman: "another Jade Snow Wong Pochahontas yellow." According to him, Chinese American women sold out—are contemptuous of their culture, pathetically strain all their lives to be white, hate Asian American men, and so marry white men (the John Smiths)—or just like Pochahontas: we rescue white men while betraying our fathers; then marry white men, get baptized, and go to dear old England to become curiosities of the civilized world. Whew! Now, that's an indictment! (Of all women of color.) Some of the male writers in the Asian American community seem never to support us. They always expect us to support them, and you know what? We almost always do. Anti-Yellow men? Are they kidding? We go to [19] their readings, buy and read and comment on their books, and try to keep up a dialogue. And they accuse us of betrayal, are resentful because we do readings together as Women, and so often do not come to our performances. And all the while we hurt because we are rejected by our brothers. The Pochahontas image used by a Chinese American man points out a tragic truth: the white man and his ideology are still over us and between us. These men of color, with clear vision, fight the racism in white society, but have bought the white male definition of "masculinity": men only should take on the leadership in the community because the qualities of "originality, daring, physical courage, and creativity" are "traditionally masculine."[2]

Some Asian men don't seem to understand that by supporting Third World women and fighting sexism, they are helping themselves as well. I understand all too clearly how dehumanized Dad was in this country. To be a Chinese man in America is to be a victim of both racism and sexism. He was made to feel he was without strength, identity, and purpose. He was made to feel soft and weak, whose only job was to serve whites. Yes, Ma, at one time I was ashamed of him because I thought he was "womanly." When those two white cops said, "Hey, fat boy, where's our meat?" he left me standing there on Grant Avenue while he hurried over to his store to get it; they kept complaining, never satisfied, "That piece isn't good enough. What's the matter with you, fat boy? Don't you have respect? Don't wrap that meat in newspapers, either; use the good stuff over there." I didn't know that he spent a year and a half on Angel Island; that we could never have our right names; that he lived in constant fear of being deported; that, like you, he worked two full-time jobs most of his life; that he was mocked and ridiculed because he speaks "broken English." And Ma, I was so ashamed after that experience when I was only six years old that I never held his hand again.

Today, as I write to you of all these memories, I feel even more deeply hurt when I realize how many people, how so many people, because of racism and sexism, fail to see what power we sacrifice by not joining hands.

But not all white women are racist, and not all Asian American men are sexist. And we choose to trust them, love and work with them. And there are visible changes. Real tangible, positive changes. The changes I love to see are those changes within ourselves.

Your grandchildren, my children, Emily and Paul. That makes three generations. Emily loves herself. Always has. There are shades of self-doubt but much less than in you or me. She says exactly what she thinks, most of the time, either in praise or in criticism of herself or others. And at sixteen she goes after whatever she wants, usually center stage. She trusts and loves people, regardless of race or sex (but, of course, she's cautious), loves her community and works in it, speaks up against racism and sexism at school. Did you know that she got Zora Neale Hurston and Alice Walker on her reading list for a Southern Writers class when there were only white authors?

2. *AIIEEEEE! An Anthology of Asian American Writers*, editors Frank Chin, Jeffery Paul Chan, Lawson Fusao Inada, Shawn Wong (Washington, D.C.: Howard University Press, 1974). [Author's note]

That she insisted on changing a script done by an Asian American man when she saw that the depiction of the character she was playing was sexist? That she went to a California State House Conference to speak out for Third World students' needs?

And what about her little brother, Paul? Twelve years old. And remember, Ma? At one of our Saturday Night Family Dinners, how he lectured Ronnie (his uncle, yet!) about how he was a male chauvinist? Paul told me once how he knew he had to fight to be Asian American, and later he added that if it weren't for Emily and me, he wouldn't have to think about feminist stuff too. He says he can hardly enjoy a movie or TV program anymore because of the sexism. Or comic books. And he is very much aware of the different treatment he gets from adults: "You have to do everything right," he said to Emily, "and I can get away with almost anything."

Emily and Paul give us hope, Ma. Because they are proud of who they are, and they care so much about our culture and history. Emily was the first to write your biography because she knows how crucial it is to get our stories in writing.

Ma, I wish I knew the histories of the women in our family before you. I bet that would be quite a story. But that may be just as well, because I can say that *you* started something. Maybe you feel ambivalent or doubtful about it, but you did. Actually, you should be proud of what you've begun. I am. If my reaction to being a Yellow Woman is different than yours was, please know that that is not a judgment on you, a criticism or a denial of you, your worth. I have always supported you, and as the years pass, I think I begin to understand you more and more.

In the last few years, I have realized the value of Homework: I have studied the history of our people in this country. I cannot tell you how proud I am to be a Chinese / Korean American Woman. We have such a proud heritage, such a courageous tradition. I want to tell everyone about that, all the particulars that are left out in the schools. And the full awareness of being a woman makes me want to sing. And I do sing with other Asian Americans and women, Ma, anyone who will sing with me.

I feel now that I can begin to put our lives in a larger framework. Ma, a larger framework! The outlines for us are time and blood, but today there is breadth possible through making connections with others involved in community struggle. In loving ourselves for who we are—American women of color—we can make a vision for the future where we are free to fulfill our human potential. This new framework will not support repression, hatred, exploitation and isolation, but will be a human and beautiful framework, created in a community, bonded not by color, sex or class, but by love and the common goal for the liberation of mind, heart, and spirit.

Ma, today, you are as beautiful and pure to me as the picture I have of you, as a little girl, under my dresser-glass.

I love you,
Merle

STUDY QUESTIONS

1. What facts are we given about the circumstances Woo's mother and father faced? How did each of them respond to discrimination or abuse? What responses and attitudes does Woo's mother seem to be sensitive about? Which anecdote seems to you most powerful in suggesting the problems faced by the older generation?

2. State as precisely as you can the differences between generations of Asian-Americans, as Woo presents them. What differences of attitude between men and women in the Asian-American community does Woo emphasize?

3. Against whom is the anger directed? What subjects seem to generate the most powerful emotions? What attitudes in others upset her most?

4. Note the variations in TONE from paragraph to paragraph. Describe how the letter moves from personal to political concerns; from frustration to anger to compassion. What devices and principles of organization does Woo use to structure the letter?

5. What strategies does Woo use to make her mother feel loved and appreciated even in the face of strong criticism? List all of the places in which she expresses love; in which she expresses respect; in which she expresses concern about being misunderstood; in which she expresses common cause with her mother's concerns.

   Do you ever feel that the mother is being patronized? Are there places where Woo seems too hard on her mother? too easy? Do you think she establishes an appropriate balance in her attitudes toward her mother? Does her rhetoric seem effective?

   How do you think you would feel if you were to receive such a letter from a child of yours when you are old? Do you feel like sending such a letter to one of your parents?

6. Are there parts of the letter with which you disagree? If so, state clearly your reasons for disagreeing. Which parts do you agree with most strongly?

Marie G. Lee

M arie G. Lee is a second-generation Korean American. Born and raised in Hibbing, Minnesota, she is the author of the novel *Finding My Voice*, which won the 1993 Friends of American Writers Award. Her other novels include *If It Hadn't Been for Yoon Jun* and a forthcoming novel, *Saying Goodbye*. Her work has also appeared in the *New York Times* and *Seventeen*, among others. She currently resides in New York City where she is a member of the Asian American Writers Workshop.

MY TWO DADS

I am a first-generation Korean-American. On my first trip to Korea at age twenty-six, I found that I had two fathers. One was the Dad I'd always known, but the second was a Korean father I'd never seen before—one surprising and familiar at the same time, like my homeland.

I was born and raised in the Midwest, and to me, my Dad was like anyone else's. He taught my brothers to play baseball, fixed the garage door, and pushed the snowblower on chilly February mornings. If there was anything different about him, to my child's eyes, it was that he was a doctor.

Growing up, my siblings and I rarely came into contact with our Korean heritage. Mom and Dad spoke Korean only when they didn't want us to know what they were saying. We didn't observe Korean customs, except for not wearing shoes in the house, which I always assumed was plain common sense. I'd once seen a photograph of Dad in a traditional Korean costume, and I remember thinking how odd those clothes made him look.

With my parents' tacit encouragement, I "forgot" that I was Korean. I loved pizza and macaroni and cheese, but I had never so much as touched a slice of kimchi.[1] All my friends, including my boyfriend, were Caucasian. And while I could explain in detail everything I thought was wrong with Ronald Reagan's policies, I had to strain to remember the name of Korea's president.

Attempting to learn the Korean language, *hangukmal*, a few years ago was a first step in atoning for my past indifference. I went into it feeling smug because of my fluency in French and German, but learning Korean knocked me for a loop. This was a language shaped by Confucian rules of reverence, where the speaker states her position (humble, equal, superior) in relation to the person she is addressing. Simultaneously humbling myself and revering the person with whom I was speaking seemed like a painful game of verbal Twister. To further complicate the process, I found there are myriad titles of reverence, starting with the highest, *sansengnim*, which loosely means "teacher/doctor," down to the ultra-specific, such as *waysukmo*, "wife of mother's brother."

Armed, then, with a year's worth of extension-school classes, a list of polite phrases and titles, and a Berlitz tape in my Walkman, I was as ready as I'd ever be to travel with my family to Korea last year.

When we arrived at Kimpo Airport in Seoul, smiling relatives funneled us into the customs line for *wayguksalam*, "foreigners." I was almost jealous watching our Korean flight attendants breeze through the line for *hanguksalam*, "Korean nationals." With whom did I identify more—the flight attendants or the retired white couple behind us, with their Bermuda shorts and

---

1. A food made from fermented cabbage.

Midwestern accents? My American passport stamped me as an alien in a land where everyone looked like me.

I got my first glimpse of my second father when we began trying to hail 8 cabs in downtown Seoul. Because the government enforces low taxi fares, the drivers have developed their own system of picking up only individual passengers, then packing more in, to increase the per-trip profit. The streets are clogged not only with traffic but also with desperately gesticulating pedestrians and empty taxis.

Even my mother was stymied by the cab-hailing competition. When 9 Mom and I traveled alone, cabs zoomed blithely past us. When we finally got one, the driver would shut off his meter, brazenly charge us triple the usual fare and ignominiously dump us somewhere not very close to our destination.

But traveling with Dad was different. He would somehow stop a taxi 10 with ease, chitchat with the driver (using very polite language), then shovel us all in. Not only would the cabbie take us where we wanted to go, but some of the usually-taciturn drivers would turn into garrulous philosophers.

I began to perceive the transformation of my father from American dad 11 to functioning urban Korean. When we met with relatives, I noticed how Dad's conversational Korean moved easily between the respect he gave his older sister to the joviality with which he addressed Mom's younger cousin. My brother Len and I and our Korean cousins, however, stared shyly and mutely at each other.

Keeping company with relatives eased my disorientation, but not my 12 alienation. Korea is the world's most racially and culturally homogeneous country, and although I was of the right race, I felt culturally shut out. It seemed to me that Koreans were pushy, even in church. When they ate, they slurped and inhaled their food so violently that at least once during every meal, someone would have a sputtering fit of coughing.

Watching my father "turn Korean" helped me as I tried to embrace the 13 culture. Drinking *soju*[2] in a restaurant in the somewhat seedy Namdaemun area, he suddenly lit into a story of the time when Communists from North Korea confiscated his parents' assets. Subsequently, he became a medical student in Seoul, where each day he ate a sparse breakfast at his sister's house, trekked across towering Namsan Mountain (visible from our room in the Hilton), and studied at Seoul National University until night, when he would grab a few hours of sleep in the borrowed bed of a friend who worked the night shift.

I have always lived in nice houses, gone on trips, and never lacked for 14 pizza money. But as my father talked, I could almost taste the millet-and-water gruel he subsisted on while hiding for months in cellars during the North Korean invasion of Seoul. Suddenly, I was able to feel the pain of the Korean people, enduring one hardship after another: Japanese colonial rule,

2. A traditional potato vodka popular in Korea.

North Korean aggression, and dependence on American military force. For a brief moment, I discerned the origins of the noble, sometimes harsh, Korean character. Those wizened women who pushed past me at church were there only because they had fought their way to old age. The noises people made while eating began to sound more celebratory than rude.

And there were other things I saw and was proud of. When we visited 15 a cemetery, I noticed that the headstones were small and unadorned, except for a few with small, pagoda-shaped "hats" on them. The hats (*chinsa*), Dad told me, were from a time when the country's leaders awarded "national Ph.D.'s," the highest civilian honor.

"Your great-grandfather has one of those on his grave," Dad mentioned 16 casually. I began to admire a people who place such a high value on hard work and scholarship. Even television commercials generally don't promote leisure pursuits, such as vacations or Nintendo, but instead proclaim the merits of "super duper vitamin pills" to help you study longer and work harder.

After two weeks, as we prepared to return to the U.S., I still in many 17 ways felt like a stranger in Korea. While I looked the part of a native, my textbook Korean was robotic, and the phrases I was taught—such as, "Don't take me for a five-won plane ride"—were apparently very dated. I tried to tell my Korean cousins an amusing anecdote: in the Lotte department store in Seoul, I asked for directions to the restroom and was directed instead to the stereo section. But the story, related once in English and once in halting Korean, became hopelessly lost in the translation.

Dad decided he would spend an extra week in Korea, savoring a culture 18 I would never fully know, even if I took every Berlitz course I could afford. When I said good-bye to him, I saw my Korean father; but I knew that come February, my American dad would be back out in our driveway, stirring up a froth of snow with his big yellow snowblower.

STUDY QUESTIONS

1. Describe the "character" of the NARRATOR. Which of the details she gives about herself are the most helpful in determining what kind of person she is? How is she different from the other characters in her narrative? What experiences seem most influential in determining her "American-ness"?

2. Exactly how is the narrator's "second" father—in Korea—different from the father she knows in America? What surprises her most about his conduct in Korea? What connections do you see between his behavior in Korea and in America?

3. What role does hierarchy play in Korean life? in Korean language? Does the father's being a doctor have anything to do with the narrator's understanding of Korean life? of language? Does his profession have anything to do with the focus of the narrative?

4. In what specific ways is the narrator a "stranger" in Korea? Are there clues that

the father feels like a stranger in America? What does seeming to be a stranger feel like to the narrator? How important are "looks" to the feeling of being a stranger in this narrative?

Fenton Johnson

Born and reared in Kentucky, Fenton Johnson now lives in San Francisco where he writes and teaches creative writing at San Francisco State University. His first novel, *Crossing the River*, was published in 1989. The following autobiographical narrative appeared in the "About Men" column of the *New York Times Magazine*, June 23, 1991.

THE LIMITLESS HEART

It is late March—the Saturday of Passover, to be exact—and I am driving an oversize rented car through west Los Angeles. I have never seen this side of the city except in the company of my companion, who died of AIDS-related complications in a Paris hospital in autumn of last year. He was an only child and often asked that I promise to visit his parents after his death. As the youngest son of a large family and a believer in brutal honesty, I refused. I have too much family already, I said. There are limits to how much love one can give.

Now I am here, driving along San Vicente Boulevard, one of the lovelier streets of Santa Monica, Calif., west from Wilshire to the Pacific. The street is divided by a broad green median lined with coral trees, which the city has seen fit to register as landmarks. They spread airy, elegant crowns against a movie-set heaven, a Maxfield Parrish blue. Each branch bleeds at its end an impossibly scarlet blossom, as if the twigs themselves had pierced the thin-skinned sky.

My friend's parents are too old to get about much. They are survivors of the Holocaust, German Jews who spent the war years hiding in a Dutch village a few miles from Germany itself. Beaten by Nazis before the war, my friend's father hid for four years with broken vertebrae, unable to see a doctor. When he was no longer able to move, his desperate wife descended to the street to find help, and saw falling from the sky the parachutes of their liberators.

After the war they came to California, promised land of this promised land. Like Abraham and Sarah,[1] they had a single son in their advanced years, proof that it is possible, in the face of the worst, to pick up sticks and start again.

At his home in Santa Monica, my friend's father sits in chronic pain, uncomplaining. Unlike his wife, he is reserved; he does not talk about his son with the women of his life—his wife or his surviving sister. No doubt he fears giving way before his grief, and his life has not allowed for much giving way. This much he and I share: as a gay man who grew up in the rural South, I am no stranger to hiding.

His wife always goes to bed early—partly as a way of coping with grief—but tonight he all but asks her to retire. After she leaves he begins talking of his son, and I listen and respond with gratefulness. We are two men in control, who permit ourselves to speak to each other of these matters because we subscribe implicitly, jointly, unconditionally to this code of conduct.

He tells of a day when his son, then 8 years old, wanted to go fishing. The quintessential urban Jew, my friend's father nonetheless bought poles and hooks and drove 50 miles to Laguna Beach. There they dropped their lines from a pier to discover the hooks dangled some 10 feet above the water. ("Thank God," he says. "Otherwise we might have caught something.") A passer-by scoffed. "What the hell do you think you're trying to catch?" My friend's father shrugged, unperturbed. "Flying fish," he replied.

I respond with my most vivid memory of his son. He was a wiser man than I, and spoke many times across our years together of his great luck, his great good fortune. Denial pure and simple, or so I told myself at first. AZT, DDI, ACT-UP, CMV, DHPG, and what I came to think of as the big "A" itself—he endured this acronymed life, while I listened and learned and participated and helped when I could.

Until our third and last trip to Paris, the city of his dreams. On what would be his last night to walk about the city we sat in the courtyard of the Picasso Museum. There at dusk, under a deep sapphire sky, I turned to him and said, "I'm so lucky," and it was as if the time allotted to him to teach this lesson, the time for me to learn it, had been consumed, and there were nothing left but the facts of things to play out.

A long silence after this story—I have ventured beyond what I permit myself, what I am permitted.

I change the subject, asking my friend's father to talk of the war years. He does not allow himself to speak of his beatings or of murdered family and friends. Instead he remembers moments of affection, loyalty, even humor,

4

5

6

7

8

9

10

11

1. Father and mother of the Hebrew people through Isaac, who was born to them late in life fulfilling a promise from God.

until he talks of winters spent immobilized with pain and huddled in his wife's arms, their breaths freezing on the quilt as they sang together to pass the time, to stay warm.

Another silence; now he has ventured too far. "I have tried to forget   12
these stories," he says in his halting English.

In the presence of these extremes of love and horror I am reduced to   13
cliché. "It's only by remembering them that we can hope to avoid repeating them."

"They are being repeated all the time," he says. "It is bad sometimes to   14
watch too much television. You see these things and you know we have learned nothing."

Are we so dense that we can learn nothing from all this pain, all this   15
death? Is it impossible to learn from experience? The bitterness of these questions I can taste, as I drive east to spend the night at a relative's apartment.

Just south of the seedier section of Santa Monica Boulevard, I stop at a   16
bar recommended by a friend. I need a drink, and I need the company of men like myself—survivors, for the moment anyway, albeit of a very different struggle.

The bar is filled with Latinos wearing the most extraordinary clothes.   17
Eighty years of B movies have left Hollywood the nation's most remarkable supply of secondhand dresses, most of which, judging from this evening, have made their ways to these guys' closets.

I am standing at the bar, very Anglo, very out of place, very much   18
thinking of leaving, when I am given another lesson:

A tiny, wizened, gray-haired Latina approaches the stage, where under   19
jerry-rigged lights (colored cellophane, Scotch tape) a man lip-syncs to Brazilian rock. His spike heels raise him to something above six feet; he wears a floor-length sheath dress, slit up the sides and so taut, so brilliantly silver, so lustrous that it catches and throws back the faces of his audience. The elderly Latina raises a dollar bill. On tottering heels he lowers himself, missing not a word of his song while half-crouching, half-bending so that she may tuck her dollar in his cleavage and kiss his cheek.

"*Su abuelita*," the bartender says laconically. "His grandmother."   20

One A.M. in the City of Angels—the streets are clogged with cars. Stuck   21
in traffic, I am haunted by voices and visions: the high thin songs of my companion's parents as they huddle under their frozen quilt, singing into their breath; a small boy and his father sitting on a very long pier, their baitless fishhooks dangling above the vast Pacific; the face of *su abuelita*, uplifted, reverent, mirrored in her grandson's dress.

Somewhere a light changes; the traffic unglues itself. As cars begin mov-   22
ing I am visited by two last ghosts—my companion and myself, sitting in the courtyard of the Hôtel Salé,[2] transfigured by the limitless heart.

---

2. The site of the Picasso Museum in Paris.

STUDY QUESTIONS

1. What bonds does the author find with the father of his companion? How does he discover their common sense of "hiding"? What "code" do they share?

2. Describe the conversation between the NARRATOR and the companion's father. What is the point of the father's stories? Why does the mother retreat from the conversation?

3. Explain the "need" the narrator feels for "the company of men like myself." Why does he feel "out of place" at the bar? Explain the attitudes behind the grandmother's gift? What do the grandmother and the father of the narrator's companion have in common? How does the memory of the Picasso Museum fit with the scene in the Los Angeles bar? What does the title mean?

CHARACTERIZATION

Most literature is about people, but works that center on families focus on the similarities and differences between individuals with special intensity. The particular traits (or *characteristics*) of a person suggest that person's CHARACTER—what it is that makes him or her distinctive. Individuals portrayed in literature are often referred to as *characters*. The way in which the author describes them and the process of defining them is usually called CHARACTERIZATION. Among the means of characterization, in addition to direct analysis, is describing the way characters look (their physical appearance and their clothing, bearing, makeup, and so on); the way they speak; the way they think, or what they think; what they do; and what other people say about them.

Cynthia Kadohata tells us that Charlie-O is always cheerful and has a "childlike joie de vivre." The mother in "My Mother's Stories" is friendly, we are told, with a compulsion to please; she's big-hearted and makes others laugh. The father in "The Gift" shows himself to be gentle and loving by the action he performs in removing a splinter.

But characterization is not always that direct. In life, we often conclude something about a person's character from the way he or she looks. In literature, the author is responsible for the character's appearance, or at least for how that appearance is conveyed to us. Probably more often than in life, the physical characteristics are fairly good indications of the inner person. That Charlie-O is only five-foot-three seems consistent with, maybe even a contributing factor to, his role as victim. The father in "The Gift" has a "lovely" face and "low" voice that seem to predict his caring and "tenderness." But the father in "Ancestor" has hands that chiefly remind the speaker of what they cannot, or do not, do.

It seems natural to assume that descriptions of the physical qualities or appearance of a character present the reader with a clear mental image of that character, but that's often not the case. Try to remember the appearance of even the main character in a poem, story, nonfictional prose piece, or the play in this chapter. Write it down. If you are able to draw, you might want to make a portrait of the character. Compare your description or drawing with those done by your classmates. The range of differences may astound you. You may have a very clear picture of Rhoda Schwartz's father, but someone else in your class may have quite a different image. You might want to ask what clues in the work he or she has used to make the description or drawing. Go back to the poem. You may be surprised to find that just about the only physical details are his slightness and shortness and, when young, his black curly hair.

Nor is this paucity of physical detail limited to poems. The mother is the central character in Tony Ardizzone's story, yet what do we know about her appearance? As a young girl she is skinny, as a bride slim, beautiful, and brown-haired, as an older woman brown-eyed and round like a fruit. They are the only details we are given.

Clothes or ornament often supplement or modify physical description. In Ardizzone's story, for example, the narrator's father as a young man is muscled, tanned, with a thin waist and dark hair; when his future wife first sees him, he is wearing a sleeveless undershirt and, around his neck, "golden things glistening on a thin chain" (paragraph 7).

Especially after we hear his "What's up?" and "How you doin', Mom, Auntie?" and his " *'Gao sai'* to you, too." For a character's language tells us much about him or her. Even though we know little about the contents of "My Father's Song," the fact that it is a "song" the way his voice sounds (stanza 1) makes the relationship to the son clear.

But in characterization, action often speaks louder than words. In Rhoda Schwartz's "Old Photographs," the father's rowing across the Dnieper River in a tiny boat against all advice gives some idea of his courage, his love of life and adventure, his independence. When he comes to America he rows across the St. Lawrence in a rowboat. His habitual actions—reading hidden books in the hayloft, arguing with what he reads—also tell you something about him. The action does not have to be habitual; it can be an instance that seems signally indicative, as in Li-Young Lee's "The Gift," in which the father's soft, deep voice and tender hands as he removes a splinter from the boy's palm and presents it to him engrave themselves on the boy's memory and on his character.

Sometimes a character will act "out of character," or so it seems, only to reveal more of his or her inner self. So the father in "My Mother's Stories," who always seems to be reading the newspaper or joking, tells his son, when his wife is desperately ill, how much he loves her, what the thirty-four years of their married life have meant to him.

These are but a few of the ways and means by which an author characterizes people. He or she counts on us and on our experience to fill in some of the gaps, to bring to life in our minds a sense of what the text implies—not the same image but one with approximately the same values and significance. To be aware of the means of characterization may make us more attentive to and appreciative of the traits, the psychological and moral suggestiveness of the people in the stories, poems, and plays we read. Such awareness may also sharpen our vision of the people we meet, even, perhaps, our understanding of ourselves.

WRITING ABOUT THE READING

PERSONAL ESSAYS AND NARRATIVES

1. What family doesn't have a thousand stories? Are you old enough to enjoy stories about yourself when you were very, very small? Like when your father and uncles used to gather in the big bathroom and smoke because your grandmother wouldn't let anyone smoke in the house, and you were two and used to knock on the door and they'd say, "Who's there?" and you'd say, "Me," and they'd say, "Who's 'me'?" and you'd say, "Me . . . me, the baby." Or stories about your mother as a child. Or your uncle's stories about the Vietnam War, or your memories of a death in the family.

   Write, for other family members, your favorite family stories. Or, for someone outside the family, write up the stories that best define—or explain or defend—your family.

2. Write an essay on family reunions, citing a few instances of the kinds of things that can happen based on your family's reunions over the past ten years or so. Or you could just remember one, perhaps the first one, and how excited you were and what happened. (Or you could make one up.)

3. Write a narrative depicting or honoring a parent or sibling in an incident or a series of incidents. You might want to embellish it a bit with a few made-up incidents or details or responses of your own. If you want to be true to your understanding of the character, make sure you invent episodes or details that are consistent with what you believe to be true of that person. Be aware, however, that sometimes the most revealing incidents or details are those that seem at first "out of character."

IMITATIONS AND PARODIES

1. Using Merle Woo's "Letter to Ma" as a guide, write a letter to your own mother explaining your differences of opinion about some major issue or attitude. Use family anecdotes or stories to illustrate the differences between your attitudes and those of older generations.

2. Try to change the point of view in one of the poems and stories in the chapter and write a new version or a piece of a new version. How does Charlie-O's wife see him? What does she think of their marriage? What is the grown child in Naomi Long Madgett's "Offspring" thinking of her and of home?

3. Write the poem you imagine the mother of the SPEAKER in Jimmy Santiago Baca's "Ancestor" would write about her husband.

ANALYTICAL PROSE

1. Choose one work, or a group of short works, from the chapter and analyze the ways in which the subjects are characterized, or compare how one story or poem characterizes—say, predominantly by actions—whereas another uses description or analysis of thoughts. It may be useful in this regard to look very closely at the selection of words and the kinds of metaphors or figures of speech that are used. Or you may be interested in analyzing all the ways in which mothers or fathers are characterized by the variety of attitudes on the part of the son or daughter.

2. Do the tributes or sketches or stories from different ethnic or cultural groups have something in common? Do they differ? If so, how?

3. Analyze the nature of family gatherings or reunions. Based on your own experience or observation, analyze the typical American (or Chinese- or Italian- or Jewish- or African- or Native American) family. Concern yourself with such questions as, What is the typical family size? How "close" is the family? How many aunts, uncles, cousins habitually visit? To what extent are friends and neighbors of the same background? Who "rules" the family? Are the children obedient? independent? What language is spoken in the house?

COMPARISON-CONTRAST PAPERS

1. Compare the ways in which fathers are eulogized by these authors—the qualities their children choose to remember with love; those qualities that one would wish had been otherwise. Or compare and contrast the ways in which mothers are treated as opposed to fathers.

2. Compare the "typical" family or family dynamics of two ethnic groups that you know.

ARGUMENTATIVE PAPER

Reread "Letter to Ma." Write a letter to one of your parents in which you try to explain, politely and lovingly, your position on some emotional issue on which you disagree. Then write a second letter in which you try to persuade the same person to change his or her position. Finally, write a third letter, on the same issue, to someone your own age, arguing the *opposite* position from the one you took in the previous letter.

RESEARCH PAPERS

1. We hear a good deal about the breakup of the American family, the frequency of divorce, and so on. Just what are the statistics? How many "nuclear" families are

there in the 1990s? Are divorce statistics skewed (some people having five or six marriages/divorces)? How do the figures break down by urban/suburban/small town/rural setting? by ethnic group? by a combination of ethnic and urban/rural factors?

2. Interview someone of the oldest living generation in your family about the ethnic makeup of the family, in as many branches as possible.

3. Interview a classmate or friend who is from an ethnic background different from your own, and gather as much detail as you can about the differences in your families and upbringing as possible.

Student Writing

"LETTER TO MA": THE CHASMS BETWEEN MOTHERS AND DAUGHTERS

Maria Albertsen

In the story "Letter to Ma" Merle Woo writes with bitterness and anger in reaction to the racism and sexism she has encountered in the United States, not only from white male society but also from white women and Asian brothers. Woo's mother is separated from her by the "chasms" created by their different generations and by her mother's habit of accepting oppression. Woo loves her mother deeply, understands that her own radical activism scares her mother, and is grateful for all the sacrifices her mother made in order to raise her. Besides the bitterness and anger that separate her from her mother, she is left with the conviction that Third World women are strong survivors. Woo gives a picture of her mother, who struggled and sacrificed herself to raise a daughter in America. She also describes her own wonderfully liberated and unprejudiced children, and in between these generations she describes herself: frustrated, hurt, furious from the pain caused by being labeled a "Yellow Feminist" in America, damaged by alcoholism she used to kill the pain. The message that Woo is sending us comes from deep inside her heart. Often you have to have been the target or victim yourself to understand the pain of others.

I was deeply touched as I read this story: it connected me with feelings about my own mother and my past that I've held onto since early childhood. Wow! Woo was able to put down on paper all these powerful feelings and echo many aspects of my life. Not only did I appreciate her analysis of the situation but I was also really moved.

The differences in our cultural backgrounds seem unimportant. Oppression is an international language and the victims of it become one victim. I am the daughter of a victim. An important contrast between Woo's mother and mine is that though her mom's life was drudgery she was able to earn enough to support her daughter and was available to her emotionally. My mother was one of an entire nation of rural Colombian women who have had no chance beyond hand-to-mouth survival and who simply do not know any other way to live. No matter how she slaved she never got ahead and could not provide for me materially. More devastating to me was that she had to abandon me emotionally in order to survive. From birth female children are valued much less than males and are set on a path that never varies: cooking, cleaning, being sexual objects, and breeding more children. Neither birth control, education, nor solidarity with other oppressed women is available. Women who break out of this cycle of poverty and despair are lucky, few, and very determined. I am proud to be one of them and this makes my mother's situation both clearer and more painful to me. I believe now that my mother had no other choice than to exist as she did; but when I was a child I was angry and terrified to feel my mother's attention drawn away by her hard life and almost constant pregnancy.

She had to take the lowest jobs, where she was treated like a slave seven   4
days and seven nights a week. She couldn't speak for herself and say "I'm tired." She did what she was told and on the nights when the master came sneaking quietly into her room she didn't even realize she was being abused. That was just life. She bore children for different masters while my loud voice was calling her for love and affection. I was terrified and frustrated seeing my mother getting pregnant by different men. I felt I was trying to swim and that something was pulling me under. I remember at age seven screaming at my mother, "How could you do this to yourself? How could you do this to me?"

Today I am dealing with my childhood pain, trying to reclaim my life   5
and make it better, and working to create possibilities for my own daughter that I never had. Sadly, my mother and my sisters in Colombia are still living as victims, still not seeing any way out of the trap of their lives. I feel that I escaped the trap of my beginnings really on my own power, but Woo gives her mother credit for getting her started. Her mother survived a terribly abusive childhood and worked constantly to provide Woo with material things and education. Her mother obviously wants the best for her, but the fact that Woo has become a radical "Yellow Feminist" really frightens her mother. She quotes her in the second paragraph of the story as saying, "I support you, honey, in everything you do except . . . except. . . ." Woo knows this means "except for your speaking and writing your anger." Since expressing herself is Woo's real life's work, this fear on her mother's part is very bitter to her. At the same time she stresses over and over that she does not blame her mother, but views her as a victim of oppression. Her mother has grown up with fear and has always lived with it. In paragraph 6 Woo affirms her love and understanding for her mother and all the sacrifices she has made throughout the years on Woo's behalf:

Now, I know you are going to think that I hate and despise you for your self-hatred, for your isolation. But I don't. Because in spite of your withdrawal, in spite of your loneliness, you have not only survived, but been beside me in the worst of times when your company meant everything in the world to me. I just need more than that now, Ma. I have taken and taken from you in terms of needing you to mother me, to be by my side, and I need, now, to take from you two more things: understanding and support for who I am now and my work.

This passage sums up the heart of this bittersweet "Letter."

Woo acknowledges here that she relates to her mother's isolation and self-hatred; Woo feels these debilitating emotions herself. In fact, "Letter to Ma" gives the reader the feeling that fighting against these "demons inside" is her life's work. All the discrimination and oppression aimed at us from the outside world are not as cunning and deadly an enemy as our own self-criticism. Women are taught that they are good enough only when they are serving or doing for others. Though we all fight against this condition daily, female artists and writers are made to feel especially wrong and bad for pursuing their talent or craft instead of taking care of others. Merle Woo seems to be trying to nurture herself into accepting herself as a writer and in this passage asking her blood mother to be mother also to the artist and writer, uncomfortable as that may be.

We are different from our mothers but also like them in many ways: our vulnerability to men and male-dominated society, our capacity for hard work, our deep sadness, and our dreams for something better for our own daughters. This is a story and a theme that women from any culture can understand.

3

HERITAGE

W here there's a will, someone once said, there's a relative, but material possessions are not the only things we inherit. We inherit physical traits, mannerisms, attitudes, tastes, and customs. Many things we inherit from our parents, but sometimes heredity skips a generation, so that we walk more like Grandma than our mother. Once in a while we are told that we do something—smile, frown, gesture—like someone we never knew, grandmother's grandfather, perhaps. Heritage, then, goes back more than a generation or two, even beyond memory.

Some of the things that make us what we are are so pervasive in our family and our community that they cannot be attributed to some *one;* they are cultural heritages. Our "self" is something more than the space between our head and toes and the time span between our birth and death. Our identity reaches back through generations, even centuries; who we are is conditioned by our familial and cultural heritage.

Cultural heritage comes to us through the older generations of our families and our community in stories, myths, art, decoration, dress, food, all sorts of daily practices, conscious or unconscious values, traditional wisdom or "lore." Much of this we take for granted, unaware that it is an intimate part of us, part of what makes us *us.* Sometimes our culture and its lore come into conflict with that of others, with "newfangled" ideas, and some of it, like some of our culture's language, has to be abandoned, or is rebelled against as we seek to join our peers from other cultures. We cannot comfortably cast it all aside, however; it all remains part of our being, some just below the surface of our "new" selves, much in the form of nostalgia and longing.

Heritage in the New World, the Americas, means something different from what it does in older and more stable societies. Our cultural heritage is both American and Other. Even those who are full-blooded Native Americans have a heritage that is not "American" in anything but the geographical sense: the dominant society on the American continents now is not that of those who were here before 1492, whatever it may have inherited from them. Nor are those whose families came from England in the seventeenth century to settle the East Coast of what is now the United States the "real Americans." Modern America includes a mix of all kinds of English, Scottish, German, Spanish, African, Jewish, and Asian ancestors. The most recent Americans—Haitians, Vietnamese, Cubans, Mexicans, Hungarians, Iranians, and so on—are in one sense more American by their very newness: their blend of old culture and new is typical of the New World. We are a significantly mixed-up people, both as individuals and as a society. American culture is a quilt, or perhaps a tightly woven fabric, intricate and various.

But most of us have a major affinity, if not an identity, with some Other culture, a "foreign" culture in time or space. When that heritage is fairly recent and identifiable, it sometimes has much of the same attractive power as home and family. But our American heritage, the pull toward more recent, polygenetic, American ways, is powerful, too. These contrary pulls and pushes can cause us pain or a sense of loss as well as pride and joy. We love our grandparents and often admire aspects of their old ways; yet we cannot be like them. Sometimes we feel we have gone on to better things and a better way of life, and resent their disapproval and their attempt to pull us back to a way of life they chose to abandon in coming here.

The poems, stories, and nonfiction prose pieces in this chapter focus on heritage, that which has been passed on to us from the recent and the remote past and is part of us in the present, in our identity and daily lives. Nostalgia, admiration, and pride; regret, embarrassment, and pain are all here, part of our heritage.

William Saroyan

Author of stories—his first collection, *The Daring Young Man on the Flying Trapeze*, was published in 1934; plays—*The Time of Your Life* won the Pulitzer Prize in 1939, though he refused the award on principle (he did not believe in literary "prizes"); and novels—the best known of which is *The Human Comedy* (1943); William Saroyan (1908–81) was born in Fresno, California. His belief in the basic goodness of humanity, his positive pictures of the innocence of the poor, popular in the socially conscious 1930s and early 1940s, seemed untenable in the darker days of World War II and the Cold War that followed, but there are recent signs of a revival of interest in Saroyan's works. Several of his works have been published posthumously, including *The Man with the Heart in the Highlands and Other Early Stories* (1989) and *Warsaw Visitor and Tales from the Vienna Streets: The Last Two Plays of William Saroyan* (1991).

NAJARI LEVON'S OLD COUNTRY ADVICE TO THE YOUNG AMERICANS ON HOW TO LIVE WITH A SNAKE

Najari Levon went to Aram's house on Van Ness Avenue for some legal advice about a private matter, but Aram hadn't come home yet, so the old man with the gargoyle face was asked to make himself at home somewhere. 1

He saw Aram's two small sons and two small daughters on the linoleum floor of a glassed-in porch, playing a board game and keeping score on a small pad with a small pencil, and so he went there and sat down to watch. 2

A metal arrow at the center of the large board was spun, and if it stopped in the space where there was a picture of a bright star, for instance, the player was given ten points, but just beside the picture of the star, there was a space in which there was a picture of a small green snake, and if the needle stopped there, ten points were taken away from the player's score. 3

The scorekeeper was Aram's firstborn, a boy of ten or eleven. 4

"Star," Aram's secondborn, a daughter, said, but the scorekeeper told his sister the needle was on the *line*, and *nearer* to the snake than to the star. 5

"Snake," he said, picking up the small pencil to put the score on the 6 pad. His sister knocked the pad and pencil out of his hand, saying, "Star." And they began to fight.

Najari Levon said in Armenian, "In our house in Bitlis lived a very large black snake, which was our family snake." 7

The fighters stopped to listen, and he said, "No proper family was without its proper snake. A house was not complete without a snake, because the long snake crawling back of the walls held the house together." 8

The fighters relaxed, and he said, "Our snake had great wisdom. It was the oldest house snake in Bitlis." 9

The scorekeeper sprawled belly down on the floor, not far from the corner of the room where the small pencil had fallen during the fight. 10

"Did you *see* the snake?" he said. 11

The storyteller glanced at the small green pencil and then at the boy, and he said, "Yes, I saw the snake. His door into the house was at the top of the stone wall in the room where I slept, a door just big enough for the snake to pass through, about the size of a saucer. In the evening as soon as I got into my bed, I looked up at the snake's door, and there I would see him looking down at me." 12

"*How much* of him would you see?" 13

"Only the head, because it was nighttime now, and he would soon go to sleep, too." 14

"Did you ever see *all* of him?" 15

"Oh, yes." 16

"How big was he?" 17

"As big around as a saucer, with a very sensitive face, very large eyes— not the little eyes of English people, but the large eyes of Armenian people. And Kurdish people. And a very thoughtful mouth, like the mouth of John D. Rockefeller, but of course with a different kind of tongue, although I can't be sure of this, because I have seen in a newspaper only a picture of John D. Rockefeller, but not a picture of his tongue." 18

"Did you see the snake's tongue?" 19

"Many times, in and out, like words, but of course in his own language, not ours." 20

"How long was he?" 21

"Ten times the length of a walking stick. He was not small." 22

"What would he do back there?" 23

"He lived there. His house was on that side of the stone wall, our house was on our side. But of course there was no such thing as his and ours. The whole house was ours and the whole house was his, but he *lived* back of the wall. In the wintertime I would not see him, and I would almost forget he was there. And then one evening in the springtime I would look up at his door, and there he would be again. He would speak, but I would say, 'Not now, because it's night and time to sleep, but in the morning come down and I will bring you something to eat.' So in the morning . . ." 24

"What did he eat?" 25

"Milk. In the morning I filled a bowl with milk—not one of those little   26
bowls soup is served in for a small man, but one of those large bowls for a
large man. My mother asked where I was taking the bowl of milk, and I said,
'Mama, I am taking the bowl of milk to the snake.' Everybody in our family,
every man, every woman, and every child comes to my room to see the
snake, because to have a snake in a house is baracat.[1] Everybody stands in
the room and waits to see the snake. Thirty-three men, women, and children, instead of thirty-four, because during the winter my grandfather Setrak
died."

"Did the snake come out?" the boy sprawled on the floor said.   27

"I took the bowl of milk, and put it in the corner straight across from   28
the snake's door so that all of the snake would be able to come out of the
door, down the wall, and across the floor. And then the thirty-three of us
would be able to see *all* of the snake, from the head with the mouth like John
D. Rockefeller's mouth, and with the eyes that are not the little eyes of English
people, but the large eyes of Armenian people, and Kurdish people. I put
the bowl down and look up at the snake's door, but the snake is not there, so
I speak to the snake, I say to him, 'Sevavor, I have put the bowl of milk on
the floor in the corner of the room, so come out of your door and down the
wall and across the floor and have something to eat; it is no longer wintertime, it is springtime.' "

"Did he come down?"   29

"The snake came to the door to see who it was who was speaking to   30
him, he came to see, he came to see who it was, was it me or was it somebody
else, so when he came to see, I said, 'Don't worry, Sevavor, it is me, Levon,
your friend. I am the one who is speaking, Najari Levon.' The snake looked
at me, and then he looked at each of the others in the room, but he did not
come down, the snake did not come down because we had been thirty-four
and now were thirty-three, so the snake did not come down. I said, 'Sevavor,
in the wintertime my grandfather Setrak died—that is why we are no longer
thirty-four, we are now only thirty-three, but two of the wives are pregnant
and in August we will be more than thirty-four, we will be thirty-five, and
if one of the wives has twins, we will be thirty-six, and if both of the wives
have twins, we will be thirty-seven, the Najari people will be thirty-seven,
Sevavor, so come out of the door, and down the wall, and across the floor to
the bowl of milk in the corner.' "

"Did he?"   31

"Very slowly, like this, like my arm, the snake came out of the door,   32
slowly, down the wall, like this, one walking-stick length of the black body
like this, slowly, down the wall, two walking-stick lengths, very hungry,
very old, very wise, three walking-stick lengths, very black, four lengths,
five lengths, six lengths, and now the snake's head is on the floor like this,
but his tail is still behind the wall, and all of the Najari people are watching

---

1. "Baracat" is "good fortune" in Arabic. [Author's note]

and waiting, and slowly the snake pushes himself forward on the floor a little nearer to the bowl of milk in the corner, seven lengths out of the door, seven lengths down the wall, eight lengths, nine lengths, and now all thirty-three of the Najari people are almost not breathing, to see better the Najari snake, the snake of the Najari people, from the head to the tail, and now there is only one more length. As soon as the snake moves one more length toward the bowl of milk in the corner, every man, woman, and child in the room will see *all* of the snake of our house, of our family, of the Najari people. But the snake stops. With only one more length to go the black snake moving to the white bowl of milk in the corner stops."

"Why?" the boy said, and the storyteller said, "An old snake who does not see an old man in the springtime because the old man is dead, an old snake who does not see an old man he saw in the summertime, because in the wintertime the old man died, an old snake stops to think about a thing like that. I said, 'Sevavor, do not be unhappy about my grandfather Setrak who died in the cold of wintertime; it is good for an old man to go to sleep in the snow, it is good for him to go home; if nobody went to sleep, if nobody went home, the house would soon be crowded and there would not be food enough for everybody. Do not be sorry for the old man, he is asleep, he has gone home, go and have the milk I have put in the bowl for you.' "

"Did he go?"

"The snake did not move, the black snake with his head and two walking-stick lengths on the floor, and seven lengths up the wall, and one length behind the wall, did not move, because when my grandfather Setrak was born the snake saw him, and every year of Setrak's life the snake saw him, but now the old man was dead, and the snake was on his way to the bowl of milk in the corner, but the snake did not want to move any more and all of the Najari people did not want to breathe. I said, 'Sevavor, do not worry about the old man, he is home, he is asleep, he is a small boy again running in the meadows, go and have your milk.' And then the snake, slowly, like a big black snake with eyes not like the little eyes of English people . . .'"

"Yes, Yes," the boy said. "Don't stop."

The old storyteller glanced at the small stub of green pencil on the floor, and then back at the boy, directly this time, scaring him a little, and then in English he said, "Dat your pancil?"

At that moment Aram came in and said, "What is it, Levon?"

The old man got up and chuckled deeply in the manner for which he was famous all over Fresno, and he said, "Aram Sevavor, I came for advice about a private matter. I came all the way from my house on L Street to your house on Van Ness Avenue, past the place where they have those red fire engines, all the way up Eye Street, where the police have their building, all the way up Forthcamp Avenue, I came, Aram Sevavor, one foot after the other, from my house to your house, I came, and now I go, I go all the way back, Aram Sevavor, because I can't remember the question I came to ask."

He went out the back, and down the alley, and the boy with the green pencil stood in the alley and watched him go, taking with him forever the end of the story about the snake.

STUDY QUESTIONS

1. "Snake" is mentioned in the title. Where does the first reference to a snake appear in the story? How does it lead (or mislead) your expectations of how a snake will figure in the story?

2. Why does Levon tell the story of the snake? What is its immediate effect upon the children? What sort of questions does the boy "scorekeeper" ask? Do these questions imply a certain amount of skepticism about the story? What skeptical or challenging questions does the boy *not* ask?

3. Why, according to Levon, does the snake, at one point, not come down to get his milk? How does Levon convince him to come down? Why, according to Levon, does the snake stop with only one length of a walking stick yet to go?

4. Describe the actions that Levon is demonstrating when he says "like this . . . like this" (paragraph 32).

5. What is the effect of the repetitions in the story? In paragraph 35, Levon begins to repeat again, "with eyes not like the little eyes of English people . . . ," but he is interrupted by the boy. What seems to have been the effect of the repetition on the boy? Why does he not want to hear it now?

6. In paragraph 37, Levon says, *in English*, "Dat your pancil?" This suggests, of course, that until now he has been speaking in Armenian. Compare the language of the story with the language in paragraph 39, when he tells Aram Sevavor that he forgot what he came for, a passage that also must have been spoken in Armenian. Compare the broken English to the language of the story. Can you see "foreign" elements in it—rhythms, for example? What does the contrast in language suggest about language and heritage?

   Look back at the title. Notice "Advice to the Young *Americans*." What is Levon's "advice"? How should one live with a snake? What does it seem to suggest about old country and American ways? In what sense is Levon passing on a "heritage"?

Maxine Hong Kingston

The Woman Warrior, Maxine Hong Kingston's first book and the one from which "No Name Woman" is taken, won the National Book Critics Circle Award in 1976. Born in California in 1940, Kingston published another volume, *China Men*, in 1980. Hers is a mixed genre or a new genre, neither fully fiction nor nonfiction, which

indeterminacy pleases her, for she wants her work to be beyond or outside categories—including ethnic and feminist categories—and to be identified merely as "human."
In 1989, she published a novel, *Tripmaster Monkey: His Fake Book*. She currently lives
in Oakland, California.

NO NAME WOMAN

"You must not tell anyone," my mother said, "what I am about to tell you.   1
In China your father had a sister who killed herself. She jumped into the
family well. We say that your father has all brothers because it is as if she
had never been born.

"In 1924 just a few days after our village celebrated seventeen hurry-up   2
weddings—to make sure that every young man who went 'out on the road'
would responsibly come home—your father and his brothers and your
grandfather and his brothers and your aunt's new husband sailed for America, the Gold Mountain. It was your grandfather's last trip. Those lucky
enough to get contracts waved good-bye from the decks. They fed and guarded
the stowaways and helped them off in Cuba, New York, Bali, Hawaii. 'We'll
meet in California next year,' they said. All of them sent money home.

"I remember looking at your aunt one day when she and I were dressing;   3
I had not noticed before that she had such a protruding melon of a stomach.
But I did not think, 'She's pregnant,' until she began to look like other pregnant women, her shirt pulling and the white tops of her black pants showing.
She could not have been pregnant, you see, because her husband had been
gone for years. No one said anything. We did not discuss it. In early summer
she was ready to have the child, long after the time when it could have been
possible.

"The village had also been counting. On the night the baby was to be   4
born the villagers raided our house. Some were crying. Like a great saw,
teeth strung with lights, files of people walked zigzag across our land, tearing
the rice. Their lanterns doubled in the disturbed black water, which drained
away through the broken bunds. As the villagers closed in, we could see that
some of them, probably men and women we knew well, wore white masks.
The people with long hair hung it over their faces. Women with short hair
made it stand up on end. Some had tied white bands around their foreheads,
arms, and legs.

"At first they threw mud and rocks at the house. Then they threw eggs   5
and began slaughtering our stock. We could hear the animals scream their
deaths—the roosters, the pigs, a last great roar from the ox. Familiar wild
heads flared in our night windows; the villagers encircled us. Some of the
faces stopped to peer at us, their eyes rushing like searchlights. The hands
flattened against the panes, framed heads, and left red prints.

"The villagers broke in the front and the back doors at the same time,   6 even though we had not locked the doors against them. Their knives dripped with the blood of our animals. They smeared blood on the doors and walls. One woman swung a chicken, whose throat she had slit, splattering blood in red arcs about her. We stood together in the middle of the house, in the family hall with the pictures and tables of the ancestors around us, and looked straight ahead.

"At that time the house had only two wings. When the men came back, we would build two more to enclose our courtyard and a third one to begin a second courtyard. The villagers pushed through both wings, even your grandparents' rooms, to find your aunt's, which was also mine until the men returned. From this room a new wing for one of the younger families would grow. They ripped up her clothes and shoes and broke her combs, grinding them underfoot. They tore her work from the loom. They scattered the cooking fire and rolled the new weaving into it. We could hear them in the kitchen breaking our bowls and banging the pots. They overturned the great waist-high earthenware jugs; duck eggs, pickled fruits, vegetables burst out and mixed in acrid torrents. The old woman from the next field swept a broom through the air and loosed the spirits-of-the-broom over our heads. 'Pig.' 'Ghost.' 'Pig,' they sobbed and scolded while they ruined our house.

"When they left, they took sugar and oranges to bless themselves. They cut pieces from the dead animals. Some of them took bowls that were not broken and clothes that were not torn. Afterward we swept up the rice and sewed it back up into sacks. But the smells from the spilled preserves lasted. Your aunt gave birth in the pigsty that night. The next morning when I went for the water, I found her and the baby plugging up the family well.

"Don't let your father know that I told you. He denies her. Now that you have started to menstruate, what happened to her could happen to you. Don't humiliate us. You wouldn't like to be forgotten as if you had never been born. The villagers are watchful."

Whenever she had to warn us about life, my mother told stories that ran like this one, a story to grow up on. She tested our strength to establish realities. Those in the emigrant generations who could not reassert brute survival died young and far from home. Those of us in the first American generations have had to figure out how the invisible world the emigrants built around our childhoods fit in solid America.

The emigrants confused the gods by diverting their curses, misleading them with crooked streets and false names. They must try to confuse their offspring as well, who, I suppose, threaten them in similar ways—always trying to get things straight, always trying to name the unspeakable. The Chinese I know hide their names; sojourners take new names when their lives change and guard their real names with silence.

Chinese-Americans, when you try to understand what things in you are Chinese, how do you separate what is peculiar to childhood, to poverty, insanities, one family, your mother who marked your growing with stories, from what is Chinese? What is Chinese tradition and what is the movies?

If I want to learn what clothes my aunt wore, whether flashy or ordinary, I would have to begin, "Remember Father's drowned-in-the-well sister?" I cannot ask that. My mother has told me once and for all the useful parts. She will add nothing unless powered by Necessity, a riverbank that guides her life. She plants vegetable gardens rather than lawns; she carries the odd-shaped tomatoes home from the fields and eats food left for the gods.

Whenever we did frivolous things, we used up energy; we flew high   14
kites. We children came up off the ground over the melting cones our parents brought home from work and the American movie on New Year's Day—*Oh, You Beautiful Doll* with Betty Grable one year, and *She Wore a Yellow Ribbon* with John Wayne another year. After the one carnival ride each, we paid in guilt; our tired father counted his change on the dark walk home.

Adultery is extravagance. Could people who hatch their own chicks and   15
eat the embryos and the heads for delicacies and boil the feet in vinegar for party food, leaving only the gravel, eating even the gizzard lining—could such people engender a prodigal aunt? To be a woman, to have a daughter in starvation time was a waste enough. My aunt could not have been the lone romantic who gave up everything for sex. Women in the old China did not choose. Some man had commanded her to lie with him and be his secret evil. I wonder whether he masked himself when he joined the raid on the family.

Perhaps she encountered him in the fields or on the mountain where the   16
daughters-in-law collected fuel. Or perhaps he first noticed her in the marketplace. He was not a stranger because the village housed no strangers. She had to have dealings with him other than sex. Perhaps he worked an adjoining field, or he sold her the cloth for the dress she sewed and wore. His demand must have surprised, then terrified her. She obeyed him; she always did as she was told.

When the family found a young man in the next village to be her hus-   17
band, she stood tractably beside the best rooster, his proxy, and promised before they met that she would be his forever. She was lucky that he was her age and she would be the first wife, an advantage secure now. The night she first saw him, he had sex with her. Then he left for America. She had almost forgotten what he looked like. When she tried to envision him, she only saw the black and white face in the group photograph the men had had taken before leaving.

The other man was not, after all, much different from her husband.   18
They both gave orders: she followed. "If you tell your family, I'll beat you. I'll kill you. Be here again next week." No one talked sex, ever. And she might have separated the rapes from the rest of living if only she did not have to buy her oil from him or gather wood in the same forest. I want her fear to have lasted just as long as rape lasted so that the fear could have been contained. No drawn-out fear. But women at sex hazarded birth and hence lifetimes. The fear did not stop but permeated everywhere. She told the man, "I think I'm pregnant." He organized the raid against her.

On nights when my mother and father talked about their life back home,   19
sometimes they mentioned an "outcast table" whose business they still seemed

to be settling, their voices tight. In a commensal tradition, where food is precious, the powerful older people made wrongdoers eat alone. Instead of letting them start separate new lives like the Japanese, who could become samurais and geishas, the Chinese family, faces averted but eyes glowering sideways, hung on to the offenders and fed them leftovers. My aunt must have lived in the same house as my parents and eaten at an outcast table. My mother spoke about the raid as if she had seen it, when she and my aunt, a daughter-in-law to a different household, should not have been living together at all. Daughters-in-law lived with their husbands' parents, not their own; a synonym for marriage in Chinese is "taking a daughter-in-law." Her husband's parents could have sold her, mortgaged her, stoned her. But they had sent her back to her own mother and father, a mysterious act hinting at disgraces not told me. Perhaps they had thrown her out to deflect the avengers.

She was the only daughter; her four brothers went with her father, husband, and uncles "out on the road" and for some years became western men. When the goods were divided among the family, three of the brothers took land, and the youngest, my father, chose an education. After my grandparents gave their daughter away to her husband's family, they had dispensed all the adventure and all the property. They expected her alone to keep the traditional ways, which her brothers, now among the barbarians, could fumble without detection. The heavy, deep-rooted women were to maintain the past against the flood, safe for returning. But the rare urge west had fixed upon our family, and so my aunt crossed boundaries not delineated in space. [20]

The work of preservation demands that the feelings playing about in one's guts not be turned into action. Just watch their passing like cherry blossoms. But perhaps my aunt, my forerunner, caught in a slow life, let dreams grow and fade and after some months or years went toward what persisted. Fear at the enormities of the forbidden kept her desires delicate, wire and bone. She looked at a man because she liked the way the hair was tucked behind his ears, or she liked the question-mark line of a long torso curving at the shoulder and straight at the hip. For warm eyes or a soft voice or a slow walk—that's all—a few hairs, a line, a brightness, a sound, a pace she gave up family. She offered us up for a charm that vanished with tiredness, a pigtail that didn't toss when the wind died. Why, the wrong lighting could erase the dearest thing about him. [21]

It could very well have been, however, that my aunt did not take subtle enjoyment of her friend, but, a wild woman, kept rollicking company. Imagining her free with sex doesn't fit, though. I don't know any woman like that, or men either. Unless I see her life branching into mine, she gives me no ancestral help. [22]

To sustain her being in love, she often worked at herself in the mirror, guessing at the colors and shapes that would interest him, changing them frequently in order to hit on the right combination. She wanted him to look back. [23]

On a farm near the sea, a woman who tended her appearance reaped a [24] reputation for eccentricity. All the married women blunt-cut their hair in flaps about their ears or pulled it back in tight buns. No nonsense. Neither style blew easily into heart-catching tangles. And at their weddings they displayed themselves in their long hair for the last time. "It brushed the backs of my knees," my mother tells us. "It was braided, and even so, it brushed the backs of my knees."

At the mirror my aunt combed individuality into her bob. A bun could 25 have been contrived to escape into black streamers blowing in the wind or in quiet wisps about her face, but only the older women in our picture album wear buns. She brushed her hair back from her forehead, tucking the flaps behind her ears. She looped a piece of thread, knotted into a circle between her index fingers and thumbs, and ran the double strand across her forehead. When she closed her fingers as if she were making a pair of shadow geese bite, the string twisted together catching the little hairs. Then she pulled the thread away from her skin, ripping the hairs out neatly, her eyes watering from the needles of pain. Opening her fingers, she cleaned the thread, then rolled it along her hairline and the tops of her eyebrows. My mother did the same to me and my sisters and herself. I used to believe that the expression "caught by the short hairs" meant a captive held with a depilatory string. It especially hurt at the temples, but my mother said we were lucky we didn't have to have our feet bound when we were seven. Sisters used to sit on their beds and cry together, she said, as their mothers or their slaves removed the bandages for a few minutes each night and let the blood gush back into their veins. I hope that the man my aunt loved appreciated a smooth brow, that he wasn't just a tits-and-ass man.

Once my aunt found a freckle on her chin, at a spot that the almanac 26 said predestined her for unhappiness. She dug it out with a hot needle and washed the wound with peroxide.

More attention to her looks than these pulling of hairs and pickings at 27 spots would have caused gossip among the villagers. They owned work clothes and good clothes, and they wore good clothes for feasting the new seasons. But since a woman combing her hair hexes beginnings, my aunt rarely found an occasion to look her best. Women looked like great sea snails—the corded wood, babies, and laundry they carried were the whorls on their backs. The Chinese did not admire a bent back; goddesses and warriors stood straight. Still there must have been a marvelous freeing of beauty when a worker laid down her burden and stretched and arched.

Such commonplace loveliness, however, was not enough for my aunt. 28 She dreamed of a lover for the fifteen days of New Year's, the time for families to exchange visits, money, and food. She plied her secret comb. And sure enough she cursed the year, the family, the village, and herself.

Even as her hair lured her imminent lover, many other men looked at 29 her. Uncles, cousins, nephews, brothers would have looked, too, had they been home between journeys. Perhaps they had already been restraining their curiosity, and they left, fearful that their glances, like a field of nesting birds, might be startled and caught. Poverty hurt, and that was their first reason for leaving. But another, final reason for leaving the crowded house was the never-said.

She may have been unusually beloved, the precious only daughter, spoiled [30] and mirror gazing because of the affection the family lavished on her. When her husband left, they welcomed the chance to take her back from the in-laws; she could live like the little daughter for just a while longer. There are stories that my grandfather was different from other people, "crazy ever since the little Jap bayoneted him in the head." He used to put his naked penis on the dinner table, laughing. And one day he brought home a baby girl, wrapped up inside his brown western-style greatcoat. He had traded one of his sons, probably my father, the youngest, for her. My grandmother made him trade back. When he finally got a daughter of his own, he doted on her. They must have all loved her, except perhaps my father, the only brother who never went back to China, having once been traded for a girl.

Brothers and sisters, newly men and women, had to efface their sexual [31] color and present plain miens. Disturbing hair and eyes, a smile like no other threatened the ideal of five generations living under one roof. To focus blurs, people shouted face to face and yelled from room to room. The immigrants I know have loud voices, unmodulated to American tones even after years away from the village where they called their friendships out across the fields. I have not been able to stop my mother's screams in public libraries or over telephones. Walking erect (knees straight, toes pointed forward, not pigeon-toed, which is Chinese-feminine) and speaking in an inaudible voice, I have tried to turn myself American-feminine. Chinese communication was loud, public. Only sick people had to whisper. But at the dinner table, where the family members came nearest one another, no one could talk, not the outcasts nor any eaters. Every word that falls from the mouth is a coin lost. Silently they gave and accepted food with both hands. A preoccupied child who took his bowl with one hand got a sideways glare. A complete moment of total attention is due everyone alike. Children and lovers have no singularity here, but my aunt used a secret voice, a separate attentiveness.

She kept the man's name to herself throughout her labor and dying; she [32] did not accuse him that he be punished with her. To save her inseminator's name she gave silent birth.

He may have been somebody in her own household, but intercourse [33] with a man outside the family would have been no less abhorrent. All the village were kinsmen, and the titles shouted in loud country voices never let kinship be forgotten. Any man within visiting distance would have been neutralized as a lover—"brother," "younger brother," "older brother"—one hundred and fifteen relationship titles. Parents researched birth charts probably not so much to assure good fortune as to circumvent incest in a population that has but one hundred surnames. Everybody has eight million relatives. How useless then sexual mannerisms, how dangerous.

As it came from an atavism deeper than fear, I used to add "brother" [34] silently to boys' names. It hexed the boys, who would or would not ask me to dance, and made them less scary and as familiar and deserving of benevolence as girls.

But, of course, I hexed myself also—no dates. I should have stood up, both arms waving, and shouted out across libraries, "Hey, you! Love me back." I had no idea, though, how to make attraction selective, how to control its direction and magnitude. If I made myself American-pretty so that the five or six Chinese boys in the class fell in love with me, everyone else—the Caucasian, Negro, and Japanese boys—would too. Sisterliness, dignified and honorable, made much more sense.

Attraction eludes control so stubbornly that whole societies designed to organize relationships among people cannot keep order, not even when they bind people to one another from childhood and raise them together. Among the very poor and the wealthy, brothers married their adopted sisters, like doves. Our family allowed some romance, paying adult brides' prices and providing dowries so that their sons and daughters could marry strangers. Marriage promises to turn strangers into friendly relatives—a nation of siblings.

In the village structure, spirits shimmered among the live creatures, balanced and held in equilibrium by time and land. But one human being flaring up into violence could open up a black hole, a maelstrom that pulled in the sky. The frightened villagers, who depended on one another to maintain the real, went to my aunt to show her a personal, physical representation of the break she had made in the "roundness." Misallying couples snapped off the future, which was to be embodied in true offspring. The villagers punished her for acting as if she could have a private life, secret and apart from them.

If my aunt had betrayed the family at a time of large grain yields and peace, when many boys were born, and wings were being built on many houses, perhaps she might have escaped such severe punishment. But the men—hungry, greedy, tired of planting in dry soil, cuckolded—had had to leave the village in order to send food-money home. There were ghost plagues, bandit plagues, wars with the Japanese, floods. My Chinese brother and sister had died of an unknown sickness. Adultery, perhaps only a mistake during good times, became a crime when the village needed food.

The round moon cakes and round doorways, the round tables of graduated size that fit one roundness inside another, round windows and rice bowls—these talismans had lost their power to warn this family of the law: a family must be whole, faithfully keeping the descent line by having sons to feed the old and the dead, who in turn look after the family. The villagers came to show my aunt and her lover-in-hiding a broken house. The villagers were speeding up the circling of events because she was too shortsighted to see that her infidelity had already harmed the village, that waves of consequences would return unpredictably, sometimes in disguise, as now, to hurt her. This roundness had to be made coin-sized so that she would see its circumference: punish her at the birth of her baby. Awaken her to the inexorable. People who refused fatalism because they could invent small resources insisted on culpability. Deny accidents and wrest fault from the stars.

After the villagers left, their lanterns now scattering in various directions toward home, the family broke their silence and cursed her. "Aiaa, we're going to die. Death is coming. Death is coming. Look what you've done. You've killed us. Ghost! Dead ghost! Ghost! You've never been born." She ran out into the fields, far enough from the house so that she could no longer hear their voices, and pressed herself against the earth, her own land no more. When she felt the birth coming, she thought that she had been hurt. Her body seized together. "They've hurt me too much," she thought. "This is gall, and it will kill me." Her forehead and knees against the earth, her body convulsed and then released her onto her back. The black well of sky and stars went out and out and out forever; her body and her complexity seemed to disappear. She was one of the stars, a bright dot in blackness, without home, without a companion, in eternal cold and silence. An agoraphobia rose in her, speeding higher and higher, bigger and bigger; she would not be able to contain it; there would be no end to fear.

Flayed, unprotected against space, she felt pain return, focusing her body. This pain chilled her—a cold, steady kind of surface pain. Inside, spasmodically, the other pain, the pain of the child, heated her. For hours she lay on the ground, alternately body and space. Sometimes a vision of normal comfort obliterated reality: she saw the family in the evening gambling at the dinner table, the young people massaging their elders' backs. She saw them congratulating one another, high joy on the mornings the rice shoots came up. When these pictures burst, the stars drew yet further apart. Black space opened.

She got to her feet to fight better and remembered that old-fashioned women gave birth in their pigsties to fool the jealous, pain-dealing gods, who do not snatch piglets. Before the next spasms could stop her, she ran to the pigsty, each step a rushing out into emptiness. She climbed over the fence and knelt in the dirt. It was good to have a fence enclosing her, a tribal person alone.

Laboring, this woman who had carried her child as a foreign growth that sickened her every day, expelled it at last. She reached down to touch the hot, wet, moving mass, surely smaller than anything human, and could feel that it was human after all—fingers, toes, nails, nose. She pulled it up on to her belly, and it lay curled there, butt in the air, feet precisely tucked one under the other. She opened her loose shirt and buttoned the child inside. After resting, it squirmed and thrashed and she pushed it up to her breast. It turned its head this way and that until it found her nipple. There, it made little snuffling noises. She clenched her teeth at its preciousness, lovely as a young calf, a piglet, a little dog.

She may have gone to the pigsty as a last act of responsibility: she would protect this child as she had protected its father. It would look after her soul, leaving supplies on her grave. But how would this tiny child without family find her grave when there would be no marker for her anywhere, neither in the earth nor the family hall? No one would give her a family hall name. She had taken the child with her into the wastes. At its birth the two of them had felt the same raw pain of separation, a wound that only the family pressing tight could close. A child with no descent line would not soften her life but only trail after her, ghostlike, begging her to give it purpose. At dawn the villagers on their way to the fields would stand around the fence and look.

Full of milk, the little ghost slept. When it awoke, she hardened her breasts against the milk that crying loosens. Toward morning she picked up the baby and walked to the well. 45

Carrying the baby to the well shows loving. Otherwise abandon it. Turn its face into the mud. Mothers who love their children take them along. It was probably a girl; there is some hope of forgiveness for boys. 46

"Don't tell anyone you had an aunt. Your father does not want to hear her name. She has never been born." I have believed that sex was unspeakable and words so strong and fathers so frail that "aunt" would do my father mysterious harm. I have thought that my family, having settled among immigrants who had also been their neighbors in the ancestral land, needed to clean their name, and a wrong word would incite the kinspeople even here. But there is more to this silence: they want me to participate in her punishment. And I have. 47

In the twenty years since I heard this story I have not asked for details nor said my aunt's name; I do not know it. People who can comfort the dead can also chase after them to hurt them further—a reverse ancestor worship. The real punishment was not the raid swiftly inflicted by the villagers, but the family's deliberately forgetting her. Her betrayal so maddened them, they saw to it that she would suffer forever, even after death. Always hungry, always needing, she would have to beg food from other ghosts, snatch and steal it from those whose living descendants give them gifts. She would have to fight the ghosts massed at crossroads for the buns a few thoughtful citizens leave to decoy her away from village and home so that the ancestral spirits could feast unharassed. At peace, they could act like gods, not ghosts, their descent lines providing them with paper suits and dresses, spirit money, paper houses, paper automobiles, chicken, meat, and rice into eternity— essences delivered up in smoke and flames, steam and incense rising from each rice bowl. In an attempt to make the Chinese care for people outside the family, Chairman Mao encourages us now to give our paper replicas to the spirits of outstanding soldiers and workers, no matter whose ancestors they may be. My aunt remains forever hungry. Goods are not distributed evenly among the dead. 48

My aunt haunts me—her ghost drawn to me because now, after fifty years of neglect, I alone devote pages of paper to her, though not origamied into houses and clothes. I do not think she always means me well. I am telling 49 on her, and she was a spite suicide, drowning herself in the drinking water. The Chinese are always very frightened of the drowned one, whose weeping ghost, wet hair hanging and skin bloated, waits silently by the water to pull down a substitute.

STUDY QUESTIONS

1. Paragraphs 4 through 9 describe in detail the attack on the NARRATOR's* grandparents' home. What is the tone of that description? Where are your sympathies at this point?

2. What is "the invisible world the emigrants built around our childhoods" (paragraph 10)? How is it related to the story of the sacking of the house?

3. What is the purpose of the emigrants' using false names, living on crooked streets, trying to confuse their children (paragraph 11)?

4. Why does the narrator find it difficult to find out what is the Chinese tradition?

5. What does it mean that the narrator's mother is "powered by Necessity" (paragraph 13)? What does that have to do with the way she tells stories? with the "prodigal aunt"? with the way her Chinese people eat chicken?

6. How were young women married in China? What was the "outcast table" (paragraph 19)? How did the moral standards for young men and women differ?

7. How did Chinese women get a smooth brow? What did the narrator's aunt do when she found a freckle on her chin? What does the narrator imagine her aunt's position in the family might have been before her "fall"?

8. How did the narrator's grandfather get the little girl baby he brought back inside his raincoat one day (paragraph 30)? How did he feel about his daughter (the narrator's aunt) when she was a little girl and while she was growing up?

9. What effect did the housing arrangement—"five generations living under one roof" (paragraph 31)—have on the way young people dressed, fixed their hair, looked at each other, spoke? What is the effect on mores of everybody having "eight million relatives" (paragraph 33)?

10. How did the Chinese villages attempt to control sexual relationships? What were the economic and social conditions among the Chinese at the time the aunt "fell"? How did the living arrangements, the sexual taboos, and the contemporary conditions contribute to the fierceness of the attack on the narrator's aunt? How did the family treat her after the raid?

11. Why did the aunt go to the pigsty to give birth?

12. Why does the narrator feel that she has participated in her aunt's punishment? What was the aunt's "real punishment"?

13. What paper offerings are given to the dead? What paper offering does the narrator give her dead aunt?

*Words in small capitals are defined in the Glossary.

Leslie Marmon Silko

B orn in 1948 in Albuquerque, New Mexico, Leslie Marmon Silko grew up on the Laguna Pueblo reservation. Her heritage is mixed—part Laguna, part Mexican, part white—and she refuses to apologize for it, believing that her storytelling ability "rise[s] out of this source." She is a graduate of the University of New Mexico and now teaches at the University of Arizona. Her best-known work, *Storyteller* (1981), is a collection of many of her best poems and stories. Her most recent work, *Almanac of the Dead: A Novel*, was published in 1991. Her writing, in both prose and poetry, is highly regarded, and she is the recipient of a prestigious MacArthur Fellowship.

PRIVATE PROPERTY

All Pueblo Tribes have stories about such a person—a young child, an orphan. 1
Someone has taken the child and has given it a place by the fire to sleep. The child's clothes are whatever the people no longer want. The child empties the ashes and gathers wood. The child is always quiet, sitting in its place tending the fire. They pay little attention to the child as they complain and tell stories about one another. The child listens although it has nothing to gain or lose in anything they say. The child simply listens. Some years go by and great danger stalks the village—in some versions of the story it is a drought and great famine, other times it is a monster in the form of a giant bear. And when all the others have failed and even the priests doubt the prayers, this child, still wearing old clothes, goes out. The child confronts the danger and the village is saved. Among the Pueblo people the child's reliability as a narrator is believed to be perfect.

Etta works with the wind at her back. Sand and dust roll down the road. She 2
feels scattered drops of rain and sometimes flakes of snow. What they have been saying about her all these years is untrue. They are angry because she left. Old leaves and weed stalks lie in gray drifts at the corners of the old fence. Part of an old newspaper is caught in the tumbleweeds; the wind presses it into brittle yellow flakes. She rakes the debris as high as her belly. They continue with stories about her. Going away has changed her. Living with white people has changed her. Fragments of glass blink like animal eyes.

The wind pushes the flames deep into the bones and old manure heaped under the pile of dry weeds. The rake drags out a shriveled work shoe and then the sleeve torn from a child's dress. They burn as dark and thick as hair. The wind pushes her off balance. Flames pour around her and catch the salt bushes. The yard burns bare. The sky is the color of stray smoke. The next morning the wind is gone. The ground is crusted with frost and still the blackened bones smolder.

The horses trot past the house before dawn. The sky and earth are the same color then—dense gray of the night burned down. At the approach of the sun, the east horizon bleeds dark blue. Reyna sits up in her bed suddenly and looks out the window at the horses. She has been dreaming she was stolen by Navajos and was taken away in their wagon. The sound of the horses' hooves outside the window had been the wagon horses of her dreams. The white one trots in the lead, followed by the gray. The little sorrel mare is always last. The gray sneezes at their dust. They are headed for the river. Reyna wants to remember this, and gets up. The sky is milky. Village dogs are barking in the distance. She dresses and finds her black wool cardigan. The dawn air smells like rain but it has been weeks since the last storm. The crickets don't feel the light. The mockingbird is in the pear tree. The bare adobe yard is swept clean. A distance north of the pear tree there is an old wire fence caught on gray cedar posts that lean in different directions. Etta has come back after many years to live in the little stone house. 3

The sound of the hammer had been Reyna's first warning. She blames herself for leaving the old fence posts and wire. The fence should have been torn down years ago. The old wire had lain half-buried in the sand that had drifted around the posts. Etta was wearing men's gloves that were too large for her. She pulled the strands of wire up and hammered fence staples to hold the wire to the posts. Etta has made the fence the boundary line. She has planted morning glories and hollyhocks all along it. She waters them every morning before it gets hot. Reyna watches her. The morning glories and hollyhocks are all that hold up the fence posts anymore. 4

Etta is watching Reyna from the kitchen window of the little stone house. She fills the coffee pot without looking at the level of water. Reyna is walking the fence between their yards. She paces the length of the fence as if she can pull the fence down with her walking. They had been married to brothers, but the men died long ago. They don't call each other "sister-in-law" anymore. The fire in the cookstove is cracking like rifle shots. She bought a pick-up load of pinon wood from a Navajo. The little house has one room, but the walls are rock and adobe mortar two feet thick. The one who got the big house got the smaller yard. That is how Etta remembers it. Their mother-in-law had been a kind woman. She wanted her sons and daughters-in-law to live happily with each other. She followed the old ways. She believed houses and fields must always be held by the women. There had been no 5 nieces or daughters. The old woman stood by the pear tree with the daughters-in-law and gave them each a house, and the yard to divide. She pointed at the little stone house. She said the one who got the little house got the bigger share of the yard. Etta remembers that.

Cheromiah drives up in his white Ford pick-up. He walks to the gate smiling. He wears his big belly over his Levi's like an apron. Reyna is gathering kindling at the woodpile. The juniper chips are hard and smooth as flint. She rubs her hands together although there is no dust. "They came through this morning before it was even daylight." She points in the direction of the river. "They were going down that way." He frowns, then he smiles. "I've been looking for them all week," he says. The old woman shakes her head. "Well, if you hurry, they might still be there." They are his horses. His father-in-law gave him the white one when it was a colt. Its feet are as big around as pie pans. The gray is the sorrel mare's colt. The horses belong to Cheromiah, but the horses don't know that. "Nobody told them," that's what people say and then they laugh. The white horse leans against corral planks until they give way. It steps over low spots in old stone fences. The gray and little sorrel follow.

    "The old lady said to share and love one another. She said we only make use of these things as long as we are here. We don't own them. Nobody owns anything." Juanita nods. She listens to both of her aunts. The two old women are quarreling over a narrow strip of ground between the two houses. The earth is hard-packed. Nothing grows there. Juanita listens to her Aunt Reyna and agrees that her Aunt Etta is wrong. Too many years living in Winslow. Aunt Etta returns and she wants to make the yard "private property" like white people do in Winslow. Juanita visits both of her aunts every day. She visits her Aunt Etta in the afternoon while her Aunt Reyna is resting. Etta and Reyna know their grandniece must visit both her aunts. Juanita has no husband or family to look after. She is the one who looks after the old folks. She is not like her brothers or sister who have wives or a husband. She doesn't forget. She looked after Uncle Joe for ten years until he finally died. He always told her she would have the house because women should have the houses. He didn't have much. Just his wagon horses, the house and a pig. He was the oldest and believed in the old ways. Aunt Reyna was right. If her brother Joe were alive he would talk to Etta. He would remind her that this is the village, not Winslow, Arizona. He would remind Etta how they all must share. Aunt Reyna would have more space for her woodpile then.

Most people die once, but "old man Joe he died twice," that's what people said, and then they laughed. Juanita knew they joked about it, but still she held her head high. She was the only one who even tried to look after the old folks. That November, Uncle Joe had been sick with pneumonia. His house smelled of Vicks and Ben-Gay. She checked on him every morning. He was always up before dawn the way all the old folks were. They greeted the sun and prayed for everybody. He was always up and had a fire in his little pot belly stove to make coffee. But that morning she knocked and there was no answer. Her heart was beating fast because she knew what she would find. The stove was cold. She stood by his bed and watched. He did not move. She touched the hand on top of the blanket and the fingers were as cold as the room. Juanita ran all the way to Aunt Reyna's house with the news. They sent word. The nephews and the clansmen came with picks and shovels. Before they went to dress him for burial, they cooked the big meal always prepared for the gravediggers. Aunt Reyna rolled out the tortillas and cried. Joe had always been so good to her. Joe had always loved her best after their parents died.

Cheromiah came walking by that morning while Juanita was getting 9 more firewood. He was dragging a long rope and leather halter. He asked if she had seen any sign of his horses. She shook her head and then she told him Uncle Joe had passed away that morning. Tears came to her eyes. Cheromiah stood quietly for a moment. "I will miss the old man. He taught me everything I know about horses." Juanita nodded. Her arms were full of juniper wood. She looked away toward the southeast. "I saw your gray horse up in the sandhills the other day." Cheromiah smiled and thanked her. Cheromiah's truck didn't start in cold weather. He didn't feel like walking all the way up to the sand hills that morning. He took the road around the far side of the village to get home. It took him past Uncle Joe's place. The pig was butting its head against the planks of the pen making loud smacking sounds. The wagon horses were eating corn stalks the old man had bundled up after harvest for winter feed. Cheromiah wondered which of the old man's relatives was already looking after the livestock. He heard someone chopping wood on the other side of the house. The old man saw him and waved in the direction of the river. "They were down there last evening grazing in the willows." Cheromiah dropped the halter and rope and gestured with both hands. "Uncle Joe! They told me you died! Everyone thinks you are dead! They already cooked the gravediggers lunch!"

From that time on Uncle Joe didn't get up before dawn like he once did. 10 But he wouldn't let them tease Juanita about her mistake. Behind her back, Juanita's cousins and in-laws were saying that she was in such a hurry to collect her inheritance. They didn't think she should get everything. They thought all of it should be shared equally. The following spring, Uncle Joe's wagon horses went down Paguate Hill too fast and the wagon wheel hit a big rock. He was thrown from the wagon and a sheepherder found him. Uncle Joe was unconscious for two days and then he died. "This time he really *is* dead, poor thing," people would say and then they'd smile.

The trouble over the pig started on the day of the funeral. Juanita caught 11 her brother's wife at the pig pen. The wife held a large pail in both hands. The pail was full of a yellowish liquid. There were bones swimming in it. Corn tassels floated like hair. She looked Juanita in the eye as she dumped the lard pail into the trough. The pig switched its tail and made one push through the liquid with its snout. It looked up at both of them. The snout kept moving. The pig would not eat. Juanita had already fed the pigs scraps from the gravediggers' plates. She didn't want her brothers' wives feeding the pig. They would claim, they had fed the pig more than she had. They would say that whoever fed the pig the most should get the biggest share of meat. At butchering time they would show up to collect half. "It won't eat slop," Juanita said, "don't be feeding it slop."

The stories they told about Etta always came back to the same thing. 12

While the other girls learn cooking and sewing at the Indian School, Etta 13 works in the greenhouse. In the evenings the teacher sits with her on the sofa. They repeat the names of the flowers. She teaches Etta the parts of the flower. On Saturdays while the dormitory matrons take the others to town, Etta stays with the teacher. Etta kneels beside her in the garden. They press brown dirt over the gladiola bulbs. The teacher runs a hot bath for her. The teacher will not let her return to the dormitory until she has cleaned Etta's fingernails. The other girls tell stories about Etta.

The white gauze curtains are breathing in and out. The hollyhocks bend 14 around the fence posts and lean over the wire. The buds are tight and press between the green lips of the sheath. The seed had been saved in a mason jar. Etta found it in the pantry behind a veil of cobwebs. She planted it the length of the fence to mark the boundary. She had only been a child the first time, but she can still remember the colors—reds and yellows swaying above her head, tiny black ants in the white eyes of pollen. Others were purple and dark red, almost black as dried blood. She planted the seeds the teacher had given her. She saved the seeds from the only year the hollyhocks grew. Etta doesn't eat pork. She is thinking about the row of tamarisk trees she will plant along the fence so people cannot see her yard or house. She does not want to spend her retirement with everyone in the village minding her business the way they always have. Somebody is always fighting over something. The years away taught her differently. She knows better now. The yard is hers. They can't take it just because she had lived away from the village all those years. A person could go away and come back again. The village people don't understand fences. At Indian School she learned fences tell you where you stand. In Winslow, white people built fences around their houses, otherwise something might be lost or stolen. There were rumors about her the whole time she lived in Winslow. The gossip was not true. The teacher had written to her all the years Etta was married. It was a job to go to after her husband died. The teacher was sick and old. Etta went because she loved caring for the flowers. It was only a job, but people like to talk. The teacher was sick for a long time before she died.

"What do you want with those things," the clanswoman scolded, "wast- 15 ing water on something we can't eat." The old woman mumbled to herself all the way across the garden. Etta started crying. She sat on the ground by the hollyhocks she had planted, and held her face. She pressed her fingers into her eyes. The old woman had taken her in. It was the duty of the clan to accept orphans.

Etta tells her she is not coming back from Indian School in the summer. She has a job at school caring for the flowers. She and the clanswoman are cleaning a sheep stomach, rinsing it under the mulberry tree. The intestines are coiled in a white enamel pan. They are bluish gray, the color of the sky before snow. Strands of tallow branch across them like clouds. "You are not much good to me anyway. I took you because no one else wanted to. I have tried to teach you, but the white people at that school have ruined you. You waste good water growing things we cannot eat." 16

The first time Etta returned from Winslow for a visit, Reyna confided there was gossip going on in the village. Etta could tell by the details that her sister-in-law was embroidering stories about her too. They did not speak to each other after that. People were jealous of her because she had left. They were certain she preferred white people. But Etta spoke only to the teacher. White people did not see her when she walked on the street. 17

The heat holds the afternoon motionless. The sun does not move. It has parched all color from the sky and left only the fine ash. The street below is empty. Down the long dim hall there are voices in English and, more distantly, the ticking of a clock. The room is white and narrow. The shade is pulled. It pulses heat the texture of pearls. The water in the basin is the color of garnets. Etta waits in a chair beside the bed. The sheets are soaked with her fever. She murmurs the parts of the flowers—she whispers that the bud is swelling open, but that afternoon was long ago. 18

Ruthie's husband is seeing that other woman in the cornfield. The cornfield belongs to her and to her sister, Juanita. Their mother left it to both of them. In the morning her husband walks to the fields with the hoe on his shoulder. Not long after, the woman appears with a coal bucket filled with stove ashes. The woman follows the path toward the trash pile, but when she gets to the far corner of the cornfield she stops. When she thinks no one is watching she sets the bucket down. She gathers up the skirt of her dress and steps over the fence where the wire sags. 19

Ruthie would not have suspected anything if she had not noticed the rocks. He was always hauling rocks to build a new shed or corral. But this time there was something about the colors of the sandstone. The reddish pink and orange yellow looked as if they had been taken from the center of the sky as the sun went down. She had never seen such intense color in sandstone. She had always remembered it being shades of pale yellow or peppered white-colors for walls and fences. But these rocks looked as if rain 20

had just fallen on them. She watched her husband. He was unloading the
rocks from the old wagon and stacking them carefully next to the woodpile.
When he had finished it was dark and she could not see the colors of the
sandstone any longer. She thought about how good-looking he was, the kind
of man all the other women chase.

Reyna goes with them. She takes her cane but carries it ready in her   21
hand like a rabbit club. Her grandnieces have asked her to go with them.
Ruthie's husband is carrying on with another woman. The same one as before.
They are going after them together—the two sisters and the old aunt. Ruthie
told Juanita about it first. It was their mother's field and now it is theirs. If
Juanita had a husband he would work there too. "The worst thing is them
doing it in the cornfield. It makes the corn sickly, it makes the beans stop
growing. If they want to do it they can go down to the trash and lie in the
tin cans and broken glass with the flies," that's what Reyna says.

They surprise them lying together on the sandy ground in the shade of   22
the tall corn plants. Last time they caught them together they reported them
to the woman's grandmother, but the old woman didn't seem to care. They
told that woman's husband too. But he has a job in Albuquerque, and men
don't bother to look after things. It is up to women to take care of everything.
He is supposed to be hoeing weeds in their field, but instead he is rolling
around on the ground with that woman, killing off all their melons and beans.

Her breasts are long and brown. They bounce against her like potatoes.   23
She runs with her blue dress in her hand. She leaves her shoes. They are
next to his hoe. Ruthie stands between Juanita and Aunt Reyna. They gesture with their arms and yell. They are not scolding him. They don't even
look at him. They are scolding the rest of the village over husband-stealing
and corn that is sickly. Reyna raps on the fence post with her cane. Juanita
calls him a pig. Ruthie cries because the beans won't grow. He kneels to lace
his work shoes. He kneels for a long time. His fingers move slowly. They
are not talking to him. They are talking about the other woman. The red
chili stew she makes is runny and pale. They pay no attention to him. He
goes back to hoeing weeds. Their voices sift away in the wind. Occasionally
he stops to wipe his forehead on his sleeve. He looks up at the sky or over
the sand hills. Off in the distance there is a man on foot. He is crossing the
big sand dune above the river. He is dragging a rope. The horses are grazing
on yellow rice grass at the foot of the dune. They are down wind from him.
He inches along, straining to crouch over his own stomach. The big white
horse whirls suddenly, holding its tail high. The gray half-circles and joins
it, blowing loudly through its nostrils. The little sorrel mare bolts to the top
of the next dune before she turns.

Etta awakens and the yard is full of horses. The gray chews a hollyhock.   24
Red petals stream from its mouth. The sorrel mare watches her come out the
door. The white horse charges away, rolling his eyes at her nightgown. Etta
throws a piece of juniper from the woodpile. The gray horse presses hard
against the white one. They tremble in the corner of the fence, strings of

blue morning glories trampled under their hooves. Etta yells and the sorrel mare startles, crowding against the gray. They heave forward against the fence, and the posts make slow cracking sounds. The wire whines and squeaks. It gives way suddenly and the white horse stumbles ahead tangled in wire. The sorrel and the gray bolt past, and for an instant the white horse hesitates, shivering at the wire caught around its forelegs and neck. Then the white horse leaps forward, rusty wire and fence posts trailing behind like a broken necklace.

STUDY QUESTIONS

1. Twice in the story, people are said to follow the "old ways." What are the "old ways"? What values do they represent? Which characters in the story embody the "old ways" most fully?

2. In what different ways do Etta's habits and values differ from those of others in the story? What in her life history accounts for those differences? Do you think that the village people are right to assume that her "foreign" experience has corrupted her? Which characteristics of hers are least attractive? Which are most attractive? How does the narrator of the story seem to feel about Etta? How can you tell?

3. What strategies does the author use to characterize each of the people in the story?

4. Who is responsible for the fences? What do the fences mean to the different characters in the story? How effective are the fences in dealing with people's feelings of ownership and sharing? How effective are they in containing the animals?

5. Why does the NARRATOR tell us directly that the rumors about Etta at school were untrue?

6. What does the episode about the catching of Ruthie's husband with another woman in the cornfield have to do with the central THEME of the story? Why do the people who have caught the husband in the act ignore him once their mission is completed? What kinds of roles do men play in the story?

7. What does the first paragraph of the story have to do with the rest of it?

Lorna Dee Cervantes

B orn in San Francisco in 1954, Lorna Dee Cervantes is of Mexican descent. She has published two books of poems, *Emplumada* (1981) and *From the Cables of Genocide: Poems on Love and Hunger* (1991). She was educated at San Jose City College and San Jose State University and is the founder of Mango Publications, a small press that publishes books and a literary magazine. She currently teaches creative writing at the University of Colorado at Boulder.

HERITAGE

Heritage
I look for you all day in the streets of Oaxaca.
The children run to me, laughing,
spinning me blind and silly.
They call to me in words of another language.   5
My brown body searches the streets
for the dye that will color my thoughts.

But Mexico gags
"ESPUTA"[1]
on this bland pochaseed.[2]   10

I didn't ask to be brought up tonta![3]
My name hangs about me like a loose tooth.
Old women know my secret,
"Es la culpa de los antepasados"[4]
Blame it on the old ones.   15
They give me a name
that fights me.

STUDY QUESTION

How does the language of this poem reflect the cultural situation of the SPEAKER?

Linda Hogan

Linda Hogan, a Chickasaw, was born in Denver in 1947, grew up in Oklahoma, and earned an M.A. in English and Creative Writing from the University of

1. Spit; *Es puta* also means "She is a prostitute."
2. Americanized Mexican.
3. As a fool.
4. It's the fault of the ancestors.

Colorado, where she now teaches creative writing. She has published several books of poems, including *Calling Myself Home; Daughters, I Love You; Eclipse; That House;* and *Seeing Through the Sun* (which won the 1986 American Book Award from the Before Columbus Foundation). Her first novel, *Mean Spirit*, appeared in 1989.

HERITAGE

From my mother, the antique mirror
where I watch my face take on her lines.
She left me the smell of baking bread
to warm fine hairs in my nostrils,
she left the large white breasts that weigh down   5
my body.

From my father I take his brown eyes,
the plague of locusts that leveled our crops,
they flew in formation like buzzards.

From my uncle the whittled wood   10
that rattles like bones
and is white
and smells like all our old houses
that are no longer there. He was the man
who sang old chants to me, the words   15
my father was told not to remember.

From my grandfather who never spoke
I learned to fear silence.
I learned to kill a snake
when you're begging for rain.   20

And grandmother, blue-eyed woman
whose skin was brown,
she used snuff.
When her coffee can full of black saliva
spilled on me   25
it was like the brown cloud of grasshoppers
that leveled her fields.
It was the brown stain
that covered my white shirt,
my whiteness a shame.   30
That sweet black liquid like the food

she chewed up and spit into my father's mouth
when he was an infant.
It was the brown earth of Oklahoma
stained with oil.   35
She said tobacco would purge your body of poisons.
It has more medicine than stones and knives
against your enemies.

That tobacco is the dark night that covers me.

She said it is wise to eat the flesh of deer   40
so you will be swift and travel over many miles.
She told me how our tribe has always followed a stick
that pointed west
that pointed east.
From my family I have learned the secrets   45
of never having a home.

STUDY QUESTIONS

1. What are the good things the SPEAKER inherits? the undesirable things? What part
   of the heritage seems doubtful or ambiguous? Is the speaker proud of his or her
   heritage? ashamed? happy or unhappy? What, then, is the tone of the poem?

2. The grandmother uses snuff, we are told in line 23; she spits into a coffee can, and
   apparently there once was an accident involving the can and the speaker. How
   does the poem use this accident to describe how the grandmother passed on to the
   speaker the cultural heritage? What other brown and black things is the black saliva
   compared to? How do they relate to the heritage? Why is the speaker's whiteness
   "a shame" (line 30)? Line 39 stands alone; what does it mean?

3. What is the nature and location of the homeland from which the speaker comes?

4. What practices or beliefs identify the culture from which the speaker comes?

Pat Mora

Born in El Paso, Pat Mora writes poems in which her Chicana heritage and South-
western background are central. Her first book, *Chants* (1985), is composed
largely of what she calls "desert incantations." Her second, *Borders* (1986), from which
the following poem is taken, describes the two cultures that create her own "border"

life. Both books won Southwest Book awards. Her third book, *Communion*, was published in 1991. She lives in Cincinnati.

BORDERS

My research suggests that men and women may speak different languages that they assume are the same.

Carol Gilligan

If we're so bright,
why didn't we notice?

I

The side-by-side translations
were the easy ones.
Our tongues tasted *luna*   5
chanting, chanting to the words
it touched; our lips circled
moon sighing its longing.
We knew: similar but different.

II

And we knew of grown-up talk,   10
how even in our own home
like became unlike,
how the child's singsong
                        I want, I want
burned our mouth   15
when we whispered in the dark.

III

But us? You and I
who've talked for years
tossing words back and forth
                        success, happiness   20
back and forth
over coffee, over wine
at parties, in bed
and I was sure you heard,
        u n d e r s t o o d ,   25
though now I think of it
I can remember screaming
to be sure.

So who can hear
the words we speak
you and I, like but unlike,
and translate us to us
side by side?

STUDY QUESTIONS

1. To whom is the poem addressed? Who are the "we" in line 2? the "us" in line 17?

2. Who is Carol Gilligan? Why is an EPIGRAPH from her study especially significant to this poem?

3. What are "side-by-side translations" (line 3)? Why are they "easy" compared with difficulties of translation when both people use the same word differently, as in section III?

4. According to the poem, what differences are there between the talk of children and that of adults? What, exactly, are the differences between women's language and men's, according to the poem? What illustrations does the poem offer?

5. In what specific ways do the examples of speech illustrated by "luna" and "moon" contribute to the sense of intimacy and companionship in the poem? How do they contribute to the atmosphere of the poem? Contrast the TONES of sections II and III. What accounts for the differences? What is the mythological connection between women and the moon? Does the poem challenge traditional mythological associations in any way?

6. How does the sense of audience projected by the poem relate to the central problem the poem poses? In what sense does a conception of audience provide a solution?

David Mura

David Mura is a *sansei*, a third-generation Japanese American. He is the author of *Turning Japanese: Memoirs of a Sansei*, which won the 1991 Josephine Miles Oakland PEN book award; *After We Lost Our Way*, which won the 1989 National Poetry Series Contest; and *A Male Grief: Notes on Pornography and Addiction*. His poems have appeared in *The American Poetry*, *The Nation*, *The New Republic*, *New England Review*, and various anthologies. Mura has written on race and multiculturalism for a wide variety of publications, and is currently working on an autobiographical book exploring the issues of race from an Asian-American perspective. He is also a performance artist and playwright, and has taught at the University of Minnesota, The Loft, St. Olaf College, and the University of Oregon.

LISTENING

And from that village, steaming with mist, riddled with rain,
from the fishermen in the bay hauling up nets of silver flecks;
from the droning of the Buddhist priest in the morning,

incense thickening his voice, a bit other-wordly, almost sickly;
from the oysters ripped from the sea bottom by half-naked women,   5
their skin darker than the bark in the woods, their lungs

as endless as some cave where a demon dwells
(soon their harvest will be split open by a blade, moist
meaty flesh, drenched in the smell of sea bracken, the tidal winds);

from the *torrii*¹ half way up the mountain   10
and the steps to the temple where the gong shimmers
with echoes of bright metallic sound;

from the waterfall streaming, hovering in the eye, and in illusion, rising;
from the cedars that have nothing to do with time;
from the small mud-cramped streets of rice shops and fish mongers;   15

from the pebbles on the riverbed, the aquamarine stream
floating pine-trunks, felled upstream
by men with *hachimaki*² tied round their forehead

and grunts of *o-sha*³ I remember from my father in childhood;
from this mythical land of the empty sign and a thousand-thousand
      manners,   20
on the tip of this peninsula, far from Kyoto, the Shogun's palace,

in a house of *shoji*⁴ and clean cut pine, crawling onto a straw futon,
one of my ancestors lay his head as I do now on a woman's belly
and felt an imperceptible bump like the bow of a boat hitting a swell

and wondered how anything so tiny could cause such rocking unbroken
      joy.   25

1. Gate of a Shinto shrine.
2. Headband.
3. Ruler or monarch.
4. Paper screen.

STUDY QUESTIONS

1. What is the basic situation in this poem? What is the setting? What is the "bump" in line 24? What is the relationship of the SPEAKER to the woman mentioned in line 23? How can you tell?

2. How far back in time does the poem go in its memories and evocation of past culture? What kind of effect is gained by this journey into the past?

3. Why does the poem withhold for so long a description of the present? Describe the effect of the piling up of details about the past. Of the repetition of words and phrases. Of the accumulation of details about Japanese tradition.

Muriel Rukeyser

B orn in New York City in 1913, Muriel Rukeyser was trained as an aviator, worked as a journalist, and was a poet as well. She was in Spain to report on the anti-Nazi "Popular Olympiad" (Barcelona, 1936) which was interrupted by the start of the Spanish Civil War which she then covered. She was one of the reporters arrested at the famous Scottsboro Trial (1931), a crucial moment in the history of American race relations. Rukeyser's poems often reflect both her Jewish heritage and her powerful concerns for human rights. She died in 1980.

"To Be a Jew" was written during World War II; it has been included in *The Service of the Heart* (London) and *The Gates of Prayer* (New York), the Reform Jewish prayer books.

TO BE A JEW IN THE TWENTIETH CENTURY
(from LETTER TO THE FRONT)

To be a Jew in the twentieth century
Is to be offered a gift.   If you refuse,
Wishing to be invisible, you choose
Death of the spirit, the stone insanity.

Accepting, take full life, full agonies: 5
Your evening deep in labyrinthine blood
Of those who resist, fail and resist; and God
Reduced to a hostage among hostages.
The gift is torment.   Not alone the still
Torture, isolation; or torture of the flesh.   10
That may come also.   But the accepting wish,
The whole and fertile spirit as guarantee
For every human freedom, suffering to be free,
Daring to live for the impossible.

STUDY QUESTIONS

1. What, according to the poem, distinguishes being a Jew in the twentieth century from previous centuries? Why does the poem refuse to be specific about agonies, blood, and torture? What kinds of sufferings are suggested by these terms? What events does the poem seem to have in mind? What kinds of information are readers assumed already to have before reading the poem?

2. What does it mean to "refuse" the gift to be "invisible" (lines 2–3)? Why is the blood described as "labyrinthine" (line 6)? What does it mean for God to be "reduced to a hostage" (line 8)? What ideals does the poem express most forcibly?

3. Why does the poem become more direct and explicit beginning with line 9? How do the final six lines relate to the first eight? What words are repeated in the poem? Explain the effect of every instance of a repeated word.

4. What pattern of rhymes does the poem have? Where are the major structural breaks in the poem's organization? How are the breaks in thought signaled?

Maya Angelou

Maya Angelou's ongoing autobiography has now reached five volumes, and she is still a relatively young woman. But no wonder. Besides writing the autobiography, three volumes of poetry, the musical *And Still I Rise*, the BBC documentary *Trying to Make It Home*, and a ten-part television series (which she also produced), Angelou has toured Europe and Africa as an actress (in *Porgy and Bess*), studied and taught dance, served as the Northern coordinator for the Southern Christian Leadership Conference, and served on the Commission of International Women's Year and on the Board of Trustees of the American Film Institute. She was understandably named "Woman of the Year" by the *Ladies Home Journal* in 1975. Angelou read her poem "On the Pulse of Morning" at the inauguration of President Bill Clinton in January 1993.

AFRICA

Thus she had lain
sugar cane sweet
deserts her hair
golden her feet
mountains her breasts   5
two Niles her tears
Thus she has lain
Black through the years.

Over the white seas
rime white and cold   10
brigands ungentled
icicle bold
took her young daughters
sold her strong sons
churched her with Jesus   15
bled her with guns.
Thus she has lain.

Now she is rising
remember her pain
remember the losses   20
her screams loud and vain
remember her riches
her history slain
now she is striding
although she had lain.   25

STUDY QUESTIONS

1. Who is the "she" in line 1? What part of speech is "deserts" in line 3? How can you be sure? How does the structure of lines 4 and 5 help you to read line 3 accurately?

2. Describe the syntax in the poem. If you were punctuating the poem conventionally, where would you put periods? commas? What effects are created by the rapid shifts in the patterns of sentences? Where do the most radical shifts occur?

3. Why are active and passive roles played off against each other? What is the difference between the past and the present in the poem?

Ray A. Young Bear

B orn in Tama, Iowa, in 1950, Ray A. Young Bear is from the Sauk and Fox tribe of Iowa, better known as the Mesquakies, and has been writing poetry since the age of sixteen. He is the author of three collections of poems, *Winter of the Salamander* (1980), *The Bumblebee Is the Bear King* (1985), and *The Invisible Musician* (1990). He has also published a new fictional work entitled *Tamaqua* (1991) and a collection of biographical narratives concerning Midwestern Native American culture, *Black Eagle Child: The Facepaint Narratives* (1992).

IN THE FIRST PLACE OF MY LIFE

in the first place of my life
something which comes before all others
there is the sacred and holylike
recurring memory of an old teethless
bushy white-haired man   5
gesturing with his wrinkled hands
and squinty eyes for me to walk to him
sitting on the edge of his wooden
summer bed

being supported and guided along   10
like a newborn spotted fawn
who rises to the cool and minty wind
i kept looking at his yellow
and cracked fingernails
they moved back and forth against the stove   15
and they shined against the kerosene
                                        darkened
kitchen and bedroom walls

i floated over the floor towards him
and he smiled as he lifted me up to the   20
                              cardboard
ceiling and on there were symbols i later read
as that of emily
her scratched-in name alongside the face
of a lonely softball player   25

remembrance two: it was shortly after he
                              held me
or else it was a day
or a couple of months

or a couple of years later when i saw him next   30
the bodies of three young men leaned against him
as he staggered out towards the night

i never knew what closed him
why i never saw him again
he was on the floor with a blanket   35
over his still and quiet body
above me there was a mouth moving
it was the face of a woman who had opened
the door for the three young men
she pointed to his body   40
this is your grandfather

and then i remember the daylight
with the bald-headed man in overalls
he too mentioned the absence
of my grandfather   45
i understood them both
i picture the appletree and its shade
as he was talking to me i saw a group
of people on the green grass
on the ground were table and linen cloths   50
with bowls and dishes of fruits and meats

the bald-headed man in overalls stood
in the brilliance of the summer daylight
his eyebrows made his face look concerned
or worried   55

later he stood on the same grass
he had been chosen to fill my grandfather's
empty place

the new colored blankets around his waist
and chest glistened with the fresh   60
fibrous wool
the beads reflected the good weather
the earth and its people stood and danced
with the beautifully clothed man
who was my grandfather   65
standing in between time
watching the daylight pass through
his eyes

from then on i only saw him occasionally
he would stand on his tractor   70
waving to each passing car on the road
as he drove home from
the soybean fields
or else he would converse with my two uncles
that the blood which ran through their   75
                            father's veins
and theirs was unlike the rest of the tribe
in that it came from the beginnings
unlike ours

STUDY QUESTIONS

1. What does "the first place of my life" seem to represent? Is it a literal place? a state of mind? a relationship to others? How far, would you estimate, is the SPEAKER removed from the central events in the poem? Why do the memories have such a power for the speaker?

2. What accounts for the dreamlike quality of the poem? Notice how many vivid details the poem presents. How do the various details relate to one another?

3. List all of the things we know about the grandfather. What do we know about the bald-headed man in overalls? the three young men? the woman whose hand opened the door? Emily? the speaker? When in the poem do we first become aware that the "teethless / bushy white-haired man" (lines 4–5) is kin to the speaker?

4. Describe the organization of the poem. How does the poem make the move from two quite specific memories in time to a more general consideration of tribal relationships?

Agha Shahid Ali

Originally from Kashmir (and a graduate of the University of Kashmir), Agha Shahid Ali moved to New Delhi and then to the United States to receive his advanced degrees (M.A., University of Delhi, 1970; M.F.A., University of Arizona, 1985; Ph.D., Penn State, 1984). He has written poetry exclusively in English since the age of ten. A scholar as well as a poet, Ali is the author of *T. S. Eliot as Editor* (1986); his three volumes of poetry are *A Walk Through the Yellow Pages* (1986), *The Half-Inch Himalayas* (1987), and *A Nostalgist's Map of America* (1991). He has taught at Hamilton College and now teaches at the University of Massachusetts, Amherst.

SNOWMEN

My ancestor, a man
of Himalayan snow,
came to Kashmir from Samarkand,
carrying a bag
of whale bones: 5
heirlooms from sea funerals.
His skeleton
carved from glaciers, his breath
arctic,
he froze women in his embrace.   10
His wife thawed into stony water,
her old age a clear
evaporation.

This heirloom,
his skeleton under my skin, passed   15
from son to grandson,
generations of snowmen on my back.
They tap every year on my window,
their voices hushed to ice.

No, they won't let me out of winter,   20
and I've promised myself,
even if I'm the last snowman,
that I'll ride into spring
on their melting shoulders.

STUDY QUESTION

What has the SPEAKER's ancestor bequeathed to him? What is that heirloom said to be made out of? How does the speaker feel about his inheritance? What do you understand the speaker's promise to himself to be? What is its tone?

Virginia Cerenio

A second-generation Filipino-American, Virginia Cerenio grew up in San Francisco and received her B.A. from San Francisco State University. She is a member of the Kearny Street Workshop and has published both poems and fiction. Her most recent work is *Trespassing Innocence*.

[WE WHO CARRY
THE ENDLESS SEASONS]

we who carry the endless seasons
          of tropical rain in our blood
still weep our mother's tears
feel the pain of their birth
                    their growing   5
          as women in america

we wear guilt for their minor sins
                    singing lullabies
                    in foreign tongue
                              ". . . o ilaw sa gabing madilim   10
                              wangis mo'y bituin sa langit . . ."[1]

---

1. Light in the middle of the night / your face like stars in the sky.

their desires
        wanting us
        their daughters
        to marry only   15
                ". . . a boy from the islands . . .
                ang guapo lalake[2] . . . and
                from a good family too. . . ."

like shadows
attached to our feet   20
we cannot walk away

though we are oceans and dreams apart
waves carry the constant clicking of their rosary beads
                  like heartbeats
                  in our every breathing   25

STUDY QUESTIONS

1. Why are different generations said to be "oceans" apart (line 22)? "dreams" apart? Why can't the present generation walk away from the past? Explain how the shadow IMAGE (lines 19–21) works.

2. What different connections between generations does the poem articulate? Explain why the Filipino phrases are inserted in a poem that is primarily in English.

3. Describe the fundamental attitude the poem takes to the past. What is the poem's basic TONE?

Yvonne Sapia

Yvonne Sapia's family came from Puerto Rico to New York, where, in 1946, she was born. She moved to Florida in 1956 and has lived there since, attending the University of Florida and Florida State University. She currently teaches at Lake City Community College. *Valentino's Hair*, from which this poem is taken, won the Samuel French Morse Poetry Prize in 1987 and the Charles H. and N. Mildred Nilon Excellence in Minority Fiction in 1991.

2. A handsome man.

GRANDMOTHER, A CARIBBEAN INDIAN, DESCRIBED BY MY FATHER

Nearly a hundred when she died,
mi viejita[1]
was an open boat,
and I had no map
to show her the safe places.   5
There was much to grieve.
Her shoulders were stooped.
Her hands were never young.
They broke jars
at the watering holes,   10
like bones, like hearts.

When she was a girl,
she was given the island
but no wings.
She wanted wings,   15
though she bruised
like a persimmon.
She was not ruined
before her marriage.
But after the first baby died,   20
she disappeared in the middle
of days to worship
her black saint,
after the second,
to sleep with a hand towel   25
across her eyes.

I had to take care
not to exhume
from the mound of memory
these myths, these lost ones.   30
Born sleek as swans
on her river, my brother,
the man you have met
who has one arm,

1. My little old woman or mother. [Author's note]

and I glided into the sun.   35
Other children poured forth,
and by the time I was sixteen
I lost my place
in her thatched house.

She let me go,   40
and she did not come to the pier
the day the banana boat
pushed away from her shore
towards Nueva York
where I had heard   45
there would be room for me.

STUDY QUESTIONS

1. Who is the SPEAKER of the poem? Who is the grandchild referred to in the title in the first person ("my")? Who is addressed as "you" in line 33?

2. What does the speaker mean when he says that his mother was "an open boat" (line 3)?

3. What were some of the things she had to grieve over? Why did she begin to sleep with "a hand towel / across her eyes" (lines 25–26)?

4. Why was there no room at home for the speaker when he was sixteen?

Alberto Alvaro Ríos

Alberto Alvaro Ríos is the author of short stories, poems, and a novel, whose books include *The Lime Orchard Woman*, *The Warrington Poems*, *Five Indiscretions*, *The Iguana Killer*, *Whispering to the Wind*, and, most recently, *Teodoro Luna's Kisses*, published in 1991. Ríos teaches at Arizona State University, not too far from Nogales, Arizona, where, in 1952, he was born. His father was from southern Mexico, his mother from England, and his interest in language came to him early. He has degrees in English, psychology, and creative writing and for a time attended law school.

MI ABUELO

Where my grandfather is is in the ground
where you can hear the future like an

Indian with his ear at the tracks. A
pipe leads down to him so that sometimes
he whispers what will happen to a man
in town or how he will meet the best-   5
dressed woman tomorrow and how the best
man at her wedding will chew the ground
next to her. Mi abuelo is the man
who talks through all the mouths in my house. An   10
echo of me hitting the pipe sometimes
to stop him from saying "my hair is a
sieve" is the only other sound. It is a
phrase that among all others is the best,
he says, and "my hair is a sieve" is sometimes   15
repeated for hours out of the ground
when I let him, but mostly I don't. "An
abuelo should be much more than a man
like you!" He stops then, and speaks: "I am a man
who has served ants with the attitude of a   20
waiter, who has made each smile as only an
ant who is fat can, and they liked me best,
but there is nothing left." Yet, I know he ground
green coffee beans as a child, and sometimes
he will talk about his wife, and sometimes   25
about when he was deaf and a man
cured him by mail and he heard ground
hogs talking, or about how he walked with a
cane he chewed on when he got hungry. At best,
mi abuelo is a liar. I see an   30
old picture of him at nani's with an
off-white yellow center mustache and sometimes
that's all I know for sure. He talks best
about these hills, slowest waves, and where this man
is going, and I'm convinced his hair is a   35
sieve, that his fever is cool now in the ground.
Mi abuelo is an ordinary man.
I look down the pipe, sometimes, and see a
ripple-topped stream in its best suit, in the ground.

STUDY QUESTIONS

1. How long does it take the reader who does not know Spanish to know what the title means?

2. Where is the SPEAKER's grandfather? What do you understand by the grandfather's speaking through a pipe in the ground? by his talking "through all the mouths in my house" (line 10)?

3. The speaker says in the middle of the poem, "An / abuelo should be much more than a man / like you" (lines 17–19). What does that mean? How does the speaker feel at the end of the poem?

Dennis Scott

Dennis Scott, from Jamaica, is best known as a playwright and play director, but he is also a skilled poet with a wonderful ear for the rhythms of speech. In 1973 he won the International Poetry Forum Award and in 1975 the Commonwealth Poetry Award. He has taught at both the Yale School of Drama in the United States and the Jamaica School of Drama. His books include *Dreadwalk: Poems 1970–78* (1982) and *Strategies* (1989).

GRAMPA

Look him. As quiet as a July riverbed, asleep, an trim' down like a tree.
Jesus! I never know the Lord could
squeeze so dry. When I was four
foot small I used to say   5
Grampa, how come you t'in so?
an him tell me, is so I stay
me chile, is so I stay
laughing, an fine
emptying on me—   10

laughing? It running from him
like a flood, that old molasses
man. Lord, how I never see?
I never know a man could sweet so, cool
as rain, same way him laugh,   15

I cry now. Wash him. Lay him out.

I know the earth going burn
all him limb dem
as smooth as bone,

clean as a tree under the river   20
skin, an gather us
beside that distant Shore
bright as a river stone.

STUDY QUESTIONS

1. Describe, as fully as you can, the SPEAKER in the poem. How much of the characterization is provided by his patterns of speech?

2. What, exactly, is the situation in the poem? Where does it become clear what has happened?

3. Describe the effect of using early memories as a way of characterizing Grampa. Why is there so much emphasis on his laughter?

4. Describe the TONE of the poem. How do you interpret the ending?

Max Apple

Max Apple grew up in a kosher Jewish household in Grand Rapids, Michigan. He often writes about his childhood memories, including the fact that Yiddish was spoken in his home, but he says about growing up Jewish in Grand Rapids: "It's a Calvinist town. There were no movies, no dances. So being Jewish was just a different kind of craziness." Apple is regarded as an affectionate critic of American life and often writes, as in the play that follows, about conflicts between different groups in American society. His first collection of stories, *The Oranging of America and Other Stories* (1976), had a major impact, and he is probably still best known as a short-story writer, though he has also written a well-received novel, *Zip: A Novel of the Left and the Right* (1978).

TROTSKY'S[1] BAR MITZVAH

CHARACTERS

LARRY, a thirteen-year-old boy. He is dressed in a blue suit, wears a prayer shawl, and carries a prayer book. It is his Bar Mitzvah day.

---

1. Russian Communist revolutionary leader of Jewish descent. One of the principal leaders in the establishment of the Soviet Union. He lived from 1879 to 1940.

GRANDPA, a very old man dressed in baker's whites

ASSISTANT BAKER, a middle-aged black man also dressed in a baker's outfit.
    He wears Walkman earphones as he works.

VOICE OF LAVERNE, the cashier in the store section of the bakery

VOICE OF LARRY'S FATHER

SETTING

*The rear of a bakery—there is an oven, several long tables, and large racks for bread
and rolls.*

LARRY: Well, it's the big day, finally.

GRANDPA: To me it's like every other day. They earn their bread by the sweat
of my brow.

LARRY: C'mon, Grandpa, you don't have to work today, just this once, can't
you stop being a communist and come to my Bar Mitzvah?

GRANDPA: [*Gives* LARRY *a very angry look.*] We've been over this a hundred
times. When you decided to go for superstition and capitalism, you got
my answer.

LARRY: But it's just for a couple of hours, and just today. What harm can it
do?

GRANDPA: [*Gives* LARRY *angry stare and continues to knead dough.*] Everything I
taught you, you've forgotten already. Instead of me, you listened to your
father. I could have taken you to Cuba—with him you'll end up in Miami
Beach.

LARRY: But Grandpa, Stalin was an anti-Semite. In Russia they'd torture
you. Daddy says they're not even communists there. He says you're the
last communist in the world.

GRANDPA: I'm not talking Russia, I'm talking revolution. I'm talking the
worldwide brotherhood of workers.

ASSISTANT BAKER: [*Near the oven and wearing headphones.*] Hold it down, comrade, you're louder than punk—

GRANDPA: I'm talking right and wrong and distribution of goods and ownership of production. I'm not talking Russia. I'm talking about the world to
come, the one you should be leading. And instead you stand here with a
prayer book and you go out to beg bourgeoisie presents. [*Spits—wipes his
mouth with the back of his hand—goes back to the dough-kneading.*]
    [*From the front of the shop we hear the cash register ringing up sales.*]

LARRY: All right, forget the Bar Mitzvah, pretend it's a birthday party. I'm
your only grandson. I want you to come to my party.

GRANDPA: I don't go to parties.

LARRY: But I want to celebrate this.

GRANDPA: I'll celebrate when the workers are victorious.

LARRY: Grandpa [*becoming angry now*], I don't care about workers or revolutions or even about religions. I just want you to be there with me when all
this stuff about being a man happens.

GRANDPA: You'll become a man when you throw off the yoke of capitalism.

LARRY: I don't even know what that means.

GRANDPA: Of course you don't, because you live in the midst of stockbrokers and insurance salesmen. You go to the synagogue of good manners. Your God says "Have a nice day" and turns away from the Third World to watch a ball game on color TV. For this kind of celebration you've got your parents; you don't need me.

LARRY: You came to my grammar-school graduation.

GRANDPA: Because education is a weapon.

LARRY: You always come to my Little League games.

GRANDPA: Because the revolution needs strong bodies.

ASSISTANT BAKER: So do I need some strong bodies. C'mere and give this poor *shvartzer*[2] a hand.

> [GRANDPA *and* LARRY *go over to help him lift a hundred-pound sack and pour some flour into a huge bowl.*]

ASSISTANT BAKER: You can't tell this old man nothin'. I been tryin' . . . it's no use. But if you want, I'll come as a representative oppressed black man so long as I won't have to do no Yid[3] talk. All I can say is "no-good *shvartzer*" and "a *shvartz jahr*"[4] and "*shvartzer chazar.*"[5] They only use black words around me.

GRANDPA: All words are black words.

LARRY: My father said I'd be wasting my time.

GRANDPA: Your father is the one who wastes time: a stockbroker—a manipulator of capital, a bloodsucker.

LARRY: He works hard, Grandpa.

GRANDPA: Sure he does—it's not easy to rob and pillage.

LARRY: He says you're a crazy and bitter man.

GRANDPA: And I say he should choke on his Gucci loafers.

LARRY: I knew you'd never come to the party at the house, but I thought you'd come to the synagogue.

GRANDPA: Why? Do I like God's house any more than your father's? They're both in the same business.

LARRY: [*Trying another approach.*] Grandpa, I wrote a socialist speech, only the rabbi said I had to put it in religious words.

GRANDPA: [*Sarcastically.*] Oh, your rabbi says. Every time the cat farts they make a new rabbinic law.

LARRY: I said the time was coming when there would be liberty and justice for all.

VOICE OF LAVERNE: [*Offstage.*] Any more white bread? I could use some sliced whites. And a few dozen biscuits, too, they're all gone.

---

2. Black man.
3. Yiddish.
4. Black year.
5. Black pig.

ASSISTANT BAKER [*Singing.*] No more biscuits! You hear dat? The revolution done ate up the biscuits. Mammy's little baby loves de revolution, but they's eatin' up his biscuits.

GRANDPA: They suck the blood and minerals out of Africa and this man laughs. In Chicago and Oakland they eat black babies, and this wise man laughs.

LARRY: They really eat children?

GRANDPA: They suck on the knucklebones of the poor and they make soup out of our feet.

LARRY: [*Laughing nervously.*] I don't believe that. Mom says you exaggerate. She says you told her she'd give birth to monsters if she married Dad. Do you think Sheryl and I are monsters?

GRANDPA: About your sister I'll be silent. You, my sweetheart, are no monster.

LARRY: Then why can't you come to my Bar Mitzvah?

GRANDPA: Because your religion is a monster and your party will be monstrous and your father is a beast. Now leave me alone. I've got to work.

[ASSISTANT BAKER *calls* LARRY *over to him*]

ASSISTANT BAKER: Don't let him get away with that shit, Larry. He loves to have folks beggin' at him to go to stuff. If there was no communists, he'd do that anyways. You just got one mean old grandpa.

LARRY: But you know he's not mean to me. Ever since I can remember he brings me donuts and cookies, he takes me to the movies. I know he hates Dad, but still he walks through our house to get me. He's never been mean to me.

ASSISTANT BAKER: He's all talk, that old man. If it ain't commie talk, he's hatin' sports or music. When I started bringin' my stereo to work, you shoulda seen him go at rock 'n' roll. He carried on so much that I finally had to lay it on him, that when it comes to the real thing, no white, not even commie Yids, is gonna tell us *shvartzers* how to blow the lid. But until then, I'm gonna play my music, and when the trumpets of justice sound, they're gonna be right on key. That shut him up.

VOICE OF LAVERNE: Bring up those rolls, okay, fellas? They're waitin' on the rolls.

LARRY: [*Volunteering.*] I'll carry them out. [*He exits with a large basket of rolls.*]

ASSISTANT BAKER: [*To* GRANDPA.]

Why don't you just go with the kid? What kind of a fuck-face are you anyway? Look how lucky you are to have a kid like him. He could be sucking up to the rich ones. Instead, he's hanging around here—always comin' back here to you. Your daughter don't care about you, neither do the communists; nobody does but this kid. That boy, he's the only revolution you ever gonna see.

[GRANDPA *seems to think about this.*]

[LARRY *returns with the empty steel bin.*]

LARRY: They need more rolls, also gingerbread cookies. LaVerne says they're as busy as Christmas Eve up front.

[ASSISTANT BAKER *loads up more baked goods.*]

LARRY: I'm gonna talk about Noah and the flood, Grandpa. You wanna hear?

[GRANDPA *says nothing.*]

ASSISTANT BAKER: Lay it on me brother, my ancestors was there—Old Black Joe and Aunt Jemima and Noah himself, black as anything.

LARRY: Noah was the only good man during bad times. In those days nobody knew how to do the right thing so God made a flood to destroy the whole world. But he didn't destroy Noah and Noah's family because they were good. And he didn't destroy all the animals because they were just animals and didn't understand about being good.

GRANDPA: You believe there was a flood?

LARRY: [*Shrugs.*] I guess.

GRANDPA: You believe in the Ten Commandments, too?

LARRY: Yes.

ASSISTANT BAKER: [*Boogies a little.*] I looked over Jordan and what'd I see . . . ? All them Bar Mitzvahs comin' after me.

[ASSISTANT BAKER *does a tap-dance number on one of the baking tables. He takes* LARRY's *tallis[6] and uses it as a veil in a parody of a female veil dance.*]

GRANDPA: [*Aside.*] For him we need a revolution.

LARRY: So God sent the flood to destroy the world, since if everyone in it was bad, the world was already destroyed. But that left all those innocent animals who hadn't done anything bad at all.

ASSISTANT BAKER: And all of them animals they lined up to get on the ark and Noah said, "Not you, Mr. Pig, Ah'm fixin' to hate you another ten thousand years."

VOICE OF LAVERNE: Where in the hell are the rye breads?

LARRY: [*Continuing despite the interruptions.*] And then God promised that He'd never destroy the world again no matter how bad people got. So we don't have to worry anymore like they did in the old days.

GRANDPA: This is what you're going to say?

LARRY: Yes.

GRANDPA: That since the world won't be destroyed, we don't have to worry?

LARRY: We don't have to worry about that, we can worry about other things.

GRANDPA: [*Slaps his head in disbelief.*] About bombs and war and nuclear destruction, about the Holocaust and Cambodia and Vietnam, about Hiroshima and Nagasaki—about all this we don't have to worry?

VOICE OF LAVERNE: I wish to hell there were six dozen rye breads out here. Sliced.

LARRY: [*Getting flustered.*] All I know is I want you to come to my Bar Mitzvah, and I don't care about the whole world.

GRANDPA: And I want you to care about the whole world, at least about all the workers.

LARRY: I'm only thirteen. I can't care about everybody yet.

6. Prayer shawl.

ASSISTANT BAKER: You got a girlfriend?

LARRY: [*Shakes his head.*] No.

ASSISTANT BAKER: He don't even care about girls, you expect him to care about workers?

LARRY: I'm waiting, Grandpa, we've got to go now. I have to be there by nine-thirty or they'll just go ahead without me, and this part doesn't come up again for a whole year.

VOICE OF LAVERNE: Just forget it, boys, I told the customers to eat cake.

[ASSISTANT BAKER *rushes out with the loaves.*]

LARRY: Grandpa, I won't ever bug you like this again. . . . I promise—not for confirmation, graduation, not even for a wedding.

GRANDPA: [*Softening.*] Larry, my *boychik*,[7] you know I love you. [GRANDPA *hugs boy.*]

LARRY: [*Crying.*] Of course I know that.

GRANDPA: Then love me, too, and don't ask me to come there among everyone and everything I hate. Don't ask me to lie about the world even for a few hours. To me that would be the Flood—all those stockbrokers and lawyers and the rabbi and everything I turned my back on fifty years ago. Even for you I can't pretend.

LARRY: Do you hate my father that much?

GRANDPA: I don't hate that harmless *shmuck*.[8] I hate the system.

LARRY: Is my Bar Mitzvah part of the system?

GRANDPA: Yes.

VOICE OF FATHER: [*Out front.*] Larry, we can't wait any longer—please hurry.

LARRY: I'm coming, Daddy.

LARRY: [*To* GRANDPA.] You mean the words are wrong, or just going and doing it there with everyone?

GRANDPA: Not the words, in the words there is nobility.

ASSISTANT BAKER: Damn right—they got all them words for "*shvartzer*." Who knows how many words they must have for God?

LARRY: Then I'm going to do it here.

[LARRY *begins to chant his Bar Mitzvah portion in Hebrew. After a few sentences there is clapping from the front.*]

VOICE OF LAVERNE: Wonderful, sweetheart, but your daddy's out here going nuts, he says it's now or never. Your choice if you want to stay with Grandpa or have your Bar Mitzvah.

[LARRY *hugs* GRANDPA *and leaves, crying.*]

[GRANDPA *goes back to making dough.*]

GRANDPA: [*To* ASSISTANT BAKER.] C'mon, then. The revolution needs gingerbread men. It's already got enough jazz.

ASSISTANT BAKER: Screw the revolution, old man. I like the boy's singing. He

---

7. Affectionate term for boy.

8. Jerk.

sung a lotta words and I didn't hear no *"shvartzers."* I didn't know you folks could sing like that.

[LARRY *comes running back in. He now has no prayer shawl on, and his suit jacket is also removed. He has been crying.*]

LARRY: [*Hugs* GRANDPA, *getting flour on his face.*] I'm not gonna have a Bar Mitzvah. I'd rather have a revolution.

VOICE OF FATHER: [*Angry, offstage.*] I hope you're satisfied, old man—I hope you've got what you want now. [*Door slams.*]

[GRANDPA *hugs* LARRY, *and slowly takes off his apron.*]

GRANDPA: The revolution will take a while, maybe until you're in college. C'mon, George. [*He nods to* ASSISTANT BAKER] We're gonna take my Trotsky to his Bar Mitzvah.

ASSISTANT BAKER: I ain't dressed for no party.

GRANDPA: Yes you are—for this boy it's going to be a workers' Bar Mitzvah.

[LARRY *lights up.*]

ASSISTANT BAKER: Lemme hear that song again.

[*The three hustle offstage, with* LARRY *once more chanting his Hebrew song.*]

STUDY QUESTIONS

1. How quickly is the conflict set up? How soon do you get a sense of Grandpa? of Larry's father? of Larry?

2. What exactly is the situation as the play opens? What does the SETTING contribute to the effect of the drama?

3. Describe, as precisely as you can, the conflict Larry feels? To what and to whom does he feel loyal? How are the loyalties to people and to ideologies sorted out? Which kind of loyalty seems most important to Larry? to the play as a whole?

4. What role does the Assistant Baker play in the conflict? What does his blackness have to do with the play's THEMES?

5. What is the "turning point" in the play? How is the play's central conflict resolved? Describe the play's attitude toward religious tradition, toward communism, toward politics, toward ideology more generally.

Margarita M. Engle

Margarita M. Engle is the daughter of a Cuban mother and an American father. She was born and raised in California, but has traveled extensively in Cuba

and other parts of Latin America. Her opinion columns have been nationally syndi-
cated by Hispanic Link News Service since 1982, and she has published nonfiction
articles in a wide variety of magazines. Trained as an agronomist and botanist, Engle
has branched out into many other fields through her writing. Her haiku have been
included in anthologies in the United States and Japan, and her short fiction has been
published in literary magazines and anthologies.

Her first novel, *Singing to Cuba*, is being published in the fall of 1993.

DIGGING FOR ROOTS

A few years ago my son came home from kindergarten with an assignment I
couldn't do—the construction of a simple form of family tree. I was dismayed to realize that not only did I know nothing at all about my great
grandparents and their predecessors, I wasn't even sure of the surnames of
one of the most important people in my life, my maternal grandmother. My
husband, on the other hand, who is of European descent, was able to immediately name an ancestor who settled in the U.S. nearly 400 years ago.

After asking around, I learned that few Americans can name their great
grandparents. Perhaps this lack of continuity develops because few of us ever
had the chance to actually meet our great grandparents. Perhaps it happens
because we live in such a busy, goal-oriented society, where we tend to think
more of the future than of our connections to the past.

By the time we have our own children, who may eventually become
curious about their ancestors, older family members may no longer be around
to answer the questions we never got around to asking.

Unless you are related to someone very famous, researching the family
history is something you have to do yourself. Churches and governments
record significant personal events which can be of great help, but they don't
compile the records of these events into family histories.

Your family tree is a puzzle which begins with only one piece, the information you have about yourself and your parents. To complete the gaps,
you have to work backwards, asking your parents, and grandparents to fill
in details.

Four key pieces of information can help you get started. You need names,
dates, places, and relationships. In particular, you need the dates, or at least
the years, of events likely to have been recorded by church or civil registries:
births, baptisms, marriages, changes in citizenship, and deaths. Try to obtain
both surnames of every individual, especially if you will eventually be consulting documents written in Spanish-speaking countries where each child
retains both the paternal and maternal surnames. Married women simply add
their husband's surnames after marriage, creating a mini-family tree which
instantly offers the surnames of father, mother, and husband. For instance,

my maternal grandmother's surnames are Uría (from her father) and Peña (from her mother). When she married, she became Josefa Uría y Peña de Ferrer.

Search within your home first. Clues to your lineage can be found in family bibles; newspaper clippings; birth, military, and death certificates; deeds; wills; marriage licenses; diaries; baby books; letters; scrapbooks; and the notes scribbled on backs of photographs. If you are lucky enough to possess the originals or copies of old Spanish documents, genealogical libraries offer guides to the deciphering of the ornate official handwriting. 7

Visit, call, or write to anyone in your family who may already have the information you're looking for. If you have distant relatives you've never visited or called, consider looking them up. One common method of initiating a genealogical study is to place an advertisement in the local genealogical bulletins of towns, states or countries where your ancestors originated. Genealogical magazines include special ancestor "query" sections. *The Genealogical Helper*, a widely circulated magazine available in many public libraries, specializes in getting people together if they are working on the same families. 8

For military, immigration, and related federal records, you can obtain data from the National Archives in Washington, D.C. Regional archive branches located in many metropolitan areas also contain U.S. census records for every decade from 1790 to 1910. Even the inscriptions found in cemeteries can provide information on dates and relationships. 9

Both family histories and surname studies become much more than routine charts documenting chronologies and kinship. They form windows you can look through to imagine the past. For me, the longing for such windows has been strong ever since the Cuban Revolution abruptly separated the Cuban and American branches of my extended family. 10

I was born in California in 1951, of Cuban and American parents. I grew up familiar with my paternal grandparents, aunts, and cousins, the descendants of refugees who immigrated to America from the Ukraine in 1917. From my mother's side of the family, I had only fond memories of two summer-long childhood visits to Cuba. Eventually my grandmother and other close relatives came to the U.S. from Cuba as refugees on the "freedom flights" of the late '60s. I now have a cassette recording of my grandmother's oral version of her family history. I've had the chance to sit and reminisce with her over photo albums, and to hear stories about her childhood and her parents. 11

Family history is much more than a series of names and dates. Those windows of understanding bring us as close as we'll ever come to experiencing the past, and to knowing our ancestors. 12

Because it is currently impossible to obtain records from Cuba, my personal puzzle has been limited to learning the origins of surnames and researching that portion of my ancestry which I can trace through microfilm copies of records from Spain available in the genealogy section of a local public library. 13

Although most of my mother's family settled in Cuba centuries ago, one of my great grandfathers immigrated to Cuba from Barcelona during the early 1800s. His Catalán surname, Serra, is so local in origin that the difficulty of searching is immediately narrowed down to a specific province.

Even a partial family tree can become very meaningful and special. If you pass it on to your descendants, they may gaze into it someday, and marvel at the window you've built for them, with its view of your life and the lives of those who preceded you. 14

State, regional, and local institutions, libraries and historical societies are also excellent sources of information. In genealogical libraries you can even search microfilm records from Mexico and many other Latin American countries, as well as Spain. Once you have the names, dates, places, and relationships for a certain generation, you can use these keys to open doors to the preceding generations. 15

There are, of course, some serious limitations. If you or your ancestors originated from a town where records were destroyed by war or natural disasters, or if they came as refugees from regions where political upheaval prevents research, pieces of the family puzzle may be missing. In this case, you have to be content with a short version of the family tree, supplemented by whatever information can be gleaned from verbal histories and surname origins. 16

Did you ever wonder how your family ended up with a particular surname? Have you ever met someone with the same surname and wondered whether you might be distant relatives? Have you wondered what your surname means, and where it originated, or when? 17

Modern Spain consists of 17 regions. In many, unique languages are spoken. Until the end of the fifteenth century, when most of Spain was united under the reign of Fernando and Isabel, the regions were not only distinct, but politically independent as well. Few cultures are as diverse as that of Spain. Thousands of years ago, Iberians built walled cities and were known as superb horsemen and skilled artisans. The Greek historian Herodotus described indigenous Iberians as proficient in mining and processing of silver and gold. Beginning in the ninth century B.C., waves of Celtic invaders reached the Iberian Peninsula from the regions which now comprise France, Germany, the Scottish Highlands, Wales, and Cornwall. Colonists followed from Greece and Phoenicia. 18

The Roman Empire ruled Spain for four centuries, followed by invasions of the Visigoths and Vandals from northern Europe, and finally the Moors from North Africa, who dominated Iberia for nearly eight centuries. 19

As a result, many Spanish surnames can be traced directly to a particular historical period, or to a regional dialect. For instance, I have been able to trace one of my maternal grandmother's surnames to the Basque region of northern Spain, even though her family has probably been in Cuba for centuries. While consulting church registries from Spain, I noticed that virtually all the births, marriages, and deaths recorded for anyone with the surname 20

Uría were registered in Vizcaya. Then I began looking for Uría in dictionaries of surnames at a local public library. I learned that Uría is a Spanish form of a Basque topographic name for someone who lived in a village rather than the open countryside (from the Basque word *uri*, meaning settlement). I even learned that *uri* is a western dialect variation of *iri*, thereby narrowing the region of origin of the surname even further.

21   Surnames generally originated during or prior to the Middle Ages. Many, like Uría, are topographical in meaning. Obvious examples are Cuevas, Del Valle, Del Río, and Montes. My great grandfather's surname of Serra is a Catalán name for someone who lived on or near a ridge or chain of hills.

22   Other surnames may have originated from the place of habitation of an ancestor. For instance, my maternal grandmother's father had two surnames, Uría and Trujillo. Trujillo is a habitation name from places in the provinces of Cáceres and Sevilla. It is a surname thought to be of pre-Roman, indigenous Iberian origin, and was first recorded in Latin as Turgalium.

23   Another type of surname is the occupational origin. The first surname of one of my great great grandfathers was Pastor, a name indicating that at some time in the past, someone in the family was a shepherd.

24   The first surname of one of my great grandmothers was Castillo. This could have originated as a topographic name for someone living near a castle, or it could have indicated a resident, or more commonly, a servant, living and working in a castle.

25   Medieval nicknames eventually evolved into surnames as well. The second surname of one of my great grandmothers was Peregrín, meaning pilgrim, originally a nickname for someone who had been on a pilgrimage to some seat of devotion, usually as penance for a sin.

26   Not all modern Spanish surnames are Spanish in origin. My mother's first maiden surname, Ferrer, is from the French word *ferrieres*, meaning iron workings; it was the name of a Norman family which held the Earldom of Derby from 1138 to 1266. The surname spread across Europe along with the family, eventually reaching Cuba by way of Spain.

27   Although the salvaged images of my antecedents are scattered and fragmented, when pieced together they may someday provide my children with a treasured window into the Cuban portion of their ancestry.

STUDY QUESTIONS

1. What specific advice does Margarita Engle give for doing research on your ancestry? What reasons does she cite for wanting to do such research?

2. What kind of information does Engle say you must have in order to get started on the research?

3. What aspects of Engle's own research seem to you most interesting? Which problems that she encountered have the most relevance to issues you might encounter in researching your own family?

Judith Ortiz Cofer

J udith Ortiz Cofer was born in Puerto Rico in 1952 but in her early years was shuttled back and forth between her mother's and her father's families in Puerto Rico and New Jersey. Her childhood was bilingual and bicultural. "I learned to listen," she has written about herself, "to the English from the television with one ear while I heard my mother and father speaking in Spanish with the other. I thought I was an ordinary American kid—like the children in the shows I watched—and that everyone's parents spoke a secret second language at home." She is the author of two books of poetry, *Terms of Survival* (1987) and *Reaching for the Mainland* (1987), a novel, *The Line of the Sun* (1989), and of *Silent Dancing: A Partial Remembrance of a Puerto Rican Childhood* (1990), from which the following selection is taken. She teaches at the University of Georgia. Her latest work, *The Latin Deli* (1993) is a collection of poetry and essays.

MORE ROOM

My grandmother's house is like a chambered nautilus; it has many rooms, yet it is not a mansion. Its proportions are small and its design simple. It is a house that has grown organically, according to the needs of its inhabitants. To all of us in the family it is known as *la casa de Mamá*. It is the place of our origin; the stage for our memories and dreams of Island[1] life.

I remember how in my childhood it sat on stilts; this was before it had a downstairs—it rested on its perch like a great blue bird—not a flying sort of bird, more like a nesting hen, but with spread wings. Grandfather had built it soon after their marriage. He was a painter and housebuilder by trade—a poet and meditative man by nature. As each of their eight children were born, new rooms were added. After a few years, the paint didn't exactly match, nor the materials, so that there was a chronology to it, like the rings of a tree, and Mamá could tell you the history of each room in her *casa*, and thus the genealogy of the family along with it.

Her own room is the heart of the house. Though I have seen it recently— and both woman and room have diminished in size, changed by the new perspective of my eyes, now capable of looking over countertops and tall

1. Puerto Rico.

beds—it is not this picture I carry in my memory of Mamá's *casa*. Instead, I see her room as a queen's chamber where a small woman loomed large, a throneroom with a massive four-poster bed in its center, which stood taller than a child's head. It was on this bed, where her own children had been born, that the smallest grandchildren were allowed to take naps in the afternoons; here too was where Mamá secluded herself to dispense private advice to her daughters, sitting on the edge of the bed, looking down at whoever sat on the rocker where generations of babies had been sung to sleep. To me she looked like a wise empress right out of the fairy tales I was addicted to reading.

Though the room was dominated by the mahogany four-poster, it also contained all of Mamá's symbols of power. On her dresser there were not cosmetics but jars filled with herbs: *yerba*[2] we were all subjected to during childhood crises. She had a steaming cup for anyone who could not, or would not, get up to face life on any given day. If the acrid aftertaste of her cures for malingering did not get you out of bed, then it was time to call *el doctor*. 4

And there was the monstrous chifforobe she kept locked with a little golden key she did not hide. This was a test of her dominion over us; though my cousins and I wanted a look inside that massive wardrobe more than anything, we never reached for that little key lying on top of her Bible on the dresser. This was also where she placed her earrings and rosary when she took them off at night. God's word was her security system. This chifforobe was the place where I imagined she kept jewels, satin slippers, and elegant silk, sequined gowns of heartbreaking fineness. I lusted after those imaginary costumes. I had heard that Mamá had been a great beauty in her youth, and the belle of many balls. My cousins had ideas as to what she kept in that wooden vault: its secret could be money (Mamá did not hand cash to strangers, banks were out of the question, so there were stories that her mattress was stuffed with dollar bills, and that she buried coins in jars in her garden under rosebushes, or kept them in her inviolate chifforobe); there might be that legendary gun salvaged from the Spanish-American conflict over the Island. We went wild over suspected treasures that we made up simply because children have to fill locked trunks with something wonderful. 5

On the wall above the bed hung a heavy silver crucifix. Christ's agonized head hung directly over Mamá's pillow. I avoided looking at this weapon suspended over where her head would have lain; and on the rare occasions when I was allowed to sleep on that bed, I scooted down to the safe middle of the mattress, where her body's impression took me in like mother's lap. Having taken care of the obligatory religious decoration with the crucifix, Mamá covered the other walls with objects sent to her over the years by her children in the States. *Los Nueva Yores*[3] was represented by, among other things, a postcard of Niagara Falls from her son Hernán, postmarked, Buf- 6

2. Herbs.
3. New York.

falo, N.Y. In a conspicuous gold frame hung a large color photograph of her daughter Nena, her husband and their five children at the entrance to Disneyland in California. From us she had gotten a black lace fan. Father had brought it to her from a tour of duty with the Navy in Europe. (On Sundays she would remove it from its hook on the wall to fan herself at Sunday mass.) Each year more items were added as the family grew and dispersed, and every object in the room had a story attached to it, a *cuento*,[4] which Mamá would bestow on anyone who received the privilege of a day alone with her. It was almost worth pretending to be sick, though the bitter herb purgatives of the body were a big price to pay for the spirit revivals of her storytelling.

Except for the times when a sick grandchild warranted the privilege, or when a heartbroken daughter came home in need of more than herbal teas, Mamá slept alone on her large bed.   7

In the family there is a story about how this came to be.   8

When one of the daughters, my mother or one of her sisters, tells the   9
cuento of how Mamá came to own her nights, it is usually preceded by the qualification that Papá's exile from his wife's room was not a result of animosity between the couple. But the act had been Mamá's famous bloodless coup for her personal freedom. Papá was the benevolent dictator of her body and her life who had had to be banished from her bed so that Mamá could better serve her family. Before the telling, we had to agree that the old man— whom we all recognize in the family as an *alma de Dios*,[5] a saintly, soft-spoken presence whose main pleasures in life, such as writing poetry and reading the Spanish large-type editions of *Reader's Digest*, always took place outside the vortex of Mamá's crowded realm, was not to blame. It was not his fault, after all, that every year or so he planted a baby-seed in Mamá's fertile body, keeping her from leading the active life she needed and desired. He loved her and the babies. He would compose odes and lyrics to celebrate births and anniversaries, and hired musicians to accompany him in singing them to his family and friends at extravagant pig-roasts he threw yearly. Mamá and the oldest girls worked for days preparing the food. Papá sat for hours in his painter's shed, also his study and library, composing the songs. At these celebrations he was also known to give long speeches in praise of God, his fecund wife, and his beloved Island. As a middle child, my mother remembers these occasions as a time when the women sat in the kitchen and lamented their burdens while the men feasted out in the patio, their rum-thickened voices rising in song and praise of each other, *compañeros*[6] all.

It was after the birth of her eighth child, after she had lost three at birth   10
or infancy, that Mamá made her decision. They say that Mamá had had a special way of letting her husband know that they were expecting, one that

4. Story.
5. Soul of God.
6. Companions.

had begun when, at the beginning of their marriage, he had built her a house too confining for her taste. So, when she discovered her first pregnancy, she supposedly drew plans for another room, which he dutifully executed. Every time a child was due, she would demand, *More space, more space.* Papá acceded to her wishes, child after child, since he had learned early that Mamá's renowned temper was a thing that grew like a monster along with a new belly. In this way Mamá got the house that she wanted, but with each child she lost in health and energy. She had knowledge of her body and perceived that if she had any more children, her dreams and her plans would have to be permanently forgotten, because she would be a chronically ill woman, like Flora with her twelve children, asthma, no teeth; in bed more than on her feet.

And so after my youngest uncle was born, she asked Papá to build a large room at the back of the house. He did so in joyful anticipation. Mamá had asked him for special things this time: shelves on the walls, a private entrance. He thought that she meant this room to be a nursery where several children could sleep. He thought it was a wonderful idea. He painted it his favorite color—sky blue—and made large windows looking out over a green hill and the church spires beyond. But nothing happened. Mamá's belly did not grow, yet she seemed in a frenzy of activity over the house. Finally, an anxious Papá approached his wife to tell her that the new room was finished and ready to be occupied. And Mamá, they say, replied: "Good, it's for *you.*"

And so it was that Mamá discovered the only means of birth control available to a Catholic woman of her time: sacrifice. She gave up the comfort of Papá's sexual love for something she deemed greater: the right to own and control her body, so that she might live to meet her grandchildren—me among them—so that she could give more of herself to the ones already there, so that she could be more than a channel for other lives, so that even now that time has robbed her of the elasticity of her body and of her amazing reservoir of energy, she still emanates the kind of joy that can only be achieved by living according to the dictates of one's own heart.

STUDY QUESTIONS

1. Describe how Mamá's house grew. What brought about each of the additions? How does the climax of the story depend on our understanding (and Papá's) of this rationale of construction?

2. What are the most important strategies of CHARACTERIZATION in presenting Mamá? Papá? the narrator herself?

3. How important is humor to the total effect of this narrative? to our understanding of each of the characters? to our understanding of the relationship between Mamá and Papá?

4. Explain the simile in the first line of the narrative. In what way does it make the house seem more vivid?

Gail Y. Miyasaki

G ail Miyasaki, a third-generation Japanese-American born in Hawaii, has taught ethnic studies; she has also worked as a journalist for bilingual newspapers and as an editor for Hawaii Public Television. Her books include *Asian Women* (1971), *A Legacy of Diversity* (1975), and *Montage: An Ethnic History of Women in Hawaii* (1977).

OBĀCHAN[1]

Her hands are now rough and gnarled from working in the canefields. But they are still quick and lively as she sews the "futon" cover. And she would sit like that for hours Japanese-style with legs under her, on the floor steadily sewing.

She came to Hawaii as a "picture bride." In one of her rare self-reflecting moments, she told me in her broken English-Japanese that her mother had told her that the streets of Honolulu in Hawaii were paved with gold coins, and so encouraged her to go to Hawaii to marry a strange man she had never seen. Shaking her head slowly in amazement, she smiled as she recalled her shocked reaction on seeing "Ojitchan's" (grandfather's) ill-kept room with only lauhula mats as bedding. She grew silent after that, and her eyes had a faraway look.

She took her place, along with the other picture brides from Japan, beside her husband on the plantation's canefields along the Hamakua coast on the island of Hawaii. The Hawaiian sun had tanned her deep brown. But the sun had been cruel too. It helped age her. Deep wrinkles lined her face and made her skin look tough, dry, and leathery. Her bright eyes peered out from narrow slits, as if she were constantly squinting into the sun. Her brown arms, though, were strong and firm, like those of a much younger woman, and so different from the soft, white, and plump-dangling arms of so many old teachers I had had. And those arms of hers were always moving—scrubbing clothes on a wooden washboard with neat even strokes, cutting vegeta-

1. Grandmother.

bles with the big knife I was never supposed to touch, or pulling the minute weeds of her garden.

I remember her best in her working days, coming home from the cane-fields at "pauhana"[2] time. She wore a pair of faded blue jeans and an equally faded navy-blue and white checked work shirt. A Japanese towel was wrapped carefully around her head, and a large straw "papale" or hat covered that. Her sickle and other tools, and her "bento-bako" or lunch-box, were carried in a khaki bag she had made on her back.

I would be sitting, waiting for her, on the back steps of her plantation-owned home, with my elbows on my knees. Upon seeing me, she would smile and say, "Tadaima" (I come home). And I would smile and say in return, "Okaeri" (Welcome home). Somehow I always felt as if she waited for that. Then I would watch her in silent fascination as she scraped the thick red dirt off her heavy black rubber boots. Once, when no one was around, I had put those boots on, and deliberately flopped around in a mud puddle, just so I could scrape off the mud on the back steps too.

Having retired from the plantation, she now wore only dresses. She called them "makule-men doresu," Hawaiian for old person's dress. They were always gray or navy-blue with buttons down the front and a belt at the waistline. Her hair, which once must have been long and black like mine, was now streaked with gray and cut short and permanent-waved.

The only time she wore a kimono was for the "Bon"[3] dance. She looked so much older in a kimono and almost foreign. It seemed as if she were going somewhere, all dressed up. I often felt very far away from her when we all walked together to the Bon dance, even if I too was wearing a kimono. She seemed almost a stranger to me, with her bent figure and her short pigeon-toed steps. She appeared so distantly Japanese. All of a sudden, I would notice her age; there seemed something so old in being Japanese.

She once surprised me by sending a beautiful "yūkata" or summer kimono for me to wear to represent the Japanese in our school's annual May Day festival. My mother had taken pictures of me that day to send to her. I have often wondered, whenever I look at that kimono, whether she had ever worn it when she was a young girl. I have wondered too what she was thinking when she looked at those pictures of me.

My mother was the oldest daughter and the second child of the six children Obāchan bore, two boys and four girls. One of her daughters, given the name of Mary by one of her school teachers, had been disowned by her for marrying a "haole" or Caucasian. Mary was different from the others, my mother once told me, much more rebellious and independent. She had refused to attend Honokaa and Hilo High Schools on the Big Island of Hawaii, but chose instead to go to Honolulu to attend McKinley High School. She

---

2. Drudgery, tedious work.
3. The Lantern Festival, the Buddhist's All Soul's Day.

smoked cigarettes and drove a car, shocking her sisters with such unheard of behavior. And then, after graduation, instead of returning home, Mary took a job in Honolulu. Then she met a haole sailor. Mary wrote home, telling of her love for this man. She was met with harsh admonishings from her mother.

"You go with haole, you no come home!" was her mother's ultimatum.   10

Then Mary wrote back, saying that the sailor had gone home to Amer-   11
ica, and would send her money to join him, and get married. Mary said she was going to go.

"Soon he leave you alone. He no care," she told her independent daugh-   12
ter. Her other daughters, hearing her say this, turned against her, accusing her of narrow-minded, prejudiced thinking. She could not understand the words that her children had learned in the American schools; all she knew was what she felt. She must have been so terribly alone then.

So Mary left, leaving a silent, unwavering old woman behind. Who   13
could tell if her old heart was broken? It certainly was enough of a shock that Honolulu did not have gold-paved streets. Then, as now, the emotionless face bore no sign of the grief she must have felt.

But the haole man did not leave Mary. They got married and had three   14
children. Mary often sends pictures of them to her. Watching her study the picture of Mary's daughter, her other daughters know she sees the likeness to Mary. The years and the pictures have softened the emotionless face. She was wrong about this man. She was wrong. But how can she tell herself so, when in her heart, she only feels what is right?

"I was one of the first to condemn her for her treatment of Mary," my   15
mother told me. "I was one of the first to question how she could be so prejudiced and narrow-minded." My mother looked at me sadly and turned away.

"But now, being a mother myself, and being a Japanese mother above   16
all, I *know* how she must have felt. I just don't know how to say I'm sorry for those things I said to her."

Whenever I see an old Oriental woman bent with age and walking with   17
short steps, whenever I hear a child being talked to in broken English-Japanese, I think of her. She is my grandmother. I call her "Obāchan."

STUDY QUESTIONS

1. Why does the NARRATOR put on her grandmother's black rubber boots (paragraph 5)? (Make sure you take into account the last word—"too"—in the sentence describing her actions.)

2. How does the narrator's perspective on her grandmother change when "Obāchan" wears a kimono?

3. How does the reader's view of Obāchan change when we learn of her treatment of her daughter Mary? What do you understand by these two sentences: "She was wrong. But how can she tell herself so, when in her heart, she only feels what is right?" (paragraph 14)?

4. Why is the narrator's mother sorry for what she said to her mother at the time of Mary's leaving home?

5. "She is my grandmother. I call her 'Obāchan' " (paragraph 17). Why? Why isn't the story called "Grandmother"?

POINT OF VIEW

No two people see things exactly alike, and in a piece of writing everything depends on whose view of events we are given. Ordinarily, a story is not just a story; it is *someone's* story. That is, it is told by someone in particular so that rather than a story that is "objective," it is some particular person's *version* of a story. Someone else might see events differently, someone else might emphasize different things, someone else might even draw different conclusions, making the same events add up to a wholly different story. Essays, too, are usually someone's in particular; often an author feels free to be quite visible and personal in an essay in a way that he or she would not be when the distancing of fiction is used. Even in poems, which sometimes do not tell a story or involve the interaction of different people, there is usually a distinctive voice or point of view that we need to identify in order to understand the poem's perspective. Words never exist in a pure vacuum, without a context. They always belong to some VOICE that speaks them to us as readers. The kind of voice portrayed therefore influences what the words seem to say, how we interpret them, from what angle of vision their "facts" or feelings come. And the better we become at identifying that voice and its characteristic features, the better we become at interpretation.

In plays, the action takes place before our eyes, and we "know" what "really" happens: we see for ourselves. But even in a play, different perspectives on the action quickly become important. Some action takes place

246

offstage, and we are told about it by a CHARACTER whose reliability we have to evaluate. The words we hear are the words of the author, but they are spoken by actors who have chosen to interpret (perhaps with the aid of a director) the words, their roles, the whole play. And even the action we actually see involves our INTERPRETATION, built on the interpretations of director and actors as well as the playwright, of the words and gestures of the characters. By the *way* characters (or actors) express themselves, they influence what we see and what conclusions we draw about actions and events.

As soon as characters begin to speak, interpretations of actions, attitudes, and feelings assert themselves. The attributes of characters affect how we respond to them. The acting is important. So are the voice, the gestures, the words spoken, the lighting, the set. All these things help determine how we interpret and what we conclude about what is going on and why. As observers ourselves, we are influenced not just by what we see for ourselves and what we hear from others, but how we see and how we "read" what we are told. Do we believe Oka's account of his relationship with his wife in *And the Soul Shall Dance* in chapter 1? Often, as here, what we come to know about the marriage and the specifics of the marriage involve putting together what we see with what characters say or report. Almost never, even in a play or a film, are we allowed to "see" purely. Words, gestures, people intervene to color what we see, to give us a fuller, more resonant, and sometimes contradictory account to put against the testimony of our own eyes and ears. We have to interpret, we have to sort.

Stories, though, are much more specifically dependent on who tells us what, for we have no eyes of our own. There, words are the only means we have of visualizing, and what we visualize depends completely on what someone tells us to see. The reliability of the NARRATOR, therefore, is all-important, and so is the angle he or she has on the central action. Often, in stories, a character tells a story about himself or herself. We are probably least reliable when we speak of ourselves, for there is where our greatest biases exist. We are far less likely to tell something damaging about ourselves than we are to divulge negative information about someone else. People who talk about themselves, in stories as in life, are thus always somewhat suspect. It may turn out, of course, that they are telling the truth—even the basest of people may be capable of being truthful—but we have to be on our guard. We cannot, at first, be sure whether they speak the truth or judge matters properly. We have to judge for ourselves, on the basis of what the text, in all its complexity, implies.

Guardedness is, in fact, a good rule of thumb for accepting the validity of anything we are told in a piece of writing. It may, of course, turn out to be absolutely true (sometimes everything we are told in a story has finally to be taken exactly at face value), but it is usually a good idea to start out with doubt, to ask basic questions about the grounds for believing. The reliability, then, of the person speaking can be a major issue for interpretation in a story, in the dialogue of a play, in an essay, or even in a poem. For poems are not always "spoken" directly by the poet; often a kind of "character" is created in a poem to speak the words; that is, the voice in the poem is sometimes that of a fictional person the poet creates, not necessarily the voice of the poet.

Often, of course, the voice in the poem is not very distinct from the voice of the poet her- or himself, and often the SPEAKER of the poem (that is, the person who speaks the poem's words) cannot be distinguished, except technically, from the voice of the poet. In Linda Hogan's "Heritage," for example, or Ray A. Young Bear's "in the first place of my life," there is little reason to think that the speaker is not someone very like the poet, for the events described there might well have happened exactly that way to Hogan and Young Bear. But it is still a good idea to get in the habit of thinking of the words in a poem as being spoken by a "speaker" rather than by the "poet," for often there is a distinction.

Sometimes, especially in stories, writers adopt an independent or "objective" stance so that the authority of the facts will not be questioned. When a story is told directly by a character, it is said to be a *first-person* story. When a distant or "objective" view is used but the action of the story follows a single character throughout, the story is said to be *focused* on that character, or that character is said to be the FOCUS of the story. *Focus* is the viewing aspect of the story; *voice* is the verbal aspect.

Knowing who it is who speaks to us in a work of literature—recognizing the voice for what it is or what it presents itself to be—is important to understanding and interpretation. Asking basic questions about the voice we hear, who the person seems to be, what we know about him or her, the accents and nuances of the voice speaking to us, is a valuable skill to learn. Often it helps us in reading, as such a skill does also in life, to sort and decide—to know how to "read" books as well as people.

WRITING
ABOUT THE READING

PERSONAL ESSAYS AND NARRATIVES

1. Construct a family tree. Go as far as you can yourself, and then consult the oldest living relative on either side of your family. Ask about the characters of your forebears, strange or interesting incidents in their lives, ethnic or national backgrounds. Any surprises? interesting new information?

   With this as a base, write a tribute to one or more of your forebears. Note that in several of the pieces the subject is not perfect—Miyasaki's obāchan, for example, seems a little narrow, old-fashioned, rigid; "mi abuelo" is "at best" an ordinary man—yet the portraits of them are touching, even loving.

   Your essay may be a general character sketch, like "Obāchan," or stress a single revealing incident or series of incidents.

2. If you chose to honor or depict a forebear in one or a series of incidents, you could write a narrative. You might even want to embellish it a bit with a few made-up incidents or responses of your own. If you want to be true to your understanding of the CHARACTER, make sure you invent episodes or details that are consistent with what you believe to be true of the person.

3. Look through a family album for the oldest family photographs you can find, preferably those of grandparents, great-grandparents, or other forebears who lived in a different country, region, or environment from yours. Try to reconstruct something of their lives and what it meant for them and you to have moved from their / your "roots" to where you live now.

4. What characteristic habit or feature of your own personality seems to you to have come most directly from your ethnic or national origins? Write a brief description of yourself as a member of a specific ethnic or national group. Try to account for the ways you differ from others in the group, and indicate the most powerful sources of influence from the group. Did particular members of the group who were not members of your family provide models for your behavior and values? Did the largest influence of the group on you come through your family upbringing? through religion? through language? through stories that were told in the group? through games and rituals?

5. Write a short essay of no more than 500 words describing the person you most admire who comes from your own ethnic or national background. Be sure to indicate what characteristics of that person you admire most. Give examples of things he or she has accomplished that lead to your high evaluation. What values does the person embody? In what ways are those values related to the "tribe" he or she comes from?

6. Describe the moment in your life when you first remember meeting someone whose

background was very different from yours. What differences did you notice most vividly at the time? How were you made aware of the differences between the two of you? Write a brief paragraph describing, as precisely as you can remember them, your responses at the time. Did you experience the meeting as conflict? Did it seem threatening to your sense of identity? How does the episode now seem different to you than it did at the time? How much of the difference derives from difference in age and knowledge? How much just because time has gone by and you have had a chance to reflect on the experience and put your emotions into perspective? Write another paragraph in which you describe your present reflections on the episode.

7. Write a *story* about the episode you have described in #3 above.

IMITATIONS AND PARODIES

1. Change the point of view in one of the poems or stories and write a new version. How might Yvonne Sapia's Caribbean Indian grandmother describe her son? Or reverse the narrator / object of one of the poems in this chapter.

2. Write a conversation with a grandparent in the grave, in PARODY of Ríos's poem.

3. Finish Najari Levon's story of the snake in the style of the existing narrative. In a separate paragraph, or in two, discuss the difference in MEANING between the unfinished tale and your completed one.

ANALYTICAL PROSE

1. What do you think of as your own "heritage"? Do you identify with one particular branch of your family tree? Do you think of yourself as "American" through and through—without any sense of roots or even tentacles entangled with another culture? Or are you so "hybrid" that you feel you almost define what it is to be American by the diversity of your heritage?

2. Write a descriptive or analytical essay about your family tree, or an essay called "Heritage," or an analysis of your own character as you understand it in terms of heredity, deducing the heredity factors from what you know of your forebears.

ARGUMENTATIVE PAPERS

1. Young people should cherish the values and traditions of their cultural traditions.

2. Young people should be free to ignore old values and old traditions in building a new society.

RESEARCH PAPERS

1. In the reference section of the library, look up (in a dictionary of slang or unconventional English) some derogatory word you have heard used about a national, ethnic, or religious group. Compare your own sense of the word, from your experience in hearing it, with the dictionary "definitions." Have you ever heard the word used affectionately or as a term of admiration by someone within that group? In what kind of situation? How could you tell the difference between the intentions?

2. With the help of a reference librarian, find three or four reliable books that provide basic factual information about the coming to America of your own national or ethnic group. Write a paper tracing the history of your people in America.

3. Interview someone from an older generation, preferably your great-grandmother or great-grandfather or someone you know from their generation. Ask them questions about things they remember from their childhood and early life, especially events that helped shape their personal identity or that involve their moving from one place to another. Take notes on the interview. Choose what you think is the most interesting story the person tells you, and write it in narrative form. Then rate yourself as an interviewer: How good were you at getting the person to tell stories? How did you do it? What would you do differently on another similar occasion? Write a brief "how to" guide for interviewing people about their life experiences, complete with a list of good questions to ask and ones to avoid.

Student Writing

WITHHOLDING CONSENT OR THE ART OF NON-CONFORMITY

LISBETH SIVERTSEN

Maxine Hong Kingston has come to represent for me immigrants who "reclaim" 1 their past and present in the new country of the United States. In her book *Woman Warrior* she shares her experiences as a child among "ghosts" in her new country as well as her old country: China. The opening story of the book is "No Name Woman." The story of an outcasted and suicidal aunt, who gives birth to her illegitimate baby in a pigsty and drowns herself and her baby in the local well, is the background for Kingston's exploring the myths, meanings, and messages of her mother's stories. As Kingston gives a voice to her own life in America, she also offers us some Chinese' suppressed biographies, a record of some lives that she has inherited through stories and from her own participation in their defeated silences. She absorbs experiences from her two cultures and comes to understand her alienation from both. She seeks acceptance from both her family and her new country and tries to make sense of the social norms of the Chinese culture, and still be able to assert her own unique bicultural worth and identity. But here lies the contradiction and the dilemma which fascinate me: is it possible to break the silence and still be accepted among those whose lies you are revealing? Can we only do this in a new setting far away from the main stage which continues to play tragedies with whole cultures as actors? And what consequences does it have for the individual person healing from their past *and* for the ones "left behind"?

In the China that Kingston depicts, individuality is not the norm. With a population of more than a billion people, "everybody has eight million relatives" (paragraph 33). The importance of conformity is therefore, if not understandable, then at least worth keeping in mind. The particular cruelty toward women is, however, an extra baggage added to any Chinese woman on top of the rigid social norms that everyone must obey. Women who were widowed or left behind by traveling husbands were to eat at their in-laws' "outcast table" and on the day after their wedding they would cut their beautiful, long hair (which made them individually different from each other!) "in flaps about their ears or pulled it back in tight buns" (paragraph 24). If they "tended" to their appearance, they were considered eccentrics, and therefore not accepted. Kingston's aunt, however, "combed individuality into her bob" (paragraph 25). She spent time on herself and her appearance, but since "combing her hair hexes beginnings, my aunt rarely found an occasion to look her best" (paragraph 27). The Chinese condemning of attention toward appearance and someone's trying to be an individual rather than a number in a crowd is in stark contrast to the American way of life, and I think that's why I react strongly to this part of the story. It does not jibe with our commercial way of living in which we believe that everyone has the right to be who we are and to express it externally through clothes, hair styles and make-up, in short "tending" to our appearance. But to some extent, the lack of concern with one's appearance gives women in China a certain freedom. They are definitely not contributing to a multinational cosmetic industry and they are free of worries as to whether or not they are in style. The flip side of the coin is then that this is imposed on them. It is a restriction *imposed* on them, and any restriction is bound to cause rebellion. If we thoroughly analyze the subject of looks, are we not as "Western women" trying to all look the same? Is there not a "goal" or specific standard for any woman to aim for: slender, young skin, preferably blond and definitely with the hair bouncing the right way? Appearance is, however, but a small aspect of the whole idea of conformity and valuing society as a whole rather than the individual, and in this matter the Chinese culture differs from what is familiar to us in the U.S.

> In the village structure, spirits shimmered among the live creatures, balanced and held in equilibrium by time and land. But one human being flaring up into violence could open up a black hole, a maelstrom that pulled in the sky. The frightened villagers, who depended on one another to main-

tain the real, went to my aunt to show her a personal, physical representation of the break she had made in the "roundness." (paragraph 37)

The "roundness" that is so important to Chinese culture (and to many other cultures as well) is fascinating. There may be two levels of interpreting the roundness. Eastern philosophy sees time not in a linear perspective, but in circles. Everything is connected and death is not so much the end of one life, but rather the beginning of another. The family must therefore "be whole, faithfully keeping the descent line by having sons to feed the old and the dead, who in turn look after the family (paragraph 39). By breaking social laws, the No Name aunt is imposing danger on the family; she has broken the circle. Round moon cakes, round windows, round tables, and round rice bowls are all talismen to remind each family of the law. In this interpretation of "roundness," the social law becomes the circle: round and where ends meet so there is no way out. The social law is unwritten, but therefore precisely much more strictly adhered to. The aunt couldn't (or wouldn't?) comply with the talismen and the consequences of breaking the roundness reflect the severity of conformism. The fatalistic view of life puts the whole society out of control over their destiny, and the aunt must therefore pay on behalf of the whole village and awaken to "the inexorable."

The contrast to the American way of centering everything around the individual is clear. In this country of "equal opportunity for everyone" fate only exists to be turned around, from life in the slums to the successful, wealthy man who has nobody to thank but himself. In the U.S. it is encouraged to break away from the family and its norms in order to succeed on your own. This break from the family is accepted in terms of aiming for higher wealth economically as well as higher wealth spiritually. In contrast to China where one's well-being depends on how the entire family is faring, we have in this country of immigrants other definitions of wealth. Here the individual must fend for herself so she will often try to break the "roundness" of the family to liberate herself from the social norms and moral judgments of her family. It may come out in terms of "naming the unspeakable." This usually refers to "coming out" about a painful past. Throats accustomed for centuries to silence let out cries of pain asking for mercy and understanding in a society without a long history of strict social laws and talismen to build on. The sense of freedom that we acquire as immigrants in America can be seen as a whole new culture breaking the "roundness." We are here giving testimony to what we found restricting and unhealthy in our home countries. We learn about dysfunctional families and learn that healing comes from being able to speak out about the pain. Maxine Hong Kingston has chosen not to participate in the shaming of her father's family any longer by breaking the silence. With her silence she has been an accomplice in the punishment of her aunt, and by naming the unspeakable, she liberates not only herself, but also her aunt and many other women in similar situations of being outlawed as a consequence of patriarchy.

Personally I can relate to this sense of freedom as an immigrant. In my new world I feel free to explore my past in an accepting and nurturing atmosphere. I know that whatever I find that has haunted me before, I can name and I will be understood, or at least accepted, instead of being rejected as an outlaw who speaks up about unpleasant childhood memories. I cherish this new-found life without shame and guilt, and yet I also resist the almost complete lack of social graces and conformity I find here. Too much individualism sometimes implies that we don't care for others anymore. That is why I asked the question earlier about what happens to us who start to reveal uncomfortable facts from the past, and what happens to the ones we're telling on? Will we ever be able to unite again? Can we discontinue the circles of dysfunction by merely healing ourselves through talk? Will our personal healing and reaching of new potential help or hurt the culture we attack and left behind? Maxine Hong Kingston has decided that she needs to break the silence. Like her, I am weeding out experiences of my past that I don't feel comfortable with and therefore will name and let go of. I am very concerned, though, about losing identity and cutting the roots I have to my culture. My goal is not to be the arch-American who does not belong anywhere. I have seen too many people in pursuit of material wealth, move around constantly without any sense of belonging and therefore without sense of loss at each move. I have seen people be so free of cultural conformity that they lose their sense of respect for others. The price of valuing individuality so much is high in my perspective. We get a nation of individuals only pursuing what is best for them *in spite of* their surroundings, instead of *together with* their surroundings. In that sense, I do understand the value of cultural and social norms if they are not carried out in extreme ways. My perspective is how do we improve as a group or nation instead of as an individual. We may have to start like Maxine Hong Kingston with ourselves, and like rings in the water a richer and more honest life will spread around us.

4

LANGUAGE

O n the surface, language seems much less personal than do home, family, or ethnic culture, but there is a dimension of language that is even more personal—though not separate—from these. When we are inside our own heads, thinking—not necessarily rigorously or logically or intellectually, but just thinking about "things," or ourselves—what do we think in? Language, mostly. Our very consciousness, one of the basic elements of our selfhood, is made up of language. So language is one of the most, not least, personal aspects of our lives.

There is a sense, however, in which language is cultural, not personal, something that may be inside ourselves but that comes to us from the outside. We did not, after all, invent the words, the syntactical structures, or other elements of our language. Even those of us whose native language is English have lived in more than one linguistic world or culture. The language spoken at home is not exactly the same as that spoken in school, and it is not exactly the same language we speak among our peers. Part of the purpose of courses in composition and literature is to make you more fully aware of and more proficient in the language of the educated or professional culture you are entering or are about to enter. Every profession and trade has its jargon, every age group its own "language." Those speaking rural, regional, or ethnic "languages" must choose to what degree they want to change that language to "fit into" and succeed in their chosen professional and social world.

Though we all have these adjustments to make, those whose native language is not English obviously are faced with a more difficult choice. If one language is spoken in your home and another at school or work, which will be the language of your consciousness? Richard Rodriguez describes just such a dilemma in "Aria." If you are a Cuban-American poet should you write poems in Spanish or English? What will be your very own name— which for others and to some degree for yourself will be your identity? Ricardo or Richard? Carroll Arnett or Gogisgi? Tony Cade or Bambara?

Anyone whose first language is not English, or anyone who has visited a country whose language he or she does not know, has experienced not only the difficulty of getting along, of doing ordinary things like catching a train or finding a drugstore, but also the diminishment of part of the self. We're a lot "dumber"—literally and figuratively—than we are at home. The young SPEAKER* in Li-Young Lee's "Persimmons" is punished by his teacher because he does not know the word "persimmons" though he knows all about the actual fruit. To feel oneself reduced to linguistic childhood, as was Rodriguez's father because he was not fluent in English, is a humiliating experience. Even when we are fully bilingual there are times when what can be thought or said in one language cannot be expressed in the other— there are puns that cannot be made, associations that do not exist, as between hunting and courtship in Chippewa, as Louise Erdrich tells us in "Jacklight."

Because language is so central to our lives, so personal and cultural, it can cause misunderstandings and even hostility. You're living in America, we sometimes think when someone addresses us in a foreign language, so why don't you speak English? Accents and inarticulateness become the butt of jokes, derision, even enmity.

Language difference often represents cultural difference, and suspicion, uncertainty, or even prejudice runs high when there are unknown ("foreign," "alien," or even just "different") ways to deal with. The Dominican dictator Trujillo, Rita Dove reminds us, even ordered the slaughter of 20,000 Haitians "because they could not pronounce the letter 'r' in *perejil*, the Spanish word for parsley." Sometimes people do not want to understand someone who speaks, or thinks, or acts differently from what they are used to, and the "foreign tongue" that person speaks comes to stand for a whole range of unacceptable values. Thus, a Spanish-speaking family may be reluctant to accept the friends of a son or daughter who speak English or

*Words in small capitals are defined in the Glossary.

Chinese, and parents from New York City may be resistant to a potential son- or daughter-in-law from a part of the country where a different dialect is spoken or where voices have a different accent: Southerners or Midwesterners or Californians or even New Englanders or upstate New Yorkers may seem "foreign" in their ways—just because they use different terms for familiar things, or express their feelings in a different way, or have different ways of pronouncing r's or of giving rhythm to their sentences. People can be very difficult with one another when their expectations are upset or their familiar routines are interrupted. And when language difficulty combines with other ready areas of misunderstanding—between generations, between people of different religions, between people with different habits or customs—major conflicts often develop and major intolerances become evident.

The selections that follow illustrate a variety of problems—some minor, some humorous, some serious, some terrible—that occur when language barriers intrude into human situations. In the "one world" of America, with its mix of cultures, customs, habits, and backgrounds, the mix of languages sometimes seems like the Tower of Babel realized in modern dress, but the challenges of linguistic difference sometimes bring out the best and most tolerant in human beings, too, as anyone who has been treated compassionately in a "foreign" nation can testify. Unfortunately, not all collisions of language result in compassionate encounters, but they do often illustrate poignantly the differences between cultural values that lie beneath language differences. Writers often find it a challenge to use language to make sense of conflicts that derive from language itself.

Hugo Martinez-Serros

Hugo Martinez-Serros teaches Spanish at Lawrence University. He has published a collection of short fiction, *The Last Laugh and Other Stories* (1988).

"LEARN! LEARN!"

José María Rivera always read important letters with a red pencil in his hand. They were letters written in *castellano*—he sometimes called it *cristiano*, his eyes rolling, his voice serious—by people who knew or should have known the language as well or better than he did, which is what made the letters important. He read first for spelling errors, rapidly, crossing out, adding, changing, circling, then he went back for a second reading to seize anything that had escaped his initial sweep. In repeated readings, finally, he concentrated on what the letters said.

There were few of these letters in the passing of a year. The two or three of his brothers-in-law far off in Mexico wrote to his wife, letters that always provoked him to say in a louder than normal voice, "*Lástima de educación universitaria, no saben escribir.*" A pity indeed, he never tired of thinking, they were educated at the university and just didn't know how to write. He said it as much to himself as to his wife, a perceptive woman who did not answer him. Years ago, before leaving Mexico, he had already developed the habit of saying things aloud to himself. And there were the other letters, rare strikes that came into his hands from friends who did not quite understand them, and from the friends of friends.

Chema—his friends called him that—had long ago stopped "editing" the *barrio semanarios*, weeklies. They had too many errors, the same ones over and over and they held no challenge for him. Besides, his anonymous letters to their editors had gone unheeded and he was not interested in writers who did not want to be redeemed. "*Cabrones ojetes*, damned assholes," he had labeled them in the final letter, and as he wrote he shouted repeatedly to himself, "*¡Que se chinguen ésos!* Fuck them! *¡No tienen interés en aprender!* They're not interested in learning!"

The church bulletin of Our Lady of Guadalupe was another matter. The Riveras, whose destinies were in the hands of *don* José—his acquaintances called him that—were not church-going, but every Sunday *don* José sent one of his sons for the bulletin, warning him as he left, to be careful, "*Ten cuidado*," and not to get lost in that den of corruption, "*No te vayas a perder en ese recinto de perversos.*" Although the bulletin dealt exclusively with what Chema called "*cosas de beatas y maricones*, news for overly pious women and fairies"—births, marriages, deaths, baptisms, confirmations, first communions, fund-raising events, the activities of the Daughters of Our Most Holy Virgin of Guadalupe and of the Knights of the Virgin of Guadalupe— he acknowledged the excellence of its language, an excellence that was not without faults, however. The author of that bulletin was the *párroco*,[1] Father Tortas, a Spaniard whom Chema called, "that overstuffed *gachupín*,"[2] adding gleefully, "*Cuervo cargado de carnes y de cagada*, a crow bursting with flesh and shit."

José María mined every one of Father Tortas' bulletins, and every one yielded something, however small or imagined. But it was the nugget of indisputable error that filled him with intense pleasure and made him shout, "*Aprende de tu padre, sanguijuela*, learn from your master, parasite! This is your only creative act, it should be perfect! You have nothing else to do, *manos de señorita!*[3] *¡Aprende! ¡Aprende!* Learn! Learn! If I am the only one willing to kick your ass, so be it! Your voice is louder than it should be, you must answer for it!" And José María taught the priest as well as he could, in anonymous letters that went out often but not regularly, for not all bulletins merited a complete letter. His sons, feeling themselves partners in this enterprise, delivered them to the church or the rectory, clandestinely, provocatively, under cover of the large crowds that moved in and out of the former or passed slowly by the latter.

There was no question of it, Father Tortas heeded portions of the anonymous letters and this made José María a better critic. Their conflict, the tip of the iceberg of their antagonisms, took place at the level of orthography, grammar, syntax, semantics. Sometimes José María applauded the priest's responses to particular challenges, for he would counter his unknown antagonist's thrust with an ingenious verbal maze here, an extraordinarily subtle play on words there. At times the priest seemed to tweak his unknown critic by slipping into flagrant error. Chema begrudged the priest his mastery of the language and whispered to himself, "*Sí, dominas el castellano, pinche cura maricón*, you lousy fairy of a priest, you do know the language! You have this over my brothers-in-law, that wherever the hell they taught you, they taught you well, *manos de señorita*."

Juan Ginés Tortas' parishioners had never seen hands more beautiful than his. They had made José María think of the hands of figures in religious

---

1. Parish priest.

2. Spaniard.

3. Literally "hands of a young woman," it is used as a charge of effeminacy.

calendars. They were white, very white, the fingers slender and long and tapering into flat tips capped by manicured nails, a labyrinth of pale blue lines just under the skin. Hands surprisingly fleshless, firm and smooth. To his flock they seemed hands made for holding and displaying Christ, a living monstrance. Nearing fifty, Father Tortas was a big man with a bald pate. A sprinkle of white flakes fell from the hair that ringed his head, and his hands recurrently fluttered up to his shoulders to flick at the incessant snow. He dressed with an elegance that belied the notion that a priest's wardrobe is uniformly dull, and even his cassocks and robes were tailored to his personal desires. He had long ago assumed the practice, after Mass, of keeping his robes on and wearing them in his chambers. They intimidated parishioners he received there, giving him the distance he needed.

As seminarian and newly ordained priest, Juan Ginés, proud and seri-   8
ous by nature and gregarious by design, had been a competitor whose incentive was competition. He was a performer who excelled when he was surrounded by excellent performers. Drawn to material comfort, he had aspired to a position of prestige in some chancery, convinced that there he would find abundance and intellectual stimulation. But the young priest's impatience, buttressed by ambition and a knowledge of English, had driven him to the United States. He had imagined himself the Sepúlveda of the *mestizos*[4] in Anglo-America, had envisioned himself in the American Hierarchy as the exegete of the Spanish-American text.

In the United States Juan Ginés saw the Canaan of his expectations   9
crumble in the Babylon of his captivity in South Chicago. They had not told him as he would later tell himself—"*¡Me enviaron al culo de esta ciudad salchichera!*"—that South Chicago was the anus of sausage-making Chicago. He had come to a dead end when the world had seemed new to him, and for a time he had struggled to check his bitterness, winning small victories over his pride and ambition, but he could not vanquish them. He convinced himself that he had been intentionally misled, ultimately believing that they had exiled him unjustly. So it was that he made a sword of his disillusionment and a shield of what had been his expectations. His weight increased with his cynicism and his hair began to thin.

For more than twenty years Father Tortas had grieved the impatience   10
that had led him to abandon Spain for the hope of rapid advancement in a city where, he discovered, it was reserved for priests with Irish surnames. Since then he had moved cautiously, slowly weighing alternatives on the scales of his distrust to arrive at decisions of consequence and inconsequence alike. He had pondered as long over the advisability of forming a parish baseball team as he had over the need for a second assistant. He scorned young people for their immaturity and lack of judgment, making them the target of diatribes delivered from the pulpit, subjecting them to inquisitional

---

4. Sepúlveda refers to Juan Ginés de Sepúlveda (1490?–1572 or 73), a Spanish theologian and historian. His *Democrates II*, in defense of Indian slavery, provoked a long controversy with Las Casas; *mestizos*—mixed blood, Spanish and Indian.

indignities in the intimacy of the confessional. And for more than twenty years he had indulged his pride with fantasies of what he could have been had he stayed in Spain: now a cardinal's secretary, now a bishop, now a cardinal. He became aloof, solitary, performed his duties with the aid of many, but drew nobody close to him and drew close to nobody, not even his assistant priests. Alone, he lived more in the world of what could have been than in the community where he ran out his time. What little affection he could summon he bestowed on his altar boys, who, uneasy in his presence, would not have passed their thirteenth year if he could have controlled their growth. Of his pastoral concerns in recent years only the composition of the church bulletin seemed to interest him. Not even his housekeeper really knew him.

On Saturday mornings Father Tortas sat at his desk and unhurriedly wrote the weekly bulletin on oversized sheets of lined paper. Working from a pad of notes, dates, symbols, he finished it in an hour, needing more time only if the bulletin was unusually long. But it never took more than two hours. His penmanship was clear, large and angular, marked by that stiffness characteristic of certain European hands. Typed by a volunteer whom the *párroco* had trained, the copy was taken to a local printer by noon and the finished product was delivered to the rectory before five. Chema's anonymous letters effected no obvious change in his routine. The priest gradually intensified his concentration, paid greater attention to expression, turned increasingly to figurative language, adopted a more sophisticated syntax and, except for rare instances, did not need additional time to produce the bulletin. Had he known this, José María, like those who measure others against themselves, would have been astounded by the facility and speed with which Father Tortas composed the document.

Like most of the men in the neighborhood, Chema worked in the steel mill. He was skilled at executing a variety of difficult and dangerous jobs that required strength, stamina and alertness. He did the jobs superbly, with an animal intelligence and grace that were incomparable among his fellow workers. He followed his nature in what he did, and what he did and how he did it were his only security in the mill since it was not unionized. But the work did not spend him; it failed to test his physical limits. It did not drain him of that need he felt to exhaust his energies. It failed to challenge his intelligence and he knew it always would.

Even the letters he wrote in English deserved at least one draft, and Chema composed them as well as he could. Inevitably he turned to one of his sons for help, a recourse that pained them both since José María had to accept his son's judgment and the son had to suffer his father's detailed, time-consuming explanations.

"But you can't say that, that's Spanish, it's not said like that in English," his son explained to him in Spanish.

"Who says you can't? If you understand what you're doing you can do anything you want to with language. But you don't understand! *¡Lástima!*[5] *¡Aprende! ¡Aprende!*"

"I'm tellin' you, Pa, *no es inglés.*"

In some cases the son's advice was rejected. Having labored for an expression he thought poetic—"My determination to become a citizen is not different from the determination of the lion that, crippled, accepted Daniel's aid. My allegiance to the Daniel that is the United States could not be different from that of the lion to Daniel"—José María held fast to his creation over his son's protests, convinced that an adult would see what the youth had failed to appreciate. There was no antagonism between father and son, no rivalry, no dispute as to who knew English better. Both felt impatience: the father over his son's incomprehension of figurative language, the son over his father's insistence, which pulled ambivalently at the boy, who admired it even while it annoyed him. Together they hammered out a finished product and Chema then typed it, his fingers slowly pounding the keys of a winged, flightless Oliver. Chema was confident that the typewritten letter would impress its *gringo* reader.

But when José María wrote the most important letters, when he wrote letters in *castellano*—his own, his wife's—he prepared for the undertaking as carefully as Father Tortas might have readied everything for a Solemn High Mass. He spread newspaper over one end of the kitchen table to smooth its uneven surface, placed Bello's *Gramática de la lengua castellana*[6] at his left elbow, a dictionary at his right, a half dozen sharp-pointed pencils and a block of unlined paper in front of him. His hands had worn through the covers of both books and he had skillfully rebuilt them. The dictionary was small, a desk copy often inadequate to his needs.

Imagining himself the addressee, José María gave himself selfishly to his letter, writing in intense pursuit of the perfection his mind projected just beyond his pencils. Always, after several days, he came close enough to that perfection to feel satisfied; on rare occasions he achieved it. Almost as a rule of thumb, the number of drafts his letters required equaled the number of pages per letter. His prose was solid, heavy at times, but he wielded it with ease and could make it leap and turn to his wishes. An isolated sentence might seem cumbrous, but it lost this quality in the configuration of a paragraph or passage. He shaped his prose as a blacksmith from Guanajuato fashioned wrought iron, heating it in the forge of his brain, hammering it over and over on the anvil of his judgment, plunging it finally into the cold water of acceptance, piece by piece, the overall design held in the eye of his intelligence. He read all finished letters to his wife:

Priest,

I repeat what I have told you before: you have no imagination. Inasmuch as you refuse to think of your parishioners as human beings, as *her-*

---

5. What a pity!

6. A Spanish-language grammar edited by Andres Bello (1781–1865).

manos or *hijos,*[7] insisting, rather, on seeing them as animals, *ovejas,*[8] always *ovejas*, lend consistency, unity, to your vision by seeing yourself as a sheep dog rather than as a shepherd. At least give your parishioners a little variety. Call them fish, or doves, or better still, *burros*. You, of all people, must know how important, useful and docile *burros* are in the Hispanic world as well as in the bible. Read Vargas Vila,[9] for you might learn from him how . . .

On the second page of your bulletin, first paragraph of the section entitled BAPTISMS, you employ a passive construction incorrectly. I bring to your attention that in passive constructions with *se* it is the nature of the passive subject that determines the form the verb must take. . . .

The tools of Chema's mill work—hammers, pickaxes, pokers, shovels, drills, wrenches—had made his hands hard and his fingers were rooted in a ridge of calluses that spread to the base of his thick palms. His nails were dense, horny, a little longer than those of other men who did his kind of work. To shake his hand was to shake the hand of a man wearing a gauntlet. In that hand a pencil or pen seemed to grow small, almost disappearing in his fist, so that when he wrote, the script seemed to flow from a little tube he operated with the slight pressure of three fingers.

The writing was utterly controlled, swift, rhythmically winding and unwinding in fluid curves, the tall letters, all the same height, gracefully swayed from lower left to upper right, the crosses of the t's straight and slightly lengthened. It was elegant in its proportions, in the purity of its lines, in the inventiveness of its capital letters, in the almost-flourishes of occasional final letters that caught the eye with their air of effortless improvisation. The surprise of those who saw him write filled Chema with immense satisfaction, and he seized every opportunity to write that presented itself, even if it was only to sign his name. His Spanish letters were written in longhand. Nothing else would do.

He wrote with a Schaeffer fountain pen, white-dotted, medium point, in his judgment the finest writing instrument his money could buy. Several times a week he filled pages of a notebook with circles, ovals, straight and curved lines, all joined together and exactly alike. It gave him no pleasure to do these exercises. He performed them routinely, knowing that by doing them his hand would always be fully in control. On the subject of writing he spoke like a specialist:

"You hold the pen with little pressure, *apenitas*, about an inch and a half up from the point. The upper part rests in the cradle formed by the thumb and the index finger, *así*. And remember, this is the most important part, you write with the forearm, not with the wrist, *con el antebrazo*. The movement is from the elbow down, that way you never get tried. *¡Nunca!* And the test is in how loosely you hold the pen. Go ahead, pull it from between my fingers, you'll see how easy it is to do. You see! *¡Aprende, aprende!*"

7. Brethren or children.

8. Sheep.

9. Jose Maria Vargas Vila (1860–1933), a Colombian writer whose novels, ungrammatical and badly constructed, enjoyed a tremendous popularity.

The Rivera children all wrote well. José María had seen to that. They [27] regularly did exercises for him in notebooks, but none showed the signs of calligraphic precociousness he had shown when he was their age. And they spoke well enough, both languages, but especially Spanish. They spoke it better than their friends, which did not surprise José María, for he had convinced them that it was important to speak well. They had heard him dominate conversations with his friends, had heard the latter turn to their father to settle disputes about word meanings, had seen him reach for his dictionary to drive all doubt from the minds of his listeners.

As much as anything it was the dictionary test that impressed the Rivera [28] children. José María did it not to show off but as a measure of himself in the presence of his children, as a way of showing them that they could learn as he had. He handed them his dictionary and they took turns opening it at random and reading them words that looked difficult. He would define them. He did it to show them that words belonged to anyone who wanted them, and they came to believe that success in life and the power of speech were closely linked, that one could not be important without knowing words.

The penmanship of the first anonymous letter had caught Father Tortas' [29] attention. The letter's message had made him smile wryly. A man had written it, that much he could tell. But he knew that man was not one of his parishioners, for which one of them could write like that, express himself like that, have so little respect for him that he dared instruct him? *Hijo de puta*, he thought, what do you know, what do you know about me? Do you think that everyone can thrive in a sea of illiteracy? It had crushed him to learn that his parishioners were laborers, poor people of little education who had fled Mexico in search of something better. They defiled his language. He came to need those letters, anticipated them, counted on them to pique him, to make him think, to lift him from the drudgery of his daily life as did his weekly flights to the Loop,[1] where he brushed elbows with his kind of people in elegant restaurants, theatres, museums. People who dressed like him, who shared his interests, who talked like him and ate like him. *Castrado*,[2] he mused, if you had *cojones*[3] you would show them to me, you would sign your name and show me your *mestizo* face. But you half-breeds have always been cowards. Only cowards live in the *culo* of Chicago and like it. I could find you out if I wanted, but I give your letters the importance they deserve—anonymity. You amuse me, *enano*,[4] you faceless dwarf. Still, he wondered who his Momus[5] might be.

As time passed, Father Tortas became convinced that his critic had to [30] be one of the parish's heretics. Chema was his prime suspect, but without

1. Chicago business district bounded by the elevated railway.
2. Castrated male; eunuch.
3. Balls.
4. Dwarf.
5. In Greek legend, a god banished from Olympus for his continued satire and criticism.

inquiry he could not learn enough about him to confirm his suspicions. In the end he abandoned all desire to ascertain who the offender was because it did not matter that he identify his anonymous correspondent. And he did not want to deter the man.

Once, several years before the priest brought out the bulletin, the two men had met. It was in the depths of *la crisis*, the Depression, and José María had been lucky to be working one and two days a week. His family was large, his children very young, and he needed additional work. They had learned to live without gas and electricity, but they could not do without food and clothing. There was always work to be done in the church and in the church's properties. Everybody knew this. Reluctantly, José María had gone to see the priest, driven to it by need and the hope of securing employment. He found Father Tortas in the sacristy.

"*¿Señor cura?*"[6] José María said.

The priest turned to face a man in his thirties, lean and muscular, his Mexican physiognomy striking with its deepset eyes, prominent cheekbones and nose, a slight fleshiness around the mouth that drew attention away from the chin. He wore heavy work shoes, corduroy trousers, a denim shirt under a light jacket, and a wool cap pulled forward on his head. José María looked steadily into the other man's eyes.

"*Aquí se me llama padre*, around here people call me Father." The priest looked deliberately at the man's cap, as if telling him to remove it. Unruffled, José María understood but kept his hands at his sides. Then the priest asked, "*¿Eres una de mis ovejas?*" all the while thinking, whether you're mine or not you're a sheep.

"*Soy hombre*, I'm a man. *Vivo en este barrio*, I live in this neighborhood," he answered coldly, offended by the other's use of *tú*. Fucking priests, he thought, they're all alike.

"*¿Qué quieres?*" the priest asked, thinking, yes, you bastard, just what is it that you want?

Hijo de la chingada,[7] Chema thought, *van dos veces*, that's twice you've done it now. Again, the answer was cold, "*No quiero nada*, I want nothing. I have come looking for work. I am a good painter, a fair plumber, a carpenter. I can repair anything that needs repairing. I am a good electrician too. Pay me what you like, *lo que quiera usted;* if you don't like my work, don't pay me anything. I need work."

"The men in this parish donate their skills to their *párroco*. Why should I hire you?"

"*Mire usted*, look," he said pointing to a wall of blistered paint above a large radiator. His "*Ahí arriba*," accompanied by an upward thrust of the head, directed the priest's eyes to a badly cracked pane of glass just below the high ceiling. "You should hire me because my work stands up to time. Because I am not afraid of height."

---

6. Priest.

7. Loosely translates as "son of the defiled one," it is specifically Mexican and carries political connotations as well as sexual ones.

Father Tortas sat down but did not offer the man a chair. He caught his 40
right trouser leg just above the knee, pulled it up gently and crossed his legs.
The black tailored material hung in a long smooth fold above a polished black
dress shoe. "Do you have a family?"

"*Sí.*" 41

"Which is your church?" 42

"I do not have a church." 43

"*Lástima.* I do not hire heretics. If you want to work for me you must 44
attend Mass here." Waving his hands back and forth between himself and
José María he added, "Bring me your heretics. When I have made Catholics
of all of you and you become sheep in my fold, I may hire you."

"I do better work than your Catholics." 45

Impatiently, the priest stood up, crossed the room, took his black Hom- 46
burg from a rack and put it on. "*¿Cómo te llamas?*" he asked, as if knowing
his name would give him some power over him.

"*Julio César,*" he answered with a smile. "*Y tú cura,*" he continued, "*segur-* 47
amente te llamas Torquemada."[8]

"I have no time for your insolence!" Tortas reached out to smooth a 48
cassock that hung neatly on a hanger.

"Nor I for yours. I am leaving, please feel free to put on your dress." 49
And he laughed, turned and left.

Father Tortas' experience with two of the Rivera boys was no better. 50
On Sundays, after Mass, they posted themselves at the doors of his church
to sell papers. He had shooed them away many times and once had managed
to snatch their little *semanarios*, tearing them to pieces and repulsing the boys
as he might have driven money changers from his temple. But they kept
coming back and he finally asked them in a threatening voice, "*¿Cómo se llama*
vuestro padre?"[9]

"*Don* José María Rivera," they answered fearlessly. 51

Furious, the priest shouted, "*¡Entre vosotros no hay don, como no sea don* 52
Mierda! There isn't a *don* among you, unless it be *don* Shit!"

One of the boys answered him, saying, "*¡Para mierda, los curas!* If it's 53
shit you have in mind, we should be talking about priests!" Chema laughed
when the boys told him what had happened. Father Tortas kept distant from
them after that.

When Chema's eldest son, at sixteen, found a part-time job at the Wil- 54
cox and Follet Book Company, it was the dictionaries that caught his attention. "They got dictionaries up the ass on the fourth floor!" he told his brothers.
"Little ones, vest-pocket dictionaries, an' bigger'n bigger ones. The biggest
are those big fat Websters with color-plates."

"Do they have 'em in Spanish?" 55

"Yeah! On all kinds of languages. In two languages too." 56

8. "Surely your name is Torquemada." Tomas de Torquemada (1420–1498) was the first grand inquisitor in
Spain and is known for his religious bigotry and cruel fanaticism.

9. "What is your father's name?"

The plan took form slowly and when they had worked it out to the last 57 detail they executed it, on a Saturday. On Sunday, when José María's youngest son brought him Father Tortas' bulletin, his other sons each brought him a dictionary, the first real gifts they had ever given him, gifts that Chema could not afford. (Three times in the air shaft, heart and hands had followed perfectly the trajectory of the falling books, three times had calculated precisely the moment at which to catch, three times had shuddered with the explosions, the grime-encrusted windows becoming banks of eyes as Chema's sons struggled to hide the books in a Boy Scout knapsack.) Chema's eyes bulged in disbelief as he fingered the three volumes: a thick, handsome *Sopena*, a *Velázquez* bilingual, and *Webster's* unabridged complete with color-plates.

Readying his table in the kitchen, his new *Sopena* at his right elbow, José 58 María picked up the bulletin and began to read it aloud, a mocking edge in his voice:

Queridas ovejas, 59

I remind the Daughters of our Most Holy Virgin of Guadalupe and the 60 Knights of the Virgin of Guadalupe . . .

"*Ahora te chingas, cura,*" he exclaimed, "you're fucked now, priest, now 61 you'll see who's who, *sabrás que soy tu padre, tu padre,* now you'll know once and for all who your master is! *¡Aprende! ¡Aprende!* Learn! Learn!"

And José María Rivera placed his hand on his new *Sopena*. 62

STUDY QUESTIONS

1. Compare the physical writing practices of José María Rivera and Father Tortas. Compare their handwriting. Compare their physical hands.

2. What is José's job? Is he a good worker? How do you reconcile the kind of job he does and his concern for language? Are there any similarities?

3. Is Father Tortas a good priest? What were his ambitions? How does he feel about his assignment to a poor parish in America? José calls him "a fairy"; what details support José's judgment or reinforce a stereotype? How do you feel about the priest?

4. What effect do José's letters have on Father Tortas? What effect does the "contest" between them have on José? Whose side are you on in the struggle between the two? What is the net effect of the struggle on each of them?

5. Their physical makeup, their lifestyles, their social roles, and their vocations differ greatly; what comment is made on such differences or on the role of language by the fact that they seem equally concerned about precision and elegance of language, even down to the level of penmanship? In a story that is largely about the purity of language, how do you explain the profanity? What does the story seem to be saying about language?

6. Explain the title of the story.

James Alan McPherson

J ames Alan McPherson was born in Savannah, Georgia, in 1943. He graduated
from the Harvard Law School in 1968 and received an M.F.A. degree from the
University of Iowa's Writers Workshop in 1971. His stories have been collected in
Hue and Cry (1969) and *Elbow Room* (1977), the latter of which won a Pulitzer Prize.
He was awarded a MacArthur Fellowship in 1981. He currently teaches in the Writ-
ers Workshop at the University of Iowa.

I AM AN AMERICAN

It was not the kind of service one would expect, considering the quality of
the hotel. At eight o'clock both Eunice and I were awakened by a heavy
pounding on the door of our room that sounded once, loud and authorita-
tively, then decreased into what seemed a series of pulsing echoes. I staggered across the dirty rug, feeling loose grit underfoot, and opened the door.
Halfway down the hall a rotund little man, seeming no more than a blur of
blue suit and red tie, was pounding steadily on another door and shouting,
"American girlies, wake up! Breakfast!"

"Telephone?" I called to him.

"Breakfast!" he shouted cheerily, turning his face only slightly in my
direction. I could not see the details of his face, although it seemed to me his
nose was large and red, and his hair was close-cropped and iron gray. For
some reason, perhaps because of the way his suit was cut, I nursed the intu-
ition that he was a Bulgarian, although there are many other eastern Europeans who wear the same loose style of suit. Just then the door before him
opened. "Breakfast, American girlies!" he called into the room. From where
I stood in my own doorway, stalled by sleepiness as much as by lingering
curiosity, I glimpsed a mass of disarranged blond hair leaning out the door
toward the man. "We'll be right down," a tired voice said. But the man was
already moving down the hall toward the next door.

"Who was it?" Eunice asked from the bed.

"Time for breakfast," I said, and slammed the door. I had been expecting something more than a call for breakfast. We had come over from Paris
to London in hopes of making a connection. All during the hot train ride the

previous afternoon, from Gare du Nord to Calais, from Dover to Paddington Station, we had built up in our imaginations X, our only local connection, into a personage of major importance and influence in matters of London tourism. But so far he had not called.

While Eunice unpacked fresh clothes, I sat on the bed smoking a cigarette and assessed our situation. We could wander about the city on our own, call X again, or wait politely for him to call on us. But the thought of waiting in the room through the morning was distasteful. Looking around, I saw again what I had been too reluctant to perceive when we checked in the evening before. The room was drab. Its high ceiling, watermarked and cracked in places, seemed a mocking reminder of the elegance that might have once characterized the entire building. The rug was dusty and footworn from tramping tourists and the sheer weight of time. The thin mattress, during the night, had pressed into my back the history of many bodies it had borne. This was not Dick Whittington's magic London.

"Hurry up!" Eunice ordered. "They stop serving breakfast at nine o'clock." She opened the door, pulling her robe close about her neck. "I'll use that john down the hall, and then you get out until after I wash up in the face bowl." As she went out, I glanced over at the yellowing face bowl. The sight of it provided another reason for giving up the room. After digging out my toothbrush from my suitcase, I stood over the bowl brushing my teeth and trying to remember just why we had come to London.

One reason might have been our having grown tired of being mere tourists. In the Louvre two mornings before, among a crowd of American tourists standing transfixed before the Old Masters of Renaissance painting, I had suddenly found myself pointing a finger and exclaiming to Eunice, "Hey, didn't they name a cheese after that guy?"

"Leroy, they did no such a-thing!" Eunice had hissed.

The other tourists had laughed nervously.

Eunice had pulled me out of the Louvre, though not by the ear.

That same morning I had decided to wire one of a list of London people suggested to us by friends back home in Atlanta. Their advice had been the usual in such matters: "Be sure to look up X. We're good friends. He showed us a good time when we were in London, and we showed him a good time when he came to Atlanta. Be sure to tell him all the news about us." My wire to X had been humble: "We are Leroy and Eunice Foster from Atlanta, friends of Y and Z. Will be in London on weekend. Would like to see you." X's reply, which arrived the next morning, was efficient: "Call at home on arrival. X." And so we had raced from Paris to London. Upon arrival, as I instructed, I called up X.

"Y and Z who?" he asked, after I introduced myself.

I gave their full names. "They send warm regards from Atlanta," I added smoothly.

"Yes," X said. "They're fine people. I always regretted I never got to know them well."

"They're fine people," I said.   16

"Yes," X allowed. "I've got a bit of a flu right now, you know."   17

So we were in London. We located a room a few blocks from the train   18
station and were content to let be. The room was in a neat, white Georgian
house that, at some point during that time when American tourists first began
arriving en masse, had been converted into a hotel. Such places abound in
London; many of them are quite pleasant. But the interior of this one was
bleak, as was the room we secured on the fourth floor. To compound our
displeasure, the landlady had insisted that we declare exactly how long we
planned to stay, and then pay for that period in advance. This was one of
those periodic lapses of faith in the American dollar. American tourists suffered with it. But watchful landlords from Lyons to Wales refused to show
the slightest mercy. "These are class rooms, love," the landlady had declared,
inspecting our faces over the tops of her glasses. She was a plump woman
who fidgeted impatiently inside a loose gray smock. "There's lots of people
callin' for rooms," she reminded us. "All the time," she added.

We had been in no position to haggle. Having entered London on the   19
eve of a bank holiday weekend, we had no choice but to cash more traveler's
checks and pay rent through the following Monday morning. Only then did
the landlady issue us a single set of keys: one for the street door, which was
always locked, and one for our room. To further frustrate us, I found that
the lobby pay telephone did not work. This required me to walk back to the
station to ring up X and supply him with our address. He did not seem
enthusiastic about getting it, but said he might call on us the next day, if his
flu showed signs of abating. Discovering, finally, that the toilet on our floor
barely flushed, and that the bathtub was unhealthily dirty, we went to bed
with curses rumbling in us and the dust of the road still clinging to our skins.

Considering the many little frustrations that marred our arrival in Lon-   20
don, we were very pleased to have been awakened for breakfast by the house
porter. After Eunice returned to the room, I went out into the hall and waited
in line for my turn in the john. I was not even perturbed that the two Orientals, occupying the room next to ours, took long chances at the toilet.
While one occupied the stall, the other stood outside the door as if on guard.
Standing behind him, I noted that he was tall and slim and conservatively
dressed in a white shirt and black trousers. He seemed aloof, even reserved,
though not inscrutable. This I could tell from the way his brows lifted and
his ears perked, like mine, each time his companion made a vain attempt to
flush the slowly gurgling toilet. Indeed, the two of us outside the door tried
with the companion: we strained to apply our own pressures to the loose
handle, to join in his anticipation of a solid and satisfying flush. But, unlike
me, the Oriental did not shift from foot to foot each time his companion's
failure was announced by strained gurgles and hisses from behind the closed
door. Standing straight as a Samurai, he seemed more intent on studying my
movements, without seeming to, than on commandeering the john. I wanted
to communicate with him, but did not want to presume that he spoke English.

To further compound the problem, I could not tell if he was Japanese or Chinese. In Paris I had seen Chinese tourists, but they had been uniformed in the colors of Chairman Mao. This fellow wore western clothes. The problem became academic, however, when I recalled that the only Oriental phrases I knew were derived from a few sessions in a class in Mandarin I had once attended. I could never hope to master the very intricate and delicate degrees of inflection required, but I had managed to bring away from the class a few phrases lodged in memory, one of which was a greeting and the other introducing me as an American.

"Ni hau ma?" I inquired with a broad smile. 21

At first the Oriental stared at me in silence. Then he pointed a finger at 22 his chest. "I next," he said. Then he pointed a finger at my chest. "You next."

He was right. I shifted from one foot to the other until finally there 23 came the welcome sound of his companion's mastery of English hydraulics. As the companion stepped out of the stall and my acquaintance went in, I wanted to caution him that he need not be as concerned with a matter as ephemeral as decorum. But the desire died aborning. I did not have the language, and could only continue to shift from foot to foot. And sadly, very shortly afterward, while the second Oriental waited by the stairs, there came the same dry, strained sound of the very same difficulty. The situation was hopeless. I brushed past the companion and raced down the stairs to the third floor. But that stall too was in use. The one on the second floor offered even less hope: an elderly couple and a young man stood shifting in front of it.

On the ground floor, off the lobby, I ran into the same little man, still 24 seeming to me like nothing if not a Bulgarian, still knocking on doors and shouting, "Americans! Americans! Get up for breakfast!" When he saw me he turned, again ever so slightly, and said, "That way," pointing toward the door to the street. "Hurry! Hurry! Only served from eight to nine." I nodded my thanks and, seeing no stall on that floor, raced back up the stairs. Just below the third floor the two Orientals passed me on their way down. "Ni hau ma?" I called to them. They stopped and looked at each other, then at me. The taller man spoke in a high, hurried tone to the other. Then his companion nodded enthusiastically and said, "Oh!" He looked at me, pointed a finger up the stairs and said, "Open now."

He was right. 25

Going down for breakfast, finally, Eunice and I passed the little blue- 26 suited man in the lobby. He seemed about to go out the door, but as we approached he stepped aside and held the portal open for us. "Breakfast that way," he said, smiling. "In the basement." We thanked him and walked out the door, along a few feet of pavement, and down into the basement of the adjoining house. The little room was dank and smelled of rancid bacon. About a score of people, mostly Americans, were seated at the cloth-covered tables. We could tell they were Americans by the way they avoided eye contact. One girl was speaking halting French with a West Texas accent to two male companions who only listened. Over against the wall a middle-aged couple was poring over a *Herald-Tribune* stretched out beside their plates of bacon and eggs. "You just wait till we get back," the man was saying in a loud voice. "I'll *get* the sonofbitches for doin' this to me!" His wife kept looking up from her reading and saying, "Now Bob . . . now Bob . . . " Eunice and I went to a table at the far side of the room. At the table next to ours a rather attractive girl was eating rapidly and saying to the young man with her, "Cadiz was an utter bore. Madrid was an utter bore. . . . There's too many kids in Copenhagen. . . . Italian men are the *nastiest* men on earth! . . . "

"Aw, shut up and eat," her friend said. 27

Across the room, seemingly at a distance, the two Orientals ate their 28 meal in silence, looking only at each other.

The landlady's assistant brought our plates out from the kitchen. She 29 was pale and dumpy, with dull auburn hair done up in a ragged bun. She seemed immune to all of us in the room. She slid two plates onto our table, plunked down a dish of jam, and sashayed back into the kitchen.

"You know," Eunice said, inspecting the food, "it's kind of funny." 30

"What?" I asked. 31

"That a place as sloppy as this can afford to have somebody wake you 32 up for breakfast. This kind of place, the more people miss breakfast, the more food they save."

"You know," I said, after reflecting a moment, "it *is* kind of funny that 33 that little Bulgarian was heading *out* the door when we came down, but stepped back *inside* the second we went out."

Eunice laid down her fork. "It's more than funny," she said. "It's pure- 34 dee suspicious."

"It's more than suspicious," I added. "It could be downright slick." 35

Both of us looked round the room. Everyone was eating. 36

"I been telling you, Leroy," Eunice said. "It's good sense to riff in a 37 place where you don't know the score." She fished the keys from her purse. "Which one of us go'n go up?"

But I had already eased out of my seat and was on my way. In a few 38 seconds I had unlocked the front door and stepped quickly into the hall. Although I ran up the three flights of stairs on tiptoe, the aged boards betrayed my presence. And just as I reached the fourth floor landing, I saw the little blue-suited man backing quickly out the door of the room next to ours. I paused. He turned and smiled at me, shutting the door and giving a theatrical turn to the doorknob. Then he walked calmly over to the linen closet, opened it, and peered inside. At first he frowned in exasperation, then he patted a stack of folded sheets and smiled reassuringly at me. Turning, he waltzed slowly to the stairs and went down. By this time I had opened my own door. Nothing in the room seemed to have been disturbed. I checked our suitcases. Eunice's camera was still there, as were the gifts she had purchased in Paris. But my suspicions were not eased. After locking the door, I rushed down to the breakfast room and directly to the table where the two Orientals were eating their meals. "Ni hau mau?" I said hurriedly. Again they stared at each other, then at me. "Not open?" the one who had the better command of English, the shorter of the two, said to me. He was dressed like his companion, except that his short-sleeved shirt was light green. And he carried a row of pens on a plastic clip in the breast pocket of his shirt.

"I think you had better check your room," I said as slowly as my excitement would allow. "I-think-you-had-better-check-your-room," I repeated even more slowly. "I-just-saw-a-man-com-ing-out-of-it." 39

He screwed up his face. "English is not good to us," he said. "Please to speak more slow." 40

I pointed to my keys and then raised a finger in the direction of the other building. "I-think-your-room-may-have-been-*robbed!*" I said. 41

"*Rob?*" he said. 42

"I saw a man come out of there." 43

"Rob," he repeated slowly to his companion. 44

To avoid seeming to caricature a fine and extremely proud people, I will not attempt to relate the development of their conversation after that point. They consulted extensively across the table in their own language. From their gestures and eye movements I could tell that the discussion included references to me, Eunice, the landlady, the quality of the meal, and the lazy toilet way up on the fourth floor. Then one word of their own language, sounding like "New Sunday," seemed to come suddenly into focus. It bounded back and forth between them across the table. The word excited them, made them anxious, perhaps even angry. The spokesman repeated "New Sunday" to me with sufficient force to make me know that my suspicion had been absorbed, and then run through their own language until it settled around a corresponding thought. "New Sunday—*robbed*," I said in answer, nodding my head. 45

Both of them leaped up from the table and rushed toward the door. Most people in the room turned to look after them. Only after the two had vanished did the tourists turn their eyes on me. I slipped back to where Eunice waited at our table. By this time my eggs had hardened into a thin layer of yellow mush encrusted in bacon fat. I sipped the cup of cold tea and waited. 46

"Leroy, maybe it was a false alarm," Eunice said. 47

"Those Chinese don't think so," I told her. 48

Eunice frowned. "Those aren't Chinese." 49

"Well, they ain't Koreans," I observed. 50

"They're Japanese," Eunice said. "How could you be so dumb?" 51

"How can *you* be so sure?" 52

"All you have to do is *look* at them," Eunice told me. "Japanese are like upper-class people down home. They don't look around much because they *know* who *they* are in relation to everybody else." 53

"Bullshit," I said. "They're Chinese. Whoever saw Japanese without cameras?" 54

"Leroy, you're a black bigot," Eunice told me. "And a *dumb* one at that," she added.

"But not in *public!*" I whispered through my teeth. Over at the next table the young man was watching us intently. But soon he turned back to his companion and her complaints—this time against Etruscan art.

We waited.

In a few minutes the two Orientals came rushing back into the room. The taller one pointed at me and spoke hurriedly to his companion. Then the two of them came over to our table. "Please to say Japanese students are . . . rob in hotel."

"New Sundayed?" I asked.

The young man nodded.

I said I was sorry to hear it.

"You see doorrobber?" He breathed excitedly.

I admitted that both of us had seen the man, although I was careful not to say that to me he seemed to be a Bulgarian.

The taller student spoke to his companion.

"He complains for police," the spokesman translated.

I agreed that should be done. Leaving Eunice at the table gloating pridefully over the sharpness of her insight, I led the two students back into the kitchen. The landlady was scraping bacon fat off the top of her black range. She glanced up at the three of us over her glasses and said, "What you want, love?"

The man in the green shirt, the shorter of the two, attempted to explain; but he seemed unable to muster sufficient English, or sufficient interest on the landlady's part, to make her appreciate how seriously he viewed the situation. While he was speaking, the service lady came in from the breakfast room with a stack of plates. She squeezed past the three of us, further upsetting the student in his recital. "Pity what these blokes does to the language," she muttered.

At this point I interrupted the student with a bow intended to be polite. I explained to the landlady the ploy used in the robbery and a description of the man whom I suspected of the deed. But I did not volunteer my suspicion that he looked to me to be a Bulgarian.

"What was took off you?" the landlady asked the two, and I thought I detected suspicion in her voice. They did not understand, so I translated as best I could, using sign language and the smallest part of pig Latin. Between the three of us it was finally determined that the thief had taken two Eurail passes, two Japanese passports, and about one hundred dollars in traveler's checks drawn on the bank of Tokyo.

"Shssss!" whispered the landlady. "Don't talk so *loud*, love! You want the other guests to hear?" Then she turned to the service lady, who leaned against a cupboard with her thick arms folded, and said, "Think they'd know enough to lock up their valuables." Then she faced the three of us again and said, "We can't be *responsible* for all that, duckies. There's signs on all the doors tellin' you to keep valuables under padlock. Regulations, you know."

Even without understanding fully what had been said, both students 71 seemed to sense they could make more progress into the theft on their own. "Go search doorrobber," the short man said.

The electricity of their excitement sparked into me. As they left the 72 basement I stepped quickly behind them, recalling all the scenes dealing with personal honor I had viewed in Japanese movies. I had the feeling of being part of a posse. As one of the students was unlocking the door, his companion suddenly gave out a shrill cry and jumped several feet in the air. He kept repeating, "*Aa! Aa! Aa!*" and pointed down the street with a quick move-ment of his arm. I looked immediately where he pointed, but did not see the man whom I suspected of being the thief. But the other student looked in the same direction, and what he saw made him shout back to his comrade. Looking again, I saw the cause of their excitement: a rather chubby Oriental man was walking up the street toward us. The two students rushed toward the man. After greeting him, and after a few gestures, the three of them, shouting something that sounded like "Waa Waa! Waa!" swept past me and into the building. The spokesman paused beside me long enough to say, "Please to watch door."

Waiting excitedly on the bottom step, I imagined them searching the 73 building from attic to basement, peering into keyholes, dark stairwells, the johns on each floor, trying doors, linen closets, open windows. I pictured the little Bulgarian cornered in the hall, trying to understand what they could possibly mean when they said in cultured Japanese, "You have dishonored the hospitality of this house. You will please commit hara-kiri." And the little fellow, sneak thief that he was, would echo the countercode: "*Why?* I want to *live!*" I expected to see at any moment the little blue-suited fellow come pumping out the door, his red tie trailing in the wind he made, with the three Japanese in hot pursuit. When Eunice came up from the basement, I urged her to take a long walk around the block. I advised that I anticipated horrors from which her modesty should be protected. But Eunice refused to budge from where she stood on the sidewalk.

"Leroy, you're overreacting," she said. 74

Eunice was right as usual. 75

Instead of three samurai bearing the head of the thief, only the two 76 Japanese students and their newfound tourist ally emerged from the build-ing. They sighed and looked up and down the street, perhaps looking for additional samurai, perhaps looking for bobbies. I sighed, and looked with them. But there was nothing else on the street we could add to our resources. The three conversed among themselves in Japanese, and then the stranger turned to me. "This Japanese salaryman from Osaka," the English-speaking student announced.

"Ni hau ma?" I said, offering my hand as the man bowed smartly. 77

"You are African?" the man asked, smiling pleasantly as we shook. 78 "Nigerian, yes?"

"Woo sh Meei-gworen," I said.

He looked perplexed. "I do not know this tribe," he confessed finally. "But now I must go. They should get the officials to help them," he told me. He turned and made a short statement to the students in Japanese. Then he shook my hand again, bowed smartly to the students, and went on his way up the block.

"What was that foolishness you were talking?" Eunice asked.

The English-speaking student strolled closer to me. He looked deep into my face and said, "All *open* upstair."

"You ought to be horsewhipped for carryin' on such foolishness at a serious time like this," Eunice said.

Of course Eunice was right.

For the second time we crowded into the kitchen to register our complaint with the landlady. "Pipe *down*, love!" she muttered. "We don't want the others to hear, now do we?"

"Why not?" I asked.

She stood with her back against the black gas range. "What can *I* do?"

"Call up the bobbies."

She mumbled some more to herself, gave us a cold stare, then fished around in the pocket of her gray smock and produced a shilling and a few pence for the telephone. As we passed again through the breakfast room, the other tourists stared at us as though we were entertainers employed by the landlady to make the breakfast hour less monotonous. I wondered how many of them had been robbed while they sat leisurely over their bacon and eggs. And I wondered whether the little Bulgarian had anticipated they would have this blind spot.

I glanced at the table Eunice and I had occupied. It had been cleared and another couple, who looked German, now occupied it. They ate in silence and looked only at each other. But at the next table the little brunette was still preaching over cold tea to her companion: "Spain was *so* depressing. The French ignore you in August. Zurich looks like a big computer. Greek men . . ."

We were inside the lobby before I remembered the telephone did not work.

After getting directions from a passerby and advising Eunice to wait outside, lest the Bulgarian should be lurking in our room, the two Japanese and I walked toward a bobby station, said to be about a mile from the hotel. During the walk they managed to communicate to me their names and the outline of their dilemma. The spokesman's name was Toyohiko Kageyama. His tall companion, who apparently knew little English, was Yoshitsune Hashima. I told them to call me Lee. Toyohiko explained that without the traveler's checks, passports and rail passes they could not get to Amsterdam, where their flight back to Japan would depart in a few days. And with the bank holiday in effect, they would not be able to obtain more traveler's checks until Monday, when the banks reopened. Unfortunately, Monday was also the day their flight was to leave Amsterdam.

They talked between themselves in Japanese, working through the problem. They decided that with help from the Japanese embassy they might be able to obtain money for a flight to Amsterdam. But there was still the matter of the missing passports. I did not learn this by listening to their conversation, but through the pains taken by Toyohiko Kageyama to explain the problem to me in English. So far as I could tell, neither of them made any unkind remarks about the thief. Instead, they seemed to have accepted the loss and were working toward solution of the problem it caused. As we talked, Yoshitsune Hashima looked at the two of us, nodding occasional, though hesitant, agreement with whatever Kageyama said to me. But neither one of them smiled.

When we arrived at the bobby station, a bleak little building containing almost no activity, I excused myself and sat in the waiting room while the two Japanese stood at the reception desk and reported the robbery to the desk officer. He was a pale, elderly man with a gray-speckled pencil-line mustache. He listened carefully, occasionally drumming his pen on a report form, while suggesting words to Toyohiko Kageyama. The student had difficulty making the bobby recognize the name of the hotel and the street on which it was located, as well as the items that had been stolen. After many trials and errors by the bobby, Kageyama came over to me. "Please tell," he said.

I went to the desk and reported to the bobby as much as I knew about the robbery. I gave him a description of the man whom I suspected of being the thief, but I did not volunteer my suspicion that to me he seemed to be a Bulgarian. The bobby wrote it all down on a report form, then questioned us again for corroboration. Afterward, he wrote something of his own at the bottom of the form, perhaps a private comment, perhaps his own name. Then the students and I sat in the waiting room, while a pair of bobbies was summoned to accompany us back to the hotel. These were somewhat younger men, although one of them sported the same kind of thin mustache as the bobby at the desk. The other was plump, with tufts of bright red hair showing beneath his tall hat. He had a cold manner that became evident when he motioned us out of the building and into the back seat of their patrol car. The gesture was one of professional annoyance.

During the drive back to the hotel, the students and I were silent, but the two bobbies in the front seat discussed a recent rally of homosexuals in Trafalgar Square.

"What a hellish sight that one was," the redhead observed.

"No doubt," the other said. "No doubt."

"At least five hundred of them parading round like the Queens of Elfin."

"No doubt," said the other. "Any trouble?"

The redhead laughed. "No," he said grimly.

The two Japanese students sat next to each other, their eyes looking past the bobbies and through the windshield of the car. Only I concentrated on the conversation. And after a while, I found myself wondering about how I had come to be driving through the streets of London in the back seat of a bobby car listening to commentary on a rally of homosexuals, when my major purpose in coming over from Paris had been to contact X, that elusive knower of London nightlife, and give him the warm regards of Y and Z, friends of his who lived in Atlanta.

The two bobbies searched the hotel from top to bottom, but they did not find the man. No one else had reported anything missing. The landlady flitted around with a great show of sympathy, explaining to the bobbies that this sort of thing had not happened in her place since the boom in American tourists back in '65. Both bobbies were cool and efficient, asking questions in a manner that suggested their suspicion of everyone and of no one in particular. But the redhead, it seemed to me, was more than probing in his questions concerning the part Eunice and I had played in the drama. He said finally, "There's little else we can do now except get a notice out. You'll have to go over to the station for the Paddington district and make a report there. This isn't our district, you know; so they'll need a bit of a report over there." 103

"People should be careful of these things," the landlady said, wiping her hands on her apron. 104

"It's ten-thirty," Eunice said. "We want to go sightseeing." 105

The redhead smiled cryptically. "He'll have to go along to make a proper description," he advised Eunice. "It would be quite helpful to these two chaps here." 106

"I'm sick and tired of all the running around," Eunice said. 107

The bobby smiled. 108

The two Orientals stood watching all of us. 109

The drive to the other district station was short. The bobbies did not talk more about the rally of homosexuals. They let us out in front of the station and wished us luck. I wished them a happy bank holiday. Inside the station the routine was the same as before: while the students explained their predicament as best they could, I stayed in the waiting room until I was needed. Waiting, I amused myself by studying the wanted posters on the bulletin board hanging between the windows. Walking close to the board for a closer inspection, I saw that four of the seven wanted men were black. Moreover, one of them, a hardcase named Wimberly Lane, priced at fifty pounds and wanted for extortion, looked somewhat familiar. I studied his face. Lane had high cheekbones, prominent eyes, and a dissolute look about him. I looked closer and saw that he resembled, especially in profile, my cousin Freddy Tifton back home in Atlanta. But Lane was a desperado, probably hiding out in the London underworld, and my cousin was a world away in Atlanta, probably at that moment eating fried chicken on Hunter Street. 110

"Please tell about . . . doorrobber," someone said. Toyohiko Kageyama was standing behind me. 111

I turned and followed him back to the desk. This bobby's pale blue eyes   112
flickered over my face. He and another man, a clerk who had obviously been
helping him piece together the story told by the students, glanced quickly at
each other and then back at me. "You saw the alleged robber?" the bobby
asked.

"I did."   113

"Can you describe him?"   114

I gave what I thought was an accurate description. But this time I was   115
sure not to venture my suspicion that he seemed to me to be a Bulgarian.
The bobby wrote with his left hand. He wrote beautiful script with his pen
turned inward toward his wrist. I watched his hands.

The two students stood behind me, one on each side.   116

"Just what is your relation to the complainants?" the bobby asked.   117

"I am an American," I said. "My room is next to theirs."   118

The bobby stopped writing and frowned. "You are the only person who   119
actually *saw* this man, you know?" His eyes narrowed.

"What about it?" I said.   120

"A friend indeed, what?" the clerk said. He looked at the bobby and   121
winked.

The two students stood behind me, conversing between themselves.   122

"Not let's go through this *once* more," the bobby said.   123

Suddenly Yoshitsune Hashima stepped from behind me and up to the   124
desk. "Lee . . . good . . . de*tail*," he said, pointing firmly at me. "Japanese
students . . . take Lee de*tail . . . doorrobber.*"

The bobby stopped smiling and began writing again. He wrote a beau-   125
tiful script.

Yoshitsune Hashima did not speak again.   126

The bobby advised them to go quickly to the Japanese embassy.   127

I wanted to go quickly and see the rest of London.   128

We saw the two students again in the late afternoon at Madame Tus-   129
saud's. Eunice and I had wandered down into one of the lower chambers
with exhibits commemorating the French Revolution. When I saw them I
was standing beside a rusty guillotine that had been used to behead Marie
Antoinette. The Japanese were standing together, peering into a lighted
showcase containing wax replicas of famous murderers who had once plagued
London. I motioned to Eunice, then walked over and touched Kageyama on
the shoulder. He started, as if intruded upon too much by the mood of the
place. But when they saw who we were, both of them smiled nervously and
bowed. Toyohiko Kageyama reported that the Japanese embassy had secured
temporary passports for them, had ordered the checks cancelled, and had
lent them enough money for living expenses and a flight to Amsterdam. Now
that business had been taken care of, they were seeing the sights of London.
Both of them thanked us for our help. Kageyama in English and Hashima in
Japanese. Both of them bowed politely. Then Yoshitsune Hashima pulled a
notebook from the pocket of his trousers, leafed through it to a certain page,

and read in a slow voice, "Please-to-give-Japanese-students-name-and-house-number."

I wrote them for him. 130

Yoshitsune Hashima accepted back the notebook, leafed through several 131 more pages, and read in an uncertain voice: "I thank you kindness at New Sunday to help Japanese students. . . . I hope Lee visit Nihon one day. . . . Please visit home of Yoshitsune Hashima in suburb of Tokyo."

Then he handed me a packet of Japanese stamps. 132

The two of them bowed again. 133

"You see?" Eunice said, as we walked away. "The Japanese ain't nothing 134 but part-time Southerners."

I had to concede that once again Eunice was right. 135

But it was too dark inside the wax museum. The colored lights shining 136 on the exhibits did not improve the mood of the place. "Let's get out," I said to Eunice.

Toward dusk we stood in a crowd of tourists on a green outside the 137 Tower of London. We had spent about ten minutes inside the tower. Before us on the green was an old man, encased in a white sack crisscrossed with chains and padlocks. He wriggled and moaned inside the sack while the crowd laughed. Standing beside him was a muscular, bald-headed man who beat himself on the naked chest with a sledge-hammer. In certain respects this man resembled the thief, but he not at all resembled a Bulgarian. From time to time this strong man marched with a tin cup around the inside of the circle, holding it out to onlookers. He collected pence and shillings from some of those standing closest to the recreation. He said things like, "Me old daddy left near a thousand pound when he died; but I ain't yet found out where he left it." When the crowd laughed, he laughed with them. But he cursed those who put slugs and very small change in his cup. He seemed to be a foreigner, but he spoke with the accents of the British lower class. "A man 'as got to live!" he shouted at us while rattling the cup. "The old man there can't get out the sack till you pay up."

"Leroy," Eunice said beside me. "I don't think X will ever call. Now 138 that we've seen London, let's please go home."

As usual, Eunice was right. 139

STUDY QUESTIONS

1. If you only knew Americans from those in the breakfast room, what would your impressions of Americans be? What do Leroy and Eunice become suspicious of at breakfast? Why? What does Eunice mean when she says that it is "good sense to riff in a place where you don't know the score" (paragraph 37)?

2. What is the first indication you have of the ethnic identity of Leroy and Eunice? Does that make you reevaluate in any way what has gone before in the story? Does it change your anticipation of what is to come?

3. Explain the title of the story. Why does the NARRATOR, long after he recognizes that the two students are not Chinese, continue to use the only Mandarin phrases he knows?

4. Why does the narrator insist, repeatedly, that Eunice is right? About what in particular is Eunice always right? Why does the narrator keep repressing his conclusion that the burglar is Bulgarian? On what different STEREOTYPES of behavior does the plot depend?

5. Why does the story put so much emphasis on people watching other people? How self-conscious is the narrator about his observations of others? How conscious is he that he moves toward national stereotypes based on his observations? Explain the force of the policemen's suspicion about him.

6. How fully does the narrator ultimately communicate with the Japanese students? When words fail, what other kinds of language do the three men use? What eye, face, and body gestures reinforce the meanings of the words they speak?

7. In how many different situations does the narrator have difficulty communicating with other people who speak English? What are the sources of difficulty? What CONVENTIONS of language are illuminated by the miscommunications with X? Is the narrator more comfortable speaking to the Japanese students than to other native speakers of English? If so, why?

8. Explain the IRONY of the service lady's observation "Pity what these blokes does to the language" (paragraph 67).

9. Explain the irony that the PLOT turns on unexpected behavior, given the fact that stereotypical behavior is under examination throughout the story.

Salli Benedict

Salli Benedict (Kawennotakie) is director of the Akwesasne Museum on the reserve of the Mohawk Nation in upstate New York.

＊

TAHOTAHONTANEKENT-SERATKERONTAKWENHAKIE

Deep in the woods, there lived a man and his wife, and their newborn baby boy. The baby was so young that his parents had not yet given him a name.

Hunting was very bad that winter and they had very little to eat. They were very poor.

One day around suppertime, a little old man came to their door. He was selling rabbits. 2

"Do you wish to buy a rabbit for your supper?" he asked. 3

The woman who met him at the door replied that they were very poor and had no money to buy anything. 4

It was growing dark and the man looked very tired. The woman knew that he had travelled very far just to see if they would buy a rabbit from him. She invited him to stay for supper and share what little they had to eat. 5

"What is your name?" the husband asked as he got up to meet the old man. 6

"I have no name," the little man replied. "My parents were lost before they could name me. People just call me Tahotahontanekentseratkerontakwenhakie which means, 'He came and sold rabbits.' " 7

The husband laughed. "My son has not been named yet either. We just call him The Baby." 8

The old man said, "You should name him so that he will know who he is. There is great importance in a name." The old man continued, "I will give you this last rabbit of mine for a good supper, so that we may feast in honor of the birth of your new son." 9

In the morning, the old man left. The parents of the baby still pondered over a name for the baby. 10

"We shall name the baby after the generous old man who gave him a feast in honor of his birth. But he has no name," the mother said. 11

"Still, we must honor his gift to our son," the husband replied. "We will name our son after what people call the old man, Tahotahontanekentseratkerontakwenhakie which means, 'He came and sold rabbits.' " 12

"What a long name that is," the mother said. "Still, we must honor the old man's wish for a name for our son and his feast for our son." 13

So the baby's name became Tahotahontanekentseratkerontakwenhakie which means, "He came and sold rabbits," in honor of the old man. 14

The baby boy grew older and became very smart. He had to be, to be able to remember his own name. Like all other children he was always trying to avoid work. He discovered that by the time his mother had finished calling his name for chores, he could be far, far away. 15

Sometimes his mother would begin telling him something to do, "Tahotahontanekentseratkerontakwenhakie . . . hmmmm . . ." She would forget what she wanted to have him do, so she would smile and tell him to go and play. 16

Having such a long important name had its disadvantages too. When his family travelled to other settlements to visit friends and other children, the other children would leave him out of games. They would not call him to play or catch ball. They said that it took more energy to say his name than it did to play the games. 17

News of this long, strange name travelled to the ears of the old man, 18
Tahotahontanekentseratkerontakwenhakie. "What a burden this name must
be for a child," the old man thought. "This name came in gratitude for my
feast for the birth of the boy. I must return to visit them."

The old man travelled far to the family of his namesake, Tahotahonta- 19
nekentseratkerontakwenhakie. The parents met the old man at the door and
invited him in. He brought with him food for another fine meal.

"You are very gracious to honor me with this namesake," he said. "But 20
we should not have two people wandering this world, at the same time, with
the same name. People will get us confused, and it may spoil my business.
Let us call your son Oiasosonaion which means, 'He has another name.' If
people wish to know his other name, then he can tell them."

Oiasosonaion smiled and said, "I will now have to call you Tahotahon- 21
tanekentseratkerontakwenhakie tanon Oiasahosonnon which means, 'He came
and sold rabbits and gave the boy another name.' "

Everyone laughed. 22

STUDY QUESTIONS

1. What do you think the point of the story is? Is the story an ALLEGORY? a FABLE? a
   PARABLE? a fairy tale? Can you think of a more appropriate label to describe the
   story's mode?

2. What does the story imply about the importance of names? What is the significance
   of the lack of names for the little man and the baby at the story's beginning? In
   what ways are the names invented here like "real" names in English or in another
   language you know? What traditions of naming are suggested by the process of
   naming depicted here?

3. Describe the TONE of the story. In what places is the story funny? Against whom
   is the laughter at the end directed? Are the poor people without names ever made
   fun of?

G. S. Sharat Chandra

Born in Mysore, India, G. S. Sharat Chandra has been living in America since
the early 1960s. Educated to be a lawyer, he gave up law to attend the University of Iowa Writers' Workshop, where he obtained an M.F.A. A biculturalist, he
has always written in English and his books are published in England, India, and the
United States. His books are *Heirloom* (1982), *Immigrants of Loss* (1993), and *Family of
Mirrors* (1993). He lives in Overland Park, Kansas.

STILL KICKING IN AMERICA

Nothing changes in America
for Asians who write in English.
Now that I'm older,
the old ones ask
the same questions   5
the young ones asked
when I was younger.
Where did you learn such good English?
A Polish wife of a travelling professor
dangles her earrings vehemently,   10
lifts the hem of her dainty skirt
to show me thighs that withstood
long lines, dictators,
before she kicked them for good.

Kicking a country   15
with such strong legs
is some kind of victory.
I look at my own
vegetarian calves,
so starved and tubular   20
even Gandhi[1] would be ashamed.
But these are calves
that never kicked anyone
but their owner
in dreams or desperation,   25
hoping for words
to come out right in English.

STUDY QUESTIONS

1. Explain "before she kicked them for good" (line 14).

2. Why are the SPEAKER's calves described as "vegetarian"?

3. What does kicking have to do with language?

4. What is the relation between the question in line 8 and the final sentence of the poem (lines 22–27)?

1. Mohandas Karamchand (Mahatma) Gandhi (1869–1948). Well-known leader of the Indian nationalist movement against British rule and esteemed for his doctrine of nonviolent protest, which included self-imposed fasts, he had notoriously skinny legs.

Gustavo Perez-Firmat

Born in Cuba in 1950, Gustavo Perez-Firmat was educated at Miami-Dade Community College, the University of Miami, and the University of Michigan where he received a Ph.D. in 1979. He currently teaches at Duke University. His books of poetry include *Carolina Cuban* (1987) and *Equivocaciones* (1989), and his literary scholarship includes *Literature and Liminality* (1986) and *The Cuban Condition: Translation and Identity in Modern Cuban Literature* (1989).

LIMEN

We took David back up just when
he was beginning to learn to speak,
to say agua[1] and mamá and galletica.[2]
(Miami es mar y calor y comida.)[3]
Just when he was on the threshold,   5
at the limen,
perinatal to his past, to me,
we delivered him to y'alls and drawls,
to some place I've never lived in all these years
I have been living there.   10
(My words are also agua and mamá and galletica
and a few improper names like El Farito,[4]
Chirino,[5] and Dadeland,[6] which is not English
now though it used to be.)
Just as David was beginning to learn to say   15
the language I breathe in,
we moved him up and inland away

1. Water.
2. Small biscuit or cookie.
3. "Miami is ocean and heat and food."
4. Lighthouse on Key Biscayne in Miami.
5. Willie Chirino, popular Cuban singer.
6. Shopping mall, and its surrounding neighborhood, in southern Miami.

from warmth and water,
knotting his tongue—my tongue—with distance.

STUDY QUESTIONS

1. What is the effect of using such relatively rare English words as "limen" and "perinatal"? of using Spanish words? of "Dadeland" that is "not English / now though it used to be" (lines 13–14)? Why does he call El Farito and Chirino "improper names"?

2. Where was it that David began to learn to speak? Where is the family moving? We can see why the move will "knot" David's tongue, but why will it have a similar effect on the SPEAKER?

Lorna Dee Cervantes

Born in San Francisco in 1954, Lorna Dee Cervantes is of Mexican descent. She has published two books of poems, *Emplumada* (1981) and *From the Cables of Genocide: Poems on Love and Hunger* (1991). She was educated at San Jose City College and San Jose State University and is the founder of Mango Publications, a small press that publishes books and a literary magazine. She currently teaches creative writing at the University of Colorado at Boulder.

REFUGEE SHIP

like wet cornstarch
I slide past *mi abuelita's*[1] eyes
bible placed by her side
she removes her glasses
the pudding thickens   5

mamá raised me with no language
I am an orphan to my spanish name
the words are foreign, stumbling on my tongue
I stare at my reflection in the mirror
brown skin, black hair   10

---

1. My grandmother's.

I feel I am a captive
aboard the refugee ship
a ship that will never dock
a ship that will never dock

STUDY QUESTIONS

1. What does it mean to be "an orphan to my spanish name" (line 7)? to be "a captive / aboard the refugee ship" (lines 11–12)?

2. Explain the "cornstarch" image in line 1. What does the fifth line mean?

3. What is the source of the SPEAKER's alienation? Why will the ship "never dock" (lines 13–14)?

4. What does the reflection in the mirror (lines 9–10) mean? Explain the meaning of the objects in lines 3 and 4.

Rita Dove

Rita Dove, born in 1952 in Akron, Ohio, is from a family that replicated the mythic migration of Southern blacks to the North. She is a *summa cum laude* graduate of Miami University (Ohio), holds an M.F.A. from the University of Iowa Writers' Workshop, and was a Fulbright Fellow at the University of Tübingen, Germany. She has been both a Guggenheim Fellow and a Fellow of the National Endowment for the Arts, and she now teaches at the University of Virginia. Her books include *The Yellow House on the Corner* (1980), *Museum* (1983), *Thomas and Beulah* (1986), for which she won the Pulitzer Prize, and *Grace Notes* (1989). Dove has also published two works of fiction, *Fifth Sunday* (1985) and *Through the Ivory Gates: A Novel* (1992).

PARSLEY[1]

1. The Cane Fields

There is a parrot imitating spring
in the palace, its feathers parsley green.
Out of the swamp the cane appears

---

1. On October 2, 1957, Rafael Trujillo (1891–1961), dictator of the Dominican Republic, ordered 20,000 blacks killed because they could not pronounce the letter "r" in *perejil*, the Spanish word for parsley. [Author's note]

to haunt us, and we cut it down. El General
searches for a word; he is all the world
there is. Like a parrot imitating spring,

we lie down screaming as rain punches through
and we come up green. We cannot speak an R—
out of the swamp, the cane appears

and then the mountain we call in whispers *Katalina*.[2]
The children gnaw their teeth to arrowheads.
There is a parrot imitating spring.

El General has found his word: *perejil*.
Who says it, lives. He laughs, teeth shining
out of the swamp. The cane appears

in our dreams, lashed by wind and streaming.
And we lie down. For every drop of blood
there is a parrot imitating spring.
Out of the swamp the cane appears.

2. The Palace
The word the general's chosen is parsley.
It is fall, when thoughts turn
to love and death; the general thinks
of his mother, how she died in the fall
and he planted her walking cane at the grave
and it flowered, each spring stolidly forming
four-star blossoms. The general

pulls on his boots, he stomps to
her room in the palace, the one without
curtains, the one with a parrot
in a brass ring. As he paces he wonders
Who can I kill today. And for a moment
the little knot of screams
is still. The parrot, who has traveled

all the way from Australia in an ivory
cage, is, coy as a widow, practising
spring. Ever since the morning
his mother collapsed in the kitchen
while baking skull-shaped candies

2. I.e., "Katarina."

for the Day of the Dead,[3] the general
has hated sweets. He orders pastries   40
brought up for the bird; they arrive

dusted with sugar on a bed of lace.
The knot in his throat starts to twitch;
he sees his boots the first day in battle
splashed with mud and urine   45
as a soldier falls at his feet amazed—
how stupid he looked!—at the sound
of artillery. *I never thought it would sing*
the soldier said, and died. Now

the general sees the fields of sugar   50
cane, lashed by rain and streaming.
He sees his mother's smile, the teeth
gnawed to arrowheads. He hears
the Haitians sing without R's
as they swing the great machetes: 55
Katalina, they sing, *Katalina*,

mi madle, mi amol en muelte.[4] God knows
his mother was no stupid woman; she
could roll an R like a queen. Even
a parrot can roll an R! In the bare room   60
the bright feathers arch in a parody
of greenery, as the last pale crumbs
disappear under the blackened tongue. Someone

calls out his name in a voice
so like his mother's, a startled tear   65
splashes the tip of his right boot.
My mother, my love in death.
The general remembers the tiny green sprigs
men of his village wore in their capes
to honor the birth of a son. He will   70
order many, this time, to be killed

for a single, beautiful word.

STUDY QUESTIONS

1. Why is "El General" said to be "all the world / there is" (lines 5–6)? Why does he
keep a parrot in the palace? Why does the parrot imitate spring?

3. All Souls' Day, November 1.
4. See line 67 for a translation.

2. What does the general's hatred of sweets (line 40) have to do with "The Cane Fields" section? How much do we know about the general? What details are especially important in CHARACTERIZING him?

3. How important to the poem's TONE are the greenness and lush tropical setting? Beyond the contrast between the fields and the palace, what other sharp contrasts does the poem contain? Why are the parrot's feathers said to be "a parody / of greenery" (lines 61–62)?

4. What effects are produced by the repeated contrasts between beauty and ugliness?

5. Why are the "we," juxtaposed with "he" in the first section of the poem, not mentioned explicitly in the second section? Why are the repeated, ritualistic phrases used in the first section? How is the second section of the poem structured?

6. Beyond the inability of the blacks to pronounce *r*'s, in what other ways is language important to the poem?

Louise Erdrich

Louise Erdrich is of Chippewa and German-American descent; she grew up in North Dakota and now lives in New Hampshire with her husband and five children. Her best-known novel, *Love Medicine* (1984), won the National Book Critics Circle Award and was a national bestseller. It was followed by *The Beet Queen* (1986) and *Tracks* (1988). Although primarily known as a novelist and story writer, she is also a poet of distinction. Her poetry has been collected in *Jacklight* (1984) and *Baptism of Desire* (1989).

JACKLIGHT

The same Chippewa word is used both for flirting and hunting game, while another Chippewa word connotes both using force in intercourse and also killing a bear with one's bare hands.

—DUNNING 1959

We have come to the edge of the woods,
out of brown grass where we slept, unseen,
out of knotted twigs, out of leaves creaked shut,
out of hiding.

At first the light wavered, glancing over us.   5
Then it clenched to a fist of light that pointed,
searched out, divided us.
Each took the beams like direct blows the heart answers.
Each of us moved forward alone.

We have come to the edge of the woods,   10
drawn out of ourselves by this night sun,
this battery of polarized acids,
that outshines the moon.

We smell them behind it
but they are faceless, invisible.   15
We smell the raw steel of their gun barrels,
mink oil on leather, their tongues of sour barley.
We smell their mother buried chin-deep in wet dirt.

We smell their fathers with scoured knuckles,
teeth cracked from hot marrow.   20
We smell their sisters of crushed dogwood, bruised apples,
of fractured cups and concussions of burnt hooks.

We smell their breath steaming lightly behind the jacklight.
We smell the itch underneath the caked guts on their clothes.
We smell their minds like silver hammers   25
cocked back, held in readiness
for the first of us to step into the open.

We have come to the edge of the woods,
out of brown grass where we slept, unseen,
out of leaves creaked shut, out of our hiding.   30
We have come here too long.

It is their turn now,
their turn to follow us. Listen,
they put down their equipment.
It is useless in the tall brush.   35
And now they take the first steps, not knowing
how deep the woods are and lightless.
How deep the woods are.

STUDY QUESTIONS

1. What is "jacklight"? Who are "we"? Who are "they"? How does the poem make
   the differences between the two groups clear?

2. What do the woods represent to the SPEAKER and companion? What are the others afraid of? What sort of threat do the others represent? How is the threat represented in the poem's images?

3. What does the EPIGRAPH of the poem mean? How does it relate to the body of the poem?

Li-Young Lee

Li-Young Lee was born in 1957 in Jakarta, Indonesia, to Chinese parents "who were classically educated and in the habit of reciting literally hundreds of ancient Chinese poems." His father was jailed by then-dictator Sukarno for nineteen months, seventeen of them in a leper colony. After his escape, the family fled from country to country, and then settled in western Pennsylvania, where his father became a Presbyterian minister. Lee has published two volumes of poems, *Rose* (1986) and *The City in Which I Love You: Poems* (1990). "I . . . believe the King James Bible to contain some of the greatest poetry in the world," he says, "and I hope to own some of its simplicity, glory, and mystery in my own writing one day."

PERSIMMONS

In sixth grade Mrs. Walker
slapped the back of my head
and made me stand in the corner
for not knowing the difference
between *persimmon* and *precision*.   5
How to choose

persimmons. This is precision.
Ripe ones are soft and brown-spotted.
Sniff the bottoms. The sweet one
will be fragrant. How to eat: 10
put the knife away, lay down newspaper.
Peel the skin tenderly, not to tear the meat.
Chew the skin, suck it,
and swallow. Now, eat

the meat of the fruit,   15
so sweet,
all of it, to the heart.

Donna undresses, her stomach is white.
In the yard, dewy and shivering
with crickets, we lie naked,   20
face-up, face-down.
I teach her Chinese.
Crickets: *chiu chiu.* Dew: I've forgotten.
Naked: I've forgotten.
Ni, wo: you and me.   25
I part her legs,
remember to tell her
she is beautiful as the moon.

Other words
that got me into trouble were   30
fight and *fright, wren* and *yarn.*
Fight was what I did when I was frightened,
fright was what I felt when I was fighting.
Wrens are small, plain birds,
yarn is what one knits with.   35
Wrens are soft as yarn.
My mother made birds out of yarn.
I loved to watch her tie the stuff;
a bird, a rabbit, a wee man.

Mrs. Walker brought a persimmon to class   40
and cut it up
so everyone could taste
a *Chinese apple.* Knowing
it wasn't ripe or sweet, I didn't eat
but watched the other faces.   45

My mother said every persimmon has a sun
inside, something golden, glowing,
warm as my face.

Once, in the cellar, I found two wrapped in newspaper,
forgotten and not yet ripe.   50
I took them and set both on my bedroom windowsill,
where each morning a cardinal
sang, *The sun, the sun.*

Finally understanding
he was going blind,   55
my father sat up all one night
waiting for a song, a ghost.
I gave him the persimmons,
swelled, heavy as sadness,
and sweet as love.   60

This year, in the muddy lighting
of my parents' cellar, I rummage, looking
for something I lost.
My father sits on the tired, wooden stairs,
black cane between his knees,   65
hand over hand, gripping the handle.

He's so happy that I've come home.
I ask how his eyes are, a stupid question.
All gone, he answers.

Under some blankets, I find a box.   70
Inside the box I find three scrolls.
I sit beside him and untie
three paintings by my father:
Hibiscus leaf and a white flower.
Two cats preening.   75
Two persimmons, so full they want to drop from the cloth.

He raises both hands to touch the cloth,
asks, *Which is this?*

This is persimmons, Father.

Oh, the feel of the wolftail on the silk,   80
the strength, the tense
precision in the wrist.
I painted them hundreds of times
eyes closed. These I painted blind.
Some things never leave a person: 85
scent of the hair of one you love,
the texture of persimmons,
in your palm, the ripe weight.

STUDY QUESTIONS

1. What different things do persimmons represent to the SPEAKER? What different characteristics of persimmons does the poem mention? What is the significance of each to the effect of the poem?

2. How much do we know about Mrs. Walker? What is ironic about her punishment of the speaker? What does she not know about persimmons? Why does the speaker watch the other faces when the persimmon is cut up? What other instances are there in the poem of watching reactions? Why is the THEME of being a spectator appropriate to the total poem?

3. What different voices are heard in the poem? What different languages does the poem record? In what different ways are the responses of one person communicated to another? How does the cardinal's song relate to the issue of communication? How is the sight of the cardinal related to other central objects in the poem?

4. How are the various CHARACTERS in the poem—Mrs. Walker, Donna, the father, and the speaker—related to the central themes of the poem?

Ricardo Pau-Llosa

Art historian, curator, poet, and English teacher, Ricardo Pau-Llosa was born in Cuba in 1954 and came to the United States in 1960. He was educated at Miami-Dade Community College (where he currently teaches), Florida International University, Florida Atlantic University, and the University of Florida. His first book of poetry, *Sorting Metaphors* (1983), won the national Anhinga Poetry Prize; his latest collection of poetry, *Bread of the Imagined*, was published in 1991. Pau-Llosa has also published scholarship on art.

FOREIGN LANGUAGE

Every object is a room
you walk words into.
Take an apple, its windows peeling.
In your hands the apple's
door opens a crack
and the words barge through   5

like salesmen confident of a kill.
The gerund opens the mail,
the verb's hands rumble through
the refrigerator, an adverb   10
caresses the daughter's knee,
the noun, its feet on the sofa,
says everything is as it should be.
Teeth tear through the walls of the apple
like a plane crashing in the suburbs.   15
The mouth is full of a wet white word
you can't pronounce, a pronoun quietly
reading the newspaper in the living room
When you bit, you never knew what hit you.

STUDY QUESTIONS

1. What are the "windows" of an apple? its "door"? Are the words barging from inside the apple out or from the outside in? What is the "wet white word" (line 16) that filled your mouth when you bit into the apple?

2. The parts of speech (including the gerund) are used as figures of speech, more or less personified. Describe what each figures forth or "pictures"; how is the function of the part of speech related to the picture or IMAGE?

3. Notice that the title is "Foreign Language." How would the relation of objects to language differ in your native language?

Nora Dauenhauer

A native Alaskan, Nora Dauenhauer comes from a family of noted carvers and beadwork artists. She is a linguist and author of instructional materials in her own native language, Tlingit. A collection of her poems, *The Droning Shaman*, was published in 1988.

TLINGIT CONCRETE POEM

```
                              t ' a   n
                            a               i
                          a   k
                  x ' a a x ' x ' a a x ' x ' a a x ' x ' a a x ' x ' a a x
                  a a x ' x ' a a x ' x ' a a x ' x ' a a x ' x ' a a x ' x ' a a x ' x
                ' x ' a a x ' x ' a a x ' x ' a a x ' x ' a a x ' x ' a a x ' x ' a a x ' x ' a
              x ' x ' a a x ' x ' a a x ' x ' a a x ' x ' a a x ' x ' a a x ' x ' a a x ' x ' a a x
              a a x ' x ' a a x ' x ' a a x ' x ' a a x ' x ' a a x ' x ' a a x ' x ' a a x ' x ' a a x '
            ' a a x ' x ' a a x ' x ' a a x ' x ' a a x ' x ' a a x ' x ' a a x ' x ' a a x ' x ' a a x ' x
          x ' a a x ' x ' a a x ' x ' a a x ' x ' a a x ' x ' a a x ' x ' a a x ' x ' a a x ' x ' a a x ' x '
          ' x ' a a x ' x ' a a x ' x ' a a x ' x ' a a x ' x ' a a x ' x ' a a x ' x ' a a x ' x ' a a x ' x '
          ' x ' a a x ' x ' a a x ' x ' a a x ' x ' a a x ' x ' a a x ' x ' a a x ' x ' a a x ' x ' a a x ' x ' a
          ' x ' a a x ' x ' a a x ' x ' a a x ' x ' a a x ' x ' a a x ' x ' a a x ' x ' a a x ' x ' a a x ' x ' a
        x ' x ' a a x ' x ' a a x ' x ' a a x ' x ' a a x ' x ' a a x ' x ' a a x ' x ' a a x ' x ' a a x ' x ' a
        x ' x ' a a x ' x ' a a x ' x ' a a x ' x ' a a x ' x ' a a x ' x ' a a x ' x ' a a x ' x ' a a x ' x ' a
        x ' x ' a a x ' x ' a a x ' x ' a a x ' x ' a a x ' x ' a a x ' x ' a a x ' x ' a a x ' x ' a a x ' x ' a
        x ' x ' a a x ' x ' a a x ' x ' a a x ' x ' a a x ' x ' a a x ' x ' a a x ' x ' a a x ' x ' a a x ' x ' a
          ' x ' a a x ' x ' a a x ' x ' a a x ' x ' a a x ' x ' a a x ' x ' a a x ' x ' a a x ' x ' a a x ' x ' a
          ' x ' a a x ' x ' a a x ' x ' a a x ' x ' a a x ' x ' a a x ' x ' a a x ' x ' a a x ' x ' a a x ' x '
          ' x ' a a x ' x ' a a x ' x ' a a x ' x ' a a x ' x ' a a x ' x ' a a x ' x ' a a x ' x ' a a x ' x '
          x ' a a x ' x ' a a x ' x ' a a x ' x ' a a x ' x ' a a x ' x ' a a x ' x ' a a x ' x ' a a x ' x '
            ' a a x ' x ' a a x ' x ' a a x ' x ' a a x ' x ' a a x ' x ' a a x ' x ' a a x ' x ' a a x ' x
            ' a a x ' x ' a a x ' x ' a a x ' x ' a a x ' x ' a a x ' x ' a a x ' x ' a a x ' x ' a a x '
            a a x ' x ' a a x ' x ' a a x ' x ' a a x ' x ' a a x ' tl ' u k w x̱ ' a a x ' x ' a a x '
              a x ' x ' a a x ' x ' a a x ' x ' a a x ' x ' a a x ' x ' a a x ' x ' a a x ' x ' a a x
              x ' x ' a a x   x ' a a x ' x ' a a x ' x ' a a x ' x ' a a x ' x ' a a x ' x ' a a
                ' x ' a a x ' x ' a a x ' x ' a a x ' x ' a a x ' x ' a a x ' x ' a a x ' x ' a
                  ' a a x ' x ' a a x ' x ' a a x ' x ' a a x ' x ' a a x ' x ' a a x ' x
                    a x ' x ' a a x ' x ' a a x ' x ' a a x ' x ' a a x ' x ' a a x
                      ' x ' a a x ' x ' a a x ' x ' a a x ' x ' a a x ' x ' a
                        ' a a x ' x ' a a x ' x ' a a x ' x ' a a x ' x '
                          ' x ' a a x ' x ' a a x ' x ' a a
                            ' x ' a a
```

Akat'ani = stem
x'aax' = apple
tl'ukwx̱ = worm

STUDY QUESTIONS

1. How long did it take you to spot the worm? Do you need to know anything about the Tlingit language to "understand" this poem? what do you think it "MEANS"?

2. Would the poem have a different effect if it were composed in a different language? What traditional meanings of apples seem to be alluded to in the poem? What traditions do they come from?

3. Describe the emotional effect the poem has on you. Does its effect have anything to do with its linguistic tradition? its visual appearance? religious beliefs? MYTH?

Linda Hogan

Linda Hogan, a Chickasaw, was born in Denver in 1947, grew up in Oklahoma, and earned an M.A. in English and creative writing from the University of Colorado where she now teaches creative writing. She has published several books of poems, including *Calling Myself Home; Daughters, I Love You; Eclipse; That House;* and *Seeing Through the Sun* (which won the 1986 American Book Award from the Before Columbus Foundation). Her first novel, *Mean Spirit,* appeared in 1989.

SONG FOR MY NAME

Before sunrise
think of brushing out an old woman's
dark braids.
Think of your hands,
fingertips on the soft hair.   5

If you have this name,
your grandfather's dark hands
lead horses toward the wagon
and a cloud of dust follows,
ghost of silence.   10

That name is full of women
with black hair
and men with eyes like night.
It means no money
tomorrow.   15

Such a name my mother loves
while she works gently
in the small house.
She is a white dove
and in her own land   20

mornings are pale,
birds sing into the white curtains
and show off their soft breasts.

If you have a name like this,
there's never enough water.   25
There is too much heat.
When lightning strikes, rain
refuses to follow.
It's my name,
that of a woman living   30
between the white moon
and the red sun, waiting to leave.
It's the name that goes with me
back to earth
no one else can touch.   35

STUDY QUESTIONS

1. List all of the things the SPEAKER's name means. What emotions does it provoke in those who have it? What sensuous experiences does it suggest? What history does it seem to have?

2. How much do we know about the poem's speaker? Why do you think the speaker does not give more direct information about herself? How do you know that the speaker in the poem is a woman?

3. What aspects of heritage seem attached to the name? What does the name mean to the speaker? Why does the speaker refuse to say what the name is?

Derek Walcott

Born in San Lucia in 1930, poet and playwright Derek Walcott attended the University of the West Indies in Jamaica. He has taught at Howard, Columbia, Yale, and Rutgers universities and is currently teaching at Boston University. Walcott is the author of more than a dozen books of poetry, the latest of which is *Omeros* (1989), as well as several plays. He has won many accolades for his writing, including a McArthur Foundation Award and the Queen Elizabeth II Gold Medal for Poetry in 1988. In 1992, Walcott was awarded the Nobel Prize in Literature.

A FAR CRY FROM AFRICA

A wind is ruffling the tawny pelt
Of Africa. Kikuyu,[1] quick as flies,
Batten upon the bloodstreams of the veldt.[2]
Corpses are scattered through a paradise.
Only the worm, colonel of carrion, cries: 5
"Waste no compassion on these separate dead!"
Statistics justify and scholars seize
The salients of colonial policy.
What is that to the white child hacked in bed?
To savages, expendable as Jews?   10

Threshed out by beaters,[3] the long rushes break
In a white dust of ibises whose cries
Have wheeled since civilization's dawn
From the parched river or beast-teeming plain.
The violence of beast on beast is read   15
As natural law, but upright man
Seeks his divinity by inflicting pain.
Delirious as these worried beasts, his wars
Dance to the tightened carcass of a drum,
While he calls courage still that native dread   20
Of the white peace contracted by the dead.

Again brutish necessity wipes its hands
Upon the napkin of a dirty cause, again
A waste of our compassion, as with Spain,[4]
The gorilla wrestles with the superman.   25
I who am poisoned with the blood of both,
Where shall I turn, divided to the vein?
I who have cursed
The drunken officer of British rule, how choose
Between this Africa and the English tongue I love?   30
Betray them both, or give back what they give?
How can I face such slaughter and be cool?
How can I turn from Africa and live?

1. An East African tribe whose members, as Mau Mau fighters, conducted an 8-year terrorist campaign against British colonial settlers in Kenya.

2. Open country, neither cultivated nor forest (Afrikaans).

3. In big game hunting, natives are hired to beat the brush, driving birds—such as ibises—and animals into the open.

4. The Spanish Civil War (1936–39), in which the Loyalists were supported by liberals in the West and militarily by Soviet Communists, and the rebels by Nazi Germany and Fascist Italy.

STUDY QUESTIONS

1. Look up such words as "salients" in line 8 and "worried" in line 18 as examples of the precision of Walcott's language. What do you learn from such an exercise about the meaning and effect of the poem that you did not understand when you first read it?

2. Explain the phrases "expendable as Jews" (line 10), "tightened carcass of a drum" (line 19) and the title (why "Far"? why the "Cry"?).

3. List the direct and indirect references to animals, birds, insects. How do these references function in terms of SETTING? THEME?

4. Whose side is Walcott on?

Israel Horovitz

Born in Wakefield, Massachusetts, in 1939, Israel Horovitz was educated at the Royal Academy of Dramatic Art in London, the New School for Social Research, and the City University of New York. He has been playwright-in-residence with the Royal Shakespeare Company, has won an Obie and a Grammy, and has been a Rockefeller, National Endowment for the Arts, Fulbright, and Guggenheim Fellow. He has written more than fifty plays for stage, screen, and television. *The Indian Wants the Bronx* was first produced off Broadway in 1968, ran for 177 performances, and won three Obie Awards.

THE INDIAN WANTS THE BRONX

CHARACTERS

GUPTA, *an East Indian*
MURPH
JOEY

 Place: A bus stop on upper Fifth Avenue in New York City.
 Time: A chilly September's night.
  As the curtains open the lights fade up, revealing GUPTA, *an East Indian. He is standing alone, right of center stage, near a bus stop sign. An outdoor telephone booth is to his left; several city-owned litter baskets are to his right.*

GUPTA *is in his early fifties. Although he is swarthy in complexion, he is anything but sinister. He is, in fact, meek and visibly frightened by the city.*

He is dressed in traditional East Indian garb, appropriately for mid-September.

As GUPTA *strains to look for a bus on the horizon, the voices of two boys can be heard in the distance, singing. They sing a rock-'n'-roll song, flatly, trying to harmonize.*

[FIRST BOY]
I walk the lonely streets at night,
A-lookin' for your door,
I look and look and look and look,
But, baby, you don't care.
Baby, you don't care.
Baby, no one cares.

SECOND BOY: [*Interrupting.*] Wait a minute, Joey. I'll take the harmony. Listen.

[*Singing.*]
But, baby, you don't care.
Baby, you don't care.
Baby, no one cares.

[*Confident that he has fully captured the correct harmony, boasting.*] See? I've got a knack for harmony. You take the low part.

[BOYS *sing together.*]
I walk . . . the lonely, lonely street . . .
A-listenin' for your heartbeat,
Listening for your love.
But, baby, you don't care.
Baby, you don't care.
Baby, no one cares.

[*They appear on stage.* FIRST BOY *is* JOEY. SECOND BOY *is* MURPH. JOEY *is slight, baby-faced, in his early twenties.* MURPH *is stronger, long-haired, the same age.*]

[MURPH *singing.*]
The lonely, lonely, streets, called out for lovin',
But there was no one to love . . .
'Cause, baby, you don't care . . .

[JOEY *joins in the singing.*]
Baby, you don't care . . .

[JOEY AND MURPH *singing together.*]
Baby, you don't care.
Baby, you don't care.
Baby, no one cares.
Baby, no one cares.

MURPH: [*Calls out into the audience, to the back row: across to the row of apartment houses opposite the park.*] Hey, Pussyface! Can you hear your babies singing? Pussyface. We're calling you.

JOEY: [*Joins in.*] Pussyface. Your babies are serenading your loveliness.
   [*They laugh.*]

MURPH: Baby, no one cares.

[MURPH AND JOEY *singing together.*]
Baby, no one cares.
Baby, no one cares.

MURPH: [*Screams.*] Pussyface, you don't care, you Goddamned idiot! [*Notices the* INDIAN.] Hey. Look at the Turk.
   [*JOEY stares at the* INDIAN *for a moment, then replies.*]

JOEY: Just another pretty face. Besides. That's no Turk. It's an Indian.

[MURPH *continues to sing.*]
Baby, no one cares.
[*Dances to his song, strutting in the* INDIAN's *direction. He then turns back to* JOEY *during the completion of his stanza and feigns a boxing match.*]

I walk the lonely, lonely streets.
A-callin' out for loving,
But, baby, you don't give a Christ for
Nothin' . . . not for nothin'.
[*Pretends to swing a punch at* JOEY, *who backs off laughing.*] You're nuts. It's a Turk!

JOEY: Bet you a ten spot. It's an Indian.

MURPH: It's a Turk, schmuck. Look at his fancy hat. Indians don't wear fancy hats. [*Calls across the street, again.*] Hey, Pussyface. Joey thinks we got an Indian. [*Back to* JOEY.] Give me a cigarette.

JOEY: You owe me a pack already, Murphy.

MURPH: So I owe you a pack. Give me a cigarette.

JOEY: Say "please," maybe?

MURPH: Say "I'll bust your squash if you don't give me a cigarette!"

JOEY: One butt, one noogie.

MURPH: First the butt.

JOEY: You're a Jap, Murphy.
   [*As* JOEY *extends the pack,* MURPH *grabs it.*]

MURPH: You lost your chance, baby. [*To the apartment block.*] Pussyface! Joey lost his chance!

JOEY: We made a deal. A deal's a deal. You're a Jap, Murphy. A rotten Jap. [*To the apartment.*] Pussyface, listen to me! Murphy's a rotten Jap and just Japped my whole pack. That's unethical, Pussyface. He owes me noogies, too!

MURPH: Now I'll give you twenty noogies, so we'll be even.

    [*He raps* JOEY *on the arm. The* INDIAN *looks up as* JOEY *squeals.*]

JOEY: Hey. The Indian's watching.

MURPH: [*Raps* JOEY *sharply again on the arm.*] Indian's a Turkie.

JOEY: [*Grabs* MURPH's *arm and twists it behind his back.*] Gimme my pack and it's an Indian, right?

MURPH: I'll give you your head in a minute, jerkoff.

JOEY: Indian? Indian? Say, Indian! [*Crosses.* MURPH *twists around. He twists* JOEY's *little finger, slowly.* JOEY's *in pain.*]

MURPH: Turkie? Turkie?

JOEY: Turkie. Okay. Let go. [MURPH *lets him up and laughs.* JOEY *jumps up and screams.*] Indian! [*Runs a few steps.*] Indian!

MURPH: [*Laughing.*] If your old lady would have you on Thanksgiving you'd know what a turkey was, ya' jerk. [*Hits him on the arm again.*] Here's another noogie, Turkie-head!

    [*The* INDIAN *coughs.*]

JOEY: Hey, look. He likes us. Shall I wink?

MURPH: You sexy beast, you'd wink at anything in pants.

JOEY: Come on. Do I look like a Murphy?

MURPH: [*Grabs* JOEY *and twists both of his arms.*] Take that back.

JOEY: Aw! ya' bastard. I take it back.

MURPH: You're a Turkie-lover, right?

JOEY: Right.

MURPH: Say it.

JOEY: I'm a Turkie-lover.

MURPH: You're a Turkie-humper, right?

JOEY: *You're* a Turkie-humper.

MURPH: Say, *I'm* a Turkie-humper.

JOEY: That's what I said. You're a Turkie-humper. [MURPH *twists his arms a bit further.*] Oww, ya' dirty bastard! All right, I'm a Turkie-humper! Now, leggo! [JOEY *pretends to laugh.*]

MURPH: You gonna hug him and kiss him and love him up like a mother?

JOEY: Whose mother?

MURPH: Your mother. She humps Turkies, right?

JOEY: Owww! All right, Yeah. She humps Turkies. Now leggo!

MURPH: [*Lets go.*] You're free.

JOEY: [*Breaks. Changes the game.*] Where's the bus?

MURPH: Up your mother.

JOEY: My old lady's gonna' kill me. It must be late as hell.

MURPH: So why don't you move out?

JOEY: Where to?

MURPH: Maybe we'll get our own place. Yeah. How about that, Joey?

JOEY: Yeah, sure. I move out on her and she starves. You know that.

MURPH: Let her starve, the Turkie-humper.

JOEY: [*Hits* MURPH *on the arm and laughs.*] That's my mother you're desecrating, you nasty bastard.

MURPH: How do you desecrate a whore? Call her a lady?

JOEY: Why don't you ask *your* mother?

MURPH: [*Hits* JOEY *on the arm.*] Big mouth, huh?

JOEY: Hey! Why don't you pick on som'body your own size, like Turkie, there.

MURPH: Leave Turkie out of this. He's got six elephants in his pocket, prob-ably.

JOEY: [*Laughs at the possibility.*] Hey, Turkie, you got six elephants in your pocket?

MURPH: Hey, shut up, Joey. [*Glances in the* INDIAN's *direction and the* INDIAN *glances back.*] Shut up.

JOEY: Ask him for a match.

MURPH: You ask him.

JOEY: You got the butts.

MURPH: Naw.

JOEY: Chicken. Want some seeds to chew on?

MURPH: I'll give you somethin' to chew on.

JOEY: Go on, ask him. I ain't never heard an Indian talk Turkie-talk.

MURPH: He's a Turkie, I told ya'. Any jerk can see that he's a definite Turk!

JOEY: You're a definite jerk, then. 'Cause I see a definite Indian!

MURPH: I'll show you.

[*Walks toward the* INDIAN *slowly, taking a full minute to cross the stage. He slithers from side to side and goes through pantomime of looking for matches.*]

JOEY: Hey, Murph. You comin' for dinner? We're havin' turkey tonight! Hey! Tell your Turkie to bring his elephants.

MURPH: Schmuck! How's he going to fit six elephants in a rickshaw?

JOEY: [*Flatly.*] Four in front. Three in back.

[*He reaches the* INDIAN.]

MURPH: Excuse me. May I borrow a match?

INDIAN: [*Speaking in Hindi.*] Mai toom-haree bo-lee nrh-hee bol sak-tah. Mai tum-hah-ree bah-sha nah-hee sah-maj-tah. [*I cannot speak your language. I don't understand.*]

MURPH: [*To* JOEY, *does a terrific "take," then speaks, incredulous.*] He's got to be kidding.

[JOEY *and* MURPH *laugh.*]

INDIAN: Moo-jhay mahaf kar-nah mai toom-hah-ree bah-art nah-hee sah-maj sak-tah. [*I'm sorry. I don't understand you.*]

MURPH: No speak English, huh? [*The* INDIAN *looks at him blankly. Louder.*] You can't speak English, huh?

[*The* INDIAN *stares at him, confused by the increase in volume.*]

JOEY: [*Flatly.*] Son of a bitch. Hey, Murph. Guess what? Your Turkie only speaks Indian.

MURPH: [*Moves in closer, examining the* INDIAN.] Say something in Indian, big mouth.

JOEY: [*Holds up his hand.*] How's your teepee? [*The* INDIAN *stares at him. He laughs.*] See.

    [*The* INDIAN *welcomes* JOEY's *laugh and smiles. He takes their hands and "shakes" them.*]

MURPH: [*Catches on as to why the* INDIAN *has joined the smile and feigns a stronger smile until they all laugh aloud.* MURPH *cuts off the laughter as he shakes the* INDIAN's *hand and says.*] You're a fairy, right?

INDIAN: [*Smiles harder than before.*] Mai toom-haree bah-at nah-hee sah-maj-tah. Mai ap-nay lah-kay kah gha-r dhoo-nd rah-haw hooh. Oos-nay moo-jhay mil-nah tar pahr nah-jah-nay woh cah-hah hai. Mai oos-kah mah-kan dhoo-nd rah-hah hoon. Oos-kah pah-tah yeh rah-hah k-yah. [*I don't understand you. I'm looking for my son's home. We were supposed to meet, but I could not find him. I'm looking for his home. This is his address. Am I headed in the correct direction?*]

    [*The* INDIAN *produces a slip of paper with an address typed on it. And a photograph.*]

MURPH: Gupta. In the Bronx. Big deal. [*To the* INDIAN.] Indian, right? You an Indian, Indian? [*Shakes his head up and down, smiling. The* INDIAN *smiles, confused.*] He don't know. [*Pauses, studies the picture, smiles.*] This picture must be his kid. Looks like you, Joe.

JOEY: [*Looks at the picture.*] Looks Irish to me. [*He hands the picture to* MURPH.]

BOTH: Ohhh.

MURPH: Yeah. Why'd you rape all those innocent children? [*Pause.*] I think he's the wrong kind of Indian. [*To the* INDIAN.] You work in a restaurant? [*Pauses. Speaks with a homosexual's sibilant "s."*] It's such a shame to kill these Indians. They do such superb beaded work.

    [MURPH *shakes his head up and down again, smiling.*]

INDIAN: [*Follows* MURPH's *cue.*] Mai—ay ap-nay lar-kay koh su-bah say nah-hee day-kha. Toom-hara shah-har bah-hoot bee barah hai. [*I haven't seen my son all day. Your city is so big and so busy.*]

JOEY: Ask him to show you his elephants.

MURPH: You ask. You're the one who speaks Turkie-Indian.

JOEY: White man fork with tongue. Right? [*The* INDIAN *stares at him blankly.*] Naw, he don't understand me. You ask. You got the right kind of accent. All you foreigners understand each other good.

MURPH: You want another noogie?

JOEY: Maybe Turkie wants a noogie or six?

MURPH: [*Shaking his head.*] You want a noogie, friend?

INDIAN: [*Agrees.*] Moo-jhay mahaf kar-nah. Moo-jay. Yah-han aye zyah-da sah-may na-hee hoo-ah. [*I'm sorry. I haven't been here long.*]

MURPH: Give him his noogie.

JOEY: Naw. He's your friend. You give it to him. That's what friends are for.

MURPH: [*Looks at the paper and photograph, gives them back.*] Jesus, look at that for a face.

JOEY: Don't make it.

MURPH: Don't make it. Prem Gupta. In the Bronx. Jesus, this is terrific. The Indian wants the Bronx.

JOEY: [*Sits on a trash can.*] He ain't gonna find no Bronx on this bus.

MURPH: Old Indian, pal. You ain't going to find the Bronx on this bus, unless they changed commissioners again. Now I've got a terrific idea for fun and profit. [*Pauses.*]

INDIAN: K-yah kah-ha toom-nay. [*Excuse me?*]

MURPH: Right. Now why don't you come home and meet my mother? Or maybe you'd like to meet Pussyface, huh? [*To* JOEY.] Should we bring him over to Pussyface?

JOEY: He don't even know who Pussyface is. You can't just go getting Indians blind dates without giving him a breakdown.

MURPH: Okay, Chief. Here's the breakdown on Pussyface. She's a pig. She lives right over there. See that pretty building? [*Points over the audience to the back row of seats.*] That one. The fancy one. That's Pussyface's hideaway. She's our social worker.

JOEY: That's right.

MURPH: Pussyface got assigned to us when we were tykers, right, Joe?

JOEY: Just little fellers.

MURPH: Pussyface was sent to us by the city. To watch over us. And care for us. And love us like a mother. Not because she wanted to. Because we were bad boys. We stole a car.

JOEY: We stole two cars.

MURPH: We stole two cars. And we knifed a kid.

JOEY: You knifed a kid.

MURPH: [*To* JOEY.] Tell it to the judge, Fella! [*He takes a pocketknife from his pocket and shows it to the* INDIAN, *who pulls back in fear.*]

JOEY: The Chief thinks you're going to cut him up into a totem pole.

MURPH: Easy, Chief. I've never cut up an Indian in my life.

JOEY: You've never *seen* an Indian in your life.

MURPH: Anyway, you got a choice. My mother—who happens to have a terrific personality. Or Pussyface, our beloved social lady.

JOEY: Where's the bus?

MURPH: It's coming.

JOEY: So's Christmas.

MURPH: Hey. Show Turkie my Christmas card for Pussyface. [*To the* INDIAN.] Pussyface gives us fun projects. I had to make Christmas cards last year. [*Back to* JOEY.] Go on. Show the Chief the card.

[JOEY *fishes through his wallet, finds a dog-eared photostat, hands it to the* INDIAN, *who accepts it curiously.*]

INDIAN: Yeh k-yah hai. [*What is this?*]

MURPH: I made that with my own two cheeks. Tell him, Joe.

JOEY: Stupid, he don't speak English.

MURPH: It don't matter. He's interested, ain't he?

JOEY: You're a fink-jerk.

MURPH: Oooo. I'll give you noogies up the kazzooo. [*Takes the card away from the* INDIAN *and explains.*] This is a Christmas card. I made it! I made it! Get me? Pussyface got us Christmas jobs last year. She got me one with the city. With the war on poverty. I ran the Xerox machines.

JOEY: Jesus. You really are stupid. He don't understand one word you're saying.

MURPH: [*Mimes the entire scene, slowly.*] He's interested, ain't he? That's more than I can say for most of them. [*To the* INDIAN.] Want to know how you can make your own Christmas cards with your simple Xerox 2400? It's easy. Watch. [*He mimes.*] First you lock the door to the stat room, so no one can bust in. Then you turn the machine on. Then you set the dial at the number of people you want to send cards to. Thirty, forty.

JOEY: Three or four.

MURPH: Right, fella. Then you take off your pants. And your underpants that's underneath. You sit on the glass. You push the little button. The lights flash. When the picture's developed, you write "Noel" across it! [*Pauses.*] That's how you make Christmas cards. [*Waits for a reaction from the* INDIAN, *then turns back to* JOEY, *dismayed.*] He's waiting for the bus.

JOEY: Me too. Jesus. Am I ever late!

MURPH: Tell her to stuff it. You're a big boy now.

JOEY: She gets frightened, that's all. She really don't care how late I come in, as long as I tell her when I'm coming. If I tell her one, and I don't get in until one-thirty, she's purple when I finally get in. [*Pauses.*] She's all right. Where's the Goddamned bus, huh? [*Calls across the park.*] Pussyface, did you steal the bus, you dirty old whore? Pussyface, I'm calling you! [*Pauses.*] She's all right, Murph. Christ, she's my mother. I didn't ask for her. She's all right.

MURPH: Who's all right? That Turkie-humper? [*To the* INDIAN.] His old lady humps Turkies, you know that? [*Smiles, but the* INDIAN *doesn't respond.*] Hey, Turkie's blowin' his cool a little. Least you got somebody waitin'. My old lady wouldn't know if I was gone a year.

JOEY: What? That Turkie-humper?

MURPH: [*To the* INDIAN.] Hey! [*The* INDIAN *jumps, startled.* MURPH *laughs.*] You got any little Indians runnin' around your teepee? No? Yeah? No? Aw, ya' stupid Indian. Where is the Goddamn bus?

JOEY: Let's walk it.

MURPH: Screw that. A hundred blocks? Besides, we gotta keep this old Turkie company, right? We couldn't let him stand all alone in this big ole city. Some nasty boys might come along and chew him up, right?

JOEY: We can walk it. Let the Indian starve.

MURPH: So walk it, jerk. I'm waiting with the Chief. [MURPH *stands next to the* INDIAN.]

JOEY: Come on, we'll grab the subway.

MURPH: Joe, the trains are running crazy now. Anyway, I'm waitin' with my friend the Chief, here. You wanna go, go. [*Murmurs.*] Where is it, Chief? Is that it? Here it comes, huh?

JOEY: [*Considers it.*] Yeah, we gotta watch out for Turkie.

[JOEY *stands on the other side of the* INDIAN, *who finally walks slowly back to the bus stop area.*]

MURPH: See that, Turkie, little Joe's gonna keep us company. That's nice, huh? [*The* INDIAN *looks for the bus.*] You know, Joey, this Turk's a pain in my ass. He don't look at me when I talk to him.

JOEY: He oughta look at you when you talk. He oughta be polite.

[*They pass the card in a game. The* INDIAN *smiles.*]

MURPH: I don't think he learned many smarts in Indiana. Any slob knows enough to look when they're being talked to. Huh?

JOEY: This ain't just any slob. This is a definite Turkie-Indian slob.

[*They pass the card behind their backs.*]

MURPH: He's one of them commie slobs, probably. Warmongering bastard. [*Flatly.*] Pinko here rapes all the little kids.

JOEY: Terrible thing. Too bad we can't give him some smarts. Maybe he could use a couple.

[*The game ends.* JOEY *has the card as in a magic act.*]

MURPH: We'll give him plenty of smarts. [*Calling him upstage.*] Want some smarts? Chief?

INDIAN: Bna-ee mai toom-maree bah-at nah-Hee sah-maj-sak-tah. Bus yah-han kis sa-may a-tee haj. K-yah mai sa-hee BUS STOP par shoon! [*I can't understand you. Please? When is the bus due here? Am I at the right station?*]

JOEY: Hey, look. He's talking out of the side of his mouth. Sure, that's right . . . Hey, Murph. Ain't Indian broads s'posed to have sideways breezers? Sure.

MURPH: [*Grins.*] You mean chinks, Joey.

JOEY: Naw. Indian broads too. All them foreign broads. Their breezers are sideways. That's why them foreign cars have the back seat facing the side, right?

MURPH: Is that right, Turkie? Your broads have horizontal snatches?

INDIAN: [*Stares at him nervously.*] Mai toom-haree bah-at nah-hee sah-maj sak-tah. [*I can't understand you.*]

MURPH: [*Repeating him in the same language.*] Toom-haree bah-at nah-hee sah-maj sak-tah.

INDIAN: [*Recognizing the language finally. He speaks with incredible speed.*] Toom-haree bah-sha nah-hee sah-maj-tah. Moo-jhay mah-Af kar-nah par ah-bhee moo-jhay tomm-ha-ray desh aye kuh-Chah hee din toh Hu-yay hain. Moo-jhay toom-ha-ree bah-sha see-kh-nay kah ah-bhee sah-mai hee nah-hee milah.

Mai ahp-nay lar-kay say bih-chur gah-ya hoon. Oos-say toh toom-ha-ray desh may rah-tay chai sah-al hoh Gah-ye hain. Jah-b doh mah-hee-nay pah-lay oos-kee mah kah inth-kahl moo-ah toh oos-nay moo-jhay ya-han booh-lah bheh-jha or mai ah gah-hay. Woh bah-ra hon-har lar-ka hai. Moo-jhay mah-af kar-nah kee majh-nay ah-bhee toom-ha-ree bah-sha na-hee see-kiee par mai see-kh loon-gha. [*Yes, that's correct. I can't understand your language. I'm sorry, but I've only been in your country for a few days. I haven't had time to understand your language. Please forgive me. I'm separated from my son. He's been living in your country for six years. When his mother died two months ago, he sent for me. I came immediately. He's a good son to his father. I'm sorry I haven't learned your language yet, but I shall learn.*]

MURPH: [*Does a take. Flatly.*] This Turkie's a real pain in the ass.

JOEY: Naw. I think he's pretty interesting. I never saw an Indian before.

MURPH: Oh. It's fascinating. It's marvelous. This city's a regular melting pot. Turkies. Kikes like you. [*Pause.*] I even had me a real French lady once. [*Looks at the ground. Pauses.*] I thought I saw a dime here. [*Ponders.*] I knew it. [*He picks up a dime and pockets it proudly.*]

JOEY: A French lady, huh?

MURPH: Yep. A real French broad.

JOEY: [*Holds a beat.*] You been at your mother again?

MURPH: [*Hits him on the arm.*] Wise-ass. Just what nobody likes. A wise-ass.

JOEY: Where'd you have this French lady, huh?

MURPH: I found her in the park over there. [*Points.*] Just sitting on a bench. She was great. [*Boasts.*] A real *talent.*

JOEY: Yeah, sure thing. [*Calls into the park.*] Hello, talent. Hello, talent! [*Pauses.*] I had a French girl, too. [*Turns to avoid* MURPH's *eyes, caught in a lie.*] Where the hell's that bus?

MURPH: [*Simply.*] Sure you did. Like the time you had a mermaid?

JOEY: You better believe I did. She wasn't really French. She just lived there a long time. I went to first grade with her. Geraldine. She was my first girl friend. [*Talks very quickly.*] Her old man was in the Army or some-thing, 'cause they moved to France. She came back when we were in high school.

MURPH: Then what happened?

JOEY: Nothin'. She just came back, that's all.

MURPH: I thought you said you *had* her . . .

JOEY: No, she was just my girl friend.

MURPH: In high school?

JOEY: No, ya stoop. In the first grade. I just told you.

MURPH: You had her in the first grade?

JOEY: Jesus, you're stupid. She was my girl friend. That's all.

MURPH: [*Feigns excitement.*] Hey . . . that's a *sweet little story.* [*Flatly.*] What the hell's wrong with you?

JOEY: What do ya' mean?

MURPH: First you say you had a French girl, then you say you had a girl friend in first grade, who went to France. What the hell kind of story's that?

JOEY: It's a true one, that's all. Yours is full of crap.

MURPH: What's full of crap?

JOEY: About the French lady in the park. You never had any French lady, unless you been at your own old lady again. Or maybe you've been at Pussyface?

MURPH: Jesus, you're lookin' for it, aren't you?

    [*They pretend to fistfight.*]

JOEY: I mean, if you gotta tell lies to your best buddy, you're in bad shape, that's all.

MURPH: [*Gives* JOEY *a "high-sign."*] Best buddy? You?

    [*They sign to the* INDIAN. *He returns the obscene gesture, thinking it a berserk American sign of welcome.*]

JOEY: Is that how it is in Ceylon, sir?

MURPH: Say-lon? What the hell is say-long?

JOEY: See, ya jerk, Ceylon's part of India. That's where they grow tea.

MURPH: No kiddin'? Boy it's terrific what you can learn just standin' here with a schmuck like you. Tea, huh? [*To the* INDIAN *he screams.*] Hey! [*The* INDIAN *turns around, startled.*] How's your teabags? [*No response.*] No? [*To* JOEY.] Guess you're wrong again. He don't know teabags.

JOEY: Look at the bags under his eyes. That ain't chopped liver.

    [*This is the transition scene:* MURPH *screams "Hey!"—the* INDIAN *smiles. They dance a war dance around him, beating a rhythm on the trashcans, hissing and cat-calling for a full minute.* MURPH *ends the dance with a final "Hey!" The* INDIAN *jumps in fear. Now that they sense his fear, the comedy has ended.*]

MURPH: Turkie looks like he's getting bored.

JOEY: Poor old Indian. Maybe he wants to play a game.

MURPH: You know any poor old Indian games?

JOEY: We could burn him at the stake. [*He laughs.*] That ain't such a terrible idea, you know. Maybe make an Indian stew.

MURPH: Naw, we couldn't burn a nice fellow like Turkie. That's nasty.

JOEY: We got to play a game. Pussyface always tells us to play games. [*To the apartment, the back of the audience.*] Ain't that right, Pussyface? You always want us to play games.

MURPH: I know a game . . .

JOEY: Yeah?

MURPH: Yeah. [*Screams at the* INDIAN.] "Indian, Indian, Where's the Indian?"

JOEY: That's a sweet game. I haven't played that for years.

MURPH: Wise-ass. You want to play a game, don't you?

JOEY: Indian-Indian. Where's the Indian?

MURPH: Sure. It's just like ring-a-leave-eo. Only with a spin.

JOEY: That sounds terrific.

MURPH: Look. I spin the hell out of you until you're dizzy. Then you run across the street and get Pussyface. I'll grab the Indian and hide him. Then Pussyface and you come over here and try to find us.

JOEY: We're going to spin, huh?

MURPH: Sure.

JOEY: Who's going to clean up after you? Remember the Ferris wheel, big shot? All those happy faces staring up at you?

MURPH: I ain't the spinner. You're the spinner. I'll hide the Chief. Go on. Spin.

JOEY: How about if we set the rules as we go along? [*To the* INDIAN.] How does that grab you, Chief?

INDIAN: Moo-jhay mah-af kar-nah. Mai toom-nakee bah-sha na-hee sah-maj sak-ta. [*I'm sorry, but I can't understand your language.*]

MURPH: He's talking Indian again. He don't understand. Go on. Spin. I'll grab the Chief while you're spinning . . . count to ten . . . hide the Chief, while you're after Pussyface. Go on. Spin.

JOEY: I ain't going to spin. I get sick.

MURPH: Ain't you going to play?

JOEY: I'll play. But I can't spin any better than you can. I get sick. You know that. How about if you spin and I hide the Chief? You can get Pussyface. She likes you better than me, anyhow.

MURPH: Pussyface ain't home. You know that. She's in New Jersey.

JOEY: Then what the hell's the point of this game, anyway?

MURPH: It's just a game. We can pretend.

JOEY: You can play marbles for all I care. I just ain't going to spin, that's all. And neither are you. So let's forget the whole game.

MURPH: [*Fiercely.*] Spin! Spin!

JOEY: You spin.

MURPH: Hey. I told you to spin.

[MURPH *squares off against* JOEY *and slaps him menacingly.* JOEY *looks* MURPH *straight in the eye for a moment.*]

JOEY: Okay. Big deal. So I'll spin. Then I get Pussyface, right? You ready to get the Chief?

MURPH: Will you stop talking and start spinning?

JOEY: All right. All right. Here I go. [JOEY *spins himself meekly, as* MURPH *goes toward the* INDIAN *and the trash can.* JOEY *giggles as he spins ever so slowly.* MURPH *glances at* JOEY *as* JOEY *pretends.* MURPH *is confused.*] There. I spun. Is that okay?

MURPH: That's a spin?

JOEY: Well, it wasn't a fox trot.

MURPH: I told you to spin! Any slob knows that ain't no spin! Now spin. God damn it! Spin!

JOEY: This is stupid. You want to play games. You want a decent spin. You spin.

[*He walks straight to* MURPH—*a challenge.* JOEY *slaps* MURPH. *He winces.*]

MURPH: [*Squares off viciously. Raises his arms. Looks at* JOEY *cruelly. Orders.*] Spin me.

> [JOEY *brings* MURPH'S *arms behind* MURPH'S *back and holds* MURPH'S *wrists firmly so that he is helpless.* JOEY *spins him. Slowly at first. Then faster. Faster.* JOEY'S *hostility is released; he laughs.*]

JOEY: You wanted to spin. Spin. Spin.

> [JOEY *spins* MURPH *frantically. The* INDIAN *watches in total horror, not knowing what to do; he cuddles next to the bus stop sign, his island of safety.*]

MURPH: [*Screaming.*] Enough, you little bastard.

JOEY: [*Continues to spin him.*] Now *you* get Pussyface. Go on. [*Spins* MURPH *all the faster as in a grotesque dance gone berserk.*] I'll hide the Chief. This is your game! This is your game. *You* get Pussyface. I'll hide the Chief. Go on, Murphy. You want some more spin? [JOEY *has stopped the spinning now, as* MURPH *is obviously ill.*] You want to spin some more?

MURPH: Stop it, Joey. I'm sick.

JOEY: [*Spins* MURPH *once more around.*] You want to spin some more, or are you going to get Pussyface and come find the Chief and me?

MURPH: You little bastard.

JOEY: [*Spins* MURPH *once again, still holding* MURPH *helpless with his arms behind his back.*] I'll hide the Chief. *You* get Pussyface and find us. Okay? Okay? Okay?

MURPH: Okay . . . you bastard . . . okay.

JOEY: Here's one more for good luck.

> [JOEY *spins* MURPH *three more times, fiercely, then shoves him offstage.* MURPH *can be heard retching, about to vomit, during the final spins.* JOEY *then grabs the* INDIAN, *who pulls back in terror.*]

INDIAN: Na-hee bha-yee toom ah-b k-yah kah-rogay? [*No, please, what are you going to do?*]

JOEY: Easy, Chief. It's just a game. Murph spun out on us. It's just a game. I've got to hide you now.

> [MURPH'S *final puking sounds can be heard well in the distance.*]

INDIAN: Na-hee na-hee bha-yee. Mai mah-afee mah-ng-ta. Hoon. [*No. No. Please. I beg you.*]

JOEY: Easy, Chief. Look. I promise you, this ain't for real. This is only a game. A game. Get it? It's all a game! Now I got to count to ten. [*Grabs the* INDIAN *and forces him down behind a city litter basket. He covers the* INDIAN'S *scream with his hand, as he slaps the* INDIAN—*a horrifying sound.*] One. Two. Three. Murphy? [*He laughs.*] Four. Five. Murph? Come get us. Six. Seven. Pussyface is waiting. Eight. Nine. [*Pauses.*] Murphy? Murph? Hey, buddy. [*Stands up. Speaks.*] Ten. [*Lights are narrowing on* JOEY *and the* INDIAN. *The* INDIAN *tries to escape.* JOEY *subdues him easily.* JOEY *turns slowly back to the* INDIAN, *who responds with open fear.*] Get up. Up. [*No response.*] Get up, Turkie. [*Moves to the* INDIAN, *who recoils sharply.* JOEY *persists and pulls the* INDIAN *to his feet. The* INDIAN *shudders, stands and faces his captor. The* INDIAN *shakes from fear and from a chill. There is a moment's silence as* JOEY *watches. He removes his own sweater and offers it to the* INDIAN.] Here. Here. Put it on. It's okay. [*The* INDIAN *is bewildered, but* JOEY *forces the sweater into his hands.*] Put it on. [*The* INDIAN *stares at the sweater.* JOEY *takes it from his hands and begins to cover the* INDIAN, *who is amazed.*] I hope I didn't hurt you too much. You okay? [*No response.*] You ain't sick too bad, huh? [*Pause.*] Huh? [*Checks the* INDIAN *for cuts.*] You look okay. You're okay, huh? [*No response.*] I didn't mean to rough you up like that, but . . . you know. Huh? [*The* INDIAN *raises his eyes to meet* JOEY's. JOEY *looks down to avoid the stare.*] I hope you ain't mad at me or nothin'. [*Pause.*] Boy it's gettin' chilly. I mean, it's cold, right? Sure is quiet all of a sudden. Kind of spooky, huh? [*Calls.*] Hey, Murphy! [*Laughs aloud.*] Murph ain't a bad guy. He's my best buddy, see? I mean, he gets kinda crazy sometimes, but that's all. Everybody gets kind of crazy sometime, right? [*No response.*] Jesus, you're a stupid Indian. Can't you speak any English? No? Why the hell did you come here, anyway? Especially if you can't talk any English. You ought to say something. Can't you even say "Thank you"?

   [*The* INDIAN *recognizes those words, finally, and mimics them slowly and painfully.*]

INDIAN: [*In English, very British and clipped.*] Thank you.

JOEY: I'll be Goddamned! You're welcome. [*Slowly, indicating for the* INDIAN *to follow.*] You're welcome.

   [*He waits.*]

INDIAN: [*In English.*] You are welcome.

JOEY: That's terrific. You are welcome. [*Smiles, as though all is forgiven. In relief.*] How are you?

INDIAN: You are welcome.

JOEY: No. How are ya? [JOEY *is excited. The* INDIAN *might be a second friend.*]

INDIAN: [*In English—very "Joey."*] How are ya?

JOEY: [*Joyously.*] Jesus. You'll be talking like us in no time! You're okay, huh? You ain't bleeding or anything. I didn't wanna hurt you none. But Murph gets all worked up. You know what I mean. He gets all excited. This ain't the first time, you know. No, sir!

INDIAN: [*In English.*] No, sir.

JOEY: That's right. He's especially crazy around broads.

INDIAN: [*In English.*] Broads.

JOEY: [*Forgetting that the* INDIAN *is only mimicking.*] That's right. Broads. [*Pauses and remembers, deeply.*] What am I yakking for? Tell me about India, huh? I'd like to go to India sometime. Maybe I will. You think I'd like India? India? [*No response. The* INDIAN *recognizes the word, but doesn't understand the question.*] That's where you're from, ain't it? Jesus, what a stupid Indian. India! [*Spells the word.*] I-N-D-I-A. Nothin'. Schmuck. *India!*

INDIAN: [*A stab in the dark.*] Hindi?

JOEY: Yeah! Tell me about India! [*Long pause as they stand staring at each other.*] No? You're not talking, huh? Well, what do you want to do? Murph oughta be back soon. [*Discovers a coin in his pocket.*] You wanna flip for quarters?

Flip? No? Look, a Kennedy half! [*Goes through three magic tricks with the coin: (1) He palms the coin, offers the obvious choice of hand, then uncovers the coin in his other hand. The Indian raises his hand to his turban in astonishment.*] Like that, huh? [(2) *Coin is slapped on his breast.*] This hand right? Is it this hand, this hand? No, it's *this* hand! Back to your dumb act? Here. Here's the one you liked! [*Does* (1). *This time the* INDIAN *points to the correct hand instantly.*] You're probably some kind of hustler. Okay. Double or nothing. [*Flips.*] Heads, you live. Tails, you die. Okay? [*Uncovers the coin.*] I'll be a son of a bitch. You got Indian luck. Here. [*He hands the coin to the* INDIAN.]

INDIAN: [*Stares in question.*] Na-hff? [*No?*]

JOEY: [*Considers cheating.*] Take it. You won. No, go ahead. Keep it. I ain't no Indian giver. [*Pause. He laughs at his own joke. No response.*] You ain't got no sense of humor, that's what. [*Stares upstage.*] Murph's my best buddy, you know? Me and him were buddies when we were kids. Me and Murph, all the time. And Maggie. His kid sister. [*Pause.*] I had Maggie once. Sort of. Well, kind of. Yeah, I had her. That's right. Murph don't know. Makes no difference now. She's dead, Maggie. [*Sings.*] "The worms crawl in, the worms crawl out." [*Speaks.*] What the hell difference does it make? *Right?*

INDIAN: [*In English.*] No, sir.

JOEY: [*Without noticing.*] That's why Murph is crazy. That's why he gets crazy, I mean. She died seventeen, that's all. Seventeen. Just like *that*. Appendix. No one around. There was no one around. His old lady? Forget it! The old man took off years ago. All there was really was just Murph and Maggie. That's why could take it. At home. You think my old lady's bad? She's nothing. His old lady's a pro. You know? She don't even make a living at it, either. That's the bitch of it. Not even a living. She's a dog. I mean, *I* wouldn't even pay her a nickel. Not a nickel. Not that I'd screw around with Murphy's old lady. Oh! Not that she doesn't try. She tries. Plenty. [*His fantasy begins.*] That's why I don't come around to his house much. She tries it all the time. She wouldn't charge me anything, probably. But it ain't right screwing your best buddy's old lady, right? I'd feel terrible if I did. She ain't that bad, but it just ain't right. I'd bet she'd even take Murph on. She probably tries it with him, too. That's the bitch of it. She can't even make a living. His own Goddamned mother. The other one—Pussyface. You think Pussyface is a help? That's the biggest joke yet. [*The* INDIAN *is by now thoroughly confused on all counts. He recognizes the name "Pussyface," and reacts slightly. Seeing* JOEY'S *anxiety, he cuddles him. For a brief moment they embrace—an insane father-and-son tableau. Note: Be careful here.*] Pussyface. There's a brain. You see what she gave us for Christmas? [*Fishes his knife out of his pocket.*] Knives. Brilliant, huh? Murph's up on a rap for slicing a kid, and she gives us knives for Christmas. To whittle with. She's crazier than Murphy. Hah. [*Flashes his open knife at the* INDIAN, *who misinterprets the move as spelling disaster. The* INDIAN *waits, carefully scrutinizing* JOEY, *until* JOEY *begins to look away.* JOEY *now wanders to the spot where he pushed* MURPH *offstage.*] Hey, Murph! [*The* INDIAN *moves slowly to the other side of the stage.* JOEY *sees his move at once and races after him, thinking the* INDIAN *was running away.*] Hey. Where are you going? [*The* INDIAN *knows he'll be hit. He tries to explain with mute gestures and attitude. It's futile. He knows at once and hits* JOEY *as best he can and races across the stage.* JOEY *recovers from the blow and starts after him, as the* INDIAN *murmurs one continuous frightening scream.* JOEY *dives after the* INDIAN *and tackles him on the other side of the stage. The* INDIAN *fights more strongly than ever, but* JOEY'S *trance carries him ferociously into this fight. He batters the* INDIAN *with punches to the body. The* INDIAN *squeals as* JOEY *sobs.*] You were gonna run off. Right? Son of a bitch. You were gonna tell Murphy.

> [*The* INDIAN *makes one last effort to escape and runs the length of the stage, screaming a bloodcurdling, anguished scream.* MURPH *enters, stops, stares incredulously as the* INDIAN *runs into his open arms.* JOEY *races to the* INDIAN *and strikes a karate chop to the back of his neck.* JOEY *is audibly sobbing. The* INDIAN *drops to the stage as a bull in the ring, feeling the final thrust of the sword . . .* JOEY *stands frozen above him.* MURPH *stares, first at* JOEY *and then at the* INDIAN.]

MURPH: Pussyface isn't home yet. She's still in New Jersey. Ring-a-leave-eo.

JOEY: [*Sobbing, senses his error.*] Indians are dumb.

MURPH: [*Stares again at* JOEY. *Then to the* INDIAN. *Spots* JOEY'S *sweater on the* INDIAN. *Fondles it, then stares at* JOEY *viciously.*] Pussyface isn't home. I rang her bell. She don't answer. I guess she's still on vacation. She ruined our game.

JOEY: [*Sobbing.*] Oh, jumping Jesus Christ. Jesus, Jesus. Jesus. Indians are dumb.

MURPH: Pussyface ruins everything. She don't really care about our games. She ruins our games. Just like Indians. They don't know how to play our games either.

JOEY: Indians are dumb. Dumb.

> [*He sobs.* MURPH *slaps* JOEY *across the face. He straightens up and comes back to reality.*]

MURPH: What the hell's going on?

JOEY: He tried to run. I hit him.

MURPH: Yeah. I saw that. You hit him, all right. [*Stares at the* INDIAN.] Is he alive?

> [*The* INDIAN *groans, pulls himself to his knees.*]

JOEY: He was fighting. I hit him.

MURPH: Okay, you hit him.

> [*The* INDIAN *groans again. Then he speaks in a plea.*]

INDIAN: [*Praying.*] Moo-jhay or nah sah-tao. Maih-nay toom-hara k-yah bigarah hai. Moo-jhay or nah sah-tao. Moo-jhay in-seh. [*Please. Don't hurt me anymore. What have I done? Please don't hurt me. Don't let them hurt me.*]

MURPH: He's begging for something. Maybe he's begging for his life. Maybe he is. Sure, maybe he is.

JOEY: [*Embarrassed, starts to help the* INDIAN *to his feet.*] C'mon there, Chief. Get up and face the world. C'mon, Chief. Everything's going to be all right.

MURPH: What's got into you, anyway?

JOEY: C'mon, Chief. Up at the world. Everything's okay.

[*The* INDIAN *ad libs words of pleading and pain.*]

MURPH: Leave him be. [*But* JOEY *continues to help the* INDIAN.] Leave him be. What's with you? Hey, Joey! I said leave him be!

[MURPH *pushes* JOEY *and the* INDIAN *pulls back with fear.*]

JOEY: Okay, Murph. Enough's enough.

MURPH: Just tell me what the hell's wrong with you?

JOEY: He tried to run away, that's all. Change the subject. Change the subject. It ain't important. I hit him, that's all.

MURPH: Okay, so you hit him.

JOEY: Okay! Where were you? Sick. Were you a little bit sick? I mean, you couldn't have been visiting, 'cause there ain't no one to visit, right?

MURPH: What *do* you mean?

JOEY: Where the hell were you? [*Looks at* MURPH *and giggles.*] You're a little green there, Irish.

MURPH: You're pretty funny. What the hell's so funny?

JOEY: Nothing's funny. The Chief and I were just having a little pow-wow, and we got to wondering where you ran off to. Just natural for us to wonder, ain't it? [*To the* INDIAN.] Right, Chief.

MURPH: Hey, look at that. Turkie's got a woolly sweater just like yours. Ain't that a terrific coincidence. You two been playing strip poker?

JOEY: Oh, sure. Strip poker. The Chief won my sweater and I won three of his feathers and a broken arrow. [*To the* INDIAN, *he feigns a deep authoritative voice.*] You wonder who I am, don't you? Perhaps this silver bullet will help to identify me? [*Extends his hand. The* INDIAN *peers into* JOEY's *empty palm quizzically. As he does,* MURPH *quickly taps the underside of* JOEY's *hand, forcing the hand to rise and slap the* INDIAN's *chin sharply. The* INDIAN *pulls back at the slap.* JOEY *turns on* MURPH, *quickly.*] What the hell did you do that for, ya' jerk. The Chief didn't do nothing.

MURPH: Jesus, you and your Chief are pretty buddy-buddy, ain't you? [*Mimics* JOEY.] "The Chief didn't do nothing." Jesus. You give him your sweater. Maybe you'd like to have him up for a beer . . .

JOEY: Drop it, Murph. You're giving me a pain in the ass.

MURPH: [*Retorts fiercely.*] You little pisser. Who the hell do you think you're talking to?

[*The telephone rings in the booth. They are all startled, especially the* INDIAN, *who senses hope.*]

JOEY: [*After a long wait, speaking the obvious flatly.*] It's the phone.

MURPH: [*To the* INDIAN.] The kid's a whiz. He guessed that right away.

[*The phone rings a second time.*]

JOEY: Should we answer it?

MURPH: What for? Who'd be calling here? It's a wrong number.

[*The phone rings menacingly a third time. Suddenly the* INDIAN *darts into the phone booth and grabs the receiver.* JOEY *and* MURPH *are too startled to stop him until he has blurted out his hopeless plea, in his own language.*]

INDIAN: Prem k-yah woh may-rah ar-kah hai. Prem (Pray-em) bay-tah moo-jhay bachah-low. Mai fah ns ga-yah boon yeh doh goon-day moo-jhay mar ra-hay hain. Mai ba-hoot ghah-bara gaya hoon. Pray-em. [*Prem? Is this my son? Prem? Please help me. I'm frightened. Please help me. Two boys are hurting me . . . I'm frightened. Please. Prem?*]

  [*The* INDIAN *stops talking sharply and listens. He crumbles as the voice drones the wrong reply. He drops the receiver and stares with horror at the boys.* MURPH *realizes the* INDIAN's *horror and begins to laugh hysterically.* JOEY *stares silently. The* INDIAN *begins to mumble and weep. He walks from the phone booth. The voice is heard as a drone from the receiver. The action freezes.*]

MURPH: [*Laughing.*] What's the matter, Turkie? Don't you have a dime? Give Turkie a dime, Joe. Give him a dime.

JOEY: Jesus Christ. I'd hate to be an Indian.

MURPH: Hey, the paper! C'mon, Joey, get the paper from him. We'll call the Bronx.

JOEY: Cut it out, Murph. Enough's enough.

MURPH: Get the frigging piece of paper. What's the matter with you, any-way?

JOEY: I just don't think it's such a terrific idea, that's all.

MURPH: You're chicken. That's what you are.

JOEY: Suppose his son has called the police. What do you think? You think he hasn't called the police? He knows the old man don't speak any English. He called the police. Right? And they'll trace our call.

MURPH: You're nuts. They can't trace any phone calls. Anyway, we'll be gone from here. You're nuts.

JOEY: I don't want to do it.

MURPH: For Christ's sake. They can't trace nothing to nobody. Who's going to trace. Get the paper.

JOEY: Get it yourself. Go on. Get it yourself. I ain't going to get it.

MURPH: C'mon, Joey. It's not real. This is just a game. It ain't going to hurt anybody. You know that. It's just a game.

JOEY: Why don't we call somebody else? We'll call somebody else and have the Indian talk. That makes sense. Imagine if an Indian called you up and talked to you in Indian. I bet the Chief would go for that all right. Jesus, Murphy.

MURPH: Get the paper and picture.

INDIAN: Ah-b toom k-yah kah-rogay. Moo-jhay mah-af kar-doh bha-yee maih-nay soh-cha tah key woh may-rah bay-tah pray-em hai. Moo-jhay tele-phone kar raha. Mai-nay soh-chah thah sha-yahd woh. Pray-em hoh. [*What are you going to do now? I'm sorry. I thought that was my son, Prem. I thought that it might be Prem calling me on the telephone. Prem. That's who I thought it was. Prem.*]

MURPH: Prem. That's the name. [*Plays the rhyme.*]

INDIAN: Pray-aim. [*Prem?*]

MURPH: Yes, Prem. I want to call Prem. Give me the paper with his name.

INDIAN: Toom pray-aim kay ba-ray may k-yah hah ra-hay. Ho toom-nay pray-aim koh kyah key-yah. Toom oos-kay bah-ray may k-yah jan-tay ho k-yah toom jan-tay ho woh kah-han hai. [*What are you saying about Prem? Prem is my son. What have you done to Prem? What do you know about him? Do you know where he is?*]

MURPH: Shut up already and give me the paper.

JOEY: Jesus, Murph.

MURPH: [*Turning the* INDIAN *around so that they face each other.*] This is ridiculous. [*Searches the* INDIAN, *who resists a bit at first, and then not at all. Finally,* MURPHY *finds the slip of paper.*] I got it. I got it. Terrific. "Prem Gupta." In the Bronx. In the frigging Bronx. This is terrific. [*Pushes the* INDIAN *to* JOEY.] Here. Hold him.

INDIAN: Toom k-yah kar ra-hay ho k-yah toom pray-aim k-oh boo-lah ra-hay ho. [*What are you doing? Are you going to call my son?*]

MURPH: Shut him up. [*Fishes for a dime.*] Give me a dime, God damn it. This is terrific.

JOEY: [*Finds the coins in his pocket.*] Here's two nickels. [*Hands them over.*] I think this is a rotten idea, that's what I think. [*Pauses.*] And don't forget to pay me back those two nickels either.

MURPH: Just shut up. [*Dials the information operator.*] Hello. Yeah, I want some information . . . I want a number up in the Bronx . . . Gupta . . . G-U-P-T-A . . . an Indian kid . . . His first name's Prem . . . P-R-E-M . . . No . . . I can't read the street right . . . Wait a minute. [*Reads the paper to himself.*] For Christ's sake. How many Indians are up in the Bronx? There must be only one Indian named Gupta.

JOEY: What's she saying?

MURPH: There are two Indians named Gupta. [*To the operator.*] Is the two of them named Prem? [*Pauses.*] Well, that's what I told you . . . Jesus . . . wait a minute . . . okay . . . Okay. Say that again . . . Okay . . . Okay . . . Right. Okay . . . thanks. [*Hurries quickly to return the coins to the slot.* GUPTA *mumbles. To* JOEY.] Don't talk to me. [*Dials.*] Six . . . seven-four. Oh. One. Seven, seven. [*Pauses.*] It's ringing. It's ringing. [*Pauses.*] Hello. [*Covers the phone with his hand.*] I got him! Hello! Is this Prem Gupta? Oh swell. How are you? [*To* JOEY.] I got the kid!

[*The* INDIAN *breaks from* JOEY'S *arms and runs to the telephone . . .* MURPH *sticks out his leg and holds the* INDIAN *off. The* INDIAN *fights, but seems weaker than ever.*]

INDIAN: [*Screams.*] Cree-payah moo-jhay ad-nay lar-kay say bah-at kar-nay doh. [*Please let me talk to my son.*]

[MURPH *slams the* INDIAN *aside violently.* JOEY *stands frozen, watching. The* INDIAN *wails and finally talks calmly, as in a trance.*]

INDIAN: Cree-payah moo-jhay ahd-nay lar-kay say bah-at kar-nay doh. Mai

toom-haray hah-th jor-tah hoom mai toom-hay joh mango-gay doon-gar
bus moo-jhay oos-say bah-at kar-nay doh. [*Please let me talk to my son. Oh,
Prem. Please, I beg of you. Please. I'll give you anything at all. Just tell me what
you want of me. Just let me talk with my son. Won't you, please?*]

    [MURPH *glares at the* INDIAN, *who no longer tries to interfere, as it becomes
obvious that he must listen to even the language he cannot understand.*]

MURPH: Just listen to me, will you, Gupta? I don't know where the hell your
old man is, that's why I'm calling. We found an old elephant down here
in Miami and we thought it must be yours. You can't tell for sure whose
elephant is whose. You know what I mean? [MURPH *is laughing now.*] What
was that? Say that again. I can't hear you too well. All the distance between
us, you know what I mean? It's a long way down here, you follow me?
No. I ain't got no Indian. I just got an elephant. And he's eating all my
peanuts. Gupta, you're talking too fast. Slow down.

INDIAN: Pray-aim bhai-yah moo-jhay ah-kay lay ja-oh moo-jhay ap-nay lar-
kay say bah-at kar-nay doh moo-jhay oos-say bah-at k-yohn nah-hee kar-
nay day-tay. [*Prem! Prem! Please come and get me. Please let me talk to my son,
mister. Why don't you let me talk to my son?*]

    [JOEY *leaps on the* INDIAN; *tackles him, lies on top of him in front of the telephone
booth.*]

MURPH: That was the waiter. I'm in an Indian restaurant. [*Pauses.*] Whoa.
Slow down, man. That was nobody. That was just a myth. Your imagination. [*Pauses. Screams into the receiver.*] Shut up, damn you! And listen.
Okay? Okay. Are you listening? [MURPH *tastes the moment. He silently clicks
the receiver back to the hook. To* JOEY.] He was very upset. [*To the* INDIAN.]
He was very upset. [*Pauses.*] Well, what the hell's the matter with you? I
only told him we·found an elephant, that's all. I thought maybe he lost his
elephant.

    [*The* INDIAN *whimpers.*]

INDIAN: Toom-nay ai-saw k-yohn ki-yah toom-nay may-ray lar-kay koh k-
yah ka-hah hai. [*Why have you done this? What have you said to my son?*]

MURPH: You don't have to thank me, Turkie. I only told him your elephant
was okay. He was probably worried sick about your elephant. [MURPH
laughs.] This is terrific, Joey. Terrific. You should have heard the guy
jabber. He was so excited he started talking in Indian just like the Chief.
He said that Turkie here and him got separated today. Turkie's only been
in the city one day. You're pretty stupid, Turkie. One day in the city . . .
and look at the mess you've made. You're pretty stupid. He's stupid, right?

JOEY: Yeah. He's stupid.

MURPH: Hold him. We'll try again. Sure.

    [*The* INDIAN *jumps on* MURPH. *He tries to strangle* MURPH.]

MURPH: [*Screaming.*] Get him off of me! [JOEY *pulls the* INDIAN *down to the ground
as* MURPH *pounds the booth four times, screaming hideous sounds of aggression. With
this tension released he begins to call, fierce but controlled, too controlled.* MURPH
takes the dime from his pocket, shows it to JOEY, *and recalls the number. Talking*

into receiver. He dials number again and waits for reply.] Hello? Is this Gupta again? Oh, hello there . . . I'm calling back to complain about your elephant . . . hey, slow down, will you? Let me do the talking. Okay? Your elephant is a terrific pain in the balls to me, get it? Huh? Do you follow me so far? [*Pauses.*] I don't know what you're saying, man . . . how about if I do the talking, all right? . . . Your elephant scares hell out of me and my pal here. We don't like to see elephants on the street. Spiders and snakes are okay, but elephants scare us. Elephants . . . yea, that's right. Don't you get it, pal? . . . Look, we always see spiders and snakes. But we never expect to see an elephant . . . What do you mean "I'm crazy"? I don't know nothing about your old man . . . I'm talking about your elephant. Your elephant offends the hell out of me. So why don't you be a nice Indian kid and come pick him up . . . that's right . . . wait a minute . . . I'll have to check the street sign. [*Covers the receiver.*] This is terrific. [*Talks again into the telephone.*] Jesus, I'm sorry about that. There don't seem to be no street sign . . . that's a bitch. I guess you lose your elephant . . . well, what do you expect me to do, bring your elephant all the way up to the Bronx? Come off it, pal. You wouldn't ever bring my elephant home. I ain't no kid, you know! I've lost a couple of elephants in my day. [*Listens.*] Jesus, you're boring me now . . . I don't know what the hell you're talking about. Maybe you want to talk to your elephant . . . huh? [*Turns to the* INDIAN.] Here, come talk to your "papoose."

    [*He offers the telephone. The* INDIAN *stares in disbelief, then grabs the telephone from* MURPH's *hands and begins to chatter wildly.*]

INDIAN: Pray-aim, bhai-yah Pray-aim moo-jhay ah-kay lay jah-oh k-Yah? moo-jhay nah-hee pa-tah mai kah-han hoo-n moo-jhay ah-hp-nay gha-ar lay chah-low ya-hahn do-ah bad-mash lar-Kay. Jo bah-hoot kha-tar-nahk hai-don-say mai nah-hee bah-cha sak-tah ah-pa-nay koh toom aik-dam moo-jhay ah-kay. [*Prem? Oh, Prem. Please come and take me away . . . what? I don't know where I am . . . Please come and take me to your house . . . please? There are two bad people. Two young men. They are dangerous. I cannot protect myself from them. Please . . . You must come and get me.*]

    [MURPH *takes his knife from his pocket, cuts the line. The* INDIAN *almost falls flat on his face as the line from the receiver to the phone box is cut, since he has been leaning away from* MURPH *and* JOEY *during his plea.*]

MURPH: You've had enough, Chief. [MURPH *laughs aloud.*]

INDIAN: [*Not at once realizing the line must be connected, continues to talk into the telephone in Hindi.*] Pray-aim, Pray-aim, ya-hahn aa-oh sah-rak kah nah-am hai—yeh toom-nay k-yah key-yah. [*Prem. Prem. Please come here. The street sign reads . . .*]

    [*He now realizes he has been cut off and stares dumbly at the severed cord as* MURPH *waves the severed cord in his face.*]

INDIAN: Toom-nay yeh k-yoh key-yah? [*What have you done?*]

MURPH: There it is, Turkie. Who you talkin' to?

INDIAN: [*To* JOEY, *screaming a father's fury and disgust.*] Toom-nay yeh k-yohn key-yah cri-payah may-ree mah-dah-d kah-roho. [*Why have you done this? Please. Please help me.*]

[*JOEY has been standing throughout the entire scene, frozen in terror and disgust. He walks slowly toward MURPH, who kicks the INDIAN. JOEY bolts from the stage, muttering one continuous droning sob.*]

MURPH: [*Screaming.*] Go ahead, Joey. Love him. Love him like a mother. Hey? Joey? What the hell's the matter? C'mon, buddy? [*Turns to the INDIAN, takes his knife and cuts the INDIAN's hand, so blood is on the knife.*] Sorry, Chief. This is for my buddy, Joey. And for Pussyface. [*Calls offstage.*] Joey! Buddy! What the hell's the matter? [*Races from the stage after JOEY.*] Joey! Wait up. Joey! I killed the Indian!

[*He exits. The INDIAN stares dumbly at his hand, dripping blood. He then looks to the receiver and talks into it.*]

INDIAN: Pray-aim, Pray-aim, mai ah-pa-nay lar-kay key ah-wah-az k-yon nah-hee soon sak-tah Pray-aim! Toom-nay may-ray sah-ahth aih-saw k-yohn key-yaw bay-tah Pray-aim, k-yah toom ho? [*Prem. Prem.*] [*He walks center stage, well way from the telephone booth.*] [*Why can I not hear my son, Prem? Why have you done this to me?*] [*Suddenly the telephone rings again. Once. Twice. The INDIAN is startled. He talks into the receiver, while he holds the dead line in his bleeding hand.*] [*Prem? Is that you? Prem?*] [*The telephone rings a third time.*] Pray-aim, Pray-aim, bay-tah k-yah toom ho—[*Prem. Prem? Is that you?*] [*A fourth ring. The INDIAN knows the telephone is dead.*] Pray-aim Pray-aim— moo-jhay bah-chald Pray-aim. [*Prem. Prem. Help me. Prem.*]

[*As the telephone rings a fifth time, in the silence of the night, the sounds of two boys' singing is heard.*]

[FIRST BOY:]
I walk the lonely streets at night,
A-lookin' for your door . . .
[SECOND BOY:]
I look and look and look and look . . .
[FIRST BOY *and* SECOND BOY:]
But, baby, you don't care.
But, baby, no one cares.
But, baby, no one cares.

[*Their song continues to build as they repeat the lyrics, so the effect is one of many, many voices. The telephone continues its unanswered ring. The INDIAN screams a final anguished scream of fury to the boys offstage. The telephone rings a final ring as the INDIAN screams.*]

INDIAN: [*Desperately, holding the telephone to the audience as an offer. He speaks in English into the telephone. The only words he remembers are those from his lesson.*] How are you? You're welcome. You're welcome. Thank you. [*To the front.*] Thank you!

Blackout.

STUDY QUESTIONS

1. How much do we know about the background of Joey and Murph? What personal traits do the two share? How do they differ from each other? How important are their different ethnic backgrounds? Why is it important to the play's effect that they act so much alike?

2. What does the horseplay between the two suggest about their friendship? about their feelings? about their sense of identity and security? What does the opening song suggest about their relationship?

3. How much accurate information do we have about Murph's mother? about Pussyface? How can you tell what is fact and what is fiction about the two women? Why do the boys keep calling to them or addressing them as if they were just offstage? What conclusions do you draw about Murph and Joey themselves from the way they talk about the two women?

4. Besides their abuse of Gupta, how many different other ethnic or racial slurs do Murph and Joey utter? Why do they argue about whether Gupta is an Indian or a Turk? What is the point of their mixing up Gupta's heritage with other heritages, especially that of American Indians? What indications are there that they know better? What is implied by the blurring of distinctions? What does the generalized lumping together of ethnic slurs imply about the two boys? What does the undifferentiated language of abuse imply about the CONFLICTS in the play? How does the blurring of terms used to describe or address "foreigners" relate to the identity of the two boys? to their CHARACTER? to the THEMES of the play?

5. If you were staging the play, how would you indicate to the audience what Gupta is saying (note that the English translation of the Hindi included in parentheses in the printed text would not be available to an audience)? How "serious" would you make the fight scene? How would you distinguish between the TONE of the violence between the boys and that between Joey and Gupta? How would you stage the spinning scene? What feelings toward the boys would you try to arouse in that scene?

6. How does the cutting of Gupta's hand affect your feelings toward the boys? How do you respond to their teasing of each other? to their verbal abuse of Gupta early in the play? How fully do you identity with Gupta's feelings? Why? At what point do you feel the most empathy with him? Do you ever identify with the feelings, attitudes, or values of Murph and Joey? If so, when? Why?

7. What is the central conflict in the play? How much of the conflict in the play occurs within the characters? How are the internal conflicts externalized? In what ways does the language of each character reflect his internal conflict? In what ways does the language reflect the larger conflicts in the play?

8. Describe the language spoken by Murph and Joey. In what ways is it distinctive? What indications are there that the two have developed a special language that has "private" meanings only for the two of them? How do the physical horseplay and the fighting relate to the language they share? Does the fact that Gupta speaks

virtually no English put more emphasis or less on the language the boys use? How does Gupta's lack of knowledge of English affect his body language and gestures?

9. How does the cutting of the telephone line relate to the major THEMES of the play? Describe the effect on Gupta of his inability to respond to words that urgently demand his response. Describe the effect on the audience.

10. How many different kinds of broken communication are represented in the play? How do the difficulties in communication relate to the frustrations about relationships felt by each of the characters? Compare ways the different characters respond to their frustrations.

11. What effect does the fact that Gupta is a stranger in the city have on his ability to understand what is happening to him? What other factors, besides his lack of understanding of English, affect his sense of disorientation?

12. Besides Hindi and English, what other human "languages" are used in the play— that is, by what other means do people try to communicate? How important is body language? gesture? facial expression? physical intimidation? physical touching? other physical rituals? communication through eye contact? verbal sparring? the verbal blurring of distinctions between people? the refusal to call people by their correct names? the staking out of physical territory?

Richard Rodriguez

B orn in San Francisco in 1944 of Mexican heritage, Richard Rodriguez received a B.A. from Stanford University and an M.A. from Columbia University. He is the author of *Hunger of Memory: The Education of Richard Rodriguez* (1982), in which a different version of the following essay appeared, as well as a new collection of essays, *Days of Obligation: An Argument with My Mexican Father* (1992).

ARIA: A MEMOIR OF A BILINGUAL CHILDHOOD

I remember, to start with, that day in Sacramento, in a California now nearly thirty years past, when I first entered a classroom—able to understand about fifty stray English words. The third of four children, I had been preceded by my older brother and sister to a neighborhood Roman Catholic school. But neither of them had revealed very much about their classroom experiences. They left each morning and returned each afternoon, always together, speaking Spanish as they climbed the five steps to the porch. And their mysterious books, wrapped in brown shopping-bag paper, remained on the table next to the door, closed firmly behind them.

An accident of geography sent me to a school where all my classmates were white and many were the children of doctors and lawyers and business executives. On that first day of school, my classmates must certainly have been uneasy to find themselves apart from their families, in the first institution of their lives. But I was astonished. I was fated to be the "problem student" in class.

The nun said, in a friendly but oddly impersonal voice: "Boys and girls, this is Richard Rodriguez." (I heard her sound it out: *Rich-heard Road-reeguess.*) It was the first time I had heard anyone say my name in English. "Richard," the nun repeated more slowly, writing my name down in her book. Quickly I turned to see my mother's face dissolve in a watery blur behind the pebbled-glass door.

Now, many years later, I hear of something called "bilingual education"—a scheme proposed in the late 1960s by Hispanic-American social activists, later endorsed by a congressional vote. It is a program that seeks to permit non-English-speaking children (many from lower-class homes) to use their "family language" as the language of school. Such, at least, is the aim its supporters announce. I hear them, and am forced to say no: It is not possible for a child, any child, ever to use his family's language in school. Not to understand this is to misunderstand the public uses of schooling and to trivialize the nature of intimate life.

Memory teaches me what I know of these matters. The boy reminds the adult. I was a bilingual child, but of a certain kind: "socially disadvantaged," the son of working-class parents, both Mexican immigrants.

In the early years of my boyhood, my parents coped very well in America. My father had steady work. My mother managed at home. They were nobody's victims. When we moved to a house many blocks from the Mexican-American section of town, they were not intimidated by those two or three neighbors who initially tried to make us unwelcome. ("Keep your brats away from my sidewalk!") But despite all they achieved, or perhaps because they had so much to achieve, they lacked any deep feeling of ease, of belonging in public. They regarded the people at work or in crowds as being very distant from us. Those were the others, *los gringos*. That term was interchangeable in their speech with another, even more telling: *los americanos*.

I grew up in a house where the only regular guests were my relations. On a certain day, enormous families of relatives would visit us, and there would be so many people that the noise and the bodies would spill out to the backyard and onto the front porch. Then for weeks no one would come. (If the doorbell rang, it was usually a salesman.) Our house stood apart—gaudy yellow in a row of white bungalows. We were the people with the noisy dog, the people who raised chickens. We were the foreigners on the block. A few neighbors would smile and wave at us. We waved back. But until I was seven years old, I did not know the name of the old couple living next door or the names of the kids living across the street.

In public, my father and mother spoke a hesitant, accented, and not always grammatical English. And then they would have to strain, their bodies tense, to catch the sense of what was rapidly said by *los gringos*. At home, they returned to Spanish. The language of their Mexican past sounded in counterpoint to the English spoken in public. The words would come quickly, with ease. Conveyed through those sounds was the pleasing, soothing, consoling reminder that one was at home.

During those years when I was first learning to speak, my mother and father addressed me only in Spanish; in Spanish I learned to reply. By contrast, English *(inglés)* was the language I came to associate with gringos, rarely heard in the house. I learned my first words of English overhearing my parents speaking to strangers. At six years of age, I knew just enough words for my mother to trust me on errands to stores one block away—but no more.

I was then a listening child, careful to hear the very different sounds of Spanish and English. Wide-eyed with hearing, I'd listen to sounds more than to words. First, there were English (gringo) sounds. So many words still were unknown to me that when the butcher or the lady at the drugstore said something, exotic polysyllabic sounds would bloom in the midst of their sentences. Often the speech of people in public seemed to me very loud, booming with confidence. The man behind the counter would literally ask, "What can I do for you?" But by being so firm and clear, the sound of his voice said that he was a gringo; he belonged in public society. There were also the high, nasal notes of middle-class American speech—which I rarely am conscious of hearing today because I hear them so often, but could not stop hearing when I was a boy. Crowds at Safeway or at bus stops were noisy with the birdlike sounds of *los gringos*. I'd move away from them all— all the chirping chatter above me.

My own sounds I was unable to hear, but I knew that I spoke English poorly. My words could not extend to form complete thoughts. And the words I did speak I didn't know well enough to make distinct sounds. (Listeners would usually lower their heads to hear better what I was trying to say.) But it was one thing for *me* to speak English with difficulty; it was more troubling to hear my parents speaking in public: their high-whining vowels and guttural consonants; their sentences that got stuck with "eh" and "ah" sounds; the confused syntax; the hesitant rhythm of sounds so different from the way gringos spoke. I'd notice, moreover, that my parents' voices were softer than those of gringos we would meet.

I am tempted to say now that none of this mattered. (In adulthood I am embarrassed by childhood fears.) And, in a way, it didn't matter very much that my parents could not speak English with ease. Their linguistic difficulties had no serious consequences. My mother and father made themselves understood at the county hospital clinic and at government offices. And yet, in another way, it mattered very much. It was unsettling to hear my parents struggle with English. Hearing them, I'd grow nervous, and my clutching trust in their protection and power would be weakened.

There were many times like the night at a brightly lit gasoline station (a blaring white memory) when I stood uneasily hearing my father talk to a teenage attendant. I do not recall what they were saying, but I cannot forget the sounds my father made as he spoke. At one point his words slid together to form one long word—sounds as confused as the threads of blue and green oil in the puddle next to my shoes. His voice rushed through what he had left to say. Toward the end, he reached falsetto notes, appealing to his listener's understanding. I looked away at the lights of passing automobiles. I tried not to hear any more. But I heard only too well the attendant's reply, his calm, easy tones. Shortly afterward, headed for home, I shivered when my father put his hand on my shoulder. The very first chance that I got, I evaded his grasp and ran on ahead into the dark, skipping with feigned boyish exuberance. 13

But then there was Spanish: *español*, the language rarely heard away from the house; *español*, the language which seemed to me therefore a private language, my family's language. To hear its sounds was to feel myself specially recognized as one of the family, apart from *los otros*.[1] A simple remark, an inconsequential comment could convey that assurance. My parents would say something to me and I would feel embraced by the sounds of their words. Those sounds said: *I am speaking with ease in Spanish. I am addressing you in words I never use with los gringos. I recognize you as someone special, close, like no one outside. You belong with us. In the family. Ricardo.* 14

At the age of six, well past the time when most middle-class children no longer notice the difference between sounds uttered at home and words spoken in public, I had a different experience. I lived in a world compounded of sounds. I was a child longer than most. I lived in a magical world, surrounded by sounds both pleasing and fearful. I shared with my family a language enchantingly private—different from that used in the city around us. 15

Just opening or closing the screen door behind me was an important experience. I'd rarely leave home all alone or without feeling reluctance. Walking down the sidewalk, under the canopy of tall trees, I'd warily notice the (suddenly) silent neighborhood kids who stood warily watching me. Nervously, I'd arrive at the grocery store to hear there the sounds of the gringo, reminding me that in this so-big world I was a foreigner. But if leaving home was never routine, neither was coming back. Walking toward our house, climbing the steps from the sidewalk, in summer when the front door was 16

---

1. The others.

open, I'd hear voices beyond the screen door talking in Spanish. For a second or two I'd stay, linger there listening. Smiling, I'd hear my mother call out, saying in Spanish, "Is that you, Richard?" Those were her words, but all the while her sounds would assure me: *You are home now. Come closer inside. With us.* "*Sí,*" I'd reply.

Once more inside the house, I would resume my place in the family. The sounds would grow harder to hear. Once more at home, I would grow less conscious of them. It required, however, no more than the blurt of the doorbell to alert me all over again to listen to sounds. The house would turn instantly quiet while my mother went to the door. I'd hear her hard English sounds. I'd wait to hear her voice turn to soft-sounding Spanish, which assured me, as surely as did the clicking tongue of the lock on the door, that the stranger was gone. 17

Plainly it is not healthy to hear such sounds so often. It is not healthy to distinguish public from private sounds so easily. I remained cloistered by sounds, timid and shy in public, too dependent on the voices at home. And yet I was a very happy child when I was at home. I remember many nights when my father would come back from work, and I'd hear him call out to my mother in Spanish, sounding relieved. In Spanish, his voice would sound the light and free notes that he never could manage in English. Some nights I'd jump up just hearing his voice. My brother and I would come running into the room where he was with our mother. Our laughing (so deep was the pleasure!) became screaming. Like others who feel the pain of public alienation, we transformed the knowledge of our public separateness into a consoling reminder of our intimacy. Excited, our voices joined in a celebration of sounds. *We are speaking now the way we never speak out in public—we are together*, the sounds told me. Some nights no one seemed willing to loosen the hold that sounds had on us. At dinner we invented new words that sounded Spanish, but made sense only to us. We pieced together new words by taking, say, an English verb and giving it Spanish endings. My mother's instructions at bedtime would be lacquered with mock-urgent tones. Or a word like *sí*, sounded in several notes, would convey added measures of feeling. Tongues lingered around the edges of words, especially fat vowels. And we happily sounded that military drum roll, the twirling roar of the Spanish *r*. Family language, my family's sounds: the voices of my parents and sisters and brother. Their voices insisting: *You belong here. We are family members. Related. Special to one another. Listen!* Voices singing and sighing, rising and straining, then surging, teeming with pleasure which burst syllables into fragments of laughter. At times it seemed there was steady quiet only when, from another room, the rustling whispers of my parents faded and I edged closer to sleep. 18

Supporters of bilingual education imply today that students like me miss a great deal by not being taught in their family's language. What they seem not to recognize is that, as a socially disadvantaged child, I regarded Spanish as a private language. It was a ghetto language that deepened and strength- 19 ened my feeling of public separateness. What I needed to learn in school was that I had the right, and the obligation, to speak the public language. The odd truth is that my first-grade classmates could have become bilingual, in the conventional sense of the word, more easily than I. Had they been taught early (as upper middle-class children often are taught) a "second language" like Spanish or French, they could have regarded it simply as another public language. In my case, such bilingualism could not have been so quickly achieved. What I did not believe was that I could speak a single public language.

Without question, it would have pleased me to have heard my teachers 20 address me in Spanish when I entered the classroom. I would have felt much less afraid. I would have imagined that my instructors were somehow "related" to me; I would indeed have heard their Spanish as my family's language. I would have trusted them and responded with ease. But I would have delayed—postponed for how long?—having to learn the language of public society. I would have evaded—and for how long?—learning the great lesson of school: that I had a public identity.

Fortunately, my teachers were unsentimental about their responsibility. 21 What they understood was that I needed to speak public English. So their voices would search me out, asking me questions. Each time I heard them I'd look up in surprise to see a nun's face frowning at me. I'd mumble, not really meaning to answer. The nun would persist. "Richard, stand up. Don't look at the floor. Speak up. Speak to the entire class, not just to me!" But I couldn't believe English could be my language to use. (In part, I did not want to believe it.) I continued to mumble. I resisted the teacher's demands. (Did I somehow suspect that once I learned this public language my family life would be changed?) Silent, waiting for the bell to sound, I remained dazed, diffident, afraid.

Because I wrongly imagined that English was intrinsically a public lan- 22 guage and Spanish was intrinsically private, I easily noted the difference between classroom language and the language of home. At school, words were directed to a general audience of listeners. ("Boys and girls . . .") Words were meaningfully ordered. And the point was not self-expression alone, but to make oneself understood by many others. The teacher quizzed: "Boys and girls, why do we use that word in this sentence? Could we think of a better word to use there? Would the sentence change its meaning if the words were differently arranged? Isn't there a better way of saying much the same thing?" (I couldn't say. I wouldn't try to say.)

Three months passed. Five. A half year. Unsmiling, ever watchful, my 23 teachers noted my silence. They began to connect my behavior with the slow progress my brother and sisters were making. Until, one Saturday morning, three nuns arrived at the house to talk to our parents. Stiffly they sat on the blue living-room sofa. From the doorway of another room, spying on the visitors, I noted the incongruity, the clash of two worlds, the faces and voices of school intruding upon the familiar setting of home. I overheard one voice gently wondering, "Do your children speak only Spanish at home, Mrs. Rodriguez?" While another voice added, "That Richard especially seems so timid and shy."

That Rich-heard!   24

With great tact, the visitors continued, "Is it possible for you and your   25
husband to encourage your children to practice their English when they are home?" Of course my parents complied. What would they not do for their children's well-being? And how could they question the Church's authority which those women represented? In an instant they agreed to give up the language (the sounds) which had revealed and accentuated our family's closeness. The moment after the visitors left, the change was observed. "*Ahora,* speak to us only *en inglés,*"[2] my father and mother told us.

At first, it seemed a kind of game. After dinner each night, the family   26
gathered together to practice "our" English. It was still then *inglés,* a language foreign to us, so we felt drawn to it as strangers. Laughing, we would try to define words we could not pronounce. We played with strange English sounds, often over-anglicizing our pronunciations. And we filled the smiling gaps of our sentences with familiar Spanish sounds. But that was cheating, somebody shouted, and everyone laughed.

In school, meanwhile, like my brother and sisters, I was required to   27
attend a daily tutoring session. I needed a full year of this special work. I also needed my teachers to keep my attention from straying in class by calling out, "*Rich-heard!*"—their English voices slowly loosening the ties to my other name, with its three notes, *Ri-car-do.* Most of all, I needed to hear my mother and father speak to me in a moment of seriousness in "broken"—suddenly heartbreaking—English. This scene was inevitable. One Saturday morning I entered the kitchen where my parents were talking, but I did not realize that they were talking in Spanish until, the moment they saw me, their voices changed and they began speaking English. The gringo sounds they uttered startled me. Pushed me away. In that moment of trivial misunderstanding and profound insight, I felt my throat twisted by unsounded grief. I simply turned and left the room. But I had no place to escape to where I could grieve in Spanish. My brother and sisters were speaking English in another part of the house.

Again and again in the days following, as I grew increasingly angry, I   28
was obliged to hear my mother and father encouraging me: "Speak to us *en inglés.*" Only then did I determine to learn classroom English. Thus, sometime afterward it happened: one day in school, I raised my hand to volunteer an answer to a question. I spoke out in a loud voice and I did not think it remarkable when the entire class understood. That day I moved very far from being the disadvantaged child I had been only days earlier. Taken hold at last was the belief, the calming assurance, that I *belonged* in public.

Shortly after, I stopped hearing the high, troubling sounds of *los gringos.*   29

2. Now . . . in English.

A more and more confident speaker of English, I didn't listen to how strangers sounded when they talked to me. With so many English-speaking people around me, I no longer heard American accents. Conversations quickened. Listening to persons whose voices sounded eccentrically pitched, I might note their sounds for a few seconds, but then I'd concentrate on what they were saying. Now when I heard someone's tone of voice—angry or questioning or sarcastic or happy or sad—I didn't distinguish it from the words it expressed. Sound and word were thus tightly wedded. At the end of each day I was often bemused, and always relieved, to realize how "soundless," though crowded with words, my day in public had been. An eight-year-old boy, I finally came to accept what had been technically true since my birth: I was an American citizen.

But diminished by then was the special feeling of closeness at home. 30 Gone was the desperate, urgent, intense feeling of being at home among those with whom I felt intimate. Our family remained a loving family, but one greatly changed. We were no longer so close, no longer bound tightly together by the knowledge of our separateness from *los gringos.* Neither my older brother nor my sisters rushed home after school any more. Nor did I. When I arrived home, often there would be neighborhood kids in the house. Or the house would be empty of sounds.

Following the dramatic Americanization of their children, even my par- 31 ents grew more publicly confident—especially my mother. First she learned the names of all the people on the block. Then she decided we needed to have a telephone in our house. My father, for his part, continued to use the word gringo, but it was no longer charged with bitterness or distrust. Stripped of any emotional content, the word simply became a name for those Americans not of Hispanic descent. Hearing him, sometimes, I wasn't sure if he was pronouncing the Spanish word *gringo,* or saying gringo in English.

There was a new silence at home. As we children learned more and 32 more English, we shared fewer and fewer words with our parents. Sentences needed to be spoken slowly when one of us addressed our mother or father. Often the parent wouldn't understand. The child would need to repeat himself. Still the parent misunderstood. The young voice, frustrated, would end up saying, "Never mind"—the subject was closed. Dinners would be noisy with the clinking of knives and forks against dishes. My mother would smile softly between her remarks; my father, at the other end of the table, would chew and chew his food while he stared over the heads of his children.

My mother! My father! After English became my primary language, I 33 no longer knew what words to use in addressing my parents. The old Spanish words (those tender accents of sound) I had earlier used—*mamá* and *papá*— I couldn't use any more. They would have been all-too-painful reminders of how much had changed in my life. On the other hand, the words I heard neighborhood kids call their parents seemed equally unsatisfactory. "Mother" and "father," "ma," "papa," "pa," "dad," "pop" (how I hated the all-American sound of that last word)—all these I felt were unsuitable terms of address for *my* parents. As a result, I never used them at home. Whenever I'd speak to my parents, I would try to get their attention by looking at them. In public conversations, I'd refer to them as my "parents" or my "mother" and "father."

My mother and father, for their part, responded differently, as their children spoke to them less. My mother grew restless, seemed troubled and anxious at the scarceness of words exchanged in the house. She would question me about my day when I came home from school. She smiled at my small talk. She pried at the edges of my sentences to get me to say something more. ("What . . .?") She'd join conversations she overheard, but her intrusions often stopped her children's talking. By contrast, my father seemed to grow reconciled to the new quiet. Though his English somewhat improved, he tended more and more to retire into silence. At dinner he spoke very little. One night his children and even his wife helplessly giggled at his garbled English pronunciation of the Catholic "Grace Before Meals." Thereafter he made his wife recite the prayer at the start of each meal, even on formal occasions when there were guests in the house.

Hers became the public voice of the family. On official business it was she, not my father, who would usually talk to strangers on the phone or in stores. We children grew so accustomed to his silence that years later we would routinely refer to his "shyness." (My mother often tried to explain: both of his parents died when he was eight. He was raised by an uncle who treated him as little more than a menial servant. He was never encouraged to speak. He grew up alone—a man of few words.) But I realized my father was not shy whenever I'd watch him speaking Spanish with relatives. Using Spanish, he was quickly effusive. Especially when talking with other men, his voice would spark, flicker, flare alive with varied sounds. In Spanish he expressed ideas and feelings he rarely revealed when speaking English. With firm Spanish sounds he conveyed a confidence and authority that English would never allow him.

The silence at home, however, was not simply the result of fewer words passing between parents and children. More profound for me was the silence created by my inattention to sounds. At about the time I no longer bothered to listen with care to the sounds of English in public, I grew careless about listening to the sounds made by the family when they spoke. Most of the time I would hear someone speaking at home and didn't distinguish his sounds from the words people uttered in public. I didn't even pay much attention to my parents' accented and ungrammatical speech—at least not at home. Only when I was with them in public would I become alert to their accents. But even then their sounds caused me less and less concern. For I was growing increasingly confident of my own public identity.

I would have been happier about my public success had I not recalled, sometimes, what it had been like earlier, when my family conveyed its intimacy through a set of conveniently private sounds. Sometimes in public, hearing a stranger, I'd hark back to my lost past. A Mexican farm worker approached me one day downtown. He wanted directions to some place.

"*Hijito*, . . ."[3] he said. And his voice stirred old longings. Another time I was standing beside my mother in the visiting room of a Carmelite convent, before the dense screen which rendered the nuns shadowy figures. I heard several of them speaking Spanish in their busy, singsong, overlapping voices, assuring my mother that, yes, yes, we were remembered, all our family was remembered, in their prayers. Those voices echoed faraway family sounds. Another day a dark-faced old woman touched my shoulder lightly to steady herself as she boarded a bus. She murmured something to me I couldn't quite comprehend. Her Spanish voice came near, like the face of a never-before-seen relative in the instant before I was kissed. That voice, like so many of the Spanish voices I'd hear in public, recalled the golden age of my childhood.

Bilingual educators say today that children lose a degree of "individuality" by becoming assimilated into public society. (Bilingual schooling is a program popularized in the seventies, that decade when middle-class "ethnics" began to resist the process of assimilation—the "American melting pot.") But the bilingualists oversimplify when they scorn the value and necessity of assimilation. They do not seem to realize that a person is individualized in two ways. So they do not realize that, while one suffers a diminished sense of *private* individuality by being assimilated into public society, such assimilation makes possible the achievement of *public* individuality. 38

Simplistically again, the bilingualists insist that a student should be reminded of his difference from others in mass society, of his "heritage." But they equate mere separateness with individuality. The fact is that only in private—with intimates—is separateness from the crowd a prerequisite for individuality; an intimate "tells" me that I am unique, unlike all others, apart from the crowd. In public, by contrast, full individuality is achieved, paradoxically, by those who are able to consider themselves members of the crowd. Thus it happened for me. Only when I was able to think of myself as an American, no longer an alien in gringo society, could I seek the rights and opportunities necessary for full public individuality. The social and political advantages I enjoy as a man began on the day I came to believe that my name is indeed *Rich-heard Road-ree-guess*. It is true that my public society today is often impersonal; in fact, my public society is usually mass society. But despite the anonymity of the crowd, and despite the fact that the individuality I achieve in public is often tenuous—because it depends on my being one in a crowd—I celebrate the day I acquired my new name. Those middle-class ethnics who scorn assimilation seem to me filled with decadent self-pity, obsessed by the burden of public life. Dangerously, they romanticize public separateness and trivialize the dilemma of those who are truly socially disadvantaged. 39

If I rehearse here the changes in my private life after my Americaniza- 40

3. Little boy, little son.

tion, it is finally to emphasize a public gain. The loss implies the gain. The house I returned to each afternoon was quiet. Intimate sounds no longer greeted me at the door. Inside there were other noises. The telephone rang. Neighborhood kids ran past the door of the bedroom where I was reading my schoolbooks—covered with brown shopping-bag paper. Once I learned the public language, it would never again be easy for me to hear intimate family voices. More and more of my day was spent hearing words, not sounds. But that may only be a way of saying that on the day I raised my hand in class and spoke loudly to an entire roomful of faces, my childhood started to end.

I grew up the victim of a disconcerting confusion. As I became fluent in   41
English, I could no longer speak Spanish with confidence. I continued to understand spoken Spanish, and in high school I learned how to read and write Spanish. But for many years I could not pronounce it. A powerful guilt blocked my spoken words; an essential glue was missing whenever I would try to connect words to form sentences. I would be unable to break a barrier of sound, to speak freely. I would speak, or try to speak, Spanish, and I would manage to utter halting, hiccuping sounds which betrayed my unease. (Even today I speak Spanish very slowly, at best.)

When relatives and Spanish-speaking friends of my parents came to the   42
house, my brother and sisters would usually manage to say a few words before being excused. I never managed so gracefully. Each time I'd hear myself addressed in Spanish, I couldn't respond with any success. I'd know the words I wanted to say, but I couldn't say them. I would try to speak, but everything I said seemed to me horribly anglicized. My mouth wouldn't form the sounds right. My jaw would tremble. After a phrase or two, I'd stutter, cough up a warm, silvery sound, and stop.

My listeners were surprised to hear me. They'd lower their heads to   43
grasp better what I was trying to say. They would repeat their questions in gentle, affectionate voices. But then I would answer in English. No, no, they would say, we want you to speak to us in Spanish *("en español")*. But I couldn't do it. Then they would call me *pocho*. Sometimes playfully, teasing, using the tender diminutive—*mi pochito*. Sometimes not so playfully but mockingly, *pocho*. (A Spanish dictionary defines that word as an adjective meaning "colorless" or "bland." But I heard it as a noun, naming the Mexican-American who, in becoming an American, forgets his native society.) *"¡Pocho!"* my mother's best friend muttered, shaking her head. And my mother laughed, somewhere behind me. She said that her children didn't want to practice "our Spanish" after they started going to school. My mother's smiling voice made me suspect that the lady who faced me was not really angry at me. But searching her face, I couldn't find the hint of a smile.

Embarrassed, my parents would often need to explain their children's   44
inability to speak fluent Spanish during those years. My mother encountered the wrath of her brother, her only brother, when he came up from Mexico

one summer with his family and saw his nieces and nephews for the very first time. After listening to me, he looked away and said what a disgrace it was that my siblings and I couldn't speak Spanish, *"su propria idioma."*[4] He made that remark to my mother, but I noticed that he stared at my father.

One other visitor from those years I clearly remember: a long-time friend of my father from San Francisco who came to stay with us for several days in late August. He took great interest in me after he realized that I couldn't answer his questions in Spanish. He would grab me, as I started to leave the kitchen. He would ask me something. Usually he wouldn't bother to wait for my mumbled response. Knowingly, he'd murmur, *"¿Ay pocho, pocho, dónde vas?"*[5] And he would press his thumbs into the upper part of my arms, making me squirm with pain. Dumbly I'd stand there, waiting for his wife to notice us and call him off with a benign smile. I'd giggle, hoping to deflate the tension between us, pretending that I hadn't seen the glittering scorn in his glance.

I recount such incidents only because they suggest the fierce power that Spanish had over many people I met at home, how strongly Spanish was associated with closeness. Most of those people who called me a *pocho* could have spoken English to me, but many wouldn't. They seemed to think that Spanish was the only language we could use among ourselves, that Spanish alone permitted our association. (Such persons are always vulnerable to the ghetto merchant and the politician who have learned the value of speaking their clients' "family language" so as to gain immediate trust.) For my part, I felt that by learning English I had somehow committed a sin of betrayal. But betrayal against whom? Not exactly against the visitors to the house. Rather, I felt I had betrayed my immediate family. I knew that my parents had encouraged me to learn English. I knew that I had turned to English with angry reluctance. But once I spoke English with ease, I came to feel guilty. I sensed that I had broken the spell of intimacy which had once held the family so close together. It was this original sin against my family that I recalled whenever anyone addressed me in Spanish and I responded, confounded.

Yet even during those years of guilt, I was coming to grasp certain consoling truths about language and intimacy—truths that I learned gradually. Once, I remember playing with a friend in the backyard when my grandmother appeared at the window. Her face was stern with suspicion when she saw the boy (the *gringo* boy) I was with. She called out to me in Spanish, sounding the whistle of her ancient breath. My companion looked up and watched her intently as she lowered the window and moved (still visible) behind the light curtain, watching us both. He wanted to know what she had said. I started to tell him, to translate her Spanish words into English. The problem was, however, that though I knew how to translate exactly

---

4. Their own language.

5. *Pocho,* where are you?

45

46

47

what she had told me, I realized that any translation would distort the deepest meaning of her message; it had been directed only to me. This message of intimacy could never be translated because it did not lie in the actual words she had used but passed through them. So any translation would have seemed wrong; the words would have been stripped of an essential meaning. Finally I decided not to tell my friend anything—just that I didn't hear all she had said.

This insight was unfolded in time. As I made more and more friends outside my house, I began to recognize intimate messages spoken in English in a close friend's confidential tone or secretive whisper. Even more remarkable were those instances when, apparently for no special reason, I'd become conscious of the fact that my companion was speaking *only to me*. I'd marvel then, just hearing his voice. It was a stunning event to be able to break through the barrier of public silence, to be able to hear the voice of the other, to realize that it was directed just to me. After such moments of intimacy outside the house, I began to trust what I heard intimately conveyed through my family's English. Voices at home at last punctured sad confusion. I'd hear myself addressed as an intimate—in English. Such moments were never as raucous with sound as in past times, when we had used our "private" Spanish. (Our English-sounding house was never to be as noisy as our Spanish-sounding house had been.) Intimate moments were usually moments of soft sound. My mother would be ironing in the dining room while I did my homework nearby. She would look over at me, smile, and her voice sounded to tell me that I was her son. *Richard.*

Intimacy thus continued at home; intimacy was not stilled by English. Though there were fewer occasions for it—a change in my life that I would never forget—there were also times when I sensed the deep truth about language and intimacy: *Intimacy is not created by a particular language; it is created by intimates.* Thus the great change in my life was not linguistic but social. If, after becoming a successful student, I no longer heard intimate voices as often as I had earlier, it was not because I spoke English instead of Spanish. It was because I spoke public language for most of my day. I moved easily at last, a citizen in a crowded city of words.

As a man I spend most of my day in public, in a world largely devoid of speech sounds. So I am quickly attracted by the glamorous quality of certain alien voices. I still am gripped with excitement when someone passes me on the street, speaking in Spanish. I have not moved beyond the range of the nostalgic pull of those sounds. And there is something very compelling about the sounds of lower-class blacks. Of all the accented versions of English that I hear in public, I hear theirs most intently. The Japanese tourist stops me downtown to ask me a question and I inch my way past his accent to concentrate on what he is saying. The eastern European immigrant in the neighborhood delicatessen speaks to me and, again, I do not pay much attention to his sounds, nor to the Texas accent of one of my neighbors or the

Chicago accent of the woman who lives in the apartment below me. But when the ghetto black teenagers get on the city bus, I hear them. Their sounds in my society are the sounds of the outsider. Their voices annoy me for being so loud—so self-sufficient and unconcerned by my presence, but for the same reason they are glamorous: a romantic gesture against public acceptance. And as I listen to their shouted laughter, I realize my own quietness. I feel envious of them—envious of their brazen intimacy.

I warn myself away from such envy, however. Overhearing those teenagers, I think of the black political activists who lately have argued in favor of using black English in public schools—an argument that varies only slightly from that of foreign-language bilingualists. I have heard "radical" linguists make the point that black English is a complex and intricate version of English. And I do not doubt it. But neither do I think that black English should be a language of public instruction. What makes it inappropriate in classrooms is not something in the language itself but, rather, what lower-class speakers make of it. Just as Spanish would have been a dangerous language for me to have used at the start of my education, so black English would be a dangerous language to use in the schooling of teenagers for whom it reinforces feelings of public separateness.

This seems to me an obvious point to make, and yet it must be said. In recent years there have been many attempts to make the language of the alien a public language. "Bilingual education, two ways to understand . . ." television and radio commercials glibly announce. Proponents of bilingual education are careful to say that above all they want every student to acquire a good education. Their argument goes something like this: Children permitted to use their family language will not be so alienated and will be better able to match the progress of English-speaking students in the crucial first months of schooling. Increasingly confident of their ability, such children will be more inclined to apply themselves to their studies in the future. But then the bilingualists also claim another very different goal. They say that children who use their family language in school will retain a sense of their ethnic heritage and their family ties. Thus the supporters of bilingual education want it both ways. They propose bilingual schooling as a way of helping students acquire the classroom skills crucial for public success. But they likewise insist that bilingual instruction will give students a sense of their identity apart from the English-speaking public.

Behind this scheme gleams a bright promise for the alien child: one can become a public person while still remaining a private person. Who would not want to believe such an appealing idea? Who can be surprised that the scheme has the support of so many middle-class ethnic Americans? If the barrio or ghetto child can retain his separateness even while being publicly educated, then it is almost possible to believe that no private cost need be paid for public success. This is the consolation offered by any of the number of current bilingual programs. Consider, for example, the bilingual voter's ballot. In some American cities one can cast a ballot printed in several languages. Such a document implies that it is possible for one to exercise that most public of rights—the right to vote—while still keeping oneself apart, unassimilated in public life.

It is not enough to say that such schemes are foolish and certainly doomed. 54 Middle-class supporters of public bilingualism toy with the confusion of those Americans who cannot speak standard English as well as they do. Moreover, bilingual enthusiasts sin against intimacy. A Hispanic-American tells me, "I will never give up my family language," and he clutches a group of words as though they were the source of his family ties. He credits to language what he should credit to family members. This is a convenient mistake, for as long as he holds on to certain familiar words, he can ignore how much else has actually changed in his life.

It has happened before. In earlier decades, persons ambitious for social 55 mobility, and newly successful, similarly seized upon certain "family words." Workingmen attempting to gain political power, for example, took to calling one another "brother." The word as they used it, however, could never resemble the word (the sound) "brother" exchanged by two people in intimate greeting. The context of its public delivery made it at best a metaphor; with repetition it was only a vague echo of the intimate sound. Context forced the change. Context could not be overruled. Context will always protect the realm of the intimate from public misuse. Today middle-class white Americans continue to prove the importance of context as they try to ignore it. They seize upon idioms of the black ghetto, but their attempt to appropriate such expressions invariably changes the meaning. As it becomes a public expression, the ghetto idiom loses its sound, its message of public separateness and strident intimacy. With public repetition it becomes a series of words, increasingly lifeless.

The mystery of intimate utterance remains. The communication of inti- 56 macy passes through the word and enlivens its sound, but it cannot be held by the word. It cannot be retained or ever quoted because it is too fluid. It depends not on words but on persons.

My grandmother! She stood among my other relations mocking me when 57 I no longer spoke Spanish. *Pocho*, she said. But then it made no difference. She'd laugh, and our relationship continued because language was never its source. She was a woman in her eighties during the first decade of my life— a mysterious woman to me, my only living grandparent, a woman of Mexico in a long black dress that reached down to her shoes. She was the one relative of mine who spoke no word of English. She had no interest in gringo society and remained completely aloof from the public. She was protected by her daughters, protected even by me when we went to Safeway together and I needed to act as her translator. An eccentric woman. Hard. Soft.

When my family visited my aunt's house in San Francisco, my grand- 58 mother would search for me among my many cousins. When she found me, she'd chase them away. Pinching her granddaughters, she would warn them away from me. Then she'd take me to her room, where she had prepared for my coming. There would be a chair next to the bed, a dusty jellied candy nearby, and a copy of *Life en Español* for me to examine. "There," she'd say. And I'd sit content, a boy of eight. *Pocho*, her favorite. I'd sift through the pictures of earthquake-destroyed Latin-American cities and blonde-wigged Mexican movie stars. And all the while I'd listen to the sound of my grandmother's voice. She'd pace around the room, telling me stories of her life. Her past. They were stories so familiar that I couldn't remember when I'd heard them for the first time. I'd look up sometimes to listen. Other times she'd look over at me, but she never expected a response. Sometimes I'd smile or nod. (I understood exactly what she was saying.) But it never seemed to matter to her one way or the other. It was enough that I was there. The words she spoke were almost irrelevant to that fact. We were content. And the great mystery remained: intimate utterance.

I learn nothing about language and intimacy listening to those social activists who propose using one's family language in public life. I learn much more simply by listening to songs on a radio, or hearing a great voice at the opera, or overhearing the woman downstairs at an open window singing to herself. Singers celebrate the human voice. Their lyrics are words, but, animated by voice, those words are subsumed into sounds. (This suggests a central truth about language: all words are capable of becoming sounds as we fill them with the "music" of our life.) With excitement I hear the words yielding their enormous power to sound, even though their meaning is never totally obliterated. In most songs, the drama or tension results from the way that the singer moves between words (sense) and notes (song). At one moment the song simply "says" something; at another moment the voice stretches out the words and moves to the realm of pure sound. Most songs are about love: lost love, celebrations of loving, pleas. By simply being occasions when sounds soar through words, however, songs put me in mind of the most intimate moments of life.

Finally, among all types of music, I find songs created by lyric poets most compelling. On no other public occasion is sound so important for me. Written poems on a page seem at first glance a mere collection of words. And yet, without musical accompaniment, the poet leads me to hear the sounds of the words that I read. As song, a poem moves between the levels of sound and sense, never limited to one realm or the other. As a public artifact, the poem can never offer truly intimate sound, but it helps me to recall the intimate times of my life. As I read in my room, I grow deeply conscious of being alone, sounding my voice in search of another. The poem serves, then, as a memory device; it forces remembrance. And it refreshes; it reminds me of the possibility of escaping public words, the possibility that awaits me in intimate meetings.

The child reminds the adult: to seek intimate sounds is to seek the company of intimates. I do not expect to hear those sounds in public. I would dishonor those I have loved, and those I love now, to claim anything else. I would dishonor our intimacy by holding on to a particular language and calling it my family language. Intimacy cannot be trapped within words; it passes through words. It passes. Intimates leave the room. Doors close. Faces move away from the window. Time passes, and voices recede into the dark. Death finally quiets the voice. There is no way to deny it, no way to stand in the crowd claiming to utter one's family language.

The last time I saw my grandmother I was nine years old. I can tell you some of the things she said to me as I stood by her bed, but I cannot quote the message of intimacy she conveyed with her voice. She laughed, holding my hand. Her voice illumined disjointed memories as it passed them again. She remembered her husband—his green eyes, his magic name of Narcissio, his early death. She remembered the farm in Mexico, the eucalyptus trees nearby (their scent, she remembered, like incense). She remembered the family cow, the bell around its neck heard miles away. A dog. She remembered working as a seamstress, how she'd leave her daughters and son for long hours to go into Guadalajara to work. And how my mother would come running toward her in the sun—in her bright yellow dress—on her return. "MMMMAAAAMMMMÁÁÁÁÁ," the old lady mimicked her daughter (my mother) to her daughter's son. She laughed. There was the snap of a cough. An aunt came into the room and told me it was time I should leave. "You can see her tomorrow," she promised. So I kissed my grandmother's cracked face. And the last thing I saw was her thin, oddly youthful thigh, as my aunt rearranged the sheet on the bed.

At the funeral parlor a few days after, I remember kneeling with my relatives during the rosary. Among their voices I traced, then lost, the sounds of individual aunts in the surge of the common prayer. And I heard at that moment what since I have heard very often—the sound the women in my family make when they are praying in sadness. When I went up to look at my grandmother, I saw her through the haze of a veil draped over the open lid of the casket. Her face looked calm—but distant and unyielding to love. It was not the face I remembered seeing most often. It was the face she made in public when the clerk at Safeway asked her some question and I would need to respond. It was her public face that the mortician had designed with his dubious art.

STUDY QUESTIONS

1. To what extent was Rodriguez's early life defined by the intimacy of the family? How was "family" defined? What role did language play in the family's self-definition? To what extent was his identity defined by the hostility of "los gringos"? In what ways was his family different from others in the neighborhood? Why is "los Americanos" a more "telling" term than "los gringos" (paragraph 6)?

2. In what ways does the language used, by Rodriguez and others, in the early paragraphs of this memoir help to define the problems of living in self-contained worlds? How does Rodriguez describe the sounds of the language used in his

house? How does he connect sound to the sense of security he felt in his family? Explain what he means later in the memoir, about the sounds of the outsider (paragraph 50). How do you reconcile these two observations?

3. How did the young Rodriguez react to his parents' efforts to speak English? Explain why he comes to think of Spanish as a "private" language. How accurate does the distinction turn out to be for him in later life? How does his opinion of "bilingual education" relate to his initial experiences at school? to his view of the difference between public and private language?

4. What does the difference between the way people call his name—"Rich-heard" or "Ri-car-do"—come to mean to Rodriguez as a boy? How does his acceptance of himself as "Rich-heard" later help him to define stages in his life?

5. Why does Rodriguez, as a boy, think that English is "intrinsically" a public language? How does his view change as he grows older? Why does it change?

6. Why does the family become more silent as the children learn more and more English? What seems to happen psychologically to the mother and father?

7. How does Rodriguez define the "necessity" (paragraph 38) of assimilation? List all of the arguments and examples he uses to support his position. What counterarguments can you think of?

8. What effect does the gradual loss of Spanish have on Rodriguez? Why does he call the speaking of English the "original sin against my family" (paragraph 46)?

9. Explain fully what Rodriguez means when he describes the "deep truth" (paragraph 49) about language and intimacy.

10. Explain the statement "Context will always protect the realm of the intimate from public misuse" (paragraph 55).

11. Why is the "sound of my grandmother's voice" (paragraph 58) so important to Rodriguez, even many years later when he remembers his childhood experiences from such a distance? Why does the sound blur or drown out other perceptions? How do you explain the preoccupation with sound and aural IMAGES throughout the memoir? Do you agree with Rodriguez that "a poem moves between the levels of sound and sense, never limited to one realm or the other"? On what principles does he base his argument?

12. Beyond his sensitivity to sound, Rodriguez is also a keen visual observer. Explain how he gives meaning to the visual image (paragraph 63) of his grandmother's face in the casket. Explain the meaning of the image (paragraph 3) of his mother's face dissolving behind the door. What other visual images in the memoir seem to you especially effective? How does each one work?

13. In what different ways are people's names important in this selection?

Gloria Naylor

G loria Naylor is the author of four highly acclaimed novels—*The Women of Brewster Place* (1982, for which she won the American Book Award for first fiction), *Linden Hills* (1985), *Mama Day* (1988), and *Bailey's Cafe* (1992)—and was awarded a Guggenheim Fellowship for 1988–89. She is a native of New York City, where she still lives, and was educated at Brooklyn College and Yale University. She has taught at George Washington University, New York University, and Boston University.

"MOMMY, WHAT DOES 'NIGGER' MEAN?"

Language is the subject. It is the written form with which I've managed to keep the wolf away from the door and, in diaries, to keep my sanity. In spite of this, I consider the written word inferior to the spoken, and much of the frustration experienced by novelists is the awareness that whatever we manage to capture in even the most transcendent passages falls far short of the richness of life. Dialogue achieves its power in the dynamics of a fleeting moment of sight, sound, smell and touch.

I'm not going to enter the debate here about whether it is language that shapes reality or vice versa. That battle is doomed to be waged whenever we seek intermittent reprieve from the chicken and egg dispute. I will simply take the position that the spoken word, like the written word, amounts to a nonsensical arrangement of sounds or letters without a consensus that assigns "meaning." And building from the meanings of what we hear, we order reality. Words themselves are innocuous; it is the consensus that gives them true power.

I remember the first time I heard the word "nigger." In my third-grade class, our math tests were being passed down the rows, and as I handed the papers to a little boy in back of me, I remarked that once again he had received a much lower mark than I did. He snatched his test from me and spit out that word. Had he called me a nymphomaniac or a necrophiliac, I couldn't have been more puzzled. I didn't know what a nigger was, but I knew that whatever it meant, it was something he shouldn't have called me. This was verified when I raised my hand, and in a loud voice repeated what he had said and watched the teacher scold him for using a "bad" word. I was later to go home and ask the inevitable question that every black parent must face—"Mommy, what does 'nigger' mean?"

And what exactly did it mean? Thinking back, I realize that this could 4 not have been the first time the word was used in my presence. I was part of a large extended family that had migrated from the rural South after World War II and formed a close-knit network that gravitated around my maternal grandparents. Their ground-floor apartment in one of the buildings they owned in Harlem was a weekend mecca for my immediate family, along with countless aunts, uncles and cousins who brought along assorted friends. It was a bustling and open house with assorted neighbors and tenants popping in and out to exchange bits of gossip, pick up an old quarrel or referee the ongoing checkers game in which my grandmother cheated shamelessly. They were all there to let down their hair and put up their feet after a week of labor in the factories, laundries and shipyards of New York.

Amid the clamor, which could reach deafening proportions—two or three 5 conversations going on simultaneously, punctuated by the sound of a baby's crying somewhere in the back rooms or out on the street—there was still a rigid set of rules about what was said and how. Older children were sent out of the living room when it was time to get into the juicy details about "you-know-who" up on the third floor who had gone and gotten herself "p-r-e-g-n-a-n-t!" But my parents, knowing that I could spell well beyond my years, always demanded that I follow the others out to play. Beyond sexual misconduct and death, everything else was considered harmless for our young ears. And so among the anecdotes of the triumphs and disappointments in the various workings of their lives, the word "nigger" was used in my presence, but it was set within contexts and inflections that caused it to register in my mind as something else.

In the singular, the word was always applied to a man who had distin- 6 guished himself in some situation that brought their approval for his strength, intelligence or drive:

"Did Johnny really do that?" 7

"I'm telling you, that nigger pulled in $6,000 of overtime last year. Said 8 he got enough for a down payment on a house."

When used with a possessive adjective by a woman—"my nigger"—it 9 became a term of endearment for husband or boyfriend. But it could be more than just a term applied to a man. In their mouths it became the pure essence of manhood—a disembodied force that channeled their past history of struggle and present survival against the odds into a victorious statement of being: "Yeah, that old foreman found out quick enough—you don't mess with a nigger."

In the plural, it became a description of some group within the com- 10 munity that had overstepped the bounds of decency as my family defined it: Parents who neglected their children, a drunken couple who fought in public, people who simply refused to look for work, those with excessively dirty mouths or unkempt households were all "trifling niggers." This particular circle could forgive hard times, unemployment, the occasional bout of depression—they had gone through all of that themselves—but the unforgivable sin was lack of self-respect.

A woman could never be a "nigger" in the singular, with its connotation of confirming worth. The noun "girl" was its closest equivalent in that sense, but only when used in direct address and regardless of the gender doing the addressing. "Girl" was a token of respect for a woman. The one-syllable word was drawn out to sound like three in recognition of the extra ounce of wit, nerve or daring that the woman had shown in the situation under discussion.

"G-i-r-l, stop. You mean you said that to his face?"

But if the word was used in a third-person reference or shortened so that it almost snapped out of the mouth, it always involved some element of communal disapproval. And age became an important factor in these exchanges. It was only between individuals of the same generation, or from an older person to a younger (but never the other way around), that "girl" would be considered a compliment.

I don't agree with the argument that use of the word nigger at this social stratum of the black community was an internalization of racism. The dynamics were the exact opposite: the people in my grandmother's living room took a word that whites used to signify worthlessness or degradation and rendered it impotent. Gathering there together, they transformed "nigger" to signify the varied and complex human beings they knew themselves to be. If the word was to disappear totally from the mouths of even the most liberal of white society, no one in that room was naïve enough to believe it would disappear from white minds. Meeting the word head-on, they proved it had absolutely nothing to do with the way they were determined to live their lives.

So there must have been dozens of times that the word "nigger" was spoken in front of me before I reached the third grade. But I didn't "hear" it until it was said by a small pair of lips that had already learned it could be a way to humiliate me. That was the word I went home and asked my mother about. And since she knew that I had to grow up in America, she took me in her lap and explained.

STUDY QUESTIONS

1. Why does the author, as a third grader, at first misunderstand a word she has heard so many times before? What is there about the word, as she hears it at school, that is different? According to Naylor, what controls the meaning of a particular word?

2. How does Naylor explain what happens when a community decides to take over a word and renegotiate its meaning?

3. What devices does Naylor use to suggest, in writing, the *oral* nuances of a word? How does her attempt to duplicate oral speech relate to the THEMES of her essay? Why, according to Naylor, is oral speech superior to writing?

4. Describe the organization of the essay. What function does the childhood anecdote perform? Why does the essay move from large generalization to specific anecdote to an again more general account of communal usage? How does the form of Naylor's essay reflect her view of how language works?

Rudolph Chelminski

Born in 1934 in Wilton, Connecticut, Rudolph Chelminski graduated from Harvard University in 1956. A reporter for *Life* magazine for many years, Chelminski served as bureau chief in Moscow. Since 1972, he has worked as a freelance writer.

NEXT TO BRZEZINSKI, CHELMINSKI'S A CINCH

"Mr. Joe Minski to see you, sir."   1

There it was: they were doing it again. I thought I had pronounced my   2
name slowly and clearly enough, but the receptionist came up with Variant
12-B of the dozens of exotic appellations I have encountered over the years.
Nothing particularly exciting or original about this one; I get it four or five
times a year, easy. Much more interesting was the guy who went for close
to a decade persuaded that my first name was Chet. He was an accountant,
too. He'd say, "Hi, Chet," then sit down with me and for half an hour or so
go over papers with my name spelled out clear as day.

It's baffling at first, but eventually you get used to it, and it finally becomes   3
something of a game, and you wonder what they'll find next in those three
syllables. Observing human creativity at work is one of the pleasures of being
born with a difficult name, a pleasure that you boring Browns and Youngs
and Norths will never be able to share. You don't know what you're missing.

On the surface—we're being purely objective now, you understand—   4
my name never struck me as being insuperably difficult: Chel-min-ski. Three
crisp syllables, bang-bang-bang, pronounced just the way they look. But
there's something about a Slavic name, especially one ending in -*ski* (the Polish way) or -*sky* (the Russian way), that panics Americans. Names equally
rich in syllabic content will trip from their tongues with the greatest of ease.
Any switchboard operator can pronounce Frankenstein, O'Mahoney, Pas-
qualini, Von Dittersdorf or Okamoto and chew gum at the same time. But
give them a whiff of the steppes of Eastern Europe and they melt into terrified stammerers, their brains frozen, everything previously heard erased as
soon as they encounter the magical -*ski*.

So it was the other day for Variant 12-B, Joe Minski.   5

I'm not sure where the Joe comes from, but it is a pattern, so I have to   6
assume that it's the only one-syllable name they can think of after their tape
has been erased. About the only Polish name I can think of that people feel
comfortable with is Stanley Kowalski, thanks to Marlon Brando and Tennessee Williams, but then they expect us to wear ripped T-shirts and mumble. Thanks a lot, boys. And what were *your* names before they changed
them?

It happens all the time, of course. I just recently heard of a Vladimir or   7
Casimir Something-or-other-ski who is now called Matt Conan, and I have
grave suspicions about all those Tab Hunters and Rock Hudsons. When I
was a senior in high school, a well-meaning teacher seriously suggested I
change my name to Chalmers or Chamberlain, and to this day my bisyllabic
pal John Neary simplifies life for himself by calling me Cholmondeley and
pronouncing it Chumley.

When I was a kid, Chiminski or Shiminski were about as close as my   8
little playmates could come to getting it right, but what could I expect from
a band of Colliers, Middlebrooks, Roscoes and Lounsberys? With a name
like mine, I might have been from another planet. Now, that was distinction.

In the Army I gave roll-call sergeants fits, of course, and if my company   9
commander in Korea had himself a little bit of innocent fun by dubbing me
Chimpanski, I was able to get some of the fun back by the Great Nameplate
Ploy. We all wore nameplates then, both the American G.I.'s and the ROK[1]
troops stationed in camp with us, our names emblazoned above the left pocket
of our fatigue shirts. Like me, the Koreans were invariably trisyllabic in
name, beginning with their patronymic and then going on to the "first" names.
Most of them were Kims, but there were exceptions.

Like me. I found me a nameplate printer and a tailor in the local village,   10
did a little presto-chango number, and for the rest of my tour of duty became
what the Koreans always called me anyway: Cho Min Sik.

I had to abandon my Oriental name when I returned to the States and   11

---

1. Republic of Korea.

became a grown-up, but I'm still able to play around a little with my sylla-bles. A few years ago I was in Finland, doing some reporting for a bureau chief in Paris named Milt Orshefsky. Naturally I checked into the Hotel Marski in the capital city because I already had worked out the first lines of the telex I wanted to send to Paris: Pro-Orshefsky Ex-Chelminski, Marski, Helsinki . . .

A few years after that memorable moment in literature, I went on a   12
story assignment to Poland, and in cold, gray, Communist Warsaw received the shock of my life when I learned that, after all those years of amused tolerance of my fellow Americans who mispronounced my name, *I had been mispronouncing it myself.*

It all has to do with the arcana of the Polish -*ch* sound, you see, and the   13
hard *l* and the soft *l*. Don't ask me why the Poles have two *l*s, but they do. You just have to accept that. The result, I discovered to my amazement, is that my name should be pronounced (are you ready?): Hey-you-mean-ski.

Oh, dear. I can't expect people to even *try* to say that, so now I just   14
stick with the same old three syllables I grew up with, even if they come out Joe Minski or Chet Nucci from time to time. After all, things could be worse. I could be named Zbigniew Brzezinski. Now, there is a guy with problems. Maybe he should change his name to Sam Brzezinski.

STUDY QUESTIONS

1. Have you had experiences in which your name has been distorted or misunder-stood at all comparable to Chelminski's? Have you been in a foreign country where your name was never pronounced quite right? (I had a friend named Bowen who, some years ago, married a Parisienne; her friends were willing to excuse her mar-rying a Yank, but, they said, "Couldn't you have married someone whose name was possible to pronounce?") If you have a common name have you run into dif-ferent but equally frustrating experiences? (An Emory graduate student named Johnson had terrible trouble opening an account with a local department store because someone with the same name had not paid her long-overdue bill.)

2. Have you or your family changed names? Do you know anyone who has? Has the purpose in either case been not just to simplify communication and relationships but to disguise ethnic origin? What public figures are you aware of who have changed their names? (Pagnozzi of the Cardinals fifty years ago would probably have been Paine—cp. Billy Martin; and Brunansky of [today] the Milwaukee Brewers would no doubt have been Brown—cp. Joe Collins of the old Yankees.)

WORDS

W hen we talk about the language someone speaks, we usually literally mean Spanish, or French, or Russian, or Japanese, or English. But those who know well any one of these major languages know that within each are dozens, perhaps hundreds, of distinct variations. "American" is different from the "English" of England, and both are different from "Canadian" or "Caribbean." But there are other refinements as well. People from Boston speak one way, people from San Antonio another. People from Toronto one way, from Vancouver another. Jamaica one way, Barbados another. Some of the difference involves urban versus rural distinctions, some involves regionalism. And there are differences, in speech and in written language, of race, class, occupation, neighborhood, income group. There is a language of farmers and one of truckers; computer technicians use a very different language, not just because they need special terms for things other people may not talk about at all, but because they think differently and share a particular system of expression that depends on shared values. English teachers tell you not to use (or certainly not to *over*use) the passive voice, and though many of them think that is because such use is "wrong" or "awkward" or "uneconomical," it is actually because the world, the value system they (we) live in assumes agency—that is, someone or something doing or acting; electrical engineers, I am told, prefer passives because they more accurately reflect the world of unnamed or unknown forces with which they deal.

There is street language, rap, the language of family, of church, of "the club" (whatever club it may be), of the classroom, the museum, the ball-park, the playground, the factory, the dance class, the game show, the kindergarten, the singles bar. All of us speak several of these languages, in addition to the English or Spanish or Arabic that we regard as our native language. We speak one way when we speak to people we know to be from a particular group—school friends, concertgoers, cousins, or lovers—and another way when we speak to others, not because we are phony with some people and not with others, but because even if all the languages are English, we are speaking different languages. Just as we would not speak French to a non-French-speaking American friend, so we would not speak "Wayne's World" lingo to our grandparents (or at least not to my grandparents). It is not just that we frame some abstract or intellectual thought and translate it into our audience's language, but when we are in that world we speak that language. Otherwise we have no dialogue; for part of our utterance is the CONTEXT—the time, place, and person we're speaking to (see the Afterword to chapter 8)—and, in a sense, part of it is that person's presumed or anticipated response, which is then another utterance leading to our response. People come from different places, literally and emotionally, and to speak with anyone, we have to speak in a common language.

Though that common language must involve some commonality of context, and a certain common competence in the syntax or structure of phrases and sentences, the basic unit of language is the word. The search for a common language must begin with words, but that is not as easy as it sounds. Words perhaps never mean quite the same thing to someone who hears them as they do to the person speaking them. They disappear into thin air, and we may misremember, or we may have misheard in the first place. Or the speaker may have misspoken or not gotten the emphasis just right. And even words firmly printed on a page do not always have definitive, discoverable, unimpeachable meaning. Nuances in the ways words are spoken change things; hearers filter words through their own consciousness, sometimes hearing only what they want to hear and sometimes mistaking intentions.

Writers work hard to make their meanings clear and solid, but often the words do not exactly express what writers wanted to say or thought they wanted to say. Words are, by definition, ambiguous. Every individual word, in any language, means more than one simple, specifiable thing, and when we string words together in phrases, sentences, and paragraphs, their possible meanings multiply and ramify. The process sounds hopeless when we think about all the things that can go wrong. And those things *do* often go wrong—in conversation, in writing, or in reading what someone else has written. Interpretations become ambiguous; confusions occur; misunderstandings result. The world of words, in life or in art, is often a frustrating and uncertain place. But it is also exciting. The excitement results in part from uncertainties and ambiguities, in part from the creative challenge. Communication does sometimes, miraculously, take place; speakers and writers, formally or in a conversation or a letter, find ways to get to us, to touch us. Words are power; they are explosive, sometimes dangerous.

Words are, first of all, things. Spoken words are sounds, and we assume poems are read aloud and sounded out as well as seen on the page. In Rita Dove's "Parsley" the sound of "r" is a matter of life and death. The SPEAKER in "Persimmons" recalls how in school his confusion about English words like "fight" and "fright" got him into trouble, and shows that those words were and are still related in his mind: "Fight was what I did when I was frightened, / fright was what I felt when I was fighting" (lines 32–33). Even in prose there is an element of sound: in " 'Learn! Learn!' " the repeated sound of "in" plus a consonant in "inquisitional indignities in the intimacy of the confessional" (paragraph 10) intensifies the vehemence of the priest's attack on the young people in his parish. This ALLITERATION, the repetition of initial sounds, also involves the look of the words as well, and written words have shapes. In the same story, José María Rivera forms his letters "in fluid curves, the tall letters, all the same height, gracefully swayed from lower left to upper right, the crosses of the t's straight and slightly lengthened" (paragraph 24). The letters in Nora Dauerhauer's concrete poem form the shape of an apple. Reading literature we need to pay attention to the sounds and shapes of the words, phrases, and even whole works.

Words are not, however, merely things, sounds in the air or marks on the page. For those who know the language, they also point outward to things, events, ideas, "meanings." The literary use of language, particularly in poetry, is economical—that is, each word or phrase is packed with meanings as well as with effective sounds or shapes—precise (without being pedestrian), suggestive, and affectively as well as intellectually effective. Notice in "Still Kicking in America," for example, how "Polish wife" and "withstood . . . dictators" call up both Hitler and Stalin; how "dangles" suggests swinging loosely, and "vehemently," which usually is applied to feelings, here suggests the woman's feelings but also incorporates its basic meaning of moving violently, so that in a few lines we have a graphic image and a sense of history, geography, politics. Later in the poem the self-deprecatory "vegetarian calves," compressing the idea of "thin legs of someone who does not eat meat," contrasts with the Polish wife's strong legs, and may even include a pun, "calves" referring to young cows, veal, and the carnivorous (puns are not beneath the dignity of poets).

Sometimes words are not used literally or referentially, but figuratively. Something unfamiliar, abstract, or emotive is written about as if it were something familiar or concrete, which helps us understand the former. The priest in " 'Learn! Learn!' " who thought he was going to rise in the Church hierarchy in Spain winds up in a Mexican-American parish; to protect his self-image and control his disappointment he "made a sword of his disillusionment and a shield of what had been his expectations" (paragraph 9).

The process of reading is a process of becoming self-conscious about words, of learning their limits, their hazards, the ways they can be misused as well as the ways they can help us to be more human and lead richer and more connected emotional and intellectual lives. Some of the misunderstandings words cause in life are from carelessness, the using of words without adequate consideration or control. In the selections in this chapter and throughout the book, the writers have ordinarily thought through very carefully exactly what they want to say and what they want to do. This does not mean that what they have written is perfect in every detail, but it does mean that the words have been carefully chosen and their effects upon us as readers have been planned, one might even say calculated.

The formal study of how language works is called RHETORIC. One can speak of the rhetoric of a given story—what effects it is calculated to produce—or more generally of the rhetoric of an author (what particular strategies of persuasion he or she uses) or the rhetoric of fiction or poetry (the way a particular literary mode uses language to accomplish its particular ends). Within rhetoric, certain standard features develop over a period of time, and when such features become commonly accepted and frequently imitated, they are called CONVENTIONS. There is, for example, a convention of giving descriptive or suggestive or symbolic names to CHARACTERS (Lily Goode, Dr. Stern) in order to give readers some idea of what they may be like. In life, nicknames often actually work the same way, but in literature, writers sometimes take a certain *license* with names, inventing names that help to characterize a person. Too egregious a use of descriptive or symbolic names would, of course, seem overdone, artificial, or just plain silly, and writers tend to husband such tricks carefully, if they are wise, so that readers will still find their work believable and enjoyable.

Writers, even the best professional writers, do sometimes make mistakes—either calculating their effects too precisely and becoming overingenious, or planning them insufficiently and becoming careless. But it is a good rule of thumb to assume that a good writer always has a reason for doing a particular thing—that every word is carefully chosen, and that the word used is exactly the one needed to make a particular point rather than some other almost equivalent word. Paying close attention to the language of a story, play, essay, or poem is usually quite rewarding, and one of the best habits a reader can develop is to ask, repeatedly, the questions: Why this word? Why in this place? What would the difference be if another word were used instead?

Words are the building blocks of writers, and writers with pride in their craft use what they have in the best possible way. The selections here have been chosen with an eye to finding examples of writing that show how language can be used effectively, how it can be used to make particular points, and, more important, how it can make us as readers feel, as well as think, in a particular way.

WRITING ABOUT THE READING

PERSONAL NARRATIVE

1. What forbidden words were considered most shocking in your home? in your community? in your school? among your friends? What kinds of people were willing to violate the taboo? What were their motivations? What price did they pay for the violation? What kinds of violations were most severely punished? Under what conditions, if any, were people allowed to use these forbidden words?

   Choose one incident from your childhood or teenage years in which community standards of language were violated. Describe the episode in detail, making clear just what kinds of standards—religious, moral, ethnic, or standards of "good" taste—were at issue in the incident.

2. Choose an incident or a repeated pattern in which your name or a friend's name has caused difficulty, or an incident in which you had great or repeated difficulty in dealing with someone's name or the names in a group. (Teachers will have no difficulty with this.)

IMITATIONS AND PARODIES

1. Using Gloria Naylor's essay as a model, discuss STEREOTYPICAL words or phrases that your own national, ethnic, or community group finds the most offensive when used by someone *outside* the group.

2. See the personal narrative suggestion regarding difficult names. Parody Rudolph Chelminski's personal narrative—perhaps by giving yourself a common name that no one gets right or a name so difficult no one could get it right but you who have that name—in which you are complaining about the ignorance or carelessness of everyone else.

3. See the second Research Paper suggestion (regarding Congressman Gingrich's list) below and construct a similar list for giving advice about courses or professors or potential dates.

4. Imitate or parody G. S. Sharat Chandra's poem by writing a poem or prose paragraph on language using a figure—and gerund—other than "kicking"—that is, "Still _____ing in America" (but see paragraph on forbidden words above).

COMPARISON-CONTRAST PAPERS

1. Note the relationshp of the repetitions in the title of " 'Learn! Learn!' " in this chapter and "Abalone, Abalone, Abalone" in chapter 9. Compare and contrast the

aspect of obsessiveness that the repetition seems to suggest in the two stories.

2. Note the common element in such titles as "Borders" in chapter 3 and "Limen" here, *Fences* in chapter 6, and those of other works you find, and compare how these boundary lines or obstructions are defined, what they suggest, how they are treated in the work, and whether they seem permanent or subject to human action and change.

ARGUMENTATIVE PAPER

On the basis of your own experiences or those of your friends, write an essay attacking Richard Rodriguez's position on the use of English in American schools. Be sure you read the Rodriguez piece carefully and understand exactly what his position is before you begin. Make clear what kinds of human values are at stake in the controversy.

Alternative essay: Write an essay based on your own experiences in which you support Rodriguez.

ANALYTICAL ESSAY

Using *The Indian Wants the Bronx*, " 'Learn! Learn!' " and "Borders" (in chapter 3) as examples, analyze the relationship between the uses of language and the everyday behavior that goes with the language use. In an essay of no more than 1,000 words, show how behavior and words are linked in the portrayal of CHARACTERS in these selections, and suggest what psychological insights are explored in the way these characters are presented.

RESEARCH PAPERS

1. List ten "forbidden" words from your childhood—words that family, friends, church groups, or school officials considered offensive. Using dictionaries of slang and other materials that reference librarians can help you find, look up the words' etymologies. Attempt to discover which words, if any, have always been considered objectionable and which, if any, have changed in their acceptability.

2. Congressman Newt Gingrich put out two lists of words—one that generates favorable response, the other unfavorable—and recommended that Republican candidates use the first about themselves or their program or party and the other about the D_____. Get the list from the library, newspaper, etc.; read the news and editorial pages of several different papers or of randomly selected issues of the same paper over a period of time; and report to what extent and how these lists seem to have been used. (You might want to go back to papers or magazines published during the election campaign of the summer and fall of 1992; in this case you could also indicate, if there is enough evidence, how effective or ineffective such tactics were.)

Student Writing

LANGUAGE, IDENTITY, AND VIOLENCE IN ISRAEL HOROVITZ'S *THE INDIAN WANTS THE BRONX*

Steven Krueger

In Israel Horovitz's *The Indian Wants the Bronx* Joey and Murph search for definitions. They try to define each other and the Indian, but the inadequacies of these definitions lead to violence and blur distinctions. Joey and Murph's use of repetition in language also reflects their failure to find meaning in words and identity. They perceive the conflicts which arise from disputes over identity as games. Throughout the drama, these characters play games, and they argue over definitions of essential words in the rules. They dispute the definitions not only of the rules, but also of the word "game" itself. This conflict reveals these characters' lack of ability to differentiate between reality and imagination. Through Joey and Murph's linguistic games and definitions, Horovitz explores the relationships between language, identity, and violence.

Joey and Murph create linguistic games in their attempts to define each other. In the beginning of this drama, they play a game which involves a pack of cigarettes. After cheating Joey out of the cigarettes, Murph tells Joey that he "lost his chance" (page 306). Joey protests Murph's victory: "We made a deal. A deal's a deal. You're a Jap, Murphy. A rotten Jap. Pussyface, listen to me! Murphy's a rotten Jap and just Japped my whole pack. That's unethical" (page 306). Joey's name-calling is an extension of this game. Although on the surface this reaction seems childish and playful, Joey's use of language has a deeper significance. While definition and heritage should create distinction, Joey's speech blends Murph's heritage and Japanese heritage. This ambiguity undermines the importance of heritage and confuses identity. In another game, Joey and Murph dispute each other's sexual identity. Murph accuses Joey of homosexuality: "You sexy beast, you'd wink at anything in pants" (page 306). Murph not only questions Joey's sexuality, but also dehumanizes him. Murph's verbal attack blurs the distinctions between animals and humans. Joey defends himself in this linguistic war by turning this attack back upon the aggressor: "Come on. Do I look like a Murphy?" (page 306). In response to this retaliation, Murph introduces violence into the game. He twists Joey's arm and demands that Joey admit that he is a "Turkie-humper" (page 306). Although he struggles momentarily, Joey surrenders to this use of force: "Oww, ya' dirty bastard! All right, I'm a Turkie-humper! Now, leggo!" (page 306). Murph wins the game, but fails to truly define Joey. Instead, Murph uses violence to force Joey to accept a false definition of himself.

Joey and Murph's use of repetition in language also reveals their inability to find meaning in identity or language. Throughout the drama, they imitate each other's language and mannerisms. Joey tells the Indian, for example, that he "ain't gonna find no Bronx on this bus" (page 309). Murph mimics Joey's statement: "You ain't going to find the Bronx on this bus" (page 309). Despite the fact that they are speaking the same words, Horovitz questions whether or not repetition reveals meaning. Murph, for example, imitates the Indian: "Toom-haree bah-at nah-hee sah-maj sak-tah" (page 311). Although he is speaking Hindi, Murph does not find meaning in the words. Similarly, the Indian repeats Joey in English. When the Indian starts imitating Joey, Joey creates a linguistic game. He says a phrase in English and then waits for the Indian to repeat it (page 316). When the Indians succeeds at this game, Joey tells him that he will "be talking like us in no time" (page 316). Joey believes that through the game the Indian will learn to speak the repetitive language which the two boys speak. Like Murph's imitation of the Indian, the Indian's mimicry does not reveal meaning. Repetition not only fails to establish meaningful communication, but also confuses individual identities. Joey and Murph's explanation of their relationship with Pussyface exemplifies the repetitive nature of their language. Joey explains that they were assigned to Pussyface, a social worker, because "we stole two cars" (page 309). Murph repeats Joey's speech: "We stole two cars. And we knifed a kid" (page 309). When Joey points out that Murph knifed the kid alone, Murph replies, "Tell it to the judge" (page 309). By mimicking Joey, Murph loses the ability to distinguish between his past and Joey's past. The line between the two boys' identities becomes practically indeterminate, and Murph suggests that only an external judge can discriminate between them. Repetition in language results in meaningless words and leads to the destruction of individual identity.

Joey and Murph dispute and confuse not only each other's identities, but also the Indian's identity. When they first meet Gupta, Joey transforms the question of the Indian's heritage into a game: "Bet you a ten spot. It's an Indian" (page 305). Joey defines Gupta as an American Indian. As in the game involving Joey and Murph's identities, this game escalates into a physical confrontation. Murph hits Joey on the arm and declares that "Indian's a Turkie" (page 306). Joey retaliates by grabbing Murph's arm, twisting it behind his back, and demanding that "it's an Indian" (page 306). Neither of these conflicting definitions are correct, and they blur the distinctions between Native American, East Indian, and Turkish heritage. Like Joey and Murph's failed attempts to define each other, their definitions of the Indian confuse identity, destroy distinction, and lead to violence.

In games Joey and Murph fight not only over identity, but also over words. For example, they debate the meanings of the words which are fundamental elements to game language—the rules. Murph establishes the regulations of one of these games: "I spin the hell out of you until you're dizzy. Then you run across the street and get Pussyface. I'll grab the Indian and hide him. Then Pussyface and you come over and try to find us" (page 314). As the spinner, Joey realizes that he will suffer pain and nausea. With this realization, he questions the nature of the rules: "How about if we set the rules as we go along?" (page 314). Murph ignores this inquiry concerning the stability of the language which governs the game, and commands Joey to "stop talking and start spinning" (page 314). Joey complies, but spins himself slowly. Murph reacts violently to Joey's performance of the spin: "I told you to spin! Any slob knows that ain't no spin" (page 314). Murph questions Joey's definition of the word "spin." In an attempt to define the word correctly, Murph orders Joey to spin him. By spinning Murph, Joey offers an alternative definition of this word: "You wanted to spin. Spin. Spin. . . . Here's one more for good luck" (page 315). While these words seem harmless, Horovitz reveals the violent nature of Joey's revised definition of the word "spin" in his stage directions: "Joey spins Murph three more times, fiercely, then shoves him offstage. Murph can be heard retching, about to vomit, during the final spins" (page 315). Like the introduction of violence into the identity games, the dispute over the definition of "spin" ends in violence. Neither of Joey's definitions satisfy Murph. In this game, Joey and Murph use the same word, but fail to agree upon a stable, universal meaning.

Joey and Murph fail to define not only the words used in the rules of the games, but also the word "game" itself. Murph appeals to Joey's definition of this word in order to convince him to participate: "C'mon, Joey. It's not real. This is just a game. It ain't going to hurt anybody. You know that. It's just a game" (page 320). Murph suggests that there is a distinction between what is real and what is a game. By defining their present situation as a game, Murph denies that their actions have real consequences. However, the impacts of the game upon the Indian reveal a blurring of the distinction between reality and game. The playwright states in the stage directions that "Murph takes his knife from his pocket, cuts the line" (page 323). When he severs the phone line, Murph causes the Indian intense psychological pain by separating him from two sources of meaning in his life—his son and his language. Murph harms the Indian not only psychologically, but also physically. Horovitz describes in the stage directions how Murph "takes his knife and cuts the Indian's hand, so blood is on the knife" (page 324). Murph's definition and usage of "game" lead to violence and the inability to distinguish between reality and imagination.

Joey and Murph fail in their painful search for definitions in language. Through their linguistic search, the playwright explores the nature of language. Language develops from and depends upon certain fundamental elements—signs, referents, sign users, and sign receivers. Joe and Murph are sign users and receivers. However, these characters cannot find a meaningful way of relating signs to referents. They fail, for example, to define each other and the words of their language. The discontinuities between the signs and the referents blur distinctions and end in violence. These characters' inability to differentiate between heritages and between game and reality exemplify these discontinuities. In *The Indian Wants the Bronx*, Horovitz suggests that the destruction of the foundations of language results in violence and loss of identity.

5

ALIENS

Not all of the people we meet are part of "our" crowd; not all share our heritage, or speak our language. Some, in fact, are so very different that it sometimes seems they might as well be men or women from another planet.

Such encounters with the "Other"—people who are totally different socially and culturally—are common in the American experience. Think of what the Native Americans must have thought when they first saw Columbus or Cortés or de Soto. Think of what some New Yorkers of a hundred years ago must have thought as they saw the stream of eastern and central Europeans pour onto the streets of the city from Ellis Island, or what Californians a little earlier must have been thinking when Chinese were brought in to build the railroads.

But even today, someone with dreadlocks or earlocks or someone wearing a turban, a sari, or a dashiki can turn heads in many towns and on many campuses. Though television and movies have made us more or less familiar with everyone from Watusi to Laplanders, and many of them with us, there is often something unsettling when someone from a dramatically different culture walks into our everyday lives. These dramatic differences in language, dress, and customs may create all kinds of misunderstandings or problems. The Japanese, for example, make the kind of slurping noises when they eat that many American mothers send children away from the table for making, though in Japan such behavior is perfectly acceptable. On the other hand, the Japanese (and Chinese as well) cannot stand the smell or taste of butter or cheese and wonder how we can manage to eat such loathsome stuff. To them, many Americans—big, blond, hairy, and boisterous—seem a bit like creatures from outer space.

"Aliens"—what we call such space creatures—is also what we call foreigners among us; but in the United States, Canada, and elsewhere in the hemisphere, aliens may be "naturalized" and become Americans. Indeed, all but a few of us are from families that came to this continent as "aliens," no matter whether that was last year, fifty, a hundred, or four hundred years ago or whether our people came as explorers, settlers, missionaries, refugees, draft evaders, or slaves. Meeting "aliens" is part of our everyday American experience; America has been a favorite landing place for "foreigners."

But the "aliens" we meet may not be aliens in fact. They may be as American as we are but from a different background and heritage, living a life so remote from ours it seems as if they inhabited another planet, but living still what is an American life. Have you ever walked into a strange neighborhood in a city, perhaps your own city, and suddenly noticed that all the older women were wearing black? Or, in another neighborhood, that all the men had beards and hair curled around their ears and were wearing round black hats and all black clothes? Or, when you visited another neighborhood, city, or region, that everyone seemed to be yelling at the tops of their voices, or in another that no one said "Hi" or smiled?

When you first meet someone from another culture, these differences may be exotic, exciting, and attractive, but they are just as likely to be puzzling, frightening, or offensive. These strange encounters interrupt our routines, our ordinary ways of speaking and behaving. Putting into question things we have taken for granted, they can be occasions for growth and expansion of our horizons. But sometimes they seem threatening, and we back off or reject the invader. Or, instead of responding to the new experience—positively or negatively, but as a new experience—we may fall back on what we have read or been told. We may have a ready-made attitude generated by a STEREOTYPE* that does not open us up to the new but closes us off from the Other. For, more often than not, these stereotypes are not very flattering or reassuring, unless it is to flatter ourselves and reassure ourselves of what we believe to be our own superiority.

The stories, poems, and nonfiction prose pieces here offer a range of

---

*Words in small capitals are defined in the Glossary.

encounters: Americans abroad who learn wonderful or troubling things about another "planet"; Americans who go abroad to find their roots only to discover that they are considered by their relatives not as siblings but as Americans, creatures from another planet; foreigners who come here as conquerors or as refugees and meet various receptions; Americans of various ethnic groups who confront other Americans from other groups with anxiety, insensitivity, or perplexity.

American society is so complex and so fluid that we are all aliens to some other Americans, and we encounter new aliens every day.

Margaret Atwood

Born in Ottawa in 1939, Margaret Atwood was educated at Victoria College of the University of Toronto and at Harvard University. Best known for her six novels, including the widely admired *Surfacing* (1972) and the best-selling *The Handmaid's Tale* (1985), she has published more than a dozen other books: poetry, nonfiction, short stories, and books for children. Her collection of poetry *The Circle Game* (1966) received the Governor-General's Award. Her most recent book, *Wilderness Tips* (1991), is her third collection of short stories.

THE MAN FROM MARS

A long time ago Christine was walking through the park. She was still wearing her tennis dress; she hadn't had time to shower and change, and her hair was held back with an elastic band. Her chunky reddish face, exposed with no softening fringe, looked like a Russian peasant's, but without the elastic band the hair got in her eyes. The afternoon was too hot for April; the indoor courts had been steaming, her skin felt poached.

The sun had brought the old men out from wherever they spent the winter: she had read a story recently about one who lived for three years in a manhole. They sat weedily on the benches or lay on the grass with their heads on squares of used newspaper. As she passed, their wrinkled toadstool faces drifted towards her, drawn by the movement of her body, then floated away again, uninterested.

The squirrels were out too, foraging; two or three of them moved towards her in darts and pauses, eyes fixed on her expectantly, mouths with the rat-like receding chins open to show the yellowed front teeth. Christine walked faster, she had nothing to give them. People shouldn't feed them, she thought, it makes them anxious and they get mangy.

Halfway across the park she stopped to take off her cardigan. As she bent over to pick up her tennis racquet again someone touched her on her freshly-bared arm. Christine seldom screamed; she straightened up suddenly, gripping the handle of her racquet. It was not one of the old men, however: it was a dark-haired boy of twelve or so.

"Excuse me," he said, "I search for Economics Building. It is there?" He motioned towards the west.

Christine looked at him more closely. She had been mistaken: he was not young, just short. He came a little above her shoulder, but then, she was above the average height; "statuesque," her mother called it when she was straining. He was also what was referred to in their family as "a person from another culture": oriental without a doubt, though perhaps not Chinese. Christine judged he must be a foreign student and gave him her official welcoming smile. In high school she had been President of the United Nations Club; that year her school had been picked to represent the Egyptian delegation at the Mock Assembly. It had been an unpopular assignment—nobody wanted to be the Arabs—but she had seen it through. She had made rather a good speech about the Palestinian refugees.

"Yes," she said, "that's it over there. The one with the flat roof. See it?"

The man had been smiling nervously at her the whole time. He was wearing glasses with transparent plastic rims, through which his eyes bulged up at her as though through a goldfish bowl. He had not followed where she was pointing. Instead he thrust towards her a small pad of green paper and a ballpoint pen.

"You make map," he said.

Christine set down her tennis racquet and drew a careful map. "We are here," she said, pronouncing distinctly. "You go this way. The building is here." She indicated the route with a dotted line and an X. The man leaned close to her, watching the progress of the map attentively; he smelled of cooked cauliflower and an unfamiliar brand of hair grease. When she had finished Christine handed the paper and pen back to him with a terminal smile.

"Wait," the man said. He tore the piece of paper with the map off the pad, folded it carefully and put it in his jacket pocket; the jacket sleeves came down over his wrists and had threads at the edges. He began to write something; she noticed with a slight feeling of revulsion that his nails and the ends of his fingertips were so badly bitten they seemed almost deformed. Several of his fingers were blue from the leaky ballpoint.

"Here is my name," he said, holding the pad out to her.

Christine read an odd assemblage of G's, Y's and N's, neatly printed in block letters. "Thank you," she said.

"You now write *your* name," he said, extending the pen.

Christine hesitated. If this had been a person from her own culture she would have thought he was trying to pick her up. But then, people from her own culture never tried to pick her up: she was too big. The only one who had made the attempt was the Moroccan waiter at the beer parlour where they sometimes went after meetings, and he had been direct. He had just intercepted her on the way to the Ladies' Room and asked and she said no;

that had been that. This man was not a waiter though but a student; she didn't want to offend him. In his culture, whatever it was, this exchange of names on pieces of paper was probably a formal politeness, like saying Thank You. She took the pen from him.

"That is a very pleasant name," he said. He folded the paper and placed it in his jacket pocket with the map.   16

Christine felt she had done her duty. "Well, goodbye," she said, "it was nice to have met you." She bent for her tennis racquet but he had already stooped and retrieved it and was holding it with both hands in front of him, like a captured banner.   17

"I carry this for you."   18

"Oh no, please. Don't bother, I am in a hurry," she said, articulating clearly. Deprived of her tennis racquet she felt weaponless. He started to saunter along the path; he was not nervous at all now, he seemed completely at ease.   19

"Vous parlez français?"[1] he asked conversationally.   20

"Oui, un petit peu," she said. "Not very well." How am I going to get my racquet away from him without being rude, she was wondering.   21

"Mais vous avez un bel accent." His eyes goggled at her through the glasses: was he being flirtatious? She was well aware that her accent was wretched.   22

"Look," she said, for the first time letting her impatience show, "I really have to go. Give me my racquet please."   23

He quickened his pace but gave no sign of returning the racquet. "Where are you going?"   24

"Home," she said. "My house."   25

"I go with you now," he said hopefully.   26

"No," she said: she would have to be firm with him. She made a lunge and got a grip on her racquet; after a brief tug of war it came free.   27

"Goodbye," she said, turning away from his puzzled face and setting off at what she hoped was a discouraging jog-trot. It was like walking away from a growling dog, you shouldn't let on you were frightened. Why should she be frightened anyway? He was only half her size and she had the tennis racquet, there was nothing he could do to her.   28

Although she did not look back she could tell he was still following. Let there be a streetcar, she thought, and there was one, but it was far down the line, stuck behind a red light. He appeared at her side, breathing audibly, a moment after she reached the stop. She gazed ahead, rigid.   29

"You are my friend," he said tentatively.   30

Christine relented: he hadn't been trying to pick her up after all, he was a stranger, he just wanted to meet some of the local people; in his place she would have wanted the same thing.   31

"Yes," she said, doling him out a smile.   32

1. Do you speak French? . . . Yes, a little bit. . . . But you have a good accent.

"That is good," he said, "My country is very far."   33

Christine couldn't think of an apt reply. "That's interesting," she said.   34
"Très intéressant."[2] The streetcar was coming at last; she opened her purse
and got out a ticket.

"I go with you now," he said. His hand clamped on her arm above the   35
elbow.

"You . . . stay . . . *here*," Christine said, resisting the impulse to shout   36
but pausing between each word as though for a deaf person. She detached
his hand—his hold was quite feeble and could not compete with her tennis
biceps—and leapt off the curb and up the streetcar steps, hearing with relief
the doors grind shut behind her. Inside the car and a block away she permitted herself a glance out a side window. He was standing where she had left
him; he seemed to be writing something on his little pad of paper.

When she reached home she had only time for a snack, and even then   37
she was almost late for the Debating Society. The topic was, "Resolved:
That War Is Obsolete." Her team took the affirmative, and won.

Christine came out of her last examination feeling depressed. It was not   38
the exam that depressed her but the fact that it was the last one: it meant the
end of the school year. She dropped into the coffee shop as usual, then went
home early because there didn't seem to be anything else to do.

"Is that you, dear?" her mother called from the livingroom. She must   39
have heard the front door close. Christine went in and flopped on the sofa,
disturbing the neat pattern of the cushions.

"How was your exam, dear?" her mother asked.   40

"Fine," said Christine flatly. It had been fine, she had passed. She was   41
not a brilliant student, she knew that, but she was conscientious. Her professors always wrote things like "A serious attempt" and "Well thought out
but perhaps lacking in *élan*" on her term papers; they gave her B's, the occasional B$^+$. She was taking Political Science and Economics, and hoped for a
job with the Government after she graduated; with her father's connections
she had a good chance.

"That's nice."   42

Christine felt, resentfully, that her mother had only a hazy idea of what   43
an exam was. She was arranging gladioli in a vase; she had rubber gloves on
to protect her hands as she always did when engaged in what she called
"housework." As far as Christine could tell her housework consisted of
arranging flowers in vases: daffodils and tulips and hyacinths through gladioli, iris and roses, all the way to asters and mums. Sometimes she cooked,
elegantly and with chafing-dishes, but she thought of it as a hobby. The girl
did everything else. Christine thought it faintly sinful to have a girl. The
only ones available now were either foreign or pregnant; their expressions
usually suggested they were being taken advantage of somehow. But her

---

2. Very interesting.

mother asked what they would do otherwise, they'd either have to go into a
Home or stay in their own countries, and Christine had to agree this was
probably true. It was hard anyway to argue with her mother, she was so
delicate, so preserved-looking, a harsh breath would scratch the finish.

"An interesting young man phoned today," her mother said. She had   44
finished the gladioli and was taking off her rubber gloves. "He asked to speak
with you and when I said you weren't in we had quite a little chat. You
didn't tell me about him, dear." She put on the glasses which she wore on a
decorative chain around her neck, a signal that she was in her modern, intelligent mood rather than her old-fashioned whimsical one.

"Did he leave his name?" Christine asked. She knew a lot of young men   45
but they didn't often call her, they conducted their business with her in the
coffee shop or after meetings.

"He's a person from another culture. He said he would call back later."   46

Christine had to think a moment. She was vaguely acquainted with sev-   47
eral people from other cultures, Britain mostly; they belonged to the Debating Society.

"He's studying Philosophy in Montreal," her mother prompted. "He   48
sounded French."

Christine began to remember the man in the park. "I don't think he's   49
French, exactly," she said.

Her mother had taken off her glasses again and was poking absentmind-   50
edly at a bent gladiolus. "Well, he sounded French." She meditated, flowery
sceptre in hand. "I think it would be nice if you had him to tea."

Christine's mother did her best. She had two other daughters, both of   51
whom took after her. They were beautiful, one was well married already and
the other would clearly have no trouble. Her friends consoled her about
Christine by saying, "She's not fat, she's just big-boned, it's the father's side,"
and "Christine is so healthy." Her other daughters had never gotten involved
in activities when they were at school, but since Christine could not possibly
ever be beautiful even if she took off weight, it was just as well she was so
athletic and political, it was a good thing she had interests. Christine's mother
tried to encourage her interests whenever possible. Christine could tell when
she was making an extra effort, there was a reproachful edge to her voice.

She knew her mother expected enthusiasm but she could not supply it.   52
"I don't know, I'll have to see," she said dubiously.

"You look tired, darling," said her mother. "Perhaps you'd like a glass   53
of milk."

Christine was in the bathtub when the phone rang. She was not prone   54
to fantasy but when she was in the bathtub she often pretended she was a
dolphin, a game left over from one of the girls who used to bathe her when
she was small. Her mother was being bell-voiced and gracious in the hall;
then there was a tap at the door.

"It's that nice young French student, Christine," her mother said.   55

"Tell him I'm in the bathtub," Christine said, louder than necessary. "He isn't French."

She could hear her mother frowning. "That wouldn't be very polite, Christine. I don't think he'd understand."

"Oh all right," Christine said. She heaved herself out the bathtub, swathed her pink bulk in a towel and splattered to the phone.

"Hello," she said gruffly. At a distance he was not pathetic, he was a nuisance. She could not imagine how he had tracked her down: most likely he went through the phone book, calling all the numbers with her last name until he hit on the right one.

"It is your friend."

"I know," she said, "How are you?"

"I am very fine." There was a long pause, during which Christine had a vicious urge to say, "Well, goodbye then," and hang up; but she was aware of her mother poised figurine-like in her bedroom doorway. Then he said, "I hope you also are very fine."

"Yes," said Christine. She wasn't going to participate.

"I come to tea," he said.

This took Christine by surprise. "You do?"

"Your pleasant mother ask me. I come Thursday, four o'clock."

"Oh," Christine said, ungraciously.

"See you then," he said, with conscious pride of one who has mastered a difficult idiom.

Christine set down the phone and went along the hall. Her mother was in her study, sitting innocently at her writing desk.

"Did you ask him to tea on Thursday?"

"Not exactly, dear," her mother said. "I did mention he might come round to tea *some*time, though."

"Well, he's coming Thursday. Four o'clock."

"What's wrong with that?" her mother said serenely. "I think it's a very nice gesture for us to make. I do think you might try to be a little more co-operative." She was pleased with herself.

"Since you invited him," said Christine, "you can bloody well stick around and help me entertain him. I don't want to be left making nice gestures all by myself."

"Christine *dear*," her mother said, above being shocked. "You ought to put on your dressing gown, you'll catch a chill."

After sulking for an hour Christine tried to think of the tea as a cross between an examination and an executive meeting: not enjoyable, certainly, but to be got through as tactfully as possible. And it *was* a nice gesture. When the cakes her mother had ordered arrived from *The Patisserie* on Thursday morning she began to feel slightly festive; she even resolved to put on a dress, a good one, instead of a skirt and blouse. After all, she had nothing against him, except the memory of the way he had grabbed her tennis racquet and then her arm. She suppressed a quick impossible vision of herself pursued around the livingroom, fending him off with thrown sofa cushions and vases of gladioli; nevertheless she told the girl they would have tea in the garden. It would be a treat for him, and there was more space outdoors.

She had suspected her mother would dodge the tea, would contrive to be going out just as he was arriving: that way she could size him up and then leave them alone together. She had done things like that to Christine before; her mother carefully mislaid her gloves and located them with a faked murmur of joy when the doorbell rang. Christine relished for weeks afterwards the image of her mother's dropped jaw and flawless recovery when he was introduced: he wasn't quite the foreign potentate her optimistic, veil-fragile mind had concocted. [77]

He was prepared for celebration. He had slicked on so much hair cream that his head seemed to be covered with a tight black patent-leather cap, and he had cut the threads off his jacket sleeves. His orange tie was overpoweringly splendid. Christine noticed however as he shook her mother's suddenly-braced white glove that the ballpoint ink on his fingers was indelible. His face had broken out, possibly in anticipation of the delights in store for him; he had a tiny camera slung over his shoulder and was smoking an exotic-smelling cigarette. [78]

Christine led him through the cool flowery softly-padded livingroom and out by the French doors into the garden. "You sit here," she said. "I will have the girl bring tea." [79]

This girl was from the West Indies: Christine's parents had been enraptured with her when they were down at Christmas and had brought her back with them. Since that time she had become pregnant, but Christine's mother had not dismissed her. She said she was slightly disappointed but what could you expect, and she didn't see any real difference between a girl who was pregnant before you hired her and one who got that way afterward. She prided herself on her tolerance; also there was a scarcity of girls. Strangely enough, the girl became progressively less easy to get along with. Either she did not share Christine's mother's view of her own generosity, or she felt she had gotten away with something and was therefore free to indulge in contempt. At first Christine had tried to treat her as an equal. "Don't call me 'Miss Christine,'" she had said with an imitation of light, comradely laughter. "What you want me to call you then?" the girl had said, scowling. They had begun to have brief, surly arguments in the kitchen, which Christine decided were like the arguments between one servant and another: her mother's attitude towards each of them was similar, they were not altogether satisfactory but they would have to do. [80]

The cakes, glossy with icing, were set out on a plate and the teapot was standing ready; on the counter the electric kettle boiled. Christine headed for it, but the girl, till then sitting with her elbows on the kitchen table and watching her expressionlessly, made a dash and intercepted her. Christine waited until she had poured the water into the pot. Then, "I'll carry it out, [81]

Elvira," she said. She had just decided she didn't want the girl to see her visitor's orange tie; already, she knew, her position in the girl's eyes had suffered because no-one had yet attempted to get *her* pregnant.

"What you think they pay me for, Miss Christine?" the girl said inso-   82
lently. She swung toward the garden with the tray; Christine trailed her, feeling lumpish and awkward. The girl was at least as big as she was but she was big in a different way.

"Thank you, Elvira," Christine said when the tray was in place. The   83
girl departed without a word, casting a disdainful backward glance at the frayed jacket sleeves, the stained fingers. Christine was now determined to be especially kind to him.

"You are very rich," he said.   84

"No," Christine protested, shaking her head; "we're not." She had never   85
thought of her family as rich, it was one of her father's sayings that nobody made any money with the Government.

"Yes," he repeated, "You are very rich." He sat back in his lawn chair,   86
gazing about him as though dazed.

Christine set his cup of tea in front of him. She wasn't in the habit of   87
paying much attention to the house or the garden; they were nothing special, far from being the largest on the street; other people took care of them. But now she looked where he was looking, seeing it all as though from a different height: the long expanses, the border flowers blazing in the early-summer sunlight, the flagged patio and walks, the high walls and the silence.

He came back to her face, sighing a little. "My English is not good," he   88
said, "but I improve."

"You do," Christine said, nodding encouragement.   89

He took sips of his tea, quickly and tenderly as though afraid of injuring   90
the cup. "I like to stay here."

Christine passed him the cakes. He took only one, making a slight face   91
as he ate it; but he had several more cups of tea while she finished the cakes. She managed to find out from him that he had come over on a Church fellowship—she could not decode the denomination—and was studying Philosophy or Theology, or possibly both. She was feeling well-disposed towards him: he had behaved himself, he had caused her no inconvenience.

The teapot was at last empty. He sat up straight in his chair, as though   92
alerted by a soundless gong. "You look this way, please," he said. Christine saw that he had placed his miniature camera on the stone sundial her mother had shipped back from England two years before: he wanted to take her picture. She was flattered, and settled herself to pose, smiling evenly.

He took off his glasses and laid them beside his plate. For a moment she   93
saw his myopic, unprotected eyes turned towards her, with something tremulous and confiding in them she wanted to close herself off from knowing about. Then he went over and did something to the camera, his back to her. The next instant he was crouched beside her, his arm around her waist as far as it could reach, his other hand covering her own hands which she had

folded in her lap, his cheek jammed up against hers. She was too startled to move. The camera clicked.

He stood up at once and replaced his glasses, which glittered now with a sad triumph. "Thank you, Miss," he said to her. "I go now." He slung the camera back over his shoulder, keeping his hand on it as though to hold the lid on and prevent escape. "I send to my family; they will like." 94

He was out the gate and gone before Christine had recovered; then she laughed. She had been afraid he would attack her, she could admit it now, and he had; but not in the usual way. He had raped, *rapeo, rapere, rapui, to seize and carry off*, not herself but her celluloid image, and incidentally that of the silver tea service, which glinted mockingly at her as the girl bore it away, carrying it regally, the insignia, the official jewels. 95

Christine spent the summer as she had for the past three years: she was the sailing instructress at an expensive all-girls camp near Algonquin Park. She had been a camper there, everything was familiar to her; she sailed almost better than she played tennis. 96

The second week she got a letter from him, postmarked Montreal and forwarded from her home address. It was printed in block letters on a piece of the green paper, two or three sentences. It began, "I hope you are well," then described the weather in monosyllables and ended, "I am fine." It was signed "Your friend." Each week she got another of these letters, more or less identical. In one of them a colour print was enclosed: himself, slightly crosseyed and grinning hilariously, even more spindly than she remembered him against her billowing draperies, flowers exploding around them like fire-crackers, one of his hands an equivocal blur in her lap, the other out of sight; on her own face, astonishment and outrage, as though he was sticking her in the behind with his hidden thumb. 97

She answered the first letter, but after that the seniors were in training for the races. At the end of the summer, packing to go home, she threw all the letters away. 98

When she had been back for several weeks she received another of the green letters. This time there was a return address printed at the top which Christine noted with foreboding was in her own city. Every day she waited for the phone to ring; she was so certain his first attempt at contact would be a disembodied voice that when he came upon her abruptly in mid-campus she was unprepared. 99

"How are you?" 100

His smile was the same, but everything else about him had deteriorated. 101
He was, if possible, thinner; his jacket sleeves had sprouted a lush new crop of threads, as though to conceal hands now so badly bitten they appeared to have been gnawed by rodents. His hair fell over his eyes, uncut, ungreased; his eyes in the hollowed face, a delicate triangle of skin stretched on bone, jumped behind his glasses like hooked fish. He had the end of a cigarette in the corner of his mouth and as they walked he lit a new one from it.

"I'm fine," Christine said. She was thinking, I'm not going to get involved again, enough is enough, I've done my bit for internationalism. "How are you?"

"I live here now," he said. "Maybe I study Economics."

"That's nice." He didn't sound as though he was enrolled anywhere.

"I come to see you."

Christine didn't know whether he meant he had left Montreal in order to be near her or just wanted to visit her at her house as he had done in the spring; either way she refused to be implicated. They were outside the Political Science building. "I have a class here," she said. "Goodbye." She was being callous, she realized that, but a quick chop was more merciful in the long run, that was what her beautiful sisters used to say.

Afterwards she decided it had been stupid of her to let him find out where her class was. Though a timetable was posted in each of the colleges: all he had to do was look her up and record her every probable movement in block letters on his green notepad. After that day he never left her alone.

Initially he waited outside the lecture rooms for her to come out. She said Hello to him curtly at first and kept on going, but this didn't work; he followed her at a distance, smiling his changeless smile. Then she stopped speaking altogether and pretended to ignore him, but it made no difference, he followed her anyway. The fact that she was in some way afraid of him— or was it just embarrassment?—seemed only to encourage him. Her friends started to notice, asking her who he was and why he was tagging along behind her; she could hardly answer because she hardly knew.

As the weekdays passed and he showed no signs of letting up, she began to jog-trot between classes, finally to run. He was tireless, and had an amazing wind for one who smoked so heavily: he would speed along behind her, keeping the distance between them the same, as though he was a pull-toy attached to her by a string. She was aware of the ridiculous spectacle they must make, galloping across campus, something out of a cartoon short, a lumbering elephant stampeded by a smiling, emaciated mouse, both of them locked in the classic pattern of comic pursuit and flight; but she found that to race made her less nervous than to walk sedately, the skin on the back of her neck crawling with the feel of his eyes on it. At least she could use her muscles. She worked out routines, escapes: she would dash in the front door of the Ladies' Room in the coffee shop and out the back door, and he would lose the trail, until he discovered the other entrance. She would try to shake him by detours through baffling archways and corridors, but he seemed as familiar with the architectural mazes as she was herself. As a last refuge she could head for the women's dormitory and watch from safety as he was skidded to a halt by the receptionist's austere voice: men were not allowed past the entrance.

Lunch became difficult. She would be sitting, usually with other members of the Debating Society, just digging nicely into a sandwich, when he would appear suddenly as though he'd come up through an unseen manhole.

She then had the choice of barging out through the crowded cafeteria, sandwich half-eaten, or finishing her lunch with him standing behind her chair, everyone at the table acutely aware of him, the conversation stilting and dwindling. Her friends learned to spot him from a distance; they posted lookouts. "Here he comes," they would whisper, helping her collect her belongings for the sprint they knew would follow.

Several times she got tired of running and turned to confront him. "What do you want?" she would ask, glowering belligerently down at him, almost clenching her fists; she felt like shaking him, hitting him.

"I wish to talk with you."

"Well, here I am," she would say. "What do you want to talk about?"

But he would say nothing; he would stand in front of her, shifting his feet, smiling perhaps apologetically (though she could never pinpoint the exact tone of that smile, chewed lips stretched apart over the nicotine-yellowed teeth, rising at the corners, flesh held stiffly in place for an invisible photographer), his eyes jerking from one part of her face to another as though he saw her in fragments.

Annoying and tedious though it was, his pursuit of her had an odd result: mysterious in itself, it rendered her equally mysterious. No-one had ever found Christine mysterious before. To her parents she was a beefy heavyweight, a plodder, lacking in flair, ordinary as bread. To her sisters she was the plain one, treated with an indulgence they did not give to each other: they did not fear her as a rival. To her male friends she was the one who could be relied on. She was helpful and a hard worker, always good for a game of tennis with the athletes among them. They invited her along to drink beer with them so they could get into the cleaner, more desirable Ladies and Escorts side of the beer parlour, taking it for granted she would buy her share of the rounds. In moments of stress they confided to her their problems with women. There was nothing devious about her and nothing interesting.

Christine had always agreed with these estimates of herself. In childhood she had identified with the False Bride or the ugly sister; whenever a story had begun, "Once there was a maiden as beautiful as she was good," she had known it wasn't her. That was just how it was, but it wasn't so bad. Her parents never expected her to be a brilliant social success and weren't overly disappointed when she wasn't. She was spared the manoeuvering and anxiety she witnessed among others her age, and she even had a kind of special position among men: she was an exception, she fitted none of the categories they commonly used when talking about girls, she wasn't a cockteaser, a cold fish, an easy lay or a snarky bitch; she was an honorary person. She had grown to share their contempt for most women.

Now however there was something about her that could not be explained. A man was chasing her, a peculiar sort of man, granted, but still a man, and he was without doubt attracted to her, he couldn't leave her alone. Other men examined her more closely than they ever had, appraising her, trying to find out what it was those twitching bespectacled eyes saw in her. They started to ask her out, though they returned from these excursions with their curiosity unsatisfied, the secret of her charm still intact. Her opaque dumpling face, her solid bear-shaped body became for them parts of a riddle no-one could solve. Christine knew this and began to use it. In the bathtub she no longer imagined she was a dolphin; instead she imagined she was an elusive water-nixie, or sometimes, in moments of audacity, Marilyn Monroe. The daily chase was becoming a habit; she even looked forward to it. In addition to its other benefits she was losing weight.

All those weeks he had never phoned her or turned up at the house. He must have decided however that his tactics were not having the desired result, or perhaps he sensed she was becoming bored. The phone began to ring in the early morning or late at night when he could be sure she would be there. Sometimes he would simply breathe (she could recognize, or thought she could, the quality of his breathing), in which case she would hang up. Occasionally he would say again that he wanted to talk to her, but even when she gave him lots of time nothing else would follow. Then he extended his range: she would see him on her streetcar, smiling at her silently from a seat never closer than three away; she could feel him tracking her down her own street, though when she would break her resolve to pay no attention and would glance back he would be invisible or in the act of hiding behind a tree or hedge. 118

Among crowds of people and in daylight she had not really been afraid of him; she was stronger than he was and he had made no recent attempt to touch her. But the days were growing shorter and colder, it was almost November, often she was arriving home in twilight or a darkness broken only by the feeble orange streetlamps. She brooded over the possibility of razors, knives, guns; by acquiring a weapon he could quickly turn the odds against her. She avoided wearing scarves, remembering the newspaper stories about girls who had been strangled by them. Putting on her nylons in the morning gave her a funny feeling. Her body seemed to have diminished, to have become smaller than his. 119

Was he deranged, was he a sex maniac? He seemed so harmless, yet it was that kind who often went berserk in the end. She pictured those ragged fingers at her throat, tearing at her clothes, though she could not think of herself as screaming. Parked cars, the shrubberies near her house, the driveways on either side of it, changed as she passed them from unnoticed background to sinisterly-shadowed foreground, every detail distinct and harsh: they were places a man might crouch, leap out from. Yet every time she saw him in the clear light of morning or afternoon (for he still continued his old methods of pursuit), his aging jacket and jittery eyes convinced her that it was she herself who was the tormentor, the persecuter. She was in some sense responsible; from the folds and crevices of the body she had treated for so long as a reliable machine was emanating, against her will, some potent invisible odour, like a dog's in heat or a female moth's, that made him unable to stop following her. 120

Her mother, who had been too preoccupied with the unavoidable fall   121
entertaining to pay much attention to the number of phone calls Christine
was getting or to the hired girl's complaints of a man who hung up without
speaking, announced that she was flying down to New York for the weekend;
her father decided to go too. Christine panicked: she saw herself in the bathtub with her throat slit, the blood drooling out of her neck and running in a
little spiral down the drain (for by this time she believed he could walk through
walls, could be everywhere at once). The girl would do nothing to help; she
might even stand in the bathroom door with her arms folded, watching.
Christine arranged to spend the weekend at her married sister's.

When she arrived back Sunday evening she found the girl close to hys-   122
terics. She said that on Saturday she had gone to pull the curtains across the
French doors at dusk and had found a strangely contorted face, a man's face,
pressed against the glass, staring in at her from the garden. She claimed she
had fainted and had almost had her baby a month too early right there on
the livingroom carpet. Then she had called the police. He was gone by the
time they got there but she had recognized him from the afternoon of the tea;
she had informed them he was a friend of Christine's.

They called Monday evening to investigate, two of them; they were   123
very polite, they knew who Christine's father was. Her father greeted them
heartily; her mother hovered in the background, fidgeting with her porcelain
hands, letting them see how frail and worried she was. She didn't like having
them in the livingroom but they were necessary.

Christine had to admit he'd been following her around. She was relieved   124
he'd been discovered, relieved also that she hadn't been the one to tell, though
if he'd been a citizen of the country she would have called the police a long
time ago. She insisted he was not dangerous, he had never hurt her.

"That kind don't hurt you," one of the policemen said. "They just kill   125
you. You're lucky you aren't dead."

"Nut cases," the other one said.   126

Her mother volunteered that the thing about people from another   127
culture was that you could never tell whether they were insane or not
because their ways were so different. The policeman agreed with her, defer-
ential but also condescending, as though she was a royal halfwit who had to
be humoured.

"You know where he lives?" the first policeman asked. Christine had   128
long ago torn up the letter with his address on it; she shook her head.

"We'll have to pick him up tomorrow then," he said. "Think you can   129
keep him talking outside your class if he's waiting for you?"

After questioning her they held a murmured conversation with her father   130
in the front hall. The girl, clearing away the coffee cups, said if they didn't
lock him up she was leaving, she wasn't going to be scared half out of her
skin like that again.

Next day when Christine came out of her Modern History lecture he   131
was there, right on schedule. He seemed puzzled when she did not begin to

run. She approached him, her heart thumping with treachery and the prospect of freedom. Her body was back to its usual size; she felt herself a giant-
ess, self-controlled, invulnerable.

"How are you?" she asked, smiling brightly.   132

He looked at her with distrust.   133

"How have you been?" she ventured again. His own perennial smile   134
faded; he took a step back from her.

"This the one?" said the policeman, popping out from behind a notice   135
board like a Keystone Cop and laying a competent hand on the worn jacket
shoulder. The other policeman lounged in the background; force would not
be required.

"Don't *do* anything to him," she pleaded as they took him away. They   136
nodded and grinned, respectful, scornful. He seemed to know perfectly well
who they were and what they wanted.

The first policeman phoned that evening to make his report. Her father   137
talked with him, jovial and managing. She herself was now out of the picture;
she had been protected, her function was over.

"What did they *do* to him?" she asked anxiously as he came back into   138
the livingroom. She was not sure what went on in police stations.

"They didn't do anything to him," he said, amused by her concern.   139
"They could have booked him for Watching and Besetting, they wanted to
know if I'd like to proffer charges. But it's not worth a court case: he's got a
visa that says he's only allowed in the country as long as he studies in Montreal, so I told them to just ship him up there. If he turns up here again
they'll deport him. They went around to his rooming house, his rent's two
weeks overdue; the landlady said she was on the point of kicking him out.
He seems happy enough to be getting his back rent paid and a free train
ticket to Montreal." He paused. "They couldn't get anything out of him
though."

"*Out* of him?" Christine asked.   140

"They tried to find out why he was doing it; following you, I mean."   141
Her father's eyes swept her as though it was a riddle to him also. "They said
when they asked him about that he just clammed up. Pretended he didn't
understand English. He understood well enough, but he wasn't answering."

Christine thought this was the end, but somehow between his arrest and   142
the departure of the train he managed to elude his escort long enough for one
more phone call.

"I see you again," he said. He didn't wait for her to hang up.   143

Now that he was no longer an embarrassing present reality he could be   144
talked about, he could become an amusing story. In fact he was the only
amusing story Christine had to tell, and telling it preserved both for herself
and for others the aura of her strange allure. Her friends and the men who
continued to ask her out speculated about his motives. One suggested he had

wanted to marry her so he could remain in the country; another said that oriental men were fond of well-built women: "It's your Rubens quality."

Christine thought about him a lot. She had not been attracted to him, 145 rather the reverse, but as an idea only he was a romantic figure, the one man who had found her irresistible; though she often wondered, inspecting her unchanged pink face and hefty body in her full-length mirror, just what it was about her that had done it. She avoided whenever it was proposed the theory of his insanity: it was only that there was more than one way of being sane.

But a new acquaintance, hearing the story for the first time, had a dif- 146 ferent explanation. "So he got you too," he said, laughing. "That has to be the same guy who was hanging around our day camp a year ago this summer. He followed all the girls like that. A short guy, Japanese or something, glasses, smiling all the time."

"Maybe it was another one," Christine said. 147

"There couldn't be two of them, everything fits. This was a pretty 148 weird guy."

"What . . . *kind* of girls did he follow?" Christine asked. 149

"Oh, just anyone who happened to be around. But if they paid any 150 attention to him at first, if they were nice to him or anything, he was unshakeable. He was a bit of a pest, but harmless."

Christine ceased to tell her amusing story. She had been one among 151 many, then. She went back to playing tennis, she had been neglecting her game.

A few months later the policeman who had been in charge of the case 152 telephoned her again.

"Like you to know, Miss, that fellow you were having the trouble with 153 was sent back to his own country. Deported."

"What for?" Christine asked. "Did he try to come back here?" Maybe 154 she had been special after all, maybe he had dared everything for her.

"Nothing like it," the policeman said. "He was up to the same tricks in 155 Montreal but he really picked the wrong woman this time—a Mother Superior of a convent. They don't stand for things like that in Quebec—had him out of here before he knew what happened. I guess he'll be better off in his own place."

"How old was she?" Christine asked, after a silence. 156

"Oh, around sixty, I guess." 157

"Thank you very much for letting me know," Christine said in her best 158 official manner. "It's such a relief." She wondered if the policeman had called to make fun of her.

She was almost crying when she put down the phone. What *had* he 159 wanted from her then? A Mother Superior. Did she really look sixty, did she look like a mother? What did convents mean? Comfort, charity? Refuge? Was it that something had happened to him, some intolerable strain just from being in this country; her tennis dress and exposed legs too much for him, flesh and money seemingly available everywhere but withheld from him wherever he turned, the nun the symbol of some final distortion, the robe and the veil reminiscent to his nearsighted eyes of the women of his homeland, the ones he was able to understand? But he was back in his own country, remote from her as another planet; she would never know.

He hadn't forgotten her though. In the spring she got a postcard with a 160
foreign stamp and the familiar block-letter writing. On the front was a picture of a temple. He was fine, he hoped she was fine also, he was her friend. A month later another print of the picture he had taken in the garden arrived, in a sealed manila envelope otherwise empty.

Christine's aura of mystery soon faded; anyway, she herself no longer 161
believed in it. Life became again what she had always expected. She graduated with mediocre grades and went into the Department of Health and Welfare; she did a good job, and was seldom discriminated against for being a woman because nobody thought of her as one. She could afford a pleasant-sized apartment, though she did not put much energy into decorating it. She played less and less tennis; what had been muscle with a light coating of fat turned gradually to fat with a thin substratum of muscle. She began to get headaches.

As the years were used up and the war began to fill the newspapers and 162
magazines, she realized which eastern country he had actually been from. She had known the name but it hadn't registered at the time, it was such a minor place; she could never keep them separate in her mind.

But though she tried, she couldn't remember the name of the city, and 163
the postcard was long gone—had he been from the North or the South, was he near the battle zone or safely far from it? Obsessively she bought the magazines and poured over the available photographs, dead villagers, soldiers on the march, colour blowups of frightened or angry faces, spies being executed; she studied maps, she watched the late-night newscasts, the distant country and terrain becoming almost more familiar to her than her own. Once or twice she thought she could recognize him but it was no use, they all looked like him.

Finally she had to stop looking at the pictures. It bothered her too much, 164
it was bad for her; she was beginning to have nightmares in which he was coming through the French doors of her mother's house in his shabby jacket, carrying a packsack and a rifle and a huge bouquet of richly-coloured flowers. He was smiling in the same way but with blood streaked over his face, partly blotting out the features. She gave her television set away and took to reading nineteenth century novels instead; Trollope and Galsworthy were her favourites. When, despite herself, she would think about him, she would tell herself that he had been crafty and agile-minded enough to survive, more or less, in her country, so surely he would be able to do it in his own, where he knew the language. She could not see him in the army, on either side; he wasn't the type, and to her knowledge he had not believed in any particular ideology. He would be something nondescript, something in the background, like herself; perhaps he had become an interpreter.

STUDY QUESTIONS

1. When you finish the story, go back and look at the first four words; why does the story begin that way?

2. Christine's face is described in the first paragraph—it "looked like a Russian peasant's." She is there being seen from the outside; both FOCUS and VOICE are someone else's, that is, a NARRATOR's. In the second paragraph, we learn that she had read a story about an old man who had lived in a manhole, so we are inside her mind. When the old men look at her as she's passing, their faces float "away again, uninterested." Is this an authoritative statement by the narrator, or is it Christine's opinion? If it is Christine's, what does it tell you about her? Look in the story for other places where the focus and voice seem to move from narrator to character or to be partly the narrator's, partly Christine's.

3. Christine remembers that her mother calls her "statuesque" "when she was straining" (paragraph 6). Straining for what? How would Christine describe herself?

4. Why does Christine give the stranger her name?

5. Why is Christine frightened (paragraph 28)?

6. That first day, Christine's team wins a debate in which they argue that war is obsolete (paragraph 37). Having read the story to the end, you may want to think about why that detail is included.

7. What does the description of Christine's mother's "housework" and how the house is run contribute to the story? How is it related to the central incident, the advent of "the man from Mars"?

8. Why does Christine's mother invite the stranger to tea?

9. What is Christine's mother's reaction when the stranger comes to the door? Why?

10. What is the relationship between the maid Elvira and Christine?

11. When "the man from Mars" takes off his glasses, Christine sees "his myopic, unprotected eyes turned towards her, with something tremulous and confiding in them she wanted to close herself off from knowing about" (paragraph 93). What do you think that "something" is? Why does Christine want not to know about it?

12. When the stranger returns to Christine's city, he follows her around; when her friends ask her why, "she could hardly answer because she hardly knew" (paragraph 108). Does the reader know? Or are we so confined to Christine's focus that we are as puzzled as she? What are the possible reasons? Which seem more likely?

13. Christine begins running between classes, taking evasive shortcuts, does everything to avoid him, with no results; she confronts him but can get him neither to stop nor explain. At that point, paragraphs 115–17, there is a surprising

twist. What happens to Christine's image in the eyes of the other students, especially male students, and of her friends?

14. Trace the stages both of the stranger's pursuit of Christine and of her feelings and yours about his actions.

15. When Elvira calls in the police, Christine is relieved, glad she did not have to do so herself, but admits to herself that "if he'd been a citizen of the country she would have called the police a long time ago" (paragraph 124). Why? What does this suggest about Christine's feelings about "Martians," those "from another culture"?

16. In what sense is the stranger "a romantic figure" (paragraph 145)?

17. Why is he deported? When Christine is told the reason he is deported, what is the effect on her?

18. The story does not end with "the man from Mars" being deported. Why? What would be the difference in the meaning and effect of the story had it ended there?

19. What country is the man from? How do you know? Why is it not mentioned earlier in the story? Why is it not specifically identified even at the end? Which part of that country do you think he comes from? What difference would that make? How does the final section of the story, in which the man does not himself appear at all, nevertheless change Christine's attitude toward him? your own?

20. The last clause in the story is "perhaps he had become an interpreter." Is there a sense in which that is true?

Becky Birtha

Becky Birtha, who lives in Philadelphia, is a poet and writer of fictional narratives. She received a fellowship from the Pennsylvania Council on the Arts in 1985, and she has published two collections of stories, *For Nights Like This One: Stories of Loving Women* (1983) and *Lover's Choice* (1987), in which the following story appears.

JOHNNIERUTH

Summertime. Nighttime. Talk about steam heat. This whole city get like the bathroom when somebody in there taking a shower with the door shut. Nights like that, can't nobody sleep. Everybody be outside, sitting on they steps or else dragging half they furniture out on the sidewalk—kitchen chairs, card tables—even bringing TVs outside.

Womenfolks, mostly. All the grown women around my way look just the same. They all big—stout. They got big bosoms and big hips and fat legs, and they always wearing runover house-shoes, and them shapeless, flowered numbers with the buttons down the front. Cept on Sunday. Sunday morning they all turn into glamour girls, in them big hats and long gloves, with they skinny high heels and they skinny selves in them tight girdles—wouldn't nobody ever know what they look like the rest of the time.

When I was a little kid I didn't wanna grow up, cause I never wanted to look like them ladies. I heard Miz Jenkins down the street one time say she don't mind being fat cause that way her husband don't get so jealous. She say it's more than one way to keep a man. Me, I don't have me no intentions of keeping no man. I never understood why they was in so much demand anyway, when it seem like all a woman can depend on em for is making sure she keep on having babies.

We got enough children in my neighborhood. In the summertime, even the little kids allowed to stay up till eleven or twelve o'clock at night—playing in the street and hollering and carrying on—don't never seem to get tired. Don't nobody care, long as they don't fight.

Me—I don't hang around no front steps no more. Hot nights like that, I get out my ten speed and I be gone.

That's what I like to do more than anything else in the whole world. Feel that wind in my face keeping me cool as a air conditioner, shooting along like a snowball. My bike light as a kite. I can really get up some speed.

All the guys around my way got ten speed bikes. Some of the girls got em too, but they don't ride em at night. They pedal around during the day, but at nighttime they just hang around out front, watching babies and running they mouth. I didn't get my Peugeot to be no conversation piece.

My mama don't like me to ride at night. I tried to point out to her that she ain't never said nothing to my brothers, and Vincent a year younger than me. (And Langston two years older, in case "old" is the problem.) She say, "That's different, Johnnieruth. You're a girl." Now I wanna know how is anybody gonna know that. I'm skinny as a knifeblade turned sideways, and all I ever wear is blue jeans and a Wrangler jacket. But if I bring that up, she liable to get started in on how come I can't be more of a young lady, and fourteen is old enough to start taking more pride in my appearance, and she gonna be ashamed to admit I'm her daughter.

I just tell her that my bike be moving so fast can't nobody hardly see me, and couldn't catch me if they did. Mama complain to her friends how I'm wild and she can't do nothing with me. She know I'm gonna do what I want no matter what she say. But she know I ain't getting in no trouble, neither.

Like some of the boys I know stole they bikes, but I didn't do nothing like that. I'd been saving my money ever since I can remember, every time I could get a nickel or a dime outta anybody.

When I was a little kid, it was hard to get money. Seem like the only time they ever give you any was on Sunday morning, and then you had to put it in the offering. I used to hate to do that. In fact, I used to hate everything about Sunday morning. I had to wear all them ruffly dresses—that shiny slippery stuff in the wintertime that got to make a noise every time you move your ass a inch on them hard old benches. And that scratchy starchy stuff in the summertime with all them scratchy crinolines. Had to carry a pocketbook and wear them shiny shoes. And the church we went to was all the way over on Summit Avenue, so the whole damn neighborhood could get a good look. At least all the other kids'd be dressed the same way. The boys think they slick cause they get to wear pants, but they still got to wear a white shirt and a tie; and them dumb hats they wear can't hide them baldheaded haircuts, cause they got to take the hats off in church.

There was one Sunday when I musta been around eight. I remember it was before my sister Corletta was born, cause right around then was when I put my foot down about the whole sanctimonious routine. Anyway, I was dragging my feet along Twenty-fifth Street in back of Mama and Vincent and them, when I spied this lady. I only seen her that one time, but I still remember just how she look. She don't look like nobody I ever seen before. I *know* she don't live around here. She real skinny. But she ain't no real young woman, either. She could be old as my mama. She ain't nobody's mama—I'm sure. And she ain't wearing Sunday clothes. She got on blue jeans and a man's blue working shirt, with the tail hanging out. She got patches on her blue jeans, and she still got her chin stuck out like she some kinda African royalty. She ain't carrying no shiny pocketbook. It don't look like she care if she got any money or not, or who know it, if she don't. She ain't wearing no house-shoes, or stockings or high heels neither.

Mama always speak to everybody, but when she pass by this lady she make like she ain't even seen her. But I get me a real good look, and the lady stare right back at me. She got a funny look on her face, almost like she think she know me from some place. After she pass on by, I had to turn around to get another look, even though Mama say that ain't polite. And you know what? She was turning around, too, looking back at me. And she give me a great big smile.

I didn't know too much in them days, but that's when I first got to thinking about how it's got to be different ways to be, from the way people be around my way. It's got to be places where it don't matter to nobody if you all dressed up on Sunday morning or you ain't. That's how come I started saving money. So, when I got enough, I could go away to some place like that.

Afterwhile I begun to see there wasn't no point in waiting around for handouts, and I started thinking of ways to earn my own money. I used to

be running errands all the time—mailing letters for old Grandma Whittaker
and picking up cigarettes and newspapers up the corner for everybody. After
I got bigger, I started washing cars in the summer, and shoveling people
sidewalk in the wintertime. Now I got me a newspaper route. Ain't never
been no girl around here with no paper route, but I guess everybody got it
figured out by now that I ain't gonna be like nobody else.

The reason I got me my Peugeot was so I could start to explore. I figured   16
I better start looking around right now, so when I'm grown, I'll know exactly
where I wanna go. So I ride around every chance I get.

Last summer, I used to ride with the boys a lot. Sometimes eight or ten   17
of us'd just go cruising around the streets together. All of a sudden my mama
decide she don't want me to do that no more. She say I'm too old to be
spending so much time with boys. (That's what they tell you half the time,
and the other half the time they worried cause you ain't interested in spending more time with boys. Don't make much sense.) She want me to have
some girl friends, but I never seem to fit in with none of the things the girls
doing. I used to think I fit in more with the boys.

But I seen how Mama might be right, for once. I didn't like the way the   18
boys was starting to talk about girls sometimes. Talking about what some
girl be like from the neck on down, and talking all up underneath somebody
clothes and all. Even though I wasn't really friends with none of the girls, I
still didn't like it. So now I mostly just ride around by myself. And Mama
don't like that neither—you just can't please her.

This boy that live around the corner on North Street, Kenny Hender-   19
son, started asking me one time if I don't ever be lonely, cause he always see
me by myself. He say don't I ever think I'd like to have me somebody special
to go places with and stuff. Like I'd pick him if I did! Made me wanna laugh
in his face. I do be lonely, a lotta times, but I don't tell nobody. And I ain't
met nobody yet that I'd really rather be with than be by myself. But I will
someday. When I find that special place where everybody different, I'm gonna
find somebody there I can be friends with. And it ain't gonna be no dumb
boy.

I found me one place already, that I like to go to a whole lot. It ain't   20
even really that far away—by bike—but it's on the other side of the Avenue.
So I don't tell Mama and them I go there, cause they like to think I'm right
around the neighborhood someplace. But this neighborhood too dull for me.
All the houses look just the same—no porches, no yards, no trees—not even
no parks around here. Every block look so much like every other block it
hurt your eyes to look at, afterwhile. So I ride across Summit Avenue and
go down that big steep hill there, and then make a sharp right at the bottom
and cross the bridge over the train tracks. Then I head on out the boulevard—that's the nicest part, with all them big trees making a tunnel over the
top, and lightning bugs shining in the bushes. At the end of the boulevard
you get to this place call the Plaza.

It's something like a little park—the sidewalks is all bricks and they got   21 flowers planted all over the place. The same kind my mama grow in that painted-up tire she got out from masquerading like a garden decoration—only seem like they smell sweeter here. It's a big high fountain right in the middle, and all the streetlights is the real old-fashion kind. That Plaza is about the prettiest place I ever been.

Sometimes something going on there. Like a orchestra playing music or some man or lady singing. One time they had a show with some girls doing some kinda foreign dances. They look like they were around my age. They all had on these fancy costumes, with different color ribbons all down they back. I wouldn't wear nothing like that, but it looked real pretty when they was dancing.

I got me a special bench in one corner where I like to sit, cause I can see just about everything, but wouldn't nobody know I was there. I like to sit still and think, and I like to watch people. A lotta people be coming there at night—to look at the shows and stuff, or just to hang out and cool off. All different kinda people.

This one night when I was sitting over in that corner where I always be at, there was this lady standing right near my bench. She mostly had her back turned to me and she didn't know I was there, but I could see her real good. She had on this shiny purple shirt and about a million silver bracelets. I kinda liked the way she look. Sorta exotic, like she maybe come from California or one of the islands. I mean she had class—standing there posing with her arms folded. She walk away a little bit. Then turn around and walk back again. Like she waiting for somebody.

Then I spotted this dude coming over. I spied him all the way cross the Plaza. Looking real fine. Got on a three piece suit. One of them little caps sitting on a angle. Look like leather. He coming straight over to this lady I'm watching and then she seen him too and she start to smile, but she don't move till he get right up next to her. And then I'm gonna look away, cause I can't stand to watch nobody hugging and kissing on each other, but all of a sudden I see it ain't no dude at all. It's another lady.

Now I can't stop looking. They smiling at each other like they ain't seen one another in ten years. Then the one in the purple shirt look around real quick—but she don't look just behind her—she sorta pull the other one right back into the corner where I'm sitting at, and then they put they arms around each other and kiss—for a whole long time. Now I really know I oughtta turn away, but I can't. And I know they gonna see me when they finally open they eyes. And they do.

They both kinda gasp and back up, like I'm the monster that just rose up outta the deep. And then I guess they can see I'm only a girl, and they look at one another—and start to laugh! Then they just turn around and start to walk away like it wasn't nothing at all. But right before they gone, they both look around again, and see I still ain't got my eye muscles and my jaw muscles working right again yet. And the one lady wink at me. And the other one say, "Catch you later."

I can't stop staring at they backs, all the way across the Plaza. And then, all of a sudden, I feel like I got to be doing something, got to be moving. 28

I wheel on outta the Plaza and I'm just concentrating on getting up my speed. Cause I can't figure out what to think. Them two women kissing and then, when they get caught, just laughing about it. And here I'm laughing too, for no reason at all. I'm sailing down the boulevard laughing like a lunatic, and then I'm singing at the top of my lungs. And climbing that big old hill up to Summit Avenue is just as easy as being on a escalator. 29

STUDY QUESTIONS

1. How quickly does the NARRATOR characterize herself? By what means? Exactly when do you discover how old she is at the time of the story's action? What else do you know about her by that time?

2. How good of an observer is the narrator? What kinds of value judgments does she make about adults? What does she think about adult women? about men? about girls and boys?

3. Describe the language the narrator uses to describe herself; to describe others. How conscious is she of her abilities with language? How self-conscious is she in her evaluation of her own feelings and values?

4. What does her "ten-speed" represent for the narrator? Where, exactly, does it take her? What kind of language does she use to describe where she is "looking around right now"? What does she discover as a result of her explorations? Where is the dividing line between the world she knows and that of the "other"? Explain what the "Plaza" comes to represent to the narrator. Exactly what does she see in the Plaza?

5. Why does the narrator go to so much trouble to explain that observers cannot tell, from her appearance, that she is a girl? How important is her age to the discovery of varieties of adult relationships? to the theme of the story?

6. Explain the title of the story. Does it mean the same thing at the end that it seemed to mean at the beginning?

7. Reread very carefully the account of Johnnieruth's Sunday meeting with the "skinny" lady on an earlier Sunday. In what specific ways does this episode anticipate her climactic discovery of the two women at the end of the story? What does her "funny look" mean to Johnnieruth at the time? What does it mean in the context of the story?

8. Explain the unmasking of the "dude" at the end. Why can't Johnnieruth stop looking? Why does one lady say, "Catch you later"?

9. Explain the sense of relief and exhilaration Johnnieruth feels at the end of the story. Why does she feel "like I got to be doing something, got to be moving" (paragraph 28)?

Neil Bissoondath

Neil Bissoondath was born in Trinidad in 1955 into a family who originally came to the West Indies from India. His is a famous literary family: he is the nephew of V. S. and Shiva Naipaul, both well-known writers. Bissoondath has published three volumes of stories, *Digging Up the Mountains*, (1986), *A Casual Brutality* (1989), and *On the Eve of the Uncertain Tomorrows* (1990). He now lives in Toronto, having moved there in 1973 to study French at York University.

THERE ARE A LOT OF WAYS TO DIE

It was still drizzling when Joseph clicked the final padlocks on the door. The name-plate, home-painted with squared gold letters on a black background and glazed all over with transparent varnish to lend a professional tint, was flecked with water and dirt. He took a crumpled handkerchief from his back pocket and carefully wiped the lettering clean: JOSEPH HEAVEN: CARPET AND RUG INSTALLATIONS. The colon had been his idea and he had put it in over his wife's objections. He felt that it provided a natural flow from his name, that it showed a certain reliability. His wife, in the scornful voice she reserved for piercing his pretensions, had said, "That's all very well and good for Toronto, but you think people here care about that kind of thing?" But she was the one people accused of having airs, not him. As far as he was concerned, the colon was merely good business; and as the main beneficiary of the profits, she should learn to keep her mouth shut.

He had forgotten to pick up his umbrella from just inside the door where he had put it that morning. Gingerly, he extended his upturned palm, feeling the droplets, warm and wet, like newly spilled blood. He decided they were too light to justify reopening the shop, always something of an event because of the many locks and chains. This was another thing she didn't like, his obsession, as she called it, with security. She wanted a more open storefront, with windows and showcases and well-dressed mannequins smiling blankly at the street. She said, "It look just like every other store around here, just a wall and a door. It have nothing to catch the eye." He replied, "You want windows and showcases? What we going to show? My tools? The

1

2

tacks? The cutter?" Besides, the locks were good for business, not a week went by without a robbery in the area. Displaying the tools would be a blatant invitation, and a recurrent nightmare had developed in which one of his cutters was stolen and used in a murder.

Across the glistening street, so narrow after the generosity of those he had known for six years, the clothes merchants were standing disconsolately in front of their darkened stores, hands in pockets, whistling and occasionally examining the grey skies for the brightening that would signal the end of the rain and the appearance of shoppers. They stared blankly at him. One half-heartedly jabbed his finger at a stalactitic line of umbrellas and dusty rain-coats, inviting a purchase. Joseph showed no interest. The merchant shrugged and resumed his tuneless whistling, a plaintive sound from between clenched front teeth.

Joseph had forgotten how sticky the island could be when it rained. The heat, it seemed, never really disappeared during the night. Instead, it retreated just a few inches underground, only to emerge with the morning rain, con-densing, filling the atmosphere with steam. It put the lie to so much he had told his Canadian friends about the island. The morning rain wasn't as refreshing as he'd recalled it and the steam had left his memory altogether. How could he have sworn that the island experienced no humidity? Why had he, in all honesty, recalled tender tropical breezes when the truth, as it now enveloped him, was the exact, stifling opposite? Climate was not so drastically altered, only memory.

He walked to the end of the street, his shirt now clinging to his shoul-ders. The sidewalk, dark and pitted, seemed to glide by under his feet, as if it were itself moving. He squinted, feeling the folds of flesh bunching up at the corner of his eyes, and found he could fuzzily picture himself on Bloor Street, walking past the stores and the bakeries and the delicatessens pungent with Eastern European flavors, the hazy tops of buildings at Bloor and Yonge far away in the distance. He could even conjure up the sounds of a Toronto summer: the cars, the voices, the rumble of the subway under the feet as it swiftly glided towards downtown.

Joseph shook himself and opened his eyes, not without disappointment. He was having this hallucination too often, for too long. He was ashamed of it and couldn't confess it even to his wife. And he mistrusted it, too: might not even this more recent memory also be fooling him, as the other had done? Was it really possible to see the tops of buildings at Yonge from Bathurst? He wanted to ask his wife, pretending it was merely a matter of memory, but she would see through this to his longing and puncture him once more with that voice. She would call him a fool and not be far wrong. Were not two dislocations enough in one man's lifetime? Would not yet a third prove him a fool?

Their return had been jubilant. Friends and relatives treated it as a vic-tory, seeking affirmation of the correctness of their cloistered life on the island, the return a defeat for life abroad. The first weeks were hectic, parties, dinners, get-togethers. Joseph felt like a curiosity, an object not of reverence but of silent ridicule, his the defeat, theirs the victory. The island seemed to close in around him.

They bought a house in the island's capital. The town was not large. Located at the extreme north-western edge of the island, having hardly expanded from the settlement originally established by Spanish adventurers as a depot in their quest for mythic gold, the town looked forever to the sea, preserving its aura of a way-station, a point at which to pause in brief respite from the larger search.

At first, Joseph had tried to deny this aspect of the town, for the town was the island and, if the island were no more than a way-station, a stopover from which nothing important ever emerged, then to accept this life was to accept second place. A man who had tasted of first could accept second only with delusion: his wife had taken on airs, he had painted his black-and-gold sign.

Then the hallucination started, recreating Bloor Street, vividly recalling the minute details of daily life. He caught himself reliving the simple things: buying milk, removing a newspaper from the box, slipping a subway token into the slot, sitting in a park. A chill would run through him when he realized they were remembrances of things past, possibly lost forever. The recollected civility of life in Toronto disturbed him, it seemed so distant. He remembered what a curious feeling of well-being had surged through him whenever he'd given directions to a stranger. Each time was like an affirmation of stability. Here, in an island so small that two leisurely hours in a car would reveal all, no one asked for directions, no one was a stranger. You couldn't claim the island: it claimed you.

The street on which their house stood used to be known all over the island. It was viewed with a twinge of admired notoriety and was thought of with the same fondness with which the islanders regarded the government ministers and civil servants who had fled the island with pilfered cash: an awed admiration, a flawed love. The cause of this attention was a house, a mansion in those days, erected, in the popular lore, by a Venezuelan general who, for reasons unknown, had exiled himself to a life of darkly rumored obscurity on the island. As far as Joseph knew, no one had ever actually seen the general: even his name, Pacheco, had been assumed. Or so it was claimed; no one had ever bothered to check.

Eventually the house became known as Pacheco House, and the street as Pacheco Street. It was said that the house, deserted for as long as anyone could remember and now falling into neglect, had been mentioned passingly in a book by an Englishman who had been looking into famous houses of the region. It was the island's first mention in a book other than a history text, the island's first mention outside the context of slavery.

The house had become the butt of schoolboys' frustration. On their way home after school, Joseph and his friends would detour to throw stones at the windows. In his memory, the spitting clank of shattering glass sounded distant and opaque. They had named each window for a teacher, thus adding thrust and enthusiasm to their aim. The largest window, high on the third floor—the attic, he now knew, in an island which had no attics—they named LeNoir, after the priest who was the terror of all students unblessed by fair skin or athletic ability. They were more disturbed by the fact that the priest himself was black; this seemed a greater sin than his choice of vocation. They had never succeeded in breaking the LeNoir window. Joseph might have put this down to divine protection had he not lost his sense of religion early on. It was a simple event: the priest at his last try at communion had showered him with sour breath the moment the flesh of Christ slipped onto Joseph's tongue. Joseph, from then on, equated the wafer with decaying flesh.

The LeNoir window went unscathed for many years and was still intact   14
when, after the final exams, Joseph left the island for what he believed to be forever.

The raindrops grew larger, making a plopping sound on the sidewalk.   15
A drop landed on his temple and cascaded down his cheek. He rubbed at it, feeling the prickly stubble he hadn't bothered to shave that morning.

Pacheco House was just up ahead, the lower floors obscured by a jungle   16
of trees and bush, the garden overgrown and thickening to impenetrability. Above the treeline, the walls—a faded pink, pockmarked by the assault of stones and mangoes—had begun disintegrating, the thin plaster falling away in massive chunks to reveal ordinary grey brick underneath. The remaining plaster was criss-crossed by cracks and fissures created by age and humidity.

During his schooldays, the grounds had been maintained by the govern-   17
ment. The house had been considered a tourist attraction and was displayed in brochures and on posters. An island-wide essay competition had been held, "The Mystery of Pacheco House," and the winning essay, of breathless prose linked by words like *tropical* and *verdant* and *lush* and *exotic*, was used as the text of a special brochure. But no tourists came. The mystery withered away to embarrassment. The government quietly gave the house up. The Jaycees, young businessmen who bustled about in the heat with the added burden of jackets and ties, offered to provide funds for the upkeep. The offer was refused with a shrug by the Ministry of Tourism, with inexplicable murmurings of "colonial horrors" by the Ministry of Culture. The house was left to its ghosts.

From the street Joseph could see the LeNoir window, still intact and   18
dirt-streaked. He was surprised that it still seemed to mock him.

Joseph had asked his nephew, a precocious boy who enjoyed exhibiting   19
his scattered knowledge of French and Spanish and who laughed at Joseph's clumsy attempts to resurrect the bits of language he had learnt in the same classes, often from the same teachers, if the boys still threw stones at Pacheco House. No, his nephew had informed him, after school they went to the sex movies or, in the case of the older boys, to the whorehouses. Joseph, stunned, had asked no more questions.

The rain turned perceptibly to a deluge, the thick, warm drops pene- 20
trating his clothes and running in rivulets down his back and face. The wild
trees and plants of the Pacheco garden nodded and drooped, leaves glistening
dully in the half-light. The pink walls darkened as the water socked into
them, eating at the plaster. The LeNoir window was black; he remembered
some claimed to have seen a white-faced figure in army uniform standing
there at night. The story had provided mystery back then, a real haunted
house, and on a rainy afternoon schoolboys could feel their spines tingle as
they aimed their stones.

On impulse Joseph searched the ground for a stone. He saw only peb- 21
bles; the gravel verge had long been paved over. Already the sidewalk had
cracked in spots and little shoots of grass had fought their way out, like
wedges splitting a boulder.

He continued walking, oblivious of the rain. 22

Several cars were parked in the driveway of his house. His wife's friends 23
were visiting. They were probably in the living room drinking coffee and
eating pastries from Marcel's and looking through *Vogue* pattern books. Joseph
made for the garage so he could enter, unnoticed, through the kitchen door.
Then he thought, "Why the hell?" He put his hands into his pockets—his
money was soaked and the movement of his fingers ripped the edge off a
bill—and calmly walked in through the open front door.

His wife was standing in front of the fake fireplace she had insisted on 24
bringing from Toronto. The dancing lights cast multicolored hues on her
caftan. She almost dropped her coffee cup when she saw him. Her friends,
perturbed, stared at him from their chairs which they had had grouped around
the fireplace.

His wife said impatiently, "Joseph, what are you doing here?" 25

He said, "I live here." 26

She said, "And work?" 27

He said, "None of the boys show up this morning." 28

"So you just drop everything?" 29

"I postponed today's jobs. I couldn't do all the work by myself." 30

She put her cup down on the mantelpiece. "Go dry yourself off. You 31
wetting the floor."

Her friend Arlene said, "Better than the bed." 32

They all laughed. His wife said, "He used to do that when he was a 33
little boy, not so, Joseph?"

She looked at her friends and said, "You know, we having so much 34
trouble finding good workers. Joseph already fire three men. Looks like we're
going to have to fire all these now."

Arlene said, "Good help so hard to find these days." 35

His wife said, "These people like that, you know, girl. Work is the last 36
thing they want to do."

Arlene said, "They 'fraid they going to melt if rain touch their skin." 37

His wife turned to him. "You mean not one out of twelve turned up this 38
morning?"

"Not one."   39

Arlene, dark and plump, sucked her teeth and moved her tongue around,   40
pushing at her cheeks and making a plopping sound.

Joseph said, "Stop that. You look like a monkey."   41

His wife and Arlene stared at him in amazement. The others sipped   42
their coffee or gazed blankly at the fireplace.

Arlene said witheringly, "I don't suffer fools gladly, Joseph."   43

He said, "Too bad. You must hate being alone."   44

His wife said, "Joseph!"   45

He said, "I better go dry off." Still dripping, he headed for the bed-   46
room. At the door he paused and added, "People should be careful when
they talking about other people. You know, glass houses . . ." He was suddenly exhausted: what was the point? They all knew Arlene's story. She had
once been a maid whose career was rendered transient by rain and imagined
illness; she had been no different from his employees. Her fortune had
improved only because her husband—who was referred to behind his back
as a "sometimes worker" because sometimes he worked and sometimes he
didn't—had been appointed a minister without portfolio in the government.
He had lost the nickname because now he never worked, but he had gained
a regular cheque, a car and a chauffeur, and the tainted respectability of
political appointment.

Joseph slammed the bedroom door and put his ear to the keyhole: there   47
was a lot of throat-clearing; pages of a *Vogue* pattern book rustled. Finally his
wife said, "Come look at this pattern." Voices oohed and ahhed and cooed.
Arlene said, "Look at this one." He kicked the door and threw his wet shirt
on the bed.

The rain had stopped and the sky had cleared a little. His wife and her   48
friends were still in the living room. It was not yet midday. His clothes had
left a damp patch on the bed, on his side, and he knew it would still be wet
at bedtime. He put on a clean set of clothes and sat on the bed, rubbing the
dampness, as if this would make it disappear. He reached up and drew the
curtains open; grey, drifting sky, vegetation drooping and wet, like wash on
a line; the very top of Pacheco House, galvanized iron rusted through, so
thin in parts that a single drop of rain might cause a great chunk to go crashing into the silence of the house. Except maybe for the bats, disintegration
was probably the only sound now to be heard in Pacheco House. The house
was like a dying man who could hear his heart ticking to a stop.

Joseph sensed that something was missing. The rainflies, delicate ant-   49
like creatures with brown wings but no sting. Defenceless, wings attached
to their bodies by the most fragile of links, they fell apart at the merest touch.
After a particularly heavy rainfall, detached wings, almost transparent, would
litter the ground and cling to moist feet like lint to wool. As a child, he used
to pull the wings off and place the crippled insect on a table, where he could
observe it crawling desperately around, trying to gain the air. Sometimes he

would gingerly tie the insect to one end of a length of thread, release it, and control its flight. In all this he saw no cruelty. His friends enjoyed crushing them, or setting them on fire, or sizzling them with the burning end of a cigarette. Joseph had only toyed with the insects; he could never bring himself to kill one.

There was not a rainfly in sight. The only movement was that of the clouds and dripping water. In the town, the insects had long, and casually, been eradicated. He felt the loss. 50

He heard his wife call her friends to lunch. He half expected to hear his name but she ignored him: he might have not been there. He waited a few more minutes until he was sure they had all gone into the dining room, then slipped out the front door. 51

Water was gurgling in the drains, rushing furiously through the iron gratings into the sewers. In the street, belly up, fur wet and clinging, lay a dead dog, a common sight. Drivers no longer even bothered to squeal their tires. 52

Joseph walked without direction, across streets and through different neighborhoods, passing people and being passed by cars. He took in none of it. His thoughts were thousands of miles away, on Bloor Street, on Yonge Street, among the stalls of Kensington Market. 53

He was at National Square when the rain once more began to pound down. He found a dry spot under the eaves of a store and stood, arms folded, watching the rain and the umbrellas and the raincoats. A man hurried past him, a handkerchief tied securely to his head the only protection from the rain. It was a useless gesture, and reminded Joseph of his grandmother's warnings to him never to go out at night without a hat to cover his head, "because of the dew." 54

National Square was the busiest part of town. Cars constantly sped by, horns blaring, water splashing. After a few minutes a donkey cart loaded with fresh coconuts trundled by on its way to the Savannah, a wide, flat park just north of the town where the horse races were held at Christmas. A line of impatient cars crept along behind the donkey cart, the leaders bobbing in and out of line in search of an opportunity to pass. 55

Joseph glanced at his watch. It was almost twelve-thirty. He decided to have something to eat. Just around the corner was a cheap restaurant frequented by office workers from the government buildings and foreign banks which enclosed the square. Holding his hands over his head, Joseph dashed through the rain to the restaurant. 56

Inside was shadowed, despite the cobwebby fluorescent lighting. The walls were lined with soft-drink advertisements and travel posters. One of the posters showed an interminable stretch of bleached beach overhung with languid coconut-tree branches. Large, cursive letters read: Welcome To The Sunny Caribbean. The words were like a blow to the nerves. Joseph felt like ripping the poster up. 57

A row of green metal tables stretched along one wall of the rectangular 58 room. A few customers sat in loosened ties and shirt-sleeves, sipping beer and smoking and conversing in low tones. At the far end, at a table crowded with empty bottles and an overflowing ashtray, Joseph noticed a familiar face. It was lined and more drawn than when he'd known it, and the eyes had lost their sparkle of intelligence; but he was certain he was not mistaken. He went up to the man. He said, "Frankie?"

Frankie looked up slowly, unwillingly, emerging from a daydream. He said, "Yes?" Then he brightened. "Joseph? Joseph!" He sprang to his feet, knocking his chair back. He grasped Joseph's hand. "How you doing, man? It's been years and years. How you doing?" He pushed Joseph into a chair and loudly ordered two beers. He lit a cigarette. His hand shook. 59

Joseph said, "You smoking now, Frankie?" 60

"For years, man. You?" 61

Joseph shook his head. 62

Frankie said, "But you didn't go to Canada? I thought somebody tell me . . ." 63

"Went and came back. One of those things. How about you? How the years treat you?" 64

"I work in a bank. Loan officer." 65

"Good job?" 66

"Not bad." 67

Joseph sipped his beer. The situation wasn't right. There should have been so much to say, so much to hear. Frankie used to be his best friend. He was the most intelligent person Joseph had ever known. This was the last place he would have expected to find him. Frankie had dreamt of university and professorship, and it had seemed, back then, that university and professorship awaited him. 68

Frankie took a long pull on his cigarette, causing the tube to crinkle and flatten. He said, "What was Canada like?" Before Joseph could answer, he added, "You shouldn't have come back. Why did you come back? A big mistake." He considered the cigarette. 69

The lack of emotion in Frankie's voice distressed Joseph. It was the voice of a depleted man. He said, "It was time." 70

Frankie leaned back in his chair and slowly blew smoke rings at Joseph. He seemed to be contemplating the answer. He said, "What were you doing up there?" 71

"I had a business. Installing carpets and rugs. Is a good little business. My partner looking after it now." 72

Frankie looked away, towards the door. He said nothing. 73

Joseph said, "You ever see anybody from school?" 74

Frankie waved his cigarette. "Here and there. You know, Raffique dead. And Jonesy and Dell." 75

Joseph recalled the faces: boys, in school uniform. Death was not an event he could associate with them. "How?" 76

"Raffique in a car accident. Jonesy slit his wrists over a woman. Dell 77

. . . who knows? There are a lot of ways to die. They found him dead in the washroom of a cinema. A girl was with him. Naked. She wasn't dead. She's in the madhouse now."

"And the others?" Joseph couldn't contemplate the death roll. It seemed to snuff out a little bit of his own life. 78

"The others? Some doing something, some doing nothing. It don't matter." 79

Joseph said, "You didn't go to university." 80

Frankie laughed. "No, I didn't." 81

Joseph waited for an explanation. Frankie offered none. 82

Frankie said, "Why the hell you come back from Canada? And none of this 'It was time' crap." 83

Joseph rubbed his face, feeling the stubble, tracing the fullness of his chin. "I had some kind of crazy idea about starting a business, creating jobs, helping my people." 84

Frankie laughed mockingly. 85

Joseph said, "I should have known better. We had a party before we left. A friend asked me the same question, why go back. I told him the same thing. He said it was bullshit and that I just wanted to make a lot of money and live life like a holiday. We quarrelled and I threw him out. The next morning he called to apologize. He was crying. He said he was just jealous." Joseph sipped the beer, lukewarm and sweating. "Damn fool." 86

Frankie laughed again. "I don't believe this. You mean to tell me you had the courage to leave *and* the stupidity to come back?" He slapped the table, rocking it and causing an empty beer bottle to fall over. "You always used to be the idealist, Joseph. I was more realistic. And less courageous. That's why I never left." 87

"Nobody's called me an idealist for years." The word seemed more mocking than Frankie's laugh. 88

Frankie said, "And now you're stuck back here for good." He shook his head vigorously, drunkenly. "A big, idealistic mistake, Joseph." 89

"I'm not stuck here." He was surprised at how much relief the thought brought him. "I can go back any time I want." 90

"Well, go then." Frankie's voice was slurred, and it held more than a hint of aggressiveness. 91

Joseph shook his head. He glanced at his watch. He said, "It's almost one. Don't you have to get back to work?" 92

Frankie called for another beer. "The bank won't fall down if I'm not there." 93

"We used to think the world would fall down if not for us." 94

"That was a long time ago. We were stupid." Frankie lit another cigarette. His hand shook badly. "In this place, is nonsense to think the world, the world out there, have room for you." 95

Joseph said, "You could have been a historian. History was your best subject, not so?" 96

"Yeah."   97

"You still interested in history?"   98

"Off and on. I tried to write a book. Nobody wanted to publish it."   99

"Why not?"   100

"Because our history doesn't lead anywhere. It's just a big, black hole.   101
Nobody's interested in a book about a hole."

"You know anything about Pacheco House?"   102

"Pacheco House? A little."   103

"What?"   104

"The man wasn't a Venezuelan general. He was just a crazy old man   105
from Argentina. He was rich. I don't know why he came here. He lived in
the house for a short time and then he died there, alone. They found his
body about two weeks later, rotting and stinking. They say he covered
himself with old cocoa bags, even his head. I think he knew he was going to
die and after all that time alone he couldn't stand the thought of anyone
seeing him. Crazy, probably. They buried him in the garden and put up a
little sign. And his name wasn't really Pacheco either, people just called him
that. They got it from a cowboy film. I've forgot what his real name was but
it don't matter. Pacheco's as good as any other."

"That's all? What about the house itself?"   106

"That's all. The house is just a house. Nothing special." Frankie popped   107
the half-finished cigarette into his beer bottle, it sizzled briefly. He added,
"R.I.P. Pacheco, his house and every damn thing else." He put another cigarette between his lips, allowing it to droop to his chin, pushing his upper
lip up and out, as if his teeth were deformed. His hands shook so badly he
couldn't strike the match. His eyes met Joseph's.

Joseph couldn't hold the gaze. He was chilled. He said, "I have to go."   108

Frankie waved him away.   109

Joseph pushed back his chair. Frankie looked past him with bloodshot   110
eyes, already lost in the confusion of his mind.

Joseph, indicating the travel poster, offered the barman five dollars for   111
it. The man, fat, with an unhealthy greasiness, said, "No way."

Joseph offered ten dollars.   112

The barman refused.   113

Joseph understood: it was part of the necessary lie.   114

Grey clouds hung low and heavy in the sky. The hills to the north, their   115
lower half crowded with the multicolored roofs of shacks, poverty plain from
even so great a distance, were shrouded in mist, as if an inferno had recently
burned out and the smoke not yet cleared away.

Some of his workers lived there, in tiny, crowded one-room shacks,   116
with water sometimes a quarter-mile away at a mossy stand-pipe. There was
a time when the sight of these shacks could move Joseph to pity. They were,
he believed, his main reason for returning to the island. He really had said,
"I want to help my people." Now the sentence, with its pomposity, its naive-

ty, was just an embarrassing memory, like the early life of the minister's wife.

But he knew that wasn't all. He had expected a kind of fame, a continual 117 welcome, the prodigal son having made good, having acquired skills, returning home to share the wealth, to spread the knowledge. He had anticipated a certain uniqueness but this had been thwarted. Everyone knew someone else who had returned from abroad—from England, from Canada, from the States. He grew to hate the stock phrases people dragged out: "No place like home, this island is a true Paradise, life's best here." The little lies of self-doubt and fear.

The gate to Pacheco House was chained but there was no lock: a casual 118 locking-up, an abandonment. The chain, thick and rusted, slipped easily to the ground, leaving a trace of gritty oxide on his fingertips. He couldn't push the gate far; clumps of grass, stems long and tapering to a lancet point, blocked it at the base. He squeezed through the narrow opening, the concrete pillar rough and tight on his back, the iron gate leaving a slash of rust on his shirt. Inside, wild grass, wet and glistening, enveloped his legs up to his knees. The trees were further back, thick and ponderous, unmoving, lending the garden the heavy stillness of jungle.

Walking, pushing through the grass, took a little effort. The vegetation 119 sought not so much to prevent intrusion as to hinder it, to encumber it with a kind of tropical lassitude. Joseph raised his legs high, free of the tangle of vines and roots and thorns, and brought his boots crashing down with each step, crushing leaves into juicy blobs of green and brown, startling underground colonies of ants into frenzied scrambling. Ahead of him, butterflies, looking like edges of an artist's canvas, fluttered away, and crickets, their wings beating like pieces of stiff silk one against the other, buzzed from tall stalk to tall stalk, narrowly avoiding the grasshoppers which also sought escape. A locust, as long as his hand and as fat, sank its claws into his shirt, just grazing the surface of his skin. He flicked a finger powerfully at it, knocking off its head; the rest of the body simply relaxed and fell off.

Once past the trees, Joseph found himself at the house. The stone foun- 120 dation, he noticed, was covered in green slime and the wall, the monotony of which was broken only by a large cavity which must once have been a window, stripped of all color. He made his way to the cavity and peered through it into the half-darkness of a large room. He carefully put one leg through, feeling for the floor. The boards creaked badly but held.

The room was a disappointment. He didn't know what he had expected— 121 he hadn't really thought about it—but its emptiness engendered an atmosphere of uncommon despair. He felt it was a room that had always been empty, a room that had never been peopled with emotion or sound, like a dried-up old spinster abandoned at the edge of life. He could smell the pungency of recently disturbed vegetation but he didn't know whether it came from him or through the gaping window.

He made his way to another room, the floorboards creaking under the 122 wary tread of his feet; just another empty space, characterless, almost shapeless in its desertion. A flight of stairs led upwards, to the second floor and yet another empty room, massive, dusty, cobwebs tracing crazy geometric patterns on the walls and the ceiling. In the corners the floorboards had begun to warp. He wondered why all the doors had been removed and by whom. Or had the house ever had doors? Might it not have been always a big, open, empty house, with rooms destined to no purpose, with a façade that promised mystery but an interior that took away all hope?

He had hoped to find something of Pacheco's, the merest testament to his having existed, a bed maybe, or a portrait, or even one line of graffiti. But were it not for the structure itself, a vacuous shell falling steadily to ruin, and the smudges of erroneous public fantasy fading like the outer edges of a dream, Pacheco might never have existed. Whatever relics might have been preserved by the government had long been carted away, probably by the last workmen, those who had so cavalierly slipped the chain around the gate, putting a period to a life. 123

Joseph walked around the room, his footsteps echoing like drumbeats. Each wall had a window of shattered glass and he examined the view from each. Jumbled vegetation, the jungle taking hold in this one plot of earth in the middle of the town: it was the kind of view that would have been described in the travel brochures as *lush* and *tropical*, two words he had grown to hate. Looking through the windows, recalling the manicured grounds of his youth, he felt confined, isolated, a man in an island on an island. He wondered why anyone would pay a lot of money to visit such a place. The answer came to him: for the tourist, a life was not to be constructed here. The tourist sought no more than an approximation of adventure; there was safety in a return ticket and foreign passport. 124

There was no way to get to the attic, where the LeNoir window was. Another disappointment: the object of all that youthful energy was nothing more than an aperture to a boxed-in room, airless and musty with age and probably dank with bat mess. 125

He made his way back down the stairs and out the gaping front door. The air was hot and sticky and the smell of vegetation, acrid in the humidity, was almost overpowering. 126

Frankie had said that Pacheco was buried in the garden and that a marker had been erected. Joseph knew there was no hope of finding it. Everything was overgrown: the garden, the flowers, the driveway that had once existed, Pacheco's grave, Pacheco himself, the mysterious South American whose last act was to lose his name and his life in sterile isolation. 127

Joseph began making his way back to the gate. Over to the left he could see the path he had made when going in, the grass flat and twisted, twigs broken and limp, still dripping from the morning rain. He felt clammy, and steamy perspiration broke out on his skin. 128

At the gate, he stopped and turned around for a last look at the house: he saw it for what it was, a deceptive shell that played on the mind. He 129 looked around for something to throw. The base of the gate-pillars was cracked and broken and moss had begun eating its way to the centre. He broke off a piece of the concrete and flung it at the LeNoir window. The glass shattered, scattering thousands of slivers into the attic and onto the ground below.

His wife wasn't home when he returned. The house was dark and silent. Coffee cups and plates with half-eaten pastries lay on the side-tables. The false fireplace had been switched off. On the mantelpiece, propped against his wife's lipstick-stained cup, was a notepad with a message: "Have gone out for the evening with Arlene. We have the chauffeur and the limo coz Brian's busy in a cabinet meeting. Don't know what time I'll be back." She hadn't bothered to sign it.

He ripped the page from the notepad: he hated the word "coz" and the word "limo" and he felt a special revulsion for "Arlene" and "Brian," fictitious names assumed with the mantle of social status. As a transient domestic, Arlene had been called Thelma, the name scribbled on her birth certificate, and Brian's real name was Balthazar. Joseph avoided the entire issue by simply referring to them as the Minister and the Minister's Wife. The sarcasm was never noticed.

He took the notepad and a pencil and sat down. He wrote *Dear* then crossed it out. He threw the page away and started again. He drew a circle, then a triangle, then a square: the last disappointment, it was the most difficult act. Finally, in big square letters, he wrote, *I am going back.* He put the pad back on the mantelpiece, switched on the fireplace lights, and sat staring into their synchronized dance.

STUDY QUESTIONS

1. What reasons does the NARRATOR give for having returned to the island? What do others assume about his reasons for returning? What other "reasons" are implied by the story?

2. Describe Joseph's CHARACTER. Which memories of his childhood mean most to him? What does he care about most in his present life? What memories of Toronto does he cherish most? What characteristics in his friends does he care most about? How does he feel about his wife's life-style? What bothers him most about the habits of her friends? What bothers him most about their values?

3. What does the episode in which he returns to his house unannounced demonstrate about Joseph's values? about his degree of success? about his attitudes toward the people on the island? Why does he dislike Arlene so intensely?

4. How much do we know about Joseph's marriage? What strategies does the story use to undermine Joseph's wife? Which of her characteristics are particularly objectionable? On what sorts of values does the marriage seem to be based?

5. Explain Joseph's "hallucinations" about the fashionable areas of Toronto. How do his memories of his childhood relate to his feelings about Toronto? How does

his sense of Pacheco House relate to his idea of Toronto? How does his discovery of the "real" history of Pacheco House relate to the main THEME of the story? to Joseph's other discoveries about his beliefs and illusions? How would you state the theme of the story?

6. What do the fates of Joseph's boyhood friends have to do with his sense of himself now? What does Joseph's "memory," when he lived in Toronto, of Caribbean weather have to do with his character? with his ideas of "home"? with his values? with his ability to handle the implied criticisms of his friends?

7. What does the chance encounter with Frankie "prove" to Joseph about his memories? about his values? about his self-perceptions?

8. Where is "home" to Joseph? What characteristics of home are most important in his scheme of values? Does his idea of home change during the story? Does his sense of values change?

9. What does the apparent permanence of "LeNoir" mean to Joseph when he first mentions his childhood adventures at Pacheco House? What does the breaking of the window seem to mean to Joseph once his illusions begin to break? How do the various details that Joseph observes during his invasion of Pacheco House help him to define his changing notion of himself?

10. How critical is the story of island habits and practices? What kinds of behavior are criticized most heavily? Does the story sympathize with Joseph's idealism? make fun of it? regard it as unrealistic? How do you feel about Joseph by the end of the story? What strategies does the author use to make you feel that way? What word best describes the attitude of the author toward Joseph? What word best describes the TONE of the story?

11. How important to the story's effects is the rain during Joseph's return home? How important is the heat? Describe the effect upon the story's MEANING of its time SETTING. In what ways is the remembered time in Toronto different in quality?

12. What values does Canada come to stand for in the story? What values does the island stand for? What values does each of the characters stand for? How important to the story is Joseph's profession?

13. What does the title of the story mean?

Diane Burns

A painter and illustrator, Diane Burns was educated at the Institute of American Indian Art in Santa Fe, New Mexico, and at Barnard College. Her first volume of poetry, *Riding the One-Eyed Ford* (1981), was nominated for the William Carlos

Williams Award. Her latest, *Sugaring Season* (1990), was named a Notable Children's Book in Social Studies by the Children's Book Council and the National Council for Social Studies. Burns was elected vice-president of the Northern Arts Council in 1991 and belongs to the Third World Writers Association and the Feminist Writers Guild. She currently resides in New York City.

SURE YOU CAN ASK ME A PERSONAL QUESTION

How do you do?
 No, I am not Chinese.
No, not Spanish.
 No, I am American Indi-uh, Native American.
No, not from India.   5
 No, not Apache.
No, not Navajo.
 No, not Sioux.
No, we are not extinct.
 Yes, Indin.   10
Oh?
 So that's where you got those high cheekbones.
Your great grandmother, huh?
 An Indian Princess, huh?
Hair down to there?   15
 Let me guess. Cherokee?
Oh, so you've had an Indian friend?
 That close?
Oh, so you've had an Indian lover?
 That tight?   20
Oh, so you've had an Indian servant?
 That much?
Yeah, it was awful what you guys did to us.
 It's real decent of you to apologize.
No, I don't know where you can get peyote.   25
 No, I don't know where you can get Navajo rugs real cheap.
No, I didn't make this. I bought it at Bloomingdale's.
 Thank you. I like your hair too.
I don't know if anyone knows whether or not Cher is really Indian.
 No, I didn't make it rain tonight.   30
Yeah. Uh-huh. Spirituality.
 Uh-huh. Yeah. Spirituality. Uh-huh. Mother
Earth. Yeah. Uh'huh. Uh'huh. Spirituality.

No, I didn't major in archery.
Yeah, a lot of us drink too much.
    Some of us can't drink enough.
This ain't no stoic look.
    This is my face.

35

STUDY QUESTIONS

1. Identify which lines are spoken by the "I" and which by someone else.

2. What are some of the STEREOTYPES indicated by the implied questions?

3. What is the TONE of the poem? How does the title contribute to the tone?

Perry Brass

Born in 1947, Perry Brass has published several books, including *Survival Kit: A Complete Guidance Manual for Gay Men* (1988), which he coedited, *Mirage* (1991), and *Works: Smoky George and Other Stories* (1992). The following poem was published in the *Penguin Book of Homosexual Verse* (1986).

I THINK THE NEW TEACHER'S A QUEER

'I think the new teacher's a queer,'

I turned around
and saw that
they were talking about me,

one false move
and it would all be over,
I could not drop my wrists
or raise my voice.

5

so I stood there up against the board
arms folded   10
pressed against my chest
and looked without seeing
or hearing until
the children became a noiseless pattern

and all those years   15
from when I sat among them
stopped dead and I feared
that they'd beat me up

in the boys' room.

STUDY QUESTIONS

1. Exactly what is the SETTING of the poem, and what is the situation when the first line of the poem is spoken? What kind of expectations for the rest of the poem does the first line provide? How do the situation and setting relate to the remembrance of the past in the final five lines of the poem?

2. What habits and gestures does the SPEAKER fear might betray him? What body movements has he cultivated to keep from betraying his homosexual identity? Why does he describe himself as "up against the board" (line 9)?

3. Describe as precisely as you can the speaker's exact feelings. How is the "other" here made to seem so ominous? What exact threat does the "other" represent here?

4. What details in the poem make it clear that the speaker is in fact homosexual? Why is he so fearful of being labeled? Why is the threat articulated (lines 18–19) in physical terms?

Mitsuye Yamada

Born in Kyushu, Japan, raised in Seattle, interned with her family in a concentration camp in Idaho during World War II, Mitsuye Yamada went on to attend New York University and the University of Chicago. After 23 years of teaching English and literature in California, she is now retired but still teaches creative writing and Asian-American literature in southern California. Her first book of poems, *Camp Notes and Other Poems* (1976), was in part written during her years in the concentration camp. Her most recent work, *Desert Run: Poems and Stories*, was published in 1988.

LOOKING OUT

It must be odd
to be a minority
he was saying.
I looked around
and didn't see any.   5
So I said
Yeah
it must be.

STUDY QUESTIONS

1. Why doesn't the SPEAKER see any minority?

2. What does the title mean?

Marcela Christine Lucero-Trujillo

Born in Colorado, Marcela Christine Lucero-Trujillo (1931–1984) taught Chicano / Chicana studies at the University of Minnesota. Her poetry has appeared in a variety of publications (such as *La Luz*) and has been included in such anthologies as *The Third Woman*.

ROSEVILLE, MINN., U.S.A.

In Roseville, one notices
    a speck on a white wall
    a moustache on a brown face
and listens to right wing dilemmas
    of another race.

Turn that corrido[1] record down,
    walk softly in ponchos,
Speak Spanish in whispers
    or they'll approach you to say,
    "I've been to Spain too, ¡Ole!"   10
    (even if you never have),
In Roseville, U.S.A.

Start the stove fan,
    close the windows on a summer day,
    'cause the neighbors might say,   15
    "Do they eat beans every day, even on Sundays?"
In Roseville, U.S.A.

At the sign of the first snowflake
    Inquiring eyes will pursue you,
    asking why you haven't returned with the migrant stream   20
    that went back in June, or even in September,
In Roseville, U.S.A.

My abuela[2] would turn in her grave
    to think that the culmination
    of her cultural perpetuation   25
    is Marcela at Target's food section
    searching desperately for flour tortillas,
No way—I live in ROSEVILLE, U.S.A.
My modus vivendi
of New Mexico piñon and green chili   30
and my Colorado Southwest mentality
are another reality
in ROSEVILLE, U.S.A.

STUDY QUESTIONS

1. What facets of "racial perpetuation" are endangered in Roseville?

2. How does Marcela respond?

1. Border folksong.
2. Grandmother.

Sharon Olds

B orn in San Francisco in 1942 and educated at Stanford and Columbia universities, Sharon Olds has published four volumes of poetry, *Satan Says* (1980), *The Dead and the Living* (1983), *The Gold Cell* (1987), from which this poem is taken, and *The Father* (1992). She has won many awards, including the National Book Critics Circle Award, a National Endowment for the Arts Grant, and a Guggenheim Foundation Fellowship.

ON THE SUBWAY

The boy and I face each other.
His feet are huge, in black sneakers
laced with white in a complex pattern like a
set of intentional scars. We are stuck on
opposite sides of the car, a couple of   5
molecules stuck in a rod of light
rapidly moving through darkness. He has the
casual cold look of a mugger,
alert under hooded lids. He is wearing
red, like the inside of the body   10
exposed. I am wearing dark fur, the
whole skin of an animal taken and
used. I look at his raw face,
he looks at my fur coat, and I don't
know if I am in his power—   15
he could take my coat so easily, my
briefcase, my life—
or if he is in my power, the way I am
living off his life, eating the steak
he does not eat, as if I am taking   20
the food from his mouth. And he is black
and I am white, and without meaning or
trying to I must profit from his darkness,

the way he absorbs the murderous beams of the
nation's heart, as black cotton   25
absorbs the heat of the sun and holds it. There is
no way to know how easy this
white skin makes my life, this
life he could take so easily and
break across his knee like a stick the way his   30
own back is being broken, the
rod of his soul that at birth was dark and
fluid and rich as the heart of a seedling
ready to thrust up into any available light.

STUDY QUESTIONS

1. Why does the SPEAKER call the boy's face "raw" (line 13)?

2. The boy is obviously bigger and stronger than the speaker, and so she is "in his
   power" (line 15); in what sense, however, is he in her power? What does she mean
   by "without meaning or / trying to I must profit from his darkness" (lines 22–23)?
   What did you anticipate would happen?

3. Is the CONFLICT in the poem between the boy and the speaker? within the speaker
   herself? neither? both? Define that conflict. How did you expect it to come out?

4. List the IMAGES and figures of speech from "like a / set of intentional scars" in lines
   3–4 to "the heart of a seedling" in the next-to-last line. What categories do they
   fall into? What one or two catergories predominate? How do these images contribute to the TONE and effect of the poem?

Tato Laviera

"Tato" Laviera (his full name is Jesus Abraham Laviera) was born in Puerto
Rico in 1950 and moved with his family to New York just before his tenth
birthday. He is the author of five critically acclaimed volumes of poetry, including
Enclave (1981) which won a Before Columbus Foundation American Book Award.
Before he began to publish poetry, he was a social services administrator, and his
writing is characterized by a strong analytical interest in social and cultural habits.
Laviera's poems are oral and colloquial—his work has been called "bilingual *salsa*
poetry"—and often celebrate heroic features of Latino life in the United States. "Tito
Madera Smith" is a fictional character—half Puerto Rican, half African American—
portrayed in *Enclave* among a series of other imagined and real cultural heroes, including Miriam Makeba and John Lennon.

TITO MADERA SMITH

for Dr. Juan Flores

he claims he can translate palés matos'[1]
black poetry faster than i can talk,
and that if i get too smart,
he will double translate pig latin
english right out of webster's   5
dictionary, do you know him?

he claims he can walk into east harlem
apartment where langston hughes gives
spanglish classes for newly-arrived
immigrants seeking a bolitero[2]-numbers   10
career and part-time vendors of cuchi-
fritters[3] sunday afternoon in central
park, do you know him?

he claims to have a stronghold of the
only santería[4] secret baptist sect in   15
west harlem, do you know him?

he claims he can talk spanish styled in
sunday dress eating crabmeat-jueyes
brought over on the morning eastern
plane deep fried by la negra costoso[5]   20
joyfully singing puerto rican folklore:
"maría luisa no seas brava,
llévame contigo pa la cama,"[6] or
"oiga capitán delgado, hey captain delgaro,
mande a revisar la grama, please inspect   25
the grass, que dicen que un aeroplano,
they say that an airplane throws marijuana
seeds."

1. Luis Pales Matos, Puerto Rican poet (all notes supplied by author).
2. Seller of illegal lotto.
3. Puerto Rican food delicacies.
4. African / Catholic Cuban-based religion.
5. Famous East Harlem cook.
6. "Maria Luisa don't be brave, take me to the bed."

do you know him? yes you do,
i know you know him, that's right,   30
madera smith, tito madera smith:
he blacks and prieto[7] talks at the same time,
splitting his mother's santurce[8] talk,
twisting his father's south carolina soul,
adding new york scented blackest harlem   35
brown-eyes diddy[9] bops, tú sabes mami,[1]
that i can ski like a bomba[2] soul salsa
mambo[3] turns to aretha franklin stevie
wonder nicknamed patato guaguancó[4] steps,
do you know him?   40

he puerto rican talks to las mamitas[5]
outside the pentecostal church, and
he gets away with it, fast-paced i
understand-you-my-man, with clave[6]
sticks coming out of his pockets hooked   45
to his stereophonic 15-speaker indispensable
disco sounds blasting away at cold reality
struggling to say estás buena[7] baby
as he walks out of tune and out of
step with alleluia cascabells,[8]   50
puma sneakers,
pants rolled up,
shirt cut in middle chest,
santería chains,
madamo[9] pantallas,[1]   55
into the spanish social club,
to challenge elders in dominoes,
like the king of el diario's[2]

7. Black.
8. Puerto Rican town.
9. Street-walking forms.
1. You know baby.
2. Afro-Puerto Rican music.
3. Salsa dance.
4. Cuban conga drummer.
5. The pretty ladies.
6. In musical key.
7. You are fine baby.
8. Tambourine bells.
9. Spiritualist.
1. Earrings.
2. New York Spanish daily.

budweiser tournament
drinking cerveza-beer   60
like a champ,
do you know him?
well, i sure don't,
and if i did, i'd
refer him to 1960   65
social scientists
for assimilation
acculturation
digging
autopsy   70
into
their
heart
attacks,
oh,   75
oh,
there
he
comes,
you can call him tito,   80
or you can call him madera,
or you can call him smitty,
or you can call him mr. t.,
or you can call him nuyorican,[3]
or you can call him black   85
or you can call him latino,
or you can call him mr. smith,
his sharp eyes of awareness,
greeting us in aristocratic harmony:
"you can call me many things, but   90
you gotta call me something."

STUDY QUESTIONS

1. What specific kinds of "heroic" features does the poem claim for tito madera smith?
   What claims does smith make for himself? In what specific ways do his CHARACTER
   and his activities show his multicultural heritage?

2. In what ways is smith an "alien" in the culture in which he lives? How accepting
   is he of his alien status? In what ways does he resist his "otherness"? How successful is he in conquering the assumptions that surround him?

3. Puerto Rican born and raised in New York City, U.S.A.

3. In what ways do the poem's own verbal strategies imitate the habits and values of smith's self-presentation? List all the examples you can find of terms that bridge smith's heritages.

4. Why is it okay to call smith "nuyorican," "black," or "latino"? Is it okay with smith? with the poet?

Leslie Marmon Silko

Born in 1948 in Albuquerque, New Mexico, Leslie Marmon Silko grew up on the Laguna Pueblo reservation. Her heritage is mixed—part Laguna, part Mexican, part white—and she refuses to apologize for it, believing that her storytelling ability "rise[s] out of this source." She is a graduate of the University of New Mexico and now teaches at the University of Arizona. Her best-known work, *Storyteller* (1981), is a collection of many of her best poems and stories. Her most recent work, *Almanac of the Dead: A Novel*, was published in 1991. Her writing, in both prose and poetry, is highly regarded, and she is the recipient of a prestigious MacArthur Fellowship.

[LONG TIME AGO]

Long time ago
in the beginning
there were no white people in this world
there was nothing European.
And this world might have gone on like that   5
except for one thing:
witchery.
This world was already complete
even without white people.
There was everything   10
including witchery.

Then it happened.
These witch people got together.
Some came from far far away
across oceans   15
across mountains.
Some had slanty eyes

others had black skin.
They all got together for a contest
the way people have baseball tournaments nowadays   20
except this was a contest
in dark things.

So anyway
they all got together
witch people from all directions   25
witches from all the Pueblos
and all the tribes.
They had Navajo witches there,
some from Hopi, and a few from Zuni.
They were having a witches' conference,   30
that's what it was
Way up in the lava rock hills
north of Cañoncito
they got together
to fool around in caves   35
with their animal skins.
Fox, badger, bobcat, and wolf
they circled the fire
and on the fourth time
they jumped into that animal's skin.   40

But this time it wasn't enough
and one of them
maybe a Sioux or some Eskimos
started showing off.
"That wasn't anything,   45
watch this."

The contest started like that.
Then some of them lifted the lids
on their big cooking pots,
calling the rest of them over   50
to take a look:
dead babies simmering in blood
circles of skull cut away
all the brains sucked out.
Witch medicine   55
to dry and grind into powder
for new victims.

Others untied skin bundles of disgusting objects:
dark flints, cinders from burned hogans where the
dead lay   60
Whorls of skin
cut from fingertips
sliced from the penis end and clitoris tip.

Finally there was only one
who hadn't shown off charms or powers.   65
The witch stood in the shadows beyond the fire
and no one ever knew where this witch came from
which tribe
or if it was a woman or a man.
But the important thing was   70
this witch didn't show off any dark thunder charcoals
or red ant-hill beads.
This one just told them to listen:
"What I have is a story."

At first they all laughed   75
but this witch said
Okay
go ahead
laugh if you want to
but as I tell the story   80
it will begin to happen.

Set in motion now
set in motion by our witchery
to work for us.

Caves across the ocean   85
in caves of dark hills
white skin people
like the belly of a fish
covered with hair.

Then they grow away from the earth   90
then they grow away from the sun
then they grow away from the plants and animals.
They see no life
When they look
they see only objects.   95
The world is a dead thing for them
the trees and rivers are not alive

the mountains and stones are not alive.
The deer and bear are objects
They see no life. 100
They fear
They fear the world.
They destroy what they fear.
They fear themselves.

The wind will blow them across the ocean 105
thousands of them in giant boats
swarming like larva
out of a crushed ant hill.

They will carry objects
which can shoot death 110
faster than the eye can see.

They will kill the things they fear
all the animals
the people will starve.

They will poison the water 115
they will spin the water away
and there will be drought
the people will starve.

They will fear what they find
They will fear the people 120
They kill what they fear.

Entire villages will be wiped out
They will slaughter whole tribes.
Corpses for us
Blood for us 125
Killing killing killing killing.

And those they do not kill
will die anyway
at the destruction they see
at the loss 130
at the loss of the children
the loss will destroy the rest.

Stolen rivers and mountains
the stolen land will eat their hearts

and jerk their mouths from the Mother. 135
The people will starve.

They will bring terrible diseases
the people have never known.
Entire tribes will die out
covered with festered sores 140
shitting blood
vomiting blood.
Corpses for our work

Set in motion now
set in motion by our witchery 145
set in motion
to work for us.

They will take this world from ocean to ocean
they will turn on each other
they will destroy each other 150
Up here
in these hills
they will find the rocks,
rocks with veins of green and yellow and black.
They will lay the final pattern with these rocks 155
they will lay it across the world
and explode everything.

Set in motion now
set in motion
To destroy 160
To kill
Objects to work for us
objects to act for us
Performing the witchery
for suffering 165
for torment
for the stillborn
the deformed
the sterile
the dead. 170

Whirling
Whirling
Whirling
Whirling

set into motion now 175
set into motion.

So the other witches said
"Okay you win; you take the prize,
but what you said just now—
it isn't so funny 180
It doesn't sound so good.
We are doing okay without it
we can get along without that kind of thing.
Take it back.
Call that story back." 185

But the witch just shook its head
at the others in their stinking animal skins, fur
and feathers.
It's already turned loose.
It's already coming. 190
It can't be called back.

STUDY QUESTIONS

1. There are some very "flat," "unpoetic" lines in this poem, like "So anyway" (line 23). Find others. What seems to be their function?

2. How is the location of the "witches' conference" in southern Colorado made use of—and how does it become ominous—later in the poem?

3. If the "white skin people" are to be the scourge, the destroyers, why are the practices of the dark-skinned people, or their witches, shown in such horrific detail (lines 52–63, for example)?

4. What are the effect and implication of the fact that the identity of the witch who tells the prize-winning story is unknown? that the prize-winning witchcraft is a story?

5. What are the "rocks with veins of green and yellow and black" (line 154)? What is the effect of the fact that some of the "prophecy" in the story—such as the coming of the white men, guns, diseases, etc.—is already history, but that the terrible ending is not . . . yet?

6. Can you make anything out of the strange physical shape of this poem?

Carter Revard

C arter Revard, part Osage on his father's side, grew up on the Osage Reservation in Oklahoma and attended Buck Creek rural school (one room, eight grades), working as a farm laborer and a greyhound trainer before earning a B.A. in English at the University of Tulsa. In 1952 he was given his Osage name, Nompewathe, which means "fear-inspiring," and went to Oxford University (as a Rhodes Scholar), later earning a Ph.D. from Yale in Middle English literature. He is professor of English at Washington University, St. Louis, and a board member of the American Indian Center of Mid-America in St. Louis. He has published three collections of poems: *Ponca War Dancers* (1980), from which "Discovery of the New World" is taken, *Cowboys and Indians, Christmas Shopping* (1992), and *An Eagle Nation* (1993).

DISCOVERY OF THE NEW WORLD

The creatures that we met this morning
marveled at our green skins
and scarlet eyes.
They lack antennae
and can't be made to grasp   5
your proclamation that they are
our lawful food and prey and slaves,
nor can they seem to learn
their body-space is needed to materialize
our oxygen absorbers—   10
which they conceive are breathing
and thinking creatures whom they implore
at first as angels or (later) as devils
when they are being snuffed out
by an absorber swelling   15
into their space.
Their history bled from one this morning
while we were tasting his brain
in holographic rainbows

which we assembled into quite an interesting   20
            set of legends—
                that's all it came to, though
    the colors were quite lovely before we
            poured them into our time;
                    the blue shift bleached away   25
meaningless circumstance and they would not fit
            any of our truth-matrices—
                there was, however,
        a curious visual echo in their history
                of our own coming to their earth;   30
a certain General Sherman
                had said concerning a group of them
                    exactly what we were saying to you
            about these creatures:
    it is our destiny to asterize this planet,   35
            and they will not be asterized,
                so they must be wiped out.
We need their space and oxygen
        which they do not know how to use,
                yet they will not give up their gas unforced,   40
        and we feel sure,
            whatever our "agreements" made this morning,
                we'll have to kill them all:
                    the more we cook this orbit,
            the fewer next time around.   45
We've finished burning all their crops
                and killed their cattle.
                They'll have to come into our pens
        and then we'll get to study
the way our heart attacks and cancers spread among them,   50
                since they seem not immune to these.
    If we didn't have this mission it might be sad
            to see such helpless creatures die,
                but never fear,
    the riches of this place are ours   55
        and worth whatever pain others may have to feel.
                We'll soon have it cleared
    as in fact it is already, at the poles.
        Then we will be safe, and rich, and happy here forever.

STUDY QUESTIONS

1. What do you understand by "their body-space is needed to materialize / our oxygen absorbers" (lines 9–10)? What do the creatures these 1green-skinned beings

have met think the oxygen absorbers are? What do you expect to happen in this encounter?

2. What appeared in "holographic rainbows" (lines 17–21)?

3. What do these lines mean: "the blue shift bleached away / meaningless circumstance and they would not fit / any of our truth-matrices" (lines 25–27)?

4. Does the invaders' talk about not keeping "agreements" (line 42) remind you of the actions of any other discoveries of new worlds?

5. In what way is the final line of the poem IRONIC?

6. What is the literal CONFLICT in the poem? What past conflict is implied? What side are you on in each? If your heritage is European, how do you feel about the conflict? If your heritage is other than European, how do *you* feel about the conflict? about the Europeans?

Grace Nichols

B orn in 1950 in Guyana, Grace Nichols now lives in England where she is an anthologist and author of children's books. Her first book of poetry, *I Is a Long-Memoried Woman* (1983), won the Commonwealth Poetry Prize. Since then she has published, among other things, two more books of her own poetry, *The Fat Black Woman's Poems* (1984) and *Lazy Thoughts of a Lazy Woman and Other Poems* (1989), three poetry anthologies for children—in which she has introduced other black and Caribbean poets—and a collection of Caribbean nursery rhymes, *No Hickory, No Dickery, No Dock* (1991).

WE NEW WORLD BLACKS

The timbre
in our voices
betray us
however far
we've been   5

whatever tongue
we speak
the old ghost

asserts itself
in dusky echoes   10
like driftwood
traces

and in spite of
ourselves
we know the way   15
back to

the river stone

the little decayed
spirit
of the navel string   20
hiding in our back garden

STUDY QUESTIONS

1. What different features of New World blacks "betray" their origins? Exactly how
   does the poem turn these betrayals into matters of cultural pride? How does the
   poem create a sense of community among this diverse group of people?

2. What kind of tensions of identity is suggested by the phrase "in spite of / ourselves"
   (lines 13–14)? What are the sources of the competing forms of identity?

Etheridge Knight

Born in 1931 in Corinth, Mississippi, Etheridge Knight became a poet while serving a sentence in the Indiana State Prison for armed robbery. His first book,
Poems from Prison (1968), from which the poem below is taken, was published one year
before his release. The recipient of Guggenheim (1975) and NEA (1980) fellowships,
as well as the Shelley Memorial Award (1986) and The American Book Award (1987),
Knight developed a major reputation as a poet; he died in 1991. His other books
include *Belly Song and Other Poems* (1975) and *Born of a Woman* (1980).

HARD ROCK RETURNS TO PRISON FROM THE HOSPITAL FOR THE CRIMINAL INSANE

Hard Rock was "known not to take no shit
From nobody," and he had the scars to prove it:
Split purple lips, lumped ears, welts above
His yellow eyes, and one long scar that cut
Across his temple and plowed through a thick   5
Canopy of kinky hair.

The WORD was that Hard Rock wasn't a mean nigger
Anymore, that the doctors had bored a hole in his head,
Cut out part of his brain, and shot electricity
Through the rest. When they brought Hard Rock back,   10
Handcuffed and chained, he was turned loose,
Like a freshly gelded stallion, to try his new status.
And we all waited and watched, like indians at a corral,
To see if the WORD was true.

As we waited we wrapped ourselves in the cloak   15
Of his exploits: "Man, the last time, it took eight
Screws[1] to put him in the Hole."[2] "Yeah, remember when he
Smacked the captain with his dinner tray?" "He set
The record for time in the Hole—67 straight days!"
"Ol Hard Rock! man, that's one crazy nigger."   20
And then the jewel of a myth that Hard Rock had once bit
A screw on the thumb and poisoned him with syphilitic spit.

The testing came, to see if Hard Rock was really tame.
A hillbilly called him a black son of a bitch
And didn't lose his teeth, a screw who knew Hard Rock   25
From before shook him down and barked in his face.
And Hard Rock did *nothing*. Just grinned and looked silly,
His eyes empty like knot holes in a fence.

And even after we discovered that it took Hard Rock
Exactly 3 minutes to tell you his first name,   30

1. Guard.
2. Solitary confinement.

We told ourselves that he had just wised up,
Was being cool; but we could not fool ourselves for long,
And we turned away, our eyes on the ground. Crushed.
He had been our Destroyer, the doer of things
We dreamed of doing but could not bring ourselves to do,   35
The fears of years, like a biting whip,
Had cut grooves too deeply across our backs.

STUDY QUESTIONS

1. What characteristics make Hard Rock a hero to his fellow inmates? What strategies
   does the poem use to make him seem attractive to readers? How much emphasis
   does the poem put on his "alien-ness"? Exactly what is "different" about Hard
   Rock?

2. How visual is the portrait of Hard Rock after his return from the hospital? Which
   physical details seem to you the most effective in showing the contrast with his
   former self?

3. What kinds of social practices does the poem seem to be protesting against? What
   kinds of assumptions about conformity?

Jack G. Shaheen

Born in 1935 in Pittsburgh, Jack G. Shaheen teaches mass communications at
Southern Illinois University, Edwardsville. The recipient of two Fulbright-
Hays Lectureship grants, he is the author of *The TV Arab* (1984) and *Nuclear War
Films* (1978).

THE MEDIA'S IMAGE OF ARABS

America's bogeyman is the Arab. Until the nightly news brought us TV   1
pictures of Palestinian youth being punched and beaten almost all portraits
of Arabs seen in America were dangerously threatening. Arabs were either
billionaires, bombers, bedouin bandits, belly dancers or bundles in black—
rarely victims. They were hardly ever seen as ordinary people practicing law,
driving taxis, singing lullabies or healing the sick. Though some TV news-

casts may portray them more sympathetically now, the absence of positive media images nurtures suspicion and stereotype.

Historically, the Arab lacks a human face. Media images are almost invariably hostile and one-sided. They articulate to, perhaps are even responsible for, the negative stereotype Americans have of Arabs. As an Arab-American, I have found that ugly caricatures have had an enduring impact on Americans of Arab heritage. For the prejudiced, during the Gulf War, all Arabs, including some of the three million Americans with Arab roots, became to many, "camel jockeys," "ragheads" and "sandsuckers." Whenever there is a crisis in the Middle East Arab-Americans are subjected to vicious stereotyping and incidents of violence and discrimination. 2

I was sheltered from prejudicial portraits at first. My parents came from Lebanon in the 1920s; they met and married in America. Our home in the steel city of Clairton, Pennsylvania was a center for ethnic sharing—black, white, Jew and gentile. There was only one major source of screen images then, at the State movie theater where I was lucky enough to get a part-time job as an usher. But in the late 1940s, Westerns and war movies were popular, not Middle Eastern dramas. Memories of World War II were fresh, and the screen heavies were the Japanese and the Germans. True to the cliché of the times, the only good Indian was a dead Indian. But when I mimicked or mocked the bad guys, my mother cautioned me. She explained that stereotypes hurt; that they blur our vision and corrupt the imagination. "Have compassion for all people, Jackie," she said. Experience the joy of accepting people as they are, and not as they appear in films, she advised. 3

Mother was right. I can remember the Saturday afternoon when my son, Michael, who was seven, and my daughter, Michele, six, suddenly called out: "Daddy, Daddy, they've got some bad Arabs on TV." They were watching that great American morality play, TV wrestling. Akbar the Great, who liked to hear the cracking of bones, and Abdullah the Butcher, a dirty fighter who liked to inflict pain, were pinning their foes with "camel clutches." From that day on, I knew I had to try to neutralize the media caricatures. 4

I believe most researchers begin their investigations because they have strong feelings in their gut about the topic. To me, the stereotyping issue was so important I had to study it. For years I watched hordes of Arabs prowl across TV and movie screens. Yet, a vacuum existed in the literature: research on TV and movie Arabs did not exist. My research began with television because visual impressions from the tube indoctrinate the young. Once a stereotypical image becomes ingrained in a child's mind, it may never wither away. 5

Investigating television's Arabs began as a solo effort. But members of my family, friends, and colleagues assisted by calling attention to dramas I might otherwise have missed. For several years, I examined *TV Guide* and cable and satellite magazines. Daily, I searched for Arab plots and characters, then taped, studied, and categorized them. To go beyond personal observations, I interviewed more than thirty industry leaders, writers, and 6 producers in New York and Los Angeles. In the spirit of fairmindedness, I invited image makers, those influential purveyors of thought and imagination, to offer sparks of decency that illuminate, rather than distort, our perception of others.

It hasn't been easy. Images teach youngsters whom to love, whom to hate. With my children, I have watched animated heroes Heckle and Jeckle pull the rug from under "Ali Boo-Boo, the Desert Rat," and Laverne and Shirley stop "Sheik Ha-Mean-ie" from conquering "the U.S. and the world." I have read more than 250 comic books like the "Fantastic Four" and "G.I. Combat" whose characters have sketched Arabs as "lowlifes" and "human hyenas." Negative stereotypes were everywhere. A dictionary informed my youngsters that an Arab is a "vagabond, drifter, hobo and vagrant." Whatever happened, my wife wondered, to Aladdin's good genie?

To a child, the world is simple: good versus evil. But my children and others with Arab roots grew up without ever having seen a humane Arab on the silver screen, someone to pattern their lives after. To them, it seems easier for a camel to go through the eye of a needle than for a screen Arab to appear as a genuine human being?

Hollywood producers employ an instant Ali Baba kit that contains scimitars, veils, sunglasses and such Arab clothing as chadors and kufiyahs. In the mythical "Ay-rab-land," oil wells, tents, mosques, goats and shepherds prevail. Between the sand dunes, the camera focuses on a mock-up of a palace from "Arabian Nights"—or a military air base. Recent movies suggest that Americans are at war with Arabs, forgetting the fact that out of 21 Arab nations, America is friendly with 19 of them.

Audiences are bombarded with rigid, repetitive and repulsive depictions that demonize and delegitimize the Arab. One reason is because since the early 1900s more than 500 feature films and scores of television programs have shaped Arab portraits.

I recently asked 293 secondary school teachers from five states—Massachusetts, North Carolina, Arkansas, West Virginia, and Wisconsin—to write down the names of any humane or heroic screen Arab they had seen. Five cited past portraits of Ali Baba and Sinbad; one memtioned Omar Sharif and "those Arabs" in *Lion of the Desert* and *The Wind and the Lion*. The remaining 287 teachers wrote "none."

Nicholas Kadi, an actor with Iraqi roots, makes his living playing terrorists in such films as the 1990 release "Navy Seals." Kadi laments that he does "little talking and a lot of threatening—threatening looks, threatening gestures." On screen, he and others who play Arab villains say "America," then spit. "There are other kinds of Arabs in the world," says Kadi. "I'd like to think that some day there will be an Arab role out there for me that would be an honest portrayal."

The Arab remains American culture's favorite whipping boy. In his memoirs, Terrel Bell, Ronald Reagan's first secretary of education, writes about an "apparent bias among mid-level, right-wing staffers at the White House" who dismissed Arabs as "sand niggers."

Sadly, the racial slurs continue. Posters and bumper stickers display an 14 Arab's skull and an atomic explosion. The tag: "Nuke their ass and take their gas."

At a recent teacher's conference, I met a woman from Sioux Falls, South 15 Dakota, who told me about the persistence of discrimination. She was in the process of adopting a baby when an agency staffer warned her that the infant had a problem. When she asked whether the child was mentally ill, or physically handicapped, there was silence. Finally, the worker said: "The baby is Jordanian."

To me, the Arab demon of today is much like the Jewish demon of 16 yesterday. We deplore the false portrait of Jews as a swarthy menace. Yet a similar portrait has been accepted and transferred to another group of Semites—the Arabs. Print and broadcast journalists have started to challenge this stereotype. They are now revealing more humane images of Arabs, a people who traditionally suffered from ugly myths. Others could follow that lead and retire the stereotypical Arab to a media Valhalla.

The civil rights movement of the 1960s not only helped bring about 17 more realistic depictions of various groups; it curbed negative images of the lazy black, the wealthy Jew, the greasy Hispanic and the corrupt Italian. These images are mercifully rare on today's screens. Conscientious image-makers and citizens worked together to eliminate the racial mockery that had been a shameful part of the American cultural scene.

It would be a step in the right direction if movie and TV producers 18 developed characters modeled after real-life Arab-Americans. We could then see a White House correspondent like Helen Thomas, whose father came from Lebanon, in "The Golden Girls," a lawyer patterned after Ralph Nader on "L.A. Law," or a Syrian-American playing tournament chess like Yasser Seirawan, the Seattle grandmaster.

Politicians, too, should speak out against the cardboard caricatures. They 19 should refer to Arabs as friends, not just as moderates. And religious leaders could state that Islam, like Christianity and Judaism, maintains that all mankind is one family in the care of God. When all imagemakers rightfully begin to treat Arabs and all other minorities with respect and dignity, we may begin to unlearn our prejudices. The ultimate result would be an image of the Arab as neither saint nor devil, but as a fellow human being, with all the potentials and frailties that condition implies.

STUDY QUESTIONS

1. Can you remember "images" of Arabs in recent movies that fit Shaheen's accusations? Can you remember any who were portrayed sympathetically? Watch television news for the next two or three evenings; what Arabs are shown there? How are they shown?

2. What Arab-Americans do you know or know of? What have they achieved? What mistreatment or misunderstanding have they suffered?

3. What STEREOTYPES other than those Arab ones Shaheen describes have you seen recently in films? on television?

James Fallows

James Fallows is Washington editor for *The Atlantic* and lived in Kuala Lumpur, Malaysia, where he wrote a series of articles on Asia for the magazine. He has published two recent works which relate differences in the educational and economic conditions of Japan and the United States, *More Like Us—Making America Great Again* (1989) and *Japanese Education: What Can It Teach American Schools?* (1990).

THE JAPANESE ARE DIFFERENT FROM YOU AND ME

Japan is turning me into Mrs. Trollope. She was the huffy Englishwoman who viewed the woolly American society of the 1820s and found it insufficiently refined. ("The total and universal want of good, or even pleasing, manners, both in males and females, is so remarkable, that I was constantly endeavoring to account for it," and so forth.) Her mistake, as seems obvious in retrospect, was her failure to distinguish between things about America that were merely different from the ways of her beloved England and things that were truly wrong. The vulgar American diction that so offended her belongs in the first category, slavery in the second.

I will confess that this distinction—between different and wrong— sometimes eludes me in Japan. Much of the time I do keep it in mind. I observe aspects of Japanese life, note their difference from standard practice in the West, and serenely say to myself, who cares? Orthodontia has never caught on in Japan, despite seemingly enormous potential demand, because by the local canon of beauty overlapping and angled-out teeth look fetching, especially in young girls. It was barely a century ago that Japanese women deliberately blackened their teeth in the name of beauty. The delicate odor of decaying teeth was in those days a standard and alluring reference in romantic poetry. This is not how it's done in Scarsdale, but so what? For their part, the Japanese can hardly conceal their distaste for the "butter smell" that they say wafts out of Westerners or for our brutish practice of wearing the same shoes in the dining room and the toilet.

Similarly, child psychologists and family therapists have told me that   3
the Japanese parent's way of persuading his children to stop doing something is not to say "It's wrong" or "It's unfair" but rather to tell the child, "People will laugh at you." This is not my idea of a wholesome child-rearing philosophy, but I'm not preparing my children for membership in a society that places such stress on harmonious social relations. Several American psychologists have recently claimed that the Japanese approach may in fact equip children for more happiness in life than American practices do. Americans are taught to try to control their destiny; when they can't, they feel they've failed. Japanese children, so these psychologists contend, are taught to adjust themselves to an externally imposed social order, which gives them "secondary control"—that is, a happy resignation to fate.

Now that Japan has become so notoriously successful, American visitors   4
often cannot help feeling, This is different—and better. Practically anything that has to do with manufacturing and economic organization falls into this category. Recently I toured a Nissan factory an hour outside Tokyo, escorted by a manager who seemed almost embarrassed by the comparisons I asked him to make between his company's standards and GM's or Ford's. Yes, Nissan did insist on a higher grade of steel for its cars. No, the foreign companies had not matched its level of automation. Yes, the gap between managers' earnings and those of assembly workers was tiny compared with that in Detroit. No, the company did not expect trouble surmounting the challenge of the higher yen.

From what I have seen, a tight-knit, almost tribal society like Japan is   5
better set up for straightforward productive competition than is the West. It places less emphasis on profit than on ensuring that every company and every worker will retain a place in the economic order. (Apart from raw materials and American movies, most Japanese would be content, I think, if the country imported nothing at all. Who cares about high prices, as long as everyone is at work?) Its politics is ridden with factions—because of certain peculiarities of the electoral system, politicians can win seats in the Diet with only 10 or 12 percent of their district's vote. (Each district elects several representatives to the Diet, but each voter has only one vote. In a four-member district, for example, the leading candidate might get 35 percent of the total vote, and the next three might get 15, 12, and 8 percent. All four of them would be winners.) But there are few seriously divisive political issues, and the country has a shared sense of national purpose, as the United States last did between 1941 and 1945.

Even beyond the measurable signs of its productive success, Japan seems   6
different and better in those details of daily life that reflect consideration and duty. During my first week here another American journalist told me that only when I had left would I realize how thoroughly Japan had had me. At

the time, I was still reeling from exchange-rate shock and thought she was crazy. But I am beginning to understand what she meant. A thousand times a day in modern society your life is made easier or harder, depending on the care with which someone else has done his job. Are the newspapers delivered on time? Are vending machines fixed when they break? Are the technocrats competent? Do the captains of industry really care about their companies, not just about feathering their own nests? In general, can you count on others to do their best? In Japan you can. Mussolini gave trains that ran on time a bad name. After seeing Japan, I think that on this one point Mussolini had the right idea.

From bureaucrats at the Ministry of Foreign Affairs (who, I am told, average six hours of overtime a *day*) to department-store package-wrappers, the Japanese seem immune against the idea that discharging their duty to others might be considered "just a job." Tipping is virtually unknown in Japan; from the Japanese perspective it seems vulgar, because it implies that the recipient will not do his best unless he is bribed. The no-tipping custom is something you get used to very quickly, because it seems so much more dignified and honorable, not—at least in Japan—because it's a way of gypping the working class. Japan is famous for the flatness of its income distribution. Year in and year out more than 90 percent of the Japanese tell pollsters that they think of themselves as "middle class"—and here the perception seems accurate, not a delusion as it might be in the United States. Indeed, from the Japanese perspective America seems fantastically wrapped up in and bound by class. American commercials are basically targeted along class lines: one kind of person drinks Miller beer, another buys Steuben glass. Japanese commercials are not—or so I am told by people who produce them. They may aim at different age groups—new mothers, teenage boys, and so forth—but otherwise they address the Japanese as one.

I can't say exactly, but I would bet that 100,000 people live within half a mile of the apartment where I live with my family. Yet in the evening, when I walk home through the alleyways from the public baths, the neighborhoods are dead quiet—unless my own children are kicking a can along the pavement or noisily playing tag. The containedness and reserve of Japanese life can seem suffocating if you're used to something different, but they are also admirable, and necessary, if so many people are to coexist so harmoniously in such close quarters. Because the Japanese have agreed not to get on one another's nerves (and because so much of Tokyo is built only two or three stories high), the city, though intensely crowded, produces nothing like the chronic high-anxiety level of New York. The very low crime rate obviously has something to do with this too. "Is this not, truly, Japan's golden age?" one American businessman exclaimed, spreading his arms in non-Japanese expansiveness and nearly knocking over the passersby, as we walked near the Imperial Place on a brilliant sunny day recently. Everyone was working, Japan was taking a proud place in the world, there were no serious domestic divisions, and the drugs, dissoluteness, and similar disorders that

7

8

blight the rest of the world barely existed here. Wasn't it obvious that Japan had figured out what still puzzled everybody else?

On the whole, I had to agree. What most Americans fear about Japan is precisely that it works so well. Foreigners who have lived for years in Japan tell me that the legendary Japanese hospitality toward visitors suddenly disappears when you stop being an "honored guest" and slide into the "resident alien" category. In effect, the country is like an expensive, very well run hotel, making the guest comfortable without ever tempting him to think he's found a home. But while it lasts, the hospitality is a delight. Those I interview at least feign more attention and courtesy than their counterparts in the United States have done. A few people have moved beyond the tit-for-tat ritualistic exchange of favors to displays of real generosity. Still, after making all appropriate allowances for the debts I owe them, and all disclaimers about the perils of generalizing after a few months on the scene, I find that two aspects of Japanese life bring out the Mrs. Trollope in me.

One is the prominence of pornography in daily life. I realize that no one from the land that created *Hustler* and *Deep Throat* can sound pious about obscene material. The difference is the degree of choice. In the United States pornography did not enter my life unless I invited it in, and I had no trouble keeping it from my grade-school children. Here it enters unbidden all the time.

Like most other residents of Tokyo, I spend a lot of time on the trains— about three hours a day. There I am surrounded not just by people but also by printed matter—advertising placards all over the trains, and books, magazines, and newspapers in everyone's hands. The dedicated literacy of Japan is yet another cause for admiration, but the content of the reading matter— especially on the trains, where no one knows his neighbor and in principle everyone is unobserved—is not. Some of the men are reading books, but more are reading either "sports papers" or thick volumes of comics, the size of telephone books, known as *manga*. What these two media have in common is the porno theme. Sports papers carry detailed coverage of baseball games or sumo tournaments on the outside pages and a few spreads of nearly nude women inside. (The only apparent restriction is that the papers must not display pubic hair.) The comic books, printed on multicolored paper and popular with every segment of the population, are issued weekly and sell in the millions. They run from innocent kids' fare to hard-core pornography.

To some degree the sports papers and the more prurient *manga* exist to display female bodies, no more and no less, and they differ from their counterparts in other cultures only in the carefree spirit with which men read them in public. I don't know whether Japanese men consume any more pornography than American ones, but in the United States men look guilty as they slink out of dirty movies, and they rarely read skin magazines in front of women. Japanese men are far less inhibited—perhaps because of the anonymity of the crowded train car, or perhaps because their society is, as often claimed, more matter-of-fact about sex. In any case, the trains and subways are awash in pornography, as are television shows starting as early as 8 P.M. My sons, ages nine and six, very quickly figured out this new aspect of Japanese culture. On train rides they stare goggle-eyed at the lurid fare now available to them.

In addition to its pervasiveness, Japanese subway pornography differs 13 from the *Playboys* and *Penthouses* of the West in the graphic nastiness of its themes. Voyeurism plays a big part in the *manga*, and in a lot of advertisements too. One new publication recently launched a huge advertising campaign billing itself as "the magazine for watchers." Its posters showed people peeping out from under manhole covers or through venetian blinds. In the comics women—more often, teenage girls—are typically peeped up at, from ground level. A major weekly magazine recently published two pages of telephoto-lens shots of couples in advanced stages of love-making in a public park. Most of the teenage girls in Japan spend their days in severe, dark, sailor-style school uniforms, with long skirts. As in Victorian-era fantasies, in the comics the skirts are sure to go. But before the garments are ripped off, the girls are typically spied upon by ecstatic men.

The comics are also quite violent. Women are being accosted, surprised, 14 tied up, beaten, knifed, tortured, and in general given a hard time. Many who are so treated are meant to be very young—the overall impression is as if the Brooke Shields of five years ago had been America's exclusive female sexual icon, with no interference from Bo Derek or other full-grown specimens. One advertising man, who has been here for ten years and makes his living by understanding the Japanese psyche, says that everything suddenly fell into place for him when he thought of a half-conscious, low-grade pedophilia as the underlying social motif. It affects business, he said, where each year's crop of fresh young things, straight out of high school, are assigned seats where the senior managers can look at them—until the next year, when a newer and younger crop are brought in. It affects TV shows and commercials, which feature girls with a teenage look. The most sought-after description in Japan is *kawaii*, or "cute" (as opposed to "beautiful" or "sexy"), often pronounced in a way equivalent to "Cuu-uuuute!" The *kawaii* look is dominant on television and in advertising, giving the impression that Japanese masculinity consists primarily of yearning for a cute little thing about fifteen years old. "A director can shoot an act of sodomy or rape for a TV drama programmed for the dinner hour with impunity so long as he allows no pubic hair to be shown," a recent article by Sarah Brickman in the *Far Eastern Economic Review* said. "He is, of course, particularly assured of immunity from legal repercussions if the female star of the scene is prepubescent."

A few years ago Ian Buruma, a Dutch writer who had lived here for 15 years and has a Japanese wife, published *Behind the Mask*, a wonderful book that closely analyzed the *manga*, soap operas, low-brow movies, and other aspects of Japanese popular culture. He richly illustrated how the Japanese, in many ways so buttoned up and contained, sought outlandish fantasy releases. Buruma attempted to trace the oddities of *manga*-style fantasy to the deep bond between Japanese boys and their mothers, who typically raise their children with little help from the father. I don't know enough to judge Buruma's theory, or otherwise to make sense of Japan's standards of pornographic display. My point is that they rest on theories and values at odds with the West's. According to the *Far Eastern Review* article, the director-general of Japan's Agency for Cultural Affairs once endorsed physical exercise this way: "When asked my reasons for jogging, I used to answer 'although it is shameful for a gentleman to rape a woman, it is also shameful for a man not to have the physical strength necessary to rape a woman!' "

In the United States more and more people are claiming that pornography contributes to sex crimes. If you look at Japan—with its high level of violent stimulation but reportedly low incidence of rape and assault—you have your doubts. But even if it leads to few indictable offenses, and even if Japanese women themselves do not complain, the abundance of violent pornography creates an atmosphere that gives most Westerners the creeps. 16

The other off-putting aspect of Japan is the ethnic—well, racial—exclusion on which the society is built. I hesitated to say "racial" or "racist," because the terms are so loaded and so irritating to the Japanese. I can understand why they are annoyed. In their dealings with the West the Japanese have traditionally seen themselves as the objects of racial discrimination—the little yellow men looked down on by the great white fathers. A new book by the historian John W. Dower, called *War Without Mercy*, provides hair-raising illustrations of the racism with which both Japanese and Japanese-Americans were viewed during the war. For instance, Ernie Pyle explained to the readers of his famous battlefront column that the difference between the Germans and the Japanese was that the Germans "were still people." 17

Rather than talking about race—as white Americans did when enslaving blacks and excluding "inferior" immigrants—the Japanese talk about "purity." Their society is different from others in being purer; it consists of practically none but Japanese. What makes the subject so complicated is the overlap between two different kinds of purity, that of culture and that of blood. 18

That the Japanese have a distinct culture seems to me an open-and-shut case. Some economists here have given me little speeches about the primacy of economic forces in determining people's behavior. Do the Japanese save more, stick with their companies longer, and pay more attention to quality? The explanations are all to be found in tax incentives, the "lifetime-employment" policy at big firms, and other identifiable economic causes. I'm sure there is something to this outlook, but I am also impressed by what it leaves out. We do not find it remarkable that the past 250 years of American history, which include revolution, settling the frontier, subjugating Indians, creating and then abolishing slavery, and absorbing immigrant groups, have 19 given the United States a distinctive set of values. Is it so implausible that 2,500 years of isolation on a few small islands might have given the Japanese some singular traits?

Japan is different from certain "old" Western cultures because it has been left to itself so much. In the same 2,500 years the British Isles were invaded by Romans, Angles, Saxons, and Normans—and after that the British themselves went invading and exploring. Blood was mixed, and culture was opened up. During all that time the Japanese sat at home, uninvaded and disinclined to sail off to see what the rest of the world might hold. The effect of this long isolation was a distinctive culture *and* the isolation of a "pure" racial group, which tempted people to think that race and culture were the same.

I'm sure that someone could prove that the Japanese are not really monoracial, or not clearly separate from the Koreans or the Chinese. The significant point is that as far as the Japanese are concerned, they *are* inherently different from other people, and are all bound together by birth and blood. The standard Japanese explanation for their horror of litigation and their esteem for consensus is that they are a homogeneous people, who understand one another's needs. When I've asked police officials and sociologists why there is so little crime, their explanations have all begun, "We are a homogenous race . . ." Most people I have interviewed have used the phrase "We Japanese . . ." I have rarely heard an American say "We Americans . . ."

The Japanese sense of separateness rises to the level of race because the Japanese system is closed. The United States is built on the principle of voluntary association; in theory anyone can become an American. A place in Japanese society is open only to those who are born Japanese.

When I say "born," I mean with the right racial background, not merely on rocky Japanese soil. One of Japan's touchiest problems is the second- or even third-generation Koreans, descended from people who were brought to Japan for forced labor in the fascist days. They are still known as Koreans even though they were born here, speak the language like natives, and in many cases are physically indistinguishable from everyone else. They have long-term "alien residence" permits but are not citizens—and in principle they and their descendants never will be. (Obtaining naturalized Japanese citizenship is not impossible but close to it.) They must register as aliens and be fingerprinted by the police. The same prospect awaits the handful of Vietnamese refugees whom the Japanese, under intense pressure from the United States, have now agreed to accept for resettlement.

The Japanese public has a voracious appetite for *Nihonjinron*—the study of traits that distinguish them from everyone else. Hundreds of works of self-examination are published each year. This discipline involves perfectly reasonable questions about what makes Japan unique as a social system, but it easily slips into inquiries about what makes the Japanese people special as a race. Perhaps the most lunatic work in this field is *The Japanese Brain*, by a Dr. Tadanobu Tsunoda, which was published to wide acclaim and vast sales in the late 1970s. The book contends that the Japanese have brains that are organized differently from those of the rest of humanity, their internal wiring optimized for the requirements of the Japanese language. (Tsunoda claims that all non-Japanese—including "Chinese, Koreans, and almost all Southeast Asian peoples"—hear vowels in the right hemispheres of their brains, while the Japanese hear them in the left. Since the Japanese also handle consonants in the left hemisphere, they are able to attain a higher unity and coherence than other races.)

I haven't heard anyone restate the theory in precisely this form. And in fairness, during the war British scientists advanced a parallel unique-Japanese-brain theory (as John Dower points out), asserting that Japanese thought was permanently impaired by the torture of memorizing Chinese characters at an early age. But British scientists don't say this any longer, while Tsunoda is still a prominent, non-ridiculed figure in Japan. Whatever the Japanese may think of his unique-brain theory, large numbers of them seem comfortable with the belief that not just their language but also their thoughts and emotions are different from those of anyone else in the world.

The Japanese language is the main evidence for this claim. It is said to foster the understatement for which the Japanese are so famous, and to make them more carefully attuned to nuance, nature, unexpressed thoughts, and so forth, than other people could possibly be. Most of all, it is a convenient instrument of exclusion. Mastering it requires considerable memory work. Japanese businessmen posted to New York or London often fret about taking their children with them, for fear that three or four years out of the Japanese school system will leave their children hopelessly behind. It's not that the overall intellectual standards are so different but that in Japan children spend much of their time memorizing the Chinese characters, *kanji*, necessary for full literacy—and for success on the all-important university-entrance tests.

Until a few years ago only a handful of foreigners had bothered to become fully fluent in Japanese, and they could be written off as exceptions proving the general rule: that Japanese was too complicated and subtle for non-Japanese to learn. Now the situation is changing—many of the Americans I meet here are well into their Japanese-language training—but the idea of uniqueness remains. Four years ago an American linguist named Roy Andrew Miller published a splenetic book titled *Japan's Modern Myth*, designed to explode the idea that Japanese was unique, any more than Urdu or German or other languages are. Edward Seidensticker, a renowned translator of Japanese literature, makes the point concisely: " 'But how do you manage the nuances of Japanese?' the Japanese are fond of asking, as if other languages did not have nuances, and as if there were no significance in the fact that the word 'nuance' had to be borrowed from French."

As Roy Miller pointed out, the concept of an unlearnable language offers a polite outlet for a more deeply held but somewhat embarrassing belief in racial uniqueness. In a passage that illustrated this book's exasperated tone but also his instinct for the home truth, Miller wrote:

Japanese race consists in using the Japanese language. But how does one become a member of the Japanese race? By being born into it, of course, just as one becomes a member of any other race. . . . But what if someone not a Japanese by right of race . . . does manage to acquire some proficiency in the Japanese language? Well, in that case, the system literally makes no intellectual provision at all for his or her very existence. Such a person is a nonperson within the terms and definitions of Japanese social order. . . . The society's assumption [is] that the Japanese-speaking foreigner is for some unknown reason involved in working out serious logical contradictions in his or her life. . . . He or she had better be watched pretty carefully; obviously something is seriously amiss somewhere, otherwise why would this foreigner be speaking Japanese?

As applied to most other races of the world—especially other Asians, 29 with whom the Japanese have been in most frequent contact—the Japanese racial attitude is unambiguous: Southeast Asians and Koreans are inferior to Japanese. Koreans are more closely related to the Japanese than are any other Asians, but they are held in deep racial contempt by the Japanese. (A hilarious, long-running controversy surrounds excavations in central Honshu that seemed to indicate that the Imperial Family was originally . . . Korean! The digs were soon closed up, for reasons that are continually debated in the English-language but not, I am told, the Japanese-language press.) Recent opinion polls show that the nation the Japanese most fear is not the United States, on which they depend for their export market, nor the Soviet Union, which still occupies four of their northern islands, but Korea—which threatens to beat them at their own hard-work game and which fully reciprocates Japan's ill will. China—the source of Japan's written language and the model for much of its traditional culture—presents a more difficult case. The Australian journalist Murray Sayle offers the model of China as the "wastrel older brother," who forfeited his natural right of prominence through his dissolute behavior, placing the family burden on the steadfast younger brother, Japan. This is one reason why stories of Chinese opium dens were so important in pre-war Japan: the older brother had gone to hell and needed the discipline of Japanese control.

For Westerners the racial question is more confusing than even for the 30 Chinese. For a few weeks after arrival I seized on the idea that being in Japan might, for a white American, faintly resemble the experience of being black in America. That is, my racial identity was the most important thing about me, and it did not seem to be a plus.

I am just beginning to understand how complicated the racial attitude 31 toward Westerners really is. Whereas Southeast Asians in Japan are objects of unrelieved disdain, Westerners are seen as both better and worse than the Japanese. One timeless argument in Japan is whether the Japanese feel inferior to Westerners, or superior to them, or some combination of the two. Feeling equal to them—different in culture, but equal as human beings—

somehow does not emerge as a possibility, at least in the talks I have had so far.

There is evidence for both propositions—that the Japanese feel superior to Westerners, and that they feel inferior to them. On the one hand, Japanese culture is simply awash in Western—mainly American—artifacts. The movies and music are imported straight from America; the fashion and commercial models are disproportionately Caucasian; the culture seems to await its next signal from the other side of the Pacific. A hundred years ago, Japan began its Meiji-era drive to catch up with the West's industrial achievements. Prominent figures urged Japanese to interbreed with Westerners, so as to improve the racial stock, and to dump the character-based Japanese language in favor of English, which was the mark of a more advanced race. To judge by the styles they affect and the movies and music they favor, today's young Japanese seem to take Europe as the standard of refinement and America as the source of pop-cultural energy. Even when nothing earthshaking is happening in America, the TV news has extensive what's-new-in-New-York segments.

Herbert Passin, a professor of sociology at Columbia University, who came to Japan during the Occupation and has been here off and on ever since, contends that the sense of inferiority is so deep-seated that a few years of economic victories cannot really have dislodged it. The longer I have been here, and the better I've gotten to know a few Japanese, the more frequently I've seen flashes of the old, nagging fear of inferiority. Americans often talk, with good reason, about the defects of their "system." Many Japanese take pride in their economic and social system but still act as if something is wrong with them as a race. I talked with a group of teenage entrepreneurs, who had set up a mildly rebellious magazine. We talked about Japan's economic success, and then one of them burst out: "We're just like a bunch of ants. We all teem around a biscuit and carry it off. That's the only way we succeed." A famous scientist who has directed successful research projects for the Ministry of International Trade and Industry—precisely the kind of man American industrialists most fear—described Japan's impressive scientific work-in-progress. Then he sighed and said, "Still, my real feeling is, Everything new comes from the States. We can refine it and improve it, but the firsts always come from outside."

On the other hand, many Japanese can barely conceal their disdain for the West's general loss of economic vigor. Many people I have interviewed have talked about the United States the way many Americans talk about England: it had its day, but now that's done. One influential businessman in his early forties told me that members of his generation were not even daunted by the wartime defeat. Our fathers were beaten, he told me with a fierce look—not us. This is shaping up as the year of "economic-adjustment" plans: every week a new ministry comes out with a scheme for reducing Japan's trade surplus. I have yet to see the word *fairness* in the English versions of these documents. Instead they are all designed to promote "harmony." The stated premise is that Japan has to give foreigners a break, so that it doesn't make needless enemies overseas. The unstated but obvious corollary is that Japan could crush every indolent Western competitor if it tried. Even the things some Japanese still claim to admire about America suggest racial condescension. Among the American virtues that Japanese have mentioned to me are a big army, a sense of style and rhythm, artistic talent and energy, and raw animal (and supposedly sexual) strength. In their eyes we are big, potent, and hairy.

The Japanese have obviously profited, in purely practical terms, from   35
their racial purity. Many of the things that are most admirable about the society—its shared moral values, its consideration for all its members' interests, the attention people pay to the collective well-being as well as to their own—are easier to create when everyone is ethnically the same. Three years ago, at a commemoration for those killed by the atomic bomb at Hiroshima, Prime Minister Nakasone made this point as crudely as possible. He said, "The Japanese have been doing well for as long as 2,000 years because there are no foreign races."

I have always thought that, simply in practical terms, the United States   36
had a big edge because it tried so hard, albeit inconsistently and with limited success, to digest people from different backgrounds and parts of the world. Didn't the resulting cultural collisions give us extra creativity and resilience? Didn't the ethnic mixture help us at least slightly in our dealings with other countries? The Japanese, in contrast, have suffered grievously from their lack of any built-in understanding of foreign cultures. Sitting off on their own, it is easy for them to view the rest of the world as merely a market—an attitude harder to hold if your population contains a lot of refugees and immigrants. This perspective has as much to do with "trade frictions" as does their admirable management style. I am exaggerating for effect here—the most cosmopolitan Japanese I have met have a broader view than most people I know in America—but in general a homogeneous population with no emotional ties to the rest of the world acts even more narcissistically than do others. When the United States threatened to drown the world in its trade surpluses, it started the Marshall Plan. The Japanese, to put it mildly, have been less eager to share their wealth.

Practicalities aside, the United States, like the rest of Western society,   37
has increasingly in the twentieth century considered it morally "right" to rise above differences of race, inconvenient and uncomfortable as that may sometimes be. Few Western societies, and few people, may succeed in so rising— but they feel guilty when they fail. The Japanese do not.

The integrationist dream has few supporters in this half of the globe.   38
The Japanese are unusual in having so large a population with so little racial diversity, but their underlying belief that politics and culture should run on racial lines is held in many other parts of Asia. Directly or indirectly, the politics of most Asian countries revolve around racial or tribal divisions, especially those between the numerous Chinese expatriates and the Malays,

Vietnamese, Indonesians, and others among whom the Chinese live. It's hard to think of a really stable or happy multi-racial Asian state. Asians look at the Hindu-Moslem partition of India and see acquiescence to fate. Japanese look at America and see a mongrel race.

Edward Seidensticker, now a professor at Columbia, lived here for many years after the war—and then, in 1962, announced his intention to depart. "The Japanese are just like other people," he wrote in a *sayonara* newspaper column. "But no. They are not like other people. They are infinitely more clannish, insular, parochial, and one owes it to one's self-respect to preserve a feeling of outrage at the insularity. To have the sense of outrage go dull is to lose the will to communicate; and that, I think, is death. So I am going home."

I've just gotten here, but I think I understand what Seidensticker was talking about. And it is connected with my only real reservation about the Japanese economic miracle. Even as Japan steadily rises in influence, the idea that it should be the new world model is hard for me to swallow. I know it is not logical to draw moral lessons from economics. But everyone does it— why else did Richard Nixon brag to Nikita Khrushchev about our big refrigerators—and the Japanese are naturally now drawing lessons of their own. Their forty-year recovery represents the triumph of a system and a people, but I think many Japanese see it as the victory of a *pure* people, which by definition no inferior or mixed-blood race can match. The Japanese have their history and we have ours, so it would not be fair to argue that they "should" be a multi-racial, immigrant land. Most of the world, with greater or lesser frankness, subscribes to the Japanese view that people must be ethnically similar to get along. But to me, its ethic of exclusion is the least lovable thing about this society. And I hope, as the Japanese reflect upon their victories, that they congratulate themselves for diligence, sacrifice, and teamwork, not for remaining "pure."

STUDY QUESTIONS

1. What things did Mrs. Trollope fail to distinguish in her criticism of America in the 1820s?

2. How do Japanese and American attitudes toward teeth and toward butter differ?

3. Why do Japanese parents tell their children, "People will laugh at you" rather than "It's unfair" or "It's wrong"?

4. What are some of the differences between Japanese and American automobile production according to the Nissan factory manager?

5. What are some of the ways in which details of daily life seem better in Japan than in America? What are the two aspects of Japanese life about which Fallows is most critical?

6. What do the sports pages and the thick comic books (*manga*) have in common? What is the *kawaii* look, and what is it symptomatic of in Japanese popular culture? To what in the Japanese culture does the Dutch writer Ian Buruma attribute the *manga*-style fantasies?

7. What do the Japanese mean when they speak of national "purity"? How is that accounted for historically? What is *Nihonjinron*? What effect does Dr. Tadanobu Tsunoda say the Japanese language has had on the Japanese brain? What happens to Japanese theories of the uniqueness and impossible difficulty of their language, according to Roy Miller, when a foreigner manages to learn Japanese well?

8. What is the Japanese attitude toward Korea and Koreans? What is the Japanese attitude toward the West, especially America? What is the Japanese STEREOTYPE of an American?

9. Is the Japanese assumption that politics and culture should be run on racial lines unique in Asia?

10. What is the basic CONFLICT between the American and Japanese ways of life?

Mark Salzman

Interested in Chinese martial arts, calligraphy, and ink paintings from the age of thirteen, Mark Salzman graduated with highest honors from Yale in 1982 with a degree in Chinese language. His senior essay, a translation of Chinese poems, won a prize for the best paper on an East Asian subject. He taught English at Hunan Medical College in Changsha from 1982 to 1984 and at that time studied with various martial arts masters, returning to China in 1985 by invitation to participate with honor in the National Martial Arts Competition and Conference. In 1987 he began work on a feature film based on his first book, *Iron and Silk* (1986); he starred in the film, and this piece is taken from the book. His second book, a novel entitled *The Laughing Sutra*, was published in 1991. Salzman lives in Los Angeles.

TEACHER WEI

I did not like riding the buses in Changsha; they were always terribly crowded, sometimes with passengers squeezed partway out of the doors and windows. I once rode a bus which stopped at a particularly crowded streetcorner. Women were holding their children above their heads so they would not be crushed in the shoving, and I saw a man desperately grab onto something inside the bus while most of his body was not yet on board. The bus attendant screamed at him to let go, but he would not, so she pressed the button operating the doors and they crashed shut on him, fixing him exactly half inside and half out. The bus proceeded to its destination, whereupon the doors opened and the man stepped down, cheerfully paid the attendant half the usual fare, and went on his way.

To avoid having to ride the buses, I decided to follow the example of the three senior Yale-China teachers in Changsha, Bill, Bob and Marcy, and buy a bicycle. Because I was a foreigner, I was allowed to choose the model I wanted, pay for it on the spot with foreign currency certificates and take it home right away. I walked it out of the store with most of the store following me, got on, and rode away feeling acutely self-conscious, as if I had walked into a car dealer, paid for a Porsche in cash, and driven it out of the showroom right through the floor-to-ceiling windows.

When I got back to the house I felt grimy from all the dust on the roads, so I went upstairs to take a bath. Foreigners were not supposed to take showers in the public bathhouse, so our building was equipped with its own bathtub on the second floor, with an electric water heater attached to the wall above it. The hot water passed from the tank, which was at head level, through an iron pipe into the tub. The first time I used the tub, not realizing that the iron pipe conducted the heat of the heating element, I leaned my backside against it while drying off. As soon as the pain struck I reached out and grabbed the only object within reach—the wire supplying electricity to the heater, which stretched across the room over the tub. As soon as I had pulled myself free, I remembered my parents' command never to touch wires or electrical devices when standing in a bathtub. I let go in a panic, lost my balance and fell back onto the pipe. After that I got in the habit of drying off in my room.

This time, as I ran downstairs with a towel around my waist, I was met in my room by Teacher Wu and a silver-haired lady who looked about the same age as Teacher Wu, but was very thin and had fiercely bright eyes. Teacher Wu, who seemed not to notice that I was half-naked and dripping wet, introduced us.

"Mark, this is Teacher Wei, my colleague. The college has assigned her to be your teacher, in case you would like to continue your study of Chinese. Since you have a background in classical Chinese, she offered to teach you; she taught classical Chinese in our middle school here for many years. She is a very good teacher." Teacher Wei shook her head and said, "No, no. I'm a bad teacher," but she grinned. Teacher Wu wanted to arrange a schedule then and there, but Teacher Wei pulled her out of the room saying, "He's wet now. I will come again some other time." She looked at me. "I will come tomorrow and bring the books you will need."

After they left I remembered that I had met Teacher Wei before, at a welcoming party thrown the day after I arrived. One of the Middle-Aged

English Teachers had taken me aside and said, "Teacher Wei is a widow and has the reputation of being the strictest teacher in our college. It is said that she never smiles and has never laughed out loud!"

I did not have much time to worry about how I would get along with mirthless Teacher Wei, however—that night I was scheduled to give a lecture for which I had yet to prepare. My predecessors at the college had begun a Wednesday night "Western Culture Lecture Series" held in the largest hall in the college and open to anyone interested in learning English. Virtually everyone in our college was interested in learning English, so we usually drew a crowd of three to five hundred. Past topics had ranged from "Medical Schools in America" to "The American Legal System," and each lecture, an hour and a half in length, was given twice—once to the doctors and teachers and once to the students. I was to give my first lecture that night to the doctors and teachers; my topic was "E.T."

For starters, I wrote out the events of the movie as I remembered them. Then I figured out what vocabulary I would have to introduce—like "spaceship," "alien," "ouch," and "phone home." I adopted a distinct facial expression, walk, or tone of voice for each character, to make it easier for the audience to know right away who was who, and decided to alternate between narrating and acting out the scenes. I worried that the audience might not appreciate this sort of storytelling and think it childish or uninteresting, but I did not have to worry long. When I introduced E.T. by jumping on the lab table and hopping the length of it with my knees under my chin and my hands dragging on the table, the audience rose to its feet and cheered.

The next day Teacher Wei arrived after xiuxi[1] with a cloth bag and her glasses case. She walked into my room, sat down and accepted a cup of tea, put on her glasses, and took a book from her bag.

"We'll begin with this collection of classical essays prepared for Chinese high school students." She handed it to me and took out another copy for herself. I noticed that her copy was filled with pencil notes, smudged from her habit of following the text with her fingertip as she read.

"We'll begin with an essay by Tao Qian. You are familiar with him, aren't you? Then of course you know that he was a hermit and a famous drinker, almost fifteen hundred years ago. Most of the great Chinese authors were drinkers and dreamers."

She stopped, took off her glasses, and looked closely at me.

"I saw your lecture last night, the one called 'E.T.' You are a very naughty boy!" She took from her bag a small medicine jar and handed it to me. I opened it and found that it contained a shot of *baijiu*—Chinese rice liquor.

"Since we will be reading the works of drinkers and dreamers, and since you are clearly an eccentric yourself, I think it only fitting that you appreciate their essays like this. From now on I will bring a small bottle of baijiu when I come. You will finish it, then we will have our lesson."

1. The Chinese version of siesta. [Author's note]

I thought she was kidding, so I laughed, but she really meant for me to 15 drink it. She reached into her bag and pulled out a container of fried peanuts, still warm from the wok.

"You must have something to eat with it, of course. I brought some 16 peanuts for you. If you don't finish the wine, no lesson for you."

I finished the baijiu and peanuts, to her great satisfaction. Then she put 17 on her glasses and began the lesson.

Not long after our first lesson Teacher Wei happened to walk by our 18 house while I was practicing *wushu* out front. *Wushu* is the Chinese word for martial arts, and refers to any of hundreds of schools of armed and unarmed combat practiced in China for more than two thousand years. These schools range from the slow, graceful Taijiquan, or T'ai Chi Ch'uan, to the explosive Northern and Southern schools of Shaolin boxing. In the West, Chinese martial arts are called "kung fu" or "gong fu," but the word *gong fu* actually means skill that transcends mere surface beauty. A martial artist whose technique is decorative but without power "has no gong fu," whereas, say, a calligrapher whose work is not pretty to look at but reflects a strong, austere taste certainly "has gong fu."

Teacher Wei walked over and asked what I was doing. When I told her 19 that wushu had been an interest of mine for many years, she nodded with approval.

"In classical Chinese we have a saying that to be a true gentleman it is 20 important to be 'well-versed in the literary and the martial.' Wushu is an excellent sport. Have you found a teacher here yet?"

At this I became very excited. I told her that I would love to find a 21 teacher but had no idea where to look for one, and that even if I found one, I wouldn't know how to approach him. I also expressed my doubts that a wushu teacher would accept a foreign student, as I had heard that they were usually secretive and old-fashioned in their thinking. She shook her head vigorously.

"That may be true of the mediocre fighters, but you will find that the 22 best fighters in China are not superstitious or close-minded. If you want to learn wushu, you will have a teacher—I can guarantee it, because you are a friendly boy. That is most important. Besides,"—she allowed herself a giggle—"you are exotic. Your big nose alone will open doors! You have blond hair, blue eyes, and you are very strong—you're a 'model foreigner'! Teachers will find you." I asked her if she knew anyone who might be able to help me, but she just smiled and said to be patient, then continued on her way.

As I walked back into the house to take a bath and have breakfast, I 23 noticed a man with close-cropped white hair squatting on the steps of our building. I said good morning to him and he answered politely, complimenting my Chinese. I asked him if he had come to see one of the American teachers, and he said no, then explained that he was staying in the one empty room in our building, which the college offered to guests when the regular guest house was full. He was a doctor of rehabilitative therapy and tradi- tional Chinese medicine at a hospital on the outskirts of the city, and had come to represent his specialty at a conference our college was sponsoring. His name was Dr. Li. When he stood up to introduce himself, I noticed that he was taller than I, had broad shoulders, and held back his head slightly, which gave him an extraordinarily distinguished appearance.

"I saw you exercising," he said, "and overheard your conversation with 24 the lady. There are several good teachers in Hunan."

"Do you know any of them?" 25

"Yes, I know one or two." 26

"Do you think any of them would be willing to teach me?" 27

"Hard to say," he said, then wished me good morning and left for break- 28 fast.

Dr. Li stayed for one week. Every morning he squatted in front of the 29 house, watched me exercise, talked for a little while, then left to get break- fast. The afternoon before he left he happened to return to the house while I was sitting out front working on a charcoal and ink sketch. He sat next to me until I finished, then took it in his hands to have a better look. He seemed to like it, so I asked him please to keep it.

"Thank you very much—it is a beautiful drawing," he said, then got up 30 to leave. "Will you be exercising tomorrow morning?" he asked casually.

"Probably." 31

"I'll tell you something. The reason you haven't seen anyone practicing 32 wushu is that you get up too late. You are out here at 6:30 every morning. The wushu people have already finished practicing by then! Get up a little earlier tomorrow; you might see something then." He thanked me again for the drawing and went into the house.

At five o'clock the next morning my alarm went off. I scrambled outside 33 and sat down on the steps. It was still dark out, and I didn't see anyone else up yet, much less practicing wushu. Then it occurred to me how unlikely it would be for a wushu expert to choose to practice in the north campus of Hunan Medical College, and I cursed myself for not asking Dr. Li where I should go. I stood up to go back to bed when I noticed an unfamiliar shape next to a bamboo tree planted against the south end of the house. I walked over and saw that it was Dr. Li, balanced on one leg in an impossible posture, his body so still I could not even see him breathe.

After an interminable length of time he suddenly straightened up, nod- 34 ding to acknowledge my presence. He then practiced a Taijiquan form that lasted some twenty minutes. He moved so slowly I felt hypnotized watching him. When he finished, he gestured for me to stand next to him.

"Of the wushu I practice," he said, "my favorite is called the Xuan Men 35 Sword. *Xuan* means dark, or mysterious; *men* means gate." He had me stay put while he quickly found two sticks of equal length, perhaps two and a half feet long, then gave one to me.

"Do what I do," he said, and began teaching me the form. 36

After half an hour or so, he said it was time for breakfast and told me   37
that this was the last day he would be living in our house, so unfortunately
he could not teach me every morning.

"But I will come here every three days or so until you learn the form.   38
Wait for me here, in front of your house, early in the morning."

He kept his promise and I was able to learn all the movements of the   39
form in a month, but he insisted that something was still missing. Although
I performed the techniques well, he could see I was not concentrating in a
manner appropriate for the form: "You look good, but you have no gong fu."
At last he invited me to his home for dinner, saying that he could teach me
better there. When I followed the directions he gave me to his house, I realized that he had been riding forty-five minutes each way to teach me for the
past month. He lived well outside the center of the city on a small hill surrounded by lush, irrigated fields. As soon as I arrived his wife offered me a
hot towel to wipe the dust off my hands and face. The three of us sat down
to a simple but delicious meal of pork strips over noodles in broth, steamed
fish, and plenty of rice.

When we had finished, Dr. Li's wife took what was left over and carried   40
it into the adjacent bedroom where, I discovered, his son and two daughters,
all in their teens or twenties, were sitting. When I asked why they hadn't
eaten with us, Dr. Li seemed puzzled. "That would be rude, wouldn't it?
You are our guest, after all."

He apparently sensed my discomfort, because he invited them to join   41
us for dessert—a few oranges and apples, and more tea. Dr. Li's children
were far too shy to carry on a conversation with me, but one of them did
manage to ask me if American food was the same as Chinese food. I tried to
describe a typical American meal for them, but it proved difficult: how do
you explain pizza to someone who has never seen cheese, tomato sauce, or a
pie crust?

After dessert Dr. Li took two swords from another room, tied them   42
together with some string, and asked me to follow him. We got on our bicy-
cles and rode to nearby Mawangdui, the site of the hole that had contained
the two-thousand-year-old corpse.[2] We walked past that hole to a second
mound, which Dr. Li told me was supposed to contain the tomb of either
the marquise's husband or her son. The top of the mound was nearly flat and
had patches of grass growing here and there on its packed dirt surface. As
Dr. Li unfastened the two swords and handed me one, I realized that the flat
part of the mound was just the right size for the form he had taught me.

The sun had not yet gone down, and it cast a glittering reflection over   43
the Xiang River a few miles away. The vegetable plots in all directions around
us caught the light as well and glowed brightly, in sharp contrast to the deep
red earth of the paths between the fields.

"Just think," he said, "under your feet is so much history! There are all   44

2. The body of a Changsha noblewoman who died about 2100 years ago. Sealed in a series of six airtight
coffins, it was so well preserved that scientists were able to perform an autopsy, which was filmed and
shown throughout China in 1973.

sorts of treasures in this mound—probably even swords like these, only real ones that were used in ancient wars. With all this history under you, don't you feel moved? Now, practice the form, and this time don't fuss over the technique. Just enjoy it, as if this mound gave you power. That is the kind of feeling that makes wushu beautiful—it is tradition passing through you. Isn't that a kind of power?"

After the lesson at Mawangdui Dr. Li said there was no need for him to come in the mornings to teach me anymore, but that if I wanted any further information I could visit him anytime. Since very few people in China have telephones, about the only way to arrange to visit someone is to walk to his house and knock on the door. If it's a friend, you can often dispense with the knocking and just walk in. My students told me again and again that if I ever wanted to see them I could walk into their homes any time of day or night.

"But what if you are busy?"

"It doesn't matter! If you come, I won't be busy anymore!"

"But what if you are asleep?"

"Then wake me up!"

No matter how often I was given these instructions, though, I could not bring myself to follow them. Whenever someone banged on my door unexpectedly, or simply appeared in my room, I always felt slightly nervous, and I only visited my friends when I felt I had a good reason.

So I did not call upon Dr. Li for more lessons, but contented myself with practicing the Xuan Men Sword and trying to recreate the feeling invoked by dancing with the sword on the Han dynasty tomb.

By that time Teacher Wei was helping me through a classical novel, *The Water Margin*, the story of a hundred and eight renegade heroes, all martial arts experts, who band together and perform deeds similar to those of Robin Hood and the men of Sherwood Forest. Teacher Wei and I agreed that our favorite character was Lu Zhishen, known as the Phony Monk, a man with a righteous soul but a powerful temper, who was on the run from the law after killing an evil merchant to redress an injustice. To escape execution he became a Buddhist monk, but was unsuited to the monk's abstemious way of life. He would sneak out of the monastery at night to drink superhuman amounts of baijiu and eat roast dogs, bones and all, then return to the monastery where the other monks would scold him for drinking and eating meat. In a drunken rage, he would beat them all up, reduce a few buildings to rubble, then throw up in the meditation hall. Of course, the next day he would feel very bad and fix everything he had broken.

My lessons with Teacher Wei had come to involve more than reading and writing assignments. She was a teacher in the Chinese tradition, taking responsibility not only for my academic progress but for my development as a person. She had advice for me concerning my family and friends, my diet, my clothing, my study and exercise habits, and my attitude toward life. At times I got impatient with her and explained that in America, children become adults around the time they leave for college and like to make decisions for themselves after that. She was appalled. "Don't your parents and teachers care about you?"

"Of course they do, but—" 54

"Then how can they leave you stranded when you are only a child?" 55

"Well, we—" 56

"And how can you possibly think you understand everything? You are 57 only twenty-two years old! You are so far away from home, and I am your teacher; if I don't care about you, won't you be lonely?"

She pointed out that the close relationship between teacher and student 58 has existed in China since before the time of Confucius and should not be underestimated—besides, she was older than me and knew better. I couldn't help respecting her conviction, and she seemed to get such pleasure out of trying to figure and then to straighten me out that I stopped resisting and let her educate me.

I learned how to dress to stay comfortable throughout the year (a useful 59 skill in a place without air conditioning or heat in most buildings), how to prevent and treat common illness, how to behave toward teachers, students, strangers and bureaucrats, how to save books from mildew and worms, and never to do anything to excess.

"Mark, you laugh a great deal during your lectures. Why?" 60

"Because, Teacher Wei, I am having fun." 61

"I see. Laugh less. It seems odd that a man laughs so hard at his own 62 jokes. People think you are a bit crazy, or perhaps choking."

"Teacher Wei, do you think it is bad to laugh?" 63

"No, not at all. In fact, it is healthy to laugh. In Chinese we have a 64 saying that if you laugh you will live long. But you shouldn't laugh too much, or you will have digestive problems."

Teacher Wei also encouraged me to travel. She knew I was homesick; 65 she said that travel gives experience, helps cope with sadness, and in any case is fun. I disagreed with her. My last trip, from Hong Kong to Changsha, had given me unwelcome experience and was no fun at all. She let the issue drop until I told her one day that Bob, Marcy and Bill were planning a trip to Wuhan to spend a holiday weekend with the Yale-China teachers living there. Actually, I had already decided to join them, but I did not want to rob Teacher Wei of the opportunity to talk me into it. After I promised her that I would go to Wuhan if she really thought I should, she wanted to know who was going to arrange our travel.

"Teacher Wei, it is only a six-hour train ride." 66

"Yes, but who will buy the tickets for you? Who will see you to the 67 train station? Who will see to it that you get seats?"

"Teacher Wei, we will just take the bus to the station, get in line, buy 68 the tickets, and find seats ourselves."

She could not understand why I would not allow her to get all of her 69 relatives in Changsha and Wuhan to arrange our passage.

"It is my duty to help you!" 70

"We will be all right, Teacher Wei. It is only for a weekend." 71

"Well, when will you be back?" 72

"Monday night." 73

"Which train will you take?" 74

"Probably this one—the one that arrives at dinner time." 75

"I see." 76

The weekend in Wuhan turned out to be fun, although I did not enjoy 77
the train ride either way. Going up we sat on pieces of newspaper on the
floor between two cars, knee to knee with three exhausted men traveling
from South to North China. On the way down it was so crowded there was
not even room on the floor between cars, so we stood, packed like cattle,
with our faces pressed against a mountain of cabbages stacked up to the ceiling of the train. Bob had the clever idea of anchoring his arms in the pile of
cabbages and leaning against it so he could sleep, so I followed his example
and managed to doze for a few hours. When we got back to Changsha we
stopped at a shop for some noodles in broth as the sun went down, before
going home.

By the time we reached the gate of our college it was nearly dark. As I 78
passed through it I heard someone calling my name and turned to see Teacher
Wei waving at me from under a tree. I walked over and asked if she was on
her way somewhere.

"No—I am waiting for you." 79

"Why are you waiting for me?" 80

"This was your first trip in China. How shameful it would be if no one 81
greeted you when you came home."

STUDY QUESTIONS

1. What do you conclude about Chinese life and attitudes from the opening episode
   about the crowded buses in Changsha? (Be sure you take into account the words
   "cheerfully" and "half" in the final sentence of the first paragraph.) What do you
   expect the attitude of the writer to be toward things Chinese after reading this
   first paragraph?

2. What is Salzman's topic for his lecture on Western culture? How does it compare
   with the topics of previous lectures that he mentions? What does it reveal about
   his CHARACTER? What did you expect the response to be? What is it? What does
   that suggest about the Chinese doctors and teachers who make up the audience?
   What does Teacher Wei think of it? of him? Is her opinion of him justified? How
   does she begin the lesson? What is your impression of her at this point (paragraphs 9–17)?

3. What does *gong fu* ("kung fu") mean literally in Chinese? How is the term used?
   What, according to Teacher Wei, is the attitude of the best fighters in China
   toward foreigners who want to learn the sport? Compare this attitude with the
   Japanese attitude toward foreigners learning their language and toward foreigners
   in general as James Fallows describes those attitudes in "The Japanese Are Different from You and Me."

4. What is there about Salzman that Teacher Wei finds "exotic"?

5. When Salzman asks Teacher Wei if she knows anyone who might teach him the martial arts, she just smiles and asks him to be patient; when he asks Dr. Li, the doctor responds, "Hard to say" (paragraph 28). What did you think of their friendliness at that point? What did you expect to happen? What does happen? Who teaches him? What does he discover his teacher must do to come to teach him? What do you make of the reticence and the silent, almost secret effort to be helpful? What qualities in the Chinese character or culture does that suggest?

6. Why do Li's son and daughters not eat with their parents and Salzman when he is a guest? What is the Chinese practice when coming to someone's door to visit (paragraphs 45–50)? What do you feel about these practices? Do they surprise you? Do you admire them? dislike them? Do they make you uncomfortable? Is there an implied conflict between their practices and manners and the Western reader's? Does it make you think about our customs?

7. When Dr. Li and Salzman go to practice on the mound at Mawangdui, what does Li advise him to do? What does he claim makes the martial arts (wushu) beautiful?

8. What is the Phony Monk in the classical Chinese novel *The Water Margin* like (paragraph 52)? Why do you think he is the favorite character of Salzman and Teacher Wei (remember what Teacher Wei said about Salzman after hearing his lecture)? What impression of their characters does their choice of favorite give you?

9. What are Chinese parents' and teachers' attitude and behavior toward grown-up children, people in their twenties, for example?

10. What does Salzman learn about laughter?

11. What is your final impression about Chinese attitudes and manners? How would you compare them with our own?

Maya Angelou

Maya Angelou's ongoing autobiography has now reached five volumes, and she is still a relatively young woman. But no wonder. Besides writing the autobiography, three volumes of poetry, the musical *And Still I Rise*, the BBC documentary *Trying to Make It Home*, and a ten-part television series (which she also produced), Angelou has toured Europe and Africa as an actress (in *Porgy and Bess*), studied and taught dance, served as the Northern coordinator for the Southern Christian Leadership Conference, and served on the Commission of International Women's Year and on the Board of Trustees of the American Film Institute. She was understandably named "Woman of the Year" by the *Ladies Home Journal* in 1975. Angelou read her poem "On the Pulse of Morning" at the inauguration of President Bill Clinton in January 1993.

"My Brother Bailey and Kay Francis" (editors' title) is from the first volume of the autobiography, *I Know Why the Caged Bird Sings*. It is set in Stamps, Arkansas, where her mother had sent her and her older brother, Bailey, to live with their grandmother (whom she calls Momma), who, with (Great-) Uncle Willie, kept a store.

MY BROTHER BAILEY
AND KAY FRANCIS

Weekdays revolved on a sameness wheel. They turned into themselves so steadily and inevitably that each seemed to be the original of yesterday's rough draft. Saturdays, however, always broke the mold and dared to be different. [1]

Farmers trekked into town with their children and wives streaming around them. Their board-stiff khaki pants and shirts revealed the painstaking care of a dutiful daughter or wife. They often stopped at the Store to get change for bills so they could give out jangling coins to their children, who shook with their eagerness to get to town. The young kids openly resented their parents' dawdling in the Store and Uncle Willie would call them in and spread among them bits of sweet peanut patties that had been broken in shipping. They gobbled down the candies and were out again, kicking up the powdery dust in the road and worrying if there was going to be time to get to town after all. [2]

Bailey played mumbledypeg with the older boys around the chinaberry tree, and Momma and Uncle Willie listened to the farmers' latest news of the country. I thought of myself as hanging in the Store, a mote imprisoned on a shaft of sunlight. Pushed and pulled by the slightest shift of air, but never falling free into the tempting darkness. [3]

In the warm months, morning began with a quick wash in unheated well water. The suds were dashed on a plot of ground beside the kitchen door. It was called the bait garden (Bailey raised worms). After prayers, breakfast in summer was usually dry cereal and fresh milk. Then to our chores (which on Saturday included weekday jobs)—scrubbing the floors, raking the yards, polishing our shoes for Sunday (Uncle Willie's had to be shined with a biscuit) and attending to the customers who came breathlessly, also in their Saturday hurry. [4]

Looking through the years, I marvel that Saturday was my favorite day in the week. What pleasures could have been squeezed between the fan folds of unending tasks? Children's talent to endure stems from their ignorance of alternatives. [5]

After our retreat from St. Louis, Momma gave us a weekly allowance. Since she seldom dealt with money, other than to take it in and to tithe to the church, I supposed that the weekly ten cents was to tell us that even she realized that a change had come over us, and that our new unfamiliarity caused her to treat us with a strangeness.

I usually gave my money to Bailey, who went to the movies nearly every Saturday. He brought back Street and Smith cowboy books for me.

One Saturday Bailey was late coming back from the Rye-al-toh. Momma had begun heating water for the Saturday-night baths, and all the evening chores were done. Uncle Willie sat in the twilight on the front porch mumbling or maybe singing, and smoking a ready-made. It was quite late. Mothers had called in their children from the group games, and fading sounds of "Yah . . . Yah . . . you didn't catch me" still hung and floated into the Store.

Uncle Willie said, "Sister, better light the light." On Saturdays we used the electric lights so that last-minute Sunday shoppers could look down the hill and see if the Store was open. Momma hadn't told me to turn them on because she didn't want to believe that night had fallen hard and Bailey was still out in the ungodly dark.

Her apprehension was evident in the hurried movements around the kitchen and in her lonely fearing eyes. The Black woman in the South who raises sons, grandsons and nephews had her heartstrings tied to a hanging noose. Any break from routine may herald for them unbearable news. For this reason, Southern Blacks until the present generation could be counted among America's arch conservatives.

Like most self-pitying people, I had very little pity for my relatives' anxiety. If something indeed had happened to Bailey, Uncle Willie would always have Momma, and Momma had the Store. Then, after all, we weren't their children. But I would be the major loser if Bailey turned up dead. For he was all I claimed, if not all I had.

The bath water was steaming on the cooking stove, but Momma was scrubbing the kitchen table for the umpteenth time.

"Momma," Uncle Willie called and she jumped. "Momma." I waited in the bright lights of the Store, jealous that someone had come along and told these strangers something about my brother and I would be the last to know.

"Momma, why don't you and Sister walk down to meet him?"

To my knowledge Bailey's name hadn't been mentioned for hours, but we all knew whom he meant.

Of course. Why didn't that occur to me? I wanted to be gone. Momma said, "Wait a minute, little lady. Go get your sweater, and bring me my shawl."

It was darker in the road than I'd thought it would be. Momma swung the flashlight's arc over the path and weeds and scary tree trunks. The night suddenly became enemy territory, and I knew that if my brother was lost in this land he was forever lost. He was eleven and very smart, that I granted, but after all he was so small. The Bluebeards and tigers and Rippers could eat him up before he could scream for help.

Momma told me to take the light and she reached for my hand. Her voice came from a high hill above me and in the dark my hand was enclosed in hers. I loved her with a rush. She said nothing—no "Don't worry" or "Don't get tender-hearted." Just the gentle pressure of her rough hand conveyed her own concern and assurance to me.

We passed houses which I knew well by daylight but couldn't recollect in the swarthy gloom.

"Evening, Miz Jenkins." Walking and pulling me along.

"Sister Henderson? Anything wrong?" That was from an outline blacker than the night.

"No ma'am. Not a thing. Bless the Lord." By the time she finished speaking we had left the worried neighbors far behind.

Mr. Willie Williams' Do Drop Inn was bright with furry red lights in the distance and the pond's fishy smell enveloped us. Momma's hand tightened and let go, and I saw the small figure plodding along, tired and old-mannish. Hands in his pockets and head bent, he walked like a man trudging up the hill behind a coffin.

"Bailey." It jumped out as Momma said, "Ju," and I started to run, but her hand caught mine again and became a vise. I pulled, but she yanked me back to her side. "We'll walk, just like we been walking, young lady." There was no chance to warn Bailey that he was dangerously late, that everybody had been worried and that he should create a good lie or, better, a great one.

Momma said, "Bailey, Junior," and he looked up without surprise. "You know it's night and you just now getting home?"

"Yes, ma'am." He was empty. Where was his alibi?

"What you been doing?"

"Nothing."

"That's all you got to say?"

"Yes, ma'am."

"All right, young man. We'll see when you get home."

She had turned me loose, so I made a grab for Bailey's hand, but he snatched it away. I said, "Hey, Bail," hoping to remind him that I was his sister and his only friend, but he grumbled something like "Leave me alone."

Momma didn't turn on the flashlight on the way back, nor did she answer the questioning Good evenings that floated around us as we passed the darkened houses.

I was confused and frightened. He was going to get a whipping and maybe he had done something terrible. If he couldn't talk to me it must have been serious. But there was no air of spent revelry about him. He just seemed sad. I didn't know what to think.

Uncle Willie said, "Getting too big for your britches, huh? You can't come home. You want to worry your grandmother to death?" Bailey was so far away he was beyond fear. Uncle Willie had a leather belt in his good hand but Bailey didn't notice or didn't care. "I'm going to whip you this time." Our uncle had only whipped us once before and then only with a peach-tree switch, so maybe now he was going to kill my brother. I screamed and grabbed for the belt, but Momma caught me. "Now, don't get uppity, miss, 'less you want some of the same thing. He got a lesson coming to him. You come on and get your bath."

From the kitchen I heard the belt fall down, dry and raspy on naked skin. Uncle Willie was gasping for breath, but Bailey made no sound. I was too afraid to splash water or even to cry and take a chance of drowning out Bailey's pleas for help, but the pleas never came and the whipping was finally over.

I lay awake an eternity, waiting for a sign, a whimper or a whisper, from the next room that he was still alive. Just before I fell exhausted into sleep, I heard Bailey: "Now I lay me down to sleep, I pray the Lord my soul to keep, if I should die before I wake, I pray the Lord my soul to take."

My last memory of that night was the question, Why is he saying the baby prayer? We had been saying the "Our Father, which art in heaven" for years.

For days the Store was a strange country, and we were all newly arrived immigrants. Bailey didn't talk, smile or apologize. His eyes were so vacant, it seemed his soul had flown away, and at meals I tried to give him the best pieces of meat and the largest portion of dessert, but he turned them down.

Then one evening at the pig pen he said without warning, "I saw Mother Dear."

If he said it, it was bound to be the truth. He wouldn't lie to me. I don't think I asked him where or when.

"In the movies." He laid his head on the wooden railing. "It wasn't really her. It was a woman named Kay Francis. She's a white movie star who looks just like Mother Dear."

There was no difficulty believing that a white movie star looked like our mother and that Bailey had seen her. He told me that the movies were changed each week, but when another picture came to Stamps starring Kay Francis he would tell me and we'd go together. He even promised to sit with me.

He had stayed late on the previous Saturday to see the film over again. I understood, and understood too why he couldn't tell Momma or Uncle Willie. She was our mother and belonged to us. She was never mentioned to anyone because we simply didn't have enough of her to share.

We had to wait nearly two months before Kay Francis returned to Stamps. Bailey's mood had lightened considerably, but he lived in a state of expectation and it made him more nervous than he was usually. When he told me that the movie would be shown, we went into our best behavior and were the exemplary children that Grandmother deserved and wished to think us.

It was a gay light comedy, and Kay Francis wore long-sleeved white silk shirts with big cuff links. Her bedroom was all satin and flowers in vases, and her maid, who was Black, went around saying "Lawsy, missy" all the time. There was a Negro chauffeur too, who rolled his eyes and scratched his head, and I wondered how on earth an idiot like that could be trusted with her beautiful cars.

The whitefolks downstairs laughed every few minutes, throwing the discarded snicker up to the Negroes in the buzzards' roost. The sound would jag around in our air for an indecisive second before the balcony's occupants accepted it and sent their own guffaws to riot with it against the walls of the theater. 47

I laughed, too, but not at the hateful jokes made on my people. I laughed because, except that she was white, the big movie star looked just like my mother. Except that she lived in a big mansion with a thousand servants, she lived just like my mother. And it was funny to think of the whitefolks' not knowing that the woman they were adoring could be my mother's twin, except that she was white and my mother was prettier. Much prettier. 48

The movie star made me happy. It was extraordinary good fortune to be able to save up one's money and go see one's mother whenever one wanted to. I bounced out of the theater as if I'd been given an unexpected present. But Bailey was cast down again. (I had to beg him not to stay for the next show.) On the way home he stopped at the railroad track and waited for the night freight train. Just before it reached the crossing, he tore out and ran across the tracks. 49

I was left on the other side in hysteria. Maybe the giant wheels were grinding his bones into a bloody mush. Maybe he tried to catch a boxcar and got flung into the pond and drowned. Or even worse, maybe he caught the train and was forever gone. 50

When the train passed he pushed himself away from the pole where he had been leaning, berated me for making all that noise and said, "Let's go home." 51

One year later he did catch a freight, but because of his youth and the inscrutable way of fate, he didn't find California and his Mother Dear—he got stranded in Baton Rouge, Louisiana, for two weeks. 52

STUDY QUESTIONS

1. Why is Bailey late coming home? Why doesn't he tell his grandmother or Uncle Willie the reason? Why is his grandmother, given the time and place, particularly worried? Why, according to Angelou, have Southern blacks, until the present generation, been "among America's arch conservatives" (paragraph 10)? What does it mean that Angelou says Bailey "was all I claimed, if not all I had" (paragraph 11)? Why is Momma "scrubbing the kitchen table for the umpteenth time" (paragraph 12)? Why does Angelou suddenly love Momma?

2. Why does Bailey say a "baby prayer" that night instead of the "Our Father" (paragraph 38)? Why was the Store for several days "a strange country, and we were all newly arrived immigrants" (paragraph 39)? Why, two months later, are the children on their best behavior?

3. What is the response of the blacks in the balcony to the laughter of the whites below at the idiotic antics of the blacks on the screen? (Why are all the blacks sitting upstairs?) Why does Angelou laugh? What is her response to Kay Francis, the white actress? What is Bailey's response? Why does Bailey rush across the tracks in front of the oncoming train? What happens to him?

AFTERWORD

EXPECTATION

Reading is a *re-creational activity*. A text should stir your mind into activity from the time you read the title, even if you are just reading the title of a chapter in a textbook: "Aliens." Even a title suggests connections with things we already know about—from science fiction, perhaps, or from sociology—and leads us to expect specific topics, ideas, or themes.

What do you do when your interest is aroused, your curiosity piqued? You read on, of course, but, whether you are aware of it or not, your mind probably scans the possible meanings of that which has aroused it. You mentally flip through other reading experiences that might have to do with aliens or strangers, and you remember what has gone before in the text. The preceding chapters, you recall, have concerned such things as home, heritage, foreign languages. What sort of pattern does that suggest? The most obvious pattern seems to consist in a movement away both in space and time: farther and farther from home toward the remote, the foreign. If the pattern holds, the chapter called "Aliens" will no doubt leave the earth and the present for space and the future; there will probably be lots of science fiction.

All of this speculation happens, if it does happen—and not everyone's mind works exactly the same way—in a matter of seconds, and, unless you're watching yourself actively read, it happens without your being aware of it. You will be aware, however, of what it is you anticipate.

Meanwhile, or in a few heartbeats, you are reading on. When you read the headnote, you might not be too sure about the science fiction: there are other kinds of "aliens," the headnote reminds you—foreign, but earthmen and -women. If you then read through the works in the order in which they appear, you will probably abandon the notion that the chapter is about Martians; the "aliens" are human: an African-American man on a subway, Latinos in Minnesota, Arabs, homosexuals, people who have left their homelands and *become* different. All of them *seem* alien to those who expect homogeneity.

Reading a literary work is a much richer experience than reading the table of contents of a chapter in an anthology of literary works, but the activity of reading is in outline much the same. There is anticipation or EXPECTATION generated by the words you are reading (even when they are just titles), recollection of what you read before, and the tentative formation of a pattern out of the past and present so that you can project it forward to anticipate what will be coming next. Reading *is* an activity; and it does *re-create*.

The activity of reading a tightly woven literary text is more complex than a simple recording, recalling, anticipating. Because of the complexity of the work and of the process, reading beyond the title is a much more global and mentally muscular activity. And there is even more to the process of reading and anticipating along with the text than just absorbing, recalling, and projecting on the basis of the words and determining signals in the text. Each of us understands the words in a slightly different way; each of us recalls selectively, and projects differently. We have had different reading and different life experiences, and it is these as well as the words of the text that trigger expectations and condition our interpretations of the text. This does not mean that we cannot learn from a text, that we can only extract from it what we already know or feel. Nor does this mean that we can make the text say anything we want. There are grossly distortive, "wrong" readings, but there is more than one right reading.

No single account of a reading, therefore, will be applicable to everyone, but, in order to bring our unconscious act of reading to consciousness, let us look very briefly and selectively at how one reader might engage a piece of one work.

Look at the beginning of Margaret Atwood's "The Man from Mars." The first words of the story are "A long time ago." How long ago? At first we may still be beguiled by the title; the present of the story may be far in the future, and the story may be being told by a Martian years and years from now. But Christine's coming away from playing tennis, wearing a tennis dress, her hair held back by an elastic band, makes it seem not so long ago—our present or recent past, perhaps (the story was first published in 1977).

We probably dismiss those first four words after a while; they seem totally irrelevant. But they are stored somewhere at the back of our mind. We have been prepared, whether we know it or not, to recognize what nation it is that is "Mars," though the name of that nation is never given in the story.

The function of holding the revelation—not, notice, just an event or action or matter of plot—to near the end is not only to intensify the surprise for its own sake but to intensify its power to engage our deepest feelings. Some of us will have felt repulsed by "the man from Mars"; his annoying relentlessness and his increasingly threatening presence will have engendered something close to disgust, perhaps mixed with a little fear and something approaching hate. But in the end, after he has been shipped back to his own country, we can imagine what he is facing or going through. The hatred is replaced by pity, the disgust with understanding. And, note, the story makes it clear that it is not going to specify whether he is our ally, from the South, or our designated enemy, from the North—for the man's plight and behavior and our responses are not to be partisan, are to be political only in the sense of deploring the inhumanity of war. Sympathy transcends argument, human feeling transcends even patriotism.

Expectation, recall, patterning, surprise or modification of expectations, new expectations and new patterning—this dynamics of reading does not only operate on details that embrace the whole work or its central themes or emotional impact. It operates locally, on smaller issues and effects, and on other tangential though important contributing concerns. In the second paragraph of Atwood's story, for example, Christine passes the old men sunning themselves: "their wrinkled toadstool faces drifted towards her, drawn by the movement of her body, then floated away again, uninterested." Almost casually we are led to expect there may be a sexual encounter of some sort; at the same time, we are made aware of Christine's lack of sexual attractiveness, which later we will recall. It will make the pursuit by "the man from Mars" more incomprehensible, even mysterious, and will arouse our curiosity. Because she is not used to sexual attention, she may be more vulnerable when "the man from Mars" pursues her, and the reader wishing her well will be more apprehensive about what might happen to her.

The third paragraph describes the squirrels foraging in the park: "two or three of them moved towards her in darts and pauses, eyes fixed on her expectantly, mouths with the ratlike receding chins open to show the yellowed front teeth. Christine walked faster, she had nothing to give them. People shouldn't feed them, she thought, it makes them anxious and they get mangy." Some will want to say that the squirrels "symbolize" "the man from Mars," but it is just as useful to see them as preparing the reader for expectations of the ominous and the threatening and for noticing a parallel with Christine's skittishness. The squirrels do not reappear in the story; they have served their purpose. They are immediately replaced by "the man from Mars," the stranger who touches her on the arm, a man she and her mother do feed.

It is sometimes useful to concentrate on one piece and a small section of that piece—in this case, the first three paragraphs of a story—in order to show the scope, nature, interaction, and complexity of expectations in a literary work. To pull out for examination only one thread, no matter how central or important, is to misrepresent the reading experience. For we respond moment by moment to detail after detail, sometimes word after word, taking words and details in, threading them together with what has gone before and projecting the pattern forward. But there is not just one pattern we project; and some projections are more conscious and enduring than others. Here we "store" or keep in the background "A long time ago," while we keep close to the forefront of our minds the sexual attention—or inattention—of the old men, and transfer immediately our, and Christine's, response to the squirrels from them to the touch on her arm and the man who touches her. We weave and unweave the story through the expectations aroused, much as Penelope unweaves at night what she weaves during the day until Ulysses comes home and the story is over.

In the rather superficial example of trying to guess what kind of story, essay, poem, or play is coming next in the chapter, you probably noticed that the "education" of your expectations did not always do you much good—that is, it did not help you guess correctly what was going to come next. And the title of Atwood's story is in many ways as misleading in indicating what that story is to be about as the title of this chapter is in preparing you for what the chapter is going to be about. But guessing wrong often yields the greater rewards in the reading experience.

The effect of a wrong guess is surprise, but surprise not just in the sense of an unexpected turn of events—though we enjoy being outwitted by a clever plot—but also in the sense of a revelation or shock of recognition, an intensification of our attention to details, a new way of looking at things. Thus Carter Revard's poem "Discovery of the New World" gets you to expect something about the discovery of America, gets you to put aside that expectation when the poem opens with space creatures, and then gets you to return to the initial expectation that you pushed into the background but were not entirely able to dismiss from your mind—the poem does have something to do with the discovery of America. Surprise, then, at the beginning and at the end makes you see the discovery and settling of America in a new light—new to those who are not Native Americans, that is— and to *feel* the inhumanity of the settling of the Americas in a way no argument and probably no documentary history could achieve. Similarly, "A long time ago," pushed into the background by the events of the Atwood story, may resurface when you recognize that the man is not literally from Mars, that the unnamed country he comes from was the setting for a war that changed our world. The time before that war now seems another epoch, a long time ago, and that unnamed country another world, another planet.

WRITING
ABOUT THE READING

PERSONAL ESSAYS AND NARRATIVES

1. Recount your experiences with strangers whose national, ethnic, or cultural origins you could not at first determine. Include encounters in which you never determined the cultural identity of the stranger. Be honest about your responses, from puzzlement to impatience, repulsion, sentimental patronizing, etc. What did you expect to happen or think or fear or hope might happen? How did it turn out?

2. Describe in detail your thoughts and feelings in an encounter—whether casual, social, or other—with a stranger from a different cultural, national, or ethnic background (not necessarily a strange or rare one), using, if you wish, Sharon Olds's poem "On the Subway" as a model, and concentrating on your expectations.

3. Recount or invent an experience in which you met someone whose national, ethnic, or cultural background puzzled you, and tell how the relationship developed. (You can be either the alien or the one "visited" by him or her.)

IMITATIONS AND PARODIES

1. In a short short story, rewrite Atwood's "The Man from Mars" as if you were the man. You need not conclude the story with the episode in Montreal or even with the war but, if you wish, with details, episodes, and explanations of your own invention. Try to keep your reader guessing.

2. Imagine (if necessary) yourself a member of a rare minority in an ethnically homogeneous town like "Roseville, Minn., U.S.A." (you need not imagine the same ethnic majority). Write a brief poem, essay, or story about your life there.

ANALYTICAL ESSAYS

1. "The _____ Are Different." Using James Fallows's article as a possible model, write an essay on a national, cultural, or ethnic group.

2. Basing your understanding of Chinese culture on the Salzman selection, compare Chinese customs to those of the Japanese as described by Fallows, to those of Americans, or to those of any culture with which you are familiar.

ARGUMENTATIVE ESSAY

Defend Joseph's "alien" values (in Neil Bissoondath's "There Are a Lot of Ways to Die") against the assumptions in his homeland. Or, alternatively, defend the values of Joseph's wife and show how Joseph's values deviate from them.

Student Writing

CARTER REVARD'S "DISCOVERY"

Jennifer Johns

One of the most disgraceful episodes in American history was the removal of Native Americans from their land in the West during the nineteenth century. According to Francis Jennings, "It is an old and shameful wound, still open, a story largely fabled in the popular mind and seldom taught honestly in American schools, a history of murder and cultural suppression and displacement from native lands" (30). It is this reprehensible action that is the focus of Carter Revard's poem, "Discovery of the New World." Revard was born in 1931 to an Osage father and a white mother. He earned degrees from the University of Tulsa and Oxford, and received his doctorate at Yale (Dodge and McCullough, 136–137). His poem appears to be simply about the conflict between creatures from two different worlds; however, as Jerome Beaty and J. Paul Hunter write, "The strangers in the poem . . . are almost literally men from Mars, but despite their green skins, scarlet eyes, and antennae, they are revealed to be uncomfortably like certain humans" (649). It is this revelation that makes Revard's poem so startling. In Carter Revard's poem, "Discovery of the New World," the treatment of humans by martians is ironically similar to the treatment of Native Americans by white settlers in the late nineteenth century.

Throughout the poem, images occur which suggest similarities between the plights of humans and Native Americans. The martians think they are superior beings who have the right to take humans as "food and prey and slaves" (line 7), just as settlers felt they had the right to possess Native American land. According to *The National Experience*, in the 1850s, a mass westward migration occurred and politicians demanded that Native Americans move aside to clear the way for settlement (Blum et al, 398). The Native Americans were not regarded as important, and there was some question as to whether they were actually human. Revard's use of the word "legends" (line 21) is a reminder of Native American legends and traditions which have never been taken seriously by the white man. Revard reveals something about human nature when he writes these crucial lines:

the blue shift bleached away
meaningless circumstance and they would not fit
any of our truth-matrices— . . . . (lines 25–27)

Revard is saying that humans have a way of justifying their action by claiming it was the best they could do under the circumstances. When one looks
at their actions alone, it appears that humans are not as morally upright as
they would like to believe.

The "curious visual echo" (line 29) that the martians see is the biggest   3
clue to the poem's irony. The mention of "a certain General Sherman" (line
31) brings to mind the Indian wars. The fact that the martians compare their
actions to those of General Sherman illustrates their own cruelty. Sherman's
ruthlessness is exemplified in the following speech:

> I will urge General Sheridan to push his measures for the utter destruction
> and subjugation of all who are outside the reservations in a hostile attitude.
> . . . I propose that he shall prosecute the war with vindictive earnestness
> against all hostile Indians, till they are obliterated or beg for mercy. (quoted
> in Blum et al., 400)

The next lines of the poem echo Sherman's words in a similarly blunt way.
The martians say,

it is our destiny to asterize this planet,
and they will not be asterized,
so they must be wiped out. (lines 35–37)

The settlers felt the same way towards Native Americans, based on Blum's
account of the wars of "extermination," which lasted from 1869 through 1874
(400). The martians have a habit of going back on their promises, much like
the white man's broken treaties. President Rutherford B. Hayes once said,
" 'Many, if not most, of our Indian wars have had their origin in broken
promises and acts of injustice on our part' " (quoted in Tindall, 766). Sarcastically, Chief Spotted Tail commented about the white man's lack of honor:
" 'Tell your people that since the Great Father promised that we should
never be removed, we have been moved five times. . . . I think you had
better put the Indians on wheels and you can run them about wherever you
wish" (quoted in Rosenstiel, 139). Though the Native Americans were not
completely blameless, their treatment was unjustified and barbaric.

The actions of the United States government were carried out in the   4
same detached, heartless way as the actions of the martians in the poem. The
following lines seem to be an exact account of the treatment of Native Americans:

We've finished burning all their crops
and killed their cattle.
They'll have to come into our pens
and then we'll get to study
the way our heart attacks and cancers spread among them,
since they seem not immune to these. (lines 46–51)

Revard's references are confirmed by Kenneth Lincoln, who writes that the government, from 1881 to 1883, employed marksmen to slaughter the remaining two and a half million buffalo. These animals were the "life-support" of the plains tribes. The migrations of the Indians that followed the game were disrupted forever. Soldiers forced the survivors onto barren reservations, issued a dress of coat and trousers, and tried to civilize them. The Secretary of the Interior commented in 1872 on killing the buffalo to starve the Indians onto reservations (20). Amazingly, the martians believe they have a "mission" (line 52) to destroy the human way of life. White people were blinded in the same way by their own Christian beliefs. They felt it was their duty to civilize the Indians. The cruelty of these martians seems incomprehensible, but they rationalize it by saying, "the riches of this place are . . . / . . . worth whatever pain others may have to feel" (lines 55–56). The attitude of the settlers toward Native Americans was barbaric, and very much the same as the attitude of these creatures. According to George Brown Tindall, the West was called the "Great American Desert," unfit for habitation. For this reason it was the perfect refuge for the Indians. This kind of thinking changed in the latter part of the nineteenth century when gold, silver, and other minerals were discovered (756–757). Greed was a good reason for whites to take land away from the Native Americans. The martians commit their acts of aggression because they "need their space and oxygen / which they do not know how to use" (lines 38–39).

The last line sums up the irony of Revard's poem. There is no doubt settlers believed that once they eliminated the Indian problem, they would live in peace and contentment. In the poem, this peace is disrupted by invaders who also believe they "will be safe, and rich, and happy here forever" (line 59). If there is a sequel to "Discovery of the New World," it might include another invasion, with the martians as the victims. The last line is a premonition, or even a warning. Revard seems to be mocking the false sense of security the martians, like the settlers, have. 5

The similarities between the two conflicts make Carter Revard's "Discovery of the New World" ironic. White Americans, like the martians in the poem, have the mistaken belief that they are untouchable and superior to others. Jennings expresses this idea: 6

The American land was more like a widow than a virgin. Europeans did not find a wilderness here; rather, however involuntarily, they made one. . . . The so-called settlement of America was a resettlement, a reoccupation of a land made waste by the diseases and demoralization introduced by the new-comers. (30)

It is this belief that led to the slaughter of humans in the poem and, more importantly, Native Americans in the late 1800s. According to Blum, the most sickening incident of the Indian wars was the so called "Battle" of Wounded Knee in 1890, in which United States troops "mowed down" two hundred Dakota men, women, and children (401). It is this kind of outrage that Revard does not want to be forgotten. More importantly, he is awakening our minds to the reality that this kind of violence is an endless cycle that occurs today, and will continue tomorrow.

WORKS CITED

Beaty, Jerome and J. Paul Hunter, eds. *New Worlds of Literature*. New York: W. W. Norton & Company, 1989.

Blum, John M., et al. *The National Experience: A History of the United States Since 1865*. San Diego: Harcourt Brace Jovanovich, 1989.

Dodge, Robert K. and Joseph B. McCullough. *New and Old Voices of Wah-Kon-Tah*. New York: International Publishers Incorporated, 1985.

Jennings, Francis. *The Invasion of America: Indians, Colonialism, and the Cant of Conquest*. Chapel Hill: University of North Carolina Press, 1975.

Lincoln, Kenneth. *Native American Renaissance*. Los Angeles: The Regents of the University of California, 1983.

Revard, Carter. "Discovery of the New World." *New Worlds of Literature*. Ed. Jerome Beaty and J. Paul Hunter. New York: W. W. Norton & Company, 1989. 649–650.

Rosenstiel, Annette. *Red and White: Indian Views of the White Man: 1492–1982*. New York: Universe Books, 1983.

Tindall, George Brown. *America: A Narrative History*. New York: W. W. Norton & Company, 1988.

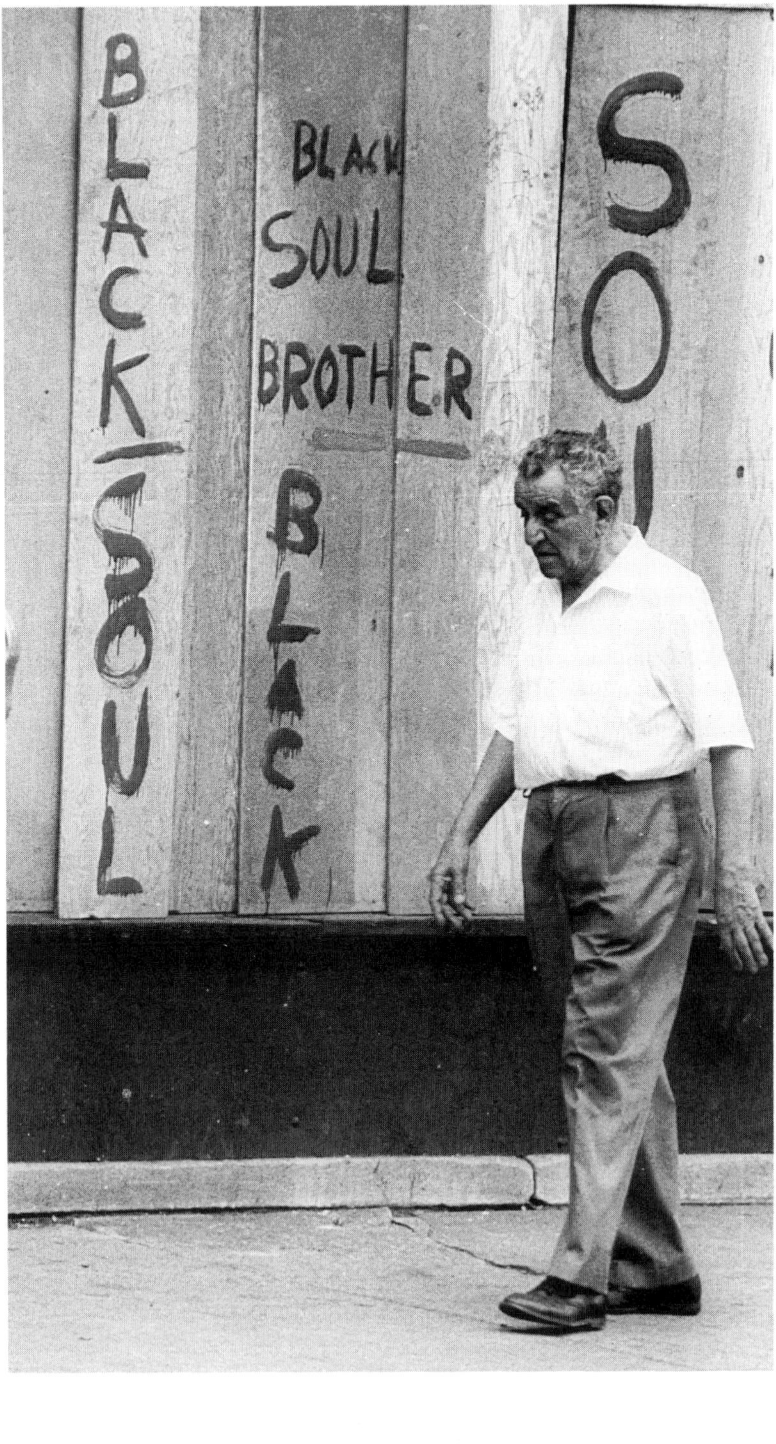
BLACK
SOUL
BLACK
SOUL
BROTHER
BLACK
SO

6

FENCES

"Good fences make good neighbors," a crusty old New England character says in one of Robert Frost's poems, reflecting a common sense of keeping things straight and insisting on distances between people so that they don't become confused about boundaries. Fences mark things—private yards from public sidewalks, pastures from fields, my property from yours—and the marking may feel good or ill depending on how satisfied we are with our own property and place or how desirous of exploring or conquering other worlds. But once fences are constructed, it is hard to pull them down, for even if they are only symbolic objects, they create difference as well as mark it.

The "fences" we construct to separate our own kind from others, even though mainly intended to keep out strangers or someone different from ourselves, also hold us in. Feelings of being confined, cut off, fenced in, are often felt especially strongly by those of us who want adventure, novelty, new experience. Families, ethnic groups, nationality groups, tribes, social and religious groups, gangs, fraternities and sororities, neighborhood groups, political parties, our "circles" of friends—all build fences around themselves both to keep others out and to keep "members" in. Often these fences are constructed for laudable motives of identity or loyalty, but sometimes they end up seeming, even to the people they are meant to benefit with security and identity, horribly confining and limiting.

Fences—literal fences—do not actually prevent the crossing of borders.

Hunters can climb over fences, and predatory beasts get over, under, or through. Cattle find holes or sometimes knock down the fence. Fences intimidate more than they actually repel or contain. The function of a fence is to mark the border and discourage crossing it. It is a sign to outsiders not to enter, an impediment to invaders, a restraint upon insiders, a reminder to anyone who tends to ignore borders or resist control. It is not a wall, a bar, an absolute barrier. A fence *articulates* difference, insists on the recognition between us and them, mine and yours, what is "in" and what is "out": it draws a line.

The risk in crossing a fence is always substantial, perhaps the more so when fences are social and metaphoric rather than physical and actual. The outsider who dares to marry into a family or ethnic group that has fenced out outsiders takes a very large risk. So does an insider who dares to leave the farm or village to try life in a big city or a foreign country. But history is full of individuals who have dared to challenge barriers and cross lines, sometimes because they were courageous and heroic, sometimes because they were just headstrong and foolish. The selections in chapter 6 will explore what happens when people cross fences.

The poems, stories, essays, and play in this chapter sometimes celebrate barriers as providing protection and definition; sometimes they denounce them as authoritarian and constricting. Mainly, though, they explore the reasons that we construct barriers, whether to keep our "own kind" in or the "other kind" out. The human conflicts described here are considerable, and the difficulties run deep. Every human step out of an ordinary path challenges, in one way or another, the limits of all established paths and patterns, and if such challenges represent necessary human growth, they also represent the crucial battlegrounds of human history.

Toni Morrison

B orn in 1931, Toni Morrison grew up in Lorrain, Ohio, and was educated at Howard and Cornell universities. For many years, she was an editor at Random House; she taught at Howard and Texas Southern universities, held the prestigious Albert Schweitzer Chair at the State University of New York, Albany, and now teaches at Princeton University. Her novels include *The Bluest Eye* (1969), *Sula* (1973), *Song of Solomon* (1977), *Tar Baby* (1981), *Beloved* (1988), for which she was awarded the Pulitzer Prize, and *Jazz* (1992). She won the Nobel Prize for Literature in 1993.

"RECITATIF"

My mother danced all night and Roberta's was sick. That's why we were taken to St. Bonny's. People want to put their arms around you when you tell them you were in a shelter, but it really wasn't bad. No big long room with one hundred beds like Bellevue. There were four to a room, and when Roberta and me came, there was a shortage of state kids, so we were the only ones assigned to 406 and could go from bed to bed if we wanted to. And we wanted to, too. We changed beds every night and for the whole four months we were there we never picked one out as our own permanent bed.

It didn't start out that way. The minute I walked in and the Big Bozo introduced us, I got sick to my stomach. It was one thing to be taken out of your own bed early in the morning—it was something else to be stuck in a strange place with a girl from a whole other race. And Mary, that's my mother, she was right. Every now and then she would stop dancing long enough to tell me something important and one of the things she said was that they never washed their hair and they smelled funny. Roberta sure did. Smell funny, I mean. So when the Big Bozo (nobody ever called her Mrs. Itkin, just like nobody ever said St. Bonaventure)—when she said "Twyla, this is Roberta. Roberta, this is Twyla. Make each other welcome." I said, "My mother won't like you putting me in here."

"Good," said Bozo. "Maybe then she'll come and take you home."

How's that for mean? If Roberta had laughed I would have killed her, but she didn't. She just walked over to the window and stood with her back to us.

"Turn around," said the Bozo. "Don't be rude. Now Twyla. Roberta. ⁵
When you hear a loud buzzer, that's the call for dinner. Come down to the
first floor. Any fights and no movie." And then, just to make sure we knew
what we would be missing, *"The Wizard of Oz."*

Roberta must have thought I meant that my mother would be mad about ⁶
my being put in the shelter. Not about rooming with her, because as soon as
Bozo left she came over to me and said, "Is your mother sick too?"

"No," I said. "She just likes to dance all night." ⁷

"Oh," she nodded her head and I liked the way she understood things ⁸
so fast. So for the moment it didn't matter that we looked like salt and pepper
standing there and that's what the other kids called us sometimes. We were
eight years old and got F's all the time. Me because I couldn't remember
what I read or what the teacher said. And Roberta because she couldn't read
at all and didn't even listen to the teacher. She wasn't good at anything except
jacks, at which she was a killer: pow scoop pow scoop pow scoop.

We didn't like each other all that much at first, but nobody else wanted ⁹
to play with us because we weren't real orphans with beautiful dead parents
in the sky. We were dumped. Even the New York City Puerto Ricans and
the upstate Indians ignored us. All kinds of kids were in there, black ones,
white ones, even two Koreans. The food was good, though. At least I thought
so. Roberta hated it and left whole pieces of things on her plate: Spam, Sal-
isbury steak—even jello with fruit cocktail in it, and she didn't care if I ate
what she wouldn't. Mary's idea of supper was popcorn and a can of Yoo-
Hoo. Hot mashed potatoes and two weenies was like Thanksgiving for me.

It really wasn't bad, St. Bonny's. The big girls on the second floor pushed ¹⁰
us around now and then. But that was all. They wore lipstick and eyebrow
pencil and wobbled their knees while they watched TV. Fifteen, sixteen,
even, some of them were. They were put-out girls, scared runaways most of
them. Poor little girls who fought their uncles off but looked tough to us,
and mean. God did they look mean. The staff tried to keep them separate
from the younger children, but sometimes they caught us watching them in
the orchard where they played radios and danced with each other. They'd
light out after us and pull our hair or twist our arms. We were scared of
them, Roberta and me, but neither of us wanted the other one to know it.
So we got a good list of dirty names we could shout back when we ran from
them through the orchard. I used to dream a lot and almost always the orchard
was there. Two acres, four maybe, of these little apple trees. Hundreds of
them. Empty and crooked like beggar women when I first came to St. Bonny's but fat with flowers when I left. I don't know why I dreamt about that
orchard so much. Nothing really happened there. Nothing all that important, I mean. Just the big girls dancing and playing the radio. Roberta and
me watching. Maggie fell down there once. The kitchen woman with legs
like parentheses. And the big girls laughed at her. We should have helped
her up, I know, but we were scared of those girls with lipstick and eyebrow
pencil. Maggie couldn't talk. The kids said she had her tongue cut out, but I

think she was just born that way: mute. She was old and sandy-colored and she worked in the kitchen. I don't know if she was nice or not. I just remember her legs like parentheses and how she rocked when she walked. She worked from early in the morning till two o'clock, and if she was late, if she had too much cleaning and didn't get out till two-fifteen or so, she'd cut through the orchard so she wouldn't miss her bus and have to wait another hour. She wore this really stupid little hat—a kid's hat with ear flaps—and she wasn't much taller than we were. A really awful little hat. Even for a mute, it was dumb—dressing like a kid and never saying anything at all.

"But what about if somebody tries to kill her?" I used to wonder about that. "Or what if she wants to cry? Can she cry?"   11

"Sure," Roberta said. "But just tears. No sounds come out."   12

"She can't scream?"   13

"Nope. Nothing."   14

"Can she hear?"   15

"I guess."   16

"Let's call her," I said. And we did.   17

"Dummy! Dummy!" She never turned her head.   18

"Bow legs! Bow legs!" Nothing. She just rocked on, the chin straps of   19
her baby-boy hat swaying from side to side. I think we were wrong. I think she could hear and didn't let on. And it shames me even to think there was somebody in there after all who heard us call her those names and couldn't tell on us.

We got along all right, Roberta and me. Changed beds every night, got   20
F's in civics and communication skills and gym. The Bozo was disappointed in us, she said. Out of 130 of us state cases, 90 were under twelve. Almost all were real orphans with beautiful dead parents in the sky. We were the only ones dumped and the only ones with F's in three classes including gym. So we got along—what with her leaving whole pieces of things on her plate and being nice about not asking questions.

I think it was the day before Maggie fell down that we found out our   21
mothers were coming to visit us on the same Sunday. We had been at the shelter twenty-eight days (Roberta twenty-eight and a half) and this was their first visit with us. Our mothers would come at ten o'clock in time for chapel, then lunch with us in the teachers' lounge. I thought if my dancing mother met her sick mother it might be good for her. And Roberta thought her sick mother would get a big bang out of a dancing one. We got excited about it and curled each other's hair. After breakfast we sat on the bed watching the road from the window. Roberta's socks were still wet. She washed them the night before and put them on the radiator to dry. They hadn't, but she put them on anyway because their tops were so pretty—scalloped in pink. Each of us had a purple construction-paper basket that we had made in craft class. Mine had a yellow crayon rabbit on it. Roberta's had eggs with wiggly lines of color. Inside were cellophane grass and just the jelly beans because I'd eaten the two marshmallow eggs they gave us. The Big Bozo

came herself to get us. Smiling she told us we looked very nice and to come downstairs. We were so surprised by the smile we'd never seen before, neither of us moved.

"Don't you want to see your mommies?" 22

I stood up first and spilled the jelly beans all over the floor. Bozo's smile 23 disappeared while we scrambled to get the candy up off the floor and put it back in the grass.

She escorted us downstairs to the first floor, where the other girls were 24 lining up to file into the chapel. A bunch of grownups stood to one side. Viewers mostly. The old biddies who wanted servants and the fags who wanted company looking for children they might want to adopt. Once in a while a grandmother. Almost never anybody young or anybody whose face wouldn't scare you in the night. Because if any of the real orphans had young relatives they wouldn't be real orphans. I saw Mary right away. She had on those green slacks I hated and hated even more now because didn't she know we were going to chapel? And that fur jacket with the pocket linings so ripped she had to pull to get her hands out of them. But her face was pretty—like always, and she smiled and waved like she was the little girl looking for her mother—not me.

I walked slowly, trying not to drop the jelly beans and hoping the paper 25 handle would hold. I had to use my last Chiclet because by the time I finished cutting everything out, all the Elmer's was gone. I am left-handed and the scissors never worked for me. It didn't matter, though; I might just as well have chewed the gum. Mary dropped to her knees and grabbed me, mashing the basket, the jelly beans, and the grass into her ratty fur jacket.

"Twyla, baby. Twyla, baby!" 26

I could have killed her. Already I heard the big girls in the orchard the 27 next time saying, "Twyyyyyla, baby!" But I couldn't stay mad at Mary while she was smiling and hugging me and smelling of Lady Esther dusting powder. I wanted to stay buried in her fur all day.

To tell the truth I forgot about Roberta. Mary and I got in line for the 28 traipse into chapel and I was feeling proud because she looked so beautiful even in those ugly green slacks that made her behind stick out. A pretty mother on earth is better than a beautiful dead one in the sky even if she did leave you all alone to go dancing.

I felt a tap on my shoulder, turned, and saw Roberta smiling. I smiled 29 back, but not too much lest somebody think this visit was the biggest thing that ever happened in my life. Then Roberta said, "Mother, I want you to meet my roommate, Twyla. And that's Twyla's mother."

I looked up it seemed for miles. She was big. Bigger than any man and 30 on her chest was the biggest cross I'd ever seen. I swear it was six inches long each way. And in the crook of her arm was the biggest Bible ever made.

Mary, simple-minded as ever, grinned and tried to yank her hand out 31 of the pocket with the raggedy lining—to shake hands, I guess. Roberta's mother looked down at me and then looked down at Mary too. She didn't say anything, just grabbed Roberta with her Bible-free hand and stepped out of line, walking quickly to the rear of it. Mary was still grinning because she's not too swift when it comes to what's really going on. Then this light bulb goes off in her head and she says "That bitch!" really loud and us almost in the chapel now. Organ music whining; the Bonny Angels singing sweetly. Everybody in the world turned around to look. And Mary would have kept it up—kept calling names if I hadn't squeezed her hand as hard as I could. That helped a little, but she still twitched and crossed and uncrossed her legs all through service. Even groaned a couple of times. Why did I think she would come there and act right? Slacks. No hat like the grandmothers and viewers, and groaning all the while. When we stood for hymns she kept her mouth shut. Wouldn't even look at the words on the page. She actually reached in her purse for a mirror to check her lipstick. All I could think of was that she really needed to be killed. The sermon lasted a year, and I knew the real orphans were looking smug again.

We were supposed to have lunch in the teachers' lounge, but Mary didn't bring anything, so we picked fur and cellophane grass off the mashed jelly beans and ate them. I could have killed her. I sneaked a look at Roberta. Her mother had brought chicken legs and ham sandwiches and oranges and a whole box of chocolate-covered grahams. Roberta drank milk from a thermos while her mother read the Bible to her. 32

Things are not right. The wrong food is always with the wrong people. Maybe that's why I got into waitress work later—to match up the right people with the right food. Roberta just let those chicken legs sit there, but she did bring a stack of grahams up to me later when the visit was over. I think she was sorry that her mother would not shake my mother's hand. And I liked that and I liked the fact that she didn't say a word about Mary groaning all the way through the service and not bringing any lunch. 33

Roberta left in May when the apple trees were heavy and white. On her last day we went to the orchard to watch the big girls smoke and dance by the radio. It didn't matter that they said "Twyyyyyla, baby." We sat on the ground and breathed. Lady Esther. Apple blossoms. I still go soft when I smell one or the other. Roberta was going home. The big cross and the big Bible was coming to get her and she seemed sort of glad and sort of not. I thought I would die in that room of four beds without her and I knew Bozo had plans to move some other dumped kid in there with me. Roberta promised to write every day, which was really sweet of her because she couldn't read a lick so how could she write anybody. I would have drawn pictures and sent them to her but she never gave me her address. Little by little she faded. Her wet socks with the pink scalloped tops and her big serious-looking eyes—that's all I could catch when I tried to bring her to mind. 34

I was working behind the counter at the Howard Johnson's on the Thruway just before the Kingston exit. Not a bad job. Kind of a long ride from Newburgh, but okay once I got there. Mine was the second night shift—eleven to seven. Very light until a Greyhound checked in for breakfast around 35 six-thirty. At that hour the sun was all the way clear of the hills behind the restaurant. The place looked better at night—more like shelter—but I loved it when the sun broke in, even if it did show all the cracks in the vinyl and the speckled floor looked dirty no matter what the mop boy did.

It was August and a bus crowd was just unloading. They would stand around a long while: going to the john, and looking at gifts and junk-for-sale machines, reluctant to sit down so soon. Even to eat. I was trying to fill the coffee pots and get them all situated on the electric burners when I saw her. She was sitting in a booth smoking a cigarette with two guys smothered in head and facial hair. Her own hair was so big and wild I could hardly see her face. But the eyes. I would know them anywhere. She had on a powder-blue halter and shorts outfit and earrings the size of bracelets. Talk about lipstick and eyebrow pencil. She made the big girls look like nuns. I couldn't get off the counter until seven o'clock, but I kept watching the booth in case they got up to leave before that. My replacement was on time for a change, so I counted and stacked my receipts as fast as I could and signed off. I walked over to the booth, smiling and wondering if she would remember me. Or even if she wanted to remember me. Maybe she didn't want to be reminded of St. Bonny's or to have anybody know she was ever there. I know I never talked about it to anybody.

I put my hands in my apron pockets and leaned against the back of the booth facing them.

"Roberta? Roberta Fisk?"

She looked up. "Yeah?"

"Twyla."

She squinted for a second and then said, "Wow."

"Remember me?"

"Sure. Hey. Wow."

"It's been a while," I said, and gave a smile to the two hairy guys.

"Yeah. Wow. You work here?"

"Yeah," I said. "I live in Newburgh."

"Newburgh? No kidding?" She laughed then a private laugh that included the guys but only the guys, and they laughed with her. What could I do but laugh too and wonder why I was standing there with my knees showing out from under that uniform. Without looking I could see the blue and white triangle on my head, my hair shapeless in a net, my ankles thick in white oxfords. Nothing could have been less sheer than my stockings. There was this silence that came down right after I laughed. A silence it was her turn to fill up. With introductions, maybe, to her boyfriends or an invitation to sit down and have a Coke. Instead she lit a cigarette off the one she'd just finished and said. "We're on our way to the Coast. He's got an appointment with Hendrix." She gestured casually toward the boy next to her.

"Hendrix? Fantastic," I said. "Really fantastic. What's she doing now?"

Roberta coughed on her cigarette and the two guys rolled their eyes up at the ceiling.

"Hendrix. Jimi Hendrix, asshole. He's only the biggest—Oh, wow. Forget it." 50

I was dismissed without anyone saying goodbye, so I thought I would do it for her. 51

"How's your mother?" I asked. Her grin cracked her whole face. She swallowed. "Fine," she said. "How's yours?" 52

"Pretty as a picture," I said and turned away. The backs of my knees were damp. Howard Johnson's really was a dump in the sunlight. 53

James is as comfortable as a house slipper. He liked my cooking and I liked his big loud family. They have lived in Newburgh all of their lives and talk about it the way people do who have always known a home. His grandmother has a porch swing older than his father and when they talk about streets and avenues and buildings they call them names they no longer have. They still call the A & P Rico's because it stands on property once a mom and pop store owned by Mr. Rico. And they call the new community college Town Hall because it once was. My mother-in-law puts up jelly and cucumbers and buys butter wrapped in cloth from a dairy. James and his father talk about fishing and baseball and I can see them all together on the Hudson in a raggedy skiff. Half the population of Newburgh is on welfare now, but to my husband's family it was still some upstate paradise of a time long past. A time of ice houses and vegetable wagons, coal furnaces and children weeding gardens. When our son was born my mother-in-law gave me the crib blanket that had been hers. 54

But the town they remembered had changed. Something quick was in the air. Magnificent old houses, so ruined they had become shelter for squatters and rent risks, were bought and renovated. Smart IBM people moved out of their suburbs back into the city and put shutters up and herb gardens in their backyards. A brochure came in the mail announcing the opening of a Food Emporium. Gourmet food it said—and listed items the rich IBM crowd would want. It was located in a new mall at the edge of town and I drove out to shop there one day—just to see. It was late in June. After the tulips were gone and the Queen Elizabeth roses were open everywhere. I trailed my cart along the aisle tossing in smoked oysters and Robert's sauce and things I knew would sit in my cupboard for years. Only when I found some Klondike ice cream bars did I feel less guilty about spending James's fireman's salary so foolishly. My father-in-law ate them with the same gusto little Joseph did. 55

Waiting in the check-out line I heard a voice say, "Twyla!" 56

The classical music piped over the aisles had affected me and the woman leaning toward me was dressed to kill. Diamonds on her hand, a smart white summer dress. "I'm Mrs. Benson," I said. 57

"Ho. Ho. The Big Bozo," she said. 58

For a split second I didn't know what she was talking about. She had a bunch of asparagus and two cartons of fancy water. 59

"Roberta!"   60

"Right."   61

"For heaven's sake. Roberta."   62

"You look great," she said.   63

"So do you. Where are you? Here? In Newburgh?"   64

"Yes. Over in Annandale."   65

I was opening my mouth to say more when the cashier called my atten-   66
tion to her empty counter.

"Meet you outside." Roberta pointed her finger and went into the express   67
line.

I placed the groceries and kept myself from glancing around to check   68
Roberta's progress. I remembered Howard Johnson's and looking for a chance
to speak only to be greeted with a stingy "wow." But she was waiting for me
and her huge hair was sleek now, smooth around a small, nicely shaped head.
Shoes, dress, everything lovely and summery and rich. I was dying to know
what happened to her, how she got from Jimi Hendrix to Annandale, a
neighborhood full of doctors and IBM executives. Easy, I thought. Everything is so easy for them. They think they own the world.

"How long," I asked her. "How long have you been here?"   69

"A year. I got married to a man who lives here. And you, you're married   70
too, right? Benson, you said."

"Yeah. James Benson."   71

"And is he nice?"   72

"Oh, is he nice?"   73

"Well, is he?" Roberta's eyes were steady as though she really meant the   74
question and wanted an answer.

"He's wonderful, Roberta. Wonderful."   75

"So you're happy."   76

"Very."   77

"That's good," she said and nodded her head. "I always hoped you'd be   78
happy. Any kids? I know you have kids."

"One. A boy. How about you?"   79

"Four."   80

"Four?"   81

She laughed. "Step kids. He's a widower."   82

"Oh."   83

"Got a minute? Let's have a coffee."   84

I thought about the Klondikes melting and the inconvenience of going   85
all the way to my car and putting the bags in the trunk. Served me right for
buying all that stuff I didn't need. Roberta was ahead of me.

"Put them in my car. Its right here."   86

And then I saw the dark blue limousine.   87

"You married a Chinaman?"   88

"No," she laughed. "He's the driver."   89

"Oh, my. If the Big Bozo could see you now." 90

We both giggled. Really giggled. Suddenly, in just a pulse beat, twenty 91
years disappeared and all of it came rushing back. The big girls (whom we
called gar girls—Roberta's misheard word for the evil stone faces described
in a civics class) there dancing in the orchard, the ploppy mashed potatoes,
the double weenies, the Spam with pineapple. We went into the coffee shop
holding on to one another and I tried to think why we were glad to see each
other this time and not before. Once, twelve years ago, we passed like strangers.
A black girl and a white girl meeting in a Howard Johnson's on the road and
having nothing to say. One in a blue and white triangle waitress hat—the
other on her way to see Hendrix. Now we were behaving like sisters separated for much too long. Those four short months were nothing in time.
Maybe it was the thing itself. Just being there, together. Two little girls who
knew what nobody else in the world knew—how not to ask questions. How
to believe what had to be believed. There was politeness in that reluctance
and generosity as well. Is your mother sick too? No, she dances all night.
Oh—and an understanding nod.

We sat in a booth by the window and fell into recollection like veterans. 92

"Did you ever learn to read?" 93

"Watch." She picked up the menu. "Special of the day. Cream of corn 94
soup. Entrées. Two dots and a wriggly line. Quiche. Chef salad, scal-
lops . . ."

I was laughing and applauding when the waitress came up. 95

"Remember the Easter baskets?" 96

"And how we tried to *introduce* them?" 97

"Your mother with that cross like two telephone poles." 98

"And yours with those tight slacks." 99

We laughed so loudly heads turned and made the laughter hard to sup- 100
press.

"What happened to the Jimi Hendrix date?" 101

Roberta made a blow-out sound with her lips. 102

"When he died I thought about you." 103

"Oh, you heard about him finally?" 104

"Finally. Come on, I was a small-town country waitress." 105

"And I was a small-town country dropout. God, were we wild. I still 106
don't know how I got out of there alive."

"But you did." 107

"I did. I really did. Now I'm Mrs. Kenneth Norton." 108

"Sounds like a mouthful." 109

"It is." 110

"Servants and all?" 111

Roberta held up two fingers. 112

"Ow! What does he do?" 113

"Computers and stuff. What do I know?" 114

"I don't remember a hell of a lot from those days, but Lord, St. Bonny's   115
is as clear as daylight. Remember Maggie? The day she fell down and those
gar girls laughed at her?"

Roberta looked up from her salad and stared at me. "Maggie didn't fall,"   116
she said.

"Yes, she did. You remember."   117

"No, Twyla. They knocked her down. Those girls pushed her down   118
and tore her clothes. In the orchard."

"I don't—that's not what happened."   119

"Sure it is. In the orchard. Remember how scared we were?"   120

"Wait a minute. I don't remember any of that."   121

"And Bozo was fired."   122

"You're crazy. She was there when I left. You left before me."   123

"I went back. You weren't there when they fired Bozo."   124

"What?"   125

"Twice. Once for a year when I was about ten, another for two months   126
when I was fourteen. That's when I ran away."

"You ran away from St. Bonny's?"   127

"I had to. What do you want? Me dancing in that orchard?"   128

"Are you sure about Maggie?"   129

"Of course I'm sure. You've blocked it, Twyla. It happened. Those girls   130
had behavior problems, you know."

"Didn't they, though. But why can't I remember the Maggie thing?"   131

"Believe me. It happened. And we were there."   132

"Who did you room with when you went back?" I asked her as if I   133
would know her. The Maggie thing was troubling me.

"Creeps. They tickled themselves in the night."   134

My ears were itching and I wanted to go home suddenly. This was all   135
very well but she couldn't just comb her hair, wash her face and pretend
everything was hunky-dory. After the Howard Johnson's snub. And no
apology. Nothing.

"Were you on dope or what that time at Howard Johnson's?" I tried to   136
make my voice sound friendlier than I felt.

"Maybe, a little. I never did drugs much. Why?"   137

"I don't know, you acted sort of like you didn't want to know me then."   138

"Oh, Twyla, you know how it was in those days: black—white. You   139
know how everything was."

But I didn't know. I thought it was just the opposite. Busloads of blacks   140
and whites came into Howard Johnson's together. They roamed together
then: students, musicians, lovers, protesters. You got to see everything at
Howard Johnson's and blacks were very friendly with whites in those days.
But sitting there with nothing on my plate but two hard tomato wedges
wondering about the melting Klondikes it seemed childish remembering the
slight. We went to her car, and with the help of the driver, got my stuff into
my station wagon.

"We'll keep in touch this time," she said.   141

"Sure," I said. "Sure. Give me a call."   142

"I will," she said, and then just as I was sliding behind the wheel, she   143
leaned into the window. "By the way. Your mother. Did she ever stop dancing?"

I shook my head. "No. Never."   144

Roberta nodded.   145

"And yours? Did she ever get well?"   146

She smiled a tiny sad smile. "No. She never did. Look, call me, okay?"   147

"Okay," I said, but I knew I wouldn't. Roberta had messed up my past   148
somehow with that business about Maggie. I wouldn't forget a thing like
that. Would I?

Strife came to us that fall. At least that's what the paper called it. Strife.   149
Racial strife. The word made me think of a bird—a big shrieking bird out of
1,000,000,000 B.C. Flapping its wings and cawing. Its eye with no lid always
bearing down on you. All day it screeched and at night it slept on the roof-
tops. It woke you in the morning and from the *Today* show to the eleven
o'clock news it kept you an awful company. I couldn't figure it out from one
day to the next. I knew I was supposed to feel something strong, but I didn't
know what, and James wasn't any help. Joseph was on the list of kids to be
transferred from the junior high school to another one at some far-out-of-the-
way place and I thought it was a good thing until I heard it was a bad thing.
I mean I didn't know. All the schools seemed dumps to me, and the fact that
one was nicer looking didn't hold much weight. But the papers were full of
it and then the kids began to get jumpy. In August, mind you. Schools
weren't even open yet. I thought Joseph might be frightened to go over there,
but he didn't seem scared so I forgot about it, until I found myself driving
along Hudson Street out there by the school they were trying to integrate
and saw a line of women marching. And who do you suppose was in line,
big as life, holding a sign in front of her bigger than her mother's cross?
MOTHERS HAVE RIGHTS TOO! it said.

I drove on, and then changed my mind. I circled the block, slowed   150
down, and honked my horn.

Roberta looked over and when she saw me she waved. I didn't wave   151
back, but I didn't move either. She handed her sign to another woman and
came over to where I was parked.

"Hi."   152

"What are you doing?"   153

"Picketing. What's it look like?"   154

"What for?"   155

"What do you mean, 'What for?' They want to take my kids and send   156
them out of the neighborhood. They don't want to go."

"So what if they go to another school? My boy's being bussed too, and   157
I don't mind. Why should you?"

"It's not about us, Twyla. Me and you. It's about our kids."   158

"What's more *us* than that?"   159

"Well, it is a free country."   160

"Not yet, but it will be."   161

"What the hell does that mean? I'm not doing anything to you."   162

"You really think that?"   163

"I know it."   164

"I wonder what made me think you were different."   165

"I wonder what made me think you were different."   166

"Look at them," I said. "Just look. Who do they think they are? Swarm-   167
ing all over the place like they own it. And now they think they can decide
where my child goes to school. Look at them, Roberta. They're Bozos."

Roberta turned around and looked at the women. Almost all of them   168
were standing still now, waiting. Some were even edging toward us. Roberta
looked at me out of some refrigerator behind her eyes. "No, they're not.
They're just mothers."

"And what am I? Swiss cheese?"   169

"I used to curl your hair."   170

"I hated your hands in my hair."   171

The women were moving. Our faces looked mean to them of course and   172
they looked as though they could not wait to throw themselves in front of a
police car, or better yet, into my car and drag me away by my ankles. Now
they surrounded my car and gently, gently began to rock it. I swayed back
and forth like a sideways yo-yo. Automatically I reached for Roberta, like
the old days in the orchard when they saw us watching them and we had to
get out of there, and if one of us fell the other pulled her up and if one of us
was caught the other stayed to kick and scratch, and neither would leave the
other behind. My arm shot out of the car window but no receiving hand was
there. Roberta was looking at me sway from side to side in the car and her
face was still. My purse slid from the car seat down under the dashboard.
The four policemen who had been drinking Tab in their car finally got the
message and strolled over, forcing their way through the women. Quietly,
firmly they spoke. "Okay, ladies. Back in line or off the streets."

Some of them went away willingly; others had to be urged away from   173
the car doors and the hood. Roberta didn't move. She was looking steadily
at me. I was fumbling to turn on the ignition, which wouldn't catch because
the gear shift was still in drive. The seats of the car were a mess because the
swaying had thrown my grocery coupons all over it and my purse was sprawled
on the floor.

"Maybe I am different now, Twyla. But you're not. You're the same   174
little state kid who kicked a poor old black lady when she was down on the
ground. You kicked a black lady and you have the nerve to call me a bigot."

The coupons were everywhere and the guts of my purse were bunched   175
under the dashboard. What was she saying? Black? Maggie wasn't black.

"She wasn't black," I said.   176

"Like hell she wasn't, and you kicked her. We both did. You kicked a black lady who couldn't even scream."   177

"Liar!"   178

"You're the liar! Why don't you just go on home and leave us alone, huh?"   179

She turned away and I skidded away from the curb.   180

The next morning I went into the garage and cut the side out of the carton our portable TV had come in. It wasn't nearly big enough, but after a while I had a decent sign: red spray-painted letters on a white background—AND SO DO CHILDREN****. I meant just to go down to the school and tack it up somewhere so those cows on the picket lines across the street could see it, but when I got there, some ten or so others had already assembled—protesting the cows across the street. Police permits and everything. I got in line and we strutted in time on our side while Roberta's group strutted on theirs. That first day we were all dignified, pretending the other side didn't exist. The second day there was name calling and finger gestures. But that was about all. People changed signs from time to time, but Roberta never did and neither did I. Actually my sign didn't make sense without Roberta's. "And so do children what?" one of the women on my side asked me. Have rights, I said, as though it was obvious.   181

Roberta didn't acknowlege my presence in any way and I got to thinking maybe she didn't know I was there. I began to pace myself in the line, jostling people one minute and lagging behind the next, so Roberta and I could reach the end of our respective lines at the same time and there would be a moment in our turn when we would face each other. Still, I couldn't tell whether she saw me and knew my sign was for her. The next day I went early before we were scheduled to assemble. I waited until she got there before I exposed my new creation. As soon as she hoisted her MOTHERS HAVE RIGHTS TOO I began to wave my new one, which said, HOW WOULD YOU KNOW? I know she saw that one, but I had gotten addicted now. My signs got crazier each day, and the women on my side decided that I was a kook. They couldn't make heads or tails out of my brilliant screaming posters.   182

I brought a painted sign in queenly red with huge black letters that said, IS YOUR MOTHER WELL? Roberta took her lunch break and didn't come back for the rest of the day or any day after. Two days later I stopped going too and couldn't have been missed because nobody understood my signs anyway.   183

It was a nasty six weeks. Classes were suspended and Joseph didn't go to anybody's school until October. The children—everybody's children—soon got bored with that extended vacation they thought was going to be so great. They looked at TV until their eyes flattened. I spent a couple of mornings tutoring my son, as the other mothers said we should. Twice I opened a text from last year that he had never turned in. Twice he yawned in my face. Other mothers organized living room sessions so the kids would keep up. None of the kids could concentrate so they drifted back to *The Price Is*   184

Right and *The Brady Bunch*. When the school finally opened there were fights once or twice and some sirens roared through the streets every once in a while. There were a lot of photographers from Albany. And just when ABC was about to send up a news crew, the kids settled down like nothing in the world had happened. Joseph hung my HOW WOULD YOU KNOW? sign in his bedroom. I don't know what became of AND SO DO CHILDREN****. I think my father-in-law cleaned some fish on it. He was always puttering around in our garage. Each of his five children lived in Newburgh and he acted as though he had five extra homes.

I couldn't help looking for Roberta when Joseph graduated from high school, but I didn't see her. It didn't trouble me much what she had said to me in the car. I mean the kicking part. I know I didn't do that, I couldn't do that. But I was puzzled by her telling me Maggie was black. When I thought about it I actually couldn't be certain. She wasn't pitch-black, I knew, or I would have remembered that. What I remember was the kiddie hat, and the semicircle legs. I tried to reassure myself about the race thing for a long time until it dawned on me that the truth was already there, and Roberta knew it. I didn't kick her; I didn't join in with the gar girls and kick that lady, but I sure did want to. We watched and never tried to help her and never called for help. Maggie was my dancing mother. Deaf, I thought, and dumb. Nobody inside. Nobody who would hear you if you cried in the night. Nobody who could tell you anything important that you could use. Rocking, dancing, swaying as she walked. And when the gar girls pushed her down, and started roughhousing, I knew she wouldn't scream, couldn't—just like me—and I was glad about that.

We decided not to have a tree, because Christmas would be at my mother-in-law's house, so why have a tree at both places? Joseph was at SUNY New Paltz and we had to economize, we said. But at the last minute, I changed my mind. Nothing could be that bad. So I rushed around town looking for a tree, something small but wide. By the time I found a place, it was snowing and very late. I dawdled like it was the most important purchase in the world and the tree man was fed up with me. Finally I chose one and had it tied onto the trunk of the car. I drove away slowly because the sand trucks were not out yet and the streets could be murder at the beginning of a snowfall. Downtown the streets were wide and rather empty except for a cluster of people coming out of the Newburgh Hotel. The one hotel in town that wasn't built out of cardboard and Plexiglas. A party, probably. The men huddled in the snow were dressed in tails and the women had on furs. Shiny things glittered from underneath their coats. It made me tired to look at them. Tired, tired, tired. On the next corner was a small diner with loops and loops of paper bells in the window. I stopped the car and went in. Just for a cup of coffee and twenty minutes of peace before I went home and tried to finish everything before Christmas Eve.

"Twyla?"

There was she. In a silvery evening gown and dark fur coat. A man and another woman were with her, the man fumbling for change to put in the cigarette machine. The woman was humming and tapping on the counter with her fingernails. They all looked a little bit drunk. 188

"Well. It's you." 189

"How are you?" 190

I shrugged. "Pretty good. Frazzled. Christmas and all." 191

"Regular?" called the woman from the counter. 192

"Fine," Roberta called back and then, "Wait for me in the car." 193

She slipped into the booth beside me. "I have to tell you something 194 Twyla. I made up my mind if I ever saw you again, I'd tell you."

"I'd just as soon not hear anything, Roberta. It doesn't matter now, 195 anyway."

"No," she said. "Not about that." 196

"Don't be long," said the woman. She carried two regulars to go and the 197 man peeled his cigarette pack as they left.

"It's about St. Bonny's and Maggie." 198

"Oh, please." 199

"Listen to me. I really did think she was black. I didn't make that up. I 200 really thought so. But now I can't be sure. I just remember her as old, so old. And because she couldn't talk—we, you know, I thought she was crazy. She'd been brought up in an institution like my mother was and like I thought I would be too. And you were right. We didn't kick her. It was the gar girls. Only them. But, well, I wanted to. I really wanted them to hurt her. I said we did it, too. You and me, but that's not true. And I don't want you to carry that around. It was just that I wanted to do it so bad that day—wanting to is doing it."

Her eyes were watery from the drinks she'd had, I guess. I know it's 201 that way with me. One glass of wine and I start bawling over the littlest thing.

"We were kids, Roberta." 202

"Yeah. Yeah. I know, just kids." 203

"Eight." 204

"Eight." 205

"And lonely." 206

"Scarced, too." 207

She wiped her cheeks with the heel of her hand and smiled. "Well, that's 208 all I wanted to say."

I nodded and couldn't think of any way to fill the silence that went from 209 the diner past the paper bells on out into the snow. It was heavy now. I thought I'd better wait for the sand trucks before starting home.

"Thanks, Roberta." 210

"Sure." 211

"Did I tell you? My mother, she never did stop dancing." 212

"Yes. You told me. And mine, she never got well." Roberta lifted her 213 hands from the tabletop and covered her face with her palms. When she took them away she really was crying. "Oh shit, Twyla. Shit, shit, shit. What the hell happened to Maggie?"

STUDY QUESTIONS

1. What does the title mean? Why is it in quotation marks? How does it relate to the story?

2. The two girls have four beds and change every night, never making a permanent claim to one bed. Why do you think that is? What does it suggest about their situation, their lives, their feelings?

3. In the second paragraph we learn that the two girls are of different races, and the SPEAKER* says her mother told her those others "never washed their hair and they smelled funny." Which race do we then assume is the speaker's and which the other girl's? When do you know which is which? Find several other instances, in which STEREOTYPES, one's perceptions of another group, are modified or reversed. How does this reversal relate to the narrative and thematic elements of the story?

4. The speaker several times refers to "beautiful dead parents in the sky" (paragraphs 6 and 17, for example). Does that expression seem consistent with Twyla's language and character? Where do you imagine it comes from? What does it suggest about Twyla's feelings about her mother?

5. What are the early signs in the story that racism will be a factor? How would you describe the relationship between the girls during their stay at the shelter? How would you describe the part racism does or does not play in what happens in their encounters in Howard Johnson's? later, in the Food Emporium? in the school integration picketing? in the diner near the Newburg Hotel? Are there any traces of racism in Twyla?

6. Deduce as best you can the dates of the action of the story. What evidence are you basing your deduction on? Would the events involving race and the attitudes toward race be different now? How much? How? What does your answer tell you about what you think of the "progress" or lack of it in race relations over the years? of prospects for the future? of the time periods involved in making attitudinal changes?

7. Compare the different versions of Maggie and the incident involving her throughout the story. What do you deduce is the "real" story? Is there a real story? What do the different versions say about memory? about the way our inner feelings during an incident affect how we remember what "actually" happened? How do the discrepancies affect the authority of the speaker? How does the Maggie episode relate to or modify the theme of racism? How does it relate to the girls' situations and their relations with their mothers? What is the effect of its being referred to so often in the story? What are the effects and implications of the story's ending with the question about Maggie?

*Words in small capitals are defined in the Glossary.

David Leavitt

D avid Leavitt is the author of three novels, *The Lost Language of Cranes* (1987), *Equal Affections* (1990), and *While England Sleeps* (1993), and two collections of short fiction, *Family Dancing* (1984) and *A Place I've Never Been* (1990). He was born in Pittsburgh in 1961 and attended Yale University. He has received a National Endowment for the Arts Grant and a Guggenheim Fellowship, and has been the writer-in-residence at the Institute of Catalan Letters in Barcelona, Spain, for several years.

A PLACE I'VE NEVER BEEN

I had known Nathan for years—too many years, since we were in college— so when he went to Europe I wasn't sure how I'd survive it; he was my best friend, after all, my constant companion at Sunday afternoon double bills at the Thalia, my ever-present source of consolation and conversation. Still, such a turn can prove to be a blessing in disguise. It threw me off at first, his not being there—I had no one to watch *Jeopardy!* with, or talk to on the phone late at night—but then, gradually, I got over it, and I realized that maybe it was a good thing after all, that maybe now, with Nathan gone, I would be forced to go out into the world more, make new friends, maybe even find a boyfriend. And I had started: I lost weight, I went shopping. I was at Bloomingdale's one day on my lunch hour when a very skinny black woman with a French accent asked me if I'd like to have a makeover. I had always run away from such things, but this time, before I had a chance, this woman put her long hands on my cheeks and looked into my face—not my eyes, my face—and said, "You're very beautiful. You know that?" And I absolutely couldn't answer. After she was through with me I didn't even know what I looked like, but everyone at my office was amazed. "Celia," they said, "you look great. What happened?" I smiled, wondering if I'd be allowed to go back every day for a makeover, if I offered to pay.

There was even some interest from a man—a guy named Roy who works downstairs, in contracts—and I was feeling pretty good about myself again, when the phone rang, and it was Nathan. At first I thought he must have been calling me from some European capital, but he said no, he was back in

New York. "Celia," he said, "I have to see you. Something awful has happened."

Hearing those words, I pitched over—I assumed the worst. (And why 3
not? He had been assuming the worst for over a year.) But he said, "No, no.
I'm fine. I'm perfectly healthy. It's my apartment. Oh, Celia, it's awful.
Could you come over?"

"Were you broken into?" I asked. 4

"I might as well have been!" 5

"Okay," I said. "I'll come over after work." 6

"I just got back last night. This is too much." 7

"I'll be there by six, Nathan." 8

"Thank you," he said, a little breathlessly, and hung up. 9

I drummed my nails—newly painted by another skinny woman at 10
Bloomingdale's—against the black Formica on my desk, mostly to try out the
sound. In truth I was a little happy he was back—I had missed him—and
not at all surprised that he'd cut his trip short. Rich people are like that, I've
observed; because they don't have to buy bargain-basement tickets on weird
charter airlines, they feel free to change their minds. Probably he just got
bored tooting around Europe, missed his old life, missed *Jeopardy!*, his friends.
Oh, Nathan! How could I tell him the Thalia had closed?

I had to take several buses to get from my office to his neighborhood— 11
a route I had once traversed almost daily, but which, since Nathan's departure, I hadn't had much occasion to take. Sitting on the Madison Avenue
bus, I looked out the window at the rows of unaffordable shops, some still
exactly what they'd been before, others boarded up, or reopened under new
auspices—such a familiar panorama, unfolding, block by block, like a Chinese
scroll I'd once been shown on a museum trip in junior high school. It was
raining a little, and in the warm bus the long, unvarying progress of my love
for Nathan seemed to unscroll as well—all the dinners and lunches and arguments, and all the trips back alone to my apartment, feeling ugly and fat,
because Nathan had once again confirmed he could never love me the way
he assured me he would someday love a man. How many hundreds of times
I received that confirmation! And yet, somehow, it never occurred to me to
give up that love I had nurtured for him since our earliest time together, that
love which belonged to those days just past the brink of childhood, before I
understood about Nathan, or rather, before Nathan understood about himself. So I persisted, and Nathan, in spite of his embarrassment at my occasional outbursts, continued to depend on me. I think he hoped that my feeling
for him would one day transform itself into a more maternal kind of affection, that I would one day become the sort of woman who could tend to him
without expecting anything in return. And that was, perhaps, a reasonable
hope on his part, given my behavior. But: "If only," he said to me once, "you
didn't have to act so crazy, Celia—" And that was how I realized I had to get
out.

I got off the bus and walked the block and a half to his building—its 12 façade, I noted, like almost every façade in the neighborhood, blemished by a bit of scaffolding—and, standing in that vestibule where I'd stood so often, waited for him to buzz me up. I read for diversion the now familiar list of tenants' names. The only difference today was that there were ragged ends of Scotch tape stuck around Nathan's name; probably his subletter had put his own name over Nathan's, and Nathan, returning, had torn the piece of paper off and left the ends of the tape. This didn't seem like him, and it made me suspicious. He was a scrupulous person about such things.

In due time—though slowly, for him—he let me in, and I walked the 13 three flights of stairs to find him standing in the doorway, unshaven, looking as if he'd just gotten out of bed. He wasn't wearing any shoes, and he'd gained some weight. Almost immediately he fell into me—that is the only way to describe it, his big body limp in my arms. "Oh, God," he murmured into my hair, "am I glad to see you."

"Nathan," I said. "Nathan." And held him there. Usually he wriggled 14 out of physical affection; kisses from him were little nips; hugs were tight, jerky chokeholds. Now he lay absolutely still, his arms slung under mine, and I tried to keep from gasping from the weight of him. But finally—reluctantly—he let go, and putting his hand on his forehead, gestured toward the open door. "Prepare yourself," he said. "It's worse than you can imagine."

He led me into the apartment. I have to admit, I was shocked by what 15 I saw. Nathan, unlike me, is a chronically neat person, everything in its place, all his perfect furniture glowing, polished, every state-of-the-art fountain pen and pencil tip-up in the blue glass jar on his desk. Today, however, the place was in havoc—newspapers and old Entenmann's cookie boxes spread over the floor, records piled on top of each other, inner sleeves crumpled behind the radiator, the blue glass jar overturned. The carpet was covered with dark mottlings, and a stench of old cigarette smoke and sweat and urine inhabited the place. "It gets worse," he said. "Look at the kitchen." A thick, yellowing layer of grease encrusted the stovetop. The bathroom was beyond the pale of my descriptive capacity for filth.

"Those bastards," Nathan was saying, shaking his head. 16

"Hold on to the security deposit," I suggested. "Make them pay for it." 17

He sat down on the sofa, the arms of which appeared to have been 18 ground with cigarette butts, and shook his head. "There *is* no security deposit," he moaned. "I didn't take one because supposedly Denny was my friend, and this other guy—Hoop, or whatever his name was—he was Denny's friend. And look at this!" From the coffee table he handed me a thick stack of utility and phone bills, all unopened. "The phone's disconnected," he said. "Two of the rent checks have bounced. The landlord's about to evict me. I'm sure my credit rating has gone to hell. Jesus, why'd I do it?" He stood, marched into the corner, then turned again to face me. "You know what? I'm going to call my father. I'm going to have him sick every one of his bastard lawyers on those assholes until they pay."

"Nathan," I reminded, "they're unemployed actors. They're poor." 19

"Then let them rot in jail!" Nathan screamed. His voice was loud and sharp in my ears. It had been a long time since I'd had to witness another person's misery, a long time since anyone had asked of me what Nathan was now asking of me: to take care, to resolve, to smooth. Nonetheless I rallied my energies. I stood. "Look," I said. "I'm going to go out and buy sponges, Comet, Spic and Span, Fantastik, Windex. Everything. We're going to clean this place up. We're going to wash the sheets and shampoo the rug, we're going to scrub the toilet until it shines. I promise you, by the time you go to sleep tonight, it'll be what it was."   20

He stood silent in the corner.   21

"Okay?" I said.   22

"Okay."   23

"So you wait here," I said. "I'll be right back."   24

"Thank you."   25

I picked up my purse and closed the door, thus, once again, saving him from disaster.   26

But there were certains things I could not save Nathan from. A year ago, his ex-lover Martin had called him up and told him he had tested positive. This was the secret fact he had to live with every day of his life, the secret fact that had brought him to Xanax and Halcion, Darvon and Valium—all crude efforts to cut the fear firing through his blood, exploding like the tiny viral time bombs he believed were lying in wait, expertly planted. It was the day after he found out that he started talking about clearing out. He had no obligations—he had quit his job a few months before and was just doing free-lance work anyway—and so, he reasoned, what was keeping him in New York? "I need to get away from all this," he said, gesturing frantically at the air. I believe he really thought back then that by running away to somewhere where it was less well known, he might be able to escape the disease. This is something I've noticed: The men act as if they think the power of infection exists in direct proportion to its publicity, that in places far from New York City it can, in effect, be outrun. And who's to say they were wrong, with all this talk about stress and the immune system? In Italy, in the countryside, Nathan seemed to feel he'd feel safer. And probably he was right; he would feel safer. Over there, away from the American cityscape with its streets full of gaunt sufferers, you're able to forget the last ten years, you can remember how old the world is and how there was a time when sex wasn't something likely to kill you.   27

It should be pointed out that Nathan had no symptoms; he hadn't even had the test for the virus itself. He refused to have it, saying he could think of no reason to give up at least the hope of freedom. Not that this made any difference, of course. The fear itself is a brutal enough enemy.   28

But he gave up sex. No sex, he said, was safe enough for him. He bought a VCR and began to hoard pornographic videotapes. And I think he was having phone sex too, because once I picked up the phone in his apartment   29 and before I could say hello, a husky-voiced man said, "You stud," and then, when I said "Excuse me?" got flustered-sounding and hung up. Some people would probably count that as sex, but I'm not sure I would.

All the time, meanwhile, he was frenzied. I could never guess what time he'd call—six in the morning, sometimes, he'd drag me from sleep. "I figured you'd still be up," he'd say, which gave me a clue to how he was living. It got so bad that by the time he actually left I felt as if a great burden had been lifted from my shoulders. Not that I didn't miss him, but from that day on my time was, miraculously, my own. Nathan is a terrible correspondent—I don't think he's sent me one postcard or letter in all the time we've known each other—and so for months my only news of him came through the phone. Strangers would call me, Germans, Italians, nervous-sounding young men who spoke bad English, who were staying at the YMCA, who were in New York for the first time and to whom he had given my number. I don't think any of them actually wanted to see me; I think they just wanted me to tell them which bars were good and which subway lines were safe—information I happily dispensed. Of course, there was a time when I would have taken them on the subways, shown them around the bars, but I have thankfully passed out of that phase.

And of course, as sex became more and more a possibility, then a likelihood once again in my life, I began to worry myself about the very things that were torturing Nathan. What should I say, say, to Roy in contracts, when he asked me to sleep with him, which I was fairly sure he was going to do within a lunch or two? Certainly I wanted to sleep with him. But did I dare ask him to use a condom? Did I dare even broach the subject? I was frightened that he might get furious, that he might overreact, and I considered saying nothing, taking my chances. Then again, for me in particular, it was a very big chance to take; I have a pattern of falling in love with men who at some point or other have fallen in love with other men. All trivial, selfish, this line of worry, I recognize now, but at that point Nathan was gone, and I had no one around to remind me of how high the stakes were for other people. I slipped back into a kind of women's-magazine attitude toward the whole thing: for the moment, at least, *I* was safe, and I cherished that safety without even knowing it, I gloried in it. All my speculations were merely matters of prevention; that place where Nathan had been exiled was a place I'd never been. I am ashamed to admit it, but there was even a moment when I took a kind of vengeful pleasure in the whole matter—the years I had hardly slept with anyone, for which I had been taught to feel ashamed and freakish, I now wanted to rub in someone's face: I was right and you were wrong! I wanted to say. I'm not proud of having had such thoughts, and I can only say, in my defense, that they passed quickly—but a strict accounting of all feelings, at this point, seems to me necessary. We have to be rigorous with ourselves these days.

In any case, Nathan was back, and I didn't dare think about myself. I went to the grocery store, I bought every cleaner I could find. And when I

got back to the apartment he was still standing where he'd been standing, in
the corner. "Nate," I said, "here's everything. Let's get to work."

"Okay," he said glumly, even though he is an ace cleaner, and we began.

As we cleaned, the truth came out. This Denny to whom he'd sublet
the apartment, Nathan had had a crush on. "To the extent that a crush is a
relevant thing in my life anymore," he said, "since God knows, there's nothing to be done about it. But there you are. The libido doesn't stop, the heart
doesn't stop, no matter how hard you try to make them."

None of this—especially that last part—was news to me, though Nathan
had managed to overlook that aspect of our relationship for years. I had
understood from the beginning about the skipping-over of the security payment, the laxness of the setup, because these were the sorts of things I would
have willingly done for Nathan at a different time. I think he was privately
so excited at the prospect of this virile young man, Denny, sleeping, and
perhaps having sex, between his sheets, that he would have taken any number of risks to assure it. Crush: what an oddly appropriate word, considering
what it makes you do to yourself. His apartment was, in a sense, the most
Nathan could offer, and probably the most Denny would accept. I understood: You want to get as close as you can, even if it's only at arm's length.
And when you come back, maybe, you want to breathe in the smell of the
person you love loving someone else.

Europe, he said, had been a failure. He had wandered, having dinner
with old friends of his parents, visiting college acquaintances who were busy
with exotic lives. He'd gone to bars, which was merely frustrating; there was
nothing to be done. "What about safe sex?" I asked, and he said, "Celia,
please. There is no such thing, as far as I'm concerned." Once again this
started a panicked thumping in my chest as I thought about Roy, and Nathan
said, "It's really true. Suppose something lands on you—you know what I'm
saying—and there's a microscopic cut in your skin. Bingo."

"Nathan, come on," I said. "That sounds crazy to me."

"Yeah?" he said. "Just wait till some ex-lover of yours calls you up with
a little piece of news. Then see how you feel."

He returned to his furious scrubbing of the bathroom sink. I returned
to my furious scrubbing of the tub. Somehow, even now, I'm always stuck
with the worst of it.

Finally we were done. The placed looked okay—it didn't smell anymore—though it was hardly what it had been. Some long-preserved pristine-
ness was gone from the apartment, and both of us knew without saying a
word that it would never be restored. We breathed in exhausted—no, not
exhausted triumph. It was more like relief. We had beaten something back,
yet again.

My hands were red from detergents, my stomach and forehead sweaty.
I went into the now-bearable bathroom and washed up, and then Nathan
said he would take me out to dinner—my choice. And so we ended up, as
we had a thousand other nights, sitting by the window at the Empire Sze-

chuan down the block from his apartment, eating cold noodles with sesame sauce, which, when we had finished them, Nathan ordered more of. "God, how I've missed these," he said, as he scooped the brown slimy noodles into his mouth. "You don't know."

In between slurps he looked at me and said, "You look good, Celia. 42 Have you lost weight?"

"Yes, as a matter of fact," I said. 43

"I thought so." 44

I looked back at him, trying to recreate the expression of the French 45 woman's face, and didn't say anything, but as it turned out I didn't need to. "I know what you're thinking," he said, "and you're right. Twelve pounds since you last saw me. But I don't care. I mean, you lose weight when you're sick. At least this way, gaining weight, I know I don't have it."

He continued eating, I looked outside. Past the plate-glass window that 46 separated us from the sidewalk, crowds of people walked, young and old, good-looking and bad-looking, healthy and sick, some of them staring in at our food and our eating. Suddenly—urgently—I wanted to be out among them, I wanted to be walking in that crowd, pushed along in it, and not sitting here, locked into this tiny two-person table with Nathan. And yet I knew that escape was probably impossible. I looked once again at Nathan, eating happily, resigned, perhaps, to the fate of his apartment, and the knowledge that everything would work out, that this had, in fact, been merely a run-of-the-mill crisis. For the moment he was appeased, his hungry anxiety sated; for the moment. But who could guess what would set him off next? I steadied my chin on my palm, drank some water, watched Nathan eat like a happy child.

The next few weeks were thorny with events. Nathan bought a new sofa, 47 had his place recarpeted, threw several small dinners. Then it was time for Lizzie Fischman's birthday party—one of the few annual events in our lives. We had known Lizzie since college—she was a tragic, trying sort of person, the sort who carries with her a constant aura of fatedness, of doom. So many bad things happen to Lizzie you can't help but wonder, after a while, if she doesn't hold out a beacon for disaster. This year alone, she was in a taxi that got hit by a bus; then she was mugged in the subway by a man who called her an "ugly dyke bitch"; then she started feeling sick all the time, and no one could figure out what was wrong, until it was revealed that her building's heating system was leaking small quantities of carbon monoxide into her awful little apartment. The tenants sued, and in the course of the suit, Lizzie, exposed as an illegal subletter, was evicted. She now lived with her father in one half of a two-family house in Plainfield, New Jersey, because she couldn't find another apartment she could afford. (Her job, incidentally, in addition to being wretchedly low-paying, is one of the dreariest I know of: proofreading accounting textbooks in an office on Forty-second Street.)

Anyway, each year Lizzie threw a big birthday party for herself in her 48 father's house in Plainfield, and we all went, her friends, because of course we couldn't bear to disappoint her and add ourselves to her roster of world-wide enemies. It was invariably a miserable party—everyone drunk on bourbon, and Lizzie, eager to recreate the slumber parties of her childhood, dancing around in pink pajamas with feet. We were making s'mores over the gas stove—shoving the chocolate bars and the graham crackers onto fondue forks rather than old sticks—and *Beach Blanket Bingo* was playing on the VCR and no one was having a good time, particularly Nathan, who was overdressed in a beige Giorgio Armani linen suit he'd bought in Italy, and was standing in the corner idly pressing his neck, feeling for swollen lymph nodes. Lizzie's circle dwindled each year, as her friends moved on, or found ways to get out of it. This year eight of us had made it to the party, plus a newcomer from Lizzie's office, a very fat girl with very red nails named Dorrie Friedman, who, in spite of her heaviness, was what my mother would have called dainty. She ate a lot, but unless you were observant, you'd never have noticed it. The image of the fat person stuffing food into her face is mythic: I know from experience, when fat you eat slowly, chew methodically, in order not to draw attention to your mouth. Over the course of an hour I watched Dorrie Friedman put away six of those s'mores with a tidiness worthy of Emily Post, I watched her dab her cheek with her napkin after each bite, and I understood: This was shame, but also, in some peculiar way, this was innocence. A state of envy.

There is a point in Lizzie's parties when she invariably suggests we play Deprivation, a game that had been terribly popular among our crowd in college. The way you play it is you sit in a big circle, and everyone is given ten pennies. (In this case the pennies were unceremoniously taken from a huge bowl that sat on top of Lizzie's mother's refrigerator, and that she had upended on the linoleum floor—no doubt, a long-contemplated act of desecration.) You go around the circle, and each person announces something he or she has never done, or a place they've never been—"I've never been to Borneo" is a good example—and then everyone who has been to Borneo is obliged to throw you a penny. Needless to say, especially in college, the game generates rather quickly to matters of sex and drugs.

I remembered the first time I ever played Deprivation, my sophomore year, I had been reading Blake's *Songs of Innocence* and *Songs of Experience*. Everything in our lives seemed a question of innocence and experience back then, so this seemed appropriate. There was a tacit assumption among my friends that "experience"—by that term we meant, I think, almost exclusively sex and drugs—was something you strove to get as much of as you could, that innocence, for all the praise it received in literature, was a state so essentially tedious that those of us still stuck in it deserved the childish recompense of shiny new pennies. (None of us, of course, imagining that five years from now the "experiences" we urged on one another might spread a murderous germ, that five years from now some of our friends, still in their youth, would be lost. Youth! You were supposed to sow your wild oats,

49

50

weren't you? Those of us who didn't—we were the ones who failed, weren't we?)

One problem with Deprivation is that the older you get, the less interesting it becomes; every year, it seemed, my friends had fewer gaps in their lives to confess, and as our embarrassments began to stack up on the positive side, it was what we *had* done that was titillating. Indeed, Nick Walsh, who was to Lizzie what Nathan was to me, complained as the game began, "I can't play this. There's nothing I haven't done." But Lizzie, who has a naive faith in ritual, merely smiled and said, "Oh come on, Nick. No one's done *everything*. For instance, you could say, 'I've never been to Togo.' or 'I've never been made love to simultaneously by twelve Arab boys in a back alley on Mott Street.' "

"Well, Lizzie," Nick said, "it *is* true that I've never been to Togo." His leering smile surveyed the circle, and of course, there *was* someone there—Gracie Wong, I think—who had, in fact, been to Togo.

The next person in the circle was Nathan. He's never liked this game, but he also plays it more cleverly than anyone. "Hmm," he said, stroking his chin as if there were a beard there, "let's see . . . Ah, I've got it. I've never had sex with anyone in this group." He smiled boldly, and everyone laughed—everyone, that is, except for me and Bill Darlington, and Lizzie herself—all three of us now, for the wretched experiments of our early youth, obliged to throw Nathan a penny.

Next was Dorrie Friedman's turn, which I had been dreading. She sat on the floor, her legs crossed under her, her very fat fingers intertwined, and said, "Hmm . . . Something I've never done. Well—I've never ridden a bicycle."

An awful silence greeted this confession, and then a tinkling sound, like wind chimes, as the pennies flew. "Gee," Dorrie Friedman said, "I won big that time." I couldn't tell if she was genuinely pleased.

And as the game went on, we settled, all of us, into more or less parallel states of innocence and experience, except for Lizzie and Nick, whose piles had rapidly dwindled, and Dorrie Friedman, who, it seemed, by virtue of lifelong fatness, had done nearly nothing. She had never been to Europe; she had never swum; she had never played tennis; she had never skied; she had never been on a boat. Even someone else's turn could be an awful moment for Dorrie, as when Nick said, "I've never had a vaginal orgasm." But fortunately, there, she did throw in her penny. I was relieved; I don't think I could have stood it if she hadn't.

After a while, in an effort not to look at Dorrie and her immense pile of pennies, we all started trying to trip up Lizzie and Nick, whose respective caches of sexual experience seemed limitless. "I've never had sex in my parents' bed," I offered. The pennies flew. "I've never had sex under a dry-docked boat." "I've never had sex with more than one other person." "Two other people." "Three other people." By then Lizzie was out of pennies, and declared the game over.

"I guess I won," Dorrie said rather softly. She had her pennies neatly 58 piled in identically sized stacks.

I wondered if Lizzie was worried. I wondered if she was thinking about 59 the disease, if she was frightened, the way Nathan was, or if she just assumed death was coming anyway, the final blow in her life of unendurable misfortunes. She started to gather the pennies back into their bowl, and I glanced across the room at Nathan, to see if he was ready to go. All through the game, of course, he had been looking pretty miserable—he always looks miserable at parties. Worse, he has a way of turning his misery around, making me responsible for it. Across the circle of our nearest and dearest friends he glared at me angrily, and I knew that by the time we were back in his car and on our way home to Manhattan he would have contrived a way for the evening to be my fault. And yet tonight, his occasional knowing sneers, inviting my complicity in looking down on the party, only enraged me. I was angry at him, in advance, for what I was sure he was going to do in the car, and I was also angry at him for being such a snob, for having no sympathy toward this evening, which, in spite of all its displeasures, was nevertheless an event of some interest, perhaps the very last hurrah of our youth, our own little big chill. And that was something: Up until now I had always assumed Nathan's version of things to be the correct one, and cast my own into the background. Now his perception seemed meager, insufficient: Here was an historic night, after all, and all he seemed to want to think about was his own boredom, his own unhappiness.

Finally, reluctantly, Lizzie let us go, and relinquished from her grip, we 60 got into Nathan's car and headed onto the Garden State Parkway. "Never again," Nathan was saying, "will I allow you to convince me to attend one of Lizzie Fischman's awful parties. This is the last." I didn't even bother answering, it all seemed so predictable. Instead I just settled back into the comfortable velour of the car seat and switched on the radio. Dionne Warwick and Elton John were singing "That's What Friends Are For," and Nathan said, "You know, of course, that that's the song they wrote to raise money for AIDS."

"I'd heard," I said. 61

"Have you seen the video? It makes me furious. All these famous singers 62 up there, grinning these huge grins, rocking back and forth. Why the hell are they smiling, I'd like to ask?"

For a second, I considered answering that question, then decided I'd 63 better not. We were slipping into the Holland Tunnel, and by the time we got through to Manhattan I was ready to call it a night. I wanted to get back to my apartment and see if Roy had left a message on my answering machine. But Nathan said, "It's Saturday night, Celia, it's still early. Won't you have a drink with me or something?"

"I don't want to go to any more gay bars, Nathan, I told you that." 64

"So we'll go to a straight bar. I don't care. I just can't bear to go back to 65 my apartment at eleven o'clock." We stopped for a red light, and he leaned closer to me. "The truth is, I don't think I can bear to be alone. Please."

"All right," I said. What else could I say? 66

"Goody," Nathan said. 67

We parked the car in a garage and walked to a darkish café on Green- 68
wich Avenue, just a few doors down from the huge gay bar Nathan used to
frequent, and which he jokingly referred to as "the airport." No mention was
made of that bar in the café, however, where he ordered latte machiato for
both of us. "Aren't you going to have some dessert?" he said. "I know I am.
Baba au rhum, perhaps. Or tiramisu. You know 'tirami su' means 'pick me
up,' but if you want to offend an Italian waiter, you say 'I'll have the *tiramilo
su*,' which means " 'pick up my dick.' "

"I'm trying to lose weight, Nathan," I said. "Please don't encourage me 69
to eat desserts."

"Sorry." He coughed. Our latte machiatos came, and Nathan raised his 70
cup and said. "Here's to us. Here's to Lizzie Fischman. Here's to never playing that dumb game again as long as we live." These days, I noticed, Nathan
used the phrase "as long as we live" a bit too frequently for comfort.

Reluctantly I touched my glass to his. "You know," he said, "I think 71
I've always hated that game. Even in college, when I won, it made me jealous. Everyone else had done so much more than me. Back then I figured I'd
have time to explore the sexual world. Guess the joke's on me, huh?"

I shrugged. I wasn't sure. 72

"What's with you tonight, anyway?" he said. "You're so distant." 73

"I just have things on my mind, Nathan, that's all." 74

"You've been acting weird ever since I got back from Europe, Celia. 75
Sometimes I think you don't even want to see me."

Clearly he was expecting reassurances to the contrary. I didn't say any- 76
thing.

"Well," he said, "is that it? You don't want to see me?" 77

I twisted my shoulders in confusion. "Nathan—" 78

"Great," he said, and laughed so that I couldn't tell if he was kidding. 79
"Your best friend for nearly ten years. Jesus."

"Look, Nathan, don't melodramatize," I said. "It's not that simple. It's 80
just that I have to think a little about myself. My own life, my own needs. I
mean, I'm going to be thirty soon. You know how long it's been since I've
had a boyfriend?"

"I'm not against your having a boyfriend," Nathan said. "Have I ever 81
tried to stop you from having a boyfriend?"

"But, Nathan," I said, "I never get to meet anyone when I'm with you 82
all the time. I love you and I want to be your friend, but you can't expect
me to just keep giving and giving and giving my time to you without anything in return. It's not fair."

I was looking away from him as I said this. From the corner of my vision 83
I could see him glancing to the side, his mouth a small, tight line.

"You're all I have," he said quietly. 84

"That's not true, Nathan," I said. 85

"Yes it is true, Celia." 86

"Nathan, you have lots of other friends." 87

"But none of them count. No one but you counts." 88

The waitress arrived with his goblet of tiramisu, put it down in front of 89
him. "Go on with your life, you say," he was muttering. "Find a boyfriend.
Don't you think I'd do the same thing if I could? But all those options are
closed to me, Celia. There's nowhere for me to go, no route that isn't dangerous. I mean, getting on with my life—I just can't talk about that simply
anymore, the way you can." He leaned closer, over the table. "Do you want
to know something?" he said. "Every time I see someone I'm attracted to I
go into a cold sweat. And I imagine that they're dead, that if I touch them,
the part of them I touch will die. Don't you see? It's bad enough to be afraid
you might get it. But to be afraid you might give it—and to someone you
loved—" He shook his head, put his hand to his forehead.

What could I say to that? What possibly was there to say? I took his 90
hand, suddenly, I squeezed his hand until the edges of his fingers were white.
I was remembering how Nathan looked the first time I saw him, in line at a
college dining hall, his hands on his hips, his head erect, staring worriedly at
the old lady dishing out food, as if he feared she might run out, or not give
him enough. I have always loved the boyish hungers—for food, for sex—
because they are so perpetual, so faithful in their daily revival, and even
though I hadn't met Nathan yet, I think, in my mind, I already understood:
I wanted to feed him, to fill him up; I wanted to give him everything.

Across from us, now, two girls were smoking cigarettes and talking about 91
what art was. A man and a woman, in love, intertwined their fingers. Nathan's
hand was getting warm and damp in mine, so I let it go, and eventually he
blew his nose and lit a cigarette.

"You know," he said after a while, "it's not the sex, really. That's not 92
what I regret missing. It's just that— Do you realize, Celia, I've never been
in love? Never once in my life have I actually been in love?" And he looked
at me very earnestly, not knowing, not having the slightest idea, that once
again he was counting me for nothing.

"Nathan," I said, "Oh, my Nathan." Still, he didn't seem satisfied, and 93
I knew he had been hoping for something better than my limp consolation.
He looked away from me, across the café, listening, I suppose, for that wind-
chime peal as all the world's pennies flew his way.

STUDY QUESTIONS

1. Explain the title. Explain the final sentence. Explain the relationship between the
   two.

2. Where would you locate the climax of this story? Describe the STRUCTURE of the
   story.

3. How would you describe the relationship between sex and love in this story? How
   would you describe the relationship between Celia and Nathan? What are her

feelings about him? his about her? How do you as reader from your vantage point of gender and sexual preference view the relationship? Nathan's situation? What are the advantages of making Celia the SPEAKER?

Wayne D. Johnson

Wayne Johnson grew up in Minnesota and lived for many years in the West. In 1990, his novel *The Snake Game* was published. A portion of the book was awarded an O. Henry Prize.

WHAT HAPPENED TO RED DEER

Red Deer turned the ball in his hand.   1

They were yelling in the bleachers now. "Chief! Go home, Chief!"   2

The ball fit in his palm like a stone. He caught the stitching with his   3
nails, then raised his eyes to the catcher. The catcher thrust two fingers at
the ground.

A slider.   4

Red Deer nodded, coiled himself back, leg raised, stretching, and hurled   5
the ball. The ball went low, looked like a gutter ball, then rose and smacked
into the catcher's mitt. The umpire jerked his hand over his head, thumb up,
and the batter shook his head.

"Out!" the umpire shouted.   6

There was a chorus of booing from the bleachers.   7

Red Deer watched them out of the corner of his eye.   8

Since the beginning of the game they had jeered, and when the game   9
had gone into overtime, they began yelling "Chief! Go home, Chief!"

He had ridden on the crest of it, letting it carry him through the game.   10
But something was happening now and he didn't know what it was. It was
as if something were dissolving in him, dissolving and going flat.

Darius, the coach, walked to the mound from the dugout.   11

"How's your arm holding up?" he said.   12

"Okay," Red Deer offered.   13

"We'll have her licked if you can hang in there."   14

Red Deer pulled the bill of his cap down.   15

"Don't mind those sons-of-bitches. They're just a bunch of drunks. You're   16

pitching like a pro. Just get back in there and kill 'em." Darius slapped Red
Deer on the back, then strode past third, up toward the bleachers.

"What the hell are you waiting for, Chief?" the loudest of the drunks   17
yelled from the stands.

A batter stepped up to the plate. He practiced his swing, dipping in   18
mid-stroke and pulling up. He tapped the bat on his shoes and positioned
himself. The umpire and catcher squatted; the catcher pointed to the ground
with his index finger. Knuckle. Red Deer turned the ball in his hand, found
the stitching with his nails again, drew back like the hammer of a gun and
hurled the ball. The ball went straight and fast, right down the pipe. The
batter uncoiled, the bat scooped down into the ball, there was a loud crack,
and the ball went high, up and back into the bleachers, a foul.

"Whooa, Chief!" the drunks yelled.   19

Red Deer turned to face the bleachers.   20

He could see the men who were doing the yelling. They were wearing   21
white shirts and colored ties, and they had brought women with them.
Attractive women, who laughed and pushed and when the men yelled laughed
into their hands.

"Go home, Chief!" the biggest yelled, standing, a beer in his fist. The   22
woman at his side laughed, pulling at his pants leg.

Red Deer shook his head. He turned to the other side of the field. There   23
his father, Osada, sat with the boy, Bear. A few rows up from them a lot of
men from the reservation stood. Red Deer had not asked them to come, and
when he had run out onto the playing field, he had been startled to see them.
Joe Big Otter had waved and Red Deer had felt something in him sad and
old and hurtful.

"Hey! Chief! You missing the Lone Ranger?" There was a cackle of   24
laughter.

The men from the reservation glared across the field.   25

Red Deer turned the ball in his hand.   26

He wished the ball were a stone.   27

He took the sign from the catcher, eyed the batter, drew his body and   28
arm back, and hurled the ball again. The batter swung around, connected,
and then it was all moving, Red Deer carried across the field, the ball sizzling
by his head, his mitt out, the hard break of the ball against his hand, then
opening the mitt and lobbing the ball to first, the baseman reaching, throwing to third, the runner coming on hard, then sliding, the umpire charging,
the ball, the baseman, the runner and the umpire all converging there. In the
dust, you couldn't see at all.

"Safe!" the umpire yelled, spreading his arms wide at his waist. "Safe!"   29

An organ broke into a frenzy of scales and the scoreboard flashed. Bot-   30
tom of the tenth. Six to five, visitor's lead.

Red Deer swung back to the mound.   31

"Go home, Chief!" the drunks yelled.   32

The shortstop caught him on the way. The man on third kicked the   33
base, watching the two men.

"Two outs. Anything goes home, okay?" 34

Red Deer nodded. 35

"Just give 'em some of the old Buck stuff," the shortstop said. He spit 36
through his teeth and slapped Red Deer on the back.

"Buck!" he said. 37

But Red Deer was staring off over the bleachers. 38

In grade school, when they ran the races on the playground, he never 39
pushed himself and still he could beat them all, even the straining, grunting
boys who couldn't stand to lose to an Indian.

It wasn't a hard thing to do. 40

He loved to run, and he ran to school and back home again and wherever 41
else it was he went. Somehow rather than tiring him, as it did the others, it
set him free. He loved the feel of the ground under his feet, the trees flashing
by, the pumping of his lungs, the pain he pushed through into a solid rhythm
that carried him away from everything. If he wanted he would change the
rhythm, his legs working harder, the ground beating up with more power,
but always the ground carried him, and he was surprised, when one day at
school a man watched him run the circumference of the football field, a watch
in his hand.

The man stopped Red Deer back of the goalposts, his face swollen with 42
excitement, his thumb held down on the watch. "Wait! Stop there!" he said.

Red Deer had looked back to see where the others were. They weren't 43
around the field yet.

"I can't believe it," the man said. 44

Red Deer's teacher came over. "Didn't I tell you he was fast?" he said. 45
"Didn't I tell you?"

"Is that as fast as you can run?" 46

"No," Red Deer said. 47

"How old are you?" 48

"Fifteen." 49

The man held out his hand. "I just can't believe it," he said. "Jim Thorpe 50
couldn't have done that at your age."

The others ran by, breathing hard, and Red Deer stepped into the stream 51
of bodies. Halfway around the field he looked back. The two men were still
talking, the man with the watch gesturing with his hands.

Red Deer heaved the ball down the baseline to the catcher. 52

"No!" the shortstop yelled. "Goddammit! Throw it around the horn." 53

Red Deer turned to face the shortstop. 54

"Haven't you ever played baseball?" The shortstop pointed to the sec- 55
ond baseman with his mitt, then shook his head. "What the hell is he doing
out here?"

Red Deer shrugged his shoulders. They had him on first, and he didn't 56
know what plays to make. He didn't like standing around so much, and they
were always yelling at him.

"Hey! Chief!" Joe Fossen, the catcher, yelled. He threw the ball and   57
Red Deer caught it, tossed it to second, and then it went around again.

It was the first time anyone on the team had called him "Chief." It was   58
the first time *anyone* had called him "Chief."

He wasn't sure he liked it.   59

But he wasn't sure he liked playing baseball either. It hadn't been his   60
idea.

They had called him down to the principal's office not long after the   61
man with the watch had been on the field, and Red Deer had wondered what
they had singled him out for now. After the business with his father and the
shooting, it seemed the teachers were afraid of him, or afraid that something
would happen to them if they had anything to do with him. And the other
Indians didn't know what to make of him, either—he was too big for his age,
and there was still a general bad feeling on the reservation about the incident.
He had gained notoriety without wanting it in any way.

In the office the principal, a short, baldheaded man behind a desk, had   62
asked Red Deer to sit.

"Well, we've got it all fixed," he said.   63

"Did I do something?" Red Deer said. His heard was pounding. He felt   64
uncomfortable and crossed his legs and uncrossed them, pressing his feet into
the floor so his toes curled under.

"We thought you'd want to play baseball," the man said. He adjusted   65
his glasses, then leaned back in his chair.

Red Deer crossed his legs again.   66

"Joe Bradley's going to be driving up to Kenora just about every day.   67
We thought you'd like to be playing on the team."

Outside the room a typewriter was snapping.   68

Red Deer didn't know what to say, so he stood. The principal stood   69
with him.

"So what do you think?" he said.   70

Red Deer pushed his hands into his pockets, then looked over the man's   71
shoulder, through the window. The wind was blowing and the poplars in
the schoolyard swayed.

"Okay," he said. "Sure."   72

The ball came around the horn again.   73

"Hey Chief!" Sampson, the shortstop, yelled. "For Christ's sake don't   74
just stand there!"

Red Deer caught the ball and carefully set it beside the base bag. He   75
covered the distance between first and shortstop and there Joe Sampson stood,
his fists tight at his sides. Red Deer hadn't realized how big Joe was until he
got right up to him; he was the only boy on the team that could stand head
to head with Red Deer.

"Hey!" the coach yelled.   76

"Don't call me that," Red Deer said.   77

"Make me," the boy said. He leaned toward Red Deer, so that Red Deer could smell his breath.   78

The coach headed across the field, then was running.   79

"Make me, *Chief!*" the boy said.   80

It made Red Deer think of his father, Osada, and how the men he had   81
been a guide for had called him "Chief." Sometimes, when Red Deer had
been out in the boat with him, he could see Osada was enraged when it
happened, and other times he didn't seem to care at all. Sometimes, with the
men who had had a sense of humor, he even seemed to like it.

"Break it up!" the coach yelled. He was nearly across the field now.   82

"Tonto," the boy said.   83

The word worked like a key in Red Deer's brain, and then as with a   84
stone he hammered at the boy's face, and even when the boy was on the
ground and bleeding Red Deer couldn't stop hitting him.

They called him "Buck" after that, and they were all a little afraid   85
of him. He got bigger, his shoulders broadening, his legs getting longer.
The boy he had beaten didn't come back; his jaw had been broken and one
of his eyes damaged. No one said anything about it, but Red Deer felt
badly.

Somehow they all seemed to feel bad.   86

They drank a good deal and had girl friends and every now and then as   87
they got older a boy would disappear from the team.

"Where's Freddie?" Red Deer had asked one afternoon at practice. Fred-   88
die had become a friend of his, though a silent one.

"Didn't you hear?"   89

"No."   90

"He's not playing anymore. They got him down at the supermarket in   91
Fort Francis."

"What the hell's he doing down there?"   92

"Gettin' married, I guess," the boy said, a wry grin on his face.   93

It puzzled Red Deer. And not long after, when he was down in Fort   94
Francis to see Osada, he stopped by the new supermarket to see if Freddie
was there. It really was super. Huge. A long, low, cinderblock building with
a giant red and blue sign in front. Red Deer stepped through the doors and
it was cold inside and smelled of floor wax, like when they had had dances
at the old school. The lights were bluish and buzzed and there were three
women in yellow dresses at the registers.

"Is there a Fred Levine who works here?"   95

The women looked at him suspiciously.   96

"You mean a young guy? Eighteen or so?" the biggest said, tossing her   97
head back.

A door opened off to one side and Freddie came out. He was wearing a   98
green apron and had his hair slicked back.

"Hey! Freddie!" Red Deer said.   99

Freddie's eye puckered and his eyebrows drew down and then he smiled,   100
too broadly.

"Come on back," he said.   101

Red Deer went up the aisle. There were all kinds of beans on the shelves,   102
beans he had never even heard of.

"How's it goin'?" Freddie said.   103

He seemed nervous and stood on one leg and then on the other.   104

"How's the team? I heard you guys wupped shit out Fond Du Lac."   105

"Nine to three," Red Deer said.   106

"I heard you were pitchin', too. Is that right?"   107

Red Deer nodded. Something was wrong. Freddie was the one guy who'd   108
gotten the others to lay off the "Chief" stuff, and they had been friends in
the way a pitcher and first baseman can be friends if they are both good at
it.

"So what's this all about, Freddie?" Red Deer said. He was so tall now   109
his head was even with the top shelf.

Freddie looked up the aisle one way and down it the other.   110

"You heard, didn't you?" he said.   111

"You're getting married."   112

"That's it," he said.   113

Red Deer braced himself against the aisle divider. "So what about all   114
that other stuff? Chicago and that school down there?"

"I'm just makin' some money now. See? Then I can go later."   115

He dusted the shelf Red Deer leaned on, rearranging the cans.   116

"So," Red Deer said.   117

The girls laughed up at the registers.   118

Freddie carefully straightened the cans, his hands shaking. He reminded   119
Red Deer of a squirrel caught in a snare, his eyes wild.

"You don't have to get married, you know," Red Deer said.   120

Freddie looked up the aisle again and back.   121

"Look, I gotta go, Buck. I can't just stand around here talking. . . ."   122

A heavy-set man with shiny black shoes stepped around the end of the   123
aisle.

"Can I help you?" he said.   124

"Just a minute," Freddie said.   125

"Freddie," the man said.   126

Freddie's face had reddened. "Just let me explain," he said. "It's not   127
what you think. . ."

"It's okay," Red Deer said. Though it was not okay.   128

"Hang on. Just wait a—"   129

The manager was coming up the aisle now. Red Deer could not stand   130
to see Freddie this way.

"See you around, Freddie," he said.   131

He didn't toss up the tuft of Freddie's hair the way he always had, and ₁₃₂
walking across the parking lot in the bright sun, the new gravel sharp under
his feet, Red Deer felt a hollow in his chest.

It seemed to Red Deer that they were all liars. And he had become a ₁₃₃
liar, too, though he lied in a different way. He said nothing, or as little as
possible. It wasn't that there wasn't anything to say, but to say it would have
torn up the fabric of all the lies and Red Deer knew none of them would
stand for it. So he pretended he didn't feel the discomfort of the whites
around him, or the hatred and bad feeling of the other Indians. It got so the
only place he could escape the lies was playing baseball, and for that reason
he came to love the game. On the field the ball moved, and they played. He
could walk out onto the field, the mitt snug on his hand, and win or lose, he
would pitch his best and whether his teammates hated him or not, they needed
him up there on the mound. Slider. Curveball. Greaseball. Knuckleball. Fast
pitch. He could get his fingers on the fine stitching of the ball and it fit into
his palm like a planet. Or a shooting star. It was all a game and he saw the
line he wanted the ball to take, up to and past the batter. He got to know the
boys on the other teams, how they batted, how they ran.

There seemed to be no end to it. It happened so fast he could only do a ₁₃₄
little at a time, test what his hand could do to the line. But he came along
fast, and people knew him.

"Let him have it, Buck!" they'd yell from the stands. "Give it to 'im, ₁₃₅
Buck!"

But after the games he went home. If he was near the reservation he ₁₃₆
stayed at his mother's, even though he didn't like his stepfather. He liked
playing with the boy, though. Bear was like a little animal, only smarter,
and faster, and they'd tumble in the dirt in the yard and the boy loved to
play catch. On hot summer afternoons they listened to Minnesota Twins
games on the radio, drinking root beer—Red Deer would buy cases of it—
and when the Hamm's commercials came on, sung as though by Indians,
with a drum pounding in the background, Red Deer and Bear burst out
laughing.

It was on one of those afternoons that Red Deer and his stepfather, Joe ₁₃₇
Big Otter, got to fighting. They were sitting outside the house, drinking
under the shade of an umbrella Joe had bought at the supermarket in Fort
Francis.

"You see a guy there with slicked back hair?" Red Deer said. "Big nose?" ₁₃₈
"No," Joe said. ₁₃₉
Red Deer looked up into the umbrella. The umbrella had been on sale. ₁₄₀
On it Huey, Louie, and Dewey marched with sand buckets, pink, yellow,
and candy blue.

The Twins were on the radio. ₁₄₁

"I want to hear a story," Bear said. 142

"Shhh," Martha Blue Feather said. She reached under Bear's armpit and 143
tickled him.

"What kind of story do you want to hear?" Red Deer said. 144

"I want to hear a story about cowboys," the boy said. 145

It made Red Deer sad to hear him say this, and he looked up into the 146
umbrella again and took a sip of his beer.

"Why don't you tell him the one about Litani?" Joe said. 147

Litani had been shot in the altercation with the marshals, when Osada 148
had gotten the men to take their boys out of the new school. Litani had been
Joe's younger brother.

Red Deer did not answer. It was hot and he could tell nothing good 149
would come of this. He noticed how whoever it was who had drawn the
ducks on the umbrella had put smiles on their bills. They looked funny holding the pails.

"Tell him that one," Joe Big Otter said. "There's a *cowboy* story." 150

Red Deer looked across the table. Joe smiled. Martha put her hand on 151
Joe's forearm, gripped him around the wrist.

"You see," Joe said, his drunken eyes on the boy, "there was this proud 152
man—"

"Shut up," Red Deer said. 153

"He should hear it," Joe said. 154

"Not the way you're telling it," Red Deer said. He set his beer on the 155
table. He was hoping this would just pass.

Martha pulled at the bottle in Joe's hand. "You've had enough," she 156
said.

"Don't," he said. 157

"You've had too much. Let go." 158

"Tell it," Joe said. 159

Red Deer looked away. He didn't want to tell Bear the story, and he 160
didn't want Joe to tell it either.

"Coward," Joe said. 161

"Not as big a coward as you with your bottle," Red Deer replied. 162

Joe stood. The boy's eyes widened. The boy could not understand what 163
they were saying, and when they began to yell, he crawled under the table.

Joe punched Red Deer in the mouth and then Red Deer had Joe by his 164
ponytail and slammed his face into the picnic table. Blood ran down Joe's
nose and Red Deer, trying to pull away, got hit in the mouth again. He tried
to pin Joe down but Joe was hollering now.

"Your goddamned cowboy—" 165

Red Deer hit him in the mouth. He felt the teeth give way under his 166
knuckles. Martha's eyes were wide and Joe stumbled back from the table.
Martha held her hand to her mouth, and Joe ran inside. Bear was crying
under the table. Then Joe swung by the kitchen window with his rifle, and

Red Deer was over the garden fence, out across the field, and he didn't stop running until he was miles out of the reservation.

He didn't tell them where he was staying. He'd made himself a lean-to   167
down by the fish hatchery, and at night he'd swim and catch brown trout, and bake them in the hillside behind the lean-to. He knew he couldn't do this very long, but he also knew something would come up. They were playing a game down in Fort Francis, against a Toronto team, and some big name scouts were supposed to be there.

"They're waiting for you," the coach had said.   168

The morning of the game with Toronto Red Deer got up early. He   169
swam in the clean, bitter cold water, then knocked down the lean-to. The fishery people were getting wise to him anyway, and he'd have to find someplace else. He walked into town, spent his last dollar on a plate of eggs and hash browns and coffee. At two he met the others at the school, and then everything was all right.

The basement was cool, and they suited up, the others snapping each   170
other with their towels and joking.

"Hey! Buckeroo!" one of the boys said, thumping him on the back.   171

Red Deer took his uniform from his locker, set his clothes out as he   172
always did. He dressed quickly, his hands sure, finally pulling the laces of his tennis shoes tight. He reached into his locker for his cleats and swung them over his shoulder. If he could keep it out of his mind, he thought, everything would be fine.

The game went terribly. The new first baseman was slow, and Red   173
Deer wished Freddie were there. He missed him now, though it didn't occur to him why. He pitched badly, and he watched the scouts in the bleachers. The two men wore wide-brimmed hats and pointed, nodded, and scribbled on note pads.

It seemed it was all coming to a grinding end.   174

They forced their way through a miserable third inning and headed for   175
the dugout.

"What the hell is wrong with you?" the coach said. Everyone else in the   176
dugout looked the other way. "Huh? What's going on?"

Red Deer stared out across the field. Meyers was up to bat. He swung   177
in short choppy strokes.

"Are you listening to me?" the coach said.   178

"I don't know," Red Deer said.   179

The coach slapped his hand on his knees. "Well, you goddamned well   180
better know. Do you have any idea how important this game is?" He lowered his voice. "It's your goddamned baby. They didn't come out here to see Hodges."

Beside him Hodges stiffened.   181

Red Deer felt badly that he had heard. He wasn't a good first baseman and he knew it. 182

There was a crack of a bat, and everyone in the dugout stood. Red Deer sat on the bench. 183

"Get up," the coach yelled, but Red Deer wasn't about to. Not like that. 184

On the mound again he couldn't force the ball down the line, and the game had all gone away somewhere. He was tired, dirty, and hungry. He had lost something, and a deep sadness was setting in. It wasn't this damn game, he thought. It was Bear. He'd lost Bear, and he figured he'd lost his mother, too, only now he could see he'd never really had her, and maybe that hurt the worst. 185

A big kid named Donnelly got up to bat, kicking his cleats into the dirt like a rooster. They were leading nine / five into the sixth inning and now their batters were all getting cocky. 186

"Come on, Chief, throw me a fast one," he said. 187

Red Deer looked into the stands, then at the boy. 188

"Come on, Chief," he said. 189

Red Deer tightened his grip on the ball. 190

"Put her right here, Chief," the boy said, tapping the base with his bat. 191

Red Deer found the stitches on the ball, gripped it in his hand. He got a kind of tunnel vision, and when Steadman, the catcher, signalled for him to throw a curve, he shook his head. He knew what to do with this one. He settled onto his legs, then stretched as if to break himself, and when he threw the ball it hissed out of his hand, went low, then broke into the catcher's mitt with a dusty thud. The batter's mouth dropped open. 192

"Steeerike!" the umpire called. 193

Red Deer caught the ball, tossed it around the horn. 194

No one said anything. 195

When it was over, and they had won by two runs, Red Deer dropped the ball on the mound and walked to the dugout. 196

"Jesus Christ!" the coach said. "That was really something." 197

Red Deer wiped his face with a towel. He never wanted to play another game like that. He had wanted to kill the boy Donnelly, and had prodded himself along with him, remembering his face and what he had said. And when the boy was up to bat again, and he sensed something dangerous in Red Deer, Red Deer imagined him saying the things he had said over again. 198

He wasn't happy now—he was drained, and felt ugly. 199

The two scouts came down to the dugout. 200

"Hell of a game you pitched." 201

Red Deer nodded. 202

They had turned the lights off on the field and now the dugout was dark but for the light coming in from the parking lot. The bigger man's glasses shone in the dark. 203

"Anything you'd like to say?" 204

All he wanted now was to be alone. 205

"I've pitched better," he said. It was what he was supposed to say. And 206
it was true, only now he wished they would leave.

"We'll be getting in touch," the bigger of the two men said. 207

Red Deer watched them cross the parking lot to the car. The lights came 208
on, and the car crackled out of the lot with the others, dust billowing behind
them. Red Deer settled down onto the dirt floor, the cement cool against his
sides, the dugout just long enough to hold him. It was all he wanted now.

The rest was easy. It was like falling. A small league team picked him 209
up as a relief pitcher, and then he was playing, and had some jack in his
pocket. He traveled a lot, and he forgot about what happened. He learned to
forget a lot of things, and he learned how to fight too.

"Hey, Chief," someone would say. 210

It was like a button they pushed. 211

He learned to hit first, and hit hard, and it wasn't until later that he got 212
into fights with men bigger than he was. He had his nose broken three times
and lost a tooth, a canine, so when he smiled it gave him the look of someone
who would take the caps off beer bottles with his teeth for fun.

And on the mound he felt it get bigger in him, like a stone, and he held 213
on to it tighter. He learned to focus it, and he thought of it as being like a
train or a bulldozer. All he had to think of was that boy, and it started again.

"Chief," he'd think to himself. 214

He got to love it, and it was precious. 215

He found it had all kinds of uses. 216

On nights when things were going badly, when he felt a slagging in his 217
desire to throw the ball, he could pump himself up with it. It got to be such
a thing with him he was afraid he would lose it, and then he nursed it when
he wasn't on the field, and soon after he was thrown in jail for nearly killing
a man in a bar.

"Don't mess with him," they said. 218

Red Deer thought it was funny. He was just playing the game. But 219
something had happened, and one night, when he came in from a drunk, he
had looked in the mirror in the bathroom of his hotel room and had seen
somebody he didn't know staring out at him—a big, fierce-looking Indian
with a crooked nose and hard eyes. It scared him so badly that he covered all
the mirrors in his room with towels and lay on his bed, his arms pulled tight
over his chest.

The morning after, Harvey, his first baseman, had spoken to him in the 220
dugout. It was a hot day at the end of August and Red Deer was tying the
laces of his cleats.

His hands shook on the laces. 221

"You'd better slow down on the sauce," Harvey said. 222

It occurred to Red Deer to knock Harvey's teeth out, but the look on 223
his face was so concerned that he laughed instead.

"Nothing that doesn't grease the old joints," Red Deer said.   224

Harvey brushed the dirt off his glove. He shook his head. "I'll tell you   225
something," he said. "Just between the two of us."

Red Deer busied himself with his shoes. He didn't want to hear it.   226

"I got an ulcer the size of a half-dollar in my gut," Harvey said, "and if   227
it gets any worse they say they're gonna have to cut some out and sew me
up. Now I thought that was pretty funny, until they said it might kill me,
see." He put his face down by Red Deer's. "Do you see what I'm saying?"

Red Deer grunted, double-tying his laces, pulling on them. He could   228
hardly control his hands now.

"Hey, do you hear what—"   229

"Shut up, Harve," Red Deer said. There was a buzzing in his brain. He   230
shot to his feet and grabbed Harvey by his shirt and twisted it. "Shut up
before I knock out your teeth."

The season ended well enough, and Red Deer got himself a job in a   231
meat packing plant in Ohio, where he had played his last game. He hated
the noises and smells at first. He hated the gray walls and the fluorescent
lights. He hated his foreman and he hated Vinny, the boy he worked with.

But as with everything else, he learned to shut it out.   232

"Don't you just love it?" Vinny said. They were cutting the heads off   233
pigs. A fine line of blood squirted up Vinny's rubber smock while he cut
with the saw.

Vinny smiled.   234

He had a few teeth mising, and Red Deer saw himself in the mirror for   235
a second.

"Cut that shit out, Vinny," he said.   236

But then it was baseball season again, the job and the winter shucked   237
off. He took the train down to Tampa and the tryouts started. The weather
was warm and there were birds all over and it was hard to pitch at first.

But it always happened.   238

"Chief," someone said "Tonto."   239

And he was throwing hot again. His arm swollen and hard. He built it   240
up slowly, added Vinny to it, but there were so many now it didn't matter.
He didn't even have to think of any specific one, it just came to him in a
knotted, hard bundle. A bundle he would spit out his arm and over the bag.

"Jesus," they said. "He throws a real killer-ball."   241

He was throwing like that in his fifth pick-up game. Hurling himself   242
into it, when a scout for the Cleveland Aces spotted him. He'd never been
hotter, and like that, a month later he was in Chicago for an exhibition game
against the Cubs, and somehow, someone had found out on the reservation
and there they were, Osada and Bear and Joe Big Otter and his friends.

The lights burned.   243

A brown bottle sailed up over the netting, turning end over end, flash-   244 ing, and landed on the field. One of the men in the white shirts and colored ties stood.

"Chief! Go home, Chief!" he shouted.   245

A bat boy ran out to the bottle.   246

Darius marched to the mound from the dugout, and the umpires came   247
up from the bases.

"What the hell is going on?" Darius said.   248

Red Deer glanced up into the lights. Everything seemed so bright now,   249
the field an electric green.

"We got a goddamned game goin' on here. You can't just stand the fuck   250
out here and pick your nose. What the hell is wrong with you? Are you on
the sauce or what?"

Red Deer kicked at the mound with his cleats.   251

"Answer me!"   252

"I don't know," Red Deer said.   253

"I'm going to put our relief in if you don't get your ass in gear."   254

Red Deer turned to Darius, looked down into his eyes.   255

Darius could tell something was wrong.   256

"I'm not on the sauce," Red Deer lied.   257

But it didn't matter now. There was no stopping what was opening. It   258
was just a matter of finishing now. He had to finish it.

"I got it," Red Deer said.   259

"Well, you better have it," Darius said.   260

He crossed the field to the dugout and climbed down.   261

Red Deer pushed his mitt on his hand. He remembered what the man   262
with the watch had said:

"Jim Thorpe couldn't have done that at your age."   263

Red Deer positioned himself on the mound. Now they had done it to   264
him, too.

"Come on, goddammit!" Darius yelled from the dugout.   265

"Chief! Hey, you! You old lady, Chief!" the man in the stands yelled.   266

Red Deer felt the anger flare in him.   267

The batter was holding his hands up and looking into the sky.   268

The catcher gave him the sign again, and Red Deer jabbed himself with   269
his anger. Now it hardly moved him at all. It was alternately terrifying, and
a relief. And when the anger came again, he gripped the ball, stared down
the pipe, got his nails on the stitching of the ball, and heaved the ball down
the line as hard as he could. The ball floated, dipped, then slammed into the
catcher's mitt and the batter coiled around.

"Steeeeerike!" the umpire called.   270

The crowd roared.   271

The tribesmen stood, and when the others took their seats again, they   272
remained standing. Someone started the others banging their feet on the stands,
and the booming got louder, a harsh, crushing banging.

With the tribesmen standing, Red Deer could not see Osada, and he   273
wondered whether he was sitting back there or if he had gone.

"Go home, Chief!" the drunk yelled. 274

Red Deer felt the ball in his hand. 275

The batter swung around, practicing. He stepped up to the plate, and 276
the catcher gave Red Deer two fingers. It pushed out of him now, and he
saw the batter grinning there. "Come on, Chief," the batter was saying. "Come
on, Chief."

Red Deer gripped the ball, a stone. 277

In a flash that burned him, Red Deer saw that he might really do it this 278
time. He saw the ball, hurling down the pipe, no curve, no spin, just hurling,
the batter's skull shattering. He could kill him now, and he could call it an
accident. It had come to this. And he knew, with absolute certainty, when
he stepped onto the mound that he was going to kill the batter. He was going
to throw the ball through the side of his head. He would crush him with his
hatred, and it would be gone, he would be free maybe, and when he got the
signal from the catcher the batter said it again, and Red Deer felt everything
in him screaming toward that pitch, the crowd roaring, the blood in his head
pounding, and sharper than ever, he saw the line the ball would take, the
point where the ball would contact the batter's head, above and back of the
ear—it was like tunnel vision, and there was only in front of him the ear and
the hair over the man's temple, the ball in his hand, the tremendous power
that moved his limbs like iron, threatening to burst him, the crowd roaring
like steam and the mound pushing up beneath him. He drew his arm back,
then farther, the weight of his rage there compressed, and in an explosion
the ball arced around, hard, heavy, and as it shot from his hand, Red Deer
caught the stitching with his thumb, and the ball, as though it were on a
track, swung wide across the field and smacked square into the batter's startled face.

The umpire burst out from behind the catcher. 279

The field came alive, the crowd roaring, and Darius scrambled from the 280
dugout. The batter kicked on the ground, and the umpire tried to hold him
down.

Red Deer turned his back to it, and tugging at his mitt, walked to the 281
mound. He stared up into the bleachers, at the big man with the bright blue
tie, the one who had started it all. The man raised his fist, opened his mouth
to shout. Something settled home in Red Deer's chest, found bottom, and
he held his eyes on the big man until he turned away. He remembered his
father's scream when Litani had been shot, and what the officers had said
after the commotion died down.

"It was a *terrible mistake*. We're sorry," the man Harris had said. 282

Red Deer drew back the bill of his cap. Without the cover for his eyes 283
the stadium lights were blinding.

They were coming up behind him now, he could hear their feet on the 284
dry grass.

He remembered his father's face, how when he had screamed it was as 285 though something had shattered in him, and when the noise had stopped and his mouth had closed, something had gone away.

"Buck!" Darius said.   286

Red Deer turned to face him. He puffed along, swinging his arms, two press men behind him with cameras.   287

Darius reached out, grasped Red Deer's forearm. "Buck," he said. "Buck, just tell them—"   288

Red Deer bent low, and as if to confide in Darius, pulled him closer. He could smell the oil in Darius' hair, his aftershave.   289

"Buck, you gotta—"   290

"Let go," Red Deer said, his voice quiet and sure as death now. "Let go of my arm, Darie," he said.   291

STUDY QUESTIONS

1. This story uses a *flashback*—that is, it shifts the scene back in time and then comes forward—rather than the more usual form of EXPOSITION in which the past is suggested or filled in. How does this affect the usual ordering of the STRUCTURE (rising action, climax, falling action, conclusion) of the story?

2. Who is Litani? How do we learn what happened to him? How is the piecemeal presentation of that story related to the story of Red Deer? How is the Litani story relevant to the final episode in the story? What is the meaning of the final sentence of the story?

3. Alcoholism is part of the STEREOTYPE of the Native American. How is it used in this story?

4. Red Deer is full of anger. How much seems due to the oppression of Native Americans? to racism? What is the nature of his encounters with whites? Is Red Deer a racist—that is, does he hate whites?

Pat Mora

Born in El Paso, Pat Mora writes poems in which her Chicana heritage and South-western background are central. Her first book, *Chants* (1985), is composed largely of what she calls "desert incantations." Her second, *Borders* (1986), from which the following poem is taken, describes the two cultures that create her own "border" life. Both books won Southwest Book awards. Her third book, *Communion*, was published in 1991. She lives in Cincinnati.

SONRISAS

I live in a doorway
between two rooms. I hear
quiet clicks, cups of black
coffee, *click*, *click* like facts
    budgets, tenure, curriculum,   5
from careful women in crisp beige
suits, quick beige smiles
that seldom sneak into their eyes.

I peek
in the other room señoras   10
in faded dresses stir sweet
milk coffee, laughter whirls
with steam from fresh *tamales*
    sh, sh, mucho ruido,[1]
they scold one another,   15
press their lips, trap smiles
in their dark, Mexican eyes.

STUDY QUESTIONS

1. What is the SPEAKER's relationship to the two worlds described in the poem? How much are we told about the speaker specifically? Why do we not need to know more? What does it mean that the speaker "lives[s] in a doorway" (line 1)?

2. How precise are the contrasts between activities in the two STANZAS? Compare the differences in word choice between the two stanzas. Why are the Anglo women said to have "beige" (line 7) smiles? Why, in stanza one, do smiles "sneak," whereas the women "trap" smiles into their eyes in stanza two? Why are the eyes in stanza two "dark," while the eyes in stanza one have no color? Compare the syntax in the two stanzas: Why do the women in stanza one perform no specific actions? What differences are suggested in the way the two groups take their coffee?

3. Which world seems to the poet to have superior human values? How can you tell? What specific values are ascribed to each world?

1. A lot of noise.

Cathy Song

B orn in 1955 in Hawaii, Cathy Song attended the University of Hawaii, Welles-ley College, and Boston University. She is the author of *Picture Bride* (winner of the Yale Younger Poets Award in 1982), in which the title poem tells the story of her Korean grandmother, who was sent for as a mail-order bride in Hawaii on the basis of her photograph. Her book *Frameless Windows, Squares of Light* was published in 1988. In 1991 she cooperated with Juliet Kono on a literary collection entitled *Sister Stew: Fiction and Poetry by Women*.

LOST SISTER

1

In China,
even the peasants
named their first daughters
Jade—
the stone that in the far fields   5
could moisten the dry season,
could make men move mountains
for the healing green of the inner hills
glistening like slices of winter melon.

And the daughters were grateful: 10
they never left home.
To move freely was a luxury
stolen from them at birth.
Instead, they gathered patience,
learning to walk in shoes   15
the size of teacups,
without breaking—
the arc of their movements
as dormant as the rooted willow,
as redundant as the farmyard hens.   20
But they traveled far
in surviving,

learning to stretch the family rice,
to quiet the demons,
the noisy stomachs.   25

                                        2

There is a sister
across the ocean,
who relinquished her name,
diluting jade green
with the blue of the Pacific.   30
Rising with a tide of locusts,
she swarmed with others
to inundate another shore.
In America,
there are many roads   35
and women can stride along with men.

But in another wilderness,
the possibilities,
the loneliness,
can strangulate like jungle vines.   40
The meager provisions and sentiments
of once belonging—
fermented roots, Mah-Jongg tiles and firecrackers—
set but a flimsy household
in a forest of nightless cities.   45
A giant snake rattles above,
spewing black clouds into your kitchen.
Dough-faced landlords
slip in and out of your keyholes,
making claims you don't understand,   50
tapping into your communication systems
of laundry lines and restaurant chains.

You find you need China:
your one fragile identification,
a jade link   55
handcuffed to your wrist.
You remember your mother
who walked for centuries,
footless—
and like her,   60
you have left no footprints,
but only because

there is an ocean in between,
the unremitting space of your rebellion.

STUDY QUESTIONS

1. Why do so many Chinese families name their first daughter Jade?

2. How were the girl children restricted in their movements? What did they achieve?

3. What advantages does the sister who comes to America find? What is the "giant snake" that rattles above the immigrant's household (line 46)? Why are the landlords called "dough-faced" (line 48)?

4. Why does the "lost sister" need a "jade link" (line 55) to China and her heritage? Why has she, like her mother, "left no footprints" (line 61)?

5. Summarize sections 1 and 2 separately. How does the division into sections suggest the STRUCTURE of the poem?

nila northSun

Born in Schurz, Nevada, in 1951 of Shoshoni-Chippewa heritage, nila northSun is coauthor of *After the Drying Up of the Water* and *Diet Pepsi and Nacho Cheese.*

UP & OUT

we total it up for
income tax
hoping to get a little
something back
but it seems we've moved ourselves   5
out of the poverty level
we made more money than
we've ever made before
but felt poorer
we made better money cause we   10
moved to the city

left the reservation where
there were no jobs
the city had jobs but
it also had high rent   15
high food high medical
high entertainment
we made better money but
it got sucked up by
the city by cable tv   20
by sparklettes water by
lunches in cute places
by drinking in quaint bars
instead of home like we did
on the reservation   25
there we lived in gramma's old house
no rent
the wood stove saved electricity &
heating bills
we only got one tv channel but   30
we visited with relatives more
there was no place to eat on the res
'cept a pool hall with chips & coke
there was only one movie house in town
& nothing good ever showed   35
we got government commodities that
tasted like dog food but
it was free
we got government doctors at i.h.s.[1]
that graduated last in their class   40
but they were free
if a car broke down there was the
old pick-up truck or a cousin with
a little mechanical know-how
god how i hated living on the reservation   45
but now
it doesn't look so bad.

STUDY QUESTIONS

1. What positive values does life on the reservation have, according to the poem? what frustrations? What indications are there that the SPEAKER's attitudes are colored by nostalgia?

1. Indian Health Services.

2. What does the image of getting sucked up by modern civilization (line 19) suggest about alien values? In what specific ways are the customs and values of the city contrasted with those of the reservation?

3. About what specific matters does the speaker feel most strongly?

Ricardo Pau-Llosa

Art historian, curator, poet, and English teacher, Ricardo Pau-Llosa was born in Cuba in 1954, and came to the United States in 1960. He was educated at Miami-Dade Community College (where he currently teaches), Florida International University, Florida Atlantic University, and the University of Florida. His first book of poetry, *Sorting Metaphors* (1983), won the national Anhinga Poetry Prize; his latest collection of poetry, *Bread of the Imagined*, was published in 1992. Pau-Llosa has also published scholarship on art.

SORTING METAPHORS

"We are like water spilled on the ground that can never be gathered up again."
                                                                2 Samuel 14:14

I open the glass and it hovers out
and back from the garden, a few feet,
inches at first, then more ambitious,
and back to knock against the screen,
until the fly is free of the thought   5
of this screen between us. We may
live a whole life between
two unyielding and unseen boundaries,
until something opens and,
reluctantly, we swing out and then   10
there is the metaphor of looking
at urban maps, those two lines
are Domínguez Street where I walked
as a child to the Covadonga's
white colonnades and lush   15
gardens, more a palace than

a hospital to my eyes, my ears
filled with the baroque lamentations
of its fountains. There
white robes recline on terraces,   20
healing in the Tropic of Cancer.
Only a map is left of that Havana,
major buildings towering
pencil marks on a grid,
half the city fitting under my spread hand   25
moving back from P-K4,[1] lightly
arched fingers, the opponents
intense sight and clicking of his time,
then suddenly a gesture and my clock
starts again, Q-Q7, Check,   30
and again my hand hovers back
from the move, not too certain,
a fatal miscalculation? My arm's
silhouette across the board
as dawn breaks over Quatre Bras[2]   35
and cumulus shadows move
toward a soldier half-dressed
stepping from a ruined barn,
the weather advancing
from the Sambre River[3] to his darkness.   40
It is a time of retreat, of tricolors
drowned in summer mud, of possible
misfortune, says the seeress,
when the ace of clubs comes together
with the four and six of clubs   45
it is almost certain death. Sad,
I know, but not irreversible;
we have our cards to warn us.
The six is separation, the ace
a long, long journey, and the four   50
is your deathbed, its four posts
you see, or at times the four
legs of your writing table,
which could mean, perhaps but unlikely,
that you are an author and will write   55
about death and journeys, and so

1. P-K4; Q-Q7: chess moves indicating piece and final position: pawn to king row 4; queen to queen row 7.

2. Village in central Belgium, about 20 miles south southeast of Brussels; battlefield where Wellington defeated the French under Ney, June 16, 1815, just before the Battle of Waterloo.

3. River in northern France and southern Belgium; scene of British victory in November 1918 in the last days of the First World War.

there is nothing to fear, no cause
for your hands to tremble.

STUDY QUESTIONS

1. In the context of the poem, to whom does the "We" in the epigraph refer? How does the situation of the fly in the opening lines relate to the "We"?

2. The METAPHOR in the poem abruptly shifts in line 11, again in line 26, again between lines 36 and 41, and once more at lines 52–53. Describe the metaphors and how they structure the poem. What is the effect of having the metaphors shift, most of the time, in mid-sentence?

Rita Mae Brown

Novelist, poet, and political activist, Rita Mae Brown was born in Hanover, Pennsylvania, in 1944 and educated at the University of Florida, New York University, the New York School of the Visual Arts, and the Institute of Policy Studies, where she received a Ph.D. in 1976. Her many novels include *Rubyfruit Jungle* (1973), *Southern Discomfort* (1982), and *Wish You Were Here* (1990). Her poems are collected in *The Hand that Cradles the Rock* (1971), *Songs to a Handsome Woman* (1973), and *Poems* (1987). Brown has also published nonfiction on the craft of writing and feminist / lesbian politics, and is a member of the National Gay Task Force.

SAPPHO'S REPLY

My voice rings down through thousands of years
To coil around your body and give you strength,
You who have wept in direct sunlight,
Who have hungered in invisible chains,
Tremble to the cadence of my legacy: 5
An army of lovers shall not fail.

STUDY QUESTIONS

1. Who is the SPEAKER? Who is being addressed?

2. Who is the "you" described as weeping specifically in "direct" sunlight? What are the "invisible chains"? What is "my" legacy?

Madeline Coopsammy

Originally from Trinidad and Tobago, Madeline Coopsammy studied in India and Canada. She currently teaches English to immigrant children in Winnipeg. Her poetry has been published in such collections as *A Shapely Fire: Changing Literary Landscape* and in *Other Voices: Writings by Blacks in Canada.*

IN THE DUNGEON OF MY SKIN

In Suez they thought I was Egyptian
In Manitoba they wonder if I'm native-born
In India they said derisively:
Indian Christian! Goan! Anglo-Indian!
In the Bronx, wayside vendors spoke to me   5
In the guttural music of Cervantes and Borges
A long time ago, in my native place
on coral shores beside the Pirate's Main[1]
they said, "You surely must be Spanish."
In a country famous for its indiscriminate racial copulation   10
ethnic nomenclature was the order of the day
and "Spanish"
was a mantle that gathered in its folds
all who bore or seemed to bear some trace,
however faint, of European ancestry.   15
It labelled you a cut above
the blacks and Hindus, low men on the totem pole;
rendered you a more pleasing place in the racial mosaic.

Now though the landscape of my being
negates the burnished faces of my youth   20
while molten rhythms
forged from the heart of Africa and India
elude me now

---

1. More commonly known as the Spanish Main, refers to the northern coast of South America from Panama on the west to Trinidad on the east and the waters and islands along that coast; notorious region for pirating activity beginning in the sixteenth century.

and I have cast from consciousness
satiric folk-songs spawned from the tortured metres of our   25
bastard English tongue
have clipped the bonds of cultures and boundaries
and made myself a universal woman
yet this poor frame, no castle
proves itself no fortress, but a dungeon from which   30
there can be no release.

STUDY QUESTIONS

1. Why is the SPEAKER's skin a dungeon rather than a fortress?

2. What is the difference between the "universal woman" she says she has made herself (line 28) and her having been mistaken for an Egyptian, Anglo-Indian, and Latina?

Dwight Okita

Dwight Okita was born in Chicago in 1958 and educated at the University of Illinois at Chicago. Active in that city's performance / poetry community, he has written music and written for the theater. His first book of poetry, *Crossing with the Light*, was published in 1992.

During World War II, both his parents were sent to relocation camps for Japanese-Americans. His father gained his release by agreeing to fight in Europe with other Japanese-Americans in the famous 442nd Battalion. His mother stayed in the camp.

IN RESPONSE TO EXECUTIVE ORDER 9066: ALL AMERICANS OF JAPANESE DESCENT MUST REPORT TO RELOCATION CENTERS

Dear Sirs:
Of course I'll come. I've packed my galoshes

and three packets of tomato seeds. Janet calls them
"love apples." My father says where we're going
they won't grow.   5

I am a fourteen-year-old girl with bad spelling
and a messy room. If it helps any, I will tell you
I have always felt funny using chopsticks
and my favorite food is hot dogs.
My best friend is a white girl named Denise—   10
we look at boys together. She sat in front of me
all through grade school because of our names:
O'Connor, Ozawa. I know the back of Denise's head very well.
I tell her she's going bald. She tells me I copy on tests.
We're best friends.   15

I saw Denise today in Geography class.
She was sitting on the other side of the room.
"You're trying to start a war," she said, "giving secrets away
to the Enemy. Why can't you keep your big mouth shut?"
I didn't know what to say.   20
I gave her a packet of tomato seeds
and asked her to plant them for me, told her
when the first tomato ripens
she'd miss me.

STUDY QUESTIONS

1. What details do we know about the SPEAKER of the poem? Which details emphasize
   her Japanese heritage? Which emphasize her likeness to "typical" American teenagers?

2. Describe the speaker's relationship to Denise. What details in the poem provide
   evidence that the speaker and Denise are "best friends"? What seems to be responsible for Denise's accusation in line 18?

3. What possessions are most important to the speaker? Why are the tomato seeds
   significant for her? Explain the appropriateness of her final gift to Denise.

R. T. Smith

R. T. Smith, Scotch-Irish and Tuscarora, was born in Washington, D.C., in
1947 and educated at the University of North Carolina at Charlotte and

Appalachian State University. He is now Alumni Writer-in-Residence and director of creative writing at Auburn University. He is the author of ten books of poetry, including *Waking Under Snow* (1975), *Good Water* (1979), *Rural Route* (1981), *Banish Misfortune* (1988), *The Cardinal Heart*, and *The Names of Trees* (1991) and has won many prizes for his work.

RED ANGER

The reservation school is brown and bleak
with bugs' guts mashed against walls
and rodent pellets reeking in corners.
Years of lies fade into the black chalk board.
A thin American flag with 48 stars   5
hangs lank over broken desks.
The stink of stale piss haunts the halls.

Tuscarora.

My reservation home is dusty.
My mother grows puffy with disease,   10
her left eye infected open forever.
Outside the bedroom window
my dirty, snotty brother Roy
claws the ground,
scratching like the goat who gnaws the garden.   15

Choctaw.

My father drinks
pale moonshine whiskey
and gambles recklessly at the garage,
kicks dust between weeds in the evening   20
and dances a fake-feathered rain dance
for tourists and a little cash.
Even the snakes have left.
Even the sun cannot stand to watch.

Cherokee.   25

Our limping dog sniffs a coil of hot shit
near the outhouse where
my sister shot herself with a .22.

So each day I march
two miles by meagre fields   30
to work in a tourist lunch stand
in their greasy aprons.
I nurse my anger like a seed,
and the whites would wonder why
I spit in their hamburgers.   35

Tuscarora, Choctaw, Cherokee . . .
the trail of tears never ends.

STUDY QUESTIONS

1. Why does the American flag have only forty-eight stars? What other outdated and leftover objects are mentioned in the first STANZA? What does the presence of such objects imply about government attitudes toward Native Americans?

2. What kinds of IMAGES characterize lines 9–15? How do they differ from those in the first stanza? What patterns and images unify the different activities described in lines 17–24? in lines 26–35?

3. Which lines suggest the most powerful emotions of the SPEAKER? What kinds of incidents or situations seem to generate the strongest feelings? Explain the image of "nurs[ing] anger like a seed" (line 33).

August Wilson

Born in 1945, August Wilson grew up in a poor family in Pittsburgh and dropped out of school at the age of sixteen. While working at menial jobs, he began to write poetry. In 1968, he founded the Black Horizons Theatre Company in St. Paul, Minnesota, but he continued to think of himself primarily as a poet until he started writing for the theater in the 1980s. In 1982, his first short play, *Jitney*, was produced in Pittsburgh, and two years later *Ma Rainey's Black Bottom* (1984) opened on Broadway. *Fences* (1985) opened on Broadway in 1987, and won several awards, including the Tony Award for best play and the Pulitzer Prize for drama. His recent plays are *Joe Turner's Come and Gone* (1986), *The Piano Lesson* (1987), and *Two Trains Running* (1990).

FENCES

CHARACTERS

TROY MAXSON
JIM BONO, Troy's friend
ROSE, Troy's wife
LYONS, Troy's oldest son by previous marriage
GABRIEL, Troy's brother
CORY, Troy and Rose's son
RAYNELL, Troy's daughter

SETTING

The setting is the yard which fronts the only entrance to the MAXSON household, an ancient two-story brick house set back off a small alley in a big-city neighborhood. The entrance to the house is gained by two or three steps leading to a wooden porch badly in need of paint.

A relatively recent addition to the house and running its full width, the porch lacks congruence. It is a sturdy porch with a flat roof. One or two chairs of dubious value sit at one end where the kitchen window opens onto the porch. An old-fashioned icebox stands silent guard at the opposite end.

The yard is a small dirt yard, partially fenced, except for the last scene, with a wooden sawhorse, a pile of lumber, and other fence-building equipment set off to the side. Opposite is a tree from which hangs a ball made of rags. A baseball bat leans against the tree. Two oil drums serve as garbage receptacles and sit near the house at right to complete the setting.

THE PLAY

Near the turn of the century, the destitute of Europe sprang on the city with tenacious claws and an honest and solid dream. The city devoured them. They swelled its belly until it burst into a thousand furnaces and sewing machines, a thousand butcher shops and bakers' ovens, a thousand churches and hospitals and funeral parlors and money-lenders. The city grew. It nourished itself and offered each man a partnership limited only by his talent, his guile, and his willingness and capacity for hard work. For the immigrants of Europe, a dream dared and won true.

The descendants of African slaves were offered no such welcome or participation. They came from places called the Carolinas and the Virginias, Georgia, Alabama, Mississippi, and Tennessee. They came strong, eager, searching. The city rejected them and they fled and settled along the riverbanks and under bridges in shallow, ramshackle houses made of sticks and tar-paper. They collected rags and wood. They sold the use of their muscles and their bodies. They cleaned houses and washed clothes, they shined shoes, and in quiet desperation and vengeful pride, they stole, and lived in pursuit of their own dream. That they could breathe free, finally, and stand to meet life with the force of dignity and whatever eloquence the heart could call upon.

By 1957, the hard-won victories of the European immigrants had solid-ified the industrial might of America. War had been confronted and won with new energies that used loyalty and patriotism as its fuel. Life was rich, full, and flourishing. The Milwaukee Braves won the World Series, and the hot winds of change that would make the sixties a turbulent, racing, danger-ous, and provocative decade had not yet begun to blow full.

ACT I

Scene 1

It is 1957. TROY *and* BONO *enter the yard, engaged in conversation.* TROY *is fifty-three years old, a large man with thick, heavy hands; it is this largeness that he strives to fill out and make an accommodation with. Together with his blackness, his largeness informs his sensibilities and the choices he has made in his life.*

Of the two men, BONO *is obviously the follower. His commitment to their friend-ship of thirty-odd years is rooted in his admiration of* TROY's *honesty, capacity for hard work, and his strength, which* BONO *seeks to emulate.*

It is Friday night, payday, and the one night of the week the two men engage in a ritual of talk and drink. TROY *is usually the most talkative and at times he can be crude and almost vulgar, though he is capable of rising to profound heights of expres-sion. The men carry lunch buckets and wear or carry burlap aprons and are dressed in clothes suitable to their jobs as garbage collectors.*

BONO: Troy, you ought to stop that lying!
TROY: I ain't lying! The nigger had a watermelon this big. [*He indicates with his hands.*] Talking about . . . "What watermelon, Mr. Rand?" I liked to fell out! "What watermelon, Mr. Rand?" . . . And it sitting there big as life.
BONO: What did Mr. Rand say?
TROY: Ain't said nothing. Figure if the nigger too dumb to know he carrying a watermelon, he wasn't gonna get much sense out of him. Trying to hide that great big old watermelon under his coat. Afraid to let the white man see him carry it home.
BONO: I'm like you . . . I ain't got no time for them kind of people.

TROY: Now what he look like getting mad cause he see the man from the union talking to Mr. Rand?

BONO: He come to me talking about . . . "Maxson gonna get us fired." I told him to get away from me with that. He walked away from me calling you a troublemaker. What Mr. Rand say?

TROY: Ain't said nothing. He told me to go down the Commissioner's office next Friday. They called me down there to see them.

BONO: Well, as long as you got your complaint filed, they can't fire you. That's what one of them white fellows tell me.

TROY: I ain't worried about them firing me. They gonna fire me cause I asked a question? That's all I did. I went to Mr. Rand and asked him "Why. Why? Why you got the white mens driving and the colored lifting?" Told him, "what's the matter, don't I count? You think only white fellows got sense enough to drive a truck. That ain't no paper job! Hell, anybody can drive a truck. How come you got all whites driving and the colored lifting?" He told me "take it to the union." Well, hell, that's what I done! Now they wanna come up with this pack of lies.

BONO: I told Brownie if the man come and ask him any questions . . . just tell the truth! It ain't nothing but something they done trumped up on you cause you filed a complaint on them.

TROY: Brownie don't understand nothing. All I want them to do is change the job description. Give everybody a chance to drive the truck. Brownie can't see that. He ain't got that much sense.

BONO: How you figure he be making out with that gal be up at Taylors' all the time . . . that Alberta gal?

TROY: Same as you and me. Getting just as much as we is. Which is to say nothing.

BONO: It is, huh? I figure you doing a little better than me . . . and I ain't saying what I'm doing.

TROY: Aw, nigger, look here . . . I know you. If you had got anywhere near that gal, twenty minutes later you be looking to tell somebody. And the first one you gonna tell . . . that you gonna want to brag to . . . is gonna be me.

BONO: I ain't saying that. I see where you be eyeing her.

TROY: I eye all the women. I don't miss nothing. Don't never let nobody tell you Troy Maxson don't eye the women.

BONO: You been doing more than eyeing her. You done bought her a drink or two.

TROY: Hell yeah, I bought her a drink! What that mean? I bought you one, too. What that mean cause I buy her a drink? I'm just being polite.

BONO: It's alright to buy her one drink. That's what you call being polite. But when you wanna be buying two or three . . . that's what you call eyeing her.

TROY: Look here, as long as you known me . . . you ever known me to chase after women?

BONO: Hell yeah! Long as I done known you. You forgetting I knew you when.

TROY: Naw, I'm talking about since I been married to Rose?

BONO: Oh, not since you been married to Rose. Now, that's the truth, there. I can say that.

TROY: Alright then! Case closed.

BONO: I see you be walking up around Alberta's house. You supposed to be at Taylors' and you be walking up around there.

TROY: What you watching where I'm walking for? I ain't watching after you.

BONO: I seen you walking around there more than once.

TROY: Hell, you liable to see me walking anywhere! That don't mean nothing cause you see me walking around there.

BONO: Where she come from anyway? She just kinda showed up one day.

TROY: Tallahassee. You can look at her and tell she one of them Florida gals. They got some big healthy women down there. Grow them right up out the ground. Got a little bit of Indian in her. Most of them niggers down in Florida got some Indian in them.

BONO: I don't know about that Indian part. But she damn sure big and healthy. Woman wear some big stockings. Got them great big old legs and hips as wide as the Mississippi River.

TROY: Legs don't mean nothing. You don't do nothing but push them out of the way. But them hips cushion the ride!

BONO: Troy, you ain't got no sense.

TROY: It's the truth! Like you riding on Goodyears!

[ROSE *enters from the house. She is ten years younger than* TROY, *her devotion to him stems from her recognition of the possibilities of her life without him: a succession of abusive men and their babies, a life of partying and running the streets, the Church, or aloneness with its attendant pain and frustration. She recognizes* TROY's *spirit as a fine and illuminating one and she either ignores or forgives his faults, only some of which she recognizes. Though she doesn't drink, her presence is an integral part of the Friday night rituals. She alternates between the porch and the kitchen, where supper preparations are under way.*]

ROSE: What you all out here getting into?

TROY: What you worried about what we getting into for? This is men talk, woman.

ROSE: What I care what you all talking about? Bono, you gonna stay for supper?

BONO: No, I thank you, Rose. But Lucille say she cooking up a pot of pigfeet.

TROY: Pigfeet! Hell, I'm going home with you! Might even stay the night if you got some pigfeet. You got something in there to top them pigfeet, Rose?

ROSE: I'm cooking up some chicken. I got some chicken and collard greens.

TROY: Well, go on back in the house and let me and Bono finish what we was talking about. This is men talk. I got some talk for you later. You know what kind of talk I mean. You go on and powder it up.

ROSE: Troy Maxson, don't you start that now!

TROY: [*Puts his arm around her.*] Aw, woman . . . come here. Look here, Bono . . . when I met this woman . . . I got out that place, say, "Hitch up my pony, saddle up my mare . . . there's a woman out there for me somewhere. I looked here. Looked there. Saw Rose and latched on to her." I latched on to her and told her—I'm gonna tell you the truth—I told her, "Baby, I don't wanna marry, I just wanna be your man." Rose told me . . . tell him what you told me, Rose.

ROSE: I told him if he wasn't the marrying kind, then move out the way so the marrying kind could find me.

TROY: That's what she told me. "Nigger, you in my way. You blocking the view! Move out the way so I can find me a husband." I thought it over two or three days. Come back—

ROSE: Ain't no two or three days nothing. You was back the same night.

TROY: Come back, told her . . . "Okay, baby . . . but I'm gonna buy me a banty rooster and put him out there in the backyard, and when he see a stranger come, he'll flap his wings and crow . . ." Look here, Bono, I could watch the front door by myself . . . it was that back door I was worried about.

ROSE: Troy, you ought not talk like that. Troy ain't doing nothing but telling a lie.

TROY: Only thing is . . . when we first got married . . . forget the rooster . . . we ain't had no yard!

BONO: I hear you tell it. Me and Lucille was staying down there on Logan Street. Had two rooms with the outhouse in the back. I ain't mind the outhouse none. But when that goddamn wind blow through there in the winter . . . that's what I'm talking about! To this day I wonder why in the hell I ever stayed down there for six long years. But see, I didn't know I could do no better. I thought only white folks had inside toilets and things.

ROSE: There's a lot of people don't know they can do no better than they doing now. That's just something you got to learn. A lot of folks still shop at Bella's.

TROY: Ain't nothing wrong with shopping at Bella's. She got fresh food.

ROSE: I ain't said nothing about if she got fresh food. I'm talking about what she charge. She charge ten cents more than the A&P.

TROY: The A&P ain't never done nothing for me. I spends my money where I'm treated right. I go down to Bella, say, "I need a loaf of bread, I'll pay you on Friday." She give it to me. What sense that make when I got money to go and spend it somewhere else and ignore the person who done right by me? That ain't in the Bible.

ROSE: We ain't talking about what's in the Bible. What sense it make to shop there when she overcharge?

TROY: You shop where you want to. I'll do my shopping where the people been good to me.

ROSE: Well, I don't think it's right for her to overcharge. That's all I was saying.

BONO: Look here . . . I got to get on. Lucille going be raising all kind of hell.

TROY: Where you going, nigger? We ain't finished this pint. Come here, finish this pint.

BONO: Well, hell, I am . . . if you ever turn the bottle loose.

TROY: [*Hands him the bottle.*] The only thing I say about the A&P is I'm glad Cory got that job down there. Help him take care of his school clothes and things. Gabe done moved out and things getting tight around here. He got that job . . . He can start to look out for himself.

ROSE: Cory done went and got recruited by a college football team.

TROY: I told that boy about that football stuff. The white man ain't gonna let him get nowhere with that football. I told him when he first come to me with it. Now you come telling me he done went and got more tied up in it. He ought to go and get recruited in how to fix cars or something where he can make a living.

ROSE: He ain't talking about making no living playing football. It's just something the boys in school do. They gonna send a recruiter by to talk to you. He'll tell you he ain't talking about making no living playing football. It's a honor to be recruited.

TROY: It ain't gonna get him nowhere. Bono'll tell you that.

BONO: If he be like you in the sports . . . he's gonna be alright. Ain't but two men ever played baseball as good as you. That's Babe Ruth and Josh Gibson. Them's the only two men ever hit more home runs than you.

TROY: What it ever get me? Ain't got a pot to piss in or a window to throw it out of.

ROSE: Times have changed since you was playing baseball, Troy. That was before the war. Times have changed a lot since then.

TROY: How in hell they done changed?

ROSE: They got lots of colored boys playing ball now. Baseball and football.

BONO: You right about that, Rose. Times have changed, Troy. You just come along too early.

TROY: There ought not never have been no time called too early! Now you take that fellow . . . what's that fellow they had playing right field for the Yankees back then? You know who I'm talking about, Bono. Used to play right field for the Yankees?

ROSE: Selkirk?

TROY: Selkirk! That's it! Man batting .269, understand? .269. What kind of sense that make? I was hitting .432 with thirty-seven home runs! Man batting .269 and playing right field for the Yankees! I saw Josh Gibson's daughter yesterday. She walking around with raggedy shoes on her feet. Now I bet you Selkirk's daughter ain't walking around with raggedy shoes on her feet. I bet you that!

ROSE: They got a lot of colored baseball players now. Jackie Robinson was the first. Folks had to wait for Jackie Robinson.

TROY: I done seen a hundred niggers play baseball better than Jackie Robinson. Hell, I know some teams Jackie Robinson couldn't even make! What you talking about Jackie Robinson. Jackie Robinson wasn't nobody. I'm talking about if you could play ball then they ought to have let you play. Don't care what color you were. Come telling me I come along too early. If you could play . . . then they ought to have let you play. [TROY *takes a long drink from the bottle.*]

ROSE: You gonna drink yourself to death. You don't need to be drinking like that.

TROY: Death ain't nothing. I done seen him. Done wrassled with him. You can't tell me nothing about death. Death ain't nothing but a fastball on the outside corner. And you know what I'll do to that! Lookee here, Bono . . . am I lying? You get one of them fastballs, about waist high, over the outside corner of the plate where you can get the meat of the bat on it . . . and good god! You can kiss it goodbye. Now, am I lying?

BONO: Naw, you telling the truth there. I seen you do it.

TROY: If I'm lying . . . that 450 feet worth of lying! [*Pause.*] That's all death is to me. A fastball on the outside corner.

ROSE: I don't know why you want to get on talking about death.

TROY: Ain't nothing wrong with talking about death. That's part of life. Everybody gonna die. You gonna die, I'm gonna die. Bono's gonna die. Hell, we all gonna die.

ROSE: But you ain't got to talk about it. I don't like to talk about it.

TROY: You the one brought it up. Me and Bono was talking about baseball . . . you tell me I'm gonna drink myself to death. Ain't that right, Bono? You know I don't drink this but one night out of the week. That's Friday night. I'm gonna drink just enough to where I can handle it. Then I cuts it loose. I leave it alone. So don't you worry about me drinking myself to death. 'Cause I ain't worried about Death. I done seen him. I done wrestled with him. Look here, Bono . . . I looked up one day and Death was marching straight at me. Like Soldiers on Parade! The Army of Death was marching straight at me. The middle of July, 1941. It got real cold just like it be winter. It seem like Death himself reached out and touched me on the shoulder. He touch me just like I touch you. I got cold as ice and Death standing there grinning at me.

ROSE: Troy, why don't you hush that talk.

TROY: I say . . . What you want, Mr. Death? You be wanting me? You done brought your army to be getting me? I looked him dead in the eye. I wasn't fearing nothing. I was ready to tangle. Just like I'm ready to tangle now. The Bible say be ever vigilant. That's why I don't get but so drunk. I got to keep watch.

ROSE: Troy was right down there in Mercy Hospital. You remember he had pneumonia? Laying there with a fever talking plumb out of his head.

TROY: Death standing there staring at me . . . carrying that sickle in his hand. Finally he say, "You want bound over for another year?" See, just like that . . . "You want bound over for another year?" I told him, "Bound over hell! Let's settle this now!" It seem like he kinda fell back when I said that, and all the cold went out of me. I reached down and grabbed that sickle and threw it just as far as I could throw it . . . and me and him commenced to wrestling. We wrestled for three days and three nights. I can't say where I found the strength from. Every time it seemed like he was gonna get the best of me, I'd reach way down deep inside myself and find the strength to do him one better.

ROSE: Every time Troy tell that story he find different ways to tell it. Different things to make up about it.

TROY: I ain't making up nothing. I'm telling you the facts of what happened. I wrestled with Death for three days and three nights and I'm standing here to tell you about it. [*Pause.*] Alright. At the end of the third night we done weakened each other to where we can't hardly move. Death stood up, throwed on his robe . . . had him a white robe with a hood on it. He throwed on that robe and went off to look for his sickle. Say, "I'll be back." Just like that. "I'll be back." I told him, say, "Yeah, but . . . you gonna have to find me!" I wasn't no fool. I wasn't going looking for him. Death ain't nothing to play with. And I know he's gonna get me. I know I got to join his army . . . his camp followers. But as long as I keep my strength and see him coming . . . as long as I keep up my vigilance . . . he's gonna have to fight to get me. I ain't going easy.

BONO: Well, look here, since you got to keep up your vigilance . . . let me have the bottle.

TROY: Aw hell, I shouldn't have told you that part. I should have left out that part.

ROSE: Troy be talking that stuff and half the time don't even know what he be talking about.

TROY: Bono know me better than that.

BONO: That's right. I know you. I know you got some Uncle Remus in your blood. You got more stories than the devil got sinners.

TROY: Aw hell, I done seen him too! Done talked with the devil.

ROSE: Troy, don't nobody wanna be hearing all that stuff.

[LYONS *enters the yard from the street. Thirty-four years old,* TROY's *son by a previous marriage, he sports a neatly trimmed goatee, sport coat, white shirt, tieless and buttoned at the collar. Though he fancies himself a musician, he is more caught up in the rituals and "idea" of being a musician than in the actual practice of the music. He has come to borrow money from* TROY, *and while he knows he will be successful, he is uncertain as to what extent his lifestyle will be held up to scrutiny and ridicule.*]

LYONS: Hey, Pop.

TROY: What you come "Hey, Popping" me for?

LYONS: How you doing, Rose? [*He kisses her.*] Mr. Bono, how you doing?

BONO: Hey, Lyons . . . how you been?

TROY: He must have been doing alright. I ain't seen him around here last week.

ROSE: Troy, leave your boy alone. He come by to see you and you wanna start all that nonsense.

TROY: I ain't bothering Lyons. [*Offers him the bottle.*] Here . . . get you a drink. We got an understanding. I know why he come by to see me and he know I know.

LYONS: Come on, Pop . . . I just stopped by to say hi . . . see how you was doing.

TROY: You ain't stopped by yesterday.

ROSE: You gonna stay for supper, Lyons? I got some chicken cooking in the oven.

LYONS: No, Rose . . . thanks. I was just in the neighborhood and thought I'd stop by for a minute.

TROY: You was in the neighborhood alright, nigger. You telling the truth there. You was in the neighborhood cause it's my payday.

LYONS: Well, hell, since you mentioned it . . . let me have ten dollars.

TROY: I'll be damned! I'll die and go to hell and play blackjack with the devil before I give you ten dollars.

BONO: That's what I wanna know about . . . that devil you done seen.

LYONS: What . . . Pop done seen the devil? You too much, Pops.

TROY: Yeah, I done seen him. Talked to him too!

ROSE: You ain't seen no devil. I done told you that man ain't had nothing to do with the devil. Anything you can't understand, you want to call it the devil.

TROY: Look here, Bono . . . I went down to see Hertzberger about some furniture. Got three rooms for two-ninety-eight. That what it say on the radio. "Three rooms . . . two-ninety-eight." Even made up a little song about it. Go down there . . . man tell me I can't get no credit. I'm working every day and can't get no credit. What to do? I got an empty house with some raggedy furniture in it. Cory ain't got no bed. He's sleeping on a pile of rags on the floor. Working every day and can't get no credit. Come back here—Rose'll tell you—madder than hell. Sit down . . . try to figure what I'm gonna do. Come a knock on the door. Ain't been living here but three days. Who know I'm here? Open the door . . . devil standing there bigger than life. White fellow . . . got on good clothes and everything. Standing there with a clipboard in his hand. I ain't had to say nothing. First words come out of his mouth was . . . "I understand you need some furniture and can't get no credit." I liked to fell over. He say "I'll give you all the credit you want, but you got to pay the interest on it." I told him, "Give me three rooms worth and charge whatever you want." Next day a truck pulled up here and two men unloaded them three rooms. Man what drove the truck give me a book. Say send ten dollars, first of every month to the address in the book and everything will be alright. Say if I miss a payment the devil was coming back and it'll be hell to pay. That was fifteen years ago. To this day . . . the first of the month I send my ten dollars, Rose'll tell you.

ROSE: Troy lying.

TROY: I ain't never seen that man since. Now you tell me who else that could have been but the devil? I ain't sold my soul or nothing like that, you understand. Naw, I wouldn't have truck with the devil about nothing like that. I got my furniture and pays my ten dollars the first of the month just like clockwork.

BONO: How long you say you been paying this ten dollars a month?

TROY: Fifteen years!

BONO: Hell, ain't you finished paying for it yet? How much the man done charged you.

TROY: Aw hell, I done paid for it. I done paid for it ten times over! The fact is I'm scared to stop paying it.

ROSE: Troy lying. We got that furniture from Mr. Glickman. He ain't paying no ten dollars a month to nobody.

TROY: Aw hell, woman. Bono know I ain't that big a fool.

LYONS: I was just getting ready to say . . . I know where there's a bridge for sale.

TROY: Look here, I'll tell you this . . . it don't matter to me if he was the devil. It don't matter if the devil give credit. Somebody has got to give it.

ROSE: It ought to matter. You going around talking about having truck with the devil . . . God's the one you gonna have to answer to. He's the one gonna be at the Judgment.

LYONS: Yeah, well, look here, Pop . . . let me have that ten dollars. I'll give it back to you. Bonnie got a job working at the hospital.

TROY: What I tell you, Bono? The only time I see this nigger is when he wants something. That's the only time I see him.

LYONS: Come on, Pop, Mr. Bono don't want to hear all that. Let me have the ten dollars. I told you Bonnie working.

TROY: What that mean to me? "Bonnie working." I don't care if she working. Go ask her for the ten dollars if she working. Talking about "Bonnie working." Why ain't you working?

LYONS: Aw, Pop, you know I can't find no decent job. Where am I gonna get a job at? You know I can't get no job.

TROY: I told you I know some people down there. I can get you on the rubbish if you want to work. I told you that the last time you came by here asking me for something.

LYONS: Naw, Pop . . . thanks. That ain't for me. I don't wanna be carrying nobody's rubbish. I don't wanna be punching nobody's time clock.

TROY: What's the matter, you too good to carry people's rubbish? Where you think that ten dollars you talking about come from? I'm just supposed to haul people's rubbish and give my money to you cause you too lazy to work. You too lazy to work and wanna know why you ain't got what I got.

ROSE: What hospital Bonnie working at? Mercy?

LYONS: She's down at Passavant working in the laundry.

TROY: I ain't got nothing as it is. I give you that ten dollars and I got to eat beans the rest of the week. Naw . . . you ain't getting no ten dollars here.

LYONS: You ain't got to be eating no beans. I don't know why you wanna say that.

TROY: I ain't got no extra money. Gabe done moved over to Miss Pearl's paying her the rent and things done got tight around here. I can't afford to be giving you every payday.

LYONS: I ain't asked you to give me nothing. I asked you to loan me ten dollars. I know you got ten dollars.

TROY: Yeah, I got it. You know why I got it? Cause I don't throw my money away out there in the streets. You living the fast life . . . wanna be a musician . . . running around in them clubs and things . . . then, you learn to take care of yourself. You ain't gonna find me going and asking nobody for nothing. I done spent too many years without.

LYONS: You and me is two different people, Pop.

TROY: I done learned my mistake and learned to do what's right by it. You still trying to get something for nothing. Life don't owe you nothing. You owe it to yourself. Ask Bono. He'll tell you I'm right.

LYONS: You got your way of dealing with the world . . . I got mine. The only thing that matters to me is the music.

TROY: Yeah, I can see that! It don't matter how you gonna eat . . . where your next dollar is coming from. You telling the truth there.

LYONS: I know I got to eat. But I got to live too. I need something that gonna help me to get out of the bed in the morning. Make me feel like I belong in the world. I don't bother nobody. I just stay with my music cause that's the only way I can find to live in the world. Otherwise there ain't no telling what I might do. Now I don't come criticizing you and how you live. I just come by to ask you for ten dollars. I don't wanna hear all that about how I live.

TROY: Boy, your mama did a hell of a job raising you.

LYONS: You can't change me, Pop. I'm thirty-four years old. If you wanted to change me, you should have been there when I was growing up. I come by to see you . . . ask for ten dollars and you want to talk about how I was raised. You don't know nothing about how I was raised.

ROSE: Let the boy have ten dollars, Troy.

TROY: [*To* LYONS.] What the hell you looking at me for? I ain't got no ten dollars. You know what I do with my money. [*To* ROSE.] Give him ten dollars if you want him to have it.

ROSE: I will. Just as soon as you turn it loose.

TROY: [*Handing* ROSE *the money.*] There it is. Seventy-six dollars and forty-two cents. You see this, Bono? Now, I ain't gonna get but six of that back.

ROSE: You ought to stop telling that lie. Here, Lyons. [*She hands him the money.*]

LYONS: Thanks, Rose. Look . . . I got to run . . . I'll see you later.

TROY: Wait a minute. You gonna say, "thanks, Rose" and ain't gonna look to see where she got that ten dollars from? See how they do me, Bono?

LYONS: I know she got it from you, Pop. Thanks. I'll give it back to you.

TROY: There he go telling another lie. Time I see that ten dollars . . . he'll be owing me thirty more.

LYONS: See you, Mr. Bono.

BONO: Take care, Lyons!

LYONS: Thanks, Pop. I'll see you again. [LYONS *exits the yard.*]

TROY: I don't know why he don't go and get him a decent job and take care of that woman he got.

BONO: He'll be alright, Troy. The boy is still young.

TROY: The *boy* is thirty-four years old.

ROSE: Let's not get off into all that.

BONO: Look here . . . I got to be going. I got to be getting on. Lucille gonna be waiting.

TROY: [*Puts his arm around* ROSE.] See this woman, Bono? I love this woman. I love this woman so much it hurts. I love her so much . . . I done run out of ways of loving her. So I got to go back to basics. Don't you come by my house Monday morning talking about time to go to work . . . 'cause I'm still gonna be stroking!

ROSE: Troy! Stop it now!

BONO: I ain't paying him no mind, Rose. That ain't nothing but gin-talk. Go on, Troy. I'll see you Monday.

TROY: Don't you come by my house, nigger! I done told you what I'm gonna be doing.

[*The lights go down to black.*]

Scene 2

The lights come up on ROSE *hanging up clothes. She hums and sings softly to herself. It is the following morning.*

ROSE: [*Sings*] Jesus, be a fence all around me every day
        Jesus, I want you to protect me as I travel on my way.
        Jesus, be a fence all around me every day.

[TROY enters from the house]

ROSE [*continued*]: Jesus, I want you to protect me
        As I travel on my way.

[*To* TROY]

ROSE: 'Morning. You ready for breakfast? I can fix it soon as I finish hanging up these clothes?

TROY: I got the coffee on. That'll be alright. I'll just drink some of that this morning.

ROSE: That 651 hit yesterday. That's the second time this month. Miss Pearl hit for a dollar . . . seem like those that need the least always get lucky. Poor folks can't get nothing.

TROY: Them numbers don't know nobody. I don't know why you fool with them. You and Lyons both.

ROSE: It's something to do.

TROY: You ain't doing nothing but throwing your money away.

ROSE: Troy, you know I don't play foolishly. I just play a nickel here and a nickel there.

TROY: That's two nickels you done thrown away.

ROSE: Now I hit sometimes . . . that makes up for it. It always comes in handy when I do hit. I don't hear you complaining then.

TROY: I ain't complaining now. I just say it's foolish. Trying to guess out of six hundred ways which way the number gonna come. If I had all the money niggers, these Negroes, throw away on numbers for one week— just one week—I'd be a rich man.

ROSE: Well, you wishing and calling it foolish ain't gonna stop folks from playing numbers. That's one thing for sure. Besides . . . some good things come from playing numbers. Look where Pope done bought him that restaurant off of numbers.

TROY: I can't stand niggers like that. Man ain't had two dimes to rub together. He walking around with his shoes all run over bumming money for cigarettes. Alright. Got lucky there and hit the numbers . . .

ROSE: Troy, I know all about it.

TROY: Had good sense, I'll say that for him. He ain't throwed his money away. I seen niggers hit the numbers and go through two thousand dollars in four days. Man bought him that restaurant down there . . . fixed it up real nice . . . and then didn't want nobody to come in it! A Negro go in there and can't get no kind of service. I seen a white fellow come in there and order a bowl of stew. Pope picked all the meat out the pot for him. Man ain't had nothing but a bowl of meat! Negro come behind him and ain't got nothing but the potatoes and carrots. Talking about what numbers do for people, you picked a wrong example. Ain't done nothing but make a worser fool out of him than he was before.

ROSE: Troy, you ought to stop worrying about what happened at work yesterday.

TROY: I ain't worried. Just told me to be down there at the Commissioner's office on Friday. Everybody think they gonna fire me. I ain't worried about them firing me. You ain't got to worry about that.

[Pause.]

Where's Cory? Cory in the house? [Calls.] Cory?

ROSE: He gone out.

TROY: Out, huh? He gone out 'cause he know I want him to help me with this fence. I know how he is. That boy scared of work.

[GABRIEL enters. He comes halfway down the alley and, hearing Troy's voice, stops.]

TROY [continues]: He ain't done a lick of work in his life.

ROSE: He had to go to football practice. Coach wanted them to get in a little extra practice before the season start.

TROY: I got his practice . . . running out of here before he get his chores done.

ROSE: Troy, what is wrong with you this morning? Don't nothing set right with you. Go on back in there and go to bed . . . get up on the other side.

TROY: Why something got to be wrong with me? I ain't said nothing wrong with me.

ROSE: You got something to say about everything. First it's the numbers . . . then it's the way the man runs his restaurant . . . then you done got on Cory. What's it gonna be next? Take a look up there and see if the weather suits you . . . or is it gonna be how you gonna put up the fence with the clothes hanging in the yard.

TROY: You hit the nail on the head then!

ROSE: I know you like I know the back of my hand. Go on in there and get you some coffee . . . see if that straighten you up. 'Cause you ain't right this morning.

[*Troy starts into the house and sees* GABRIEL. GABRIEL *starts singing.* TROY's *brother, he is seven years younger than* TROY. *Injured in World War II, he has a metal plate in his head. He carries an old trumpet tied around his waist and believes with every fiber of his being that he is the Archangel Gabriel. He carries a chipped basket with an assortment of discarded fruits and vegetables he has picked up in the strip district and which he attempts to sell.*]

[GABRIEL *singing.*]
Yes, ma'am, I got plums
You ask me how I sell them
Oh ten cents apiece
Three for a quarter
Come and buy now
'Cause I'm here today
And tomorrow I'll be gone

[GABRIEL *enters.*]

GABRIEL: Hey, Rose!

ROSE: How you doing, Gabe?

GABRIEL: There's Troy . . . Hey, Troy!

TROY: Hey, Gabe. [*Exit into kitchen.*]

ROSE: [*To* GABRIEL.] What you got there?

GABRIEL: You know what I got, Rose. I got fruits and vegetables.

ROSE: [*Looking in basket.*] Where's all these plums you talking about?

GABRIEL: I ain't got no plums today, Rose. I was just singing that. Have some tomorrow. Put me in a big order for plums. Have enough plums tomorrow for St. Peter and everybody. [TROY *re-enters from kitchen, crosses to steps.*] [*To* ROSE.] Troy's mad at me.

TROY: I ain't mad at you. What I got to be mad at you about? You ain't done nothing to me.

GABRIEL: I just moved over to Miss Pearl's to keep out from in your way. I ain't mean no harm by it.

TROY: Who said anything about that? I ain't said anything about that.

GABRIEL: You ain't mad at me, is you?

TROY: Naw . . . I ain't mad at you, Gabe. If I was mad at you I'd tell you about it.

GABRIEL: Got me two rooms. In the basement. Got my own door too. Wanna see my key? [*He holds up a key.*] That's my own key! Ain't nobody else got a key like that. That's my key! My two rooms!

TROY: Well, that's good, Gabe. You got your own key . . . that's good.

ROSE: You hungry, Gabe? I was just fixing to cook Troy his breakfast.

GABRIEL: I'll take some biscuits. You got some biscuits? Did you know when I was in heaven . . . every morning me and St. Peter would sit down by the gate and eat some big fat biscuits? Oh, yeah! We had us a good time. We'd sit there and eat us them biscuits and then St. Peter would go off to sleep and tell me to wake him up when it's time to open the gates for the judgment.

ROSE: Well, come on . . . I'll make up a batch of biscuits. [ROSE *exits into the house.*]

GABRIEL: Troy . . . St. Peter got your name in the book. I seen it. It say . . . Troy Maxson. I say . . . I know him! He got the same name like what I got. That's my brother!

TROY: How many times you gonna tell me that, Gabe?

GABRIEL: Ain't got my name in the book. Don't have to have my name. I done died and went to heaven. He got your name though. One morning St. Peter was looking at his book . . . marking it up for the judgment . . . and he let me see your name. Got it in there under M. Got Rose's name . . . I ain't seen it like I seen yours . . . but I know it's in there. He got a great big book. Got everybody's name what was ever been born. That's what he told me. But I seen your name. Seen it with my own eyes.

TROY: Go on in the house there. Rose going to fix you something to eat.

GABRIEL: Oh, I ain't hungry. I done had breakfast with Aunt Jemimah. She come by and cooked me up a whole mess of flapjacks. Remember how we used to eat them flapjacks?

TROY: Go on in the house and get you something to eat now.

GABRIEL: I got to go sell my plums. I done sold some tomatoes. Got me two quarters. Wanna see? [*He shows* TROY *his quarters.*] I'm gonna save them and buy me a new horn so St. Peter can hear me when it's time to open the gates. [GABRIEL *stops suddenly. Listens.*] Hear that? That's the hell-hounds. I got to chase them out of here. Go on get out of here! Get out!

[GABRIEL *exits singing.*]
Better get ready for the judgment
Better get ready for the judgment
My Lord is coming down

[ROSE *enters from the house.*]

TROY: He gone off somewhere.

GABRIEL: (Offstage)

Better get ready for the judgment

Better get ready for the judgment morning
Better get ready for the judgment
My God is coming down

ROSE: He ain't eating right. Miss Pearl say she can't get him to eat nothing.

TROY: What you want me to do about it, Rose? I done did everything I can for the man. I can't make him get well. Man got half his head blown away . . . what you expect?

ROSE: Seem like something ought to be done to help him.

TROY: Man don't bother nobody. He just mixed up from that metal plate he got in his head. Ain't no sense for him to go back into the hospital.

ROSE: Least he be eating right. They can help him take care of himself.

TROY: Don't nobody wanna be locked up, Rose. What you wanna lock him up for? Man go over there and fight the war . . . messin' around with them Japs, get half his head blown off . . . and they give him a lousy three thousand dollars. And I had to swoop down on that.

ROSE: Is you fixing to go into that again?

TROY: That's the only way I got a roof over my head . . . cause of that metal plate.

ROSE: Ain't no sense you blaming yourself for nothing. Gabe wasn't in no condition to manage that money. You done what was right by him. Can't nobody say you ain't done what was right by him. Look how long you took care of him . . . till he wanted to have his own place and moved over there with Miss Pearl.

TROY: That ain't what I'm saying, woman! I'm just stating the facts. If my brother didn't have that metal plate in his head . . . I wouldn't have a pot to piss in or a window to throw it out of. And I'm fifty-three years old. Now see if you can understand that! [TROY *gets up from the porch and starts to exit the yard.*]

ROSE: Where you going off to? You been running out of here every Saturday for weeks. I thought you was gonna work on this fence?

TROY: I'm gonna walk down to Taylors'. Listen to the ball game. I'll be back in a bit. I'll work on it when I get back.

[*He exits the yard. The lights go to black.*]

Scene 3

The lights come up on the yard. It is four hours later. ROSE *is taking down the clothes from the line.* CORY *enters carrying his football equipment.*

ROSE: Your daddy liked to had a fit with you running out of here this morning without doing your chores.

CORY: I told you I had to go to practice.

ROSE: He say you were supposed to help him with this fence.

CORY: He been saying that the last four or five Saturdays, and then he don't never do nothing, but go down to Taylors'. Did you tell him about the recruiter?

ROSE: Yeah, I told him.

CORY: What he say?

ROSE: He ain't said nothing too much. You get in there and get started on your chores before he gets back. Go on and scrub down them steps before he gets back here hollering and carrying on.

CORY: I'm hungry. What you got to eat, Mama?

ROSE: Go on and get started on your chores. I got some meat loaf in there. Go on and make you a sandwich . . . and don't leave no mess in there.

[CORY *exits into the house.* ROSE *continues to take down the clothes.* TROY *enters the yard and sneaks up and grabs her from behind.*]

Troy! Go on, now. You liked to scared me to death. What was the score of the game? Lucille had me on the phone and I couldn't keep up with it.

TROY: What I care about the game? Come here, woman. [*He tries to kiss her.*]

ROSE: I thought you went down Taylors' to listen to the game. Go on, Troy! You supposed to be putting up this fence.

TROY: [*Attempting to kiss her again.*] I'll put it up when I finish with what is at hand.

ROSE: Go on, Troy. I ain't studying you.

TROY: [*Chasing after her.*] I'm studying you . . . fixing to do my homework!

ROSE: Troy, you better leave me alone.

TROY: Where's Cory? That boy brought his butt home yet?

ROSE: He's in the house doing his chores.

TROY: [*Calling.*] Cory! Get your butt out here, boy!

[ROSE *exits into the house with the laundry.* TROY *goes over to the pile of wood, picks up a board, and starts sawing.* CORY *enters from the house.*]

TROY: You just now coming in here from leaving this morning?

CORY: Yeah, I had to go to football practice.

TROY: Yeah, what?

CORY: Yessir.

TROY: I ain't but two seconds off you noway. The garbage sitting in there overflowing . . . you ain't done none of your chores . . . and you come in here talking about, "Yeah."

CORY: I was just getting ready to do my chores now, Pop . . .

TROY: Your first chore is to help me with this fence on Saturday. Everything else come after that. Now get that saw and cut them boards.

[CORY *takes the saw and begins cutting the boards.* TROY *continues working. There is a long pause.*]

CORY: Hey, Pop . . . why don't you buy a TV?

TROY: What I want with a TV? What I want one of them for?

CORY: Everybody got one. Earl, Ba Bra . . . Jesse!

TROY: I ain't asked you who had one. I say what I want with one?

CORY: So you can watch it. They got lots of things on TV. Baseball games and everything. We could watch the World Series.

TROY: Yeah . . . and how much this TV cost?

CORY: I don't know. They got them on sale for around two hundred dollars.

TROY: Two hundred dollars, huh?

CORY: That ain't that much, Pop.

TROY: Naw, it's just two hundred dollars. See that roof you got over your head at night? Let me tell you something about that roof. It's been over ten years since that roof was last tarred. See now . . . the snow come this winter and sit up there on that roof like it is . . . and it's gonna seep inside. It's just gonna be a little bit . . . ain't gonna hardly notice it. Then the next thing you know, it's gonna be leaking all over the house. Then the wood rot from all that water and you gonna need a whole new roof. Now, how much you think it cost to get that roof tarred?

CORY: I don't know.

TROY: Two hundred and sixty-four dollars . . . cash money. While you thinking about a TV, I got to be thinking about the roof . . . and whatever else go wrong around here. Now if you had two hundred dollars, what would you do . . . fix the roof or buy a TV?

CORY: I'd buy a TV. Then when the roof started to leak . . . when it needed fixing . . . I'd fix it.

TROY: Where you gonna get the money from? You done spent it for a TV. You gonna sit up and watch the water run all over your brand new TV.

CORY: Aw, Pop. You got money. I know you do.

TROY: Where I got it at, huh?

CORY: You got it in the bank.

TROY: You wanna see my bankbook? You wanna see that seventy-three dol- lars and twenty-two cents I got sitting up in there.

CORY: You ain't got to pay for it all at one time. You can put a down payment on it and carry it on home with you.

TROY: Not me. I ain't gonna owe nobody nothing if I can help it. Miss a payment and they come and snatch it right out your house. Then what you got? Now, soon as I get two hundred dollars clear, then I'll buy a TV. Right now, as soon as I get two hundred and sixty-four dollars, I'm gonna have this roof tarred.

CORY: Aw . . . Pop!

TROY: You go on and get you two hundred dollars and buy one if ya want it. I got better things to do with my money.

CORY: I can't get no two hundred dollars. I ain't never seen two hundred dollars.

TROY: I'll tell you what . . . you get you a hundred dollars and I'll put the other hundred with it.

CORY: Alright, I'm gonna show you.

TROY: You gonna show me how you can cut them boards right now.

[CORY *begins to cut the boards. There is a long pause.*]

CORY: The Pirates won today. That makes five in a row.

TROY: I ain't thinking about the Pirates. Got an all-white team. Got that boy

. . . that Puerto Rican boy . . . Clemente. Don't even half-play him. That boy could be something if they give him a chance. Play him one day and sit him on the bench the next.

CORY: He gets a lot of chances to play.

TROY: I'm talking about playing regular. Playing every day so you can get your timing. That's what I'm talking about.

CORY: They got some white guys on the team that don't play every day. You can't play everybody at the same time.

TROY: If they got a white fellow sitting on the bench . . . you can bet your last dollar he can't play! The colored guy got to be twice as good before he get on the team. That's why I don't want you to get all tied up in them sports. Man on the team and what it get him? They got colored on the team and don't use them. Same as not having them. All them teams the same.

CORY: The Braves got Hank Aaron and Wes Covington. Hank Aaron hit two home runs today. That makes forty-three.

TROY: Hank Aaron ain't nobody. That's what you supposed to do. That's how you supposed to play the game. Ain't nothing to it. It's just a matter of timing . . . getting the right follow-through. Hell, I can hit forty-three home runs right now!

CORY: Not off no major-league pitching, you couldn't.

TROY: We had better pitching in the Negro leagues. I hit seven home runs off of Satchel Paige. You can't get no better than that!

CORY: Sandy Koufax. He's leading the league in strikeouts.

TROY: I ain't thinking of no Sandy Koufax.

CORY: You got Warren Spahn and Lew Burdette. I bet you couldn't hit no home runs off of Warren Spahn.

TROY: I'm through with it now. You go on and cut them boards. [*Pause.*] Your mama tells me you got recruited by a college football team? Is that right?

CORY: Yeah. Coach Zellman say the recruiter gonna be coming by to talk to you. Get you to sign the permission papers.

TROY: I thought you supposed to be working down there at the A&P. Ain't you suppose to be working down there after school?

CORY: Mr. Stawicki say he gonna hold my job for me until after the football season. Say starting next week I can work weekends.

TROY: I thought we had an understanding about this football stuff? You suppose to keep up with your chores and hold that job down at the A&P. Ain't been around here all day on a Saturday. Ain't none of your chores done . . . and now you telling me you done quit your job.

CORY: I'm gonna be working weekends.

TROY: You damn right you are! And ain't no need for nobody coming around here to talk to me about signing nothing.

CORY: Hey, Pop . . . you can't do that. He's coming all the way from North Carolina.

TROY: I don't care where he coming from. The white man ain't gonna let you get nowhere with that football noway. You go on and get your book-learning so you can work yourself up in that A&P or learn how to fix cars or build houses or something, get you a trade. That way you have something can't nobody take away from you. You go on and learn how to put your hands to some good use. Besides hauling people's garbage.

CORY: I get good grades, Pop. That's why the recruiter wants to talk with you. You got to keep up your grades to get recruited. This way I'll be going to college. I'll get a chance . . .

TROY: First you gonna get your butt down there to the A&P and get your job back.

CORY: Mr. Stawicki done already hired somebody else 'cause I told him I was playing football.

TROY: You a bigger fool than I thought . . . to let somebody take away your job so you can play some football. Where you gonna get your money to take out your girlfriend and whatnot? What kind of foolishness is that to let somebody take away your job?

CORY: I'm still gonna be working weekends.

TROY: Naw . . . naw. You getting your butt out of here and finding you another job.

CORY: Come on, Pop! I got to practice. I can't work after school and play football too. The team needs me. That's what Coach Zellman say . . .

TROY: I don't care what nobody else say. I'm the boss . . . you understand? I'm the boss around here. I do the only saying what counts.

CORY: Come on, Pop!

TROY: I asked you . . . Did you understand?

CORY: Yeah . . .

TROY: What?!

CORY: Yessir.

TROY: You go down there to that A&P and see if you can get your job back. If you can't do both . . . then you quit the football team. You've got to take the crookeds with the straights.

CORY: Yessir. [*Pause.*] Can I ask you a question?

TROY: What the hell you wanna ask me? Mr. Stawicki the one you got the questions for.

CORY: How come you ain't never liked me?

TROY: Liked you? Who the hell say I got to like you? What law is there say I got to like you? Wanna stand up in my face and ask a damn fool-ass question like that. Talking about liking somebody. Come here, boy, when I talk to you.

[CORY *comes over to where* TROY *is working. He stands slouched over and* TROY *shoves him on his shoulder.*] Straighten up, goddammit! I asked you a question . . . what law is there say I got to like you?

CORY: None.

TROY: Well, alright then! Don't you eat every day? [*Pause.*] Answer me when I talk to you! Don't you eat every day?

CORY: Yeah.

TROY: Nigger, as long as you in my house, you put that sir on the end of it when you talk to me!

CORY: Yes . . . sir.

TROY: You eat every day.

CORY: Yessir!

TROY: Got a roof over your head.

CORY: Yessir!

TROY: Got clothes on your back.

CORY: Yessir.

TROY: Why you think that is?

CORY: Cause of you.

TROY: Aw, hell I know it's 'cause of me . . . but why do you think that is?

CORY: [*Hesitant.*] Cause you like me.

TROY: Like you? I go out of here every morning . . . bust my butt . . . putting up with them crackers every day . . . cause I like you? You about the biggest fool I ever saw. [*Pause.*] It's my job. It's my responsibility! You understand that? A man got to take care of his family. You live in my house . . . sleep you behind on my bedclothes . . . fill you belly up with my food . . . cause you my son. You my flesh and blood. Not 'cause I like you! Cause it's my duty to take care of you. I owe a responsibility to you! Let's get this straight right here . . . before it go along any further . . . I ain't got to like you. Mr. Rand don't give me my money come payday cause he likes me. He gives me cause he owe me. I done give you everything I had to give you. I gave you your life! Me and your mama worked that out between us. And liking your black ass wasn't part of the bargain. Don't you try and go through life worrying about if somebody like you or not. You best be making sure they doing right by you. You understand what I'm saying, boy?

CORY: Yessir.

TROY: Then get the hell out of my face, and get on down to that A&P.

[ROSE *has been standing behind the screen door for much of the scene. She enters as* CORY *exits.*]

ROSE: Why don't you let the boy go ahead and play football, Troy? Ain't no harm in that. He's just trying to be like you with the sports.

TROY: I don't want him to be like me! I want him to move as far away from my life as he can get. You the only decent thing that ever happened to me. I wish him that. But I don't wish him a thing else from my life. I decided seventeen years ago that boy wasn't getting involved in no sports. Not after what they did to me in the sports.

ROSE: Troy, why don't you admit you was too old to play in the major leagues? For once . . . why don't you admit that?

TROY: What do you mean too old? Don't come telling me I was too old. I just wasn't the right color. Hell, I'm fifty-three years old and I can do better than Selkirk's .269 right now!

ROSE: How's was you gonna play ball when you were over forty? Sometimes I can't get no sense out of you.

TROY: I got good sense, woman. I got sense enough not to let my boy get hurt over playing no sports. You been mothering that boy too much. Worried about if people like him.

ROSE: Everything that boy do . . . he do for you. He wants you to say "Good job, son." That's all.

TROY: Rose, I ain't got time for that. He's alive. He's healthy. He's got to make his own way. I made mine. Ain't nobody gonna hold his hand when he get out there in that world.

ROSE: Times have changed from when you was young, Troy. People change. The world's changing around you and you can't even see it.

TROY: [Slow, methodical.] Woman . . . I do the best I can do. I come in here every Friday. I carry a sack of potatoes and a bucket of lard. You all line up at the door with your hands out. I give you the lint from my pockets. I give you my sweat and my blood. I ain't got no tears. I done spent them. We go upstairs in that room at night . . . and I fall down on you and try to blast a hole into forever. I get up Monday morning . . . find my lunch on the table. I go out. Make my way. Find my strength to carry me through to the next Friday. [Pause.] That's all I got, Rose. That's all I got to give. I can't give nothing else.

[TROY exits into the house. The lights go down to black.]

Scene 4

It is Friday. Two weeks later. CORY starts out of the house with his football equipment. The phone rings.

CORY: [Calling.] I got it! [He answers the phone and stands in the screen door talking.] Hello? Hey, Jesse. Naw . . . I was just getting ready to leave now.

ROSE: [Calling.] Cory!

CORY: I told you, man, them spikes is all tore up. You can use them if you want, but they ain't no good. Earl got some spikes.

ROSE: [Calling.] Cory!

CORY: [Calling to ROSE.] Mam? I'm talking to Jesse. [Into phone.] When she say that? [Pause.] Aw, you lying, man. I'm gonna tell her you said that.

ROSE: [Calling.] Cory, don't you go nowhere!

CORY: I got to go to the game, Ma! [Into the phone.] Yeah, hey, look, I'll talk to you later. Yeah, I'll meet you over Earl's house. Later. Bye, Ma.

[CORY exits the house and starts out the yard.]

ROSE: Cory, where you going off to? You got that stuff all pulled out and thrown all over your room.

CORY: [In the yard.] I was looking for my spikes. Jesse wanted to borrow my spikes.

ROSE: Get up there and get that cleaned up before your daddy gets back in here.

CORY: I got to go to the game! I'll clean it up *when I get back.* [CORY *exits.*]

ROSE: That's all he need to do is see that room all messed up.

[ROSE *exits into the house.* TROY *and* BONO *enter the yard.* TROY *is dressed in clothes other than his work clothes.*]

BONO: He told him the same thing he told you. Take it to the union.

TROY: Brownie ain't got that much sense. Man wasn't thinking about nothing. He wait until I confront them on it . . . then he wanna come crying seniority. [*Calls.*] Hey, Rose!

BONO: I wish I could have seen Mr. Rand's face when he told you.

TROY: He couldn't get it out of his mouth! Liked to bit his tongue! When they called me down there to the Commissioner's office . . . he thought they was gonna fire me. Like everybody else.

BONO: I didn't think they was gonna fire you. I thought they was gonna put you on the warning paper.

TROY: Hey, Rose! [*To* BONO.] Yeah, Mr. Rand like to bit his tongue. [TROY *breaks the seal on the bottle, takes a drink, and hands it to* BONO.]

BONO: I see you run right down to Taylors' and told that Alberta gal.

TROY: [*Calling.*] Hey Rose! [*To* BONO.] I told everybody. Hey, Rose! I went down there to cash my check.

ROSE: [*Entering from the house.*] Hush all that hollering, man! I know you out here. What they say down there at the Commissioner's office?

TROY: You supposed to come when I call you, woman. Bono'll tell you that. [*To* BONO.] Don't Lucille come when you call her?

ROSE: Man, hush your mouth. I ain't no dog . . . talk about "come when you call me."

TROY: [*Puts his arm around* ROSE.] You hear this, Bono? I had me an old dog used to get uppity like that. You say, "C'mere, Blue!" . . . and he just lay there and look at you. End up getting a stick and chasing him away trying to make him come.

ROSE: I ain't studying you and your dog. I remember you used to sing that old song.

TROY: [*He sings.*] Hear it ring! Hear it ring! I had a dog his name was Blue.

ROSE: Don't nobody wanna hear you sing that old song.

TROY: [*Sings.*] You know Blue was mighty true.

BONO: Hell, I remember that song myself.

TROY: [*Sings.*] You know Blue was a good old dog. Blue treed a possum in a hollow log. That was my daddy's song. My daddy made up that song.

ROSE: I don't care who made it up. Don't nobody wanna hear you sing it.

TROY: [*Makes a song like calling a dog.*] Come here, woman.

ROSE: You come in here carrying on, I reckon they ain't fired you. What they say down there at the Commissioner's office?

TROY: Look here, Rose . . . Mr. Rand called me into his office today when I got back from talking to them people down there . . . it come from up top

. . . he called me in and told me they was making me a driver.

ROSE: Troy, you kidding!

TROY: No I ain't. Ask Bono.

ROSE: Well, that's great, Troy. Now you don't have to hassle them people no
more.

[LYONS *enters from the street.*]

TROY: Aw hell, I wasn't looking to see you today. I thought you was in jail.
Got it all over the front page of the *Courier* about them raiding Sefus' place
. . . where you be hanging out with all them thugs.

LYONS: Hey, Pop . . . that ain't got nothing to do with me. I don't go down
there gambling. I go down there to sit in with the band. I ain't got nothing
to do with the gambling part. They got some good music down there.

TROY: They got some rogues . . . is what they got.

LYONS: How you been, Mr. Bono? Hi, Rose.

BONO: I see where you playing down at the Crawford Grill tonight.

ROSE: How come you ain't brought Bonnie like I told you. You should have
brought Bonnie with you, she ain't been over in a month of Sundays.

LYONS: I was just in the neighborhood . . . thought I'd stop by.

TROY: Here he come . . .

BONO: Your daddy got a promotion on the rubbish. He's gonna be the first
colored driver. Ain't got to do nothing but sit up there and read the paper
like them white fellows.

LYONS: Hey, Pop . . . if you knew how to read you'd be alright.

BONO: Naw . . . naw . . . you mean if the nigger knew how to *drive* he'd be
all right. Been fighting with them people about driving and ain't even got
a license. Mr. Rand know you ain't got no driver's license?

TROY: Driving ain't nothing. All you do is point the truck where you want it
to go. Driving ain't nothing.

BONO: Do Mr. Rand know you ain't got no driver's license? That's what I'm
talking about. I ain't asked if driving was easy. I asked if Mr. Rand know
you ain't got no driver's license.

TROY: He ain't got to know. The man ain't got to know my business. Time
he find out, I have two or three licenses.

LYONS: [*Going into his pocket.*] Say, look here, Pop . . .

TROY: I knew it was coming. Didn't I tell you, Bono? I know what kind of
"Look here, Pop" that was. The nigger fixing to ask me for some money.
It's Friday night. It's my payday. All them rogues down there on the
avenue . . . the ones that ain't in jail . . . and Lyons is hopping in his shoes
to get down there with them.

LYONS: See, Pop . . . if you give somebody else a chance to talk sometime,
you'd see that I was fixing to pay you back your ten dollars like I told you.
Here . . . I told you I'd pay you when Bonnie got paid.

TROY: Naw . . . you go ahead and keep that ten dollars. Put it in the bank.
The next time you feel like you wanna come by here and ask me for something . . . you go on down there and get that.

LYONS: Here's your ten dollars, Pop. I told you I don't want you to give me nothing. I just wanted to borrow ten dollars.

TROY: Naw . . . you go on and keep that for the next time you want to ask me.

LYONS: Come on, Pop . . . here go your ten dollars.

ROSE: Why don't you go on and let the boy pay you back, Troy?

LYONS: Here you go, Rose. If you don't take it I'm gonna have to hear about it for the next six months. [*He hands her the money.*]

ROSE: You can hand yours over here too, Troy.

TROY: You see this, Bono. You see how they do me.

BONO: Yeah, Lucille do me the same way.

[GABRIEL *is heard singing offstage. He enters.*]

GABRIEL: Better get ready for the Judgment. Better get ready for . . . Hey! . . . Hey! . . . There's Troy's boy!

LYONS: How you doing, Uncle Gabe?

GABRIEL: Lyons . . . The King of the Jungle! Rose . . . hey, Rose. Got a flower for you. [*He takes a rose from his pocket.*] Picked it myself. That's the same rose like you is!

ROSE: That's right nice of you, Gabe.

LYONS: What you been doing, Uncle Gabe?

GABRIEL: Oh, I been chasing hellhounds and waiting on the time to tell St. Peter to open the gates.

LYONS: You been chasing hellhounds, huh? Well . . . you doing the right thing, Uncle Gabe. Somebody got to chase them.

GABRIEL: Oh, yeah . . . I know it. The devil's strong. The devil ain't no pushover. Hellhounds snipping at everybody's heels. But I got my trumpet waiting on the judgment time.

LYONS: Waiting on the Battle of Armageddon, huh?

GABRIEL: Ain't gonna be too much of a battle when God get to waving that Judgment sword. But the people's gonna have a hell of a time trying to get into heaven if them gates ain't open.

LYONS: [*Putting his arm around* GABRIEL.] You hear this, Pop. Uncle Gabe, you alright!

GABRIEL: [*Laughing with* LYONS.] Lyons! King of the Jungle.

ROSE: You gonna stay for supper, Gabe. Want me to fix you a plate?

GABRIEL: I'll take a sandwich, Rose. Don't want no plate. Just wanna eat with my hands. I'll take a sandwich.

ROSE: How about you, Lyons? You staying? Got some short ribs cooking.

LYONS: Naw, I won't eat nothing till after we finished playing. [*Pause.*] You ought to come down and listen to me play, Pop.

TROY: I don't like that Chinese music. All that noise.

ROSE: Go on in the house and wash up, Gabe . . . I'll fix you a sandwich.

GABRIEL: [*To* LYONS, *as he exits.*] Troy's mad at me.

LYONS: What you mad at Uncle Gabe for, Pop.

ROSE: He thinks Troy's mad at him cause he moved over to Miss Pearl's.

TROY: I ain't mad at the man. He can live where he want to live at.

LYONS: What he move over there for? Miss Pearl don't like nobody.

ROSE: She don't mind him none. She treats him real nice. She just don't allow all that singing.

TROY: She don't mind that rent he be paying . . . that's what she don't mind.

ROSE: Troy, I ain't going through that with you no more. He's over there cause he want to have his own place. He can come and go as he please.

TROY: Hell, he could come and go as he please here. I wasn't stopping him. I ain't put no rules on him.

ROSE: It ain't the same thing, Troy. And you know it. [GABRIEL *comes to the door*.] Now, that's the last I wanna hear about that. I don't wanna hear nothing else about Gabe and Miss Pearl. And next week . . .

GABRIEL: I'm ready for my sandwich, Rose.

ROSE: And next week . . . when that recruiter come from that school . . . I want you to sign that paper and go on and let Cory play football. Then that'll be the last I have to hear about that.

TROY: [*To* ROSE *as she exits into the house*.] I ain't thinking about Cory nothing.

LYONS: What . . . Cory got recruited? What school he going to?

TROY: That boy walking around here smelling his piss . . . thinking he's grown. Thinking he's gonna do what he want, irrespective of what I say. Look here, Bono . . . I left the Commissioner's office and went down to the A&P . . . that boy ain't working down there. He lying to me. Telling me he got his job back . . . telling me he working weekends . . . telling me he working after school . . . Mr. Stawicki tell me he ain't working down there at all!

LYONS: Cory just growing up. He's just busting at the seams trying to fill out your shoes.

TROY: I don't care what he's doing. When he get to the point where he wanna disobey me . . . then it's time for him to move on. Bono'll tell you that. I bet he ain't never disobeyed his daddy without paying the consequences.

BONO: I ain't never had a chance. My daddy came on through . . . but I ain't never knew him to see him . . . or what he had on his mind or where he went. Just moving on through. Searching out the New Land. That's what the old folks used to call it. See a fellow moving around from place to place . . . woman to woman . . . called it searching out the New Land. I can't say if he ever found it. I come along, didn't want no kids. Didn't know if I was gonna be in one place long enough to fix on them right as their daddy. I figured I was going searching too. As it turned out I been hooked up with Lucille near about as long as your daddy been with Rose. Going on sixteen years.

TROY: Sometimes I wish I hadn't known my daddy. He ain't cared nothing about no kids. A kid to him wasn't nothing. All he wanted was for you to learn how to walk so he could start you to working. When it come time for eating . . . he ate first. If there was anything left over, that's what you got. Man would sit down and eat two chickens and give you the wing.

LYONS: You ought to stop that, Pop. Everybody feed their kids. No matter how hard times is . . . everybody care about their kids. Make sure they have something to eat.

TROY: The only thing my daddy cared about was getting them bales of cotton in to Mr. Lubin. That's the only thing that mattered to him. Sometimes I used to wonder why he was living. Wonder why the devil hadn't come and got him. "Get them bales of cotton in to Mr. Lubin" and find out he owe him money . . .

LYONS: He should have just went on and left when he saw he couldn't get nowhere. That's what I would have done.

TROY: How he gonna leave with eleven kids? And where he gonna go? He ain't knew how to do nothing but farm. No, he was trapped and I think he knew it. But I'll say this for him . . . he felt a responsibility toward us. Maybe he ain't treated us the way I felt he should have . . . but without that responsibility he could have walked off and left us . . . made his own way.

BONO: A lot of them did. Back in those days what you talking about . . . they walk out their front door and just take on down one road or another and keep on walking.

LYONS: There you go! That's what I'm talking about.

BONO: Just keep on walking till you come to something else. Ain't you never heard of nobody having the walking blues? Well, that's what you call it when you just take off like that.

TROY: My daddy ain't had them walking blues! What you talking about? He stayed right there with his family. But he was just as evil as he could be. My mama couldn't stand him. Couldn't stand that evilness. She run off when I was about eight. She sneaked off one night after he had gone to sleep. Told me she was coming back for me. I ain't never seen her no more. All his women run off and left him. He wasn't good for nobody. When my turn come to head out, I was fourteen and got to sniffing around Joe Canewell's daughter. Had us an old mule we called Greyboy. My daddy sent me out to do some plowing and I tied up Greyboy and went to fooling around with Joe Canewell's daughter. We done found us a nice little spot, got real cozy with each other. She about thirteen and we done figured we was grown anyway . . . so we down there enjoying ourselves . . . ain't thinking about nothing. We didn't know Greyboy had got loose and wandered back to the house and my daddy was looking for me. We down there by the creek enjoying ourselves when my daddy come up on us. Surprised us. He had them leather straps off the mule and commenced to whupping me like there was no tomorrow. I jumped up, mad and embarrassed. I was scared of my daddy. When he commenced to whupping on me . . . quite naturally I run to get out of the way. [*Pause.*] Now I thought he was mad cause I ain't done my work. But I see where he was chasing me off so he could have the gal for himself. When I see what the matter of it was, I lost all fear of my daddy. Right there is where I become a man . . . at fourteen years of age. [*Pause.*] Now it was my turn to run him off. I picked up them same reins that he had used on me. I picked up them reins and commenced to whupping on him. The gal jumped up and run off, and when my daddy turned to face me, I could see why the devil had never come to get him . . . cause he was the devil himself. I don't know what happened. When I woke up, I was laying right there by the creek, and Blue . . . this old dog we had . . . was licking my face. I thought I was blind. I couldn't see nothing. Both my eyes were swollen shut. I layed there and cried. I didn't know what I was gonna do. The only thing I knew was the time had come for me to leave my daddy's house. And right there the world suddenly got big. And it was a long time before I could cut it down to where I could handle it. Part of that cutting down was when I got to the place where I could feel him kicking in my blood and knew that the only thing that separated us was the matter of a few years.

[GABRIEL *enters from the house with a sandwich.*]

LYONS: What you got there, Uncle Gabe?

GABRIEL: Got me a ham sandwich. Rose gave me a ham sandwich.

TROY: I don't know what happened to him. I done lost touch with everybody except Gabriel. But I hope he's dead. I hope he found some peace.

LYONS: That's a heavy story, Pop. I didn't know you left home when you was fourteen.

TROY: And didn't know nothing. The only part of the world I knew was the forty-two acres of Mr. Lubin's land. That's all I knew about life.

LYONS: Fourteen's kinda young to be out on your own. [*Phone rings.*] I don't even think I was ready to be out on my own at fourteen. I don't know what I would have done.

TROY: I got up from the creek and walked on down to Mobile. I was through with farming. Figured I could do better in the city. So I walked the two hundred miles to Mobile.

LYONS: Wait a minute . . . you ain't walked no two hundred miles, Pop. Ain't nobody gonna walk no two hundred miles. You talking about some walking there.

BONO: That's the only way you got anywhere back in them days.

LYONS: Shhh. Damn if I wouldn't have hitched a ride with somebody!

TROY: Who you gonna hitch it with? They ain't had no cars and things like they got now. We talking about 1918.

ROSE: [*Entering.*] What you all out here getting into?

TROY: [*To* ROSE.] I'm telling Lyons how good he got it. He don't know nothing about this I'm talking.

ROSE: Lyons, that was Bonnie on the phone. She say you supposed to pick her up.

LYONS: Yeah, okay, Rose.

TROY: I walked on down to Mobile and hitched up with some of them fellows that was heading this way. Got up here and found out . . . not only couldn't you get a job . . . you couldn't find no place to live. I thought I was in freedom. Shhh. Colored folks living down there on the riverbanks in whatever kind of shelter they could find for themselves. Right down there under the Brady Street Bridge. Living in shacks made of sticks and tarpaper. Messed around there and went from bad to worse. Started stealing. First it was food. Then I figured, hell, if I steal money I can buy me some food. Buy me some shoes too! One thing led to another. Met your mama. I was young and anxious to be a man. Met your mama and had you. What I do that for? Now I got to worry about feeding you and her. Got to steal three times as much. Went out one day looking for somebody to rob . . . that's what I was, a robber. I'll tell you the truth. I'm ashamed of it today. But it's the truth. Went to rob this fellow . . . pulled out my knife . . . and he pulled out a gun. Shot me in the chest. It felt just like somebody had taken a hot branding iron and laid it on me. When he shot me, I jumped at him with my knife. They tell me I killed him and they put me in the penitentiary and locked me up for fifteen years. That's where I met Bono. That's where I learned how to play baseball. Got out that place and your mama had taken you and went on to make life without me. Fifteen years was a long time for her to wait. But that fifteen years cured me of that robbing stuff. Rose'll tell you. She asked me when I met her if I had gotten all that foolishness out of my system. And I told her, "Baby, it's you and baseball all what count with me." You hear me, Bono? I meant it too. She say, "Which one comes first?" I told her, "Baby, there ain't no doubt it's baseball . . . but you stick and get old with me and we'll both outlive this baseball." Am I right, Rose? And it's true.

ROSE: Man, hush your mouth. You ain't said no such thing. Talking about, "Baby, you know you'll always be number one with me." That's what you was talking.

TROY: You hear that, Bono? That's why I love her.

BONO: Rose'll keep you straight. You get off the track, she'll straighten you up.

ROSE: Lyons, you better get on up and get Bonnie. She waiting on you.

LYONS: [*Gets up to go.*] Hey, Pop, why don't you come on down to the Grill and hear me play?

TROY: I ain't going down there. I'm too old to be sitting around in them clubs.

BONO: You got to be good to play down at the Grill.

LYONS: Come on, Pop . . .

TROY: I got to get up in the morning.

LYONS: You ain't got to stay long.

TROY: Naw, I'm gonna get my supper and go on to bed.

LYONS: Well, I got to go. I'll see you again.

TROY: Don't you come around my house on my payday!

ROSE: Pick up the phone and let somebody know you coming. And bring Bonnie with you. You know I'm always glad to see her.

LYONS: Yeah, I'll do that, Rose. You take care now. See you, Pop. See you, Mr. Bono. See you, Uncle Gabe.

GABRIEL: Lyons! King of the Jungle!

[LYONS *exits*.]

TROY: Is supper ready, woman? Me and you got some business to take care of. I'm gonna tear it up too!

ROSE: Troy, I done told you now!

TROY: [*Puts his arm around* BONO.] Aw hell, woman . . . this is Bono. Bono like family. I done known this nigger since . . . how long I done know you?

BONO: It's been a long time.

TROY: I done known this nigger since Skippy was a pup. Me and him done been through some times.

BONO: You sure right about that.

TROY: Hell, I done know him longer than I known you. And we still standing shoulder to shoulder. Hey, look here, Bono . . . a man can't ask for no more than that. [*Drinks to him*.] I love you, nigger.

BONO: Hell, I love you too . . . but I got to get home to see my woman. You got yours in hand. I got to go get mine.

[BONO *starts to exit as* CORY *enters the yard, dressed in his football uniform. He gives* TROY *a hard, uncompromising look*.]

CORY: What you do that for, Pop? [*He throws his helmet down in the direction of* TROY.]

ROSE: What's the matter? Cory . . . what's the matter?

CORY: Papa done went up to the school and told Coach Zellman I can't play football no more. Wouldn't even let me play the game. Told him to tell the recruiter not to come.

ROSE: Troy . . .

TROY: What you Troying me for. Yeah, I did it. And the boy know why I did it.

CORY: Why you wanna do that to me? That was the one chance I had.

ROSE: Ain't nothing wrong with Cory playing football, Troy.

TROY: The boy lied to me. I told the nigger if he wanna play football . . . to keep up his chores and hold down that job at the A&P. That was the conditions. Stopped down there to see Mr. Stawicki . . .

CORY: I can't work after school during football season, Pop! I tried to tell you that Mr. Stawicki's holding my job for me. You don't never want to listen to nobody. And then you wanna go and do this to me!

TROY: I ain't done nothing to you. You done it to yourself.

CORY: Just cause you didn't have a chance! You just scared I'm gonna be better than you, that's all.

TROY: Come here.

ROSE: Troy . . .

[CORY *reluctantly crosses over to* TROY.]

TROY: Alright! See. You done made a mistake.

CORY: I didn't even do nothing!

TROY: I'm gonna tell you what your mistake was. See . . . you swung at the ball and didn't hit it. That's strike one. See, you in the batter's box now. You swung and you missed. That's strike one. Don't you strike out!

[*Lights fade to black.*]

ACT II

Scene 1

The following morning. CORY *is at the tree hitting the ball with the bat. He tries to mimic* TROY, *but his swing is awkward, less sure.* ROSE *enters from the house.*

ROSE: Cory, I want you to help me with this cupboard.

CORY: I ain't quitting the team. I don't care what Poppa say.

ROSE: I'll talk to him when he gets back. He had to go see about your Uncle Gabe. The police done arrested him. Say he was disturbing the peace. He'll be back directly. Come on in here and help me clean out the top of this cupboard.

[CORY *exits into the house.* ROSE *sees* TROY *and* BONO *coming down the alley.*]

Troy . . . what they say down there?

TROY: Ain't said nothing. I give them fifty dollars and they let him go. I'll talk to you about it. Where's Cory?

ROSE: He's in there helping me clean out these cupboards.

TROY: Tell him to get his butt out here.

[TROY *and* BONO *go over to the pile of wood.* BONO *picks up the saw and begins sawing.*]

TROY: [*To* BONO] All they want is the money. That makes six or seven times I done went down there and got him. See me coming they stick out their *hands*.

BONO: Yeah, I know what you mean. That's all they care about . . . that money. They don't care about what's right. [*Pause.*] Nigger, why you got to go and get some hard wood? You ain't doing nothing but building a little old fence. Get you some soft pine wood. That's all you need.

TROY: I know what I'm doing. This is outside wood. You put pine wood inside the house. Pine wood is inside wood. This here is outside wood. Now you tell me where the fence is gonna be?

BONO: You don't need this wood. You can put it up with pine wood and it'll stand as long as you gonna be here looking at it.

TROY: How you know how long I'm gonna be here, nigger? Hell, I might just live forever. Live longer than old man Horsely.

BONO: That's what Magee used to say.

TROY: Magee's a damn fool. Now you tell me who you ever heard of gonna pull their own teeth with a pair of rusty pliers?

BONO: The old folks . . . my granddaddy used to pull his teeth with pliers. They ain't had no dentists for the colored folks back then.

TROY: Get clean pliers! You understand? Clean pliers! Sterilize them! Besides we ain't living back then. All Magee had to do was walk over to Doc Goldblums.

BONO: I see where you and that Tallahassee gal . . . that Alberta . . . I see where you all done got tight.

TROY: What you mean "got tight"?

BONO: I see where you be laughing and joking with her all the time.

TROY: I laughs and jokes with all of them, Bono. You know me.

BONO: That ain't the kind of laughing and joking I'm talking about.

[CORY *enters from the house.*]

CORY: How you doing, Mr. Bono?

TROY: Cory? Get that saw from Bono and cut some wood. He talking about the wood's too hard to cut. Stand back there, Jim, and let that young boy show you how it's done.

BONO: He's sure welcome to it.

[CORY *takes the saw and begins to cut the wood.*]

Whew-e-e! Look at that. Big old strong boy. Look like Joe Louis. Hell, must be getting old the way I'm watching that boy whip through that wood.

CORY: I don't see why Mama want a fence around the yard noways.

TROY: Damn if I know either. What the hell she keeping out with it? She ain't got nothing nobody want.

BONO: Some people build fences to keep people out . . . and other people build fences to keep people in. Rose wants to hold on to you all. She loves you.

TROY: Hell, nigger, I don't need nobody to tell me my wife loves me, Cory . . . go on in the house and see if you can find that other saw.

CORY: Where's it at?

TROY: I said find it! Look for it till you find it!

[CORY *exits into the house.*]

What's that supposed to mean? Wanna keep us in?

BONO: Troy . . . I done known you seem like damn near my whole life. You and Rose both. I done know both of you all for a long time. I remember when you met Rose. When you was hitting them baseball out the park. A lot of them old gals was after you then. You had the pick of the litter. When you picked Rose, I was happy for you. That was the first time I knew you had any sense. I said . . . My man Troy knows what he's doing . . . I'm gonna follow this nigger . . . he might take me somewhere. I been following you too. I done learned a whole heap of things about life watching you. I done learned how to tell where the shit lies. How to tell it from the alfalfa. You done learned me a lot of things. You showed me how to not make the same mistakes . . . to take life as it comes along and keep putting one foot in front of the other. [*Pause.*] Rose a good woman, Troy.

TROY: Hell, nigger, I know she a good woman. I been married to her for eighteen years. What you got on your mind, Bono?

BONO: I just say she a good woman. Just like I say anything. I ain't got to have nothing on my mind.

TROY: You just gonna say she a good woman and leave it hanging out there like that? Why you telling me she a good woman?

BONO: She loves you, Troy. Rose loves you.

TROY: You saying I don't measure up. That's what you trying to say. I don't measure up cause I'm seeing this other gal. I know what you trying to say.

BONO: I know what Rose means to you, Troy. I'm just trying to say I don't want to see you mess up.

TROY: Yeah, I appreciate that, Bono. If you was messing around on Lucille I'd be telling you the same thing.

BONO: Well, that's all I got to say. I just say that because I love you both.

TROY: Hell, you know me . . . I wasn't out there looking for nothing. You can't find a better woman than Rose. I know that. But seems like this woman just stuck onto me where I can't shake her loose. I done wrestled with it, tried to throw her off me . . . but she just stuck on tighter. Now she's stuck on for good.

BONO: You's in control . . . that's what you tell me all the time. You responsible for what you do.

TROY: I ain't ducking the responsibility of it. As long as it sets right in my heart . . . then I'm okay. Cause that's all I listen to. It'll tell me right from wrong every time. And I ain't talking about doing Rose no bad turn. I love Rose. She done carried me a long ways and I love and respect her for that.

BONO: I know you do. That's why I don't want to see you hurt her. But what you gonna do when she find out? What you got then? If you try and juggle both of them . . . sooner or later you gonna drop one of them. That's common sense.

TROY: Yeah, I hear what you saying, Bono. I been trying to figure a way to work it out.

BONO: Work it out right, Troy. I don't want to be getting all up between you and Rose's business . . . but work it so it come out right.

TROY: Aw hell, I get all up between you and Lucille's business. When you gonna get that woman that refrigerator she been wanting? Don't tell me you ain't got no money now. I know who your banker is. Mellon don't need that money bad as Lucille want that refrigerator. I'll tell you that.

BONO: Tell you what I'll do . . . when you finish building this fence for Rose . . . I'll buy Lucille that refrigerator.

TROY: You done stuck your foot in your mouth now!

[TROY *grabs up a board and begins to saw.* BONO *starts to walk out the yard.*]
Hey, nigger . . . where you going?

BONO: I'm going home. I know you don't expect me to help you now. I'm protecting my money. I wanna see you put that fence up by yourself. That's what I want to see. You'll be here another six months without me.

TROY: Nigger, you ain't right.

BONO: When it comes to my money . . . I'm right as fireworks on the Fourth of July.

TROY: Alright, we gonna see now. You better get out your bankbook.

[BONO *exits, and* TROY *continues to work.* ROSE *enters from the house.*]

ROSE: What they say down there? What's happening with Gabe?

TROY: I went down there and got him out. Cost me fifty dollars. Say he was disturbing the peace. Judge set up a hearing for him in three weeks. Say to show cause why he shouldn't be re-committed.

ROSE: What was he doing that cause them to arrest him?

TROY: Some kids was teasing him and he run them off home. Say he was howling and carrying on. Some folks seen him and called the police. That's all it was.

ROSE: Well, what's you say? What'd you tell the judge?

TROY: Told him I'd look after him. It didn't make no sense to recommit the man. He stuck out his big greasy palm and told me to give him fifty dollars and take him on home.

ROSE: Where's he at now? Where'd he go off to?

TROY: He's gone on about his business. He don't need nobody to hold his hand.

ROSE: Well, I don't know. Seem like that would be the best place for him if they did put him into the hospital. I know what you're gonna say. But that's what I think would be best.

TROY: The man done had his life ruined fighting for what? And they wanna take and lock him up. Let him be free. He don't bother nobody.

ROSE: Well, everybody got their own way of looking at it I guess. Come on and get your lunch. I got a bowl of lima beans and some cornbread in the oven. Come on get something to eat. Ain't no sense you fretting over Gabe.

[ROSE *turns to go into the house.*]

TROY: Rose . . . got something to tell you.

ROSE: Well, come on . . . wait till I get this food on the table.

TROY: Rose!

[*She stops and turns around.*]

I don't know how to say this. [*Pause.*] I can't explain it none. It just sort of grows on you till it gets out of hand. It starts out like a little bush . . . and the next thing you know it's a whole forest.

ROSE: Troy . . . what are you talking about?

TROY: I'm talking, woman, let me talk. I'm trying to find a way to tell you . . . I'm gonna be a daddy. I'm gonna be somebody's daddy.

ROSE: Troy . . . you're not telling me this? You're gonna be . . . what?

TROY: Rose . . . now . . . see . . .

ROSE: You telling me you gonna be somebody's daddy? You telling your *wife* this?

[GABRIEL *enters from the street. He carries a rose in his hand.*]

GABRIEL: Hey, Troy! Hey, Rose!

ROSE: I have to wait eighteen years to hear something like this.

GABRIEL: Hey, Rose . . . I got a flower for you. [*He hands it to her.*] That's a rose. Same rose like you is.

ROSE: Thanks, Gabe.

GABRIEL: Troy, you ain't mad at me is you? Them bad mens come and put me away. You ain't mad at me is you?

TROY: Naw, Gabe, I ain't mad at you.

ROSE: Eighteen years and you wanna come with this.

GABRIEL: [*Takes a quarter out of his pocket.*] See what I got? Got a brand new quarter.

TROY: Rose . . . it's just . . .

ROSE: Ain't nothing you can say, Troy. Ain't no way of explaining that.

GABRIEL: Fellow that give me this quarter had a whole mess of them. I'm gonna keep this quarter till it stop shining.

ROSE: Gabe, go on in the house there. I got some watermelon in the frigidaire. Go on and get you a piece.

GABRIEL: Say, Rose . . . you know I was chasing hellhounds and them bad mens come and get me and take me away. Troy helped me. He come down there and told them they better let me go before he beat them up. Yeah, he did!

ROSE: You go on and get you a piece of watermelon, Gabe. Them bad mens is gone now.

GABRIEL: Okay, Rose . . . gonna get me some watermelon. The kind with the stripes on it. [GABRIEL *exits into the house.*]

ROSE: Why, Troy? Why? After all these years to come dragging this in to me now. It don't make no sense at your age. I could have expected this ten or fifteen years ago, but not now.

TROY: Age ain't got nothing to do with it, Rose.

ROSE: I done tried to be everything a wife should be. Everything a wife could be. Been married eighteen years and I got to live to see the day you tell me you been seeing another woman and done fathered a child by her. And you know I ain't never wanted no half nothing in my family. My whole family is half. Everybody got different fathers and mothers . . . my two sisters and my brother. Can't hardly tell who's who. Can't never sit down and talk about Papa and Mama. It's your papa and your mama and my papa and my mama . . .

TROY: Rose . . . stop it now.

ROSE: I ain't never wanted that for none of my children. And now you wanna drag your behind in here and tell me something like this.

TROY: You ought to know. It's time for you to know.

ROSE: Well, I don't want to know, goddamn it!

TROY: I can't just make it go away. It's done now. I can't wish the circumstance of the thing away.

ROSE: And you don't want to either. Maybe you want to wish me and my boy away. Maybe that's what you want? Well, you can't wish us away. I've got eighteen years of my life invested in you. You ought to have stayed upstairs in my bed where you belong.

TROY: Rose . . . now listen to me . . . we can get a handle on this thing. We can talk this out . . . come to an understanding.

ROSE: All of a sudden it's "we." Where was "we" at when you was down there rolling around with some godforsaken woman? "We" should have come to an understanding before you started making a damn fool of yourself. You're a day late and a dollar short when it comes to an understanding with me.

TROY: It's just . . . She gives me a different idea . . . a different understanding about myself. I can step out of this house and get away from the pressures and problems . . . be a different man. I ain't got to wonder how I'm gonna pay the bills or get the roof fixed. I can just be a part of myself that I ain't never been.

ROSE: What I want to know . . . is do you plan to continue seeing her? That's all you can say to me.

TROY: I can sit up in her house and laugh. Do you understand what I'm saying. I can laugh out loud . . . and it feels good. It reaches all the way down to the bottom of my shoes. [*Pause.*] Rose, I can't give that up.

ROSE: Maybe you ought to go on and stay down there with her . . . if she a better woman than me.

TROY: It ain't about nobody being a better woman or nothing. Rose, you ain't the blame. A man couldn't ask for no woman to be a better wife than you've been. I'm responsible for it. I done locked myself into a pattern trying to take care of you all that I forgot about myself.

ROSE: What the hell was I there for? That was my job, not somebody else's.

TROY: Rose, I done tried all my life to live decent . . . to live a clean . . . hard . . . useful life. I tried to be a good husband to you. In every way I knew how. Maybe I come into the world backwards, I don't know. But . . . you born with two strikes on you before you come to the plate. You got to guard it closely . . . always looking for the curve-ball on the inside corner. You can't afford to let none get past you. You can't afford a call strike. If you going down . . . you going down swinging. Everything lined up against you. What you gonna do. I fooled them, Rose. I bunted. When I found you and Cory and a halfway decent job . . . I was safe. Couldn't nothing touch me. I wasn't gonna strike out no more. I wasn't going back to the penitentiary. I wasn't gonna lay in the streets with a bottle of wine. I was safe. I had me a family. A job. I wasn't gonna get that last strike. I was on first looking for one of them boys to knock me in. To get me home.

ROSE: You should have stayed in my bed, Troy.

TROY: Then, when I saw that gal . . . she firmed up my backbone. And I got to thinking that if I tried . . . I just might be able to steal second. Do you understand after eighteen years I wanted to steal second.

ROSE: You should have held me tight. You should have grabbed me and held on.

TROY: I stood on first base for eighteen years and I thought . . . well, goddamn it . . . go on for it!

ROSE: We're not talking about baseball! We're talking about you going off to lay in bed with another woman . . . and then bring it home to me. That's what we're talking about. We ain't talking about no baseball.

TROY: Rose, you're not listening to me. I'm trying the best I can to explain it to you. It's not easy for me to admit that I been standing in the same place for eighteen years.

ROSE: I been standing with you! I been right here with you, Troy. I got a life too. I gave eighteen years of my life to stand in the same spot with you. Don't you think I ever wanted other things? Don't you think I had dreams and hopes? What about my life? What about me? Don't you think it ever crossed my mind to want to know other men? That I wanted to lay up somewhere and forget about my responsibilities? That I wanted someone to make me laugh so I could feel good? You not the only one who's got wants and needs. But I held on to you, Troy. I took all my feelings, my wants and needs, my dreams . . . and I buried them inside you. I planted a seed and watched and prayed over it. I planted myself inside you and waited to bloom. And it didn't take me no eighteen years to find out the soil was hard and rocky and it wasn't never gonna bloom. But I held on to you, Troy. I held you tighter. You was my husband. I owed you everything I had. Every part of me I could find to give you. And upstairs in that room . . . with the darkness falling in on me . . . I gave everything I had to try and erase the doubt that you wasn't the finest man in the world. And wherever you was going . . . I wanted to be there with you. Cause you was my husband. Cause that's the only way I was gonna survive as your wife. You always talking about what you give . . . and what you don't have to give. But you take too. You take . . . and don't even know nobody's giving!

[ROSE *turns to exit into the house;* TROY *grabs her arm.*]

TROY: You say I take and don't give!

ROSE: Troy! You're hurting me.

TROY: You say I take and don't give.

ROSE: Troy . . . you're hurting my arm! Let go!

TROY: I done give you everything I got. Don't you tell that lie on me.

ROSE: Troy!

TROY: Don't you tell that lie on me!

[CORY *enters from the house.*]

CORY: Mama!

ROSE: Troy. You're hurting me.

TROY: Don't you tell me about no taking and giving.

[CORY *comes up behind* TROY *and grabs him.* TROY, *surprised, is thrown off balance just as* CORY *throws a glancing blow that catches him on the chest and knocks him down.* TROY *is stunned, as is* CORY.]

ROSE: Troy. Troy. No!

[TROY *gets to his feet and starts at* CORY.]

Troy . . . no. Please! Troy!

[ROSE *pulls on* TROY *to hold him back.* TROY *stops himself.*]

TROY: [*To* CORY.] Alright. That's strike two. You stay away from around me, boy. Don't you strike out. You living with a full count. Don't you strike out.

[TROY *exits out the yard as the lights go down.*]

Scene 2

It is six months later, early afternoon. TROY *enters from the house and starts to exit the yard.* ROSE *enters from the house.*

ROSE: Troy, I want to talk to you.

TROY: All of a sudden, after all this time, you want to talk to me, huh? You ain't wanted to talk to me for months. You ain't wanted to talk to me last night. You ain't wanted no part of me then. What you wanna talk to me about now?

ROSE: Tomorrow's Friday.

TROY: I know what day tomorrow is. You think I don't know tomorrow's Friday? My whole life I ain't done nothing but look to see Friday coming and you got to tell me it's Friday.

ROSE: I want to know if you're coming home.

TROY: I always come home, Rose. You know that. There ain't never been a night I ain't come home.

ROSE: That ain't what I mean . . . and you know it. I want to know if you're coming straight home after work.

TROY: I figure I'd cash my check . . . hang out at Taylors' with the boys . . . maybe play a game of checkers . . .

ROSE: Troy, I can't live like this. I won't live like this. You livin' on borrowed time with me. It's been going on six months now you ain't been coming home.

TROY: I be here every night. Every night of the year. That's 365 days.

ROSE: I want you to come home tomorrow after work.

TROY: Rose . . . I don't mess up my pay. You know that now. I take my pay and I give it to you. I don't have no money but what you give me back. I just want to have a little time to myself . . . a little time to enjoy life.

ROSE: What about me? When's my time to enjoy life?

TROY: I don't know what to tell you, Rose. I'm doing the best I can.

ROSE: You ain't been home from work but time enough to change your clothes and run out . . . and you wanna call that the best you can do?

TROY: I'm going over to the hospital to see Alberta. She went into the hospital this afternoon. Look like she might have the baby early. I won't be gone long.

ROSE: Well, you ought to know. They went over to Miss Pearl's and got Gabe today. She said you told them to go ahead and lock him up.

TROY: I ain't said no such thing. Whoever told you that is telling a lie. Pearl ain't doing nothing but telling a big fat lie.

ROSE: She ain't had to tell me. I read it on the papers.

TROY: I ain't told them nothing of the kind.

ROSE: I saw it right there on the papers.

TROY: What it say, huh?

ROSE: It said you told them to take him.

TROY: Then they screwed that up, just the way they screw up everything. I ain't worried about what they got on the paper.

ROSE: Say the government send part of his check to the hospital and the other part to you.

TROY: I ain't got nothing to do with that if that's the way it works. I ain't made up the rules about how it work.

ROSE: You did Gabe just like you did Cory. You wouldn't sign the paper for Cory . . . but you signed for Gabe. You signed that paper.

[*The telephone is heard ringing inside the house.*]

TROY: I told you I ain't signed nothing, woman! The only thing I signed was the release form. Hell, I can't read, I don't know what they had on that paper! I ain't signed nothing about sending Gabe away.

ROSE: I said send him to the hospital . . . you said let him be free . . . now you done went down there and signed him to the hospital for half his money. You went back on yourself, Troy. You gonna have to answer for that.

TROY: See now . . . you been over there talking to Miss Pearl. She done got mad cause she ain't getting Gabe's rent money. That's all it is. She's liable to say anything.

ROSE: Troy, I seen where you signed the paper.

TROY: You ain't seen nothing I signed. What she doing got papers on my brother anyway? Miss Pearl telling a big fat lie. And I'm gonna tell her about it too! You ain't seen nothing I signed. Say . . . you ain't seen nothing I signed.

[ROSE *exits into the house to answer the telephone. Presently she returns.*]

ROSE: Troy . . . that was the hospital. Alberta had the baby.

TROY: What she have? What is it?

ROSE: It's a girl.

TROY: I better get on down to the hospital to see her.

ROSE: Troy . . .

TROY: Rose . . . I got to go see her now. That's only right . . . what's the matter . . . the baby's alright, ain't it?

ROSE: Alberta died having the baby.

TROY: Died . . . you say she's dead? Alberta's dead?

ROSE: They said they done all they could. They couldn't do nothing for her.

TROY: The baby? How's the baby?

ROSE: They say it's healthy. I wonder who's gonna bury her.

TROY: She had family, Rose. She wasn't living in the world by herself.

ROSE: I know she wasn't living in the world by herself.

TROY: Next thing you gonna want to know if she had any insurance.

ROSE: Troy, you ain't got to talk like that.

TROY: That's the first thing that jumped out your mouth. "Who's gonna bury her?" Like I'm fixing to take on that task for myself.

ROSE: I am your wife. Don't push me away.

TROY: I ain't pushing nobody away. Just give me some space. That's all. Just give me some room to breathe.

[ROSE *exits into the house.* TROY *walks about the yard.*]

TROY: [*With a quiet rage that threatens to consume him.*] Alright . . . Mr. Death. See now . . . I'm gonna tell you what I'm gonna do. I'm gonna take and build me a fence around this yard. See? I'm gonna build me a fence around what belongs to me. And then I want you to stay on the other side. See? You stay over there until you're ready for me. Then you come on. Bring your army. Bring your sickle. Bring your wrestling clothes. I ain't gonna fall down on my vigilance this time. You ain't gonna sneak up on me no more. When you ready for me . . . when the top of your list say Troy Maxson . . . that's when you come around here. You come up and knock on the front door. Ain't nobody else got nothing to do with this. This is between you and me. Man to man. You stay on the other side of that fence until you ready for me. Then you come up and knock on the front door. Anytime you want. I'll be ready for you.

[*The lights go down to black.*]

Scene 3

The lights come up on the porch. It is late evening three days later. ROSE *sits listening to the ball game waiting for* TROY. *The final out of the game is made and* ROSE *switches off the radio.* TROY *enters the yard carrying an infant wrapped in blankets. He stands back from the house and calls.*

[ROSE *enters and stands on the porch. There is a long, awkward silence, the weight of which grows heavier with each passing second.*]

TROY: Rose . . . I'm standing here with my daughter in my arms. She ain't but a wee bittie little old thing. She don't know nothing about grownups' business. She innocent . . . and she ain't got no mama.

ROSE: What you telling me for, Troy? [*She turns and exits into the house.*]

TROY: Well . . . I guess we'll just sit out here on the porch. [*He sits down on the porch. There is an awkward indelicateness about the way he handles the baby.*

His largeness engulfs and seems to swallow it. He speaks loud enough for ROSE *to hear.*] A man's got to do what's right for him. I ain't sorry for nothing I done. It felt right in my heart. [*To the baby.*] What you smiling at? Your daddy's a big man. Got these great big old hands. But sometimes he's scared. And right now your daddy's scared cause we sitting out here and ain't got no home. Oh, I been homeless before. I ain't had no little baby with me. But I been homeless. You just be out on the road by your lonesome and you see one of them trains coming and you just kinda go like this . . .

[*He sings as a lullaby.*]
    Please, Mr. Engineer let a man ride the line
    Please, Mr. Engineer let a man ride the line
    I ain't got no ticket please let me ride the blinds
[ROSE *enters from the house.* TROY *hearing her steps behind him, stands and faces her.*]

She's my daughter, Rose. My own flesh and blood. I can't deny her no more than I can deny them boys. [*Pause.*] You and them boys is my family. You and them and this child is all I got in the world. So I guess what I'm saying is . . . I'd appreciate it if you'd help me take care of her.

ROSE: Okay, Troy . . . you're right. I'll take care of your baby for you . . . cause . . . like you say . . . she's innocent . . . and you can't visit the sins of the father upon the child. A motherless child has got a hard time. [*She takes the baby from him.*] From right now . . . this child got a mother. But you a womanless man.

[ROSE *turns and exits into the house with the baby. Lights go down to black.*]

Scene 4

It is two months later. LYONS *enters from the street. He knocks on the door and calls.*

LYONS: Hey, Rose! [*Pause.*] Rose!

ROSE: [*From inside the house.*] Stop that yelling. You gonna wake up Raynell. I just got her to sleep.

LYONS: I just stopped by to pay Papa this twenty dollars I owe him. Where's Papa at?

ROSE: He should be here in a minute. I'm getting ready to go down to the church. Sit down and wait on him.

LYONS: I got to go pick up Bonnie over her mother's house.

ROSE: Well, sit it down there on the table. He'll get it.

LYONS: [*Enters the house and sets the money on the table.*] Tell Papa I said thanks. I'll see you again.

ROSE: Alright, Lyons. We'll see you.

[LYONS *starts to exit as* CORY *enters.*]

CORY: Hey, Lyons.

LYONS: What's happening, Cory. Say man, I'm sorry I missed your graduation. You know I had a gig and couldn't get away. Otherwise you know I would have been there. So what you doing?

CORY: I'm trying to find a job.

LYONS: Yeah I know how that go, man. It's rough out here. Jobs are scarce.

CORY: Yeah, I know.

LYONS: Look here, I got to run. Talk to Papa . . . he know some people. He'll be able to help get you a job. Talk to him . . . see what he say.

CORY: Yeah . . . alright, Lyons.

LYONS: You take care. I'll talk to you soon. We'll find some time to talk.

[LYONS *exits the yard.* CORY *wanders over to the tree, picks up the bat and assumes a batting stance. He studies an imaginary pitcher and swings. Dissatisfied with the result, he tries again.* TROY *enters. They eye each other for a beat.* CORY *puts the bat down and exits the yard.* TROY *starts into the house as* ROSE *exits with* RAYNELL. *She is carrying a cake.*]

TROY: I'm coming in and everybody's going out.

ROSE: I'm taking this cake down to the church for the bakesale. Lyons was by to see you. He stopped by to pay you your twenty dollars. It's laying in there on the table.

TROY: [*Going into his pocket.*] Well . . . here go this money.

ROSE: Put it in there on the table, Troy. I'll get it.

TROY: What time you coming back?

ROSE: Ain't no use in you studying me. It don't matter what time I come back.

TROY: I just asked you a question, woman. What's the matter . . . can't I ask you a question?

ROSE: Troy, I don't want to go into it. Your dinner's in there on the stove. All you got to do is heat it up. And don't you be eating the rest of them cakes in there. I'm coming back for them. We having a bakesale at the church tomorrow.

[ROSE *exits the yard.* TROY *sits down on the steps, takes a pint bottle from his pocket, opens it and drinks. He begins to sing.*]

TROY: Hear it ring! Hear it ring!
           Had an old dog his name was Blue
           You know Blue was mighty true.
           You know Blue as a good old dog
           Blue trees a possum in a hollow log
           You know from that he was a good old dog

[BONO *enters the yard.*]

BONO: Hey, Troy.

TROY: Hey, what's happening, Bono?

BONO: I just thought I'd stop by to see you.

TROY: What you stop by and see me for? You ain't stopped by in a month of Sundays. Hell, I must owe you money or something.

BONO: Since you got your promotion I can't keep up with you. Used to see you everyday. Now I don't even know what route you working.

TROY: They keep switching me around. Got me out in Greentree now . . . hauling white folks' garbage.

BONO: Greentree, huh? You lucky, at least you ain't got to be lifting them barrels. Damn if they ain't getting heavier. I'm gonna put in my two years and call it quits.

TROY: I'm thinking about retiring myself.

BONO: You got it easy. You can *drive* for another five years.

TROY: It ain't the same, Bono. It ain't like working the back of the truck. Ain't got nobody to talk to . . . feel like you working by yourself. Naw, I'm thinking about retiring. How's Lucille?

BONO: She alright. Her arthritis get to acting up on her sometime. Saw Rose on my way in. She going down to the church, huh?

TROY: Yeah, she took up going down there. All them preachers looking for somebody to fatten their pockets. [*Pause.*] Got some gin here.

BONO: Naw, thanks. I just stopped by to say hello.

TROY: Hell, nigger . . . you can take a drink. I ain't never known you to say no to a drink. You ain't got to work tomorrow.

BONO: I just stopped by. I'm fixing to go over to Skinner's. We got us a domino game going over his house every Friday.

TROY: Nigger, you can't play no dominoes. I used to whup you four games out of five.

BONO: Well, that learned me. I'm getting better.

TROY: Yeah? Well, that's alright.

BONO: Look here . . . I got to be getting on. Stop by sometime, huh?

TROY: Yeah, I'll do that, Bono. Lucille told Rose you bought her a new refrigerator.

BONO: Yeah, Rose told Lucille you had finally built your fence . . . so I figured we'd call it even.

TROY: I knew you would.

BONO: Yeah . . . okay. I'll be talking to you.

TROY: Yeah, take care, Bono. Good to see you. I'm gonna stop over.

BONO: Yeah. Okay, Troy. [BONO *exits.* TROY *drinks from the bottle and sings.*]

TROY: Old Blue died and I dig his grave
            Let him down with a golden chain
            Every night when I hear old Blue bark
            I know Blue treed a possum in Noah's Ark.
            Hear it ring! Hear it ring!

[CORY *enters the yard. They eye each other for a beat.* TROY *is sitting in the middle of the steps.* CORY *walks over.*]

CORY: I got to get by.

TROY: Say what? What's you say?

CORY: You in my way. I got to get by.

TROY: You got to get by where? This is my house. Bought and paid for. In full. Took me fifteen years. And if you wanna go in my house and I'm sitting on the steps . . . you say excuse me. Like your mama taught you.

CORY: Come on, Pop . . . I got to get by.

[CORY *starts to maneuver his way past* TROY. TROY *grabs his leg and shoves him back.*]

TROY: You just gonna walk over top of me?

CORY: I live here too!

TROY: [*Advancing toward him.*] You just gonna walk over top of me in my own house?

CORY: I ain't scared of you.

TROY: I ain't asked if you was scared of me. I asked you if you was fixing to walk over top of me in my own house? That's the question. You ain't gonna say excuse me? You just gonna walk over top of me?

CORY: If you wanna put it like that.

TROY: How else am I gonna put it?

CORY: I was walking by you to go into the house cause you sitting on the steps drunk, singing to yourself. You can put it like that.

TROY: Without saying excuse me???

[CORY *doesn't respond.*]

I asked you a question. Without saying excuse me???

CORY: I ain't got to say excuse me to you. You don't count around here no more.

TROY: Oh, I see . . . I don't count around here no more. You ain't got to say excuse me to your daddy. All of a sudden you done got so grown that your daddy don't count around here no more . . . Around here in his own house and yard that he done paid for with the sweat of his brow. You done got so grown to where you gonna take over. You gonna take over my house. Is that right? You gonna wear my pants. You gonna go in there and stretch out on my bed. You ain't got to say excuse me cause I don't count around here no more. Is that right?

CORY: That's right. You always talking this dumb stuff. Now, why don't you just get out my way.

TROY: I guess you got someplace to sleep and something to put in your belly. You got that, huh? You got that? That's what you need. You got that, huh?

CORY: You don't know what I got. You ain't got to worry about what I got.

TROY: You right! You one hundred percent right! I done spent the last seventeen years worrying about what you got. Now it's your turn, see? I'll tell you what you do. You grown . . . we done established that. You a man. Now, let's see you act like one. Turn your behind around and walk out this yard. And when you get out there in the alley . . . you can forget about this house. See? Cause this is my house. You go on and be a man and get your own house. You can forget about this. Cause this is mine. You go on and get yours cause I'm through with doing for you.

CORY: You talking about what you did for me . . . what'd you ever give me?

TROY: Them feet and bones! That pumping heart, nigger! I give you more than anybody else is ever gonna give you.

CORY: You ain't never gave me nothing! You ain't never done nothing but hold me back. Afraid I was gonna be better than you. All you ever did was try and make me scared of you. I used to tremble every time you called my name. Every time I heard your footsteps in the house. Wondering all the time . . . what's Papa gonna say if I do this? . . . What's he gonna say if I do that? . . . what's Papa gonna say if I turn on the radio? And Mama, too . . . she tries . . . but she's scared of you.

TROY: You leave your mama out of this. She ain't got nothing to do with this.

CORY: I don't know how she stand you . . . after what you did to her.

TROY: I told you to leave your mama out of this! [*He advances toward* CORY.]

CORY: What you gonna do . . . give me a whupping? You can't whup me no more. You're too old. You just an old man.

TROY: [*Shoves him on his shoulder.*] Nigger! That's what you are. You just another nigger on the street to me!

CORY: You crazy! You know that?

TROY: Go on now! You got the devil in you. Get on away from me!

CORY: You just a crazy old man . . . talking about I got the devil in me.

TROY: Yeah, I'm crazy! If you don't get on the other side of that yard . . . I'm gonna show you how crazy I am! Go on . . . get the hell out of my yard.

CORY: It ain't your yard. You took Uncle Gabe's money he got from the army to buy this house and then you put him out.

TROY: [TROY *advances on* CORY.] Get your black ass out of my yard!

[TROY's *advance backs* CORY *up against the tree.* CORY *grabs up the bat.*]

CORY: I ain't going nowhere! Come on . . . put me out! I ain't scared of you.

TROY: That's my bat!

CORY: Come on!

TROY: Put my bat down!

CORY: Come on, put me out.

[CORY *swings at* TROY, *who backs across the yard.*]

What's the matter? You so bad . . . put me out!

[TROY *advances toward* CORY.]

CORY: [*Backing up.*] Come on! Come on!

TROY: You're gonna have to use it! You wanna draw that bat back on me . . . you're gonna have to use it.

CORY: Come on! . . . Come on!

[CORY *swings the bat at* TROY *a second time. He misses.* TROY *continues to advance toward him.*]

TROY: You're gonna have to kill me! You wanna draw that bat back on me. You're gonna have to kill me.

[CORY, *backed up against the tree, can go no farther.* TROY *taunts him. He sticks out his head and offers him a target.*]

Come on! Come on!

[CORY *is unable to swing the bat.* TROY *grabs it.*]

TROY: Then I'll show you.

[CORY *and* TROY *struggle over the bat. The struggle is fierce and fully engaged.* TROY *ultimately is the stronger, and takes the bat from* CORY *and stands over him ready to swing. He stops himself.*]

Go on and get away from around my house.

[CORY, *stung by his defeat, picks himself up, walks slowly out of the yard and up the alley.*]

CORY: Tell Mama I'll be back for my things.

TROY: They'll be on the other side of that fence.

[CORY *exits.*]

TROY: I can't taste nothing. Helluljah! I can't taste nothing no more. [TROY *assumes a batting posture and begins to taunt Death, the fastball in the outside corner.*] Come on! It's between you and me now! Come on! Anytime you want! Come on! I be ready for you . . . but I ain't gonna be easy.

[*The lights go down on the scene.*]

Scene 5

The time is 1965. The lights come up in the yard. It is the morning of TROY's *funeral. A funeral plaque with a light hangs beside the door. There is a small garden plot off to the side. There is noise and activity in the house as* ROSE, LYONS *and* BONO *have gathered. The door opens and* RAYNELL, *seven years old, enters dressed in a flannel nightgown. She crosses to the garden and pokes around with a stick.* ROSE *calls from the house.*

ROSE: Raynell!

RAYNELL: Mam?

ROSE: What you doing out there?

RAYNELL: Nothing.

[ROSE *comes to the door.*]

ROSE: Girl, get in here and get dressed. What you doing?

RAYNELL: Seeing if my garden growed.

ROSE: I told you it ain't gonna grow overnight. You got to wait.

RAYNELL: It don't look like it never gonna grow. Dag!

ROSE: I told you a watched pot never boils. Get in here and get dressed.

RAYNELL: This ain't even no pot, Mama.

ROSE: You just have to give it a chance. It'll grow. Now you come on and do what I told you. We got to be getting ready. This ain't no morning to be playing around. You hear me?

RAYNELL: Yes, mam.

[ROSE *exits into the house.* RAYNELL *continues to poke at her garden with a stick.* CORY *enters. He is dressed in a Marine corporal's uniform, and carries a duffel bag. His posture is that of a military man, and his speech has a clipped sternness.*]

CORY: [*To* RAYNELL.] Hi.

    [*Pause.*]

I bet your name is Raynell.

RAYNELL: Uh huh.

CORY: Is your mama home?

    [RAYNELL *runs up on the porch and calls through the screen door.*]

RAYNELL: Mama . . . there's some man out here. Mama?

    [ROSE *comes to the door.*]

ROSE: Cory? Lord have mercy! Look here, you all!

    [ROSE *and* CORY *embrace in a tearful reunion as* BONO *and* LYONS *enter from the house dressed in funeral clothes.*]

BONO: Aw, looka here . . .

ROSE: Done got all grown up!

CORY: Don't cry, Mama. What you crying about?

ROSE: I'm just so glad you made it.

CORY: Hey Lyons. How you doing, Mr. Bono.

    (LYONS *goes to embrace* CORY.)

LYONS: Look at you, man. Look at you. Don't he look good, Rose. Got them Corporal stripes.

ROSE: What took you so long.

CORY: You know how the Marines are, Mama. They got to get all their paper-work straight before they let you do anything.

ROSE: Well, I'm sure glad you made it. They let Lyons come. Your Uncle Gabe's still in the hospital. They don't know if they gonna let him out or not. I just talked to them a little while ago.

LYONS: A Corporal in the United States Marines.

BONO: Your daddy knew you had it in you. He used to tell me all the time.

LYONS: Don't he look good, Mr. Bono?

BONO: Yeah, he remind me of Troy when I first met him. [*Pause.*] Say, Rose, Lucille's down at the church with the choir. I'm gonna go down and get the pallbearers lined up. I'll be back to get you all.

ROSE: Thanks, Jim.

CORY: See you, Mr. Bono.

LYONS: [*With his arm around* RAYNELL.] Cory . . . look at Raynell. Ain't she precious? She gonna break a whole lot of hearts.

ROSE: Raynell, come and say hello to your brother. This is your brother, Cory. You remember Cory.

RAYNELL: No, Mam.

CORY: She don't remember me, Mama.

ROSE: Well, we talk about you. She heard us talk about you. [*To* RAYNELL.] This is your brother, Cory. Come on and say hello.

RAYNELL: Hi.

CORY: Hi. So you're Raynell. Mama told me a lot about you.

ROSE: You all come on into the house and let me fix you some breakfast. Keep up your strength.

CORY: I ain't hungry, Mama.

LYONS: You can fix me something, Rose. I'll be in there in a minute.

ROSE: Cory, you sure you don't want nothing. I know they ain't feeding you right.

CORY: No, Mama . . . thanks. I don't feel like eating. I'll get something later.

ROSE: Raynell . . . get on upstairs and get that dress on like I told you.

[ROSE *and* RAYNELL *exit into the house.*]

LYONS: So . . . I hear you thinking about getting married.

CORY: Yeah, I done found the right one, Lyons. It's about time.

LYONS: Me and Bonnie been split up about four years now. About the time Papa retired. I guess she just got tired of all them changes I was putting her through. [*Pause.*] I always knew you was gonna make something out yourself. Your head was always in the right direction. So . . . you gonna stay in . . . make it a career . . . put in your twenty years?

CORY: I don't know. I got six already, I think that's enough.

LYONS: Stick with Uncle Sam and retire early. Ain't nothing out here. I guess Rose told you what happened with me. They got me down the workhouse. I thought I was being slick cashing other people's checks.

CORY: How much time you doing?

LYONS: They give me three years. I got that beat now. I ain't got but nine more months. It ain't so bad. You learn to deal with it like anything else. You got to take the crookeds with the straights. That's what Papa used to say. He used to say that when he struck out. I seen him strike out three times in a row . . . and the next time up he hit the ball over the grand-stand. Right out there in Homestead Field. He wasn't satisfied hitting in the seats . . . he want to hit it over everything! After the game he had two hundred people standing around waiting to shake his hand. You got to take the crookeds with the straights. Yeah, Papa was something else.

CORY: You still playing?

LYONS: Cory . . . you know I'm gonna do that. There's some fellows down there we got us a band . . . we gonna try and stay together when we get out . . . but yeah, I'm still playing. It still helps me to get out of bed in the morning. As long as it do that I'm gonna be right there playing and trying to make some sense out of it.

ROSE: [*Calling.*] Lyons, I got these eggs in the pan.

LYONS: Let me go on and get these eggs, man. Get ready to go bury Papa. [*Pause.*] How you doing? You doing alright?

[CORY *nods.* LYONS *touches him on the shoulder and they share a moment of silent grief.* LYONS *exits into the house.* CORY *wanders about the yard.* RAYNELL *enters.*]

RAYNELL: Hi.

CORY: Hi.

RAYNELL: Did you used to sleep in my room?

CORY: Yeah . . . that used to be my room.

RAYNELL: That's what Papa call it. "Cory's room." It got your football in the closet.

[ROSE *comes to the door.*]

ROSE: Raynell, get in there and get them good shoes on.

RAYNELL: Mama, can't I wear these. Them other one hurt my feet.

ROSE: Well, they just gonna have to hurt your feet for a while. You ain't said they hurt your feet when you went down to the store and got them.

RAYNELL: They didn't hurt then. My feet done got bigger.

ROSE: Don't you give me no backtalk now. You get in there and get them shoes on. [RAYNELL *exits into the house.*] Ain't too much changed. He still got that piece of rag tied to that tree. He was out here swinging that bat. I was just ready to go back in the house. He swung that bat and then he just fell over. Seem like he swung it and stood there with this grin on his face . . . and then he just fell over. They carried him on down to the hospital, but I knew there wasn't no need . . . why don't you come on in the house?

CORY: Mama . . . I got something to tell you. I don't know how to tell you this . . . but I've got to tell you . . . I'm not going to Papa's funeral.

ROSE: Boy, hush your mouth. That's your daddy you talking about. I don't want hear that kind of talk this morning. I done raised you to come to this? You standing there all healthy and grown talking about you ain't going to your daddy's funeral?

CORY: Mama . . . listen . . .

ROSE: I don't want to hear it, Cory. You just get that thought out of your head.

CORY: I can't drag Papa with me everywhere I go. I've got to say no to him. One time in my life I've got to say no.

ROSE: Don't nobody have to listen to nothing like that. I know you and your daddy ain't seen eye to eye, but I ain't got to listen to that kind of talk this morning. Whatever was between you and your daddy . . . the time has come to put it aside. Just take it and set it over there on the shelf and forget about it. Disrespecting your daddy ain't gonna make you a man, Cory. You got to find a way to come to that on your own. Not going to your daddy's funeral ain't gonna make you a man.

CORY: The whole time I was growing up . . . living in his house . . . Papa was like a shadow that followed you everywhere. It weighed on you and sunk into your flesh. It would wrap around you and lay there until you couldn't tell which one was you anymore. That shadow digging in your flesh. Trying to crawl in. Trying to live through you. Everywhere I looked, Troy Maxson was staring back at me . . . hiding under the bed . . . in the closet. I'm just saying I've got to find a way to get rid of that shadow, Mama.

ROSE: You just like him. You got him in you good.

CORY: Don't tell me that, Mama.

TROY: You Troy Maxson all over again.

CORY: I don't want to be Troy Maxson. I want to be me.

ROSE: You can't be nobody but who you are, Cory. That shadow wasn't nothing but you growing into yourself. You either got to grow into it or cut it down to fit you. But that's all you got to make life with. That's all you got to measure yourself against that world out there. Your daddy wanted you to be everything he wasn't . . . and at the same time he tried to make you into everything he was. I don't know if he was right or wrong . . . but I do know he meant to do more good than he meant to do harm. He wasn't always right. Sometimes when he touched he bruised. And sometimes when he took me in his arms he cut.

When I first met your daddy I thought . . . Here is a man I can lay down with and make a baby. That's the first thing I thought when I seen him. I was thirty years old and had done seen my share of men. But when he walked up to me and said, "I can dance a waltz that'll make you dizzy," I thought, Rose Lee, here is a man that you can open yourself up to and be filled to bursting. Here is a man that can fill all them empty spaces you been tipping around the edges of. One of them empty spaces was being somebody's mother.

I married your daddy and settled down to cooking his supper and keeping clean sheets on the bed. When your daddy walked through the house he was so big he filled it up. That was my first mistake. Not to make him leave some room for me. For my part in the matter. But at that time I wanted that. I wanted a house that I could sing in. And that's what your daddy gave me. I didn't know to keep up his strength I had to give up little pieces of mine. I did that. I took on his life as mine and mixed up the pieces so that you couldn't hardly tell which was which anymore. It was my choice. It was my life and I didn't have to live it like that. But that's what life offered me in the way of being a woman and I took it. I grabbed hold of it with both hands.

By the time Raynell came into the house, me and your daddy had done lost touch with one another. I didn't want to make my blessing off of nobody's misfortune . . . but I took on to Raynell like she was all them babies I had wanted and never had. [*The phone rings.*] Like I'd been blessed to relive a part of my life. And if the Lord see fit to keep up my strength . . . I'm gonna do her just like your daddy did you . . . I'm gonna give her the best of what's in me.

RAYNELL: [*Entering, still with her old shoes.*] Mama . . . Reverend Tollivier on the phone.

[ROSE *exits into the house.*]

RAYNELL: Hi.

CORY: Hi.

RAYNELL: You in the Army or the Marines?

CORY: Marines.

RAYNELL: Papa said it was the Army. Did you know Blue?

CORY: Blue? Who's Blue?

RAYNELL: Papa's dog what he sing about all the time.

CORY: [*Singing.*] Hear it ring! Hear it ring!

I had a dog his name was Blue

You know Blue was mighty true
You know Blue was a good old dog
Blue treed a possum in a hollow log
You know from that he was a good old dog.
Hear it ring! Hear it ring!
    [RAYNELL *joins in singing.*]
CORY and RAYNELL: Blue treed a possum out on a limb
Blue looked at me and I looked at him
Grabbed that possum and put him in a sack
Blue stayed there till I came back
Old Blue's feets was big and round
Never allowed a possum to touch the ground.

Old Blue died and I dug his grave
I dug his grave with a silver spade
Let him down with a golden chain
And every night I call his name
Go on Blue, you good dog you
Go on Blue, you good dog you
RAYNELL: Blue laid down and died like a man
Blue laid down and died . . .
BOTH: Blue laid down and died like a man
Now he's treeing possums in the Promised Land
I'm gonna tell you this to let you know
Blue's gone where the good dogs go
When I hear old Blue bark
When I hear old Blue bark
Blue treed a possum in Noah's Ark
Blue treed a possum in Noah's Ark.
    [ROSE *comes to the screen door.*]
ROSE: Cory, we gonna be ready to go in a minute.
CORY: [*To* RAYNELL.] You go on in the house and change them shoes like
    Mama told you so we can go to Papa's funeral.
RAYNELL: Okay, I'll be back.
    [RAYNELL *exits into the house.* CORY *gets up and crosses over to the tree.* ROSE
    stands in the screen door watching him. GABRIEL *enters from the alley.*]
GABRIEL: [*Calling.*] Hey, Rose!
ROSE: Gabe?
GABRIEL: I'm here, Rose. Hey Rose, I'm here!
    [ROSE *enters from the house.*]
ROSE: Lord . . . Look here, Lyons!
LYONS: See, I told you, Rose . . . I told you they'd let him come.
CORY: How you doing, Uncle Gabe?
LYONS: How you doing, Uncle Gabe?

GABRIEL: Hey, Rose. It's time. It's time to tell St. Peter to open the gates. Troy, you ready? You ready, Troy. I'm gonna tell St. Peter to open the gates. You get ready now.

> [*Gabriel, with great fanfare, braces himself to blow. The trumpet is without a mouthpiece. He puts the end of it into his mouth and blows with great force, like a man who has been waiting some twenty-odd years for this single moment. No sound comes out of the trumpet. He braces himself and blows again with the same result. A third time he blows. There is a weight of impossible description that falls away and leaves him bare and exposed to a frightful realization. It is a trauma that a sane and normal mind would be unable to withstand. He begins to dance. A slow, strange dance, eerie and life-giving. A dance of atavistic signature and ritual.* LYONS *attempts to embrace him.* GABRIEL *pushes* LYONS *away. He begins to howl in what is an attempt at song, or perhaps a song turning back into itself in an attempt at speech. He finishes his dance and the gates of heaven stand open as wide as God's closet.*]

That's the way that go!

[*BLACKOUT.*]

STUDY QUESTIONS

1. How does the SETTING relate to the play's title? If you were staging the play, how prominent would you make the fence-building materials? How would you indicate, visually, their temporariness and potential to add another dimension to the scene? What other visual aspects of the setting help to set up the THEMES of the play? Why do you think the author takes the trouble to describe the setting in so much detail? What does each of the items mentioned in the description of setting suggest about the CHARACTERS in the play?

2. Why is each of the characters described, in the list of characters, strictly in his or her relationship to Troy? What other indications are there, early on, that Troy is to be considered the center of the play? How much of the ACTION do we experience from Troy's POINT OF VIEW? What early indications are there of Troy's weakness? of flaws in his perceptions of reality?

3. What events from the past seem to have been most important in shaping Troy's character? What indications are there in the text that Troy's treatment of Cory replicates patterns of previous generations? Describe fully Troy's character; what aspects of his character and personality are explicable in terms of his past experiences? How important is family history in explaining his behavior? How important are economic and social conditions?

4. In what ways does the language of the play reflect Troy's past life? How thoroughly does the past infiltrate conceptions of the present in the play's language? What indications are there that behavior is passed down from generation to generation?

5. What characteristics of Troy are held in common by all of his children? What position does the play seem to take on the question of inherited characteristics? What gender roles seem to be important to the play's sorting out of issues? In

what ways is history important to the behavior of the various characters?

6. In what ways are the characters' ages important to events in the play? How fully do different characters seem to reflect roles "characteristic" of their age groups? How are age behaviors distinguished from actions dependent on individual character?

7. What STEREOTYPES of white behavior are referred to in the play? How are these stereotypes represented? Which of the stereotypes seem to be upheld by the play's action? Which are undercut or corrected? What kind of attitude does the play take toward stereotypes based on race? on social position? on age? on economic conditions?

8. What different CONFLICTS does the play represent? Which ones seem most important to the play's dramatic focus? How do the conflicts reflect one another? What seems to you to be the central conflict of the play? Who is the central character? How can you tell?

9. What function does the idea of the fence perform for the central characters? How do their notions of the significance of the fence differ from one another? How does the function of the fence change as the play goes on? By the end, what significance does the fence take on? Whose ideas of "fencing" does the play ultimately seem to support?

10. What value does Troy's life seem to have had by the play's end? What characters seem most closely to embody the play's human values? What attitude does the play ultimately establish toward Lyons? toward Gabriel? toward Bono? toward men? toward women?

11. On what principles are Troy's values based? What attitude does the total play take toward those values? How important is the past to the behavior of the various characters? According to the play, how does one free oneself from the influence of the past?

12. Which characters in the play are the most attractive? What characteristics make them attractive? What kinds of behavior are we, as audience, led to disapprove of most fully? How are we made to disapprove? What values does the play ultimately seem to support most fully? What values does it disapprove of? How can you tell?

13. In what ways are the values of the white world brought to bear on the lives of the people in the play? What attitudes does the play support toward these values? How responsible do the characters in the play seem for their own destiny? What results seem to have been determined by larger social forces?

14. Toward what characters do you feel most sympathetic by the end of the play? Toward which do you feel the least sympathetic? What accounts for your feelings?

15. Describe the TONE of the ending of the play. What does the repetition of the song suggest about attitudes toward Troy? What issues are resolved satisfactorily by the death of Troy? What issues are left unresolved?

James Seilsopour

J ames Seilsopour was born in California in 1962, the son of an Iranian father. He spent most of his early life in Iran but returned to the United States with his family in 1979 at the time when the Ayatollah Khomeini came to power. He was in high school in California during the "hostage crisis" that began in 1979 when Iranians took control of the American embassy in Teheran.

I FORGOT THE WORDS TO THE NATIONAL ANTHEM

The bumper sticker read, "Piss on Iran." 1

To me, a fourteen-year-old living in Teheran, the Iranian revolution 2 was nothing more than an inconvenience. Although the riots were just around the corner, although the tanks lined the streets, although a stray bullet went through my sister's bedroom window, I was upset because I could not ride at the Royal Stable as often as I used to. In the summer of 1979 my family— father, mother, brothers, sister, aunt, and two cousins—were forced into exile. We came to Norco, California.

In Iran, I was an American citizen and considered myself an American, 3 even though my father was Iranian. I loved baseball and apple pie and knew the words to the "Star-Spangled Banner." That summer before high school, I was like any other kid my age; I listened to rock'n'roll, liked fast cars, and thought Farrah Fawcett was a fox. Excited about going to high school, I was looking forward to football games and school dances. But I learned that it was not meant to be. I was not like other kids, and it was a long, painful road I traveled as I found this out.

The American embassy in Iran was seized the fall I started high school. 4 I did not realize my life would be affected until I read that bumper sticker in the high school parking lot which read, "Piss on Iran." At that moment I knew there would be no football games or school dances. For me, Norco High consisted of the goat ropers, the dopers, the jocks, the brains, and one quiet Iranian.

I was sitting in my photography class after the hostages were taken. The 5 photography teacher was fond of showing travel films. On this particular day, he decided to show a film about Iran, knowing full well that my father was Iranian and that I grew up in Iran. During the movie, this teacher encouraged the students to make comments. Around the room, I could hear "Drop the bomb" and "Deport the mothers." Those words hurt. I felt dirty, guilty. However, I managed to laugh and assure the students I realized they were just joking. I went home that afternoon and cried. I have long since forgiven those students, but I have not and can never forgive that teacher. Paranoia set in. From then on, every whisper was about me: "You see that lousy son of a bitch? He's Iranian." When I was not looking, I could feel their pointing fingers in my back like arrows. Because I was absent one day, the next day I brought a note to the attendance office. The secretary read the note, then looked at me. "So you're Jim Seilsopour?" I couldn't answer. As I walked away, I thought I heard her whisper to her co-worker, "You see that lousy son of a bitch? He's Iranian." I missed thirty-five days of school that year.

My problems were small compared to those of my parents. In Teheran, my mother had been a lady of society. We had a palatial house and a maid. Belonging to the women's club, she collected clothes for the poor and arranged Christmas parties for the young American kids. She and my father dined with high government officials. But back in the States, when my father could not find a job, she had to work at a fast-food restaurant. She was the proverbial pillar of strength. My mother worked seventy hours a week for two years. I never heard her complain. I could see the toll the entire situation was taking on her. One day my mother and I went grocery shopping at Stater Brothers Market. After an hour of carefully picking our food, we proceeded to the cashier. The cashier was friendly and began a conversation with my mother. They spoke briefly of the weather as my mother wrote the check. The cashier looked at the check and casually asked, "What kind of name is that?" My mother said, "Italian." We exchanged glances for just a second. I could see the pain in her eyes. She offered no excuses; I asked for none.

Because of my father's birthplace, he was unable to obtain a job. A naturalized American citizen with a master's degree in aircraft maintenance engineering from the Northrop Institute of Technology, he had never been out of work in his life. My father had worked for Bell Helicopter International, Flying Tigers, and McDonnell Douglas. Suddenly, a man who literally was at the top of his field was unemployable. There is one incident that haunts me even today. My mother had gone to work, and all the kids had gone to school except me. I was in the bathroom washing my face. The door was open, and I could see my father's reflection in the mirror. For no particular reason I watched him. He was glancing at a newspaper. He carefully folded the paper and set it aside. For several long moments he stared blankly into space. With a resigned sigh, he got up, went into the kitchen, and began doing the dishes. On that day, I know I watched a part of my father die.

My father did get a job. However, he was forced to leave the country. 8
He is a quality control inspector for Saudi Arabian Airlines in Jeddah, Saudi
Arabia. My mother works only forty hours a week now. My family has
survived, financially and emotionally. I am not bitter, but the memories are.
I have not recovered totally; I can never do that.

And no, I have never been to a high school football game or dance. The 9
strike really turned me off to baseball. I have been on a diet for the last year,
so I don't eat apple pie much anymore. And I have forgotten the words to
the national anthem.

STUDY QUESTIONS

1. Describe the author's social and political background. Do his habits and affluent
   life-style make his adjustment to American life more or less difficult? In what ways
   does he feel that he fits in? In what ways is he "different"?

2. Who seems to be responsible for the barriers raised against Seilsopour in high
   school? Who is responsible for the bumper sticker and the comments following the
   taking of hostages at the American embassy?

3. Why does Seilsopour feel "dirty, guilty" (paragraph 5)? Describe his attitude toward
   his Iranian heritage.

4. How do you account for the calm TONE of his description of a bullet passing through
   his sister's room? Which events are the most upsetting to him? Why?

5. What does learning "The Star-Spangled Banner" mean to Seilsopour? What does
   his "forgetting" the words mean to him? In what other ways has he changed by
   the end of the essay?

Laurence Thomas

Laurence Thomas teaches in the philosophy, political science, and Judaic studies
departments at Syracuse University. He is the author of two books, *Living Morally* (1989) and *Vessels of Evil* (1993), and of numerous articles in moral theory and
social philosophy. He is the recipient of numerous awards and fellowships, including
the Andrew W. Mellon Faculty appointment at Harvard University.

NEXT LIFE, I'LL BE WHITE

In my next life, I shall certainly aim to come back a white person—make that 1
a white male.

You see, while white males have committed more evil cumulatively than any other class of people in the world, this fact is often lost on both them and others. The Crusades, American slavery and the two World Wars, including the Holocaust, should clinch this point.

When it comes to evil on a grand scale, black men do not hold a candle to white men. But notwithstanding this painfully obvious—and, I should think, embarrassing—truth, not only do white males generally regard themselves as morally superior to all others; moreover, whites generally regard white males in this way.

My 40-year journey through life has revealed to me that more often than not, I need only to be in the presence of a white woman and she will begin clutching her pocketbook. My sheer presence has reminded more white people—female and male alike—to lock their car doors than I care to think about. I suppose it can be said here that I make an unwitting contribution to public safety.

I rarely enjoy what is properly called the public trust of whites. That is to say, the white person on the street who does not know me from Adam or Eve is much more likely to judge me negatively on account of my skin color, however much my attire and mannerisms (including gait) conform to the traditional standards of well-off white males.

And the absurdity of doing so is no barrier here. I was recently walking down a supermarket aisle with a hand-basket full of groceries, one in each hand. A white woman saw me and rushed for her pocketbook, which she had left in her cart. I would have had to put my own groceries down in order to take her pocketbook.

No doubt she thought to herself: "He won't fool me with that old basket-in-each-hand trick." By contrast, I suspect that there are very few white males who, when traditionally attired and mannered, fail to enjoy the trust of other whites or anyone else for that matter.

If a 150-pound, well-groomed white man wearing a tweed jacket, tie and wool slacks were reading the bulletin board outside a university conference hall, I cannot imagine him being reported to the police as a suspicious character—let alone one requiring four police officers to attend to the matter, as happened to me at a Midwestern university. Four officers! What on earth was I reported as:—10 feet tall in military garb? Or, "There is a black man . . ."?

Many of my well-placed black friends in the academy report similar mind-boggling stories. We could support a "Believe-It-Or-Not" column for years. Now if we, well-groomed and mannered blacks, do not enjoy the public trust, it is discomforting to think how less-well-off blacks fare.

If white people generally think white men are morally superior, given the moral track record of white men, it is simply unimaginable what white people would think if this unenviable record were held by the males of another ethnic group.

I have committed no crimes; and it seems rather unlikely that I shall turn to a criminal life in the future. No, I intend to go on living morally as best I can. But it sure would be nice to enjoy on a much more frequent basis one of the benefits that come with living morally—namely, the public trust. And this I would most certainly do if I were white.

Now, I can hear white people, especially white males, telling me that 12 the truly moral person is indifferent to the public trust. Plato and Kant are among the great defenders of this claim.

I would not dream of thinking that I could show either of these great 13 minds to be wrong. So let me just respond with the observation that the public trust that white men claim to be irrelevant is something that they have always enjoyed and take for granted. People generally do not appreciate the role of a good in their lives when they are able to take it for granted. Indeed, in such instances they often discount its significance.

Psychology is constantly telling us that being affirmed by others is indis- 14 pensable to our flourishing. It would be stunning if psychology were right, but in general enjoying the public trust was irrelevant to humankind flourishing, Plato and Kant notwithstanding. As is the case so often with oppression, the victims are made to feel inadequate for insisting upon what their oppressors enjoy and routinely take for granted.

STUDY QUESTIONS

1. How do the first two and final three paragraphs frame the central argument?

2. Why does Thomas introduce Plato and Kant into the essay? What other evidence is there in the essay that he is educated, middle class? How much do you learn about Thomas in the essay (height? vocation? etc.)? What strength, if any, does this lend to his argument?

3. The essay frequently uses the word "moral" and at some points talks of "crime" and "criminal"? How synonymous are these terms? Is all immorality criminal? Are all crimes immoral?

Michelle Cliff

Born in Kingston, Jamaica, Michelle Cliff was educated at Wagner College and the Warburg Institute (London). A novelist, poet, and essayist, she has been a MacDowell Fellow, an Eli Kantor Fellow at Yaddo, and a Fellow of the National Endowment for the Arts. She has also worked as a reporter, researcher, and editor, and has taught at the New School for Social Research, Hampshire College, the University of Massachusetts at Amherst, and Vista College. She now lives in Santa Cruz, California, and holds an appointment as Allan K. Smith Visiting Writer at Trinity College in Hartford, Connecticut. Her most recent novel, *Free Enterprise*, was published in 1993.

IF I COULD WRITE THIS IN FIRE
I WOULD WRITE THIS IN FIRE[1]

I

We were standing under the waterfall at the top of Orange River. Our chests were just beginning to mound—slight hills on either side. In the center of each were our nipples, which were losing their sideways look and rounding into perceptible buttons of dark flesh. Too fast it seemed. We touched each other, then, quickly and almost simultaneously, raised our arms to examine the hairs growing underneath. Another sign. Mine was wispy and light-brown. My friend Zoe had dark hair curled up tight. In each little patch the river-water caught the sun so we glistened.

———

The waterfall had come about when my uncles dammed up the river to bring power to the sugar mill. Usually, when I say "sugar mill" to anyone not familiar with the Jamaican countryside or for that matter my family, I can tell their minds cast an image of tall smokestacks, enormous copper cauldrons, a man in a broad-brimmed hat with a whip, and several dozens of slaves—that is, if they have any idea of how large sugar mills once operated. It's a grandiose expression—like plantation, verandah, outbuilding. (Try substituting farm, porch, outside toilet.) To some people it even sounds romantic.

Our sugar mill was little more than a round-roofed shed, which contained a wheel and woodfire. We paid an old man to run it, tend the fire, and then either bartered or gave the sugar away, after my grandmother had taken what she needed. Our canefield was about two acres of flat land next to the river. My grandmother had six acres in all, one donkey, a mule, two cows, some chickens, a few pigs, and stray dogs and cats who had taken up residence in the yard.

1. For this piece I owe a debt to Ama Ata Aidoo and her brilliant book *Our Sister Killjoy or Reflections from a Black-Eyed Squint* (Lagos and New York: Nok Publishers, 1979). [Author's note]

Her house had four rooms, no electricity, no running water. The kitchen
was a shed in the back with a small pot-bellied stove. Across from the stove
was a mahogany counter, which had a white enamel basin set into it. The
only light source was a window, a small space covered partly by a wooden
shutter. We washed our faces and hands in enamel bowls with cold water
carried in kerosene tins from the river and poured from enamel pitchers. Our
chamber pots were enamel also, and in the morning we carefully placed them
on the steps at the side of the house where my grandmother collected them
and disposed of their contents. The outhouse was about thirty yards from
the back door—a "closet" as we called it—infested with lizards capable of
changing color. When the door was shut it was totally dark, and the lizards
made their presence known by the noise of their scurrying through the torn
newspaper, or the soft shudder when they dropped from the walls. I remember most clearly the stench of the toilet, which seemed to hang in the air in
that climate.

But because every little piece of reality exists in relation to another little
piece, our situation was not that simple. It was to our yard that people came
with news first. It was in my grandmother's parlor that the Disciples of Christ
held their meetings.

———

Zoe lived with her mother and sister on borrowed ground in a place called
Breezy Hill. She and I saw each other almost every day on our school vacations over a period of three years. Each morning early—as I sat on the cement
porch with my coffee cut with condensed milk—she appeared: in her straw
hat, school tunic faded from blue to gray, white blouse, sneakers hanging
around her neck. We had coffee together, and a piece of hard-dough bread
with butter and cheese, waited a bit and headed for the river. At first we
were shy with each other. We did not start from the same place.

There was land. My grandparents' farm. And there was color. (My family
was called "red." A term which signified a degree of whiteness. "We's just a
flock of red people," a cousin of mine said once.) In the hierarchy of shades
I was considered among the lightest. The countrywomen who visited my
grandmother commented on my "tall" hair—meaning long. Wavy, not curly.
I had spent the years from three to ten in New York and spoke—at first—
like an American. I wore American clothes: shorts, slacks, bathing suit. Because
of my American past I was looked upon as the creator of games. Cowboys
and Indians. Cops and Robbers. Peter Pan.

(While the primary colonial identification for Jamaicans was English, American colonialism was a strong force in my childhood—and of course continues
today. We were sent American movies and American music. American aluminum companies had already discovered bauxite on the island and were
shipping the ore to their mainland. United Fruit bought our bananas. White

Americans came to Montego Bay, Ocho Rios, and Kingston for their vacations and their cruise ships docked in Port Antonio and other places. In some ways America was seen as a better place than England by many Jamaicans. The farm laborers sent to work in American agribusiness came home with dollars and gifts and new clothes; there were few who mentioned American racism. Many of the middle class who emigrated to Brooklyn or Staten Island or Manhattan were able to pass into the white American world—saving their blackness for other Jamaicans or for trips home; in some cases, forgetting it altogether. Those middle-class Jamaicans who could not pass for white managed differently—not unlike the Bajans in Paule Marshall's *Brown Girl, Brownstones*—saving, working, investing, buying property. Completely separate in most cases from Black Americans.)

I was someone who had experience with the place that sent us triple features   10
of B-grade westerns and gangster movies. And I had tall hair and light skin. And I was the granddaughter of my grandmother. So I had power. I was the cowboy, Zoe was my sidekick, the boys we knew were Indians. I was the detective, Zoe was my "girl," the boys were the robbers. I was Peter Pan, Zoe was Wendy Darling, the boys were the lost boys. And the terrain around the river—jungled and dark green—was Tombstone, or Chicago, or Never-Never Land.

This place and my friendship with Zoe never touched my life in Kingston.   11
We did not correspond with each other when I left my grandmother's home.

I never visited Zoe's home the entire time I knew her. It was a given: never   12
suggested, never raised.

————

Zoe went to a state school held in a country church in Red Hills. It had been   13
my mother's school. I went to a private all-girls school where I was taught by white Englishwomen and pale Jamaicans. In her school the students were caned as punishment. In mine the harshest punishment I remember was being sent to sit under the *lignum vitae* to "commune with nature." Some of the girls were out-and-out white (English and American), the rest of us were colored—only a few were dark. Our uniforms were blood-red gabardine, heavy and hot. Classes were held in buildings meant to recreate England: damp with stone floors, facing onto a cloister, or quad as they called it. We began each day with the headmistress leading us in English hymns. The entire school stood for an hour in the zinc-roofed gymnasium.

Occasionally a girl fainted, or threw up. Once, a girl had a grand mal seizure.   14
To any such disturbance the response was always "keep singing." While she flailed on the stone floor, I wondered what the mistresses would do. We sang "Faith of Our Fathers," and watched our classmate as her eyes rolled back in her head. I thought of people swallowing their tongues. This student

was dark—here on a scholarship—and the only woman who came forward to help her was the gamesmistress, the only dark teacher. She kneeled beside the girl and slid the white web belt from her tennis shorts, clamping it between the girl's teeth. When the seizure was over, she carried the girl to a tumbling mat in a corner of the gym and covered her so she wouldn't get chilled.

Were the other women unable to touch this girl because of her darkness? I think that now. Her darkness and her scholarship. She lived on Windward Road with her grandmother; her mother was a maid. But darkness is usually enough for women like those to hold back. Then, we usually excused that kind of behavior by saying they were "ladies." (We were constantly being told we should be ladies also. One teacher went so far as to tell us many people thought Jamaicans lived in trees and we had to show these people they were mistaken.) In short, we felt insufficient to judge the behavior of these women. The English ones (who had the corner on power in the school) had come all this way to teach us. Shouldn't we treat them as the missionaries they were certain they were? The creole Jamaicans had a different role: they were passing on to those of us who were light-skinned the creole heritage of collaboration, assimilation, loyalty to our betters. We were expected to be willing subjects in this outpost of civilization.   15

The girl left school that day and never returned.   16

After prayers we filed into our classrooms. After classes we had games: tennis, field hockey, rounders (what the English call baseball), netball (what the English call basketball). For games we were divided into "houses"—groups named for Joan of Arc, Edith Cavell, Florence Nightingale, Jane Austen. Four white heroines. Two martyrs. One saint. Two nurses. (None of us knew then that there were black women with Nightingale at Scutari.) One novelist. Three involved in white men's wars. Two dead in white men's wars. *Pride and Prejudice.*   17

Those of us in Cavell wore red badges and recited her last words before a firing squad in W.W. I: "Patriotism is not enough. I must have no hatred or bitterness toward anyone."   18

Sorry to say I grew up to have exactly that.   19

———

Looking back: To try and see when the background changed places with the foreground. To try and locate the vanishing point: where the lines of perspective converge and disappear. Lines of color and class. Lines of history and social context. Lines of denial and rejection. When did *we* (the light-skinned middle-class Jamaicans) take over for *them* as oppressors? I need to see when and how this happened. When what should have been reality was   20 overtaken by what was surely unreality. When the house nigger became master.

"What's the matter with you? You think you're white or something?" 21

"Child, what you want to know 'bout Garvey for? The man was nothing but a damn fool."

"They not our kind of people."

Why did we wear wide-brimmed hats and try to get into Oxford? Why did 22
we not return?

Great Expectations: a novel about origins and denial. about the futility and 23
tragedy of that denial. about attempting assimilation. We learned this novel from a light-skinned Jamaican woman—she concentrated on what she called the "love affair" between Pip and Estella.

Looking back: Through the last page of *Sula.* "And the loss pressed down on 24
her chest and came up into her throat. 'We was girls together,' she said as though explaining something." It was Zoe, and Zoe alone, I thought of. She snapped into my mind and I remembered no one else. Through the greens and blues of the riverbank. The flame of red hibiscus in front of my grand-mother's house. The cracked grave of a former landowner. The fruit of the ackee which poisons those who don't know how to prepare it.

"What is to become of us?" 25
We borrowed a baby from a woman and used her as our dolly. Dressed and undressed her. Dipped her in the riverwater. Fed her with the milk her mother had left with us: and giggled because we knew where the milk had come from.

———

A letter: "I am desperate. I need to get away. I beg you one fifty-dollar." 26

I send the money because this is what she asks for. I visit her on a trip back 27
home. Her front teeth are gone. Her husband beats her and she suffers black-outs. I sit on her chair. She is given birth-control pills which aggravate her "condition." We boil up sorrel and ginger. She is being taught by Peace Corps volunteers to embroider linen mats with little lambs on them and gives me one as a keepsake. We cool off the sorrel with a block of ice brought from the shop nearby. The shopkeeper immediately recognizes me as my grand-mother's granddaughter and refuses to sell me cigarettes. (I am twenty-seven.) We sit in the doorway of her house, pushing back the colored plastic strands which form a curtain, and talk about Babylon and Dred. About Manley and what he's doing for Jamaica. About how hard it is. We walk along the railway tracks—no longer used—to Crooked River and the post office. Her little

daughter walks beside us and we recite a poem for her: "Mornin' buddy/Me no buddy fe wunna/Who den', den' I saw?" and on and on.

I can come and go. And I leave. To complete my education in London. 28

II

Their goddam kings and their goddam queens. Grandmotherly Victoria 29
spreading herself thin across the globe. Elizabeth II on our t.v. screens. We
stop what we are doing. We quiet down. We pay our respects.

1981: In Massachusetts I get up at 5 a.m. to watch the royal wedding. I tell 30
myself maybe the IRA will intervene. It's got to be better than starving
themselves to death. Better to be a kamikaze in St. Paul's Cathedral than a
hostage in Ulster. And last week Black and white people smashed storefronts
all over the United Kingdom. But I really don't believe we'll see royal blood
on t.v. I watch because they once ruled us. In the back of the cathedral a
Maori woman sings an aria from Handel and I notice that she is surrounded
by the colored subjects.

To those of us in the commonwealth the royal family was the perfect symbol 31
of hegemony. To those of us who were dark in the dark nations the prime
minister, the parliament barely existed. We believed in royalty—we were
convinced in this belief. Maybe it played on some ancestral memories of
West Africa—where other kings and queens had been. Altars and castles and
magic.

The faces of our new rulers were everywhere in my childhood. Calendars, 32
newsreels, magazines. Their presences were often among us. Attending test
matches between the West Indians and South Africans. They were our landlords. Not always absentee. And no matter what Black leader we might elect—
were we to choose independence—we would be losing something almost holy
in our impudence.
WE ARE HERE BECAUSE YOU WERE THERE 33
BLACK PEOPLE AGAINST STATE BRUTALITY
BLACK WOMEN WILL NOT BE INTIMIDATED
WELCOME TO BRITAIN . . . WELCOME TO SECOND-CLASS
CITIZENSHIP
(slogans of the Black movement in Britain)

Indian women cleaning the toilets in Heathrow airport. This is the first thing 34
I notice. Dark women in saris trudging buckets back and forth as other dark
women in saris—some covered by loosefitting winter coats—form a line to
have their passports stamped.

The triangle trade: molasses/rum/slaves. Robinson Crusoe was on a slave- 35
trading journey. Robert Browning was a mulatto. Holding pens. Jamaica

was a seasoning station. Split tongues. Sliced ears. Whipped bodies. The constant pretense of civility against rape. Still. Iron collars. Tinplate masks. The latter a precaution: to stop the slaves from eating the sugar cane.

A pregnant woman is to be whipped—they dig a hole to accommodate her belly and place her face down on the ground. Many of us became light-skinned very fast. Traced ourselves through bastard lines to reach the duke of Devonshire. The earl of Cornwall. The lord of this and the lord of that. Our mothers' rapes were the thing unspoken.   36

You say: But Britain freed her slaves in 1834. Yes.   37

Tea plantations in India and Ceylon. Mines in Africa. The Cape-to-Cairo Railroad. Rhodes scholars. Suez Crisis. The white man's bloody burden. Boer War. Bantustans. Sitting in a theatre in London in the seventies. A play called *West of Suez*. A lousy play about British colonials. The finale comes when several well-known white actors are machine-gunned by several lesser-known Black actors. (As Nina Simone says: "This is a show tune but the show hasn't been written for it yet.")   38

The red empire of geography classes. "The sun never sets on the British empire and you can't trust it in the dark." Or with the dark peoples. "Because of the Industrial Revolution European countries went in search of markets and raw materials." Another geography (or was it a history) lesson.   39

Their bloody kings and their bloody queens. Their bloody peers. Their bloody generals. admirals. explorers. Livingstone. Hillary. Kitchener. All the bwanas. And all their beaters, porters, sherpas. Who found the source of the Nile. Victoria Falls. The tops of mountains. Their so-called discoveries reek of untruth. How many dark people died so they could misname the physical features in their blasted gazetteer. A statistic we shall never know. Dr. Livingstone, I presume you are here to rape our land and enslave our people.   40

There are statues of these dead white men all over London.   41

An interesting fact: The swearword "bloody" is a contraction of "by my lady"—a reference to the Virgin Mary. They do tend to use their ladies. Name ages for them. Places for them. Use them as screens, inspirations, symbols. And many of the ladies comply. While the national martyr Edith Cavell was being executed by the Germans in Belgium in 1915 (Belgium was called "poor little Belgium" by the allies in the war), the Belgians were engaged in the exploitation of the land and peoples of the Congo.   42

And will we ever know how many dark peoples were "imported" to fight in white men's wars. Probably not. Just as we will never know how many hearts were cut from African people so that the Christian doctor might be a suc-   43 cess—i.e., extend a white man's life. Our Sister Killjoy observes this from her black-eyed squint.

Dr. Schweitzer—humanitarian, authority on Bach, winner of the Nobel Peace 44 Prize—on the people of Africa: "The Negro is a child, and with children nothing can be done without the use of authority. We must, therefore, so arrange the circumstances of our daily life that my authority can find expression. With regard to Negroes, then, I have coined the formula: 'I am your brother, it is true, but your elder brother.' " (*On the Edge of the Primeval Forest*, 1961)

They like to pretend we didn't fight back. We did: with obeah, poison, rev- 45 olution. It simply was not enough.

"Colonies . . . these places where 'niggers' are cheap and the earth is rich."— 46 W. E. B. DuBois, "The Souls of White Folk"

A cousin is visiting me from M.I.T. where he is getting a degree in engi- 47 neering. I am learning about the Italian Renaissance. My cousin is recogniz- ably Black and speaks with an accent. I am not and I do not—unless I am back home, where the "twang" comes upon me. We sit for some time in a bar in his hotel and are not served. A light-skinned Jamaican comes over to our table. He is an older man—a professor at the University of London. "Don't bother with it, you hear. They don't serve us in this bar." A run-of- the-mill incident for all recognizably Black people in this city. But for me it is not.

Henry's eyes fill up, but he refuses to believe our informant. "No, man, the 48 girl is just busy." (The girl is a fifty-year-old white woman, who may just be following orders. But I do not mention this. I have chosen sides.) All I can manage to say is, "Jesus Christ, I hate the fucking English." Henry looks at me. (In the family I am known as the "lady cousin." It has to do with how I look. And the fact that I am twenty-seven and unmarried—and for all they know, unattached. They do not know that I am really the lesbian cousin.) Our informant says—gently, but with a distinct tone of disappointment— "My dear, is that what you're studying at the university?"

You see—the whole business is very complicated. 49

Henry and I leave without drinks and go to meet some of his white colleagues 50 at a restaurant I know near Covent Garden Opera House. The restaurant caters to theatre types and so I hope there won't be a repeat of the bar scene— at least they know how to pretend. Besides, I tell myself, the owners are Italian *and* gay; they *must* be halfway decent. Henry and his colleagues work for an American company which is paying their way through M.I.T. They mine bauxite from the hills in the middle of the island and send it to the United States. A turnaround occurs at dinner: Henry joins the white men in a sustained mockery of the waiters: their accents and the way they walk. He whispers to me: "Why you want to bring us to a battyman's den, lady?" (*Battyman* = *faggot* in Jamaican.) I keep quiet.

We put the white men in a taxi and Henry walks me to the underground   51
station. He asks me to sleep with him. (It wouldn't be incest. His mother was a maid in the house of an uncle and Henry has not seen her since his birth. He was taken into the family. She was let go.) I say that I can't. I plead exams. I can't say that I don't want to. Because I remember what happened in the bar. But I can't say that I'm a lesbian either—even though I want to believe his alliance with the white men at dinner was forced: not really him. He doesn't buy my excuse. "Come on, lady, let's do it. What's the matter, you 'fraid?" I pretend I am back home and start patois to show him somehow I am not afraid, not English, not white. I tell him he's a married man and he tells me he's a ram goat. I take the train to where I am staying and try to forget the whole thing. But I don't. I remember our different skins and our different experiences within them. And I have a hard time realizing that I am angry with Henry. That to him—no use in pretending—a queer is a queer.

———

1981: I hear on the radio that Bob Marley is dead and I drive over the Mohawk   52
Trail listening to a program of his music and I cry and cry and cry. Someone says: "It wasn't the ganja that killed him, it was poverty and working in a steel foundry when he was young."

I flashback to my childhood and a young man who worked for an aunt I lived   53
with once. He taught me to smoke ganja behind the house. And to peel an orange with the tip of a machete without cutting through the skin—"Love" it was called: a necklace of orange rind the result. I think about him because I heard he had become a Rastaman. And then I think about Rastas.

We are sitting on the porch of an uncle's house in Kingston—the family and   54
I—and a Rastaman comes to the gate. We have guns but they are locked behind a false closet. We have dogs but they are tied up. We are Jamaicans and know that Rastas mean no harm. We let him in and he sits on the side of the porch and shows us his brooms and brushes. We buy some to take back to New York. "Peace, missis."

There were many Rastas in my childhood. Walking the roadside with their   55
goods. Sitting outside their shacks in the mountains. The outsides painted bright—sometimes with words. Gathering at Palisadoes Airport to greet the

Conquering Lion of Judah. They were considered figures of fun by most middle-class Jamaicans. Harmless: like Marcus Garvey.

Later: white American hippies trying to create the effect of dred in their straight white hair. The ganja joint held between their straight white teeth. "Man, the grass is good." Hanging out by the Sheraton pool. Light-skinned Jamaicans also dredlocked, also assuming the ganja. Both groups moving to the music but not the words. Harmless. "Peace, brother." 56

III

My grandmother: "Let us thank God for a fruitful place." My grandfather: "Let us rescue the perishing world." 57

This evening on the road in western Massachusetts there are pockets of fog. Then clear spaces. Across from a pond a dog staggers in front of my headlights. I look closer and see that his mouth is foaming. He stumbles to the side of the road—I go to call the police. 58

I drive back to the house, radio playing "difficult" piano pieces. And I think about how I need to say all this. This is who I am. I am not what you allow me to be. Whatever you decide me to be. In a bookstore in London I show the woman at the counter my book and she stares at me for a minute, then says: "You're a Jamaican." "Yes." "You're not at all like our Jamaicans." 59

Encountering the void is nothing more nor less than understanding invisibility. Of being fogbound. 60

It is up to me to sort out these connections—to employ anger and take the consequences. To choose not to be harmless. To make it impossible for them to think me harmless. 61

Then: It was never a question of passing. It was a question of hiding. Behind Black and white perceptions of who we were—who they thought we were. Tropics. Plantations. Calypso. Cricket. We were the people with the musical voices and the coronation mugs on our parlor tables. I would be whatever figure these foreign imaginations cared for me to be. It would be so simple to let others fill in for me. So easy to startle them with a flash of anger when their visions got out of hand—but never to sustain the anger for myself. 62
It could become a life lived within myself. A life cut off. I know who I am but you will never know who I am. I may in fact lose touch with who I am.

I hid from my real sources. But my real sources were hidden from me. 63

Now: It is not a question of relinquishing privilege. It is a question of grasp- 64
ing more of myself. I have found that in the real sources are concealed
my survival. My speech. My voice. To be colonized is to be rendered
insensitive. To have those parts necessary to sustain life numbed. And
this is in some cases—in my case—perceived as privilege. The test of
a colonized person is to walk through a shantytown in Kingston and
not bat an eye. This I cannot do. Because part of me lives there—and
as I grasp more of this part I realize what needs to be done with the
rest of my life.

———

Sometimes I used to think we were like the Marranos—the Sephardic Jews 65
forced to pretend they were Christians. The name was given to them by the
Christians, and meant "pigs." But once out of Spain and Portugal, they became
Jews openly again. Some settled in Jamaica. They knew who the enemy was
and acted for their own survival. But they remained Jews always.

We also knew who the enemy was—I remember jokes about the English. 66
Saying they stank. saying they were stingy. that they drank too much and
couldn't hold their liquor. that they had bad teeth. were dirty and dishonest.
were limey bastards. and horse-faced bitches. We said the men only wanted
to sleep with Jamaican women. And that the women made pigs of themselves
with Jamaican men.

But of course this was seen by us—the light-skinned middle class—with a 67
double vision. We learned to cherish that part of us that was them—and to
deny the part that was not. Believing in some cases that the latter part had
ceased to exist.

None of this is as simple as it may sound. We were colorists and we aspired 68
to oppressor status. (Of course, almost any aspiration instilled by western
civilization is to oppressor status: success, for example.) Color was the symbol of our potential: color taking in hair "quality," skin tone, freckles, nose-
width, eyes. We did not see that color symbolism was a method of keeping
us apart: in the society, in the family, between friends. Those of us who
were light-skinned, straight-haired, etc., were given to believe that we could
actually attain whiteness—or at least those qualities of the colonizer which
made him superior. We were convinced of white supremacy. If we failed we
were not really responsible for our failures: we had all the advantages—but
it was that one persistent drop of blood, that single rogue gene that made us
unable to conceptualize abstract ideas, made us love darkness rather than
despise it, which was to be blamed for our failure. Our dark part had taken
over: an inherited imbalance in which the doom of the creole was sealed.

I am trying to write this as clearly as possible, but as I write I realize that 69
what I say may sound fabulous, or even mythic. It is. It is insane.

Under this system of colorism—the system which prevailed in my childhood   70
in Jamaica, and which has carried over to the present—rarely will dark and
light people co-mingle. Rarely will they achieve between themselves an intimacy informed with identity. (I should say here that I am using the categories light and dark both literally and symbolically. There are dark Jamaicans
who have achieved lightness and the "advantages" which go with it by their
successful pursuit of oppressor status.)

Under this system light and dark people will meet in those ways in which   71
the light-skinned person imitates the oppressor. But imitation goes only so
far: the light-skinned person becomes an oppressor in fact. He / she will have
a dark chauffeur, a dark nanny, a dark maid, and a dark gardener. These
employees will be paid badly. Because of the slave past, because of their dark
skin, the servants of the middle class have been used according to the traditions of the slavocracy. They are not seen as workers for their own sake, but
for the sake of the family who has employed them. It was not until Michael
Manley became prime minister that a minimum wage for houseworkers was
enacted—and the indignation of the middle class was profound.

During Manley's leadership the middle class began to abandon the island in   72
droves. Toronto. Miami. New York. Leaving their houses and businesses
behind and sewing cash into the tops of suitcases. Today—with a new regime—
they are returning: "Come back to the way things used to be" the tourist
advertisement on American t.v. says. "Make it Jamaica again." "Make it your
own."

But let me return to the situation of houseservants as I remember it: They   73
will be paid badly, but they will be "given" room and board. However, the
key to the larder will be kept by the mistress in her dresser drawer. They
will spend Christmas with the family of their employers and be given a length
of English wool for trousers or a few yards of cotton for dresses. They will
see their children on their days off: their extended family will care for the
children the rest of the time. When the employers visit their relations in the
country, the servants may be asked along—oftentimes the servants of the
middle class come from the same part of the countryside their employers
have come from. But they will be expected to work while they are there.
Back in town, there are parts of the house they are allowed to move freely
around; other parts they are not allowed to enter. When the family watches
the t.v. the servant is allowed to watch also, but only while standing in a
doorway. The servant may have a radio in his / her room, also a dresser and
a cot. Perhaps a mirror. There will usually be one ceiling light. And one
small square louvered window.

A true story: One middle-class Jamaican woman ordered a Persian rug from   74
Harrod's in London. The day it arrived so did her new maid. She was going

downtown to have her hair touched up, and told the maid to vacuum the rug. She told the maid she would find the vacuum cleaner in the same shed as the power mower. And when she returned she found that the fine nap of her new rug had been removed.

The reaction of the mistress was to tell her friends that the "girl" was back-   75
ward. She did not fire her until she found that the maid had scrubbed the teflon from her new set of pots, saying she thought they were coated with "nastiness."

_____

The houseworker / mistress relationship in which one Black woman is the   76
oppressor of another Black woman is a cornerstone of the experience of many Jamaican women.

I remember another true story: In a middle-class family's home one Christ-   77
mas, a relation was visiting from New York. This woman had brought gifts for everybody, including the housemaid. The maid had been released from a mental institution recently, where they had "treated" her for depression. This visiting light-skinned woman had brought the dark woman a bright red rayon blouse, and presented it to her in the garden one afternoon, while the family was having tea. The maid thanked her softly, and the other woman moved toward her as if to embrace her. Then she stopped, her face suddenly covered with tears, and ran into the house, saying, "My God, I can't, I can't."

_____

We are women who come from a place almost incredible in its beauty. It is   78
a beauty which can mask a great deal, and which has been used in that way. But that the beauty is there is a fact. I remember what I thought the freedom of my childhood, in which the fruitful place was something I took for granted. Just as I took for granted Zoe's appearance every morning on my school vacations—in the sense that I knew she would be there. That she would always be the one to visit me. The perishing world of my grandfather's graces at the table, if I ever seriously thought about it, was somewhere else.

Our souls were affected by the beauty of Jamaica, as much as they were   79
affected by our fears of darkness.

There is no ending to this piece of writing. There is no way to end it. As I   80
read back over it, I see that we / they / I may become confused in the mind of the reader: but these pronouns have always co-existed in my mind. The Rastas talk of the "I and I"—a pronoun in which they combine themselves with Jah. Jah is a contraction of Jahweh and Jehova, but to me always sounds like the beginning of Jamaica. I and Jamaica is who I am. No matter how far I travel—how deep the ambivalence I feel about ever returning. And Jamaica is a place in which we / they / I connect and disconnect—change place.

STUDY QUESTIONS

1. In what ways, according to the author, did her family and its traditions influence her later life and attitudes? How important was the influence of childhood friends? childhood experiences? social standing? the physical beauty of Jamaica? the traditions of social hierarchy?

2. What experiences in London and the United States seem, in retrospect, the most memorable? Describe the author's attitude toward England; toward the United States; toward Jamaica.

3. What specific effects are accomplished by the following writing strategies?
   —the use of many anecdotes, told succinctly and quickly
   —the rapid pace of the essay, with its refusal to dwell long on individual experiences
   —the extraordinary willingness to talk about strong feelings of distrust and dislike
   —the extensive allusions to historical events and political figures
   —the extensive allusions to books
   —the frequent use of quotations

4. Which anecdote seems to you most powerful in its effects? Analyze carefully how the story is told. What devices account for the power of the anecdote?

5. What "fences" encountered by the author seem to have produced the most bitter memories? the most powerful results?

CONFLICT AND STRUCTURE

C onflict, however unpleasant, seems a constant in human history. Most people try hard to avoid conflict, preferring that their lives be serene and their relationships with other people smooth and without complication. No one, however, escapes conflict for long. Even without wars or large-scale disagreements among nations or religions or ethnic groups or political parties or gangs, human beings seldom are successful in avoiding conflict in their daily lives. In school, the desire to learn or excel often becomes competition among people; in the marketplace, people compete for jobs or profits or success. Men find themselves in conflict with the interests of women, blacks in conflict with the interests of whites, Native Americans with Hispanics, Chinese-Americans with Vietnamese-Americans, poor with rich, people from one part of town with people from another, Cub fans with White Sox fans, pedestrians with drivers, teachers with students, children with parents, friends with friends. Even those who avoid conflict with others at all cost—those who are solitary or who stay passive in the face of any difficulty or opposition—find conflict, if not between themselves and another, then within themselves. Many psychologists think that conflict is necessary, if not to life itself, at least to growth, change, and emotional development. Necessary or not, it is a part of the human condition as we know it.

And literature thrives on it. Conflict is at the base of almost all literature—at least narrative and dramatic literature. Plots are structured on the
basis of conflict, and emotional identifications with characters in literature
almost always depend on the reader's choosing someone's side in a disagreement. In plays, one can usually chart, quite regularly and predictably,
where the conflict will occur. The introduction of conflict (and other elements of an unfolding plot) is so predictable in a play that it has become
conventional to speak of plays as having five regular units or steps:

1. Exposition, in which the situation at the beginning of the play is explained,
   characters are introduced and their interrelationships explained, the setting is presented, and the plot begins to be introduced.
2. Rising Action, in which a series of events occur to complicate the original
   situation and create conflict among the characters.
3. Climax (sometimes called Turning Point). During the rising action, the
   flow or movement of the play is in one direction; the climax introduces
   some crucial moment that changes the direction of the action.
4. Falling Action, in which the complications begin to unwind.
5. Conclusion (also sometimes called Catastrophe or Denouement), in which
   a stable situation is reestablished so that the drama may end.

Ordinarily, in a five-act play, the acts correspond (at least roughly) to
these five units. When a play is divided into two or three acts, as most modern plays are, the five stages are included but divided up differently. Some
plays use multiple scenes rather than "acts" as such, but almost always one
can trace a progressive movement rather like that described in the five units
above.

A good deal of the exposition of *Fences* appears for the reader of the
play in the author's headnotes—"Characters," "Setting," "The Play"—and
in the stage directions (the two paragraphs in italics at the head of Act I,
Scene 1). The audience at the play must get the information from program
notes or fill in if possible from details in the later portions of the play. The
Rising Action involves Troy's success in becoming the first African-American garbage truck driver in a conflict with the company and union, his telling the high school coach that Cory is not to play football, his affair with
Alberta. When Alberta dies in childbirth and Rose agrees to raise Alberta
and Troy's daughter but not to be a wife to Troy any longer, the play has
reached its Climax and Troy's descent and the Falling Action begin. Cory
faces him down and leaves home. Years pass, Troy retires, Rose dominates
the house, and Troy dies. Cory comes home a sergeant in the Marines (he

left eight years earlier). He says he will not go to the funeral. Lyons is on leave from jail; Gabe is on leave from the mental institution and silently blows his trumpet opening heaven's gates for Troy. Cory and Raynell sing Troy's song about the dog Blue, Cory is getting married and has replaced his father. The situation is stabilized and the play has reached its Conclusion.

In the conventional organization of plays, the centrality of conflict is readily apparent. Nothing much gets started until conflict develops; conflict is at the heart of the action, and in fact no action of any meaningful sort takes place until some conflict is introduced. Conflict is just as crucial to short stories and to other kinds of narrative, such as autobiography. There are several conflicts in the short story " 'Recitatif,' " between Twyla and Roberta and Bozo and the gar girls, between Twyla and her mother, between Twyla and Roberta, and the larger conflict between the races. The very title of the autobiographical essay "If I Could Write This in Fire I Would Write This in Fire," suggests conflict. Poems, too, are often (though not always) characterized by conflict; conflict there, however, may just as easily involve a conflict within a person's mind as conflict that manifests itself in physical confrontation or overt action. In Pat Mora's "Sonrisas," for example, though it is not stated directly, there is clearly an implied conflict in the SPEAKER who "stands in the doorway" between her Chicana ethnic identity and her white-collar or executive position that separates her from "her people."

Other, more formal features may also help to STRUCTURE a piece of writing. Just as the act and scene divisions in a play or the dialogue between characters provide visual divisions on a page (divisions that have a visual and aural counterpart onstage when the play is produced), so stories, essays, and poems have divisions marked by numbers—"In the American Society" (chapter 8, the divisions also having titles), "Lost Sister," "If I Could Write This in Fire . . ."—white space on the page (that is, skipped lines)—"A Place I've Never Been," "Sonrisas," and "Teacher Wei" (in chapter 5).

Prose is almost always divided into paragraphs. Paragraph division helps to mark the stages of transition in an argument or discourse and in a story provides breaks (rather like scene divisions in a play) in the narrative that may mark changes in time, place, mood, or perspective. The sections of a poem divided by white space are called *verse paragraphs*, but when they repeat patterns such as length of lines ("Roseville, Minn., U.S.A.," in chapter 5) or of rhyme ("I'm sitting in my history class," in Chapter 8) they are called STANZAS. Individual lines are often "broken" at what seem to be illogical places, recording instead sounds and rhythms, the cadences of a human voice. Poetry is closely related to music and often is structured by sound in addition to content. Poems, in fact, often play off their crucial elements of sound and sense against one another, creating their effects through a tension between meaning and musical vehicle. Line breaks and the way words are arranged on the page provide a guide to reading. To an experienced reader, they are like a musical score that signals the reader where to pause, how fast to proceed, and what tone to strike, offering a visual equivalent of the rhythms of the human voice.

Writers, in fact, use all kinds of devices to organize their materials in ways that will produce in their audience a certain effect, for they are concerned not only to "make sense" but to produce feelings in readers, to drive them to conclusions, to persuade them to hold new attitudes, sometimes even to take some kind of action. The strategies of persuasion that literature uses are collectively called RHETORICAL DEVICES, and the rhetoric of a poem, story, essay, or play crucially involves the work's STRUCTURE—the sum of all the devices of organization and shape. Some of those devices are logical (involving meaning), some are formal (involving shape, visual or otherwise). All are important in influencing the way a work affects us as we read it from beginning to end.

WRITING
ABOUT THE READING

PERSONAL ESSAYS AND NARRATIVES

1. What "fences" have you encountered in your school, community, church, clubs, or social groups? Have you ever felt excluded from some group you wished to be in because of race, nationality, or gender? because of personal characteristics that were considered odd or undesirable? because of your economic status, political beliefs, or social class? because of language or your lack of knowledge of "the code"? How did you sort out the reasons for your exclusion? How could you tell what the "real" reasons were? Did you try to change yourself or hide facts about yourself to make you more suitable to the group you wished to join? How did you feel about the incident? In what ways would you handle it differently if a similar thing were to happen again?

   To get some perspective on the effects—emotional, personal, psychological, and social—of the episode, create a CHARACTER who is in some crucial way different from yourself, and write a short story about an episode similar to the one in your own life. Tell the story from the POINT OF VIEW of the character who is excluded, and try to make clear the complexities of the sorting-out process as the character assesses the reasoning of the in-group and the feelings he or she experiences as a result of the exclusion.

2. What experiences have you had as the excluder? Consider episodes in which, for one reason or another, you have kept someone out of a social organization, and choose one such episode to concentrate on. What was the person you excluded like? What were your reasons for excluding him or her? Did you have second thoughts about the exclusion? Did you ever distrust your reasons? suspect yourself of some categorical kind of prejudice? regret your decision?

   Write a straightforward autobiographical NARRATIVE of the episode in which you try to explain yourself and indicate what kind of long-range effects the episode had on your self-analysis and on your behavior.

3. What experiences have you had as the "friend" outside a love relationship? How have your feelings shifted or varied during that experience? What did you consider your role? What were the difficulties? Were you closer to one of the two people involved?

   Write an autobiographical NARRATIVE of that experience in which you analyze the positive and negative effects on you and on the others.

4. How has AIDS affected your attitudes towards sex? Have you had a friend or schoolmate who has AIDS or who has tested positive for HIV virus?

   Write an essay on the change in sexual attitudes and behavior or a personal narrative about an experience with someone afflicted with AIDs, including the variety of emotions you have experienced.

IMITATIONS AND PARODIES

1. Using R. T. Smith's "Red Anger" as your model, write a short poem in which you explore some powerful emotion you have experienced as a member of a particular national, ethnic, religious, or other group.

2. Using " 'Recitatif' " as a model, write a story in which someone who is "not prejudiced" and has an equally unprejudiced friend comes to recognize a latent STEREOTYPING or prejudgment in him or herself and / or in the other. The basis of the prejudice can be race, religion, social class, gender, or sexual orientation.

ARGUMENTATIVE PAPER

Construct both sides of a debate on the following topic: Resolved, that a church or political group organized primarily for religious or political purposes has no right to exclude people who do not agree with its goals and should be legally prosecuted for such exclusions.

RESEARCH PAPERS

1. How were Iranians treated in North America during and after the hostage crisis of 1979–81? Using newspaper and magazine articles in your library (a reference librarian can show you how to use the appropriate indexes), find out as much as you can about the public and private treatment of people of Iranian descent. How much anger did Americans express about Iran's actions? In what ways did the anger manifest itself toward individuals who seemed to be of Iranian descent? How did Iranians in America respond?

2. Using the guidelines in #1, do the same kind of research on:

   a) the treatment of people of Japanese or Italian descent in the United States or Canada during World War II.
   b) the treatment of people of German descent in the United States or Canada during World War I.
   c) the treatment of people of Russian descent in the late 1950s in the United States or Canada.
   d) the treatment of people of Iraqi descent during the Persian Gulf War.

Student Writing

ALONE IN THE MIDST OF 100,000 PEOPLE

BETH HECHT

Upward mobility: Movement to a higher economic or social status.
—Oxford American Dictionary, *1980*

In nila northSun's poem "up & out," life in the city is contrasted with life on the reservation in a manner which clearly conveys the speaker's conclusions as to which lifestyle is preferable. Typically, when one decides to bite at the dangling carrot, one must expect to pay a price. Such is the case with the family depicted in "up & out." While the costs accompanying seemingly desirable change may not always outweigh its benefits, all too often, as in this poem, the odds seem to tilt in that direction.

Ms. northSun's use of language in the poem helps to create a subtle undercurrent which leads the reader's mind through a partially prenavigated journey. To illustrate her descriptions of the transition from reservation life to modern city life, the author employs words such as up, out, better, money, and high. In contrast, key words chosen to convey the realities of existence on the "res" are poverty, no, only, except, nothing, down, old, and little. Even without further analysis of Ms. northSun's poem, her audience has already absorbed "propaganda" which must influence its perception of the work in question. One's associations with post-reservation life suggest abundance and improvement, paralleling the "Amerikan" philosophy that "more is better." In sharp contrast to these associations, but still reaffirming the school of thought that accompanies materialistic dogma, the impressions painted around reservation life through nila's use of words allude to deprivation and inadequacy.

The wording of the poem is deliberately paradoxical; the city is equated with money and higher living, the reservation with poverty and substandard existence. When we take a closer look, however, we must examine how better versus worse is being qualified in the writing. The supposed improvements attained by moving to the city revolve around Americanized standards of wealth and social position. Jobs, more money, cable TV, bottled water, high costs of food, medical bills, rent and entertainment, all are meant to symbolize a better standard of living. Notice that all of these symbols of a good life are just that, materialistic representations of that which constitutes the successful family in America. Notice, too, that there is no mention in the above list of anything relating to spiritual or emotional well-being. It is only through the speaker's nostalgic reflections on reservation life that we feel the color, the warm glow emanating from the essential parts of her past existence. She speaks of a wood stove (which connotes warmth and familial centrality), visiting with relatives, free food, rent, and medical attention, help from a cousin, and living in an ancestor's house. Life on the reservation is depicted as being flavored with, but not overpowered by, scarcity, yet life there comes across as rich and full with that which is truly important in life, simplicity complemented by the support of community and family.

Native Americans differ from many immigrants to the United States in that they are not arriving here from another country. However, their reality is as if they actually live on foreign territory within America. America to the Native American must seem to be a foreign land—Native Americans are treated as foreigners, have many restrictions placed on their personal liberties, and are barred from many opportunities to seek success on several levels in this country. Just as immigrants often fall victim to the illusions surrounding this capitalist nation, this "Gold Mountain," so, too, must the Native American attempt to eradicate her feelings of alienation by striving for material wealth. It is primarily wealth and power that define success in America. Emotional well-being and spiritual contentment are discredited and devalued here. It becomes clear almost immediately to any foreigner who arrives here that money is what matters most to Americans, not feeling or spirituality. All too quickly, when this foreigner jumps the fence for the dollar sign, she realizes that what she has lost in this process is not just her native land, but its ideology as well.

The speaker's matter-of-fact conveyance of a loss of cultural values and sense of familial community is subtle yet agitating in "up & out." Clearly, for her family, the grass is not greener in the city. In a monetary sense, and perhaps in society's eye, these Native Americans are on an upwardly mobile path. Yet, as the author writes, "we made better money but / it got sucked up . . ." (lines 18–19). The notion that as we have more, we spend more seems to hold true—it is virtually impossible to save one's money when suddenly the power of acquisition lies at one's fingertips. There are always so many things to buy, things that one didn't even know one needed so desperately. northSun writes, "we made more money than / we've ever made before / but felt poorer . . ." (lines 7–9). The money that is earned gets consumed by the invisible forces of industrialized society; meanwhile, the price of selling out by moving off of the reservation is far too costly. Gone are the visits with relatives, as well as the unceasing companionship of friends and family to eat chips and drink Coke with, or see B-grade movies with. Gone with these things are the true jewels of life, the priceless treasures previously found in those ordinary hours chatting with sisters and brothers around the wood stove. When we leave the wisdom of following that which is true to ourselves in pursuit of monetary gain, we enter into an emotional abyss. Suddenly, we are alone in the midst of 100,000 people, alone because our spirituality and emotional contentment have been vacuumed up by the unavoidable emptiness pervading city life. We, and the family in the poem, are left completely high and dry. We probably have no more money than we had before; what's more, we have lost our true source of happiness, the ideology of our own people, and in that sense, we are inestimably poorer.

The speaker recalls, "god how i hated living on the reservation / but now / it doesn't look so bad" (lines 45–47). Often, when we look back on the past, we have a tendency to remember things as prettier than they really were. Maybe this tendency influences the speaker's remembrance of days gone by. Even so, she has stumbled upon the wisdom that often can only be obtained through costly experience. She realizes that, for her family, supposed "upward mobility" projected her family into an emotional and spiritual "downward spiral." Perhaps this family can in time regain that which it lost through moving to the city. The speaker, at least, has taken the first step towards that end, as she has acknowledged the unforeseen and costly sacrifices that were made in the attempt to reach financial security and higher social standing. The speaker sees now, just as Joni Mitchell sings, "Don't it always seem to go / that you don't know what you've got 'til it's gone." Sometimes our greatest gifts go unnoticed until the moment that they disappear from our lives.

7

CROSSING

Whether a group is as small as a family or a fraternity or as large and diverse as a nation or ethnic community, the sense of togetherness, familiarity, and belonging is, for many people, comforting. Within the group we feel secure, for we know its customs, rules, and rituals, its language and its limits. Within the group we know our place; we know who we are. Other members are like us—"our kind of people." Our very sense of who we are is bound up with our place in the group.

An outsider is an unknown quantity, *not* like us, *not* one of "our people," a threat not only to the group but to our sense of ourselves. For our safety and sanity and sense of self, then, as well as for the protection of the homogeneity of the group, it sometimes seems necessary to repel the outsider who tries to cross over the boundary line and into our group, even if we have to use force. At its worst, this fear of the Other becomes prejudice against all outsiders, or even xenophobia—fear or hatred of anything or anyone "foreign." It is the dangerous other side of feelings of familiarity and security within the group.

In growing up, however, it is often necessary to rebel against the familiar and secure, to assert our own sense of individuality, freedom, difference, by separating ourselves from our parents and their values, and to define ourselves by our differences from them. The more adventurous—or rebellious—of us, or those with the greater opportunity, often step across the boundaries of the larger group: the neighborhood, the ethnic or cultural community. If we attempt to cross the fences, however, we must be prepared not only to be criticized, restrained, perhaps even cast out by our own, but to be rebuffed and ridiculed, even attacked, by the group toward which we are reaching out. In leaving the "narrow" and "provincial" tribe, we may think of ourselves as seeking growth, breadth of experience, and knowledge. We may see ourselves as generously "tolerating" the differences of the Other, and therefore entitled to admiration by our own who stay at home and the Other whom we flatter with our acceptance and attention. That may be what we think, but it may not be what others think of our venturing abroad; indeed, we risk rootlessness and rejection.

Not all rebellion arises from curiosity, adventurousness, or generous motives. Rejection of those nearest to us—parents, friends, compatriots—may at times be the result of callow notions of greener grass on the other side, or of conceited notions of our own importance and potential being restricted by the ignorance of those around us. If we were only free, we think, of the foolish restraints of "home," we would at last be treated in the manner we know we deserve.

But "crossing" is not only the action of the strong, adventurous individual defying the repressive power of the group. For there are societies, from families to tribes, that may need to be strengthened by bringing in new ideas and blood. The young in such a society must sometimes be kicked out of the nest; they may be permitted to marry, for example, only outside the group.

Courtship and marriage are, of course, the ultimate and thus most controversial of crossing experiences. Many of the pieces in this chapter, therefore, have to do with sexual relationships. When the most intimate and emotional of private feelings clash with the most primordial sense of the group, the conflict may threaten the security and identity of both the individual and the group. Both sides will fight with passionate intensity, but there are also values to be claimed by the crossing itself, the bringing together in creative conflict of two powerful forces and sources of value and belief.

Sandra Cisneros

Sandra Cisneros was born in Chicago, the daughter of a Mexican father and a Mexican-American mother. She is the author of *The House on Mango Street* (1983), which was awarded the Before Columbus Foundation Book Award in 1985 and *My Wicked Wicked Ways* (1987). Her short story collection, *Woman Hollering Creek* (1991), from which "Bread" is taken, received the Lannan Award for Fiction and the PEN Center West Award for Fiction. Cisneros lives in San Antonio, Texas.

BREAD

We were hungry. We went into a bakery on Grand Avenue and bought bread. Filled the backseat. The whole car smelled of bread. Big sourdough loaves shaped like a fat ass. Fat-ass bread, I said in Spanish, *Nalgona* bread. Fat-ass bread, he said in Italian, but I forget how he said it.

We ripped big chunks with our hands and ate. The car a pearl blue like my heart that afternoon. Smell of warm bread, bread in both fists, a tango on the tape player loud, loud, loud, because me and him, we're the only ones who can stand it like that, like if the bandoneón, violin, piano, guitar, bass, were inside us, like when he wasn't married, like before his kids, like if all the pain hadn't passed between us.

Driving down streets with buildings that remind him, he says, how charming this city is. And me remembering when I was little, a cousin's baby who died from swallowing rat poison in a building like these.

That's just how it is. And that's how we drove. With all this new city memories and all my old. Him kissing me between big bites of bread.

STUDY QUESTIONS

1. Who is the "We" in the first and second sentences? Exactly when do you discover the identity of the CHARACTERS*? How much do you know about each? Where does the story take place? How important is the SETTING?

2. How is the ethnic identity of two characters made clear?

*Words in small capitals are defined in the Glossary.

3. How well do the two know each other? For how long? How much are we told about their past? How much do we know about the man's life now?

4. Explain the role of the bread in the relationship; in the episode. How important is the music? the memories of each's past?

5. What emotions does the NARRATOR feel? What is the primary emotion that she feels now?

Tobias Wolff

Born in 1945, Tobias Wolff is the author of several books, including *The Barracks Thief* (1984), *Back in the World* (1986), *In the Garden of the North American Martyrs* (1990), and, most recently, *This Boy's Life: A Memoir* (1990). Formerly a reporter for the Washington Post, he currently teaches at Syracuse University.

SAY YES

They were doing the dishes, his wife washing while he dried. He'd washed the night before. Unlike most men he knew, he really pitched in on the housework. A few months earlier he'd overheard a friend of his wife's congratulate her on having such a considerate husband, and he thought, *I try.* Helping out with the dishes was a way he had of showing how considerate he was.

They talked about different things and somehow got on the subject of whether white people should marry black people. He said that all things considered, he thought it was a bad idea.

"Why?" she asked.

Sometimes his wife got this look where she pinched her brows together and bit her lower lip and stared down at something. When he saw her like this he knew he should keep his mouth shut, but he never did. Actually it made him talk more. She had that look now.

"Why?" she asked again, and stood there with her hand inside a bowl, not washing it but just holding it above the water.

"Listen," he said, "I went to school with blacks, and I've worked with blacks and lived on the same street with blacks, and we've always gotten along just fine. I don't need you coming along now and implying that I'm a racist."

"I didn't imply anything," she said, and began washing the bowl again, turning it around in her hand as though she were shaping it. "I just don't see what's wrong with a white person marrying a black person, that's all."

"They don't come from the same culture as we do. Listen to them sometime—they even have their own language. That's okay with me, I *like* hearing them talk"—he did; for some reason it always made him feel happy—"but it's different. A person from their culture and a person from our culture could never really *know* each other."

"Like you know me?" his wife asked.

"Yes. Like I know you."

"But if they love each other," she said. She was washing faster now, not looking at him.

Oh boy, he thought. He said, "Don't take my word for it. Look at the statistics. Most of those marriages break up."

"Statistics." She was piling dishes up on the drainboard at a terrific rate, just swiping at them with the cloth. Many of them were greasy, and there were flecks of food between the tines of the forks. "All right," she said, "what about foreigners? I suppose you think the same thing about two foreigners getting married."

"Yes," he said, "as a matter of fact I do. How can you understand someone who comes from a completely different background?"

"Different," said his wife. "Not the same, like us."

"Yes, different," he snapped, angry with her for resorting to this trick of repeating his words so that they sounded crass, or hypocritical. "These are dirty," he said, and dumped all the silverware back into the sink.

The water had gone flat and gray. She stared down at it, her lips pressed together, then plunged her hands under the surface. "Oh!" she cried, and jumped back. She took her right hand by the wrist and held it up. Her thumb was bleeding.

"Ann, don't move," he said. "Stay right there." He ran upstairs to the bathroom and rummaged in the medicine chest for alcohol, cotton, and a Band-Aid. When he came back down she was leaning against the refrigerator with her eyes closed, still holding her hand. He took the hand and dabbed at her thumb with the cotton. The bleeding had stopped. He squeezed it to see how deep the wound was and a single drop of blood welled up, trembling and bright, and fell to the floor. Over the thumb she stared at him accusingly. "It's shallow," he said. "Tomorrow you won't even know it's there." He hoped that she appreciated how quickly he had come to her aid. He'd acted out of concern for her, with no thought of getting anything in return, but now the thought occurred to him that it would be a nice gesture on her part not to start up that conversation again, as he was tired of it. "I'll finish up here," he said. "You go and relax."

"That's okay," she said. "I'll dry."

He began to wash the silverware again, giving a lot of attention to the forks.

"So," she said, "you wouldn't have married me if I'd been black."

"For Christ's sake, Ann!" 22

"Well, that's what you said, didn't you?" 23

"No, I did not. The whole question is ridiculous. If you had been black 24 we probably wouldn't even have met. You would have had your friends and I would have had mine. The only black girl I ever really knew was my partner in the debating club, and I was already going out with you by then."

"But if we had met, and I'd been black?" 25

"Then you probably would have been going out with a black guy." He 26 picked up the rinsing nozzle and sprayed the silverware. The water was so hot that the metal darkened to pale blue, then turned silver again.

"Let's say I wasn't," she said. "Let's say I am black and unattached and 27 we meet and fall in love."

He glanced over at her. She was watching him and her eyes were bright. 28 "Look," he said, taking a reasonable tone, "this is stupid. If you were black you wouldn't be you." As he said this he realized it was absolutely true. There was no possible way of arguing with the fact that she would not be herself if she were black. So he said it again: "If you were black you wouldn't be you."

"I know," she said, "but let's just say." 29

He took a deep breath. He had won the argument but he still felt cor- 30 nered. "Say what?" he asked.

"That I'm black, but still me, and we fall in love. Will you marry me?" 31

He thought about it. 32

"Well?" she said, and stepped close to him. Her eyes were even brighter. 33 "Will you marry me?"

"I'm thinking," he said. 34

"You won't, I can tell. You're going to say no." 35

"Let's not move too fast on this," he said. "There are lots of things to 36 consider. We don't want to do something we would regret for the rest of our lives."

"No more considering. Yes or no." 37

"Since you put it that way—" 38

"Yes or no." 39

"Jesus, Ann. All right. No." 40

She said, "Thank you," and walked from the kitchen into the living 41 room. A moment later he heard her turning the pages of a magazine. He knew that she was too angry to be actually reading it, but she didn't snap through the pages the way he would have done. She turned them slowly, as if she were studying every word. She was demonstrating her indifference to him, and it had the effect he knew she wanted it to have. It hurt him.

He had no choice but to demonstrate his indifference to her. Quietly, 42 thoroughly, he washed the rest of the dishes. Then he dried them and put them away. He wiped the counters and the stove and scoured the linoleum where the drop of blood had fallen. While he was at it, he decided, he might as well mop the whole floor. When he was done the kitchen looked new, the way it looked when they were first shown the house, before they had ever lived here.

He picked up the garbage pail and went outside. The night was clear and he could see a few stars to the west, where the lights of the town didn't blur them out. On El Camino the traffic was steady and light, peaceful as a river. He felt ashamed that he had let his wife get him into a fight. In another thirty years or so they would both be dead. What would all that stuff matter then? He thought of the years they had spent together, and how close they were, and how well they knew each other, and his throat tightened so that he could hardly breathe. His face and neck began to tingle. Warmth flooded his chest. He stood there for a while, enjoying these sensations, then picked up the pail and went out the back gate.

The two mutts from down the street had pulled over the garbage can again. One of them was rolling around on his back and the other had something in her mouth. Growling, she tossed it into the air, leaped up and caught it, growled again and whipped her head from side to side. When they saw him coming they trotted away with short, mincing steps. Normally he would heave rocks at them, but this time he let them go.

The house was dark when he came back inside. She was in the bathroom. He stood outside the door and called her name. He heard bottles clinking, but she didn't answer him. "Ann, I'm really sorry," he said. "I'll make it up to you, I promise."

"How?" she asked.

He wasn't expecting this. But from a sound in her voice, a level and definite note that was strange to him, he knew that he had to come up with the right answer. He leaned against the door. "I'll marry you," he whispered.

"We'll see," she said. "Go on to bed. I'll be out in a minute."

He undressed and got under the covers. Finally he heard the bathroom door open and close.

"Turn off the light," she said from the hallway.

"What?"

"Turn off the light."

He reached over and pulled the chain on the bedside lamp. The room went dark. "All right," he said. He lay there, but nothing happened. "All right," he said again. Then he heard a movement across the room. He sat up, but he couldn't see a thing. The room was silent. His heart pounded the way it had on their first night together, the way it still did when he woke at a noise in the darkness and waited to hear it again—the sound of someone moving through the house, a stranger.

STUDY QUESTIONS

1. Describe the CHARACTER of the speaker and his wife as presented in the first paragraph. Why is the speaker so proud of his reputation as a "considerate husband"? What kind of investment does he have in his reputation?

2. In what specific ways does your sense of the two main characters change as the narrative proceeds? What events are most important in modifying your sense of the character of each?

3. What techniques of argument does the wife use in setting up her hypothetical situation? What kind of investment does she have in the hypothesis? What textual evidence is there that she cares deeply about the issue?

4. Explain the episode of the injured thumb. How does each character respond to the event? How does each interpret it? Why is the husband so proud of his response? How do you interpret the re-reversal of the washing and drying roles?

5. Where does the story take place? What textual evidence is there of the SETTING? What does the setting have to do with the THEME of the story?

6. What does the "darkness" of the setting have to do with the issues when the narrator returns from his garbage errand? What does it have to do with the story's theme?

7. How do you interpret the darkness when the narrator turns out the light? Who is the author of the light / dark experiment here?

8. Why is the wife suddenly described as a stranger when the narrator returns from taking out the garbage? What accounts for the changes in the two characters at the end of the story?

9. What do you think is going to be revealed in the "darkness"? What textual evidence can you cite to support your position?

Robbie Clipper Sethi

R obbie Clipper Sethi's stories have appeared in such magazines as the *Literary Review*, *Mademoiselle*, and the *Atlantic Monthly*. She teaches English at Rider College in New Jersey. "Grace" was first published in 1991.

GRACE

She should have known that her marriage of convenience would be anything but. She had seduced him easily enough. Their love affair was all a big cliché: they'd met at a party near the University of Pennsylvania campus; he was one of the few people there who cared anything about design, perspective, and re-creation of life in two dimensions; she had asked him if he'd care to see her paintings.

He liked her geometric heads, their crossed eyes and twisted lips. "I wanted to study photography," he said, "but we were middle class."   2

"*We're* middle class." Worse: her father worked the line at Campbell's Soup.   3

"In India only the rich can take a chance on not making money." He had come to Wharton for an M.B.A.   4

"I can't support myself with this," Grace said. She was looking for an assistant professorship; meanwhile, she was waiting tables, which paid more than part-time teaching.   5

In some ways marrying a well-paid man seemed easier than supporting herself, as long as he was willing to spend his salary on paint and canvases, and save Grace the time she would otherwise have had to waste taking orders, wiping tables, and picking up tips.   6

Living together might have been enough if she had known what to call him: "boyfriend" seemed too immature, and when she referred to her "lover," everyone assumed that she was living with a woman, so thoroughly had homosexuals expropriated the term.   7

Her parents didn't like the obvious cohabitation without papers, but they had spent all their lives avoiding conflict; they went out of their way not to mention marriage. "What is he," her mother asked, "a Hindu?"   8

Her father said, "At least he's not a Catholic."   9

When Inder finished his degree, his parents and his sister wrote him letters asking him to come back and "settle down" with "a good girl of your own choice."   10

"That means they're finding me a wife," he said.   11

"Don't they know about me?"   12

"Are you kidding? They don't even know I've given up the turban, or shaved my beard! They'd be over here in a minute, trying to persuade me that I'd been seduced, that you were only interested in my money."   13

"You have been seduced," she said, "and your money is keeping me out of the bars six nights a week."   14

"I can't go anyway," he said. "Immigration would never let me back."   15

They were married in city hall, the statue of tolerant, immigrant William Penn standing over them. They didn't dare tell Grace's parents. Only after Inder was sure that he could get back into the country did he write a letter to his mother and father: 16

> I am planning a trip to India in January. I have met someone I very much respect. I would like to bring her with me to meet the family, according to your wishes.
>
> With highest respect, your loving son,
>
> Inder Singh

The first call came in three weeks: Inder's mother was ill, he had to [17] come right away; his father was weak, only God could say whether he would live to see his son again; his sister shouted so loud that Grace could hear her voice across the room.

In the end they got on a plane together, watched four movies, ate five [18] meals, and leafed through every magazine in the racks.

At the airport Inder's mother clung to his neck and wailed while big [19] tears disappeared into his father's beard. Until they could pry his mother off him and lead her to the taxi—hordes of people were watching this display— Inder's sister crushed Grace in her fleshy arms. Grace was glad her parents had not had the money to come and be on hand to witness this display of excessive emotion.

Days passed on the string cots and jute mats in the courtyard of Inder's [20] parents' house. His mother shouted in Punjabi[1] while Inder sat, hardly reacting, on one of the steel-and-linoleum chairs of their dinette set.

"My brother was so handsome with the turban and the beard," his sister [21] said. "Bibiji and Darji[2] cannot accept."

Inder's uncles came, their wives, their grown-up sons. Everybody had [22] something to say, mostly in Punjabi.

Grace finally saw Inder alone, on his way out of the bathroom, which [23] was separated from the house by the open courtyard. "What's going on?" she asked.

"We're getting married." [24]

"Here you are!" his sister said, walking across the courtyard. "I've been [25] looking all over for you."

Grace wore one of Inder's sister's saris, rose silk embroidered with silver [26] marigolds, wrapped around her own black leotard. She stood before a crowd of people in their temple and heard a bearded priest say something like her name—Ga-race Mad-i-son. Then she and Inder walked four times around the holy book and stood under a shower of flowers, the like of which were used to decorate their marriage bed, the only double in the house.

"This is the first time I've been alone with you the whole trip," Grace [27] said.

"We've got our whole lives to be alone," he said. [28]

She didn't see much of Inder, either. She got up to the smell of dung [29] smoke every morning, the sound of vegetable hawkers and prayers. She sat in the courtyard and sketched the sunlight coloring the cement walls of the house. "What are you drawing?" people asked, and they looked from her sketch pad to the walls and back again.

"We would have had the whole house painted," her father-in-law said, [30] "but you gave so little notice."

She dressed in brilliant skirts, saris, or baggy pants, rode taxis through [31]

---

1. Language spoken in the Punjab state in India.
2. Mother; father.

streets teeming with oranges, golds, yellows, and reds, and then slept for an hour or two. Inder's sister would wake them up, saying that it was time to visit some relative.

She couldn't wait to get home. 32

Back in the bigger and sunnier bedroom of their new two-bedroom 33 apartment, she painted the evil eyes of peacock feathers, the stripes of the Bengal tiger. She framed the batiks and Rajasthani[3] paintings she had bought, and painted Philadelphia girls, their breasts bulging out of midriff tops.

Inder let her paint. He was the only man who had ever let her paint. 34 Other men had interfered, tried to finish the paintings for her, tried to out-paint her. Inder told her what he thought only when she asked for it.

"This is the most productive summer I have ever had," she said. 35

In the fall his mother came. She cleaned the apartment every day, from 36 time to time bursting in on Grace with a handful of corner dust for her inspection. In the afternoons she sat behind Grace, coughing every time Grace opened a tube of paint. Toward evening she banged pots loudly. The smell of cooking oil seeped into Grace's oil paints.

Grace watched, speechless. Unlike Inder's sister and father, his mother 37 spoke no English, and Grace was far too busy painting to learn Punjabi. The closest language to it that she could have studied was Hindi-Urdu,[4] and the University of Pennsylvania was so expensive that she couldn't afford to take the course anyway.

"Why doesn't your mother go home?" she asked. "Two months is long 38 enough to visit anyone."

"She has a four-month visa," Inder said. 39

"I can't take another two months!" 40

"I can't tell her to leave. In India a parent is always welcome." 41

"But this is not India!" 42

"She doesn't care about that. I'm her only son. She wants to make sure 43 I'm well settled."

"Well, tell her. You're very well settled. She can go home and get on 44 with her own life."

"She will. She's worried, anyway, about my father and sister." 45

And she did go home, but not until six months later, after her visa had 46 been extended for four more months.

Another summer, and Grace painted folds of fabric, cascading hair, the 47 sun on russet skin. She and Inder bought a house and made love on the screened porch, waking to the songs of birds. "This is even better than last summer," Grace said, and she wished it could go on forever, but just as the nights were turning cold, Bibiji came back, with Inder's father.

3. State in northwest India bordering Pakistan.
4. Hindi: national language of India. Urdu: official language of Pakistan.

"I cannot live alone," he said. "I am infirm." 48

"What is he talking about?" Grace asked. "They live with your sister." 49

"He's retired." Inder said. "His pension won't even pay the taxes, let 50
alone the bills, and in India you don't take money from your daughter. People say you're stealing from her dowry."

"Your sister's forty-four years old!" 51

"They tried for fifteen years to have me," Inder said. "When my father 52
lost the business, Behanji had to go to work. Her dowry went to pay for my school."

"You already stole from her dowry! Are you saying this is it? They're 53
here to stay?"

"Of course not. They're happy in India." 54

In the mornings, after Inder went to work, Grace would go downstairs 55
for her coffee. Her father-in-law always joined her at the table. Her mother-in-law went right on cleaning. One morning her mother-in-law shouted from the family room, where she was on her hands and knees, dusting the floor.

"Bibiji wants a baby," her father-in-law said, almost blushing. 56

"Isn't she a little old?" Grace asked. 57

He laughed. "Not hers," he said. "She is impatient for a grandson to 58
carry on the name."

"It's your name," Grace said. 59

She told Inder, in the bathroom, the only place she could get to him 60
alone when he came home from work, "If I thought you wanted babies, I wouldn't have tied you down with me."

"What are you talking about?" he said. "I don't want babies." 61

"Well, your mother does." 62

"Of course she does. She has no other chance for grandchildren, and in 63
India children are everything. Don't you remember all the jokes my aunts made about American grandchildren?"

"I couldn't understand your aunts. Do you want babies?" 64

"I don't know," he said. "I've never thought about it." 65

"Because if you do, you never should have married me. If I had a baby, 66
I'd never get any work done. Even now I can't concentrate on a simple sketch with them shouting at each other—"

"What do you want me to do? I can't tell my parents what to do." 67

"But you can tell your wife she can't live the way she wants to in her 68
own house."

"You can do anything you want," he said. "I've never told you what to 69
do. Have I? Have I?"

She had to admit that he never had. 70

"It's only temporary, Grace. A few more months." She tried to turn 71
away. "Grace? Please let me handle this. I just don't want to hurt them."

She stuffed her ears with wax, couldn't even hear when Darji knocked 72
on the door. He would come upstairs to the third bedroom and stand behind

her, for how long she never knew. She'd turn, jump, sometimes let out a little scream, which he would return, and Bibiji would shout from the kitchen. He would tell Grace, every day, "We have no milk, no eggs. What are you cooking for dinner?"

When Inder came home, she would corner him in the bathroom. "They're mature adults. Why can't they get their own groceries?"

"They can't drive."

"Teach them."

"Me teach my father how to drive? He never even drove in India."

"This is not India."

"They'll only be here a few more months," Inder said. "If they need groceries, I can buy them on the way home."

She could never get them to complain to him directly. Darji would wait until Inder had gone off to work. "Your mother-in-law is not feeling well," he'd say. "She must see a doctor."

"What's wrong?" she asked—once. After that she learned.

"Some pains in the neck," her father-in-law said.

"Have you mentioned this to Inder?"

"She does not want to worry her son."

She took them to a doctor she had confided in when she was still supporting herself serving double scotches to medical students. Darji translated Bibiji's complaints; then he told the doctor about his own muscle pains, fatigue, indigestion, confusion with the fast talk on the television.

"Get a little exercise," Joel said. "Your wife, too. Walk an hour every day."

"We cannot walk," Darji said. "Our legs are weak."

Joel sent them out into the waiting room. "I could order tests," he told Grace, "but my suspicion is it's arthritis, lack of exercise, old age. And tests can be expensive. Do they have insurance?"

"I don't know." She felt like crying—if only Joel had specialized in psychiatry.

"Yo," he said. "Where's the Grace who used to get me drunk? Professionally speaking, that is." She had to leave, she knew it. He had other patients. Besides, she scared herself with a sudden urge to rub her face against the auburn stubble on his pasty cheek.

On the way home Darji asked if they could do a little shopping. With whose money, Grace wondered. She had just dropped sixty bucks for their medical hallucinations. Their very presence in her Japanese subcompact depressed her—Darji on the seat beside her with his turban pressed against the roof, Bibiji in the back in her polyester pantaloons and 1940s dress. Even the Philadelphia boys in their tight black pants and tank tops made her want to stop the car, get out, and hang out on the corner. She was, she realized with a touch of alarm, beginning to prefer her own kind.

Grace had never been able to approach a conflict with anything more flammable than paint, but arguing with Inder had given her practice. "Darji," she said, "why don't I enroll you in a driving school, so you don't have to keep asking me to take Bibiji shopping?"

"I cannot drive," he said. "My legs are too short!" The old man's eyes filled with tears, and he shouted, his voice breaking, "It is for the children to care for the old. What is time to them? We have little time left. How much trouble can it be to take your Bibiji and Darji to the shopping center so we will have some time outside our stinking, paint-smelling house?" *92*

Grace tore home, left them in the driveway, and backed out again to scream at the highway. "The bastard! It's bad enough I was stupid enough to marry one man. Now I have to deal with two. Who is he to expect me to walk him around the local mall? How does he know how much time I have? I wouldn't put it past him to outlive me!" *93*

When she came home in the evening, they were sitting in front of the television, watching a situation comedy with a laugh track so loud that Grace could hear it even before she touched the doorknob. Darji turned around, a smile stretched across his face. "Hello, daughter!" he shouted. "Did you buy the milk? Potatoes? Cooking oil?" *94*

She found Inder in the bathroom. "Send a letter to your sister," she said. "Tell her that we just can't take it anymore. She has to take them back." *95*

"I can't say that!" *96*

"Well, you'll have to say something. I drive around for hours not wanting to come home and face the noise, the demands, the expectations. When does their visa run out?" *97*

"It doesn't matter. They've applied for permanent residency." *98*

"What? They can't stay here! Are you crazy?" *99*

"It's not to stay here. It's just so they can come back any time without being hassled by Immigration." *100*

"I'm not sure I want them to come back any time." *101*

"They won't," Inder said. "They're bored. That's why they have so many aches and pains. Do you think they like being dependent on us?" *102*

"I don't know what they like," Grace said. "Except for afternoon TV, shopping, and—oh, yes—babies." *103*

"It's hard for them," Inder said. "Everyone they know is dying." *104*

"It's hard for me," Grace said. "I'm dying—" *105*

"Don't say that!" *106*

"I'm dying, you're dying, we're all dying!" *107*

He put his arms around her. "Don't even say it. If I ever lose you, I'll lose everything." *108*

She wanted to believe it. She even thought she wanted to have his baby—someday, when she'd done enough work, had enough success. His arms still felt good. Even with his parents downstairs, he was sexy, dark like the Philadelphia boys, but different—educated, on his way to wealth, exotic. *109*

"I need a place to work," Grace said. "I'm going to have to rent a studio." *110*

"How much will that cost? They'll be here for only a few more months." 111

After another month he finally sent the letter. His sister answered it by telephone, collect. "What? You have the whole house to yourself," Inder said. 112

And his sister said all the rest: she was bankrupt; the house was a mess; she had nothing to repair it with, so she had rented it to Uncleji, who had moved in with a woman of a different caste and questionable morals; Bibiji had told her that Inder had three bedrooms, air-conditioning; she had no place to go; she had no husband, no children of her own. She threatened to commit suicide if she could not see her mother and father again, her brother and his wife. 113

They put her in the third bedroom. Grace moved her canvases into the basement. While she carried a still life down the stairs, Inder's sister stood in the doorway, apologizing. "Do not worry. When you start your family, I will sleep in the room with the baby. When he cries, I will get up and bring him to you in the bed." 114

"I can't stand this," Grace told Inder. "We've got to get them an apartment." 115

"Behanji will go back," he said. "She'll never be able to live without doing business, and this country operates so differently from India, she'll never get a job." 116

But she stayed for weeks, months. She sat up all hours with her mother, sobbing. "When are they going to take her back?" Grace asked. "I thought Bibiji wanted to go back and kick her brother out of the house." 117

"It's difficult to get rid of a tenant in India," Inder said, "especially if the tenant is a relative. Besides, none of them have an income." 118

"Well, send them cashier's checks," she said. "I'm looking for a job. At a college or a school—where I can use the studio. I can't work in this house anymore." 119

"Anyone will hire you," Inder said. "Your stuff is ten times better than it's ever been." 120

"I haven't painted in weeks." 121

"It hasn't been that bad, has it? You can paint in the basement." 122

Inder put track lights in the basement, his father supervising. The effort was wasted. Her colors came out wrong. The dampness warped the canvases. She bought a dehumidifier. The noise helped to drown out the TV, the floorboards groaning under Behanji's weight, Bibiji's shouting from the kitchen. The smell of onions, spices, and simmering meat drifted down the steps every day. 123

Still she tried to paint. She'd trace a perfect jawline, dead set on re-creating that face in her mind. 124

Behanji would knock on the door. "Am I disturbing you?" 125

Grace would hold the image just behind her eyes. Unlocking the door, 126
she'd tell Behanji, "Yes. Later. I can't."

"One second," she'd say. "Mummy is afraid you will ruin your eyes, so 127
I have ground up almonds with milk. You must drink it. I will bring it to
you. I will not disturb you. One second only."

"Okay, put it there." She would go back to her canvas. 128

"I will, only you must drink it. Mummy told me, 'Make sure she drinks 129
her milk,' and I must. She worries. Even I worry."

It would be hours before Grace could even think of that face again, and 130
by then the jaw was ruined.

She spent the night, whenever she ran out of tolerance, with her par- 131
ents. They were no help. "Those Indians," her father said, "they're just like
the Italians. One of them gets over here, they bring the whole family."

Grace's ancestors, a hundred years ago, had each come over from Europe 132
alone, forgetting even the countries they came from.

"Why don't you get them an apartment?" her mother said. "How old is 133
Inder's sister? They're hiring at the K-mart."

"In India," Grace said, "it's just not done." 134

She sent résumés to every college and private school within a hundred- 135
mile radius. Sometimes she wondered why she didn't look for schools a thousand miles away.

"When you're working full time," Inder said, "it won't be all that bad. 136
You won't have to come home until the evening, and they're all in bed by
nine."

"I've got a better idea: why don't we blow my first three months' pay 137
on three one-way tickets?"

"It's not the money. If it was the money, they would leave. Grace, 138
you've got to get used to them living with us."

"Can you get used to them living with us?" 139

"They're my family! Behanji gave up her life to send me to school." 140

"To study something you didn't particularly want," she reminded him. 141
"In America you give up your family to take a wife. I thought you could do
that."

"I did do that." 142

"No," Grace said. "No." 143

With a full-time salary at last, she had enough to rent a studio across the 144
river, in the city they had moved away from when they needed the room
that Inder's family had filled. She set her easel in front of a long, bare window overlooking the street, and furnished the room with chairs and tables
she found by the curbs on her way to work. She bought a mattress for one
corner; then she went out and bought sheets, a comforter, and two feather
pillows. Her own bed, filling up one corner of the room, scared her, but she
lay on it and almost fell asleep. Then she made a cup of coffee and stared at
her half-done portrait, pretty bad, in the waning light of the afternoon.

Through the window she watched the men and women in their winter coats. How lonely she had felt in the house in the suburbs, but with no peace to justify the loneliness! She would have preferred the trees, even the lawn mowers, to the traffic, but the city was the place where she had started with Inder, so it was the only place she could return to. Besides, the campus was a block away. From a phone booth across the street she called Inder at work. 145

"I've got a studio," she said. 146

"That's great!" 147

"Move out with me." 148

"Are you crazy? We can't." 149

"It's the perfect solution. Let them have the house. We can go back to being lovers. I married you, not a whole damned household." 150

"Don't say that. I'd like to be irresponsible too, but we can't." 151

"We can be anything we want. You told me that." 152

"I meant it. I'll be getting six figures by the time I'm forty, and you'll have so many shows you'll have to hire someone—" 153

"I don't want to hire anyone," she said, sobbing. 154

She unwrapped her palette and stroked a little paint onto the canvas. Then she walked to the bank where Inder worked and waited for him. "Let's go home," he said. "They'll stay up all night if we don't come home." 155

"Don't you ever make a move unless they make it first?" 156

"What do you want me to do? Give up my family?" 157

"You don't have to give them up," she said. "Just put them up. Somewhere else." 158

"They wouldn't go," he said, "even if I asked them to move out. They made a pilgrimage to every temple in India just to have me. They sacrificed themselves to send me to the best schools." 159

"So now you must sacrifice yourself," Grace said. "But you can't sacrifice me." 160

"I'm not asking you to sacrifice." 161

He looked as gray as the paints she'd been pushing around that afternoon. "Come home with me," she said. 162

"You come home." 163

"Couldn't you take them out some night, so I can come and pack my clothes?" 164

"I don't have to take them away," he said. "They forgive everything." 165

He could have called her any time, but she could understand. She might even have welcomed the silence if it hadn't left her staring at the phone, lunging for it on the first ring, dialing him at work and then hanging up before his secretary could answer. She didn't dare call him at home, even at night. 166

She threw her energy into teaching, spent too much time with her students, though she couldn't wait to get home and work on her painting: long, lugubrious faces, their complexions gray, their eyes mere holes. 167

After three weeks he called. "I wish I'd never supported you in the first place," he said. "You might not have left as soon as you got some money of your own." 168

"It's not the money," she said. "I thought you understood." 169

"I do. They don't. You've got to come over." 170

"Are you alone?" 171

"I thought you'd rather see them here. They're talking about looking for you at the college." 172

"They wouldn't!" 173

"They need to feel like they tried to reconcile us. That's how things are done in India." 174

"This is *not* India," Grace said. "Don't they know that their 'little India' split us apart?" 175

"You won't say that, will you?" 176

"Neither one of us says anything," she said. "That's the problem!" 177

When she walked through the door, Darji took off his turban and laid it at her feet. Bibiji, kicking it out of the way, threw her arms around her and made kissing noises in the air. Behanji wept: "I will give you my gold, all my diamonds, if you will return." 178

Inder stood in front of the door, his face blank, as if he had never had anything to do with any one of them. Grace stared at him and remembered her painting. She wanted to slap him; then she wanted to comfort him— anything to shock him into loving her again, but not in this place. She pushed Bibiji away. "I haven't come to take your gold or your turban—" 179

"You must come back," Behanji said. "This is ridiculous. You and my brother have no differences that cannot be reconciled. If you wish, you can sleep in the room with me. Look at you, you are young, you are healthy. You will have many children. It is true what I say, no?" 180

"No," Grace said. She stared at Inder, unable to find words. "Tell them, damn it." 181

"Grace needs some time alone for a while," he said. 182

"No!" she said. "No. What Grace needs is a house of her own. If you want to stay with them—" 183

"I can't!" he said. 184

"I can't either." She pushed him aside and opened the door. 185

"Wait!" Darji said. "I am elder of this family. I forbid you to divorce my son." 186

Grace laughed. His mouth fell open. Inder said, "No one said anything about divorce." 187

"Do not go," Behanji cried. "You will stay tonight, have some food. Leave that place in Philadelphia. I will give you new clothes." 188

"I left my clothes here," Grace said. "All I have in Philadelphia are my paints." She turned and walked out the door. 189

"Grace!" Inder said. 190

Darji stood up and fell on his face on the threshold. "I have humbled   191
myself!" he cried. "Witness: I have touched my daughter-in-law's feet!"

Grace drove away before he could throw himself in front of the car. The   192
silence of the road felt almost warm, like the comforting silence of her mother
when as a child she was too sick to go to school, and lay on the sofa all day,
sipping ginger ale. Her studio was even quieter. She lay on the mattress
sipping wine until the voices stopped ringing in her ears.

Inder had seemed not to be there at all. Turning himself off was the   193
only way he'd managed to accept the situation. Grace understood that. But
she could never have learned to ignore what was going on right in front of
her face. For one thing, it would have killed her work.

Living without him wasn't easy. She taught. She painted. Sometimes   194
she spent a weekend with her parents, but after a night outside the studio
she began to miss the smell of paint, the incomplete portrait, the hours spent
looking into space while the lines and figures flashed before her eyes. Within
a few more weeks she had almost grown to like missing Inder.

For months she heard about him. Behanji sent accusatory letters to her   195
at the college. At first Darji was dying, Bibiji had lost ten years off her life.
Inder lost weight daily and snapped at his family all the time. Then Darji
was better, but would never smile again; Bibiji was eating, but only small-
small bites. Inder was developing a horrible temper and would listen to no
one.

The last letter shunted all the blame: 196

> I have been blind, my sister. Now I see. He is cold. He is my own
> brother, but I call him cold. I do not see how you could have made a love
> marriage. When he was born, the only son, he was spoiled by too much
> love. I tell you, they are my mother and father, but they are wrong. He
> grew up expecting everything and getting everything he wanted. And because
> of him—this boy—because he went to the best schools, wore the best cloth-
> ing, and had more toys than I got in my lifetime, because of this I have had
> no dowry. I did not marry and have sons of my own because my brother
> got everything. It is a fact. That is why I am forced to live on his charity,
> to share his home. If I had any other choice, I would not.

So, Grace thought, a six-year-old child is supposed to prevent his family   197
from killing itself for him. That would make a good mythic triptych. No: a
twenty-one-year-old woman is supposed to know she can't give up her future
for a six-year-old brother, who will one day leave the family and find a woman
of his own. No doubt in India people had different ideas. She wrote a letter:

> Look here, Behanji, maybe he is cold, though for a time I thought he gave
> me all the warmth I need. Maybe you should blame your parents. But blam-
> ing anybody after twenty-five years is no way to get on with your life. Get
> a job, for God's sake. Learn to drive. You're only forty-five. Lose a little

weight and you might meet some lonely divorcé a damn sight warmer than your little brother.

Her letter may have been a bit harsh, but absence had made Grace's heart a good deal harder, and though the same absence told her that she'd never again live with Inder, she thought the least she could do was leave him with a better life than they had lived when they had tried to live together. 198

She avoided other men. Men had always gotten her into trouble. Why had she expected Inder to be any different? She went to the campus. She came home. She painted. She was happy with her latest. It portrayed a gray-faced man, abstractly outlined with a skeletal jaw, a hanging, startled mouth, and big, uncomprehending eyes. A little derivative, but it worked. Her current canvas was so far nothing but a blur of the same grayish white. 199

As the months went by, she put off the decision to file for divorce. She knew Inder was putting it off too. That had always been his way. She loved him. She always would. But she had loved other men, still loved some of them, and had gotten over them, except in memory. Such memories were often sweet. 200

In the corner that she had turned into a rudimentary kitchen, she watched half a pot of coffee materialize, feeling as if with this little space that no one else trod, no one else dirtied, no one else cleaned, she owned the world. Pouring a cup, she unwrapped her paints and began to put the finishing touches on a piece she liked even better than her last—two gray-white faces this time, with just a touch of yellow. Elongated, the figures stretched from crown to abdomen as if they were hanging from the skyline behind them. They wore the same wide-eyed stare as their frightened brother, but she'd managed to work a touch of comprehension into their eyes, like the reconciliation to fate she envisioned in the heart of Christ, hanging on the cross, right after he had cried out to his Father, "Why have You forsaken me?" and understood the silence of God's reply. 201

Someone knocked on the door. She hesitated. This was her day to paint, and she'd been saving the whole day to finish this portrait, *Grace*. She'd begrudged every minute spent showering, brewing coffee, getting dressed. 202

She opened the door. Behanji stood there, lugging two big bags. She dropped the suitcases and threw her fat arms around Grace. 203

"Sister! We will not be alone." 204

"Are you crazy? What is this?" 205

"All that I own in the world." 206

"I told you," Grace said. "I don't want it. Inder and I are no longer together. There's no changing our minds." 207

"I know, sister. Oi! So many steps! I must sit." 208

Her big haunches spread out on the mattress. "We need furniture, sister." From the mattress she could see *Grace*. Its dual stare turned her face as gray as the paint. "You made that?" she said. 209

"I haven't made it yet. I was about to make it when you came in. How did you find my studio?" 210

"Telephone, sister." 211

"I never got your call." 212

"The address book." 213

"Inder told you? I'll kill him." 214

"No, no, you can't do that," she said. "Listen, I will tell you. I know that you and Inder are divorced." 215

"We're not divorced." 216

"Do not worry, I am reconciled. Even Mummy and Daddy are reconciled. Perhaps it is too soon to say, but when he is ready, they will find him another wife." 217

"Another wife?" 218

"He will be happy. Don't worry, sister. I will lose weight, I promise. As for marriage, what is a woman when she is too old to have children? We will find for you, my sister. I have wasted my life for my brother, but I will not waste it with my sister!" 219

"I'm not—" Grace started, but what Behanji wanted to call her was not entirely the point. "You're forty-five years old! When are you going to live your own life?" 220

"I will find a job," Behanji said. "You will paint." 221

"I can't paint! I can't even breathe when you're around. I need privacy. I need to be alone." 222

"Paint. I won't disturb you. I'll unpack quietly. Like a little mouse." 223

"No! No, no. I want my own home, my own space, not just to work, to live in." 224

"But we feel it is the same house," she said. "My brother's house is my house. Just as it is your house. You see, it is the same house, brothers, sisters, mothers, husbands, and wives. Just because you are divorcing my brother does not mean you are not still my sister. I think of you that way. And my sister's home is my home. See?" 225

"No," Grace said. Behanji would never understand. Grace wished she had learned Punjabi; maybe it would have been easier to communicate with them, even Inder. "Would you like a cup of tea?" She remembered that they always took tea in the afternoon. Behanji shook her head. 226

"Well, I'm going to tell you, even if you don't understand. My problem was never with Inder. It was with you." 227

"Me! What have I done?" 228

"I can't work with you around. I can't work with anyone around, and I need to work, all the time, even if it's only in my head. Even if it looks like I'm not working." 229

"Everyone works too hard in America." Behanji sat, staring at the painting. 230

Grace started too and found herself longing, more than ever, to get back to it. "Shall I call you a cab?" 231

"I can manage," Behanji said. "There are many taxis on the corner." 232

Grace kept staring at her painting after Behanji had left. She didn't like 233
it nearly as much. She dialed Inder's office. "Your sister was here."

"Oh?" 234

It was the first she'd heard his voice in months. She almost forgot what 235
she wanted, hearing that voice. "She wanted to move in with me."

"I take it you didn't let her." 236

"I'm sorry it took me so long to call," Grace said. "I didn't want to 237
bother you."

"That's news." 238

"I made a big mistake. I'm sorry." 239

"Is there anything else? Because if that's all you wanted to tell me, you 240
could have told me months ago."

"I haven't exactly been out of touch," she said. "Your sister has been 241
writing me letters."

"That's not all she's been doing." 242

"I think you ought to pay her back that dowry." 243

"What?" 244

"It wouldn't take much: her own apartment, driving lessons, and if you're 245
feeling generous, a car, some employment counseling."

"Are you coming home?" 246

"I am home. And even here I can't get away from your family. They 247
should hate me. Why don't they hate me?"

"In India a marriage is for life." 248

"Is that why we haven't filed for divorce?" 249

"Do you want a divorce?" 250

"It's not why I called." 251

"Come home," he said. 252

"You come here." 253

"I have a meeting in two minutes." 254

"I've got work to do myself." 255

But neither one of them hung up. 256

"If your sister can stop by," she said, "I don't see why you can't." 257

"If I stop by," he said, "I'll be caught in the middle again." 258

"You are in the middle." 259

"I've got to go." 260

"Good-bye." 261

She cursed her stupid luck. The lines of her portrait blurred in front of 262
her. She tried a wash. By nightfall she had managed to blend the foreheads
of the figures into the city scape behind them. The painting needed something. She opened a tube of primary red, put a dab of paint on the tip of her
finger, and touched a dot above each figure's eyes.

STUDY QUESTIONS

1. How likable a CHARACTER is Grace? At what points do you feel the most sympathy for her? At what points do you feel the least? Describe the most dominant traits in her character. How devoted is she to her art? In what particular ways?

2. How fully do you identify with Grace as NARRATOR? Are there points where you think she should be more understanding of those with different cultural assumptions? Does your attitude toward Grace shift in the course of the story? Do you think that your own ethnic background makes a difference in how you respond to her as a character? Does your gender make a difference?

3. What were Grace's original intentions in getting involved with Inder? When did they change? What plans does she have for her life? What values seem most important to her in the first part of the story, before she meets her new in-laws?

4. Describe Inder as a character. How sensitive is he to Grace's needs early in their relationship? How does he feel about her art? What are his own ambitions? What values seem most important to him? Do his values change in the course of the story? How do you feel about what happens to him? Do you identify with his difficulties? When do you sympathize most with him?

5. What is the story *about*? Using terms defined in the Afterword, try to come up with a description of the story's specific subject; its general subject; its theme.

6. One way of talking about the story is to emphasize the several difficulties of *communication* between the characters. What role does language difficulty play in the failures of communication? Which characters willfully refuse to speak each other's language? Which ones refuse to translate their words into terms others can understand? Which retreat into silence or distance? Which ones metaphorically refuse to speak in a language others can understand? Which characters try hardest to understand values and habits across language barriers?

7. Compare the parents of Grace and Inder. What ingrained habits do Grace's parents have? Does the story give any reason for their apparently greater "tolerance"?

8. How fully is Behanji characterized? Can you generalize anything about generations and generational differences in Indian culture by comparing her values with those of Inder? How fully is Inder Americanized? What features of his Indian heritage continue to operate powerfully in his behavior?

9. Art. Privacy. Love. Family. Key terms such as these help to define both cultural assumptions and individual attitudes. Trace the meaning of each of these terms for the major characters in the story.

10. What kind of values seem to characterize America as a culture, according to this story?

Paula Gunn Allen

S ioux-Laguna and Lebanese-Jewish, Paula Gunn Allen was born in 1939 in Cu-
bero, New Mexico. Her family spoke five languages when she was growing up.
It is to this mixture she attributes her being a poet. She believes that poetry should
be useful, and that the use-full is the beauty-full. "Language, like a woman, can bring
into being what was not in being; it can, like food, transform one set of materials into
another set of materials." She is a professor of English at the University of California,
Los Angeles. She has published a novel, *The Woman Who Owned the Shadows* (1983); a
collection of essays, *The Sacred Hoop: Recovering the Feminine in American Indian Tradition* (1992); and several books of poetry. She is editor of *Spider Woman's Granddaughters:
Traditional Tales and Contemporary Writing by Native American Women* (1989), which
won an American Book Award in 1990. Her latest effort, *Grandmothers of the Light*
(1991), is an anthology of stories written by Native Americans.

POCAHONTAS TO HER ENGLISH HUSBAND, JOHN ROLFE

Had I not cradled you in my arms,
oh beloved   perfidious one,
you would have died.
And how many times did I pluck you
from certain death in the wilderness—   5
my world through which you stumbled
as though blind?
Had I not set you tasks
your masters far across the sea
would have abandoned you—   10
did abandon you, as many times they
left you to reap the harvest of their lies;
still you survived   oh my fair husband
and brought them gold
wrung from a harvest I taught you   15
to plant: Tobacco.   It
is not without irony that by this crop

your descendants die, for other powers
than those you know take part in this.
And indeed I did rescue you   20
not once but a thousand thousand times
and in my arms you slept, a foolish child,
and beside me you played,
chattering nonsense about a God
you had not wit to name;   25
and wondered you at my silence—
simple foolish wanton maid you saw,
dusky daughter of heathen sires
who knew not the ways of grace—
no doubt, no doubt.   30
I spoke little, you said.
And you listened less.
But played with your gaudy dreams
and sent ponderous missives to the throne
striving thereby to curry favor   35
with your king.   I saw you well.   I
understood the ploy and still protected you,
going so far as to die in your keeping—
a wasting, putrifying death, and you,
deceiver, my husband, father of my son,   40
survived, your spirit bearing crop
slowly from my teaching, taking
certain life from the wasting of my bones.

STUDY QUESTIONS

1. When is Pocahontas speaking this poem?

2. What did Pocahontas die of?

3. How would you describe the TONE of this speech to her husband? (You may want
   to try reading it aloud, as if you were acting the part.)

Wendy Rose

E ditor (*American Indian Quarterly*), anthropologist (*Aboriginal Tattooing in California*), professor (Native American studies, University of California, Berkeley),

artist, and poet (*Lost Copper*—nominated for the American Book Award in 1981—and *Halfbreed Chronicles*, from which "Julia" is taken), Hopi / Miwok Wendy Rose is a major force in Native American culture.

JULIA

Julia Pastrana, 1832–60, was a singer and dancer billed in the circus as "The Ugliest Woman in the World" or "Lion Lady." She was a Mexican Indian, born with a deformed bone structure of the face and hair growing from her entire body. Her manager, in an attempt to maintain control over her professional life, married her. She believed in him and was heard to say on the morning of her wedding, "I know he loves me for my own sake." When she gave birth to her son, she saw that he had inherited her own deformities plus some lethal gene that killed him at the age of six hours. In less than a week, Julia also died. Her husband, unwilling to abandon his financial investment, had Julia and her infant son stuffed and mounted in a wood and glass case. As recently as 1975 they were exhibited at locations in the United States and Europe.

Tell me it was just a dream,
my husband, a clever trick
made by some tin-faced village god
or ghost-coyote pretending
to frighten me with his claim   5
that our marriage is made
of malice and money. Oh tell me again
how you admire my hands, how
my jasmine tea is rich and strong,
my singing sweet, my eyes so dark   10
you would lose yourself swimming,
man into flesh, as you mapped the pond
you would own. That was not all.
The room grew cold
as if to joke with these   15
warm days; the curtains blew out
and fell back against
the moon-painted sill.
I rose from my bed like a spirit
and, not a spirit at all, floated   20
slowly to my great glass oval

to see myself reflected
as the burnished bronze woman,
skin smooth and tender,
I know myself to be in the dark   25
above the confusion
of French perfumes and
I was there in the mirror
and I was not.
I had become hard   30
as the temple stones of Otomi,
hair grown over my ancient face
like black moss, gray
as jungle fog soaking green
the tallest tree tops.   35
I was frail as
the breaking dry branches
of my winter wand canyons
standing so still as if
to stand forever. Oh   40
such a small room—
no bigger than my elbows outstretched
and just as tall as my head.
A small room from which
to sing open the doors   45
with my cold graceful mouth,
my rigid lips, silences
dead as yesterday, cruel as what
the children say, cold
as the coins that glitter   50
in your pink fist.
And another terrifying magic
in the cold of that tall box: in my arms
or standing next to me
on a tall table by my right shoulder   55
a tiny doll that
looked like me . . . oh my husband
tell me again
this is only a dream
I wake from warm   60
and today is still today,
summer sun and quick rain;
tell me, husband, how you love me
for my self one more time.
It scares me so

to be with child
lioness
with cub.

STUDY QUESTIONS

1. To what does "it" in the first line refer?

2. How does Julia in the dark imagine herself to be?

3. Explain lines 28–29—"I was there in the mirror / and I was not."

4. In lines 53–57, Julia says there's a doll that looks like her standing near her; who or what is that "doll"? In the last four lines of the poem, Julia says she is with child. Is that true? When is the poem being spoken by Julia? Where is she?

Lynn Nelson

Lynn Nelson lives with her family in the northeast.

SEQUENCE

His Mother
For months the letters from his mother came,
that first year of our lawful wedded life.
She didn't even want to know my name,
much less what I was like, his nightmare wife.
He wouldn't read them to me, but I knew   5
her letters told him that she'd been betrayed
by his transgression of her worst taboo.
She begged him to renege the vows he'd made.
Dumbstruck with pain, he struggled toward a choice
between love for his mother and for me,   10
turning from both of us without a voice
to ask either of us for sympathy.
Its tongue cut out by my guilt and his loss,
our love hung silent on his mother's cross.

How Did I Love Him?

I loved him with a passion put to use   15
in childhood's longing for identity.
I loved him for his detailed and profuse
remembered past: It gave a past to me.
I loved him for the thin potato soup,
the push-meat sandwiches after the war,   20
his mother's sneaking up on him, to swoop
him up and wrestle him to the floor.
I loved his college and his army days,
his trips to capitols I'd never seen;
the operas and concerts, films and plays   25
I saw as he described them, with a keen
and narcissistic vision: With what grace
I bent to kiss his sky, and saw my face!

Frogs

That spring I dreamed incessantly of frogs.
Their silly croaking lulled me every night;   30
sometimes they swam through me as polliwogs
or sperm bearing the chromosome for blight.
They wanted me to kiss their ugliness,
beseeching me with staring, swollen eyes.
Caught in the dream, I had to acquiesce: 35
My children, in dream-logic's weird disguise,
they wanted me to love them and conceive.
In autumn when the test read positive,
he told me if I had it, he would leave.
I loved him: That's the thing I can't forgive.   40
Feet in the stirrups, riding on my back,
I loved him. Even as my world went black.

The Circus

The woman whom I hoped to make my friend
invited us to meet her and her kids
three hours' drive away, so we could spend   45
an evening at the circus. There, amid
the awe and shouts of laughter, I forgot
how miserable I'd been an hour before.
Like Guinevere in love in Camelot,
I was enchanted by the lions' roar,   50
the trained pigs, and this woman's youngest son
whose giggle was a melody of bells
which shivered joy through every ganglion
of my unhappy body, made me swell

almost to bloom. Then he said he'd prefer   55
if I drove her kids home: He'd ride with her.

What I Knew

The clash of cultures—of my ignorance
and his clear, European intellect—
embarrassed and enraged me. What a dunce
I thought I was. My fledgling self-respect   60
disintegrated daily. He was shocked
by my miseducation, so I'd shrink
when he made any overture to talk,
because I was afraid of what he'd think.
The insecurity I'd felt at school—   65
where I got A's, I thought, for being black
when all the time I knew I was a fool—
and deeply buried in myself, came back.
My habit of surrender grew so strong
he never knew when I knew he was wrong.   70

Everyday

I never felt the ordinary rage
my friends confess to over coffee cups.
I never had to go on a rampage
as they do, when their husbands won't clean up
the bathroom, when they don't take out the trash,   75
when they leave dirty laundry on the floor.
My husband whipped up dinners with panache;
he gladly tackled any household chore.
We went for months without an argument,
without a missed beat in our clockwork life,   80
with nothing to take ill, or to resent:
my perfect husband and his perfect wife.
For months, I could have nothing to complain
to him about, except my constant pain.

Sisters

The schoolbus drove us home from highschool, where   85
we got off in the Negro neighborhood
and several times a week there was a fight:
One sister called another sister "hoe,"
pulled out black handfuls of her straightened hair,
clawed at her face and hands, and ripped her shirt.   90
I walked home. I believed in sisterhood.
I still do, after thirty years, although
I'll never understand why several white

sisters walked on me as if I was dirt.
We were all sisters, feminists, I thought,   95
forgetting what those cat-fights should have taught.
I was too well brought-up, too middle class
to call a heifer out, and whup her ass.

By the Track

We came home to our lives, and home to all
the friends we'd half-forgotten. Home to her.   100
She was unhappy; at midnight, she'd call
to talk with him. I listened: a voyeur.
I saw her notes to him, counted her gifts,
and plotted routes by which I could escape.
It wasn't her fault: She'd been set adrift,   105
and had no sextant other than her shape.
One day, we walked beside the railroad track.
I thinking *murder, lawyers, money, death.*
He reached his goal, decided to turn back,
and mused, "I think, before my fortieth   110
birthday, I might like to have a child . . ."
He didn't understand why I ran wild.

Color

For him, I gave away my father's name.
He gave away his mother's love for me.
So each of us was partially to blame   115
for the other's lost, and found identity.
I tried to find myself, in our old car,
by looking at his profile as he drove
to see if we were somehow similar,
had more in common than the kitchen stove   120
and our Breughel print, which only shared a room.
I asked him once what he was thinking of;
I should have known his answer spelled our doom,
for nothing I could think of sounded duller:
He said, "Of Goethe's writings about color."   125

Recurrent Dream

My father came back regularly, to see
how I was doing, long after he died.
He came in dreams in which he lovingly
explained that he'd returned to be my guide
through the important shadows. I awoke   130
and all day saw day's light intensified.
The last time, in an aureole of smoke

that somehow shone, he stood outside the door.
I didn't open it. Instead, I spoke:
"I'm grown up; I don't need you any more."   135
He smiled and nodded, saying, "Yes, I know."
Last night I had another visitor:
Love's ghost, as though compelled by need, as though
it knew the way. My love, I'm grown. Let go.

STUDY QUESTIONS

1. Why according to the first poem in the sequence ("His Mother"), is the SPEAKER a "nightmare wife" (line 4)? Where, in the sequence of poems, does the exact nature of that nightmare become clear? Exactly what is the "worst taboo" (line 7) of the speaker's mother-in-law?

2. Characterize the husband. What are his strongest character traits? What, according to the speaker, are his biggest weaknesses? In what specific ways are his weaknesses the vehicle for the speaker's new maturity as described in the tenth poem, "Recurrent Dream"?

3. Characterize the speaker. What aspects of her past (as she relates it) seem to have the most to do with her present character? How important is race as an influence on her behavior? In what specific ways? What kinds of experiences seem to stir the strongest personal feelings? Why does the speaker not feel the "ordinary rage" (line 71) of other wives?

4. In what basic ways are the speaker and her husband different? In what ways are they similar? How strong is the speaker's love? How strong is the husband's love? In what different ways are his mother's rivalry a measure of the problems they face?

5. How important is race as a factor in the marriage? How much are the speaker and her husband affected by the attitudes of their parents? of their childhoods?

6. Describe the patterns of rhythm in each line of the first poem. What pattern do you find in the alternation between stressed and unstressed syllables? Describe the patterns in the second poem; in the third. What variations in the basic pattern do you see in other poems? How do these variations relate to what is happening at the time in the content of the poems?

7. Describe the rhyme scheme in the first poem—that is, describe which words, in which lines, rhyme with each other, and note the patterns of repetition. How similar is the scheme in the second poem ("How Did I Love Him?")? Describe the rhyme scheme in the third and fourth poems. In what ways does the rhyme scheme in the seventh poem ("Sisters") differ from that in the first six poems? How is the rhyme scheme in the tenth (and final) poem different? How does the content of poems 7 and 10 differ from that of the other poems in the sequence? What connections do you see between content and rhyme scheme in the sequence?

Elizabeth Alexander

A s the following poem suggests, Elizabeth Alexander has a complex Jamaican heritage. Her mother is a writer, and her father (Clifford L. Alexander, Jr.) is a lawyer and public servant who was once chairman of the Equal Employment Opportunity Commission and who served in the cabinet under President Jimmy Carter. Her first collection of poems, *The Venus Hottentot* (1990), was highly praised. She teaches literature and creative writing at the University of Chicago.

WEST INDIAN PRIMER

for Clifford L. Alexander, Sr.
1898–1989

"On the road between Spanish Town
and Kingston," my grandfather said,
"I was born." His father a merchant,
Jewish, from Italy or Spain.

In the great earthquake the ground split   5
clean, and great-grandfather fell
in the fault with his goat. I don't know
how I got this tale and do not ask.

His black mother taught my grandfather figures, fixed codfish cakes   10
and fried plantains, drilled cleanliness,
telling the truth, punctuality.

"There is no man more honest,"
my father says. Years later
I read that Jews passed through my   15
grandfather's birthplace frequently.

I know more about Toussaint[1]
and Hispaniola[2] than my own
Jamaica and my family tales
I finger the stories like genie   20

lamps. I write this West Indian primer.

STUDY QUESTIONS

1. Characterize the speaker's great-grandfather. Her great-grandmother. How much specific detail are we given about each? What qualities does the grandfather seem to take from each? How do they fit together?

2. What does the anecdote of the earthquake and the goat add to the poem? How does it relate to the poem's ending?

3. Why does the SPEAKER contrast her lack of knowledge of family history with what she knows about political history? Why does she "finger" (line 20) the family stories? What kind of magic do they embody?

4. Explain the poem's title.

Juliet Kono

Born and reared in Hilo, Hawaii, Juliet Kono is the author of *Hilo Rains* and the forthcoming *Tsunami Years*. She cooperated with Cathy Song on a literary collection, *Sister Stew: Fiction and Poetry by Women*, published in 1991.

SASHIMI

You call
eating sashimi
primitive.

1. Self-educated, Haitian black soldier and liberator who lived from 1743 to 1803.

2. The first island claimed by Columbus for Spain in 1492. It houses the modern nations of Haiti and the Dominican Republic.

I slice pieces
from a slab   5
of my favorite fish,
abura shibi,
from Kekaulike Market.
Upon a blue plate,
on a bed of shredded *daikon*   10
and *chiso* leaves,
I fashion
thin, red slivers
of raw fish
into a pinwheel.   15
In the center
of this wheel,
I place a dollop
of *wasabi* mustard,
into a flower cup   20
cut from a carrot.

I dissolve
the pungent mustard
into the shoyu sauce,
the aroma exciting   25
my ancestors—
they dance
on my tongue.
I pierce
a slice of fish   30
with my chopstick,
dip it into
the sauce.
I close my eyes.
I let the smooth fish   35
slide over my teeth,
my tongue,
then swim down
my gullet.
I chase this fish
with a mouthful   40
of hot rice,
some green tea,
and smack my lips
in ancient noises
of satisfaction.   45

I take another piece.
Looking up,
I toast you
with this trembling
delicacy.   50
Soon you will come
to appreciate
the years
behind my palate.
And I am patient   55
as all love is patient,
for you will learn
as you once learned
with women—
to close your eyes   60
and take
flesh
to mouth.

STUDY QUESTIONS

1. Who is the "You" in line 1? How much do we get to know about him? What is his relationship to the SPEAKER?

2. What makes this poem so sensuous? Which words emphasize the feeling of the food? What is meant by "the years behind my palate" (lines 54–55)? How does this line relate to the charge (in line 3) that eating sashimi is "primitive"? How do we know that the man to whom the poem is addressed lacks those years of experience? Why is the speaker confident that his lack of experience can be overcome? Is the poem sensual as well as sensuous?

3. How much do we know about the speaker? Draw as complete a picture of her as you can from what is revealed in the text. How much does the poem tell us about the nature of her relationship with the "You" of line 1? What indications are there that the two have found previous bridges across their cultural divide?

Yusef Komunyakaa

Yusef Komunyakaa served in Vietnam as a correspondent and editor of *The Southern Cross*. He now teaches literature at the University of California, Berkeley.

His latest book is *DIEN CAI DAU*, published in 1988. "Tu Do Street" was included in the Pushcart Prize anthology, volume 13.

TU DO STREET

Searching for love, a woman,
someone to help ease down the cocked hammer
of my nerves & senses. The music
divides the evening into black
& white—soul, country & western,   5
acid rock, & Frank Sinatra.
I close my eyes & can see
men drawing lines in the dust,
daring each other to step across.
America pushes through the membrane   10
of mist & smoke, & I'm a small boy
again in Bogalusa skirting tough talk
coming out of bars with *White Only*
signs & Hank Snow. But tonight,
here in Saigon, just for the hell of it,   15
I walk into a place with Hank Williams
calling from the jukebox. The bar girls
fade behind a smokescreen, fluttering
like tropical birds in a cage, not
speaking with their eyes & usual   20
painted smiles. I get the silent
treatment. We have played Judas
for each other out in the boonies
but only enemy machinegun fire
can bring us together again.   25
When I order a beer, the mama-san
behind the counter acts as if she
can't understand, while her
eyes caress a white face;
down the street the black GIs   30
hold to their turf also.
An off-limits sign pulls me
deeper into alleys; I look
for a softness behind these voices
wounded by their beauty & war.   35
Back in the bush at Dak To
& Khe Sahn, we fought

the brothers of these women
we now run to hold in our arms.
There's more than a nation divided   40
inside us, as black & white
soldiers touch the same lovers
minutes apart, tasting
each other's breath,
without knowing these rooms   45
run into each other like tunnels
leading to the underworld.

STUDY QUESTIONS

1. Where, exactly, do you become aware of the SETTING for the present action of the poem? of the full situation? When does the basic action of the poem take place?

2. How do memories of the past figure in the poem? Where did the SPEAKER grow up? When does the poem make clear that the speaker is black? What specific memories are relevant to the theme of the poem? How does the off-limits sign (line 32) relate in the speaker's mind to the "*White Only* signs" in lines 13–14?

3. How early in the poem is the black versus white THEME introduced? How does the civil situation in Vietnam relate to the American civil divisions represented by the speaker's racial experiences?

4. Explain the simile in lines 18–19. Explain the metaphor in lines 22–23. Explain how the situation of interlocked rooms, entered from opposite streets and alleys, works metaphorically in the poem.

Gogisgi

Born in Oklahoma City in 1927, Carroll Arnett (who often writes under his Cherokee name, "Gogisgi") was educated at Beloit College, the University of Oklahoma, and the University of Texas. He has taught at Knox College, Stephens College, Wittenberg University, and Nasson College; he is now professor of English at Central Michigan University. He is the author of ten volumes of poetry and has been awarded a National Endowment for the Arts Fellowship.

SONG OF THE BREED

Don't offend
the fullbloods,
don't offend
the whites,
stand there in   5
the middle
of the god-
damned road
and get hit.

STUDY QUESTIONS

1. To whom is the poem addressed? What do the "fullbloods" (line 2) and the "whites" (line 4) have in common, as far as the narrator is concerned?

2. Describe the frustrations the NARRATOR feels. Does the fact that we have no particulars about his circumstances diminish the poem's potential effect? How much can we justifiably infer about the narrator's circumstances? What indications are there of his strength of feeling?

Cyn. Zarco

Cyn. Zarco was born in Manila, Philippines, in 1950, raised in Miami from the age of nine and now lives in California. She won the Before Columbus Foundation's American Book Award in 1986 for her book *Cir'cum-nav'i-ga'tion*.

FLIPOCHINOS

when a brown person
gets together
with a yellow person
it is something like

the mating of a chico[1] and a banana 5
the brown meat of the chico
plus the yellow skin of the banana
take the seed of the chico for eyes
peel the banana for sex appeal
lick the juice from your fingers 10
and watch your step

STUDY QUESTIONS

1. The line endings of this poem serve as punctuation in some cases. Where would you end the sentences in this poem? If you look closely, you will notice that many of the lines are parallel—lines 1 and 3, for example: "w——a brown person," "w——a yellow person." What other parallel structures can you find? How do these structures reflect the subject matter of the poem?

2. Who is the "you" in the poem ("your," in the final line)?

Alice Bloch

Alice Bloch has written two books, a memoir called *Lifetime Guarantee* (1981) and a novel called *The Law of Return* (1983). Her work has also appeared in *The Penguin Book of Homosexual Verse*.

SIX YEARS

for Nancy

A friend calls us
an old married couple

I flinch
you don't mind

1. Greasewood; a thorny plant with fleshy leaves and dry papery fruit found in the deserts of the American West.

On the way home   5
you ask why I got upset
We are something
like what she said
you say   I say
No   10

We aren't married
No one has blessed
this union   no one
gave us kitchen gadgets
We bought our own blender   15
We built our common life
in the space between the laws

Six years
What drew us together
a cartographer   a magnetic force   20
our bodies   our speech
the wind   a hunger

Listeners both
we talked

I wanted: your lean wired energy   25
control   decisiveness
honesty   your past
as an athlete

You wanted:
my 'culture'   30
gentleness   warmth

Of course that was doomed
You brought out
my anger   I resist
your control   your energy   35
exhausts me   my hands
are too hot for you   you gained
the weight I lost   my gentleness
is dishonest   your honesty
is cruel   you hate   40
my reading   I hate
your motorcycle

Yet something has changed
You have become gentler
I more decisive   45
We walk easily
around our house
into each other's language
There is nothing
we cannot say together   50

Solid ground
under our feet
we know this landscape
We have no choice
of destination   only the route   55
is a mystery   every day
a new map of the same terrain

STUDY QUESTIONS

1. In what ways is this "union" (line 13) different from others? How quickly does the PLOT of this poem reveal itself? What does it literally mean that "No one has blessed / this union" (lines 12–13)?

2. What differences are there between the "you" in the poem and the SPEAKER? What different attitudes do they have toward the other people's responses to them? What needs did each bring to their union? How have they each changed? In what ways are they now alike?

3. Describe the sense of destiny and determinism in the poem? Where does the faith in forces beyond the personal seem to come from? Find all the places in the poem where fate or destiny seem to have an effect on their relationship. Explain the map imagery in lines 20 and 57.

4. Describe the effects of stanzas 8 and 9 (lines 32–50) on the opening description of "an old married couple" (line 2). Does the speaker seem to know that her lover has a more realistic view of the relationship than she does? What are the textual indications?

Michael Lassell

Michael Lassell was born in 1947 in New York City and now lives in New York. He holds degrees from Colgate University, California Institute of the

Arts, and the Yale School of Drama; he works as a writer, editor, and photographer. Lassell writes poetry and fiction; his book of poems, *Poems for Lost and Unlost Boys*, won the Amelia Chapbook Award for 1985, and his most recent book, *Decade Dance*, won the Lambda Literary Award of 1990.

HOW TO WATCH YOUR BROTHER DIE

For Carl Morse

When the call comes, be calm.
Say to your wife, "My brother is dying. I have to fly
to California."
Try not to be shocked that he already looks like
a cadaver.   5
Say to the young man sitting by your brother's side,
"I'm his brother."
Try not to be shocked when the young man says,
"I'm his lover. Thanks for coming."

Listen to the doctor with a steel face on.   10
Sign the necessary forms.
Tell the doctor you will take care of everything.
Wonder why doctors are so remote.

Watch the lover's eyes as they stare into
your brother's eyes as they stare into
space.   15
Wonder what they see there.
Remember the time he was jealous and
opened your eyebrow with a sharp stick.
Forgive him out loud   20
even if he can't
understand you.
Realize the scar will be
all that's left of him.

Over coffee in the hospital cafeteria   25
say to the lover, "You're an extremely good-looking
young man."
Hear him say,

"I never thought I was good enough looking to
deserve your brother."   30

Watch the tears well up in his eyes. Say,
"I'm sorry. I don't know what it means to be
the lover of another man."
Hear him say,
"It's just like a wife, only the commitment is   35
deeper because the odds against you are so much
greater."
Say nothing, but
take his hand like a brother's.

Drive to Mexico for unproven drugs that might   40
help him live longer.
Explain what they are to the border guard.
Fill with rage when he informs you,
"You can't bring those across."
Begin to grow loud.   45
Feel the lover's hand on your arm
restraining you. See in the guard's eye
how much a man can hate another man.
Say to the lover, "How can you stand it?"
Hear him say, "You get used to it."   50
Think of one of your children getting used to
another man's hatred.

Call your wife on the telephone. Tell her,
"He hasn't much time.
I'll be home soon." Before you hang up say,   55
"How could anyone's commitment be deeper than
a husband and wife?" Hear her say,
"Please. I don't want to know all the details."

When he slips into an irrevocable coma,
hold his lover in your arms while he sobs,   60
no longer strong. Wonder how much longer
you will be able to be strong.
Feel how it feels to hold a man in your arms
whose arms are used to holding men.
Offer God anything to bring your brother back.   65
Know you have nothing God could possibly want.
Curse God, but do not
abandon Him.

Stare at the face of the funeral director
when he tells you he will not   70
embalm the body for fear of
contamination. Let him see in your eyes
how much a man can hate another man.

Stand beside a casket covered in flowers,
white flowers. Say,   75
"Thank you for coming," to each of several hundred
    men
who file past in tears, some of them
holding hands. Know that your brother's life
was not what you imagined. Overhear two   80
mourners say, "I wonder who'll be next?" and
"I don't care anymore,
as long as it isn't you."

Arrange to take an early flight home.
His lover will drive you to the airport.   85
When your flight is announced say,
awkwardly, "If I can do anything, please
let me know." Do not flinch when he says,
"Forgive yourself for not wanting to know him
after he told you. He did."   90
Stop and let it soak in. Say,
"He forgave me, or he knew himself?"
"Both," the lover will say, not knowing what else
to do. Hold him like a brother while he
kisses you on the cheek. Think that   95
you haven't been kissed by a man since
your father died. Think,
"This is no moment not to be strong."

Fly first class and drink Scotch. Stroke
your split eyebrow with a finger and   100
think of your brother alive. Smile
at the memory and think
how your children will feel in your arms,
warm and friendly and without challenge.

STUDY QUESTIONS

1. How do the last five lines tie the details and emotions of the poem together?

2. Explain the final two words of the poem.

Joseph Bruchac

Publisher of the *Greenfield Review*, poet, novelist, editor, and anthologist, Joseph Bruchac was born in Saratoga Springs, New York, in 1942 of Slovakian and Abenaki (Native American) heritage. He did not wander too far away to go to college, earning a B.A. from Cornell University and an M.A. from Syracuse University. He still lives in nearby Greenfield Center, New York. He is the author of five collections of traditional Abenaki and Iroquois tales, two novels, fourteen collections of poetry, and two books of nonfiction, among them *Entering Onandaga, Turkey Brother*, and *There Are No Trees Inside the Prison.*

ELLIS ISLAND

Beyond the red brick of Ellis Island
where the two Slovak children
who became my grandparents
waited the long days of quarantine,
after leaving the sickness,   5
the old Empires of Europe,
a Circle Line ship slips easily
on its way to the island
of the tall woman, green
as dreams of forests and meadows   10
waiting for those who'd worked
a thousand years
yet never owned their own.

Like millions of others,
I too come to this island,   15
nine decades the answerer
of dreams.

Yet only one part of my blood loves that memory.
Another voice speaks
of native lands   20

within this nation.
Lands invaded
when the earth became owned.
Lands of those who followed
the changing Moon,   25
knowledge of the seasons
in their veins.

STUDY QUESTIONS

1. Who is the "tall woman" (line 9)?

2. Why is Ellis Island referred to in lines 16–17 as "nine decades the answerer / of dreams"?

3. What part of the SPEAKER's heritage seems the more desirable?

Alice Childress

Her 1955 play *Trouble in Mind* won an Obie Award and her novel *A Hero Ain't Nothing but a Sandwich* was nominated for both the Newbery Medal and the National Book Award, yet Alice Childress (born in Charleston, South Carolina, in 1920) still seems relatively neglected. Her work, *Happy Birthday Mrs. Craig*, a video-recording which presents five generations of a black family and their role in the American experience, was published in 1990. She died in August 1994.

Wedding Band is set in 1918, during World War I, when, after decades of Jim Crow racist laws, blacks expected that their service in the war would earn them greater rights at war's end. The play was first performed (at the University of Michigan) in 1966, in the middle of the Vietnam War and just after the passage of the Civil Rights Act of 1965, which raised similar hopes for the future of racial harmony and justice in America. It was performed in New York, directed by the author and Joseph Papp, in 1972 and the following year was on national television (ABC).

WEDDING BAND

A LOVE / HATE STORY IN BLACK AND WHITE

CHARACTERS
(In Order of Appearance)

JULIA AUGUSTINE

TEETA

MATTIE

LULA GREEN

FANNY JOHNSON

NELSON GREEN

THE BELL MAN

PRINCESS

HERMAN

ANNABELLE

HERMAN'S MOTHER

ACT I

Scene I

TIME: *Summer 1918 . . . Saturday morning. A city by the sea . . . South Carolina, U.S.A.*

SCENE: *Three houses in a backyard. The center house is newly painted and cheery looking in contrast to the other two which are weather-beaten and shabby. Center house is gingerbready . . . odds and ends of "picked up" shutters, picket railing, wrought iron railing, newel posts, a Grecian pillar, odd window boxes of flowers . . . everything clashes with a beautiful, subdued splendor; the old and new mingle in defiance of style and period. The playing areas of the houses are raised platforms furnished according to the taste of each tenant. Only one room of each house is visible.* JULIA AUGUSTINE *(tenant of the center house) has recently moved in and there is still unpacking to be done. Paths are worn from the houses to the front yard entry. The landlady's house and an outhouse are offstage. An outdoor hydrant supplies water.*

JULIA *is sleeping on the bed in the center house.* TEETA, *a girl about eight years old, enters the yard from the Stage Right house. She tries to control her weeping as she examines a clump of grass. The muffled weeping disturbs* JULIA'S *sleep. She starts up, half rises from her pillow, then falls back into a troubled sleep.* MATTIE, TEETA'S *mother, enters carrying a switch and fastening her clothing. She joins the little girl in the search for a lost quarter. The search is subdued, intense.*

MATTIE: You better get out there and get it! Did you find it? Gawd, what've I done to be treated this way! You gon' get a whippin' too.

FANNY: [*Enters from the front entry. She is landlady and the self-appointed, fifty-year-old representative of her race.*] Listen, Mattie . . . I want some quiet out here this mornin'.

MATTIE: Dammit, this gal done lost the only quarter I got to my name.

    [LULA *enters from the direction of the outhouse carrying a covered slop jar. She is forty-five and motherly.*]

    "Teeta," I say, "Go to the store, buy three cent grits, five cent salt pork, ten cent sugar; and keep your hand closed 'roun' my money." How I'm gonna sell any candy if I got no sugar to make it? You little heifer! [*Goes after* TEETA *who hides behind* LULA.]

LULA: Gawd, help us to find it.

MATTIE: Your daddy is off sailin' the ocean and you got nothin' to do but lose money! *I'm gon' put you out in the damn street, that's what!*

    [TEETA *cries out.* JULIA *sits up in the bed and cries out.*]

JULIA: No . . . no . . .

FANNY: You disturbin' the only tenant who's paid in advance.

LULA: Teeta, retrace your steps. Show Lula what you did.

TEETA: I hop-hop-hop . . . [*Hops near a post-railing of* JULIA's *porch.*]

MATTIE: What the hell you do that for?

LULA: There 'tis! That's a quarter . . . down in the hole . . . Can't reach it . . .

    [JULIA *is now fully awake. Putting on her house-dress over her camisole and petticoat.* MATTIE *takes an axe from the side of the house to knock the post out of the way.*]

MATTIE: Aw, *move*, move! That's all the money I got. I'll tear this damn house down and you with it!

FANNY: And I'll blow this police whistle.

    [JULIA *steps out on the porch. She is an attractive brown woman about thirty-five years old.*]

MATTIE: Blow it . . . blow it . . . blow it . . . hot damn—[*Near tears. She decides to tell* JULIA *off also.*] I'll tear it down—that's right. If you don't like it—come on down here and whip me.

JULIA: [*Nervous but determined to present a firm stand.*] Oh, my . . . Good mornin' ladies. My name is Julia Augustine. I'm not gonna move.

LULA: My name is Lula. Why you think we wantcha to move?

FANNY: Miss Julia, I'm sorry your first day starts like this. Some people are ice cream and others just cow-dung. I try to be ice cream.

MATTIE: Dammit, I'm ice cream, too. Strawberry. [*Breaks down and cries.*]

FANNY: That's Mattie. She lost her last quarter, gon' break down my house to get it.

JULIA: [*Gets a quarter from her dresser.*] Oh my, dear heart, don't cry. Take this twenty-five cents, Miss Mattie.

MATTIE: No thank you, ma'm.

JULIA: And I have yours under my house for good luck.

FANNY: Show your manners.

TEETA: Thank you. You the kin'est person in the worl'.

   [LULA *enters her house.* TEETA *starts for home, then turns to see if her mother is coming.*]

MATTIE: [*To* JULIA.] I didn't mean no harm. But my husband October's in the Merchant Marine and I needs my little money. Well, thank you. [*To* TEETA.] Come on, honey bunch.

   [*She enters her house Stage Right.* TEETA *proudly follows.* LULA *is putting* NELSON's *breakfast on the table at Stage Left.*]

FANNY: [*Testing strength of post.*] My poor father's turnin' in his grave. He built these rent houses just 'fore he died . . . And he wasn't a carpenter. Shows what the race can do when we wanta. [*Feels the porch railing and tests its strength.*] That loud-mouth Mattie used to work in a white cathouse.

JULIA: A what?

FANNY: Sportin' house, house of . . . A whore house. Know what she used to do?

JULIA: [*Embarrassed.*] Not but so many things *to* do, I guess.

   [FANNY *wants to follow her in the house but* JULIA *fends her off.*]

FANNY: Used to wash their joy-towels. Washin' joy-towels for one cent apiece. I wouldn't work in that kinda place—would you?

JULIA: Indeed not.

FANNY: Vulgarity.

JULIA: [*Trying to get away.*] I have my sewing to do now, Miss Fanny.

FANNY: I got a lovely piece-a blue serge. Six yards. [*She attempts to get into the house but* JULIA *deftly blocks the door.*]

JULIA: I don't sew for people. [FANNY *wonders why not.*] I do homework for a store . . . hand-finishin' on ladies' shirt-waists.

FANNY: You 'bout my age . . . I'm thirty-five.

JULIA: [*After a pause.*] I thought you were younger.

FANNY: [*Genuinely moved by the compliment.*] Thank you. But I'm not married 'cause nobody's come up to my high standard. Where you get them expensive-lookin', high-class shoes?

JULIA: In a store. I'm busy now, Miss Fanny.

FANNY: Doin' what?

JULIA: First one thing then another. Good-day.

   [*Thinks she has dismissed her. Goes in the house.* FANNY *quickly follows into the room . . . picks up a teacup from the table.*]

FANNY: There's a devil in your teacup . . . also prosperity. Tell me 'bout yourself, don't be so distant.

JULIA: It's all there in the tea-leaves.

FANNY: Oh, go on! I'll tell you somethin' . . . that sweet-face Lula killed her only child.

JULIA: No, she didn't.

FANNY: In a way-a speakin'. And then Gawd snatched up her triflin' husband. One nothin' piece-a man. Biggest thing he ever done for her was to lay down and die. Poor woman. Yes indeed, then she went and adopted this fella from the colored orphan home. Boy grew too big for a lone woman to keep in the house. He's a big, strappin', over-grown man now. I wouldn't feel safe livin' with a man that's not blood kin, 'doption or no 'doption. It's 'gainst nature. Oughta see the muscles on him.

JULIA: [Wearily.] Oh, my . . . I think I hear somebody callin' you.

FANNY: Yesterday the white-folks threw a pail-a dirty water on him. A black man on leave got no right to wear his uniform in public. The crackers don't like it. That's flauntin' yourself.

JULIA: Miss Fanny, I don't talk about people.

FANNY: Me neither. [Giving her serious advice.] We high-class, quality people oughta stick together.

JULIA: I really do stay busy.

FANNY: Doin' what? Seein' your beau? You have a beau haven't-cha?

JULIA: [Realizing she must tell her something in order to get rid of her.] Miss Johnson . . .

FANNY: Fanny.

JULIA: [Managing to block her toward the door.] My mother and father have long gone on to Glory.

FANNY: Gawd rest the dead and bless the orphan.

JULIA: Yes, I do have a beau . . . But I'm not much of a mixer. [She now has FANNY out on the porch.]

FANNY: Get time, come up front and see my parlor. I got a horsehair settee and a four piece, silver-plated tea service.

JULIA: Think of that.

FANNY: The first and only one to be owned by a colored woman in the United States of America. Salesman told me.

JULIA: Oh, just imagine.

[MATTIE enters wearing a blue calico dress and striped apron.]

FANNY: My mother was a genuine, full-blooded, qualified, Seminole Indian.

TEETA: [Calls to her mother from the doorway.] Please . . . Mama . . . Mama . . . Buy me a hair ribbon.

MATTIE: All right! I'm gon' buy my daughter a hair ribbon.

FANNY: Her hair is so short you'll have to nail it on. [FANNY exits to her house.]

MATTIE: That's all right about that, Fanny. Your father worked in a stinkin' phosphate mill . . . yeah, and didn't have a tooth in his head. Then he went and married some half Portuguese woman. I don't call that bein' in no damn society. I works for my livin'. I makes candy and I takes care of a little white girl. Hold this nickel 'til I get back. Case of emergency I don't like Teeta to be broke.

JULIA: I'll be busy today, lady.

MATTIE: [*As she exits carrying a tray of candy.*] Thank you, darlin'.

TEETA: Hey lady, my daddy helps cook food on a big war boat. He peels potatoes. You got any children?

JULIA: No . . . Grace-a Gawd. [*Starts to go in house.*]

TEETA: Hey, lady! Didja ever hear of Philadelphia? After the war that's where we're goin' to live. Philadelphia!

JULIA: Sounds like heaven.

TEETA: Jesus is the President of Philadelphia.

> [TEETA *sweeps in front of* JULIA'*s house. Lights come up in* LULA'*s house.* NELSON *is eating breakfast. He is a rather rough-looking muscly fellow with a soft voice and a bittersweet sense of humor. He is dressed in civilian finery and his striped silk shirt seems out of place in the drab little room.* LULA *makes paper flowers, and the colorful bits of paper are seen everywhere as finished and partially finished flowers and stems, also a finished funeral piece. A picture of Abraham Lincoln hangs on the upstage wall.* LULA *is brushing* NELSON'*s uniform jacket.*]

LULA: Last week the Bell Man came to collect the credit payment he says . . . "Auntie, whatcha doin' with Abraham Lincoln's pitcher on the wall? He was such a poor president."

NELSON: Tell the cracker to mind his damn business.

LULA: It don't pay to get mad. Remember yesterday.

NELSON: [*Studying her face for answers.*] Mama, you supposed to get mad when somebody throw a pail-a water on you.

LULA: It's their country and their uniform, so just stay out the way.

NELSON: Right. I'm not goin' back to work in that coal-yard when I get out the army.

LULA: They want you back. A bird in the hand, y'know.

NELSON: A bird in the hand ain't always worth two in the bush.

LULA: This is Saturday, tomorrow Sunday . . . thank Gawd for Monday; back to the army. That's one thing . . . Army keeps you off the street.

> [*The sound of the* SHRIMP MAN *passing in the street.*]

SHRIMP MAN: [*Offstage.*] Shrimp-dee-raw . . . I got raw shrimp.

> [NELSON *leaves the house just as* JULIA *steps out on her porch to hang a rug over the rail.* TEETA *enters* GREEN *house.*]

NELSON: Er . . . howdy-do, er . . . beg pardon. My name is Nelson. Lula Green's son, if you don't mind. Miss . . . er . . . Mrs.?

JULIA: [*After a brief hesitation.*] Miss . . . Julia Augustine.

NELSON: Miss Julia, you the best-lookin' woman I ever seen in my life. I declare you look jus' like a violin sounds. And I'm not talkin' 'bout pretty. You look like you got all the right feelin's, you know?

JULIA: Well, thank you, Mr. Nelson.

NELSON: See, you got me talkin' all outta my head.

> [LULA *enters,* TEETA *follows eating a biscuit and carrying a milk pail . . . she exits toward street.*]

Let's got for a walk this evenin', get us a lemon phosphate.

JULIA: Oh, I don't care for any, Mr. Nelson.

LULA: That's right. She say stay home.

JULIA: [*To* NELSON.] I'm sorry.

NELSON: Don't send me back to the army feelin' bad 'cause you turn me down. Orange-ade tonight on your porch. I'll buy the oranges, you be the sugar.

JULIA: No, thank you.

NELSON: Let's make it—say—six o'clock.

JULIA: No, I said no!

LULA: Nelson, go see your friends. [*He waves goodbye to* JULIA *and exits through the back entry.*] He's got a lady friend, her name is Merrilee Jones. And he was just tryin' to be neighborly. That's how me and Nelson do. But you go on and stay to yourself. [*Starts toward her house.*]

JULIA: Miss Lula! I'm sorry I hurt your feelin's. Miss Lula! I have a gentleman friend, that's why I said no.

LULA: I didn't think-a that. When yall plan to cut the cake?

JULIA: Not right now. You see . . . when you offend Gawd you hate for it to be known. Gawd might forgive but people never will. I mean . . . when a man and a woman are not truly married . . .

LULA: Oh, I see.

JULIA: I live by myself . . . but he visits . . . I declare I don't know how to say . . .

LULA: Everybody's got some sin, but if it troubles your heart you're a gentle sinner, just a good soul gone wrong.

JULIA: That's a kind thought.

LULA: My husband, Gawd rest the dead, used to run 'round with other women; it made me kind-a careless with my life. One day, many long years ago, I was sittin' in a neighbor's house tellin' my troubles; my only child, my little boy, wandered out on the railroad track and got killed.

JULIA: That must-a left a fifty pound weight on your soul.

LULA: It did. But if we grow stronger . . . and rise higher than what's pullin' us down . . .

JULIA: Just like Climbin' Jacob's Ladder . . . [*Sings.*] Every round goes higher and higher . . .

LULA: Yes, rise higher than the dirt . . . that fifty pound weight will lift and you'll be free, free without anybody's by-your-leave. Do something to wash out the sin. That's why I got Nelson from the orphanage.

JULIA: And now you feel free?

LULA: No, no yet. But I believe Gawd wants me to start a new faith; one that'll make our days clear and easy to live. That's what I'm workin' on now. Oh, Miss Julia, I'm glad you my neighbor.

JULIA: Oh, thank you, Miss Lula! Sinners or saints, didn't Gawd give us a beautiful day this mornin'!

[*The sound of cow-bells clanking and the thin piping of a tin and paper flute.* TEETA *backs into the yard carefully carrying the can of milk.* THE BELL MAN *follows humming "Over There" on the flute. He is a poor white about thirty years old but time has dealt him some hard blows. He carries a large suitcase; the American flag painted on both sides, cowbells are attached.* THE BELL MAN *rests his case on the ground. Fans with a very tired-looking handkerchief. He cuts the fool by dancing and singing a bit of a popular song as he turns corners around the yard.*]

THE BELL MAN: [*As* LULA *starts to go in the house.*] Stay where you at, Aunty! You used to live on Thompson Street. How's old Thompson Street?

JULIA: [*A slightly painful memory.*] I moved 'bout a year ago, moved to Queen Street.

THE BELL MAN: Move a lot, don'tcha? [*Opens suitcase.*] All right, everybody stay where you at! [*Goes into a fast sales spiel.*] Lace-trim ladies' drawers! Stockin's, ladies stockin's . . . gottem for the knock-knees and the bow-legs too . . . white, black and navy blue! All right, no fools no fun! The joke's on me! Here we go! [*As he places some merchandise in front of the* WOMEN, *does a regular minstrel walk-around.*] Anything in the world . . . fifty cent a week and one long, sweet year to pay . . . Come on, little sister!

[TEETA *doing the walk-around with* THE BELL MAN.]

And a-ring-ting-tang
And-a shimmy-she-bang
While the sun am a-shinin' and the sky am blue . . .
And a-ring-ting-tang
And-a shimmy-she-bang
While the sun am a-shinin' and the sky am blue . . .

LULA: [*Annoyed with* TEETA's *dancing with* THE BELL MAN.] Stop all that shimmy she-bang and get in the house! [*Swats at* TEETA *as she passes.*]

THE BELL MAN: [*Coldly.*] Whatcha owe me, Aunty?

LULA: Three dollars and ten cent. I don't have any money today.

THE BELL MAN: When you gon' pay?

LULA: Monday, or better say Wednesday.

JULIA: [*To divert his attention from* LULA.] How much for sheets?

THE BELL MAN: For you they on'y a dollar.

[JULIA *goes to her house to get the money.* THE BELL MAN *moves toward her house as he talks to* LULA.]

Goin' to the Service Men's parade Monday?

LULA: Yes sir. My boy's marchin'. [*She exits.*]

THE BELL MAN: Uh-huh, I'll getcha later. Lord, Lord, Lord, how'dja like to trot 'round in the sun beggin' the poorest people in the world to buy somethin' from you. This is nice. Real nice. [*To* JULIA.] A good friend-a mine was a nigra boy. Me 'n' him was jus' like that. Fine fella, he couldn't read and he couldn't write.

JULIA: [*More to herself than to him.*] When he learns you're gon' lose a friend.

THE BELL MAN: But talkin' serious, what is race and color? Put a paper bag over your head and who'd know the difference. Tryin' to remember me ain'tcha. I seen you one time coming out that bakery shop on Thompson Street, didn' see me.

JULIA: Is that so?

THE BELL MAN: [*Sits on the bed and bounces up and down.*] Awwww, Great Gawd-a-mighty! I haven't been on a high-built bed since I left the back woods.

JULIA: Please don't sit on my bed!

THE BELL MAN: Old country boy, that's me! Strong and healthy country boy . . . [*Not noticing any rejection.*] Sister, Um in need for it like I never been before. Will you 'commodate me? Straighten me, fix me up, will you? Wouldn't take but five minutes. Um quick like a jack rabbit. Wouldn't nobody know but you and me.

[*She backs away from him as he pants and wheezes out his admiration.*]

Um clean, too. Clean as the . . . Board-a Health. Don't believe in dip-pin' inta everything. I got no money now, but Ladies always need stock-in's.

JULIA: [*Trying to keep her voice down, throws money at his feet.*] Get out of my house! Beneath contempt, that's what you are.

THE BELL MAN: Don't be lookin' down your nose at me . . . actin' like you Mrs. Martha Washington . . . Throwin' one chicken-shit dollar at me and goin' on . . .

JULIA: [*Picking up wooden clothes hanger.*] Get out! Out, before I take a stick to you.

THE BELL MAN: [*Bewildered, gathering his things to leave.*] Hell, what I care who you sleep with! It's your nooky. Give it 'way how you want to. I don't own no run-down bakery shop but I'm good as those who do. A baker ain' nobody . . .

JULIA: I wish you was dead, you just oughta be dead, stepped on and dead.

THE BELL MAN: Bet that's what my mama said first time she saw me. I was a fourteenth child. Damn women! . . . that's all right . . . Gawd bless you, Gawd be with you and let his light shine on you. I give you good for evil . . . God bless you! [*As he walks down the porch steps.*] She must be goin' crazy. Unfriendly, sick-minded bitch!

[TEETA *enters from* LULA'*s house.* THE BELL MAN *takes a strainer from his pocket and gives it to* TEETA *with a great show of generosity.*]

Here, little honey. You take this sample. You got nice manners.

TEETA: Thank you, you the kin'est person in the world.

[THE BELL MAN *exits to the tune of clanking bells, and* LULA *enters.*]

JULIA: I hate those kind-a people.

LULA: You mustn't hate white folks. Don'tcha believe in Jesus? He's white.

JULIA: I wonder if he believes in me.

LULA: Gawd says we must love everybody.

JULIA: Just lovin' and lovin', no matter what? There are days when I love, days when I hate.

FANNY: Mattie, Mattie, mail!

JULIA: Your love is worthless if nobody wants it.

[FANNY *enters carrying a letter. She rushes over to Mattie's house.*]

FANNY: I had to pay the postman two cent. No stamp.

TEETA: [*Calls to* JULIA.] Letter from Papa! Gimmie my mama's five cents!

FANNY: [*To* TEETA.] You gon' end your days in the Colored Women's Jail-house.

[PRINCESS, *a little girl, enters skipping and jumping. She hops, runs and leaps across the yard.* PRINCESS *is six years old.* TEETA *takes money from* JULIA's *outstretched hand and gives it to* FANNY.]

TEETA: [*To* MATTIE.] Letter from Papa! Gotta pay two cent!

FANNY: Now I owe you three cent . . . or do you want me to read the letter?
[PRINCESS *gets wilder and wilder, makes Indian war whoops.* TEETA *joins the noise-making. They climb porches and play follow-the-leader.* PRINCESS *finally lands on* JULIA's *porch after peeping and prying into everything along the way.*]

PRINCESS: [*Laughing merrily.*] Hello . . . hello . . . hello.

JULIA: [*Overwhelmed by the confusion.*] Well—hello.

FANNY: Get away from my new tenant's porch!

PRINCESS: [*Is delighted with* FANNY's *scolding and decides to mock her.*] My new tennis porch!
[MATTIE *opens the letter and removes a ten-dollar bill. Lost in thought she clutches the letter to her bosom.*]

FANNY: [*To* MATTIE.] Ought-a mind w-h-i-t-e children on w-h-i-t-e property!

PRINCESS: [*Now swinging on* JULIA's *gate.*] . . . my new tennis porch!

FANNY: [*Chases* PRINCESS *around the yard.*] You Princess! Stop that!
[JULIA *laughs but she is very near tears.*]

MATTIE: A letter from October.

FANNY: Who's gon' read it for you?

MATTIE: Lula!

PRINCESS: My new tennis porch!

FANNY: Princess! Mattie!

MATTIE: Teeta! In the house with that drat noise!

FANNY: It'll take Lula half-a day. [*Snatches letter.*] I won't charge but ten cent.
[*Reads.*] "Dear, Sweet Molasses, My Darlin' Wife . . ."

MATTIE: No, I don't like how you make words sound. You read too rough.
[*Sudden offstage yells and screams from* TEETA *and* PRINCESS *as they struggle for possession of some toy.*]

PRINCESS: [*Offstage.*] Give it to me!

TEETA: No! It's mine!

MATTIE: [*Screams.*] Teeta! [*The* CHILDREN *are quiet.*]

FANNY: Dear, Sweet Molasses—how 'bout that?

JULIA: [*To* FANNY.] Stop that! Don't read her mail.

FANNY: She can't read it.

JULIA: She doesn't want to. She's gonna go on holdin' it in her hand and never know what's in it . . just 'cause it's hers!

FANNY: Forgive 'em Father, they know not.

JULIA: Another thing, you told me it's quiet here! You call this quiet? I can't stand it!

FANNY: When you need me come and humbly knock on my *back* door. [*She exits.*]

MATTIE: [*Shouts to* FANNY.] I ain't gonna knock on no damn back door! Miss Julia, can you read? [*Offers the letter to* JULIA.] I'll give you some candy when I make it.

JULIA: [*Takes the letter.*] All right.

[LULA *takes a seat to enjoy a rare social event. She winds stems for the paper flowers as* JULIA *reads.*]

Dear, sweet molasses, my darlin' wife.

MATTIE: Yes, honey. [*To* JULIA.] Thank you.

JULIA: [*Reads.*] Somewhere, at sometime, on the high sea, I take my pen in hand . . . well, anyway, this undelible pencil.

LULA: Hope he didn't put it in his mouth.

JULIA: [*Reads.*] I be missin' you all the time.

MATTIE: And we miss you.

JULIA: [*Reads.*] Sorry we did not have our picture taken.

MATTIE: Didn't have the money.

JULIA: [*Reads.*] Would like to show one to the men and say this is my wife and child . . . They always be showin' pictures.

MATTIE: [*Waves the ten-dollar bill.*] I'm gon' send you one, darlin'.

JULIA: [*Reads.*] I recall how we used to take a long walk on Sunday afternoon . . . [*Thinks about this for a moment.*] . . . then come home and be lovin' each other.

MATTIE: I recall.

JULIA: [*Reads.*] The Government people held up your allotment.

MATTIE: Oh, do Jesus.

JULIA: [*Reads.*] They have many papers to be sign, pink, blue and white also green. Money can't be had 'til all papers match. Mine don't match.

LULA: Takes a-while.

JULIA: [*Reads.*] Here is ten cash dollars I hope will not be stole.

MATTIE: [*Holds up the money.*] I got it.

JULIA: [*Reads.*] Go to Merchant Marine office and push things from your end.

MATTIE: Monday. Lula, le's go Monday.

LULA: I gotta see Nelson march in the parade.

JULIA: [*Reads.*] They say people now droppin' in the street, dying' from this war-time influenza. Don't get sick—buy tonic if you do. I love you.

MATTIE: Gotta buy a bottle-a tonic.

JULIA: [*Reads.*] Sometimes people say hurtful things 'bout what I am, like color and race . . .

MATTIE: Tell 'em you my brown-skin Carolina daddy, that's who the hell you are. Wish I was there.

JULIA: [*Reads.*] I try not to hear 'cause I do want to get back to your side. Two

things a man can give the woman he loves . . . his name and his protection
. . . The first you have, the last is yet to someday come. The war is here,
the road is rocky. I am *ever* your lovin' husband, October.
MATTIE: So-long, darlin'. I wish I had your education.
JULIA: I only went through eighth grade. Name and protection. I know you
love him.
MATTIE: Yes'm I do. If I was to see October in bed with another woman, I'd
never doubt him 'cause I trust him more than I do my own eyesight. Bet
yall don't believe me.
JULIE: I know how much a woman can love. [*Glances at the letter again.*] Two
things a man can give . . .
MATTIE: Name and protection. That's right, too. I wouldn't live with no man.
Man got to marry me. Man that won't marry you thinks nothin' of you.
Just usin' you.
JULIA: I've never allowed anybody to *use* me!
LULA: [*Trying to move her away Stage Right.*] Mattie, look like rain.
MATTIE: A man can't use a woman less she let him.
LULA: [*To* MATTIE.] You never know when to stop.
JULIA: Well, I read your letter. Good day.
MATTIE: Did I hurtcha feelin's? Tell me, what'd I say.
JULIA: I—I've been keepin' company with someone for a long time and . . .
we're not married.
MATTIE: For how long?
LULA: [*Half-heartedly tries to hush* MATTIE *but she would also like to know.*] Ohhh,
Mattie.
JULIA: [*Without shame*]. Ten years today, ten full, faithful years.
MATTIE: He got a wife?
JULIA: [*Very tense and uncomfortable.*] No.
MATTIE: Oh, a man don't wanta get married, work on him. Cut off piece-a
his shirt-tail and sew it to your petticoat. It works. Get Fanny to read the
tea leaves and tell you how to move. She's a old bitch but what she sees in
a teacup is true.
JULIA: Thank you, Mattie.
LULA: Let's pray on it, Miss Julia. Gawd bring them together, in holy matri-
mony.
JULIA: Miss Lula, please don't . . . You know it's against the law for black
and white to get married, so Gawd nor the tea leaves can help us. My
friend is white and that's why I try to stay to myself.
[*After a few seconds of silence.*]
LULA: Guess we shouldn't-a disturbed you.
JULIA: But I'm so glad you did. Oh, the things I can tell you 'bout bein'
lonesome and shut-out. Always movin', one place to another, lookin' for
some peace of mind. I moved out in the country . . . Pretty but quiet as
the graveyard; so lonesome. One year I was in such a *lovely* colored neighborhood but they couldn't be bothered with me, you know? I've lived near

sportin' people . . . they were very kindly but I'm not a sporty type person. Then I found this place hid way in the backyard so quiet, didn't see another soul . . . And that's why I thought yall wanted to tear my house down this mornin' . . . 'cause you might-a heard 'bout me and Herman . . . and some people are . . . well, they judge, they can't help judgin' you.

MATTIE: [*Eager to absolve her of wrong doing.*] Oh, darlin', we all do things we don't want sometimes. You grit your teeth and take all he's got; if you don't somebody else will.

LULA: No, no, you got no use for 'em so don't take nothin' from 'em.

MATTIE: He's takin' somethin' from her.

LULA: Have faith, you won't starve.

MATTIE: Rob him blind. Take it all. Let him froth at the mouth. Let him die in the poorhouse—bitter, bitter to the gone!

LULA: A white man is somethin' else. Everybody knows how that low-down slave master sent for a different black woman every night . . . for his pleasure. That's why none of us is the same color.

MATTIE: And right now today they're mean, honey. They can't help it; their nose is pinched together so close they can't get enough air. It makes 'em mean. And their mouth is set back in their face so hard and flat . . . no roundness, no sweetness, they can't even carry a tune.

LULA: I couldn't stand one of 'em to touch me intimate no matter what he'd give me.

JULIA: Miss Lula, you don't understand. Mattie, the way you and your husband feel that's the way it is with me 'n' Herman. He loves me . . . We love each other, that's all, we just love each other. [*After a split second of silence.*] And someday, as soon as we're able, we have to leave here and go where it's right . . . Where it's legal for everybody to marry. That's what we both want . . . to be man and wife—like you and October.

LULA: Well I have to cut out six dozen paper roses today. [*Starts for her house.*]

MATTIE: And I gotta make a batch-a candy and look after Princess so I can feed me and Teeta 'til October comes back. Thanks for readin' the letter. [*She enters her house.*]

JULIA: But Mattie, Lula—I wanted to tell you why it's been ten years—and why we haven't—

LULA: Good day, Miss Julia. [*Enters her house.*]

JULIA: Well, that's always the way. What am I doing standin' in a backyard explainin' my life? Stay to yourself, Julia Augustine. Stay to yourself. [*Sweeps her front porch.*]

> I got to climb my way to glory
> Got to climb it by myself
> Ain't nobody here can climb it for me
> I got to climb it for myself.

Curtain.

Scene 2

TIME: *That evening. Cover closed Scene 1 curtain with song and laughter from* MAT-
TIE, LULA *and* KIDS.

    As curtain opens, JULIA *has almost finished the unpacking. The room now looks quite cozy. Once in a while she watches the clock and looks out of the window.* TEETA *follows* PRINCESS *out of* MATTIE'*s house and ties her sash.* PRINCESS *is holding a jump-rope.*

[MATTIE *offstage. Sings.*]

My best man left me, it sure do grieve my mind
When I'm laughin', I'm laughin' to keep from cryin' . . .

PRINCESS: [*Twirling the rope to one side.*] Ching, ching, China-man eat dead
    rat . . .
TEETA: [*As* PRINCESS *jumps rope.*] Knock him in the head with a baseball bat . . .
PRINCESS: You wanta jump?
TEETA: Yes.
PRINCESS: Say "Yes, M'am."
TEETA: No.
PRINCESS: Why?
TEETA: You too little.
PRINCESS: [*Takes bean bag from her pocket.*] You can't play with my bean bag.
TEETA: I 'on care, play it by yourself.
PRINCESS: [*Drops rope, tosses the bag to* TEETA.] Catch.
    [TEETA *throws it back.* HERMAN *appears at the back-entry. He is a strong, forty-year-old working man. His light brown hair is sprinkled with gray. At the present moment he is tired.* PRINCESS *notices him because she is facing the back fence. He looks for a gate or opening but can find none.*]
    Hello.
TEETA: Mama! Mama!
HERMAN: Hello, children. Where's the gate?
    [HERMAN *passes several packages through a hole in the fence; he thinks of climbing the fence but it is very rickety. He disappears from view.* MATTIE *dashes out of her house, notices the packages, runs into* LULA'*s house, then back into the yard.* LULA *enters in a flurry of excitement; gathers a couple of pieces from the clothes-line.* MATTIE *goes to inspect the packages.*]
LULA: Don't touch 'em, Mattie. Might be dynamite.
MATTIE: Well, I'm gon' get my head blowed off, 'cause I wanta see.
    [NELSON *steps out wearing his best civilian clothes; neat fitting suit, striped silk shirt and bulldog shoes in ox-blood leather. He claps his hands to frighten* MAT-
TIE.]
MATTIE: Oh, look at him. Where's the party?
NELSON: Everywhere! The ladies have heard Nelson's home. They waitin'
    for me!

LULA: Don't get in trouble. Don't answer anybody that bothers you.

NELSON: How come it is that when I carry a sack-a coal on my back you don't worry, but when I'm goin' out to enjoy myself you almost go crazy.

LULA: Go on! Deliver the piece to the funeral.

[*Hands him a funeral piece.* MATTIE *proceeds to examine the contents of a paper bag.*]

NELSON: Fact is, I was gon' stay home and have me some orange drink, but Massa beat me to it. None-a my business no-how, dammit.

[MATTIE *opens another bag.* HERMAN *enters through the front entry.* FANNY *follows at a respectable distance.*]

MATTIE: Look, rolls and biscuits!

LULA: Why'd he leave the food in the yard?

HERMAN: Because I couldn't find the gate. Good evening. Pleasant weather. Howdy do. Cool this evenin'. [*Silence.*] Err—I see where the Allies suffered another set-back yesterday. Well, that's the war, as they say.

[*The* WOMEN *answer with nods and vague throat clearings.* JULIA *opens her door, he enters.*]

MATTIE: That's the lady's husband. He's a light colored man.

PRINCESS: What is a light colored man?

[CHILDREN *exit with* MATTIE *and* NELSON. FANNY *exits by front entry,* LULA *to her house.*]

JULIA: Why'd you pick a conversation? I tell you 'bout that.

HERMAN: Man gotta say somethin' stumblin' round in a strange back yard.

JULIA: Why didn't you wear your good suit? You know how people like to look you over and sum you up.

HERMAN: Mama and Annabelle made me so damn mad tonight. When I got home Annabelle had this in the window. [*Removes a cardboard sign from the bag . . . printed with red, white and blue crayon . . .* WE ARE AMERICAN CITIZENS . . .]

JULIA: We are American Citizens. Why'd she put it in the window?

HERMAN: Somebody wrote cross the side of our house in purple paint . . . "Krauts . . . Germans live here"! I'd-a broke his arm if I caught him.

JULIA: It's the war. Makes people mean. But didn't she print it pretty.

HERMAN: Comes from Mama boastin' 'bout her German grandfather, now it's no longer fashionable. I snatched that coward sign outta the window . . . Goddamit, I says . . . Annabelle cryin', Mama hollerin' at her. Gawd save us from the ignorance, I say . . . Why should I see a sign in the window when I get home? That Annabelle got flags flyin' in the front yard, the backyard . . . and red, white and blue flowers in the grass . . . confound nonsense . . . Mama is an ignorant woman . . .

JULIA: Don't say that . . .

HERMAN: A poor ignorant woman who is mad because she was born a sharecropper . . . outta her mind 'cause she ain't high class society. We're redneck crackers, I told her, that's what.

JULIA: Oh, Herman . . . no you didn't . . .

HERMAN: I did.

JULIA: [*Standing.*] But she raised you . . . loaned you all-a-her three thousand dollars to pour into that bakery shop. You know you care about her.

HERMAN: Of course I do. But sometimes she makes me so mad . . . Close the door, lock out the world . . . all of 'em that ain't crazy are coward. [*Looks at sign.*] Poor Annabelle—Miss War-time Volunteer . . .

JULIA: She's what you'd call a very Patriotic Person, wouldn't you say?

HERMAN: Well, guess it is hard for her to have a brother who only makes pies in time of war.

JULIA: A brother who makes pies and loves a nigger!

HERMAN: Sweet Kerist, there it is again!

JULIA: Your mama's own words . . . according to you—I'll never forget them as long as I live. Annabelle, you've got a brother who makes pies and loves a nigger.

HERMAN: How can you remember seven or eight years ago, for Gawd's sake? Sorry I told it.

JULIA: I'm not angry, honeybunch, dear heart. I just remember.

HERMAN: When you say honeybunch, you're angry. Where do you want your Aunt Cora?

JULIA: On my dresser!

HERMAN: An awful mean woman.

JULIA: Don't get me started on your mama and Annabelle. [*Pause.*]

HERMAN: Julia, why did you move into a backyard?

JULIA: [*Goes to him.*] Another move, another mess. Sometimes I feel like fightin' . . . and there's nobody to fight but you . . .

HERMAN: Open the box. Go on. Open it.

JULIA: [*Opens the box and reveals a small but ornate wedding cake with a bride and groom on top and ten pink candles.*] Ohhh, it's the best one ever. Tassels, bells, roses . . .

HERMAN: . . . Daffodils and silver sprinkles . . .

JULIA: You're the best baker in the world.

HERMAN: [*As she lights the candles.*] Because you put up with me . . .

JULIA: Gawd knows that.

HERMAN: . . . because the palms of your hands and the soles of your feet are pink and brown . . .

JULIA: Jus' listen to him. Well, go on.

HERMAN: Because you're a good woman, a kind, good woman.

JULIA: Thank you very much, Herman.

HERMAN: Because you care about me.

JULIA: Well, I do.

HERMAN: Happy ten years . . . Happy tenth year.

JULIA: And the same to you.

[HERMAN *tries a bit of soft barbershop harmony.*]

I love you as I never loved before [JULIA *joins him.*]
When first I met you on the village green

Come to me ere my dream of love is o'er
I love you as I loved you
When you were sweet—Take the end up higher—
When you were su-weet six-ateen.
Now blow!

[*They blow out the candles and kiss through a cloud of smoke.*]

JULIA: [*Almost forgetting something.*] Got something for you. Because you were my only friend when Aunt Cora sent me on a sleep-in job in the white-folks kitchen. And wasn't that Miss Bessie one mean white woman? [*Gives present to* HERMAN.]

HERMAN: Oh, Julia, just say she was mean.

JULIA: Well yes, but she was white too.

HERMAN: A new peel, thank you. A new pastry bag. Thank you.

JULIA: [*She gives him a sweater.*] I did everything right but one arm came out shorter.

HERMAN: That's how I feel. Since three o'clock this morning, I turned out twenty ginger breads, thirty sponge cakes, lady fingers, Charlotte Russe . . . loaf bread, round bread, twist bread and water rolls . . . and—

JULIA: Tell me about pies. Do pies!

HERMAN: Fifty pies. Open apple, closed apple, apple-crumb, sweet potato and pecan. And I got a order for a large wedding cake. They want it in the shape of a battleship. [HERMAN *gives* JULIA *ring box.* JULIA *takes out a wide, gold wedding band—it is strung on a chain.*] It's a wedding band . . . on a chain . . . To have until such time as . . . It's what you wanted, Julia. A damn fool present.

JULIA: Sorry I lost your graduation ring. If you'd-a gone to college what do you think you'd-a been?

HERMAN: A baker with a degree.

JULIA: [*Reads.*] Herman and Julia 1908 . . . and now it's . . . 1918. Time runs away. A wedding band . . . on a chain. [*She fastens the chain around her neck.*]

HERMAN: A damn fool present. [JULIA *drops the ring inside of her dress.*]

JULIA: It comforts me. It's your promise. You hungry?

HERMAN: No.

JULIA: After the war, the people across the way are goin' to Philadelphia.

HERMAN: I hear it's cold up there. People freeze to death waitin' for a trolley car.

JULIA: [*Leans back beside him, rubs his head.*] In the middle of the night a big bird flew cryin' over this house—then he was gone, the way time goes flyin' . . .

HERMAN: Julia, why did you move in a back yard? Out in the country the air was so sweet and clean. Makes me feel shame . . .

JULIA: [*Rubbing his back.*] Crickets singin' that lonesome evenin' song. Any kind-a people better than none a-tall.

HERMAN: Mama's beggin' me to hire Greenlee again, to help in the shop, "Herman, sit back like a half-way gentleman and just take in money."

JULIA: Greenlee! When white-folks decide . . .

HERMAN: People, Julia, people.

JULIA: When people decide to give other people a job, they come up with the biggest Uncle Tom they can find. The *people* I know call him a "white-folks-nigger." It's a terrible expression so don't you ever use it.

HERMAN: He seems dignified, Julia.

JULIA: Jus' 'cause you're clean and stand straight, that's not dignity. Even speakin' nice might not be dignity.

HERMAN: What's dignity? Tell me. Do it.

JULIA: Well, it . . . it . . . It's a feeling—It's a spirit that rises higher than the dirt around it, without any by-your-leave. It's not proud and it's not 'shamed . . . Dignity "Is" . . . and it's never Greenlee . . . I don't know if it's us either, honey.

HERMAN: [*Standing.*] It still bothers my mother that I'm a baker. "When you gonna rise in the world!" A baker who rises . . . [*Laughs and coughs a little.*] Now she's worried 'bout Annabelle marryin' a sailor. After all, Annabelle is a concert pianist. She's had only one concert . . . in a church . . . and not many people there.

JULIA: A sailor might just persevere and become an admiral. Yes, an admiral and a concert pianist.

HERMAN: Ten years. If I'd-a known what I know now, I wouldn't-a let Mama borrow on the house or give me the bakery.

JULIA: Give what? Three broken stoves and all-a your papa's unpaid bills.

HERMAN: I *got* to pay her back. And I can't go to Philadelphia or wherever the hell you're saying to go. I can hear you thinkin', Philadelphia, Philadelphia, Phil . . .

JULIA: [*Jumping up. Pours wine.*] Oh damnation! The hell with that!

HERMAN: All right, not so much hell and damn. When we first met you were so shy.

JULIA: Sure was, wouldn't say "dog" 'cause it had a tail. In the beginnin' nothin' but lovin' and kissin' . . . and thinkin' 'bout you. Now I worry 'bout gettin' old. I do. Maybe you'll meet somebody younger. People do get old, y'know. [*Sits on bed.*]

HERMAN: There's an old couple 'cross from the bakery . . . "Mabel," he yells, "where's my keys!" . . . Mabel has a big behind on her. She wears his carpet slippers. "All right, Robbie, m'boy," she says . . . Robbie walks kinda one-sided. But they're havin' a pretty good time. We'll grow old together both of us havin' the same name. [*Takes her in his arms.*] Julia, I love you . . . you know it . . . I love you . . . [*After a pause.*] Did you have my watch fixed?

JULIA: [*Sleepily.*] Uh-huh, it's in my purse. [*Getting up.*] Last night when the bird flew over the house—I dreamed 'bout the devil's face in the fire . . . He said "I'm comin' to drag you to hell."

HERMAN: [*Sitting up.*] There's no other hell, honey. Celestine was sayin' the other day—

JULIA: How do you know what Celestine says?

HERMAN: Annabelle invited her to dinner.

JULIA: They still trying to throw that white widow-woman at you? Oh, Herman, I'm gettin' mean . . . jumpin' at noises . . . and bad dreams.

HERMAN: [*Brandishing bottle.*] Dammit, this is the big bird that flew over the house!

JULIA: I don't go anywhere, I don't know anybody, I gotta do somethin'. Sometimes I need to have company—to say . . . "Howdy-do, pleasant evenin'," do drop in." Sometimes I need other people. How you ever gonna pay back three thousand dollars? Your side hurt?

HERMAN: Schumann came in to see me this mornin'. Says he'll buy me out, ten cents on the dollar, and give me a job bakin' for him . . . it's an offer—can get seventeen hundred cash.

JULIA: Don't do it. Herman. That sure wouldn't be dignity.

HERMAN: He makes an American flag outta gingerbread. But they sell. Bad taste sells. Julia, where do you want to go? New York, Philadelphia, where? Let's try their dignity. Say where you want to go.

JULIA: Well, darlin', if folks are freezin' in Philadelphia, we'll go to New York.

HERMAN: Right! You go and size up the place. Meanwhile I'll stay here and do like everybody else, make war money . . . battleship cakes, cannon-ball cookies . . . chocolate bullets . . . they'll sell. Pay my debts. Less than a year, I'll be up there with money in my pockets.

JULIA: Northerners talk funny—"We're from New Yorrrk."

HERMAN: I'll getcha train ticket next week.

JULIA: No train. I wanta stand on the deck of a Clyde Line boat, wavin' to the people on the shore. The whistle blowin', flags flyin' . . . wavin' my handkerchief . . . So long, so long, look here—South Carolina . . . so long, hometown . . . goin' away by myself—[*Tearfully blows her nose.*]

HERMAN: You gonna like it. Stay with your cousin and don't talk to strangers. [JULIA *gets dress from her hope chest.*]

JULIA: Then, when we do get married we can have a quiet reception. My cut glass punch bowl . . . little sandwiches, a few friends . . . Herman? Hope my weddin' dress isn't too small. It's been waitin' a good while. [*Holds dress in front of her.*] I'll use all of my hope chest things. Quilts, Irish linens, the silver cups . . . Oh, Honey, how are you gonna manage with me gone?

HERMAN: Buy warm underwear and a woolen coat with a fur collar . . . to turn against the northern wind. What size socks do I wear?

JULIA: Eleven, eleven and a half if they run small.

HERMAN: . . . what's the store? Write it down.

JULIA: Coleridge. And go to King Street for your shirts.

HERMAN: Coleridge. Write it down.

JULIA: Keep payin' Ruckheiser, the tailor, so he can start your new suit.

HERMAN: Ruckheiser. Write it down.

JULIA: Now that I know I'm goin' we can take our time.

HERMAN: No, rush, hurry, make haste, do it. Look at you . . . like your old self.

JULIA: No, no, not yet—I'll go soon as we get around to it. [*Kisses him.*]

HERMAN: That's right. Take your time . . .

JULIA: Oh, Herman.

> [MATTIE *enters through the back gate with* TEETA. *She pats and arranges* TEE-TA's *hair.* FANNY *enters from the front entry and goes to* JULIA's *window.*]

MATTIE: You goin' to Lula's service?

FANNY: A new faith. Rather be a Catholic than somethin' you gotta make up. Girl, my new tenant and her—

MATTIE: [*Giving* FANNY *the high-sign to watch what she says in front of* TEETA.] . . . and her husband.

FANNY: I gotcha. She and her husband was in there havin' a orgy. Singin', laughin', screamin', crying' . . . I'd like to be a fly on that wall.

> [LULA *enters the yard wearing a shawl over her head and a red band on her arm. She carries two chairs and places them beside two kegs.*]

LULA: Service time!

> [MATTIE, TEETA *and* FANNY *enter the yard and sit down.* LULA *places a small table and a cross.*]

FANNY: [*Goes to* JULIA's *door and knocks.*] Let's spread the word to those who need it. [*Shouts.*] Miss Julia, don't stop if you in the middle-a somethin'. We who love Gawd are gatherin' for prayer. Got any time for Jesus?

ALL: [*Sing.*] When the roll is called up yonder.

JULIA: Thank you, Miss Fanny.

> [FANNY *flounces back to her seat in triumph.* JULIA *sits on the bed near* HERMAN.]

HERMAN: Dammit, she's makin' fun of you.

JULIA: [*Smooths her dress and hair.*] Nobody's invited me anywhere in a long time . . . so I'm goin'.

HERMAN: [*Standing.*] I'm gonna buy you a Clyde Line ticket for New York City on Monday . . . this Monday.

JULIA: Monday?

HERMAN: As Gawd is my judge. That's dignity. Monday.

JULIA: [*Joyfully kissing him.*] Yes, Herman! [*She enters yard.*]

LULA: My form-a service opens with praise. Let us speak to Gawd.

MATTIE: Well, I thang Gawd that—that I'm livin' and I pray my husband comes home safe.

TEETA: I love Jesus and Jesus loves me.

ALL: Amen.

FANNY: I thang Gawd that I'm able to rise spite-a-those who try to hold me down, spite-a those who are two-faceted, spite-a those in my own race who jealous 'cause I'm doin' so much better than the rest of 'em. He pre-parest a table for me in the presence of my enemies. Double-deal Fanny Johnson all you want but me 'n' Gawd's gonna come out on top.

> [ALL *look to* JULIA.]

JULIA: I'm sorry for past sin—but from Monday on through eternity—I'm gonna live in dignity accordin' to the laws of God and man. Oh, Glory!

LULA: Glory Halleluhjah!

[NELSON *enters a bit unsteadily . . . struts and preens while singing.*]

NELSON: Come here black woman . . . whoooo . . . eee . . . on daddy's knee . . . etc.

LULLA: [*Trying to interrupt him.*] We're testifyin' . . .

NELSON: [*Throwing hat on porch.*] Right! Testify! Tonight I asked the prettiest girl in Carolina to be my wife; and Merrilee Jones told me . . . I'm sorry but you got nothin' to offer. She's right! I got nothin' to offer but a hard way to go. Merrilee Jones . . . workin' for the rich white folks and better off washin' their dirty drawers than marryin' me.

LULA: Respect the church! [*Slaps him.*]

NELSON: [*Sings.*] Come here, black woman (*etc.*) . . .

JULIA: Oh, Nelson, respect your mother!

NELSON: Respect your damn self, Julia Augustine! [*Continues singing.*]

LULA: How we gonna find a new faith?

NELSON: [*Softly.*] By tellin' the truth, Mama. Merrilee ain't no liar. I got nothin' to offer, just like October.

MATTIE: You keep my husband's name outta your mouth.

NELSON: [*Sings.*] Come here, black woman . . .

FANNY AND CONGREGATION: [*Sing.*]

> Ain't gon let nobody turn me round, turn me round,
>   turn me round
> Ain't gon let nobody turn me round . . .

HERMAN: [*Staggers out to porch.*] Julia, I'm going now, I'm sorry . . . I don't feel well . . . I don't know . . . [*Slides forward and falls.*]

JULIA: Mr. Nelson . . . won'tcha please help me . . .

FANNY: Get him out of my yard.

[NELSON AND JULIA *help* HERMAN *in to bed. Others freeze in yard.*]

ACT II

Scene 1

TIME: *Sunday morning.*

SCENE: *The same as Act One except the yard and houses are neater. The clothes line is down. Off in the distance someone is humming a snatch of a hymn. Church bells are ringing.* HERMAN *is in a heavy, restless sleep. The bed covers indicate he has spent a troubled night. On the table Downstage Right are medicine bottles, cups and spoons.*

JULIA *is standing beside the bed, swinging a steam kettle; she stops and puts it on a trivet on top of her hope chest.*

FANNY: [*Seeing her.*] Keep usin' the steam-kettle.
 [HERMAN *groans lightly.*]
MATTIE: [*Picks up scissors.*] Put the scissors under the bed, open, It'll cut the pain.
FANNY: [*Takes scissors from* MATTIE.] That's for childbirth.
JULIA: He's had too much paregoric. Sleepin' his life away. I want a doctor.
FANNY: Over my dead body. It's against the damn law for him to be layin' up in a black woman's bed.
MATTIE: A doctor will call the police.
FANNY: They'll say I run a bad house.
JULIA: I'll tell 'em the truth.
MATTIE: We don't tell things to police.
FANNY: When Lula gets back with his sister, his damn sister will take charge.
MATTIE: That's his family.
FANNY: Family is family.
JULIA: I'll hire a hack and take him to a doctor.
FANNY: He might die on you. That's police. That's the work-house.
JULIA: I'll say I found him on the street!
FANNY: Walk into the jaws of the law—they'll chew you up.
JULIA: Suppose his sister won't come?
FANNY: She'll be here. [FANNY *picks up a teacup and turns it upside down on the saucer and twirls it.*] I see a ship, a ship sailin' on the water.
MATTIE: Water clear or muddy?
FANNY: Crystal clear.
MATTIE: [*Realizing she's late.*] Oh, I gotta get Princess so her folks can open their ice cream parlor. Take care-a Teeta.
FANNY: I see you on your way to Miami, Florida, goin' on a trip.
JULIA: [*Sitting on window seat.*] I know you want me to move. I will, Fanny.
FANNY: Julia, it's hard to live under these mean white-folks . . . but I've done it. I'm the first and only colored they let buy land' round here.
JULIA: They all like you, Fanny. Only one of 'em cares for me . . . just one.
FANNY: Yes, I'm thought highly of. When I pass by they can say . . . "There she go, Fanny Johnson, representin' her race in-a approved manner" . . . 'cause they don't have to worry 'bout my next move. I can't afford to mess that up on account-a you or any-a the rest-a these hard-luck, better-off-dead, triflin' niggers.
JULIA: [*Crossing up Right.*] I'll move. But I'm gonna call a doctor.
FANNY: Do it, we'll have a yellow quarantine sign on the front door . . . "INFLUENZA." Doctor'll fill out papers for the law . . . address . . . race . . .
JULIA: I . . . I guess I'll wait until his sister gets here.
FANNY: No, you call a doctor, Nelson won't march in the parade tomorrow

or go back to the army, Mattie'll be outta work, Lula can't deliver flowers . . .

JULIA: I'm sorry, so very sorry. I'm the one breakin' laws, doin' wrong.

FANNY: I'm not judgin' you. High or low, nobody's against this if it's kept quiet. But when you pickin' white . . . pick a wealthy white. It makes things easier.

JULIA: No, Herman's not rich and I've never tried to beat him out of anything.

FANNY: [*Crossing to* JULIA.] Well, he just ought-a be and you just should-a. A colored woman needs money more than anybody else in this world.

JULIA: You sell yours.

FANNY: All I don't sell I'm going to keep.

HERMAN: Julia?

FANNY: [*Very genial.*] Well, well, sir, how you feelin', Mr. Herman? This is Aunt Fanny . . . Miss Julia's landlady. You lookin' better, Mr. Herman. We've been praying for you. [FANNY *exits to* TEETA's *house.*]

JULIA: Miss Lula—went to get your sister.

HERMAN: Why?

JULIA: Fanny made me. We couldn't wake you up.

[*He tries to sit up in bed to prepare for leaving. She tries to help him. He falls back on the pillow.*]

HERMAN: Get my wallet . . . see how much money is there. What's that smell?

[*She takes the wallet from his coat pocket. She completes counting the money.*]

JULIA: Eucalyptus oil, to help you breathe; I smell it, you smell it and Annabelle will have to smell it too! Seventeen dollars.

HERMAN: A boat ticket to New York is fourteen dollars—Ohhh, Kerist! Pain . . . pain . . . Count to ten . . . one, two . . . [JULIA *gives paregoric water to him. He drinks. She puts down glass and picks up damp cloth from bowl on tray and wipes his brow.*] My mother is made out of too many . . . little things . . . the price of carrots, how much fat is on the meat . . . little things make people small. Make ignorance—y'know?

JULIA: Don't fret about your people, I promise I won't be surprised at anything and I won't have unpleasant words no matter what.

HERMAN: [*The pain eases. He is exhausted.*] Ahhh, there . . . All men are born which is—utterly untrue.

[NELSON *steps out of the house. He is brushing his army jacket.* HERMAN *moans slightly.* JULIA *gets her dress-making scissors and opens them, places the scissors under the bed.*]

FANNY: [*To* NELSON *as she nods towards* JULIA's *house.*] I like men of African descent, myself.

NELSON: Pitiful people. They pitiful.

FANNY: They common. Only reason I'm sleepin' in a double bed by myself is 'cause I got to bear the standard for the race. I oughta run her outta here for the sake-a the race too.

NELSON: It's your property. Run us all off it, Fanny.

FANNY: Plenty-a these hungry, jobless, bad-luck colored men, just-a itchin' to move in on my gravy-train. I don't want 'em.

NELSON: [*With good nature.*] Right, Fanny! We empty-handed, got nothin' to offer.

FANNY: But I'm damn tired-a ramblin' round in five rooms by myself. House full-a new furniture, the icebox forever full-a goodies. I'm a fine cook and I know how to pleasure a man . . . he wouldn't have to step outside for a thing . . . food, fun and finance . . . all under one roof. Nelson, how'd you like to be my business advisor? Fix you up a little office in my front parlor. You wouldn't have to work for white folks . . . and Lula wouldn't have to pay rent. The war won't last forever . . . then what you gonna do? They got nothin' for you but haulin' wood and cleanin' toilets. Let's you and me pitch in together.

NELSON: I know you just teasin', but I wouldn't do a-tall. Somebody like me ain't good enough for you no-way, but you a fine-lookin' woman, though. After the war I might hit out for Chicago or Detroit . . . a rollin' stone gathers no moss.

FANNY: Roll on. Just tryin' to help the race.

    [LULA *enters by front entry, followed by* ANNABELLE, *a woman in her thirties. She assumes a slightly mincing air of fashionable delicacy. She might be graceful if she were not ashamed of her size. She is nervous and fearful in this strange atmosphere. The others fall silent as they see her,* ANNABELLE *wonders if* PRINCESS *is her brother's child. Or could it be* TEETA, *or both?*]

ANNABELLE: Hello there . . . er . . . children.

PRINCESS: [*Can't resist mocking her.*] Hello there, er . . . children. [*Giggles.*]

ANNABELLE: [*To* TEETA.] Is she your sister? [ANNABELLE *looks at* NELSON *and draws her shawl a little closer.*]

TEETA: You have to ask my mama.

NELSON: [*Annoyed with* ANNABELLE'S *discomfort.*] Mom, where's the flat-iron? [*Turns and enters his house.* LULA *follows.* MATTIE *and* CHILDREN *exit.*]

FANNY: I'm the landlady. Mr. Herman had every care and kindness 'cept a doctor. Miss Juliaaaa! That's the family's concern. [FANNY *opens door, then exits.*]

ANNABELLE: Sister's here. It's Annabelle.

JULIA: [*Shows her to a chair.*] One minute he's with you, the next he's gone. Paregoric makes you sleep.

ANNABELLE: [*Dabs at her eyes with a handkerchief.*] Cryin' doesn't make sense a-tall. I'm a volunteer worker at the Naval hospital . . . I've nursed my mother . . . [*Chokes with tears.*]

JULIA: [*Pours a glass of water for her.*] Well, this is more than sickness. It's not knowin' 'bout other things.

ANNABELLE: We've known for years. He is away all the time and when old Uncle Greenlee . . . He's a colored gentleman who works in our neighborhood . . . and he said . . . he told . . . er, well, people do talk. [ANNABELLE

spills water, JULIA *attempts to wipe the water from her dress.*] Don't do that . . .
It's all right.

HERMAN: Julia?

ANNABELLE: Sister's here. Mama and Uncle Greenlee have a hack down the
street. Gets a little darker we'll take you home, call a physician . . .

JULIA: Can't you do it right away?

ANNABELLE: 'Course you could put him out. Please let us wait 'til dark.

JULIA: Get a doctor.

ANNABELLE: Our plans are made, thank you.

HERMAN: Annabelle, this is Julia.

ANNABELLE: Hush.

HERMAN: This is my sister.

ANNABELLE: Now be still.

JULIA: I'll call Greenlee to help him dress.

ANNABELLE: No. Dress first. The colored folk in *our* neighborhood have great
respect for us.

HERMAN: Because I give away cinnamon buns, for Kerist sake.

ANNABELLE: [*To* JULIA.] I promised my mother I'd try and talk to you. Now—
you look like one-a the nice coloreds . . .

HERMAN: Remember you are a concert pianist, that is a very dignified calling.

ANNABELLE: Put these on. We'll turn our backs.

JULIA: He can't.

ANNABELLE: [*Holds the covers in a way to keep his midsection under wraps.*] Hold
up. [*They manage to get the trousers up as high as his waist but they are twisted
and crooked.*] Up we go! There . . . [*They are breathless from the effort of lifting
him.*] Now fasten your clothing.

    [JULIA *fastens his clothes.*]

    I declare, even a dead man oughta have enough pride to fasten himself.

JULIA: You're a volunteer at the Naval hospital?

HERMAN: [*As another pain hits him.*] Julia, my little brown girl . . . Keep singing . . .

                                [JULIA.]
    We are climbin' Jacob's ladder, We are climbin' Jacob's ladder,
    We are climbin' Jacob's ladder, Soldiers of the Cross . . .

HERMAN: The palms of your hands . . .

    [JULIA *singing*]
    Every round goes higher and higher . . .

HERMAN: . . . the soles of your feet are pink and brown.

ANNABELLE: Dammit, hush. Hush this noise. Sick or not sick, hush! It's ugliness. [*To* JULIA.] Let me take care of him, please, leave us alone.

JULIA: I'll get Greenlee.

ANNABELLE: No! You hear me? No.

JULIA: I'll be outside.

ANNABELLE: [*Sitting on bed.*] If she hadn't-a gone I'd-a screamed. [JULIA *stands on the porch.* ANNABELLE *cries.*] I thought so highly of you . . . and here you are in somethin' that's been festerin' for years. [*In disbelief.*] One of the finest women in the world is pinin' her heart out for you, a woman who's pure gold. Everything Celestine does for Mama she's really doin' for you . . . to get next to you . . . But even a Saint wants some reward.

HERMAN: I don't want Saint Celestine.

ANNABELLE: [*Standing.*] Get up! [*Tries to move* HERMAN.] At the Naval hospital I've seen influenza cases tied down to keep 'em from walkin'. What're we doin' here? How do you meet a black woman?

HERMAN: She came in the bakery on a rainy Saturday evening.

ANNABELLE: [*Giving in to curiosity.*] Yes?

MATTIE: [*Offstage. Scolding* TEETA *and* PRINCESS.] Sit down and drink that lemonade. Don't bother me!

HERMAN: "I smell rye bread baking." Those were the first words . . . Every day . . . Each time the bell sounds over the shop door I'm hopin' it's the brown girl . . . pretty shirt-waist and navy blue skirt. One day I took her hand . . . "Little lady, don't be afraid of me" . . . She wasn't. . . . I've never been lonesome since.

ANNABELLE: [*Holding out his shirt.*] Here, your arm goes in the sleeve. [*They're managing to get the shirt on.*]

HERMAN: [*Beginning to ramble.*] Julia? Your body is velvet . . . the sweet blackberry kisses . . . you are the night-time, the warm, Carolina night-time in my arms . . .

ANNABELLE: [*Bitterly.*] Most excitement I've ever had was takin' piano lessons.

JULIA: [*Calls from porch.*] Ready?

ANNABELLE: No. Rushin' us out. A little longer, please. [*Takes a comb from her purse and nervously combs his hair.*] You nor Mama put yourselves out to understand my Walter when I had him home to dinner. Yes, he's a common sailor . . . I wish he was an officer. I never liked a sailor's uniform, tight pants and middy blouses . . . but they are in the service of their country . . . He's taller than I am. You didn't even stay home that one Sunday like you promised. Must-a been chasin' after some-a them blackberry kisses you love so well. Mama made a jackass outta Walter. You know how she can do. He left lookin' liked a whipped dog. Small wonder he won't live down here. I'm crazy-wild 'bout Walter even if he is a sailor. Marry Celestine. She'll take care-a Mama and I can go right on up to the Brooklyn Navy Yard. I been prayin' so hard . . . You marry Celestine and set me free. And Gawd knows I don't want another concert.

HERMAN: [*Sighs.*] Pain, keep singing.

ANNABELLE: Dum-dum-blue Danube.

   [*He falls back on the pillow. She bathes his head with a damp cloth.*]

JULIA: [*As* NELSON *enters the yard.*] Tell your mother I'm grateful for her kindness. I appreciate . . .

NELSON: Don't have so much to say to me. [*Quietly, in a straightforward man-*

ner.] They set us on fire 'bout their women. String us up, pour on kerosene and light a match. Wouldn't I make a bright flame in my new uniform?

JULIA: Don't be thinkin' that way.

NELSON: I'm thinkin' 'bout black boys hangin' from trees in Little Mountain, Elloree, Winnsboro.

JULIA: Herman never killed anybody. I couldn't care 'bout that kind-a man.

NELSON: [*Stepping, turning to her.*] How can you account for carin' 'bout him a-tall?

JULIA: In that place where I worked, he was the only one who cared . . . who really cared. So gentle, such a gentle man . . . "Yes, Ma'am," . . . "No, Ma'am," "Thank you, Ma'am . . ." In the best years of my youth, my Aunt Cora sent me out to work on a sleep-in job. His shop was near that place where I worked. . . . Most folks don't have to *account* for why they love.

NELSON: You ain't most folks. You're down on the bottom with us, under his foot. A black man got nothin' to offer you . . .

JULIA: I wasn't lookin' for anybody to do for me.

NELSON: . . . and *he's* got nothin' to offer. The one layin' on your mattress, not even if he's kind as you say. He got nothin' for you . . . but some meat and gravy or a new petticoat . . . or maybe he can give you meriny-lookin' little bastard chirrun for us to take in and raise up. We're the ones who feed and raise 'em when it's like this . . . They don't want 'em. They only too glad to let us have their kin-folk. As it is, we supportin' half-a the slave-master's offspring right now.

JULIA: Go fight those who fight you. He never threw a pail-a water on you. Why didn't you fight them that did? Takin' it out on me 'n' Herman 'cause you scared of 'em . . .

NELSON: Scared? What scared! If I gotta die I'm carryin' one 'long with me.

JULIA: No you not. You gon' keep on fightin' me.

NELSON: . . . Scared-a what? I look down on 'em, I spit on 'em.

JULIA: No, you don't. They throw dirty water on your uniform . . . and you spit on me!

NELSON: Scared, what scared!

JULIA: You fightin' me, me, me, not them . . . never them.

NELSON: Yeah, I was scared and I'm tougher, stronger, a better man than any of 'em . . . but they won't letcha fight one or four or ten. I was scared to fight a hundred or a thousand. A losin' fight.

JULIA: I'd-a been afraid too.

NELSON: And you scared right now, you let the woman run you out your house.

JULIA: I didn't want to make trouble.

NELSON: But that's what a fight is . . . trouble.

LULA: [*In her doorway.*] Your mouth will kill you. [*To* JULIA.] Don't tell Mr. Herman anything he said . . . or I'll hurt you.

JULIA: Oh, Miss Lula.

LULA: Anyway, he didn't say nothin'.

[HERMAN'S MOTHER *enters the yard. She is a "poor white" about fifty-seven years old. She has risen above her poor farm background and tries to assume the airs of "quality." Her clothes are well-kept-shabby. She wears white shoes, a shirt-waist and skirt, drop earrings, a cameo brooch, a faded blue straw hat with a limp bit of veiling. She carries a heavy-black, oil-cloth bag. All in the yard give a step backward as she enters. She assumes an air of calm well-being. Almost as though visiting friends, but anxiety shows around the edges and underneath.* JULIA *approaches and* HERMAN'S MOTHER *abruptly turns to* MATTIE.]

HERMAN'S MOTHER: How do.

[MATTIE, TEETA *and* PRINCESS *look at* HERMAN'S MOTHER. HERMAN'S MOTHER *is also curious about them.*]

MATTIE: [*In answer to a penetrating stare from the old woman.*] She's mine. I take care-a her. [*Speaking her defiance by ordering the children.*] Stay inside 'fore y'all catch the flu!

HERMAN'S MOTHER: [*To* LULA.] You were very kind to bring word . . . er . . .

LULA: Lula, Ma'am.

HERMAN'S MOTHER: The woman who nursed my second cousin's children . . . she had a name like that . . . Lul*u* we called her.

LULA: My son, Nelson.

HERMAN'S MOTHER: Can see that.

[MATTIE *and the children exit.* FANNY *hurries in from the front entry. Is most eager to establish herself on the good side of* HERMAN'S MOTHER. *With a slight bow. She is carrying the silver tea service.*]

FANNY: Beg pardon, if I may be so bold, I'm Fanny, the owner of all this property.

HERMAN'S MOTHER: [*Definitely approving of* FANNY.] I'm . . . er . . . Miss Anna-belle's mother.

FANNY: My humble pleasure . . . er . . . Miss er . . .

HERMAN'S MOTHER: [*After a brief, thoughtful pause.*] Miss Thelma.

[*They move aside but* FANNY *makes sure others hear.*]

FANNY: Miss Thelma, this is not Squeeze-gut Alley. We're just poor, hum-ble, colored people . . . and everybody knows how to keep their mouth shut.

HERMAN'S MOTHER: I thank you.

FANNY: She wanted to get a doctor. I put my foot down.

HERMAN'S MOTHER: You did right. [*Shaking her head, confiding her troubles.*] Ohhhh, you don't know.

FANNY: [*With deep understanding.*] Ohhhh, yes, I do. She moved in on me yesterday.

HERMAN'S MOTHER: Friend Fanny, help me to get through this.

FANNY: I will. Now this is Julia, she's the one . . .

[HERMAN'S MOTHER *starts toward the house without looking at* JULIA. FANNY *decides to let the matter drop.*]

HERMAN'S MOTHER: [*To* LULA.] Tell Uncle Greenlee not to worry. He's holdin' the horse and buggy.

NELSON: [*Bars* LULA'*s way*.] Mama. I'll do it.

[LULA *exits into her house.* FANNY *leads her to the chair near* HERMAN'*s bed*.]

ANNABELLE: Mama, if we don't call a doctor Herman's gonna die.

HERMAN'S MOTHER: Everybody's gon' die. Just a matter of when, where and how. A pretty silver service.

FANNY: English china. Belgian linen. Have a cup-a tea?

HERMAN'S MOTHER: [*As a studied pronouncement*.] My son comes to deliver baked goods and the influenza strikes him down. Sickness, it's the war.

FANNY: [*Admiring her cleverness*.] Yes, Ma'am, I'm a witness. I saw him with the packages.

JULIA: Now please call the doctor.

ANNABELLE: Yes, please, Mama. No way for him to move 'less we pick him up bodily.

HERMAN'S MOTHER: Then we'll pick him up.

HERMAN: About Walter . . . your Walter . . . I'm sorry . . .

[JULIA *tries to give* HERMAN *some water*.]

HERMAN'S MOTHER: Annabelle, help your brother. [ANNABELLE *gingerly takes glass from* JULIA.] Get that boy to help us. I'll give him a dollar. Now gather his things.

ANNABELLE: What things?

HERMAN'S MOTHER: His possessions, anything he owns, whatever is his. What you been doin' in here all this time?

[FANNY *notices* JULIA *is about to speak, so she hurries her through the motions of going through dresser drawers and throwing articles into a pillow case*.]

FANNY: Come on, sugar, make haste.

JULIA: Don't go through my belongings.

[*Tears through the drawers, flinging things around as she tries to find his articles.* FANNY *neatly piles them together*.]

FANNY: [*Taking inventory*.] Three shirts . . . one is kinda soiled.

HERMAN'S MOTHER: That's all right, I'll burn 'em.

FANNY: Some new undershirts.

HERMAN'S MOTHER: I'll burn them too.

JULIA: [*To* FANNY.] Put 'em down. I bought 'em and they're not for burnin'.

HERMAN'S MOTHER: [*Struggling to hold her anger in check*.] Fanny, go get that boy. I'll give him fifty cents.

FANNY: You said a dollar.

HERMAN'S MOTHER: All right, dollar it is. [FANNY *exits toward the front entry. In tense, hushed, excited tones, they argue back and forth*.] Now where's the bill-fold . . . there's papers . . . identity . . . [*Looks in* HERMAN'*s coat pockets*.]

ANNABELLE: Don't make such-a to-do.

HERMAN'S MOTHER: You got any money of your own? Yes, I wanta know where's his money.

JULIA: I'm gettin' it.

HERMAN'S MOTHER: In her pocketbook. This is why the bakery can't make it.

HERMAN: I gave her the Gawd-damned money!

JULIA: And I know what Herman wants me to do . . .

HERMAN'S MOTHER: [*With a wry smile.*] I'm sure you know what he wants.

JULIA: I'm not gonna match words with you. Furthermore, I'm too much of a lady.

HERMAN'S MOTHER: A lady oughta learn how to keep her dress down.

ANNABELLE: Mama, you makin' a spectacle outta yourself.

HERMAN'S MOTHER: You a big simpleton. Men have nasty natures, they can't help it. A man would go with a snake if he only knew how. They cleaned out your wallet.

HERMAN: [*Shivering with a chill.*] I gave her the damn money.

[JULIA *takes it from her purse.*]

HERMAN'S MOTHER: Where's your pocket-watch or did you give that too? Annabelle, get another lock put on that bakery door.

HERMAN: I gave her the money to go—to go to New York.

[JULIA *drops the money in* HERMAN'S MOTHER'*s lap. She is silent for a moment.*]

HERMAN'S MOTHER: All right. Take it and go. It's never too late to undo a mistake. I'll add more to it. [*She puts the money on the dresser.*]

JULIA: I'm not goin' anywhere.

HERMAN'S MOTHER: Look here, girl, you leave him 'lone.

ANNABELLE: Oh, Mama, all he has to do is stay away.

HERMAN'S MOTHER: But he can't do it. Been years and he can't do it.

JULIA: I got him hoo-dooed, I sprinkle red pepper on his shirt-tail.

HERMAN'S MOTHER: I believe you.

HERMAN: I have a black woman . . . and I'm gon' marry her. I'm gon' marry her . . . got that? Pride needs a paper, for . . . for the sake of herself . . . that's dignity—tell me, what is dignity—Higher than the dirt it is . . . dignity is . . .

ANNABELLE: Let's take him to the doctor, Mama.

HERMAN'S MOTHER: When it's dark.

JULIA: Please!

HERMAN'S MOTHER: Nightfall. [JULIA *steps out on the porch but hears every word said in the room.*]

I had such high hopes for him. [*As if* HERMAN *is dead.*] All my high hopes. When he wasn't but five years old I had to whip him so he'd study his John C. Calhoun speech. Oh, Calhoun knew 'bout niggers. He said, "*MEN are not born* . . . *equal, or any other kinda way* . . . *MEN are made*" . . . Yes, indeed, for recitin' that John C. Calhoun speech . . . Herman won first mention and a twenty dollar gold piece . . . at the Knights of The Gold Carnation picnic.

ANNABELLE: Papa changed his mind about the Klan. I'm glad.

HERMAN'S MOTHER: Yes, he was always changin' his mind about somethin'. But I was proud-a my men-folk that day. He spoke that speech . . . The officers shook my hand. They honored me . . . "That boy a-yours gonna be somebody." A poor baker-son layin' up with a nigger woman, a over-grown daughter in heat over a common sailor. I must be payin' for somethin' I did. Yesiree, do a wrong, God'll ship you.

ANNABELLE: I wish it was dark.

HERMAN'S MOTHER: I put up with a man breathin' stale whiskey in my face every night . . . pullin' and pawin' at me . . . always tired, inside and out . . . [*Deepest confidence she has ever shared.*] Gave birth to seven . . . five-a them babies couldn't draw breath.

ANNABELLE: [*Suddenly wanting to know more about her.*] Did you love Papa, Mama? Did you ever love him? . . .

HERMAN'S MOTHER: Don't ask me 'bout love . . . I don't know nothin' about it. Never mind love. This is my harvest . . .

HERMAN: Go home. I'm better.

[HERMAN'S MOTHER'*s strategy is to enlighten* HERMAN *and also wear him down. Out on the porch,* JULIA *can hear what is being said in the house.*]

HERMAN'S MOTHER: There's something wrong 'bout mismatched things, be they shoes, socks, or people.

HERMAN: Go away, don't look at us.

HERMAN'S MOTHER: People don't like it. They're not gonna letcha do it in peace.

HERMAN: We'll go North.

HERMAN'S MOTHER: Not a thing will change except her last name.

HERMAN: She's not like others . . . she's not like that . . .

HERMAN'S MOTHER: All right, sell out to Schumann. I want my cash-money . . . You got no feelin' for me, I got none for you . . .

HERMAN: I feel . . . I feel what I feel . . . I don't know what I feel . . .

HERMAN'S MOTHER: Don't need to feel. Live by the law. Follow the law— law, law of the land. Obey the law!

ANNABELLE: We're not obeyin' the law. He should be quarantined right here. The city's tryin' to stop an epidemic.

HERMAN'S MOTHER: Let the city drop dead and you 'long with it. *Rather* be dead than disgraced. Your papa gimme the house and little money . . . I want my money back. [*She tries to drag* HERMAN *up in the bed.*] I ain't payin' for this. [*Shoves* ANNABELLE *aside.*] Let Schumann take over. A man who knows what he's doin'. Go with her . . . Take the last step against your own! Kill us all. Jesus, Gawd, save us or take us—

HERMAN: [*Screams.*] No! No! No! No!

HERMAN'S MOTHER: Thank Gawd, the truth is the light. Oh, Blessed Savior . . . [HERMAN *screams out, starting low and ever going higher. She tries to cover his mouth.* ANNABELLE *pulls her hand away.*] Thank you, Gawd, let the fire go out . . . this awful fire.

[LULA *and* NELSON *enter the yard.*]

ANNABELLE: You chokin' him. Mama . . .

JULIA: [*From the porch.*] It's dark! It's dark. Now it's very dark.

HERMAN: One ticket on the Clyde Line . . . Julia . . . where are you? Keep singing . . . count . . . one, two . . . three. Over there, over there . . . send the word, send the word . . .

HERMAN'S MOTHER: Soon be home, son.

> [HERMAN *breaks away from the men, staggers to* MATTIE'*s porch and holds on.* MATTIE *smothers a scream and gets the children out of the way.* FANNY *enters.*]

HERMAN: Shut the door . . . don't go out . . . the enemy . . . the enemy . . . [*Recites the Calhoun speech.*] Men are not born, infants are born! They grow to all the freedom of which the condition in which they were born permits. It is a great and dangerous error to suppose that all people are equally entitled to liberty.

JULIA: Go home— Please be still.

HERMAN: It is a reward to be earned, a reward reserved for the intelligent, the patriotic, the virtuous and deserving; and not a boon to be bestowed on a people too ignorant, degraded and vicious . . .

JULIA: You be still now, shut up.

HERMAN: . . . to be capable either of appreciating or of enjoying it.

JULIA: [*Covers her ears.*] Take him . . .

HERMAN: A black woman . . . not like the others . . .

JULIA: . . . outta my sight . . .

HERMAN: Julia, the ship is sinking . . .

> [HERMAN'S MOTHER *and* NELSON *help* HERMAN *up and out.*]

ANNABELLE: [*To* JULIA *on the porch.*] I'm sorry . . . so sorry it had to be this way. I can't leave with you thinkin' I uphold Herman, and blame you.

HERMAN'S MOTHER: [*Returning.*] You the biggest fool.

ANNABELLE: I say a man is responsible for his own behavior.

HERMAN'S MOTHER: And you, you oughta be locked up . . . workhouse . . . jail! Who you think you are!?

JULIA: I'm your damn daughter-in-law, you old bitch! The Battleship Bitch! The bitch who destroys with her filthy mouth. They could win the war with your killin' mouth. The son-killer, man-killer bitch . . . She's killin' him 'cause he loved me more than anybody in the world.

> [FANNY *returns.*]

HERMAN'S MOTHER: Better off . . . He's better off dead in his coffin than live with the likes-a you . . . black thing! [*She is almost backing into* JULIA'*s house.*]

JULIA: The black thing who bought a hot water bottle to put on your sick, white self when rheumatism threw you flat on your back . . . who bought flannel gowns to warm your pale, mean body. He never ran up and down King Street shoppin' for you . . . I bought what he took home to you . . .

HERMAN'S MOTHER: Lies . . . tear outcha lyin' tongue.

JULIA: . . . the lace curtains in your parlor . . . the shirt-waist you wearin'— I made them.

FANNY: Go on . . . I got her. [*Holds* JULIA.]

HERMAN'S MOTHER: Leave 'er go! The undertaker will have-ta unlock my hands off her black throat!

FANNY: Go on, Miss Thelma.

JULIA: Miss Thelma my ass! Her first name is Frieda. The Germans are here . . . in purple paint!

HERMAN'S MOTHER: Black, sassy nigger!

JULIA: Kraut, knuckle-eater, red-neck . . .

HERMAN'S MOTHER: Nigger whore . . . he used you for a garbage pail . . .

JULIA: White trash! Sharecropper! Let him die . . . let 'em all die . . . Kill him with your murderin' mouth—sharecropper bitch!

HERMAN'S MOTHER: Dirty black nigger . . .

JULIA: . . . If I wasn't black with all-a Carolina 'gainst me I'd be mistress of your house! [*To* ANNABELLE.] Annabelle, you'd be married livin' in Brooklyn, New York . . . [*To* HERMAN'S MOTHER.] . . . and I'd be waitin' on Frieda . . . cookin' your meals . . . waterin' that damn red white and blue garden!

HERMAN'S MOTHER: Dirty black bitch.

JULIA: Daughter of a bitch!

ANNABELLE: Leave my mother alone! She's old . . . and sick.

JULIA: But never sick enough to die . . . dirty ever-lasting woman.

HERMAN'S MOTHER: [*Clinging to* ANNABELLE, *she moves toward the front entry.*] I'm as high over you as Mount Everest over the sea. White reigns supreme . . . I'm white, you can't change that.

[*They exit.* FANNY *goes with them.*]

JULIA: Out! Out! Out! And take the last ten years-a my life with you and . . . when he gets better . . . keep him home. Killers, murderers . . . Kinsmen! Klansmen! Keep him home. [*To* MATTIE.] Name and protection . . . he can't gimme either one. [*To* LULA.] I'm gon' get down on my knees and scrub where they walked . . . what they touched . . . [*To* MATTIE.] . . . with brown soap . . . hot lye-water . . . scaldin' hot . . . [*She dashes into the house and collects an armful of bedding . . .*] Clean! . . . Clean the whiteness outta my house . . . clean everything . . . even the memory . . . no more love . . . Free . . . free to hate-cha for the rest-a my life. [*Back to the porch with her arms full.*] When I die I'm gonna keep on hatin' . . . I don't want any whiteness in my house. Stay out . . . out . . . [*Dumps the things in the yard.*] . . . out . . . out . . . out . . . and leave me to my black self!

Blackout.

Scene 2

TIME: *Early afternoon the following day.*

PLACE: *The same.*

In JULIA's *room, some of the hope chest things are spilled out on the floor, bedspread, linens, silver cups. The half-emptied wine decanter is in a prominent spot. A table is set up in the yard. We hear the distant sound of a marching band. The excite-*

ment of a special day is in the air. NELSON's *army jacket hangs on his porch.* LULA *brings a pitcher of punch to table.* MATTIE *enters with* TEETA *and* PRINCESS; *she is annoyed and upset in contrast to* LULA's *singing and gala mood. She scolds the children, smacks* TEETA's *behind.*

MATTIE: They was teasin' the Chinaman down the street 'cause his hair is braided. [*To* CHILDREN.] If he ketches you, he'll cook you with onions and gravy.

LULA: [*Inspecting* NELSON's *jacket.*] Sure will.

TEETA: Can we go play?

MATTIE: A mad dog might bite-cha.

PRINCESS: Can we go play?

MATTIE: No, you might step on a nail and get lockjaw.

TEETA: Can we go play?

MATTIE: Oh, go on and play! I wish a gypsy would steal both of 'em!
    [JULIA *enters her room.*]

LULA: What's the matter, Mattie?

MATTIE: Them damn fool people at the Merchant Marine don't wanta give me my 'lotment money.

JULIA: [*Steps out on her porch with deliberate, defiant energy. She is wearing her wedding dress . . . carrying a wine glass. She is over-demonstrating a show of carefree abandon and joy.*] I'm so happy! I never been this happy in all my life! I'm happy to be alive, alive and livin' for my people.

LULA: You better stop drinkin' so much wine. [LULA *enters her house.*]

JULIA: But if you got no feelin's they can't be hurt!

MATTIE: Hey, Julia, the people at the Merchant Marine say I'm not married to October.

JULIA: Getcha license, honey, show your papers. Some of us, thang Gawd, got papers!

MATTIE: I don't have none.

JULIA: Why? Was October married before?

MATTIE: No, but I was. A good for nothin' named Delroy . . . I hate to call his name. Was years 'fore I met October. Delroy used to beat the hell outta me . . . tried to stomp me, grind me into the ground . . . callin' me such dirty names . . . Got so 'til I was shame to look at myself in a mirror. I was glad when he run off.

JULIA: Where'd he go?

MATTIE: I don't know. Man at the office kept sayin' . . . "You're not married to October" . . . and wavin' me 'way like that.

JULIA: Mattie, this state won't allow divorce.

MATTIE: Well, I never got one.

JULIA: You shoulda so you could marry October. You have to be married to get his benefits.

MATTIE: We was married. On Edisto Island. I had a white dress and flowers

. . . everything but papers. We couldn't get papers. Elder Burns knew we was doin' best we could.

JULIA: You can't marry without papers.

MATTIE: What if your husband run off? And you got no money? Readin' from the Bible makes people married, not no piece-a paper. We're together eleven years, that oughta-a be legal.

JULIA: [*Puts down glass.*] No, it doesn't go that way.

MATTIE: October's out on the icy water, in the war-time, worryin' 'bout me 'n Teeta. I say he's my husband. Gotta pay Fanny, buy food. Julia, what must I do?

JULIA: I don't know.

MATTIE: What's the use-a so much-a education if you don't know what to do?

JULIA: You may's well just lived with October. Your marriage meant nothin'.

MATTIE: [*Standing angry.*] It meant somethin' to me if not to anybody else. It means I'm ice cream, too, strawberry. [MATTIE *heads for her house.*]

JULIA: Get mad with me if it'll make you feel better.

MATTIE: Julia, could you lend me two dollars?

JULIA: Yes, that's somethin' I can do besides drink this wine.

[JULIA *goes into her room, to get the two dollars. Enter* FANNY, TEETA *and* PRINCESS.]

FANNY: Colored men don't know how to do nothin' right. I paid that big black boy cross the street . . . thirty cents to paint my sign . . . [*Sign reads* . . . GOODBYE COLORED BOYS . . . *on one side; the other reads* . . . FOR GOD AND CONTRY.] But he can't spell. I'm gon' call him a dumb darky and get my money back. Come on, children! [CHILDREN *follow laughing.*]

LULA: Why call him names!?

FANNY: 'Cause it makes him mad, that's why.

[FANNY *exits with* TEETA *and* PRINCESS. JULIA *goes into her room.* THE BELL MAN *enters carrying a display board filled with badges and flags . . . buttons, red and blue ribbons attached to the buttons . . . slogans . . .* THE WAR TO END ALL WARS. *He also carries a string of overseas caps (paper) and wears one. Blows a war tune on his tin flute.* LULA *exits.*]

BELL MAN: "War to end all wars . . ." Flags and badges! Getcha emblems! Hup-two-three . . . Flags and badges . . . hup-two-three! Hey, Aunty! Come back here! Where you at?

[*Starts to follow* LULA *into her house.* NELSON *steps out on the porch and blocks his way.*]

NELSON: My mother is in her house. You ain't to come walkin' in. You knock.

BELL MAN: Don't letcha uniform go to your head, Boy, or you'll end your days swingin' from a tree.

LULA: [*Squeezing past* NELSON *dressed in skirt and open shirt-waist.*] Please, Mister, he ain't got good sense.

MATTIE: He crazy, Mister.

NELSON: Fact is, you stay out of here. Don't ever come back here no more.

BELL MAN: [*Backing up in surprise.*] He got no respect. One them crazies. I ain't never harmed a bareassed soul but, hot damn, I can get madder and badder than you. Let your uniform go to your head.

LULA: Yessir, he goin' back in the army today.

BELL MAN: Might not get there way he's actin'.

MATTIE: [*As* LULA *takes two one dollar bills from her bosom.*] He sorry right now, Mister, his head ain' right.

BELL MAN: [*Speaks to* LULA *but keeps an eye on* NELSON.] Why me? I try to give you a laugh but they say, "Play with a puppy and he'll lick your mouth." Familiarity makes for contempt.

LULA: [*Taking flags and badges.*] Yessir. Here's somethin' on my account . . . and I'm buyin' flags and badges for the children. Everybody know you a good man and do right.

BELL MAN: [*To* LULA.] You pay up by Monday. [*To* NELSON.] Boy, you done cut off your Mama's credit.

LULA: I don't blame you, Mister. [BELL MAN *exits.*]

NELSON: Mama, your new faith don't seem to do much for you.

LULA: [*Turning to him.*] Nelson, go on off to the war 'fore somebody kills you. I ain't goin' to let nobody spoil my day.

> [LULA *puts flags and badges on punchbowl table.* JULIA *comes out of her room, with the two dollars for* MATTIE—*hands it to her. Sound of Jenkins Colored Orphan Band is heard (Record: "Ramblin" by Bunk Johnson).*]

JULIA: Listen, Lula . . . Listen, Mattie . . . it's Jenkin's Colored Orphan Band . . . Play! Play, you Orphan boys! Rise up higher than the dirt around you! Play! That's struttin' music, Lula!

LULA: It sure is!

> [LULA *struts, arms akimbo, head held high.* JULIA *joins her; they haughtily strut toward each other, then retreat with mock arrogance . . . exchange cold, hostile looks . . . A Carolina folk dance passed on from some dimly remembered African beginning. Dance ends strutting.*]

JULIA: [*Concedes defeat in the dance.*] All right, Lula, strut me down! Strut me right on down! [*They end dance with breathless laughter and cross to* LULA's *porch.*]

LULA: Julia! Fasten me! Pin my hair.

JULIA: I'm not goin' to that silly parade, with the colored soldiers marchin' at the end of it.

> [LULA *sits on the stool.* JULIA *combs and arranges her hair.*]

LULA: Come on, we'll march behind the white folks whether they want us or not. Mister Herman's people got a nice house . . . lemon trees in the yard, lace curtains at the window.

JULIA: And red, white and blue flowers all around.

LULA: That Uncle Greenlee seems to be well-fixed.

JULIA: He works for the livery stable . . . cleans up behind horses . . . in a uniform.

LULA: That's nice.

JULIA: Weeds their gardens . . . clips white people's pet dogs . . .

LULA: Ain't that lovely? I wish Nelson was safe and nicely settled.

JULIA: Uncle Greenlee is a well-fed, tale-carryin' son-of-a-bitch . . . and that's the only kind-a love they want from us.

LULA: It's wrong to hate.

JULIA: They say it's wrong to love too.

LULA: We got to show 'em we're good, got to be three times as good, just to make it.

JULIA: Why? When they mistreat us who cares? We mistreat each other, who cares? Why we gotta be so good jus' for them?

LULA: Dern you, Julia Augustine, you hard-headed thing, 'cause they'll kill us if we not.

JULIA: They doin' it anyway. Last night I dreamed of the dead slaves—all the murdered black and bloody men silently gathered at the foot-a my bed. Oh, that awful silence. I wish the dead could scream and fight back. What they do to us . . . and all they want is to be loved in return. Nelson's not Greenlee. Nelson is a fighter.

LULA: [*Standing.*] I know. But I'm tryin' to keep him from findin' it out.

[NELSON, *unseen by* LULA, *listens.*]

JULIA: Your hair looks pretty.

LULA: Thank you. A few years back I got down on my knees in the court-house to keep him off-a the chain gang. I crawled and cried, "Please white folks, yall's everything. I'se nothin, yall's everything." The court laughed— I meant for 'em to laugh . . . then they let Nelson go.

JULIA: [*Pitying her.*] Oh, Miss Lula, a lady's not supposed to crawl and cry.

LULA: I was savin' his life. Is my skirt fastened? Today might be the last time I ever see Nelson. [NELSON *goes back in house.*] Tell him how life's gon' be better when he gets back. Make up what *should* be true. A man can't fight a war on nothin' . . . would you send a man off—to die on nothin'?

JULIA: That's sin, Miss Lula, leavin' on a lie.

LULA: That's all right—some truth has no nourishment in it. Let him feel good.

JULIA: I'll do my best.

[MATTIE *enters carrying a colorful, expensive parasol. It is far beyond the price range of her outfit.*]

MATTIE: October bought it for my birthday 'cause he know I always wanted a fine-quality parasol.

[FANNY *enters through the back entry,* CHILDREN *with her. The mistake on the sign has been corrected by pasting OU over the error.*]

FANNY: [*Admiring* MATTIE'S *appearance.*] Just shows how the race can look when we wanta. I called Rusty Bennet a dumb darky and he wouldn't even get mad. Wouldn't gimme my money back either. A black Jew.

[NELSON *enters wearing his private's uniform with quartermaster insignia. He salutes them.*]

NELSON: Ladies. Was nice seein' you these few days. If I couldn't help, 'least

I didn't do you no harm, so nothin' from nothin' leaves nothin'.

FANNY: [*Holds up her punch cup;* LULA *gives* JULIA *high sign.*] Get one-a them Germans for me.

JULIA: [*Stands on her porch.*] Soon, Nelson, in a little while . . . we'll have whatsoever our hearts desire. You're comin' back in glory . . . with honors and shining medals . . . And those medals and that uniform is gonna open doors for you . . . and for October . . . for all, all of the servicemen. Nelson, on account-a you we're gonna be able to go in the park. They're gonna take down the no-colored signs . . . and Rusty Bennet's gonna print new ones . . . Everybody welcome . . . Everybody welcome . . .

MATTIE: [*To* TEETA.] Hear that? We gon' go in the park.

FANNY: Some of us ain't ready for that.

PRINCESS: Me too?

MATTIE: You can go now . . . and me too if I got you by the hand.

PRINCESS: [*Feeling left out.*] Ohhhhh.

JULIA: We'll go to the band concerts, the museums . . . we'll go in the library and draw out books.

MATTIE: And we'll draw books.

FANNY: Who'll read 'em to you?

MATTIE: My Teeta!

JULIA: Your life'll be safe, you and October'll be heroes.

FANNY: [*Very moved.*] Colored heroes.

JULIA: And at last we'll come into our own.

[ALL *cheer and applaud.* JULIA *steps down from porch.*]

NELSON: Julia, can you look me dead in the eye and say you believe all-a that?

JULIA: If you just gotta believe somethin', it may's well be that.

[*Applause.*]

NELSON: [*Steps up on* JULIA's *porch to make his speech.*] Friends, relatives and all other well-wishers. All-a my fine ladies and little ladies—all you good-lookin', tantalizin', pretty-eyed ladies—yeah, with your *kind* ways and your *mean* ways. I find myself a thorn among six lovely roses. Sweet little Teeta . . . the merry little Princess. Mattie, she so pretty 'til October better hurry up and come on back here. Fanny—uh—tryin' to help the race . . . a race woman. And Julia—my good friend. Mama—the only mama I got, I wanta thank you for savin' my life from time to time. What's hard ain't the goin', it's the comin' back. From the bottom-a my heart, I'd truly like to see y'all, each and every one-a you . . . able to go in the park and all that. I really would. So, with a full heart and a loaded mind, I bid you, as the French say, Adieu.

LULA: [*Bowing graciously, she takes* NELSON's *arm and they exit.*] Our humble thanks . . . my humble pleasure . . . gratitude . . . thank you . . .

[CHILDREN *wave their flags.*]

FANNY: [*To the* CHILDREN.] Let's mind our manners in front-a the downtown white people. Remember we're bein' judged.

PRINCESS: Me too?

MATTIE: [*Opening umbrella.*] Yes, you too.

FANNY: [*Leads the way and counts time.*] Step, step, one, two, step, step.

[MATTIE, FANNY *and the* CHILDREN *exit.* HERMAN *enters yard by far gate, takes two long steamer tickets from his pocket.* JULIA *senses him, turns. He is carelessly dressed and sweating.*]

HERMAN: I bought our tickets. Boat tickets to New York.

JULIA: [*Looks at tickets.*] Colored tickets. You can't use yours. [*She lets tickets flutter to the ground.*]

HERMAN: They'll change and give one white ticket. You'll ride one deck, I'll ride the other . . .

JULIA: John C. Calhoun really said a mouthful—men are not born—men are made. Ten years ago—that's when you should-a bought tickets. You chained me to your mother for ten years.

HERMAN: [*Kneeling, picking up tickets.*] Could I walk out on 'em? . . . Ker-ist sake. I'm that kinda man like my father was . . . a debt-payer, a plain, workin' man—

JULIA: He was a member in good standin' of The Gold Carnation. What kinda robes and hoods did those plain men wear? For downin' me and mine. You won twenty dollars in gold.

HERMAN: I love you . . . I love work, to come home in the evenin' . . . to enjoy the breeze for Gawd's sake . . . But no, I never wanted to go to New York. The hell with Goddamn bread factories . . . I'm a stony-broke, half-dead, half-way gentleman . . . But I'm what I wanta be. A baker.

JULIA: You waited 'til you was half-dead to buy those tickets. I don't want to go either . . . Get off the boat, the same faces'll be there at the dock. It's that shop. It's that shop!

HERMAN: It's mine. I did want to keep it.

JULIA: Right . . . people pick what they want most.

HERMAN: [*Indicating the tickets.*] I did . . . you threw it in my face.

JULIA: Get out. Get your things and get out of my life. [*The remarks become counterpoint. Each rides through the other's speech.* HERMAN *goes in house.*] Must be fine to *own* somethin'—even if it's four walls and a sack-a flour.

HERMAN: [JULIA *has followed him into the house.*] My father labored in the street . . . liftin' and layin' down cobblestone . . . liftin' and layin' down stone 'til there was enough money to open a shop . . .

JULIA: My people . . . relatives, friends and strangers . . . they worked and slaved free for nothin' for some-a the biggest name families down here . . . Elliots, Lawrences, Ravenals . . .

[HERMAN *is wearily gathering his belongings.*]

HERMAN: Great honor, working for the biggest name families. That's who you slaved for. Not me. The big names.

JULIA: . . . the rich and the poor . . . we know you . . . all of you . . . Who you are . . . where you came from . . . where you goin' . . .

HERMAN: What's my privilege . . . Good mornin', good afternoon . . . pies are ten cents today . . . and you can get 'em from Schumann for eight . . .

JULIA: "She's different" . . . I'm no different . . .

HERMAN: I'm white . . . did it give me favors and friends?

JULIA: . . . "Not like the others" . . . We raised up all-a these Carolina children . . . white and the black . . . I'm just like all the rest of the colored women . . . like Lula, Mattie . . . Yes, like Fanny!

HERMAN: Go here, go there . . . Philadelphia . . . New York . . . Schumann wants me to go North too . . .

JULIA: We nursed you, fed you, buried your dead . . . grinned in your face—cried 'bout your troubles—and laughed 'bout ours.

HERMAN: Schumann . . . Alien robber . . . waitin' to buy me out . . . My father . . .

JULIA: Pickin' up cobblestones . . . left him plenty-a time to wear bed-sheets in that Gold Carnation Society . . .

HERMAN: He never hurt anybody.

JULIA: He hurts me. There's no room for you to love him and me too . . . [Sits.] it can't be done—

HERMAN: The ignorance . . . he didn't know . . . the ignorance . . . mama . . . they don't know.

JULIA: But *you* know. My father was somebody. He helped put up Roper Hospital and Webster Rice Mills after the earthquake wiped the face-a this Gawd-forsaken city clean . . . a fine brick-mason he was . . . paid him one-third-a what they paid the white ones . . .

HERMAN: We were poor . . . No big name, no quality.

JULIA: Poor! My Gramma was a slave wash-woman bustin' suds for free! Can't get poorer than that.

HERMAN: [*Trying to shut out the sound of her voice.*] Not for me, she didn't!

JULIA: We the ones built the pretty white mansions . . . for free . . . the fishin' boats . . . for free . . . made your clothes, raised your food . . . for free . . . and I loved you—for free.

HERMAN: A Gawd-damn lie . . . nobody did for me . . . you know it . . . you know how hard I worked—

JULIA: If it's anybody's home down here it's mine . . . everything in the city is mine—why should I go anywhere . . . ground I'm standin' on—it's mine.

HERMAN: [*Sitting on foot of the bed.*] It's the ignorance . . . Lemme be, lemme rest . . . Ker-ist sake . . . It's the ignorance . . .

JULIA: After ten years you still won't look. All-a my people that's been killed . . . It's your people that killed 'em . . . all that's been in bondage—your people put 'em there—all that didn't go to school—your people kept 'em out.

HERMAN: But I didn't do it. Did I do it?

JULIA: They killed 'em . . . all the dead slaves . . . buried under a blanket-a this Carolina earth, even the cotton crop is nourished with hearts' blood . . . roots-a that cotton tangled and wrapped 'round my bones.

HERMAN: And you blamin' me for it . . .

JULIA: Yes! . . . For the one thing we never talk about . . . white folks killin' me and mine. You wouldn't let me speak.

HERMAN: I never stopped you . . .

JULIA: Every time I open my mouth 'bout what they do . . . you say . . . "Ker-ist, there it is again . . ." Whenever somebody was lynched . . . you 'n'me would eat a very silent supper. It hurt me not to talk . . . what you don't say you swallow down . . . [Pours wine.]

HERMAN: I was just glad to close the door 'gainst what's out there. You did all the givin' . . . I failed you in every way.

JULIA: You nursed me when I was sick . . . paid my debts . . .

HERMAN: I didn't give my name.

JULIA: You couldn't . . . was the law . . .

HERMAN: I shoulda walked 'til we came to where it'd be all right.

JULIA: You never put any other woman before me.

HERMAN: Only Mama, Annabelle, the customers, the law . . . the ignorance . . . I honored them while you waited and waited—

JULIA: You clothed me . . . you fed me . . . you were kind, loving . . .

HERMAN: I never did a damn thing for you. After ten years look at it—I never did a damn thing for you.

JULIA: Don't low-rate yourself . . . leave me something.

HERMAN: When my mother and sister came . . . I was ashamed. What am I doin' bein' ashamed of us?

JULIA: When you first came in this yard I almost died-a shame . . . so many times you was nothin' to me but white . . . times we were angry . . . damn white man . . . times I was tired . . . damn white man . . . but most times you were my husband, my friend, my lover . . .

HERMAN: Whatever is wrong, Julia . . . not the law . . . me; what I didn't do, with all-a my faults, spite-a all that . . . You gotta believe I love you . . . 'cause I do . . . That's the one thing I know . . . I love you . . . I love you.

JULIA: Ain't too many people in this world that get to be loved . . . really loved.

HERMAN: We gon' take that boat trip . . . You'll see, you'll never be sorry.

JULIA: To hell with sorry. Let's be glad!

HERMAN: Sweetheart, leave the ignorance outside . . . [Stretches out across the bed.] Don't let that doctor in here . . . to stand over me shakin' his head.

JULIA: [Pours water in a silver cup.] Bet you never drank from a silver cup. Carolina water is sweet water . . . Wherever you go you gotta come back for a drink-a this water. Sweet water, like the breeze that blows 'cross the battery.

HERMAN: [Happily weary.] I'm gettin' old, that ain' no joke.

JULIA: No, you're not. Herman, my real weddin' cake . . . I wanta big one . . .

HERMAN: Gonna bake it in a wash-tub . . .

JULIA: We'll put pieces of it in little boxes for folks to take home and dream on.

HERMAN: . . . But let's don't give none to your landlady . . . Gon' get old and funny-lookin' like Robbie m'boy and . . . and . . .

JULIA: And Mable . . .

HERMAN: [*Breathing heavier.*] Robbie says "Mable, where's my keys" . . . Mable—Robbie—Mable—

[*Lights change, shadows grow longer.* MATTIE *enters the yard.*]

MATTIE: Hey, Julia! [*Sound of carriage wheels in front of the main house.* MATTIE *enters* JULIA'*s house. As she sees* HERMAN.] They 'round there, they come to get him, Julia.

[JULIA *takes the wedding band and chain from around her neck, gives it to* MATTIE *with tickets.*]

JULIA: Surprise. Present.

MATTIE: For me?

JULIA: Northern tickets . . . and a wedding band.

MATTIE: I can't take that for nothing.

JULIA: You and Teeta are my people.

MATTIE: Yes.

JULIA: You and Teeta are my family. Be my family.

MATTIE: We your people whether we blood kin or not. [MATTIE *exits to her own porch.*]

FANNY: [*Offstage.*] No . . . No, Ma'am. [*Enters with* LULA. LULA *is carrying the wilted bouquet.*] Julia! They think Mr. Herman's come back.

[HERMAN'S MOTHER *enters with* ANNABELLE. *The old lady is weary and subdued.* ANNABELLE *is almost without feeling.* JULIA *is on her porch waiting.*]

JULIA: Yes, Fanny, he's here. [LULA *retires to her doorway.* JULIA *silently stares at them, studying each* WOMAN, *seeing them with new eyes. She is going through that rising process wherein she must reject them as the molders and dictators of her life.*] Nobody comes in my house.

FANNY: What kind-a way is that?

JULIA: Nobody comes in my house.

ANNABELLE: We'll quietly take him home.

JULIA: You can't come in.

HERMAN'S MOTHER: [*Low-keyed, polite and humble simplicity.*] You see my condition. Gawd's punishin' me . . . Whippin' me for somethin' I did or didn't do. I can't understand this . . . I prayed, but ain't no understandin' Herman's dyin'. He's almost gone. It's right and proper that he should die at home in his own bed. I'm askin' humbly . . . or else I'm forced to get help from the police.

ANNABELLE: Give her a chance . . . She'll do right . . . won'tcha?

[HERMAN *stirs. His breathing becomes harsh and deepens into the sound known as the "death rattle."* MATTIE *leads the* CHILDREN *away.*]

JULIA: [*Not unkindly.*] Do whatever you have to do. Win the war. Represent the race. Call the police. [*She enters her house, closes the door and bolts it.* HERMAN'S MOTHER *leaves through the front entry.* FANNY *slowly follows her.*] I'm here, do you hear me? [*He tries to answer but can't.*] We're standin' on the

deck-a that Clyde Line Boat . . . wavin' to the people on the shore . . .
Your mama, Annabelle, my Aunt Cora . . . all of our friends . . . the
children . . . all wavin' . . . "Don't stay 'way too long . . . Be sure and
come back . . . We gon' miss you . . . Come back, we need you" . . . But
we're goin' . . . The whistle's blowin', flags wavin' . . . We're takin' off,
ridin' the waves so smooth and easy . . . There now . . . [ANNABELLE *moves
closer to the house as she listens to* JULIA.] . . . the bakery's fine . . . all the
orders are ready . . . out to sea . . . on our way . . . [*The weight has lifted,
she is radiantly happy. She helps him gasp out each remaining breath. With each
gasp he seems to draw a step nearer to a wonderful goal.*] Yes . . . Yes . . . Yes
. . . Yes . . . Yes . . . Yes . . .

Curtain.

STUDY QUESTIONS

1. Early in the first scene, Mattie picks up an axe to knock the post out of the way
so she can get to the quarter that she had given Teeta to get some things at the
store but that Teeta had dropped. When Julia, not knowing what is going on,
steps out on the porch, Mattie thinks she is trying to stop her and says, "If you
don't like it—come down here and whip me." Julia "(*Nervous but determined to
present a firm stand.*)" says, "Oh, my . . . Good mornin' ladies. My name is Julia
Augustine. I'm not gonna move." Why does she say that?

2. What image of Julia and her CHARACTER do you get from her giving Mattie the
quarter and saying that she has Mattie's quarter under the house for good luck,
and from Julia's conversation with Fanny that follows?

3. What elements of humor do you find in the first scene?

4. When Nelson meets Julia, he tells her she's "the best-lookin' woman I ever seen
in my life." What EXPECTATIONS do you have about their relationship? How do
your expectations change or shift or grow as the play progresses? How late in the
play do you think they may still get together?

5. What issues and expectations does the scene with the Bell Man introduce? How
does the appearance of Princess reinforce some of these?

6. Now that you've read the whole play, what is there in October's letter that omi-
nously foreshadows what is to happen later? Do you remember whether you
particularly noticed the detail that will be important when you first read the
passage? Do you think this detail, dropped in so inconspicuously, helped prepare
the way for your acceptance of the later event, even if you didn't notice it? As
you read the scene a second time, what is the difference in effect between your
two readings? What significance does this sentence from the letter have later:
"Two things a man can give the woman he loves . . . his name and his protection"?

7. The first scene ends with the situation clear—Julia is in love with a white man;
they have been lovers for ten years but cannot marry because of laws against

miscegenation in South Carolina at the time. Yet the fact of the relationship is not dropped dramatically—at the curtain—but almost a page earlier. Is this a weakness or a strength in the play? What is the effect of the relatively undramatic (or untheatrical) timing of the curtain?

8. Early in Act I, scene 2, Lula tells Nelson to "Go on!" He says, "Fact is, I was gon' stay home and have me some orange drink, but Massa beat me to it. None-a my business no-how, dammit." What does he mean by all that?

9. What image of Herman's mother do you get from his first conversation with Julia? What aspects of social class are touched upon in the play, and how do these interact with the racial issues?

10. What elements in the first lengthy conversation between Herman and Julia (through the celebration of their tenth "anniversary") help define their relationship for you? Can you describe that relationship in your own words, in a paragraph, perhaps?

11. In what sense does "a wedding band . . . on a chain" encapsulate their situation?

12. Which of the two seems the more "racist"? Is this confirmed or qualified later in the play?

13. Julia defines dignity as "a spirit that rises higher than the dirt around it, without any by-your-leave. It's not proud and it's not 'shamed"; why is she uncertain whether she and Herman have dignity?

14. The first act ends more dramatically than the first scene did, with Herman collapsing, but the last line, Fanny's "Get him out of my yard," splashes the cold water of reality on its theatricality. What did you think was wrong with Herman? What did you think was going to happen in Act II?

15. Why doesn't Fanny want a doctor called in?

16. Why, after Herman wakes, takes more medicine, and groans, does Julia put her open dressmaking scissors under his bed?

17. In the first act, we learn that "the people across the way" are going to Philadelphia after the war, and early in Act II, Nelson thinks he "might hit out for Chicago or Detroit" after the war. How does this reflect on the conditions of blacks in the South? on their vision of conditions in the North? on their expectations of how things will change after the end of World War I? In Act II, scene 2, what does Lula ask Julia to tell Nelson as he heads back to active duty? What do you infer that she believes will happen after the war? What does Julia say about what Lula wants her to tell Nelson? What does she actually tell him? Can you relate the situation in 1918 to that in 1966 when the play was first performed?

18. Julia asks Annabelle to get Herman to a doctor right away; Annabelle insists on waiting until dark. What is each woman's motivation? Who is right?

19. Why does Annabelle want Herman to marry Celestine?

20. What is the relationship between Fanny and Herman's mother? Why?

21. How does Herman's mother plan to explain why Herman is where he is?

22. What is Herman's mother's attitude toward men? Why?

23. What was the gist of Herman's speech on John C. Calhoun at the Gold Carnation picnic? How old was he? What is Julia's reaction when he begins reciting it in his delirium? How much of her further actions and words are the result of his recitation?

24. What does Julia reveal to Herman's mother about what she, Julia, has done for her in the past? How does Herman's mother respond?

25. How does Act II, scene 1, end?

26. What do Herman and Julia reveal about their childhood and families and their place and experience in society in the scene in which they speak in "counterpoint" (Act II, scene 2)?

27. The "counterpoint" scene begins in hostility and with accusations and grievances. When and how does it turn around to a love scene? Is the turn effective?

28. How is the end of the play an affirmation? What is it an affirmation of? How would you project Julia's future for the next few days? years? the rest of her life?

Gary Soto

Californian Gary Soto (born 1952), who writes fiction, nonfiction, and poetry, has won many awards, including a Guggenheim Fellowship, the Academy of American Poets Award, Discovery—The Nation Prize, *Poetry*'s Bess Hoskins Prize, and, in 1985, the American Book Award for his volume of recollections, *Living Up the Street*. That was the same year *Small Faces*, from which this selection is taken, was published. He is the author of four poetry collections including *Black Hair* (1985). His most recent book, *Home Course in Religion*, was published in 1991. Soto teaches Chicano Studies and English at the University of California, Berkeley.

LIKE MEXICANS

My grandmother gave me bad advice and good advice when I was in my early teens. For the bad advice, she said that I should become a barber because they made good money and listened to the radio all day. "Honey, they don't work como burros," she would say every time I visited her. She made the sound of donkeys braying. "Like that, honey!" For the good advice, she said that I should marry a Mexican girl. "No Okies, hijo"—she would say—"Look, my son. He marry one and they fight every day about I don't know what and I don't know what." For her, everyone who wasn't Mexican, black, or Asian were Okies. The French were Okies, the Italians in suits were Okies. When I asked about Jews, whom I had read about, she asked for a picture. I rode home on my bicycle and returned with a calendar depicting the important races of the world. "Pues si, son Okies tambien!"[1] she said, nodding her head. She waved the calendar away and we went to the living room where she lectured me on the virtues of the Mexican girl: first, she could cook and, second, she acted like a woman, not a man, in her husband's home. She said she would tell me about a third when I got a little older.

I asked my mother about it—becoming a barber and marrying Mexican. She was in the kitchen. Steam curled from a pot of boiling beans, the radio was on, looking as squat as a loaf of bread. "Well, if you want to be a barber—they say they make good money." She slapped a round steak with a knife, her glasses slipping down with each strike. She stopped and looked up. "If you find a good Mexican girl, marry her of course." She returned to slapping the meat and I went to the backyard where my brother and David King were sitting on the lawn feeling the inside of their cheeks.

"This is what girls feel like," my brother said, rubbing the inside of his cheek. David put three fingers inside his mouth and scratched. I ignored them and climbed the back fence to see my best friend, Scott, a second-generation Okie. I called him and his mother pointed to the side of the house where his bedroom was a small aluminum trailer, the kind you gawk at when they're flipped over on the freeway, wheels spinning in the air. I went around to find Scott pitching horseshoes.

I picked up a set of rusty ones and joined him. While we played, we talked about school and friends and record albums. The horseshoes scuffed up dirt, sometimes ringing the iron that threw out a meager shadow like a sundial. After three argued-over games, we pulled two oranges apiece from his tree and started down the alley still talking school and friends and record albums. We pulled more oranges from the alley and talked about who we would marry. "No offense, Scott," I said with an orange slice in my mouth, "but I would never marry an Okie." We walked in step, almost touching, with a sled of shadows dragging behind us. "No offense, Gary," Scott said, "but I would *never* marry a Mexican." I looked at him: a fang of orange slice showed from his munching mouth. I didn't think anything of it. He had his girl and I had mine. But our seventh-grade vision was the same: to marry, get jobs, buy cars and maybe a house if we had money left over.

We talked about our future lives until, to our surprise, we were on the downtown mall, two miles from home. We bought a bag of popcorn at Penneys and sat on a bench near the fountain watching Mexican and Okie girls pass. "That one's mine," I pointed with my chin when a girl with eyebrows arched into black rainbows ambled by. "She's cute," Scott said about a girl

1. Well yes, they're Okies too.

with yellow hair and a mouthful of gum. We dreamed aloud, our chins busy pointing out girls. We agreed that we couldn't wait to become men and lift them onto our laps.

But the woman I married was not Mexican but Japanese. It was a surprise to me. For years, I went about wide-eyed in my search for the brown girl in a white dress at a dance. I searched the playground at the baseball diamond. When the girls raced for grounders, their hair bounced like something that couldn't be caught. When they sat together in the lunchroom, heads pressed together, I knew they were talking about us Mexican guys. I saw them and dreamed them. I threw my face into my pillow, making up sentences that were good as in the movies.

But when I was twenty, I fell in love with this other girl who worried my mother, who had my grandmother asking once again to see the calendar of the Important Races of the World. I told her I had thrown it away years before. I took a much-glanced-at snapshot from my wallet. We looked at it together, in silence. Then grandma reclined in her chair, lit a cigarette, and said, "Es pretty." She blew and asked with all her worry pushed up to her forehead: "Chinese?"

I was in love and there was no looking back. She was the one. I told my mother who was slapping hamburger into patties. "Well, sure if you want to marry her," she said. But the more I talked, the more concerned she became. Later I began to worry. Was it all a mistake? "Marry a Mexican girl," I heard my mother say in my mind. I heard it at breakfast. I heard it over math problems, between Western Civilization and cultural geography. But then one afternoon while I was hitchhiking home from school, it struck me like a baseball in the back: my mother wanted me to marry someone of my own social class—a poor girl. I considered my fiancee, Carolyn, and she didn't look poor, though I knew she came from a family of farm workers and pull-yourself-up-by-your-bootstraps ranchers. I asked my brother, who was marrying Mexican poor that fall, if I should marry a poor girl. He screamed "Yeah" above his terrible guitar playing in his bedroom. I considered my sister who had married Mexican. Cousins were dating Mexican. Uncles were remarrying poor women. I asked Scott, who was still my best friend, and he said, "She's too good for you, so you better not."

I worried about it until Carolyn took me home to meet her parents. We drove in her Plymouth until the houses gave way to farms and ranches and finally her house fifty feet from the highway. When we pulled into the drive, I panicked and begged Carolyn to make a U-turn and go back so we could talk about it over a soda. She pinched my cheek, calling me a "silly boy." I felt better, though, when I got out of the car and saw the house: the chipped paint, a cracked window, boards for a walk to the back door. There were rusting cars near the barn. A tractor with a net of spiderwebs under a mulberry. A field. A bale of barbed wire like children's scribbling leaning against an empty chicken coop. Carolyn took my hand and pulled me to my future mother-in-law who was coming out to greet us.

We had lunch: sandwiches, potato chips, and iced tea. Carolyn and her 10
mother talked mostly about neighbors and the congregation at the Japanese
Methodist Church in West Fresno. Her father, who was in khaki work clothes,
excused himself with a wave that was almost a salute and went outside. I
heard a truck start, a dog bark, and then the truck rattle away.

Carolyn's mother offered another sandwich, but I declined with a shake 11
of my head and a smile. I looked around when I could, when I was not saying
over and over that I was a college student, hinting that I could take care of
her daughter. I shifted my chair. I saw newspapers piled in corners, dusty
cereal boxes and vinegar bottles in corners. The wallpaper was bubbled from
rain that had come in from a bad roof. Dust. Dust lay on lamp shades and
window sills. These people are just like Mexicans, I thought. Poor people.

Carolyn's mother asked me through Carolyn if I would like a *sushi*. A 12
plate of black and white things were held in front of me. I took one, wide-
eyed, and turned it over like a foreign coin. I was biting into one when I saw
a kitten crawl up the window screen over the sink. I chewed and the kitten
opened its mouth of terror as she crawled higher, wanting in to paw the
leftovers from our plates. I looked at Carolyn who said that the cat was just
showing off. I looked up in time to see it fall. It crawled up, then fell again.

We talked for an hour and had apple pie and coffee, slowly. Finally, we 13
got up with Carolyn taking my hand. Slightly embarrassed, I tried to pull
away but her grip held me. I let her have her way as she led me down the
hallway with her mother right behind me. When I opened the door, I was
startled by a kitten clinging to the screen door, its mouth screaming "cat
food, dog biscuits, *sushi*. . . ." I opened the door and the kitten, still holding
on, whined in the language of hungry animals. When I got into Carolyn's
car, I looked back: the cat was still clinging. I asked Carolyn if it were possibly hungry, but she said the cat was being silly. She started the car, waved
to her mother, and bounced us over the rain-poked drive, patting my thigh
for being her lover baby. Carolyn waved again. I looked back, waving, then
gawking at a window screen where there were now three kittens clawing and
screaming to get in. Like Mexicans, I thought. I remembered the Molinas
and how the cats clung to their screens—cats they shot down with squirt
guns. On the highway, I felt happy, pleased by it all. I patted Carolyn's
thigh. Her people were like Mexicans, only different.

STUDY QUESTIONS

1. Why does the NARRATOR's grandmother want him to become a barber? Who,
   according to her, are Okies? Why does Soto say, in the first paragraph, that his
   grandmother's advice to marry a Mexican girl was good advice? What is his mother's advice? Why does she seem so uninterested?

2. What is Soto's mother's advice when he says he wants to marry a Japanese girl?
   How does that advice seem to conflict with what he hears her voice saying inside
   him? How does he reconcile the conflicting advice?

3. Why is he worried about visiting his girlfriend's parents? Why does he feel "better" when he sees the chipped paint, cracked windows, and boards used as a walkway to the back door?

4. How are Carolyn's people "like Mexicans"? How are they different?

Julia Alvarez

J ulia Alvarez has published a book of poetry, *Homecoming* (1984), and a novel, *How the Garcia Girls Lost Their Accents* (1991), about a Latino-American family. The following essay appeared in the "Hers" column in the *New York Times Magazine*.

HOLD THE MAYONNAISE

"If I die first and Papi ever gets remarried," Mami used to tease when we were kids, "don't you accept a new woman in my house. Make her life impossible, you hear?" My sisters and I nodded obediently, and a filial shudder would go through us. We were Catholics, so of course, the only kind of remarriage we could imagine had to involve our mother's death.

We were also Dominicans, recently arrived in Jamaica, Queens, in the early 60's, before waves of other Latin Americans began arriving. So, when we imagined who exactly my father might possibly ever think of remarrying, only American women came to mind. It would be bad enough having a *madrastra*,[1] but a "stepmother." . . .

All I could think of was that she would make me eat mayonnaise, a food I identified with the United States and which I detested. Mami understood, of course, that I wasn't used to that kind of food. Even a madrastra, accustomed to our rice and beans and tostones and pollo frito, would understand. But an American stepmother would think it was normal to put mayonnaise on food, and if she were at all strict and a little mean, which all stepmothers, of course, were, she would make me eat potato salad and such. I had plenty of my own reasons to make a potential stepmother's life impossible. When I

1. Stepmother.

nodded obediently with my sisters, I was imagining not just something foreign in our house, but in our refrigerator.

So it's strange now, almost 35 years later, to find myself a Latina stepmother of my husband's two tall, strapping, blond, mayonnaise-eating daughters. To be honest, neither of them is a real aficionado of the condiment, but it's a fair thing to add to a bowl of tuna fish or diced potatoes. Their American food, I think of it, and when they head to their mother's or off to school, I push the jar back in the refrigerator behind their chocolate pudding and several open cans of Diet Coke.

What I can't push as successfully out of sight are my own immigrant childhood fears of having a *gringa* stepmother with foreign tastes in our house. Except now, I am the foreign stepmother in a gringa household. I've wondered what my husband's two daughters think of this stranger in their family. It must be doubly strange for them that I am from another culture.

Of course, there are mitigating circumstances—my husband's two daughters were teen-agers when we married, older, more mature, able to understand differences. They had also traveled when they were children with their father, an eye doctor, who worked on short-term international projects with various eye foundations. But still, it's one thing to visit a foreign country, another altogether to find it brought home—a real bear plopped down in a Goldilocks house.

Sometimes, a whole extended family of bears. My warm, loud Latino family came up for the wedding: my *tía*[2] from Santo Domingo; three dramatic, enthusiastic sisters and their families; my papi, with a thick accent I could tell the girls found it hard to understand; and my mami, who had her eye trained on my soon-to-be stepdaughters for any sign that they were about to make my life impossible. "How are they behaving themselves?" she asked me, as if they were 7 and 3, not 19 and 16. "They're wonderful girls," I replied, already feeling protective of them.

I looked around for the girls in the meadow in front of the house we were building, where we were holding the outdoor wedding ceremony and party. The oldest hung out with a group of her own friends. The younger one whizzed in briefly for the ceremony, then left again before the congratulations started up. There was not much mixing with me and mine. What was there for them to celebrate on a day so full of confusion and effort?

On my side, being the newcomer in someone else's territory is a role I'm used to. I can tap into that struggling English speaker, that skinny, dark-haired, olive-skinned girl in a sixth grade of mostly blond and blue-eyed giants. Those tall, freckled boys would push me around in the playground. "Go back to where you came from!" "*No comprendo!*"[3] I'd reply, though of course there was no misunderstanding the fierce looks on their faces.

Even now, my first response to a scowl is that old pulling away. (My husband calls it "checking out.") I remember times early on in the marriage

4

5

6

7

8

9

10

2. Aunt.

3. I don't understand.

when the girls would be with us, and I'd get out of school and drive around doing errands, killing time, until my husband, their father, would be leaving work. I am not proud of my fears, but I understand—as the lingo goes—where they come from.

And I understand, more than I'd like to sometimes, my stepdaughters' pain. But with me, they need never fear that I'll usurp a mother's place. No one has ever come up and held their faces and then addressed me, "They look just like you." If anything, strangers to the remarriage are probably playing Mr. Potato Head in their minds, trying to figure out how my foreign features and my husband's fair Nebraskan features got put together into these two tall, blond girls. "My husband's daughters," I kept introducing them.

Once, when one of them visited my class and I introduced her as such, two students asked me why. "I'd be so hurt if my stepmom introduced me that way," the young man said. That night I told my stepdaughter what my students had said. She scowled at me and agreed. "It's so weird how you can call me Papa's daughter. Like you don't want to be related to me or something."

"I didn't want to presume," I explained. "So it's O.K. if I call you my stepdaughter?"

"That's what I am," she said. Relieved, I took it for a teensy inch of acceptance. The takings are small in this stepworld, I've discovered. Sort of like being a minority. It feels as if all the goodies have gone somewhere else.

Day to day, I guess I follow my papi's advice. When we first came, he would talk to his children about how to make it in our new country. "Just do your work and put in your heart, and they will accept you!" In this age of remaining true to your roots, of keeping your Spanish, of fighting from inside your culture, that assimilationist approach is highly suspect. My Latino students—who don't want to be called Hispanics anymore—would ditch me as faculty adviser if I came up with that play-nice message.

But in a stepfamily where everyone is starting a new life together, it isn't bad advice. Like a potluck supper, an American concept my mami never took to. ("Why invite people to your house and then ask them to bring the food?") You put what you've got together with what everyone else brought and see what comes out of the pot. The luck part is if everyone brings something you like. No potato salad, no deviled eggs, no little party sandwiches with you know what in them.

STUDY QUESTIONS

1. What, according to Alvarez, was the basis for her bias against stepmothers? What caused her to change her position? Why is she so opposed to mayonnaise?

2. Describe Alvarez's stepdaughters. What assumptions do they have about stepmothers? What are the sources of their different value structures?

3. What country did Alvarez grow up in? her stepdaughters? What kind of parents did each have?

4. Why does Alvarez respond as she does to a scowl? Explain the stepdaughters' response to the wedding.

5. What is a "stepworld"? Explain the difference between Alvarez's response to the term "stepdaughter" and that of her stepdaughters.

6. List all of the differences in custom between the Latino and Anglo worlds. What cultural misunderstandings are created by each?

Lynn Minton

The following selection, taken from the December 15, 1991, issue of *Parade* magazine, reflects a series of actual conversations recorded by columnist Lynn Minton.

IS IT OKAY TO DATE SOMEONE OF
ANOTHER RACE?

The teenagers at Westwood High in Mesa, Arizona—representing a broad range of [1]
cultures—were unusually open in their responses to this question. We spoke with Gary Festa, 18; Domingo Delci, 18; Wendy Burgess, 17; Teresa Zachary, 18; Tamieka Howell, 16; Jeff Arnett, 17; and Robert Johnston, 18.

Gary: It depends on the crowd you hang out with. My Italian friends where [2] I used to live were very racist. Blacks, Hispanics—anybody different that came into their neighborhood—they didn't appreciate. Your friends have a big impact on you. You're afraid of losing them. Then there's pressure from home. Me, I would want my family to stay Italian. That's the way I was brought up. Still, if I was in love with an Indian girl or a black girl, I'd marry her.

Domingo: My little sister hangs around mostly with Mexicans, and she crit- [3] icized me because I went to the prom with a white girl. My first girlfriend was white, and it took a month for my mom to accept it. And I go, "Mom, what happens, like, 10 years from now, if I want to marry a white girl?" I think it's just that she wants to keep the Mexican culture alive.

Gary: Your mother has a big impact on you. You respect what she says.   4

Wendy: What I don't understand is, if you're in love, why does it matter   5 what color or race you are? If I was in love, and he was black, I would marry him.

Teresa: Would you? Regardless of what your parents said?   6

Wendy: Yes, I would. You are in love with that person. Why should it   7 matter just because he has a different color skin?

Teresa: Can you honestly say that? I was going to go to the prom with a   8 black guy. He's one of the most popular guys on campus. I went home and told Mom. My house was in an uproar for about three days. I said, "But it's just a dance." I was told, "He's not good enough for you." And I thought, "Well, that's ridiculous. He's got better grades than I do."

    There were a million things I could give them on his good side, because   9 he's a heck of a guy. But she stereotyped him and said, "He's this and this and this. And you're going to come home from the prom and . . ." And she gave me these horror stories of what was going to happen to me on prom night. I knew better, but there was no explaining. And I was scared—what if we keep dating, and I fall in love with him, and we decide to get married? I don't have my family anymore.

Gary: And if you marry this black guy, and you divorce him a year later,   10 you're always going to have your mother on your back: "I told you he was nothing. I knew you were going to get divorced the day you married him." Then there are other pressures: Who's going to be at the wedding? Who're you going to come to when you need money?

Tamieka: I've never had a problem with who I can and cannot date. I've   11 dated a Norwegian. I've dated two African-Americans. My mom completely respects whoever I bring home. If my friends hassle me, if they don't respect what I think—they don't have to agree—it's too bad. I'm just one less friend for them.

Jeff: You might think Teresa's mom is really out of line, but I think that's so   12 true with many people around here. The older generation associates so much with their own race, they stay prejudiced.

    I think *we're* prejudiced because we're scared. The other day I see this big Mexican walking up the street who seems to be wearing a gang hat. And I'm really uneasy. Then I get up a little closer, and I see that it's a Mexican I'm real good friends with.

Domingo: Robert, don't you kind of feel weird sometimes, if you're taking out a white girl, about what her parents are going to think about you? The first girlfriend I had—what she used to tell me about what her parents would say about me, it was just frightening. I was afraid to go to her house. No, I couldn't talk to them about it. What if they'd said, "We don't like you, we don't trust you, because you're Mexican"? It's not my fault. And I'm proud to be Mexican. And then if they'd told me that I couldn't go out with their daughter, I'd have felt really bad. It's really neat, though, when you meet parents who don't care who you are.   13

Gary: I think the word "Mexican" is a big factor. Parents read stories: "White girl raped by four Mexicans." Then they're like, "Mexican people, they're bad. Black people, they're bad." They don't see your face. You could be the nicest person in he world.   14

Robert: My family on my mom's side is Creek. From Oklahoma. And when my mom began to date a Choctaw—who became my dad—that upset the whole family. And now my mom and dad are like, "Oh, let's go to this Indian event, because there'll be some nice Indian girls for you to marry." I wasn't sure how they were all going to react when my brother started dating a white girl. But within months, everything was cool. The first time she met everybody was at a big cookout. She walks in, and everyone just looks. They're used to seeing dark skin, and suddenly there's a flash of white there.   15

Teresa: My mom went to the Martin Luther King march with me. And she meant it. And when Robert or any of my other friends who are another race come over, it's okay. My mom loves them. Everybody who's met my mom knows she is just a wonderful person. But there's a difference between my being friends with someone and my dating them.   16

Gary: My parents want an Italian grandson. But my mom would not hold it against me if I married someone who wasn't Italian.   17

Domingo: I think my family is the same way. But if it's not—well, that's their problem. I'm my own person, and they're not going to stop me.   18

Robert: My parents don't say, "No, you can't go out with a non-Indian." But whenever I mention someone, the first question they ask is, "Is she white?"   19

Jeff: My mom has grown up with blacks all her life, and she loves to be around them. Both of my parents would love me to date Tamieka. They think she's great. I don't know what they'd feel about me marrying somebody black, though.   20

Gary: Would that influence you, if they were against it? 21

Jeff: It comes down to if I love her. 22

Gary: Your mom would probably turn around and say, "There's other fish 23
in the sea. You can find someone else."

Robert: If I was dating a girl, and my mom said, "I don't want you to date 24
this person anymore," I think I'd stop dating her. Because I feel indebted to
my parents. They've done so much for me.

Jeff: I don't know how we're going to learn to deal with all this. But I think 25
it's up to us. The more our generation associates with each other, the more
unscared of each other we'll get. And once that happens, things will get
better.

STUDY QUESTIONS

1. How fully do each of the participants in the conversation characterize themselves?
   Which of the people do you think you would like the most? the least? Which
   specific attitudes and expressions bother you the most?

2. Where do the values and attitudes of each of the speakers seem to come from?
   What indications do you find in the conversation of willingness to be convinced by
   the opinions or experiences of others?

Robert Anthony Watts

Robert Anthony Watts was born in 1962 and lives in Atlanta, Georgia. He is a
graduate of Harvard University and has worked as a journalist for the last
eight years. As a staff writer for the *Atlanta Journal-Constitution*, and presently for the
Associated Press, he has written extensively on race relations and civil rights. "Not
Black, Not White, But Biracial" appeared in the *Atlanta Journal-Constitution* on
December 1, 1991.

NOT BLACK, NOT WHITE, BUT BIRACIAL

Larene LaSonde lived as a black American for 37 years: She participated in civil rights protests, she read widely in black history, and she twice married black men. 1

But eight years ago, one of her sons asked her how he should identify himself racially. Ms. LaSonde, whose mother is black and father is white, instinctively told the boy that he was black. 2

Immediately, she says, she knew she was wrong. 3

"I was saying dumb things like you may have white skin, but you are 'affirmatively black.' " says Ms. LaSonde, who lives near Decatur. "Here I was telling them to find their acceptance with the black community—I, who had never found acceptance in the black or white community." 4

She now calls herself, and her children, mulatto. 5

Ms. LaSonde is one of a growing number of Americans from interracial families who are demanding a radical rethinking of the classifications that have defined race relations in this country for hundreds of years. 6

• In cities and towns across the country, biracial Americans are pressing local school systems, government agencies, hospitals and universities to create a new category that reflects their diverse heritage. 7

• On college campuses, particularly on the West Coast, multiracial students are forming their own organizations. 8

• A national push is under way to force the U.S. Census Bureau to create a "multiracial" or "biracial" category for the 2000 census. 9

Angry that our society asks them to identify themselves as black *or* white— instead of black *and* white—these people say they shouldn't have to reject the heritage that comes from either of their parents. 10

Locally, the Interracial Family Alliance of Atlanta, a support group, has formed Project RACE (Reclassify All Children Equally) to spearhead the drive to get local institutions to create a new multiracial category. The group is researching race classifications in Georgia and plans to press local institutions, such as hospitals and schools, for change. 11

The multiracial movement includes people who are a mix of Asian and white, Hispanic and white, Hispanic and Asian, and other races. But offspring of black-white marriages, such as Ms. LaSonde, are the driving force behind the movement and face the most difficult challenge in getting society to acknowledge them. 12

"It's for the self-esteem of multiracial people," said Susan Graham of Sandy Springs, the mother of two biracial children and a leader of the local 13 effort. "They have every right to call themselves biracial and for other people to recognize them as biracial, because that's what they are."

But biracial Americans face resistance from blacks, from whites and from 14
a society used to viewing anyone with the slightest trace of African ancestry as black. Further complicating the task of the biracial movement is the fact that about 75 percent of black Amerians are of mixed ancestry, many of them with African, American Indian and European blood, according to historians. Many biracial Americans are, in fact, no lighter or more noticeably mixed than African-Americans.

When Larene La Sonde speaks of her life as a mulatto, the term she 15
prefers, she speaks with an intensity born of years of wrestling with the question of her racial identity.

"You got white folks with their perceptions of black people, black people 16
with their perceptions of white folks," says Ms. LaSonde, a 45-year-old legal assistant. "We are the product of their mating. Where is that middle ground where we are comfortable? Where do we fit?"

A native of Mount Vernon, N.Y., Ms. LaSonde grew up in a black 17
neighborhood and never considered herself anything but black—despite the fact that her father was a white man, the son of Russian Jews who emigrated to the United States.

But alone, in quiet moments, Ms. LaSonde says, she sensed she was 18
different. She felt somewhat defensive because her skin was so light, and because her father was white.

These days, she expresses anger at blacks and whites for ignoring bira- 19
cial people. Determined to learn more about people with one black and one white parent, Ms. LaSonde spends her nights poring through history books in hopes of writing a book on the subject. She is seeking out other biracial people to interview.

Experts on race relations trace the emergence of the multiracial move- 20
ment to two factors: the success of the civil rights movement in breaking down rigid racial barriers, and the rise in the number of interracial marriages.

The number of black-white couples has increased from 65,000 in 1970 21
to 218,000 in 1988, according to the U.S. Census Bureau. The number of interracial marriages of all kinds—among white, black, Native American, Eskimo and Asian residents—rose from 310,000 to 956,000 during the same period.

Although the Census Bureau does not track the number of biracial 22
Americans, the annual number of multiracial births of all kinds has been rising rapidly. In 1988, the most recent year for which statistics are available, the number of births to black-white couples was 41,301, up nearly fivefold from 8,758 births in 1968, according to the National Center for Health Statistics.

Amy Nelson, a 13-year-old from Marietta, is the product of one of those 23
interracial unions.

Amy, whose mother is white and father black, was told by her parents all her life that she was mixed. 24

"That's just what I am," says Amy, an eighth grader at Marietta Junior High School, who prefers the term "biracial" or "mixed" to "mulatto." "I can't call myself black, because my mom is white. I can't call myself white, because my dad is black. I'm just biracial." 25

When Amy's mother, Deane Nelson, was pregnant, many people told her that her child would be considered black. She objected. "I was bound and determined that my child would not be raised black, would not be called black, because I'm white and half of her background is white," Mrs. Nelson says. 26

Amy says being biracial isn't as difficult as many people suspect. She says she can embrace the best of the black and white worlds. 27

Perhaps the hardest part is having to confront the issue of race so frequently. Two years ago, Amy got into a conflict on the first day of school when a white pupil stood up to count the number of black and white children in the class. The boy counted Amy as black; she objected, saying she was mixed. School officials later apologized for the incident. 28

"Things probably come up every day," Amy says. "Someone will ask me if I'm mixed or something. I think that would depress me if I weren't so confident." 29

Self-esteem, in fact, is a central issue of the biracial movement. Biracial people say that rejecting part of their heritage is emotionally damaging. 30

A small but growing body of psychological research backs their point of view. In a study of 44 young-adult offspring of interracial marriages in Southern California, psychologist Agneta Mitchell found that those who identified themselves as biracial, as opposed to black, exhibited more self-confidence. 31

The people in her study who identified themselves as biracial "had a stronger sense of who they were," Dr. Mitchell said. "They came out feeling they belonged in both worlds rather than feeling they belonged to neither." 32

Nevertheless, living with the biracial label can be stressful, Dr. Mitchell says. The adults who identified themselves as biracial reported higher levels of anxiety than those who called themselves black. 33

"A lot of them had experienced a lot of stuff from teachers and kids," said Dr. Mitchell, a clinical psychologist in Waltham, Mass. "But the outcome is that they really know who they are at the end and they came out really healthy when they got through the stress." 34

Taking on the biracial identity runs up against a pillar of American race relations: the "one-drop rule." 35

Under this rule, anyone possessing one drop of African blood, no matter how remote in their ancestry, was considered black. In the Caribbean, Latin America and even South Africa, by contrast, those who are of mixed ancestry are considered distinct from blacks. 36

For much of America's history, the one-drop rule was embedded in law, part of the network of Jim Crow laws that set blacks apart as second-class 37 citizens, particularly in the South. While the one-drop rule has all but dis-appeared as law, its cultural legacy remains, and this is what children of black and white parents like Ms. LaSonde are fighting.

The impact of the movement on the larger society remains unclear. "If a person uses the multiethnic identity as a way of creating bridges, it is pos-itive and progressive," said Reginald Daniel, a professor of Latin American and Afro-American studies at UCLA who has written extensively on multi-racial Americans. [38]

"The problem is, some people may be unwittingly wanting to escape the stigma that society still places on people of color," said Dr. Daniel, who is generally supportive of the movement. [39]

Perhaps surprisingly, given the historic pressures for black unity, some civil rights organizations speak favorably of the biracial movement. [40]

"It's an interesting development," said the Rev. Joseph Lowery, presi-dent of the Southern Christian Leadership Conference. [41]

"What's implied in labeling everybody black who has any black blood . . . is that you are contaminated," the Rev. Lowery said. By attacking this premise, he said, the multiracial movement may cause some white Ameri-cans to see the illogic of classifying people by race for the purpose of discrim-inating against them. [42]

"We're not just talking about a name in a box," says Ms. LaSonde. "We're talking about an identity, a *raison d'être*. We are the children of two mighty nations at war with each other since the beginning of time in this hemi-sphere." [43]

STUDY QUESTIONS

1. What is the traditional basis for defining blackness in the American South? What kinds of "tests" were applied? What is the "one-drop rule"?

2. What is the practical basis for supporting the category of "multiracial"? the politi-cal basis? the ideological basis? Who, according to the article, supports the use of such a category?

3. What arguments can you construct against such a "middle" or "compromising" category?

4. What kinds of psychological effects are said to occur because of the simple black-white division? What kind of research is available to suggest the different psycho-logical effects of those who are identified publicly as biracial?

5. What kinds of statistics are available to suggest the trends in interracial marriages? How many children were born to black-white couples in 1968? in 1988?

6. Describe the kinds of evidence the newspaper article uses to promote the new "multiracial" category? What kinds of people are quoted in support of the cate-gory? Who specifically speaks in favor of it? In what ways are statistics used? How strong is the case against the category, according to the article?

AFTERWORD

THEME

Literary works are, of course, about *something*. A work is always "about" something concrete: Robbie Clipper Sethi's story "Grace" is about a visit of the groom's parents to a newlywed couple's home. That is its SUB-JECT. But literature is also about things other than *specific* events and details. "Grace" is also about cross-cultural marriages and the special problems of parents and families who have different cultural expectations. This, too, is the *subject*, but stated more generally. It is therefore important to be clear when you are talking about the *specific subject* and when about the *general subject*.

Once we get beyond the particulars and into generalization, readers begin to have a larger and larger role in formulating just what the general subject is. For every generalization leaves out some details and consequently emphasizes others. Some will insist that any statement of the general subject of "Grace" will have to mention the problems of cultural "adaptation"—the stance toward the differences in the expectations of home, work, and so on.

At some point we begin to talk less about the concrete things in the "real" world that the work points to than we do about its "ideas." As we move from the things the work points toward to the stance or position it takes about those things, we move from subject to THEME. "Grace" may be said to have as its theme the necessity of building a marriage according to a new, and clearly articulated, set of guidelines for individuals rather than bowing to cultural expectations. The cultural differences here put a strain on marriage that requires unusual toleration and accommodation. When we get to the realm of ideas and theme, the reader plays an even greater part in selecting and defining; for theme, or the articulation of theme, is virtually an INTERPRETATION of the work.

That does not mean, of course, that readers "own" the work and can extract or impose any theme they choose, though there may be—indeed, probably will be—different wordings or versions of the theme of a work. Another "version" of the theme of Sethi's story, for example, may go something like this: "Grace" is about the difficulty of crossing borders in marriage. Formulating a fuller statement of the theme by bringing these two versions together means not just spinning out of our own head and experience what *we* mean by love, marriage, accommodation, and tolerance, but going back to the story itself. In doing so, with a tentative model of the theme in mind, we may discover the relevance of many details that we may have overlooked earlier, from the title of the story itself to the behavior of all the individual family members. We will also have to adjust our earlier brief statements and examine carefully the limitations of attitude in *all* the characters, including the narrator. Whose "grace" is it that the story finally validates?

It is worth struggling on for the best possible statement of the theme, testing it as it evolves against the particulars of the story, for you will learn more and more about more and more details and implications of the story. But you will never be able to frame a theme that will be a substitute for the richness of the story. That is a major reason why the term "theme" seems better than *moral* or *message*, terms that easily lead to oversimplification and give the illusion that a work of literature exists for its statement, that it is something like a Chinese fortune cookie that tempts you with sweetness of story, drama, or verse to get to the real "meaning" inside.

Another important reason for avoiding the terms "moral" and "message" is the model of literary communication they imply: the author encodes a message that you "receive," open the envelope, and read; or the author sees a great truth, which he teaches you by example. There are, in fact, such things as FABLES and PARABLES, which are short, usually familiar stories that do have as their major aim to teach a moral or religious message. There are ALLEGORIES, narratives in which every detail has reference to another structure of events or ideas. Even so subtle a writer and critic as Henry James spoke of "the figure in the carpet"—that is, a structural or thematic pattern, a pattern that controls every particular, every comma, of a work, which may seem to convey something like "hidden meaning" or a formal equivalent of "message." All of these literary examples assume the same model: (encoding) Sender-(encoded) Message-(decoding) Receiver.

There is a certain attraction, a certain clarity and common sense, even a certain amount of truth in this model. But besides having to carry such baggage as "moral," "message," "encoded message," and such embarrassingly presumptuous assertions as "what Shakespeare is trying to say," the model inevitably suggests that there is only *one* "meaning," one "interpretation" of a work, and it is the function of criticism and literary study to find that "true meaning."

Some nonfiction works do have something like a message. Personal essays or narratives, such as Gary Soto's "Like Mexicans," often make points that approach mere message—likeness of economic class is more important than ethnic identity in marriage—but they more nearly resemble fictional narrative in the importance of theme rather than message. The essays by Elena Padilla (chapter 1) and James Fallows (chapter 5) do aim to inform and convince in a more direct way than most stories, poems, or plays.

Perhaps another way of looking at the difference between theme and message is that while message seeks to inform or convince, theme seeks to have you comprehend and empathize, so that the information or the ideas are less directly articulated, or more broadly accessible. It is difficult to read Wendy Rose's "Julia," for example, without feeling, and the feeling is not empty of significance; it feels as if it means. What, precisely, does it mean? That ugly-grotesque-horrific people are nonetheless human, capable of strong human emotions and therefore also worthy of our attempting to understand them and sympathize with those strong emotions? Yes, but is that a message? Are there not other ways of coming at this poem, through the monstrous greed and inhumanity of Julia's husband, for example, another instance of the bestiality humans are capable of? Or, combining both: there are monsters with human feelings and humans with monstrous appetites. There are clearly meaning and emotions here, but not necessarily a message.

Most poets, playwrights, fiction writers—and even many essayists—do not think in terms of their messages, some easy "conclusion" that can be simply stated or summarized. Their "meaning" is their vision, and their story, poem, or play is itself "what they are trying to say" more than any summary statement would be. They embody their vision in a language that does not belong to the author but to the community and in a literary form that, whatever the work may do that is innovative and original, is part of a literary tradition. The embodied vision or perception, once put before the public, is then the property of its readers. Of course the readers, too, are constrained by the "rules" of the language, the definitions of words, the cultural assumptions of what "makes sense," and what constitutes or has constituted literature. So the readers even now do not "own" the work to make of it whatever they might fancy. But readers, in translating the communal language back to their understanding and experience, will all inevitably and legitimately have somewhat different "readings."

Think of a literary work not as a telegram, but as a musical score. For a work cannot mean until it is read, any more than a musical score can be music until it is played. And every reading and every performance is unique. No two performances of Beethoven's Fifth Symphony will be identical (even when performed by the same orchestra led by the same conductor on consecutive nights). But it will not sound like "You Ain't Nothin' but a Hound Dog" no matter who plays it. Wildly eccentric readings are constrained by the language, history, and communally agreed upon standards of reasonableness. Before you can perform a work, you have to know the score.

If one reason to concern yourself with seeking out the theme of a work and articulating it as best you can is to reimmerse yourself in the details of the work and alert yourself to relationships and implications, another is to apprehend its concerns in such a way that you can relate it to your own experience. If you find the theme of "Grace" to be something like "ethnic differences make impossible marriages," you may still see that the story is about far more than difficulty or impossibility. The story has no such easy "moral" or message. Instead, the story presents a rich account of complex individuals influenced by their cultures but not determined by them.

Articulating a theme does help you relate to the story and to relate the story to you. Though a work does not exist solely to embody a theme, theme is a useful instrument for digging into a story, poem, play, or essay. Habitual attention to theme will reveal similarities among works that you may not have noticed otherwise, and comparing how works handle similar themes will differentiate them, perhaps even help you evaluate them.

Finally, you need to put Humpty-Dumpty together again, however. A work of literature is not an embellished theme; a thematic statement is not a work of literature. Of all the elements of literature, however, theme is the most broadly inclusive, and you will probably get closer to the performed score of the work in trying to frame its theme as precisely and fully as possible than you will by exploring any other single element.

WRITING
ABOUT THE READING

PERSONAL ESSAYS AND NARRATIVES

1. Write a short paper—1,000–1,500 words—on an experience in which you were either the outsider intentionally or unintentionally invading another's turf, or a group member whose turf was being invaded by an outsider.

2. Describe a situation you have witnessed in which someone else was attempting to cross an established line or merge into a diferent group. You may have belonged to one of the groups or you may have been a disinterested observer. Try to relate the feelings of both sides with equal sympathy.

IMITATIONS AND PARODIES

1. Write a story in which an "invader" understands the values of the group she or he invades—but appears at first to be an insensitive violator.

2. Imitate "what gramma said about her grandpa" to produce a poem or sketch about an ancestor of yours.

ANALYTICAL AND ARGUMENTATIVE PAPER

Analyze the issues of community solidarity versus cosmopolitan openness. For example, should there be Irish-American clubs, or White Only (or Blacks Only) or Men Only private social organizations or schools? Is there a difference between a Whites Only club and a Blacks or Asians or Hispanics Only one?

RESEARCH PAPERS

1. How many blacks served in the armed forces during World War I? What efforts, if any, were made by blacks to avoid serving on political grounds? What promises or expectations were there about how race relations would change after World War I? What can you find in newspapers or magazines of the late 1960s about the Vietnam War, black servicemen and -women, and what they might expect after the war was over?

2. What are the legends and the historical facts surrounding Pocahontas and her relations with whites?

3. Trace the history of miscegenation laws since 1900. What races or ethnic groups were not allowed to marry in the South, the Far West, the Northeast, in 1900, 1914, 1920, 1929, 1941, 1950, and 1964?

    Or trace the history and nature of such laws in your region.

    Or trace the history of the debate over miscegenation in a relevant decade or period, detailing the arguments on both sides.

Student Writing

A LAVENDER LIFE

Juli Nishimuta

Funny you don't look Japanese,
They say.
I don't feel Japanese either.
But my name is.

They call it,   5
Multi-racial, multi-cultural, mixed, mutt.
Hey Hapa-haole, you chop suey, eh?
Mixed, chopped, blended, pureed, whipped.

I feel the blood of my ancestors,
The Samurai warrior,   10
The Spanish conquistador,
The Knights of The Round Table.
They give me strength.

My father was a farmer, a soldier,
with strong arms and beefy hands.   15
American-Japanese,
Nissei-Newspaperman.

Is she your daughter?
They ask my mother.
Funny, she doesn't have red hair and blue eyes,   20
Like you do.

She's also,
Jules the Gemini,
Mercurial, a magical pixie,
Watch out! The spell-caster   25
will sprinkle her dust upon you.

A rain-loving, forest seeking,
creature of nature,
she talks to redwoods, squirrels, sparrows.
The animals talk to her,   30
and she listens.

The cat comes to her,
calls to her, you know me.
I know you.
You help me heal, the cat smiles.   35

So,
what is a lesbian feminist perspective, anyway?
A love unknown, a world unseen.
Sisters, my sisters, call to me,
Strong women, Wise women, Witchy women.   40

Who are you?
They ask.
But the boxes don't fit,
Anglo.
Hispanic.   45
Asian.
so I write in,
All of the above.

8

AMERICANS

There is, of course, no such thing as a typical American; no single, quintessential "American" society; no single set of cultural assumptions that covers the geography from Alaska to Puerto Rico or the ethnography from Native American to Latino to Jew to Moslem to African American to Cambodian. Every American life is essentially individual, modified by the heritages and desires of an individual who lives out his or her own life story in some particular location or locations, community or communities. It is an irony that the descendants of those who first lived in this land (the United States, Canada, the Caribbean) are, in North America at least, a "minority." From about the time of the American Revolution to World War I or a bit later, the more or less official image of the typical American (citizen of the United States) was of someone of northern European ancestry. In reality, there were, in addition to Native Americans, innumerable Hispanics who had occupied large portions of South and Central America and many sections of what is now the United States. There were the French, from Quebec to Louisiana; the millions of African Americans who had been forcibly brought to the New World as slaves; the Germans of Pennsylvania; those who, from mid-nineteenth century, fled the Continental wars and revolutions; the Irish who, at the same period, fled starvation in their native land; and the Chinese who were "imported" to build U.S. railways. In the last decades of the nineteenth century southern and eastern Europeans came by the millions; between the World Wars, refugees from Nazi Germany and occupied sections of Europe; and after the Korean and Vietnam wars millions of Asians. And these are only the gross movements of peoples: there has been a steady stream of new arrivals. The image of the typical American is no longer the northern European American; it is the new arrival, the immigrant, who is ironically the most typical. Except for Native Americans the typical American is someone whose family, or part of whose family, has arrived here in the past twenty, fifty, or one hundred years.

Whoever we are and whatever we bring with us, the journey to a new place or the entry into a new culture is full of surprises. No other way of life is exactly like ours; no two cultures have exactly the same customs, habits, rituals, and expectations. Making the adjustment can be painful or exciting—or both. Learning the new rules is one thing; discovering what the way of life is really like, with all its built-in values and assumptions, is something else again. No one brings along to a life in a new place exactly what is needed and expected there, and old ways and new expectations— like exotic new possessions and treasured old ones—remain continually in contrast, often in deep conflict. The "I" that a person discovers in a new world is often a revelation—a new identity only partly descended from the old.

That is the case for most Americans in the past century or so and for many in the past couple decades. When we circumscribe parts of the American community and identify them in ethnic terms, we not only mark "them" as "different" but also as "the same." Though we know that of course there are among the African-American population rich and poor, brilliant and dull, educated and uneducated, they are assumed by many (including many within their culture) to be ethnically or culturally homogeneous. But Africa is a vast continent and was made up of many peoples; the slaves were members of many tribes and nations from different parts of the African continent, physically, historically, culturally diverse. Moreover, over the three to five centuries that Africans have lived in the Americas— despite slavery, racism, Jim Crow, and social barriers—few African Americans who descended from slaves are still "pure" blooded Africans; none, it seems safe to say, is culturally thoroughly "African."

This diversity and heterogeneity is true of any cultural group that came to America several generations ago. Europe includes Swedes and Slavs, Italians and Bretons, to mention but a few of the tribes and nations. Though many "older" European-American families think of themselves as

"English" (or "German" or "Swedish"), there are very few Americans who do not have in their genealogy three or more ethnic roots if they can *even find out what they are.* A student in one of my New World literature classes came back from spring break all excited. I had asked each student early in the term to do a genealogical profile; she had identified her heritage as "English." Now, she said, she realized she was "ethnic"; her great-grand-mother had told her of the Scots, French Huguenots, and even Danes in the family tree! All four of the "African Americans" in the class had, even within the past three generations, Native American or European "blood"; one had spent a year in Paris and was fluent in French, another grew up in Germany. Reservations have to some degree isolated Native Americans, but Joseph Bruchac is Abnaki and Slovakian, Paula Gunn Allen is Lakota and Lebanese, and Louise Erdrich is Chippewa and German American. Indeed, if one definition of an American is someone who lives on this conti-nent or on a Caribbean island but whose family came fairly recently from elsewhere, another is that anyone whose family has been here more than three or four generations probably has had several ethnic strains superadded to that which is presumed to be the predominant heritage.

Americans are new or mixed or both. And that's what a great many stories, poems, and essays about America and Americans are about: what it's like to be new, or what it's like to encounter "others." America provides a common meeting place for great varieties of people who can come together in a more or less neutral setting so that their various values can compete legitimately.

"Neutral" the setting never truly is, of course, in an absolute way. Somebody gets there first, somebody sets the rules; the talents, language skills, and material possessions give some competitors advantages and others liabilities. And people or backgrounds never do "melt"; individuals, as well as peoples, carry their baggage with them, for better or worse. America is a series of different societies made up of different kinds of Americans of dif-ferent origins, traditions, and histories, somehow intermingled. Here is where "home" comes to be after long struggle. Here is where we confront the "fences" and negotiate the "crossings"; here is where self meets other, where the old forces of family, ancestry, and language are confronted with new situations, where challenge is lived out in everyday life and work.

The writings in this chapter suggest some of the many varieties of American experience that result from the steady confrontations of culture and of self that *are* America at its most basic. Sometimes that America is an admirable place, approaching that ideal culture that its Idea—its Dream—represents at its best. Sometimes it falls far short of its ideals. The stories that result from the lives lived within it are of varied kinds and moods—there are tragedies, farces, success stories, narratives of heartbreak and disappointment, poems of aspiration and despair. All such tones and all such literary "kinds" reflect actuality as well as the desires and fears of those writing them. The history of America is a collection of the stories and perspectives of individual drives and conflicts, confrontations between individual and family or heritage, customs coming up against other customs, anxieties of belonging up against stubborn retentions of selves defined as old habits and rules. Most stories approach America in a spirit of hopefulness and idealism at the beginning; how that hope fares is the focus of most experiences about American life.

Toni Cade Bambara

Dancer, teacher, critic, editor, activist, and writer, Toni Cade Bambara was born in New York and educated there (B.A. from Queens College, M.A. from City College of the City University of New York). She has published two collections of short stories—*Gorilla, My Love* (1972) and *The Sea Birds Are Still Alive* (1977)—and a novel, *The Salt Eaters* (1980).

THE LESSON

Back in the days when everyone was old and stupid or young and foolish and me and Sugar were the only ones just right, this lady moved on our block with nappy hair and proper speech and no makeup. And quite naturally we laughed at her, laughed the way we did at the junk man who went about his business like he was some big-time president and his sorry-ass horse his secretary. And we kinda hated her too, hated the way we did the winos who cluttered up our parks and pissed on our handball walls and stank up our hallways and stairs so you couldn't halfway play hide-and-seek without a goddamn gas mask. Miss Moore was her name. The only woman on the block with no first name. And she was black as hell, cept for her feet, which were fish-white and spooky. And she was always planning these boring-ass things for us to do, us being my cousin, mostly, who lived on the block cause we all moved North the same time and to the same apartment then spread out gradual to breathe. And our parents would yank our heads into some kinda shape and crisp up our clothes so we'd be presentable for travel with Miss Moore, who always looked like she was going to church, though she never did. Which is just one of things the grown-ups talked about when they talked behind her back like a dog. But when she came calling with some sachet she'd sewed up or some gingerbread she'd made or some book, why then they'd all be too embarrassed to turn her down and we'd get handed over all spruced up. She'd been to college and said it was only right that she should take responsibility for the young ones' education, and she not even related by marriage or blood. So they'd go for it. Specially Aunt Gretchen. She was the main gofer in the family. You got some ole dumb shit foolishness you want somebody to go for, you send for Aunt Gretchen. She been screwed into the go-along for so long, it's a blood-deep natural thing with her. Which is how she got saddled with me and Sugar and Junior in the first place while our mothers were in a la-de-da apartment up the block having a good ole time.

So this one day Miss Moore rounds us all up at the mailbox and it's puredee hot and she's knockin herself out about arithmetic. And school suppose to let up in summer I heard, but she don't never let up. And the starch in my pinafore scratching the shit outta me and I'm really hating this nappy-head bitch and her goddamn college degree. I'd much rather go to the pool or to the show where it's cool. So me and Sugar leaning on the mailbox being surly, which is a Miss Moore word. And Flyboy checking out what everybody brought for lunch. And Fat Butt already wasting his peanut-butter-and jelly sandwich like the pig he is. And Junebug punchin on Q.T.'s arm for potato chips. And Rosie Giraffe shifting from one hip to the other waiting for somebody to step on her foot or ask her if she from Georgia so she can kick ass, preferably Mercedes'. And Miss Moore asking us do we know what money is, like we a bunch of retards. I mean real money, she say, like it's only poker chips or monopoly papers we lay on the grocer. So right away I'm tired of this and say so. And would much rather snatch Sugar and go to the Sunset and terrorize the West Indian kids and take their hair ribbons and their money too. And Miss Moore files that remark away for next week's lesson on brotherhood, I can tell. And finally I say we oughta get to the subway cause it's cooler and besides we might meet some cute boys. Sugar done swiped her mama's lipstick, so we ready.

So we heading down the street and she's boring us silly about what things cost and what our parents make and how much goes for rent and how money ain't divided up right in this country. And then she gets to the part about we all poor and live in the slums, which I don't feature. And I'm ready to speak on that, but she steps out in the street and hails two cabs just like that. Then she hustles half the crew in with her and hands me a five-dollar bill and tells me to calculate 10 percent tip for the driver. And we're off. Me and Sugar and Junebug and Flyboy hangin out the window and hollering to everybody, putting lipstick on each other cause Flyboy a faggot anyway, and making farts with our sweaty armpits. But I'm mostly trying to figure how to spend this money. But they all fascinated with the meter ticking and Junebug starts laying bets as to how much it'll read when Flyboy can't hold his breath no more. Then Sugar lays bets as to how much it'll be when we get there. So I'm stuck. Don't nobody want to go for my plan, which is to jump out at the next light and run off to the first bar-b-que we can find. Then the driver tells us to get the hell out cause we there already. And the meter reads eighty-five cents. And I'm stalling to figure out the tip and Sugar say give him a dime. And I decide he don't need it bad as I do, so later for him. But then he tries to take off with Junebug foot still in the door so we talk about his mama something ferocious. Then we check out that we on Fifth Avenue and everybody dressed up in stockings. One lady in a fur coat, hot as it is. White folks crazy.

"This is the place," Miss Moore say, presenting it to us in the voice she   4
uses at the museum. "Let's look in the windows before we go in."

"Can we steal?" Sugar asks very serious like she's getting the ground   5
rules squared away before she plays. "I beg your pardon," say Miss Moore,
and we fall out. So she leads us around the windows of the toy store and me
and Sugar screamin, "This is mine, that's mine, I gotta have that, that was
made for me, I was born for that," till Big Butt drowns us out.

"Hey, I'm goin to buy that there."   6

"That there? You don't even know what it is, stupid."   7

"I do so," he say punchin on Rosie Giraffe. "It's a microscope."   8

"Whatcha gonna do with a microscope, fool?"   9

"Look at things."   10

"Like what, Ronald?" ask Miss Moore. And Big Butt ain't got the first   11
notion. So here go Miss Moore gabbing about the thousands of bacteria in a
drop of water and the somethinorother in a speck of blood and the million
and one living things in the air around us is invisible to the naked eye. And
what she say that for? Junebug go to town on that "naked" and we rolling.
Then Miss Moore ask what it cost. So we all jam into the window smudgin
it up and the price tag say $300. So then she ask how long'd take for Big Butt
and Junebug to save up their allowances. "Too long," I say. "Yeh," adds
Sugar, "outgrown it by that time." And Miss Moore say no, you never out-
grow learning instruments. "Why, even medical students and interns and,"
blah, blah, blah. And we ready to choke Big Butt for bringing it up in the
first damn place.

"This here costs four hundred eighty dollars," say Rosie Giraffe. So we   12
pile up all over her to see what she pointin out. My eyes tell me it's a chunk
of glass cracked with something heavy, and different-color inks dripped into
the splits, then the whole thing put into a oven or something. But the $480
it don't make sense.

"That's a paperweight made of semi-precious stones fused together under   13
tremendous pressure," she explains slowly, with her hands doing the mining
and all the factory work.

"So what's a paperweight?" asks Rosie Giraffe.   14

"To weigh paper with, dumbbell," say Flyboy, the wise man from the   15
East.

"Not exactly," say Miss Moore, which is what she say when you warm   16
or way off too. "It's to weigh paper down so it won't scatter and make your
desk untidy." So right away me and Sugar curtsy to each other and then to
Mercedes who is more the tidy type.

"We don't keep paper on top of the desk in my class," say Junebug,   17
figuring Miss Moore crazy or lyin one.

"At home, then," she say. "Don't you have a calendar and a pencil case   18 and a blotter and a letter-opener on your desk at home where you do your homework?" And she know damn well what our homes look like cause she nosys around in them every chance she gets.

"I don't even have a desk," say Junebug. "Do we?"   19

"No. And I don't get no homework neither," say Big Butt.   20

"And I don't even have a home," say Flyboy like he do at school to keep   21
the white folks off his back and sorry for him. Send this poor kid to camp
posters, is his specialty.

"I do," says Mercedes. "I have a box of stationery on my desk and a   22
picture of my cat. My godmother bought the stationery and the desk. There's
a big rose on each sheet and the envelopes smell like roses."

"Who wants to know about your smelly-ass stationery," say Rosie Giraffe   23
fore I can get my two cents in.

"It's important to have a work area all your own so that . . ."   24

"Will you look at this sailboat, please," say Flyboy, cuttin her off and   25
pointin to the thing like it was his. So once again we tumble all over each
other to gaze at this magnificent thing in the toy store which is just big enough
to maybe sail two kittens across the pond if you strap them to the posts tight.
We all start reciting the price tag like we in assembly. "Handcrafted sailboat
of fiberglass at one thousand one hundred ninety-five dollars."

"Unbelievable," I hear myself say and am really stunned. I read it again   26
for myself just in case the group recitation put me in a trance. Same thing.
For some reason this pisses me off. We look at Miss Moore and she lookin at
us, waiting for I dunno what.

Who'd pay all that when you can buy a sailboat set for a quarter at   27
Pop's, a tube of glue for a dime, and a ball of string for eight cents? "It must
have a motor and a whole lot else besides," I say. "My sailboat cost me about
fifty cents."

"But will it take water?" say Mercedes with her smart ass.   28

"Took mine to Alley Pond Park once," say Flyboy. "String broke. Lost   29
it. Pity."

"Sailed mine in Central Park and it keeled over and sank. Had to ask   30
my father for another dollar."

"And you got the strap," laugh Big Butt. "The jerk didn't even have a   31
string on it. My old man wailed on his behind."

Little Q.T. was staring hard at the sailboat and you could see he wanted   32
it bad. But he too little and somebody'd just take it from him. So what the
hell. "This boat for kids, Miss Moore?"

"Parents silly to buy something like that just to get all broke up," say   33
Rosie Giraffe.

"That much money it should last forever," I figure.   34

"My father'd buy it for me if I wanted it."   35

"Your father, my ass," say Rosie Giraffe getting a chance to finally push   36
Mercedes.

"Must be rich people shop here," say Q.T. 37

"You are a very bright boy," say Flyboy. "What was your first clue?" 38
And he rap him on the head with the back of his knuckles, since Q.T. the
only one he could get away with. Though Q.T. liable to come up behind
you years later and get his licks in when you half expect it.

"What I want to know," I says to Miss Moore though I never talk to 39
her, I wouldn't give the bitch that satisfaction, "is how much a real boat
costs? I figure a thousand'd get you a yacht any day."

"Why don't you check that out," she says, "and report back to the group?" 40
Which really pains my ass. If you gonna mess up a perfectly good swim day
least you could do is have some answers. "Let's go in," she say like she got
something up her sleeve. Only she don't lead the way. So me and Sugar turn
the corner to where the entrance is, but when we get there I kinda hang
back. Not that I'm scared, what's there to be afraid of, just a toy store. But
I feel funny, shame. But what I got to be shamed about? Got as much right
to go in as anybody. But somehow I can't seem to get hold of the door, so I
step away for Sugar to lead. But she hangs back too. And I look at her and
she looks at me and this is ridiculous. I mean, damn, I have never ever been
shy about doing nothing or going nowhere. But then Mercedes steps up and
then Rosie Giraffe and Big Butt crowd in behind and shove, and next thing
we all stuffed into the doorway with only Mercedes squeezing past us,
smoothing out her jumper and walking right down the aisle. Then the rest
of us tumble in like a glued-together jigsaw done all wrong. And people
lookin at us. And it's like the time me and Sugar crashed into the Catholic
church on a dare. But once we got in there and everything so hushed and
holy and the candles and the bowin and the handkerchiefs on all the drooping
heads, I just couldn't go through with the plan. Which was for me to run up
to the altar and do a tap dance while Sugar played the nose flute and messed
around in the holy water. And Sugar kept givin me the elbow. Then later
teased me so bad I tied her up in the shower and turned it on and locked her
in. And she'd be there till this day if Aunt Gretchen hadn't finally figured I
was lyin about the boarder takin a shower.

Same thing in the store. We all walkin on tiptoe and hardly touchin the 41
games and puzzles and things. And I watched Miss Moore who is steady
watchin us like she waitin for a sign. Like Mama Drewery watches the sky
and sniffs the air and takes note of just how much slant is in the bird formation. Then me and Sugar bump smack into each other, so busy gazing at the
toys, 'specially the sailboat. But we don't laugh and go into our fat-lady
bump-stomach routine. We just stare at that price tag. Then Sugar run a
finger over the whole boat. And I'm jealous and want to hit her. Maybe not
her, but I sure want to punch somebody in the mouth.

"Watcha bring us here for, Miss Moore?" 42

"You sound angry, Sylvia. Are you mad about something?" Givin me 43
one of them grins like she tellin a grown-up joke that never turns out to be

funny. And she's lookin very closely at me like maybe she plannin to do my portrait from memory. I'm mad, but I won't give her that satisfaction. So I slouch around the store bein very bored and say, "Let's go."

Me and Sugar at the back of the train watchin the tracks whizzin by large then small then gettin gobbled up in the dark. I'm thinkin about this tricky toy I saw in the store. A clown that somersaults on a bar then does chin-ups just cause you yank lightly at his leg. Cost $35. I could see me askin my mother for a $35 birthday clown. "You wanna who that costs what?" she'd say, cocking her head to the side to get a better view of the hole in my head. Thirty-five dollars could buy new bunk beds for Junior and Gretchen's boy. Thirty-five dollars and the whole household could go visit Granddaddy Nelson in the country. Thirty-five dollars would pay for the rent and the piano bill too. Who are these people that spend that much for performing clowns and $1,000 for toy sailboats? What kinda work they do and how they live and how come we ain't in on it? Where we are is who we are, Miss Moore always pointin out. But it don't necessarily have to be that way, she always adds then waits for somebody to say that poor people have to wake up and demand their share of the pie and don't none of us know what kind of pie she talkin about in the first damn place. But she ain't so smart cause I still got her four dollars from the taxi and she sure ain't gettin it. Messin up my day with this shit. Sugar nudges me in my pocket and winks. 44

Miss Moore lines us up in front of the mailbox where we started from, seem like years ago, and I got a headache for thinkin so hard. And we lean all over each other so we can hold up under the draggy-ass lecture she always finishes us off with at the end before we thank her for borin us to tears. But she just looks at us like she readin tea leaves. Finally she say, "Well, what did you think of F.A.O. Schwartz?" 45

Rosie Giraffe mumbles, "White folks crazy." 46

"I'd like to go there again when I get my birthday money," says Mercedes, and we shove her out the pack so she has to lean on the mailbox by herself. 47

"I'd like a shower. Tiring day," say Flyboy. 48

Then Sugar surprises me by sayin, "You know, Miss Moore, I don't think all of us here put together eat in a year what that sailboat costs." And Miss Moore lights up like somebody goosed her. "And?" she say, urging Sugar on. Only I'm standin on her foot so she don't continue. 49

"Imagine for a minute what kind of society it is in which some people can spend on a toy what it would cost to feed a family of six or seven. What do you think?" 50

"I think," say Sugar pushing me off her feet like she never done before, cause I whip her ass in a minute, "that this is not much of a democracy if you ask me. Equal chance to pursue happiness means an equal crack at the dough, don't it?" Miss Moore is besides herself and I am disgusted with Sugar's treachery. So I stand on her foot one more time to see if she'll shove me. She shuts up, and Miss Moore looks at me, sorrowfully I'm thinkin. And somethin weird is goin on, I can feel it in my chest. 51

"Anybody else learn anything today?" lookin dead at me. I walk away 52
and Sugar has to run to catch up and don't even seem to notice when I shrug
her arm off my shoulder.

"Well, we got four dollars anyway," she says. 53

"Uh hunh." 54

"We could go to Hascombs and get half a chocolate layer and then go to 55
the Sunset and still have plenty money for potato chips and ice-cream sodas."

"Uh hunh." 56

"Race you to Hascombs," she say. 57

We start down the block and she gets ahead which is O.K. by me cause 58
I'm goin to the West End and then over to the Drive to think this day through.
She can run if she want to and even run faster. But ain't nobody gonna beat
me at nuthin.

STUDY QUESTIONS

1. What does the opening sentence tell you about the ATTITUDE* of the SPEAKER "back
   in [those] days" *and* the attitude of the speaker at the time of the writing or telling
   of the story? What else do you learn in the very first paragraph about "Miss Moore"?
   about the neighborhood? about the speaker's family? When do you know the speaker
   is a girl? that her name is Sylvia?

2. In paragraph 2, the speaker uses a "Miss Moore word": "surly." Can you find any
   other Miss Moore words in the story? What does this "double VOICE" suggest about
   what may have happened to the speaker since the time of the story? What effect
   does the double voice have (even if you did not notice the specific words and
   identify their "source" at the time you were first reading the story)?

3. How are the rest of the youngsters introduced into the story?

4. What strikes the speaker first about the "white folks" who are the "Americans" on
   Fifth Avenue?

5. Early in the story you may be amused by the youngsters' naïveté, and perhaps a
   little appalled at their amorality, but there seems to be a shift in the story's or the
   reader's relationship to the attitudes of the children when the $480 paperweight is
   introduced. Describe that shift. How long does it last? What is its effect? implication?

6. When the speaker reads for herself the price of the toy model sailboat, she says,
   "For some reason this pisses me off"; what's the reason? Then, "We look at Miss
   Moore and she lookin at us, waiting for I dunno what"; what is she waiting for?

7. Describe the speaker's hesitation in entering the store and her unarticulated reasons. What previous experience does she compare the children's behavior with
   when they first enter the store (paragraph 40)? Why does she feel like punching
   somebody in the mouth (paragraph 41)?

8. What is "the lesson"?

*Words in small capitals are defined in the Glossary.

Gish Jen

B orn in 1955 to Chinese immigrants, Gish Jen grew up in New York and was educated at Harvard University and the Iowa Writers' Workshop. Novelist, short story writer, and essayist, her stories have appeared in numerous quarterlies and have been anthologized in *The New Generation* and *Best American Short Stories*. She published a novel, *Typical American*, in 1991.

IN THE AMERICAN SOCIETY

I. His Own Society

When my father took over the pancake house, it was to send my little sister Mona and me to college. We were only in junior high at the time, but my father believed in getting a jump on things. "Those Americans always saying it," he told us. "Smart guys thinking in advance." My mother elaborated, explaining that businesses took bringing up, like children. They could take years to get going, she said, years.

In this case, though, we got rich right away. At two months we were breaking even, and at four, those same hotcakes that could barely withstand the weight of butter and syrup were supporting our family with ease. My mother bought a station wagon with air conditioning, my father an over-sized, red vinyl recliner for the back room; and as time went on and the business continued to thrive, my father started to talk about his grandfather and the village he had reigned over in China—things my father had never talked about when he worked for other people. He told us about the bags of rice his family would give out to the poor at New Year's, and about the people who came to beg, on their hands and knees, for his grandfather to intercede for the more wayward of their relatives. "Like that Godfather in the movie," he would tell us as, his feet up, he distributed paychecks. Sometimes an employee would get two green envelopes instead of one, which meant that Jimmy needed a tooth pulled, say, or that Tiffany's husband was in the clinker again.

"It's nothing, nothing," he would insist, sinking back into his chair. "Who else is going to take care of you people?"

My mother would mostly just sigh about it. "Your father thinks this is

China," she would say, and then she would go back to her mending. Once in a while, though, when my father had given away a particularly large sum, she would exclaim, outraged, "But this here is the U—S—of—A!"—this apparently having been what she used to tell immigrant stock boys when they came in late.

She didn't work at the supermarket anymore; but she had made it to the rank of manager before she left, and this had given her not only new words and phrases, but new ideas about herself, and about America, and about what was what in general. She had opinions, now, on how downtown should be zoned; she could pump her own gas and check her own oil; and for all she used to chide Mona and me for being "copycats," she herself was now interested in espadrilles, and wallpaper, and most recently, the town country club.

"So join already," said Mona, flicking a fly off her knee.

My mother enumerated the problems as she sliced up a quarter round of watermelon: There was the cost. There was the waiting list. There was the fact that no one in our family played either tennis or golf.

"So what?" said Mona.

"It would be waste," said my mother.

"Me and Callie can swim in the pool."

"Plus you need that recommendation letter from a member."

"Come *on*," said Mona. "Annie's mom'd write you a letter in a *sec.*"

My mother's knife glinted in the early summer sun. I spread some more newspaper on the picnic table.

"*Plus* you have to eat there twice a month. You know what that means." My mother cut another, enormous slice of fruit.

"No, I *don't* know what that means," said Mona.

"It means Dad would have to wear a jacket, dummy," I said.

"Oh! Oh! Oh!" said Mona, clasping her hand to her breast. "Oh! Oh! Oh! Oh! Oh!"

We all laughed: my father had no use for nice clothes, and would wear only ten-year-old shirts, with grease-spotted pants, to show how little he cared what anyone thought.

"Your father doesn't believe in joining the American society," said my mother. "He wants to have his own society."

"So go to dinner without him." Mona shot her seeds out in long arcs over the lawn. "Who cares what he thinks?"

But of course we all did care, and knew my mother could not simply up and do as she pleased. For in my father's mind, a family owed its head a degree of loyalty that left no room for dissent. To embrace what he embraced was to love; and to embrace something else was to betray him.

He demanded a similar sort of loyalty of his workers, whom he treated more like servants than employees. Not in the beginning, of course. In the beginning all he wanted was for them to keep on doing what they used to do, and to that end he concentrated mostly on leaving them alone. As the months passed, though, he expected more and more of them, with the result that for all his largesse, he began to have trouble keeping help. The cooks and busboys complained that he asked them to fix radiators and trim hedges, not only at the restaurant, but at our house; the waitresses that he sent them on errands and made them chauffeur him around. Our head waitress, Gertrude, claimed that he once even asked her to scratch his back.

"It's not just the blacks don't believe in slavery," she said when she quit.   23

My father never quite registered her complaint, though, nor those of the   24
others who left. Even after Eleanor quit, then Tiffany, then Gerald, and Jimmy, and even his best cook, Eureka Andy, for whom he had bought new glasses, he remained mostly convinced that the fault lay with them.

"All they understand is that assembly line," he lamented. "Robots, they   25
are. They want to be robots."

There *were* occasions when the clear running truth seemed to eddy, when   26
he would pinch the vinyl of his chair up into little peaks and wonder if he was doing things right. But with time he would always smooth the peaks back down; and when business started to slide in the spring, he kept on like a horse in his ways.

By the summer our dishboy was overwhelmed with scraping. It was no   27
longer just the hashbrowns that people were leaving for trash, and the service was as bad as the food. The waitresses served up French pancakes instead of German, apple juice instead of orange, spilt things on laps, on coats. On the Fourth of July some greenhorn sent an entire side of fries slaloming down a lady's *massif centrale*. Meanwhile in the back room, my father labored through articles on the economy.

"What is housing starts?" he puzzled. "What is GNP?"   28

Mona and I did what we could, filling in as busgirls and bookkeepers   29
and, one afternoon, stuffing the comments box that hung by the cashier's desk. That was Mona's idea. We rustled up a variety of pens and pencils, checked boxes for an hour, smeared the cards up with coffee and grease, and waited. It took a few days for my father to notice that the box was full, and he didn't say anything about it for a few days more. Finally, though, he started to complain of fatigue; and then he began to complain that the staff was not what it could be. We encouraged him in this—pointing out, for instance, how many dishes got chipped—but in the end all that happened was that, for the first time since we took over the restaurant, my father got it into his head to fire someone. Skip, a skinny busboy who was saving up for a sportscar, said nothing as my father mumbled on about the price of dishes. My father's hands shook as he wrote out the severance check; and he spent the rest of the day napping in his chair once it was over.

As it was going on midsummer, Skip wasn't easy to replace. We hung a   30
sign in the window and advertised in the paper, but no one called the first week, and the person who called the second didn't show up for his interview. The third week, my father phoned Skip to see if he would come back, but a friend of his had already sold him a Corvette for cheap.

Finally a Chinese guy named Booker turned up. He couldn't have been   31 more than thirty, and was wearing a lighthearted seersucker suit, but he looked as though life had him pinned: his eyes were bloodshot and his chest sunken, and the muscles of his neck seemed to strain with the effort of holding his head up. In a single dry breath he told us that he had never bussed tables but was willing to learn, and that he was on the lam from the deportation authorities.

"I do not want lie to you," he kept saying. He had come to the United 32 States on a student visa, had run out of money, and was now in a bind. He was loath to go back to Taiwan, as it happened—he looked up at this point, to be sure my father wasn't pro-KMT[1]—but all he had was a phony social security card and a willingness to absorb all blame, should anything untoward come to pass.

"I do not think, anyway, that it is against law to hire me, only to be 33 me," he said, smiling faintly.

Anyone else would have examined him on this, but my father conceived 34 of laws as speed bumps rather than curbs. He wiped the counter with his sleeve, and told Booker to report the next morning.

"I will be good worker," said Booker. 35

"Good," said my father. 36

"Anything you want me to do, I will do." 37

My father nodded. 38

Booker seemed to sink into himself for a moment. "Thank you," he said 39 finally. "I am appreciate your help. I am very, very appreciate for everything." He reached out to shake my father's hand.

My father looked at him. "Did you eat today?" he asked in Mandarin. 40

Booker pulled at the hem of his jacket. 41

"Sit down," said my father. "Please, have a seat." 42

My father didn't tell my mother about Booker, and my mother didn't 43 tell my father about the country club. She would never have applied, except that Mona, while over at Annie's, had let it drop that our mother wanted to join. Mrs. Lardner came by the very next day.

"Why, I'd be honored and delighted to write you people a letter," she 44 said. Her skirt billowed around her.

"Thank you so much," said my mother. "But it's too much trouble for 45 you, and also my husband is . . ."

"Oh, it's no trouble at all, no trouble at all. I tell you." She leaned 46 forward so that her chest freckles showed. "I know just how it is. It's a secret of course, but you know, my natural father was Jewish. Can you see it? Just look at my skin."

"My husband," said my mother. 47

"I'd be honored and delighted," said Mrs. Lardner with a little wave of 48 her hands. "Just honored and delighted."

Mona was triumphant. "See, Mom," she said, waltzing around the kitchen 49

1. Kuomintang ("National People's party"); forced from mainland China by the Communists, it has ruled Taiwan since 1949.

when Mrs. Lardner left. "What did I tell you? 'I'm just honored and delighted, just honored and delighted.' " She waved her hands in the air.

"You know, the Chinese have a saying," said my mother. "To do nothing is better than to overdo. You mean well, but you tell me now what will happen."

"I'll talk Dad into it," said Mona, still waltzing. "Or I bet Callie can. He'll do anything Callie says."

"I can try, anyway," I said.

"Did you hear what I said?" said my mother. Mona bumped into the broom closet door. "You're not going to talk anything; you've already made enough trouble." She started on the dishes with a clatter.

Mona poked diffidently at a mop.

I sponged off the counter. "Anyway," I ventured, "I bet our name'll never even come up."

"That's if we're lucky," said my mother.

"There's all these people waiting," I said.

"Good," she said. She started on a pot.

I looked over at Mona, who was still cowering in the broom closet. "In fact, there's some black family's been waiting so long, they're going to sue," I said.

My mother turned off the water. "Where'd you hear that?"

"Patty told me."

She turned the water back on, starting to wash a dish, then put it back down and shut the faucet.

"I'm sorry," said Mona.

"Forget it," said my mother. "Just forget it."

Booker turned out to be a model worker, whose boundless gratitude translated into a willingness to do anything. As he also learned quickly, he soon knew not only how to bus, but how to cook, and how to wait table, and how to keep the books. He fixed the walk-in door so that it stayed shut, reupholstered the torn seats in the dining room, and devised a system for tracking inventory. The only stone in the rice was that he tended to be sickly; but, reliable even in illness, he would always send a friend to take his place. In this way we got to know Ronald, Lynn, Dirk, and Cedric, all of whom, like Booker, had problems with their legal status and were anxious to please. They weren't all as capable as Booker, though, with the exception of Cedric, whom my father often hired even when Booker was well. A round wag of a man who called Mona and me *shou hou*—skinny monkeys—he was a professed nonsmoker who was nevertheless always begging drags off of other people's cigarettes. This last habit drove our head cook, Fernando, crazy, especially since, when refused a hit, Cedric would occasionally snitch one. Winking impishly at Mona and me, he would steal up to an ashtray, take a quick puff, and then break out laughing so that the smoke came rolling out of his mouth in a great incriminatory cloud. Fernando accused him of stealing fresh cigarettes too, even whole packs.

"Why else do you think he's weaseling around in the back of the store all the time," he said. His face was blotchy with anger. "The man is a frigging thief."

Other members of the staff supported him in this contention and joined in on an "Operation Identification," which involved numbering and initialing their cigarettes—even though what they seemed to fear for wasn't so much their cigarettes as their jobs. Then one of the cooks quit; and rather than promote someone, my father hired Cedric for the position. Rumors flew that he was taking only half the normal salary, that Alex had been pressured to resign, and that my father was looking for a position with which to placate Booker, who had been bypassed because of his health.

The result was that Fernando categorically refused to work with Cedric.

"The only way I'll cook with that piece of slime," he said, shaking his huge tattooed fist, "is if it's his ass frying on the grill."

My father cajoled and cajoled, to no avail, and in the end was simply forced to put them on different schedules.

The next week Fernando got caught stealing a carton of minute steaks. My father would not tell even Mona and me how he knew to be standing by the back door when Fernando was on his way out, but everyone suspected Booker. Everyone but Fernando, that is, who was sure Cedric had been the tip-off. My father held a staff meeting in which he tried to reassure everyone that Alex had left on his own, and that he had no intention of firing anyone. But though he was careful not to mention Fernando, everyone was so amazed that he was being allowed to stay that Fernando was incensed nonetheless.

"Don't you all be putting your bug eyes on me," he said. "*He's* the frigging crook." He grabbed Cedric by the collar.

Cedric raised an eyebrow. "Cook, you mean," he said.

At this Fernando punched Cedric in the mouth; and the words he had just uttered notwithstanding, my father fired him on the spot.

With everything that was happening, Mona and I were ready to be getting out of the restaurant. It was almost time: the days were still stuffy with summer, but our window shade had started flapping in the evening as if gearing up to go out. That year the breezes were full of salt, as they sometimes were when they came in from the East, and they blew anchors and docks through my mind like so many tumbleweeds, filling my dreams with wherries and lobsters and grainy-faced men who squinted, day in and day out, at the sky.

It was time for a change, you could feel it; and yet the pancake house was the same as ever. The day before school started my father came home with bad news.

"Fernando called police," he said, wiping his hand on his pant leg.

My mother naturally wanted to know what police; and so with much coughing and hawing, the long story began, the latest installment of which had the police calling immigration, and immigration sending an investigator. My mother sat stiff as whalebone as my father described how the man summarily refused lunch on the house and how my father had admitted, under pressure, that he knew there were "things" about his workers.

"So now what happens?" 79

My father didn't know. "Booker and Cedric went with him to the jail," 80 he said. "But me, here I am." He laughed uncomfortably.

The next day my father posted bail for "his boys" and waited apprehen- 81 sively for something to happen. The day after that he waited again, and the day after that he called our neighbor's law student son, who suggested my father call the immigration department under an alias. My father took his advice; and it was thus that he discovered that Booker was right: it was illegal for aliens to work, but it wasn't to hire them.

In the happy interval that ensued, my father apologized to my mother, 82 who in turn confessed about the country club, for which my father had no choice but to forgive her. Then he turned his attention back to "his boys."

My mother didn't see that there was anything to do. 83

"I like to talking to the judge," said my father. 84

"This is not China," said my mother. 85

"I'm only talking to him. I'm not give him money unless he wants it." 86

"You're going to land up in jail." 87

"So what else I should do?" My father threw up his hands. "Those are 88 my boys."

"Your boys!" exploded my mother. "What about your family? What 89 about your wife?"

My father took a long sip of tea. "You know," he said finally, "in the 90 war my father sent our cook to the soldiers to use. He always said it—the province comes before the town, the town comes before the family."

"A restaurant is not a town," said my mother. 91

My father sipped at his tea again. "You know, when I first come to the 92 United States, I also had to hide-and-seek with those deportation guys. If people did not helping me, I'm not here today."

My mother scrutinized her hem. 93

After a minute I volunteered that before seeing a judge, he might try a 94 lawyer.

He turned. "Since when did you become so afraid like your mother?" 95

I started to say that it wasn't a matter of fear, but he cut me off. 96

"What I need today," he said, "is a son." 97

My father and I spent the better part of the next day standing in lines at 98 the immigration office. He did not get to speak to a judge, but with much persistence he managed to speak to a judge's clerk, who tried to persuade him that it was not her place to extend him advice. My father, though, shamelessly plied her with compliments and offers of free pancakes until she finally conceded that she personally doubted anything would happen to either Cedric or Booker.

"Especially if they're 'needed workers,' " she said, rubbing at the red 99 marks her glasses left on her nose. She yawned. "Have you thought about sponsoring them to become permanent residents?"

Could he do that? My father was overjoyed. And what if he saw to it right away? Would she perhaps put in a good word with the judge?

She yawned again, her nostrils flaring. "Don't worry," she said. "They'll get a fair hearing."

My father returned jubilant. Booker and Cedric hailed him as their savior, their Buddha incarnate. He was like a father to them, they said; and laughing and clapping, they made him tell the story over and over, sorting over the details like jewels. And how old was the assistant judge? And what did she say?

That evening my father tipped the paperboy a dollar and bought a pot of mums for my mother, who suffered them to be placed on the dining room table. The next night he took us all out to dinner. Then on Saturday, Mona found a letter on my father's chair at the restaurant.

> Dear Mr. Chang,
> You are the grat boss. But, we do not like to trial, so will runing away now. Plese to excus us. People saying the law in America is fears like dragon. Here is only $140. We hope some day we can pay back the rest bale. You will getting intrest, as you diserving, so grat a boss you are. Thank you for every thing. In next life you will be burn in rich family, with no more pancaks.
>
> Yours truley,
Booker + Cedric

In the weeks that followed my father went to the pancake house for crises, but otherwise hung around our house, fiddling idly with the sump pump and boiler in an effort, he said, to get ready for winter. It was as though he had gone into retirement, except that instead of moving South, he had moved to the basement. He even took to showering my mother with little attentions, and to calling her "old girl," and when we finally heard that the club had entertained all the applications it could for the year, he was so sympathetic that he seemed more disappointed than my mother.

II. In the American Society

Mrs. Lardner tempered the bad news with an invitation to a bon voyage bash she was throwing for a friend of hers who was going to Greece for six months.

"Do come," she urged. "You'll meet everyone, and then, you know, if things open up in the spring . . ." She waved her hands.

My mother wondered if it would be appropriate to show up at a party for someone they didn't know, but "the honest truth" was that this was an annual affair. "If it's not Greece, it's Antibes," sighed Mrs. Lardner. "We really just do it because his wife left him and his daughter doesn't speak to him, and poor Jeremy just feels so *unloved.*"

She also invited Mona and me to the goings on, as *"demi-*guests" to keep   108
Annie out of the champagne. I wasn't too keen on the idea, but before I could
say anything, she had already thanked us for so generously agreeing to honor
her with our presence.

"A pair of little princesses, you are!" she told us. "A pair of princesses!"   109

The party was that Sunday. On Saturday, my mother took my father   110
out shopping for a suit. As it was the end of September, she insisted that he
buy a worsted rather than a seersucker, even though it was only ten, rather
than fifty percent off. My father protested that it was as hot out as ever,
which was true—a thick Indian summer had cozied murderously up to us—
but to no avail. Summer clothes, said my mother, were not properly worn
after Labor Day.

The suit was unfortunately as extravagant in length as it was in price,   111
which posed an additional quandary, since the tailor wouldn't be in until
Monday. The salesgirl, though, found a way of tacking it up temporarily.

"Maybe this suit not fit me," fretted my father.   112

"Just don't take your jacket off," said the salesgirl.   113

He gave her a tip before they left, but when he got home refused to   114
remove the price tag.

"I like to asking the tailor about the size," he insisted.   115

"You mean you're going to *wear* it and then return it?" Mona rolled her   116
eyes.

"I didn't say I'm return it," said my father stiffly. "I like to asking the   117
tailor, that's all."

The party started off swimmingly, except that most people were wear-   118
ing bermudas or wrap skirts. Still, my parents carried on, sharing with great
feeling the complaints about the heat. Of course my father tried to eat a
cracker full of shallots and burnt himself in an attempt to help Mr. Lardner
turn the coals of the barbecue; but on the whole he seemed to be doing all
right. Not nearly so well as my mother, though, who had accepted an entire
cupful of Mrs. Lardner's magic punch, and seemed indeed to be under some
spell. As Mona and Annie skirmished over whether some boy in their class
inhaled when he smoked, I watched my mother take off her shoes, laughing
and laughing as a man with a beard regaled her with navy stories by the pool.
Apparently he had been stationed in the Orient and remembered a few words
of Chinese, which made my mother laugh still more. My father excused
himself to go to the men's room then drifted back and dropped anchor at the
hors d'oeuvre table, while my mother sailed on to a group of women, who
tinkled at length over the clarity of her complexion. I dug out a book I had
brought.

Just when I'd cracked the spine, though, Mrs. Lardner came by to bewail   119
her shortage of servers. Her caterers were criminals, I agreed; and the next
thing I knew I was handing out bits of marine life, making the rounds as
amiably as I could.

"Here you go, Dad," I said when I got to the hors d'oeuvre table.   120

"Everything is fine," he said.   121

I hesitated to leave him alone; but then the man with the beard zeroed   122
in on him, and though he talked of nothing but my mother, I thought it
would be okay to get back to work. Just that moment, though, Jeremy Brothers lurched our way, an empty, albeit corked, wine bottle in hand. He was
a slim, well-proportioned man, with a Roman nose and small eyes and a nice
manly jaw that he allowed to hang agape.

"Hello," he said drunkenly. "Pleased to meet you."   123

"Pleased to meeting you," said my father.   124

"Right," said Jeremy. "Right. Listen. I have this bottle here, this most   125
recalcitrant bottle. You see that it refuses to do my bidding. I bid it open
sesame, please, and it does nothing." He pulled the cork out with his teeth,
then turned the bottle upside down.

My father nodded.   126

"Would you have a word with it please?" said Jeremy. The man with   127
the beard excused himself. "Would you please have a goddamned word with
it?"

My father laughed uncomfortably.   128

"Ah!" Jeremy bowed a little. "Excuse me, excuse me, excuse me. You   129
are not my man, not my man at all." He bowed again and started to leave,
but then circled back. "Viticulture is not your forte, yes I can see that, see
that plainly. But may I trouble you on another matter? Forget the damned
bottle." He threw it into the pool, and winked at the people he splashed. "I
have another matter. Do you speak Chinese?"

My father said he did not, but Jeremy pulled out a handkerchief with   130
some characters on it anyway, saying that his daughter had sent it from
Hong Kong and that he thought the characters might be some secret message.

"Long life," said my father.   131

"But you haven't looked at it yet."   132

"I know what it says without looking." My father winked at me.   133

"You do?"   134

"Yes, I do."   135

"You're making fun of me, aren't you?"   136

"No, no, no," said my father, winking again.   137

"Who are you anyway?" said Jeremy.   138

His smile fading, my father shrugged.   139

"*Who are you?*"   140

My father shrugged again.   141

Jeremy began to roar. "This is my party, *my party*, and I've never seen   142
you before in my life." My father backed up as Jeremy came toward him.
"*Who are you? WHO ARE YOU?*"

Just as my father was going to step back into the pool, Mrs. Lardner   143
came running up. Jeremy informed her that there was a man crashing his
party.

"Nonsense," said Mrs. Lardner. "This is Ralph Chang, who I invited   144 extra especially so he could meet you." She straightened the collar of Jeremy's peach-colored polo shirt for him.

"Yes, well we've had a chance to chat," said Jeremy. 145

She whispered in his ear; he mumbled something; she whispered something more. 146

"I do apologize," he said finally. 147

My father didn't say anything. 148

"I do." Jeremy seemed genuinely contrite. "Doubtless you've seen drunks before, haven't you? You must have them in China." 149

"Okay," said my father. 150

As Mrs. Lardner glided off, Jeremy clapped his arm over my father's shoulders. "You know, I really am quite sorry, quite sorry." 151

My father nodded. 152

"What can I do, how can I make it up to you?" 153

"No thank you." 154

"No, tell me, tell me," wheedled Jeremy. "Tickets to casino night?" My father shook his head. "You don't gamble. Dinner at Bartholomew's?" My father shook his head again. "You don't eat." Jeremy scratched his chin. "You know, my wife was like you. Old Annabelle could never let me make things up—never, never, never, never, never." 155

My father wriggled out from under his arm. 156

"How about sport clothes? You are rather overdressed, you know, excuse me for saying so. But here." He took off his polo shirt and folded it up. "You can have this with my most profound apologies." He ruffled his chest hairs with his free hand. 157

"No thank you," said my father. 158

"No, take it, take it. Accept my apologies." He thrust the shirt into my father's arms. "I'm so very sorry, so very sorry. Please, try it on." 159

Helplessly holding the shirt, my father searched the crowd for my mother. 160

"Here, I'll help you off with your coat." 161

My father froze. 162

Jeremy reached over and took his jacket off. "Milton's, one hundred twenty-five dollars reduced to one hundred twelve-fifty," he read. "What a bargain, what a bargain!" 163

"Please give it back," pleaded my father. "Please." 164

"Now for your shirt," ordered Jeremy. 165

Heads began to turn. 166

"Take off your shirt." 167

"I do not take orders like a servant," announced my father. 168

"Take off your shirt, or I'm going to throw this jacket right into the pool, just right into this little pool here." Jeremy held it over the water. 169

"Go ahead." 170

"One hundred twelve-fifty," taunted Jeremy. "One hundred twelve . . ." 171

My father flung the polo shirt into the water with such force that part 172 of it bounced back up into the air like a fluorescent fountain. Then it settled into a soft heap on top of the water. My mother hurried up.

"You're a sport!" said Jeremy, suddenly breaking into a smile and slapping my father on the back. "You're a sport! I like that. A man with spirit, that's what you are. A man with panache. Allow me to return to you your jacket." He handed it back to my father. "Good value you got on that, good value."   173

My father hurled the coat into the pool too. "We're leaving," he said grimly. "Leaving!"   174

"Now, Ralphie," said Mrs. Lardner, bustling up; but my father was already stomping off.   175

"Get your sister," he told me. To my mother: "Get your shoes."   176

"That was *great*, Dad," said Mona as we walked down to the car. "You were *stupendous*."   177

"Way to show 'em," I said.   178

"What?" said my father offhandedly.   179

Although it was only just dusk, we were in a gulch, which made it hard to see anything except the gleam of his white shirt moving up the hill ahead of us.   180

"It was all my fault," began my mother.   181

"Forget it," said my father grandly. Then he said, "The only trouble is I left those keys in my jacket pocket."   182

"Oh, *no*, said Mona.   183

"Oh no is right," said my mother.   184

"So we'll walk home," I said.   185

"But how're we going to get into the *house*," said Mona.   186

The noise of the party churned through the silence.   187

"Someone has to going back," said my father.   188

"Let's go to the pancake house first," suggested my mother. "We can wait there until the party is finished, and then call Mrs. Lardner."   189

Having all agreed that that was a good plan, we started walking again.   190

"God, just think," said Mona. "We're going to have to *dive* for them."   191

My father stopped a moment. We waited.   192

"You girls are good swimmers," he said finally. "Not like me."   193

Then his shirt started moving again, and we trooped up the hill after it, into the dark.   194

STUDY QUESTIONS

1. Describe the father's essential CHARACTER traits. What desires motivate him most strongly? What is the source of his values? How important to him are the opinions of others? How important is money? family? his own authority?

2. Under what conditions is the mother "licensed" to disagree with the father or trick him? In what ways do the mother's values differ from the father's?

3. How much do we learn, during the story, about the NARRATOR's values? Why does she remain an amused observer through most of the story? What are her attitudes toward the father? Which episodes demonstrate the narrator's attitudes toward the father most vividly?

4. What strategies does the author use to keep the father from seeming tyrannical and foolish? How is Jeremy Brothers characterized? What new aspects of the father's personality are revealed by his confrontation with Jeremy?

5. How can you tell what the narrator thinks of her father?

6. Why is the SETTING of the story's final episode especially appropriate? How does the mother's conduct at the party affirm aspects of her personality and character revealed earlier in the story? In what ways is the narrator like her father?

7. In what different ways are possessions and cultural "symbols" important to the PLOT of the story? Describe the effect of the final IMAGE of the daughters' diving for their father's keys in the Lardners' swimming pool. How does the previous image—the family waiting in the pancake house for the party to end—affect the final one?

8. Why does the story emphasize so strongly the father's imperfect understanding of English? What signs are there that the daughters are embarrassed by their parents' language skills? In what other ways do generational gaps stand for differences in cultural understanding?

Bharati Mukherjee

Bharati Mukherjee is the author of three novels, *The Tiger's Daughter* (1972), *Wife* (1975), and *Jasmine* (1989); and two volumes of short stories, *Darkness* (1985) and *The Middleman* (1988) which earned the National Book Critics Circle Award. She has also written, along with her husband, Clarke Blaise, two nonfiction books. Mukherjee has been awarded Guggenheim, National Endowment for the Arts, and Woodrow Wilson fellowships, and she currently teaches English at the University of California at Berkeley. Born in Calcutta in 1940, she believes she and her writing have changed since she began to see herself not as an expatriate, an exile looking back to a lost home, but as an immigrant, a citizen of a new country finding her place in that country made up largely of other immigrants.

HINDUS

I ran into Pat at Sotheby's[1] on a Friday morning two years ago. Derek and I had gone to view the Fraser Collection of Islamic miniatures at the York Avenue galleries. It bothered Derek that I knew so little about my heritage. Islam is nothing more than a marauder's faith to me, but the Mogul emperors stayed a long time in the green delta of the Ganges, flattening and reflattening a fort in the village where I was born, and forcing my priestly ancestors to prove themselves brave. Evidence on that score is still inconclusive. That village is now in Bangladesh.

Derek was a filmmaker, lightly employed at that time. We had been married three hundred and thirty-one days.

"So," Pat said, in his flashy, plummy, drawn-out intonation, "you finally made it to the States!"

It was one of those early November mornings when the woodsy smell of overheated bodies in cloth coats clogged the public stairwells. Everywhere around me I detected the plaintive signs of over-preparedness.

"Whatever are you doing here?" He engulfed me in a swirl of Liberty[2] scarf and cashmere lapels.

"Trying to get the woman there to sell me the right catalog," I said.

The woman, a very young thing with slippery skin, ate a lusty Granny Smith apple and ignored the dark, hesitant miniature-lovers hanging about like bats in the daytime.

"They have more class in London," Pat said.

"I wouldn't know. I haven't been back since that unfortunate year at Roedean."[3]

"It was always New York you wanted," Pat laughed. "Don't say I didn't warn you. The world is full of empty promises."

I didn't remember his having warned me about life and the inevitability of grief. It was entirely possible that he had—he had always been given to clowning pronouncements—but I had not seen him in nine years and in Calcutta he had never really broken through the fortifications of my shyness.

"Come have a drink with me," Pat said.

It was my turn to laugh. "You must meet Derek," I said.

Derek had learned a great deal about India. He could reel off statistics of Panchayati Raj[4] and the electrification of villages and the introduction of mass media, though he reserved his love for birds migrating through the wintry deserts of Jaisalmer. Knowledge of India made Derek more sympa-

---

1. Famous auction house for rare manuscripts, books, and art objects.
2. Fashionable London store for fabrics.
3. Elite British boarding school for women.
4. Village rule by a council of five elders.

thetic than bitter, a common trait of decent outsiders. He was charmed by
Pat's heedless, old-world insularity.

"Is this the lucky man?" he said to Derek. He did not hold out his hand.   15
He waved us outside; a taxi magically appeared. "Come have a drink with
me tomorrow. At my place."

He gave Derek his card. It was big and would not fit into a wallet made   16
to hold Visa and American Express. Derek read it with his usual curiosity.

17

H.R.H. Maharajah Patwant Singh
of
Gotlah
Purveyor and Exporter

He tucked the card in the pocket of his raincoat. "I'll be shooting in   18
Toronto tomorrow," he said, "but I'm sure Leela would like to keep it."

There was, in the retention of those final "h's"—even Indian maps and   19
newspapers now referred to Gotla and to maharajas, and I had dropped the
old "Leelah" in my first month in America—something of the reclusive
mountebank. "I'm going to the Patels for dinner tomorrow," I said, afraid
that Pat would misread the signs of healthy unpossessiveness in our marriage.

"Come for a drink before. What's the matter, Leela? Turning a prude   20
in your old age?" To Derek he explained, "I used to rock her on my knee
when she was four. She was gorgeous then, but I am no lecher."

It is true that I was very pretty at four and that Pat spent a lot of time   21
in our house fondling us children. He brought us imported chocolates in
beautiful tins and made a show of giving me the biggest. In my family, in
every generation, one infant seems destined to be the repository of the family's comeliness. In my generation, I inherited the looks, like an heirloom, to
keep in good condition and pass on to the next. Beauty teaches humility and
responsibility in the culture I came from. By marrying well, I could have
seen to the education of my poorer cousins.

Pat was in a third floor sublet in Gramercy Park South. A West Indian   22
doorman with pendulous cheeks and an unbuttoned jacket let me into the
building. He didn't give me a chance to say where I was going as I moved
toward the elevator.

"The maharaja is third floor, to the right. All the way down."   23

I had misunderstood the invitation. It was not to be an hour of wit and   24
nostalgia among exotic knick-knacks squirreled into New York from the Gotla
Palace. I counted thirty guests in the first quarter hour of my short stay.
Plump young men in tight-fitting suits scuttled from living room to kitchen,
balancing overfull glasses of gin and tonic. The women were mostly blondes,
with luridly mascaraed, brooding eyes, blonde the way South Americans are
blonde, with deep residual shading. I tried to edge into a group of three

women. One of them said, "I thought India was spellbinding. Naresh's partner managed to get us into the Lake Palace Hotel."

"I don't think I could take the poverty," said her friend, as I retreated. 25

The living room walls were hung with prints of British East India Company officials at work and play, the vestibule with mirror-images of Hindu gods and goddesses. 26

"Take my advice," a Gujarati man said to Pat in the dim and plantless kitchen. "Get out of diamonds—emeralds *won't* bottom out. These days it *has* to be rubies and emeralds." 27

In my six years in Manhattan I had not entered a kitchen without plants. There was not even a straggly avocado pushing its nervous way out of a shrivelling seed. 28

I moved back into the living room where the smell of stale turmeric hung like yellow fog from the ceiling. A man rose from the brocade-covered cushions of a banquette near me and plumped them, smiling, to make room for me. 29

"You're Pat's niece, no?" The man was francophone, a Lebanese. "Pat has such pretty nieces. You have just come from Bombay? I love Bombay. Personally, Bombay to me is like a jewel. Like Paris, like Beirut before, now like Bombay. You agree?" 30

I disclaimed all kinship to H.R.H. I was a Bengali Brahmin; maharajas—not to put too sharp a point on it—were frankly beneath me, by at least one caste, though some of them, like Pat, would dispute it. Before my marriage to Derek no one in my family since our initial eruption from Vishnu's knee had broken caste etiquette. I disclaimed any recent connection with India. "I haven't been home in ages," I told the Lebanese. "I am an American citizen." 31

"I too am. I am American," he practically squealed. He rinsed his glass with a bit of gin still left in the bottom, as though he were trying to dislodge lemon pulp stuck and drying on its sides. "You want to have dinner with me tonight, yes? I know Lebanese places, secret and intimate. Food and ambiance very romantic." 32

"She's going to the Patels." It was Pat. The Gujarati with advice on emeralds was still lodged in the kitchen, huddling with a stocky blonde in a fuchsia silk sari. 33

"Oh, the Patels," said the Lebanese. "You did not say. Super guy, no? He's doing all right for himself. Not as well as me, of course. I own ten stores and he only has four." 34

Why, I often ask myself, was Derek never around to share these intimacies? Derek would have drawn out the suave, French-speaking, soulful side of this Seventh Avenue *shmattiste.*[5] 35

It shouldn't have surprised me that the Lebanese man in the ruffled shirt should have known Mohan and Motibehn Patel. For immigrants in similar 36

5. A contrived word, joining a Yiddish root meaning "rag" with a French ending: a rag artist, or clothing manufacturer. Seventh Avenue is the main artery of New York's Garment District.

trades, Manhattan is still a village. Mohan had been in the States for eighteen years and last year had become a citizen. They'd been fortunate in having only sons, now at Cal Tech and Cornell; with daughters there would have been pressure on them to return to India for a proper, arranged marriage.

"Is he still in Queens?" 37

"No," I told him. "They've moved to a biggish old place on Central Park West." 38

"Very foolish move," said the Lebanese. "They will only spend their money now." He seemed genuinely appalled. 39

Pat looked at me surprised. "I can't believe it," he exclaimed. "Leela Lahiri actually going crosstown at night by herself. I remember when your Daddy wouldn't let you walk the two blocks from school to the house without that armed Nepali, what was his name, dogging your steps." 40

"Gulseng," I said. "He was run over by a lorry three years ago. I think his name was really something-or-other-Rana, but he never corrected us." 41

"Short, nasty and brutal," said Pat. "They don't come that polite and loyal these days. Just as likely to slit your throat as anyone else, these days." 42

The Lebanese, sensing the end of brave New World overtures, the gathering of the darknesses we shared, drifted away. 43

"The country's changed totally, you know," Pat continued. "Crude rustic types have taken over. The *dhoti-wallahs*, you know what I mean, they would wrap themselves in loincloths if it got them more votes. No integrity, no finesse. The country's gone to the dogs, I tell you." 44

"That whole life's outmoded, Pat. Obsolete. All over the world." 45

"They tried to put me in jail," he said. His face was small with bitterness and alarm. "They didn't like my politics, I tell you. Those Communists back home arrested me and threw me in jail. Me. Like a common criminal." 46

"On what charges?" 47

"Smuggling. For selling family heirlooms to Americans who understand them. No one at home understands their value. Here, I can sell off a little Pahari painting for ten thousand dollars. Americans understand our things better than we do ourselves. India wants me to starve in my overgrown palace." 48

"Did you really spend a night in jail?" I couldn't believe that modernization had finally come to India and that even there, no one was immune from consequences. 49

"Three nights!" he fumed. "Like a common *dacoit*. The country has no respect anymore. The country has nothing. It has driven us abroad with whatever assets we could salvage." 50

"You did well, I take it." I did not share his perspective; I did not feel my country owed me anything. Comfort, perhaps, when I was there; a different comfort when I left it. India teaches her children: you have seen the worst. Now go out and don't be afraid. 51

"I have nothing," he spat. "They've stripped me of everything. At night I hear the jackals singing in the courtyard of my palace." 52

But he had recovered by the time I left for the crosstown cab ride to the Patels. I saw him sitting on the banquette where not too long before the Lebanese had invited me to share an evening of unwholesomeness. On his knee he balanced a tall, silver-haired woman who looked like Candice Bergen. She wore a pink cashmere sweater which she must have put through the washing machine. Creases, like worms, curled around her sweatered bosom. 53

I didn't see Pat for another two years. In those two years I did see a man who claimed to have bounced the real Candice Bergen on his knee. He had been a juggler at one time, had worked with Edgar Bergen on some vaudeville act and could still pull off card tricks and walk on his hands up and down my dining table. I kept the dining table when Derek and I split last May. He went back to Canada which we both realized too late he should never have left and the table was too massive to move out of our West 11th Street place and into his downtown Toronto, chic renovated apartment. The ex-juggler is my boss at a publishing house. My job is menial but I have a soothing title. I am called an Administrative Assistant. 54

In the two years I have tried to treat the city not as an island of dark immigrants but as a vast sea in which new Americans like myself could disappear and resurface at will. I did not avoid Indians, but without Derek's urging for me to be proud of my heritage, I did not seek them out. The Patels did invite me to large dinners where all the guests seemed to know with the first flick of their eyes in my direction that I had married a white man and was now separated, and there our friendships hit rock. I was a curiosity, a novel and daring element in the community; everyone knew my name. After a while I began to say I was busy to Motibehn Patel. 55

Pat came to the office with my boss, Bill Haines, the other day. "I wanted you to meet one of our new authors, Leela," Bill said. 56

"Leela, *dar-ling!*" Pat cried. His voice was shrill with enthusiasm, and he pressed me histrionically against his Burberry raincoat. I could feel a button tap my collarbone. "It's been years! Where have you been hiding your gorgeous self?" 57

"I didn't realize you two knew each other," Bill said. 58

All Indians in America, I could have told him, constitute a village. 59

"Her father bailed me out when the Indian government sought to persecute me," he said with a pout. "If it hadn't been for courageous friends like her daddy, I and my poor subjects might just as well have kicked the bucket." 60

"She's told me nothing about India," said Bill Haines. "No accent, Western clothes—" 61

"Yes, a shame, that. By the way, Leela, I just found a picture of Lahiri-*sahab* on an elephant when I was going through my official papers for Bill. If you come over for drinks—after getting out of those ridiculous clothes, I must insist—I can give it to you. Lahiri-*sahab* looks like Ernest Hemingway in that photo. You tell him I said he looks like Hemingway." 62

"Daddy's in Ranikhet this month," I said. "He's been bedridden for a 63
while. Arthritis. He's just beginning to move around a bit again."

"I have hundreds of good anecdotes, Bill, about her daddy and me doing 64
shikar in the Sundarban forest. Absolutely *huge* Bengal tigers. I want to balance the politics—which as you rightly say are central—with some stirring
bits about what it was like in the good old days."

"What are you writing?" I asked. 65

"I thought you'd never ask, my dear. My memoirs. At night I leave a 66
Sony by my bed. Night is the best time for remembering. I hear the old
sounds and voices. You remember, Leela, how the palace ballroom used to
hum with dancing feet on my birthdays?"

"*Memoirs of a Modern Maharajah,*" Bill Haines said. 67

"I seem to remember the singing of jackals," I said, not unkindly, though 68
he chose to ignore it.

"Writing is what keeps me from going through death's gate. There are 69
nights . . ." He didn't finish. His posture had stiffened with self-regard; he
communicated great oceans of anguish. He'd probably do well. It was what
people wanted to hear.

"The indignities," he said suddenly. "The atrocities." He stared straight 70
ahead, at a watercooler. "The nights in jail, the hyenas sniffing outside your
barred window. I will never forget their smell, never! It is the smell of death,
Leela. The new powers-that-be are peasants. Peasants! They cannot know,
they cannot suspect how they have made me suffer. The country is in the
hands of tyrannical peasants!"

"Look, Pat," Bill Haines said, leading the writer toward his office, "I 71
have to see Bob Savage, the sub-rights man one floor down. Make yourself
at home. Just pull down any book you want to read. I'll be back in a minute."

"Don't worry about me. I shall be all right, Bill. I have my Sony in my 72
pocket. I shall just sit in a corner beside the daughter of my oldest friend,
this child I used to bounce on my knee, and I shall let my mind skip into the
nooks and crannies of Gotlah Palace. Did I tell you, when I was a young lad
my mother kept pet crocs? Big, huge gents and ladies with ugly jaws full of
nasty teeth. They were her pets. She gave them names and fed them chickens every day. Come to me, Padma. Come to me, Prem."

"It'll be dynamite," Bill Haines said. "The whole project's dynamite." 73
He pressed my hand as he eased his stubby, muscular body past the stack
of dossiers on my desk. "And *you'll* be a godsend in developing this project."

"And what's with you?" Pat asked me. I could tell he already knew the 74
essentials.

"Nothing much." But he wasn't listening anyway. 75

"You remember the thief my security men caught in the early days of 76
your father's setting up a factory in my hills? You remember how the mob
got excited and poured acid on his face?"

I remembered. Was the Sony recording it? Was the memory an illustra- 77 tion of swift and righteous justice in a collapsed Himalayan princely state, or was it the savage and disproportionate fury of a people resisting change?

"Yes, certainly I do. Can I get you a cup of coffee? Or tea?" That, of course, was an important part of my job. 78

"No thanks," he said with a flutter of his wrinkled hands. "I have given up all stimulants. I've even given up bed-tea. It interferes with my writing. Writing is everything to me nowadays. It has been my nirvana." 79

"The book sounds dynamite," I assured him. An Indian woman is brought up to please. No matter how passionately we link bodies with our new countries, we never escape the early days. 80

Pat dropped his voice, and, stooping conspiratorially, said to me in Hindi, "There's one big favor you can do for me, though. Bill has spoken of a chap I should be knowing. Who is this Edgar Bergen?" 81

"I think he was the father of a movie actress," I said. I, too, had gone through the same contortion of recognition with Bill Haines. Fortunately, like most Americans, he could not conceive of a world in which Edgar Bergen had no currency. Again in Hindi, Pat asked me for directions to the facilities, and this time I could give a full response. He left his rolled-slim umbrella propped against my desk and walked toward the fountain. 82

"Is he really a maharaja?" Lisa leaned over from her desk to ask me. She is from Rhode Island. Brown hasn't cured her of responding too enthusiastically to each call or visit from a literary personage. "He's terrific. So suave and distinguished! Have you known him from way back when?" 83

"Yes," I said, all the way from when. 84

"I had no idea you spoke Hindu. It's eerie to think you can speak such a hard language. I'm having trouble enough with French. I keep forgetting that you haven't lived here always." 85

I keep forgetting it too. I was about to correct her silly mistake—I'd learned from Derek to be easily incensed over ignorant confusions between Hindi and Hindu—but then I thought, why bother? Maybe she's right. That slight undetectable error, call it an accent, isn't part of language at all. I speak Hindu. No matter what language I speak it will come out slightly foreign, no matter how perfectly I mouth it. There's a whole world of us now, speaking Hindu. 86

The manuscript of *Memoirs* was not dynamite, but I stayed up all night to finish it. In spite of the arch locutions and the aggrieved posture that Pat had stubbornly clung to, I knew I was reading about myself, blind and groping conquistador who had come to the New World too late. 87

STUDY QUESTIONS

1. Describe how Leela thinks of herself. What kinds of clothes does she wear? What kinds of social gatherings does she like? What characteristics of other people does

she tend to emphasize? How does she talk about her own background in India? In what ways is she an "American"? in what ways is she not? In what ways does the story define or modify the concept of an American?

2. What is the significance of her changing her name from Leelah to Leela?

3. In what ways is the New York SETTING important to the story? What different aspects of New York are detailed? What particular places are mentioned? In what kinds of New York social circles does the ACTION take place?

4. What function does Derek perform in Leela's life? in the story as she presents it? Why do Candice and Edgar Bergen keep coming up in the story?

5. In what ways is the maharaja important to Leela's sense of herself? What different kinds of Hindus does the story present? What does the title of the story mean?

6. What is the historical CONTEXT of this story? What is going on in India, politically, socially, economically, at the time of the story? What effect does that have on the maharaja? What is Leela's attitude toward the changes?

Joan Murray

Joan Murray grew up in New York City and was educated at Hunter College and New York University. She has taught literature and writing at Lehman College of the City University of New York. Murray has won several awards for her poetry, including a 1989 National Endowment for the Arts grant, a 1988 New York Foundation for the Arts Fellowship, and a Pushcart Prize. She is currently an instructor for the New York State Literary Center.

COMING OF AGE ON THE HARLEM

for Kathy

I

My father would tie a life jacket
to a length of seaworn rope and dangle me
off the dock of The Harlem Boat Club float.
A strange baptism.

Down, down into the mad rushing river,   5
worm on a hook, a girl of six or seven,
I am let loose among water rats,
made sister to half-filled soda cans
floating vertically home from a picnic,
and to condoms that look like mama doll socks   10
in the unopened infant eye.
What man would toss his child to that swill?
He who can swim across the river,
whose arms churn a feud with the current.
He thinks he can hold me from any maelstrom.   15
Safe on the dock, I watch my father
float on his back from the Bronx
to Manhattan and back again.

II

Between the river edge and river park,
the New York Central tracks could fry a child.   20
How lucky to have this father with
long, strong arms to whisk me over
the wooden hooded, menacing third rail.
Can you remember when you reached your father's waist
and he told you of the serpent track where   25
only birds could land in safety?
But one day my father takes me home a different way:
up the wooden bridge above the tracks
where huge phallic shapes have been burned in black
along its walls. Don't look. Don't look.   30
That sight will fry you up like Semele.
Now my stronger father, my never ruffled father
pulls me roughly over the wooden planks.
His dark face reddened tells of great,
unspoken danger. When we reach the street,   35
he makes me promise never to come this way again,
never to go to the river shore without him.
Over my shoulder I form an opposite determination.

III

The Harlem Boat Club is the man place.
My father flips down twice a week to shower,   40
on weekends plays a sweaty game
of four wall ball. Outside in the garden,
I wander six years old among lilies
of the valley, Queen Anne's lace,

the shoreline irises and great climbing rose   45
that began as someone's potted plant.
Elmer, the muscular black cat,
drags a water rat to the front door.
I follow inside to the boat room,
run my hand along the lean flanks   50
of polished rowing sculls,
then up the stairway, pause at the wooden roster,
the names with gold stars dead in some war.
Then the sweat smell of the lockers,
the place where they held a party   55
to welcome the Beatty brothers home from Korea.
Off to the side, three men stand
naked in the steamy, tiled shower.
Quiet, I sit down on a bench
beside a girl my own age, who has also come   60
to pretend she doesn't notice.

IV

Still my close, though distant, friend,
who sat with me in the men's locker room,
whose father had a strong right arm for handball,
whose mother and mine embarrassed   65
in their forties, had pregnancies,
who accompanied me through puberty
up and down the Harlem shore,
Kathy, in your Brahmin home in Brooklyn,
you say you want to rid your sleep   70
of those dirty years along the river.
But stop for a moment, stop trying
to make the river pass genteelly,
for there'll be no weaning from those waters.
Instead come back with me and watch   75
the sun glint off the rippling surface,
bearing the shore-hugging flow of turds and
condoms north to the Hudson.
You conjectured it all came from cabin cruisers
on some far-off glory ocean.   80
Kathy, would you have even looked
if you had known it came from humble tenements
on our Highbridge[1] hill?
Could that one reflection
have darkened all your plans to sail?   85

1. Harlem neighborhood overlooking the Harlem River.

V

"Mirror Mirror"
was the name you gave him,
a dexterous man with a pocket mirror
who could catch the Sunday morning sun
and flash it on our untouched child bodies.   90
A fairy tale gone haywire, Rapunzel in reverse:
"Mirror Mirror!"
we shouted from the bridge height,
and he below us in the river park
would hold his instrument to the sky like   95
a sextant and calculate his grotesque angles.
Then we'd race down the ramp
just beyond his unknown reach and dive
behind the safety of a tree.
Oh God! Oh God! the heavy breathing,   100
ours, his, the fear, the vague desire
that was always escaped in time to
run home at one for Sunday dinner and meet our
unsuspecting fathers coming home from mass.

VI

Just before ten, just before your father's curfew,   105
you can station yourself on the highway bridge,
where it joins the ramp from the river park,
to see the couples rise up on the evening tide:
the sooty venuses with dirty hand marks
on white and fondled blouses, and   110
their boyfriends swaggering in teenage jeans.
You laugh, and send your first awakening lust
to follow them back to the neighborhood
where someday all will notice that you've grown.
And small children will stand on bridges   115
to flank your path
as you make your debut entry
to the nightly river park cotillion, on the arm
of some lanky boy with a dangling black curl,
and the cleanest, oh the cleanest hands.   120

VII

It's the boys with sprouts of pubic hair
who have the manliness to strip and jump
while tourists on the Circle Line around
Manhattan watch with Brownie cameras.

Bright faced fathers and mothers, pointing out   125
the river life to their wondering children.
They look for street kids in straw hats,
the Tom Sawyers and Huck Finns of the Harlem
but only get an upraised finger.
Behind the nude boys who perch on river rocks   130
and invite the sun to their members,
a ring of girls, in tight black shorts and
pony tails, keep a coy but glancing distance.
And behind them all, a white-haired voyeur
drops his pants to masturbate.   135
The eyes of the Circle Line sail up river, still
hopeful that Becky Thatcher in eyelet bloomers
will wave a hanky from the shore.

VIII

In Undercliff Park, below Washington Bridge,[2]
I play stretch and toe-knee-chest-nut with   140
my father's pocketed army knife.
A dangerous age. Threats are cutting through the air:
the flailing depantsings, the groping bra quests for
a wad of cotton or a nylon stocking.
A dangerous age, with the deadly fear   145
of being found a child.
To relieve it one day, we hang a tire in a tree and
swing in packs out over the cliff edge, until
the boy beside me loses grip and lies below,
as quiet as an infant in a lullabye.   150
Weeks later, we visit him at home, sign his casts
and giggle at his immature pajamas.
He lifts his mattress to show
an arsenal of thirty knives and ice picks,
and lets each girl pick a pocket lighter   155
shoplifted from Woolworth's.

IX

Hung by my hands above the water,
I am dangled by boys from the ledge
of the Washington Bridge abutment.
Twelve years old, twelve feet from the surface,   160
I do not trust boys, but love their giddy danger
like a windflaw teasing with a sail.
And while we dangle, the boys hurl rocks

2. The Washington Bridge, which crosses the Harlem River at 181 Street and links Harlem to the Bronx.

at the river, waiting for the splash that will leap
up to our blouses and clutch the outlines   165
of our forming breasts.
Soaked through, we climb the naked limbs
of a shore tree and sprawl in the afternoon sun.
Above a boy hovers in the branches,
reaches for my hand a moment and is gone,   170
leaving something growing in me
that holds me separate from my friends
as we walk together to our fathers' houses,
wearing our secret scent of the river.

                              X

My husband no more swims b.a.[3]   175
I can no longer picture his shadow
rippling across the sidewalks to the Harlem.
A swaggering, older boy, once unattainable.
Now at night I cradle his black hair
to my breast and we share the river's secrets: 180
My splashing joyride pick-up
with three strange boys in a motor boat.
His first hesitating touch of Dodie, the hillbilly
girl on the fourteen steps below Macombs Dam Bridge.[4]
The tales of all those years I was not permitted   185
at The Harlem, unless my father stood beside me,
gathering me into his safe garden.
All those years I learned the route to avoid his path.
Now I retrace it in the dark, step by step, till
again I watch The Harlem Boat Club burn,   190
and see the steps plucked from the river bridge
where no child can again take the path
that leads me nightly to this good bed.
Kathy, did we escape our fathers?
Or did they plan our turns and detours   195
just carefully enough to lead us here?

STUDY QUESTIONS

1. The title has two parts: "coming of age" is common to all; "Harlem" is a particular
CONTEXT for the SPEAKER's coming of age. Describe what is common to all experience and how the particular place in which the speaker comes of age modifies and
enriches the general theme of growing up. Does the difference between the speak-

3. Bare-assed.
4. Links Harlem to the Bronx at 155 Street.

er's context and experiences distance you from her experience? Does it make you know her better? feel closer to her?

2. Some of the physical details of the Harlem context are quite unpleasant. What is the speaker's attitude toward Harlem and her environment? Compare her acceptance of the reality of her environment and the attitude of Kathy (section IV).

Juan Felipe Herrera

B orn in Fowler, California, in 1948, Juan Felipe Herrera attended Stanford University and currently teaches Ethnic Studies at Fresno State University. His writings include *Rebozos of Love* (1974), *Exiles of Desire* (1983), and *Facegames* (1987). He has been awarded a National Endowment for the Arts Fellowship, a UCLA Chicano Cultural Center Grant, and a California Arts Council Grant.

REVOLUTION SKYSCRAPER

"Let me count the stars inside you and breathe the air in your mouth."
—*Margarita Luna Robles*

LOOK at me! I am a tux dressed crew-cut Chicano lifting an invisible curtain with my eyebrows. I walk & shuffle down this asphalt album where humans are paisley notes stretching by the neon lit fast food chicken special signs. Warm breeze on a Sunday nite. Listen to me. The Japanese are busy finishing with the Obon festival on Jackson street selling tickets for the two thousand dollar raffle. The guy calling me to buy 5 for three dollars reminds me of an old sergeant. But, deep inside he's a No-No boy. He'll never forget Manzanar, Tule Lake, the Loyalty oath in front of the Mad Salivator Recruit dog monster called America back in '42. I can see the tattoo—NISEI REVENGE—through the finely pressed khaki shirt, man! Strolling. That's what I call it. The sky is a blue-black newspaper cut out with a Marine bayonet screaming "Ban Gay Sex" in a Supreme Court accent. God's moon quivers epileptic with secret sperm. They don't want nobody cruising or dancing on the street in spicy angles. Only Soldier positions are legal in Freetown. Maxim #5: Destroy every human cell that spells Love. Everything is on a fancy ferris wheel of blood, disguise and artificial crank. Baseball idols and football heros crackle on a pyre at the center of Main Street, and the music from a lonely and heart-torn Corvette of teen resentments spills. All the bedroom windows are breaking into a confetti of hot laughter. Heterosex-Megaton Man is wearing his favorite polka-dot tie and is on a tap dance marathon with the Soviets. I think of Little Manuel in second grade. Logan Heights Varrio. 1957. I see Ms. Simmons slamming him in the cloak room. Manuel is frozen. Looking into a red liquid mirror on the oak grain floor. You ain't nothing but a hound dog. *Elvis and Chevys Forever* is written on every classroom wall. The horrible cloak room shrinks and disappears into a yellow knot with the face of Csilla Molnar; a seventeen year old blonde beauty queen that committed suicide today because she couldn't handle all the attention that the public was giving her. Csilla and the public and in-between, the Mad Salivator Recruit Dog counts the dollars in his pin-stripe jacket. Csilla, your hair is olive oil pouring from the Hyatt Regency, slowly, covering all the escape ladders with feverish glass. Pink fingernail polish floods the dining rooms. Olive tar webs stream down the Manikin panty hose empire legs twitching in the Department store. Csilla, Miss Hungary 1986, can you hear me? My uncle Beto Quintana taught us all about rage in a Mexican way. I never thought I would tell you this. In the 20's we migrated North with thousands carrying splinters and old vases. My mother, Lucha, my aunt, Lela, my grandmother, Juanita: three in black silent mourning of a life past crucified with brick beds and long walks through *La Colonia Roma* looking for food and Destiny. Later, somehow, in El Paso, my uncle put together a comedy show—El Barco de La Illusión—where he showed *Tin-Tan* how to crack a joke and where *El Charro Avitia* made his first debut. Then, one day he came here, made tortillas on a tortilla machine, Mexican candy in dark kettles and spun Mexican oldies for Radio KOFY. We followed. His hands were made of anise and basil. He took us to the wharf where the illegal boats docked. And he opened up the crate of smuggled songs and literature. I'll never forget you. I'll never forget you. And we scattered about, on an infinite orange shore looking for each other, again. My love, come closer, now. I need you. Weave your arms through me. Pour your burning opal breasts into me; spin their twin halos inside me, glowing closer above the ruby forests of my soul. Forever. Kiss me. Listen to me. This is the most elegant nation in the world. I love the new fashions for '88. Don't you? All the floors are clean. Waxed properly. The aisle glistens. The Mayor dances to the numbers that are predictable. Minority Matthew says he will sell you the Real Last Letters of Slavery. The Rock top hit of the year—*Afrikan Murder*—blasts out. Everyone is feeling romantic. The hands of Victor Jara and the flayed heart of Rodrigo Rojas fall out of Nowhere, like phosphorescent meteors and explode into Red palm trees spurting gold honey on the plaza. At the dark hour of five. *A las cinco de la tarde. ¡Eran las cinco en todos relojes! ¡Ay que terribles cinco de la tarde! ¡Que no quiero verla! Díle a la luna que no quiero ver la sangre de Rodrigo sobre la arena.*[1] Can you hear the scream from the basement of the General Hospital? A brown baby is crying, standing, pointing at you. A wave of bees crashes out of the billion watt Gibson amp in her chest.

STUDY QUESTIONS

1. Why is this a poem? or is it?

2. Explain the relevance to the poem of both words in the title.

3. What is the ethnic image of "Americans" projected in the poem?

4. What is the historical CONTEXT of the poem?

Fran Winant

Born in Brooklyn, New York, in 1943, Fran Winant received a B.A. degree in studio art from Fordham University. She has published three volumes of poetry, *Looking at Women* (1971), *Dyke Jacket* (1976), and *Goddess of Lesbian Dreams* (1980), and is the editor of one of the earliest lesbian/gay anthologies. *We Are All Lesbians* (1975). Her poems have appeared in several anthologies, including *The Penguin Book of Homosexual Verse, Mountain Moving Day, We Become New, The Political Palate,* and in *The Sexual Politics of Meat,* a book of feminist theory. Winant's paintings were in the 1982 New Museum show "Extended Sensibilities: Homosexual Presence in Contemporary Art," and are reproduced and discussed in *The Sexual Perspective: Homosexuality and Art in the Last 100 Years in the West,* by Emmanuel Cooper. She is the recipient of a New York State Arts Council CAPS Grant in poetry and a National Endowment for the Arts Visual Artists Fellowship in Painting.

CHRISTOPHER ST. LIBERATION DAY, JUNE 28, 1970

with our banners and our smiles
we're being photographed

---

1. "At five o'clock in the afternoon. It said five o'clock on all clocks! It's terrible that it's five o'clock in the evening! Because I don't want to see it! Tell the moon that I don't want to see the blood of Rodrigo all over the arena."

by tourists police and leering men
we fill their cameras
with 10,000 faces   5
bearing witness
to our own existence
in sunlight
from Washington Maryland
Massachusetts Pennsylvania   10
Connecticut Ohio
Iowa Minnesota
from Harlem and the suburbs
the universities
and the world   15
we are women who love women
we are men who love men
we are lesbians and homosexuals
we cannot apologize
for knowing   20
what others refuse to know
for affirming
what they deny
we might have been
the women and men   25
who watched us and waved
and made fists
and gave us victory signs
and stood there after we had passed
thinking of all they had to lose   30
and of how society punishes
its victims
who are all of us
in the end
but we are sisters and sisters   35
brothers and brothers
workers and lovers
we are together

we are marching
past the crumbling old world   40
that leans toward us
in anguish from the pavement
our banners are sails
pulling us through the streets
where we have always been   45
as ghosts

now we are shouting our own words
we are a community
we are society
we are everyone   50
we are inside you
remember
all you were taught to forget
we are part of the new world

photographers   55
grim behind precise machines
wait to record
our blood and sorrow
and revolutionaries beside them
remark   60
love is not political
when we stand against our pain
they say
we are not standing against anything
when we demand our total lives   65
they wonder
what we are demanding
cant you lie
cant you lie
they whisper they hiss   70
like fire in grass
cant you lie
and get on with the real work

our line winds
into Central park   75
and doubles itself
in a snakedance
to the top of a hill
we cover the Sheep Meadow
shouting   80
lifting our arms
we are marching into ourselves
like a body
gathering its cells
creating itself   85
in sunlight
we turn to look back
on the thousands behind us
it seems we will converge

until we explode   90
sisters and sisters
brothers and brothers
together

STUDY QUESTIONS

1. Explain the title, locating the poem in its historical CONTEXT.

2. Line 8, "in sunlight," is repeated as line 86. Why is the phrase significant? Relate it to lines 30 and 45–46.

3. What is the objection of the political revolutionaries to the march? What course of action do they advise?

Linda Hogan

Linda Hogan, a Chickasaw, was born in Denver in 1947, grew up in Oklahoma, and earned an M.A. in English and creative writing from the University of Colorado where she now teaches creative writing. She has published several books of poems, including *Calling Myself Home; Daughters, I Love You; Eclipse; That House;* and *Seeing Through the Sun* (which won the 1986 American Book Award from the Before Columbus Foundation). Her first novel, *Mean Spirit*, appeared in 1989.

In 1981, a group of Native Americans, ranchers, and environmentalists gathered over several weeks to protest development in the Black Hills of South Dakota.

BLACK HILLS SURVIVAL GATHERING, 1980

Bodies on fire
the monks in orange cloth
sing morning into light.

Men wake on the hill.
Dry grass blows from their hair.
B52's blow over their heads   5

leaving a cross on the ground.
Air returns to itself and silence.

Rainclouds are disappearing
with fractures of light in the distance.   10
Fierce gases forming,
the sky bending
where people arrive
on dusty roads that change
matter to energy.   15

My husband wakes.
My daughter wakes.
Quiet morning, she stands
in a pail of water
naked, reflecting light   20
and this man I love,
with kind hands
he washes her slim hips,
narrow shoulders, splashes
the skin containing   25
wind and fragile fire,
the pulse in her wrist.

My other daughter wakes
to comb warm sun across her hair.
While I make coffee I tell her   30
this is the land of her ancestors,
blood and heart.
Does her hair become a mane
blowing in the electric breeze,
her eyes dilate and darken?   35

The sun rises on all of them
in the center of light
hills that have no boundary,
the child named Thunder Horse,
the child named Dawn Protector   40
and the man
whose name would mean home in Navajo.

At ground zero
in the center of light we stand.
Bombs are buried beneath us,   45
destruction flies overhead.

We are waking
in the expanding light
the sulphur-colored grass.
A red horse standing on a distant ridge   50
looks like one burned
over Hiroshima,
silent, head hanging in sickness.
But look
she raises her head   55
and surges toward the bluing sky.

Radiant morning.
The dark tunnels inside us carry life.
Red.
Blue.   60
The children's dark hair against my breast.
On the burning hills
in flaring orange cloth
men are singing and drumming
Heartbeat.   65

STUDY QUESTIONS

1. What different kinds of survival is the poem about? How does the sense of family and the passing on of personal values relate to the threats posed by war machines?

2. What different ways is the sun reflected in people, animals, and landscape? In what sections of the poem does bright light suggest hope and possibility? Where does it suggest potential disaster?

3. Explain the effect of portraying simple family rituals in the middle of the poem. How are IMAGES from the beginning and the ending of the poem reflected in family scenes?

4. What different meanings does "cross" have in line 7? Explain how its SYMBOLISM relates to the THEMES of the poem.

5. How many different images of life and energy does the poem contain? What effect does each create? How are they differentiated? How are human bodies made to seem vessels of life and transmitters of tradition? In what ways is the SETTING of the poem significant? How have political events since 1980 made the CONTEXT of this poem seem more "historical"?

Pat Mora

Born in El Paso, Pat Mora writes poems in which her Chicana heritage and South-western background are central. Her first book, *Chants* (1985), is largely composed of what she calls "desert incantations." Her second, *Borders* (1986), from which the following poem is taken, describes the two cultures that create her own "border" life. Both books won Southwest Book awards. Her third book, *Communion*, was published in 1991. She lives in Cincinnati.

IMMIGRANTS

wrap their babies in the American flag,
feed them mashed hot dogs and apple pie,
name them Bill and Daisy,
buy them blonde dolls that blink blue
eyes or a football and tiny cleats   5
before the baby can even walk,
speak to them in thick English,
     hallo, babee, hallo,
whisper in Spanish or Polish
when the babies sleep, whisper   10
in a dark parent bed, that dark
parent fear, "Will they like
our boy, our girl, our fine american
boy, our fine american girl?"

STUDY QUESTIONS

1. What, according to the poem, does being an "American" consist of? What are "typical" Americans like? What do they do? What do they look like? What does the poem imply about American tolerance for difference or individuality?

2. Who is the "their" in line 1? the "they" in line 12?

3. Explain the implied differences between "speak" (line 7) and "whisper" (lines 9, 10). What is the source of the parents' "dark" fears?

4. What ATTITUDE does the poem ultimately take toward conformity? toward assimilation? How, exactly, does the IRONY of the poem work?

Gregory Orfalea

G regory Orfalea is the author of *Before The Flames: A Quest for the History of Arab Americans* (1988), and co-editor of *Grapes Leaves: A Century of Arab American Poetry* (1988). He lives with his family in Washington, D.C.

ARAB AND JEW IN ALASKA

for Gordon Massman

. . . on the surface of the desert were fine
flakes like hoarfrost. The Israelites asked
one another, "What is this?" Moses told them,
"This is the bread which the Lord has given you to eat."

Exodus 16:14–15

God's light is an olive
that is neither of the East nor of the West
whose oil wellnigh would shine, even if no fire touched it.

Koran, Sura XXIV

1

Two sons of Sem,[1] called by an unknown
we drove separate over gravel—North.
Leaves shuddered down. Gold
radiated up to our faces and went cold.

In no-man's land we met. You pulled   5
out sheaves of poems, and your voice quavered.
My feet pawed on the other side
of the table as you read

---

1. Shem, one of Noah's sons, from whom Semites, Arabs, and Jews are said to have descended.

from the Book of Lamentations,[2]
twentieth century-style: aborted   10
life, walled death—Rothschild's screeching[3]
fiddle, I thought. And when you threatened
to kill off the reader, I bristled.
Did you have the whole corner
on suffering? I wondered,   15
wondered, and watched the snow
drop into blistering
cold dunes . . .

2

Winter fell hard on the harder earth,
aged it quiet   20
and did its work on the warm-blooded.

Hoarfrost did not discriminate
between our moustaches. White
ice clung to our eyebrows, lashes
and dripped from our noses, so that our mouths   25
shut. We joined in Fairbanks
from opposite directions, shivering
breath-clouds
indoors, gasping
with poems.   30

3

Warm and lone as wolves, barking
our art, we withdrew
each boiling his own despair
on the crossed logs.
                Waiting . . .   35
At night in the woods
Moses and Joshua trailed past my cabin,
pointing—and Ishmael,
father of Bedouins.
The desert does things to people   40
like latitude. But the heart
beats in longitude.
A Bedouin is born on a dune—
if it doesn't crest and crash
to shore, he will burn   45

2. Book of the Bible that mourns the destruction of Jerusalem.

3. The name of a great European Jewish banking family whose empire was plundered in World War II.

his soles to get to another dune.
He will tell his feet: *Water*
even if they rupture. Like Aaron's rod:[4]
Water is my flower that splits the rocks!

4

Cold tar poured over the North 50
and I begged God spare the last
quivering light . . .

                          outside, huge in parka,
inflated shoes, I banged the empty
oil drums—darkness 55
hit my face
like sand. Darkness felt: *khamsin*,[5]
the Pharoah's Ninth Plague,[6]
a dark to be rubbed by the hands.

5

And how does one row 60
in a black vortex?
—Straight back into the soul,
flaring the wick of rare life
where others, too, are raw.

From separate vigils, we brought each other 65
what glowed in the dark:
the blue of snow that pulls
the soul out of the lung,
a woman's sequins on the moonlit branches.
I walked a long way from the lost 70
gold mines at Ester,[7] legs block-ice,
to tell you there was no gold
but the Aurora, our new Ark of the Covenant.

For here—in the tremor of discovering
the other—Arab and Jew 75
disappear.

---

4. From the Book of Exodus, the rod cast by Aaron before Pharoah, which became a serpent, and was later used by Moses to split the rock that brought forth water.

5. A hot south wind from the Sahara that blows in the Near East from late March to early May.

6. Of the ten plagues brought down against the Pharoah and his people in the Book of Exodus, the ninth was a thick darkness lasting three days.

7. Small village west of Fairbanks, Alaska.

6

The next year we camped near
an ice-filled port. Anchorage
mornings you'd trudge in the dark
grasping poems, gray sparrows, breathing   80
on the wings and calling, "Here! Quickly!"

Goliath gloves held the poem like a membrane:
This is the best one yet, hot off the griddle.
The mercury held forty-below zero.

That year a dagger rose from the snow   85
you recognized, helped pull it out
of me, scarred birch, brother.
Frozen sparrows of your life you held as evidence
and began laughing so strangely
I understood. We kicked up snow   90
with our *dabkah*,[8] our *hora*,[9]

a laughing dance to fill the abyss!

7

If I could sculpt the world
the path we wore back and forth in the snow
under the dark, over the skeptic ice,   95
poems on their toes
with our breath—
If I could hold that feet-on-feet way
in the white that sees a light
that vaults the past—   100

I would take the sculpture,
call it Minimal Art—
and place it in Sinai, the Golan Heights,[1]
Jerusalem, leading from temple to church to mosque—
A wave sculpture like a ray   105
that would freeze the hearts of men
such they would want melting
over anything
without country, religion, any claim but:

"Heat us—light."   110

8. Ritual Arab rain dance.
9. Israeli folk dance.
1. A disputed territory in southwest Syria, annexed by Israel in 1981.

8

It is raining today on the Pacific
and you are on the gulf, rain-years away.
I hold over the cloud of tea and marvel
at such a cold California day.

Friend, where is our homeland?   115
We were born in America, set adrift
on what it started.
Our veins often wander
at the smell of mint,
the sound of a goat . . . but   120
where, dear friend, where?

I know, at times, even in the hottest
blood, I hear an echo,
a thin icy rasping, the sash
of the sky undoing—   125

the sound of color, all together,
and alone. Someday, again,

home.

STUDY QUESTIONS

1. What is the SPEAKER's attitude toward the other (Jewish) "Son of Sem" in the first
   section of the poem?

2. How does the CONTEXT (especially the weather in Alaska) bring them together in
   sections, 2, 4, and 5? What is the implied effect of "latitude" on people (section 3,
   line 41)? Explain your understanding of lines 41 and 42 in that section: "but the
   heart / beats in longitude." Where is the speaker in the final section of the poem?
   Where is his Jewish friend?

3. In what way are the speaker and his friend "Americans"? in what ways not? The
   last word and line in the poem is "home"; where is "home"?

Mitsuye Yamada

B orn in Kyushu, Japan, raised in Seattle, interned with her family in a concentration camp in Idaho during World War II, Yamada went on to attend New York

University and the University of Chicago. After 23 years of teaching English and
literature in California, she is now retired but still teaches creative writing and Asian-
American literature in southern California. Her first book of poems, *Camp Notes and
Other Poems* (1976), was in part written during her years in the camp. Her most recent
work, *Desert Run: Poems and Stories*, was published in 1988.

THE QUESTION OF LOYALTY

I met the deadline
for alien registration
once before
was numbered fingerprinted
and ordered not to travel   5
without permit.

But alien still they said I must
forswear allegiance to the emperor.
for me that was easy
I didn't even know him   10
but my mother who did cried out
    If I sign this
    What will I be?
    I am doubly loyal
    to my American children   15
    also to my own people.
    How can double mean nothing?
    I wish no one to lose this war.
    Everyone does.

I was poor   20
at math.
I signed
my only ticket out.

STUDY QUESTIONS

1. What is the historical CONTEXT of the poem? How much are we told about the
SPEAKER? When did the events of the poem occur? What do the earlier events in
her life suggest about her background? her feelings? about the way she perceives
her place in American society? What indications are there of her age? What suggestions are there that the "present" of the poem is long after the central event
described in it?

2. Explain the different generational responses to the question of loyalty. How does each interpret what loyalty means? What is the speaker's motivation for her decision to sign? How does she feel about her decision?

3. How does the poem make use of contrasts between human feelings and routine, impersonal, and "numbered" outlooks on human life? How does the speaker respond to such choices? In what sense is her signature a "ticket" (line 23)?

4. What, exactly, does the final word of the poem mean?

Richard Olivas

[I'M SITTING IN MY HISTORY CLASS]

I'm sitting in my history class,
The instructor commences rapping,
I'm in my U.S. History class,
And I'm on the verge of napping.

The Mayflower landed on Plymouth Rock.   5
Tell me more! Tell me more!
Thirteen colonies were settled.
I've heard it all before.

What did he say?
Dare I ask him to reiterate?   10
Oh why bother
It sounded like he said,
George Washington's my father.

I'm reluctant to believe it,
I suddenly raise my mano.[1]   15
If George Washington's my father,
Why wasn't he Chicano?

1. Hand.

STUDY QUESTIONS

1. What special effects are created by the mixture of formal and colloquial language in the poem? Explain the IRONIES in using the term "rapping" to describe the instructor's talk. What does "rapping" first suggest to you now? Does its use in the poem simply to mean to talk make the language seem dated? What does that suggest about slang?

2. Why does the poem repeat the simplest "facts" from class, then jump to the level of METAPHOR and MYTH in its reference to George Washington? What does the poem imply about the CONTEXT of the classroom and its relation to out-of-class reality?

3. How much do we know about the NARRATOR of the poem? Describe the poem's TONE.

Mari Evans

Born in Toledo, Ohio, Mari Evans now lives in Indianapolis. She attended the University of Toledo, has taught at Indiana University, Purdue, Northwestern, Cornell, and Washington University in St. Louis, and has also worked as a television writer, producer, and director. She is the author of several plays, four books of poetry, and several children's books, and she is the editor of *Black Women Writers 1950–80: A Critical Perspective* (1984). Her most recent book, of poetry, is *A Dark and Splendid Mass* (1993). She has won many awards for her writing, including a MacDowell Fellowship, a Copeland Fellowship, a John Hay Whitney Fellowship, a Yaddo Fellowship, and a National Endowment for the Arts Award.

THE FRIDAY LADIES OF THE PAY ENVELOPE

they take
stations
in the broken doorways
the narrow alcoves

and the flaking   5
gray paint
the rainandsoot paint
clings
to their limpworn
sweaters clings   10
hair and limpworn souls they
wait
for the sullen
triumph
for the crumpled lifeblood   15
wet with reluctance
thrust
   at them
in the direction
of them   20
  of their reaching
of their drydamp
 limpworn hands

STUDY QUESTIONS

1. What details are we given about the SETTING? In what ways does the setting contribute to the MOOD of the poem? to its THEME? Why are the "ladies" described collectively rather than individually?

2. Describe the TONE of the poem. How do you account for the intensity of the poem? Why are certain words ("limpworn," for example) repeated?

3. Why does the arrival of the pay envelope involve "sullen / triumph" (lines 13–14)? Why are the envelopes "thrust / at them" (lines 17–18)? Why are the envelopes "wet with reluctance" (line 16)?

4. What ATTITUDE does the poem take toward the "ladies"? What strategies are used to produce in readers an attitude toward them? What attitude does the poem take toward those who bring the envelopes? Why are the women said to "take / stations" (lines 1–2)?

Jimmy Santiago Baca

Born in New Mexico in 1952, Jimmy Santiago Baca wrote the poems in his collection *Immigrants in Our Own Land* (1979), from which this poem is taken, while he was in prison. His second collection, *Martin & Meditations on the South Valley* (1987), won the 1987 Before Columbus Foundation American Book Award. His most recent work, *Black Mesa Poems*, was published in 1989. He now lives on a small farm outside Albuquerque.

SO MEXICANS ARE TAKING JOBS FROM AMERICANS

O Yes? Do they come on horses
with rifles, and say,
                Ese gringo, gimmee your job?
And do you, gringo, take off your ring,
drop your wallet into a blanket   5
spread over the ground, and walk away?

I hear Mexicans are taking your jobs away.
Do they sneak into town at night,
and as you're walking home with a whore,
do they mug you, a knife at your throat,   10
saying, I want your job?

Even on TV, an asthmatic leader
crawls turtle heavy, leaning on an assistant,
and from a nest of wrinkles on his face,
a tongue paddles through flashing waves   15
of lightbulbs, of cameramen, rasping
"They're taking our jobs away."

Well, I've gone about trying to find them,
asking just where the hell are these fighters.

The rifles I hear sound in the night   20
are white farmers shooting blacks and browns
whose ribs I see jutting out
and starving children,
I see the poor marching for a little work,
I see small white farmers selling out   25
to clean-suited farmers living in New York,
who've never been on a farm,
don't know the look of a hoof or the smell
of a woman's body bending all day long in fields.

I see this, and I hear only a few people   30
got all the money in this world, the rest
count their pennies to buy bread and butter.

Below that cool green sea of money,
millions and millions of people fight to live,
search for pearls in the darkest depths   35
of their dreams, hold their breath for years
trying to cross poverty to just having something.

The children are dead already. We are killing them,
that is what America should be saying;
on TV, in the streets, in offices, should be saying,
  "We aren't giving the children a chance to live."   40

  Mexicans are taking our jobs, they say instead.
  What they really say is, let them die,
  and the children too.

STUDY QUESTIONS

1. How many different ways does the poem literalize the notion that jobs are being "taken" from Americans? Which literalization seems to you the most effective? Why?

2. Describe the STRUCTURE of the poem. Where does the TONE change? At what point does the poem begin to concentrate on human needs? on the lives of the disadvantaged? How many different ways does the poem use the principle of contrast?

3. Which details in the poem are the most vivid? What strategies account for the vividness? Which IMAGES seem to you especially effective?

4. What value system does the poem accuse America of having? What value system does the poem itself support?

5. How does the CONTEXT of recent arguments over the Mexican-American Free Trade
   Agreement modify or reinforce the tone and relevance of the poem?

Lee Ki Chuck

B orn in Seoul, Korea, "Lee Ki Chuck" (a pseudonym) came to the United States
with his family in 1973. They first settled in a Los Angeles suburb but later
moved to the New York metropolitan area. The following "autobiography" is taken
from an oral interview in 1975.

FROM KOREA TO HEAVEN COUNTRY

Before, I was Oriental guy, right? But different society—everything is dif-   1
ferent—like girl friend and study and spending money and riding car.

I came here and I bought Pinto car. I was driving very crazy. One day   2
my friend was driving crazy, Mustang, make follow me. I thought, "Americans are very lucky, they are always having good time." I was kind of hating
inside. I never want to lose *anything*—even studies, sports, anything—I didn't
want to lose to American. So I just beat him. After that time people know I
am driving crazy. People just come to me, racing, so I raced every time.
Then during last year, I wrecked up one car, first car, and I was *crazy*. I was
racing with friend. I hit a tree. I have so many tickets from the police. [Laughs.]
In a twenty-five-mile [zone], sixty miles I drove. I had so many warning
tickets. I know that is very bad. You can't go to Harvard with these kind of
tickets. I don't drive now anymore.

I have matured a lot since I got to this country. I smoke a lot, too. I used   3
to smoke because I was curious—now one day, one pack. Every time I get
up in the morning is so pain. And drinking. I found I like rock concert. So
interesting, different. Like I go in the morning, 4:00. Those are nice guys I
get drunk with, whiskey, go down to the beach and go swimming. Found a
lot of crazy.

Actually my immigration was very hard. I had so many times crying.   4
That was really a terrible time. I guess is all right now, really. I am so happy.
And then, after my mother came here, my father was getting all right. They
found I skip school so many times, getting bad, but they didn't tell anything

to me. "Do whatever you want, but just don't be bad about it." They gave me another chance.

I'm still Korean. I was really trying to make good friend with American. I have a friend but I never think he is my best friend. American friend I can never make best friend. They just like "hi" friends. "Hi." "Hi."

What was your reaction to girls in this country?

Oh yeh, girls. When I was in Korea—like if I have girl friend—very innocent, talking about philosophy, society, politics, every time. It is hard to even touch hand there. You understand? Very innocent. This is Korea.

I met these few girls in this country, but I don't like them. They are more strong on the physical than I am. [Laughs.] Every time, is physical. Every time I try to talk to them about life, they say, "I think you are too smart. I don't think I can follow you." That's what everybody says.

I tried suicide. When I hit the tree, I was almost dead—fifty miles, I hit. But I didn't die. I was lucky—just a scratch and sore on the face. That was my fault. My friend, he couldn't stop his car, and he hit my car and the breaking window and spread out the glass. Insurance paid for car. Was total. And then after that, when I was getting really bad in the school—skipping school, drinking, doing marijuana outside—I come by home about 1:00. During school days, too. Sometimes I work. I make a lot of money. Like moonlight can make thirty, forty dollars, busboy, tips and they pay check, too, at the hotel. Make a lot of money, and then I can get whatever I want.

I can't face my principal. He's very nice but I couldn't face him so I just took twenty pills. Slept, but I didn't die. My mother didn't tell it to my father. Twenty, that's what I only regret, and my mother said, "You can die with twenty pills." But in the America, if you take sleeping pills a lot, you never die, but just the body inside is changed.

All of my friends in the Korea they still think I am having very good time. I don't tell them what happened to me. I have a car, and they think I am very rich.

If I come to America, I thought that America was really heaven country. I saw so many movie. I saw cars, everyone drives car. If I go to America, I can drive. I can watch TV, everything. I thought I was really heading to heaven. But that's wrong. You have to try to make heaven. Everybody still, everybody think all immigration come to this country. Before they come here they think of this country as heaven. This country, if you try, if you walk out, you can make money, you can be rich here. It's a really nice country, actually.

I used to be with a lot of friends, but now I am alone always. I didn't know what I am searching. I used a lot of philosophy book, but I can't find any answers. That's all American way. Everyone says I try too hard. Really, I want to make a lot of experience; I thought experience was good. If there is bad, don't even try. That's all I wanted to say to young people. I didn't expect I would smoke a lot like this. If there is a bad, don't even try, like racing cars, don't even try. You are going to have an accident. Is very bad.

You say I look like a quiet boy—but outside. Inside is very different. 116

STUDY QUESTIONS

1. What does the first sentence of the interview suggest about Lee Ki Chuck's sense of identity? Are there signs by the end of the piece that he has begun to develop a new identity? What evidence is there that he has begun to grow up after the suicide attempts?

2. In what different ways do the opinions—or presumed opinions—of those left behind in Korea affect Lee's attitudes? his behavior? What evidence is there that Lee cares deeply about the opinions of others?

3. What is Lee's attitude toward his principal? toward his father? (The mother he mentions in paragraph 4 is really his stepmother; his mother remained in Korea.) toward authority figures more generally?

4. For Lee when he arrives, what does "America" represent? What are the values of "home"?

Jesse G. Monteagudo

A regular contributor to *The Community Voice* of West Palm Beach, Florida, Jesse G. Monteagudo's articles and reviews have been featured in a variety of lesbian-gay and mainstream publications as well as in several anthologies, including *Gay Life*, *Lavender Lists*, and *Hometowns*, from which the following essay is taken. A long-time activist, Monteagudo lives in Fort Lauderdale.

MIAMI, FLORIDA

I grew up in Miami's Little Havana, a community like no other. Here, in the 1 southern half of a once-sleepy Miami, a community of Cuban immigrants, refugees from a revolution, created, within the confines of American society, a mirror image of a Havana that they believed existed before Fidel Castro and his minions did away with the things they once held dear.

Though waves of Cubans have landed in the United States since the 2 nineteenth century, they were largely limited to members of the political opposition or the intelligentsia. The revolution of 1959, by changing Cuba from a capitalist country dependent on the United States to a communist country dependent on the U.S.S.R., let loose a series of migrations that rid the island of much of its upper and upper-middle classes and that incidentally spared Castro an organized base of opposition. While the American government welcomed this massive exodus as a weapon in the Cold War, it sought to avoid its consequences by resettling the refugees throughout the fifty states and Puerto Rico. It did not work. Most Cuban exiles chose to settle in Miami, a city with a tropical climate and a proximity to the homeland. By the mid-sixties a sizable Cuban exile community had emerged in south Florida, a bilingual society that centered around South West Eighth Street, the old Tamiami Trail whose name, like that of almost everything else in the new Miami, was soon Hispanicized into the now familiar nickname of Calle Ocho.

Though Calle Ocho has changed in the last twenty years, it will always 3 remind me of my formative years, the turbulent sixties. Many of the old sights and sounds remain: old men playing dominoes, coffee shops dispensing rivers of *cafe Cubano*, statues of the saints beaming from store windows and car windshields, and fiery speeches shot from street corners or the airwaves. Other aspects of Calle Ocho are more "typically" American; huge U.S. flags waving (along with Cuban flags) from used-car lots, smartly dressed yuccas (young, upwardly mobile Cuban-Americans) driving BMWs, politicians of all ethnic origins seeking the Cuban vote in perfect or fractured Spanish. The language of Calle Ocho is like no other: a driven, fast-lane Spanish, now diluted into Spanglish, that leaves other Spanish speakers amused and everyone else amazed.

Critics complain that Miami's Cuban community refuses to assimilate. 4 Actually, Cuban-Americans have adopted the American Dream with a vengeance. People who arrived in Miami with just the clothes on their backs became, within a decade, prosperous business owners with homes in Westchester or Kendall, brand-new cars, and a voice in government. Since the once dominant Democratic Party is too liberal for their tastes, most Cuban-Americans are registered Republicans, a development that made the Grand Old Party a force in local and Florida state politics.

When I first moved to Little Havana (1964), Calle Ocho was a street in 5 transition, where some of the older, "Anglo-owned" businesses stubbornly held out against the Cuban tide. I remember walking home from school among a variety of supermarkets, pharmacies, and dime stores that tried to outdo each other in their devotion to *La Causa* by displaying large Cuban flags, maps of the island, and portraits of Cuban heroes Jose Martí and Antonio Maceo.[1] My parents' generation then took it for granted that *el exilio* was only a temporary condition and that they would soon be able to return to *la Cuba libre*,[2] there to start anew where they left off.

1. Jose Martí (1853–95), Antonio Maceo (1845–96): leaders of the Cuban independence movement against Spanish rule.
2. "Free Cuba."

Little Havana was largely a self-contained community, which meant   6
that I seldom had to deal with the problems of belonging to an ethnic minority. Where I lived, we were the majority. The world was divided between the Cubans and the *Americanos*, a category in which we dumped all native-born whites (blacks were in a class by themselves). Some of the older Cubans made it a point of patriotism not to learn English, even when they sought public office. More typical of their generation are my parents who, though naturalized and English-speaking at work, spend all of their nonworking hours surrounded by Spanish, whether emanating from their relatives or friends or from radio or television sets constantly tuned to Spanish-language stations.

Having created a replica of Old Havana in their new home, Miami's   7
Cuban community sought to prevent the emergence of a progressive movement that it believed was responsible for the revolution. Seeing itself as a community at war, Little Havana refused to tolerate diversity within its ranks. Political dissent was (and to some extent still is) taboo, and any form of liberalism, progressivism, or socialism is frowned upon as being tantamount to aiding the "enemy." The Cuban-American media broadcasts the party line with no pretense at impartiality, and anyone who dares to disagree is (they believe) either a communist or an idiot. I remember being called communist (at the age of twelve!) for speaking out in favor of the Civil Rights Movement. Calle Ocho did not "go conservative" with Reagan's election in 1980; conservative politics there were a given, even (especially) during the activist sixties. Reagan himself is acclaimed as a hero in Little Havana (as in nearby Little Managua), even if his crusade against communism was more talk than action.

Politics were the least of my problems. As a budding gayboy, I could   8
not fit in, either with my parents' generation or with my own. My parents worried that I lacked the masculine qualities needed to carry on the family name and genes and, perhaps, to share in the liberation of *La Patria*.[3] My peers saw in me a nerdy bookworm who was undoubtedly queer and thus deserving of their constant harassment. I am still amazed that these boys were able to guess my sexual orientation long before I knew it myself, though here perhaps I am allowing them more insight than they really had. The fact that I was different was enough to convince these boys, raised as they were on machismo and the herd instinct, that I was a sexual deviate.

Miami's Cuban community, with roots planted deep in the soil of Span-   9
ish machismo and Roman Catholicism (and politically conservative to boot), is still unwilling to accept its gay population. Twenty years ago, things were even worse, especially for gay adolescents struggling to understand themselves. When I turned thirteen my father sat me down and gave me a stern lecture warning me to watch out for prowling perverts. I was the person my parents were warning me against! Whenever change could not be blamed on communism, it was attributed to homosexuals. My father swore that all rock

3. The fatherland.

singers were queer, while the kids in school were certain that their male teachers, especially those who gave them less than satisfactory grades, were *maricones*. Male homosexuals were perennial objects of abuse in a community that worshipped virility and equated dissent with effeminacy.

With such attitudes to deal with, it's not surprising that most of Little Havana's gay population prefers the safety of the closet to the risks of gay activism. The only noticeable homosexuals are those whose looks and mannerisms seem to confirm their community's most cherished beliefs and worst expectations. One such character lived in the apartment building my family and I dwelled in around 1968. The man in question was an *artista*, a word which is Spanish for an artist or an entertainer but which, as it was used by my parents, left no doubt as to what the man's sexual orientation was. A bit player in community theater and local television shows, our neighbor, who, to make things worse, bore the androgynous name of Angel, was lean and fastidious and spoke Spanglish with a pronounced lisp (as did I!). I remember the impression Angel invariably gave as he sashayed down the hall, greeting my bemused parents before vanishing into the apartment he shared with his elderly mother and maiden aunt. Though a charming and doubtlessly courageous man, Angel appeared to be rarely happy and always alone. He was definitely not a good role model for a confused teenager who was trying to deal with feelings that he knew would outrage everyone around him (save one).

Though Calle Ocho was not without its share of obviously gay men, they seemed to gather around such professions as hairdressing, studio photography and show business. The prevalence of *maricones* in Little Havana's theatrical industry is somewhat ironic since gay men are popular targets of ridicule in Cuban-American vaudeville, even (especially) in comedies produced by gay-owned theater companies, directed by gay directors and acted out by gay actors. During my formative years Little Havana's leading playhouse, which naturally specialized in gay-baiting farces, was run by an obvious (but discreet) gay couple who apparently saw no conflict between their personal lives and the prejudices they perpetuated on the stage.

Cuban parents would go to any length to save their sons from a fate they believed was worse than death. Many a Cuban boy of uncertain sexuality was subjected to hormone shots, a practice that led to a crop of hirsute, deep-voiced gay men who walk the streets of Miami today. My parents chose a less drastic (though equally popular) measure. Every afternoon after school I would dutifully walk to the local YMCA—where, naturally, Spanish was spoken—and take judo classes, as if my erotic interest in my own gender could be extinguished through physical contact with other males. When that didn't seem to work, my parents sent me to a psychiatrist, an equally futile gesture but one popular with many concerned Cuban parents at that time.

By the time I graduated from high school in 1972, Little Havana had changed. It had expanded its horizons westward as affluent, now naturalized Cuban-Americans began to move to the suburbs. Calle Ocho itself underwent a transformation as the last of the old Anglo-owned businesses closed down and were replaced by Cuban enterprises. Cuban-Americans were ready to assume leadership of the city of Miami from the retreating Anglos, who were now migrating north into Broward and Palm Beach counties.

I turned twenty in 1973. That year I became both an American citizen and a practicing homosexual, no small feat for a man who is naturally reluctant to take chances. My parents had moved into a house just outside of Little Havana and I had moved along with them, commuting to and from college and a part-time job selling shoes at a Hialeah shoe store owned by a Cuban Danny De Vito. I also worked as a dishwasher for a greasy spoon whose manager was a notorious chicken hawk who invariably invited all his young employees to his apartment for some tea and sympathy. Finding both job and boss unattractive, I quit after a few weeks.

Determined to work my way through college, I got a job in the school library, which helped my coming out process in two ways. First, the library carried all the latest "gay liberation" books, which I, an incorrigible bookworm, did not fail to read. Second, the library had a very cruisy men's room, which I used to good benefit during my student years. From tearooms I "graduated" to adult bookstores and then, in 1974, to gay bars.

Though my parents had long suspected, they did not have to face my sexual orientation outright until one night when I, my inhibitions dulled by alcohol, finally blurted it out to them (so much for my education). I offered to move out then and there but my parents, for whom the family unit is paramount, wouldn't hear of it. Apparently they thought that my reputation (and theirs) would be safer if I remained under parental supervision.

Most twenty-year-olds would have taken this opportunity to leave an increasingly uncomfortable parental nest and set up a place of their own. But Little Havana, like big Havana, is a family-oriented society that expects its sons and daughters to reside with their parents until they get, heterosexually, a means of escape that is unavailable to most lesbian or gay Cubans. *La familia* comes first, which means that "little" Jesse (or everyone else in his predicament) was expected to drop everything in order to assist his parents, straight siblings, aunts, uncles, and cousins.

In the Cuban community a façade of heterosexuality must be maintained while living at home. If one's sexual orientation is known it is treated as, at best, an unfortunate vice that should only be indulged elsewhere. It's no wonder that, once away from their parents, many young gay Cubans went wild. This system of repression and hypocrisy also applied to heterosexual singles, though they have the privilege of eventually getting married, thus adding respectability (and children) to their sexual relations.

An institution that developed in order to deal with the plight of the Cuban single was the *posada*, a drive-in motel which rented by the hour. During the early seventies Calle Ocho was home to several *posadas*, places where Cuban gays and straight singles alike went for sexual release before going home to *Mama y Papa*. A couple would check in, do their business, and check out, after which the motel attendant would come in to change the bed and clean up a bit before renting the same room to another couple. To their credit *posada* managers and attendants were very accepting of sexual diversity, though I once tried their sense of tolerance by bringing in a dirty-looking, *Americano hippiado* ("hippyish" American) I picked up somewhere. In any case, with Cuban libidos (my own included) running high, *posada* owners made a tidy profit. I remember trying to find a room on New Year's Eve 1974 only to find an especially long waiting list and impatient couples lining up round the block.

Not having a car or a place of my own, my sex life depended upon the   20
kindness of strangers. Still, I was able to enjoy Little Havana's lively but furtive gay male social scene, one that centered around bars, beaches, a few private homes (for not all gay Cubans lived with their parents), and the newly opened Club Miami baths. Camp humor combined with Latin high spirits to create a light and lively atmosphere, which, within its limitations, offered Cuban gay men a break from the problems of living in a society that hated them. Some gay Cubans stood machismo on its head by adopting outrageously effeminate behavior, at least within the confines of gay space, while others sought to let off steam through heavy drug or alcohol use and promiscuous sex.

Being a relatively handsome and newly uninhibited young guy in his   21
early twenties, I was able to enjoy many of the pleasures Little Havana's gay demimonde had to offer. From other gay Cubans I learned how to dress (bell-bottom pants and platform shoes were then the rage), to stay up late, to hold my liquor, to cruise and deal with rejection (nonchalantly). I even "learned" to adopt an effeminate pose and to refer to myself and others as "she," though this was something I never cared for. Though I did not have a car, I joined friends who did for joyrides to the gay beach on Virginia Key and north to Fort Lauderdale's hot spots. My sex partners—and I was seldom without one—ranged from my first lover, a Cuban eighteen years older than me who eventually left me to join a Pentecostal church, to a Mexican doctor on vacation and the above-mentioned *Americano hippiado*.

To many Cubans, gay men want to be women. Many gay Cubans took   22
them at their word and got as close to being women as finances and opportunities allowed. Some went into female impersonation, an art form that flourishes in South Florida. Others went the whole route, becoming genital females through hormones and surgery. Many of these were unhappy and confused gay kids who, growing up in an atmosphere of self-hatred, saw a sex change as the only alternative to suicide. They should not be confused with the true transsexuals, people who knew what they wanted and usually got it.

The most memorable of the gender benders who inhabited Little Hav-   23
ana's demimonde was Silvia, who, when I first met her, was a large and imposing *transformista* who lip-synched in straight and gay bars in the neighborhood. (Her impressions of La Lupe, a salsa singer known for throwing

her shoes and her wig at the audience, were legendary.) Silvia's goal was to save enough money to have a sex change operation, a goal that she eventually accomplished. I remember the party Silvia's friends gave her the night before she checked into the hospital, a combination victory party and wake that I, a friend of a friend, was invited to. The operation was a success and Silvia, "the woman who became a legend" (as the title of a never-produced stage rendition of her life proclaimed), settled down as a lesbian, eventually moving in with a tough dyke who managed a Cuban lesbian bar on Miami Beach.

Though gay life in Little Havana was fun while it lasted, this shallow   24
and somewhat neurotic scene became ponderous after a while. I was never happy with the excessive effeminacy, the heavy drug and alcohol use, the backstabbing and catfighting (I was once robbed by a so-called friend), the self-hatred, and the need to pretend. I wanted to break with my surroundings, to finish college and find a place of my own. I also wanted to find a permanent lover and get involved in gay activism, two commodities that were scarce on Calle Ocho. By 1978, a year after Little Havana joined the rest of Dade County in overturning a gay rights ordinance, I accomplished all of these goals and moved out of Little Havana, not because of the vote but to be with my lover. I moved to Broward County and a chapter in my life came to an end.

In some ways, I never "left" Little Havana. Fort Lauderdale, where I   25
now live, is only an hour's drive from Miami, in the same state and in the next county. As it turned out, I now live in a section of Fort Lauderdale that is becoming increasingly Hispanic, with a social and commercial life reminiscent of Calle Ocho during the sixties. Fort Lauderdale seems to be a near-perfect compromise between living at home and living away from home. Even my parents have accepted my living arrangements—though they still expect me to visit them.

Calle Ocho has changed much during the past decade. It is now a tourist   26
attraction along the lines of New Orleans' French Quarter, though without the *Vieux Carré*'s historical authenticity and artistic reputation. Miami's Cuban community has changed as well, though they might not admit it. If Miami is now "a Cuban city"—a majority of the city's commissioners, municipal employees, business owners, and residents are Hispanic—it is equally true that an overwhelming majority of Miami's Cubans have been Americanized, though not assimilated enough to please their critics. My generation of Cuban-Americans, who has now come of age, is largely U.S.-educated, speaks fluent English, and enjoys American careers, tastes, and often American-born, non-Hispanic spouses.

As for me, I have changed my first name, my religion, and my address,   27
and I profess political views and a sexual orientation that are at odds with those held dear by most Cuban-Americans. My English is even more fluent than my Spanish, though I still speak both with a telltale accent (and a lisp!). My lover, most of my friends, and my economic, social, and cultural life are

largely non-Hispanic, and I cannot visit Calle Ocho these days without realizing that I do not belong there anymore.

Still, I am Cuban by birth, descent, and upbringing, my surname is still 28 Monteagudo (a name that remains unpronounceable for most non-Hispanics), and at times I still count and curse in Spanish. I am proud of the way Miami's Cuban community *(mi gente)*[4] has changed the social and economic life of Dade County, even while electing politicians who held political views that are diametrically opposed to my own. One of the buttons on my car radio remains tuned to a Miami-based Spanish-language station, which I always play whenever I drive down Calle Ocho.

As an openly gay man, I can never be reconciled with Little Havana, as 29 it is personified by my relatives and by other Cubans and Cuban-Americans with whom I come in contact. I recently made a very reluctant appearance at my sister's second wedding, an event to which my lover was not invited. Many of my relatives were there, accompanied, of course, by their heterosexual spouses and their children. Though my sister and cousins have lifestyles that are vastly different from those of their parents—most of them are married to non-Cubans and most of them have been divorced—their views on homosexuality remain similar to those of the generation before them.

In spite of it all, I have made my peace with my past and do not regret 30 having liked it. Calle Ocho will always be a street of memories that, with the flight of time, become increasingly better. Growing up in Little Havana has made me what I am today, and that can't be all bad.

STUDY QUESTIONS

1. What are the geographical and historical CONTEXTS of this autobiographical essay? Is the information the author supplies sufficient to make the environment—physical and spiritual—in which he grew up clear? What do you infer are his political positions—conservative or liberal? How do the differences between him and the dominant culture of Cuban-American Miami relate to his difference in sexual orientation?

2. How is the fact that he is gay introduced? What is its effect? (This essay was published in a collection of gay autobiographical essays related to the hometowns of the authors; the context, then, would have given the introduction of this information a quite different—or negligible—effect.)

3. How does Monteagudo explain the fact that most of the acknowledged gays of Cuban Miami actually do fit the STEREOTYPE? What is the IRONY of the prevalence of gays in Little Havana's theatrical community? What is the irony of his parents' means of trying to "cure" him of his orientation?

4. The essay is quite candid about cruising and apparently casual pick-ups. What effect does this candor have on you as reader? Does the publishing history of this

4. "My people."

essay (see queston 2 above) help explain the nature of the candor? What does the range of his lovers suggest?

5. In what sense is Monteagudo "conventional" in his sexual morality?

Adrienne Rich

B orn in Baltimore, Maryland, in 1929, Adrienne Rich is one of the best-known poets of this day. Her life has been one of change—first as "faculty wife" and mother, then as civil-rights and antiwar activist, then as lesbian in the women's liberation movement, teacher, and lecturer—as she describes in her famous autobiographical essay "When We Dead Awaken: Writing as Re-Vision" (1972, 1976). She is a prolific writer, having published 16 books, most of them collections of poems, and has won many awards, including the Brandeis University Creative Arts Medal and the Ruth Lilly Poetry Prize. Her book *Diving into the Wreck* (1973) received the National Book Award in 1974. Her most recent books are *An Atlas of the Difficult World* (1991), for which she received the *Los Angeles Times* Book Prize for poetry, *Collected Early Poems* (1993), and *What Is Found There* (1993). The following essay is taken from *Blood, Bread, and Poetry* (1986).

IF NOT WITH OTHERS, HOW? (1985)

I have been reflecting on what feels so familiar about this: to identify actively as a woman and ask what that means; to identify actively as a Jew and ask what that means. It is feminist politics—the efforts of women trying to work together as women across sexual, class, racial, ethnic, and other lines—that have pushed me to look at the starved Jew in myself; finally, to seek a path to that Jewishness still unsatisfied, still trying to define its true homeland, still untamed and unsuburbanized, still wandering in the wilderness. Over and over, the work of Jewish feminists has inspired and challenged me to educate myself, culturally and politically and spiritually, from Jewish sources, to cast myself into the ancient and turbulent river of disputation which is Jewish culture.

Jews, like women, exist everywhere, our existence often veiled by history; we have been "the Jewish question" or "the woman question" at the margins of Leftist politics, while Right Wing repressions have always zeroed

in on us. We have—women and Jews—been the targets of biological determinism and persistent physical violence. We have been stereotyped both
viciously and sentimentally by others and have often taken these stereotypes
into ourselves. Of course, the two groups interface: women are Jews, and
Jews are women; but what this means for the Jewish vision, we are only
beginning to ask. We exist everywhere under laws we did not make; speaking
a multitude of languages; excluded by law and custom from certain spaces,
functions, resources associated with power; often accused of wielding too
much power, of wielding dark and devious powers. Like Black and other
dark-skinned people, Jews and women have haunted white Western thought
as Other, as fantasy, as projected obsession.

My hope is that the movement we are building can further the conscious 3
work of turning Otherness into a keen lens of empathy, that we can bring
into being a politics based on concrete, heartfelt understanding of what it
means to be Other. We are women and men, *Mischlings* (of mixed parentage)
and the sons and daughters of rabbis, Holocaust survivors, freedom fighters,
teachers, middle- and working-class Jews. We are gay and straight and bisex-
ual, older and younger, differently able and temporarily able-bodied; and we
share an unquenched hope for the survival and sanity of the human community. Believing that no single people can survive being only for itself, we
want a base from which to act on our hope.

I feel proud to be identified as a Jew among Jews, not simply a progres- 4
sive among progressives, a feminist among feminists. And I ask myself, What
does that mean? What is this pride in tribe, family, culture, heritage? Is it a
feeling of being better than those outside the tribe? The medieval philosopher Judah ha-Levi claimed a hierarchy of all species, places on earth, races,
families, and even languages. In this hierarchy, the land, language, and people of Israel are naturally superior to all others. As a woman, I reject all such
hierarchies.

Then is pride merely a cloak I pull around me in the face of anti-Semi- 5
tism, in the face of the contempt and suspicion of others? Do I invoke pride
as a shield against my enemies, or do I find its sources deeper in my being,
where I define myself for myself?

Difficult questions for any people who for centuries have met with der- 6
ogation of identity. Pride is often born in the place where we refuse to be
victims, where we experience our own humanity under pressure, where we
understand that we are not the hateful projections of others but intrinsically
ourselves. Where does this take us? It helps us fight for survival, first of all,
because we know, from somewhere, we deserve to survive. "I am not an
inferior life form" becomes "There is sacred life, energy, plenitude in me and
in those like me you are trying to destroy." And if, in the example of others
like me, I learn not only survival but the plenitude of life, if I feel linked by
a texture of values, history, words, passions to people long dead or whom I
have never met, if I celebrate these linkages, is this what I mean by pride?
Or am I really talking about love?

Pride is a tricky, glorious, double-edged feeling. I don't feel proud of everything Jews have done or thought, nor of everything women have done or thought. The poet Irena Klepfisz has confronted in her long poem "Bashert" the question of sorting out a legacy without spurning any of it, a legacy that includes both courage and ardor, and the shrinking of the soul under oppression, the damages suffered. In any one like me, I have to see mirrored my own shrinkings of soul, my own damages. 7

Yet I must make my choices, take my positions according to my conscience and vision now. To separate from parts of a legacy in a conscious, loving, and responsible way in order to say "This is frayed and needs repair; that no longer serves us; this is still vital and usable" is not to spurn tradition, but to take it very seriously. Those who refuse to make these distinctions— and making distinctions has been a very Jewish preoccupation—those who suppress criticism of the Jewish legacy suppress further creation. 8

As an American Jew, I fear the extent to which both Americans and Israelis, in their national consciousness, are captives of denial. Denial, first, of the existence of the peoples who, in the creation of both nations, have been swept aside, their communities destroyed, pushed into reservations and camps, traumatized by superior might calling itself destiny. I fear that this denial, this unaccountability for acts which are still continuing, is a deep infection in the collective life and conscience of both nations. 9

America wants to forget the past, and the past in the present; and one result of that was Bitburg. Israeli denial is different. Years ago, I remember seeing, with great emotion, on the old Jerusalem–Tel Aviv road, rusted tanks left from the 1948 war, on one of which was painted "If I forget thee, O Jerusalem . . ." But Palestinian memory has been violently obliterated. I fear for the kind of "moral autism" (Amos Oz's phrase) out of which both the United States and Israel, in their respective capacities of power, have made decisions leading to physical carnage and to acute internal disequilibrium and suffering. 10

I say this here, knowing my words will be understood or at least not heard as anti-Semitism. But many of us have experienced a censorship in American Jewish communities, where dissent from official Israeli policies and actions is rebuked and Jewish critical introspection is silenced. "The armored and concluded mind" (Muriel Rukeyser's phrase)[1] is not what the Jewish mind has been overall. Torah itself is not a closed system; we have been a people unafraid of argument, a people of many opinions. Our forebears were instructed to commit suicide rather than idolatry; yet Israel has become a kind of idol for many American Jews. Israel is not seen and cared about as an unfinished human effort, harrowed and flawed and full of gashes between dreams and realities, but as an untouchable construct: The Place Where Jews Can Be Safe. I think that the taboo on dissent among American Jews damages all Jews who, in the wake of the Holocaust and the birth of a 11

1. *The Collected Poems of Muriel Rukeyser* (New York: McGraw-Hill, 1978), p. 102. [Author's note.]

Jewish state, are trying to imagine a Jewish future and a Jewish consciousness that does not stop with Hillel's first question.[2]

The word *safe* has two distinct connotations: one, of a place in which we can draw breath, rest from persecution or harassment, bear witness, lick our wounds, feel compassion and love around us rather than hostility or indifference. The safety of the mother's lap for the bullied child, of the battered-women's shelter, the door opened to us when we need a refuge. Safety in this sense implies a place to gather our forces, a place to move from, not a destination. But there is also the safety of the "armored and concluded mind," the safety of the barricaded door which will not open for the beleaguered Stranger, the psychotic safety of the underground nuclear-bomb shelter, the walled and guarded crime-proof condominium, the safety bought with guns and money at no matter what cost, the safety bought and sold at the cost of shutting up. And this safety becomes a dead end in the mind and in the mapping of a life or a collective vision. I want to say that though the longing for safety has been kept awake in us by centuries of danger, mere safety has not been the central obsession of the Jewish people. It has not been an ultimate destination. How to live in compassion, pursue justice, create a society in which "what is hateful to you, do not do to your neighbor," how to think, praise, celebrate life—these have been fundamental to Jewish vision. Even if strayed from, given lip service, even if in this vision Jewish women have remained Other, even if many Jews have acted on this vision as social reformists and radicals without realizing how Jewish—though not exclusively Jewish—a vision it is. And I don't believe that the Jewish genius has completed itself on this earth: I think it may be on the verge of a new, if often painful and disorienting, renascence.

All of us here live in two dissonant worlds. There is the world of this community and others like it in America: Jewish and gentile, men and women, Black and brown and red and yellow and white, old and young, educated in books and educated in what Tillie Olsen has named "the college of work," in poverty or in privilege—the communities of those who are trying to "turn the century," in Black activist musician Bernice Reagon's words.[3] In this world of vision and struggle, there is still myopia, division, anti-Semitism, racism, sexism, heterosexism. But there is also passion, and persistence, and memory, and the determination to build what we need, and the refusal to buy safety or comfort by shutting up. We affirm the diversity out of which we come, the clashes and pain we experience in trying to work together, the unglamorous ongoing labors of love and necessity.

And there is that other world, that America whose history is Disneyland, whose only legitimized passion is white male violence, whose people

---

2. "If I am not for myself, who will be for me?" See *Sayings of the Fathers, or Pirke Aboth, the Hebrew text, with a New English Translation and a Commentary by the Very Rev. Dr. Joseph H. Hertz* (New York: Behrman House, 1945), p. 25. [Author's note.]

3. Bernice Reagon, "Turning the Century," in *Home Girls: A Black Feminist Anthology*, ed. Barbara Smith (New York: Kitchen Table / Women of Color Press, 1981), pp. 356–368. [Author's note.]

are starving for literal food and also for intangible sustenance they cannot always name, whose opiate is denial. As progressives, we live in this America, too, and it affects us. Even as we try to change it, it affects us. This America that has never mourned or desisted in or even acknowledged the original, deliberate, continuing genocide of the indigenous American people now called the Indians. This America that has never acknowledged or mourned or desisted in the ordinary, banal murderousness of its racism—murderous of the individuals and groups targeted by skin color, and murderous of the spiritual integrity of all of us.

As Jews, we have tried to comprehend the losses encompassed by the Holocaust, not just in terms of numbers or communities or families or individuals, but in terms of unknown potentialities—voices, visions, spiritual and ethical—of which we and the world are irreparably deprived. As American Jews, our losses are not from the Holocaust alone. We are citizens of a country deprived of the effective moral, ethical, and aesthetic visions of those whom white racism has tried to quench in both subtle and violent ways; whose capacity, nonetheless, to insist on their humanity, to persevere and resist, to educate their fellow citizens in political reality, to carry their "message for the world," as W. E. B. Du Bois called it, should be supported and celebrated by Jews everywhere.

For progressive American Jews, racism as it exists here in America, around and also within us, in the air we breathe, has both an ethical and a pragmatic urgency. We cannot continue to oppose the racism of Kahane and his like or of South African apartheid and take less oppositional stands on the malignancy of racism here where we live. The depth of the work we do depends on its rootedness—in our knowledge of who we are and also of where we are—a country which has used skin color as the prime motive for persecution and genocide, as Europe historically used religion. As Elly Bulkin indicates in a mindstretching essay, "Hard Ground": "In terms of anti-Semitism and racism, a central problem is how to acknowledge their differences without contributing to the argument that one is important and the other is not, one is worthy of serious attention and the other is not."[4] It is difficult to move beyond these polarizations, but we are learning to do so and will, I believe, continue to help each other learn.

We must continue to insist that the concepts of Jewish survival and "what is good for the Jews" have an expanding, not a constricting, potential. I long to see the widest range of progressive issues defined as Jewish issues everywhere in this country. I long to see the breaking of encrustations of fear and caution, habits of thought engrained by centuries of endangerment and by the spiritual sterility of white mainstream America. I long to see Jewish energy, resources, passion, our capacity to celebrate life pouring into a gathering of thousands of American Jews toward "turning the century." I believe the

4. Elly Bulkin, "Hard Ground: Jewish Identity, Racism, and Anti-Semitism," in Elly Bulkin, M. B. Pratt, and B. Smith, *Yours in Struggle: Three Feminist Perspectives on Anti-Semitism and Racism* (Brooklyn, N.Y.: Long Haul, 1984; distributed by Firebrand Books, Ithaca, N.Y.).

potential is there; I long to see it stirred into glowing life. I believe we may be at the watershed for such a movement. And I would like to end by reading Hillel's three questions, which can never really be separated, and by adding a fourth, which is implicit in what we are doing:

> *If I am not for myself, who will be for me?*
> *If I am only for myself, what am I?*
> *If not now, when?*
>
> *If not with others, how?*

STUDY QUESTIONS

1. What are some of the similarities Rich sees between the treatment and roles of women and Jews? Rich distinguished Jews from Western whites; do you make that distinction? What seems to be her strategy (this is not to suggest that she does not believe it) in doing so? What does she mean by her "conscious work of turning Otherness into a keen lens of empathy" (paragraph 3)? Why does she reject "hierarchies" (paragraph 4)? In the course of the essay how many other groups does she identify as, like the Jews, Other?

2. In what way do the meanings of pride and love overlap? What are the "two edges" of pride?

3. How does she justify criticizing portions of the "Jewish legacy"? (Note that the audience to which this speech was originally addressed was the attendees of the New Jewish Agenda National Convention.) From what directions does she expect to be attacked for "anti-Semitism"?

4. What does she suggest are the two different ways of defining "safety"?

5. What do you infer from this essay is her view of that other world, the Disneyland "America"?

6. Explain the essay's title.

AFTERWORD

CONTEXTS

In face-to-face spoken language there is always a physical context. If you say, "Please close the door," the person you are speaking to knows what you mean and either does or does not do what you ask. If there is more than one other person present, your eyes or gestures will usually indicate which of those present you are addressing. The context is actually part of the "text," part of the language rather than a wrapper or ornament. If you were in an open field and you said to someone "Please close the door," your words would have no meaning. Your auditor would think you were either crazy, joking, or making some kind of figurative statement—meaning, for example, shut your mouth, button your buttons, or zip your zipper.

Written language does not have a physical context, but it does have a context—or, rather, contexts—nonetheless.

Just as no person is an island, so is no text. All texts are connected to something beyond themselves, usually to several things at once. Texts are connected to the events they describe or reflect, and individuals often need to know facts from outside the text to understand what is going on. Reading "[I'm sitting in my history class]," you need to know about the *Mayflower*, Plymouth Rock, and George Washington as the father of his country in order to understand the poem; reading "Black Hills Survival Gathering, 1980," you will need to know what B52's are. Most of us will not need footnotes to understand these references to things "outside" the poems. But what about the references to "Bitburg" and "Amos Oz" in Adrienne Rich's "If Not with Others, How?"?

Texts are connected to the languages in which they are written, and the habits and conventions of those languages—as well as the vocabulary, grammar, and syntax—determine what the texts can do and how they can do it. Texts are connected to the cultures and value systems from which they derive, and they are connected to concepts and larger patterns of thought, so that a reader's understanding and appreciation of the text will often be enhanced by a recognition of the idea. Texts come from specific authors and are read by specific readers. No text, however "complete" and "formal" in itself, exists alone as a totally separate world. Those things beyond the text that may be relevant to reading the text itself are called CONTEXTS, literally things that go with, but which may be considered part of, the text. Often it is important to think about the various contexts that relate to a text. And sometimes it is crucial.

What a reader needs to know to read pleasurably and usefully varies considerably from text to text. Some texts are very demanding in what they expect readers to bring to them; others are "user friendly" to virtually any reader. One thing that every text requires its reader to bring to it is some knowledge of the language (or languages) in which it is written. Selections in this book were chosen specifically for readers who know the English language, and they draw on the reader's knowledge of how English works in a variety of ways. But many of them draw on other languages as well. Toward the end of "Revolution Skyscraper" there are several sentences in Spanish; the reader who does not know Spanish may get the gist of these sentences even without the footnotes, but the full meaning requires some knowledge of the language. Many of the other selections included here contain some words or phrases in a language other than English (French, Japanese, Yiddish, and several Indian languages, for example), primarily because they deal with situations in which one culture confronts another or people from one kind of national or linguistic background meet people with other traditions and knowledge.

Generally speaking, the more you know as a reader, about language or anything else, the better a reader you have the potential to be. Some texts use language in surprising and even confusing ways in order to disorient readers or make them adjust to very special uses of language; many of the selections in chapter 4 subvert reader expectations in that way. More often, texts explore the complex possibilities readers know in the vocabulary or syntax of language used in a conventional way. And sometimes—though rarely—writings try to "educate" a reader in a particular language from a dead stop: that is, they assume no reading ability at all in a particular language. Nora Dauenhauer's "Tlingit Concrete Poem" tells us in an authorial footnote what the three words of the poem mean, and then asks us to savor their sounds and "look" by arranging them in strange ways on the page.

Historical contexts or *cultural contexts* are often the most demanding in a text, and they can be the most difficult for a reader to discover and apply. Many texts are specifically *referential*, that is, they refer to specific events, people, or things in the "real" world, and references to these things (to Iran's holding of American hostages, for example, in James Seilsopour's "I Forgot the Words to the National Anthem" in chapter 6) assume that a reader will know, or be willing to find out, the facts involved in a specific situation.

Getting beyond factual references to the more subtle attitudes toward facts, people, and events is often far more difficult, for readers never quite know when they know enough, and sometimes no single reference in the text, or no single errand in the library, produces just the right key. To understand Fran Winant's "Christopher Street Liberation Day, June 28, 1970," you have to learn about the event itself, but you must also understand enough about the times to reconstruct the joy and excitement of those who had been feeling lonely and nearly unique (as well as cursed) when they came "out of the closet" to find 10,000 others marching with them. The *cultural context* of a particular text may ask us not only to know but to empathize with a whole set of circumstances and traditions of a particular people in a particular place, and the text does not always give us a specific signal—the name of a person, place, or thing—that we have to look up in order to understand.

Another kind of context is the *generic context*. The kind of writing that the writer chooses—a poem, a play, or a story, for example—brings with it some quite specific expectations, for every *literary form* (or GENRE or *literary mode*) has a tradition of use, and this involves specific habits and expectations. A play, for example, involves the assumption that it can be produced on a stage, and one expects it to include CHARACTERS (who are going to be "played by" actors, thus adding an additional dimension of interpretation), and physical SETTING (another interpretive dimension determined beyond the text), and ACTION that can be successfully represented on a stage of a certain size and with specific physical limitations. Stories, poems, autobiographies, essays—all forms of literature—have CONVENTIONS of their own.

Poems, for example, depend for some of their effects on rhythms and the sound of a voice reading them, stories move in a more or less chronological direction, etc. Of course, there are many different varieties within any genre—there are lyric poems, narrative poems, satirical poems, and many others, each with specific conventions that lead a reader to have specific EXPECTATIONS—and knowledge about kinds and subkinds can often lead a reader more deeply or more meaningfully into a particular text.

There are all kinds of other contexts as well. *Authorial contexts,* for example, involve a reader's potential knowledge of other works by the same writer or knowledge of biographical information that may or may not be relevant to interpretation. Anything that has a tradition behind it, or that develops specific, expectable habits and conventions, offers some kind of context. Setting, for example, often participates in general expectations about mood, and characterization in a particular text often participates in characterization that has gone before, drawing on particular STEREOTYPES in order to get a "quick fix" on a character before developing more individual-istic traits through additional details and further action.

There is no simple rule of thumb to bring to bear on context. The more one knows the better, but skill, experience, and good personal judg-ment are necessary for the reader in figuring out just what he or she needs to know and how to apply it. Texts often give signals, referring to events or people that one has to look up, but not always. The best thing a reader can do is to be flexible and a bit humble in the face of a new text, for it will often ask more than it appears to ask of readers—sensitivity to the traditions of others, curiosity about the larger world, human wisdom as well as factual knowledge.

WRITING
ABOUT THE READING

PERSONAL ESSAYS AND NARRATIVES

1. Write a short personal account in which you describe the most important compromise you have made in order to feel as if you belonged in some community, club, or group. How were you changed by the experience? Do you regret the compromise? Do you feel as if understanding the needs and expectations of others helped you grow? made you feel cheap? Do you feel that you were permanently affected by the experience? Be sure to organize your account of the experience so that you make clear what the personal and moral issues were for you at the time you entered into the compromise, and indicate clearly whether your feelings changed after the fact.

2. Make a list of the "typical" qualities shared by people of your age group in your neighborhood. Make another list of qualities that are devalued or distrusted. Then create an "inside" character and an "outside" character, and construct a dialogue in which the two characters argue about the appropriateness of peer values in your community.

3. Who is the person you have known who seems to have had the most trouble "fitting in" to a particular group? Write a story in which that person is the main character; construct a situation in which the person's inability to fulfill the expectations of others causes him or her pain. Construct the story and characterize the person in such a way that the reader is made to sympathize with his or her problem.

IMITATIONS AND PARODIES

1. Using Pat Mora's "Immigrants" as a model, write a poem in which you give advice to an outsider about fitting in.

2. Using Adrienne Rich's "If Not with Others, How?" prepare a speech to be delivered to your classmates in which you outline your ideals for American society.

3. Write a poem—or prose poem—using Joan Murray's poem as a model, entitled "Coming of Age in _____." This can be either a serious imitation or a parody.

COMPARISON-CONTRAST PAPER

Compare the attitudes and alternatives of exiles in Edward Said's essay in chapter 1 and Bharati Mukherjee's in "Hindus," or of exiles in Elena Padilla's essay in chapter 1 with Jesse G. Monteagudo's "Miami, Florida."

ANALYTICAL PAPERS

1. Write a critical essay analyzing the father's values in "In the American Society." (Alternative: Analyze the mother's values.)

2. Answer the questions in the final three lines of "Coming of Age on the Harlem" by analyzing the details in the poem.

ARGUMENTATIVE PAPER

In Fran Winant's poem, lines 19–23 and 50–53 suggest that everyone is, "inside," gay or lesbian (or both?). Interpret how you understand these lines in the most (to you) acceptible way possible, and argue the issue pro or con.

RESEARCH PAPER

Go to the library and research the events surrounding Christopher Street Liberation Day and the origins of the Gay and Lesbian Liberation movements. Find three or four editorials or essays responding to the "coming out of the closet" and the growing militancy of the movement in the early 1970s. Find three or four recent articles or editorials about gays and lesbians (not exclusively devoted to AIDS, though not ignoring that identification). Write a paper on the continuities and changes in the public response to gays and lesbians, including the controversy surrounding gays in the military.

Student Writing

THE CONTEXT OF "HINDUS": BHARATI MUKHERJEE'S VOLUME OF SHORT STORIES, *DARKNESS*

Laura Johnson

Bharati Mukherjee, born in India and now residing in the United States,   1
provides a unique look at the assimilation experience through her literature. Like most immigrant writers of the course, Mukherjee's characters mirror her own attitudes about expatriatism, immigration, and assimilation; the short stories of *Darkness* reflect her own changing experiences and variant feelings about life in a new world. Some of the stories in this collection were written in Canada, where assimilation is impossible and as Mukherjee writes, "immigrants were lost souls, put upon and pathetic" (1). One such work, "Hindus,"

is the story of Pat, who epitomizes an unassimilated immigrant, and his failed attempt to relive his Indian life. By understanding the author's personal experiences, the reader pities Pat's character and may understand his actions in the context of cultural pressures. The other Canadian works, such as "Isolated Incidents" and "Courtly Vision," are also "uneasy stories of expatriation" (2).

In contrast to her Canadian experience, Mukherjee encountered a more accepting society in the United States; in the introduction to *Darkness* Mukherjee suggests that American society embraces immigrants and provides each a home where their uniqueness is an asset not a stigma. Mukherjee describes herself as a semi-assimilated Indian who possesses "sentimental attachments to a distant homeland but no real desire for permanent return." The elderly H.R.H. Maharajah Patwant Singh in "Hindus" pretends to want to return to India, but he only wants to return to the past, to the India that was, and thus his desire is sentimental nostalgia. Leela, the protagonist in that story, is perhaps the most assimilated Indian in the volume: she's married a white Canadian, wears Western clothes, does not like to hang out with other Indians. However, she's still conscious of her caste and of her inability to assimilate (she is divorced from her husband) and so no longer speaks Hindi, but the language Americans confuse with the nationality—"Hindu": "There's a whole world of us now, speaking Hindu." This is one of the stories in the volume *Darkness* that, along with "The Lady from Lucknow," "A Father," "Nostalgia," and "Visitors," is about, as Mukherjee says, "broken identities and discarded languages, and the will to bond oneself to a new community, against the ever present fear of failure and betrayal" (3). These four stories in their similar focus and their variation place the characters in "Hindus" on something like a scale or chart representing the inner turmoil brought about by the immigrant experience and make it easier to understand the different way in which they deal with being "an island of dark immigrants" in the "vast sea" of America which contained many new peoples.

As mentioned earlier, Mukherjee's characters appear to be content or appeased by their American lives rather than intensely longing to return to their homeland. Their sense of security in the New World has been acquired through material possessions, high social status, and respectable, well-paying jobs: Mukherjee has chosen to examine only one immigration experience which includes Indians of apparently high birth who are afforded even more luxurious lives in America. As a portrait of materialism, Dr. Patel of "Nostalgia" describes himself as a "patriot" for America, though his devotion is presumedly the result of his success: "He was grateful that there were so many helpless, mentally disabled people in New York State, and that they afforded him . . . a nice living" (98). Dr. Patel continues to note aspects of his life in monetary terms and he is constantly aware of the value of the material goods around him.

Although he is content with his new life, Dr. Patel does not forget New Delhi: "America had been very good to him, no question; but there were things that he had given up. There were some boyhood emotions, for instance, that he could no longer retrieve" (99). When speaking of his childhood and his homeland, Dr. Patel is matter-of-fact and slightly regretful: ironically, he describes himself as being "not one of nostalgia" (98). However, it becomes evident through his actions that Dr. Patel's characterization of himself is untrue: "In crisis, he seemed to regress, to reach automatically for the miracle cures of his Delhi youth, though normally he had no patience with nostalgia" (105). Furthermore, the affair with a Bengali woman seems to be a manifestation of his homesickness: "The Indian food, an Indian woman in bed, made him nostalgic" (111). Finally, in a vulgar reaction to his betrayal, Dr. Patel defecates "squatting the way he had done in his father's home" (113).

Dr. Patel seems to be a man of contradictions, portraying the "broken 5
identities" as a result of immigration of which Mukherjee spoke: "But he knew he would forever shuttle between the old world and the new. He couldn't pretend he had been reborn when he became an American citizen in a Manhattan courthouse" (105). As most immigrants do, Dr. Patel struggles to assimilate and there is some evidence that the affair he pursued may have subconsciously been an attempt at 'Americanization.' When speaking of the ensuing union between himself and the young Bengali girl, the narrator reveals, "for the first time in years he felt a kind of agitated discovery, as though if he let up for a minute, his reconstituted, instant American life would not let him back" (103). When Dr. Patel registers at the hotel the narrator comments, "He had laid claim to America," further suggesting ironically that this act of illicit passion with an Indian woman would suture Dr. Patel into the American society (110).

Yet another paradox of Dr. Patel's character, which may also be a man- 6
ifestation of his broken identity, is an underlying desire to find and experience consuming, passionate love. The normally calm, rational man described to the reader in his occupational and family situations was shaken and excited by the idea of initiating an illicit affair: "Nothing could diminish the thrill he felt in taking a chance" (111). The passion and excitement of living life on the edge through this one evening contrasts everything identifiable with his current life—a job which has become routine, a wife he does not love, and memories from which he cannot escape. On the whole, this is an important, albeit unfulfilled, aspect of his identity. It is also interesting to note that after his experience, Dr. Patel's life continues in the same routine manner which has characterized it.

Sexual desire impels the plot of "The Lady from Lucknow" as well. The 7
story is centered upon an affair Nafeesa has with an older American man. With him she experiences the passion which seems to be lacking in the rest of her life: "James flatters me indefatigably; he makes me beautiful, exotic, responsive. . . . When he is with me, the world seems a happy enough place" (25). Like Dr. Patel, Nafeesa's life is obviously unsatisfying but good and comfortable: "I married a good man. . . . Now we live in Atlanta, Georgia, in a wide, new house with a deck and a backyard that runs into a golf course. We expect to pass on this good and decent life to our children" (24).

As a memory from her homeland, Lucknow, Nafeesa brings the legend 8 of Husseina's torn heart and thus a standard of perfect love. Nafeesa appears to long for this kind of love which she does not share with her own husband: "I have fancied myself in love many times since, but never enough for the emotions to break through tissue and muscle" (24). Ironically, the reader realizes by the end of the story that James Beamish, her lover, has given her this passion. After the startling end to their affair, Nafeesa relates that "the pain in my chest will not go away. I should be tasting blood in my throat by now" (34).

The passion which Nafeesa longs for is on the surface physical but may be incorporated into a stronger, subconscious desire to belong and thus assimilate. Nafeesa has traveled from place to place throughout her life and thus lacks something concrete with which to identify: "I have lived a life perched on the edge of ripeness and decay. The traveler feels at home everywhere, because she is never at home anywhere" (31). Nafeesa hopes to find the answer to her broken identity through the passion, attention, and sense of attachment she acquires through her affair. All of these feelings are shattered, however, when James' wife discovers the lovers: "I was a shadow without depth or color, a shadow-temptress who would float back to the city of teeming millions when the affair with James had ended" (33). The depth of Nafeesa's identity struggle is painfully revealed as well as the isolation she experiences as an immigrant: "I had thought myself provocative and fascinating. . . . I was just another involvement of a white man in a pokey little outpost" (33). Nafeesa does not fall apart, however, as one might expect. On the contrary, her life continues on its monotonous course, ironically suggesting, just as the ending of "Nostalgia" might, that her experience is just one in the unending struggle to assimilate: "It wasn't the end of the world. It was humorous, really" (33).

Nafeesa seems to have broken from her homeland and to be more assimilated into the American culture than Dr. Patel. The reader may conclude this by virtue of the fact that Nafeesa has an affair with a white man and by the fact that she is rarely nostalgic. Nafeesa does attend receptions for foreign students at Emory even though her husband "thinks of them as excuses for looking back when we should be looking forward" (25). Her assimilation is further evident, however, when she is speaking with a newly immigrated dentist who is describing the calamities in West Beirut: "I wonder when aphasia sets in. When does a dentist, even a Palestinian dentist, decide it's time to cut losses" (27). Unlike Dr. Patel, Nafeesa seems to be coldly frank about her homeland, without any of the sense of the loss Dr. Patel displays in "Nostalgia."

Yet another of Mukherjee's characters who has chosen an American way of life though he has been unable to release himself from the old world values, religion, and customs, is Mr. Bhowmick of "A Father." Mr. Bhowmick is very frank about his decision to immigrate: "There was no question of going back where he'd come from. He hated Ranchi. . . . Mr. Bhowmick had dreamed of success abroad. Success had meant to him escape from the constant plotting and bitterness that wore out India's middleclass" (65). Like the two characters previously mentioned, the acquisition of material things and providing a comfortable life for one's family is equivalent to success for Mr. Bhowmick. However, he describes his life as routine, his wife as nagging and his daughter as disappointing; Mukherjee has also portrayed Mr. Bhowmick as unfulfilled, and to a degree unsatisfied, with the life he has created for himself in America.

One aspect of his heritage which Mr. Bhowmick is unable to dismiss is the rituals and superstitions of his religion. For example, in his Detroit apartment Mr. Bhowmick has erected a shrine for the goddess Kali-Mata; in many ways he is fanatical about his religion and his prayers are a constant source of strife between him and his wife. Furthermore, one morning on the way to work he debates whether he can risk the bad omen suggested in his neighbor's sneeze, and he finally decides not to go to work. As part of his semi-assimilation, Mr. Bhowmick has learned to compromise his beliefs and he says that everyday he makes "small trade-offs between new-world reasonableness and old-world beliefs" (64). In addition, Mr. Bhowmick misses many of the customs and values of India which his wife and daughter seem to mock: "But Babli could never comfort him. She wasn't womanly or tender the way that unmarried girls had been in the wistful days of his adolescence" (63).

Mr. Bhowmick's life appears to be completely void of passion, except that which he feels for the goddess Kali-Mata. When he first realizes Babli is pregnant, "the idea excited him" that some man had taken the time to make love to the daughter he has been unable to love (66). Mr. Bhowmick envies her passion: "At twenty-six Babli had found the man of her dreams; whereas at twenty-six Mr. Bhowmick had given up on truth, beauty and poetry and exchanged them for two years at Carnegie Tech" (66). When Mr. Bhowmick learns the truth, that Babli's impregnation is by artificial means, his dreams are shattered. Babli has mocked his values and beliefs, even the tradition of arranged marriages, through her act. Mr. Bhowmick not only blames his wife because she made them move to America, but he also sees this fate as punishment from the goddess Kali-Mata. Both Mr. Bhowmick and his daughter are pitiable characters. Mr. Bhowmick, lonely and unimportant in the American world, is trapped in his routine, passionateless life and controlled by the customs of the old world. Babli, on the other hand, while being fully assimilated, is still a victim of her parents', specifically her father's, homeland ties.

Probably the least assimilated character in *Darkness* is Vinita of "Visitors." As a new bride who has only recently moved to America, Vinita epitomizes Indian womanhood and cultural values. However, this is not to suggest that she is not willing to break her ties to her homeland, and in fact she embraces America and all the new opportunities open to her: "[She] wanted all along to exchange her native world for an alien one. . . . She is grateful Salien agreed to her father's proposal of marriage and that she is now cut off from her moorings" (164,166). An arranged marriage has afforded Vinita a wealthy husband and a life of comfort and luxury, but one lacking in passion and true love. Her encounter with a "maladjusted failed American" stirs in her a passion she remembers from her youth (174).

Her confrontation with Mr. Khanna forces Vinita to confront her ideal-   15
izations of America and assimilation. Vinita seems to suggest that in some way it is American to be involved in something unconventional: "Here one has to size up one's own rules. Or is it, here, that one has to seize the situation?" (167). She was excited by the fact that he was completely assimilated, an American with whom she would not have to act out old-world rules; in fact she envies him as "the looter of American culture" (172). However, when he becomes a frenzy of passion and blames his behavior on her betrayal of Indian standards she is confronted with the fact of her heritage as a "crazy emblem" (172).

The behavior and essentially the passion expressed by the young man is   16
not in keeping with her new way of life: "But this is America, she insists. There is no place for feelings here" (172). In many ways Vinita is deeply affected by this experience and she admires the young man's courage and wonders if that is "the same torment she too would have suffered if she had the courage to fall in love" (174). The theme of a void which needs to be filled with passionate love recurs in "Visitors." Vinita also experiences a desire to leave the security of her present life in search of her desire: "Why then is she moved by an irresistible force to steal out of his bed in the haven of his expensive condominium, and run off into the alien American night where only shame and disaster can await her?" (176).

These four short stories are representative of a particular presentation   17
of the immigrant experience related in *Darkness*. In keeping with Mukherjee's own experiences, her characters do not pine away for their motherland, rather they are comfortable in their new home and new culture. Old-world values and customs are not extinct, however, which makes complete assimilation into American culture impossible. Most, if not all, of Mukherjee's characters feel secure in their roles as American wives or breadwinners. On the other hand, each character also demonstrates an emptiness which they attempt to fill with illicit love and chance. Some are tormented by passion while others are controlled by superstitions. Broken identities and dissatisfaction are subtly manifested in each short story. Characters are motivated by a desire to belong and to love as well as to maintain their comfortable lifestyles. The irony of the immigration experience as well as the trials of assimilation are made even more real because Mukherjee brings her personal experiences to her writing.

WORK CITED

Mukherjee, Bharati. *Darkness*. Ontario, Canada: Penguin books, 1985.

9

BELIEFS

The individual, the self, is situated within widening gyres of time and space. Each of us is part of a family, of a culture both present and past, and of a larger society that has its own traditions and culture. We are related as well to the human race and human history. But even then we have not necessarily reached the widest, deepest, or highest sphere in which we are located: we play our part within the animal kingdom, the planet Earth, the cosmos. And many of us see ourselves in relation to some Higher Being, a spiritual entity or concept that has dominion over our world and ourselves.

Often our spiritual relationship to the universe is situated within our cultural heritage; our religion is that of our parents, or sometimes—especially when our parents have taken a different spiritual route from that of their own parents—that of our more remote forebears. Sometimes, however, as we move into another culture, we adopt the spiritual or cosmological orientation of that culture, or we are caught between two cultures, two ways of looking at the world and the universe.

Over the past several centuries, there has been an increasing, though not uniform, secularization of Western society. Some of us are a generation or two removed from any real spiritual or religious roots, though there may be residual cultural identities that have religious connections and can, in time, exert a pull back toward our religious heritage.

The search for a cosmological vision does not necessarily stop at the

boundary lines of our own heritage. Those of us who no longer have traditional roots may search elsewhere, may "shop around" for a worldview that
satisfies our needs and perspectives. In America, this search is no longer
confined to the major Western religions—Catholicism, Protestantism, Judaism. With the increased communication between the Western and Eastern
and Southern worlds, with increasing numbers of immigrants from Asia,
the Middle East, and other Third World countries, there are cosmologies
and religious orientations that not only have their own traditional followers
in America but also offer options to others seeking a way of looking at the
world and the cosmos. Moslems, Hindus, and Buddhists, and the various
sects related to those major religions, abound. Those who find one or
another of these sects—the Hare Krishna, for example—somehow too
strange and therefore unacceptable, call these sects "cults," just as we sometimes call our beliefs "religion" and others' beliefs "myths."

Since the end of World War II especially, there seems to have been a
revival of religious yearning, not only among the young. This spiritual
quest may have something to do with the threat of a nuclear holocaust and
the consequent loss of faith in science as the infallible guide to the good life
and a better world. The vast movements of peoples, the stirring of dormant
societies by the last war, the Holocaust and other religious persecutions of
various kinds, have also contributed to the revival of religion, particularly
the more fundamentalist sects within the major religions: Chasidic Judaism,
Shiite Islam, evangelical, charismatic, and other fundamentalist forms of
Christianity. Sometimes this revival is associated with the revival of cultural
or nationalist feeling, as with Iranian fundamentalists, Black Muslims,
Native American totemists.

Regardless of cause or even of form, there is undeniably a spiritual
"revival" or search in progress, taking us back to our roots here or in our
native European, Asian, African, or other heritage, to ancient but hitherto
strange or foreign creeds and practices.

The works in this chapter exemplify the relationships of our contempo-
raries to the cosmic, the universal, the eternal, the supernatural. The texts
here do not investigate all the possibilities, but they give some notion of the
kinds of search, within and without, that are going on, and the kinds of
resting places or "homes" that some have found. This volume ends, then, as
it began, with home and family devotion, but with the emphasis in this
final chapter on *devotion*.

Toshio Mori

B orn in California in 1910 of Japanese ancestry, Toshio Mori is the author of the
novel *Woman from Hiroshima* (1979). He is, however, best known for his short
stories, which have been collected in the volumes *Yokahama, California* (1949) and *The
Chauvinist and Other Stories* (1979).

ABALONE, ABALONE, ABALONE

Before Mr. Abe went away I used to see him quite often at his nursery. He   1
was a carnation grower just as I am one today. At noontime I used to go to
his front porch and look at his collection of abalone shells.

They were lined up side by side against the side of his house on the   2
front porch. I was curious as to why he bothered to collect them. It was a lot
of bother polishing them. I had often seen him sit for hours on Sundays and
noon hours polishing each one of the shells with the greatest of care. Of
course I knew these abalone shells were pretty. When the sun strikes the
insides of these shells it is something beautiful to behold. But I could not
understand why he continued collecting them when the front porch was
practically full.

He used to watch for me every noon hour. When I appeared he would   3
look out of his room and bellow, "Hello, young man!"

"Hello, Abe-*san*," I said. "I came to see the abalone shells."   4

Then he came out of the house and we sat on the front porch. But he   5
did not tell me why he collected these shells. I think I have asked him dozens
of times but each time he closed his mouth and refused to answer.

"Are you going to pass this collection of abalone shells on to your chil-   6
dren?" I said.

"No," he said. "I want my children to collect for themselves. I wouldn't   7
give it to them."

"Why?" I said. "When you die?"   8

Mr. Abe shook his head. "No. Not even when I die," he said. "I couldn't   9
give the children what I see in these shells. The children must go out for
themselves and find their own shells."

"Why, I thought this collecting hobby of abalone shells was a simple affair," I said.

"It is simple. Very simple," he said. But he would not tell me further.

For several years I went steadily to his front porch and looked at the beautiful shells. His collection was getting larger and larger. Mr. Abe sat and talked to me and on each occasion his hands were busy polishing shells.

"So you are still curious?" he said.

"Yes," I said.

One day while I was hauling the old soil from the benches and replacing it with new soil I found an abalone shell half buried in the dust between the benches. So I stopped working. I dropped my wheelbarrow and went to the faucet and washed the abalone shell with soap and water. I had a hard time taking the grime off the surface.

After forty minutes of cleaning and polishing the old shell it became interesting. I began polishing both the outside and the inside of the shell. I found after many minutes of polishing I could not do very much with the exterior side. It had scabs of the sea which would not come off by scrubbing and the surface itself was rough and hard. And in the crevices the grime stuck so that even with a needle it did not become clean.

But on the other side, the inside of the shell, the more I polished the more lustre I found. It had me going. There were colors which I had not seen in the abalone shells before or anywhere else. The different hues, running berserk in all directions, coming together in harmony. I guess I could say they were not unlike a rainbow which men once symbolized. As soon as I thought of this I thought of Mr. Abe.

I remember running to his place, looking for him. "Abe-*san!*" I said when I found him. "I know why you are collecting the abalone shells!"

He was watering the carnation plants in the greenhouse. He stopped watering and came over to where I stood. He looked me over closely for awhile and then his face beamed.

"All right," he said. "Do not say anything. Nothing, mind you. When you have found the reason why you must collect and preserve them, you do not have to say anything more."

"I want you to see it, Abe-*san*," I said.

"All right. Tonight," he said. "Where did you find it?"

"In my old greenhouse, half buried in the dust," I said.

He chuckled. "That is pretty far from the ocean," he said, "but pretty close to you."

At each noon hour I carried my abalone shell and went over to Mr. Abe's front porch. While I waited for his appearance I kept myself busy polishing the inside of the shell with a rag.

One day I said, "Abe-*san*, now I have three shells."

"Good!" he said. "Keep it up!"

"I have to keep them all," I said. "They are very much alike and very much different."

"Well! Well!" he said and smiled. 29

That was the last I saw of Abe-*san*. Before the month was over he sold 30 his nursery and went back to Japan. He brought his collection along and thereafter I had no one to talk to at the noon hour. This was before I discovered the fourth abalone shell, and I should like to see Abe-*san* someday and watch his eyes roll as he studies me whose face is now akin to the collectors of shells or otherwise.

STUDY QUESTIONS

1. Why doesn't Mr. Abe tell the NARRATOR* why he collects abalone shells? Why will he not leave them to his children?

2. Mr. Abe says that collecting abalone shells is a very simple affair, yet it seems puzzling at first to the narrator. What is the explanation?

3. What is the TURNING POINT in the story?

4. The colors of the polished abalone shell, the narrator says, "were not unlike a rainbow which men once symbolized" (paragraph 17). What does he mean that men "once symbolized" the rainbow?

5. Explain the repetitions in the title of the story.

6. Does this story not appear to have more meaning than its simple narrative? What elements make it seem to have larger implications or wider applications?

Helena Maria Viramontes

Born in East Los Angeles in 1954, Helena Maria Viramontes has published widely and has been frequently anthologized, chiefly in Chicano/Chicana publications. Some of the stories have been collected in her 1985 volume *The Moths and Other Stories*. She has recently co-edited, with Maria Herrera Sobek, *Chicana Creativity and Criticism: Charting New Frontiers in American Literature* (1988). She lives in Irvine, California.

---

*Words in small capitals are defined in the Glossary.

THE MOTHS

I was fourteen years old when Abuelita requested my help. And it seemed only fair. Abuelita had pulled me through the rages of scarlet fever by placing, removing and replacing potato slices on the temples of my forehead; she had seen me through several whippings, an arm broken by a dare jump off Tío Enrique's toolshed, puberty, and my first lie. Really, I told Amá, it was only fair.

Not that I was her favorite granddaughter or anything special. I wasn't even pretty or nice like my older sisters and I just couldn't do the girl things they could do. My hands were too big to handle the fineries of crocheting or embroidery and I always pricked my fingers or knotted my colored threads time and time again while my sisters laughed and called me bull hands with their cute waterlike voices. So I began keeping a piece of jagged brick in my sock to bash my sisters or anyone who called me bull hands. Once, while we all sat in the bedroom, I hit Teresa on the forehead, right above her eyebrow and she ran to Amá with her mouth open, her hand over her eye while blood seeped between her fingers. I was used to the whippings by then.

I wasn't respectful either. I even went so far as to doubt the power of Abuelita's slices, the slices she said absorbed my fever. "You're still alive, aren't you?" Abuelita snapped back, her pasty gray eye beaming at me and burning holes in my suspicions. Regretful that I had let secret questions drop out of my mouth, I couldn't look into her eyes. My hands began to fan out, grow like a liar's nose until they hung by my side like low weights. Abuelita made a balm out of dried moth wings and Vicks and rubbed my hands, shaped them back to size and it was the strangest feeling. Like bones melting. Like sun shining through the darkness of your eyelids. I didn't mind helping Abuelita after that, so Amá would always send me over to her.

In the early afternoon Amá would push her hair back, hand me my sweater and shoes, and tell me to go to Mama Luna's. This was to avoid another fight and another whipping, I knew. I would deliver one last direct shot on Marisela's arm and jump out of our house, the slam of the screen door burying her cries of anger, and I'd gladly go help Abuelita plant her wild lilies or jasmine or heliotrope or cilantro or hierbabuena in red Hills Brothers coffee cans. Abuelita would wait for me at the top step of her porch holding a hammer and nail and empty coffee cans. And although we hardly spoke, hardly looked at each other as we worked over root transplants, I always felt her gray eye on me. It made me feel, in a strange sort of way, safe and guarded and not alone. Like God was supposed to make you feel.

On Abuelita's porch, I would puncture holes in the bottom of the coffee cans with a nail and a precise hit of a hammer. This completed, my job was to fill them with red clay mud from beneath her rose bushes, packing it softly, then making a perfect hole, four fingers round, to nest a sprouting avocado pit, or the spidery sweet potatoes that Abuelita rooted in mayonnaise jars with toothpicks and daily water, or prickly chayotes that produced vines that twisted and wound all over her porch pillars, crawling to the roof, up and over the roof, and down the other side, making her small brick house look like it was cradled within the vines that grew pear-shaped squashes ready for the pick, ready to be steamed with onions and cheese and butter. The roots would burst out of the rusted coffee cans and search for a place to connect. I would then feed the seedlings with water.

But this was a different kind of help, Amá said, because Abuelita was dying. Looking into her gray eye, then into her brown one, the doctor said it was just a matter of days. And so it seemed only fair that these hands she had melted and formed found use in rubbing her caving body with alcohol and marihuana, rubbing her arms and legs, turning her face to the window so that she could watch the Bird of Paradise blooming or smell the scent of clove in the air. I toweled her face frequently and held her hand for hours. Her gray wiry hair hung over the mattress. Since I could remember, she'd kept her long hair in braids. Her mouth was vacant and when she slept, her eyelids never closed all the way. Up close, you could see her gray eye beaming out the window, staring hard as if to remember everything. I never kissed her. I left the window open when I went to the market.

Across the street from Jay's Market there was a chapel. I never knew its denomination, but I went in just the same to search for candles. I sat down on one of the pews because there were none. After I cleaned my fingernails, I looked up at the high ceiling. I had forgotten the vastness of these places, the coolness of the marble pillars and the frozen statues with blank eyes. I was alone. I knew why I had never returned.

That was one of Apá's biggest complaints. He would pound his hands on the table, rocking the sugar dish or spilling a cup of coffee and scream that if I didn't go to mass every Sunday to save my goddamn sinning soul, then I had no reason to go out of the house, period. Punto final. He would grab my arm and dig his nails into me to make sure I understood the importance of catechism. Did he make himself clear? Then he strategically directed his anger at Amá for her lousy ways of bringing up daughters, being disrespectful and unbelieving, and my older sisters would pull me aside and tell me if I didn't get to mass right this minute, they were all going to kick the holy shit out of me. Why am I so selfish? Can't you see what it's doing to Amá, you idiot? So I would wash my feet and stuff them in my black Easter shoes that shone with Vaseline, grab a missal and veil, and wave good-bye to Amá.

I would walk slowly down Lorena to First to Evergreen, counting the cracks on the cement. On Evergreen I would turn left and walk to Abuelita's. I liked her porch because it was shielded by the vines of the chayotes and I could get a good look at the people and car traffic on Evergreen without them knowing. I would jump up the porch steps, knock on the screen door as I wiped my feet and call Abuelita? mi Abuelita? As I opened the door and stuck my head in, I would catch the gagging scent of toasting chile on the placa.[1] When I entered the sala,[1] she would greet me from the kitchen, wringing her hands in her apron. I'd sit at the corner of the table to keep from being in her way. The chiles made my eyes water. Am I crying? No, Mama Luna, I'm sure not crying. I don't like going to mass, but my eyes watered anyway, the tears dropping on the tablecloth like candle wax. Abuelita lifted the burnt chiles from the fire and sprinkled water on them until the skins began to separate. Placing them in front of me, she turned to check the menudo.[2] I peeled the skins off and put the flimsy, limp looking green and yellow chiles in the molcajete and began to crush and crush and twist and crush the heart out of the tomato, the clove of garlic, the stupid chiles that made me cry, crushed them until they turned into liquid under my bull hand. With a wooden spoon, I scraped hard to destroy the guilt, and my tears were gone. I put the bowl of chile next to a vase filled with freshly cut roses. Abuelita touched my hand and pointed to the bowl of menudo that steamed in front of me. I spooned some chile into the menudo and rolled a corn tortilla thin with the palms of my hands. As I ate, a fine Sunday breeze entered the kitchen and a rose petal calmly feathered down to the table.

I left the chapel without blessing myself and walked to Jay's. Most of the time Jay didn't have much of anything. The tomatoes were always soft and the cans of Campbell soups had rusted spots on them. There was dust on the tops of cereal boxes. I picked up what I needed: rubbing alcohol, five cans of chicken broth, a big bottle of Pine Sol. At first Jay got mad because I thought I had forgotten the money. But it was there all the time, in my back pocket.

When I returned from the market, I heard Amá crying in Abuelita's kitchen. She looked up at me with puffy eyes. I placed the bags of groceries on the table and began putting the cans of soup away. Amá sobbed quietly. I never kissed her. After a while, I patted her on the back for comfort. Finally: "¿Y mi Amá?"[3] she asked in a whisper, then choked again and cried into her apron.

Abuelita fell off the bed twice yesterday, I said, knowing that I shouldn't have said it and wondering why I wanted to say it because it only made Amá cry harder. I guess I became angry and just so tired of the quarrels and beatings and unanswered prayers and my hands just there hanging helplessly by my side. Amá looked at me again, confused, angry, and her eyes were filled with sorrow. I went outside and sat on the porch swing and watched the people pass. I sat there until she left. I dozed off repeating the words to myself like rosary prayers: when do you stop giving when do you start giving when do you . . . and when my hands fell from my lap, I awoke to catch

10

11

12

1. Living room. *Placa:* griddle.
2. Tripe soup. *Molcajete:* Mexican mortar.
3. And my mother?

them. The sun was setting, an orange glow, and I knew Abuelita was hungry.

There comes a time when the sun is defiant. Just about the time when moods change, inevitable seasons of a day, transitions from one color to another, that hour or minute or second when the sun is finally defeated, finally sinks into the realization that it cannot with all its power to heal or burn, exist forever, there comes an illumination where the sun and earth meet, a final burst of burning red orange fury reminding us that although endings are inevitable, they are necessary for rebirths, and when that time came, just when I switched on the light in the kitchen to open Abuelita's can of soup, it was probably then that she died. 13

The room smelled of Pine Sol and vomit and Abuelita had defecated the remains of her cancerous stomach. She had turned to the window and tried to speak, but her mouth remained open and speechless. I heard you, Abuelita, I said, stroking her cheek, I heard you. I opened the windows of the house and let the soup simmer and overboil on the stove. I turned the stove off and poured the soup down the sink. From the cabinet I got a tin basin, filled it with lukewarm water and carried it carefully to the room. I went to the linen closet and took out some modest bleached white towels. With the sacredness of a priest preparing his vestments, I unfolded the towels one by one on my shoulders. I removed the sheets and blankets from her bed and peeled off her thick flannel nightgown. I toweled her puzzled face, stretching out the wrinkles, removing the coils of her neck, toweled her shoulders and breasts. Then I changed the water. I returned to towel the creases of her stretch-marked stomach, her sporadic vaginal hairs, and her sagging thighs. I removed the lint from between her toes and noticed a mapped birthmark on the fold of her buttock. The scars on her back which were as thin as the life lines on the palms of her hands made me realize how little I really knew of Abuelita. I covered her with a thin blanket and went into the bathroom. I washed my hands, and turned on the tub faucets and watched the water pour into the tub with vitality and steam. When it was full, I turned off the water and undressed. Then, I went to get Abuelita. 14

She was not as heavy as I thought and when I carried her in my arms, her body fell into a V, and yet my legs were tired, shaky, and I felt as if the distance between the bedroom and bathroom was miles and years away. Amá, where are you? 15

I stepped into the bathtub one leg first, then the other. I bent my knees slowly to descend into the water slowly so I wouldn't scald her skin. There, there, Abuelita, I said, cradling her, smoothing her as we descended, I heard you. Her hair fell back and spread across the water like eagle's wings. The water in the tub overflowed and poured onto the tile of the floor. Then the moths came. Small, gray ones that came from her soul and out through her mouth fluttering to light, circling the single dull light bulb of the bathroom. Dying is lonely and I wanted to go to where the moths were, stay with her 16 and plant chayotes whose vines would crawl up her fingers and into the clouds; I wanted to rest my head on her chest with her stroking my hair, telling me about the moths that lay within the soul and slowly eat the spirit up; I wanted to return to the waters of the womb with her so that we would never be alone again. I wanted. I wanted my Amá. I removed a few strands of hair from Abuelita's face and held her small light head within the hollow of my neck. The bathroom was filled with moths, and for the first time in a long time I cried, rocking us, crying for her, for me, for Amá, the sobs emerging from the depths of anguish, the misery of feeling half born, sobbing until finally the sobs rippled into circles and circles of sadness and relief. There, there, I said to Abuelita, rocking us gently, there, there.

STUDY QUESTIONS

1. How does the first paragraph prepare the reader for the last one?

2. How would you describe the NARRATOR? her CHARACTER?

3. How are the narrator's "bull hands" (paragraph 2) made normal?

4. Why does the narrator's grandmother make her feel "like God was supposed to make you feel" (paragraph 4)?

5. How does the detailed description of the transplanting of roots (paragraph 5) prepare for the final episode in the story? How does it relate to the "supernatural" or fantastic elements in the story?

6. Why doesn't the narrator go to Mass? Where does she go instead?

Louise Erdrich

Although primarily known as a novelist and story writer, Louise Erdrich is also a poet of distinction. She is of Chippewa and German-American descent; she grew up in North Dakota and now lives in New Hampshire with her husband and five children. Her best-known novel, *Love Medicine* (1984), won the National Book Critics Circle Award and was a national bestseller. It was followed by *The Beet Queen* (1986) and *Tracks* (1988). Her poetry has been collected in *Jacklight* (1984) and *Baptism of Desire* (1989).

FLEUR

The first time she drowned in the cold and glassy waters of Lake Turcot, Fleur Pillager was only a girl. Two men saw the boat tip, saw her struggle in the waves. They rowed over to the place she went down, and jumped in. When they dragged her over the gunwales, she was cold to the touch and stiff, so they slapped her face, shook her by the heels, worked her arms back and forth, and pounded her back until she coughed up lake water. She shivered all over like a dog, then took a breath. But it wasn't long afterward that those two men disappeared. The first wandered off, and the other, Jean Hat, got himself run over by a cart.

It went to show, my grandma said. It figured to her, all right. By saving Fleur Pillager, those two men had lost themselves.

The next time she fell in the lake, Fleur Pillager was twenty years old and no one touched her. She washed onshore, her skin a dull dead gray, but when George Many Women bent to look closer, he saw her chest move. Then her eyes spun open, sharp black riprock, and she looked at him. "You'll take my place," she hissed. Everybody scattered and left her there, so no one knows how she dragged herself home. Soon after that we noticed Many Women changed, grew afraid, wouldn't leave his house, and would not be forced to go near water. For his caution, he lived until the day that his sons brought him a new tin bathtub. Then the first time he used the tub he slipped, got knocked out, and breathed water while his wife stood in the other room frying breakfast.

Men stayed clear of Fleur Pillager after the second drowning. Even though she was good-looking, nobody dared to court her because it was clear that Misshepeshu, the waterman, the monster, wanted her for himself. He's a devil, that one, love-hungry with desire and maddened for the touch of young girls, the strong and daring especially, the ones like Fleur.

Our mothers warn us that we'll think he's handsome, for he appears with green eyes, copper skin, a mouth tender as a child's. But if you fall into his arms, he sprouts horns, fangs, claws, fins. His feet are joined as one and his skin, brass scales, rings to the touch. You're fascinated, cannot move. He casts a shell necklace at your feet, weeps gleaming chips that harden into mica on your breasts. He holds you under. Then he takes the body of a lion or a fat brown worm. He's made of gold. He's made of beach moss. He's a thing of dry foam, a thing of death by drowning, the death a Chippewa cannot survive.

Unless you are Fleur Pillager. We all knew she couldn't swim. After the first time, we thought she'd never go back to Lake Turcot. We thought she'd keep to herself, live quiet, stop killing men off by drowning in the lake. After the first time, we thought she'd keep the good ways. But then, after the second drowning, we knew that we were dealing with something much more serious. She was haywire, out of control. She messed with evil, laughed at the old women's advice, and dressed like a man. She got herself into some half-forgotten medicine, studied ways we shouldn't talk about. Some say she kept the finger of a child in her pocket and a powder of unborn rabbits in a leather thong around her neck. She laid the heart of an owl on her tongue so she could see at night, and went out, hunting, not even in her own body. We know for sure because the next morning, in the snow or dust, we followed the tracks of her bare feet and saw where they changed, where the claws sprang out, the pad broadened and pressed into the dirt. By night we heard her chuffing cough, the bear cough. By day her silence and the wide grin she threw to bring down our guard made us frightened. Some thought that Fleur Pillager should be driven off the reservation, but not a single person who spoke like this had the nerve. And finally, when people were just about to get together and throw her out, she left on her own and didn't come back all summer. That's what this story is about.

During that summer, when she lived a few miles south in Argus, things 7 happened. She almost destroyed that town.

When she got down to Argus in the year of 1920, it was just a small grid 8 of six streets on either side of the railroad depot. There were two elevators, one central, the other a few miles west. Two stores competed for trade of the three hundred citizens, and three churches quarreled with one another for their souls. There was a frame building for Lutherans, a heavy brick one for Episcopalians, and a long narrow shingled Catholic church. This last had a tall slender steeple, twice as high as any building or tree.

No doubt, across the low, flat wheat, watching from the road as she 9 came near Argus on foot, Fleur saw that steeple rise, a shadow thin as a needle. Maybe in that raw space it drew her the way a lone tree draws lightning. Maybe, in the end, the Catholics are to blame. For if she hadn't seen that sign of pride, that slim prayer, that marker, maybe she would have kept walking.

But Fleur Pillager turned, and the first place she went once she came 10 into town was to the back door of the priest's residence attached to the landmark church. She didn't go there for a handout, although she got that, but to ask for work. She got that too, or the town got her. It's hard to tell which came out worse, her or the men or the town, although the upshot of it all was that Fleur lived.

The four men who worked at the butcher's had carved up about a thou- 11 sand carcasses between them, maybe half of that steers and the other half pigs, sheep, and game animals like deer, elk, and bear. That's not even mentioning the chickens, which were beyond counting. Peter Kozka owned the place, and employed Lily Veddar, Tor Grunewald, and my stepfather, Dutch James, who had brought my mother down from the reservation the year before she disappointed him by dying. Dutch took me out of school to take her place. I kept house half the time and worked the other in the butcher shop, sweeping floors, putting sawdust down, running a hambone across the street to a customer's bean pot or a package of sausage to the corner. I was a good one to have around because until they needed me, I was invisible. I blended into the stained brown walls, a skinny, big-nosed girl with staring eyes. Because I could fade into a corner or squeeze beneath a shelf, I knew everything, what the men said when no one was around, and what they did to Fleur.

Kozka's Meats served farmers for a fifty-mile area, both to slaughter, for   12
it had a stock pen and chute, and to cure the meat by smoking it or spicing it in sausage. The storage locker was a marvel, made of many thicknesses of brick, earth insulation, and Minnesota timber, lined inside with sawdust and vast blocks of ice cut from Lake Turcot, hauled down from home each winter by horse and sledge.

A ramshackle board building, part slaughterhouse, part store, was fixed   13
to the low, thick square of the lockers. That's where Fleur worked. Kozka hired her for her strength. She could lift a haunch or carry a pole of sausages without stumbling, and she soon learned cutting from Pete's wife, a string-thin blonde who chain-smoked and handled the razor-sharp knives with nerveless precision, slicing close to her stained fingers. Fleur and Fritzie Kozka worked afternoons, wrapping their cuts in paper, and Fleur hauled the packages to the lockers. The meat was left outside the heavy oak doors that were only opened at 5:00 each afternoon, before the men ate supper.

Sometimes Dutch, Tor, and Lily ate at the lockers, and when they did   14
I stayed too, cleaned floors, restoked the fires in the front smokehouses, while the men sat around the squat cast-iron stove spearing slats of herring onto hardtack bread. They played long games of poker or cribbage on a board made from the planed end of a salt crate. They talked and I listened, although there wasn't much to hear since almost nothing ever happened in Argus. Tor was married, Dutch had lost my mother, and Lily read circulars. They mainly discussed about the auctions to come, equipment, or women.

Every so often, Peter Kozka came out front to make a whist, leaving   15
Fritzie to smoke cigarettes and fry raised doughnuts in the back room. He sat and played a few rounds but kept his thoughts to himself. Fritzie did not tolerate him talking behind her back, and the one book he read was the New Testament. If he said something, it concerned weather or a surplus of sheep stomachs, a ham that smoked green or the markets for corn and wheat. He had a good-luck talisman, the opal-white lens of a cow's eye. Playing cards, he rubbed it between his fingers. That soft sound and the slap of cards was about the only conversation.

Fleur finally gave them a subject.   16

Her cheeks were wide and flat, her hands large, chapped, muscular.   17
Fleur's shoulders were broad as beams, her hips fishlike, slippery, narrow. An old green dress clung to her waist, worn thin where she sat. Her braids were thick like the tails of animals, and swung against her when she moved, deliberately, slowly in her work, held in and half-tamed, but only half. I

could tell, but the others never saw. They never looked into her sly brown eyes or noticed her teeth, strong and curved and very white. Her legs were bare, and since she padded around in beadwork moccasins they never saw that her fifth toes were missing. They never knew she'd drowned. They were blinded, they were stupid, they only saw her in the flesh.

And yet it wasn't just that she was a Chippewa, or even that she was a woman, it wasn't that she was good-looking or even that she was alone that made their brains hum. It was how she played cards. 18

Women didn't usually play with men, so the evening that Fleur drew a chair up to the men's table without being so much as asked, there was a shock of surprise. 19

"What's this," said Lily. He was fat, with snake's cold pale eyes and precious skin, smooth and lily-white, which is how he got his name. Lily had a dog, a stumpy mean little bull of a thing with a belly drum-tight from eating pork rinds. The dog liked to play cards just like Lily, and straddled his barrel thighs through games of stud, rum poker, vingt-un.[1] The dog snapped at Fleur's arm that first night, but cringed back, its snarl frozen, when she took her place. 20

"I thought," she said, her voice soft and stroking, "you might deal me in." 21

There was a space between the heavy bin of spiced flour and the wall where I just fit. I hunkered down there, kept my eyes open, saw her black hair swing over the chair, her feet solid on the wood floor. I couldn't see up on the table where the cards slapped down, so after they were deep in their game I raised myself up in the shadows, and crouched on a sill of wood. 22

I watched Fleur's hands stack and ruffle, divide the cards, spill them to each player in a blur, rake them up and shuffle again. Tor, short and scrappy, shut one eye and squinted the other at Fleur. Dutch screwed his lips around a wet cigar. 23

"Gotta see a man" he mumbled, getting up to go out back to the privy. The others broke, put their cards down, and Fleur sat alone in the lamplight that glowed in a sheen across the push of her breasts. I watched her closely, then she paid me a beam of notice for the first time. She turned, looked straight at me, and grinned the white wolf grin a Pillager turns on its victims, except that she wasn't after me. 24

"Pauline there," she said, "how much money you got?" 25

We'd all been paid for the week that day. Eight cents was in my pocket. 26

"Stake me," she said, holding out her long fingers. I put the coins in her palm and then I melted back to nothing, part of the walls and tables. It was a long time before I understood that the men would not have seen me no matter what I did, how I moved. I wasn't anything like Fleur. My dress hung loose and my back was already curved, an old woman's. Work had roughened me, reading made my eyes sore, caring for my mother before she 27

1. Twenty-one.

died had hardened my face. I was not much to look at, so they never saw me.

When the men came back and sat around the table, they had drawn 28 together. They shot each other small glances, stuck their tongues in their cheeks, burst out laughing at odd moments, to rattle Fleur. But she never minded. They played their vingt-un, staying even as Fleur slowly gained. Those pennies I had given her drew nickels and attracted dimes until there was a small pile in front of her.

Then she hooked them with five-card draw, nothing wild. She dealt, 29 discarded, drew, and then she sighed and her cards gave a little shiver. Tor's eye gleamed, and Dutch straightened in his seat.

"I'll pay to see that hand," said Lily Veddar. 30

Fleur showed, and she had nothing there, nothing at all. 31

Tor's thin smile cracked open, and he threw his hand in too. 32

"Well, we know one thing," he said, leaning back in his chair, "the 33 squaw can't bluff."

With that I lowered myself into a mound of swept sawdust and slept. I 34 woke up during the night, but none of them had moved yet, so I couldn't either. Still later, the men must have gone out again, or Fritzie come out to break the game, because I was lifted, soothed, cradled in a woman's arms and rocked so quiet that I kept my eyes shut while Fleur rolled me into a closet of grimy ledgers, oiled paper, balls of string, and thick files that fit beneath me like a mattress.

The game went on after work the next evening. I got my eight cents 35 back five times over, and Fleur kept the rest of the dollar she'd won for a stake. This time they didn't play so late, but they played regular, and then kept going at it night after night. They played poker now, or variations, for one week straight, and each time Fleur won exactly one dollar, no more and no less, too consistent for luck.

By this time, Lily and the other men were so lit with suspense that they 36 got Pete to join the game with them. They concentrated, the fat dog sitting tense in Lily Veddar's lap, Tor suspicious, Dutch stroking his huge square brow, Pete steady. It wasn't that Fleur won that hooked them in so, because she lost hands too. It was rather that she never had a freak hand or even anything above a straight. She only took on her low cards, which didn't sit right. By chance, Fleur should have gotten a full or flush by now. The irritating thing was she beat with pairs and never bluffed, because she couldn't, and still she ended up each night with exactly one dollar. Lily couldn't believe, first of all, that a woman could be smart enough to play cards, but even if she was, that she would then be stupid enough to cheat for a dollar a night. By day I watched him turn the problem over, his hard white face dull, small fingers probing at his knuckles, until he finally thought he had Fleur figured out as a bit-time player, caution her game. Raising the stakes would throw her.

More than anything now, he wanted Fleur to come away with some- 37 thing but a dollar. Two bits less or ten more, the sum didn't matter, just so he broke her streak.

Night after night she played, won her dollar, and left to stay in a place that just Fritzie and I knew about. Fleur bathed in the slaughtering tub, then slept in the unused brick smokehouse behind the lockers, a windowless place tarred on the inside with scorched fats. When I brushed against her skin I noticed that she smelled of the walls, rich and woody, slightly burnt. Since that night she put me in the closet I was no longer afraid of her, but followed her close, stayed with her, became her moving shadow that the men never noticed, the shadow that could have saved her.

August, the month that bears fruit, closed around the shop, and Pete and Fritzie left for Minnesota to escape the heat. Night by night, running, Fleur had won thirty dollars, and only Pete's presence had kept Lily at bay. But Pete was gone now, and one payday, with the heat so bad no one could move but Fleur, the men sat and played and waited while she finished work. The cards sweat, limp in their fingers, the table was slick with grease, and even the walls were warm to the touch. The air was motionless. Fleur was in the next room boiling heads.

Her green dress, drenched, wrapped her like a transparent sheet. A skin of lakeweed. Black snarls of veining clung to her arms. Her braids were loose, half-unraveled, tied behind her neck in a thick loop. She stood in steam, turning skulls through a vat with a wooden paddle. When scraps boiled to the surface, she bent with a round tin sieve and scooped them out. She'd filled two dishpans.

"Ain't that enough now?" called Lily. "We're waiting." The stump of a dog trembled in his lap, alive with rage. It never smelled me or noticed me above Fleur's smoky skin. The air was heavy in my corner, and pressed me down. Fleur sat with them.

"Now what do you say?" Lily asked the dog. It barked. That was the signal for the real game to start.

"Let's up the ante," said Lily, who had been stalking this night all month. He had a roll of money in his pocket. Fleur had five bills in her dress. The men had each saved their full pay.

"Ante a dollar then," said Fleur, and pitched hers in. She lost, but they let her scrape along, cent by cent. And then she won some. She played unevenly, as if chance was all she had. She reeled them in. The game went on. The dog was stiff now, poised on Lily's knees, a ball of vicious muscle with its yellow eyes slit in concentration. It gave advice, seemed to sniff the lay of Fleur's cards, twitched and nudged. Fleur was up, then down, saved by a scratch. Tor dealt seven cards, three down. The pot grew, round by round, until it held all the money. Nobody folded. Then it all rode on one last card and they went silent. Fleur picked hers up and blew a long breath. The heat lowered like a bell. Her card shook, but she stayed in.

Lily smiled and took the dog's head tenderly between his palms.

"Say, Fatso," he said, crooning the words, "you reckon that girl's bluff- 46
ing?"

The dog whined and Lily laughed. "Me too," he said, "let's show." He 47
swept his bills and coins into the pot and then they turned their cards over.

Lily looked once, looked again, then he squeezed the dog up like a fist 48
of dough and slammed it on the table.

Fleur threw her arms out and drew the money over, grinning that same 49
wolf grin that she'd used on me, the grin that had them. She jammed the
bills in her dress, scooped the coins up in waxed white paper that she tied
with string.

"Let's go another round," said Lily, his voice choked with burrs. But 50
Fleur opened her mouth and yawned, then walked out back to gather slops
for the one big hog that was waiting in the stock pen to be killed.

The men sat still as rocks, their hands spread on the oiled wood table. 51
Dutch had chewed his cigar to damp shreds, Tor's eye was dull. Lily's gaze
was the only one to follow Fleur. I didn't move. I felt them gathering, saw
my stepfather's veins, the ones in his forehead that stood out in anger. The
dog had rolled off the table and curled in a knot below the counter, where
none of the men could touch it.

Lily rose and stepped out back to the closet of ledgers where Pete kept 52
his private stock. He brought back a bottle, uncorked and tipped it between
his fingers. The lump in his throat moved, then he passed it on. They drank,
quickly felt the whiskey's fire, and planned with their eyes things they couldn't
say out loud.

When they left, I followed. I hid out back in the clutter of broken boards 53
and chicken crates beside the stock pen, where they waited. Fleur could not
be seen at first, and then the moon broke and showed her, slipping cautiously
along the rough board chute with a bucket in her hand. Her hair fell, wild
and coarse, to her waist, and her dress was a floating patch in the dark. She
made a pig-calling sound, rang the tin pail lightly against the wood, froze
suspiciously. But too late. In the sound of the ring Lily moved, fat and nim-
ble, stepped right behind Fleur and put out his creamy hands. At his first
touch, she whirled and doused him with the bucket of sour slops. He pushed
her against the big fence and the package of coins split, went clinking and
jumping, winked against the wood. Fleur rolled over once and vanished in
the yard.

The moon fell behind a curtain of ragged clouds, and Lily followed into 54
the dark muck. But he tripped, pitched over the huge flank of the pig, who
lay mired to the snout, heavily snoring. I sprang out of the weeds and climbed
the side of the pen, stuck like glue. I saw the sow rise to her neat, knobby
knees, gain her balance, and sway, curious, as Lily stumbled forward. Fleur
had backed into the angle of rough wood just beyond, and when Lily tried
to jostle past, the sow tipped up on her hind legs and struck, quick and hard
as a snake. She plunged her head into Lily's thick side and snatched a mouthful of his shirt. She lunged again, caught him lower, so that he grunted in

pained surprise. He seemed to ponder, breathing deep. Then he launched his huge body in a swimmer's dive.

The sow screamed as his body smacked over hers. She rolled, striking out with her knife-sharp hooves, and Lily gathered himself upon her, took her foot-long face by the ears and scraped her snout and cheeks against the trestles of the pen. He hurled the sow's tight skull against the iron post, but instead of knocking her dead, he merely woke her from her dream. 55

She reared, shrieked, drew him with her so that they posed standing upright. They bowed jerkily to each other, as if to begin. Then his arms swung and flailed. She sank her black fangs into his shoulder, clasping him, dancing him forward and backward through the pen. Their steps picked up pace, went wild. The two dipped as one, boxstepped, tripped each other. She ran her split foot through his hair. He grabbed her kinked tail. They went down and came up, the same shape and then the same color, until the men couldn't tell one from the other in that light and Fleur was able to launch herself over the gates, swing down, hit gravel. 56

The men saw, yelled, and chased her at a dead run to the smokehouse. And Lily too, once the sow gave up in disgust and freed him. That is where I should have gone to Fleur, saved her, thrown myself on Dutch. But I went stiff with fear and couldn't unlatch myself from the trestles or move at all. I closed my eyes and put my head in my arms, tried to hide, so there is nothing to describe but what I couldn't block out, Fleur's hoarse breath, so loud it filled me, her cry in the old language, and my name repeated over and over among the words. 57

The heat was still dense that next morning when I came back to work. Fleur was gone but the men were there, slack-faced, hung over. Lily was paler and softer than ever, as if his flesh had steamed on his bones. They smoked, took pulls off a bottle. It wasn't noon yet. I worked awhile, waiting shop and sharpening steel. But I was sick, I was smothered, I was sweating so hard that my hands slipped on the knives, and I wiped my fingers clean of the greasy touch of the customers' coins. Lily opened his mouth and roared once, not in anger. There was no meaning to the sound. His boxer dog, sprawled limp beside his foot, never lifted its head. Nor did the other men. 58

They didn't notice when I stepped outside, hoping for a clear breath. And then I forgot them because I knew that we were all balanced, ready to tip, to fly, to be crushed as soon as the weather broke. The sky was so low that I felt the weight of it like a yoke. Clouds hung down, witch teats, a tornado's green-brown cones, and as I watched one flicked out and became a delicate probing thumb. Even as I picked up my heels and ran back inside, the wind blew suddenly, cold, and then came rain. 59

Inside, the men had disappeared already and the whole place was trembling as if a huge hand was pinched at the rafters, shaking it. I ran straight through, screaming for Dutch or for any of them, and then I stopped at the heavy doors of the lockers, where they had surely taken shelter. I stood there 60 a moment. Everything went still. Then I heard a cry building in the wind, faint at first, a whistle and then a shrill scream that tore through the walls and gathered around me, spoke plain so I understood that I should move, put my arms out, and slam down the great iron bar that fits across the hasp and lock.

Outside, the wind was stronger, like a hand held against me. I struggled forward. The bushes tossed, the awnings flapped off storefronts, the rails of porches rattled. The odd cloud became a fat snout that nosed along the earth and sniffled, jabbed, picked at things, sucked them up, blew them apart, rooted around as if it was following a certain scent, then stopped behind me at the butcher shop and bored down like a drill.   61

I went flying, landed somewhere in a ball. When I opened my eyes and looked, stranger things were happening.   62

A herd of cattle flew through the air like giant birds, dropping dung, their mouths opened in stunned bellows. A candle, still lighted, blew past, and tables, napkins, garden tools, a whole school of drifting eyeglasses, jackets on hangers, hams, a checkerboard, a lampshade, and at last the sow from behind the lockers, on the run, her hooves a blur, set free, swooping, diving, screaming as everything in Argus fell apart and got turned upside down, smashed, and thoroughly wrecked.   63

Days passed before the town went looking for the men. They were bachelors, after all, except for Tor, whose wife had suffered a blow to the head that made her forgetful. Everyone was occupied with digging out, in high relief because even though the Catholic steeple had been torn off like a peaked cap and sent across five fields, those huddled in the cellar were unhurt. Walls had fallen, windows were demolished, but the stores were intact and so were the bankers and shop owners who had taken refuge in their safes or beneath their cash registers. It was a fair-minded disaster, no one could be said to have suffered much more than the next, at least not until Fritzie and Pete came home.   64

Of all the businesses in Argus, Kozka's Meats had suffered worst. The boards of the front building had been split to kindling, piled in a huge pyramid, and the shop equipment was blasted far and wide. Pete paced off the distance the iron bathtub had been flung—a hundred feet. The glass candy case went fifty, and landed without so much as a cracked pane. There were other surprises as well, for the back rooms where Fritzie and Pete lived were undisturbed. Fritzie said the dust still coated her china figures, and upon her kitchen table, in the ashtray, perched the last cigarette she'd put out in haste. She lit it up and finished it, looking through the window. From there, she could see that the old smokehouse Fleur had slept in was crushed to a reddish sand and the stockpens were completely torn apart, the rails stacked helter-skelter. Fritzie asked for Fleur. People shrugged. Then she asked about the others and, suddenly, the town understood that three men were missing.   65

There was a rally of help, a gathering of shovels and volunteers. We   66 passed boards from hand to hand, stacked them, uncovered what lay beneath the pile of jagged splinters. The lockers, full of the meat that was Pete and Fritzie's investment, slowly came into sight, still intact. When enough room was made for a man to stand on the roof, there were calls, a general urge to hack through and see what lay below. But Fritzie shouted that she wouldn't allow it because the meat would spoil. And so the work continued, board by board, until at last the heavy oak doors of the freezer were revealed and people pressed to the entry. Everyone wanted to be the first, but since it was my stepfather lost, I was let go in when Pete and Fritzie wedged through into the sudden icy air.

Pete scraped a match on his boot, lit the lamp Fritzie held, and then the three of us stood still in its circle. Light glared off the skinned and hanging carcasses, the crates of wrapped sausages, the bright and cloudy blocks of lake ice, pure as winter. The cold bit into us, pleasant at first, then numbing. We must have stood there a couple of minutes before we saw the men, more rightly, the humps of fur, the iced and shaggy hides they wore, the bearskins they had taken down and wrapped around themselves. We stepped closer and tilted the lantern beneath the flaps of fur into their faces. The dog was there, perched among them, heavy as a doorstop. The three had hunched around a barrel where the game was still laid out, and a dead lantern and an empty bottle, too. But they had thrown down their last hands and hunkered tight, clutching one another, knuckles raw from beating at the door they had also attacked with hooks. Frost stars gleamed off their eyelashes and the stubble of their beards. Their faces were set in concentration, mouths open as if to speak some careful thought, some agreement they'd come to in each other's arms.

Power travels in the bloodlines, handed out before birth. It comes down through the hands, which in the Pillagers were strong and knotted, big, spidery, and rough, with sensitive fingertips good at dealing cards. It comes through the eyes, too, belligerent, darkest brown, the eyes of those in the bear clan, impolite as they gaze directly at a person.

In my dreams, I look straight back at Fleur, at the men, I am no longer the watcher on the dark sill, the skinny girl.

The blood draws us back, as if it runs through a vein of earth. I've come home and, except for talking to my cousins, live a quiet life. Fleur lives quiet too, down on Lake Turcot with her boat. Some say she's married to the waterman, Misshepeshu, or that she's living in shame with white men or windigos, or that she's killed them all. I'm about the only one here who ever goes to visit her. Last winter, I went to help out in her cabin when she bore the child, whose green eyes and skin the color of an old penny made more talk, as no one could decide if the child was mixed blood or what, fathered in a smokehouse, or by a man with brass scales, or by the lake. The girl is bold, smiling in her sleep, as if she knows what people wonder, as if she hears the old men talk, turning the story over. It comes up different every time and has no ending, no beginning. They get the middle wrong too. They only know that they don't know anything.

STUDY QUESTIONS

1. How early in your reading do you know that you are in for some unusual events? When do you begin to suspend your normal sense of probability and cause and effect?

2. How much do we know about Fleur Pillager? Which details about her help to "explain" the central events in the story? What events in the story are the most challenging to your normal sense of probability?

3. How do you feel about Fleur? At what points in the story do you feel the most sympathy for her? the most anxiety for what might happen to her? Do you ever feel sympathy for the other card players? Why?

4. Which of the surprising events in the story can be explained by natural causes? Which cannot? How do you interpret the story of Misshepeshu?

5. How fully is the NARRATOR characterized? What is her role in the story? How fully does she interpret the saga? What issues in the story remain for you unresolved at the end?

6. How do you explain the compelling power of the narrative here? What kinds of beliefs does the community share?

Barry Targan

Barry Targan was born in Atlantic City, New Jersey, and educated at Rutgers University, the University of Chicago, and Brandeis University. He currently teaches creative writing at the State University of New York at Binghamton. He is the author of three collections of short stories—*Harry Belten and the Mendelssohn Violin Concerto* (winner of the Iowa School of Letters Award in short fiction), *Surviving Adverse Seasons* (winner of the Saxifrage Award from the University of North Carolina), and *Falling Free*, from which "Dominion" is taken; two collections of poetry—*Thoreau Stalks the Land Disguised as a Father* and *Let the Wild Rumpus Start*; and two novels—*Kingdoms* (winner of the Associated Writing Programs Award in the novel) and *The Tangarine Tango Equation*.

DOMINION

In a moment, in the twinkling of an eye, at the last trump: for the trumpet shall sound, and the dead shall be raised incorruptible, and we shall be changed.

I Corinthians 15:52

He played absently with the tiny party hat in his hand, a hat such as a leprechaun in a movie cartoon might wear, a truncated cone of metallic green paper board with a flat silver brim and a black paper buckle. He pulled at the thin rubber band that would hold the hat in place and listened carefully to what the men were explaining. Sometimes he would nod in comprehension. Last night he and Sandra had gone to the Balmuths' New Year's Eve party. And now, January the first, suddenly a lifetime later, he listened to the two men, the accountant and the lawyer, explain what had happened.

What had happened was that Poverman and Charney, a small manufacturer of lightweight women's clothing, was ruined, embezzled into insolvency by Charney, who even now sat in Florida in the noonday sun. Morton Poverman sat here, at his chilling dining room table cloaked with the fabric of his loss, the neat stacks of paper—bills, letters, invoices, bank statements, memoranda, and packets of canceled checks—that chronicled Charney's wretched course, his wicked testament.

Poverman said, "And all this could have happened without my knowing? Amazing."

In a corner off from the table, Poverman's wife, Sandra, sat in a stuffed chair with her right leg raised up on an ottoman. Her leg, up to the middle of the calf, was in a cast, her ankle broken. "Oh," she said like a moan, a curse, a threat. "Oh God." It was all she could say now, though later, Poverman knew, she would say more, her vehemence strident, hot, and deep. For twenty years she had disliked Phil Charney, distrusted him always, his flamboyance, his fancy women and his fancy ways, the frivolous instability of his unmarried state. And now to be right! To be helplessly confirmed! She put her head back against the chair and closed her eyes as she clogged with rage nearly to fainting. "Oh God."

"Not so amazing," Friedsen, the accountant, snapped. "You never looked at the books. You never asked a question." He slapped at some figures on a pad before him. "Five thousand dollars for the material for the chemises? When is the last time you made a chemise? Who buys chemises any more? And this?" He looked down at the pad. "The bias tape? Forty cases? and here," he jabbed at the entry with his finger, his nail piercing at the numbers like the beak of a ravening bird. "The printing bill on the new boxes? You weren't suspicious of that?" Friedsen was angry. He had done their books from the start, had managed them well. And now he held them in his hands like smudged ashes. Like dirt. Like an affront. If one was a thief, then the other was a fool.

"I never looked at the books," Poverman told him, though Friedsen knew that already, knew everything. "If I had looked, so what would I have known? I did the selling, Philly did the rest. For twenty-five years it worked okay."

"The bastard," Friedsen said.

Poverman could not find his own anger. Perhaps he was still too startled. What Phil Charney had done, he had done quickly, in less than a year altogether, but conclusively in the last quarter before the Christmas season, when their money moved about most rapidly and in the largest amounts. Friedsen, for his own orderly reasons, liked to see his client's fiscal shape at the end of the calendar year. He had gotten to Poverman and Charney two days ago and, hour by hour, he had tumbled ever more quickly through the shreds that Charney had made of the once solid company. Friedsen had gone to no New Year's Eve party. And this morning he had pulled the lawyer, Kuhn, to this dreadful meeting. It had not taken him long to explain and demonstrate the bankruptcy and its cause. Now Kuhn explained the rest, the mechanism of foreclosure and collection, the actual bankruptcy petition to the courts, the appointment of the referee, the slim possibility of criminal action against Charney. He went on, but to Poverman, the intricacies of his disaster like the details of his success were equally abstractions. He could not contain them. He could understand the results, of course. He could understand purposes and conclusions. Consequences. But he had always been the man in front, the one to whom you spoke when you called Poverman and Charney. Morton Poverman, a man of good will and even humor who had put in his working years directly, flesh on flesh, voice against voice, eye to eye. Let Friedsen and Kuhn do what must be done in their rigorous and judicial way. But let him do what he could do in his.

"So what's left?" he asked, first to one then the other. "Anything?"

Of the business there was not much. He would lose the factory and everything in it and connected to it, including the dresses, housecoats, and nightgowns already on the racks. There were two outlet stores, the largest, the newer store in Fairlawn Shopping Mall he would have to close. The older store in the business strip just off of North Broadway, he could probably keep. Where he and Phil had begun.

Personally, there was the paid-up life insurance, fifty-thousand. That was safe. There was also about twenty thousand in cash. There were things like the cars and all that was in the house. The house itself might be a question. Kuhn said the house would depend on too many variables to discuss now. And there was the trust fund for Robert's education. Twenty-five thousand dollars. Nothing could touch that. There were some small investments, mostly stocks. Those would probably have to be called in, for one reason or another. For one bill or another, like Friedsen's perhaps, or Kuhn's. Or merchandise for the store. At this point who could say?

"So? That's it?" 12

"That's about it," Kuhn said. 13

"Well, it's not nothing, is it?" Poverman said. 14

"No," Kuhn said. "It's not nothing." 15

Sandra Poverman sobbed high and quietly at the top of her voice, still 16
unable to open her eyes to what she would have to look at forever after.

When the men left he did some small figuring of his own. Immediately 17
there would be no Florida vacation this winter. Perhaps he would sell one
car. The membership in the country club? What did he need that for, he
didn't even play golf. He started to write down numbers—mortgage payment, property tax, homeowner's insurance, the car payments, but after these
he could not say. He did not know what his heating bill was, his electricity,
food, clothing. And the rest. Did Sandra? Did anyone in this house know
such things? Probably not. He had earned, each year a little more, and in
the last five years nearly, though not quite, a lot. Yesterday the future was
all before him various with pleasures just about to come within his grasp, the
long-planned trips to Europe, to South America the year after that, Hawaii.
The house in the semi-retirement village at Seadale, a hundred miles north
of Miami. Gone. Today only the future itself was waiting, empty and dangerous. The little store on North Broadway with the old lighting fixtures and
the cracked linoleum flooring from twenty-five years ago. That was waiting.

He had earned and they all had spent what they needed, and each year 18
they had needed a little more. So now they would need less. They would
make an accommodation. Tomorrow he would go to the outlet store and take
stock and make arrangements. Begin. He was fifty-three.

The phone rang. It was Phil Charney calling from Miami. He knew that 19
Friedsen would find him in the year-end audit.

"Morty, this is Phil. You know why I'm calling?" 20

"Friedsen was here. Just now. And Kuhn. They just left." 21

"Morty, this is so terrible, I can't say how terrible." 22

Sandra stiffened. "That's him?" she hissed. He nodded. "Give me." She 23
motioned the phone to her. "Give me. I'll tell him something. I'll tell that
filth something. Give me. Give me." She waved for the phone, her voice
rising. He covered the mouthpiece. She tried to stand up.

"Morty, I'm sitting here weeping. I didn't sleep all night. Not for two 24
nights. Not for three nights. I couldn't help it. I still can't. She wants and
wants and I must give. *Must!* Who knows where it ends. There's not so much
money I can go on like this. Then what? But what can I do? *Morty*, what can
I do, kill myself?"

"No, no, of course not." 25

He scrambled for his outrage like a weapon, but a weapon with which 26
to defend himself and not attack. He was embarrassed for the man sobbing
at the other end of the line, his agony. He summoned his hatred for protection, but it would not come. But he had always lacked sufficient imagination,
and what he felt now was more the loss of his life-long friend, the swoop and

gaiety of his presence as he would click about the factory, kidding the women on the machines, hassling in mocking fights the blacks on the loading platforms. He had even picked up enough Spanish to jabber back at the volatile Puerto Ricans. Even the Puerto Ricans Phil could make laugh and work.

That would be gone. And the flitting elegance, the Cadillacs and the women. The clothing and the jewelry. The flights to anywhere, to Timbuktu. He would miss the women. They were an excitement, these strenuous pursuits of Phil Charney's, these expensive pursuits. He was a tone, an exuberant vibrato that pushed into and fluttered the lives of anyone near him. Battered floozies or sometimes women much younger, but often enough recently divorced or widowed women ready at last for madder music, headier wine. Sandra Poverman condemned it, but her husband could afford his own small envy, safe enough within his wife's slowly thickening arms to tease her with his short-reined lust. That would be gone. Tomorrow he would go to work as he had known he would even before Friedsen, but now in silence with no edge of scandal or tightly-fleshed surprise.

"Filth. Murderer," Sandra shouted into the phone. She had gotten up and hobbled over to him. "Liar. Dog."

"She's right, Morty. She's right. I'm no better than a murderer."

"No. Stop this, Phil. Get a hold."

"Die," Sandra screamed. "Die in hell. Bastard. Scum." She pulled at the phone in his hand but he forced it back.

"Oh Morty, Morty, what I've done to you! Oh Morty, forgive me."

"Yes, Phil. OK. I do." He hung up before either could say more.

What more? That time had come to take away their life together, abandoning Phil Charney more severely than himself? But if he had said that, would he be certain enough himself what he meant? That only the sorrow was left, enough of that to go around for them all, so what did the rest of anything else matter?

"What?" Sandra demanded. "What did he want? 'I do' you said. You 'do' what?" He told her. And then she screamed, raised her fists to her ears to block his words, but too late. She fell against him, staggered by the shaking that was bringing down upon her the castles they had built. And now he had even taken from her the solid and pure energy of revenge.

The large, good, sustaining thing that happened in January was that his son, Robert, received the report of his Scholastic Aptitude Tests: 690 in Verbal, 710 in Math. In the achievement tests he did comparably well. The rest of the month, however, was not unexpected as what he had come to do grew clearer. The store had made economic sense as an outlet for the factory, a nice way of taking some retail profit right off the top. But without the factory as the primary supplier, the store was just another women's clothing store, in competition everywhere. That situation would be impossible. But Morton Poverman had his accrued advantages from twenty-five years in both ends of the business. He knew enough to know where he could get overruns, returns, seconds from other manufacturers, small producers such as he had been. What credit he needed, at least with some cash down, he could still get from them.

By the end of January he could at least begin to think seriously about his spring line; various enough and inexpensive as it was, he had a chance to exist. Not much more. But already the stock was coming into the storeroom in the back faster than he could handle it. Still, that was not so bad. Better more than not enough. He would put in the time to inventory and price and mark it all.   37

In January he had let go all the workers in the store, three of them, and handled the front himself. Only on Saturday, dashing back and forth from customer to cash register, was it too difficult. The stock he worked on at night. At first until nine o'clock and now until midnight. But it was coming together, the store brightening with variety and loading up with goods. And people were still shopping downtown, he could tell. He would get by on his low pricing and his long hours. And now he was bringing in a whole line of Playtex girdles and bras, all kinds of pantyhose and lingerie. In a year maybe he would bring in sewing articles, fabrics, patterns. In a year. Or two.   38

It was easier to say that twenty-five years ago when there was still a year or two or three or five to invest. And two of them to do it. But he could say it now, nonetheless, again and alone. His flame burned, steadily if low, even by the end of January when, like fuel for the flame, Bobby's SAT's had arrived. 690 / 710. Fuel enough. Then Morton Poverman would crush back in the large cardboard boxes under the dim, bare-bulbed lighting of the storeroom with his supper sandwich and the last of his thermos of coffee and think that though he was bone-weary and hard-pressed, he was not without intelligent purpose and a decent man's hope. More he did not ask. Or need.   39

February, March—a time for clinging to the steep, roughly-grained rock face of his endeavor, seeking the small, icy handholds, the cracks and fissures of little victories to gain a purchase on, by which to lever himself up an inch: he picked up one hundred assorted dusters for nearly nothing, garbage from South Korea with half their buttons gone. He would replace the buttons. Kurtlanger's, the largest women's clothing store in the area, was dropping its entire line of womens' nylons. It was not worth the bother to Kurtlanger's to supply the relatively few women who still wore separate stockings. It was all pantyhose now. For Poverman the bother could become his business. He stocked the nylons and put an ad in the newspaper saying so. Seeds for springtime. He put money into a new floor, found bags in Waltham, Massachusetts, at a ten percent saving, joined the Downtown Merchants Association protesting for increased side-street lighting and greater police surveillance. He checked three times a day the long-range weather reports. Would winter freeze him shut, March blow his straw house down?   40

At first Sandra had gone mad with anger calling everyone to behold her suffering. She called her friends and relatives, *Charney's* friends and relatives, the police. Worse than the stunning death of a loved one in a car crash or by the quick, violent blooming of a cancer in the lymph, where you could curse   41

God and be done with it, this that Charney had done to her was an unshared burden, separate from life and others' fate, and unsupportable for being so. If we all owe life a death and perhaps even pain, certainly we do not owe it bankruptcy and humiliation. She cried out, howled, keening in the ancient way of grief and lamentation.

And then she dropped into silence like a stone. 42

She would hardly speak to him, as if his failure to share her intensity of 43 anger had separated them. Or to speak to anyone. She grew hard and dense with her misery, imploded beneath the gravity of her fury and chagrin. At first she had fought with her simple terrifying questions: Who could she face? What was the rest of her life to be like? But then, far beyond her questions, she grew smaller yet until at the last she atomized into the vast unspecific sea of justice and worth, and there she floated like zero.

Late at night Poverman would come home and get into bed beside her 44 and chafe her arms and rub her back. Sometimes he would kiss her gently on the neck as she had always liked. But she was wood. Still, he would talk to her, tell her the good things that were happening, his incremental progress, prepare her for the future. But she would not go with him. The future, like her past, had betrayed her, had disintegrated. She would trust in no future again.

Robert Poverman said to his father, "I'll come in after school. You'll 45 show me how to mark the clothing, and that will be a help."

"No," his father said. "By the time you come in after school, get down- 46 town, it would already be late. What could you do in an hour?"

"What do you mean, 'an hour'? I'd work with you at night. I'd come 47 home with you. If I helped, then we'd both get home earlier."

"No. Absolutely not. You're in school. You do the school, I'll do the 48 business. In the summer, we'll see. Not now, Sonny. Not now."

"Are you kidding, Dad? School's over. I'm a second semester senior. It's 49 all fun and games, messing around. It's nothing."

"So do fun and games. Mess around. That's part of school, too. Next 50 year you'll be in college, with no messing around. And what about your activities, the Photography Club, the Chess Club, Current Events Club, Student Council, French Club, the math team. Your guitar. And soon it's track season. So what about track?" Poverman knew it all, remembered everything.

"Dad, listen. I'm a third-string miler. Sometimes they don't even run 51 me. I struggle to break six minutes. And the clubs are strictly baloney. Nothing. Believe me, *nothing*. Let me help you, please. Let me *do* something."

"No. NO. If you want to do something, Sonny, do school, *all* of it just 52 the way you always did. Do it the way you would have before . . . *this*." He smeared his hand in the air.

His son took his hand out of the air and kissed it. "OK, Daddy," he said 53 softly. "OK. And I'll pray for you, too."

That night, turning the handle of the machine that ground out the 54 gummed pricing tags, Poverman recalled what his son had said, that he would pray for him. The machine clicked on: size, stock number, price. What could that mean? But Poverman had enough to think about without adding prayer. He had ten crates of L'Eggs to unpack by morning, two dozen bathrobes that had arrived that day without belts, and all the leather accessories that he still had to stick these tags on. He turned the crank faster.

February, March, and now, somehow, April. Already the first wavelets of Easter buying had lapped at his shore, eroded slightly the cloth of his island. Good. Let it all be washed away in a flood of gold. Poverman walked about. He was working harder than ever, but accomplishing more. The hard, heaving work was mostly done, and there was a shape to everything now, his possibilities limited but definite, and definite perhaps because they were limited. So be it. He had started in quicksand and had built this island. The rest now was mostly up to the weather and the caprice of the economy. At least it was out of the hands of men like Phil Charney.

Poverman seldom thought of him even though he had to meet often enough with Friedsen and Kuhn. He had even made a joke once that he had to work for Charney twice, before and after. Friedsen had not laughed. But what did it matter? What mattered was what *could* matter.

It was six o'clock. He walked about in the crisp store, straightening a few boxes, clothes loosely strewn in bins, the merchandise hanging on the racks. Tonight, for the first time in months, he was closing now. Tonight he was going home early. To celebrate. Let the three hundred pairs of slaps from the Philippines wait. Let the gross of white gloves wait. Tonight he was going home to celebrate. Today, all on the same day, Robert Poverman had been accepted at Yale, Cornell, and the State University of New York at Binghamton, a university center. He had until May fifteenth to make his decision and send in his deposit. They would talk about it tonight. And everything.

Poverman turned out all the lights after checking the locks on the back door. He walked out of the store pulling the door to and double locking it. He looked up at the sign recently painted on the door, the new name he had decided upon: The Fashion Center. Nothing too fancy. Nothing too smart. But what did he need with fancy or smart? He had Robert Poverman of Yale or Cornell. *That* was fancy. *That* was smart.

After supper Poverman spread out on the diningroom table the various catalogues and forms and descriptive literature from the three colleges. He had also added to that, clippings from magazines and newspapers. They had seen most of it all before, when Robert had applied, but now it was to be examined differently as one seriously considered the tangibilities of life in Harkness Memorial Hall or Mary Donlon Hall. Here, this material, was what they had from which to read the auguries of Robert Poverman's future. Even Sandra leavened as they discussed (As always. Again.) what he would study. Which school might be best for what. Neither Poverman nor his wife knew how to make their comparisons. It would, now as before, be their son's

choice. But who could refrain from the talking? The saying of such things as
law or medicine or physics or international relations? Poverman again looked
up the size of the libraries. Yale: 6,518,848. Cornell: 4,272,959. SUNY at
Binghamton: 729,000. 6,518,848 books. How could he imagine that? Still, it
was one measure. But what did Robert Poverman want? His interests were
so wide, his accomplishments so great, what could he *not* decide for? What
could he not illimitably cast for and catch?

They drank tea and talked. In two days Sandra would go for a small   60
operation on the ankle to adjust a bone that had drifted slightly. Even with
his medical coverage it would cost him a thousand dollars. But okay. Of
course. Let her walk straight. Let her life go on. He had hoped that she
would be able to help him in the store now that the Easter push was happening, but instead he had hired someone part time.

He looked at the pictures in the college catalogues, the jungle of glass   61
tubes in the laboratories, the pretty girls intensely painting things on large
canvases, the professor standing at the blackboard filled with lines and numbers and signs like a magical incantation, smiling young men like Robert
flinging frisbees across the wide Commons, the view of Cayuga Lake, the
wondrous glowing cube of the Beinecke Library at Yale (*another* library, a
special library for the rare books alone). Yale. Yale began to creep into Morton
Poverman's heart. He would say nothing. What did he know? It was up to
Robert. But he hoped for Yale. 6,518,848 books.

"I don't know," Robert said. "What's the rush?" He turned to Sandra.   62

"This is an important decision, right? And he's got a month. Think   63
about it, that's the smart thing," he said to his son. "Sure. Don't jump before
you look." He gathered up the evidence of what was to come, the scattered
materials about one of Robert Poverman's schools, and put it all back into
the reddish brown paper portfolio. He took the letters of acceptance and the
letters to be returned with the deposit and put them elsewhere. He wished
that he could have sent one back in the morning with a check enclosed, a
down payment on his son's happiness, a bond, a covenant.

That night in bed he held his wife's hand.   64

"Which do you like?" he asked.   65

"Cornell, I think."   66

"Not Yale? Why not Yale?"   67

"The bulldog," she said. "It's so ugly. What kind of animal is that for a   68
school?"

The weather was warm and balmy. Good for light cotton prints. Easter   69
did well by him and spring, too. Business was beating through the veins of
the store. Sandra's ankle was fixed for good now, mending correctly, though
she would still need more weeks of resting it. This Sunday he had asked
Robert to come to the store with him to help him catch up on some stock
work. Also he wanted to describe what Robert would do in the store that
summer, his job. Robert would work in the store and his pay, except for

some spending money, would be put into a bank account for his use in college. And today Poverman would push his son, slightly, toward his decision. Time was now growing short. Ten days till the deadline. He would like to have this settled.

At three o'clock they sat down to some sandwiches that Sandra had packed for them.

"So? What do you think?" he asked his son. "Do you think you can last the summer? Listen, this is the easy part. The stock don't talk back. The stock don't complain. You think you can explain to a size twelve lady why she don't fit into a size ten dress? Hah? Let me tell you sweetheart, everything to know is not in books." Then he reached across and stroked his son's softly stubbled cheek. His oldest gesture. "But Sonny, all of this is nothing to know. What you're going to learn, compared to this, you could put all this into a little nut shell." Then, "Did you choose a college yet?"

Robert Poverman said, "I don't know."

"There's only ten days," his father said. "What can you know in ten more days that you don't know already? What do you want to know? Who can you ask? Sonny, maybe you think you have to be certain. Well let me tell you, you can't be certain of nothing. And with any one of these schools, you can't go so far wrong. You can't lose anyway."

"It's about college," Robert Poverman said. "I'm not so sure about that."

His father did not understand.

"Maybe college isn't for me. Just yet, anyway. I don't know."

"Know?" his father said. "Know what? What is there to know? You think you want *this?*" he indicated the store around them. "Maybe you want to go into the Army? Shoot guns? Maybe you want to be a fireman and ride on a red truck?" He was filling out.

"Don't be angry, Dad. Please." But it wasn't anger ballooning in Morton Poverman now, it was panic.

"Then what are you talking about? *What* don't you know? You go to college to find out what you don't know. Ah," it occurred to him, "it's the money. Is that it? You're worried about the money, about me and your mother. But I told you, the money is already there. Twenty-five thousand and that will make interest. Plus a little more I've got. Plus what you'll earn. Don't worry about the money, Bobby, please. I swear to you, your mother and I are going to be okay that way. Look, look. The store is working out, Sonny."

"Daddy, it's not that. Maybe there's another way." They were silent.

"So?" Poverman finally asked. "What other way?"

"I've been thinking about religion." He looked at his father evenly. "There's a religious retreat down at this place in Nyack this summer, from the middle of July to the middle of August. I think maybe I should go there." He looked down away from his reflection in his father's brightening eyes.

"Why?"

"Yes, *why*. I need to find out the meaning of things. Not *what* I want to do or where I want to go to college, but *why*. Is that unreasonable?"

But what did Morton Poverman know about reasonableness? What he   85
knew about was hanging on, like a boxer after he has been hit very hard.

"So what has this to do with college? Why can't I send in the deposit?"   86

"I might not go to college right away. I can't honestly say now. Or I   87
might not want to go to one of those colleges. Where I was accepted. I might
find out that I want to go to a . . . a religious type of college. I just don't
know. I've got to think about it. I don't want you wasting the money. If I
change my mind, I can probably still get into a good college somewhere."

"Money again," Poverman roared. He stood. "I'm telling you, money is   88
shit. I know. I've lost money before. That's nothing."

Driving home from the store Robert told his father that for the past six   89
months he had been attending weekly meetings organized by the Society of
the Holy Word for high school age people. Driving down Pearl Street, he
pointed to a store with many books in the window and the name of the
organization neatly lettered on the panes of glass.

"So everybody's in business," Poverman said as he drove by. "Do they   90
belong to the Downtown Businessmen's Association?"

"They're not selling," his son said.   91

"Oh no? Aren't they? So what's that, a church?"   92

"No, Dad. It isn't a business and it isn't a church. It's a place for people   93
to meet to discuss things."

"Yeah? Like what?"   94

"Religion, meaning of life, ethical conduct. The Bible, mostly. The Bible   95
as the word of God."

"Is that right? The Bible tells you what college to go to? Yale or Cornell?   96
Amazing. I never knew. But then, there's so much I don't know."

"Daddy, please don't be angry. Don't be bitter."   97

"No? So what should I be, happy? For eighteen years I'm thinking Chief   98
Justice of the Supreme Court and now my son tells me he's thinking of
becoming a monk. Wonderful. Terrific." He drove faster.

"Ah Daddy, come on. It's not that way at all. We sit and talk about how   99
religion can give a full and wonderful meaning to our lives. It's raised some
important questions for me about my future. And it's offered some possible
answers and solutions."

"Solutions? Why? You've got problems?"   100

"We've all got problems, Daddy."   101

"Like?"   102

"Like our souls," Robert Poverman said. "Like the fate of our immortal   103
souls."

"Souls? *Souls*? You're eighteen and you're worried about your soul? What   104
about your body?"

But his son closed down then, as did he, each caught in the other's orbit   105
as they would ever be, but as silent now and awesomely distant as Venus to

Pluto. And what could the earthbound Morton Poverman breathe in such empty space?

"Yes? Can I help you?" the tall man asked. He was very clean, scrubbed 106 so that he was pink and white. He did not seem to need to shave, his skin as smooth as thin polished stone, nearly translucent. His steel gray hair was combed straight back over his head. He wore small octagonal rimless glasses.

"Just looking," Poverman said. He walked about in the converted store. 107 Converted to what? All he saw were arrangements of books with such titles as *Satan in the Sanctuary* and *Which Will You Believe*. There were piles of small folded tracts and pamphlets on different color paper, pink, green, blue. Newspapers called the *New Word Times* and *Revelation Tribune*. On the walls were large, poster-sized photographs of people, mostly healthy young people, working at good deeds in foreign countries, in ghettos, in hospitals, in old folks' homes. Even Poverman could quickly see that the young people in the photographs were shining with pleasure in the midst of the misery and needs they were serving, gleaming and casting light so that, behold, their light warmed and illuminated the rheumy-eyed old woman in the wheelchair smiling toothlessly; the bloated-bellied eczema-scabbed children in the jungle clearing; the slit-eyed hoodlum sucking deeply on his joint of dope. All down the wall—growing, building, feeding, helping. Hallelujah.

Past the main room, behind a partition, was another room. He turned 108 and walked back to the pink and white man.

"I'm Morton Poverman," he said, and put out his hand. 109

"I'm George Fetler," the pink and white man said, and took the hand. 110

"I've got a son, Robert Poverman. He comes here." 111

"Oh yes. Robert. A wonderful boy. Brilliant. Absolutely brilliant. I'm 112 very pleased to meet you. You must be very proud of such a son."

But Poverman did not have time for this playing. Even now, four blocks 113 away in his own store, United Parcel trucks would be arriving with goods he must pay for and he had not yet made the deposit in the bank that would cover them, and Francine Feynman (now working full time) would be on two customers at once (or worse, none), and the phone would ring with the call from Philadelphia about the slightly faded orlon sweaters. And what had he come here for, this man's opinions?

"Yes," Poverman said. "Proud." But he did not know what to say, nor 114 what to do. What he *wanted* to do was dump five gallons of gasoline over everything—the books, the newspapers, the green pamphlets—and put a match to it. But there were too many other empty store fronts downtown for that to matter. So he was stuck.

George Fetler said, "You're probably here because you're worried about 115 Robert."

"Yes. That's right. Exactly." Poverman beat down the small loop of 116 gratitude.

"Robert's such a thoughtful fellow. He's quite uncertain about college now, about his future. I suppose you and Mrs. Poverman must be concerned." 117

"Yes," Poverman said again, eagerly, even before he could stop himself. Oh this guy was smooth. He was a salesman, all right, as soft as Poverman was hard. 118

"You're probably upset with the Society of the Holy Word, too." 119

Poverman clamped his lips but nodded. 120

"You must think that we've probably poisoned your son's mind." 121

Poverman nodded again. What else? 122

"Let's sit down, Mr. Poverman, and let me tell you about us. Briefly. You're probably anxious to get back to your business." 123

Oh good, good. Oh terrific. All his life Morton Poverman wished he could have been so smooth with customers—buying, selling, complaints, but with him it had always been a frontal attack. A joke, a little screaming or a quick retreat into a deal for twenty percent off. But never like this, quiet, slick as oil, full of probabilities, the ways so easily greased. Yes yes yes where do I sign? 124

He took Poverman into the back room. Half the room was set up like a small class, rows of metal chairs facing a small table and blackboard. The other half of the room was soft chairs drawn around in a circle. They sat there. 125

George Fetler described simply and directly what the Society of the Holy Word did as far as Robert Poverman was concerned. On Thursday evening it conducted, right here, right in these soft chairs, discussions about religion generally, Christianity specifically, and most of all the idea that the Bible was the exact word of God. 126

"That's it?" Poverman asked. 127

"Let's be frank. Let *me* be frank. If you believe that the Bible is the exact word of God, then that can certainly raise some important questions about how you lead your life henceforth. I think this is what has happened to Robert. He came to us six months ago with two friends. I'm sure he came because his two friends, already Christians, wanted him to come. Like many before him, he came more as a lark, skeptical and doubting. But he read the Bible and he discussed what he read and the questions arose, Mr. Poverman, they just arose. And Mr. Poverman, I just wish you could see him, his openness, his honesty, his intelligence. It is very gratifying. Very." Fetler sat back and locked his hands together in front of him. 128

"You'll pardon me for asking," Poverman asked anyway, "but how does this all get paid for?" 129

George Fetler smiled, unlocked his hands, and stood up. "Here. This will explain it in detail." He went out to the tables in the front and returned with a booklet. "This will tell you what you probably want to know, including a financial statement. The Society of the Holy Word is but one arm of 130 the Church of the Resurrection, Incorporated. We're based in Chicago. We've got our printing operation there and headquarters for our evangelical units. The Church also has two colleges, one in San Diego, the other . . ."

"In Nyack?"   131

"Yes. Has Robert mentioned that? He's thinking of going on our sum-   132
mer retreat there."

"But sooner or later, it all comes down to them—what do you call it?—   133
coming out for Jesus? Right?"

"One need not declare for Christ, but that is what we hope will hap-   134
pen." George Fetler and Morton Poverman were coming closer now to what
they thought of the other. "Yes. That is what we hope and pray for."

"Why?"   135

"It is," George Fetler said, not such a soft guy anymore (no sale here),   136
"the only way to avoid the everlasting torments of Hell."

Morton Poverman had never been able to handle the Christian's Hell. It   137
looked to him like the answer to everything and to nothing. And what did
they need it for, this endless knife at the throat? Besides, about Hell—here,
now, right away—he had his own ideas. No. Not ideas. Necessities.

His week went on, all his life became a tactical adventure now, no crease   138
in it without its further unexpected bend, no crack that might not open up
suddenly into an abyss from which he could not scramble back. This is what
he slept with now. Battle. War.

On Thursday evening at seven o'clock he went to the discussion meeting   139
at 183 Pearl Street, to the Society of the Holy Word. And he had studied.
From the array of pamphlets and tracts on the tables in the Society's store he
had taken copiously. And he had read them, late at night in the back of the
store, later than ever, he had read slowly in the bad light, bent to this new
labor as the unopened cartons piled up on each other and each morning Francine Feynman would complain of empty this and replaced that.

THE BIBLE SAYS YOU HAVE SINNED!   140

For all have sinned, and come short of the glory of God (*Rom. 3:23*)   141

THE BIBLE SAYS YOU DESERVE HELL!   142

For the wages of sin is death: but the gift of God is eternal life through   143
Jesus Christ our Lord (*Rom. 6:23*)

THE BIBLE SAYS YOU HAVE A CHOICE!   144

And if it seem evil unto you to serve the Lord, choose you this day   145
whom ye will serve . . . (*Joshua 24:15*)

THE BIBLE SAYS JESUS DIED FOR YOU!   146

But God commendeth his love toward us, in that while we were yet   147
sinners, Christ died for us (*Rom. 5:8*)

THE BIBLE SAYS YOU MUST BELIEVE JESUS!   148

For whosoever shall call upon the name of the Lord shall be saved (*Rom.*   149
10:13)

THE BIBLE SAYS YOU HAVE ETERNAL LIFE!   150

And this is the record, that God hath given to us eternal life, and this   151
life is in his Son. He that hath the Son hath life. *(I John 5:11)* Poverman got
himself a Bible and checked it out. It was all there.

There were ten people at the Thursday night meeting, all as young   152
as Robert or a little older, all regulars, except for the new member,
Morton Poverman, who was introduced all around. Also attending were
George Fetler and the Reverend Julius Meadly, who more or less conducted
things.

It went well enough. After Poverman explained to them that he had   153
come out of interest in his son's interest and his talk with Mr. Fetler, the
discussion picked up where, apparently, it had left off last week.

The point of concern, always a tough one, Reverend Meadly told them,   154
was whether those born before Christ, before, that is, the opportunity to
receive Christ, would go to Hell. The Reverend drew the distinction between
Pagans, who had not had the chance to embrace Christ, and the Heathens,
those born since Christ who did and do have the opportunity but reject it.
Heathens were unquestionably doomed to Hell, but about Pagans there was
still some serious debate, for surely Abraham and the Prophets were in Heaven
already, and Moses as well as Adam.

They all discussed at length the fairness of this, that those who had had   155
no choice should be so grievously punished. The Reverend said that indeed
the ways of the Lord were not always apparent to Man, and they were certainly unfathomable, but it did no good to question what was *not* going to
happen to the Pagans, and one should concentrate instead on the glory of
what *was* going to happen to the Saved. And he concluded, "You know,
sometimes I think that the last chapter and verse isn't completed. That on
Judgment Day, God in his infinite wisdom and mercy will raise up even the
unfortunate Pagans." They closed on that high note. Through the evening
Robert Poverman had said nothing.

Driving home he said, "What are you doing?"   156
"What do you mean?" his father said.   157
"You know what I mean. Why did you come tonight?"   158
"What's the matter, suddenly it's not a free country? A man can't wor-   159
ship how he wants anymore?"
"Cut it out, Dad. You know what I mean."   160
"You go to this place because you've got questions, right?" Poverman   161
said. "Well, I've got questions too."
"Like what?"   162
"Like have you declared for Jesus, or whatever you call it?"   163
"No."   164
"Are you going to?"   165
"I don't know. I can't say."   166
"Do you believe in all that . . . stuff?"   167
"I think about it." They drove on in silence. "Are you going back? To   168
another meeting?" Robert asked.

"Yeah. Sure. I still got my questions. What about you? Are you going back?" 169

Robert did not answer that. "You're not sincere," he said. 170

But there, Morton Poverman knew, without any doubt at all, his son was wrong. 171

He hacked at his store and grew bleary with fatigue. What he sold in front he brought in through the back and touched everything once, twice, thrice in its passage. Slips, underwear, dresses, bandanas, now bathing suits and beach or pool ensembles. From passing over all that plastic, his fingertips were sanded as smooth as a safecracker's. And doggedly he studied the Word of the Lord. Bore up his wife. Bore his son. 172

At the second meeting that Poverman attended, Fetler understood. Robert Poverman, once so animated and involved, would not participate, not in the presence of his father. And the blunt intensity of his father's questions caused the Reverend Meadly to veer about, put his helm over frequently to avoid the jutting rocks of Morton Poverman's intent, not that he was making an argument. He was polite enough, whatever that cost him. But his questions, they were so fundamental. 173

Almost all of the group had been together for months and had already covered the ecclesiastical ground that was new to him. It was not fair to the group to have to pause so often while the Reverend Meadly (the soul of patience) answered in detail what they all had heard and discussed before. This is what Fetler explained to Poverman after the meeting. 174

"You're throwing me out?" Poverman said. "You're telling me to go elsewhere with my soul in danger of eternal perdition?" He had studied well. He had the lingo, like in every line of work. 175

"No no no," Fetler said, growing more pink than ever. Close to him, Poverman could see the blue fretwork of his veining. His whole face was like a stained-glass window. "That would be unthinkable, of course. What I had in mind was our Sunday afternoon group for older people." Poverman shook his head at Sunday afternoon. "Or private instruction," Fetler followed up. "Perhaps you could come to us, the Reverend Meadly or me, on another evening? Then we could give you a 'cram course,' so to speak?" 176

"OK," Poverman said. They agreed on Tuesday night. 177

On Tuesday night Poverman met with Reverend Meadly and after two hours of explaining—starting with Genesis (oh it would be a long time before he would be able to rejoin the young group already well into Corinthians), Poverman leaned back and said, 178

"But it's all faith, isn't it? All this reasoning, all this explaining, if you've got the faith that's all that matters." 179

"Yes," the Reverend said. "Faith more than anything else." 180

"And if you get the faith, then what?" 181

"You must declare it. You must stand forth and join God through His Son, Jesus Christ." 182

"Yes, but how? I mean could I just say it to you now? Is that enough? Would God know?"   183

"If you declare yourself through us, the Church of the Resurrection, there are certain formalities."   184

"A ceremony?"   185

"Yes, that's right. You must answer certain questions, take certain vows before a congregation."   186

"What about this?" Poverman produced one of the pamphlets that the Society of the Holy Word published. "Wherever I look, I'm always on trial. Some trial. Listen." He read the fiery, imprescriptible indictment through to the end. " 'Verdict: Guilty as charged. Appeal: None. Sentence: Immediately eternal, conscious, tormenting, separational death in a burning lake of fire and brimstone.' "   187

"Well?" Reverend Meadly asked. Nothing else.   188

"So that's it for me? For Robert?"   189

"Unless you embrace the Lord Jesus as your Savior, that is your fate and Robert's fate, yes."   190

"No either / or huh?"   191

"Either Love or Damnation," Reverend Meadly said. Kindly.   192

On Thursday Poverman showed up at the meeting. Fetler called him aside. "I thought we agreed that you would work privately?"   193

"I wouldn't say a single word," Poverman promised. "I'll listen. I'll watch. I can learn a lot that way, and I won't interrupt. Not one word."   194

But there were no longer any words to say, for Morton Poverman had decided that at long last the time and event had come for God to stand forth and defend Himself, make good his terrible threat and vaunt or scram. He had paid enough with good faith and would not bargain now. He had reached his sticking price. Take it or leave it. What was his, was his, and what belonged to his son, the legacy of his life, for all his—Poverman's—own clumsiness on this earth, *that* he would not let be stolen easily. And whatsoever should raise his hand or voice against his son must answer for that to him.   195

Thus girded, midway through the meeting Poverman suddenly stood up. The Reverend Meadly had just finished an intricate restatement of Paul's words: 196

> In a moment, in the twinkling of an eye, at the last trump: for the trumpet shall sound, and the dead shall be raised incorruptible, and we shall be changed.

Poverman stood up and said:

"Me too. I have seen the way and the light. I want to declare for Jesus." There was commotion.   197

"Mr. Poverman!" George Fetler said, standing too, quickly in his alarm.   198

"Now," Poverman said. "Right now. The spirit is in me." He stepped   199 away from the group of seated young people and then turned to them. "Be ye followers of me, even as I also am of Christ," he intoned, trying to get it right. One of the group clapped. "I've been thinking and so this is what I want to do, thanks to Reverend Meadly." Reverend Meadly smiled, but Fetler curdled, his pink now blotched redness.

"So what's next?" Poverman asked. "What do I got to do?" 200

There was a happy excitement in the young people at this immanence 201
of spirit, all the thick words of the past months came true like a miracle. Fetler urged a later time, a more appropriate time for the declaration, but "Now," Poverman insisted. "Between now and later, who knows what could happen? And *then* what about my soul?" He looked at Fetler. "Now."

Robert Poverman, stiff and frozen, watched his father don white robes 202
(cotton / polyester—60 / 40, not silk) that drooped to the floor and take in either hand a large Bible and a heavy brass crucifix. The classroom was turned into a chapel, the lights dimmed. The Reverend Meadly took his place behind the table. From a drawer in the table he took out a paper.

"Wait," Poverman said. "I want my son Robert to stand next to me. He 203
should see this up close." He motioned Robert to him.

The Reverend said, "You must be delivered to Christ by one who has 204
already received Him. Robert has not yet."

"That's okay," Poverman said. "Let Mr. Fetler deliver me. I just want 205
my son to stand by. This is a big thing for me." And so it was arranged, George Fetler, crimson and his eyes like thin slivers, on Poverman's right, Robert Poverman, cast into numb darkness, on his father's left. "Okay," Poverman said. "Let's go."

It was simple enough. The Reverend would read statements that Pov- 206
erman would repeat. After a brief preamble in which Reverend Meadly explained the beauty and importance of this glorious step toward Salvation, the ceremony began.

"Oh Lord I have offended thee mightily," Poverman echoed the Rever- 207
end Meadly flatly.

"Oh Lord I am an infection of evil that I ask you to heal and make 208
clean," he went on.

"Oh Lord I ask you to break open my hard and selfish heart to allow 209
your mercy into it that I might learn love."

"Oh Lord I have made the world foul with my pride." 210

"Oh Lord I am a bad man and stained with sin." 211

"No," Robert Poverman said out of his darkness. 212

"Sha,"[1] his father said. He motioned for the Reverend Meadly with his 213
cross to go on.

"Daddy, please. Stop this. Don't." He wept. 214

"I am an abomination in Your eyes," the Reverend read from his paper. 215

---

1. Be quiet (Yiddish).

"NO!" Robert Poverman shouted. Demanded. "NO!" He stepped forward, but his father held out his Bible-loaded hand like a rod.

"Don't you be afraid," he said to his son. "Don't you worry *now*, Sonny," he said. "I'm here." And unsheathing the great sword of his love, he waved it about his balding, sweaty head and advanced upon his Hosts in dubious battle. And fought.

Not without glory.

STUDY QUESTIONS

1. How is the word "testament" being used at the end of the second paragraph? What other meanings does the word suggest? What other words could have been used instead of "testament"? Why does this word seem the best possible choice in this passage?

2. After the first five paragraphs, what image of Poverman's character do you have? How is that confirmed or modulated by the telephone conversation with Charney in paragraphs 20–25? How is your image of Poverman changed later in the story?

3. The first part of the story centers on Poverman's bankruptcy and his attempt to make a new start. Why does Targan begin the story this way? What new complication and focus of attention is introduced in the midst of the details of Poverman's beginning again?

4. Why are Bobby's SAT scores described as fuel for Poverman's flame (paragraph 39)?

5. Paragraph 40 goes into considerable detail about Poverman's business dealings in the store; what does that contribute to your view of him? What image is used to describe his actions in this paragraph? Does the image seem too dramatic? What does it add to your view of Poverman? How does it contribute to your expectations?

6. Why does Poverman not want his son Robert to help him in the store at night? What does Robert mean when he says he will pray for his father (paragraph 53)? What is Poverman's reaction?

7. ". . . what did he [Mr. Poverman] need with fancy or smart? He had Robert Poverman of Yale or Cornell. *That* was fancy. *That* was smart" (paragraph 58). Is this selfish of Poverman? Is he trying to live through or succeed through his son? Why does he "hope for Yale" (paragraph 61)? Why does Mrs. Poverman prefer Cornell?

8. Do you recognize the descriptions of the college catalogue in paragraph 61? Do you remember looking at such catalogues? What is the effect of having had emotional experiences similar to the one you are reading about? How does it influence your reading or judgment of the story?

9. What sudden turn does the story take around paragraphs 72–82?

10. Poverman is not "reasonable," paragraph 85 suggests; he just knows how to hang on. Which seems the greater virtue? Where are your sympathies and loyalties at this point, with the father or son?

11. What does Poverman think about George Fetler during their first conversation? What do you think of him? What did you expect would happen from this point on?

12. Why is Poverman's life now described as a battle, a war (paragraph 138)? A battle or war for or against what?

13. Coming home from the meeting of the Society of the Holy Word, Robert accuses his father of not being sincere. "But there, Morton Poverman knew, without any doubt at all, his son was wrong" (paragraph 171). Why is Robert wrong?

14. "At the second meeting that Poverman attended, Fetler understood" (paragraph 173). What did he understand?

15. Poverman decides (paragraph 195) "that at long last the time and event had come for God to stand forth and defend Himself, make good his terrible threat and vaunt or scram." What "threat"? What "vaunt"? Is this blasphemous? What, if anything, justifies the vehemence or daring of Poverman's decision?

16. Why does Fetler "curdle" (paragraph 199) when Poverman declares for Jesus?

17. Why does Poverman want Robert to stand next to him during the ceremony?

18. Why does Robert say "No," ask his father to stop, and weep (pars. 212–14)?

19. Explain the last two paragraphs of the story, especially the sword, the Hosts, the glory.

N. Scott Momaday

Poet, editor, novelist, and adapter of Indian tales, N. Scott Momaday was born in Lawton, Oklahoma, in 1934 of Kiowa parents. He earned a B.A. at the University of New Mexico, the state in which he grew up, and an M.A. and Ph.D. from Stanford University. In 1969, he published both *The Way to Rainy Mountain*, which contained personal memories, Kiowa myth, and expository prose, and his first novel, *House Made of Dawn*, which won the Pulitzer Prize for fiction. Again in 1976 he struck twice—with a volume of poems, *The Gourd Dancer*, and *The Names: A Memoir*. He published *The Ancient Child: A Novel* in 1990, and contributes to the *New York Times Book Review* pieces on American Indian subjects. He currently lives in Tucson, Arizona, and teaches at the University of Arizona.

THE EAGLE-FEATHER FAN

The eagle is my power,
And my fan is an eagle.
It is strong and beautiful
In my hand. And it is real.
My fingers hold upon it   5
As if the beaded handle
Were the twist of bristlecone.
The bones of my hand are fine
And hollow; the fan bears them.
My hand veers in the thin air   10
Of the summits. All morning
It scuds on the cold currents;
All afternoon it circles
To the singing, to the drums.

STUDY QUESTIONS

1. What does "it" in line 4 refer to? What does the SPEAKER mean when he says that "it" is "real"?

2. In lines 8 and 9 the speaker says the bones of his hands are hollow. How do you read that statement? In the last five lines, the speaker's hand seems to fly away like an eagle but is responsive to the songs and drums. Is there a way of reading the description in these lines that gives a more "realistic" or secular sense to the lines? Must you choose one reading or the other? Must you believe in the literalness of the ritual in order to appreciate the poem?

Stephen Shu-Ning Liu

Born in Fu-Ling, China, in 1930, Stephen Shu-Ning Liu was in an expeditionary army in World War II, emigrated to America in 1952, and, while working his way toward a doctorate in English (from the University of North Dakota), was a dishwasher, hamburger cook, white mice caretaker, and janitor. Liu won a National Endowment for the Arts Award in 1981–82 and the PEN fiction contest in 1983. He has contributed poetry to over 200 literary magazines and published a bilingual volume of poems (written in English and translated by himself into Chinese) called *Dream Journeys to China* (1982). He teaches at Community College of Southern Nevada in Las Vegas.

MY FATHER'S MARTIAL ART

When he came home Mother said he looked
like a monk and stank of green fungus.
At the fireside he told us about life
at the monastery: his rock pillow,
his cold bath, his steel-bar lifting   5
and his wood-chopping. He didn't see
a woman for three winters, on Mountain O Mei.

"My Master was both light and heavy.
He skipped over treetops like a squirrel.
Once he stood on a chair, one foot tied   10
to a rope. We four pulled; we couldn't move him a
bit. His kicks could split
a cedar's trunk."

I saw Father break into a pumpkin
with his fingers. I saw him drop a hawk   15
with bamboo arrows. He rose before dawn, filled
our backyard with a harsh sound *hah, hah, hah:*
there was his Black Dragon Sweep, his Crane Stand,
his Manti Walk, his Tiger Leap, his Cobra Coil. . . .
Infrequently he taught me tricks and made me   20
fight the best of all the village boys.

From a busy street I brood over high cliffs
on O Mei, where my father and his Master sit:
shadows spread across their faces as the smog
between us deepens into a funeral pyre.   25

But don't retreat into night, my father.
Come down from the cliffs. Come
with a single Black Dragon Sweep and hush
this oncoming traffic with your *hah, hah, hah.*

STUDY QUESTIONS

1. Where is the SPEAKER's father now?

2. Was the speaker close to his father? What evidence is there about how he feels about his father?

Ishmael Reed

Ishmael Reed was born in Chattanooga, Tennessee, in 1938 and was educated at the University of Buffalo. One of the most outrageous—and humorous—of the writers of the counterculture that flourished in the 1960s and early 1970s, he is the author of eight novels, three collections of essays, four volumes of poetry, has edited numerous anthologies, and is a songwriter, publisher, playwright, and founder of the Before Columbus Foundation. He is perhaps best known for his novels, such as *The Freelance Pallbearers, Mumbo Jumbo,* and *Yellow Back Radio Broke-Down,* though his poetry shows the same bite, the same mixture of real and surreal, present and past, the same brilliant wordplay. He currently teaches at the University of California at Berkeley.

I AM A COWBOY IN THE
BOAT OF RA

"The devil must be forced to reveal any such physical evil (potions, charms, fetishes, etc.) still outside the body and these must be burned."
   RITUALE ROMANUM, *published 1947, endorsed by the coat of arms and introduction letter from Francis Cardinal Spellman*

I am a cowboy in the boat of Ra,[1]
sidewinders in the saloons of fools
bit my forehead   like   O

---

1. Chief of the ancient Egyptian gods, creator and protector of humans and vanquisher of Evil.

the untrustworthiness of Egyptologists
Who do not know their trips. Who was that   5
dog-faced man?[2] they asked, the day I rode
from town.

School marms with halitosis cannot see
the Nefertiti[3] fake chipped on the run by slick
germans, the hawk behind Sonny Rollins' head or   10
the ritual beard of his axe,[4] a longhorn winding
its bells thru the Field of Reeds.

I am a cowboy in the boat of Ra. I bedded
down with Isis,[5] Lady of the Boogaloo, dove
down deep in her horny, stuck up her Wells-Far-ago   15
in daring midday get away. "Start grabbing the
blue," i said from top of my double crown.

I am a cowboy in the boat of Ra. Ezzard Charles[6]
of the Chisholm Trail. Took up the bass but they
blew off my thumb. Alchemist in ringmanship but a   20
sucker for the right cross.

I am a cowboy in the boat of Ra. Vamoosed from
the temple i bide my time. The price on the wanted
poster was a-going down, outlaw alias copped my stance
and moody greenhorns were making me dance; while my mouth's 25
shooting iron got its chambers jammed.

I am a cowboy in the boat of Ra. Boning-up in
the ol West i bide my time. You should see
me pick off these tin cans whippersnappers. I
write the motown long plays for the comeback of   30
Osiris.[7] Make them up when stars stare at sleeping
steer out here near the campfire. Women arrive
on the backs of goats and throw themselves on
my Bowie.[8]

2. The Egyptian god of the dead Anubis was usually depicted as a man with the head of a dog or jackal.

3. Fourteenth-century B.C. Egyptian queen; elsewhere Reed says that German scholars are responsible for the notion that her dynasty was white.

4. Musical instrument. *Sonny Rollins:* jazz great of the late 1950s and early 1960s.

5. Principal goddess of ancient Egypt.

6. World heavyweight boxing champion, 1949–51.

7. Husband of Isis and constant foe of his brother Set (line 48). Tricked by Set, he died violently but later rose from the dead.

8. Large hunting knife.

I am a cowboy in the boat of Ra. Lord of the lash,   35
the Loup Garou[9] Kid. Half breed son of Pisces and
Aquarius. I hold the souls of men in my pot. I do
the dirty boogie with scorpions. I make the bulls
keep still and was the first swinger to grape the taste.

I am a cowboy in his boat. Pope Joan[1] of the   40
Ptah Ra. C / mere a minute willya doll?
Be a good girl and
Bring me my Buffalo horn of black powder
Bring me my headdress of black feathers
Bring me my bones of Ju-Ju snake   45
Go get my eyelids of red paint.
Hand me my shadow
I'm going into town after Set

I am a cowboy in the boat of Ra
look out Set   here i come Set   50
to get Set   to sunset Set
to unseat Set   to Set down Set
   usurper of the Royal couch
   imposter RAdio of Moses' bush[2]
   party pooper O hater of dance   55
   vampire outlaw of the milky way

STUDY QUESTIONS

1. In lines 11–12, there are, among other puns, references to musical instruments (once Sonny Rollins is mentioned) in "longhorn," "bells," "Reeds" (the last with a bow in the direction of the poet himself, no doubt). What other wordplay do you find in the poem? What is its effect on the TONE? In what ways is it appropriate to the strange juxtaposition of cowboy and Ra, the old Far West and the old (Middle) East?

2. In lines 31–32, there is some sound-play to reinforce the wordplay—"stars stare at sleeping / steer out here near the campfire." What other examples can you find? What is the effect of such devices?

3. Reed, as one footnote suggests, believes European Egyptologists misleadingly identify the Egyptian rulers as white. What elements in the poem celebrate blackness and the identification of the Egyptian culture with that of the rest of Africa and Africans?

9. French for werewolf; in voodoo, a priest who has run amok or gone mad.

1. Mythical female pope, supposed to have succeeded to the papacy in 855. *Ptah Ra:* chief god of Memphis, capital of ancient Egypt.

2. Which, according to Exodus 3:2, burned but was not consumed and from which Moses heard the voice of God telling him to lead the Israelites out of Egypt.

Olive Senior

Born in Jamaica, Olive Senior was educated in her homeland and in Canada. She has worked in publishing, public relations, journalism, and as a free-lance writer and researcher. She is both a poet and a story writer and is the author of *A–Z of Jamaican Heritage* (1983).

ANCESTRAL POEM

I

My ancestors are nearer
than albums of pictures
I tread on heels thrust
into broken-down slippers

II

My mother's womb impulsed   5
harvests perpetually. She
deeply breathed country air
when she laboured me.

III

The pattern woven by my
father's hands lulled me   10
to sleep. Certain actions
moved me so: my father
planting.

When my father planted
his thoughts took flight.   15
He did not need to think.
The ritual was ingrained
in the blood, embedded
in the centuries of dirt
beneath his fingernails   20

encased in the memories
of his race.

(Yet the whiplash of my
father's wrath rever-
berated days in my   25
mind with the inten-
sity of tuning forks.
He did not think.
My mother stunned wept
and prayed Father   30
Forgive Them knowing not
what she prayed for.)

One day I did not pray.
A gloss of sunlight through
the leaves betrayed me so   35
abstracted me from rituals.
And discarded prayers and
disproven myths
confirmed me freedom.

IV

Now against the rhythms   40
of subway trains my
heartbeats still drum
worksongs. Some wheels
sing freedom, the others:
home.   45

Still, if I could balance
water on my head I can
juggle worlds
on my shoulders.

STUDY QUESTIONS

1. Describe the syntax of the poem. In what ways do the rhythms of speech contribute to the poem's THEME?

2. What does it mean that "The ritual was ingrained / in the blood" (lines 17–18)? How fully are the mother and father characterized? What specific details do we have about them? How do these details relate to the central issues of the poem?

3. How fully is the SPEAKER characterized? Where does her central act of rebellion take place?

4. How completely is the speaker "free" of her rituals and her heritage? Explain the effect of the next-to-last stanza of the poem?

5. Explain the two images in the final stanza.

Cathy Song

Born in 1955 in Hawaii, Cathy Song attended the University of Hawaii, Wellesley College (B.A., 1977), and Boston University (M.A., 1981). She is the author of *Picture Bride* (winner of the Yale Younger Poets Award in 1982), in which the title poem tells the story of her Korean grandmother, who was sent for as a mail-order bride in Hawaii on the basis of her photograph. Her book *Frameless Windows, Squares of Light* was published in 1988. In 1991 she cooperated with Juliet Kono on a literary collection, *Sister Stew: Fiction and Poetry by Women*.

HEAVEN

He thinks when we die we'll go to China.
Think of it—a Chinese heaven
where, except for his blond hair,
the part that belongs to his father,
everyone will look like him.   5
China, that blue flower on the map,
bluer than the sea
his hand must span like a bridge
to reach it.
An octave away.   10

I've never seen it.
It's as if I can't sing that far.
But look—
on the map, this black dot.
Here is where we live,   15
on the pancake plains
just east of the Rockies,
on the other side of the clouds.

A mile above the sea,
the air is so thin, you can starve on it.   20
No bamboo trees
but the alpine equivalent,
reedy aspen with light, fluttering leaves.
Did a boy in Guangzhou[1] dream of this
as his last stop?   25

I've heard the trains at night
whistling past our yards,
what we've come to own,
the broken fences, the whiny dog, the rattletrap cars.
It's still the wild west,   30
mean and grubby,
the shootouts and fistfights in the back alley.
With my son the dreamer
and my daughter, who is too young to walk,
I've sat in this spot   35
and wondered why here?
Why in this short life,
this town, this creek they call a river?

He had never planned to stay,
the boy who helped to build   40
the railroads for a dollar a day.[2]
He had always meant to go back.
When did he finally know
that each mile of track led him further away,
that he would die in his sleep,   45
dispossessed,
having seen Gold Mountain,
the icy wind tunneling through it,
these landlocked, makeshift ghost towns?

It must be in the blood,   50
this notion of returning.
It skipped two generations, lay fallow,
the garden an unmarked grave.
On a spring sweater day
it's as if we remember him.   55
I call to the children.
We can see the mountains

1. Usually called Canton, a seaport city in southeastern China.

2. The railroads used immigrant day labor (most of it Chinese) to lay the tracks in the nineteenth century.

shimmering blue above the air.
If you look really hard
says my son the dreamer,   60
leaning out from the laundry's rigging,
the work shirts fluttering like sails,
you can see all the way to heaven.

STUDY QUESTIONS

1. Explain the "notion of returning" (line 51) that seems so powerful in the boy. How does the SPEAKER herself feel about China as homeland?

2. How much do we find out about the grandfather who first came to the U.S. mainland? How much do we know about what became of him?

3. Why are we given so many details of the speaker's present location "just east of the Rockies" (line 17)? What is the meaning of "dispossessed" (line 46)?

4. Describe the sense of the past that the poem creates. Describe the mood of the poem. What kind of picture does the speaker present of herself? of her children? What else do we know about the immediate family?

Walter K. Lew

Born and raised in Baltimore after his parents immigrated to the United States soon after the Korean War, Walter K. Lew is now a New York–based poet, multimedia performance artist, and scholar of Asian-American and Korean literature who has also worked as a television news and documentary producer. Awarded fellowships for his writing and performances, including one from the National Endowment for the Arts, Lew has taught at Brown and Cornell universities, and is currently co-editing a comprehensive anthology of recent Asian-American writing. "Leaving Seoul: 1953" is from a series of poems in which the speaker attempts to communicate with ancestors who perished during the tragedies of Korean history.

LEAVING SEOUL: 1953

We have to bury the urns,
Mother and I. We tried to leave them in a back room,
Decoyed by a gas lamp, and run out

But they landed behind us here, at the front gate.
It is 6th hour, early winter, black cold: 5
Only, on the other side of the rice-paper doors

The yellow *ondol*[1] stone-heated floors
Are still warm. I look out to the blue
Lanterns along the runway, the bright airplane.

Off the back step, Mother, disorganized   10
As usual, has devised a clumsy rope and pulley
To bury the urns. I wonder out loud

How she ever became a doctor.
Get out, she says   *Go to your father: he too*
Does not realize what is happening. You see,   15

Father is waiting at the airfield in a discarded U.S. Army
Overcoat. He has lost his hat, lost
His father, and is smoking Lucky's like crazy . . .

We grab through the tall weeds and wind
That begin to shoot under us like river ice.   20
It is snowing. We are crying, from the cold

Or what? It is only decades
Later that, tapping the tall glowing jars,
I find they contain all that has made
The father have dominion over hers.   25

STUDY QUESTIONS

1. Line 1 suggests there is some sort of obligation to bury the urns; what sort of obligation do you imagine there is? In line 2, the SPEAKER and his mother, despite the obligation, try to leave the urns behind. Why? What does the phrase "Decoyed by a gas lamp" (line 3) suggest is happening?

2. The poem does not say how it was that the urns arrived at the front gate. How do you think they did?

3. The father is waiting at the airfield, but the mother, somewhat disorganized herself, says he does not know what is happening (lines 14–15). What *is* happening?

4. The first twenty-one and a half lines are written in the present tense, yet the last lines suggest that the event described occurred "decades" before. What is the effect of the present tense in the first part of the poem? What is the effect when you realize that it all happened some time ago?

---

1. Korean under-floor heating system.

5. Were the urns buried?

6. Explain the last two lines.

Mary Stewart Hammond

M ary Stewart Hammond is a product both of the mountains of Virginia and of Baltimore. A graduate of Goucher College, she has worked as a print and broadcast journalist and critic. Her book of poems, *Out of Canaan*, was published in 1993. She lives in New York City.

CANAAN

1

And we grazed in the first ridges
behind the Piedmont, toward the uttermost
part of the South creek. Lo,

wood smoke weaves ribbons
through fall days and the sun   5
skitters on tin roofs

like fat in a skillet. Here,
even the serpent is reluctant, dozes
in the sparse warmth

at the foot of tree stumps. Blessed   10
were the least of our brethren
for they ate with the wrong fork,

chased gravy around thick plates
with Wonder bread, didn't know
the Sabbath from Shinola, therefore   15

were we holy. They shall move
their lips when they read this
and ignite the words with an index finger

run under the lines. If you know you can leave
in the middle of the night in the middle of the war   20
with a full tank of gas,

ye will never know them.

2

That the call may come forth like Jedidiah,[1]
fear not. In those mountain hollows,
we grew eggs and beets, lifted up our eyes   25

for wild mushrooms. And King James
opened and closed on us, seven days,
with the ecstasy of pump organs.

So it is, cabbage roses flare
on cold slipcovers and Mamma's shotgun   30
pauses on its peg leg

back of the door. For when you went forth
on visitations, your male flock
drew to the manse, thirsty for salt,

scared Mamma like daughters. Thus   35
were sour mash jars lined up
at the edge of the yard for targets.

And the steeple inched three times its length
across the onion grass, pointing East
to home. And the shadow of death   40

danced on good days in the corncrib,
by sunset had crept under the fence,
reaching for the root cellar. Only

the fast dark saved us.

3

And on the sixth day so also   45
did you labor, upstairs
preparing sermons, far from babies

---

1. Beloved by God. Name which Nathan bestowed upon the baby Solomon.

congregating before Mamma
for mashed bananas, turnips, the wrong
salvation, our mouths open like fish   50

hungry for the hook. There, in an oak
swivel chair, you rocked the Bible,
your feet crossed on the desk. Whence

you went on your knees by the cot,
pressing your forehead into your fists.   55
We watched through the keyhole.

Come Sundays, I was old enough
to sit in your lap, count seeds,
the lumps of coal, the signed cuffs

in the collection plate. After, I rose up   60
magnified as the angels, soared
over Galilee down to Mamma,

never touching the stairs, anointed
by the lot of their inheritance,
by the smell of your shirt.   65

I think Mamma was jealous your coin
tethered her, made her belly so swollen
her footsteps rattled china. She would

press the small of her back
when the sun fell in windowpanes   70
across Deuteronomy and the yellow pine floor

I didn't need, calling.

STUDY QUESTIONS

1. What region of the United States is the SETTING of "Canaan"? What locations in
the poem provide clues? What details of life make the region clear? How important
are these details to the effect of the poem? How important is the regional setting
to the effects the poem creates?

2. What does the title of the poem mean? How does the land of Canaan in the Christian Bible (note that the King James version is mentioned directly in line 26) relate
to the setting of the poem?

3. How much do we know about the SPEAKER? What kind of home did she grow up in? Who is the "you" of line 46? What is his profession? How central is "Mamma" to the poem?

4. Are there places in the poem where the speaker seems to patronize the people she grew up with? What, do you think, is the TONE in these passages? What is the poem's attitude toward the people from her home region? How can you be sure?

Pat Mora

Born in El Paso, Pat Mora writes poems in which her Chicana heritage and South-western background are central. Her first book, *Chants* (1985), is composed largely of what she calls "desert incantations." Her second, *Borders* (1986), from which the following poem is taken, describes the two cultures that create her own "border" life. Both books won Southwest Book awards. Her third book, *Communion*, was published in 1991. She lives in Cincinnati.

GENTLE COMMUNION

Even the long-dead are willing to move.
Without a word, she came with me from the desert.
Mornings she wanders through my rooms
making beds, folding socks.

Since she can't hear me anymore,   5
Mamande[1] ignores the questions I never knew
to ask, about her younger days, her red
hair, the time she fell and broke her nose
in the snow. I will never know.

When I try to make her laugh,   10
to disprove her sad album face, she leaves
the room, resists me as she resisted
grinning for cameras, make-up, English.

---

1. A child's conflation of *mama grande* ("grandmother").

While I write, she sits and prays,
feet apart, legs never crossed,   15
the blue housecoat buttoned high
as her hair dries white, girlish
around her head and shoulders.

She closes her eyes, bows her head,
and like a child presses her hands together,   20
her patient flesh steeple, the skin
worn, like the pages of her prayer book.

Sometimes I sit in her wide-armed
chair as I once sat in her lap.
Alone, we played a quiet I Spy.   25
She peeled grapes I still taste.

She removes the thin skin, places
the luminous coolness on my tongue.
I know not to bite or chew. I wait
for the thick melt,   30
our private green honey.

STUDY QUESTIONS

1. Who is the "she" in line 2? Why does she have a "sad album face" (line 11)? When do you become aware that the situation in the poem is a fantasy? What facts about "Mamande" does the speaker not know?

2. What differences are there between "Mamande" and the SPEAKER? in language? in background? in habits? in cultural assumptions? Exactly when does the poem make you aware of each?

3. What does the poem's title mean? Where in the poem does the fullness of the ritual take place? How do earlier events in the poem prepare us for this ritual?

Rafael Jesús González

B orn in El Paso in 1935 and educated in Texas, Mexico, and Oregon, Rafael Jesús González teaches creative writing and literature at Laney College. He is the author of a collection of poems, *El Hacedor de Juegos*, and the recipient of National Endowment for the Arts and Woodrow Wilson fellowships.

SESTINA: SANTA PRISCA

One would think that these
Dry standards of pink stone
Would whip the wind with iron
Tongues and speak the word
Kept by their chiseled, gesticulating saints   5
Weeping dust tears upon the courtyard floor.

From the chequered, knee-rubbed floor
Rise supplications cast with wings of iron
To perch with gentle claws upon the word
"God" carved with gold upon the pimpled stone.   10
Futile as this chasuble of rock, these
Prayers can never tame the gestures of the saints.

Now the sun strikes with glory the cold saints
Forcing their lips to simulate a word
Voiced in silver by the bells of iron.   15
Each note a silver globule floats to crack these
Shallow crystals of the morning hours lying on the floor
And scatter their potions of tranquility on the stone.

It is not time for winds to ruffle the starched stone
Which clothes the rock-ribbed bosoms of the saints   20
And checks the pulses of the word.
It will never be time to resuscitate these
Dead theologies groveling on the vestry floor
Rehearsing one-time truths from vellums bound in iron.

The lace work of the sun-forged iron   25
Is not wide enough to let the saints
Escape wearing their still phylacteries of stone.
The bougainvillaea climbs its progress from the floor
To leave its purple kisses on the saints' lips; these
Let the bits of passion drop, but keep the precious word.   30

But it is there, the tongue-tied word
Encapsuled in its throats of iron,
To shake to truth the rock hinged saints
Hanging like dead murmurs above the ocean floor.
The matutinal orations will rise on plumes of stone   35
And the loud tongues of candles whisper: "Listen to these."

The bells of iron will testify their love and these
Flowers on the floor become testaments from which the saints
Will preach the golden word and the green life-stone.

STUDY QUESTIONS

1. The sestina is a very elaborate form. It contains six six-line STANZAS, in which the words ending each line of the first stanza are repeated in changed order in the following stanzas, and a final three-line stanza, with three of the end words at the ends of the lines and the other three within the lines. In what ways is the elaborateness of the poetic form justified by the SUBJECT MATTER? by the ideas of the poem?

2. Describe the church as precisely as you can, citing lines or passages to support your description.

3. How do the carved saints "[weep] dust tears" (line 6)? The prayers, the poem says, "can never tame the gestures of the saints" (line 12). What do you imagine those gestures to be? Why do they need to be tamed?

4. The poem begins with "One would think" that the saints would speak. Why have they not done so? What, does the poem say at the end, will make them finally speak?

Alice Walker

Alice Walker was born in Eatonville, Georgia, in 1944, and now lives in San Francisco where she is a consulting editor to *MS* magazine and to *Freedomways*, a black political quarterly. She is probably best known for her novel *The Color Purple* (1983), which won the Pulitzer Prize, but over the years she has also been a prolific and celebrated poet, publishing four volumes of poems. Her most recent novel, *Possessing the Secret of Joy*, was published in 1992.

REVOLUTIONARY PETUNIAS

Sammy Lou of Rue
sent to his reward

the exact creature who
murdered her husband,
using a cultivator's hoe   5
with verve and skill;
and laughed fit to kill
in disbelief
at the angry, militant
pictures of herself   10
the Sonneteers quickly drew:
not any of them people that
she knew.
A backwoods woman
her house was papered with   15
funeral home calendars and
faces appropriate for a Mississippi
Sunday School. She raised a George,
a Martha, a Jackie and a Kennedy. Also
a John Wesley Junior.   20
"Always respect the word of God,"
she said on her way to she didn't
know where, except it would be by
electric chair, and she continued
"Don't yall forgit to *water*   25
my purple petunias."

STUDY QUESTIONS

1. Exactly what is the situation at the beginning of the poem? Where do the events take place?

2. Who are the "Sonneteers" (line 11) who characterize Sammy Lou as "angry" and "militant" (line 9)? Why does Sammy Lou laugh at their portrayal of her?

3. What is the exact meaning of the "reward" in line 2? What is the TONE of the poem at this point? How does Sammy Lou regard the "reward" she sends the murderer to? How do you know? Compare the destination ("she didn't / know where," lines 22–23) of Sammy Lou? How do you explain the different kinds of terminology employed here?

4. How religious, do you think, is Sammy Lou? How patriotic? What is the basis of her belief? What do you make of her final statement?

Estela Portillo

D irector of the arts at El Paso Community College in the city in which she was born (1936) and where she has taught in high school, conducted a television talk show, and helped found a bilingual theater, Estela Portillo is best known for her play *The Day of the Swallows* (1972), though her work also includes *Sor Juana and Other Plays* (1983), *Rain of Scorpions* (short stories, 1975), and *Trini* (novel, 1986).

THE DAY OF THE SWALLOWS

THE CHARACTERS
(IN ORDER OF APPEARANCE)

ALYSEA

CLEMENCIA

JOSEFA

TOMÁS

EDUARDO

CLARA

DON ESQUINAS

FATHER PRADO

The tierra of Lago de San Lorenzo is within memory of mountain sweet pine. Then the maguey thickens with the ferocity of chaotic existence; here the desert yawns. Here it drinks the sun in madness.

The village of Lago de San Lorenzo is a stepchild; it is a stepchild to the Esquinas hacienda, for the hacienda has been a frugal mother and a demanding father. Its name comes from the yearly ritual of the saint-day of San Lorenzo when all the young women gather around the lake to wash their hair and bathe in promise of a future husband. The tempo of life, unbroken, conditioned, flavors its heartbeat with dreams and myths. The hacienda is the fiber upon which existence hangs. The church, the fluid rose, assures the future promise of Elysium fields. No one dares ask for life.

What is this footfall beyond ritual, beyond livelihood? What is this faint unknown ache in the heart? It's more than just the rasp of hope. . . . The young know this; and they go to the spring with lyrical intimacy. By the lake, eyes burn and feet dig the mud of the spring; someone traces mountain against sky and gulf expands drowning, drowning. The obligation is remembered back in the village; the toll of the church bell offering sanctuary is a relief; the lake becomes too much for them.

At daybreak the fiesta day is sanctified with a misa[1] at sunrise; the choir rejoices the promise of day. A holy procession is led by the priest and an "honored member" of the church. Offerings to the patron saint are generous amidst frugality. The animals are blessed; the people are blessed; all is washed clean.

Perhaps secretly each villager senses the werewolf moon inside him; the bite into passions will be hard and fierce after sunset.

On the day of San Lorenzo, in the heat of July, everybody goes to the lake; this day the lake is invaded by village life. When the church bells toll eleven in the sun, the late morning is the sole witness to the bathing of the virgins. The lake becomes a sacred temple. The high priestesses talk of hopes, lovers, and promises. In earnest belief, they wash their hair in spring water to insure future marriages in heaven. It is true, no one has seen a marriage made in heaven, but each girl hugs the private truth that hers will be the one.

Two hundred years before the Esquinas family had settled in Lago de San Lorenzo on a Spanish grant of fifty thousand acres, the Indians were pushed out further into the desert. This was the way of the bearded gachupín,[2] with his hot grasp and his hot looks. Their greedy vitality was a wonder to the Indian. It was also death.

But now the barrio clustered itself around the hacienda. The conquered conquered the conquerors.

There is a house, the only house close to the edge of the lake. Here our story begins. . . .

ACT I

Scene 1

JOSEFA's *sitting room; it is an unusually beautiful room, thoroughly feminine and in good taste; the profusion of lace everywhere gives the room a safe, homey look. The lace pieces are lovely, needlepoint, hairpin, limerick, the work of patience and love. Upstage left is a large French window; from it one can view a large tree. On the tree is a freshly painted tree house of unusual size and shape. It is an orb that accommodates a great number of birds. The room faces south, so it is flooded with light; the light, the lace, the open window all add to the beauty of the room, a storybook beauty of serenity. To the right is a door leading to the kitchen; there is another door leading to a bedroom; downstage left there is a door leading to the outside.*

ALYSEA *is sitting on the floor when the curtain rises. It is before dawn; but a few minutes after the curtain rises, light begins to fill the room.* ALYSEA *is cleaning the sitting room carpet, an unusual task for this hour. Next to her is a pail; she uses a piece*

1. Mass.
2. Spaniard who settled in Spanish America.

of cloth with quick frantic movements, rinses, and continues the scrubbing. After a while she looks at the cloth in her hand intently, as in realization of what she is doing. Suddenly she drops it seemingly in horror. She looks helpless and lost. Still sitting on the floor she leans her head against a chair and cries silently staring up into the now streaming light from the window. There is the sound of the milk bell. It is CLEMENCIA *delivering. When she hears it,* ALYSEA *jumps up, wipes away traces of tears with her apron, then opens the French window and looks out.*

ALYSEA: She'll come right in if I'm not at the door to pay her.

[*She looks around the room. Her eyes fall on a small side table next to the couch. She goes to the table and stares at a long kitchen knife with traces of blood on it. Hurriedly, she picks up the cleaning cloth, and uses it to pick up the knife gingerly. She wraps the cloth around the knife and places it in a side table drawer. During this interval,* CLEMENCIA's *noisy arrival is heard. The kitchen door is opened; there is a tug of milk can, then a pouring of milk. Several sighs and ejaculations about hard work are heard.* ALYSEA *looks around the room one last time as* CLEMENCIA *walks in.*]

CLEMENCIA: Josefa! Alysea! My centavos for the week are not on the kitchen table. Hombre . . . do I have to beg for my money? Oye. . . ¿dónde están?[3]

ALYSEA: Buenos días, Clemencia . . . early?

CLEMENCIA: [*Staring at* ALYSEA.] Que horror! What is the matter? You look terrible. Have you been up all night?

ALYSEA: [*Smooths her hair; looks at her hands guiltily.*] Yes . . . I stayed up late. A new pattern in lace.

CLEMENCIA: You work hard to please Josefa, don't you? [*She notices* ALYSEA *looking at her hands.*] What's the matter with your hands? Not rheumatism . . . you're just a girl . . . Look at mine! Life has eaten them up . . . I feel pain . . . ay! . . . it is my destiny to suffer . . . You owe me seven pesos.

ALYSEA: Yes, of course. [*She goes to the household money box, takes a set of keys from her apron pocket and opens it. She counts out the money.*] Cinco . . . seis . . . siete.[4]

CLEMENCIA: Gracias . . . [*Looks at* ALYSEA *again and shakes her head.*] Rest in the afternoon . . . you look all in. You can in this house. There is beautiful peace here.

ALYSEA: Yes . . . here it stretches itself out to breathe. . . .

CLEMENCIA: You begin to talk like Josefa now . . . you like her . . . eh? She doesn't want you to work yourself to death . . . she is too kind.

ALYSEA: The most considerate of persons . . . but there is so much to do.

CLEMENCIA: Of course, San Lorenzo . . . mañana . . . Josefa will be so grand leading the procession with the Father to the church . . . a happy day for the barrio . . . we all share Josefa's honor like we have shared her goodness . . . a great lady.

3. Where are they?
4. Five . . . six . . . seven.

ALYSEA: I had forgotten . . . the procession tomorrow.

CLEMENCIA: What's the matter with you? Forgotten?

ALYSEA: Don't mind me . . . I'm not myself today . . . Clemencia.

CLEMENCIA: Doña Josefa is an angel. All her life, she goes around . . . with that walking stick of hers . . . always she goes . . . like an avenging angel . . . helping . . . what a sight she must be . . . pounding with her stick on those evil people . . . One, two . . . that's for wickedness! [*She makes motions of one pounding away.*] She takes care of the devil all right . . . eh? Yes . . . she saved you from the sickness. . . .

ALYSEA: Saved me . . . from the sickness . . . what is shadow? What is sickness?

CLEMENCIA: Talk sense, child! . . . you need rest. [*She looks at lace work on table.*] My . . . you are making lace as beautiful as Josefa's! You are lucky.

ALYSEA: Lucky? [*She goes to the window.*] This room is beautiful . . . isn't it? I'm lucky to be here . . . aren't I? [*Pause.*] Appearances . . . they are very funny! Tomorrow the church will honor Josefa . . . how very funny! [*She begins to laugh; then, the laugh is eventually lost in sobbing.*] Oh, God!

CLEMENCIA: What is the matter? [*She looks around.*] Where is Josefa. . . . Josefa! [*She goes to* ALYSEA *and feels her forehead.*] Are you feverish?

[*At this point,* JOSEFA *enters. She is a tall regal woman about thirty-five. Her bones are Indian's; her coloring is Aryan. She wears her hair back severely. Her movements are graceful and quiet. The cuffs and collar of her dress are of exquisite lace. She walks up to* ALYSEA *and puts her arm around her.*]

JOSEFA: Alysea, quiet! [*She turns to* CLEMENCIA.] She's not feeling well, I suppose.

CLEMENCIA: She worked all night.

JOSEFA: Oh?

CLEMENCIA: You must make her rest.

JOSEFA: You're right, of course. . . .

CLEMENCIA: Well . . . I must be going . . . I'm late on my rounds . . . [*She sighs.*] I wish I could stay here. [*She looks around.*] What heavenly peace . . .

JOSEFA: [*Smiling.*] You are welcome . . . this is your home . . .

CLEMENCIA: Doña Josefa . . . you are an angel!

JOSEFA: No . . . just happy! . . . Did you get your money?

[JOSEFA *escorts* CLEMENCIA *to the door.* CLEMENCIA *gives a last anxious look at* ALYSEA.]

CLEMENCIA: She'll be all right in your hands, Josefa.

JOSEFA: I'll see that she rests.

[CLEMENCIA *leaves through the kitchen door.* JOSEFA *remains silent as the sounds of departure from the kitchen are heard.*]

JOSEFA: You should rest . . . Clemencia's right.

[ALYSEA *shakes her head.*]

JOSEFA: Do you think it's wise. . . .

ALYSEA: Wise! the way you word it . . . wise!

JOSEFA: Very well, I'll put it another way . . . is this the time to break down?

Beautiful days demand our strength . . . We must be faithful to loveliness.

ALYSEA: [*Incredulously.*] You believe that? [*She walks up to* JOSEFA *almost menacingly.*] How can you justify in that way? You!

JOSEFA: [*Softly.*] There are things we must do . . . to keep a sanity . . . to make the moment clear. [*Pause.*] Any signs of the swallows? Isn't the tree lovely?

ALYSEA: Have you forgotten? . . . how can you! . . . Josefa, last night . . .

[ALYSEA *is overwhelmed with the memory; she runs out of the room.* JOSEFA *looks for a moment after her; then she touches the lace curtains on the window.*]

JOSEFA: We pattern our lives for one beautiful moment . . . like this lace . . . little bits and pieces come together . . . to make all this . . . my world . . . a crystal thing of light; Alysea must understand . . . she must!

[*There is a knock to the door leading outside.* JOSEFA *goes to the door; she opens it; it is* TOMÁS, *her shiftless uncle.*]

TOMÁS: Oh . . . it is you, Josefa! You're not at the hacienda this morning.

JOSEFA: What are you doing here?

TOMÁS: The pump. . . .

JOSEFA: You fixed that already . . . I've told you not to come around here at this time of day. . . .

TOMÁS: You do not appreciate . . . always suspicious. . . .

JOSEFA: I don't want you bothering Alysea . . . ever. . . .

TOMÁS: It is like you . . . to think the worse of me.

JOSEFA: [*With resignation.*] How are the children? Your wife Anita?

TOMÁS: They manage better than me . . . thanks to you . . . there is little steady work . . . I need a few centavos . . . Josefa . . . you're rich!

JOSEFA: What for . . . Tequila?

TOMÁS: Just a little money . . . look, my hands . . . they shake . . . I need it, Josefa . . . please!

JOSEFA: Don't beg!

TOMÁS: You let Clara have all she wants. . . .

JOSEFA: That is none of your business.

TOMÁS: [*Noticing the pail.*] Eh . . . what's this? Looks like blood!

JOSEFA: Go to the kitchen . . . help yourself to meal and beans . . . for the family.

[TOMÁS *is still staring at the pail.*]

JOSEFA: Did you hear me?

TOMÁS: Yes . . . yes, Doña Perfecta . . . Doña Perfecta . . . so charitable . . . ha! ha!

JOSEFA: I'm not in the mood for your sarcasm.

TOMÁS: You will lead the procession tomorrow like the queen of the world . . . eh? You can spare a few centavos? a bottle? Do you keep some in the house when you get it for Clara?

JOSEFA: You're not getting any money.

TOMÁS: [*Starting to leave.*] What's in that pail?

JOSEFA: [*Indignant.*] I don't have to satisfy your curiosity.

TOMÁS: Cálmate[5] . . . I was just asking. . . .

[JOSEFA *turns her back to him; he leaves through the kitchen door; his grumbling is heard as he helps himself to the food offered by* JOSEFA. JOSEFA *stares at the contents of the pail; she looks away and touches her temples with her fingertips. She sits in a rocking chair; leans back, closes her eyes, and grips the arms of the chair; she rocks back and forth.*]

JOSEFA: There is no desert here . . . only light . . . to live each day with nothing . . . to sink . . . [*She closes her eyes and rocks.*] The lonely, lonely struggle . . . then to emerge . . . to find the light . . . I have so much now . . . I want to give so much now . . . Alysea must understand! We must keep this world of light at all costs. . . . [*She rises and walks to the window and stands absorbing the light; one can sense an obvious union between the light and* JOSEFA.]

JOSEFA: [*Softly.*] How moist your lips, my light . . . Through me . . . through me . . . you live. [*She comes back from her intimate world and looks at the bird house with pleasure.*] The long flight . . . how tired they will be; how thirsty after the desert . . . here my swallows will find peace . . . home.

[*As she looks at the tree,* TOMÁS *comes through the patio outside the window. He has a sack over his shoulder.* JOSEFA *does not seem to be mindful of him.* TOMÁS *calls.*]

TOMÁS: Hey, Josefa! Are you casting a spell . . . so early? You don't scare me . . . I know you, querida[6] . . . I know many things . . . you burn inside. . . .

[JOSEFA *stares at him unbelievingly, as if he has destroyed a beauty; then she turns away from the window.*]

TOMÁS: Hey, Josefa . . . don't run away . . . great Doña Perfecta runs away from her good-for-nothing uncle . . . that's funny . . . ha, ha!

JOSEFA: [*Firmly, but in an ominous tone.*] Go home, Tomás, go home.

[*She closes the window and walks to an unfinished damask close to the window. She sits down, unhooks the needle, and begins to work on it. Her concentration is a fiery intensity; this is obvious in her finger movements.* ALYSEA *comes back into the room; she is now composed and refreshed; she has put on a pretty dress. She sees the pail and removes it; taking it into the kitchen; all this time* JOSEFA *remains absorbed in the damask.* ALYSEA *comes back.* JOSEFA *looks up.*]

JOSEFA: You look so nice! Every morning now . . . you look like the garden. . . .

ALYSEA: Nothing is as beautiful as your garden . . . paradise must look like that.

JOSEFA: A garden of light . . . perhaps it has a sense of paradise. . . .

ALYSEA: Tomás was here?

JOSEFA: Sneaking around as usual. [*Pause.*] The pretty dress . . . for Eduardo again?

---

5. Calm down.
6. Dear.

ALYSEA: Yes . . . I'll bring in the morning coffee . . . scones?

JOSEFA: Fine . . . and honey . . . suddenly I'm hungry . . . [*She leaves the damask, and begins to clear the coffee table.*] By the way . . . ask Eduardo to have some morning coffee with us today . . . don't run off for your usual morning walk.

ALYSEA: May I? Thank you . . . he's been coaxing me . . . he's absolutely fascinated by you.

JOSEFA: Do invite him.

[ALYSEA *seems to be holding back tears, although she has pretended calm through the conversation.*]

JOSEFA: What's the matter?

[ALYSEA *is not able to answer; she just shakes her head.* JOSEFA *walks up to her.* ALYSEA *stands still and helpless.* JOSEFA *takes* ALYSEA'S *face in her hands.*]

JOSEFA: You are so dear to me . . . I don't like to see you like this . . . Alysea, don't dwell on what happened . . . things will be all right. Haven't I always made things all right?

[ALYSEA *still doesn't answer.*]

JOSEFA: The tragic things in my life taught me one thing . . . calm. The waiting . . . that is harder than struggle . . . Alysea, learn how . . . to find a strength . . . this loveliness here . . . our world . . . isn't it worth it?

[ALYSEA *begins to cry gently.* JOSEFA *comforts her.* ALYSEA *becomes limp; she places her head on* JOSEFA'S *shoulder like a child.* JOSEFA *strokes her hair.*]

JOSEFA: Your hair . . . your beautiful hair . . . here, let me comb it. . . .

[*Suddenly* ALYSEA *breaks away. She seems at a loss, then remembers the coffee.*]

ALYSEA: I'll get things started in the kitchen . . . Eduardo will be here any moment now.

JOSEFA: About last night, Alysea . . . we must have a story.

ALYSEA: [*She seems to shiver.*] Story?

JOSEFA: When I took David to the hospital . . . the doctors . . . everyone was sympathetic . . . I told them someone had broken in. . . .

ALYSEA: And David?

JOSEFA: He will be all right.

ALYSEA: I can never believe that. . . .

JOSEFA: I will take care of him always. . . .

ALYSEA: You killed him!

JOSEFA: Don't! He'll be back with us in a few weeks . . . I will make a fine life for him always. . . .

ALYSEA: He'll never . . . he'll never. . . .

[*She is overcome by emotion; she walks out of the room into the kitchen.* JOSEFA *looks after her. She remains standing for a moment; then she picks up a book of poetry from the lamp table.*]

JOSEFA: Santa Teresita . . .

"El hombre toma . . . toma y hiere,
La flor desnuda . . . temblorosa . . ."[7]

In her world of God . . . she saw what I see . . . she knew the light . . . beauty . . . truth . . . yes . . . in a cloister. [*She looks around the room. Then she walks up to a workbasket and picks up a piece of lace. She holds it to the light and intently traces the pattern.*] The web . . . the beautiful web we weave! Anything . . . anything is worth this!

Scene 2

A few minutes later; ALYSEA *comes from the kitchen with a morning tray; coffee, scones, juice. She places the tray on the coffee table. There is a knock.* ALYSEA *goes to the door. It is* EDUARDO, *a young man of mixed heritage.*

EDUARDO: I came through the path. . . .

ALYSEA: [*Drawing him in.*] I'm glad. Josefa wants you to have morning coffee . . . in here . . . with her. You always come for me in such a hurry . . . you hadn't seen this room . . . had you?

EDUARDO: No . . . never! [*Looking around.*] Well . . . you were right . . . what a room! . . . for women.

ALYSEA: What do you mean?

EDUARDO: It is a dream of gentleness . . . peace; it is not a man's room . . . but it is beautiful.

ALYSEA: You're right . . . Josefa made this haven . . . away from the world of men.

EDUARDO: [*Looking at her quizzically.*] You like that?

ALYSEA: After what I've lived through . . . yes; this was heaven . . . when she brought me here. Sit down . . . she'll be here any moment.

[EDUARDO *watches* ALYSEA *as she arranges napkins, spoons.*]

EDUARDO: Have you told her . . . about our plans?

ALYSEA: No . . . she suspects something between us.

EDUARDO: And?

ALYSEA: It is hard to understand her feelings . . . there is a stillness in her.

EDUARDO: She dotes on you . . . I don't think she will be pleased . . . after all, I'm taking you away to a wilderness . . . mountain, pines. My squaw . . . living and loving in the open.

[*He goes to her, gathers her in his arms; they kiss;* ALYSEA *clings to him.*]

EDUARDO: It won't be like this . . . you know!

ALYSEA: I'll be with you . . . isn't that everything?

EDUARDO: And the gentle life you love?

7. From a poem by Saint Theresa of Ávila (1515–82): "Man takes . . . . takes and wounds / The stripped flower . . . shivering . . ."

ALYSEA: What you will share with me . . . will be so much more.

[*They embrace again.*]

EDUARDO: Say! Have you seen the morning? It is a conspiracy . . . sun, clouds, green fields . . . and the pines from the distance . . . I can hardly wait. Let's leave right now . . . pack the horses . . . take the mountain trail past the lake . . . the way of my people.

ALYSEA: Not now . . . you crazy Indian!

EDUARDO: We'll find a clearing . . . plow . . . build a cabin . . . have babies. . . .

ALYSEA: Sometimes I think you have to be out in the open . . . no matter what. . . .

EDUARDO: That's where my God is.

[EDUARDO *sits down.* ALYSEA *stands behind his chair and gently traces his cheek.*]

ALYSEA: Your world! A beautiful God exists . . . in your world . . . when you talk . . . He is free . . . green . . . open. You know something?

EDUARDO: [*Catching her hand and kissing it.*] What?

ALYSEA: Father Prado understands your God too. At confession . . . I told him about not attending Mass because we go exploring . . . to find the tallest pines . . . I told him about your God . . . he smiled and told me I had found a holier temple.

EDUARDO: Let's take him with us.

ALYSEA: [*Laughing.*] You know better . . . his life is the barrio . . . the people.

EDUARDO: He will marry us . . . before we leave. . . .

ALYSEA: [*Pulling away.*] No . . . we must wait. . . .

EDUARDO: Why? Listen, woman . . . no one in her right mind turns down a marriage proposal. . . .

ALYSEA: I want you to be sure . . . after a while . . . after we have shared. . . .

EDUARDO: [*In jest.*] You shameless hussy . . . you wish to live in sin, eh?

ALYSEA: Don't jest . . . there was so much ugliness . . . before Josefa brought me here . . . I remember . . . they brought a bunch of us from the country . . . they promised jobs as seamstresses; my barrio was poor . . . we went hungry . . . so I came . . . the city was a nightmare . . . they locked us up in an old house . . . they gave us disgusting soiled dresses to wear . . . then we found out.

EDUARDO: Stop torturing yourself.

ALYSEA: No . . . let me finish . . . I've never told you . . . I hid in the closet of the room; an ugly man with fat hands asked the girls where I was . . . they didn't know . . . he cursed; I was trembling underneath a pile of dirty dresses suffering with the sweat of lust . . . I closed my eyes. Then, I decided to run . . . I simply got up . . . and ran . . . down the stairs . . . into an open hall . . . where men . . . men with hard dead looks stared . . . no one expected me to try and escape through the front door . . . but I did . . . I got as far as the street . . . then he caught up with me; his hands were at my throat. . . .

EDUARDO: That's enough. . . .

ALYSEA: All of a sudden . . . Josefa appeared . . . with her walking stick. She raised it over her head and beat the man . . . he cried out in pain . . . she never faltered . . . then, she brought me to this world of light. . . .

EDUARDO: We shall marry tomorrow night . . . that's it!

ALYSEA: No . . . no . . . there's something else . . . [*She becomes very agitated.*] Eduardo . . . last night . . .

[JOSEFA *enters.*]

JOSEFA: Good morning . . . am I late? Is the coffee cold?

ALYSEA: No . . . no . . . you are just in time.

EDUARDO: [*Drawing out a chair for her.*] Our great lady!

[ALYSEA *becomes busy with the food.*]

ALYSEA: [*To* JOSEFA.] Juice?

JOSEFA: Yes . . . thank you. Eduardo, what are you up to . . . charming the women so early in the morning?

EDUARDO: What better time?

JOSEFA: You are different! Alysea . . . give Eduardo . . . some of this orange . . . it's delicious. . . .

EDUARDO: No! No! just coffee . . . and what's this? [*He picks up a scone, tastes it.*] Wonderful! I had heard about all your wonders . . . but . . . cooking too!

JOSEFA: Alysea baked them . . . from an old recipe of mine. . . .

[ALYSEA *hands* EDUARDO *some coffee.*]

EDUARDO: Thank you, Linda. . . .

[ALYSEA *serves herself.* JOSEFA *looks intently from one to the other.*]

JOSEFA: All these walks you two take . . . into forbidden country. . . .

EDUARDO: How can beauty be forbidden. . . .

JOSEFA: I feel the same way . . . but the desert mind forbids it . . . many times.

ALYSEA: It won't be forbidden tomorrow . . . all the young girls will bathe in the lake at noontime . . . the promise of a perfect love. . . .

EDUARDO: I hear it is your year. Josefa . . . you will lead the church procession. . . .

JOSEFA: My people enjoy planning for it. . . .

ALYSEA: Josefa is as bad as Father Prado about the barrio people . . . all is to please them. . . .

EDUARDO: And what pleases you, Josefa?

JOSEFA: To make them happy!

EDUARDO: I can see why they talk of you with awe. . . .

JOSEFA: I am Indian you know . . . yet not of desert, not of them, in a way. Yet . . . totally theirs.

ALYSEA: [*Rising.*] Well . . . I shall leave you for a few moments; Josefa . . . the lace for the capitol . . . must make the morning express . . . excuse me.

[ALYSEA *leaves.* EDUARDO *finishes his coffee.*]

JOSEFA: She's falling in love with you. . . .

EDUARDO: It's mutual. . . .

JOSEFA: For how long, Eduardo?

EDUARDO: [*Stands, hands in pocket, somewhat ill at ease.*] Love is not timed.

JOSEFA: Isn't it?

EDUARDO: What do you mean?

JOSEFA: Clara.

EDUARDO: You know?

JOSEFA: She has described to me . . . your every mood . . . your every gesture . . . in love. . . .

EDUARDO: I don't know what to say!

JOSEFA: Guilt?

EDUARDO: Ridiculous . . . there's no guilt in love!

JOSEFA: [*Laughing as if to herself.*] The way you men justify . . . the word "love" doesn't it really mean . . . take? . . . destroy?

EDUARDO: It isn't that. . . .

JOSEFA: Of course not! Disguised in a man's words . . . in a man's promises . . . oh, I know, you make a dream of your deadly game.

EDUARDO: Alysea's happy.

JOSEFA: Is she? For how long . . . until you find another fancy?

EDUARDO: What I feel for her is different. . . .

JOSEFA: I remember Clara telling me the same things about you and her . . . how easily you put her out of your life.

EDUARDO: Clara understands.

JOSEFA: No, Eduardo . . . she just accepts . . . she knows nothing else.

EDUARDO: You make me feel guilty . . . why?

JOSEFA: I'll tell you why . . . Alysea has love here; she is happy . . . she has found her place in the world . . . safe with me . . . there is a constancy here. . . .

EDUARDO: All right! I don't think one should have Conditions . . . I know I love her now . . . I want to love her forever . . . but it is not for me to know. . . .

JOSEFA: She belongs here . . . with me . . . You men explain away all your indiscretions, so easily . . . after all, you make the rules and enjoy the abuses!

EDUARDO: That's not fair. . . .

JOSEFA: That's funny . . . When has a man been fair to . . . women?

EDUARDO: You are distorting. . . .

JOSEFA: What I offer her is not a violence . . . Man's love is always a violence.

EDUARDO: I'm sorry.

JOSEFA: For what . . . the evil in the world?

EDUARDO: I love Alysea.

JOSEFA: Oh, yes . . . you love, he loves, they love . . . how convenient the word "love"!

[EDUARDO *remains silent.* JOSEFA *suddenly realizes he is a guest.*]

JOSEFA: [*In an even pleasant voice.*] Come, Eduardo, you must forgive me for such an outburst . . . What a terrible hostess I am! Don't mind me, when there is concern for the people you love . . . Here let me refill your cup!

[*She pours him some coffee and hands it to him.*] There is a special happiness in this house, you know. . . .

EDUARDO: [*Reassured.*] I know . . . it is the soaring sea in you.

JOSEFA: What?

EDUARDO: You carry things, people with you . . . when your strength is washed away . . . you leave beauty behind.

JOSEFA: How lovely . . . you are easy to fall in love with. . . .

EDUARDO: So are you . . . if a man is brave enough.

JOSEFA: Brave?

EDUARDO: You are a whirlwind. . . .

JOSEFA: I have always sought the calm. . . .

EDUARDO: Ah . . . but your depths! Josefa, I sense them . . . you are not in the barrio.

JOSEFA: [*Amused.*] Such discernment! . . . but then, you are right . . . I am of the lake.

EDUARDO: I've heard . . . I hear you dare the lake alone . . . in solitude. . . .

JOSEFA: The barrio stories are myth . . . primitive fears . . . what most of the people fear is instinctive. . . .

EDUARDO: In what way?

JOSEFA: Out in the lake . . . out in the pines . . . they see themselves too well . . . they have become the desert . . . it is too much to accept . . . so monsters are created. . . . but for me . . . ah . . . for me!

EDUARDO: Tell me. . . .

JOSEFA: When I was young . . . when I refused to go bathe on San Lorenzo's day, when I chose the moonlight in any season . . . it was defiance. . . .

EDUARDO: What did you defy?

JOSEFA: What defied me . . . the world! Yes, I would go . . . to defy . . . then . . . but it became something else.

EDUARDO: [*Looking at her intently.*] Why didn't you ever marry? No one good enough?

JOSEFA: [*Shrugs it off.*] I never saw the dream . . . I never felt the hope . . . there was always too much clarity for me . . . [*Pause.*] . . . Do you think me beautiful?

EDUARDO: Yes . . . very . . . mixed in with a dangerous excitement. . . .

JOSEFA: You are making love to me. . . .

EDUARDO: I make love to all things beautiful . . . don't you?

JOSEFA: [*In a whisper.*] Yes . . . oh, yes. . . .

[ALYSEA *comes in breathless.*]

ALYSEA: Well . . . you two . . . that wasn't long was it? [*Looks at both of them.*] You two must have found marvelous things to talk about . . . it shows!

JOSEFA: I tell you Eduardo . . . this girl has possibilities. . . .

EDUARDO: I know. . . .

ALYSEA: Did she tell you about her magicians?

EDUARDO: She was about to . . . when you came.

JOSEFA: [*Looking at him intently.*] How did you know . . . I was about to?

EDUARDO: The light in your eyes . . . the sudden magic in you. . . .

ALYSEA: I know what you mean, Eduardo . . . such a mystical thing. . . .

JOSEFA: You have laid the setting . . . so kindly. [*She walks to the window and looks out with her eyes closed as she speaks.*]

JOSEFA: The magicians are real, you know! I found them . . . long ago . . . the night of the Festival of San Lorenzo. The virgins had bathed by the noon day sun . . . I . . . I went after the Rosary bell . . . I went when they were all celebrating; the silence was perfumed . . . desire was heavy . . . painful. Does it surprise you that I speak of desire? Oh, yes . . . I felt it . . . to my fingertips . . . it was so real, the beautiful need . . . the lights of the barrio were far off in another world . . . this always affected me . . . I became another being far from my kind . . . even my desire was a special suffering. . . .

EDUARDO: You still did not marry.

JOSEFA: What does that have to do with desire? My desire . . . like my being . . . became a purer grain. It was more than someone to see or touch . . . or embrace . . . it was a need for a pouring of self . . . a gentleness . . . a faith. I did not want the callous Indian youth . . . with hot breath and awkward hands . . . a taking without feeling . . . no, not that! I wanted so much more. . . . [*She turns to look at* ALYSEA *and* EDUARDO *caught in her spell.*] Look at you . . . children . . . listening to fairy tales. . . .

EDUARDO: Children believe. . . .

JOSEFA: So do I! . . . isn't it funny?

EDUARDO: No . . . it is like that with some people.

JOSEFA: For me . . . it came true! . . . the wonder was my magicians. That night at the lake there was a different music . . . the stillness sung inside me . . . the moonlight grew in me . . . it became my lover . . . There by the lake, I felt the light finding its way among the pines . . . to me . . . It took me . . . then . . . perhaps it was my imagination . . . it said to me . . . "We are one . . . make your beauty . . . make your truth." Deep, I felt a burning spiral . . . it roared in my ears . . . my heart . . . [*Pause.*] It was too much to bear . . . so I ran, and ran and ran until I fell . . . not knowing where; I lay there in utter quiet . . . then I opened my eyes and found myself calmly looking up at the stars . . . sisters of my love! The moon had followed me; it lay a lake around me, on the grass. . . .

EDUARDO: Were you afraid?

JOSEFA: Afraid! There was no room . . . the joy was too great. I had the secret of the magicians . . . the wine of love . . . the light was me; I knew that I would bear the children of light . . . the moon . . . the burning lake.

ALYSEA: [*In a whisper.*] I believe her . . . look around you, the children of light . . . her garden . . . the lace . . . her love for the barrio people . . . her bright, bright calm. . . .

EDUARDO: [*Taking up the pace.*] Her person. . . .

JOSEFA: Hush . . . you two . . . don't go on so!

[*The voice of* TOMÁS *from the outside window breaks the spell.*]

TOMÁS: Josefa! . . . David's horse! . . . I found it out in the pasture . . . without a bridle . . . Josefa!

JOSEFA: [*Goes to the window.*] David's horse?

EDUARDO: [*Going to the window.*] Need any help?

JOSEFA: He didn't hear you . . . he's coming in. . . .

[ALYSEA *all of a sudden loses all her brightness; she seems frightened and lost. She looks at* JOSEFA'*s every move;* JOSEFA *shows no reaction; she calmly begins to pick up cups, napkins.*]

JOSEFA: It is getting late . . . my! The morning has flown . . . such wonderful time . . . I hope it isn't too late for you two to go for your walk.

EDUARDO: No . . . no . . . there's plenty of time.

[TOMÁS *comes in through the kitchen door.*]

TOMÁS: He must have broken out from the stable . . . I thought I would tell you before I took him back to the hacienda. . . .

JOSEFA: Yes . . . take him back . . . horses will do that.

[EDUARDO *takes* ALYSEA *by the hands. He looks at her intently.*]

EDUARDO: What on earth is the matter? You need some morning air . . . I'll tell you what . . . I'll take you to a place where I can trace the path of the swallows any day now. . . .

[ALYSEA *doesn't seem to be listening to him;* JOSEFA *notices this and promptly suggests.*]

JOSEFA: Yes . . . I insist on it . . . take her; right now . . . enjoy this lovely day. . . .

[EDUARDO *takes* ALYSEA *by the shoulder.*]

EDUARDO: Come on. . . .

[*He stirs her to the door;* ALYSEA *does not resist. They exit.*]

TOMÁS: [*Shyly.*] I guess she feels bad about David . . . what happened last night. . . .

JOSEFA: What?

TOMÁS: I heard the talk in the barrio . . . someone broke into the house . . . that is . . . that is what you claim.

JOSEFA: What do you mean?

TOMÁS: You didn't tell me earlier. . . .

JOSEFA: Tell you? Why should I tell you anything.

TOMÁS: The blood in the pail . . . you didn't tell me anything about that either. . . .

JOSEFA: So?

TOMÁS: Well . . . I remember . . . all those times . . . you save the poor; innocent, helpless ones . . . you never say anything . . . it's always the barrio who puts the story together . . . you are clever. . . .

JOSEFA: Don't be ridiculous. . . .

TOMÁS: Yes . . . people have no idea how clever you really are . . . la doña Perfecta! You saved Alysea from the evil man . . . you saved David from

a drunken father, the barrio tells the story of an angel . . . but it's funny
. . . somehow . . . they never remember to tell that you crippled one man
and the other died on the road where you left him. . . .

JOSEFA: You are pitiful . . . like those two men . . . destructive and pitiful. . . .

TOMÁS: Perhaps you'll get your hands on me too.

JOSEFA: [*Calmly, with disdain.*] Hadn't you better see about that horse?

TOMÁS: Now the town is busy making you out a heroine . . . an intruder?
That's hard to believe . . . the girl looked too guilty a while ago . . . [*He
studies* JOSEFA *who is straightening up.*] But you . . . it's amazing! . . . such
grace . . . such pious silence . . . yes . . . you are a dangerous one, all
right!

JOSEFA: All this . . . this foolishness, I know, is leading up to some sort of
blackmail . . . you want money . . . don't you?

TOMÁS: You know me so well! . . . after all, I'm on your side . . . we are of
the same blood. . . .

JOSEFA: Get out of here . . . and be careful about what you say . . . you
clown! . . . who's going to believe anything you say? Be careful . . . or I
may let you starve.

TOMÁS: Didn't work . . . eh? No money?

JOSEFA: You've tried my patience long enough . . . I have better things to do
with my time . . . go and see about that horse. . . . [*She picks up the tray
and starts toward the kitchen.*]

TOMÁS: Not even a few pesos?

[JOSEFA *looks at him contemptuously and walks out into the kitchen without a
word.*]

TOMÁS: She'll break! She'll break . . . once I lay all my cards on the table.
. . . stupid women! . . . [*He looks around the room.*] I know they keep the
household money somewhere around here . . . yes.

[*He begins to look in the drawers.*]

Scene 3

Later the same morning. The room is empty, full of light, when CLARA *enters. She is
the wife of* DON ESQUINAS, *owner of the hacienda. She has the grace and elegance of
good living. But, at closer scrutiny, one can see that this once beautiful woman is
dissipated. Her blond beauty, although meticulously enhanced by great care, has the
flavor of fading youth. She carries a knitting bag. Although she has been in this room
many times, she is each time overwhelmed by the unusual light. She walks up to the
table, lays her bag on it, opens it, searches for a cigarette; she finds one, lights it, and
draws its flavor leisurely. She catches sight of* JOSEFA'S *workbasket; she also sees the
damask; she traces the design; then she picks up a piece of lace from the workbasket and
examines it admiringly.*

CLARA: Angel filigree . . . how lovely . . . it's unearthly. . . .

[*As she examines the lace,* ALYSEA *walks into the room breathlessly. Her arms are full of freshly cut flowers. She glances at Doña Clara apologetically.*]

ALYSEA: Doña Clara . . . am I late?

CLARA: No, no . . . I just got here.

ALYSEA: [*Going to the vase and setting the flowers next to it.*] I always linger too long in the garden. . . .

CLARA: What a garden . . . what incantations does Josefa use?

ALYSEA: It's marvelous, the way she does it. . . .

CLARA: She talks to the flowers. . . .

ALYSEA: She talks to all living things. . . .

CLARA: [*Looking at* ALYSEA *as she arranges the flowers in the vase.*] You too . . . how you have blossomed in this house.

ALYSEA: Me?

CLARA: [*In a deliberately contained voice.*] Of course, this time it could be Eduardo . . . I hear he loves you.

ALYSEA: Love does that . . . doesn't it?

CLARA: It's true then! . . . and you love him too?

ALYSEA: Yes.

CLARA: Well . . . [*She puts out her cigarette.*] That's that! . . . where is my dress?

ALYSEA: [*Coming out of her reverie.*] Oh, I'm sorry . . . of course, your fitting. [ALYSEA *goes to a wardrobe and takes out a simple gown. She hands it to* CLARA. CLARA *goes behind the screen.*]

CLARA: I suppose you'll go away with him?

ALYSEA: He wants me to . . . I haven't quite decided. . . .

CLARA: About love?

ALYSEA: Am I good enough for him? I have to use reason. . . .

CLARA: [*Almost impatiently.*] You don't have to reason love . . . my God!

ALYSEA: Will it be fair to him!

CLARA: What love there is . . . you take . . . don't reason it away . . . take it! [*She comes from around the screen and gives her back to* ALYSEA *so* ALYSEA *will fasten the dress. Both are facing the mirror.* CLARA *looks* ALYSEA *directly in the eyes.*]

CLARA: Love is always fair just because it is. [*She can't look in the mirror any longer.*] What's the matter with me . . . look at me . . . an expert on love . . . ha! [*She bites her lip.*]

ALYSEA: You are beautiful and wise.

[CLARA *doesn't answer; she deliberately becomes absorbed with the gown. She surveys herself in the mirror.*]

CLARA: It seems to lack something . . . Alysea . . . what do you think?

ALYSEA: Of course . . . Josefa made something very special for it . . . [*She looks around.*] Where is it? Oh, yes . . . I'll be back in a minute. [ALYSEA *goes through the bedroom door.* CLARA *goes to the mirror and traces the lines on her face. She then walks up to her knitting bag; takes a flask, opens it.*]

CLARA: [*Bitterly.*] Here's to youth! [*She drinks long draughts. She does it three times; then, she puts the flask away. She walks up to the mirror again.*]

CLARA: Well, my girl . . . what's in store for you? He's left you . . . you always knew he would leave you . . . what is there now, my girl . . . except time? . . . [*She covers her face with her hands.*]

[ALYSEA *comes in from the bedroom with a beautiful lace shawl.* CLARA *quickly recovers and looks at the shawl.*]

ALYSEA: Look . . . isn't it beautiful . . . a duende[8] design.

CLARA: Andalucian?

ALYSEA: Yes . . . Josefa copied it!

CLARA: Superb!

[ALYSEA *drapes it over one shoulder and claps it on* CLARA'*s waist.*]

CLARA: Oh, thank you . . . but . . . these days I need the right lights . . . not all things are kind to me anymore . . . Yes, it is beautiful. . . . [*She turns and contemplates* ALYSEA.] Look at you . . . you are so young . . . your beauty so sharp . . . only yesterday, my dear, only yesterday, I was young like you . . . mark that well!

[JOSEFA *comes in through the outside door.* CLARA *sees her. She goes to* JOSEFA *and kisses her cheek.*]

CLARA: I missed you this morning . . . you didn't come.

JOSEFA: Didn't I tell you? . . . there's a million things to do before tomorrow.

CLARA: The shawl . . . it's beautiful . . . only Josefa!

JOSEFA: [*Surveying her handiwork.*] The design . . . the delicacy against the dark dress . . . it is impressive . . . you wear it well. [*She notices that* CLARA *is somewhat too gay; a little bit unsteady.*]

ALYSEA: Shall I get the combs?

CLARA: Combs?

JOSEFA: Mantilla combs . . . made by the gypsies. . . .

CLARA: To go with the gown.

ALYSEA: I'll get them. [*She walks back to the bedroom.* JOSEFA *looks at* CLARA, *realizing what the matter is.*]

JOSEFA: You must have started early. . . .

CLARA: What? [*She busies herself at the mirror.*] You worry too much . . . just a little courage . . . I needed a little courage. . . .

JOSEFA: Eduardo?

CLARA: [*Turns and faces* JOSEFA; *pain in her eyes.*] He loves her.

JOSEFA: I know. . . .

CLARA: You see . . . I needed a little courage this morning.

JOSEFA: If you start again . . . promise me you won't!

CLARA: [*With false gaiety.*] I promise! [*She closes her eyes.*] I wish . . . I wish I were young for one day . . . just one day . . . so he would love me the way I love him.

JOSEFA: Men don't love . . . they take . . . haven't you learned that by now?

CLARA: Oh, Josefa . . . you are wrong . . . you are wrong . . . a woman was made to love a man . . . to love is enough for a woman . . . if only they

8. Elf.

would let us love them without negating, without negating. . . .

JOSEFA: Why, Clara? Why must you give . . . so easily? Not to them . . . Clara . . . not to men!

CLARA: [*Shrugs.*] My downfall? [*In a whisper.*] My life?

JOSEFA: Here . . . enough of that . . . there are beautiful things to love. . . .

    [ALYSEA *returns with the combs. She hands them to* JOSEFA, *who goes to* CLARA *and expertly places them in her hair.*]

CLARA: Without mantilla?

JOSEFA: It would be too much with the shawl. . . .

CLARA: Yes . . . of course . . . you're right . . . a gypsy with majesty!

ALYSEA: Yes . . . That's what you look like . . . a gypsy queen.

JOSEFA: El espíritu duende. . . .

CLARA: Like your magicians?

JOSEFA: Perhaps. . . .

    [*The church bell rings midday; suddenly two swallows are seen outside the window.*]

ALYSEA: Look!

JOSEFA: They're coming . . . the advance guard . . . every year.

CLARA: You love them . . . don't you? . . . your magicians let you find so many things to love . . . lucky . . . lucky Josefa.

JOSEFA: The swallows are safe here . . . after the long, long, lonely flight. . . .

CLARA: Lonely? . . . they come in droves. . . .

    [*The three look outside the window for a minute. Choir practice begins.*]

JOSEFA: Look at the lake . . . it shimmers with love . . . [*Turns to Clara.*] I said lonely, Clara, because finding direction . . . is lonely . . . it is too personal a thing. . . .

CLARA: I see what you mean . . . Josefa [*Looks out the window pensively.*] why don't I see the love shimmering in your lake?

    [JOSEFA *smiles.*]

ALYSEA: Her magicians . . . isn't it, Josefa?

JOSEFA: Yes . . . my magicians.

ACT II

It is early afternoon of the same day. JOSEFA *comes through the outside door. There is a small injured bird in her hands. She cradles it gently and examines it.*

JOSEFA: You poor little thing . . . a broken wing . . . don't worry, you'll be fine in a little while . . . [*She puts the soft piece of life against her cheek.*] There will be no second pain . . . Alysea!

ALYSEA: [*Comes in through the kitchen door.*] Yes?

JOSEFA: Look . . . I found it in the garden . . . it lay there . . . small, helpless . . . look, he's thirsty . . . quick get some water and an eye-dropper.

    [ALYSEA *goes into the bedroom.* JOSEFA *sits in her rocking chair and places the bird gently on her lap. . . .* ALYSEA *comes back with a cup and an eye-dropper.*]

JOSEFA *picks up the bird, fills the eye-dropper and patiently feeds the bird water. The bird drinks.*]

JOSEFA: See . . . oh, he has life . . . this one!

ALYSEA: Just a baby . . . let us set the wing . . . I'll get some small twigs and a bandage. . . .

[*She leaves again;* JOSEFA *continues feeding the bird.*]

JOSEFA: How did you find the bird-house . . . eh? My magicians must have led you here . . . before the others . . . every year . . . the sky is black with their wings . . . here they rest . . . and eat . . . you will be safe . . . until you join your brothers and sisters . . . yes. . . .

[ALYSEA *comes back; together they carefully set the small wing.*]

JOSEFA: There!

ALYSEA: Let's put him in the bird-house . . . he's tired. . . .

[JOSEFA *kisses the bird; then both of them go to the window, lean out to the tree, and place the bird in the tree house. Satisfied,* JOSEFA *and* ALYSEA *look at each other.* JOSEFA *reaches out and begins to stroke* ALYSEA's *hair.*]

JOSEFA: [*Softly.*] We share so much . . . just wait . . . the magicians will come to you . . . I know. . . .

ALYSEA: What?

JOSEFA: Remember how much you wished for the magicians?

ALYSEA: No . . . no . . . I don't want them anymore. . . .

JOSEFA: But. . . .

ALYSEA: When you brought me here . . . all that's happened . . . it is so unreal . . . a year of mists and deep sinking dreams . . . but not any more!

JOSEFA: Hush . . . you're just upset . . . that's all. . . .

ALYSEA: No . . . last night . . . no . . . never again. . . .

JOSEFA: Poor little girl . . . you've tired yourself out all morning . . . I forgot . . . I don't know why . . . but I just forgot about . . . about last night.

ALYSEA: [*Looking at her with horror.*] Josefa . . . no! Forgot? How could you.

JOSEFA: [*Becoming slightly agitated.*] Habit . . . to keep strong . . . since I was little . . . to keep strong . . . I put ugliness away.

ALYSEA: Where? Where?

JOSEFA: What do you mean?

ALYSEA: If you have a conscience . . . where could you put it away?

JOSEFA: There will be atonement. . . .

ALYSEA: No. . . . that's impossible . . . you think . . . it will . . . disappear? The blood . . . the knife . . . [*She runs to the table where she had placed the knife.*] Look . . . I'll show you . . . you make it disappear! [*She opens the drawer and stares unbelievingly.*] The knife . . . it's gone! [*She begins to look frantically everywhere.*] Did you hear me?

[JOSEFA *seems almost unaware of* ALYSEA's *frenzy.*]

JOSEFA: Yes . . . of course. . . .

[ALYSEA *begins to look again and this time finds the money box gone.*]

ALYSEA: The money box . . . it's gone too.

JOSEFA: Tomás . . . of course . . . he took the money and the knife.

[ALYSEA *collapses into a chair and covers her face with her hands.* TOMÁS's *voice is heard singing a barrio love song;* ALYSEA *looks up in fright.* JOSEFA *goes to the door of the kitchen and calls out into the patio behind the kitchen.*]

JOSEFA: Tomás! Come in here. . . .

[TOMÁS *comes into the kitchen still singing. He walks into the room.* JOSEFA *watches him warily.* ALYSEA *in terror.*]

TOMÁS: Well . . . well . . . Did you call me, querida? [*He strokes* JOSEFA's *arm intimately. She breaks away.*]

JOSEFA: Don't you ever put your hands on me!

TOMÁS: Ha! ha! ha! . . . Doña Perfecta . . . [*He looks around the room.*] You know . . . I think I'll move over here . . . I like this house . . . ah! . . . it is time I had a little elegance in my life . . . yes. [*He sprawls out in a chair.*]

JOSEFA: You've been drinking. . . .

TOMÁS: Yes . . . I have been drinking . . . and I shall drink some more . . . you can afford it. . . .

[ALYSEA *begins to cry.*]

TOMÁS: What's the matter with her?

JOSEFA: She is tired . . . and I . . . have had enough of your insolence. . . .

TOMÁS: Que maravilla[9] . . . How long . . . Josefa . . . how long . . . can you keep it up? [*He paces in front of her; she remains calm.*]

TOMÁS: [*Practically shouting in her face.*] I took the knife! Do you understand . . . I took the knife! . . . aren't you afraid, Josefa?

[ALYSEA *begins to cry desperately.* JOSEFA *goes to her. She tries to comfort her.*]

JOSEFA: Don't, Alysea . . . remember . . . it's late . . . we have to pack for David . . . he'll need his things in the hospital . . . compose yourself . . . Why don't you go and start packing . . . I'll talk to Tomás.

[ALYSEA *nods her head in agreement; she rises and leaves as if she wanted escape.*]

JOSEFA: [*Turns and faces* TOMÁS.] Have you ever . . . have you ever . . . done anything kind for anybody?

TOMÁS: [*Sarcastically.*] No . . . just you . . . querida . . . you are the angel. . . .

JOSEFA: All right . . . what do you intend to do?

TOMÁS: Nothing . . . you see . . . we . . . you and I . . . must have a clearer understanding . . . I know much more than you think . . . about you and [*Nods towards bedroom.*] her!

JOSEFA: [*Stiffens.*] All right . . . you win . . . I'll give you money. . . .

TOMÁS: No more crumbs . . . dear niece . . . I call the play . . . from now on.

JOSEFA: You're bluffing . . . lying . . . as usual.

TOMÁS: Am I?

[*There is a knock at the door; with alacrity* TOMÁS *springs up and goes to the door and opens it. It is* DON ESQUINAS, CLARA's *husband.*]

9. Amazing.

TOMÁS: Ah . . . Don Esquinas, won't you come in?

> [DON ESQUINAS *brushes past* TOMÁS, *totally ignoring him.* TOMÁS *makes a mock gesture of humility.*]

DON ESQUINAS: Josefa . . . the worst has happened . . . I warned you!

JOSEFA: [*Placing her hands on her heart.*] Clara . . . let me go to her. [*She starts to go;* DON ESQUINAS *stops her.*]

DON ESQUINAS: It's too late. . . .

JOSEFA: [*Savagely.*] It isn't . . . I can take care of her.

DON ESQUINAS: How? By giving her more drink . . . you've done enough harm. . . .

JOSEFA: Harm? I have been her sole companion for years . . . I have suffered with her . . . nursed her . . . Harm?

DON ESQUINAS: Do you know how I found my wife this afternoon when I got home? She was lying in bed . . . stark naked . . . screaming about crawling . . . crawling, dark . . . she slashed everything in sight . . . broke the mirror . . . there were bottles . . . everywhere. . . .

JOSEFA: My poor, poor darling. . . .

DON ESQUINAS: I . . . the servants . . . we were helpless . . . it was dreadful . . . she kept screaming and sobbing that your magicians had . . . had no faces. . . .

JOSEFA: She's so alone. . . .

DON ESQUINAS: Your lies . . . the liquor and your lies . . . both supplied by you! I'm taking her to the sanitorium . . . this time for good.

JOSEFA: She is so alone. . . .

DON ESQUINAS: Stop saying that! You . . . you supplied her with liquor. . . .

JOSEFA: All that unhappiness . . . she is so lost . . . there was nothing else . . . She promised me this afternoon.

DON ESQUINAS: Promised? You stupid woman . . . you know she wouldn't keep the promise. . . .

JOSEFA: [*Suddenly in anger.*] I tell you . . . you won't listen . . . you men never listen . . . all she had was hopelessness. . . .

DON ESQUINAS: You don't know what you are talking about . . . she always had everything . . . since the day she was born . . . never, never did she have to lift a finger . . . anything she desires. . . .

JOSEFA: Except her husband!

DON ESQUINAS: What in damnation?

JOSEFA: She wanted you to love her. . . .

DON ESQUINAS: Love her? You women are insane! I married her . . . didn't I?

JOSEFA: She knew all about your . . . your women. . . .

DON ESQUINAS: That is a man's way! You have no right to question . . . Tell me, how much liquor did you give her? When did you give it to her?

> [JOSEFA *remains silent.*]

DON ESQUINAS: Well?

JOSEFA: She wanted a baby. . . .

DON ESQUINAS: Nonsense! We settled that long ago . . . that was past and forgotten. . . .

JOSEFA: No . . . it was never forgotten . . . she cried every night. . . .

DON ESQUINAS: Silly tears of a drunken woman . . . adopt a baby . . . a baby not of the Esquinas blood? For my heir? Absurd!

JOSEFA: [*Bitterly.*] Which of your bastards are you going to choose as your heir?

DON ESQUINAS: You ungrateful peasant . . . let me tell you . . . you influenced her too much . . . this is probably all your fault . . . I don't want you around the hacienda now that she is gone . . . do you hear?

[JOSEFA *turns her back on him;* DON ESQUINAS *is somewhat at a loss. Her calm toward his anger is disconcerting. He stands for a moment, then, he walks out of the room. On his way out,* TOMÁS *follows him, still assuming a pose of mock humility.*]

TOMÁS: It is terrible, Don Esquinas, what my niece has done . . . if I can make up for it in any way . . . please call on me. . . .

[DON ESQUINAS *ignores him and leaves.* TOMÁS *turns to* JOSEFA.]

TOMÁS: See what you have done to your friend . . . the wife of our Don?

[JOSEFA *too ignores him.* TOMÁS's *attitude of humility is now gone. His attitude is again cunning and sly. He walks up to* JOSEFA.]

TOMÁS: Tch, tch, tch . . . Doña Perfecta is not perfecta . . . eh?

JOSEFA: [*Not listening to him.*] She's gone . . . the light of my magicians never came to her . . . poor, poor lost child.

TOMÁS: You are insane about those magicians. [JOSEFA *walks away from him;* TOMÁS *grabs her arm angrily.*] I'm sick and tired of you ignoring me! You think I'm scum? I don't matter . . . do I? Well, you listen. Doña Perfecta, you listen to me!

JOSEFA: [*Waits silently for him to let go of her arm. When he does, she touches her temples with her fingertips.*] I have a headache. . . .

TOMÁS: None of your tricks . . . listen to me! I saw you . . . do you hear . . . I saw you. Last San Lorenzo's Day, I remember. I left the fiesta . . . I was too drunk; I walked toward the lake . . . I remember, it was a clear, clear night; the moon lighted everything . . . as I came near the lake past the back of this house . . . I saw two figures come from the water's edge . . . they ran . . . one caught up with the other! [*He watches her maliciously and intently wishing to get a reaction; her surface is still calm as he scrutinizes her face.*]

JOSEFA: What are you trying to do?

TOMÁS: [*Laughing slyly and triumphantly.*] It was you and the girl . . . you and the girl . . . wasn't it? Now . . . I begin to put things together . . . it all fits!

JOSEFA: Your drunken hallucinations. . . .

TOMÁS: I know better, reina del barrio[1] . . . you are a. . . .

---

1. Queen of the barrio.

JOSEFA: If you have nothing else to threaten me with. . . . [*She walks away from him with disdain.*]

TOMÁS: [*Practically screaming with exasperation.*] You think you can always win, with your calm; you're not made of stone . . . you'll break, milady . . . I'll be back. Inside you're trembling with fear. . . .

[*She turns abruptly and faces him haughtily.* TOMÁS *falters first; he turns and leaves. As* JOSEFA *looks after him,* ALYSEA *comes from the bedroom wearing street clothes.*]

JOSEFA: [*Turns and sees her.*] Finished?

ALYSEA: Yes, I'm ready.

JOSEFA: [*Walks up to her and puts her arm around her.*] The ride will do you good; after you come back from the hospital . . . after you see my little David, we'll have supper here . . . then, we can have one of our little chats.

ALYSEA: [*Gently breaks away from Josefa.*] I'm not coming back.

JOSEFA: Not coming back?

ALYSEA: I meant to tell you earlier . . . I'm going away with Eduardo.

JOSEFA: Because of what happened last night?

ALYSEA: Many reasons, but mostly because I want to be with him.

JOSEFA: You are like all the rest . . . you insist on being a useless, empty sacrifice!

ALYSEA: I love him.

JOSEFA: Love him? Tell me, how long will your precious Eduardo love you? [*Pause.*] You know who was here? Don Esquinas! Clara drank herself insane because your Eduardo left her. What do you think he'll do to you?

ALYSEA: I can't believe that . . . there's more to love.

JOSEFA: [*Ironically and bitterly.*] Love! Remember the brothel? No different . . . you choose darkness . . . all your pains are still to come! Haven't I taught you anything?

ALYSEA: It all fell apart . . . last night. All I can remember are David's eyes. [*She breaks down sobbing.*]

JOSEFA: He'll be all right . . . I'll take care of my little love . . . as long as he lives. . . .

ALYSEA: His eyes told me. You and I were all the terror in the world.

JOSEFA: No . . . the terror is in the world out there . . . don't say that!

ALYSEA: The violence . . . the useless violence. . . .

JOSEFA: I forbid you to go on like this. [*She walks to the window and reaches into the bird house until she finds the crippled bird. She picks it up; fondles him and holds him against her cheek.*]

JOSEFA: [*With eyes closed.*] Remember how he came . . . crippled, starved, half dead?

ALYSEA: The way I came?

JOSEFA: It will be safe here and happy; you have always been safe and happy! We have so much, Alysea.

[ALYSEA *remains silent.*]

JOSEFA: You know why I built the bird-house? [*She seems to be remembering something painful; she goes to the rocking chair; places the bird on her lap and strokes it gently.*] When I was seven . . . the swallows came . . . they came one hot dry dawn . . . and continued all day . . . on the edge of the desert that still hotter afternoon . . . I saw noisy boys with desert time on their hands . . . playing . . . I watched the playing become a violence . . . they were catching birds . . . now it became a killing . . . they stoned them . . . plucked them . . . laughing with a fearful joy . . . the sand was a sea of dead birds . . . I . . . I . . . couldn't stand it . . . I ran . . . I hit them . . . I said, "Stop! Stop!" [*Pause.*] They laughed; then for a joke . . . for a joke they said . . . they held me down, the burning sand against my back . . . In spite of all my terror, I opened my eyes . . . a boy . . . a big boy . . . held a swallow over me; he took a knife . . . cut the bird . . . Oh, God! so much blood . . . all that blood. [JOSEFA *strokes the bird gently and shakes her head, closes her eyes.*] It spilled . . . spilled into my face . . . ran into my mouth . . . warm . . . warm . . . salt warm . . . was it my tears? the blood? [*She stands and goes to the window still with the bird; she caresses the bird with her cheek and places it gently in the bird house. The rosary bell begins to toll. It is sunset.* JOSEFA *looks out in silence.*] Alysea . . . look, the lake is screaming with life . . . look . . . the colors of love . . . then . . . the day went . . . [*She turns to* ALYSEA.] Out there . . . the beauty is lost in fears . . . what do you expect out there? Stay with the radiance . . . Alysea, stay with me?

ALYSEA: I won't be coming back.

[ALYSEA *turns and leaves, going into the bedroom;* JOSEFA *looks after her for a moment; seems to start after* ALYSEA, *then changes her mind. She turns to the unfinished damask; she unhooks the needle and begins to work on it in deep concentration.* ALYSEA *returns with a suitcase.* JOSEFA *does not look up although she is aware of* ALYSEA. ALYSEA *comes close to* JOSEFA *rather hesitantly.* JOSEFA *looks up and smiles.*]

JOSEFA: [*In a casual tone.*] Look . . . do you think I ought to give the design a name? I saw it in a dream the other night . . . so vivid! Perhaps I should call it "Swallow Song." What do you think?

ALYSEA: [*Looking intently at the design over* JOSEFA's *shoulder.*] It looks like flowing grain . . . with . . . with a streak of lightning . . . so well intermingled . . . how strange! . . . beauty and terror as one . . . see? [*She traces the pattern with her finger.*]

JOSEFA: How foolish of you . . . that is not lightning . . . it is . . . it is sweet rain.

[ALYSEA *looks intently at the pattern, then at* JOSEFA.]

ALYSEA: [*Softly.*] Lovely Josefa . . . no, no . . . you could never see the lightning . . . only your gentle lights. [*She picks up her suitcase and starts to leave.*] Goodbye, sweet lady of light!

[JOSEFA *looks up but does not answer.* ALYSEA *moves toward the outside door.*]

JOSEFA: [*As if in afterthought.*] Alysea?

ALYSEA: Yes?

JOSEFA: On the way . . . please stop by the rectory . . . will you? Tell Father Prado I cannot make rosary tonight. Tell him . . . if he would be so kind . . . to come later this evening. . . .

ALYSEA: Of course.

[*She hesitates for a moment, as if at a loss for words. Then with one last look of love for* JOSEFA *and the room, she departs. After* ALYSEA *leaves,* JOSEFA *continues putting the final stitches on the damask.*]

JOSEFA: There! finished . . . another birth of light! [*She stands and stretches as if very tired. She rubs the back of her neck and breathes deep. She goes to the window again. It is now dark.*] My lover! You look morning crystal in the water . . . so still . . . so deep . . . I ache for you so! You beckon me shamelessly. . . . [*She stands at the window as the curtain drops for Act II.*]

ACT III

Late the same evening. The church bells are announcing the end of rosary. JOSEFA *is sitting in her rocking chair saying her prayer beads. Every so often she pauses in thought. There is a knock at the door.* JOSEFA *rises and goes to the door.* FATHER PRADO *enters.*

FATHER PRADO: [*Kissing her on the cheek.*] My dear . . . how are you this evening? We missed you at rosary . . . you always lead prayer with the confidence of an angel . . . a hundred things to do before tomorrow . . . eh?

JOSEFA: It's good to see you! [*She leads him by the arm to a settee.*]

FATHER PRADO: Tell me . . . can I help with anything?

JOSEFA: You are here . . . that is more than enough.

FATHER PRADO: You must give me a chance . . . you do so much for the church, for me . . . now let me do something for you.

JOSEFA: Father . . . you are my kindred spirit . . . the oasis in the middle of the desert.

FATHER PRADO: You spoil me. . . .

JOSEFA: I finished the boys' surplices for tomorrow. . . .

FATHER PRADO: See what I mean? Your lovely little hands [*Kisses them.*] produce such lovely wondrous things for us . . . [*Looks around.*] And this place! A sanctuary . . . who would think? To find such a place as this in our desert barrio? Ah . . . all things and all people here are too mindful of the desert . . . except you.

JOSEFA: My magicians, Father!

FATHER PRADO: [*In jest.*] Of course, your magicians!

JOSEFA: I wonder if you take me seriously? Come . . . would you like some coffee? tea?

FATHER PRADO: No . . . no, it is late; I ate too much at supper . . . I tell myself every night it seems . . . but I go on eating just the same.

JOSEFA: The way you work for the barrio people! Every church festival is such a chore for you . . . you work yourself to death. . . .

FATHER PRADO: So do you!

JOSEFA: We can't help it . . . can we, Father? You love the people as much as I do.

FATHER PRADO: It means so much to them . . . these festivals . . . they are just ritual to you . . . aren't they?

JOSEFA: Maybe . . . but what blossoms from the barrio people because of the festival . . . that is not ritual . . . there is a rebirth . . . they come to life for a little while.

FATHER PRADO: Tomorrow will be very special for them . . . a day to honor their Josefa. Such a legend you are!

JOSEFA: If it makes them happy.

FATHER PRADO: [*Looks at her intently.*] Are you feeling all right? You look a little pale . . . of course! How stupid of me . . . so many things have been happening today . . . even in the rectory life seeps in. . . .

JOSEFA: You know about Clara?

FATHER PRADO: Unfortunate . . . pobrecita[2] . . . such a beautiful child.

JOSEFA: She won't be coming back this time. [*She begins to cry softly. She brushes a tear from her cheek.*]

FATHER PRADO: There . . . there, don't cry! [*Comforts her.*] I know how you feel . . . you two were so close . . . she depended on you so!

JOSEFA: When life is a farce. . . .

FATHER PRADO: In her own way . . . there was so much meaning . . . Alysea has found something special too . . . she and Eduardo stopped by the rectory.

JOSEFA: One by one . . . like leaves from a tree. . . .

FATHER PRADO: I know! Then . . . the terrible thing . . . I heard in the village . . . the terrible thing that happened to David . . . I hope they catch. . . .

JOSEFA: [*Interrupts violently.*] Father!

FATHER PRADO: What is it, child?

JOSEFA: May I have confession now?

FATHER PRADO: [*Puzzled.*] Here?

JOSEFA: Please, Father!

FATHER PRADO: Of course, if that's what you want. . . . [*He comes near her; as he does, she falls to her knees and leans her head against his body.*] What is wrong?

JOSEFA: Forgive me, Father, for I have sinned. . . . [FATHER *remains silent.*] I have sinned . . . I have sinned. . . .

FATHER PRADO: God forgives. . . .

JOSEFA: Oh, Father . . . I'm lost! I'm lost. . . .

FATHER PRADO: All of us . . . at one time. . . .

JOSEFA: I am guilty of grievous sins . . . they are beyond forgiveness . . . people will judge them so! Father . . . before I tell you . . . you must know . . . I do not feel sorry . . . I want . . . I need . . . the calm . . . to keep things as they are.

2. Poor little one.

[FATHER *simply nods his head.*]

JOSEFA: David was hurt last night . . . I lied about the intruder. There was no intruder . . . I was the one.

FATHER PRADO: [*Incredulously.*] You . . . did that to David?

JOSEFA: Yes . . . [*She braces herself as if to accept the fact.*] I did that to David.

FATHER PRADO: I can't believe it . . . you! Not you!

JOSEFA: Me, Father, Me!

FATHER PRADO: It was inhuman. . . .

JOSEFA: Oh, Father! I . . . I don't know . . . why? why?

FATHER PRADO: Tell me, my child, there must have been a reason. . . .

JOSEFA: Last night . . . last night . . . after supper . . . David helped Alysea and me put the last touches on the bird house. David was so excited . . . [*Pause.*] The moon . . . the reflection of diamonds on the lake . . . life . . . all were too much for me . . . I was overflowing . . . I felt the sweetness of the night with every fiber . . . every fiber . . . [*Lost in memory; then she resumes her story.*] David didn't want to go to bed . . . he insisted on staying up all night to wait for the swallows . . . Of course I said, "No!" He left for bed reluctantly . . . [*Pause.*] Father?

FATHER PRADO: Yes?

JOSEFA: Have you ever felt as if you were one total yearning . . . it roars and spills. . . .

[FATHER PRADO *remains silent.*]

JOSEFA: Alysea and I are lovers.

FATHER PRADO: What?

JOSEFA: A year ago tonight we became lovers . . . if you remember she had been with me for some months before San Lorenzo's Day . . . she was something new in my life . . . she felt and responded to my every mood . . . my every act . . . Oh! To have someone in your life! I had repulsed all the men in the barrio . . . the coarseness! The taking! No . . . no . . . I could never surrender to that . . . but when she came, she filled my life in so many ways . . . so many ways . . . it was natural that the yearning grow for more . . . the body too is master. . . .

FATHER PRADO: Yes, my child, of course it is!

JOSEFA: A year ago I took Alysea to the lake on the eve of San Lorenzo . . . She had heard about the Bathing of the Virgins at noon the next day . . . Could she go . . . she asked! I was angry . . . I knew all the hope . . . all the dreams of those girls would turn to jagged violence . . . it was a lie . . . The whole ritual is a lie!

FATHER PRADO: No . . . no, Josefa . . . to those girls the dream of a perfect love is true as long as it gives meaning to their lives. . . .

JOSEFA: I know what men are!

[FATHER PRADO *remains silent.*]

JOSEFA: I told her . . . go with me when the moon comes out . . . when the lake waits for just me . . . it is my lover! [*Pause.*] She believed me . . . It is true, Father . . . the lake is my lover. . . .

FATHER PRADO: Oh, my child!

JOSEFA: We bathed . . . and then . . . it happened . . . [*Pause.*] Last night after David went to bed . . . I felt the nymph magic . . . I took Alysea . . . Suddenly . . . there was David . . . in the middle of the room. The horror in his eyes . . . Why? Why? There was horror in his eyes. . . .

FATHER PRADO: He did not understand. . . .

JOSEFA: Oh, Father! Now . . . I can see why . . . now! But . . . last night . . . it was not the Josefa he loved that David saw . . . I could not stand what he saw! I could not!

FATHER PRADO: God forgive you!

JOSEFA: Something happened in me . . . I don't know what it was . . . I ran . . . I ran into the kitchen and found a kitchen knife . . . Somehow . . . somehow I knew David would tell . . . the barrio people would look at me that way too. . . .

FATHER PRADO: I never thought you would care about what people. . . .

JOSEFA: Oh, Father . . . until last night I never knew my fears . . . I went back to where Alysea was holding the frightened child . . . then . . . then I made Alysea hold him tight . . . Father, it was not her fault! There have been so many furies in her life . . . she drowned in my agony . . . she trusted me . . . what else could she do? [*She goes to the window, looks out at the lake for a moment.*] Father . . . look . . . come look at the lake . . . maybe you can understand the power it has over me . . . Look. . . .

[FATHER PRADO *goes somewhat reluctantly to the window. He also looks out, but remains silent.*]

JOSEFA: I took the knife and cut David's tongue. . . .

FATHER PRADO: Jesucristo, perdona a tu hija. . . .[3]

JOSEFA: I was silencing the world from reprimand . . . I knew I had to silence the world from reprimand . . . I felt no guilt . . . all I knew . . . the life I had . . . the faith of the barrio people . . . this house of light . . . must be preserved . . . I silenced all reprimand with my terrible deed . . . [*She covers her face for a moment. Then, she gathers strength and continues talking.*] With the light of day . . . I knew better . . . others had not my eyes . . . others had not my eyes . . . others had not my reasons . . . or my magicians . . . [*She looks at* FATHER PRADO *intently.*] Can you ever understand?

FATHER PRADO: [*As if talking to himself.*] I don't understand . . . I don't understand why I didn't see . . . detect what was happening to you. . . .

JOSEFA: [*Puzzled.*] Happening to me?

FATHER PRADO: All your beauty . . . your calm . . . your giving was . . . your talent . . . what a splendid canopy for the twisted fears of so many years . . . so many years . . . I'm an old fool . . . forgive me, my daughter, I have never really seen you . . . I pride myself in knowing you so well . . . I claimed I loved you . . . how blind . . . how blind. . . .

JOSEFA: Don't blame yourself, Father . . . I am what you see . . . that is

3. (Praying) Jesus Christ, forgive your daughter.

really what I am . . . Not what you discovered this moment. . . .

FATHER PRADO: My poor, poor child. . . .

JOSEFA: No . . . Father . . . don't pity me . . . anything but that! That is one thing I shall never suffer. . . .

FATHER PRADO: I have never seen you cry . . . Josefa . . . until tonight. . . .

JOSEFA: The past . . . the dark gnawing . . . such hungers! I must not be a desert . . . now they are harmless ghosts. . . .

FATHER PRADO: Are they?

JOSEFA: You don't understand . . . do you?

FATHER PRADO: I want to. . . .

JOSEFA: The magicians created "me!" . . . the blight of meniality never touched me . . . The magicians gave me the purity of light . . . and the wisp of beauties at my fingertips . . . so . . . I really am . . . what you always thought I was. . . .

FATHER PRADO: There is so much God in you! . . .

JOSEFA: God in me? . . . no, Father, . . . no . . . I failed goodness . . . I wanted, I prayed . . . to save my soul as the church instructed . . . as your faith believed. . . .

FATHER PRADO: [*Somewhat taken aback.*] But . . . you are the most pious . . . the most constant . . . in the barrio . . . Faith shines in you . . . all the beauty you create. . . .

JOSEFA: Faith? Oh, no, Father . . . no . . . It was not faith, it was the light of my magicians . . . I bear the children of light! I am its high priestess. . . .

FATHER PRADO: I . . . I . . .

[*He can't go on; he sits down and places his head in his hands.* JOSEFA *looks at him and is full of concern. She goes to comfort him.*]

JOSEFA: [*She says this as if she does not believe it herself.*] Don't grieve for me, Father . . . for what I have done, I am willing to atone . . . David will be my whole life . . . I will create beauty for him . . . for you . . . for the barrio people . . . longings will fade away with commitment . . . Father . . . Father. [*She kneels in front of him.*] Forgive me, Father, for I have sinned . . . I have grievously sinned.

FATHER PRADO: [*With tears in his eyes . . . He strokes her hair in silence.*]

Final Scene

Dawn the next morning; the sitting room is a pastel paradise; there is life in the bird house, a roar of bird sounds; JOSEFA *comes from the bedroom with a white gown over her arm. It is the gown to be worn at the procession. She goes to the window and looks at the tree with great happiness.*

JOSEFA: I waited for you . . . before dawn I heard the flurry of the sea . . . oh, what a sight you were over my burning lake . . . straight . . . straight

. . . you came to me . . . to this temple of peace . . . no more songs of pain for you. . . .

[*Church bells sound morning vigil. The procession will follow in the freshness of the early morning.* JOSEFA *remembers the barrio world.*]

JOSEFA: My day . . . my day . . . but, oh my people! . . . it was not meant to be shared with you . . . my day was planned by my magicians . . . long before you planned this one for me . . . I must get ready. . . . [*She goes behind the screen; puts on her gown, comes back and looks in the mirror. Her dress is white. She looks unusually young and beautiful. All of a sudden she touches her rather severe hair-do. Then she lets down her hair.*]

JOSEFA: [*Looking at herself intently in the mirror.*] Yes . . . yes . . . this way . . . there is a wildness in me . . . [*She laughs in joyous delirium. Then she becomes the usual* JOSEFA *for a moment. She remembers the boys' surplices. She goes to the wardrobe and takes them out. She lays them carefully over a chair.*] There . . . something of me will be at the procession . . . yes, even that . . . the boys will find them here . . . . [*She takes a final look in the mirror, then she goes to the window and looks out to the lake.*] So still your water . . . but I know your passions underneath . . . deep . . . deep . . . for all time . . . Hush! I'm coming. . . . [*As she turns to leave, she touches the lace, the damask now finished, the fresh flowers on the table . . . with love . . . with a tender regret . . . but a secret within her. . . .*] My magicians will let me come back as light . . . yes, yes! [*She goes to the door and gives the room one final glance.*]

JOSEFA: [*In a whisper.*] Wait for me. . . .

[*Church bells begin to toll for the gathering of the procession. Voices are heard outside the window.*]

VOICES: "Here! the starting will be here . . . in front of Josefa's garden." "Has anyone seen Josefa this morning?"

[*The sitting room seems alive even without people; then, two boys enter. They have come for the surplices.*]

1ST BOY: Hey . . . look . . . they're over there. [*Each of the boys takes one. . . .*]

2ND BOY: Aren't they something . . . grand . . . like at the cathedral. . . .

1ST BOY: That's what he said. . . .

2ND BOY: Who said?

1ST BOY: Father Prado . . . he said Josefa was like a Cathedral. . . .

2ND BOY: 'Cause she makes all this grand stuff?

1ST BOY: I guess so . . . 'cause she's different . . . don't you think?

2ND BOY: Ah . . . ha! She made all the altar linen. . . .

1ST BOY: Yeah . . . Father Prado said she was like the silence of the cathedral . . . and you know those glass-stained windows?

2ND BOY: Yeah. . . .

1ST BOY: That's her soul. . . .

2ND BOY: You think something is wrong with Father Prado?

[*They laugh in jest; shove each other around in horse play, then stop when the church bells ring again.*]

1ST BOY: Hey, come on . . . the procession is going to start. . . .

[*The room is empty again; this time the voices of the choir beginning the procession hymns are heard . . . They are as ethereal as the room. Combined, the room and the voices have a cathedral-like awesomeness.* CLEMENCIA *breaks the atmosphere. She is in her Sunday best.*]

CLEMENCIA: Josefa! . . . Where are you? [*She looks in the bedroom; then, she peeks through the kitchen door.*] Mnnnn . . . where could she be? Everybody's waiting. Josefa! Oh, dear, oh, dear! They've started without her. . . . [*She goes to the window.*] Look at those birds! Every year! . . . they come straight to this tree. Ah . . . God's morning . . . the lake . . . the green pines . . . [*Suddenly something out in the lake catches her eye.*] What is that . . . floating in the lake? Mmmmmmm . . . looks like a girl dressed in white . . . That's foolish! It is too early for the Bathing of the Virgins, yet . . . yes, wearing clothes? [*As she hears the choir, she loses interest and goes to the mirror and straightens her hat.*]

CLEMENCIA: [*With a sigh.*] Why do we all end up looking like scarecrows? [*She turns to leave and catches sight of the open window.*] I better close the window . . . the room will be covered with birds! [*She goes to the window again; as she starts to close it, she gazes out into the lake again fascinated by what she saw before.*] Yes . . . it is a body! A body floating in the lake . . . I'm sure of it! [*She gasps, but at this moment the church bells ring again. Out of habit, she starts to hurry off, shrugging off what she has seen.*] The sun is too bright . . . it is my imagination! I better hurry . . . what a day this will be. . . .

[*She leaves the room. The voices of the choir, the church bells, the birds on the tree in full life, and the almost unearthly light streaming through the windows give the essence of a presence in the room . . . of something beautiful.*]

STUDY QUESTIONS

1. What is the annual ritual in the village of Lago de San Lorenzo on their saint's day?

ACT I

1. Why does Alysea, while she is cleaning the sitting room carpet in scene 1, "[look] at the cloth in her hand intently"?

2. What does the conversation with Clemencia add to your expectations? How does it characterize Josefa? What questions about Alysea's attitude toward Josefa does it leave in your mind? What contradictory information or feelings do you have about Josefa? Are these clarified or intensified by the first scene between Alysea and Josefa? Can you recall what possibilities ran through your mind about what had happened on the night before the opening scene?

3. What do you make of Josefa's references in this scene to the swallows? to light?

4. Summarize what you know of the CHARACTERS and the situation at the end of this first scene.

5. Explain Josefa's final line (curtain speech) in this scene. What images have been planted in your mind during this scene?

6. Since neither the place nor, except for a few moments, the time has changed since the ending of the first scene, why is scene 2 a separate scene?

7. Eduardo is described as of "mixed heritage"; what does that mean to you? How was Josefa described in the stage directions in scene 1? How does ethnic heritage condition your view of and expectations about the characters? What does Eduardo mean when he describes the room as a room "for women"? What gender STEREO-TYPES are suggested? To what extent does the play seem to endorse his stereotyp-ical view? to criticize it? How are the ethnic and sexual stereotypes related?

8. Eduardo says his "God" is in the open, Alysea adds that Eduardo's God is beau-tiful, "free . . . green," and that Father Prado approves of that God. How is this a commentary on Josefa's room? on gender?

9. Describe how it was that Alysea came to live with Josefa.

10. Josefa has been described as an angel, and Alysea here compares her with Father Prado in her concern for the poor, yet Alysea has, at the end of scene 1, accused her of killing someone named David. There has been talk of gods and rooms for women and the open air. What kind of moral struggles and themes do you see beginning to form in this first act?

11. Who is Clara? What do we learn about her in the conversation between Josefa and Eduardo when they are alone? Has your opinion of Eduardo been changed by this conversation?

12. Josefa says to Eduardo that people out in the lake or among the pines see them-selves too well, cannot accept what they see, and "so monsters are created." Explain.

13. How would you play Eduardo in the tête-à-tête with Josefa? Is he flirting with her? trying to impress her? trying to seduce her? simply trying to get her approval of his courting Alysea? To what degree is the decision about how to play his scene here an interpretation of this character?

14. How would you play Josefa in her conversation with Eduardo? Is she defying him and his "male" ways as a feminist? Is she impressed with him despite herself? Is she trying to taunt him? tease him?

15. How does Josefa define what she means by "desire"? Describe her experience out in the lake on the night of the Festival of San Lorenzo.

16. In what way has Josefa given birth to "the children of light"?

17. When, in response to Doña Clara's questions in scene 3, Alysea admits that she loves Eduardo and he her, Doña Clara puts out a cigarette and says, "Well . . . That's that!" What does she mean by the remark?

18. When Alysea leaves them alone, Josefa says to Clara, "You must have started early." What does she mean?

19. What is Clara's view of love? Josefa's?

20. Who or what are Josefa's "magicians"?

21. What does she mean when she says the swallows, even though they are in flocks, are "lonely"?

ACT II

1. What does Doña Clara mean when she says that Josefa's magicians have no faces?

2. How does Don Esquinas "justify" his philandering?

3. What does Tomás say he saw the night of the previous San Lorenzo Festival?

4. David's eyes, Alysea says, told her that she and Josefa were "all the terror in the world"? What did he—or she—mean by this?

5. Describe Josefa's childhood experience with a bird. Why does she tell Alysea the story at this point?

6. Whom does Josefa address as her lover at the end of the act?

7. What action ends this act?

ACT III

1. What does Father Prado mean when he says the festival is "just ritual" to Josefa?

2. Why does Josefa confess to Father Prado? What does she confess?

3. What reason does Josefa give for her violence toward David?

4. Why does Father Prado ask Josefa to forgive him?

5. It was not faith that made her create beauty and do good, Josefa says, but "the light of my magicians." But at the end of the act, she asks forgiveness, "for . . . I have grievously sinned." Does this suggest that she has been reunited with her religious faith? What is meant by the stage directions that say what she says here is said "as if she does not believe it herself"? Does she or doesn't she?

FINAL SCENE

1. What does Josefa mean when she says that her magicians will let her come back as light? that they planned this day for her long before the people did?

2. What does Clemencia see on the lake?

3. Explain the implications of Clemencia's last words; of the final stage direction.

GENERAL QUESTIONS

1. Is this a feminist play?

2. Is this play "religious"? If so, does it support the Catholic religion? an ancient, "pagan," perhaps Native American religion? both? neither?

3. How do such IMAGES or SYMBOLS as the lake, the swallows, light, function in the play?

Leonard Begay

Leonard Begay, a member of the Navajo Nation, credits his writing inspiration to his grandparents Helen Bighouse and Helen A. Begay. He wrote the following essay while he was a student at Northern Arizona University, and later received his Bachelor of Science in American politics. He lives in Nazlini, Arizona.

BEYOND SACRED MOUNTAINS

In the beginning everything was dark. Mystic beings existed in the first underworld of the Navajo. The second world was red in which insects of many different beings existed. The third world was yellow in which many types of birds lived. In the fourth world the Navajos were transformed from insects, birds and mystic beings into the body form of their gods. It was here that First Man and First Woman were created and their daughter, Changing Woman, was born unto them. Changing Woman, a mother figure of the Navajo people, is a symbol of everlasting and eternal life. The newly created beings, Dine (The People), were expelled from the fourth world by a great flood due to incestuous behavior, stealing from one another and committing wrong doings which went against the values of the gods. Being forced into the fifth world, the gods set boundaries for the Navajo people which were marked with four sacred mountains. Sisnaajini, Blanca Peak in Colorado, was the sacred mountain of the east; Soodzil, Mount Taylor in New Mexico, was the sacred mountain of the south; Dook'o'oosliid, the San Francisco Peak in Arizona, was the sacred mountain of the west; and Dibentsaa, La Plata Mountain in Colorado, was the sacred mountain of the north. The Navajo people were instructed never to exist outside their sacred mountains and to live in harmony and balance with Mother Earth. Not doing so would result in the destruction of the present world of the Navajo.

Changing Woman bore a pair of twins, often referred to as the Hero Twins because of the many monsters (human-devouring creatures that roamed the fifth world) that they slew. The twins left Mother Earth and traveled on holy trails, made of rainbow, lightning, pollen and sunbeam, to visit their father the Sun. Upon arriving at the house of their father, the twins were put through many tests to test their endurance, commitment, faith and respect for their father, mother, religion and environment. Successfully completing their tests, the Sun asked them what they sought. The twins replied that they sought the assistance of their father, and the means with which they could destroy the monsters that were devouring their people. The Sun granted their wish and provided them with powerful arms, such as armor made of flint, lightning arrows, bows of rainbow, streaks of sunbeams and clubs made of rainbow. They descended back to earth and destroyed the creatures that were devouring their people. In this way the Hero Twins saved their people from the monsters. Navajos have taken these teachings to heart and today remain within their four sacred mountains.

In time the Navajo people flourished and spread about within their homeland, Dinetah. The Navajos made a tradition of adopting those aspects of foreign societies that was appealing and rejected those that did not appeal to them. An important example of this was when Navajos embraced the sheep and horse with the coming of the Spaniards, yet they really never accepted the Spaniards. The Navajos did not realize that the coming of the white man would change their way of life forever. Unlike the Spaniards, and later the Mexicans, the white man would impose a foreign form of education, economy, social and political structure upon them. All Navajos were affected to a certain degree, depending on their geographic location. Those who lived within a few miles from towns, forts and settlements were directly affected by this change. Families that lived in rugged localities such as Fluted Rock, Black Mountain and the Chuska Mountains carried on their traditional life-styles well into the mid-twentieth century. This meant that they still lived in octagonal-shaped wooden structures with dirt floors, called hogans. These families depended upon livestock raising, mainly sheep, for their survival. A majority of these remote families still spoke their native tongue. They were not literate and had no modern conveniences such as running water, heating, cooling and sewage systems. Roads inaccessible by buses or cars left many Navajo children uneducated. The rugged terrain kept a majority of Navajos virtually untouched by modern technology. This was the case with the King-saai (Bighouse) family who lived at Fluted Rock. Fluted Rock, named after the long vertical black lava rock formations that tower hundreds of feet above the ponderosa pine covered mountain, is located in northeastern Arizona on the Navajo reservation. Navajo families have lived around Fluted Rock, a sacred shrine, for generations. The families are all blood related in one way or another by clans, which are traced down through the mother. The Big-house family was one of these families who lived at Fluted Rock.

The year was 1968, January, and the snow drifts rose above hogans and corrals. Many sheep, horses and cattle perished during the early, unexpectedly harsh winter. Livestock had to be fed hay and corn that had been harvested the previous fall or that had been purchased at the trading post. Families in the Fluted Rock area were isolated from the outside world by blinding snow that had accumulated quickly into snow drifts. Nellie, a young Navajo woman of the Bighouse family, was nearing labor during the early morning hours with the hospital thirty miles away. Horses were saddled up much to the protest of great grandmother who argued that the baby could be delivered in the hogan by her. Nellie's mother Helen would not hear of it, so Nellie, her mother, and Uncle James headed out in two feet of snow for Sawmill.

Nellie's Aunt Grace lived in Sawmill, ten miles from their home. Grace had a truck that could transport them to the hospital in Fort Defiance. The way was difficult, especially for Nellie, whose labor pains seemed to be coming closer. When it seemed that they would never reach their destination, Sawmill appeared just a few miles at the base of the ridge. Smoke from houses down below was wafting toward the sky as they slowly rode down to the little settlement. They tethered their horses to the lightposts outside the house. Grace was shocked to see them when they entered the house. The family quickly started for the hospital, with roads barely visible and covered with ice. The family arrived at Fort Defiance within a few hours. Early the next morning the family was greeted by a healthy baby; their prayers had been answered. I came into the fifth world in this way.

I lived with my grandparents throughout my early childhood at Fluted Rock. I enjoyed the freedom and immense space I had. My immediate family consisted of my grandparents, aunt, uncle and myself. I had no playmates except the lambs, dogs, cats and horses. I had a carefree and happy childhood. I grew up herding sheep, riding horses, raising cattle and planting and harvesting corn, squash, melons, alfalfa and fruit trees. We moved according to the seasons. My favorite time of year was the spring. Everything seemed to be bursting with new life, especially at the sheep corral. There would be hundreds of clumsy little lambs struggling to get up and walk. The curly little goats would be jumping and kicking up their heels running around the corral. The little goats would prance around with their small heads held high and their pink noses proudly pointed upward. My grandparents would take turns throughout the night and walk to the sheep corral to see if any new lambs or goats were born. The early morning April frost would often claim the life of a lamb or goat.

In time my grandparents encouraged me to skin and butcher the little dead lambs and goats, so that I may learn how to butcher a sheep. At first I was scared and could not bring myself to cut the throat. I eventually got over my fear and became more serious about my learning. I tried so hard to prevent cutting the skin during the skinning process, but my efforts were rewarded with cuts that spotted the skin.

My grandmother would hold it up and laugh out loud. Spring was also a time for shearing the wool and mohair off the sheep and goats. Relatives and friends would come from miles around and shear our flock. It took about a month. Every morning I would wake to the laughter of family and to the smell of mutton stew, fry bread and coffee. Every day I would watch the mountains of wool grow larger and larger. They resembled big puffs of white clouds that drifted across the sky. I would usually give in to temptation and climb the mountains of wool. I would pretend that I was atop a big white cloud floating across the sky and imagine that I was floating over the earth. By month's end the wool would be sacked in huge gunny sacks and loaded onto pickup trucks. The wool was sold in Gallup and my grandparents would buy groceries, clothes, farming supplies and of course candy, which I would not let them forget.

As the days grew hot and dry our family would load the truck and begin to move to our summer mountain camp. We would travel with the sheep and horses through desert plateau and eventually ascend onto the mountaintop. We would spend the summer months grazing our sheep on lush green grass on the mountain sides and valleys. I loved to watch the ducks at Fluted Rock lake and play in the creek that ran through Oak Valley. I would hear my uncle listening to the radio at night. I would try and make out the strange sounds on the radio that seemed so rapid and loud. I would sit outside and count the stars on a clear night; to my surprise a star would wink at me. I would wonder if another little boy or girl somewhere on earth saw that very star. My parents would come out every two or three weeks with my sister Cathy, who was born a year after I was, and we would all go to Gallup. I enjoyed the time I spent with my family, but Fluted Rock was my home. My grandfather would often instruct me to herd the sheep to the lake during early morning, before the day grew too hot, to water the flock. I would tell them that I was going to take the sheep to Toniteel (The big water or ocean) to water them and then graze them at Toohonani (Across the ocean). My grandparents, aunt and uncle would laugh at me and tell me that the ocean was farther than Gallup. Ignoring their laughter, I would hold up my head and march off after the sheep telling myself that someday I would show them. I would go to see the ocean and the land on the other side.

Fall was a time of harvesting corn, squash, melons and alfalfa. This was the time to take the lambs and steers to the market in Gallup or the auction in Ganado. We would search the mountain valleys and springs for cattle. The cattle would be rounded up and herded into the corral that was made of large ponderosa pine laid one on top of the other. My uncles and father would rope and drag the reluctant steers into the truckbed. Lambs were easier to handle; they just had to be caught by the hind legs and put into the truck. By fall the lambs were big and fat; some even had little horns that stuck out like flints. I would run after the lambs and try to catch one. More than often I was dragged and run over. After the livestock was sold my grandparents would buy large quantities of groceries and feed for the livestock to sustain us through the winter months. Once they bought a brand new truck from Rico Motor Company in Gallup.

Winter usually came early to the mountains in Fluted Rock and there would be low-lying fog that blanketed the valleys. As the fog slowly lifted skyward it would leave behind thick frost that looked like tiny stars glittering in the early morning dew. The frost would soon vanish like the stars as the sun rose higher in the east. The days would grow shorter and colder. The sheep and goats began to look like round balls of cotton as their wool and mohair grew. I liked the goats better than I did the sheep because of their long silky hair. When the snows came and the watering holes froze over we would melt snow in big water barrels over open fire, to water our livestock. Winter was a time for learning. Grandpa and I would sit long into the night talking about legends, myths, prayers and songs. I was taught to sing ceremonial and social songs about myself, history and people, so that I may learn to walk in beauty throughout my life. Sometimes we would make up funny songs about cats, dogs and one another. This was the life cycle in which I lived during the early part of my childhood.

One afternoon in late fall, when the oak trees were exploding with vibrant colors, my parents and sister came to visit us. They lived over one hundred miles away from home in Tuba City, located on the western half of the Navajo reservation. My grandparents and parents talked for a long time in the house. My sister and I ran through the oaks and tumbled in the leaves of orange, gold, yellow and red. We ran home when we heard our mother calling us. I knew I was in for it when my grandmother told me to sit down. She said, "My child, you are a big boy now and the time has come for you to get an education." Tears blinded me, for I knew that I was leaving the only home I had known, and I could feel a painful swelling in my throat. My grandfather spoke to me and said that education was important in order for me to survive in the white man's world. I reluctantly got into the truck with my parents and headed for Tuba City. I was amazed at the sights I saw. I had never been beyond Black Mountain and I always thought that the ocean lay behind this great mountain. I was so used to my mountain home and immense flocks of sheep, that I assumed that all Navajos lived the way we did.

Tuba City was virtually a desert. We arrived in the evening; the sun was setting. My mother told me that I was going to school, beginning the next morning, where I would see many little kids just like me. All I could do was wait and wonder.

I soon found out that the many little kids were not just like me. They talked about things I was not familiar with. I spoke predominantly Navajo, while they spoke English. I was surprised that some did not even understand me, yet I was filled with wonder. In school I learned how to write, read and speak English. I learned to color. That became my favorite pastime. Once my teacher asked me to color a picture of a cow purple, but I refused to listen to her. I kept telling her that cows were not purple; eventually she gave in, and she let me color it brown. I was sure my teacher was crazy. I was thrilled when I learned to count and spell my name. I could count to twenty in Navajo, but now I could count in English. Time seemed to pass quickly, yet at times I would become depressed. I would think of the sheep, horses and my grandparents. I was often homesick, so we had to go home every two weeks. Upon my first visit home to Fluted Rock, I jumped out of the truck and ran for my grandparents. I clung to them. My dogs ran about and barked and the sheep bleated from the corral. It was good to be home again. Sunday came to be a dreaded day for me because that was when we left and headed on that long stretch of road for Tuba City. I once told my grandmother during one of my visits that Tuba City was the place of hell. The land was so dry and barren, there were little flocks of sheep, if any, and there was a strange race of people there that spoke a weird language. She laughed and said that I should be more positive and that the strange people were Hopis. Grandmother told me that Fluted Rock will always be here and that it would always be my home.

We soon moved closer to home in Chinle, which is about thirty miles   15
from Fluted Rock. It was during this time that I excelled and came to enjoy school. My vacations were spent at home with my grandparents. I missed the spring time when lambing season came around. I loved my summer vacations because this is when I spent time with my grandparents. I remember one time during the fall when my grandmother and I took a truck load of lambs to the market in Fort Defiance. The trader unloaded the lambs when we arrived at the trading post. I sat in the truck and watched through the window as the trader spoke to my grandmother. I noticed that my grandmother was shaking her head saying that she did not understand him. There was no interpreter around to translate, so I got out of the truck and walked over to my grandmother. The trader turned to me and asked me about my grandmother's name, social security number and address. I turned to my grandmother and translated her reply. We followed the trader inside the store and my grandmother was paid. The trader gave me some bubble gum and through a customer he told my grandmother that he was very proud of me. I chewed gum and blew bubbles on the way home. My grandmother told my family what I had done, and I felt extremely proud that I was in school. Through this experience I realized the importance of education.

We eventually moved back to Tuba City when my father transferred to   16
a higher paying job with the Bureau of Indian Affairs. High school was a time of growing and learning, physically, mentally and emotionally. I became interested in business and extracurricular activities, such as student government and FBLA. I had many friends that made high school enjoyable. By this time many of my friends had come to realize that I was different from them. They would tell me that I was calm and never seemed to stress out. I was never ashamed or embarrassed about my home, way of life and the way I grew up in Fluted Rock. My friends respected me for my honesty.

There were many things that I did not know when I reached high school.   17
Once after cross country practice my friends called me at home and asked if I wanted to "cruise." I said okay, but while I waited I wondered just what "cruise" meant. When my friends arrived we went cruising. I sat there and thought, "So this is cruising." It seemed to be a waste of time and gas to drive around for no particular reason. When my friends dropped me off, I stood at the gate with a smile on my face and said to myself "I went cruising." This was one story to tell my grandparents.

Whenever possible, I returned home to Fluted Rock during holidays, 18
vacations and some weekends. On my return trips home, my grandparents
would tell me traditional Navajo stories and relate this to my education. I
would listen attentively as they stressed the importance of education. Grandfather would tell me that anything worthwhile in life is not easy, and education was one of them. He would tell me that the Hero Twins came into
contact with many obstacles, such as hunger, poverty and hardships of many
kinds, which they overcame. They were rewarded with arms of many types
with which they destroyed the monsters.

"The Hero Twins," grandfather would say, "were young men just like 19
you who returned to Dinetah to help and save their people." Grandfather
would tell me that education was my coat of flint, sunbeam bow and arrow
of lightning, with which I could protect myself and my people. My grandparents would often tell me, "Navajos have many resources that the white
men desire and wish to behold. It is up to you, my grandson, to help and
educate our people in the ways of the white man."

Grandfather became sick during the late summer in 1984. The doctor 20
in Fort Defiance told grandfather that he had pneumonia. He had to stay
indoors to avoid exposure and to rest. Keeping grandfather inside was like
trying to cage water. We would find him outside chopping wood and sad-
dling the horse. Grandmother urged him to stay in bed so that he may recover,
which only upset grandfather. In a few weeks he was confined to a hospital
bed in Fort Defiance and spent about two weeks in the hospital. Grandfather
recovered quite well, yet I worried about him while I was in school. I could
imagine grandmother struggling alone and trying to contain grandfather at
the same time. Grandfather was sick throughout the fall. During Christmas
vacation I returned home to learn that his lungs had collapsed and he was
now on a respirator.

When my family and I visited grandfather at the hospital, I was shocked 21
to see his condition. He was once a tall and husky man, but now he was this
large frame covered with sagging skin. As I hugged grandfather I could hear
his heavy breathing. We talked with grandfather, but it was difficult to
understand him. We stayed until visiting hours were over. As we were leaving, grandfather motioned for me to stay. Grandfather took my hand in his,
like he always did many times before a serious talk, and looked at me with
his weak eyes. I had a feeling in my stomach that made me want to throw
up.

Grandfather said, "My grandchild, my baby, listen to me. I have grown 22
old and my time has come for me to depart from this world. My strength is
drained from me and this makes me very tired. I often have dreams of my
mother and father; they await me in the next world. As a medicine man who
specializes in the Blessing Way ceremony, I have always tried to live and
walk in beauty for my family, relatives and people. This path is not an easy
one to travel. I have tried to teach you all I know, but I have yet to teach you
many things. Do not weep for me my grandson, for the many people who

dislike our family will be happy to see you weep. I am a medicine man, and I will always be here for you. I will exist within the sacred mountains, I will be in the soft rains, I will be in the mist that covers the mountain valleys, and I will dwell in the house of the holy people. The holy ones will come for me soon, and I shall leave in a snow storm. Stay in school my grandson, and help your people like the Hero Twins have done and complete the cycle. With this I shall leave you; go my grandson, walk the path of the corn pollen and old age, walk in beauty, walk in everlasting beauty."

I clenched my jaw tight and shut my eyes and hugged my grandfather 23 for the last time. Four days later grandmother came to the house during the early morning hours and said that grandfather died in the night. I walked to the corral and did the best I could to hold back my tears. I could not believe that my grandfather had passed away. Just as grandfather had said, there was a snow storm. The family had a difficult time during the burial process. We all stood there in the snow with grey dark clouds racing overhead. We placed the last flower over grandfather's grave and departed. We returned home and tried to adjust to life without grandfather.

I completed my high school education in Tuba City. My senior year I 24 was elected president of my class. I remember that hot stuffy May evening in the gym. Three hundred graduating students crowded on the basketball court, along with hundreds of proud parents, families, friends and teachers. I sat up in the front row with mixed emotions of fear, anxiety and happiness. Being the student body president, I was to give a speech. I sat there wondering what I was going to say. As I heard my name called I rose and took off my cap and gown to expose my traditional Navajo outfit: a velvet shirt, turquoise and silver jewelry, moccasins and a Navajo blanket thrown over the shoulder, much to the shock of my graduating class and audience. I walked up to the podium and greeted, introduced and delivered my speech in the Navajo language. I proceeded to translate my speech into English. I was overwhelmed and touched when the crowd rose and applauded as I walked back to my seat. We received our diplomas and filed outside. On my way out, there at the door was my grandmother, standing like a hundred times before waiting to receive me upon my return home from school. Drawn by love and emotion I embraced her and cried. We had completed a part of the long and difficult trail of education together. I only wished that grandfather could have been there. I guess he was there in his own special way. Grandfather was in the laughter and happiness of the people in the gym that night.

I returned to Fluted Rock after graduation. I felt different as I stood 25 there looking at the weather-worn grey corrals and the earth-colored hogans that seemed to be a part of the earth. I felt as if I stood out with an unnatural color that wasn't part of the place where I grew up. Throughout the summer I herded sheep alone. I would saddle the horse and round up the cattle, which would take a couple of days. I had applied to Northern Arizona University and to the Navajo Tribe for a scholarship back in January. I wondered how college life was going to be. This was going to be another long and difficult trail. I did a lot of thinking about my life, such as who I am, where I came from and where I was going. It was mid-summer when my father drove up to the house. Grandmother stood outside shading her eyes from the sun with her small palm. My father got out of the truck and he shook our hands. He took a letter from his coat pocket and handed it to me. I took the letter and read it. I had been awarded a scholarship from the Navajo Tribe and I was accepted at NAU. Grandmother impatiently asked me what the letter said. She clapped her aged hands together and hugged me when I told her. Personally I really did not know how to respond because I could not comprehend the idea of going to a university.

In early August sheep dipping is an annual event, where people from miles around brought their flocks of sheep to be dipped in vaccine to rid them of lice. Once again many families and relatives came together. This was an exciting social event. Riding horseback grandmother and I set out for the event during the early morning hours before dawn with the family flock. We would arrive at the sheep dipping corrals at sunrise. Already people would be camped out by the corrals. These families lived a day's trip away, maybe ten miles. Families greeted one another with terms of endearment, such as my grandchild, mother, father and son. We were usually invited to eat. As we sat there people would compliment grandmother on the immense flock we had or they would admire the big healthy lambs. Grandmother would laugh modestly at the compliments that she received. As the sun rose higher the rest of the family would come in trucks, bringing with them pots, pans, firewood and food. While grandmother was butchering a sheep, my aunts would immediately start a fire and begin cooking. 26

Flocks of sheep would be driven into the adjacent corral as each flock was dipped. Big rams and goats would be dragged into the small square corral right before they would be thrown into the vaccine. The sheep would plunge into the vaccine as the people stood alongside them and pushed their heads under. Sheep dipping was an exciting and very colorful event. Through the dust and glazing August sun, one would be able to hear shouting and laughter, one would smell the sweet smell of cedar smoke rising from family fires, boiling coffee, and roasting mutton, and see the colorful attire of the elderly men and women in shining silver and turquoise jewelry. After each flock was dipped, the owners would drive their bleating and dripping animals homeward. 27

School was drawing closer and closer. I began to feel scared and anxious at the same time. The week before school I saddled up the horse and went riding. I rode down through Oak Valley across the stream and up to Fluted Rock lake. As I approached Fluted Rock lake the ducks flapped their wings across the silver surface and flew skyward, quacking as they went. I rode through the green meadows above the lake and eventually ended up at Fluted Rock. The horse was breathing heavily and was white with sweat as we climbed the black lava rocks to the top of Fluted Rock. When we reached the top I could see rolling ponderosa pines for miles around in all directions. 28

Lukachukai, Black Rock, Canyon de Chelly and Fuzzy Mountain were all in view. It was from here that I prayed for my family and the new life that I was about to take on. I prayed and meditated; as evening approached I mounted my horse and rode homeward. I felt cleansed, calm and at peace with myself and the environment.

Arriving at NAU was confusing. Registration, moving into my hall, and adjusting to the environment was stressful. I forced myself to approach students and try to start a conversation in hopes of finding a friend. I became involved with the Native Americans United organization here on campus. It was very helpful. I found many students whom I could relate to. My first semester went surprisingly well, but during my second semester I did not do as well. I have noticed that people at NAU are very time oriented; they are not in touch with nature and do not understand it. Back home our clock was the sun. We rose with the sun and lay down to sleep when darkness came. 29

In the years I have spent here at NAU I have gained much knowledge about myself and the dominant society. I have been challenged and questioned about my belief and religion. At times I felt defensive. I have come to realize this is just one of many tests that I will encounter by being an individual and being one of my people, Dine. I am still gradually adjusting to college life and at times I do not understand it. Upon my return trips home, I realize that I look at my grandmother, uncle, parents and aunt through different eyes. They have noticed that education has taken up most of my time. I do not go home as often as I used to and when I do go home I spend it doing homework. I rarely have time to sit down and talk to my grandmother about traditional Navajo teachings and culture any more. 30

I realize that I am a singular functioning part of a whole in my family, environment and religion. My foundation is made up of my belief in my religion, my culture, which my grandparents are a part of, and the environment in which I grew up. Education is presently playing an active role in my life and it will determine my future. I realize the long and difficult road of education will take me far. I will encounter new horizons and walk among unknown people, with the knowledge and teachings that I received from my grandparents, but I shall walk with confidence and dignity. I am still the child of First Man, First Woman; and Changing Woman and the Hero Twins are my protectors. My dreams are that of my people of adopting those favorable aspects of foreign societies and returning to my homeland to help my people. Like the Hero Twins, I will leave my homeland and travel on paths of pollen, rainbow, sunbeam and lightning to reach my dreams and visions. In beauty I shall travel beyond Sacred Mountains. 31

STUDY QUESTIONS

1. The narrative begins as an account of Navajo history and belief and then, in paragraph 4, becomes a personal history of the author and his family. What are the advantages of organizing the narrative in this way? In what specific ways does

Leonard Begay's personal story draw on traditional Navajo narratives? Are there disadvantages to this organization?

2. What does the title mean? Explain its significance to the end of the narrative.

3. In what ways does the story of creation and early history here resemble the stories told of origins in other religions? How might such similarities be accounted for? In what ways is the Navajo story unique? How do you interpret the story of the Hero Twins?

4. Near the end of the narrative Begay describes himself as having taken on "an unnatural color." What does his sense of being "unnatural" mean to him at this point in his narrative? by the end of his account of himself? How does the use of color imagery here relate to the story of creation in paragraph 1? How does the story of the Hero Twins relate to Begay's own experience and aspirations?

5. What is a "hogan"? What is the significance of its dirt floor? How is the importance of the hogan as a symbol emphasized near the end of the narrative?

6. What are the most important events so far in Begay's life? Why is education so important to his grandparents? to Begay himself? What specific conflicts does Begay feel as a result of his education?

7. What are the various signs of pride in his heritage in Begay's account of himself? In what way have the attitudes changed as he has grown older?

8. How significant are the place names in the area near Begay's birthplace? What different histories are suggested by the names "Sawmill, "Fort Defiance," and "Fluted Rock"?

Garrison Keillor

B orn in Anoka, Minnesota, in 1942, Garrison Keillor, largely through his weekly radio program, "The Prairie Home Companion," made Lake Wobegon the heart of America's heartland, located not far from the funny bone. This excerpt from *Protestant* was originally published in *Lake Wobegon Days* (1985), Keillor's bestseller. He is currently the host of "The Prairie Home Companion." Keillor received a gold medal for spoken English from the American Academy of Arts and Letters. His latest novel, *WLT: A Radio Romance*, was published in 1991.

PROTESTANT

Our family was dirt poor, which I figured out as a child from the fact we had   1
such a bad vacuum. When you vacuumed the living room, it would groan
and stop and you had to sit and wait for it to groan and start up, then vacuum
like mad before it quit again, but it didn't have good suction either. You had
to stuff the hairballs into it. I also knew it because Donald Hoglund told me.
He asked me how much my dad earned, and I said a thousand dollars, the
most money I could imagine, and he shrieked, "You're poor! You're poor!"
So we were. And, in a town where everyone was either Lutheran or Catholic, we were neither one. We were Sanctified Brethren, a sect so tiny that
nobody but us and God knew about it, so when kids asked what I was, I just
said Protestant. It was too much to explain, like having six toes. You would
rather keep your shoes on.

Grandpa Cotten was once tempted toward Lutheranism by a preacher   2
who gave a rousing sermon on grace that Grandpa heard as a young man
while taking Aunt Esther's dog home who had chased a Model T across
town. He sat down on the church steps and listened to the voice boom out
the open windows until he made up his mind to go in and unite with the
truth, but he took one look from the vestibule and left. "He was dressed up
like the pope of Rome," said Grandpa, "and the altar and the paintings and
the gold candlesticks—my gosh, it was just a big show. And he was reading
the whole darn thing off a page, like an actor."

Jesus said, "Where two or three are gathered together in my name, there   3
am I in the midst of them," and the Brethren believed that was enough. We
met in Uncle Al's and Aunt Flo's bare living room with plain folding chairs
arranged facing in toward the middle. No clergyman in a black smock. No
organ or piano, for that would make one person too prominent. No uphol-
stery, it would lead to complacency. No picture of Jesus, He was in our
hearts. The faithful sat down at the appointed hour and waited for the Spirit
to move one of them to speak or to pray or to give out a hymn from our Little
Flock hymnal. No musical notation, for music must come from the heart and
not off a page. We sang the texts to a tune that fit the meter, of the many
tunes we all knew. The idea of reading a prayer was sacrilege to us—"If a
man can't remember what he wants to say to God, let him sit down and
think a little harder," Grandpa said.

"There's the Lord's Prayer," said Aunt Esther meekly. We were sitting   4
on the porch after Sunday dinner. Esther and Harvey were visiting from
Minneapolis and had attended Lake Wobegon Lutheran, she having turned
Lutheran when she married him, a subject that was never brought up in our
family.

"You call that prayer? Sitting and reciting like a bunch of schoolchil-   5
dren?"

Harvey cleared his throat and turned to me with a weak smile. "Speaking of school, how are you doing?" he asked.

There was a lovely silence in the Brethren assembled on Sunday morning as we waited for the Spirit. Either the Spirit was moving someone to speak who was taking his sweet time or else the Spirit was playing a wonderful joke on us and letting us sit, or perhaps silence was the point of it. We sat listening to rain on the roof, distant traffic, a radio playing from across the street, kids whizzing by on bikes, dogs barking, as we waited for the Spirit to inspire us. It was like sitting on the porch with your family, when nobody feels that they have to make talk. So quiet in church. Minutes drifted by in silence that was sweet to us. The old Regulator clock ticked, the rain stopped and the room changed light as the sun broke through—shafts of brilliant sun through the windows and motes of dust falling through it—the smell of clean clothes and floor wax and wine and the fresh bread of Aunt Flo which was Christ's body given for us. Jesus in our midst, who loved us. So peaceful, and we loved each other too. I thought perhaps the Spirit was leading me to say that, but I was just a boy, and children were supposed to keep still. And my affections were not pure. They were tainted with a sneaking admiration of Catholics—Catholic Christmas, Easter, the Living Rosary, and the Blessing of the Animals, all magnificent. Everything we did was plain, but they were regal and gorgeous—especially the Feast Day of St. Francis, which they did right out in the open, a feast for the eyes. Cows, horses, some pigs, right on the church lawn. The turmoil, animals bellowing and barking and clucking and cats scheming how to escape and suddenly leaping out of the girl's arms who was holding on tight, the cat dashing through the crowd, dogs straining at the leash, and the ocarina band of third-graders playing Catholic dirges, and the great calm of the sisters, and the flags, and the Knights of Columbus decked out in their handsome black suits—I stared at it until my eyes almost fell out, and then I wished it would go on much longer.

"Christians," my uncle Al used to say, "do not go in for show," referring to the Catholics. We were sanctified by the blood of the Lord, therefore we were saints, like St. Francis, but we didn't go in for feasts or ceremonies, involving animals or not. We went in for sitting, all nineteen of us, in Uncle Al's and Aunt Flo's living room on Sunday morning and having a plain meeting and singing hymns in our poor thin voices while not far away the Catholics were whopping it up. I wasn't allowed inside Our Lady, of course, but if the Blessing of the Animals on the Feast Day of St. Francis was any indication, Lord, I didn't know but what they had elephants in there and acrobats. I sat in our little group and envied them for the splendor and gorgeousness, as we tried to sing without even a harmonica to give us the pitch. Hymns, Uncle Al said, didn't have to be sung perfect, because God looks on the heart, and if you are In The Spirit, then all praise is good.

The Brethren, also known as the Saints Gathered in the Name of Christ Jesus, who met in the living room were all related to each other and raised in the Faith from infancy except Brother Mel who was rescued from a life of drunkenness, saved as a brand from the burning, a drowning sailor, a sheep on the hillside, whose immense red nose testified to his previous condition. I envied his amazing story of how he came to be with us. Born to godly parents, Mel left home at fifteen and joined the Navy. He sailed to distant lands in a submarine and had exciting experiences while traveling the downward path, which led him finally to the Union Gospel Mission in Minneapolis where he heard God's voice "as clear as my voice speaking to you." He was twenty-six, he slept under bridges and in abandoned buildings, he drank two quarts of white muscatel every day, and then God told him that he must be born again, and so he was, and became the new Mel, except for his nose.

Except for his nose, Mel Burgess looked like any forty-year-old Brethren 10 man: sober, preferring dark suits, soft-spoken, tending toward girth. His nose was what made you look twice: battered, swollen, very red with tiny purplish lines, it looked ancient and very dead on his otherwise fairly handsome face, the souvenir of what he had been saved from, the "Before" of his "Before . . . and After" advertisement for being born again.

For me, there was nothing before. I was born among the born-again. 11 This living room so hushed, the Brethren in their customary places on folding chairs (the comfortable ones were put away on Sunday morning) around the end-table draped with a white cloth and the glass of wine and loaf of bread (unsliced) was as familiar to me as my mother and father, the founders of my life. I had always been here.

Our family sat in one row against the picture window. Al and Florence 12 and their three, Janet and Paul and Johnny, sat opposite us, I saw the sky and the maple tree reflected in my uncle's glasses. To our left, Great-Aunt Mary sat next to Aunt Becky and Uncle Louie, and to our right were Grandma and Grandpa and Aunt Faith, and behind them was Mel, sitting on the piano bench. His wife, Rita, was a Lutheran. She only came occasionally and when she did, she stood out like a brass band. She used lipstick and had plucked eyebrows and wore bright hats. Brethren women showed only a faint smudge of powder on their cheeks and their hats were small and either black or navy blue. Once Rita spoke up in the meeting—Al had stood up to read from the Lord's Word, and she said, "Pardon me, which chapter did you say?"—and we all shuddered as if she had dropped a plate on the floor: *women did not speak in meeting.* Another time, Sunday morning, she made as if to partake of the bread as it was passed, and Grandpa snatched it away from her. It had to be explained to Rita later that she could not join in the Lord's Supper with us because she was not in fellowship.

We were "exclusive" Brethren, a branch that believed in keeping itself 13 pure of false doctrine by avoiding association with the impure. Some Brethren assemblies, mostly in larger cities, were not so strict and broke bread with strangers—we referred to them as "the so-called Open Brethren," the "so-called" implying the shakiness of their position—whereas we made sure that any who fellowshiped with us were straight on all the details of the Faith, as set forth by the first Brethren who left the Anglican Church in 1865 to worship on the basis of correct principles. In the same year, they posed for a photograph: twenty-one bearded gentlemen in black frock coats, twelve sitting on a stone wall, nine standing behind, gazing solemnly into a sunny day in Plymouth, England, united in their opposition to the pomp and corruption of the Christian aristocracy.

Unfortunately, once free of the worldly Anglicans, these firebrands were not content to worship in peace but turned their guns on each other. Scholarly to the core and perfect literalists every one, they set to arguing over points that, to any outsider, would have seemed very minor indeed but which to them were crucial to the Faith, including the question: if Believer *A* is associated with Believer *B* who has somehow associated himself with *C* who holds a False Doctrine, must *D* break off association with *A*, even though *A* does not hold the Doctrine, to avoid the taint? 14

The correct answer is: Yes. Some Brethren, however, felt that *D* should only speak with *A* and urge him to break off with *B*. The Brethren who felt otherwise promptly broke off with them. This was the Bedford Question, one of several controversies that, inside of two years, split the Brethren into three branches. 15

Once having tasted the pleasure of being Correct and defending True Doctrine, they kept right on and broke up at every opportunity, until, by the time I came along, there were dozens of tiny Brethren groups, none of which were speaking to any of the others. 16

Our Lake Wobegon bunch was part of a Sanctified Brethren branch known as the Cox Brethren, which was one of a number of "exclusive" Brethren branches—that is, to *non*-Coxians, we were known as "Cox Brethren"; to ourselves, we were simply *The* Brethren, the last remnant of the true Church. Our name came from Brother Cox in South Dakota who was kicked out of the Johnson Brethren in 1932—for preaching the truth! So naturally my grandpa and most of our family went with Mr. Cox and formed the new fellowship. 17

The split with the Johnsons was triggered by Mr. Johnson's belief that what was abominable to God in the Old Testament must be abominable still, which he put forward at the Grace & Truth Bible Conference in Rapid City in 1932. Mr. Cox stood up and walked out, followed by others. The abomination doctrine not only went against the New Covenant of Grace principle, it opened up rich new areas of controversy in the vast annals of Jewish law. Should Brethren then refrain from pork, meat that God had labeled "Unclean"? Were we to be thrown into the maze of commandments laid out in Leviticus and Deuteronomy, where we are told to smite our enemies with the sword and stone to death rebellious children? 18

Mr. Johnson's sermon was against women's slacks, and he had quoted Deuteronomy 22:5, "The woman shall not wear that which pertaineth unto a man, neither shall a man put on a woman's garment: for all that do so are abomination unto the Lord thy God," but Mr. Cox, though he was hardly pro-slacks, felt Mr. Johnson failed to emphasize grace as having superseded 19 the law, and when Mr. Johnson said, "An abomination to God under the law is still an abomination to God under grace," Mr. Cox smelled the burning rubber of Error and stood up and marched. He and the other walkouts proceeded to a grove of trees and prayed for Mr. Johnson's soul, and Mr. Johnson and those seated inside did the same for them. The split was never repaired, though as a result of being thought in favor of slacks, the Cox Brethren became death on the subject. My mother never wore slacks, though she did dress my sister in winter leggings, which troubled Grandpa. "It's not the leggings so much as what they represent and what they could lead to," he told her. He thought that baby boys should not wear sleepers unless they were the kind with snaps up the legs. Mother pointed out that the infant Jesus was wrapped in swaddling clothes. "That doesn't mean he wore a dress," Grandpa said. "They probably wrapped his legs separately."[1]

Intense scholarship was the heart of the problem. We had no ordained clergy, believing in the priesthood of all believers, and all were exhorted to devote themselves to Bible study. Some did, Brother Louie and Brother Mel in particular. In Wednesday-night Bible reading, they carried the ball, and some nights you could see that the Coxes of Lake Wobegon might soon divide into the Louies and Mels.   20

One summer night, they set to over the issue of speaking in tongues, Louie arguing that the manifestation of the Spirit was to be sought earnestly, Mel holding that it was a miraculous gift given to the early Church but not given by God today. I forget the Scripture verses each of them brought forward to defend his position, but I remember the pale faces, the throat-clearing, the anguished looks, as those two voices went back and forth, straining at the bit, giving no ground—the poisoned courtesy ("I think my brother is overlooking Paul's very *clear* message to the Corinthians . . . ," "Perhaps my brother needs to take a closer look, a *prayerful* look, at this verse in Hebrews . . .") as the sun went down, neighbor children were called indoors, the neighbors turned out their lights, eleven o'clock came—they wouldn't stop!   21

"Perhaps," Grandpa offered, "it would be meet for us to pray for the Spirit to lead us," hoping to adjourn, but both Louie and Mel felt that the Spirit *had* led, that the Spirit had written the truth in big black letters—if only some people could see it.   22

The thought of Uncle Louie speaking in tongues was fascinating to me. Uncle Louie worked at the bank, he spoke to me mostly about thrift and hard work. What tongue would he speak? Spanish? French? Or would it   23

1. Brethren history is confusing, even to those of us who heard a lot on the subject at a young age—the Dennis Brethren, for example: I have no idea whether they left us or we left them. Ditto the Reformed Sanctified, and the Bird Brethren, though I think that Sabbath observance was involved in our (i.e., the *Beale* Brethren, what we were called before 1932 when we Coxes left the Johnson wing) dispute with the Birds, who tended to be lax about such things as listening to the radio on Sunday and who went in for hot baths to an extent the Beales considered sensual. The Beale, or Cold Water, Brethren felt that the body was a shell or a husk that the spirit rode around in and that it needed to be kept in line with cold baths. But by the time I came along, we listened to the radio on Sunday and ran the bath hot, and yet we never went back and patched things up with the Birds. Patching up was not a Brethren talent. As my grandpa once said of the Johnson Brethren, "Anytime they want to come to us and admit their mistake, we're perfectly happy to sit and listen to them and then come to a decision about accepting them back." [Author's note]

sound like gibberish? Louie said that speaking in tongues was the true sign, that those who believed *heard* and to those who didn't it was only gabble—what if he stood up and said, "Feemalator, jasperator, hoo ha ha, Wamala-magamanama, zis boom bah!" and everyone else said, "Amen! That's right, brother! Praise God!" and *I was the only one who said, "Huh?"*

Bible reading finally ended when Flo went up to bed. We heard her 24
crying in the bathroom. Al went up to comfort her. Grandpa took Louie aside in the kitchen. Mel went straight home. We all felt shaky.

It was soon after the tongues controversy that the Lake Wobegon Breth- 25
ren folded their tent and merged into another Cox Assembly in St. Cloud, thirty-two miles away. Twenty-eight Brethren worshiped there, in a large bare rented room on the second floor of the bus depot. We had often gone there for special meetings, revivals, and now we made the long drive every Sunday and every Wednesday night. Grandpa fought for this. "It is right for Brethren to join together," he said. Louie agreed. Mel didn't. He felt God had put us in Lake Wobegon to be a witness. But finally he gave in. "Think of the children," Grandpa said. One fear of Grandpa's was that we children would grow up and marry outside the Faith if only because we knew nobody in the Faith except for relatives. Faced with the lonely alternative, we'd marry a Lutheran, and then, dazzled by the splendid music and vestments and stained glass, we'd forsake the truth for that carnival down the street. Grandpa knew us pretty well. He could see us perk up on Sunday morning when the Lutheran organ pealed out at ten-thirty. The contrast between the church of Aunt Flo's living room and the power and glory of Lutheranism was not lost on him. Among other Brethren boys and girls, nature would take its course, and in due time, we'd find someone and make a Brethren family. Grandpa was looking to the future.

The shift to St. Cloud changed things, all right, and not all for the 26
better.

My mother hated the move from the start. She had no Scripture to 27
quote, only a feeling that we had taken a step away from the family, from ourselves. We had walked to Flo's house, we had sat in Sunday school class in her kitchen and celebrated the Lord's death in the living room. The bread we broke was bread Flo baked, and she also made the wine, in a pickle crock in the basement. Flo's two cats, Ralph and Pumpkin, walked in and out of the service, and along toward the end, having confessed our unworthiness and accepted our redemption by Christ, the smell of Flo's pot roast, baking at low heat, arose to greet us. Before it was Flo's and Al's, the house had been Grandpa's and Grandma's—Mother had known this room since she was tiny, and though she bowed to Grandpa's wishes, she felt in her heart that she was leaving home. Sunday in St. Cloud meant a long drive, and Mother was a nervous rider who saw death at every turn. She arrived at the St. Cloud Assembly in a frazzled state. The second-floor room was huge and bare and held no associations for her. The long silences were often broken

by the roar of bus engines and rumble of bus announcements downstairs. Waiting for the Spirit to guide us to a hymn, a prayer, a passage from Scripture, we heard, *"Now boarding at Gate One . . . Greyhound Bus service to Waite Park . . . St. Joseph . . . Collegeville . . . Avon . . . Albany . . . Freeport . . . Melrose . . . and Sauk Center. All aboard, please!"*

Whenever a special Bible study meeting was scheduled for Sunday afternoon at three, we couldn't drive home after morning meeting, have dinner, and get back to St. Cloud in time, so one Sunday our family traipsed over to a restaurant that a friend of Dad's had recommended, Phil's House of Good Food. The waitress pushed two tables together and we sat down and studied the menus. My mother blanched at the prices. A chicken dinner went for $2.50, the roast beef for $2.75. "It's a nice place," Dad said, multiplying the five of us times $2.50. "I'm not so hungry, I guess," he said, "maybe I'll just have soup." We weren't restaurantgoers—"Why pay good money for food you could make better at home?" was Mother's philosophy—so we weren't at all sure about restaurant custom: could, for example, a person who had been seated in a restaurant simply get up and walk out? Would it be proper? Would it be *legal?* 28

The waitress came and stood by Dad. "Can I get you something from the bar?" she said. Dad blushed a deep red. The question seemed to imply that he looked like a drinker. "No," he whispered, as if she had offered to take off her clothes and dance on the table. Then another waitress brought a tray of glasses to a table of four couples next to us. "Martini," she said, setting the drinks down, "whiskey sour, whiskey sour, Manhattan, whiskey sour, gin and tonic, martini, whiskey sour." 29

"Ma'am? Something from the bar?" Mother looked at her in disbelief. 30

Suddenly the room changed for us. Our waitress looked hardened, rough, cheap—across the room, a woman laughed obscenely, "Haw, haw, haw"—the man with her lit a cigarette and blew a cloud of smoke—a swear word drifted out from the kitchen like a whiff of urine—even the soft lighting seemed suggestive, diabolical. To be seen in such a place on the Lord's Day— *what had we done?* 31

My mother rose from her chair. "We can't stay. I'm sorry," Dad told the waitress. We all got up and put on our coats. Everyone in the restaurant had a good long look at us. A bald little man in a filthy white shirt emerged from the kitchen, wiping his hands. "Folks? Something wrong?" he said. "We're in the wrong place," Mother told him. Mother always told the truth, or something close to it. 32

"This is *humiliating,*" I said out on the sidewalk. "I feel like a *leper* or something. Why do we always have to make such a big production out of everything? Why can't we be like regular people?" 33

She put her hand on my shoulder. "Be not conformed to this world," she said. I knew the rest by heart: ". . . but be ye transformed by the renewing of your mind, that ye may prove what is that good and acceptable and perfect will of God." 34

"Where we gonna eat?" Phyllis asked. "We'll find someplace reasonable," said Mother, and we walked six blocks across the river and found a lunch counter and ate sloppy joes (called Maid-Rites) for fifteen cents apiece. They did not agree with us, and we were aware of them all afternoon through prayer meeting and Young People's.

The Cox Brethren of St. Cloud held to the same doctrines as we did but they were not so exclusive, more trusting of the world—for example, several families owned television sets. They kept them in their living rooms, out in the open, and on Sunday, after meeting and before dinner, the dad might say, "Well, I wonder what's on," knowing perfectly well what was on, and turn it on—a Green Bay Packers game—and watch it. On Sunday.

I ate a few Sunday dinners at their houses, and the first time I saw a television set in a Brethren house, I was dumbfounded. None of the Wobegonian Brethren had one; we were told that watching television was the same as going to the movies—*no*, in other words. I wondered why the St. Cloud people were unaware of the danger. You start getting entangled in the things of the world, and one thing leads to another. First it's television, then it's worldly books, and the next thing you know, God's people are sitting around drinking whiskey sours in dim smoky bars with waitresses in skimpy black outfits and their bosoms displayed like grapefruit.[2]

That was not my view but my parents'. "Beer is the drunkard's kindergarten," said Dad. Small things led to bigger ones. One road leads up, the other down. A man cannot serve two masters. Dancing was out, even the Virginia reel: it led to carnal desires. Card-playing was out, which led to gambling, though we did have Rook and Flinch—why those and not pinochle? "Because. They're different." No novels, which tended to glamorize iniquity. "How do you know if you don't read them?" I asked, but they *knew*. "You only have to touch a stove once to know it's hot," Mother said. (Which novel had she read? She wasn't saying.) Rock 'n' roll, jazz, swing, dance music, nightclub singing: all worldly. "How about Beethoven?" I asked, having heard something of his in school. "That depends," she said. "Was he a Christian?" I wasn't sure. I doubted he was.

On the long Sunday-night drive home, leaning forward from the back seat, I pressed them on inconsistencies like a little prosecutor: if dancing leads to carnal desire, how about holding hands? Is it wrong to put your arm around a girl? People gamble on football: is football wrong? Can you say "darn"? What if your teacher told you to read a novel? Or a short story?

35

36

37

38

39

2. Clarence Bunsen: "Most Brethren I knew were death on card-playing, beer-drinking, and frowned on hand-holding, and of course they wouldn't go near a dance. They thought it brought out carnal desires. Well, maybe theirs lay closer to the surface, I don't know. Some were not only opposed to dancing but also felt that marching in formation was wrong, so we called them the Left-Footed Brethren. Some others were more liberal, Mr. Bell for example, he thought cards were okay so long as you didn't play with a full deck. The Bijou used to show good movies but the Brethren and some Lutherans ganged up on Art and made him stop, so now you have to drive to St. Cloud if you want to see unmarried people together in one room with the door closed. It's a shame. I think if the church put in half the time on covetousness that it does on lust, this would be a better world for all of us." [Author's note]

What if you were hitchhiking in a blizzard and were picked up by a guy who was listening to rock 'n' roll on the radio, should you get out of the car even though you would freeze to death? "I guess the smart thing would be to dress warmly in the first place," offered Dad. "And wait until a Ford comes along." All Brethren drove Fords.

STUDY QUESTIONS

1. How does Keillor turn the cliché "dirt poor" (paragraph 1) into a source of humor?

2. Among Keillor's other devices for achieving his tone of gentle humor and everyday flat-as-a-prairie realism are his analogies—as when he suggests that he identified himself as a Protestant chiefly because belonging to the Sanctified Brethren "was too much to explain, like having six toes. You would rather keep your shoes on" (paragraph 1). Another device is his use of "irrelevant" but realistic detail: "Grandpa Cotten was once tempted toward Lutheranism by a preacher who gave a rousing sermon on grace that Grandpa heard as a young man while taking Aunt Esther's dog home who had chased a Model T across town" (paragraph 2). (What does Aunt Esther's dog have to do with Lutheranism, religion, or anything Keillor is talking about?) Find several instances of these devices. What other devices does Keillor use to create humor or a sense of everyday reality?

3. Religion is a difficult and delicate subject, especially when the tone is somewhat humorous. Do you find anything in this selection blasphemous? offensive? Does the selection seem antifundamentalist? anti-Lutheran? anti-Catholic? anti-Christian? If you were one of the Brethren, how would you feel about this selection? Do you get any sense of what Keillor's own present religious position might be? Do you read this selection as fact or fiction (or fact slightly fictionalized)? What evidence is there for your decision? Does the factuality or fictionality of this (or any other selection) make a difference in how you read it, how you respond to it? Explain.

4. What seems to be Keillor's attitude toward the people in his family? Which relatives might have some reason to resent their portrait or Keillor's attitude toward them?

Martin Luther King, Jr.

Born in Atlanta, the son and grandson of ministers, Martin Luther King, Jr., attended Morehouse College, Crozier Theological Seminary, and Boston University, from which he received the doctorate. Eventually he became minister of the same congregation, Ebenezer Baptist Church in Atlanta, led by his father and founded by his maternal grandfather. His leadership of the Civil Rights movement through his position with the Southern Christian Leadership Conference is legendary. He died a martyr in 1968, the victim of an assassin's bullet in Memphis.

I HAVE A DREAM

I am happy to join with you today in what will go down in history as the greatest demonstration for freedom in the history of our nation.

Five score years ago, a great American, in whose symbolic shadow we stand today, signed the Emancipation Proclamation. This momentous decree came as a great beacon light of hope to millions of Negro slaves who had been seared in the flames of withering injustice. It came as a joyous daybreak to end the long night of their captivity.

But one hundred years later, the Negro still is not free; one hundred years later, the life of the Negro is still sadly crippled by the manacles of segregation and the chains of discrimination; one hundred years later, the Negro lives on a lonely island of poverty in the midst of a vast ocean of material prosperity; one hundred years later, the Negro is still languished in the corners of American society and finds himself in exile in his own land.

So we've come here today to dramatize a shameful condition. In a sense we've come to our nation's capital to cash a check. When the architects of our republic wrote the magnificent words of the Constitution and the Declaration of Independence, they were signing a promissory note to which every American was to fall heir. This note was the promise that all men, yes, black men as well as white men, would be guaranteed the unalienable rights of life, liberty, and the pursuit of happiness.

It is obvious today that America has defaulted on this promissory note in so far as her citizens of color are concerned. Instead of honoring this sacred obligation, America has given the Negro people a bad check; a check which has come back marked "insufficient funds." But we refuse to believe that the bank of justice is bankrupt. We refuse to believe that there are insufficient funds in the great vaults of opportunity of this nation. And so we've come to cash this check, a check that will give us upon demand the riches of freedom and the security of justice.

We have also come to this hallowed spot to remind America of the fierce urgency of now. This is no time to engage in the luxury of cooling off or to take the tranquilizing drug of gradualism. Now is the time to make real the promises of democracy; now is the time to rise from the dark and desolate valley of segregation to the sunlit path of racial justice; now is the time to lift our nation from the quicksands of racial injustice to the solid rock of brotherhood; now is the time to make justice a reality for all of God's children. It would be fatal for the nation to overlook the urgency of the moment. This sweltering summer of the Negro's legitimate discontent will not pass until there is an invigorating autumn of freedom and equality.

Nineteen sixty-three is not an end, but a beginning. And those who hope that the Negro needed to blow off steam and will now be content, will have a rude awakening if the nation returns to business as usual. There will be neither rest nor tranquility in America until the Negro is granted his citizenship rights. The whirlwinds of revolt will continue to shake the foundations of our nation until the bright day of justice emerges. 7

But there is something that I must say to my people, who stand on the worn threshold which leads into the palace of justice. In the process of gaining our rightful place, we must not be guilty of wrongful deeds. Let us not seek to satisfy our thirst for freedom by drinking from the cup of bitterness and hatred. We must forever conduct our struggle on the high plain of dignity and discipline. We must not allow our creative protests to degenerate into physical violence. Again and again we must rise to the majestic heights of meeting physical force with soul force. The marvelous new militancy, which has engulfed the Negro community, must not lead us to a distrust of all white people. For many of our white brothers, as evidenced by their presence here today, have come to realize that their destiny is tied up with our destiny. And they have come to realize that their freedom is inextricably bound to our freedom. We cannot walk alone. And as we walk, we must make the pledge that we shall always march ahead. We cannot turn back. 8

There are those who are asking the devotees of Civil Rights, "When will you be satisfied?" We can never be satisfied as long as the Negro is the victim of the unspeakable horrors of police brutality; we can never be satisfied as long as our bodies, heavy with the fatigue of travel, cannot gain lodging in the motels of the highways and the hotels of the cities; we cannot be satisfied as long as the Negro's basic mobility is from a smaller ghetto to a larger one; we can never be satisfied as long as our children are stripped of their selfhood and robbed of their dignity by signs stating "For White Only"; we cannot be satisfied as long as the Negro in Mississippi cannot vote and a Negro in New York believes he has nothing for which to vote. No! No, we are not satisfied, and we will not be satisfied until "justice rolls down like waters and righteousness like a mighty stream." 9

I am not unmindful that some of you have come here out of great trials and tribulations. Some of you have come fresh from narrow jail cells. Some of you have come from areas where your quest for freedom left you battered by the storms of persecution and staggered by the winds of police brutality. You have been the veterans of creative suffering. Continue to work with the faith that unearned suffering is redemptive. Go back to Mississippi. Go back to Alabama. Go back to South Carolina. Go back to Georgia. Go back to Louisiana. Go back to the slums and ghettos of our Northern cities, knowing that somehow this situation can and will be changed. Let us not wallow in the valley of despair. 10

I say to you today, my friends, so even though we face the difficulties 11 of today and tomorrow, I still have a dream. It is a dream deeply rooted in the American dream. I have a dream that one day this nation will rise up and live out the true meaning of its creed, "We hold these truths to be self-evident, that all men are created equal." I have a dream that one day on the red hills of Georgia, sons of former slaves and the sons of former slave owners will be able to sit down together at the table of brotherhood. I have a dream that one day even the state of Mississippi, a state sweltering with the heat of injustice, sweltering with the heat of oppression, will be transformed into an oasis of freedom and justice. I have a dream that my four little children will one day live in a nation where they will not be judged by the color of their skin, but by the content of their character.

I HAVE A DREAM TODAY! 12

I have a dream that one day down in Alabama—with its vicious racists, 13 with its Governor having his lips dripping with the words of interposition and nullification—one day right there in Alabama, little black boys and black girls will be able to join hands with little white boys and white girls as sisters and brothers.

I HAVE A DREAM TODAY! 14

I have a dream that one day every valley shall be exalted, every hill and 15 mountain shall be made low. The rough places will be plain and the crooked places will be made straight, "and the glory of the Lord shall be revealed, and all flesh shall see it together."

This is our hope. This is the faith that I go back to the South with. With 16 this faith we will be able to hew out of the mountain of despair, a stone of hope. With this faith we will be able to transform the jangling discords of our nation into a beautiful symphony of brotherhood. With this faith we will be able to work together, to pray together, to struggle together, to go to jail together, to stand up for freedom together, knowing that we will be free one day. And this will be the day. This will be the day when all of God's children will be able to sing with new meaning, "My country 'tis of thee, sweet land of liberty, of thee I sing. Land where my father died, land of the pilgrim's pride, from every mountainside, let freedom ring." And if America is to be a great nation, this must become true.

So let freedom ring from the prodigious hilltops of New Hampshire; let 17 freedom ring from the mighty mountains of New York; let freedom ring from the heightening Alleghenies of Pennsylvania; let freedom ring from the snow-capped Rockies of Colorado; let freedom ring from the curvaceous slopes of California. But not only that. Let freedom ring from Stone Mountain of Georgia; let freedom ring from Lookout Mountain of Tennessee; let freedom ring from every hill and mole hill of Mississippi. "From every mountainside, let freedom ring."

And when this happens, and when we allow freedom to ring, when we 18 let it ring from every village and every hamlet, from every state and every city, we will be able to speed up that day when all of God's children, black men and white men, Jews and Gentiles, Protestants and Catholics, will be able to join hands and sing in the words of the old Negro spiritual: "Free at last. Free at last. Thank God Almighty, we are free at last."

STUDY QUESTIONS

1. What, specifically, is accomplished by echoing, at the beginning, the words of Abraham Lincoln? What echoes of Lincoln do you find elsewhere in the speech?

2. What effects are produced by the frequent patterns of repetition? How is the device of repetition related to the way history is conceived in the speech? How is the repetition related to THEMES developed in the speech?

3. Explain the check / promissory note IMAGERY beginning in paragraph 4. In what different ways is the image developed? What other extended images does the speech present? Besides Lincoln, what other familiar sources are echoed or alluded to?

4. Why is it significant that the most forceful part of the speech is presented through the imagery of a dream?

MYTH AND SYMBOL

MYTH is a communal narrative about the unknown or unknowable, the remote in time or space, the spiritual universe, or our place in that universe. For some, a myth is a fiction: *their* view of the universe is myth; *ours* is a religious truth. For the past century or more, however, many have seen in myths of highly diverse and far-flung cultures an underlying unity. They therefore consider myths each culture's attempt to understand and articulate the same underlying truths. All such attempts, then, are valuable and "true" in one way or another. If nothing else, many believe, myth reveals the way the human mind universally confronts and interprets the mysterious aspects of its surroundings.

A RITUAL—a rite or ceremony in which an act or series of acts is exactly repeated on specific occasions—is, like a myth, communal. It is, indeed, usually part of the communal religion. Sometimes its purpose is to seek some sort of blessing or gift from a Higher Power. In *The Day of the Swallows*, for example, each year on the saint day of San Lorenzo at eleven in the morning, the young women of the village "gather around the lake to wash their hair and bathe in promise of a future husband." Other rituals may involve a confession of sin, a recognition of some group or cultural triumph, a desire for supernatural intervention into a pattern of history.

Ritual is a symbolic representation in action—often including music and words. A SYMBOL at its simplest is something (often something concrete) that stands for something else (often abstract, indefinite, religious).

Americans all know what the Stars and Stripes stand for. Usually symbols, even well-understood ones, are a bit more complex: most of us believe we know what, in a religious context, the cross represents, but in putting its MEANING in words we are likely to get into the area of INTERPRETATION, emphasizing different aspects or using words with slightly different meanings or connotations. "Communion," for example, means several different things in Mora's poem because the actors come to the action of the poem with differing assumptions.

It is sometimes difficult, especially in a ritual with which we are not familiar, to distinguish when an act, a word, a belief, is meant to be literal and when it is symbolic, something "instead of" something else, a figure of speech or metaphor. The SPEAKER in "The Eagle-Feather Fan" first says, "The eagle is my power," which many will interpret as symbolic (after all, the bald eagle is a symbol of America); then he says, "my fan is an eagle," which secular readers surely interpret to mean that the fan made of eagle feathers represents, symbolizes, stands for, is "instead of," the eagle. But later he says of the fan, "it is real," and the poem / ritual metamorphosizes the speaker's hand with the fan into the eagle itself: "The bones of my hand are fine / And hollow . . . / My hand veers in the thin air / Of the summits." The speaker's hands and fan *actually* turn into an eagle and soar above the mountains, or does he only *believe* he is soaring? Or does he not *really* believe he is, but is representing the flight of the eagle with his hands and fan, they being there "instead of" the eagle itself? Before you answer too readily, think of a ritual or a mystery in your own religion, and ask yourself similar questions; you may find the line between the real and the symbolic or mythic becoming a little shadowy and uncertain.

Though myth and ritual are communal—not the invention or property of the individual, priest or poet—and traditional, even absolutely literal, nonsymbolic beliefs or religious texts seem to require interpretation so that in order to maintain the sense of community, a certain amount of latitude must be allowed. Among Garrison Keillor's Brethren, however, "perfect literalists every one" who therefore believe in reading the Bible in absolutely literal, nonsymbolic terms, schism is rampant. Keillor tells us that the Cox Brethren split with the Johnson Brethren because the Johnsons believed "that what was abominable to God in the Old Testament must be abominable still" (paragraph 18), but Mr. Cox held to "the New Covenant of Grace." Keillor wryly reduces the principles to near-absurdity when he recounts the actual issue over which the Brethren split, Johnson's application of the controversial principle to a modern instance: "Mr. Johnson's sermon was against women's slacks, and he had quoted Deuteronomy 22:5, 'The woman shall not wear that which pertaineth unto a man . . .' " (paragraph 19). His people, the Cox Brethren, walk out. Perhaps it is a function of myth, ritual, and symbol to offer not unyielding principles, but flexible, affective, sensory images and meanings that bind rather than separate.

Though myths and rituals are most often used in a more or less religious and communal context, symbols, though they can be part of ritual or myth and certainly may be religious, may also be literary rather than religious. The literary symbols may be traditional—a rose has often been used by poets to suggest beauty and romance—or it may be invented by the writer. The abalone shell in Mori's story, for example, takes on symbolic meaning though it is not part of a mythic or ritualistic or even literary tradition.

Because it is not part of a preexistent tradition, and because it is complex and particular, the precise meaning of the symbol of the abalone shell may be difficult to paraphrase. That it does, however, have meaning—that it is symbolic—is created and insisted upon by context: something that has such value it controls one's life, something that has indescribable beauty, every example of which is equally beautiful and valuable but different, surely means *something*, either in itself or in the way it is invested with meaning by the mind of the collector of the shells. Here the individual symbol—the shell—seems to be part of a ritual that is not specifically communal (though it was passed on from one man to another) and is certainly not traditional, and, since it suggests something almost religious in its beauty and value, it seems almost to create its own myth. It is because of works like "Abalone, Abalone, Abalone" that "myth" and "ritual" have come to be used as literary terms.

WRITING
ABOUT THE READING

PERSONAL ESSAYS AND NARRATIVES

1. Tell about your experiences and your family's in your place of worship. In what ways have your own experiences expressed values different from those of your family or your ancestors?

2. Recount an experience of a ceremony or ritual in a place of worship other than your own.

3. Write about an event or experience that seems to have been or that you believe to have been supernatural.

4. Recount a conflict between you and one or more members of your family involving religion.

IMITATIONS AND PARODIES

1. Write an important scene in "Dominion" from Robert's or Mrs. Poverman's point of view.

2. Parody "Abalone, Abalone, Abalone," perhaps by adding a "y" to each word of the title, perhaps by making the object collected baseball cards or Barbie dolls.

3. Write a final scene for *The Day of the Swallows* in which the outcome is quite different. Make sure, however, that your ending is true to the earlier part of the work.

DESCRIPTIVE PAPERS

1. In prose or poetry, describe your place of worship as Rafael Jesús González does.

2. Describe a religious ritual in which you have participated or that you have witnessed; try to do so in such a way that the reader will understand and sympathize with the meaning and emotions involved in the ritual.

COMPARISON-CONTRAST PAPER

Compare a ritual or service in your religion with another that you have witnessed or with which you are familiar.

ANALYTICAL PAPERS

1. Analyze the imagery—the swallows, the lake, the light, and so on—in *The Day of the Swallows.*

2. Analyze the use of the supernatural or the apparently supernatural in at least three of the pieces in the chapter—for example, "The Moths," "Fleur," and "Gentle Communion"—with particular (but not necessarily exclusive) emphasis on to what degree the reader must accept (or deny) the irrational or supernatural in the work.

ARGUMENTATIVE PAPER

Construct both sides of a debate on one of the following topics: Resolved, that Garrison Keillor is blasphemous and makes fun of his friends and family (or his characters) in "Protestant." Or *The Day of the Swallows* is a feminist (or antifeminist) play.

RESEARCH PAPER

Go to the library and look up several (at least three) personal accounts of the Civil Rights March on Washington during which Martin Luther King, Jr., delivered his "I Have a Dream" speech. Find accounts that mention the speech specifically, and compare the reactions expressed by different hearers. Then, using periodical indexes (and getting help from a reference librarian if you need it), look up later articles commenting on and evaluating the speech. Write a paper comparing immediate and long-term responses to the speech, and try to account for the differences by looking carefully at the rhetoric of the speech itself.

Student Writing

MACARONI, MACARONI ... AND CHALCEDONY

Elizabeth Douglas

I used to accompany my mother to the grocery store nearly every week. At noontime on Saturdays, we'd take the old stationwagon to the store, which was only a mile or two away. I was always glad to go so that I could help her pick out the best foods and the ingredients for my favorite dinners.

And sometimes I'd even pass the aisle of cookies, including a variety of chocolates, to get to the deli section first. That section had innumerable meats and cheeses, and fresh pasta and sauces.

They were lined up side by side, the little packages of noodles. Impatiently, I crushed some of the broken ones into powder through the cello-phane while waiting for my mother. Sometimes I'd just sit and look around me, pretending I owned the store. I was curious as to why the noodles were always so beautifully wrapped, all twisted into woven bundles, and just so we could buy and boil them. It was a lot of bother weaving and wrapping them so carefully when they could be just thrown in a bag.

Occasionally, I had seen the grocer twisting the fresh strips, and during those times I sat watching him while my mother wasted time in frozen foods. It seemed to me he took his work seriously, and I had always admired the finished product. When the fluorescent lights hit him just right, it was some-thing beautiful to behold. But I still could not understand why he continued to contort those noodles when the shelves where practically full. 4

He used to speak to me when I came by at noon. I'd roll by on my cart and he'd bellow, "Hello, young girl!" 5

"Hello, Melvin," I said. "I came to look at the pasta." 6

Then he'd grab a pile of fresh noodles from the back room and his hands would jerk quickly to untangle every strand. I must have asked him a million times why he took the time to braid those long strands, but each time, he just closed his mouth and refused to answer. 7

I once asked if he'd pass some of the bundles on to his children when he died, but after some thought, he said, "No." When I asked why, he explained. 8

"I couldn't give the children what I see in this pasta of mine. The chil-dren must learn for themselves, get their own sense of the noodles," he said, "for there are so many different kinds." 9

I told him then that I had thought this twisting hobby of pasta was a fairly simple affair. 10

"It is simple. Very simple," he said. But he wouldn't say anything else. 11

All of this made me very curious. In fact, I didn't even like the kind of noodles he twisted. My mother always made the sauce with large chunks of onion which made my face contort. Instead, I loved the big fat packages of macaroni noodles, which could be cooked with cheese in my mother's deep-dish casseroles. So, when we went grocery shopping, I inevitably made sure she bought some macaroni, and I always wondered about Melvin. 12

I believe my deep love for macaroni stemmed from my experiences as a preschooler. I had loved kindergarten from the first day. 13

We shuffled in, a line of heads turning and talking, of arms swinging lunchboxes carelessly. We were guided single-file into a classroom with enor-mous windows, and walls covered with colorful fingerpaintings. When the kid in front of me sat down, I dropped too, and watched those behind me gravitate to the ground like dominoes in a neat semi-circle around the room. The first activity of the day was making collages out of household items, and we eyed our speaker intently. When she displayed some examples for us to see, the boy next to me whispered urgently with clenched teeth from the corner of his lips, "What! That's just macaroni . . ." 14

"Macaroni . . ." I murmured. My eyes lifted to gaze at the paintings, in 15 bright shades of green, blue, . . . every color I could imagine decorated images on the wall. I couldn't understand why we would waste time pasting macaroni on a plain piece of paper. But later, Miss Elliott came to put her hand on my shoulder as I stared at my blank paper and bowl of macaroni.

"Aren't you having fun?" she bellowed. Then she handed me some glue and glitter. "Go to it! It's simple." But she didn't tell me further.

After forty minutes of spreading blue on my paper and meticulously arranging the miniature elbows, my creation became interesting. I found after many minutes of aggravation, I could not do much with the glitter; it clung persistently to my fingers, dress, and hair, and would not come off by scrubbing. But, suddenly inspired, I gently brushed each noodle with the paints we were given. I discovered, the more I colored, the more luster I found. I took more time to blend shades, making exotic and sometimes brownish colors. Then I made polka-dots on my macaroni. I guess I could say they were not unlike a rainbow which men once symbolized.

I remember running from my mother into the grocery, looking for him. "Melvin!" I said when I found him. "I think I know why you are twisting the pasta!"

He looked at me for a long time then and I thought he might punish me, but only for a moment, for eventually, his face fell into a smile.

"All right," he said. "Do not say anything. Nothing, mind you. When you find the reason why you must work with pasta, you do not have to say anything more."

A summer ago, I packed the car and drove with a friend to New York City. The days were hot driving in late August, but grew cooler with the rain as we arrived in New York. A few of those days in the city found us roaming the streets of Greenwich Village. The brilliant sun beckoned vendors to line the avenues, and we confronted the crowds to mull over their merchandise. With what pocket change we had left, we approached some laden with jewelry, bags, tie-dyed cotton shirts and skirts, hats, and more.

We stopped first at one with a cardboard box full of cotton clothing.

"Ah, you want to try some?" he asked. "They're from Italy. I can get more if you don't like these. I have a friend who makes them."

The clothes were expensive. They were all oversized, the material was rough, and the colors were faded. After searching through the box for twenty minutes, we continued down the sidewalk.

We soon entered a small shop on the avenue when the afternoon sun had grown strong. The man inside was selling jewelry, and his table was covered with earrings, bracelets, rings, and pendants. We browsed for thirty minutes, and then he called to us.

"If you'd like to see more, I have some other things in the glass case over by the wall," he pointed. Then he showed us a basket of stones and told us we could choose one to have made into a piece of jewelry, "if you would like that." I stirred the stones in the intricately woven basket, and then said quietly to Lisa, "Strange. They're all gray. What could you do with these?"

Before leaving, we walked to the glass case to examine the remaining 27
jewelry. After gazing for a moment, my friend whispered, awed, "Oh . . .
the necklace. It's so beautiful."

I was looking at another piece, mesmerized by the combination of the 28
stone and the silver. The two contrasted, yet came together in harmony,
creating pinkish hues in an elegant style. The glare on the silver reflected
other colors. I remember thinking vaguely, the colors were strange, almost
abstract in my mind, yet in perfect unison with the piece.

I turned to ask the owner how he made the piece, but when I did, he 29
pointed to the basket of gray stones.

"I made them from those stones I showed you. I can make any design 30
you like with your choice of stone. It's simple," he said.

Puzzled that I had not recognized them as the same stones, I returned 31
to the basket. I shuffled them again and then, holding one to the light, I
asked him, "What are they?"

"They are a type of quartz," he said, "sometimes they are totally trans- 32
lucent, other times they are milky or grayish like these. I make each piece
myself. Each one is sorta similar and yet different, don't you think?"

"They are all very beautiful," said my friend. He smiled suddenly and 33
added after a moment, "The stone is chalcedony."

"Chalcedony . . ." she repeated, ". . . never heard of it." 34

On the sidewalk, the sun was hot and we walked for awhile without 35
speaking. We soon found our car and manuevered out of the cramped space;
with the speed came a cool breeze on our faces.

Only then did my friend remark, "I wish I could make jewelry. That 36
stuff was amazing."

"It's like macaroni . . ." I murmured. 37

Not listening, she answered "I guess . . ." She yawned then, and merged 38
into traffic.

I was still smiling, thinking. I should like to see Melvin someday and 39
watch his eyes roll as he studies me whose face is now akin to the creators of
art or otherwise.

WRITING ABOUT LITERATURE

Introduction

Writing about literature ought to be easier than writing about anything else. When you write about painting, for example, you have to translate shapes and colors and textures into words. When you write about music, you have to translate various aspects and combinations of sounds into words. When you write about that complex, mysterious, fleeting thing called "reality" or "life," you have an even more difficult task. Worst of all, perhaps, is trying to put into words all that is going on at any given moment inside your particular and unique self. So you ought to be relieved to know that you are going to write—that is, use words—about literature—again, words.

But writing about literature will not be easy if you haven't learned to *read* literature, for in order to write about anything you have to know that something rather well. Helping you to learn to read literature is what the rest of this book is about; this chapter is about the writing. (But, as you will see, you cannot fully separate the writing from the reading.)

Another thing keeps writing about literature from being easy: writing itself is not easy. Writing well requires a variety of language skills—a good working vocabulary, for example—and a sense of ordering your words and your ideas, of how to link one idea or statement to another, of what to put in and what to leave out. Worse, writing is not a finite or definite skill or art; you never really "know how to write," you just learn how to write a little better about a little more. These very words you are reading have been written and revised several times, even though your editors have had a good many years in which to practice.

Representing the Literary Text

COPYING

If writing about literature is using words about words, what words should you use? Since most writers work very hard to get each word exactly right and in exactly the right order, there are no better words to use in discussing what the literature is about than those of the literary work itself. Faced with writing about a story, then, you could just write the story over again, word for word:

> When I was fifteen, I was almost as tall as the man I have always thought of as my father . . .

and so on until the end. Copying texts was useful in medieval monasteries, but nowadays, what with printing, word processors, and Fax machines, it would not seem to be very useful. Besides, if you try to copy a text, you will probably find that spelling or punctuation errors, reversed word order, missing or added or just different words seem mysteriously to appear. Still, it's a good exercise for teaching yourself accuracy and attention to detail, and you will probably discover things about the text you are copying that you would be unlikely to notice otherwise. Early in a literature course, particularly, copying can serve as a useful step in the direction of learning how to read and write about narrative, poetic, or dramatic literature; later, being able to copy a passage accurately will help when you want to quote a passage to illustrate or prove a point you are making. But copying is not, in itself, writing *about* literature.

Reading aloud, a variation of copying, may be a more original and interpretive exercise than copying itself, since by tone, emphasis, and pace you are clarifying the text or indicating the way you understand the text. But it, too, is not *writing* about literature, and you will not long be satisfied with merely repeating someone else's words. You will have perceptions, responses, and ideas that you will want to express for yourself about what you are reading. And having something to say and wanting to say or write it is the first and most significant step in learning to write about literature.

PARAPHRASE

If you look away from the text for a while and then write the same material but in your own words, you are writing a **paraphrase.**

For example, let's try to paraphrase the first sentence of a story in chapter 8, Tony Cade Bambara's "The Lesson": "Back in the days when everyone was old and stupid or young and foolish and me and Sugar were the only ones just right, this lady moved on our block with nappy hair and proper speech and no makeup." We can begin by "unraveling" the first clause: "Back . . . just right." What does this *say?* "Some time ago when everyone older than Sugar and I was old and stupid and everyone younger than we were was young and foolish, and we were the only ones who were just right. . . ." We have made very few changes, but even so you can see what has happened—the statement or the narrator has been distanced from her younger self. The first version seems to reflect more accurately the language of the narrator when she was younger not only because of the ungrammatical "me," but because of the more colloquial though correct "Back in the days" and because of the overall informal structure as compared with the paraphrased version. Even the change in the order of the phrases seems to change the meaning, if emphasis and focus are aspects of meaning. Bambara's version puts us in the position of the young narrator through the word "foolish": there is no qualification of everyone either being too old or too young to be sensible, and thus are she and Sugar—the "just right" ones—introduced. Though the paraphrase seems to contain all the statement of the original, it is not only stiffer but also less ironic, less shrewd, and less amusing—a little pompous, perhaps. The paraphrase also does not set up the younger narrator's evaluation of the "lady" (think what would be lost if we changed this to "woman") who "moved on our block": "proper" not "correct" speech reinforces "lady" and the apparently critical overtone, so that wearing no makeup seems somehow wrong—not like me and Sugar. The word "nappy" raises another problem in paraphrasing. Not only is it difficult to find an adequate description equivalent ("kinky" won't quite do), but the whole cultural context would be lost. You can see that the process of paraphrase is something like translation: translating Bambara's colloquial African-American prose into a pallid formal "general American" equivalent.

What good is paraphrasing? First of all, it enables us to test whether we really understand what we are reading; does everyone reading this story know what "nappy" means? Second, certain elements of the text become clearer: we may see more clearly now that Bambara's sentence is meant to be ironic or humorous, and we may be able to define more clearly the cultural context that is being projected. Third, we can check our paraphrase with those of others, our classmates' versions, for example, to compare our understanding of the passage with theirs. Finally, we have learned how dependent literature is upon words. A paraphrase, no matter how precise, can render only an approximate equivalent of the meaning of a text—how *good* Bambara's sentence is, how *flat* our paraphrase.

Paraphrasing, like copying, is not in itself an entirely satisfactory way of writing about literature, but, like copying, it can be a useful tool when you write about literature in other ways. In trying to explain or clarify a literary text for someone, to illustrate a point you are making about that text, or to remind your readers of or to acquaint them with a text or passage you will at times want to paraphrase. Unlike an exact copy, a paraphrase, being in your own words, adds something of yours to the text or passage—your emphasis, your perspective, your understanding.

SUMMARY

Paraphrase follows faithfully the outlines of the text. But if you stand back far enough from the text so as not to see its specific words or smaller details and put down briefly in your own words what you believe the work is about, you will have a **summary.** How briefly? Well, you could summarize the 58 lines of Carter Revard's "Discovery of the New World" (chapter 5) in an approximate number of words (about 58) like this, for example:

> The speaker of Carter Revard's "Discovery of the New World" is an alien from a more advanced planet reporting to his leader about the somewhat painful necessity of absorption and enslavement of the "creatures" on this planet (that is, humans, us) who do not seem to understand that this is necessary so the "higher" life can prosper here.

Or, to choose a work that is not in the text but is likely to be familiar to all of us, you could summarize the story of the whole long play *Hamlet* in a single sentence: "A young man, seeking to avenge the murder of his father by his uncle, kills his uncle, but he himself and others die in the process." Has *too* much been left out? What do you feel it essential to add? Let's try again: "In Denmark, many centuries ago, a young prince avenged the murder of his father, the king, by his uncle, who had usurped the throne, but the prince himself was killed as were others, and a well-led foreign army had no trouble successfully invading the decayed and troubled state." A classmate may have written this summary: "From the ghost of his murdered father a young prince learns that his uncle, who has married the prince's mother, much to the young man's shame and disgust, is the father's murderer, and he plots revenge, feigning madness, acting erratically—even to insulting the woman he loves—and, though gaining his revenge, causes the suicide of his beloved and the deaths of others and, finally, of himself."

The last two, though accurate enough, sound like two different plays, don't they? To summarize means to select and emphasize and so to interpret: that is, not to replicate the text in miniature, as a reduced photograph might replicate the original, but while reducing it to change the angle of vision and even the filter, to represent the essentials as the reader or summarizer sees them. When you write a summary you should try to be as objective as possible; nevertheless, your summary will reflect not only the literary text but also your own understanding and attitudes. There's nothing wrong with your fingerprints or "mindprints" appearing on the summary, so long as you recognize that in summarizing you are doing more than copying, paraphrasing, or merely reflecting the text. You might learn something about language, literature, and yourself by comparing your summaries of, say, three or four short poems, a couple of short stories, a play, or an essay with summaries of the same works by several of your classmates. Try to measure the refraction of the text as it passes through the lens of each student's mind. You might then write a composite summary that would include all that any one reader felt important. You might try the same exercise again on different texts. Has the practice made you more careful? More inclusive? Is there a greater degree of uniformity or inclusiveness in your summaries?

A good summary can be a form of literary criticism. Though you will seldom be called upon merely to summarize a work, a good deal of writing about literature requires that at some point or other you do summarize—a whole work, a particular incident or aspect, a stanza, chapter, or scene. But beware: a mere summary, no matter how accurate, will seldom satisfy the demand for a critical essay.

Replying to the Text

IMITATION AND PARODY

While paraphrase is something like translation—a faithful following of the original text but in different words—and summary is the faithful, but inevitably interpretive, reduction of the matter, there is another kind of writing about literature that faithfully follows the manner or matter or both of a literary text, but that does so for different ends. It's called **imitation.**

Art students learn to paint by copying the Old Masters; "writing from models," was for many generations the way students were taught to write.

Many serious works are, in one way or another, imitations: Virgil's *Aeneid*, for example, may be said to be an imitation of Homer's *Odyssey*, and, in a very different way, so might James Joyce's *Ulysses*. You too may be able to learn a good deal about writing—and reading—by trying your hand at an imitation.

But how would *you* go about writing an imitation? You first analyze the original—that is, break it down into its characteristics or qualities—and decide just what you want to preserve in your version. Sometimes you can poke fun at a work by imitating it but at the same time exaggerating its style or prominent characteristics, or placing it in an inappropriate context; that kind of imitation, a kind that is still popular, is called a **parody.** The list of qualities and the model might be much the same for a serious imitation and for a parody, only in a parody you can exaggerate a little—or a lot.

Because so many of the texts in *New Worlds of Literature* are very recent, there is not an established body of parodic literature dealing with works included here, so let's use as an example a parody of a work familiar to almost all of us who had Miss Hudson in the tenth grade, Edgar Allan Poe's "The Raven." To parody "The Raven," we may decide to stick closely to Poe's rhythms, his use of repetitive mood words or of several words that mean almost the same thing, and his frequent use of alliteration (words that begin with the same sound). We might want to exaggerate the characteristic stylistic devices as C. L. Edson does in his parody; it begins,

> Once upon a midnight dreary, eerie, scary,
> I was wary, I was weary, full of worry, thinking of my lost Lenore,
> Of my cheery, airy, faerie, fierie Dearie—(Nothing more).

We may choose another kind of parody, keeping the form as close as possible to the original but applying it to a ludicrously unsuitable subject. In writing such a parody of "The Raven," we will keep the rhythm closer to Poe's and the subject matter less close. How about this?

> Once upon a midday murky, crunching on a Christmas turkey,
> And guzzling giant Jereboams of gin . . .

And maybe we could use the "Nevermore" refrain as if it were an antacid commercial. Elizabeth Douglas does something like this in the parodic title—"Macaroni, Macaroni . . . and Chalcedony"—of her imitation of Toshiro Mori's "Abalone, Abalone, Abalone."

You will have noticed that in order to write a good imitation or parody you must read and re-read the original very carefully, examine it, and identify just those elements and qualities that go to make it up and be itself. Since you admire works you wish to imitate, such close study should be a pleasure. You may or may not greatly admire a work you wish to parody, but parody itself is fun to do and fun to read. In either case, you are having fun while gaining a deeper, more intimate knowledge of the nature and details of a work of literature. Moreover, such close attention to how a professional piece of writing is put together and how its parts function together to do what it does along with your effort to reproduce the effects in your own imitation or parody are sure to help you understand the process of writing and so help you improve your own ability to write about literature knowledgeably.

RE-CREATION AND REPLY

Sometimes a story, poem, or play will seem so partial, biased, or unrealistic that it will stimulate a response that is neither an imitation nor a parody but a retort. After reading Jimmy Santiago Baca's "Ancestor" (chapter 2), one might want to imagine the grandmother's version of having to bring up the speaker and his siblings because the love "beyond the ordinary" that their father has for them includes telling their grandmother to take the children and " 'Care for them!' "

While retorts can often be witty, they are also serious. Usually they say not merely, "That's not how the story, poem, or play went," but "That's not what life is really like." We must always read literature initially with the aim of understanding it and taking it at its highest value (rather than reducing it and quibbling). We must try to "hear" what it is saying and not impose our own notions of reality prematurely upon a work but if possible learn from it and broaden our own views. We must finally, however, read it critically as well, asking, "Is this the way things *really* are?" or, more generously, "If I were standing over there, where the story (author, character) is, would things really look that way?"

Explaining the Text

DESCRIPTION

To give an account of the form of a work or passage rather than merely a brief version of its content or plot (and a plot summary, even of a poem, is usually what we mean by "summary") you may wish to write a

description. A description of Simon J. Ortiz's "Speaking," for example, may concentrate on the form of the poem. The desire to describe the form may come from a sense as we read it that there *is* form here, even though the poem lacks the conventional, formal elements of poetry: regular meter (or beat) and rhyme. A description of the somewhat unconventional form of the poem may go something like this:

> Though in Simon J. Ortiz's poem "Speaking" there is an early example of rhyme—"ground" / "sound" in lines 3 and 5—that is the only end-rhyme in the twenty lines of the poem, though two end-words are repeated—"him" in lines 10 and 17; "us" in lines 6, 13, and 14—which may have something of the effect of rhyme. A number of other words are repeated, but no repeated pairs appear at the ends of lines: "son" and "boy" are repeated, but each of them appears only once at the end of a line: "son," line 8; "boy," line 19. Similarly, a pair of words—"crickets, cicadas"—is repeated, with "crickets" at the end of the line the first time (line 4) and "cicadas" at the end the second time (line 11); "million years old" (line 5) appears as "millions of years" at the end of line 12. More notable perhaps is a repetition with change: " '. . . speaking for him' " ends line 10 and "speaking for me" ends line 20, more especially notable not only because these phrases end the stanzas but because they contain the word that is the title of the poem, "Speaking."
>
> Not all poetic form, of course, consists in rhyme or regular meter. Stanzas also have form, and though we have noted that the two stanzas here are not marked by similar rhyme schemes, both contain ten lines and both are marked by similar, almost "responsive" final lines. Not only that, but there is another comparable or contrasting similarity in the forms of the two stanzas: the first has a three-line "introduction" and the last a three-line "conclusion" which together seem to serve as a "frame" for the enclosed fourteen lines—seven in each stanza. So although there is no regularity of meter or line length and no regular rhyme, "Speaking" still has regularity in the length and shape of the stanzas, repetition, and repetition with change, all of which contribute to a sense of form.

These paragraphs show how you can describe at length and in detail certain aspects of a work without mentioning the content at all. You can describe a play in comparable terms—acts, scenes, settings, time lapses perhaps—and you might describe a novel in terms of chapters, books, summary narration, dramatized scenes. In addition to describing the narrative structure or focus and voice of a short story, you might also describe the diction (word choice), the sentence structure, the amount of description of the characters or landscape, and so on.

ANALYSIS

Like copying, paraphrase, and summary, a description of a work or passage rarely stands alone as a piece of writing about literature. It is, instead, a tool, a means of supporting a point or opinion. Even the description we have given above borders on **analysis.** To analyze is to break something down into its parts to discover what they are, and, usually, how they function in and relate to the whole. The description of the stanza structure of "Speaking" tells you what that pattern is but says nothing about how it functions in the poem. If you were to add such an account to the description, then, you would have analyzed one aspect of the poem. In order to do so, however, you would first have to decide what, in a general way, the poem is about: what its THEME is. If you defined the theme of "Speaking" as "the close relationship of an innocent child with nature," you could then write an analytical paper suggesting how the rhyme scheme reinforces that theme. You might begin something like this:

The Stanzaic Structure of Ortiz's "Speaking"

The narrative of Simon J. Ortiz's "Speaking" is a clear indication of its theme: a father takes his infant son into the woods to introduce him to nature, but the little boy can communicate with nature better than the father can. The narrative or plot and the theme are both reinforced or closely connected to the structure of the poem.

At first "Speaking" does not seem to have a formal structure, since we usually think of poetic structure in terms of rhyme and meter.

Then you could follow with the description of the stanzaic structure and continue like this:

The division into two balanced stanzas, each with three-line frames and with final lines that are similar to each other in structure and with the same verb, forces us to adjust somewhat our initial statement of the theme: the child is not just close to nature but is *closer than his father is.* In the first stanza the father tries to speak to nature for his son, to introduce him, it seems. Nature and eternity ("the millions of years") just watch, the second stanza says, until the infant boy babbles and then they listen. Not only does the father not speak to nature for the boy; the boy speaks for the father. The frame, the balance, the repetition, and the responsive final lines of the stanzas suggest that not only does the boy have a close relationship with nature but he communicates with nature and his relationship and language are superior to that of the father. The poem is not just about the relationship of the child to nature but of the superiority of innocence to experience and the superiority of the pre-verbal to the verbal.

INTERPRETATION

Principles and Procedures

If you have been reading carefully, you may have noticed what looks like a catch: to turn description into analysis, you must relate what you are describing to the theme, the overall effect and meaning of the work of literature. But how do you know what the theme is? If analysis relates the part to the whole, how can you know the "whole" before you have analyzed each part? But then, how can you analyze each part—relating it to the whole—if you don't know what that whole is?

Interpretation, or the expression of your understanding of a literary work and its meaning, involves an initial general impression that is then supported and, often, modified by analysis of the particulars. It involves looking at the whole, the part, the whole, the part, the whole, the part, in a series of approximations and adjustments. (Note, in particular, that you must keep your mind open for modifications or changes rather than forcing your analysis to confirm your first impressions.)

This procedure should in turn suggest something of the nature and even the form of the critical essay, or essay of interpretation. The essay should present the overall theme and support that generalization with close analyses of the major elements of the text (or, in some essays, an analysis of one significant element)—showing how one or more of such elements as rhyme or speaker, plot or setting reinforce, define, or modify the theme of the story. Often the conclusion of such an essay will be a fuller, more refined and more complex statement of the theme.

Both the definition of and the procedures for interpreting a work suggest that a literary text is unified, probably around a theme, a meaning and effect. In interpreting, you therefore keep asking of each element or detail, "How does it fit? How does it contribute to *the* theme or whole?" In most instances, especially when you are writing on shorter texts, if you dig hard and deep enough, you will find a satisfactory interpretation or central theme. Even after you have done your best, however, you must hold your "reading" or interpretation as a hypothesis rather than a final truth. Your experience of reading criticism has probably already shown you that more than one reading of a text is possible and that no reading exhausts the meaning and totality of a work. Nonetheless, you must begin reading a text as if it were going to make a central statement and create a single effect, no matter how complex. You must try as conscientiously as you can to "make sense" of the work, to analyze it, show how its elements work together. In analyzing elements, you kept your initial sense of the whole as hypothesis and did not try to force evidence to fit your first impression. So, too, you must hold your interpretation as a hypothesis even in its final stages, even at the end. It is, you must be sure, the fullest and best "reading" of the text you are capable of at this time, with the evidence and knowledge you have at this moment; but only that. In other words, an interpretation is "only an opinion." But just as your political and other opinions are not lightly held but are what you really feel and believe based on all you know and have experienced and all you have thought and felt, so your opinion or interpretation of a text should be as responsible as you can make it. Your opinions are a measure of your knowledge, your experience, your intelligence, and your sensibility. They should not be lightly changed but neither should they be obstinately and inflexibly held.

Reading and Theme Making

Because you need a sense of the whole text before you can analyze it, analysis and interpretation would seem to be possible only after repeated readings. Though obvious, logical, and partially true, this may not be *entirely* true. In reading, we actually anticipate theme or meaning much as we anticipate what will happen next. Often this anticipation or expectation of theme or effect begins with our first opening a book—or even before, in reading the title. If you were to read *Hamlet* in an edition that gives its full title—*The Tragedy of Hamlet, Prince of Denmark*—even if, as unlikely as it may seem, you had never heard of the play or its author before—you would have some idea or hypothesis about who the protagonist is, where the action will more than likely be set, how the play will end, and even some of the feelings it will arouse.

Such anticipation of theme and effect, projecting and modifying understanding and response, continues as you read. As soon as you read the strange title of William Savoyan's "Najari Levon's Old Country Advice to the Young Americans on How to Live with a Snake" your curiosity is aroused (living with a snake?) and you are alerted to look for a theme in the form of "advice" (though you may not be too sure whether the advice is going to be serious). We find out who Najari Levon is in the first paragraph—an "old man with [a] gargoyle face" —and, since "Aram's two small sons and two small daughters" live on Van Ness Avenue (Fresno, California—see paragraph 19), we are pretty sure early in the second short paragraph that they are the "young Americans" of the title. There is also the word "advice," but it is advice—legal advice—that Levon is seeking, although the title promises he will be giving "old country" advice. When in the next paragraph the "snake" seems to be just a picture on a board game and in the following paragraphs it becomes the subject of controversy, we expect that snake to be the snake they—and we—will be advised to live with. We are still listening for the old country advice, however. Then Najari says, " 'In our house in Bitlis lived a very large black snake, which was our family snake' " (paragraph 7), and there it is. The snake is then "real" or at least part of a tale that Najari tells as if it were real. We keep listening for advice. Aram comes home, interrupting the story, and Najari forgets what legal advice he was seeking and never finishes his story and does not give old country advice about how to live with the snake. Or does he? *We* are left to infer what Najari's advice might have been or to think about the whole question of advice, legal or "old country."

Just as we have more than one expectation of what may happen next as we read a story, poem, or play, so we may have more than one expectation of what it is going to be "about" in the more general sense: as we read along we have expectations or hypotheses of meaning, and so we consciously or unconsciously try to fit together the pieces of elements of what we are reading into a pattern of significance. By the end of our first reading we should have a fairly well-defined sense of what the work is "about," what it means, even how some of the elements have worked together to produce that meaning and effect. Indeed, isn't this the way we read when we are not reading for a class or performance? Don't most people read most stories, poems, plays only once? And don't we usually think we have understood what we have read? Shouldn't we be able to read a very short story in class just once and immediately write an interpretive paper based on that first reading?

This is not to say that we cannot understand more about a work by repeated re-readings, or that there is some virtue or purity of response in the naive first reading that is lost in closer study. Our first "reading"—"reading" in the sense of both "casting our eye over" and "interpretation"—is almost certain to be modified or refined by re-reading: if nothing else, we know from the beginning what the snake is, why Maxine Hong Kingston's "Woman" has "No Name," and what in the world "Tahotahontanekentseratkerontak-wenhakie" can possibly be. The theme or meaning is likely to be modulated by later readings, the way the elements' function in defining or embodying meaning is likely to be clearer; the effect of the second reading is certain to be different from that of the first. It may be instructive to re-read several times the short work we interpreted in class after a single reading, write a new interpretive essay, and see how our understanding has been changed and enriched by subsequent readings.

Opinions, Right and Wrong

Just as each of our separate readings is different, so naturally one reader's fullest and "final" reading, interpretation, or opinion will differ somewhat from another's. Seldom will readers agree entirely with any full statement of the theme of a literary text. Nor is one of these interpretations entirely "right" and all the others necessarily "wrong." For no thematic summary, no analysis or interpretation, no matter how full, can exhaust the affective or intellectual significance of a major literary text. There are various approximate readings of varying degrees of acceptability, various competent or "good" readings, not just one single "right" reading.

Anyone who has heard two accomplished musicians faithfully perform the same work, playing all the "same" notes; or anyone who has seen two performances of *Hamlet* will recognize how "interpretations" can be both correct and different. You might try to get hold of several recordings of one or more of Hamlet's soliloquies—by John Barrymore, Sir John Gielgud, Richard Burton, Sir Laurence Olivier, for example—and notice how each of these actors lends to identical passages his own emphasis, pacing, tone, color, his own effect, and so, ultimately, his own meaning. These actors reading the identical words are, in effect, "copying," not paraphrasing or putting Shakespeare's Elizabethan poetry into modern American prose, not "interpreting" as we have defined it, or putting his play into their own words. If merely performing or reading the words aloud generates significant differences in interpretation, it is no wonder that when you write an interpretive essay about literature, when you give your conception of the meaning and effect of the literary text in your own words, your interpretation will differ from other interpretations, even when each of the different interpretations is competent and "correct."

Any communication, even a work of literature, is refracted by the recipient, and, in one sense, it is not complete until it is received, just as, in a sense, a musical score is not "music" until it is played. Philip Roth reported, not too long ago, how perturbed he was by what the critics and other readers said of his first novel—that was not at all what he intended, what the novel really was, he thought at first. But then he realized that once he had had his say in the novel, it was "out there," and each reader had to understand it within the limits and range of his or her own perspectives and literary and life experiences. His novel, once in print, was no longer merely "his," and rightly so.

That quite different interpretations may be "correct" is not to say, with Alice's Humpty-Dumpty, that a word or a work "means just what I choose it to mean." Though there may not be one "right" reading, some readings are more appropriate and convincing than others and some readings are demonstrably wrong.

What would you say about this reading of *Hamlet?*

> The play is about the hero's sexual love for his mother. He sees his father's "ghost" because he feels guilty, somehow responsible for his father's death, more than likely because he had often wished his father dead. To free himself from this feeling of guilt, he imagines that he sees his father's ghost and that the ghost tells him that his uncle murdered his father. He focuses upon his uncle because he is fiercely jealous that it is his uncle not himself who has replaced his father in his mother's bed. He so resents his mother's choice of so unworthy a mate, he attributes it not to love but to mere lust, clearly a projection of his own lust for his mother, which he calls love. His mother's lust so disgusts him that he hates all women now, even Ophelia. When his father was alive he could be fond of Ophelia, for his sexual feeling for his mother was deflected by his father-the-king's powerful presence. Now, however, he must alienate Ophelia not only because of his new hatred of women but because he has a chance of winning his mother, especially if he can get rid of Claudius, his uncle.

Such a reading explains more or less convincingly certain details in the play, but it wrenches some out of context and it leaves a good deal out and a good deal unexplained: why, for example, do others see the ghost of Hamlet's father if it is just a figment of his imagination? What are Horatio and Fortinbras and the political elements doing in the play? *If* you accept certain Freudian premises about human psychology and see life in Freudian terms; *if* you see literary texts as the *author's* psychic fantasy stimulating your own psychic fantasies and believe that interpretation of *Hamlet* is not merely a reading of the play itself but an analysis of Shakespeare's psyche, you will find this reading convincing. You will perhaps explain away some of the details of the play that do not seem to fit your Freudian reading as a cover-up, an attempt by Shakespeare to disguise the true but hidden meaning of his dramatic fantasy from others—and from himself. Such a reading is probably neither right nor wrong but only a way of interpreting *Hamlet* based on certain assumptions about psychology and about the way literature *means* and so it would be "right" or acceptable to those who share those assumptions.

Suppose one of your ingenious classmates were to argue that the real subject of *Hamlet* is that the hero has tuberculosis. This would explain, your classmate would say, the hero's moodiness, his pretended madness that sometimes seems real, his rejection of Ophelia (he wouldn't want their children to suffer from the disease), his father's ghost (he, too, died of consumption), his anger at his uncle (who carries the disease, of course) for marrying Hamlet's mother, and so on. Your classmate might even argue that the text of the play is flawed, that it was just copied down during a performance by someone in the audience or was printed from an actor's imperfect copy. Therefore, "O that this too too *solid flesh*" should read "*sullied flesh*," as many scholars have argued (and might not "sullied flesh" suggest tuberculosis?). And, therefore, isn't it quite possible that the most famous soliloquy in the play really began or was meant to begin, "TB or not TB"? "No way!" we'd say. We would be reasonably sure that this is not just "not proved" but just plain *wrong*. It might be interesting and illuminating to rebut that reading in a paper of your own and to notice what kinds of evidence you bring to bear on an interpretive argument.

Reader and Text

If it is difficult to say exactly what a piece of literature *says*, it is usually not because it is vague or meaning*less* but because it is too specific and meaning*ful* to paraphrase satisfactorily in any language other than its own. Since no two human beings are identical and no two people can inhabit the same space at the same time, no two people can see exactly the same reality from the same angle and vantage point. Most of us get around this awkward truth by saying that we see—or by only actually seeing—what we are "supposed" to see, a generalized, common-sense approximation of reality.

Some individuals struggle to see things as fully and clearly as possible from their own unique vantage point and to communicate to others their particular—even peculiar—vision. But here too we are individuated, for though we speak of our "common language," we each speak a unique language, made up of "dialects" that are not only regional and ethnic but also conditioned by our age group, our profession, our education, travel, reading—all our experiences. Yet if we want to express our unique vision to others who have different visions and different "languages" we must find some medium that is both true to ourselves and understandable to others.

There is for these individuals—these writers of literature—a constant tug-of-war between the uniqueness of their individual visions and the generalizing nature of language. The battle does not always result in sheer loss, however. Often, in the very struggle to get their own perceptions into language, writers sharpen those perceptions or discover what they themselves did not know when they began to write. You have probably made similar discoveries some time or other in the process of writing a letter or an assigned paper. But writers also find that what they have written does not perfectly embody what they meant it to, just as you perhaps have found that your finished papers have been not quite so brilliant as your original idea.

"Understanding" is not a passive reception of a text but an active reaching out from our own experiences toward the text. At least at first we need to do so by meeting the author on the ground of a common or general language and set of conventions—things that everybody "knows." The first task of the reader, therefore, is to get not to the author's intention, but to the general statement that the work itself makes—that is, its theme or thesis. After a few readings we can usually make a stab at articulating the theme of most works. What a work says in the way of a general theme, however, is not necessarily its full or ultimate meaning; otherwise we would read theme summaries and not stories, poems, or plays. The theme is the meaning accessible to all through close reading of the text and common to all, but a literary text is not all statement. There are often cloudy areas in the text where we cannot be sure what is **implication,** the suggestion of the text, and what is our **inference,** or interpretation, of the text. How does the title of "Jacklight" fit the poem (chapter 4)? Though a jacklight is a torch or light used for attracting game at night and that seems to fit the poem well enough, why is it the title? Is it that important? Of the many meanings of "jack" or "light," are there any others that make it appropriate? Is the adjectival form of "jack" that means "man" intentionally related, or is it our (or my) inference? What is the relation of the epigraph about the Chippewa words to the poem? The details of the poem clearly concern hunting; are they supposed to relate as well to "flirting"? If so, which details do and which do not? Is there anything about rape or killing with the bare hands? Is the poem feminist? Is it about the modern ("now" in line 32) shift of the initiative of courtship from the man to the woman? If so, is there not a problem with "flirting" as a synonym for the jacklight initiative, since "flirting" is a word traditionally associated with the woman's courtship "signals"? The meaning of the poem will vary with the individual reader's inferences from these details or answers to these questions or with different questions other readers will raise.

The full meaning of a work for you is not only in its stated theme, one that everyone can agree on, but in the meaning you derive by bringing together that generalized theme, the precise language of the text, and your own applicable experiences—including reading experience—and imagination. That "meaning" is not the total meaning of the work, not what the author originally perceived and "meant to say"; it is the vision of the author as embodied in the work *and re-viewed from your own angle of vision.*

Your role in producing a meaning from the text does not free you, please note, from paying very close attention to the precise language of the text, the words and their meanings, their order, the syntax of the sentences, and even such mundane details as punctuation. You cannot impose a meaning on the text, no matter how sincerely and intensely you feel it, in defiance of the rules of grammar and the nature of the language.

Still, the reader must be an artist too, trying to experience the reality of the work as the author experienced reality, and with the same reverence and sense of responsibility for the original. To write about literature you must try to embody your reading experience—or interpretation—of the work in language. Alas, writing about literature, using words about words, is not as easy as it sounded at first. But it is more exciting, giving you a chance to see with another's eyes, to explore another's perceptions or experiences, and to explore and more fully understand your own in the process, thus expanding the horizon of your experience, perception, consciousness.

When some rich works of literature seem to have more than one meaning or no entirely satisfactory meaning or universally agreed upon single theme, it is not that they are not saying something, and saying something very specific, but that what they are saying is too specific, and complex, and profound, and true, perhaps, to be generalized or paraphrased in a few dozen words. The literary work is meaning*ful*—that is, full of meaning or meanings; but it is the reader who produces each particular meaning from the work, using the work itself, the language of the community and of the work, and his or her own language, experience, and imagination.

As readers trying to understand the unique perception and language of the author, we must translate the text as best we can into terms we can understand for ourselves. We try not to reduce the text to our own earlier, limited understanding but to stretch our minds and feelings toward its vision.

An interpretation, then, is not a clarification of what the writer "was trying to say"; it is a process that itself says, in effect, "The way I am trying to understand this work is . . ."

Deciding What to Write About

HAVING SOMETHING TO SAY

Deciding what to write about—what approach to use, which questions to ask—seems like the first step in the process of writing a paper about a work of literature. It isn't. Before that, you have to have confidence that you have something to say, which is not easy. You may feel as if you can *never* begin and want to put off the paper forever, or you may want to plunge in fast and get it over with. Either of these approaches is a mistake: the best way is to begin preparing for the paper as soon as possible—the moment you know you have one to write—but not to hurry into the writing itself.

The first step is to get close enough to the text to feel comfortable with it. Before you can tell anyone else about what you have read—and writing about literature is just another form of talking about literature—you need to "know" the work, to have a sure sense of what the text itself is like, how its parts function, what ideas it expresses, how it creates particular effects, how it makes you feel. And the only way you will get to know the work is to spend time with it, reading it carefully and thoughtfully several times and turning it over in your mind, *before* you pick up a pen and prepare to write.

Begin, then, by reading carefully the work you are going to write about. The first time, read it straight through at one sitting: read slowly, pausing at its natural divisions—between paragraphs or stanzas, or at the ends of scenes—to consider how you are responding to the work. Later, when your sense of the work is more comfortable and when you have the "feel" of the whole, you can compare your early responses with your more considered thoughts, in effect "correcting" your first impressions in whatever way seems necessary on the basis of new and better knowledge. But if you are noncommittal at first, refusing to notice what you think and feel, you will have nothing to correct, and you may cut yourself off from the most direct routes of response. Feelings are not always reliable—about texts any more than about people—but they are always the first point of contact with a literary work: you feel before you think. Try to start with your mind open, as if it were a blank sheet of paper ready to receive an impression from what you read.

When you have finished a first reading, think about your first impressions. Think about how the work began, how it gained your interest, how its conflicts and issues were resolved, how it ended, how it made you feel from beginning to end. Write down any phrases or events that you remember especially vividly, anything you are afraid you might forget. Look back at any parts that puzzled you at first. Write down in one sentence what you think the story, poem, or play is about. Then read it again, this time more slowly, making notes on any passages that seem especially significant and pausing over any features or passages that puzzle you. Then write a longer statement—three or four sentences—summarizing the work and suggesting more fully what it seems to be about. Try to write the kind of summary described above on pages 932–33.

Stop and do something else for a while, something as different as possible, but do NOT do some other reading you have been meaning to do; getting away from reading for a while will make you readier to get back to it. When you go back to the work and finish reading it for the third time—rapidly and straight through—write down in a sentence the most important thing you would want to tell someone else who was about to read it for the first time: not just whether you liked it or not, but what exactly you liked, how the whole thing seems to have worked.

Now you are ready to choose a topic.

CHOOSING A TOPIC

Once you are ready to choose a topic, the chances are that you have already—quietly and perhaps unconsciously—chosen one. The clue is in the last statement you wrote. Chances are that what you wrote down as the one thing you most wanted to say is close to the heart of the central issue in the work you are going to write about. Your statement will become, perhaps, in somewhat revised form, your thesis.

The next step is to convert your personal feelings and desire to communicate into something communicable—into some statement about the work that will mean something to someone else. Again, you may already be further along than you think. Look at the "summary" you wrote after your second reading. The summary will probably sound factual, objective, and general about the work; the personal statement you wrote after the third reading will be more emotional, subjective, and particular about some aspect of the work. In combining the two successfully lies the key to a good paper: what you want to do is write persuasively an elaboration and explanation of the last statement so that your reader comes to share the "objective" view of the whole work that your summary expresses. You want to build your essay on the basis of your first statement, taking a firm hold on the handle you have found. The summary is your limit and guide: it reminds you of where you will come out. Any good topic ultimately leads back to the crucial perceptions involved in a summary. Ultimately, any good writing about literature leads to a full sense of the central focus of the work, but the most effective way to find that center is by discovering a pathway that particularly interests you. The best writing about literature presents a clear—and well-argued—

thesis about a work or works and presents it from the perspective of personal, individual perception.

Topics often suggest themselves after a second or third reading, simply because one feature or problem stands out so prominently that it almost demands to be talked about. But if you're still looking for a topic after three or four readings, you may sometimes have to settle for the kind of topic that will be safe—more or less—for any literary work. Some topics are almost all-purpose. You can always analyze devices of characterization in a narrative, showing how descriptive detail, dialogue, and the reactions of other characters combine to present a particular character and evoke the reader's response to him or her; with a poem you can almost always write an adequate paper analyzing rhythm, or verse form, or imagery, or the connotations of key words. Such "fall-back" topics are, however, best used only as last resorts, when your instincts have failed you in a particular instance. When choice is free, a more lively and committed paper is likely to begin from a particular insight or question, something that compels you and makes you want to say something, or solve a problem, or formulate a thesis. The best papers are usually very personal in origin; even when a topic is set by the assignment, the best papers come from a sense of having personally found a persuasive answer to a significant question. To turn a promising idea into a good paper, however, personal responses usually need to be supported by a considerable mass of evidence; the process often resembles the testing of "evidence" in a laboratory or the formulation of hypotheses and arguments in a law case—and they will usually need to go through repeated written revisions that will sharpen and refine them.

CONSIDERING YOUR AUDIENCE

Thinking of your paper as an argument or an explanation will also help with one of the most sensitive issues in writing about literature: audience. To whom are you writing? The obvious answer is your instructor, but in an important sense that is the wrong answer. It is wrong because, although it could literally be true that your instructor will be the only person (besides you) who will ever read your paper, your object in writing about literature is to learn to write for an audience of peers, people a lot like yourself who are sensible, in the process of being educated, and need to have something (in this case a literary work) explained to them so that they will be able to understand it more fully. Don't be insulting and explain the obvious, but don't assume either that your reader has noticed and considered every detail. The object is to inform and convince your reader, not to try to impress.

Should you, then, altogether ignore the obvious fact that it is an instructor—probably with a master's degree or Ph.D. in literature—who is your actual reader? Not altogether: you don't want to get so carried away with speaking to people of your own age and interests that you slip into street slang, or feel the need to explain what a stanza is, or leave an allusion to a rock star unexplained. But don't become preoccupied with the idea that you are writing for someone in "authority" or someone you need to please. Most of all, don't think of yourself as writing for a captive audience, for a reader who *has* to read what you write. The tone of your paper should be serious and straightforward and its attitude respectful toward the reader, as well as toward the text. But its approach and vocabulary, while formal enough for academic writing, should be readily understandable by someone with your own background and reading experience. And it should be lively enough to interest someone like you. Try to imagine, as your ideal reader, the person in your class whom you most respect. Write to get, and hold, that person's serious attention. Try to communicate, try to *teach*.

From Topic to Rough Draft

Writing about literature is very much like talking about literature. But there is one important difference. When we talk, we organize as we go—trying to get a handle, experimenting, working toward an understanding. And the early stages of preparing a paper—the notetaking, the outlining, the rough drafts—are much like that. A "finished" paper, however, has the uncertainties and tentativeness worked out and presents an argument that moves carefully and compellingly toward a conclusion. How does one get from here to there?

Once you have decided on a topic, the process of planning is fairly straightforward, but it can be time consuming and (often) frustrating. There are three basic steps in the planning process: first you gather the evidence, then you sort it into order, and (finally) you develop it into a convincing argument. The easiest way is to take these steps one by one.

GATHERING EVIDENCE

The first step involves gathering evidence that supports the thesis statement you have chosen; this step takes you back (once more) to the text. But before you read it again, look over any notes you have already made in the margin, any passages you may have underlined, and any comments you have written down about the text. Which things that you noted earlier have something to do with the topic you have now defined? Which of them will be useful to you in making your main point? Which ones can you now set aside as irrelevant to the topic you have decided on?

Reading over the notes you have already made is a good preparation for re-reading the work again, for this time as you read it you will be looking at it in a new and quite specific way, looking for all the things in it that relate to the topic you have decided on. This time you will, in effect, be flagging everything—words, phrases, structural devices, changes of tone, anything— that bears upon your topic. Read slowly with your topic always in mind and keep your pen constantly poised to mark useful points. Be ready to say something about the points as you come upon them; it's a good idea to write down, immediately, any sentences that occur to you as you re-read this time. Consider the possibility of recording notes and comments directly into a computer so you'll have them ready at hand when you actually begin writing your paper. Some of these sentences will turn out to be useful in the paper itself.

No one can tell you exactly how to take notes, but here are five hints that you may find useful.

1. Keep your topic and your thesis about your topic constantly in mind as you re-read and take notes. Mark all passages in the work that bear on your topic, and for each one write on a note card a single sentence that describes how the passage relates to your topic and thesis. (You can, of course, create the equivalent of a series of separate cards in a computer.) Indicate, for each passage, the specific location in the text— by page or paragraph number if you are working on a narration or an essay; by line number if you are writing about a poem; by act, scene, and line number if you are writing about a play.
2. Keep re-reading and taking notes until one of five things happens:
   a. You get too tired and lose your concentration. (If that happens, stop and then start again when you are rested, preferably the next day.)
   b. You stop finding relevant passages or perceive a noticeable drying up of your ideas. (Again, time to pause; give the work at least one more reading later when your mind is fresh and see whether the juices start anew. If they don't, you may be ready to outline and write.)
   c. You begin to find yourself annotating every single sentence or line, and the evidence all begins to run together into a single blob. (Stop and sort out your thesis again, simplifying and narrowing it so that you don't try to include everything. Then go back to your notetaking and discriminate more carefully between what actually is important to your thesis and what only relates at some distance.)

       d. You become impatient with your notetaking and can't wait to get started writing. (Start writing. Be prepared to go back to systematic notetaking if your ideas or your energy fade. The chances are that the prose passages you write this way will find a place in your paper, but they may not belong exactly where you think they do when you first write them down. Writing when you are excited about what you are thinking can get energy into your paper and sometimes produce articulateness and clarity, but you will often need to reorganize for greater effectiveness.)

       e. You find that there is insufficient evidence for your thesis, that the evidence points in another direction, or that the evidence contradicts your thesis. (Revise your topic to reflect the evidence, and begin rereading once more.)

3. When you think you have finished your notetaking, read all your note cards over slowly, one by one, and jot down any further ideas as they occur to you, each one on a separate note card. (Sometimes it will seem as if note cards beget note cards. Too much is better than too little at the notetaking stage: you can always discard the extras before the final draft. Don't worry if you seem to have too many notes and too much material. But later, when you boil down to essentials, you will have to be ruthless and omit some of your favorite ideas.)

4. Transfer all of your notes to pieces of paper—or note cards—that are all the same size, one note on each. It is easier to sort them this way when you get ready to organize and outline. If you like to write notes in the margin of your text (or on the backs of envelopes, or on dinner napkins, or on shirtsleeves), systematically transfer every note to uniform sheets of paper or cards before you begin to outline. Again, you can do it on a computer, but there is often some virtue in having your ideas spatialized on cards so that you can reorganize by physically resorting the cards, especially when you change your mind (as you will) and decide to move a point from one part of your paper to another. Index cards—either 3 × 5, if you write small and make economical notes, or 4 × 6, if you need more space—are ideal for notetaking and sorting.

5. When you think you are done taking notes (because you are out of ideas, or out of time, or getting beyond a manageable number of pieces of evidence), read through the whole pile one more time, again letting any new ideas—or ideas that take on a fresh look because you combine them in a new way—spawn new sentences for new note cards.

    How many times should you read a story, poem, or play before you stop taking notes? There is no right answer. If you have read the work three times before settling on a topic, two more readings may do. Let your conscience, your judgment, and your clock be your guides.

ORGANIZING YOUR NOTES

The notes you have taken will become, in the next few hours, almost the whole content of your paper. The key to the task is getting all your ideas into the right order—that is, into a sequence that will allow them to argue your thesis most persuasively.

In order to put your notes into a proper order, you will need (ironically) to get a little distance from your notes. Set your notes aside, but not too far away. On a fresh sheet of paper, write down all the major points you want to be sure to make. Write them down randomly, as they occur to you. Now read quickly through your pack of note cards and add to your list any important points from these new notes that were not already on your cards. Then decide which ideas should go first, which should go second, and so on. The easiest way to try out an order is to take your random list and put a 1 in front of the point you will probably begin with, a 2 before the probable second point, and so on. Then copy the list, in numerical order, onto a clean sheet of paper, revising (if you need to) as you go. Do not be surprised if later you have to revise your list further. Your next task is to match up your note cards (and the examples they contain) with the points on your outline.

Putting things in a particular order is a spatial problem, and by having your notes on cards or pieces of paper of a uniform size you can do much of your organizing physically. Prepare a title card for each point in your outline, writing on it the point and its probable place in your paper, then line them up on the table or floor in order before you begin writing.

Two-thirds of this exercise is quite easy: most examples and ideas you have written down will match quite easily with a particular point. But some cards will resist classification. Some cards will seem to belong in two or more places; others will not seem to belong at all. If a card seems to belong to more than one point, put it in the pile with the lowest number (but write on it the number or numbers of other possible locations). If, for example, a card might belong in point 2 but could also belong in point 6 or 9, put it in the pile of 2's and write "maybe 6 or 9" on the card; if you don't use it in writing about point 2 move it to pile 6; if you don't use it in 6, move it to 9. Remember that you will work your way through the piles in numerical order, so that you have a safety system for notes that don't seem to belong where you first thought but that still belong somewhere in your paper. Move them to a possible later point, or put them in a special pile (marked "?" or "use in revised draft") and, once you have completed a first draft of your paper, go through this pile, carefully looking for places in your paper where these ideas may belong. Almost never will everything fit neatly into your first draft. If everything does seem to fit exactly as you had originally planned, you have either done an incredible job of planning and guessing about the organization of your paper, or you are forcing things into inappropriate places.

Don't be surprised if you have a large number of leftover note cards—that is, cards whose ideas you haven't yet used—after you have written your first draft. You will probably find places for many of these ideas later, but some just won't fit and won't be needed for the paper you ultimately write, no matter how good the ideas are.

DEVELOPING AN ARGUMENT

Once you have decided on your major points and assembled your evidence, you have to decide how you are going to present your argument and how you are going to present *yourself*. What you say is, of course, more important than how you say it, but your manner of presentation can make a world of difference. Putting your evidence together effectively—in a coherent and logical order so that your readers' curiosities and questions are answered systematically and fully—is half the task in developing a persuasive argument. The other half involves your choice of a voice and tone that will make readers want to read on—and make them favorably disposed toward what you say.

The tone of your paper is the basis of your relationship with your reader. How do you want your readers to feel about you and your argument? Being too positive can make your readers feel stupid and inadequate and can turn them into defensive, resistant readers who will rebel at your every point. Friendship with your reader is almost always better than an adversary relationship. Sounding like a nice person who is talking reasonably and sensibly is not enough if in fact you don't make sense or have nothing to say, but the purpose of the tone you choose is to make your reader receptive to your content, not hostile. The rest of the job depends on the argument itself.

It has been said that all good papers should be organized in the same way, what we call the Tell[3] method.

1. Tell 'em what you're going to tell 'em.
2. Tell 'em.
3. Tell 'em what you told 'em.

That description fits—in pretty general terms—the most common kind of organization, which includes an introduction, a body of argument, and a conclusion, but take care not to follow this rule too simplistically. The beginning does need to introduce the subject, sort out the essential issues, and suggest what your perspective will be, and the conclusion does need to sum up what you have said in the main part of your paper, but the first paragraph shouldn't give *everything* away, nor should the final one simply repeat what is already clear. Lead into your subject clearly but with a little subtlety; arrange your main points in the most effective manner you can think of, building a logical argument and supporting your general points with evidence from the text, concisely phrased and presented, and at the end show *how* your argument has added up—don't just *say* that it did.

There are, of course, other ways to organize than the basic Tell³ method, but the imagination and originality that can be exercised in a straightforward Tell³ paper are practically unlimited.

WRITING THE FIRST DRAFT

It is now time to set pen to paper—or fingers to machine. No one can help you much now for a while. The main thing is to get started right with a clear first sentence that expresses your sense of direction and arrests the attention of your readers. (If you can't think of a good first sentence, don't pause over it too long. Write down a paraphrase of what you want it to say— something like the statement you wrote down after your third reading—and go on to start writing about your main points. Your final "first" sentence may sometimes be the last one you will actually write.) And then you inch along, word by word and sentence by sentence, as you follow your outline from one paragraph to another. Keep at it. Struggle. Stare into space. Get up and stride about the room. Scratch your head. Sharpen a pencil. Run your fingers through your hair. Groan. Snap your fingers. Pray. Make coffee. But keep writing.

It is often frustrating as you search for the right word or struggle to decide how the next sentence begins, but it is satisfying when you get it right. Stay with it until you complete a draft you think you can live with. Write "The End" at the bottom and set it aside. Breathe a sigh of relief.

And try not to think about the revisions you will do tomorrow.

From Rough Draft to Completed Paper

REVISING

This final stage of the process is the most important of all, and it is the easiest one to mismanage. There is a world of difference between a bunch of ideas that present a decent interpretation of a work of literature and a cogent, coherent, persuasive essay that will stir your readers to a nod of agreement and shared pleasure in a moment of insight. If you haven't done good literary analysis and sorted out your insights earlier, nothing you do at this stage will help much, but if what you have done so far is satisfactory, this is the stage that can turn your paper from an adequate analysis into something special.

The important thing is not to allow yourself to be too easily satisfied. If you have struggled with earlier stages, it may be tempting to think you are finished when you have put a period to the last sentence in your first draft. It will often feel as if you are done: you may feel drained, tired of the subject, anxious to get on to other things, such as sleep or food or friends or another project. And it *is* a good idea to take a break once you've finished a draft and let what you have done settle for a few hours, preferably overnight. (The Roman poet and critic Horace suggested putting a draft aside for nine years, but most instructors won't wait that long.)

It may take *several* more drafts to produce your best work. Often it is tempting to cut corners—to smooth out a troublesome paragraph by obscuring the issue or by omitting the difficult point altogether instead of confronting it, or to ask a roommate or friend for help in figuring out what is wrong with a particular passage. But you will learn more in the long run if you make yourself struggle a bit. When a particular word or phrase you have used turns out to be imprecise, or misleading, or ambiguous, search until you find the *right* word or phrase. (At least put a big X in the margin so that you will come back and fix it later.) If a paragraph is incomplete or poorly organized, fill it out or reorganize it. If a transition from one point to another does not work, look again at your outline and see if another way of ordering your points would help. *Never* decide that the problem can best be solved by hoping that your reader will not notice. The satisfaction of finally solving the problem will build your confidence and sooner or later make your writing easier and better.

REVIEWING YOUR WORK AND REVISING AGAIN

Precisely how you move from one draft to another is up to you and will properly depend on the ways you work best; the key is to find all the things that bother you (and that *should* bother you) and then gradually correct them, moving toward a better paper with each succeeding draft. Here are some things to watch for.

Thesis and central thrust: Is it clear what your main point is? Do you state it straightforwardly, effectively, and early? Do you make clear what the work is about? Are you fair to the spirit and emphasis of the work? Do you make clear the relationship between your thesis and the central thrust of the work? Do you explain *how* the work creates its effect rather than just asserting it?

Organization: Does your paper move logically from beginning to end? Does your first paragraph set up the main issue you are going to discuss and suggest the direction of your discussion? Do your paragraphs follow each other in a coherent and logical order? Does the first sentence of each paragraph accurately suggest what that paragraph will contain? Does your final paragraph draw a conclusion that follows from the body of your paper? Do you resolve the issues you say you resolve?

Use of evidence: Do you use enough examples? Too many? Does each example prove what you say it does? Do you explain each example fully enough? Are the examples sufficiently varied? Are any of them labored, or over-explained, or made to bear more weight than they can stand? Have you left out any examples useful to your thesis? Do you include any gratuitous ones just because you like them? Have you achieved a good balance between examples and generalizations?

Tone: How does your voice sound in the paper? Confident? Arrogant? Boastful? Does it show off too much? Is it too timid or self-effacing? Do you ever sound smug? Too tentative? Too dogmatic? Would a neutral reader be put off by any of your assertions? By your way of arguing? By your choice of examples? By the language you use?

Sentences: Does each sentence read clearly and crisply? Have you rethought and rewritten any sentences you can't explain? Is the first sentence of your paper a strong, clear one likely to gain the interest of a neutral reader? Is the first sentence of each paragraph an especially vigorous one? Are your sentences varied enough? Do you avoid the passive voice and "there is/there are" sentences?

Word Choice: Have you used any words whose meaning you are not sure of? In any cases in which you were not sure of what word to use, did you stay with the problem until you found the exact word? Do your metaphors and figures of speech make literal sense? Are all the idioms used correctly? Is your terminology correct? Are your key words always used to mean *exactly* the same thing? Have you avoided sounding repetitive by varying your sentences rather than using several different terms to mean precisely the same thing?

Conciseness: Have you eliminated all the padding you put in when you didn't think your paper would be long enough? Have you gone through your paper, sentence by sentence, to eliminate all the unnecessary words and phrases? Have you looked for sentences (or even paragraphs) that essentially repeat what you have already said—and eliminated all repetition? Have you checked for multiple examples and pared down to the best and most vivid ones? Have you gotten rid of all inflated phrasing calculated to impress readers? Have you eliminated all roundabout phrases and rewritten long, complicated, or confusing sentences into shorter, clearer ones? Are you convinced that you have trimmed every possible bit of excess and that you cannot say what you have to say any more economically?

Mechanics: Have you checked the syntax in each *separate* sentence? Have you checked the spelling of any words that you are not sure of or that look funny? Have you examined each sentence separately for punctuation? Have you checked every quotation word by word against the original? Have you given proper credit for all material—written or oral—that you have borrowed from others? Have you followed the directions your instructor gave you for citations, footnotes, and form?

The most effective way to revise in the final stages is to read through your paper looking for one problem at a time, that is, to go through it once looking at paragraphing, another time looking at individual sentences, still another for word choice or problems of grammar. It is almost impossible to check too many things too often—although you can get so absorbed with little things that you overlook larger matters, and you may just run out of time. With practice, you will learn to watch carefully for the kinds of mistakes you are most prone to. Everyone has individual weaknesses and flaws. Here are some of the most common temptations that beginning writers fall for:

1. Haste. (Don't start too late, or finish too soon after you begin.)
2. Pretentiousness. (Don't use words you don't understand, tackle problems that are too big for you, or write sentences you can't explain; it is more important to make sense than to make a big, empty impression.)
3. Boredom. (The quickest way to bore others is to be bored yourself. If you think your paper will be a drag, you are probably right. It is hard to fake interest in something you can't get excited about; keep at it until you find a spark.)
4. Randomness. (Don't try to string together half a dozen unrelated ideas or insights and con yourself into thinking that you have written a paper.)
5. Imprecision. (Don't settle for approximation, either in words or ideas; something that is 50 percent right is also 50 percent wrong.)
6. Universalism. (Don't try to be a philosopher and make grand statements about life; stick to what is in the text you are writing about.)
7. Vagueness. (Don't settle for a general "sense" of the work you are talking about; get it detailed, get it right.)
8. Wandering. (Don't lose track of your subject or the text that you are talking about.)
9. Sloppiness. (Don't sabotage all your hard work on analysis and writing by failing to notice misspelled words, grammatical mistakes, misquotations, incorrect citations or references, or typographical errors. Little oversights make readers suspicious and make them pickier about content.)
10. Impatience. (Don't be too anxious to get done. Enjoy the experience; savor the process. Have fun watching yourself learn.)

Being flexible—being willing to rethink your ideas and reorder your argument as you go—is crucial to success in writing, especially in writing about literature. You will find different (and better) ways to express your ideas and feelings as you struggle with revisions, and you will also find that—in the course of analyzing the work, preparing to write, writing, and rewriting—your response to the work itself will have grown and shifted somewhat. Part of the reason is that you will have become more knowledgeable as a result of the time and effort you have spent, and you will have a more subtle understanding of the work. But part of the reason will also be that the work itself will not be exactly the same. Just as any text is a little different for every reader, it is also a little different with every successive reading by the *same* reader, and what you will be capturing in your words is some of the subtlety of the text, its capacity to produce effects that are alive and that are therefore always changing just slightly. You need not, therefore, feel that you must say the final word about the text you are writing about—but you do want to say whatever word you have to say in the best possible way.

Writing *will* come more easily with practice. But you needn't aspire to professional writing to take pleasure in what you accomplish. Learning to write well about literature will help you with all sorts of tasks, some of them having little to do with writing. Writing trains the mind, creates habits, teaches you procedures that will have all kinds of long-range effects that you may not immediately recognize or be able to predict. And ultimately it is very satisfying, even if it is not easy, to be able to stand back and say, "That is mine. Those are my words. I know what I'm talking about. I understand, and I can make someone else understand."

One final bit of advice: do not follow too slavishly anyone's advice, including ours. We have suggested some general strategies and listed some common pitfalls. But writing is a very personal experience, and you will have talents (and faults) that are a little different from anyone else's. Learn to play to your own strengths and avoid the weaknesses that you are especially prone to. Pay attention to your instructor's comments; learn from your own mistakes.

A Summary of the Process

Here, briefly, is a summary, step by step, of the stages we have suggested you move through in preparing a paper about literature.

STAGE ONE: DECIDING WHAT TO WRITE ABOUT

- Read the text straight through, thoughtfully. Make notes at the end on any points that caught your special attention.

- Read the text again more slowly, pausing to think through all the parts you don't understand. When you finish, write a three- or four-sentence summary.

- Read the text again, carefully but quite quickly. Decide what you feel most strongly about in the text, and write down the one thing you would most want to explain to a friend about how the narrative, essay, poem, or play works, or (if the text still puzzles you) the one question you would most like to be able to answer.

- Decide how the statement you made at the end of your third reading relates to the summary you wrote down after the second reading.

- Write a one-paragraph "promise" of what your paper is going to argue.

STAGE TWO: PLANNING YOUR PAPER

- Read the text at least twice more and make notes on anything that relates to your thesis.

- Read through all your notes so far, and for each write a sentence articulating how it relates to your thesis.

- Transfer all your notes to note cards of uniform size.

- Read through all your notes again and record any new observations or ideas on additional note cards.

- Set aside your note cards for the moment, and make a brief outline of the major points you intend to make.

- Sort the note cards into piles corresponding to the major points in your outline. Sort the cards in each separate pile into the most likely order of their use in the paper.

- Make a more detailed outline (including the most significant examples) from your pile of note cards on each point.

- Reconsider your order of presentation and make any necessary adjustments.

- Begin writing.

STAGE THREE: REWRITING

- Go over your writing, word by word, sentence by sentence, and paragraph by paragraph, in draft after draft until your writing is worthy of the ideas you want to express.

STAGE FOUR: FINAL PREPARATION

- Type or word-process. Chances are that your instructor does not have a degree in hieroglyphics.

- Proofread. Who wants to read a paper you did not care enough about to read yourself?

- Proofread again. Find your mistakes before someone else does.

- Read it one more time, pen in hand.

ACKNOWLEDGMENTS

Maria Albertson: " 'Letter to Ma': The Chasm Between Mothers and Daughters" by Maria Albertson. Reprinted with permission.

Elizabeth Alexander: "West Indian Primer" from *The Venus Hottentot*, reprinted by permission of the University Press of Virginia.

Agha Shahid Ali: "Postcard from Kashmir" and "Snowmen" from *The Half-Inch Himalayas*, copyright © 1987 by Agha Shahid Ali, Wesleyan University Press by permission of University Press of New England.

Paula Gunn Allen: "Pocahontas to Her English Husband, John Rolfe," *Skin and Bones*, Paula Gunn Allen, Albuquerque: West End Press, 1988. Reprinted by permission of Diane Cleaver, Inc.

Julia Alvarez: "Hers: Hold the Mayonnaise" by Julia Alvarez (*The New York Times*, 1 / 12 / 92). Copyright © 1992 by The New York Times Company. Reprinted by permission.

Maya Angelou: "My Brother Bailey and Kay Francis" from *I Know Why the Caged Bird Sings* by Maya Angelou. Copyright © 1969 by Maya Angelou. Reprinted by permission of Random House, Inc. "Africa" from *Oh Pray My Wings Are Gonna Fit Me Well* by Maya Angelou. Copyright © 1975 by Maya Angelou. Reprinted by permission of Random House, Inc.

Michael Anthony: "Sandra Street" by Michael Anthony from *Cricket in the Road*, 1973. Reprinted by permission of Andre Deutsch Ltd.

Max Apple: "Trotsky's Bar Mitzvah" reprinted by permission of International Creative Management, Inc. Copyright © 1981 by Max Apple.

Tony Ardizzone: "My Mother's Stories" reprinted from *The Evening News* by Tony Ardizzone. Copyright © 1986 by Tony Ardizzone. Reprinted by permission of the author.

Margaret Atwood: "The Man from Mars" from *Dancing Girls* by Margaret Atwood. Used by permission of the Canadian Publishers, McClelland & Stewart, Toronto. "The Man from Mars" from *Dancing Girls* by Margaret Atwood, copyright © 1977, 1982 by O. W. Toad, Ltd. Reprinted by permission of Simon & Schuster, Inc.

Jimmy Santiago Baca: "Ancestor" and "So Mexicans Are Taking Jobs from Americans" by Jimmy Santiago Baca from *Immigrants in Our Own Land*. Copyright © 1982 by Jimmy Santiago Baca. Reprinted by permission of New Directions Publishing Corp.

Toni Cade Bambara: "The Lesson" from *Gorilla, My Love* by Toni Cade Bambara, copyright © 1972 by Toni Cade Bambara. Reprinted by permission of Random House, Inc.

Leonard Begay: "Beyond Sacred Mountains" by Leonard Begay from *We Did It Our Way: A Collection of Native American Literary Creations*, edited by Dr. D. G. Campbell, supported by the Native American Honor Society at Northern Arizona University, Dr. Frank C. Dukepoo, Director. Reprinted by permission of Leonard Begay.

Salli Benedict: "Tahotahontanekentseratkerontakwenhakie" by Salli M. K. Benedict. Reprinted by permission of Salli M. K. Benedict.

Becky Birtha: "Johnnieruth" from *Lovers' Choice* by Becky Birtha. Reprinted by permission of The Seal Press.

Neil Bissoondath: "There Are a Lot of Ways to Die" from *Digging Up the Mountains* by Neil Bissoondath, copyright © 1986 by Neil Bissoondath. Reprinted by permission of Macmillan Canada and Viking Penguin, a division of Penguin Books USA Inc.

Alice Bloch: "Six Years" was originally published by *rara avis* magazine. Reprinted by permission of Alice Bloch.

Perry Brass: "I Think the New Teacher's a Queer" by Perry Brass, copyright © 1973 by Panjandrum Press, Inc. / Gay Sunshine Press. Reprinted by permission of Panjandrum Press, Inc.

Rita Mae Brown: "Sappho's Reply" from *Rita Mae Brown Poems*, copyright © 1971, 1973, by Rita Mae Brown, The Crossing Press, Freedom, CA. Reprinted by permission of The Crossing Press.

Joseph Bruchac: "Ellis Island" by Joseph Bruchac from *The Remembered Earth*, ed. Geary Jobson. Albuquerque: Red Earth Press, 1979.

Diane Burns: "Sure You Can Ask Me a Personal Question" by Diane Burns. Reprinted by permission of the author.

Luis Cabalquinto: "Hometown." First appeared in *Breaking Silence*, The Greenfield Review Press. Reprinted by permission of Luis Cabalquinto.

Virginia Cerenio: "We Who Carry the Endless Seasons." Reprinted by permission of Kearny Street Workshop Press from *Trespassing Innocence* by V. R. Cerenio. Kearny Street Workshop Press: 1989, San Francisco.

Lorna Dee Cervantes: "Heritage" and "Refugee Ship" from *The Americas Review* (formerly *Revista Chicano-Riqueña*), reprinted by permission of Arte Publico Press. "Freeway 280" reprinted by permission of the publisher, *Latin American Literary Review*, Vol. 15 No. 10, 1977, Pittsburgh, Pennsylvania.

G. S. Sharat Chandra: "Still Kicking in America" reprinted with permission from the author.

Rudolph Chelminski: "Next to Brzezinski, Chelminski's a Cinch" by Rudolph Chelminski (*Smithsonian*, February 1992). Reprinted by permission of *Smithsonian Magazine* and Rudolph Chelminski.

Alice Childress: *Wedding Band* by Alice Childress, copyright © 1973 by Alice Childress. Used by permission of Flora Roberts, Inc.

Eric Chock: "Chinese Fireworks Banned in Hawaii" is reprinted from *Last Days Here*, copyright © 1989 by Eric Chock.

Lee Ki Chuck: "From Korea to Heaven Country" by Lee Ki Chuck from *First Generation* by June Namias, Revised Edition, © 1978, 1992 by the Board of Trustees of the University of Illinois, used with permission from the University of Illinois Press.

Sandra Cisneros: "Bread" from *Woman Hollering Creek*. Copyright © 1991 by Sandra Cisneros. Published in the United States by Vintage Books, a division of Random House, Inc., New York and simultaneously in Canada by Random House of Canada Limited, Toronto. Originally published in hardcover by Random House, Inc., New York, in 1991. Reprinted by permission of Susan Bergholz Literary Services, New York.

Michelle Cliff: "If I Could Write This in Fire I Would Write This in Fire," from *The Land of Look Behind*, by Michelle Cliff. Copyright © 1985 by Michelle Cliff. Reprinted by permission of the author.

Lucille Clifton: "in the inner city," copyright © 1987 by Lucille Clifton. Reprinted from *Good Woman: Poems and a Memoir 1969–1980*, by Lucille Clifton, with the permission of BOA Editions, Ltd., 92 Park Ave., Brockport, NY 14420.

Judith Ortiz Cofer: "More Room" by Judith Ortiz Cofer is reprinted with permission from the publisher of *Silent Dancing: A Partial Remembrance of a Puerto Rican Childhood* (Houston: Arte Publico Press—University of Houston, 1990). "More Room" originally appeared in *Puerto del Sol* magazine.

Madeline Coopsammy: "In the Dungeon of My Skin" by Madeline Coopsammy, previously published in *Creation Fire: A CAFRA Anthology of Caribbean Women's Poetry*. Sister Vision, Black Women and Women of Colour Press, Toronto, Canada, 1990.

Nora Dauenhauer: "Tlingit Concrete Poem." Copyright © by Nora Dauenhauer. Reprinted by permission of author.

Richard Dokey: "Sánchez." Copyright © 1967 by Richard Dokey. This story first appeared in *Southwest Review*. Reprinted by permission.

Elizabeth Douglas: "Macaroni, Macaroni . . . and Chalcedony" by Elizabeth Douglas. Reprinted with permission.

Rita Dove: "Parsley." Reprinted from Rita Dove: *Museum* by permission of Carnegie Mellon University Press, copyright © 1983 by Rita Dove.

Margarita M. Engle: "Digging for Roots" (*Hispanic Magazine*, September 1991) by Margarita Engle. Reprinted with permission from *Hispanic Magazine* and Margarita Engle.

Louise Erdrich: "Jacklight" from *Jacklight* by Louise Erdrich. Copyright © 1984 by Louise Erdrich. Reprinted by permission of Henry Holt and Company, Inc. "Fleur" copyright © 1986 by Louise Erdrich. Reprinted by permission of the author.

Mari Evans: "The Friday Ladies of the Pay Envelope" from *I Am a Black Woman*, published by William Morrow & Co., 1970, by permission of the author.

James Fallows: "The Japanese Are Different from You and Me" by James Fallows from *The Atlantic Monthly* (September 1986). Reprinted by permission of James Fallows.

Gogisgi / Carroll Arnett: "Song of the Breed." Copyright © 1982 by Gogisgi / Carroll Arnett, from *Rounds* (Cross-Cultural Communications Press, 1982). Reprinted by permission.

Rafael Jesús González: "Sestina: Santa Prisca." Reprinted by permission of the author. First published in *El Grito*, Vol. 3, No. 1, Fall 1969.

Mary Stuart Hammond: "Canaan" is reprinted from *Out of Canaan: Poems* by Mary Stewart Hammond, by permission of W. W. Norton & Company, Inc. Copyright © 1991 by Mary Stewart Hammond.

Beth Hecht: "Alone in the Midst of 100,000 People" by Beth Hecht. Reprinted with permission.

Juan Felipe Herrera: "Revolution Skyscraper." We have made diligent efforts to contact the copyright holder to obtain permission to reprint this selection. If you have information that would help us, please write W. W. Norton & Company, 500 Fifth Avenue, New York, NY 10110.

Edward Hirsch: "In a Polish Home for the Aged" from *Wild Gratitude* by Edward Hirsch, copyright © 1985 by Edward Hirsch. Reprinted by permission of Alfred A. Knopf, Inc.

Linda Hogan: "Song for My Name" and "Heritage" from *Calling Myself Home*, originally published by The Greenfield Review Press; "Black Hills Survival Gathering, 1980" from *Eclipse*, published by American Indian Center Press, UCLA. Reprinted by permission of Linda Hogan.

Israel Horovitz: *The Indian Wants the Bronx* by Israel Horovitz. © Copyright 1968, by Israel Horovitz; © copyright 1967, by Israel Horovitz, as an unpublished dramatic composition. CAUTION: THE INDIAN WANTS THE BRONX, being duly copyrighted, is subject to a royalty. The amateur performance rights in the play are controlled exclusively by the Dramatists Play Service, Inc., 440 Park Avenue South, New York, N.Y. 10016. No amateur performance of the play may be given without obtaining in advance the written permission of the Dramatists Play Service, Inc. and paying the requisite fee.

Vanessa Howard: "Escape the Ghettos of New York" by Vanessa Howard. Reprinted by permission of the author.

Gish Jen: "In the American Society" by Gish Jen, copyright © 1986 by Gish Jen. First published in the *Southern Review*. Reprinted by permission of the author.

Jennifer Johns: "Carter Revard's 'Discovery' " by Jennifer Johns. Reprinted with permission.

Fenton Johnson: "About Men: The Limitless Heart" by Fenton Johnson (*The New York Times*, 6/23/91). Copyright © 1991 The New York Times Company. Reprinted by permission.

Laura Johnson: "The Context of 'Hindus': Bharati Mukherjee's Volume of Short Stories, *Darkness*" by Laura Johnson. Reprinted with permission.

Wayne D. Johnson: "What Happened to Red Deer" by Wayne Johnson reprinted by permission of the author. "What Happened to Red Deer" originally appeared in *Ploughshares*.

Cynthia Kadohata: "Charlie-O" from *The Floating World* by Cynthia Kadohata. Copyright © 1989 by Cynthia Kadohata. Used by permission of Viking Penguin, a division of Penguin Books USA Inc.

Garrison Keillor: "Protestant" from *Lake Wobegon Days* by Garrison Keillor. Copyright © 1985 by Garrison Keillor. Used by permission of Viking Penguin, a division of Penguin Books USA Inc.

Maurice Kenny: "Going Home" by Maurice Kenny from *Between Two Rivers: Selected Poems* by Maurice Kenny. Reprinted by permission of White Pine Press.

Martin Luther King, Jr.: "I Have a Dream," copyright © 1963 by Martin Luther King, Jr., copyright renewed 1991 by Coretta Scott King.

Maxine Hong Kingston: "No Name Woman" from *The Woman Warrior* by Maxine Hong Kingston, copyright © 1975, 1976 by Maxine Hong Kingston. Reprinted by permission of Alfred A. Knopf, Inc.

Etheridge Knight: "Hard Rock Returns to Prison from the Hospital for the Criminal Insane" by Etheridge Knight. Permission granted by Broadside Press.

Yusef Komunyakaa: "Tu Do Street" by Yosef Komunyakaa, reprinted from *Dien Cai Dau*, copyright © 1988 by Yusef Komunyakaa, Wesleyan University Press. Reprinted by permission of University Press of New England and Yusef Komunyakaa.

Juliet Kono: "Sashimi" by Juliet Kono, reprinted by permission of the author.

Steven Krueger: "Language, Identity, and Violence in Israel Horovitz's *The Indian Wants the Bronx*" by Steven Krueger. Reprinted with permission.

Michael Lassell: "How to Watch Your Brother Die," copyright © 1990 by Michael Lassell, reprinted from *Decade Dance* by Michael Lassell (Alyson Publications, Boston, 1990). Reprinted by permission of Michael Lassell.

Tato Laviera: "Tito Madera Smith" from *Enclave*, reprinted by permission of Arte Publico Press.

David Leavitt: "A Place I've Never Been" from *A Place I've Never Been* by David Leavitt. Copyright © 1990 by David Leavitt. Used by permission of Viking Penguin, a division of Penguin Books USA Inc.

Li-Young Lee: "The Gift" and "Persimmons" copyright © 1986 by Li-Young Lee. Reprinted from *Rose* by Li-Young Lee with the permission of BOA Editions, Ltd., 92 Park Avenue, Brockport, NY 14420.

Marie G. Lee: "My Two Dads" by Marie G. Lee, reprinted by permission of the author. "My Two Dads" first appeared in the *Brown Alumni Monthly*.

Walter K. Lew: "Leaving Seoul: 1953." First appeared in *Breaking Silence*, The Greenfield Review Press. Reprinted by permission of The Greenfield Review Press.

Stephen Shu Ning Liu: "My Father's Martial Art," copyright © 1981 by The Antioch Review, Inc. First appeared in the *Antioch Review*, Vol. 39 No. 3 (Summer, 1981).

Audre Lorde: "Home," reprinted from *Our Dead Behind Us: Poems* by Audre Lorde, by permission of W. W. Norton & Company, Inc. Copyright © 1986 by Audre Lorde.

Naomi Long Madgett: "Offspring" from *Pink Ladies in the Afternoon* by Naomi Long Madgett (Detroit: Lotus Press, Inc., 1972, 1990).

Marcela Christine Lucero-Trujillo: "Roseville, Minn., U.S.A." Copyright © 1976. Reprinted by permission of Patricia Trujillo-Villalobos.

Hugo Martinez-Serros: "Learn! Learn!" by Hugo Martinez-Serros from *The Last Laugh and Other Stories*, reprinted by permission of Arte Publico Press.

James Alan McPherson: "I Am an American" from *Elbow Room* by James Alan McPherson. Copyright © 1974 by James Alan McPherson. By permission of Little, Brown & Company.

Lynn Minton: "Is It Okay to Date Someone of Another Race?" from "Fresh Voices" column, *Parade*, December 15, 1991 by Lynn Minton. Reprinted with permission from *Parade*, copyright © 1991.

Gail Y. Miyasaki: "Obāchan." We have made diligent efforts to contact the copyright holder to obtain permission to reprint this selection. If you have information that would help us, please write W. W. Norton & Company, 500 Fifth Avenue, New York, NY 10110.

N. Scott Momaday: "The Eagle-Feather Fan" from *The Gourd Dancer* by N. Scott Momaday, reprinted by permission of the author.

Jesse G. Monteagudo: "Miami, Florida" by Jesse G. Monteagudo, originally appeared in *Hometowns: Gay Men Write About Where They Belong*, ed. John Preston. Reprinted by permission of Jesse G. Monteagudo.

Pat Mora: "Gentle Communion" by Pat Mora is reprinted with permission from the publisher of *Communion* (Houston: Arte Publico Press—University of Houston, 1991). "Borders," "Immigrants," and "Sonrisas," by Pat Mora are reprinted with permission from the publisher of *Borders* (Houston: Arte Publico Press—University of Houston, 1986).

Toshio Mori: "Abalone, Abalone, Abalone" by Toshio Mori, reprinted from *The Chauvinist and Other Stories*, Asian American Studies Center, Los

Angeles, California, copyright © Regents of the University of California, 1979.

Toni Morrison: "Recitatif" reprinted by permission of Toni Morrison. Copyright © 1983 by Toni Morrison.

Bharati Mukherjee: "Hindus" by Bharati Mukherjee, copyright © 1985, from *Darkness*, Penguin: New York. Reprinted by permission of The Elaine Markson Agency and Bharati Mukherjee.

Elías Miguel Muñoz: "Little Sister Born in This Land" and "Returning" by Elías Miguel Muñoz from *En estas tierras / In This Land*, copyright © 1989 Bilingual Press / Editorial Bilingue, Arizona State University, Tempe, AZ.

David Mura: "Listening" first appeared in *Crazyhorse* and then as a special chapbook printed by the Minnesota Center for Book Arts. The poem is used by permission of the author. Copyright © 1989, David Mura.

Joan Murray: "Coming of Age on the Harlem" by Joan Murray. Reprinted by permission from *The Hudson Review*, Vol. XXXV, No. 4 (Winter 1982–83). Copyright © 1983 by The Hudson Review, Inc.

Gloria Naylor: "Mommy, What Does Nigger Mean?" by Gloria Naylor (*The New York Times*, 2 / 20 / 86). Copyright © 1986 by The New York Times Company and Gloria Naylor. Reprinted by permission of The New York Times Company and Sterling Lord Literistic, Inc.

Lynn Nelson: "Sequence" by Lynn Nelson first published in *The New Virginia Review*. Reprinted by permission of Lynn Nelson.

Grace Nichols: "We New World Blacks," copyright © Grace Nichols 1984. Published by Virago Press 1984. Reprinted by permission of Virago Press. We have made diligent efforts to contact the author to obtain United States English-language rights to reprint this selection. If you have information that would help us, please write W. W. Norton & Company, 500 Fifth Avenue, New York, NY 10110.

Juli Nishimuta: "A Lavender Life" by Juli Nishimuta. Reprinted with permission.

nila northSun: "up & out" from *Small Bones, Little Eyes*, A Windriver Book Series, Duck Down Press 1981, reprinted by permission of nila northSun.

Dwight Okita: "In Response to Executive Order 9066: All Americans of Japanese Descent Must Report to Relocation Centers," copyright © 1983 by Dwight Okita. This poem is from Okita's first book of poems, *Crossing with the Light* published by Tia Chucha Press in Chicago, 1992.

Sharon Olds: "On the Subway" from *The Gold Cell* by Sharon Olds, copyright © 1987 by Sharon Olds. Reprinted by permission of Alfred A. Knopf, Inc.

Richard Olivas: "I'm Sitting in My History Class." We have made diligent efforts to contact the copyright holder to obtain permission to reprint this selection. If you have information that would help us, please write W. W. Norton & Company, 500 Fifth Avenue, New York, NY 10110.

Gregory Orfalea: "Arab and Jew in Alaska" reprinted by permission of the author from *The Capital of Solitude*, The Greenfield Review Press, P.O. Box 308, Greenfield Center, New York 12833.

Simon J. Ortiz: "Speaking" and "My Father's Song" reprinted by permission of the author, Simon J. Ortiz.

Elena Padilla: "Migrants: Transients or Settlers?" from *Up from Puerto Rico* by Elena Padilla, copyright © 1958, Columbia University Press, New York. Used by permission of the publisher.

Ricardo Pau-Llosa: "Sorting Metaphors" and "Foreign Language" reprinted by permission of the author, Ricardo Pau-Llosa.

Gustavo Pérez-Firmat: "Limen" by Gustavo Pérez-Firmat from *Carolina Cuban* (Bilingual Review Press, 1987). Reprinted by permission of the author.

Estela Portillo: "Day of the Swallows" by Estela Portillo, selection taken from *Contemporary Chicano Theatre*, edited by Robert Garza. Copyright © 1976 by the University of Notre Dame Press. Reprinted by permission.

Ishmael Reed: "I Am a Cowboy in the Boat of Ra" by Ishmael Reed, reprinted with permission. Reprinted with permission of Atheneum Publishers, an imprint of Macmillan Publishing Company, from *New and Collected Poems* by Ishmael Reed. Copyright © 1972 by Ishmael Reed.

Carter Revard: "Driving in Oklahoma" and "Discovery of the New World" by Carter Revard, copyright © 1975 by Carter Revard. "Discovery of the New World" appeared in print first in *Voices of the Rainbow* (ed. Kenneth Rosen, Viking, 1975), and was included with "Driving in Oklahoma" in Revard's poem-gathering, *Ponca War Dancers* (Point Riders Press, Norman, OK 73070), copyright © 1980 by Carter Revard.

Adrienne Rich: "If Not with Others, How?" is reprinted from *Blood, Bread, and Poetry: Selected Prose 1979–1985*, by Adrienne Rich, by permission of W. W. Norton & Company, Inc. Copyright © 1986 by Adrienne Rich.

Alberto Ríos: "Mi Abuelo," © 1982 by Alberto Ríos. Reprinted by permission of author. Alberto Ríos, "Mi Abuelo" from *Selections: University and College Poetry Prizes, 1973–78*, copyright © 1980 is reprinted by permission from The Academy of American Poets. "Mi Abuelo" was first published in *The Louisville Review*.

Richard Rodriguez: "Aria: A Memoir of a Bilingual Childhood" by Richard Rodriguez. Reprinted by permission of Georges Borchardt, Inc. for the author. Copyright © 1981 by Richard Rodriguez. First published in *The American Scholar*.

Wendy Rose: "Julia" from *Halfbreed Chronicles* by Wendy Rose. Copyright © 1985 by Wendy Rose. Reprinted by permission of West End Press.

Muriel Rukeyser: "From 'Letter to the Front' " or "To Be a Jew" © Muriel Rukeyser, by permission of William L. Rukeyser.

Edward Said: "Reflections on Exile," copyright © 1984 by Edward Said, reprinted with the permission of Wylie, Aitken & Stone, Inc.

Mark Salzman: "Teacher Wei" from *Iron and Silk* by Mark Salzman, copyright © 1986 by Mark Salzman. Reprinted by permission of Random House, Inc.

Yvonne Sapia: "Grandmother, a Caribbean Indian, Described by My Father" from *Valentino's Hair* by Yvonne Sapia. Copyright © 1987 by Yvonne Sapia. Reprinted with the permission of Northeastern University Press, Boston.

William Saroyan: "Najari Levon's Old Country Advice to the Young Americans" by William Saroyan from *Madness in the Family*. Copyright © 1988 by Leo Hamalian. Reprinted by permission of New Directions Publishing Corporation.

Rhoda Schwartz: "Old Photographs." Copyright © 1974 by Rhoda Schwartz. Originally appeared in *Jewish-American Literature: An Anthology*, edited by Abraham Chapman, a Mentor Book. Reprinted from manuscript by permission of author.

Dennis Scott: "Grampa" reprinted from *Uncle Time* by Dennis Scott, by permission of the University of Pittsburgh Press, © 1973 by Dennis Scott.

James Seilsopour: "I Forgot the Words to the National Anthem" by James Seilsopour, copyright © 1984 from *Student Writers and Their Work: The Bedford Prizes* by Nancy Sommers and Donald McQuade. Reprinted with permisson of St. Martin's Press, Inc.

Olive Senior: "Ancestral Poem" by Olive Senior, reprinted by permission of the author.

Robbie Clipper Sethi: "Grace" (*The Atlantic Monthly*, August 1991) by Robbie Clipper Sethi. Reprinted by permission of Robbie Clipper Sethi. "Grace" first appeared in *The Atlantic Monthly*.

Jack G. Shaheen: "The Media's Image of Arabs" reprinted by permission of Dr. Jack G. Shaheen.

Elise Sprunt Sheffield: "The Gentle Wholeness of Home" (*Brown Alumni Monthly*, 11 / 91) by Elise Sprunt Sheffield. Reprinted by permission of the author. "The Gentle Wholeness of Home" first appeared in the *Brown Alumni Monthly*.

Leslie Marmon Silko: "Long Time Ago," copyright © 1981 by Leslie Marmon Silko, reprinted by permission of Wylie, Aitken & Stone, Inc. "Private Property" copyright © Leslie Marmon Silko. Reprinted by permission of Wylie, Aitken & Stone, Inc.

Lisabeth Sivertsen: "Witholding Consent or the Art of Non-Conformity" by Lisabeth Sivertsen. Reprinted with permission.

R. T. Smith: "Red Anger" copyright © R. T. Smith. Reprinted by permission of the author.

Cathy Song: "Heaven" is reprinted from *Frameless Windows, Squares of Light: Poems* by Cathy Song, by permission of W. W. Norton & Company, Inc. Copyright © 1988 by Cathy Song. "Lost Sister" by Cathy Song from *Picture Bride*, copyright © 1983, published by Yale University Press.

Gary Soto: "Like Mexicans" from *Small Faces* by Gary Soto. Copyright © 1986 by Gary Soto. Used by permission of Delacorte Press, a division of Bantam Doubleday Dell Publishing Group, Inc.

Amy Tan: "A Pair of Tickets" reprinted by permission of The Putnam Publishing Group from *The Joy Luck Club* by Amy Tan. Copyright © 1989 by Amy Tan.

Barry Targan: "Dominion." First appeared in *The Iowa Review* (Spring 1979), vol. 10, no. 2. Reprinted by permission of author.

Laurence Thomas: "Next Life, I'll Be White," by Laurence Thomas (*The New York Times*, 8 / 8 / 90). Copyright © 1990 by The New York Times Company. Reprinted by permission.

Bao Gia Tran: "My Home" by Bao Gia Tran. Reprinted with permission.

Helena Maria Viramontes: "The Moths" by Helena Maria Viramontes from *The Moths and Other Stories*, reprinted by permission of Arte Publico Press.

Derek Walcott: "A Far Cry from Africa" from *Collected Poems 1948–1984* by Derek Walcott. Copyright © 1962, 1986 by Derek Walcott. Reprinted by permission of Farrar, Straus & Giroux, Inc.

Alice Walker: "Revolutionary Petunias" from *Revolutionary Petunias & Other Poems*, copyright © 1972 by Alice Walker, reprinted by permission of Harcourt Brace Jovanovich, Inc.

Robert Anthony Watts: "Not Black, Not White, But Biracial," by Robert Anthony Watts from *The Atlanta Journal* and *The Atlanta Constitution* (December 1, 1991, page A-1). Reprinted with permission from *The Atlanta Journal* and *The Atlanta Constitution*.

John Edgar Wideman: "Little Brother" from *Fever* by John Edgar Wideman. Copyright © 1989 by John Edgar Wideman. Reprinted by permission of Henry Holt and Company, Inc.

Sherley Williams: "Say Hello to John," *The Peacock Poems*, copyright © 1975 by Sherley Williams, Wesleyan University Press by permission of University Press of New England.

August Wilson: *Fences* by August Wilson. Copyright © 1986 by August Wilson. Used by permission of New American Library, a division of Penguin Books USA Inc.

Fran Winant: "Christopher St. Liberation Day, June 28, 1970," copyright © Fran Winant, first appeared in *Looking at Women* by Fran Winant (1971), Violet Press, P.O. Box 398, New York, NY 10009.

Tobias Wolff: "Say Yes" from *Back in the World* by Tobias Wolff. Copyright © 1985 by Tobias Wolff. Reprinted by permission of Houghton Mifflin Company. All rights reserved.

Merle Woo: "Letter to Ma" by Merle Woo from *This Bridge Called My Back: Writings By Radical Women of Color*, copyright © 1983 by Cherrie Moraga and Gloria Anzaldúa. Used with permission of the author and Kitchen Table: Women of Color Press, P.O. Box 908, Latham, NY 12110.

Mitsuye Yamada: "Looking Out" and "The Question of Loyalty" from *Camp Notes and Other Poems* (Kitchen Table: Women of Color Press) by Mitsuye Yamada. Reprinted by permission of author.

Wakako Yamauchi: *And the Soul Shall Dance*. Reprinted by permission of author.

Ray A. Young Bear: "in the first place of my life." Reprinted by permission of author.

Cyn. Zarco: "Flipochinos" from *Cir'cum-nav'i-ga'tion* by Cyn. Zarco. Reprinted by permission of author. Copyright © 1986 by Cyn. Zarco.

GLOSSARY

ACTION. What happens in a narrative, play, or other piece of writing. Action usually involves CONFLICT. In a play, action usually refers to what happens onstage (as distinguished from what has happened before the play begins or what happens offstage); in a narrative, it refers to what happens as the story unfolds (as distinguished from events that have occurred earlier or ones that are simply mentioned). PLOT is a more comprehensive term that includes events that have occurred earlier, the situation that brings about the events, the motivations that lead to the conflict, and the arrangement of the action.

ALLEGORY. In an allegory, the events usually make sense on a literal level, but a second and more complex level of meaning is also available to the reader. That special meaning is usually moral, religious, or political. An allegory is an extended form of METAPHOR and is more systematic and its meaning more paraphrasable than a SYMBOL.

ALLUSION. A brief reference to a person, place, thing, or passage in another literary work, usually for the purpose of associating the meaning or tone of one work with another. Sometimes the term *allusion* is used as the general equivalent of "reference"—to indicate any glance in a literary work at something outside itself, to an event or person or idea, as well as to another piece of writing.

ATTITUDE. The position—emotional or intellectual—assumed toward an idea, event, or person by an author or a literary work. Attitude is closely related to TONE. The tone of a work—the way its words are spoken by a human voice—derives from the attitude of the author and work and is the key device for expressing attitude, but tone of voice may express the attitude indirectly or ironically, through such devices as UNDERSTATEMENT, HYPERBOLE, or SARCASM.

CATASTROPHE. See CONCLUSION.

CHARACTER, CHARACTERIZATION. The particular traits (or characteristics) of a person suggest that person's character—what it is that makes that person distinctive from other people. Individuals portrayed in literature are often referred to as characters. Characterization is the way in which an author describes and defines characters.

969

CLIMAX, or TURNING POINT. During the RISING ACTION of a play, the flow or movement is in one direction; the climax is the crucial moment at which the direction of the action changes and the FALLING ACTION begins. The term *climax* is also used to suggest the moment in a narrative in which the flow of the action changes direction.

CONCLUSION, or CATASTROPHE or DENOUEMENT. The moment in a play (or a narrative) at which a stable situation is reestablished so that the drama (or story) may end.

CONCRETE POEM. A poem in which the words are arranged on a page so as to imitate the shape of a "concrete" or material object.

CONFLICT. The struggle between opposing forces—characters, families, nations, ideas, or ideological systems—that provides the central ACTION and interest in any literary PLOT.

CONTEXT. Anything beyond the text that may be relevant to reading the text itself. Contexts may be historical or literary or authorial or of several other kinds. Sometimes relevant contexts have to do with when a piece of writing was written or what times or events it refers to, sometimes to the wider climate of ideas a piece of writing may engage.

CONVENTION. Within traditions of rhetoric and within literary history, certain standard literary features develop over a period of time, and when such features become commonly accepted and frequently reused, they are called conventions. When such features come to seem tired, they become clichés and are useless as ways of calling up expected responses. But often conventions provide shortcuts to meaning or feeling because they rely on ways of thinking that have become established enough in the public mind to generate a specific reaction in readers. See EXPECTATION.

DENOUEMENT. See CONCLUSION.

EPIGRAPH. An inscription at the beginning of a piece of writing, usually a quotation from another literary work. An epigraph ordinarily suggests the THEME of the writing or otherwise suggests what is to be expected in what follows, or serves as an ALLUSION.

EXPECTATION. What readers think they will find in a piece of writing. Most frequently used in fiction or drama to refer to "what will happen next," it can also refer to anticipation of rhymes (in poetry), structure, character development, or development of ideas. Expectations are suggested by a variety of literary devices and strategies, including the title, epigraph, choice of literary kind, allusion, and other literary conventions.

EXPOSITION. The structural element in a play in which the situation is explained, the characters introduced, and the basis of the conflict set up. Exposition in narrative performs similar functions in order to set the plot in motion. The term *exposition* is also used to distinguish discourse that explains the nature of something—a thing, a person, an idea—from other kinds of discourse: argumentation, description, narration.

FABLE. A brief tale, told in order to illustrate a moral. See PARABLE.

FALLING ACTION. The term used to describe the structural element just after the CLIMAX in a play, when the complications begin to unwind. Sometimes the term is also used to describe the corresponding structural part of a narrative.

FOCUS. The angle of vision from which a narrative is presented, the point from which people, events, and other details are viewed. Compare POINT OF VIEW and VOICE.

GENRE. See LITERARY KIND.

HYPERBOLE, or OVERSTATEMENT. Exaggeration used for rhetorical purposes.

IMAGE, IMAGERY. Imagery visualizes something that is being described by comparing it to something else that is more familiar, through either a *simile* (in which something is compared directly and explicitly to something else) or a METAPHOR (in which something is described in terms that pretend it *is* something else). Though the term *image* literally refers to the visual, images may involve the other senses. Sometimes, however, the term *imagery* is extended to include any strategy of visualization, including straightforward description. An image is a specific visualization.

INTERPRETATION. The explanation of a piece of writing, how it works and what it means. When readers interpret a literary work, they provide what is sometimes called a *reading* of the work, that is, a specific explanation of its THEME, TONE, and MEANING.

IRONIC, IRONY. The calculated discrepancy between what something appears to mean and what it really means. *Verbal irony* is the use of words to say, deliberately, something other than what one really means. Irony is usually thought of as a tone that suggests that a word or phrase "really" means the opposite of what it seems to say, but irony does not necessarily imply the exact opposite: it can be oblique, deviating indirectly from what is apparently said rather than directly reversing meaning. Sometimes, too, an event is said to be *ironic* (in a colloquial sense) when it is surprising compared with the expected outcome, especially when there is a discrepancy between what might be expected from the way events have gone so far and what the characters seem to deserve.

LITERARY KIND, or GENRE. A traditional literary way of organizing experience. The division of literature into different *kinds* or *forms* is, in part, a convenience for purposes of description, but every literary kind develops habits, traditions, and CONVENTIONS that distinguish it from other literary ways of organizing and presenting human experience. Often writers choose to write in a particular literary kind—the short story, for example, or the lyric poem—as a way of indicating to readers what sorts of expectations to bring to the work; in that sense, the literary kind that an author chooses represents a contract with the reader, a contract that involves what the author is most likely to do because of the conventions of the *kind*. Writers often build surprise into what they do, however, using a reader's expectations to create quite unexpected effects, thus modifying a kind even as they employ it.

MEANING. The whole complex of effects produced by a work on readers. The full meaning of a work involves both its intellectual and emotional implications, a recognition of its THEME and TONE. The meaning of a work depends not only on the statements that the work makes about a particular subject or theme, but also the tone in which it makes those statements. Most works have more than a single meaning, having different effects upon different readers and sometimes several distinctive effects on a single reader; but there is usually a core or range of meaning or meanings upon which different readers can agree.

METAPHOR. A figure of speech in which something is described in terms more appropriate for something else, as if the thing really were something else. Sometimes *metaphor* is used to include all figures of speech, especially those, like *simile*, that involve comparison. See IMAGE.

MONOLOGUE. A speech, often a lengthy one, by one person. Poems are sometimes presented as monologues, often involving IRONY, because the person does not fully understand what he or she is saying. Short stories are sometimes mono-logues, too, but in plays, monologues have a special and specific function—to let the audience know (confidentially) something that is on the mind of a particular CHARACTER.

MOOD. The atmosphere that pervades a work and gives the reader or audience a sense of what to expect. In drama, it involves the set and music as well as the words; in a poem or story, it can involve the reader's inferences beyond the VOICE or NARRATOR.

MYTH. A communal narrative about the unknown or unknowable, the remote in time or space, the spiritual universe, or humankind's place in that universe. A narra-tive takes on *mythic* dimensions when it comes to speak for a common perception experienced by a coherent group—a nation, a people, or a community. Com-munal representation is crucial to the attainment of mythic status.

NARRATION, NARRATOR. Unlike drama, narrative is mediated: someone "tells" the story and therefore stands between the reader and the ACTION, CHARACTERS, and other elements of the story. The narrator—roughly the equivalent of the SPEAKER in a poem—is an integral part of the story, its effect, and its meaning. Words are the only means we have of visualizing, and what we visualize depends com-pletely on what someone tells us to see.

OVERSTATEMENT. See HYPERBOLE.

PARABLE. A short, usually familiar story that has as its major aim to teach a moral or religious message. Unlike a FABLE, a parable makes its point by directly compar-ing things or events in its narrative with actual things or events.

PARODY. Imitation of the style or prominent characteristics of a particular piece of writing, often for comic purposes. Ordinarily, HYPERBOLE (or overstatement) is used in parody to mock a subject or a work by treating common or "low" things in language that is exaggeratedly formal or high-flown.

PERSONA. The mask or representation through which an author speaks when he or she is not necessarily expressing his or her own opinion, often halfway between the personal voice of the author and the self-presentation of a named and fully developed character in a play or narrative.

PLOT. *What* happens (ACTION) and *why* in a narrative, play, or (sometimes) poem. Plot, or *plot structure*, also includes the *how*: the arrangement of events and the way the action is presented to readers or an audience.

POINT OF VIEW. The perspective from which a narrative is presented, including both the angle of vision (FOCUS) and the words in which it is communicated (VOICE). While *point of view* is usually an adequate term, in some works the focus and voice are distinct: what we are seeing from a particular vantage point may be more limited than how it is being described; the language may be more sophis-ticated and knowledgeable.

RHETORIC, RHETORICAL DEVICES. The formal study of how words work is called *rhet-oric*. One can speak of the rhetoric of a given narrative or poem or play—what effects it is calculated to produce—or more generally of the rhetoric of an author (what particular strategies of persuasion he or she uses), or the rhetoric of fiction or of poetry (the way a particular literary mode uses language to accomplish its particular ends).

RISING ACTION. The second stage in formal dramatic structure, the period between EXPOSITION and CLIMAX. During the rising action, a series of events occur to complicate the original situation and create CONFLICT among the characters.

RITUAL. A rite or ceremony in which an act or series of acts is exactly repeated on specific occasions in order to recall or celebrate an event or an idea. In ritual, the communal sharing of action or behavior stands for some common agreement about meaning or value in the society or group.

SARCASM. IRONY of a simple, snide, and derogatory kind. Sarcasm, unlike most forms of irony, is specifically directed at someone and is usually intended to wound.

SETTING. The location and context in which the ACTION of a literary work takes place. It involves both time and place; it establishes MOOD, gives particularity to the action, and often makes the action possible, believable, or meaningful.

SIMILE. See IMAGERY.

SPEAKER. The person who speaks the words of a poem. The speaker in a poem is similar to the NARRATOR in a story. See also PERSONA.

STANZA. Identifiable on a page by the spaces used to set them apart from one another, stanzas are the structural units into which many poems are divided. They suggest the rhythmic patterns of a poem, indicate the pacing, and may or may not reflect the divisions of meaning in a poem.

STEREOTYPE. A CHARACTER based upon conscious or unconscious generalizations about age, sex, national or ethnic identification, occupation, marital status, etc. Often even complex characters in a story or play have some stereotypical features. Writers sometimes build a character upon the base of a stereotype and then complicate the expectations as the plot develops. Stereotypes, though often offensive to the group on whom the stereotype is based, do not necessarily represent prejudice on the part of an author, but sometimes are used to set up some larger conclusion about easy generalizations and biases.

STRUCTURE. The framework of a piece of writing, the way it is put together, its organization. It is common to distinguish between the *structure* of a work and its *form:* the form, like the form of a physical object such as a house, has to do with external appearance and visible shape; the structure, with the principles involved in putting it together.

SUBJECT. See THEME.

SYMBOL, SYMBOLISM. A symbol in general usage is something that stands for, or signifies, something else. Often a material object, such as a cross or a flag, symbolizes something abstract, something that has been communally agreed upon over a long period of time (a *traditional symbol*). Works of literature, however, sometimes create symbols having a significance solely within the limits of the work itself, just as individuals can create symbols in their own minds. These symbols are usually not paraphrasable, not because they have no meaning, but because their meanings are complex or multiple. Owning a home, for example, may symbolize freedom, independence, stability, security, or financial worries. When symbols are used densely throughout a work to establish a frame of reference different from that of ordinary reality, the work itself is said to be symbolic. When a series of symbols is agreed upon within a culture over a long period of time so that they become established as a belief system commonly available to all members of the group, the combination of symbols is often called a MYTH.

THEME. *Theme* is closely related to *subject*, but the two terms should be distinguished for precision in specifying how writings embody ideas. Literary works—in fact, all pieces of writing, however simple or informal—are about something. A work is always "about" something concrete—a particular action, a specific event, what happens to someone, what something feels like. But literature is also about things other than specific events and details—it is about concepts, ideas, and institutions, relationships, problems. The *specific subject* of a poem might be how it feels to shoot a deer or meet a stranger; its *general subject* might involve pursuit or ritualistic killing or the question of human and animal relationships, or cultural biases against people from outside one's own group or the love or fear of the alien and exotic.

Most works of literature not only imply that individual actions and events reflect more general human patterns, they often also take stances and attitudes and express opinions. That is, they express—or, more often, imply—a position, a value judgment about behavior, relationships, institutions, about what people do and how they do it. The stance that a work takes toward something is its *theme*. Most works may be said to have more than a single theme, just as a symbol may be said to have more than one meaning. The role of the individual reader is very great in determining the theme of a work, but the general subject, TONE, and other elements in the work set limits to the reader's freedom to interpret.

TONE. The attitude of a literary work toward its subject (see THEME). To describe tone, it is customary to use words that would ordinarily be used to describe the modulations of a human voice; thus the tone of a literary work might be described as "somber," "gloomy," "sarcastic," "resigned," "celebratory," or "angry." Tone may be used to describe individual sentences, phrases, or even words as well as whole works.

TURNING POINT. See CLIMAX.

UNDERSTATEMENT. A rhetorical figure of speech in which something is represented as less important than it really is or in which something is stated less forcibly than it would be if the writer's actual feelings were expressed. Understatement (its technical name in classical rhetoric is *meiosis*) is often used when a writer wishes readers to find and state for themselves the true importance of a particular thought or value, rather than forcing upon them some strong opinion or feeling that they might resist.

VOICE. The verbal aspect of the perspective or point of view in a narrative. See FOCUS and POINT OF VIEW.

INDEX OF AUTHORS
AND TITLES